NON-LEAGUE DIRECTORY 1985

Editor
Tony Williams

NEWNES BOOKS

Published by Newnes Books
a Division of The Hamlyn Publishing Group Limited
84-88, The Centre, Feltham, Middlesex, England
and distributed for them by
The Hamlyn Publishing Group Limited
Rushden, Northants, England

ISBN 0 600 35851 8 (cased)
0 600 35784 8 (softback)

Printed in Finland

FRONT COVER

Colourful F.A. Vase action as Stamford's Steve Blades leaps ahead of Paul Gillard who scored one of Stansted's goals in their excellent Wembley victory. Photo: Bob Thomas

CONTENTS

ACKNOWLEDGEMENTS

No-one will ever understand how much an editor of a book like this owes to his contributors. I am certainly impressed more and more each year by the enthusiastic and dedicated offerings from amateur writers and photographers who write in to help with each year's publication. This year I am particularly grateful to Bill Mitchell who has been a very loyal and hardworking Assistant Editor and the incredible work achieved by such superb photographers as Mike Joss and Eric Marsh.

We have so many other excellent photographers that it would be difficult to mention all of them, but look through the book and you will see what excellent work they have done.

Special thanks also to Leo Hoenig whose all-round contributions have been quite staggering, and to Steve Clark and Adrian Titcombe at The Football Association who are always happy to give help and advice.

On the editorial side I must thank all the League secretaries for their amazing enthusiasm and loyalty to the book. I really appreciate this and I do realise how busy they are on their own business whether it's covering football, work or normal home 'duties'. Thank you very much indeed!

It is very difficult to remember all the names of people who have bothered to write in with ideas and contributions for the book, but I will list some of those who have made my job a little easier: Gordon Wallis, Roland Reeve, Sean Creedon, Darren Lovell, Peter Lynn, Colin Startup, Steve Whitney, Paul Walker, John Rooney, Ian Runham, Rupert Metcalf, F. G. Vaukins, Simon Inglis, Jeremy Biggs, Paul Newman, Steve Anderson, Derrick Linsey, Mike Berry, Michael Firth, Tony Incenzo, John Litster, David Hills, Steve Lindsell, David Shute, Andrew Bamping, Peter Wallis, Tom Webb, Yves Gonnet, Barry White, John Greenwood, David Kenard, Mark Herron, Bruce Speller, Sid Blain, Ray Spiller and David Stacey.

I treasure the letters of every one who writes in and helps the book and to all of you who obviously love the game and want to contribute — thank you very much. I hope you all get replies but thank you all the same and please carry on writing. TONY WILLIAMS

Editorial Preface

It is with particular pleasure that I write this Editorial Preface as it appeared at one time that there might not be a Non-League publication this year.

After three much appreciated years of support from Rothmans, the famous tobacco company who had already helped semi-professional football through the form of sponsorship for four major leagues, decided to concentrate on other ways of promotion.

The previous publisher didn't wish to publish another book in the same series so it was particularly pleasing to hear that Newnes Books, a Division of the Hamlyn Publishing Group should not only be prepared to publish a Non-League book without the help of a sponsor but also be willing to increase the pages and reduce the cover price.

The confindence that Newnes Books have shown in the principle of a 'Bible' for this level of the game deserves the very highest degree of loyalty from within football and I am pleased to say that thanks to the extremely efficient promotional and marketing techniques of the publishers, the response already received suggests record sales for the book.

I know the Football Association appreciate the efforts of the publishers and I would personally like to add my thanks.

This is the seventh annual Non-League publication I have edited and this year the interest, support, and indeed keenness to be included, that has been noticeable in most clubs and competitions, has been most welcome. The book can only be as good as its contributors and these include over 600 clubs, 60 competitions and an every increasing band of loyal and enthusiastic photographers and statisticians. These people are the 'salt of the earth' and I really appreciate their support.

In the game outside the Football League, because there are few livelihoods at stake, practically everything is done for the love of the game and most people involved put more into football than they take out.

In an atmosphere like this it is very difficult not to enjoy life and I must say I consider it a privilege to be part of this very happy 'world'.

TONY WILLIAMS

Editor: Tony Williams

Assistant Editor: Bill Mitchell

Editorial Committee: Tony Williams, Bill Mitchell, Adrian Titcombe, Steve Clark and Tony Bagley

Editorial Office: 4 Rosen Court, Turners Drive, Thatcham, Newbury, Berkshire RG13 4DF

HAVE THE FOOTBALL LEAGUE CLUBS CLOSED RANKS?

The exciting climax of the Alliance championship race highlighted a season which ended sadly with Maidstone United's bid for League status given no chance at all by the League club chairmen who understandably but frustratingly rallied round their colleagues in distress.

Having held off Nuneaton Borough's challenge which was spearheaded by the devastating finishing of Paul Culpin, Maidstone won their final match against Telford by a staggering six clear goals to underline the quality of their playing strength. The club's facilities have never been in doubt and it can only be assumed that, since the Alliance Premier League has established itself through excellent administration, the emergence of some very well run clubs has given many of the struggling Football League set-ups an uncomfortable sense of insecurity which has inspired them to close ranks to protect themselves from being shown up.

In a serious comparison between Maidstone United and Hartlepools United, Halifax Town or Rochdale, their facilities, quality of play, and most importantly the aura of the friendly progressiveness of a club used to success must clearly point to Maidstone being the best investment for the future. The other clubs will continue to struggle on from season to season within an atmosphere of gloom. Is that really what the Football League wants?

ENGLAND IN ITALY

At the time of the League AGM I was lucky enough to be in Italy watching England defending the Four Nations title they won with such style in Scarborough. Two Maidstone United supporters had travelled at their own expense to support the four Maidstone lads in the England squad and when discussing the club's chances of joining the Football League with all the club members it was obvious that feelings were very mixed on the subject. Would the chance of glamorous Milk Cup ties make up for the prospect of segregation on the sparse Fourth Division terraces harrassed by home supporters and police presence? Would the fun of entertaining new clubs make up for the lack of non-League hospitality on most League grounds? Would part time players have a future in Division Four?

Avon League's 'Old Boy' Gary Hackett scores for Shrewsbury Town in the F.A. Cup against Ipswich Town.

A 'loonies' re-union at Quarry Quay Nomads!

Having seen that opinion was divided there is still no doubt that whatever the advantages or disadvantages of changing their status, Maidstone United, or in the future the top Alliance club each year, deserves the right to move forward. It would obviously transform the thinking of the whole of semi-professional football overnight and all over the country senior football administrators and even top club officials agree that it would be the right move to accept promotion and relegation on a one up and one down basis. Everyone agrees — that is until the annual vote comes round and year after year club chairmen take the easy way out. There is no reason why Football League club chairmen should consider the good of the game before their own interests so presumably, however well organised and efficient the Alliance becomes, the fear of the League strugglers will always force their 'brothers' to rally round. How very sad!

Apart from the Maidstone supporters it was also good to see the Harrow Borough chairman and assistant manager in Italy despite the fact that their two squad men had little chance of winning caps. Incidently, when watching the England semi-professional squad play every year, it never ceases to amaze me that the coaches are not snapped up by League clubs. The planning, organisation and the football produced after a week's work together is always most impressive. Why can't this level of performance be achieved at higher levels where presumably the players are naturally more gifted?

PROGRESSIVE NEW CLUBS

The national pyramid as set up under the Alliance has created a fascinating pattern of football in which a number of clubs are taking advantage of the system to progress. In the Alliance it seems to be the clubs with 'senior pedigree' such as Dartford, Barrow, Bangor City and AP Leamington who 'shuttle' backwards and forwards in and out of the senior competition but progressive new names are pushing towards the top with a single minded determination. These clubs include Fisher Athletic, Shepshed Charterhouse and RS Southampton, and they are proving to be an example to all the progressive little clubs emerging from the Vase level of clubs.

Unfortunately the Isthmian League clubs, although agreeing to form part of the 'pyramid', have not yet produced a club who wants to move up. However, the main point is that the way is there should a club want to go 'national'. In the meantime the famous Yeovil Town club will be extremely pleased that no Isthmians are moving as they were saved from relegation for the second consecutive year because of this.

I must say that, while filled with only admiration for the Alliance and the high standing it has given senior football outside the Football League, I still feel that the Third and Fourth Division clubs must turn to regionalised third divisions (probably on a part time basis) and when that happens the senior Alliance clubs would be ideally suited to feed in on a North and South basis.

When one considers the quality of the Italian Football League clubs — their wealth, their facilities and the number of clubs (all with QUALIFIED COACHES) that they run each week to serve the youth of their towns, we should really sit up and take notice. Their system of two comparatively small full time First and Second Divisions backed by three regional part time third divisions works a treat. In fact Udinese, who played in the Anglo-Italian competition only eight years ago, recently broke the world transfer record when signing Brazil's star forward Zico. Steady progress from part time football can work perfectly.

This year's editorial seems to have taken on a more serious note than usual, but the Football Association and the major semi-professional Leagues in the country have sorted out an extremely effective and appreciated 'pyramid' system in which clubs at all levels are improving their facilities to prepare for possible promotion. So it seems such a shame that a sensible link with the Football League is prevented purely through the fear shown by the lowly League clubs who doubt their ability to 'bounce' back if relegated to the Alliance.

One most encouraging aspect of the game outside The Football League is the ever increasing band of 'loonies', 'travellers' or just plain fanatics who enjoy visiting new grounds and collecting new programmes. I often receive the most interesting photographs taken by these roving correspondents and they are much appreciated.

This band of football fans are the happiest of people and I'm pleased to say that from the majority of reports they receive the most warm and appreciative welcomes at most of the clubs they visit. If you truly love the game I can think of no better hobby.

You may notice that we have included some interesting Ex-Non-League players 'teams' who are now with Football League clubs. More and more players seem to be travelling this path into full time football employment and surely this reflects very well on the excellent early training, coaching and character development that they receive within part-time football.

Finally a word of thanks to Keith Wright who at the time of writing is considering retirement from the England semi-professional International managers position. He has contributed greatly to the game over the last six years at this level, one year as Howard Wilkinson's assistant and five in charge. The quality of his teams' performances on and off the field have always been a credit to him and to England and I am sure he will continue to be extremely successful in whatever coaching capacity he accepts. TONY WILLIAMS

The views and opinions given in this Directory are not necessarily those of The Football Association and of course guest writers are purely expressing their own opinions.

BRIAN THOMPSON
Player of the Year

Brian Thompson (Maidstone United and England): When Office Cleaning Services sponsored an Inter-League Representative knock out tournament in 1978, with the aim of discovering the Non League players most worthy of International recognition, Brian Thompson stepped up as captain of the Southern League side to accept the trophy. Since then Brian played for the England team that won the first Four Nations Tournament, turned full time professional with Mansfield Town and has returned to help Maidstone United reach the top of the 'pyramid'. As right back Brian has been an England regular with ?? caps to his credit and being a North Easterner it isn't surprising that his loyalty, enthusiasm and will to win has been cherished by all who have been associated with him.

MERIT AWARD WINNERS

Paul Culpin (Nuneaton Borough and England): Anyone who breaks the Gola League goalscoring record and scores over 50 goals in Senior competitive semi-professional football season must be a 'bit special'. Paul not only did this but he also won his first England cap against Wales. Unfortunately, his summer contract with his club in Finland prevented him from travelling to Italy but no doubt he will be one of the Gola League's main attractions again this season.

Tommy Robson (Stamford): So many Football League players find it difficult to give maximum effort when joining the semi-professional ranks and possibly a player with over 600 Football League appearances could be forgiven for 'going through the motions' at times. Not so Tommy Robson however; he crowned a superb season with Stamford in the United Counties League with an outstanding display of non-stop grafting to keep his side in the game despite early setbacks at Wembley. No one worked harder and he proved a fine example of real professionalism.

Mark Newsome (Maidstone United and England): Consistently impressive performances for his club brought Mark to the notice of the England selectors and having made his debut against Wales he held his place despite pressure from Blyth's Peter Robinson (one of the outstanding players of the previous International Tournament) and was one of the successes in Italy. Maidstone United's championship success was also built on his dominance in the heart of their defence and surely a Football League club will be luring him away in the very near future.

Dave Ryan (Northwich Victoria) has proved to be one of the most consistent goalkeepers in senior semi professional football since joining Northwich seven years ago after four years on Manchester United's books. In eleven Trophy ties last season's opponents only scored five times and no team scored more than once in a game. Indeed Dave kept a clean sheet for five consecutive Trophy games and gave his usual confident displays in both finals thus inspiring all in front of him with his solid dependability.

REGIONAL CLUB AWARDS

North East: Whitby Town. The impressive attendances of this little club are highlighted elsewhere in 'The Directory' but Town's cup triumphs over Bishop Auckland, Halifax Town (A), Blyth Spartans, Leytonstone-Ilford (A), and Frickley Athletic must give them the award for the 1983-84 season. Hopefully their recent triumphs and the consistency of the fine Blyth Spartans club will soon inspire a Drybroughs Northern League club to reach Wembley in a Trophy Final.

North West: South Liverpool. In a year when Liverpool and Everton dominated the senior domestic scene, it must have given everyone at South Liverpool Football Club extra satisfaction to win three very competitive cup competitions: The Liverpool Senior, The Lancashire Junior and The Northern Premier League Cup. In the Liverpool Senior Cup their beaten opponents in the final were Liverpool Reserves and not many clubs in the Central League put them in their place!

Midlands: Shepshed Charterhouse. When a club continues to win trophies and move steadily up the 'pyramid' there is always a risk that supporters and indeed officials can get complacent. Shepshed however seem to thrive on the challenge to improve and their promotion to The Premier Division of the Southern League plus the continued development of their ground should make them a power in the game for many years to come. For the record their achievements last season were:

East of England: Stansted. When you have never won more than one tie in any previous Vase competition one can hardly consider a Wembley appearance anything other than a 'pipedream'. Stansted not only got to Wembley but they beat the hot favourites to take the Vase and returned home to win the

Home Counties: Maidstone United. As the current Gola League Champions they are the undisputed top club outside the Football League. However, the manner in which they stormed through the second half of the season despite some worrying off the field publicity brings great credit to the club and their 6-0 victory on the last day of the season, against quality opposition, really underlined the class of an excellent side.

West of England: Exmouth Town. Eight years ago when the club suffered relegation from the Western League's senior strata and attendances had dropped to a depressing low no-one would have imagined that Exmouth Town would bounce back with such style and quality to win the Great Mills Western Leauge Championship in 1984. All credit should go to a fine 'club' triumph for the way this present success has been planned and achieved.

Stansted FC
Back Row (L-R): Dave Hoddle (ass. manager), Eddie Coe, John Reading, Malcolm Skingle, Steve Turner, Micky Southgate, Jamie Reeves, Lol Williams, Peter Fox (physio.), Steve Cooper, Dave Edwards (manager). Front Row (L-R): Gabby Callanan, Jeff Hilton, Dave Williams, Barry Simpson (captain), Robbie Doyle, Collin Krzoska, Ray Holt, John Hitchcock (trainer). Photo: John Behets; Bishop's Stortford Gazette

PAST NON-LEAGUE FOOTBALL YEARBOOK AWARDS 1977-83

Team of the Year

1977/78	Blyth Spartans
1978/79	Barking
1979/80	Dagenham
1980/81	Altrincham
1981/82	Leytonstone & Ilford
1982/83	England Semi-Professional XI.

FA Cup Merit Award

1977/78	Blyth Spartans
1978/79	Altrincham
1979/80	Harlow Town
1980/81	Enfield
1981/82	Altrincham
1982/83	Bishop's Stortford

Special Merit Award

1977/78	Enfield
1978/79	Worcester City
1979/80	Altrincham, Stamford
1980/81	Bishop's Stortford, Runcorn, Slough Town
1981/82	Shepshed Charterhouse, Enfield, Runcorn, Wealdstone
1982/83	Enfield, Sutton United, Gateshead, Harrow Borough

FA Vase Merit Award

1977/78	Barton Rovers
1978/79	Billericay Town
1979/80	Guisborough Town
1980/81	Willenhall
1981/82	Rainworth M.W.
1982/83	Harry Rudge (Halesowen T)

Scottish Team of the Year

1980/81	Pollok
1981/82	Inverness Caledonian
1982/83	Inverness Caledonian

Personalities of the Season

1977/78

Dave Clark (Blyth Spartans)
Gerry Stewart (Boston United)
Paul Glover (Bath City)
John King (Altrincham)
Keith Searle (Enfield)

1978/79

Jim Arnold (Stafford Rangers)
Tony Jennings (Enfield)
Billy Kellock (Kettering)
Chris Tudor (Almondsbury Greenway)
Howard Wilkinson (England Semi-Professional Manager)

1979/80

Leo Skeete (Mossley)
Graham Smith (Northwich Victoria)
Mike Roberts (Winsford United)
Ted Hardy (Enfield Manager)
Adrian Titcombe (Football Association)

1980/81

Tony Saunders (Altrincham Manager)
Larry Pritchard (Sutton United)
Terry Moore (Bishop's Stortford)
Colin Williams (Northwich Victoria)
Keith Wright (England Semi-Professional Manager)

1981/82

Micky Burns (Forest Green Rovers)
Barry Howard (Altrincham)
Graham Bennett (Bangor City)
John Williams (Runcorn Manager)
Keith Barrett (Enfield)

1982/83

John Watson (Maidstone U)
John Davison (Altrincham)
John Bartley (Maidstone U)
Ken Jones (Northwich Victoria)
Tommy Dixon (Blyth Spartans)
Bill Dellow (Southern League)

England's Semi-Professional squad represents 98 per cent of the country's footballers

By Ted Croker,
secretary of the Football Association

Ted Croker

"Non-League Football" is a term that has come to mean the layer of football below the Football League and generally involving clubs with their own self-contained ground. This Directory is long overdue and will I am sure be a very interesting guide and record of a very important level of football.

Non-League football has its two national knock-out competitions, now well established, and its own representative national team. The history of the more senior of the two club competitions, the Challenge Trophy, is scarcely a long one, dating back only to 1969. It was inaugurated to provide competition for professional or semi-professional clubs outside the Football League. These clubs were not, of course, able to enter the Amateur Challenge Cup, and the Challenge Trophy now gave a whole stratum of clubs a realistic chance of an appearance in a Wembley final.

When the status of "amateur" was abolished by the FA Council and the Amateur Cup discontinued as a result in 1974, it heralded a new interest and keenness for the Trophy competition. It became the premier non-League knock-out Cup and now included a hundred or so of the leading clubs who had previously played in the Amateur Cup. A number of these clubs had achieved some measure of fame – for example Barnet, Bishop Auckland, Crook Town and Hendon.

The impact made by these ex-"amateur" teams was not great in the first two years of their participation in the new competition, but the semi-final draw in 1977 which paired Dagenham and Slough Town ensured a first appearance in the Final for a club from the Amateur Cup. The integration was complete in 1980, with Dagenham's victory over Mossley, and then merely emphasised in the following year with Bishop's Stortford and Sutton United providing an all-Isthmian League Final.

It seems unlikely that the attendances at Trophy finals will ever match those huge Amateur Cup final gates, particularly those in the 1950s, and the present record for the Trophy is 32,000 – in 1979. Clearly there is a great deal of public interest in the Trophy competition, although publicity for it in the national newspapers is scarcely extensive, and it is interesting to note that the Final is regularly played before a larger crowd than at something like thirty Football League matches played on the same afternoon. Usually, of course, the size of the Final gate depends on the sort of home attendances that the two competing clubs are regularly able to draw.

Last April saw the Challenge Vase Final contested for the tenth time. The Vase effectively replaced the Amateur Cup in 1974 and – with the most successful Amateur Cup clubs switching to the Trophy – this second new competition provided the remaining clubs with an opportunity to grab the headlines and, of course, to play at Wembley, which they had scarcely had before.

The Vase finalists have comprised a cross-section of clubs – some long established, some recently formed — from many different areas of the country and for many the Vase has been the springboard for further success.

For five years after the abolition of the distinction between "amateur" and "professional" there had been no opportunity for players outside the Football League to earn international honours. In an endeavour to fill the gap, the Football Associaton undertook in 1979 to organise a quadrangular international tournament for semi-professional (and non-League) players and invited Scotland, Italy and Holland to send teams.

More players are now playing football in England than ever before and England's semi-professional team managed by FA Regional Coach Keith Wright is the representative side that represents 98 per cent of them. The team has enjoyed much success in the Four Nations Tournament, now an annual event, with three first places since 1979.

My interest in Non-League football started when Kingstonians, from my home town Kingston-on-Thames, were involved in the Amateur Cup Final of 1933. I remember sitting on my father's shoulders in the Market Square, along with many thousands of other people, welcoming the team back with the Amateur Cup, which they won in the Final against Stockton in Darlington.

One of my most pleasant football memories were the many matches that I played for Kingstonians in the Isthmian League. Before and after my time with Charlton Athletic in their First Division days, I played for Dartford and, much later, for Kidderminster Harriers and Headington in the Southern League, so I have strong personal memories of Non-League football and I am, therefore, especially pleased that this level of football has now become structured in a way that has added a great deal of interest to the many players, officials and supporters of this level of football. I am sure that the prospects for the future are extremely bright and I hope that the tendency will be for more players to play for their local teams, to avoid the expensive and unnecessary travel at present indulged in and the clubs themselves will become the focal point of the football development in their district.

TED CROKER
General Secretary,
The Football Association

TEN YEARS OF THE VASE

It is barely credible that today sees the Challenge Vase Final contested for the tenth time as it seems only yesterday that the Steering Committee was appointed to set up a new competition to replace the Amateur Challenge Cup, which the abolition of the amateur status had condemned to an early grave. I wonder how many of the fifteen clubs to have appeared at Wembley so far would have honestly predicted such an occurrence before the inauguration of the Vase. Certainly, the finalists have comprised a cross-section of clubs, some long established, some of recent formation, from many different areas of the country and for many the Vase has been the spring-board for further success.

The first-ever Final in 1975, paired Spartan Leaguers Hoddesdon Town, approaching their centenary, and Epsom and Ewell of the Surrey Senior who had recently experienced their share of problems off the field. However, Manager Pat O'Connoll (Ex-Fulham) had gathered together an exciting team including Tommy Tuite, now at Carshalton Athletic and approaching a career total of 400 goals, and Trevor Lee and Phil Walker, who soon joined Millwall. On the day Hoddesdon proved the more solid outfit and Dick Sedgwick's two goals were answered only by a late effort from Wales.

The following season saw Epsom's Semi-Final victims, Stamford, go one better at the expense of Friar Lane Old Boys who thus failed again at the last hurdle. The Lincolnshire outfit were unfortunate to meet Billericay Town (Essex Senior) who had enjoyed a brief but successful senior career and were blessed with a huge following of faithful supporters. In a match in which defences were generally in command, Stamford believed they had it won with Dick Walpole's 'goal' until they spotted the Linesman flagging for offside. In the event, Geoff Aslett notched Billericay's extra time winner.

Over fifteen thousand spectators witnessed Billericay's 1977 return to Wembley, where they met Sheffield of the Yorkshire League, the oldest Football Club in the world having been formed in 1857. Although Clayden wiped out skipper Coughlan's own goal, the Essex side could not clinch victory and needed a replay at Nottingham Forest to retain the Vase by a 2-1 margin. Few people would have bet against Billericay making it three in a row but Barton Rovers (South Midlands), the previous season's defeated Semi-Finalists and another relatively 'young' club, edged them out and went on to meet Wearsiders Blue Star in the Final. Both sides had an attacking pedigree and did not disappoint the 16,300 crowd with Barry Dunn's volley equalising for Blue Star after Smith had opened the scoring. The North Eastern side squandered a penalty before Crumplin's 46th goal of the season won the day.

Once again in 1979 the previous year's beaten Semi-Finalists, Almondsbury Greenway, this time made the final, but their domination of the Gloucester County League counted for little as they met Billericay in front of a seventeen thousand five hundred gate, which is still a Vase record. The latter's greater experience proved decisive and Dougie Young notched a hat-track as they recorded a 4-1 victory under the guidance of Manager Colin Searle, who had taken over from John Newman, architect of the Club's earlier triumphs.

The only FA Vase Final hat trick was scored by Douggie Young for Billericay Town against Almondsbury Greenway in 1979. Here he hooks in his second goal. Photo: Evening Echo

Billericay were to have one more season in the Vase before their League status qualified them for the Trophy and their Quarter-Final defeat by Hungerford Town made the latter favourites. However, Guisborough Town, another club with very little history, had other ideas and went on to tackle Stamford the 1976 finalists. The Northern Alliance side gambled on the fitness of key striker McElvaney but he had already been replaced when Alexander and McGowan grabbed the second half goals that took the Vase back to Lincolnshire.

Both the 1981 finalists had battled through from the Preliminary Rounds and Rainworth MW had put themselves in the record books with a Semi-Final gate in excess of five thousand. The Notts side started brightly but the Hellenic team Forest Green Rovers were full of experience and used the Wembley spaces to great effect with the gangling Leach adding two more to his impressive tally so that they had the Vase won even before Skipper Norman's chipped third goal.

1982 produced a thrilling affair as Willenhall of the West Midlands League scored twice in eleven minutes through Smith and Stringer, before Whickham full-back Scott pulled one back six minutes later. Shortly after Willenhall lost 'keeper Newton through injury, replacing him first with leading scorer Matthews and then Woodhall. Wearside pressure eventually paid off with Williamson's goal and extra time was required. Whickham's winner was a miss-hit clearance by Peck who deserved a better fate, but both teams produced 120 minutes of first-rate entertainment for the fans.

Last season's all-Midland clash was absorbing rather than exciting as hot favourites Halesowen Town were handicapped by an injury to Joinson twin, Lee, limiting their fire power. Nevertheless, VS Rugby, in existence for less than thirty years, were the better team when it mattered even if Crawley's 47th minute winner was hardly the fiercest of shots. Likewise, neither Stamford nor Stanstead will complain if today's all-important goal is not the finest ever seen at the Stadium!

ADRIAN TITCOMBE

This article was first published in the official FA Vase programme for last year's final at Wembley.

Brian Lee, Chairman of Wycombe Wanderers and Director of Bisham Abbey.

BRIDGING THE GAP (OR US AND THEM!)

As we go into the second half of the 1980's it is interesting to look back before looking forward. The reorganisation of non Football League football or senior football outside The Football League has been like a ten thousand metre athletics race in the Olympic Trials; it is all been done on the last lap. After a slow ponderous start the qualifying time was done in the end but will it be enough to qualify? You see Clubs outside The Football League have done their preparation, they have run the opening laps with thought and planning and on the insistance of others have completed the last lap in reorganisation — but will they qualify?

There are still some old runners in The Football League, some Clubs who have produced good times in the past but not now, yet they still get selected for the big race. Reputations as runners in the end are not enough because "the legs go" and in soccer terms it is usually the financial legs that go. At the moment though it is an unfair race because there are different starting places and starting times — it is not surprising that the final selection is a bit suspect. 'Suspect' may not be the right word it really is irrational I suppose.

Ambition and opportunity are two vital ingredients in life; both have to be tempered with common sense and available resources. A race is objective, you can always gauge the winner, even against a world record, with some degree of comfort and satisfaction. Our game is a combination of objectivity in terms of the results and subjectivity in assessing the quality of the competitors. At the same time it is difficult to reward or acknowledge ambition if there are no opportunities. It is a bit like the game itself, soccer is a skilful game to be played fairly (within the spirit and rules stated) but if you do not play the game fairly you cannot play it skilfully.

We have reached an impasse outside The Football League because opportunities for the ambitious Clubs are continually being stifled. Is it just, is it in the interest of the game, is it in the interests of the Clubs? I can pose several questions and from the outside, there only seems one answer — No.

Up and down the Country, Clubs have been pushed to improve the standard of their grounds, many at considerable expense, and they have organised themselves, some at considerable pain, into a progressive structured ladder. This 'feeder League' system was established to provide opportunities and reward ambition both on and off the playing field. It provides a total promotion and relegation system until you reach the top of the Gola Alliance League. Within this system a small club from the bottom providing it satisfied strict criteria can reach the top of the Alliance.

What then? It is back to our athletics race. One or two runners unable to stand the pace have been forced to drop out and sadly have not come back to run again in the same race. It is those runners who have influenced all the others since once they drop out they cannot get back no matter what their improvement. In a race, runners get over cramp or a pulled hamstring and can run again at the highest level but in our game they simply do not return nowadays.

As I said, it is the Clubs that dropped out that paint the picture for The Football League, fear that if it happens to us it could be all over. None of the deposed Clubs from The Football League in the last decade or so (Barrow, Southport, Gateshead) have been in a position to rechallenge for *their* rightful place. This does not, of course, include Bradford P.A. or Accrington Stanley who suffered worse fates.

If they had reorganised, won the Gola Alliance League and wanted to bounce back, would not that have helped the other Football League Clubs to realise that it is not the end of the World in being relegated from the Fourth Division? It appears that it is the *former* Football League Clubs who have let Non-League Football down by not being in a position to reapply for election to the Football League from outside the Football League although they succeeded several times from within the Football League before finally losing their places.

So much has been written about the expense of competing in the lower Football League divisions but there are progressive, well structured Clubs outside who are ambitious and want the opportunity to play in The Football League. It is the best League in the World, we are proud that it is English and all Clubs should have the dream to play in it but it does not make us proud to be English in running what is virtually a closed competition. Why should it be a failure or disgrace to be relegated if the opportunity is there to come back?

What more do the Gola Alliance League have to do? What more do Altrincham or Maidstone United have to do? Why cannot the Football League accept and help to bridge the gap? What have they to be afraid of?

The severest standards off the field can be set, progressive and established criteria can be met but in the end it should be the race that really matters. As I said the race should be one of skill to be played fairly but unless you do play fairly you cannot show your skill. But it could, at least, be a fair race!

ARE MOTORWAYS THE SOLUTION?

Critics of the Football League's lower echelons are constantly referring to the financial suicide of long journeys between Clubs. From Exeter to Hartlepool or Portsmouth to Newcastle may not be desirable but what about the Gola Alliance League. Does Maidstone to Barrow or Gateshead to Yeovil differ?

The only difference is that the Football League Clubs are full-time and, therefore, able to do it with time on their hands whilst the Gola Alliance League Clubs engage part-time players.

If arguments have been put to regionalise the Football League divisions, would it not be sensible, or even more sensible, to regionalise the Gola Alliance League? A logical step would be in the Football League Division Three North and South and in the Gola Alliance League a similar North and South split.

Whilst British Rail and new motorways help, there can be no denying the extra cost in money and time that threatens the financial future of many Football League Clubs and Gola Alliance League Clubs. Is a crystal ball really necessary for financial sanity to prevail or will the game continue to tread a critical path until the critical point is reached?

ANON.

CONFESSIONS OF A GROUNDHOPPER/ TRAVELLER

It was January 5th 1974 and Millwall, my main passion in life for the past fifteen years or so, had just held mighty Scunthorpe, bottom of Division Four, to a 1-1 draw in the FA Cup Third Round tie at 'The Den'. What added insult to injury was the fact that Millwall's equaliser looked highly dubious, the ball appearing to go out of play before Derek Possee crossed to Alf Wood who thumped the ball home. Justice was seen to be done when Scunthorpe won the replay and I remember thinking at the time – 'football *must* give me more pleasure than this lot are giving us long-suffering fans at present'.

Now I'd always been a fan of the non-League game. My Grandfather had taken me to see Bromley play Dulwich Hamlet in the late fifties and indeed I hardly missed a Bromley home game in 1959-60. The 'pull' of professional football took me back to the 'Den' and Charlton's 'Valley' in subsequent seasons, but I always sneaked into the odd non-League match and well remember Barnet beating Enfield in front of an 8,000 crowd in the FA Cup, 1964/5 season. Barnet were always worth watching and in the early seventies impressed me enough to want to watch them away. It was great fun. I got to know the players, a tremendous bunch (all with a great sense of humour), and it gave me a real kick going to places like Bath, Gloucester and even what I considered a real outpost at the time, Lowestoft, in the FA Cup.

After the Millwall-Scunthorpe debacle, I recalled what fun non-League soccer had been, and decided that on the following Saturday I would travel down to the New Forest to see Brockenhurst play St. Albans in an FA Amateur Cup replay. What a day! Fine beer and Lunch at the 'Morrant Arms' right outside the station, a crowd of 1,000 standing three deep round the pitch, a great atmosphere as Brockenhurst won 2-0, a new programme for my collection and not a hooligan in sight – all for 20p admission plus 5p for the programme! That was it – I was well-hooked! Non-League soccer was in my life to stay.

Having always liked the West Country, I took a fit into my head to watch Taunton play Glastonbury in the Western League at the end of 1973-74 and to my embarrassment was confronted by two journalists and a photographer from the local press. I could not have handled that every week; to me I was just doing a hobby I wanted to do, but Taunton Town FC saw things differently and I was treated to a day I'll never forget. The people who run clubs like this are the salt of the earth. I was always welcome to travel with the team if Taunton were playing away and the same happened with Bodmin Town FC when I attempted an 'assault' on the South-Western League. Other amazing experiences include getting completely 'stoned' with the Blyth Spartans players when they had won the Northern League title in 1976, seeing a Halesowen player 'booked' for leaving the field without permission after he had gone behind the goal to sort out one or two yobbos who were aiming missiles at his goalkeeper, having drink upon drink bought me at Gretna after one evening match this season and (before you all drop off to sleep) being invited to stay with the parents of the Blaenrhondda FC chairman when I did a 'double-header' (ie: two new grounds in a weekend) in that area last February.

Besides meeting club officials there have been other spin-offs from this hobby which is not as unusual these days as one might think. For instance, I met my long-suffering and thoroughly understanding wife, Gloria, in a pub prior to my attending a game at Barton Town (South Humberside). A man with a beard and glasses, better known as Wembley press officer Pete(r) Burrin, crossed my path in the waiting room at Ewell West station after a game at Epsom & Ewell and we've been mates ever since.

There are a host of other 'travellers' with whom I've become very friendly and it's all down to the marvellous world of non-League soccer.

So, after ten years on the circuit, I still get a big kick out of visiting a new ground each week. The intimacy which is lacking in the 'big-time', the new programmes, the enjoyable brand of football – still serious but not life and death – the travel, lack of thuggery, the quality food at the grounds which won't put you on the sick list for a month etc. These reasons and more I hope will explain to a few of you just why I, and others, spend so much time and money on our beloved sport.

MICK BURT

Non-League Photographs of the Year

Once again we received a vast number of photographs covering all levels of football outside The Football League and may I stress that we can never have too many. Our regular 'loonies' Mike Joss and Leo Hoenig must have covered the length and breadth of the country a few times over and their efforts are particularly appreciated.

Eric Marsh has also had a great season in the home counties and other much valued helpers are Peter Burrin, David Shute and Stan Allen, while the FA's official photographer Bob Thomas always provides top quality work.

However, the winner of this year's 'Best Action Photograph of Football outside 'The Football League' was sent to us by Maidenhead United and was taken by Chris Forsey. Chris caught United's Lance Cadogan beautifully balanced and about to crash a goal past Aveley's goalkeeper Dave Cass. Dave has come out to narrow the angle and his eyes are fixed on the ball while the covering defender looks on apprehensively. The photo catches all the goalscoring tension and the exciting action that gives us special moments to remember.

There cannot be anything in football more thrilling than scoring at Wembley and if that goal is probably making victory safe then what could be better? Here Eric Marsh shows us a jubilant John Reading, celebrating colleagues, bemused Stamford defenders and the ecstatic Stansted supporters. A wonderfully happy and exciting photo which wins the award for 'The Most Exciting Photograph of The Year'.

The Highly Recommended section this year concentrated on some great headed efforts and a couple of spectacular volleys.

The above photo isn't a particularly clear one as it was taken under floodlights but this header crashed in with unbelievable force by Harrow Borough's centre half David Howell from a driven corner was the most exciting goal I saw last season and the FA Cup replay with Fisher Athletic was certainly one of the best games that I was lucky enough to see.

On the left: Another Harrow Borough goal and this time from ace scorer George Duck who shows perfect timing, balance and power to score one of his side's nine FA Cup goals against Ware. This photo was taken by one of last year's winners, S. Allen.

A fine action shot from Mike Joss shows a flying effort by Mark Heeley for Aylesbury United just misses during his side's 3-3 League Cup draw with Milton Keynes City.

Above: Another player who regularly features amongst the goalscorers is Lewes forward Pip Parris. Here, Wembley fanatic Peter Burrin catches him volleying in mid-air as keeper Fred Smart looks on aprehensively.

Right: This photo by Oxford's Mike Allen wasn't taken last season, in fact I found it amongst some old files, but it was such a good action shot of the players both keeping their eye on the ball at Oxford City's White House ground that I thought it worth including.

Below: Weston-super-Mare replayed their drawn First Qualifying Round Trophy match on a mid-week afternoon and sure enough a large number of 'loonies' turned up to visit a new ground. In this excellent photo Eric Marsh shows a fine volleyed effort by a home forward just about to scrape the bar but Weston went on to win.

These two photographs were also worthy of some type of awards, as above, Bob Thomas's picture of Tommy Robson, who had played his heart out for Stamford, walks slowly away from the celebrating Stansted throng and this photo says more than any words could ever describe.

Some people will know why the photo below appeals to me! It's a goal for Hungerford Town and little Kevin Bright has just slid in to convert a 'knock down' from centre half Martin Turner against Molesey. Celebrations too from Simon Pentland while the Chairman and vice chairman take it all in their stride on the touchline!

Photo: Newbury Weekly News

INTERNATIONAL AND F.A. REPRESENTATIVE FOOTBALL

FA REPRESENTATIVE MATCHES

Match Committee: B. Mulrenan, Chairman; C. G. Oakes, Vice-Chairman; A. W. Brett; E. A. Brown; B. Clark; F. Hannam; Lt Cdr H. A. Sheppard; C. H. Wilcox.

As usual the Football Association completed a full programme of representative matches last season, and England manager Keith Wright and his assistant Kevin Verity were able to see many England possibles playing alongside 'strangers' in these FA XIs. It's certainly not easy to excel in representative football.

Three players who obviously impressed when their opportunities came were Harrow goalkeeper Andy Pape, Alliance record goalscorer Paul Culpin from Nuneaton Borough, and his team mate Trevor Morley, all of whom forced their way into the England squad for the first time.

However, the most spectacular success in the FA games last season as far as goalscoring was concerned must have been that of Steve Price, Almondsbury Greenway's star forward, who scored six goals in two and a half games.

Two other records were achieved during the season; the FA beat the Combined Services for the first time (ironically in the season that the Services recorded a brilliant Kentish Cup success) and the attendance at Barrow for the FA's game against the Northern Premier League was a record 647.

Wales beat England 2-1

In their first ever meeting at Semi-Professional level, Wales recorded beat England by the odd goal in three with their winner coming in the 86th minute from substitute Paul Hughes. This defeat was only the second ever for the England team at this level (the first was by Scotland in the second four nations tournament).

Keith Wright selected all the uncapped players in the squad but the team still contained plenty of experience and the Welsh victory was a surprise, although on the night the home side looked to be the more determined.

John Davison skippered England for the first time and when John Watson, last season's captain, came on as substitute they had both won a record fifteen 'caps'.

Brian Thompson sustained a nasty neck injury when acrobatically clearing off his goalline but England took the lead when Runcorn's Ossie Smith scored after 38 minutes. However, the Welsh hit back just before half time through Andy Jones and then, with just four minutes left of a scrappy second half, Wales snatched a winner amongst much jubilation in the 1,500 at the well appointed Newtown ground.

Wales: Nott (Maesteg), Redwood (Barry), Rogers (Barry), Jones, B. (Colwyn Bay), Griffiths (Barry), Morgan (Aberystwyth), Sullivan (Barry), Love (Merthyr Tydfil), Jones, A. (Rhyl), Fisher (Merthyr Tydfil).
Substitutes: Smith (Bangor) for Morgan and Hughes (Aberystwyth) for Jones, B.

England: Richardson (Maidstone United), Thompson (Maidstone United), Robinson (Blyth Spartans), Newson (Maidstone United), Davison (Altrincham), Smith (Runcorn), Morley (Nuneaton Borough), Ironton (Maidstone United), Cordice, A. (Wealdstone), Culpin (Nuneaton Borough), Ashford (Enfield).
Substitutes: Barrett (Enfield) for Thompson and Watson (Maidstone) for Ironton.

FA Representative Matches 1983-84

FA XI 0 v Middlesex County FA 0
Bowtell (Fisher Athletic), Thompson (Maidstone United), Scales (Dagenham), McAyna (Leytonstone-Ilford), Ahern (Harlow Town), Watson (Maidstone United), Crown (Barking), Dunwell (Dagenham), Bartley (Maidstone United), Stephens, Joyce (Sutton United). Substitutes: Collyer (Sutton United) for Bowtell, Margerison (Barnet) for Watson, Hill (Wycombe Wanderers) for Thompson and Dingwall (Maidstone United) for McAyna).

FA XI 2 (Sutton, Rowland) v South West Counties 3
Hards (Gloucester City), Collins (Liskeard), Pluckrose (Saltash United), Manley (Barnstaple Town), Steele (Dorchester), Batley, Thompson (Saltash United), McKelvaney (Frome Town), Rowland (Exmouth Town), Sutton (Bridgwater Town), Burford (Gloucester City). Substitutes: Evans (Trowbridge Town) for Thompson, Penwill (Saltash United) for Collins, Palmer (Barnstaple Town) for Hards and Hook (Exmouth) for Burford.

FA XI 7 (Price 3, Freegard, Sheahan, Farr, Kelly) v Oxford University 2
Teasdale (Devizes Town), Down (Bristol Manor Farm), Herring (Park), Kelly (Fairford Town), Kanes (Clanfield), Simmons (Mangotsfield United), Sheahan (Almondsbury Greenway), Freegard (Chippenham Town), Moore (Yate Town), Price (Almondsbury Greenway). Substitutes: Farr (Hungerford Town) for Moore, Alexander (Oxford City) for Kanes, Neves (Supermarine) for Herring, Hatter (Devizes Town) for Simmons, Haines (Highworth) for Teasdale.

FA XI 0 v Cambridge University 2
Cobbold (Sudbury Town), Winter (Eynesbury Rovers), Thorpe (Brantham Athletic), Hubbard, Hancocks (Cambridge City), Brett (St. Andrews), Salkeld (Combined Services), Sutton (Wroxham), Rider (Great Shelford), Mead (Dunstable Town). Substitutes: Sarll (Arlesey Town) for Cobbold, Lill (Somersham Town) for Thorpe, and Kier (Yaxley) for Brett.

FA XI 4 (Price 2, Morley, Culpin) v British Polytechnics Sports Association 2
Ogden (Cheltenham Town), Peacock (Bedworth United), McGrath (Worcester City), Glover (Nuneaton Borough), Brennan (Worcester City), Sheahan (Almondsbury Greenway), Abbley (Witney Town), Moss (Worcester City), Culpin (Nuneaton Borough). Substitutes: Price (Almondsbury Greenway) for Moss, Seacole (Witney Town) for Abbley, Collicutt (Cheltenham Town) for Cornes.

FA XI 4 (Goodwin, Lamb, Lane, Groom) v London University 1
M. Taylor (Woodford Town), Anderson (Heybridge Swifts), Cooper (Stansted), Gregory (Woodford Town), Sammons (Grays Athletic), Groom (Heybridge Swifts), Doyle (Stansted), Lane (Leyton-Wingate), G. Taylor (Grays Athletic), Goodwin (Leyton-Wingate), Lamb (Heybridge Swifts). Substitute: Galder (Grays Athletic) for M. Taylor.

FA XI 3 (Price, Emmanuel, Culpin) v Oxford County FA 1
Pape (Harrow Borough), Corbin (Wokingham Town), Mackay (Sutton United), McMahon (Wokingham Town), Glover (Nuneaton Borough), Peacock (Bedworth United), Docker (Barnet), Emmanuel (Harrow Borough), Morley, Culpin (Nuneaton Borough), Price (Almondsbury Greenway). Substitute: Sheahan (Almondsbury Greenway) for McMahon.

FX XI 5 (Smith 2, Johnson, Heathcote, Davison) v Universities Athletic Union 0
Dance, Constantine, Davison (Altrincham), Barnett (Telford United), Cuddy, Johnson (Altrincham), Meachin (Marine), Smith (Runcorn), Williams (Telford United), Heathcote (Altrincham), Whelan (Witton Albion). Substitutes: Roberts (Runcorn) for Whelan and Smith (Witton Albion) for Barnett.

Past F.A. XI Results 1975-84

FA XI 0 v Northern Premier League 2
Clarke, Robinson (Blyth Spartans), Smith (Witton Albion), Gardner, Johnson (Altrincham), Scaife, Stirk (Blyth Spartans), Heathcote (Altrincham), Reid, Chesters (Northwich Victoria), Carroll (North Shields). Substitutes: Ross (North Shields) for Chesters and Davison (Altrincham) for Smith.

FA XI 0 v Drybroughs Northern League 1
Evans (Burton Albion), Casey (Boston United), Vaughan (Burton Albion), Lukasic (Matlock Town) Taylor (Gainsborough Trinity), Gill (Stafford Rangers), Adams (Worksop Town), Carr (Stafford Rangers), Gauden (Gainsborough Trinity), Wadsworth (Barnsley), Fisher (Stafford Rangers). Substitutes: Malcolm (Chester-le-Street) for Evans, Moore (Worksop Town) for Gauden and Mountain (Matlock Town) for Fisher.

FA XI 3 (Pearce 2, Watson) v Combined Services 2
Pape (Harrow Borough), Corbin (Wokingham Town), Kinnear (Barnet), Howell (Harrow Borough), Pittaway, Stein (Barnet), Watson (Maidstone United), Docker (Barnet), Crown (Barking), Pearce (Harrow Borough), Church (Uxbridge). Substitute: Duff (Uxbridge) for Pittaway.

FA XI v Cambridge University

			FA XI	CU
1976/77	Cambridge Utd.	W	1	0
1977/78	Cambridge Utd.	W	4	0
1978/79	Cambridge Utd.	W	6	1
1979/80	Cambridge City	W	2	1
1980/81	Cambridge City	D	1	1
1981/82	Cambridge Utd.	D	1	1
1982/83	Cambridge City	L	1	2
1983/84	Cambridge Utd.	L	0	2

F.A. XI v London University

			FA XI	LU
1975/76	Kingstonian	W	4	1
1976/77	Wealdstone	W	3	0
1977/78	Met. Police	W	2	0
1978/79	Harrow Borough	W	5	1
1979/80	Hayes	W	3	0
1980/81	Sutton Utd.	W	3	1
1982/83	Tooting & M	W	7	0
1983/84	Dagenham	W	4	1

F.A. XI v British Colleges Sports Association

			FA XI	BC
1975/76	Cheltenham T.	L	0	1
1976/77	Cheltenham T.	W	4	0
1977/78	Cheltenham T.	L	0	1
1979/80	Stafford Rangers	W	2	0
1980/81	Cancelled due to bad weather			
1981/82	Nuneaton B.	W	4	3
1982/83	York City	W	4	1
1983/84	Cheltenham T.	W	4	2

FA XI v Oxford University

			FA XI	OU
1976/77	Oxford Utd.	W	1	0
1977/78	Oxford Utd.	W	4	0
1978/79	Oxford City	W	3	1
1979/80	Oxford City	W	6	1
1980/81	Witney Town	W	3	1
1981/82	Oxford City	L	0	2
1982/83	Oxford City	W	7	0
1983/84	Oxford City	W	7	2

F.A. XI v Northern League

			FA XI	NL
1976/77	Blyth Spartans	L	2	3
1977/78	Consett	L	2	3
1978/79	North Shields	L	0	2
1979/80	Blyth Spartans	L	1	3
1980/81	Consett	D	0	0
1981/82	North Shields	W	2	0
1982/83	Bishop Auckland	D	1	1
1983/84	Darlington	L	0	1

F.A. XI v British Police

			FA XI	BP
1979/80	Bramshill	D	1	1
1980/81	Bramshill	W	1	0
1982/83	Bramshill	W	2	0

F.A. XI v Northern Premier League

			FA XI	NPL
1980/81	Runcorn	D	0	0
1981/82	Gainsborough T.	D	1	1
1982/83	Burton Albion	D	3	3
1983/84	Barrow	L	0	2

F.A. XI v Amateur Football Alliance

			FA XI	AFA
1975/76	Dulwich	W	4	0
1976/77	Leytonstone	D	2	2
1977/78	Wealdstone	W	4	1
1978/79	Met. Police	W	5	2
1979/80	Met. Police	W	2	1
1980/81	Met. Police	W	5	1
1981/82	Harrow Borough	D	1	1
1982/83	Enfield	W	2	1

F.A. XI v Universities Athletic Union

			FA XI	UAU
1975/76	York City	D	2	2
1976/77	York City	D	2	2
1977/78	Altrincham	W	2	1
1978/79	Altrincham	D	1	1
1979/80	Altrincham	W	4	2
1980/81	Cancelled due to weather			
1981/82	Altrincham	W	3	0
1982/83	Nuneaton B	W	4	0
1983/84	Altrincham	W	5	0

F.A. XI v Combined Services

			FA XI	CS
1976/77	Army Stadium	D	2	2
1977/78	Aldershot	D	1	1
1978/79	Aldershot	D	1	1
1979/80	Aldershot	L	1	2
1980/81	Aldershot	D	1	1
1982/83	Aldershot	L	0	2
1983/84	Aldershot	W	3	2

F.A. XI v Royal Air Force

			FA XI	RAF
1975/76	Wealdstone	W	2	1

F.A. XI v South West Counties

			FA XI	SWC
1977/78	Exeter City	L	0	1
1978/79	Southampton	W	1	0
1979/80	Bath City	W	5	1
1981/82	Swindon	W	2	1
1983/84	Southampton	L	2	3

F.A. XI v Isthmian League

			FA XI	IL
1979/80	Dagenham	L	0	3

F.A. XI v Western League

			FA XI	WL
1980/81	Frome Town	D	0	0
1982/83	Frome Town	D	2	2

F.A. XI v Jersey F.A.

			FA XI	JFA
1980/81	St. Helier	W	3	0

F.A. XI v Lincolnshire F.A.

			FA XI	LFA
1980/81	Boston Utd.	D	0	0

F.A. XI v Middlesex F.A.

			FA XI	MCFA
1983/84	Harrow Borough		0	0

F.A. XI v Oxfordshire F.A.

			FA XI	OCFA
1983/84	Oxford City		3	1

England Semi-Professional Squad v Wales — March 27
Back Row (L-R): Derek Richardson (Maidstone Utd), Peter Robinson (Blyth Spartans), Colin Williams (Telford Utd), Nick Ironton (Maidstone Utd), Keith Barrett (Enfield), Trevor Morley (Nuneaton Borough), Derek Clarke (Blyth Spartans). Centre: Adrian Titcombe (admin officer), Ossie Smith (Runcorn), Noel Ashford (Enfield), Paul Culpin (Nuneaton Borough), Mark Newson (Maidstone Utd), Dr. Arthur Tabor (physician). Front Row: Brian Thompson (Maidstone Utd), Keith Wright (manager), John Watson (Maidstone Utd), John Davison (Altrincham), Kevin Verity (asst manager), Alan Cordice (Wealdstone).

After a disappointing result in Wales, Keith Wright's final tour selection included three uncapped players at this level. Two from Servowarm Isthmian champions Harrow Borough, goalkeeper Andy Pape and striker David Pearce and Peter Taylor the ex England, Crystal Palace and Tottenham Hotspur winger who is now with Maidstone United.

Eleven of last year's successful squad were retained plus Mark Newson and Trevor Morley who played in Wales. Paul Culpin was not available for selection as he was contracted to play in Finland during the summer and many considered Runcorn's Ossie Smith unlucky to miss the tour narrowly.

Only four players were selected from clubs outside the Alliance Premier League with two from Blyth Spartans and two from Harrow Borough while Maidstone United had most players selected (4) and Enfield and Altrincham also had two players in the squad.

Goalkeepers: David Clarke (Blyth Spartans), Andy Pape (Harrow Borough).
Defenders: Keith Barrett (Enfield), Peter Robinson (Blyth Spartans), Mark Newson (Maidstone United), Brian Thompson (Maidstone United), John Davison (Altrincham).
Mid Field: Neil Sellers (Scarborough), John Watson (Maidstone United), Trevor Morley (Nuneaton Borough), Jeff Johnson (Altrincham).
Forwards: Alan Cordice (Wealdstone), Noel Ashford (Enfield), Colin Williams (Telford United), David Pearce (Harrow Borough), Peter Taylor (Maidstone United).

A Memorable Week for us all

How many times have we read about tourists representing their countries at various sports getting into trouble in hotels with guests, with shopkeepers, barmen and indeed at times with each other.

Until one spends some time with a bunch of sportsmen in a country where English isn't readily understood, under the pressure of an International tournament, it may be difficult to understand why any such upsets should occur.

However with the touring party made up of all types of characters stuck together in a hotel for a week the onus is well and truly on the administrators to keep the party busy and happy. This was done superbly by The Football Association staff on behalf of the England Semi-Professional side in Italy and for this Adrian Titcombe must be congratulated in particular.

Selection is half the secret; however, whether it is the FA Representative Committee's selection of the coaching staff or indeed the coaching staff's selection of the touring party, both are reflected by the atmosphere of the week.

Keith Wright and Kevin Verity have always been loyal to players who have played well for England so their touring squad included few surprises although the two late replacements David Pearce and Anton Joseph may not have expected their selection.

For me, the most impressive aspects of the week, accepting that the preparation organised by the managers was again second to none, was the way the players kept their heads after some tough 'treatment' from the opposition and some very frustrating refereeing.

In the final match there seemed to be no way England were going to be allowed even into dangerous attacking positions, as every sort of infringement was spotted as England moved into the home side's half.

The fact that the referee pulled up the England players for shouting to each other (in Italy players may be penalised for any sort of talking on the field!) must have been so frustrating in a match of such importance. And all credit must go to the players for keeping 'their cool' at all times despite conceding a goal with thirty five minutes in which to battle against some very well practised time wasting.

Three England supporters, Darren Lovell and Barry Fenn from Maidstone and Martin Woodall who has worked hard for Kettering over the years, all gave the team excellent support and the lads also appreciated the enthusiastic coverage submitted to 'The Daily Star' by Paul Walker who has also kindly contributed two excellent features for this directory.

It was a happy week for everyone and even Andy Pape, who didn't win a cap on the tour, showed commendable spirit by never showing his natural disappointment in public.

I cannot imagine a more enjoyable holiday for any Non League Football follower and I am sure all those who travelled to Italy will meet up again in Holland next year.

Despite all the happy moments on the tour, however, it is a very moving memory that will probably stay with me for ever. As the final whistle went and the Italians celebrated their first Four Nations success the sight of the England players lost, forlorn and both physically and mentally shattered was too much for me. I will certainly admit to a few tears as all of us in the stand felt so hopeless at a time when the lads needed consolation.

Those of you who have played, managed or fanatically supported know what I mean!

Tony Williams

England lose the trophy but not their pride

By Paul Walker, Daily Star

Four Nations Tournament, Modena, Italy, June 5-9

England's semi-professional squad returned from Italy in June, having lost the Four Nations Trophy . . . but not their pride.

The non-league game can be justly proud of the party's dedication, commitment to their country and immaculate behaviour on and off the field.

The week-long tournament, staged on three excellent Third Division grounds — Palma, Modena and Reggio Emilia just outside Bologna, brewed up into a classic confrontation between the hosts and the holders on the last night.

Their squad was the cream of their Third Division, including many young men destined, or already signed, for Italy's giants.

Roared on by several thousand fans at Reggio Emilia, the Italians forced England to defend for much of the first half, but could have been a goal down near the break when Trevor Morley mishit after a fine four man move.

Ten minutes into the second half the Italians scored the only goal, when the pacy Pietro Puzone crossed from the left for Roberto Bordin to score from six yards.

England fought gallently for the goal that would have given them a draw, and the cup. Strikers Alan Cordice and David Pearce were thrown into the non-stop bombardment of the now virtually static Italian defence.

Cordice had one shot handled in the box . . . only to be penalised for high kicking! That was just one of an array of dubious decisions that infuriated the English contingent. The English lads were even penalised for calling for the ball!

England boss Keith Wright could have asked for no more from his brave side, but in the end the many and varied pressures of trying to win anything in Italy proved too much.

Just how much winning had meant to England was summed up at the end with skipper John Watson sobbing on assistant boss Kevin Verity's shoulder after collecting the runners-up trophy.

The knowledge that this game was the end of an era for England, with several of the older players knowing they may not play for this highly successful team again, made it a highly emotional night.

Clarke will be sadly missed. He's been England's number one 'keeper for five years and played 14 times for his country. One of non-league's true characters, he's worth a place in the squad for his humour and galvanising effect on his colleagues, alone.

Thompson played in the first tournament in '79, and also has 14 caps. A fine right back, composed and determined, he too will take some replacing!

It was against the Dutch that England opened the tournament in Palma. The game ended in a 3-3 draw, and twice England conceded a two goal lead.

Jeff Johnson, restored to the squad after being left out of the disappointing warm up defeat in Wales, justified his place with sterling displays on the left flank in all three games.

He put England ahead after only four minutes against the Dutch, and his Altrincham club mate John Davison made it two from the spot after Colin Williams had been fouled.

But a fine 20 yard drive from Edwin Goerter made it 2-1 at the break. An exceptional goal from centre back Keith Barrett — he started and finished an 80 yard move — restored the two goal advantage ten minutes after half time.

But the talented Dutch threw men forward, and in a four minute spell Roger Schouwenaar and Michel Beukers put them level.

The Scots were on next, and they battled magnificently in the face of continual provocation from the Italians to secure a deserved 0-0 draw.

Two days later in Modena, the Scots and the English clashed. Whether it's at Hampden or in a corner of Northern Italy such games mean much to all!

Scotland opened in a blaze of action, and missed several chances, but England were ahead after 35 minutes. Former Spurs star Peter Taylor — the first ever full international to win selection for the semi-pro side — produced a stunning dummy and shot, which surprisingly was given as a corner.

England made full use of the good fortune, when Williams headed in Taylor's flag kick. From then on England's better team work and composure put them in control and when Williams cleverly sent Noel Ashford through for the second it was all over. Telford's Anton Joseph came on to win his first cap as the victory was sewn up.

The Italians followed this up with a dubious 3-1 win over the Dutch. The match was seen in full on TV in the hotel the following night, and the English watched in amazement as the Dutch were 'engineered' out of a victory they deserved.

Two clear penalties were not given, a fine 20 yard free kick goal was disallowed and a string of Italian bookings — and one sending off — reduced the game to a farce.

On the last day the Dutch overcame Scotland 4-2, after being one down at the break, so the significance of their experience against the Italians was all too obvious.

England now knew just what they were up against, but their pride in wearing an England shirt almost carried them to their fourth tournament victory in six years.

A great week, then, tinged with sadness, but with the never-to-be-forgotten comradeship of true football folk the lasting memory! **PAUL WALKER, DAILY STAR**

A supporter's review of Italy '84

By Darren Lovell

"Hello lads. Great of you to come over for the week."

"That's OK Mr Wright," I said.

"No fellas, the name's Keith. Hope you have a good week."

That summed the week up for myself and travelling companion Barry Fenn. We had travelled from Maidstone to watch the 1984 Semi-Professional tournament in Italy, and before we knew it England manager Keith Wright had made us feel a little more proud to be there, and we were still only on our flight over to Milan.

Tuesday 5th June — the day of the first match for England. The weather was attrocious, but the spirit in the England party was already very strong, and it was infectious. A good day was topped off for the supporters with the offer of a lift on the team coach to and from the ground in Parma some 40 kilometres away (an offer that was to be generously repeated during the week). The lift was gratefully accepted, and already we felt a part of the squad, which in all honesty was quite unexpected, and as the week went on was very warmly appreciated.

The second game against Scotland (always a game to stir the emotions in any Englishman or Scotsman) was fascinating. The light hearted attitude so prevalent on the rest day had been professionally replaced by an insatiable urge to beat Scotland by every member of the England squad. It was very noticeable that Keith Wright and his staff (who deserve every credit for their efforts) had the ability to raise the morale and control the mood of the squad, an ability the Scots unfortunately seemed to be lacking.

Not surprisingly, once England had edged ahead in the match through Colin Williams's goal nothing was going to stop England.

The most stirring moment that week came immediately after the Italy match. Having gone 1-0 down, the team played with great character and did everything to retrieve the situation, apart from scoring a goal for the draw needed for the title.

At the final whistle the teams lined up and the trophies were presented; and it was a very touching moment when John Watson embraced Keith Wright and in turn goalkeeper Dave Clarke found it impossible to hold back the tears.

That was the true spirit and feeling in the squad. EVERY player WANTED to win for his country above everything else.

However, such was the character of the team that within a few hours the squad had turned out to a man in the hotel bar to keep the spirit of every Englishman in the party up, including two very lucky supporters, who were both very proud to be made to feel a part of the team by a group of players and officials who deserve every credit for their performances, their professionalism, their character and their generosity both on and off the field, in what was the end to a superb week for a football supporter.

The England team line up before their ill fated match in Wales. Left to right: John Davison, Brian Thompson, Noel Ashford, Alan Cordice, Ossie Smith, Peter Robinson, Mark Newsome, Derek Richardson, Paul Culpin, Nicky Ironton, Trevor Morely and substitutes on the night David Clarke, John Watson and Keith Barrett. Photo: Mike Joss

English Semi-Professional International Caps 1979-1984 (max 19)

David Adamson (Boston United) 79 v S.H. 80 v I.S.H. (5)
Jim Arnold (Stafford Rangers) 79 v S.H. (2)
Noel Ashford (Enfield) 82 v G.H.S. 83 v I.H.S. 84 v W.H.S.I. (10)
Keith Barrett (Enfield) 81 v H.S.I. 82 v G.I.H.S. 83 v I.H.S. 84 v W (sub), H.S. (13)
David Clarke (Blyth Spartans) 80 v I.S. (sub), H. 81 v H.S.I. 82 v I.H.S. 83 v H.S. 84 v H.S.I. (14)
Alan Cordice (Wealdstone) 83 v I.H.S. 84 v W.S. (sub), I. (sub) (6)
Paul Culpin (Nuneaton Borough) 84 v W. (1)
John Davison (Altrincham) 79 v S.H. 80 v I.S. 81 v H.S.I 82 v G.I.H.S. 83 v I.H.S. 84 v W.H.I.S. (18)
John Denham (Northwich Victoria) 80 v H. (1)
Phil Derbyshire (Mossley) 83 v H. (sub). S. (sub) (2)
Trevor Finnegan (Weymouth) 81 v H.S. (2)
Kenny Hill (Maidstone United) 80 v I.S.H. (3)
Keith Houghton (Blyth Spartans) 79 v S. (1)
Barry Howard (Altrincham) 81 v H.S.I. 82 v G.I.H.S. (7)
Nicky Ironton (Enfield) 83 v H. (sub) (1) 84 v W. (2)
Tony Jennings (Enfield) 79 v S.H. 80 v I.S.H. 81 v H.S.I. 82 v G.I.H.S. (12)
Jeff Johnson (Altrincham) 81 v S.I. 82 v G.I.H.S. 83 v I.H.S. 84 v H.S.I. (12)
Anton Joseph (Telford United) 84 v S. (sub) (1)
Paul Mayman (Northwich Victoria) 80 v I.S. (2)
Neil Merrick (Weymouth) 80 v I. (sub), S. (2)
Trevor Morley (Nuneaton Borough) 84 v W.H.S.I. (4)
Les Murrie (Blyth Spartans) 79 v S.H. 80 v I.S.H. (5)
Mark Newson (Maidstone United) 84 v W.H.S.I. (4)
Eamon O'Keefe (Mossley) 79 v S.H. (2)
Frank Ovard (Maidstone United) 81 v H. (sub) S. (sub) I. (sub) (3)
Brian Parker (Yeovil Town) 80 v S. (1)
Trevor Peake (Nuneaton Borough) 79 v S.H. (2)
David Pearce (Harrow Borough) 84 v I. (sub) (1)
Brendan Phillips (Nuneaton B., Kettering) 79 v S.H. 80 v S. (sub), H. (4)
Gary Phillips (Barnet) 82 v G. (1)
Derek Richardson (Maidstone United) 83 v I. 84 v W. (2)
Peter Robinson (Blyth Spartans) 83 v I.H.S. 84 v W.I. (5)
John Rogers (Altrincham) 81 v H.S.I. 82 v I. (sub), S. (5)
Neil Sellars (Scarborough) 81 v H.S.I. 82 v H. (sub), S. 83 v I.H.S. (8)
Gordon Simmonite (Boston United) 79 v S. (sub), H. (sub), 80 v I.S.H. (5)
Alan Smith (Alvechurch) 82 v G.I.S. (3)
Ian Smith (Mossley) 80 v I.S.H. (sub) (3)
Ossie Smith (Runcorn) 84 v W. (1)
Mickey Stephens (Sutton United) 82 v G.S. (sub) (2)
Bob Stockley (Nuneaton Borough) 80 v H. (1)
Brian Thompson (Yeovil Town & Maidstone United) 79 v S.H. 81 v H.S.I. 82 v I.H.S. 83 v I.H.S. 84 v W.H.S.I. (15)
David Waite (Enfield) 82 v G. (1)
Mark Ward (Northwich Victoria) 83 v S. (sub) (1)
John Watson (Wealdstone, Scarborough & Maidstone) 79 v S. (sub), H. 80 v I.S.H. 81 v H.S.I. 82 v I.H.S. 83 v I.H.S. 84 v W. (sub), H.S.I. (18)
Barry Whitbread (Runcorn, Altrincham) 79 v S.H. 80 v I.S.H. 81 v I. (6)
Colin Williams (Scarborough & Telford) 81 v H.S. 82 v I. 83 v I.H.S. 84 v H.W.I. (9)

England Goalscorers

John Davison	(Altrincham)	5 (all pens)	John Watson	(Wealdstone, Scar'bro & Maidstone U)	2
Noel Ashford	(Enfield)	4			
Colin Williams	(Scar'bro & Telford U)	4	Barry Whitbread	(Altrincham)	2
Dave Adamson	(Boston United)	3 (2 pens)	Keith Barrett	(Enfield)	1
Jeff Johnson	(Altrincham)	3	Eamonn O'Keefe	(Mossley)	1
Alan Cordice	(Wealdstone)	2	Ian Smith	(Mossley)	1
Kenny Bill	(Maidstone U)	2	Ossie Smith	(Runcorn)	1
Les Mutrie	(Blyth Spartans)	2	Kenny Stephens	(Sutton United)	1
			'Own Goal'		1

England captain John Watson, who with John Davison has won most England semi-professional International caps. Photo: Roger Price

David Clarke has showed excellent form as England's first choice goalkeeper for four years and has also lifted the side's morale as resident vocalist and dressing room character. Photo: Roger Price

FOUR NATIONS SEMI-PROFESSIONAL TOURNAMENT 1979-83

Past Winners

1979	England*
1980	Scotland
1981	England
1982	Scotland
1983	England

1983

England	3	3	0	0	10-1	6
Scotland	3	1	1	1	7-6	4
Holland	3	1	1	1	6-11	4
Italy	3	0	0	3	3-8	0

PAST RESULTS 1979-1983

England v Scotland

	E	S
1979 Stafford	5	1
1980 Zeist	2	4
1981 Empoli	0	0
1982 Aberdeen	1	1
1983 Scarborough	2	1

England v Holland

	E	H
1979 Stafford	1	0
1980 Zeist	2	1
1981 Lucca	2	0
1982 Aberdeen	1	0
1983 Scarborough	6	0

England v Italy

	E	I
1980 Zeist	2	0
1981 Montecatini	1	1
1982 Aberdeen	0	0
1983 Scarborough	2	0

Scotland v Holland

	S	H
1979	*	
1980 Zeist	3	0
1981 Montecatini	2	2
1982 Aberdeen	2	1
1983 Scarborough	3	3

Scotland v Italy

	S	I
1979 Northwich	*	
1980 Zeist	0	0
1981 Lucca	0	0
1982 Aberdeen	2	2
1983 Scarborough	3	1

Holland v Italy

	H	I
1979 Northwich	3	0
1980 Zeist	2	2
1981 Empoli	0	1
1982 Aberdeen	4	2
1983 Scarborough	3	2

* 1979 The competition was played on a knock out basis, England beating Holland 1-0 in the Final, so with a play off for third place each country only played two matches.

FOUR NATIONS TOURNAMENT FINAL TABLES 1979-83

1980

Scotland	3	2	1	0	7-2	5
England	3	2	0	0	6-5	4
Italy	3	0	2	1	2-4	2
Holland	3	0	1	2	3-7	1

1981

England	3	1	2	0	3-1	4(+2)
Italy	3	1	2	0	2-1	4(+1)
Scotland	3	0	3	0	2-2	3
Holland	3	0	0	3	1-4	1

1982

Scotland	3	1	2	0	5-4	4(+1)
England	3	1	2	0	2-1	4(+1)
Italy	3	0	2	1	4-6	2
Holland	3	1	0	2	5-5	2

Scotland won on most goals

England Semi-Professional Squad 1984 *Back Row (L-R): Newson (Maidstone), Ashford (Enfield), Pearce (Harrow), Williams (Telford), Robinson (Blyth). Middle Row (L-R): Taylor (Maidstone), Morley (Nuneaton), Davison (Altrincham), Pape (Harrow), Barrett (Enfield), Johnson (Altrincham). Front Row (L-R): Joseph (Telford), Thompson (Maidstone), Clarke (Blyth), Watson (capt) (Maidstone), A. Cordice (Wealdstone).*

Maidstone players *(L-R): Peter Taylor, Mark Newson, Trevor Morley (Nuneaton), John Watson, Brian Thompson.*

F.A. CHALLENGE TROPHY

F A CHALLENGE TROPHY
Committee: G A Jones, Chairman; E G Powell, Vice-Chairman; C D Bullen; A Clark; G T Evans; J V Hayward; S W Jacobs; T Myatt; W Secker; G Thompson; J C Thompson; N White.

Result of the Round

Preliminary Round	Forest Green Rovers v Weston-super-Mare	0-1 after 2-2
First Qualifying Round	Maidenhead United v Kings Lynn	1-0
Second Qualifying Round	Bognor Regis Town v Fisher Athletic	1-3
Third Qualifying Round	Harlow v Fareham Town City	0-7
First Round	Sutton United v Chelmsford	0-3
Second Round	Leytonstone/Ilford v Whitby Town	0-1
Third Round	AP Leamington v Chelmsford City	4-0
Fourth Round	Marine v Telford United	2-0 after 3-3

Best Attendances

Preliminary Round	Accrington Stanley v Bootle	285
First Qualifying Round	Matlock Town v Gainsborough Trinity	716
Second Qualifying Round	Chelmsford City v Clapton	747
Third Qualifying Round	Matlock Town v Alvechurch	837 (replay)
First Round	Worcester City v Nuneaton Borough	1572
Second Round	Telford United v Runcorn	2683
Third Round	Telford United v Bromsgrove Rovers	2929
Fourth Round	Whitby Town v Dagenham	2688 (replay)
Semi-Final	Marine v Northwich Victoria	2549 (2nd Leg)

It's a little different from Wembley but a lot more beautiful! Lea Hoenig recorded this lovely setting as Matlock entertained Sutton Coldfield Town in the Second qualifying round of the Trophy.

PRELIMINARY ROUND

Strength or Weakness

One of the strengths, which some clubs may consider a weakness, of the FA Trophy is that so many strong clubs from good leagues knock each other out of the competition before the end of the qualifying rounds.

The standard is indeed very high and the prestige of the Trophy improves each year. This season saw two leading west country clubs, Forest Green Rovers and Taunton Town, both knocked out of the competition in the Preliminary Round, but in general there were few upsets.

The result of the round was Forest Green Rovers 0 Weston-super-Mare 1, after a 2-2 draw, and the best attendance was 285 for Accrington Stanley v Bootle.

	Sc	Att	Rcpts
Accrington Stanley v Bootle	0-1	285	£190
Prescot Cables v Formby	0-2	60	£30
Curzon Ashton v West Auckland Town	2-0	153	£51
Alfreton Town v Eastwood Town	3-0	118	£59
Heanor Town v Willenhall Town	1-2	153	£62
Congleton Town v Radcliffe Borough	3-4	134	£92
Banbury United v St Albans City	1-1	128	£65
Milton Keynes City v Cambridge City	0-3	67	£43
Highgate United v Lye Town	0-2	60	£37
Boreham Wood v Hertford Town	3-0	161	£78
Sudbury Town v Spalding United	1-1	189	£87
Hillingdon v Feltham	2-1	89	£69
Epsom & Ewell v Hornchurch	5-0	105	£64
Sittingbourne v Ashford Town	2-3	153	£65
Dover Athletic v Thanet United	2-2	155	£110
Cheshunt v Farnborough Town	0-4	44	£25
Sheppey United v Walton & Hersham	3-3	180	£63
Taunton Town v Basingstoke Town	0-1	174	£93
Weston-super-Mare v Forest Green R	2-2	224	£95
Cinderford Town v Bridport	2-0	66	£36

REPLAYS

St Albans City v Banbury United	1-2*	218	£168
Spalding United v Sudbury Town	2-1	184	£99
Thanet United v Dover Athletic	4-3	140	£111
Walton & Hersham v Sheppey United	1-0	93	£62
Forest Green R v Weston-super-Mare	0-1	273	£171

FIRST QUALIFYING ROUND

Quality Ties

Big names start dropping out in this round with the quality of ties surprisingly high.

Penrith lost at home to South Bank, Kings Lynn away to Maidenhead United, Gainsborough Trinity in a replay at Matlock Town, Willenhall Town at Alfreton Town, Hillingdon at home to Windsor, Waterlooville in a home replay against Bognor Regis Town, and Staines Town in an away replay at Leatherhead.

The result of the round was Maidenhead United 1 Kings Lynn 0, and the best attendance was 716 for Matlock Town v Gainsborough Trinity (replay).

	Sc	Att	Rcpts
Bridlington Trinity v Southport	2-2	85	£59
Burscough v Goole Town	3-3	100	£66
Crook Town v Tow Law Town	1-1	111	£48
Curzon Ashton v Workington	0-0	217	£106
Morecambe v Ferryhill Athletic	2-1	258	£176
Penrith v South Bank	0-2	148	£75
Consett v Billingham Synthonia	4-2	86	£36
Evenwood Town v Shildon	1-1	79	£33
Ashton United v Netherfield	0-0	114	£43
Worksop Town v Emley	2-1	309	£206
North Shields v Willington	6-1	200	£79
Whitley Bay v Radcliffe Borough	1-2	66	£31
Durham City v Mexborough Town A	3-1	100	£49
Leek Town v South Liverpool	0-2	164	£93
Winsford United v Bootle	1-1	165	£106
Hyde United v Formby	4-0	377	£305
Tamworth v Nantwich Town	3-1	133	£119
Buxton v Belper Town	1-1	275	£212
Macclesfield Town v Horwich RMI	0-1	598	£418
Glossop v Oswestry Town	1-2	200	£90
Caernarfon Town v Colwyn Bay	1-0	111	£50
Hednesford Town v Rhyl	0-2	580	£307
Sutton Coldfield Town v Witney Town	1-0	254	£190
Alfreton Town v Willenhall Town	3-1	273	£133
Boston v Bedworth United	0-3	67	£43
Lye Town v Bromsgrove Rovers	1-2	383	£170
Moor Green v Redditch United	1-1	312	£163
Leicester United v Bilston	1-0	145	£94
Oldbury United v Arnold	0-3	64	£36
Dudley Town v Grantham	1-2	170	£97
Stourbridge v Sutton Town	1-2	176	£134
Gainsborough Trinity v Matlock Town	1-1	508	£323
Walthamstow Avenue v Oxford City	0-0	193	£115
Lowestoft Town v Boreham Wood	1-4	288	£163
Hayes v Cambridge City	6-1	171	£129
Fisher Athletic v Hounslow	4-0	242	£206
Chesham United v Wembley	1-1	215	£147
Spalding United v Wokingham Town	0-1	232	£144
Maidenhead United v Kings Lynn	1-0	173	£145
Dunstable v Clapton	1-5	59	£46
Billericay Town v Wellingborough T	1-0	338	£207
Hillingdon v Windsor & Eton	1-2	237	£140
Aveley v Chelmsford City	0-3	213	£199
Gravesend & Northfleet v Banbury U	2-0	498	£357
Ashford Town v Fareham Town	0-2	220	£144
Hampton v Kingstonian	2-0	265	£145
Folkestone v Epsom & Ewell	0-0	659	£465
Addlestone & Weybridge T v Crawley T	0-2	121	£94
Farnborough T v Walton & Hersham	2-2	203	£134
Bognor Regis Town v Waterlooville	1-1	479	£335
Lewes v Bromley	2-3	139	£100
Chatham v Andover	1-2	223	£163
Thanet United v Metropolitan Police	0-1	183	£113
Tonbridge AFC v Worthing	2-3	342	£252
Basingstoke Town v Canterbury City	1-1	286	£157
Staines Town v Leatherhead	0-0	145	£109
Keynsham Town v Minehead	0-1	100	£20
Barnstaple Town v Frome Town	0-3	207	£125
Cinderford Town v Bridgend Town	1-1	91	£50
Maesteg Park v Salisbury	1-1	80	£35
Bideford v Bridgwater Town	2-1	283	£138
Melksham Town v Weston-super-Mare	1-1	173	£72
Shepton Mallet Town v Poole Town	1-2	150	£66
Dawlish v Clandown	6-0	43	£19

REPLAYS

Southport v Bridlington Trinity	2-0	306	£221
Goole Town v Burscough	4-2	263	£177
Tow Law Town v Crook Town	0-1	148	£49
Workington v Curzon Ashton	2-0	293	£226
Shildon v Evenwood Town	1-0	123	£50
Netherfield v Ashton Town	2-1	79	£32
Bootle v Winsford United	0-1	120	£47
Belper Town v Buxton	2-2	267	£188
Redditch United v Moor Green	2-0	243	£138
Matlock Town v Gainsborough Trinity	1-0	716	£459
Oxford City v Walthamstow Avenue	1-2	160	£117
Wembley v Chesham United	4-0	95	£78
Epsom & Ewell v Folkestone	0-1	223	£149
Walton & Hersham v Farnborough T	1-0	178	£101
Waterlooville v Bognor Regis Town	0-3	358	£296
Canterbury City v Basingstoke Town	0-2	99	£82
Leatherhead v Staines Town	4-1	174	£133
Bridgend Town v Cinderford Town	2-0*	92	£37
Salisbury v Maesteg Park	3-0	225	£170
Weston-super-Mare v Melksham Town	3-2	159	£67

SECOND REPLAY

Belper Town v Buxton	1-0	343	£242

SECOND QUALIFYING ROUND

Only three away Winners

With two more games to win before the Competition Proper is reached the pressure is well and truly on in this round and luck in the draw is a great help. Last season quality ties such as Bognor Regis Town v Fisher Athletic, North Shields v Morecambe, Wokingham Town v Windsor & Eton, and Gravesend & Northfleet v Worthing showed just how hard it can be to qualify.

Salisbury's Ray Haysom scores with a header past Maesteg goalkeeper Trevor Nott. Salisbury drew this First Qualifying Round tie 1-1 away and won the replay 3-0. Photo: Mike Joss

Chelmsford City, who enjoyed an eventful Cup season, are seen putting pressure on the Clapton defence during their 3-0 home win in the Second Qualifying Round. Photo: Mike Joss

It was a long way to go for a First Qualifying Round Trophy tie, but Wokingham won 1-0 at Spalding so they were able to enjoy their return journey. Photo: Leo Hoenig

Only three away victories were recorded before the replays but 12 of the 32 ties were drawn with two going to two replays. In one of these North Shields showed their goal-scoring ability with 1-1, 4-4 and 4-1 results against Morecambe.

The result of the round was Bognor Regis Town 1 Fisher Athletic 3, and the best attendance was 747 for Chelmsford City v Clapton.

	Sc	Att	Rcpts
South Bank v Shildon	3-1	102	£43
Crook Town v Netherfield	4-1	69	£41
Consett v South Liverpool	1-1	168	£79
North Shields v Morecambe	1-1	192	£159
Radcliffe Borough v Workshop Town	2-2	302	£112
Durham City v Goole Town	1-0	134	£67
Workington v Southport	0-0	247	£194
Hyde United v Caernarfon Town	2-1	507	£365
Bromsgrove Rovers v Redditch United	1-0	397	£247
Rhyl v Tamworth	5-0	459	£234
Arnold v Oswestry Town	2-0	176	£64
Sutton Town v Belper Town	2-1	153	£79
Alfreton Town v Bedworth United	2-0	248	£123
Horwich RMI v Winsford United	4-1	251	£166
Grantham v Leicester United	0-0	439	£300
Matlock Town v Sutton Coldfield Town	4-0	626	£401
Boreham Wood v Bromley	1-1	185	£90
Walton & Hersham v Billericay Town	2-0	154	£100
Metropolitan Police v Wembley	1-1	80	£66
Chelmsford City v Clapton	3-0	747	£662
Maidenhead United v Fareham Town	1-1	163	£80
Bognor Regis Town v Fisher Athletic	1-3	229	£157
Walthamstow Avenue v Crawley Town	1-1	197	£141
Hampton v Basingstoke Town	2-1	150	£68
Leatherhead v Andover	2-0	162	£80
Wokingham Town v Windsor & Eton	2-2	411	£312
Gravesend & Northfleet v Worthing	2-2	537	£419
Hayes v Folkestone	2-1	249	£190
Minehead v Bideford	1-1	144	£80
Bridgend Town v Poole Town	2-3	68	£26
Salisbury v Weston-super-Mare	4-2	284	£214
Dawlish v Frome Town	0-1	42	£17

REPLAYS

South Liverpool v Consett	2-0	331	£196
Morecambe v North Shields	4-4	252	£228
Worksop Town v Radcliffe Borough	2-1*	325	£212
Southport v Workington	0-1	251	£177
Leicester United v Grantham	0-1	205	£154
Bromley v Boreham Wood	3-1	170	£122
Wembley v Metropolitan Police	2-1	76	£64
Fareham Town v Maidenhead United	3-0	170	£162
Crawley Town v Walthamstow Avenue	0-0	333	£272
Windsor & Eton v Wokingham Town	3-2*	437	£332
Worthing v Gravesend & Northfleet	2-0	598	£564
Bideford v Minehead	2-3	268	£131

SECOND REPLAYS

North Shields v Morecambe	4-1	545	£436
Walthamstow Avenue v Crawley Town	1-3	191	£143

THIRD QUALIFYING ROUND

Southern League Successes

Nearly there! It was in this round that the Southern League's improved form became noticeable. After a number of quiet seasons in cup competition with their Isthmian neighbours, a number of impressive results certainly boosted their morale. Aylesbury United beat Bromley away 3-1, Welling beat Tooting after a replay, Fareham scored seven at Harlow, Hastings United knocked out Worthing and the ever-consistent Fisher Athletic put paid to Walton & Hersham, who had battled through from the preliminary round.

The Isthmians best result came from Dulwich Hamlet, who beat Kettering Town in a 4-3 thriller, but four other Alliance clubs got through, the much improved Frickley Athletic, Yeovil Town and Trowbridge Town at home and Barnet with a good win at Hayes.

The result of the round was Harlow Town 0 Fareham Town 7, and the best attendance was 837 for Matlock Town v Alvechurch (replay).

	Sc	Att	Rcpts
Spennymoor United v Ashington	2-1	173	£82
Frickley Athletic v Worksop Town	1-0*	305	£310
Horwich RMI v Marine	0-1	225	£158
North Shields v Workington	3-1	230	£190
Durham City v Lancaster City	3-0	104	£53
South Liverpool v South Bank	4-2	145	£98
Horden CW v Crook Town	4-1	77	£39
Arnold v Burton Albion	1-0	294	£121
Alfreton Town v Sutton Town	1-1	187	£99
Ilkeston Town v Witton Albion	0-5	148	£105
Rhyl v Stalybridge Celtic	3-0	389	£229
Bromsgrove Rovers v Stafford Rangers	2-2	360	£246
Alvechurch v Matlock Town	2-2	258	£178
Hyde United v Grantham	0-4	408	£289
Bromley v Aylesbury United	1-3	341	£253
Leatherhead v Windsor & Eton	2-3	284	£216
Welling U v Tooting & Mitcham U	0-0	538	£389
Harlow Town v Fareham Town	0-7	50	£40
Carshalton Athletic v Hitchin Town	1-0	137	£103
Hampton v Wembley	1-1	246	£155
Dulwich Hamlet v Kettering Town	4-3	275	£202
Crawley Town v Chelmsford City	0-2	296	£239
Hendon v Woking	2-0	144	£112
Hastings United v Worthing	3-1	403	£262
Walton & Hersham v Fisher Athletic	1-3	—	—
Hayes v Barnet	1-3	199	£164
Barking v Tilbury	5-0	—	—
Salisbury v Gloucester City	2-2	335	£257
Trowbridge Town v Poole Town	6-2	305	—
Yeovil Town v Cheltenham Town	5-2	781	£718
Dorchester Town v Minehead	1-1	193	£160
Frome Town v Merthyr Tydfil	0-1	254	£172

REPLAYS

Sutton Town v Alfreton Town	2-1	222	£103
Stafford Rangers v Bromsgrove Rovers	1-1	725	£560
Matlock Town v Alvechurch	4-2	837	£540
Tooting & Mitcham U v Welling U	1-2	230	£197
Wembley v Hampton	0-2	98	£79
Gloucester City v Salisbury	3-3	390	£253
Minehead v Dorchester Town	1-3	212	£119

SECOND REPLAYS

Bromsgrove Rovers v Stafford Rangers	2-0	657	£404
Gloucester City v Salisbury	2-0	537	£349

First Round Proper

		Sc	Att	Rpts
1	Sutton T v Frickley Ath	1-4	322	£ 218
2	Durham C v North Shields	1-3	211	£ 153
3	Worcester C v Nuneaton Boro	0-0	1,572	£1,458
4	Witton A v AP Leamington	3-4	332	£ 251
5	Bishop Auckland v Grantham	1-1	413	£ 387
6	Bangor C v Spennymoor U	3-1	569	£ 498
7	Chorley v Rhyl	2-1	217	£ 209
8	Bromsgrove R v S Liverpool	2-1	471	£ 302
9	Gateshead v Horden CW	1-1	286	£ 199
10	Boston U v Northwich V	1-1	987	£ 940
11	Arnold v Barrow	0-1	437	£ 284
12	Runcorn v Matlock Town	1-0	605	£ 431
13	Mossley v Telford United	1-2	681	£ 513
14	Whitby T v Blyth Spartans	1-1	961	£ 838
15	Marine v Scarborough	2-1	274	£ 197
16	Altrincham v Kidderminster H	0-2	638	£ 642
17	Barnet v Dartford	3-0	760	£ 653
18	Barking v Aylesbury United	0-1	162	£ 161
19	Merthyr Tydfil v Enfield	2-0	789	£ 657
20	Yeovil Town v Wealdstone	4-3	1,397	£1,189
21	Welling U v Hastings U	2-1	539	£ 394
22	Sutton U v Chelmsford C	0-3	605	£ 533
23	Leyton/Ilford v Trowbridge T	0-0	212	£ 156
24	Weymouth v Hendon	2-3	440	£ 430
25	Carshalton Ath v Harrow Boro	2-2	205	£ 154
26	Wycombe W v Dorchester T	4-0	559	£ 391
27	Dagenham v Fareham Town	0-0	517	£ 430
28	Gloucester C v Fisher Ath	3-3	347	£ 221
29	Slough T v Dulwich Hamlet	3-4	481	£ 335
30	Croydon v Bath City	0-0	221	£ 149
31	Windsor & Eton v Bishop's S	2-1	438	£ 355
32	Hampton v Maidstone U	0-2	473	£ 399

One of the surprises of the First Round was Merthyr Tydfil's defeat of Enfield. The Londoners had won 6-1 at Merthyr two years previously, but the Welsh club gained satisfying revenge last season although the visitors' defence managed to clear this attack. Photo: Mike Joss

It's always an embarrasment when a corner swings directly into the goal and here we can see the anguish of Carshalton Athletic goalkeeper Richard Teale as Gateshead score a vital goal in their Second Round Trophy meeting in Surrey. Photo: Eric Marsh

Thanet United's Richard Hemmings (centre) beats Dover goalkeeper Joe Radford but his shot hits the bar. Photo: R. Barrett

Replays

		Sc	Att	Rpts
3	Nuneaton Boro v Worcester C	2-0	964	£ 976
5	Grantham v Bishop Auckland	1-0	576	£ 419
9	Horden CV v Gateshead	1-3*	220	£ 209
10	Northwich V v Boston U	5-1	975	£ 882
14	Blyth Spartans v Whitby T	1-2	1,140	£ 854
23	Trowbridge T v Leyton/Ilford	1-2		
25	Harrow Boro v Carshalton Ath	0-2	392	£ 195
27	Fareham Town v Dagenham	2-3	280	£ 273
28	Fisher Ath v Gloucester C	2-1	342	£ 255
30	Bath City v Croydon	6-0	382	£ 233

SECOND ROUND

Three real battles of the giants saw Nuneaton Borough and Dagenham beating Maidstone United and Yeovil Town respectively, at the second attempt, and Telford United just held on to knock out Runcorn 2-1. Poor Runcorn never seem to get much Trophy luck but there were celebrations at Bromsgrove who added Wycombe Wanderers to their list of victims.

Fisher Athletic beat Windsor & Eton after a replay just a year after the Berks & Bucks side had eliminated them in similar fashion in the FA Vase. Whitby Town came all the way down to Essex and grabbed a 1-0 win while fellow North Easterners, Gateshead, were also rewarded for their long trip when they beat Carshalton in a mid week afternoon match.

Other fine results were Frickley's 5-2 defeat of NPL leaders Barrow, Chelmsford's victory over Hendon and Marine's 3-0 win at Grantham, while Barnet and AP Leamington scored four times against North Shields and Welling United.

F.A. TROPHY — SECOND ROUND

	Sc	Att	
A.P. Leamington v Welling United	4-1	396	£270
Barnet v North Shields	4-1	1008	£704
Telford United v Runcorn	2-1	2683	£3146
Windsor & Eton v Fisher Athletic	1-1	410	£309
Maidstone U v Nuneaton Borough	2-2	1292	£1686
Carshalton Athletic v Gateshead	1-2	327	£265
Leytonstone-Ilford v Whitby Town	0-1	419	£315
Bangor City v Bath City	1-0	581	£507
Dagenham v Yeovil Town	1-1	680	£590
Merthyr Tydfil v Kidderminster Har	0-1	760	£632
Aylesbury U v Northwich Victoria	0-1	925	£659
Chelmsford City v Hendon	2-1	795	£627
Frickley Athletic v Barrow	5-2	720	£712
Dulwich Hamlet v Chorley	1-1	460	£375
Bromsgrove R v Wycombe Wand	2-0	1195	£788
Grantham v Marine	0-3	503	£353

REPLAYS

Fisher Athletic v Windsor & Eton	4-0	635	£415
Nuneaton Borough v Maidstone U	1-0	1230	£1230
Yeovil Town v Dagenham	1-4	1610	£1610
Chorley v Dulwich Hamlet	2-2	830	£814

SECOND REPLAY
(at Kettering Town)

Dulwich Hamlet v Chorley	2-0	317

FA TROPHY
Third Round

It's the end of the road for Bromsgrove Rovers whose exciting run had really lifted the club. Telford proved just a little too experienced for them but Whitby Town continued their impressive cup season with a sound 2-0 victory over high scoring Alliance club, Frickley Athletic.

Last year's runners up Northwich Victoria took three matches to eliminate the last Servowarm Isthmian club, Dulwich Hamlet, and Marine managed an unexpected win at high flying Fisher Athletic of the Southern Premier.

Five of the last eight are Alliance clubs but only Barnet and Dagenham have survived to give the South an interest in the next round.

AP Leamington 4 (Ollis 2, Campbell, 1 og) **Chelmsford City 0** Attendance: 672
AP Leamington: Conway, Rigby, Wilson, Kane, Boxall, Kavanagh, Ollis, MacKenzie, Casey, Downes, Campbell, Rhodes.
Chelmsford City: Carrick, Dudley, Johnson, Kilbey, Herbert, Cowlishaw, Powell, Devine, Bright, (Thrift), Bishop.

Whitby Town 2 (Sills 2) **Frickley Athletic 0** Attendance: 1,863
Whitby Town: Coleby, Scott, Walker, Granycome, Coleby, Gollogly, Lawrence, Smith, Sharkey, Sills, Hampton.
Frickley Athletic: Hinchcliffe, Smith, Overton, Dunn, Wright, Gill, Wilcox, Howey, Reed, Wilson, Miles.

Dulwich Hamlet 0 Northwich Victoria 0 Attendance: 670
Dulwich Hamlet: Knock, Langley, Roughan, Baldwin, Edwards P, Kingston, Carolan, Norman, Edwards A, Williams, Richards.
Northwich Victoria: Ryan, Fretwell, Dean, Jones, Forshaw, Bennett, Anderson, Abel, Reid, Chesters, Wilson.

Nuneaton Borough 2 (Culpin pen, Morley) **Dagenham 2** (McCombe 2) Attendance: 1,822
Nuneaton Borough: Pool, Carr, Jenas, Gasson, Dixey, Glover, Smithers, Hamill, Hill, Culpin, Morley, Richardson.
Dagenham: Scott, Knapman, Wade, Wells, Campbell, Dunwell, Sille, Scott, McCombe, Whitton, Maycock.

Telford United 2 (Hogan, Edwards) **Bromsgrove Rovers 0** Attendance: 2,929
Telford United: Charlton, Rutter, Turner, Joseph, Bailey, Lewis, Barnett, Mayman, Williams, Mather, Hogan.
Bromsgrove Rovers: Allen, Snape, Skeldong, O'Connell, Kurila, Lang, Allbutt, O'Meara, Kalenski, Langford, Butler.

Barnet 2 (Atkins, Stein) **Kidderminster Harriers 1** (McGowan) Attendance: 988
Barnet: Phillips, Brown, Kinnear, Millett, Baldry, Margerison, Atkins, Stein, Ragan, Evans, Mahoney.
Kidderminster Harriers: Garner, Wood, Richards, McGowan, Jones, Woodall, Powell, Gavin, Davies, Roberts, Bowater.

Gateshead 2 (Davies, Henderson) **Bangor City 2** (Morris, Carter) Attendance: 323
Gateshead: Dodds, Higgins, Pearson, Pugh, Mitchinson, Parnaby, Robson, Davies, Grady, Tweedy, Henderson.
Bangor City: Letheren, Cavanagh, Gray, Whelan, Banks, Owen, Puddle, Morris, Carter, Howat, Westwood, (Graham).

Fisher Athletic 0 Marine 1 (Williams) Attendance: 570
Fisher Athletic: Bowtell, Sault, Boulter, Shinners R, Shinners B, Hodges, Murrock, Brown, Shinners P, Sansom, Bayram.
Marine: Parkinson, Edwards, Dawson, Johnson, Wilson, Wilson, Williams, Scott, McClatchey, Meachin, Kelly.

THIRD ROUND REPLAYS

Northwich Victoria 0 Dulwich 0 a.e.t. Attendance: 1,604
Northwich Victoria: Ryan, Fretwell, Dean, Jones, Forshaw, Bennett, Anderson, Abel, Reid, Chesters, Wilson, (Bradley).
Dulwich Hamlet: Knock, Langley, Roughan, Baldwin, Morgan, Lewis, Kingston, Norman, Hewitt, Williams, Richards.

Bangor City 2 (Banks, Carter) **Gateshead 0** Attendance: 925
Bangor City: Letheren, Cavanagh, Gray, Whelan, Banks, Owen, Puddle, Morris, Carter, Howat, Westwood.
Gateshead: Dodds, Higgins, Pearson, Hibbitt, Robson, Parnaby, Pugh, Davies, Topping, Donaldson, Henderson.

Dagenham 1 (McCombe) **Nuneaton Borough 0** Attendance: 779
Dagenham: Scott, Knapman, Wade, (Oliver), Wells, Campbell, Dunwell, Sille, Scott, McCombe, Whitton, Maydock.
Nuneaton Borough:

FA TROPHY SECOND REPLAY

Northwich Victoria 1 (Forshaw) **Dulwich Hamlet 0** Attendance: 537
Northwich Victoria: Ryan, Fretwell, Dean, Jones, Forshaw, Bennett, Anderson, Abel, Reid, Bradley, (Power), Wilson.
Dulwich Hamlet: Knock, Langley, Roughan, Baldwin, Edwards, Lewis, Kingston, Hewitt, Norman, Williams, Richards.

Marine enjoyed a great Trophy run and one of their more unexpected wins was at Fisher Athletic who were on excellent form but lost to this goal scored early in the second half by ???. Photo: Eric Marsh

Having beaten Lye Town, Redditch United, Stafford Rangers, and South Liverpool, Bromsgrove Rovers were given a home draw against Isthmian 'giants' Wycombe Wanderers. Rovers rose to the occasion and won 2-0. Here Maurice O'Connell scores with a tremendous diving header. Photo: Mike Joss

Another excellent view of the Merthyr Tydfil v Enfield Trophy tie which attracted an excellent crowd. Photo: David Shute

FA TROPHY
Quarter Finals

Six goals away in a Trophy quarter final must be a great performance so with Mark Carter the hat trick hero Bangor City certainly destroyed a demoralised Leamington side and had high hopes of becoming the first Welsh club to play at Wembley since Cardiff City beat Arsenal in 1927.

Marine and Whitby Town shook Alliance opposition away from home but after forcing replays only Marine with a fine 2-0 victory over holders Telford United managed to finish the job off. Whitby Town of the Drybroughs Northern League attracted an impressive 2,688 into The Turnbull Ground for Dagenham's visit but the Londoners stormed away for a three goal success and kept up their remarkable consistency in the competition.

The departure of the holders was certainly a surprise especially after they had recovered from being three down at home but Marine, who had already beaten Scarborough kept cool and recorded a famous victory.

The fourth qualifying club turned out to be Northwich Victoria who just pipped Barnet at home and reached their third semi-final in consecutive years.

Northwich Victoria 1 (Chesters) **Barnet 0** Attendance: 1,690
Northwich Victoria: Ryan, Fretwell, Dean, Jones, Forshaw (Bradley), Bennett, Anderson, Abel, Reid, Chesters, Wilson.
Barnet: Phillips, Brown, Kinnear, Millett, Baldry, Margerison, Docker (Mahoney), Stein, Ragan, Evans, Atkins.

Telford United 3 (Mather, Hogan, Alcock) **Marine 3** (Edwards, McClathcey, Meachin) Attendance: 2,544
Telford United: Charlton, Rutter, Turner, Mayman, Bailey, Lewis, Barnett, Williams, Mather, Hogan, Edwards (Alcock).
Marine: Parkinson, Dawson, Edwards P (Wilson), Smith, Johnson, Edwards A, Williams, Scott, McClatchey, Meachin, Kelly.

Dagenham 2 (Campbell, Dunwell) **Whitby Town 2** (Smith, Sills) Attendance: 1,217
Dagenham: Scott L, Oliver, Scales, Wells, Campbell, Dunwell, Sille, Scott S, McCombe, Whitton, Smith.
Whitby Town: Coleby, Escritt, Walker, Granycome, Gallogly, Scott, Lawrence, Smith, Lilley (Sharkey), Sills, Hampton.

A.P. Leamington 1 (Casey) **Bangor City 6** (Carter 3, Banks, Urquart, Westwood) Attendance: 915
A.P. Leamington: Conway, Rigby, Britton, Boxall, Kavanagh, Ollis, MacKenzie, Casey, Griffin (Downes), Campbell, Wilson.
Bangor City: Letheran, Cavanagh, Gray, Whelan, Banks, Owen, Urquhart, Morris, Carter, Murphy, Westwood.

REPLAYS

Marine 2 (McClatchey Meachin) **Telford United 0** Attendance: 2,024
Marine: Parkinson, Dawson, Edwards P, Smith, Johnson, Edwards A, Williams, Scott, McClatchey, Meachin, Kelly.
Telford United: Charlton, Rutter, Turner, Mayman, Bailey, Lewis, Barnett, Williams, Mather, Hogan (Edwards), Alcock.

Whitby Town 0 **Dagenham 3** (Scott S, McCombe, Whitton) Attendance: 2,688
Whitby Town: Coleby D, Scott, Walker, Granycome, Coleby S, Gallogly, Lawrence, Smith (Escritt), Sharkey, Sills, Hampton.
Dagenham: Scott L, Oliver, Scales, Wells, Campbell, Dunwell, Sille, Scott, McCombe (Page), Whitton, Maycock.

FA TROPHY
Semi-Finals

Marine, the pride of the Northern Premier League, must have been thrilled with their draw at Northwich but like so many clubs before them they found the pressure of playing at home with a lead very difficult to master.

Northwich Victoria's extra Trophy experience over the last two years made all the difference and they were joined by Bangor City who edged out Dagenham by just one goal. Both finalists had endured difficult financial problems so the boost of a Wembley appearance was particularly welcome and of course poor Bangor had paid for success in cup competitions by getting behind with their League fixtures to such an extent that they had been relegated. A Welsh club at Wembley and a possible Trophy success might just make up for this dissapointment.

FIRST LEGS
Bangor City 1 (Whelan) **Dagenham 0** Attendance: 1,659
Bangor City: Letheren, Cavanagh, Gray, Whelan, Banks, Lunn, Sutcliffe, Banks, Carter, Howat (Murphy), Westwood.
Dagenham: Scott L, Oliver, Wade, Knapman, Campbell, Dunwell, Sille, Scott S, McCombe, Whitton, Maycock.

Northwich Victoria 1 (Reid) **Marine 1** (McClatchey) Attendance: 2,240
Northwich Victoria: Ryan, Fretwell, Dean, Jones, Forshaw, Bennett, Anderson, Abel (Bradley), Reid, Chesters, Wilson.
Marine: Parkinson, Dawson, Edwards P, Smith, Johnson, Edwards A, Williams, Scott, McClatchey, Meachin, Kelly.

SECOND LEG

Dagenham 2 (Dunwell 2) **Bangor City 2** (Morris, Carter) a.e.t. Attendance: 2,069
Dagenham: Scott L, Oliver, Wade, Knapman, Campbell, Dunwell, Sille (Sheringham), Scott S, McCombe, Whitton, Maycock.
Bangor City: Letheren, Cavanagh, Gray, Urquhart, Banks, Lunn, Sutcliffe, Morris, Carter, Howat (Whelan), Westwood.

Marine 0 Northwich Victoria 2 (Chesters, Edwards P own goal) Attendance: 2,549
Marine: Griffiths, Dawson, Edwards P, Smith, Johnson, Edwards A, Williams (Thornton), Scott, McClatchey, Meachin, Kelly.
Northwich Victoria: Ryan, Fretwell, Dean, Jones, Forshaw, Bennett, Anderson, Abel, Reid, Chesters, Wilson.

Dagenham are under pressure in the first-leg as Kevin Eastwood leads the foray.

Ace goalscorer Bob Mountain is seen about to open the scoring for Matlock Town at Alvechurch in a 2-2 draw.
Photo: David Shute

Joy for Marine as Mike Scott scores his side's goal in their 1-1 draw at Northwich. This was the first goal conceded by the Alliance club for five Trophy ties. Photo: Mike Joss

The greatest moment in a career — scoring at Wembley. Here, Paul Whelan gives Bangor the lead in the first half. Photo: Eric Marsh

Welsh Under 21 and 23 International Glen Letheran punches well clear from an early Northwich attack. Photo: Leo Hoenig

Bruce Urquart and Phil Lunn just stop Northwich Victoria's Paul Reid. Photo: Bob Thomas

F.A. TROPHY — ROUND-BY-ROUND TO WEMBLEY

First Round	Second Round	Third Round	Fourth Round	Semi-Final	Final
Bangor City . . 3 Spennymoor U . 1	**Bangor City . 1**				
Croydon . . . . 0,0 Bath City 0,6	Bath City 0	**Bangor C . . 2,2**			
Carshalton A . 2,2 Harrow B . . . 2,0	Carshalton Ath 1		**Bangor C . . . 6**		
Gateshead . . . 1,3 Horden CW . 1,1+	Gateshead 2	•Gateshead . . 2,0			
Witton A . . . . . 3 A P Leamington 4	AP Leam'gton 4			**Bangor C . . 1,2**	
Welling U . . . . . 2 Hastings U 1	Welling U 1	•AP Leam'gton 4			
Sutton U . . . . . . 0 Chelmsford C . . 3	Chelmsford C . 2		•AP Leam'gton 1		
Weymouth . . . . 2 Hendon 3	Hendon 1	Chelmsford C . 0		*1st Leg at Bangor 2nd Leg at Dagenham*	
Hampton . . . . . 0 Maidstone U . . 2	Maidstone U 2,0				**Bangor C . 1,*1**
Worcester C . 0,0 Nuneaton B . . 0,2	Nuneaton B . 2,1	•Nuneaton B . 2,0			
Dagenham . . . 0,3 Fareham T . . 0,2	Dagenham . . 1,4		•Dagenham . . 2,3		
Yeovil T . . . . . . 4 Wealdstone 3	Yeovil Town 1,1	Dagenham . . 2,1			
Leytonstone/I 0,1 Trowbridge T 0,0	L'stone/Ilford . 0			Dagenham . . 0,2	
Whitby T . . . 1,2 Blyth S 1,1	Whitby T 1	•Whitby T 2			
Sutton T . . . . . . 1 Frickley Ath . . . 4	Frickley Ath . . 5		Whitby T . . 2,0		
Arnold . . . . 0 Barrow 1	Barrow 2	Frickley Ath . . 0			*FA Trophy replay at Stoke City*
Mossley . . . . . . 1 Telford U 2	Telford U 2				
Runcorn . . . . . . 2 Matlock T 1	Runcorn 1	•Telford U 2			
Bromsgrove R . 2 S Liverpool 1	Bromsgrove R. 2		•Telford U . . 3,0		
Wycombe W . . . 4 Dorchester T . . 0	Wycombe W . . 0	Bromsgrove R . 0			
Windsor & Eton 2 Bishop's Stort . . 1	Windsor & E 1,0			Marine 1,0	
Gloucester C . 3,1 Fisher A 3,2	Fisher Ath . . 1,4	•Fisher Ath . . . 0			
Bishop Auck . . . Grantham	Grantham 0		Marine 3,2		
Marine . . . . 2 Scarborough . . . 1	Marine 3	Marine 1		*1st Leg at Northwich 2nd Leg at Marine*	**N'wich V . . 1,2**
Barnet . . . . 3 Dartford 0	Barnet 4				
Durham C . . . . 1 N Shields 3	North Shields . 1	•Barnet 2			
Merthyr Tydfil 2 Enfield 0	Merthyr T . . . 0		Barnet 0		
Altrincham . . . . 0 Kid'minster H . 2	Kidder'ster H . 1	Kidder'ster H . 1			
Slough T . . . . . 3 Dulwich H 4	Dulwich H 1,2,2			**N'wich V . . 1,2**	
Chorley . . . . 2 Rhyl 1	Chorley . . 1,2,0	•Dulwich H. 0,0,0			
Barking . . . . 0 Aylesbury U . . . 1	Aylesbury U . . 0		**•Northwich V . 1**		
Boston U . . . . 1,1 **Northwich V 1,5**	**Northwich V . 1**	**N'wich V 0,0,1**			

Clubs listed first were drawn at home in rounds one and two. +After extra time.

*** Indicates club drawn at home**
+ After extra time
° At Kettering Town FC
x At Nuneaton Borough

FA Challenge Trophy Final

Northwich go one better

Bangor City (0) 1 (Whelan) Northwich Victoria (0) 1 (Chesters) aet Att: 14,200

Having reached the semi-final stage in 1982 and then losing the 1983 final, Northwich were obvious favourites for this Trophy climax between two Alliance Premier League clubs. Bangor City's excellent cup results (they had already beaten Northwich in the FA Cup) had given the club a lift but they had been relegated and the constant battle against inflation was also expected to have taken it's toll.

However, it was the Welsh club who showed most initiative in a very ordinary first half in which the only incident of note was a booking for the aggressive Chesters after a wild challenge.

The second half was altogether better without being anything exceptional and the Welshmen were justifiably ahead in the fifty-eighth minute with a very good goal scored by Whelan after an excellent run and cross by Carter, the captain. Whelan and Urquhart had both come close earlier in the half and the lead was deserved. Chances to go further ahead soon fell to Carter and Whelan, but Ryan was sound in goal for Northwich and they were not accepted. With seventy-one minutes gone Dean made a skilled run down the left for the Cheshire side and his cross was missed by the entire Bangor defence, but the lively Chesters, was in position to head powerfully home and level the scores. Northwich did then make some strong attacks, but without further success, so the match went into extra-time.

By now a limping Forshaw had been replaced by Power and as the teams changed ends after a further fifteen minutes Westwood came on for Bangor's Sutcliffe, but neither player could make much difference to the scene since the other twenty were by now very tired. During the last few minutes first Banfor through Carter and then Northwich in a scramble near goal had chances but the defences at each end survived. Lunn of Bangor became the second person to be cautioned late in extra-time.

Teams:

Bangor City: G. Letheren, J. Cavanagh, M. Gray, P. Whelan, J. Banks, P. Lunn, B. Urquhart, A. Morris, M. Carter (Captain), I. Howat, P. Sutcliffe (K. Westwood 105 minutes).
Northwich Victoria: D. Ryan, D. Fretwell, M. Dean, K. Jones (Captain), J. Forshaw (P. Power 65 minutes), P. Bennett, J. Anderson, G. Abel, P. Reid, C. Chesters, P. Wilson.
Referee: John Martin.

Northwich Victoria's route from Boston to Wembley

Round	*Opponents*	*Venue*	*Result*	*Scorers*	*Attendance*
First Proper	**Boston United** (Alliance Premier)	Away	1-1	Bennett	987
Replay	**Boston United**	Home	5-1	Reid 3, Chesters, Bennett (pen)	975
Second Proper	**Aylesbury United** (Southern)	Away	1-0	Bennett (pen)	925
Third Proper	**Dulwich Hamlet** (Isthmian)	Away	0-0	–	670
Replay	**Dulwich Hamlet**	Home	0-0	–	1,804
2nd Replay	**Dulwich Hamlet**	Nuneaton	1-0	Forshaw	537
Fourth Proper	**Barnet** (Alliance Premier)	Home	1-0	Chesters	1,690
Semi-Final					
First Leg	**Marine** (Northern Premier)	Home	1-1	Reid	2,433
Second Leg	**Marine**	Away	2-0	Own goal, Chesters	2,549

Matches played: 9 goals for: 12 against: 3

Bangor City's route from Wales to Wembley

Round	*Opponents*	*Venue*	*Result*	*Scorers*	*Attendance*
First Proper	**Spennymoor United** (Northern)	Home	3-1	Carter, Westwood, Howat	569
Second Proper	**Bath City** (Alliance Premier)	Home	1-0	Carter	581
Third Proper	**Gateshead** (Alliance Premier)	Away	2-2	Morris, Carter	323
Replay	**Gateshead**	Home	2-0	Banks, Carter	925
Fourth Proper	**AP Leamington** (Alliance Premier)	Away	6-1	Carter 3, Urquhart, Westwood	915
Semi-Final					
First Leg	**Dagenham** (Alliance Premier)	Home	1-0	Whelan	1,659
Second Leg	**Dagenham**	Away	2-2*	Carter, Morris	2,069

Matches played: 7 goals for: 17 against: 6 * after extra time

Never before had a Trophy Final been drawn so this is an historic photo of both sides together after their Wembley match. Photo: Leo Hoenig

FA Challenge Trophy Replay at The Victoria Ground, Stoke

Bangor City (1) 1 (Lunn) Northwich Victoria (1) 2 Chesters, pen. Anderson Att: 5,805

This was the first Trophy Final replay in the history of the competition and, although the attendance appears disappointing, it compares reasonably with most Third or Fourth Division crowds.

Once again, it was Bangor City who took the lead after showing most of the early promise. This time it was a superb drive from outside the penalty area following a well worked free kick, with Lunn the scorer after 18 minutes. However, the Welsh club must have realised that it just wasn't their season when Urquhart was penalised for hand ball as a Wilson header crashed against his arm from short range.

It's incidents like this that can lift or demoralise a side and when Colin Chesters scored his second cup final goal from the penalty spot Northwich must have felt that their Trophy luck had changed. The game remained well balanced however until the last seconds of full time when Anderson, a quick and skillful winger, beat two defenders to a left wing cross and joyfully slipped the ball past goalkeeper Letheren.

One hopes that the income from the two games will lift each club's financial worries and to Bangor City who had such fluctuating luck during the season we can only hope they bounce back to the Alliance in the near future.

Northwich Victoria, who had shown such consistency in the competition during the last two seasons and had the character to lift themselves up after two grim disappointments, could hardly be begrudged a Trophy triumph. Their teamwork, determination and well balanced attack are admirable and always there at the back, 'conducting' proceedings, was captain Ken Jones with a mere 900 games for the club behind him.

It was a very special success to be enjoyed by a 'club' in every sense of the word. The manager and most of his players have been together some time and for their efforts off the field when clearing the club's overdraft everyone really deserved this memorable reward.

The teams were the same as those which started the match at Wembley.

Bangor again take the lead in the replay. Phil Lunn crashes home from 25 yards after a short free kick.
Photo: Leo Hoenig

An anxious Colin Chesters sees Letheran go the right way but his penalty is successful and Northwich are level again.
Photo: Bob Thomas

Everyone is looking at his watch and injury time is being played out. A centre comes over to the edge of the Bangor six yard area and it is Victoria's John Anderson who gets there first to score. The Bangor team and their supporters just can't believe it!
Photo: Leo Hoenig

Despite relegation and losing so tragically in the replay I'm sure that this happy group of Welsh supporters seen at Wembley will remember last season for the rest of their lives.
Photo: Eric Marsh

F.A. CHALLENGE TROPHY FINALS
1970-1983

1970 (*Attendance:* 28,000)
Macclesfield Town 2 (Lyons, Fidler B.) **Telford United 0** Referee: K. Walker
Macclesfield Town: Cooke; Sievwright, Bennett, Beaumont, Collins, Roberts; Lyons, Fidler B., Young, Corfield, Fidler D.
Telford United: Irvine; Harris, Croft, Flowers, Coton, Ray, Fudge, Hart, Bentley, Murray, Jagger.

1971 (*Attendance:* 29,500)
Telford United 3 (Owen, Bentley, Fudge) **Hillingdon 2** (Reeve, Bishop) Referee: D Smith
Telford United: Irvine; Harris, Croft, Ray, Coton, Carr, Fudge, Owen, Bentley, Jagger, Murray.
Hillingdon: Lowe; Batt, Langley; Higginson, Newcombe, Moore, Fairchild, Bishop, Reeve, Carter, Knox.

1972 (*Attendance:* 24,000)
Stafford Rangers 3 (Williams (2), Cullerton (1)) **Barnet 0** Referee: P Partridge
Stafford Rangers: Aleksic; Chadwick, Clayton, Sargeant, Aston, Machin, Cullerton, Chapman, Williams, Bayley, Jones.
Barnet: McClelland; Lye, Jenkins, Ward, Embrey, King, Powell, Ferry, Flatt, Easton, Plume.

1973 (*Attendance:* 23,000)
Scarborough 2 (Leask, Thompson) **Wigan Athletic 1** (Rogers) aet Referee: H Hackney
Scarborough: Garrow; Appleton, Shoulder, Dunn, Siddle, Fagan, Donoghue, Franks, Leask (Barmby), Thompson, Hewitt.
Wigan Athletic: Reeves, Morris, Sutherland, Taylor, Jackson, Gillibrand, Clements, Oates (McCunnell), Rogers, King, Worswick.

1974 (*Attendance:* 19,000)
Morecambe 2 (Richmond, Sutton) **Dartford 1** (Cunningham) Referee: B Homewood
Morecambe: Coates; Pearson, Bennett, Sutton, Street, Baldwin, Done, Webber, Roberts (Galley), Kershaw, Richmond.
Dartford: Morton; Read, Payne, Carr, Burns, Binks, Light, Glozier, Robinson (Hearne), Cunningham, Halliday.

1975 (*Attendance:* 21,000)
Matlock Town 4 (Oxley, Dawson, T. Fenoughty, N. Fenoughty) **Scarborough 0** Referee: K Styles
Matlock Town: Fell; McKay, Smith, Stuart, Dawson, Swan, Oxley, Fenoughty N., Scott, Fenoughty, T., Fenoughty M.
Scarborough: Williams: Hewitt, Pettit, Dunn, Marshall, Todd, Houghton, Woodall, Davidson, Barmby, Aveyard.

1976 (*Attendance:* 21,000)
Scarborough 3 (Woodall, Abbey, Marshall pen) **Stafford Rangers 2** (Jones 2) aet Referee: R Challis
Scarborough: Barnard; Jackson, Marshall, Dunn (H.), Ayre, (Donoghue), Dunn (H.A.), Dale, Barmby, Woodall, Abbey, Hilley.
Stafford Rangers: Arnold; Ritchie, Richards, Sargeant, Seddon, Morris, Chapman, Lowe, Jones, Hutchison, Chadwick.

1977 (*Attendance:* 20,500)
Scarborough 2 (Dunn pen, Abbey) **Dagenham 1** (Harris) Referee: G Courtney
Scarborough: Chapman; Smith, Marshall (Barmby), Dunn, Ayre, Deere, Aveyard, Donoghue, Woodall, Abbey, Dunn.
Dagenham: Huttley; Wellman, Currie P., Dunwell, Moore, Currie W., Harkins, Saul, Fox, Harris, Holder.

1978 (*Attendance:* 20,000)
Altrincham 3 (King, Johnson, Rogers) **Leatherhead 1** (Cook) Referee: A Grey
Altrincham: Eales, Allan, Crossley, Bailey, Owens, King, Morris, Heathcote, Johnson, Rogers, Davison (Flaherty).
Leatherhead: Swannell, Cooper, Eaton, Davies, Reid, Malley, Cook, Salkeld, Kelly, Baker, Doyle (Bailey).

1979 (*Attendance:* 32,000)
Stafford Rangers 2 (Wood A. 2) **Kettering Town 0** Referee: D Richardson
Stafford Rangers: Arnold, Wood F., Willis, Sargeant, Seddon, Ritchie, Seeker, Chapman, Wood A., Cullerton, Chadwick, (Jones).
Kettering Town: Lane, Ashby, Lee, Easthall, Dixey, Suddards, Flannagan, Kellock, Phipps, Clayton, Evans (Hughes).

1980 (*Attendance:* 26,000)
Dagenham 2 (Duck, Maycock) **Mossley 1** (Smith) Referee: K Baker
Dagenham: Huttley, Wellman, Scales, Dunwell, Moore, Durrell, Maycock, Horan, Duck, Kidd, Jones, (Holder).
Mossley: Fitton, Brown, Vaughan, Gorman, Salter, Polliot, Smith, Moore, Skeete, O'Connor, Keelan, (Wilson).

1981 (*Attendance:* 22,578)
Bishop's Stortford 1 (Sullivan) **Sutton United 0** Referee: J Worrall
Bishop's Stortford: Moore; Blackman (Capt), Brame, Smith (Worrell), Bradford, Avery, Sullivan, Knapman, Radford, Simmonds, Mitchell.
Sutton United: Collyer; Rogers, Green, Rains J. (Capt), Rains T, Stephens (Sunnucks), Waldon, Pritchard, Cornwell, Parsons, Dennis.

1982 (*Attendance:* 18,678)
Enfield 1 (Taylor) **Altrincham 0** Referee: B Stevens
Enfield: J. Jacobs, K. Barrett, J. Tone, J. Jennings, D. Waite, N. Ironton, N. Ashford, P. Taylor, L. Holmes, S. Oliver (D. Flint), S. King.
Altrincham: J. Connaughton, I Crossley, J. Davison, M. Bailey, P. Cuddy, J. King (B. Whitbread), S. Allan, G. Heathcote, J. Johnson, J. Rogers, B. Howard.

1983 (*Attendance:* 22,071)
Telford 2 (Mather 2) **Northwich Victoria 1** (Bennett) Referee: B Hill
Telford United: Charlton, Lewis, Turner, Mayman (Joseph), Walker (Capt), Eaton, Barnett, Williams, Mather, Hogan, Alcock.
Northwich Victoria: Ryan, Fretwell, Murphy, Jones (Capt), Forshaw, Ward, Anderson, Abel (Bennett), Reid, Chesters, Wilson.

F.A. TROPHY CLUB RECORDS

	69-70	70-71	71-72	72-73	73-74	74-75	75-76	76-77	77-78	78-79	79-80	80-81	81-82	82-83	83-84	Total
Scarborough	2	2	2	W	2	F	W	W	1	2	1	1	Q-F	3	1	48
Dagenham						Q-F	3	F	Q-F	S-F	W	2	3	S-F	S-F	44
Stafford Rangers	2	1	W	S-F	Q-F	1	F	2	2	W	1	2	1	1	—	42
Telford United	F	W	S-F	1	2	3	2	1	—	—	1	—	3	W	Q-F	42
Bangor City	3	3	1	Q-F	2	1	1	2	3	1	2	S-F	1	3	F	38
Northwich Victoria	1	2	1	—	2	2	1	1	1	2	1	3	S-F	F	W	35
Weymouth	3	2	1	2	Q-F	3	2	Q-F	2	2	3	2	1	3	1	35
Altrincham	—	1	—	2	—	1	—	S-F	W	1	3	Q-F	F	3	1	34
Dartford	2	1	Q-F	1	F	1	1	2	2	—	1	S-F	2	Q-F	1	33
Yeovil Town	1	S-F	S-F	1	1	1	1	2	1	Q-F	3	2	1	1	2	31
Matlock	3	2	1	1	1	W	3	3	3	1	2	1	—	1	1	30
Worcester City	Q-F	2	1	2	Q-F	1	1	—	1	2	1	Q-F	Q-F	2	1	30
Enfield						3	S-F	1	2	Q-F	1	1	W	Q-F	1	29
Morecambe	1	—	3	Q-F	W	2	3	Q-F	1	1	2	1	—	—	—	29
Boston United	—	2	—	1	3	2	1	1	2	3	S-F	2	1	Q-F	1	28
Mossley	Q-F	2	1	1	1	3	—	—	—	—	F	Q-F	3	2	1	28
Burton Albion	Q-F	3	2	1	1	S-F	2	2	1	—	3	1	1	1	—	27
Macclesfield Town	W	Q-F	Q-F	1	S-F	1	1	2	—	—	1	—	—	—	—	26
Runcorn	—	—	—	—	—	—	S-F	3	S-F	S-F	1	1	3	1	2	26
Chorley	—	3	3	1	1	—	—	Q-F	2	2	2	1	2	2	2	25
Hillingdon Bor.	Q-F	F	3	2	1	2	Q-F	1	1	1	—	—	—	—	—	25
Kettering Town	3	1	1	—	3	2	1	2	1	F	1	2	1	1	—	25
Nuneaton Bor.	2	1	1	2	1	—	—	Q-F	2	1	Q-F	1	1	2	3	25
Barnet	S-F	1	F	1	1	—	—	1	—	—	3	—	—	2	Q-F	24
Grantham	3	1	Q-F	2	3	2	2	1	1	1	1	—	—	—	2	23
Hastings United	1	2	2	1	2	1	2	1	—	1	3	3	1	1	1	22
Kidderminster H.	2	3	2	1	1	—	1	1	—	1	1	1	Q-F	1	3	22
Bromsgrove R.	3	2	2	1	2	1	Q-F	1	1	—	—	—	—	—	3	20
Chelmsford C.	S-F	2	3	Q-F	1	1	1	—	—	—	—	—	—	—	3	20
Merthyr Tydfil	—	—	2	2	2	1	2	1	Q-F	—	2	—	2	—	2	20
Wycombe Wanderers						—	—	2	2	3	2	2	S-F	2	2	20
Barrow				2	2	1	1	—	—	2	Q-F	1	1	3	2	19
Blyth Spartans						1	—	1	1	2	Q-F	3	2	Q-F	1	19
Buxton	2	Q-F	Q-F	3	3	1	1	—	—	—	—	—	1	—	—	19
Lancaster City	1	1	—	2	—	3	3	1	2	2	1	1	2	—	—	19
Slough Town						—	3	S-F	2	2	1	1	3	1	1	19
Leatherhead						2	2	1	F	3	2	1	1	—	—	18
Bishop's Stortford						1	2	1	—	—	—	W	Q-F	1	1	17
Marine						—	—	1	1	2	3	2	1	1	S-F	16
Sutton United						1	1	—	4	4	—	F	3	2	1	16
Tooting & Mitcham U.						1	Q-F	3	3	1	2	1	1	—	—	16
Goole T.	1	1	—	—	—	Q-F	2	—	3	1	—	2	—	1	—	15
Hendon						1	2	3	3	1	1	—	2	—	2	15
Maidstone U.				2	—	—	—	—	1	3	1	1	2	3	2	15
Spennymore U.						—	—	2	S-F	2	1	1	1	2	1	15
Witton Alb.	—	1	1	3	—	—	—	2	—	3	—	1	3	—	1	15
Bishop Auckland						1	2	1	—	Q-F	1	—	3	1	1	14
Cheltenham T.	1	—	—	1		2	—	1	1	3	2	1	1	1	—	14
Dover Ath.	1	3	1	2	1	2	1	1	—	1	1	—	—	—	—	14
Stourbridge	2	Q-F	1	3	2	1	1	—	—	—	—	—	—	—	—	14
Banbury U.	—	3	1	1	3	1	1	1	1	—	—	—	—	—	—	12
Bath C.	1	—	—	1	—	—	—	1	—	1	3	1	1	1	2	12
Dulwich H.						—	1	—	—	—	Q-F	1	1	2	3	12
Gainsborough T.	2	1	1	1	1	—	2	—	1	1	2	—	—	—	—	12
Minehead	1	1	1	—	2	—	—	2	1	2	—	1	1	—	—	12
South Liverpool	1	1	2	2	1	2	1	1	—	—	—	—	—	—	1	12
Thanet U.	—	1	1	—	2	2	2	1	—	3	—	—	—	—	—	12
Winsford U.	1	1	—	—	—	1	—	1	Q-F	1	1	2	—	—	—	12
Burscough	1	2	1	1	2	2	1	—	—	—	—	—	—	1	—	11
Woking						—	—	—	1	1	S-F	1	2	1	—	11
King's Lynn	1	1	1	1	1	1	1	—	—	2	—	—	—	1	—	10
Leytonstone/Ilford	—	—	—	—	—	3	—	—	—	—	—	3	—	2	2	10
Stalybridge Celtic	1	—	—	—	2	—	—	—	—	1	2	1	1	2	—	10
Ashford T	—	—	—	S-F	1	2	1	—	—	—	—	—	—	—	—	9
Aylesbury U.										—	1	Q-F	1	1	2	9
Dorchester T.	—	—	3	—	—	—	—	—	—	—	1	1	1	2	1	9
Hitchin T.						1	—	3	1	—	—	3	1	—	—	9
Ilkeston T.	1	1	2	1	1	—	—	—	—			—	—	3	—	9
Walthamstow Ave.						—	—	2	3	—	1	2	1	—	—	9
Ashington						—	1			—	2	2	1	2	—	8
Bridgwater T.	3	1	1	3	—	—	—	—	—	—	—	—	—	—	—	8
Carshalton Ath.						—	—	—	—	—	1	3	—	2	2	8
Crook T.						—	1	3	2	1	1	—	—	—	—	8
Harrow Boro						—	—	—	1	1	—	—	—	S-F	1	8
Tamworth	1	Q-F	1	1	1	—	—	—	—	—	—	—	—	—	—	8
Whitby T.						—	—	—	2	1	—	—	—	1	Q-F	8
Frickley Ath.	—	—	—	—	—	—	—	1	2	—	—	—	1	—	3	7
Wealdstone				—	3	—	—	—	—	—	—	—	2	1	1	7

W=7 F=6 S-F=5 Q-F=4

Bedford T. (35), Wigan Ath. (27), Romford (18), Wimbledon (18), Atherstone T. (12), Gateshead U. (12), Hereford U. (10), Bexley U. (9), Great Harwood (7) no longer compete in the FA Trophy.

F.A. Challenge Vase

FA CHALLENGE VASE
Committee: J R Plumbe, Chairman; C C Oakes, Vice-Chairman; J Barter; A Burbidge; J E Davey; W G Halsey; F Jones; R W Kiddell; P Rushton; F D Terry.

STANSTED UPHOLD VASE UNDERDOGS TRADITION

For a club who had never won more than one Vase match in any previous competition Stansted burst onto the scene in incredible fashion. They not only beat hot favourites Stamford at Wembley but they also defeated three other very well fancied clubs in Basildon, Heybridge Swifts and Whickham, all away from home!

This type of fairy story isn't new to the Vase competition as every year sees new names battling it out in the later stages with a very real chance of a Wembley place. But the very fact that little clubs can assemble teams together capable of reaching Wembley means there is hope for everyone and no doubt there will be many ambitious chairmen encouraging managers to get their team building right in the close season.

If Stansted claimed the glamour last year it was Stamford who deservedly took over at the top of the F.A. Vase consistency chart. They reached their third final and as they have had to rebuild twice during the nine years this feat shows the club must be run on the very best principles.

Round by round reviews are included with the results in this directory so on page nineteen we are pleased to reproduce Adrian Titcombe's article from this year's Wembley programme in which he looks back over the first ten years of F.A. Vase football.

'RESULT OF THE ROUND'

Preliminary Rounds	Eastbourne United	v	Midland Bank	1-5
First Round	Seaham CW Red Star	v	Chester-le-Street	2-4
Second Round	Lincoln United	v	Shepshed Charterhouse	3-1
Third Round	Chester-le-Street	v	Brandon United	3-5
Fourth Round	Hucknall CW	v	VS Rugby	2-1
Fifth Round	Leyton-Wingate	v	RS Southampton	2-1
Sixth Round	Irthlingborough Diamonds	v	Brandon United	5-0

BEST ATTENDANCES

Preliminary Rounds	Wisbech Town	v	Bridgnorth Town	292
First Round	Harrogate Town	v	Annfield Plain	replay 310
Second Round	Lincoln United	v	Shepshed Charterhouse	433
Third Round	Shifnal Town	v	Bridgnorth Town	1002
Fourth Round	Hucknall CW	v	VS Rugby	906
Fifth Round	Guiseley	v	Brandon United	780
Sixth Round	Old Georgians	v	Stansted	770
Semi-Final	Stamford	v	Irthlingborough Diamonds	(2nd leg) 1432

FA Vase

AFA CLUBS IMPRESS

Extra Preliminary and Preliminary Rounds

One hundred and sixty-five matches are played in these two preliminary rounds and it is a very depressing fact that so many losers are left with no interest in their major knock-out competition so early in the season.

Some famous names took part in the Vase including the oldest club in the country, Sheffield FC, who have contested a Vase Final; Coventry Sporting, who not so long ago hit the headlines with an FA Cup defeat of Tranmere Rovers; Harwich & Parkeston, who played in an FA Amateur Cup Final in front of 100,000 people; and Corinthian-Casuals, who were also to hit the FA Cup headlines.

An interesting feature of the round was the improved form of the AFA sides from the pure amateur leagues in London. Old Esthameians beat Rainham Town 3-1 away, Norsemen won 3-1 at Amersham Town, Old Salesians beat Shoreham 5-1 and Midland Bank travelled to Eastbourne United to record a fine 5-1 victory.

The result of the two rounds was Eastbourne United 1 Midland Bank 5, and the best attendance was 292 for Wisbech Town v Bridgnorth Town.

EXTRA PRELIMINARY ROUND	Sc	Att	Rcpts
Rowntree Mackintosh v Stockton	4-3	29	£13
Armitage v Oldswinford	0-2	35	£18
Bury Town v Northwood Town	1-2	107	£51
Lancing v Fleet Town	2-1	95	£43
Supermarine v Brislington	4-3	45	£9

PRELIMINARY ROUND			
Wigton v Annfield Plain	1-5	—	£4
Rowntree Mackintosh v South Sheilds	4-1	107	£40
Ryhope CA v Farsley Celtic	0-5	70	£32
Nunthorpe Ath v Northallerton T	2-0	11	£5
Wingate v Billingham Town	1-2	20	£6
Seaton D S T v Tadcaster Albion	1-1	20	£6
Bed'ton Terrace v Cleator Moor Celtic	8-2	50	£24
Easington Colliery v Ossett Town	7-0	87	£38
Yorkshire Amateur v Coundon T T	3-0	42	£17
Darlington RA v Esh Winning	2-2	35	£17
Chester-le-Street v Peterlee Newtown	1-1	132	£53
Hebburn Reyrolle v Harrogate Town	1-1	121	£36
Bradley Rangers v Nelson	1-1	30	£12
Haig Colliery v Norton & Stockton Anc	1-1		
Gretna v Hall Road Rangers	6-1	63	£35
York RI v Seaham CW Red Star	1-2*	20	£9
Norton Woodseats v Fryston CW	3-1	28	£15
Blackpool Mechanics v Rylands	1-3*	12	£8
Ford Motors (L'pool) v Garforth M	1-2	20	£9
Wythenshawe Amateurs v St Dominics	4-1	36	£19
North Ferriby United v BSC (Parkgate)	4-4	36	£9
Fleetwood Town v Linotype	3-1	160	£72
Prestwich Heys v Atherton LR	0-1	70	£25
Cheadle Town v Waterloo Dock	2-1	68	£22
Sheffield v Pilkington Recreation	3-2	45	£17
Atherton Collieries v Lytham	3-1	57	£26
Burnley Belvedere v Kiveton Park	0-0	35	£13
Hatfield Main v Maine Road	3-2	25	£7
Grimethorpe MW v Woolley MW	0-2	80	£41
Chadderton v Maghull	4-4	60	£19
Heswall v Bentley Victoria	3-1	60	£19
Rossendale United v North Withington	6-2	60	£36
Barton Town v Worsbro' Bridge MW	3-3	60	£22
Prescot BI v Warrington Town	2-3	21	£4
Daisy Hill v Graham St Prims	1-2*	40	£14
Clay Cross Works v Denaby United	2-3	68	£29
Kimberley Town v Long Eaton United	2-0	58	£23
Ellesmere P & Neston v Skelmersdale U	3-1	30	£12
New Mills v Immingham Town — w.o. for Im'ham			
Clipstone W v Brigg T	2-1	100	£41
Darlaston v Paget Rangers	2-4	155	£59
Oakham United v Bourne Town	5-4	32	£10
Hucknall CW v Oadby Town	3-1	110	£51
Louth United v Stapenhill	3-0	40	£15
Rothwell Town v Northfield Town	2-1	77	£31
Eastwood Hanley v Anstey Nomads	3-0	101	£34
John Player v Gresley Rovers	2-3	113	£23
Coleshill Town v Brereton Social	01-	65	£12
March Town v Newhall United	2-1	130	£35
Arnold Kingswell v Birstall United	2-1	86	£20
Oldswinford v Wolverhampton United	2-0	48	£22
Solihull Boro v Boldmere St Michaels	2-1	43	£19
Potton United v Melton Town	2-0	135	£39
Wisbech Town v Bridgnorth Town	1-2	292	£149
Blakenall v Smethwick Highfield	0-1	53	£23
Mile Oak Rovers & Youth v Cradley T	1-2	60	£16
Soham Town Rangers v Ampthill T	2-4*	75	£55
Histon v Hinckley Athletic	1-3	60	£21
Coventry Sporting v Stratford Town	3-0	42	£26
Tividale v Racing Club Warwick	0-1	65	£31
Wolverton Town v Shillington	3-0	78	£38
Rushall Olympic v Evesham United	3-1	125	£35
Ely City v Bicester Town	0-2	70	£32
Baldock Town v Milton Keynes Boro	7-0	136	£74
Holbeach U v Harwich & Parkeston	1-0	107	£38
Watton United v Chatteris Town	1-2	74	£35
Yaxley v Haverhill Rovers	1-2	58	£29
Crane Sports v Coggeshall Town	1-0	17	£6
Wootton Blue Cross v Stotfold	5-1*	88	£44
Bungay Town v Stowmarket Town	3-5	75	£33
Somersham Town v Clacton Town	0-0	84	£42
Ransomes v Sawbridgeworth Town	4-0	24	£12
Epping Town v Stanstead	0-2	88	£45
Diss Town v Mirrless Blackstone	0-1	109	£38
Hadleigh United v Newmarket Town	0-2	68	£22
Heybridge Swifts v Felixstowe Town	3-0	158	£91
Letchworth Garden City v Edgware	0-1	42	£26
Saffron Walden Town v Maldon Town	3-0	174	£82
Brightlingsea Untied v Crown & Manor	0-2	54	£20
Pirton v St Neots Town	2-1	57	£24
Finchley v Beckton United	0-2	14	£8
Northwood Town v Kempston Rovers	3-2	140	£40
Witham Town v Berkhamsted Town	0-0	48	£15
Hatfield Town v 61 (Luton)	0-2	32	£14
Stevenage Borough v Waterlows	4-1	259	£152
Thetford Town v Haringey Borough	3-2*	84	£27
Halstead Town v Beaconsfield United	1-2	98	£44
Rainham Town v Old Esthameians	1-3	38	£20
Barkingside v Slade Green	1-0	52	£16
Bowers Untied v Hoddesdon Town	3-5*	90	£36
Braintree Town v Woodford Town	2-2	136	£73
Welwyn Garden City v Tring Town	1-3	65	£28
Winchmore Hill v Malden Vale	2-1	79	£34
East Ham United v Royston Town	0-1	30	£13
Kingsbury Town v Vauxhall Motors	1-0	40	£20
Uxbridge v Tansley	6-0	60	£26
Darenth Heathside v BAC Weybridge	2-1	43	£17
Ford U (London) v Chalfont St Peter	0-5	42	£17
Amersham Town v Norsemen	1-3	45	£17
Winslow United v Ware	3-0	60	£24
Chobham v Merstham	1-0	33	£11
Eaton Bray United v Flackwell Heath	3-0	108	£22
Kew Association v Beckenham Town	1-2	10	£5
Corinthian-Casuals v Wallingford T	2-1	26	£14
Whitehawk v Haywards Heath	3-1	121	£48
Selby v Banstead Athletic	2-1	25	£4
Cobham v Erith & Belvedere	1-3	75	£22
Faversham Town v Dorking	2-2	104	£55
Old Salesians v Shoreham	5-1	34	£18
Herne Bay v Chertsey Town	1-1	110	£52
Eastbourne United v Midland Bank	1-5	67	£42
Godalming T v Burgess Hill T	3-1	137	£55
East Grinstead v Tunbridge Wells	0-1	94	£36
Swanley Town v West Wickham	1-0	16	£7
Whitstable Town v Southwick	2-3	59	£31
Redhill v Egham Town	1-1	130	£88
Crockenhill v Eastbourne Town	1-0	81	£37
Deal Town v Malden Town	3-0	67	£32
Hythe Town v Bexhill Town	4-1*	40	£15
Hastings Town v Horley Town	7-1	32	£24
Ash United v Portsmouth RN	2-0	105	£41
Hailsham Town v Ringmer	3-0	104	£37
Peacehaven & Telscombe v Horsham	1-2	102	£38
Horndean v Guildford & Worplesdon	0-3	89	£33
Eastleigh v Frimley Green	4-0	52	£19
Lancing v Horsham YMCA	2-1	76	£29
Camberley Town v Havant Town	2-1	60	£23
Portfield v Wick	1-0	44	£16
Kidlington v Maidenhead T & Youth	0-3	31	£10

Steyning Town v Littlehampton T	2-3	63	£29
Pagham v RS Southampton	1-3	62	£26
Pirelli General v Farnham Town	0-1	43	£18
Thatcham Town v Abington Town	0-1	61	£22
Arundel v Petersfield United	2-1*	38	£17
Chichester City v Wantage Town	1-4*	85	£34
Warminster Town v Romsey Town	2-2	146	£78
Yate Town v Cirencester Town	3-2	81	£22
Brockenhurst v Wimborne Town	6-1	116	£41
Flight Refuelling v Calne Town	3-3	20	£7
Didcot Town v Thame United	3-0*	28	£12
Wilton Rovers v Mangotsfield United	1-1	40	£20
Chipping Norton T v Pegasus Juniors	0-1	30	£13
Hazells (Aylesbury) v Peasedown Ath	3-0	70	£27
Lawrence Weston Hallen v Paulton R	3-2	18	£9
Moreton Town v Larkhall Athletic	0-2	72	£28
Abingdon United v Malvern Town	0-1	45	£20
Lydbrook v Old Georgians	0-2	30	£5
Amesbury v Supermarine	3-2	50	£17
Westbury United v Port of Bristol	1-4	38	£9
Clanfield v Sharpness	1-0	70	£25
Ledbury T v Fairford T – w.o. for F'ford			
Chip'ham T v Welton R	1-0	100	£43
Bristol Manor Farm v Odd Down	1-0	23	£16
Wadebridge Town v Portway-Bristol	1-2	160	£78
Glenside St Gabriels v Portishead	2-1	20	£0
Radstock Town v Avon Bradford	4-1	42	£19
Clevedon Town v Glastonbury	1-0	70	£30
Newquay v Torrington	2-0*	233	£70
Ottery St Mary v Hengrove Ath	2-1	60	£26
Backwell United v Exmouth Town	0-4	39	£24

PRELIMINARY ROUND REPLAYS

Tadcaster Albion v Seaton Terrace	2-0	51	£14
Esh Winning v Darlington RA	2-0	82	£34
Peterlee Newtown v Chester-le-Street	2-3	71	£29
Harrogate Town v Hebburn Reyrolle	3-2	150	£50
Nelson v Bradley Rangers	0-1	18	£8
BSC (Parkgate) v North Ferriby U	2-5*	25	£8
Kiveton Park v Burnley Belvedere	3-0	25	£4
Maghull v Chadderton	2-0	36	£17
Worsbrough Bridge MW v Barton T	2-2	70	£28
Clacton Town v Somersham Town	2-3	30	£12
Berkhamstead Town v Witham Town	1-2	32	£14
Woodford Town v Braintree Town	0-1	65	£58
Dorking v Faversham Town	6-0	100	£44
Chertsey Town v Herne Bay	2-1	50	£28
Egham Town v Redhill	2-1	65	£24
Romsey Town v Warminster Town	2-1	155	£56
Calne Town v Flight Refuelling	1-2	22	£10
Mangotsfield United v Wilton Rovers	3-0	75	£35

SECOND REPLAY

Worsbrough Bridge MW v Barton T	1-3	208	£87

FIRST ROUND

Casuals Score Nine

Ninety-six more ties saw many more 'names' disappear from the competition but at least fans were seeing plenty of goals. Corinthian-Casuals scored 9 at Chertsey, Bracknell Town and Newquay registered 6 away, and large home victories are achieved by Fleetwood Town 7-1 and Littlehampton 5-0. Bridgnorth Town joined fellow Southern Leaguers RS Southampton in the next round with an emphatic 8-1 away victory at Oldswinford.

A battle of the Hampshire giants saw Sholing Sports win away against arch rivals AFC Totton with the only goal of the game and Hungerford Town, twice semi-finalists, were eliminated by Chippenham Town.

The result of the round was Seaham CW Red Star 2 Chester-le-Street 4, and the best attendance was 310 for Harrogate Town v Annfield Plain (replay).

Tadcaster Albion v Esh Winning	1-3	101	£24
Seaham CW R S v Chester-le-Street	2-4	235	£80
Annfield Plain v Harrogate Town	1-1	130	£56
Billingham Town v Farsley Celtic	0-1	150	£19
Whickham v Bedlington Terriers	2-1	94	£39
Bradley Rangers v Nunthorpe Ath	0-1	48	£18
Yorks Am v Norton & Stockton Anc	1-2*	60	£23
Rowntree Mackintosh v Gretna	1-2	120	£41
Eppleton CW v Easington Colliery	1-0	138	£47
Wren Rovers v Cheadle Town	1-2	42	£14
Fleetwood Town v Norton Woodseats	7-1	203	£100
Atherton LR v Atherton Collieries	3-1	110	£51
Rossendale United v Irlam Town	0-5	76	£44
Kiveton Park v Heswall	1-3	40	£19
Thackley v Clitheroe	1-5	277	£94
Garforth Miners v Warrington Town	2-4	100	£39
Wythenshawe Amateurs v Guiseley	1-2	100	£49
Ellesmere P & N v Woolley MW	3-2	45	£19
Maghull v Rylands	2-4	47	£17
North Ferriby U v Immingham T	3-0	62	£21
Graham St Prims v Lincoln United	0-1	52	£17
Hucknall CW v Kimberley Town	3-0	114	£51
Oakham United v Barton Town	2-3	128	£50
Paget Rangers v Winterton Rangers	1-1	58	£22
Clipstone W'fare v Appleby Frod'ham	1-4	120	£52
Hatfield Main v Sheffield	3-1	30	£8
Denaby United v Louth Unted	3-2	89	£24
Oldswinford v Bridgnorth Town	1-8	41	£18
Eastwood Hanley v Desborough T	1-2	75	£27
Rothwell Town v Knowle	5-0	83	£31
Arnold Kingswell v Cradley Town	0-0	102	£41
West Midlands Police v Ampthill T	1-4	52	£19
Wolverton T v Smethwick Highfield	3-1	100	£40
Wednesfield Social v Friar Lane OB	0-1	52	£20
Gresley Rovers v Rushall Olympic	2-1	175	£75
March Town U v Walsall Borough	2-0	87	£45
Hinckley Ath v Rushden Town	2-2	245	£152
Brereton Social v Potton United	0-1	93	£43
Wigston Fields v Solihull Borough	3-0	30	£16
Racing C Warwick v Coventry Sport	1-2	67	£21
Crane Sports v Arlesey Town	2-2	9	£4
Somersham Town v Holbeach United	2-4	78	£39
Baldock Town v Mirrless Blackstone	3-1	194	£80
Wivenhoe Town v Newmarket Town	2-1	67	£23
Haverhill Rovers v Chatteris Town	4-2	110	£49
Stowmarket Town v Beckton United	2-0	128	£56
Ransomes v Brantham Athletic	3-1	87	£35
Saffron Walden Town v Norsemen	4-0	252	£127
Beaconsfield U v Tiptree U	0-1	61	£27
Edgware v Heybridge Swifts	1-1	134	£61
Wooton Blue Cross v Harefield U	2-3	81	£43
Braintree Town v Thetford Town	2-0	80	£74
Stevenage Borough v Ruislip Manor	2-1*	230	£146
Winchmore Hill v Eaton Bray United	0-1*	80	£45
Old Esthameians v Uxbridge	1-2	40	£20
Southall v Northwood Town	2-1	130	£56
Hemel Hempstead v Chalfont St Peter	2-0	116	£53
Winslow United v Royston Town	1-1	90	£38
Witham Town v Pirton	3-0	72	£22
Selby v 61 (Luton)	1-3	30	£6
Crown & Manor v Tring Town	3-1	24	£12
Kingsbury Town v Hoddesdon Town	2-0	44	£21
Stansted v Barkingside	4-1	74	£25
Hailsham Town v Swanley Town	1-1	163	£52
Littlehampton Town v Didcot Town	5-0	115	£87
Guildford & Worplesdon v Dorking T	1-2	125	£75
Newport IOW v Farnham Town	3-2	184	£94
Chobham v RS Southampton	0-5	81	£28
Lancing v Bracknell Town	1-6	105	£63
Horsham v Tunbridge Wells	2-4	90	£39
Chertsey Town v Corinthian-Casuals	2-9	120	£65
Hythe Town v Egham Town	1-0	50	£20
Darenth Heathside v Eastleigh	1-2	40	£11
Erith & Belvedere v Arundel	1-2	91	£50
Southwick v Midland Bank	1-1	151	£42
Maidenhead T & Youth v Hastings T	3-1	48	£14
Whitehawk v Godalming Town	3-2	90	£40
AFC Totton v Sholing Sports	0-1	300	£184
Beckenham Town v Alma Swanley	4-4	60	£13
Old Salesians v Ash United	1-2	38	£16
Camberley Town v Deal Town	0-4	31	£14
Crockenhill v Portfield	2-1	53	£24
Malvern Town v Amesbury Town	4-1	108	£40
Portway-Bristol v Bristol Manor Farm	2-3	60	£29
Hazells (Aylesbury) v Fairfield Town	4-4	20	£7
Brockenhurst v Port of Bristol	2-1	97	£30
Abingdon Town v Flight Refuelling	2-2	58	£24
Chippenham T v Hungerford T	2-0	142	£73
Clanfield v Bicester Town	0-3	58	£23

Mangotsfield U v Pegasus Juniors	0-0	80	£46
Yate Town v Larkhall Athletic	4-0	91	£30
O Georgians v Lawrence Weston H	1-0	64	£17
Wantage Town v Romsey Town	3-1	108	£38
Clevedon Town v Ottery St Mary	4-0	93	£38
Glenside St Gabriels v Newquay	2-6	120	£60
Exmouth v Radstock Town	1-0	150	£45
Replays			
Harrogate Town v Annfield Plain	2-1	310	£100
Winterton Rangers v Page Rangers	1-2*	87	£25
Cradley Town v Arnold Kingswell	2-4*	70	£23
Rushden Town v Hinckley Athletic	0-3	270	£163
Arlesey Town v Crane Sports	2-3	143	£58
Heybridge Swifts v Edgware	3-2*	284	£159
Royston Town v Winslow United	3-4	136	£54
Swanley Town v Hailsham Town	4-0	68	£27
Midland Bank v Southwick	2-4	54	£27
Alma Swanley v Beckenham Town	3-1		
Fairford Town v Hazells (Aylesbury)	1-0	30	£12
Flight Refuelling v Abingdon Town	2-3	38	£18
Pegasus Juniors v Mangotsfield U	1-2	132	£71

SECOND ROUND

Shepshed Charterhouse Out

All the 'big guns' are now in, but sometimes a club with a run of two Vase victories and the smell of Wembley in their nostrils can catch the exempt clubs cold.

Results in the north mostly go to form but Lincoln United's defeat of Shepshed Charterhouse raised a few eyebrows. Holders VS Rugby looked determined enough with a 7-1 victory over Skegness Town, and finalists Halesowen Town got through a difficult tie at Wigston Fields.

Fancied clubs who went out included Almondsbury Greenway and Basildon United, while Three Bridges and Burnham, who have done well in recent years, also failed to get through.

Clubs to watch, apart from last season's finalists, were, according to the grapevine, RS Southampton, Corinthian-Casuals, Brandon United and Heybridge Swifts.

The result of the round was Lincoln United 3 Shepshed Charterhouse 1, and the best attendance was 433 at Lincoln United v Charterhouse.

	Score	Att	Rcpts
Ossett Albion v Harrogate Town	0-2	140	£63
Chester-le-Street v Norton & Stockton Ancients	5-0	103	£37
Whickham v Eppleton CW	2-0	125	£52
Gretna v Brandon United	0-1	81	£45
Farsley Celtic v Guisborough Town	1-1	141	£52
Clitheroe v Guiseley	1-3	266	£186
Blue Star v Nunthorpe Athletic	1-0	71	£33
Fleetwood Town v Esh Winning	2-1	172	£102
North Ferriby United v Rainworth MW	0-1	142	£52
Barton Town v Cheadle Town (abandoned in extra time)	2-1	52	£19
Warrington Town v Hallam	1-0	80	£39
Atherton LR v Rylands	0-2	54	£25
Ellesmere Port & Neston v Appleby Frodingham	1-3	24	£12
Lincoln U v Shepshed Charterhouse	3-1	433	£197
Denaby United v Irlam Town	4-1	181	£55
Heswall v Hatfield Main	2-4	60	£29
Frecheville Community v Staveley Wks	1-1	41	£18
Coventry Sporting v Bridgnorth Town	0-1	35	£23
Paget Rangers v Hinckley Athletic	2-0	116	£60
Friar Lane OB v Hucknall CW	0-3	120	£38
Wigston Fields v Halesowen Town	0-1	337	£193
Arnold Kingswell v Shifnal Town	1-2*	65	£26
March Town United v Holbeach United	1-2	94	£50
Atherstone United v Gresley Rovers	3-0	204	£97
VS Rugby v Skegness Town	7-1	376	£272
Gorleston v Stamford	2-3*	288	£106
Desborough T v Great Yarmouth T	0-2	200	£96
Wivenhoe Town v Haverhill Rovers	2-1	87	£39
Crane Sports v Potton United	0-1	49	£21
Witham Town v Baldock Town	1-2	101	£37
Basildon United v Stansted Town	0-1	185	£85
Braintree Town v Ampthill Town	1-2*	182	£72
Irthlingborough Diamonds v 61 (Luton)	2-2	130	£58
Stowmarket Town v Crown & Manor	1-3*	134	£77
Harefield United v Southall	4-1	103	£48
Rothwell Town v Stevenage Borough	1-0	103	£42
Winslow United v Tiptree United	1-2	76	£36
Leyton-Wingate v Kingsbury Town	1-0	70	£55
Heybridge Swifts v Wolverton Town	4-0	187	£100
Barton Rovers v Uxbridge	2-2	146	£74
Buckingham Town v Ransomes	5-2	146	£74
Eaton Bray United v Saffron Waldon T	1-2*	100	£36
Grays Athletic v Burnham	1-0	117	£64
Hemel Hempstead v Marlow	4-1	102	£47
Whyteleafe v Corinthian-Casuals	0-1	127	£60
RS Southampton v Maidenhead Town	4-2*	128	£86
Crockenhill v Cray Wanderers	2-1*	171	£81
Three Bridges v Dorking	1-2	140	£74
Bracknell Town v Littlehampton Town	2-1	68	£63
Tunbridge Wells v Ash United	2-1	119	£63
Arundel v Alma Swanley	2-1	90	£29
Sholing Sports v Eastleigh	0-2	200	£53
Deal Town v Swanley Town	1-2	—	—
Southwick v Whitehawk	0-1	310	£78
Newport IOW v Hythe Town	5-2	244	£163
Malvern Town v Wantage Town	2-2	124	£50
Yate Town v Brockenhurst	1-0	125	£33
Bristol Manor Farm v Almdonsbury Greenway	2-1	159	£92
Shortwood Town v Abingdon Town	1-1	80	£33
Chippenham Town v Newbury Town	1-2*	86	£45
Bicester Town v Fairford Town	2-1	68	£17
Devizes Town v Mangotsfield United	5-0	80	£50
Old Georgians v Clevedon Town	1-0	100	£43
Newquay v Exmouth Town	0-2	260	£109

REPLAYS

Guisborough Town v Farsley Celtic	0-1	115	£55
Cheadle Town v Barton Town	1-0	62	£18
Staveley Works v Frecheville Com	3-1	40	£17
61 (Luton) v Irthlingborough Diamonds	0-1	67	£32
Uxbridge v Barton Rovers	3-1	102	£43
Wantage Town v Malvern Town	2-0	105	£32
Abingdon Town v Shortwood Town	2-0	83	£35

THIRD ROUND

Brandon Look Powerful

Suddenly the competition looks rather small! There are only 32 ties and there will not be many easy matches after this round.

Brandon United won a superb match 5-3 away to Chester-le-Street, and Blue Star went out. Past winners Whickham were lurking up in the North and in the Midlands a titanic struggle between Shifnal Town and Bridgnorth Town was won away by Shifnal in a replay (1-1, 1-2).

Stamford, Irthlingborough Diamonds and a powerful looking Buckingham Town looked a very strong United Counties representation and in the South Heybridge Swifts, Casuals and RS Southampton still looked the pick of the bunch, although Leyton Wingate and Bristol Manor Farm represented exciting outsiders.

The result of the round was Chester-le-Street 3 Brandon United 5, and the best attendance was 1,002 for Shifnal Town v Bridgnorth Town.

	Score	Att	Rcpts
Guiseley v Harrogate Town	2-0*	450	£225
Chester-le-Street v Brandon United	3-5	297	£124
Whickham v Fleetwood Town	1-0	255	£122
Blue Star v Farsley Celtic	1-1	133	£65
Warrington T v Appleby Frodingham	4-0	90	£39
Lincoln United v Hatfield Main	0-1	132	£60
Shifnal Town v Bridgnorth Town	1-1	1002	£497
Denaby United v Halesowen Town	2-1	556	£248
Staveley Works v Paget Rangers	3-1	180	£56
+ Rylands v Rainworth MW	4-1*	160	£80
Hucknall CW v Cheadle Town	4-0	260	£110
Stamford v Potton United	2-1	272	£148
Holbeach United v Crown & Manor	2-2	126	£46
Irthlingborough Diamonds v Ampthill T	2-1	185	£85
Baldock Town v Great Yarmouth Town	3-0	408	£194
VS Rugby v Atherstone United	2-1	832	£630
Stansted Town v Wivenhoe Town	2-0	146	£62
Harefield United v Heybridge Swifts	3-4	125	£50
Leyton-Wingate v Arundel	3-1	136	£111
Tunbridge Wells v Buckingham Town	2-4*	224	£123
Bracknell Town v Corinthian-Casuals	0-4	120	£130
Tiptree United v Whitehawk	1-4	144	£71
Crockenhill v Swanley Town	4-0	153	£75

Rothwell Town v Dorking	4-3*	177	£77
Uxbridge v Saffron Walden Town	2-1	156	£59
Grays Athletic v Hemel Hempstead	4-1	151	£85
Wantage Town v Abingdon Town	2-5	174	£70
RS Southampton v Exmouth Town	3-0	149	£113
Old Georgians v Devizes Town	4-1	120	£42
Newbury Town v Yate Town	3-1	165	£90
Newport IOW v Eastleigh	2-0	264	£133
Bicester Town v Bristol Manor Farm	0-1	71	£19

+ MATCH ORDERED TO BE REPLAYED

Rainworth MW v Rylands	1-0	236	£95

REPLAYS

Farsley Celtic v Blue Star	1-0	250	£96
Bridgnorth Town v Shifnal Town	1-2	463	£298
Crown & Manor v Holbeach United	1-0	97	£48

FOURTH ROUND

	Sc	Att
Whickham v Denaby United	3-2*	402
Warrington Town v Guiseley	0-3	216
Brandon United v Farsley Celtic	2-1	300
Hucknall CW v VS Rugby	2-0	906
Stamford v Shifnal Town	3-1	544
Rothwell Town v Rainworth MW	3-3	340
Staveley Works v Hatfield Main	2-1	150
Baldock Town v Grays Athletic	1-0	566
Heybridge Swifts v Stansted	1-2*	326
Leyton-Wingate v Crown & Manor	5-0	202
Buckingham Town v Crockenhill	3-1	280
Uxbridge v Irthlingborough Diams	0-2	196
Newbury T v Bristol Manor Farm	0-1	
Abingdon Town v RS Southampton	1-2*	256
Corinthian-Casuals v Whitehawk	1-0	133
Old Georgians v Newport IOW	3-2*	267

REPLAY

Rainworth MW v Rothwell Town	3-2	362

Tunbridge Wells beat Ash United 2-1 in the Second Round and here one of their defenders rises high above the visitor's Bobby Burton. Photo: Eric Marsh

Newbury Town's Graeme Gourley wins this ball against Bristol Manor Farm but his side lost 1-2 at home in the Fourth Round. Photo: Newbury Weekly News

Fifth Round

A closely fought round

With only two of the eight ties producing victories by more than one goal, it was perhaps surprising that there were no replays in this round.

Runaway leaders of the Southern League Division One (South), RS Southampton, were beaten by Leyton Wingate, and the Essex club immediately took over from their visitors as the Southern favourites in this year's competition.

Another impressive victory was recorded by Brandon United, away to Guisley, so the North East, with past winners Whickham also getting through quite comfortably, were to be strongly represented in the quarter-finals.

The most exciting tie was at Corinthian Casuals, where the famous club, having enjoyed the publicity of a fine FA Cup run, were ahead of the strong Stamford side, but allowed their visitors to take the game into extra time. It was then that Dominic Genovese proved to be the hero of the day by completing a fine hat trick.

Two outsiders made up the eight, with Old Georgians raising Bristolians' hopes by beating Baldock Town, and Stavely Works winning in fine style by 4-2 against Rainworth Miners Welfare.

Leyton Wingate 2 (Goodwin, Warwick) **RS Southampton 1** (Young) Attendance: 220
Leyton Wingate: Tucker, Thomas, McKenzie, Hamberder, Mavin, Goodwin, Rhoden, Warwick, Tippett, Trainer, Lane.
RS Southampton: Moore, Young, Farmer, Baxter, Cleveland, Bennett, Dowding, Young, Mooney, Earles, White.

Corinthian-Casuals 2 (Merron 2) **Stamford 4** (Genovese 3, Beech) *aet* Attendance: 243
Corinthian-Casuals: Chapman, Bateman, Stevenson, Coldspring, Green, Parden, Armitt, Finnigan, Merron, Rulton, Watson (Finn).
Stamford: Parslow, Smitheringale, Blades, McIlwain, Lyon, Mackin, Genovese, Waddicor, (Hines), Allen, Robson, Beech.

Stansted 2 (Reeves, Williams) **Bristol Manor Farm 1** (Micciche) Attendance: 481
Stansted: Coe, Hilton, Williams, Simpson, Cooper, Gillard, Callanan, Doyle, Reeves, Holt, Williams.
Bristol Manor Farm: Parsons, Holbrook, Savage, Sullivan, Garrett, Down, Hawkes, George, Johns, Rex, Micciche, (Bray).

Old Georgians 1 (Hudson) **Baldock Town 0** Attendance: 420
Old Georgians: Hutchings, Edmunds, Pitt, King, Trought, Hudson, House, Bedford, Jacobs, Black, (Leitch), Bell.
Baldock Town: Allinson, Simpson, Nunn, Rowncy, King, Ferguson, Armsby, Adcock, Beech, Carter, Dance.

Irthlingborough Diamonds 1 (Atkinson) **Buckingham Town 0** Attendance: 700
Irthlingborough Diamonds: Smith, Kaines, Lloyd, Ashby, Garratt, Gillespie, Phipps, Mann, Sargent, McGuire, Atkinson.
Buckingham Town: Hopps, Kingston, Folds, Liddle, Goodeve, Frost, Russell, Heap, Shrieves, Pittam, Holmes.

Stavely Works 4 (Vernon 2, Hardy, Degiralamo) **Rainworth Miners Welfare 2** (Comerford, Guy) Attendance: 685
Stavely Works: Turner, Pettifier, Hemstalk, Dennis, Hardy K, Hardy N, Degiralamo, Millard, (Quigley), Lee, Vernon, Atkinson.
Rainworth MW: Darvon, Hallam, Hodgson, Comerford, Sterland, Wright, Knowles, Raine, (Morton), Guy, Owen, Bostock.

Guisley 0 **Brandon United 1** (Thomson) Attendance: 780
Guisley: Armfield, Harney, Ford, (Birch), Kydlenitzky, Codd, Hall, Houlston, Harrison, Baker, Lawson, McPhee.
Brandon United: Charlton, Hillary, Liddle, Brown, Dixon, Forster, Kerr, Thomson, Jennings, Herczeg, (Dixon), McKenzie.

Whickham 2 (Spellman, Rafferty) **Hucknall Colliery Welfare 0** Attendance: 408
Whickham: Gutherie, Hogg, Knox, Spellman, Riley, Ward, Rafferty, Keilty, Heron, Diamond, Barker.
Hucknall CW: Bull, Beeby, Nixon, Priestley, Harrod, Nicholls, (Hickling), Ecob, Dawkins, Grantham, Freeman, Dulson.

Action during Stavely Works fine 4-2 victory over Rainworth Miners Welfare at home. Photo: David Shute

Old Georgians were one of the Vase surprises last season as they reached the quarter finals. Here they are attacking against Newport I.O.W. whom they beat 3-2 after extra time in the Fourth Round.
Photo: Mike Joss

Stamford's Lindon Parslow punches clear from Corinthian Casuals mid field player Colin Coldspring watched by John Mackin, the only Stamford survivor from their 1980 Wembley side. Photo: Eric Marsh

Tommy Robson's free kick sails over the packed Irthlingborough Diamonds defence for Russ Allan (third from right) to head the deciding semi-final goal for Stamford. Photo Stamford Photographic Services/ Stamford Mercury

Sixth Round

Traditional Vase teams do well

Two very decisive victories by the United Counties League representatives, Irthlingborough Diamonds, who thrashed the well fancied Brandon United 5-0 thanks to an excellent hat trick by Gary Sargent, and Stamford, who beat Stavely Works 3-0, dominated this round. These two clubs, with excellent Vase pedigrees, would surely wish to avoid each other in the semi-finals. Past winners Whickham qualified to represent the North-East with a last-minute winner from substitute Billy Rafferty in extra time, and they, too, had tradition on their side.

The least-known semi-finalist turned out to be Stansted from the Essex Senior League, who of course produced the most famous Vase club of all, Billericay Town. Looking at Stansted's record in this season's competition, however, proves that they certainly deserved to reach the last four.

Irthlingborough Diamonds 5 (Sargent 3, Garratt, Atkinson) **Brandon United 0** Attendance: 609
Irthlingborough Diamonds: Smith, Haines, Lloyd, Ashby, Garratt, Dunn, Phipps, Mann, Sargent, McGuire, Atkinson, (York).
Brandon United: Charlton, Hillary, Liddle, Brown, Dixon, Forster, Kerr, Thomson, Jennings, Herczeg, (McKendrie), Moat.

Old Georgians 1 (Edmonds) **Stansted 1** (Reeves) *aet* Attendance: 770
Old Georgians: Hutchings, Ratcliffe, Edmonds, King, Trought, Hudson, House, Bedford, Jacobs, Black, Bell, (Leitch).
Stansted: Coe, Williams D, Hilton, Simpson, Cooper, Callanan, Doyle, Reading, Reeves, Holt, Williams L.

Stamford 3 (Allen 2, Robson) **Stavely Works 0** Attendance: 695
Stamford: Parslow, Smitheringale, Blades, McIlwain, Lyon, Mackin, Genovese, Waddicor, Allen, Robson, Chapman.
Stavely Works: Turner, Collins, Hardy, (Quigley), Atkinson, Hemstalk, Dennis, Degiralamo, Millward, Lee, Hardy, Vernon.

Leyton Wingate 0 **Whickham 1** (Rafferty) *aet* Attendance: 500
Leyton Wingate: Tucker, Thomas, Mahoney, Sharp, Mavin, Goodwin, Jones, Bee, (Parkinson), Warwick, Rhoden, Lane.
Whickham: Guthrie, Hogg, Knox, Spellman, (Rafferty), Riley, Ward, Kielty, Mayne, Heron, Diamond, Barker.

SIXTH ROUND REPLAY

Stansted 2 (Cooper, Holt) **Old Georgians 0** Attendance: 711
Stansted: Coe, Williams D, Hilton, Simpson, Cooper, Reading, Callanan, Holt, Reeves, Doyle, Williams L.
Old Georgians: Hutchings, Ratcliffe, Pitt, King, Edmonds, Hudson, House, Bedford, Jacobs, Vaughan, (Leitch), Bell.

Semi-Finals

Stansted provide a shock

The first two results brought one surprise — the defeat of Irthlingborough Diamonds at home by Stamford — and one expected score of 1-1 at Stansted where Whickham held the little Essex club.

On closer inspection, however, Stamford could be considered to be the Diamonds' bogey side, having beaten the reigning United Counties champions twice in the league this season, and if any one were to knock out this excellent club it would certainly be the very experienced Stamford outfit.

So on to the second legs, and the shock result that took Stansted to Wembley. Their 2-0 win at Whickham, where the home side had never lost a Vase tie, was a tremendous achievement and one which needed no little amount of character and determination. The Vaux Wearside club were badly rattled and the game developed into a very physical battle.

Poor Irthlingborough, demoralised by their home defeat, were eliminated by a confident Stamford side and thus joined the unfortunate Friar Lane Old Boys, Farnborough Town and Hungerford Town, who had all lost twice at the semi-final stage.

FIRST LEGS

Stansted 1 (Doyle pen) **Whickham 1** (Mayne) Attendance: 828
Stansted: Coe, Williams D, Hilton, Simpson, Cooper, Reading, Callanan, Holt, Reeves, Doyle, Gillard.
Whickham: Guthrie, Hogg, Knox, Spellman, Riley, Ward, Keilty, Mayne, Heron, Diamond, Barker.

Irthlingborough Diamonds 1 (Ashby) **Stamford 2** (Genovese, Waddicor) Attendance: 1,332
Irthlingborough Diamonds: Smith, Haines, Lloyd, Ashby, Garratt, McGuire, Dunn, (Hamilton), Mann, Sargent, York, Atkinson.
Stamford: Parslow, Smitheringale, Blades, McIlwain, Lyon, Mackin, Genovese, Waddicor, Allen, Robson, Chapman.

SECOND LEGS

Whickham 0 **Stansted 2** (Reeves, Gillard) Attendance: 1,102
Whickham: Guthrie, Hogg, Knox, Spellman, (Rafferty), Riley, Ward, Kielty, Mayne, Heron, Diamond, Barker.
Stansted: Coe, Hilton, Williams D, Simpson, Cooper, Krsozka, Doyle, Callanan, Reeves, Holt, Gillard.

Stamford 2 (Waddicor, Allen) **Irthlingborough Diamonds 0** Attendance: 1,432
Stamford: Parslow, Smitheringale, Blades, McIlwain, Lyon, Mackin, Genovese, Waddicor, Allen, Robson, Chapman.
Irthlingborough Diamonds: Verity, Haines, Lloyd, Ashby, Garratt, McGuire, Sargent, Head, York, Phipps, (Dunn), Atkinson.

Hucknall Colliery Welfare defend in depth during their fine 2-0 home victory over the then V.S. Rugby.
Photo: Leo Hoenig

Chris King, whose goal in the last minute of extra time won the game for Old Georgians, shoots over the Newport (I.O.W.) crossbar from close range.
Photo: David Shute

Stansted attack the Whickham goal and finished up as the first team to win a Vase tie at the Vaux Wearside club's ground.
Photo: Leo Hoenig

Ace Directory photographers Eric Marsh and Mike Joss have caught some excellent action in the Vase and here above we see hero of the day Dominic Genovese, who was regularly watched by Manchester United last season, head home to complete a match winning hat trick against Casuals. Photo: Eric Marsh
Below: A great Leyton Wingate effort hit the bar with the whole Whickham defence beaten. Photo: Mike Joss
Bottom: Another great diving header, this time by R.S. Southampton's White early in the competition at Chobham. Photo: Eric Marsh

FA VASE — ROUND-BY-ROUND TO WEMBLEY

Third Round

Stamford 2
Potton U 1

Shifnal T 1 2
Bridgnorth T . 1 1

Bracknell T 0
C-Casuals 4

Tiptree U 1
Whitehawk 4

Staveley Works . . 3+
Paget Rangers . . 1

Lincoln U 0
Hatfield Main . . 1

Rothwell T . . . . 4+
Dorking 3

×Rylands 4+ 0
Rainworth MW1 1

Uxbridge 2
Saffron Walden T 1

Irthlingbro' D . . 2
Ampthill T 1

Tunbridge W . . 2+
Buckingham T . 4

Crockenhill 4
Swanley T 0

Warrington T . . 4
Appleby Frod . . 0

Guisley . . . . 2+
Harrogate T . . . 0

Chester-le-Street 3
Brandon U. 5

Blue Star. 1 0
Farsley Celtic . 1 1

Leyton-Wingate 3
Arundel 1

Holbeach 2 0
Crown&Manor 2 1

Wantage T. 2
Abingdon T. . . . 5

RS Southampton 3
Exmouth T 0

Whickham. 1
Fleetwood T . . . 0

Denaby U 2
Halesowen T . . . 1

Hucknall CW . . 4
Cheadle T 0

VS Rugby 2
Atherstone U . . . 1

Old Georgians . . 4
Devizes T 1

Newport IOW . . 2
Eastleigh 0

Baldock T 3
Gt Yarmouth T . 0

Grays Ath 4
H Hempstead . . 1

Newbury T 3
Yate T 1

Bicester T 0
Bristol MF. 1

Harefield U 3
Heybridge Swifts 4

Wivenhoe T . . . 0
Stansted. 2

Fourth Round

Stamford 3
Shifnal. 1
C-Casuals 1
Whitehawk 0
Staveley Works . 2
Hatfield Main . . 1
Rothwell T. . . 3 2
Rainworth MW3 3
Uxbridge. 0
Irthlingboro' D . 2
Buckingham T . 3
Crockenhill 1
Warrington T . . 0
Guisley 3
Brandzon U. . . . 2
Farsley Celtic . . 1
Leyton-Wingate 5
Crown & Manor 0
Abingdon T. . . . 1
RS S'hampton +2
Whickham . . . +3
Denaby U 2
Hucknall CW . . 2
VS Rugby 0
Old Georgians +3
Newport IOW . . 2
Baldock T 1
Grays Ath 0
Newbury T 0
Bristol MF. 1
Heybridge Swifts 1
Stansted. . . . +2

Fifth Round

Stamford . . . +4
C-Casuals 2
Staveley Works . 4
Rainworth MW. 2
Irthlingboro' D . 1
Buckingham T . 0
Guisley 0
Brandon U. 1
Leyton-Wingate 2
RS Southampton 1
Whickham. 2
Hucknall CW . . 0
Old Georgians . . 1
Baldock Town. . 0
Bristol MF. 1
Stansted. 2

Sixth Round

Stamford 3
Staveley Works . 0
Irthlingboro' D . 5
Brandon United 0
Leyton-Wingate 0
Whickham . . . +1
Old Georgians 1 0
Stansted 1 2

Semi Final

Stamford . . . 2 2
Irthlingboro Diamonds . . 1 0

1st Leg at Irthlingborough
2nd Leg at Stamford

Whickham . . . 1 0
Stansted 1 2

1st Leg at Stansted
2nd Leg at Whickham

Final

Stamford 2
Stansted. 3

+ Denotes after extra time (all drawn ties include extra time)
× Denotes tie ordered to be replayed

First named club at home in rounds three and four except Stansted in round three

STANSTED WIN SUPERB FINAL

By Paul Walker, Daily Star

Last season's FA Vase Final at Wembley proved to be the year of the underdog as Essex Senior League outfit Stansted beat much fancied Stamford from the United Counties 3-2 in the competition's tenth final.

Much of the interest centred on Stamford's veteran winger Tommy Robson, who retired after the final, having previously played in over 800 Football League games for Newcastle, Chelsea, Northampton and Peterborough. He certainly covered every blade of grass in a hard working display, but it was the unknowns from Essex who deservedly took the trophy.

For Stamford it was their second losing final in three appearances, with the only survivor from their previous Wembley big day being skipper John Mackin, when they beat Guisborough 2-0 in 1980.

Manager Chris Corby had rebuilt the side over the past couple of seasons and, with an impressive Vase pedigree, they were clear favourites.

But it was Stansted, with a highly organised defence, who settled first and were ahead after 20 minutes.

Jamie Reeves, who won a winners' medal with Billericay in 1979, sent Gabriel Callanan away, and his pass sent in Ray Holt to draw 'keeper Linden Parslow before scoring.

Sixteen minutes later another Callanan pass presented Paul Gillard with the chance to make it two. The favourites were stunned, but came out after the break with renewed determination.

Within four minutes of the restart Dominic Genovese and Russ Allen set up the chance for John Waddicor to pull a goal back. The final was really buzzing now, and Stansted showed their fighting spirit nine minutes later when Reeves crossed perfectly for John Reading to head in the third.

Still Stamford would not give up and Allen — son of the famous West Bromwich and England star Ronnie — kept the game alive.

Allen senior had scored for Albion in the FA Cup Final exactly 30 years previously against Preston, and Allen junior was not to be outdone.

Stamford's route from Gorleston to Wembley

Round	*Opponents*	*Venue*	*Result*	*Scorers*	*Attendance*
Second	**Gorleston** (Eastern Counties)	Away	3-2	McIlwain, Lyon, Waddicor	288
Third	**Potton United** (United Counties)	Home	2-1	Genovese (pen), Mackin	272
Fourth	**Shifnal Town** (West Midlands Regional)	Home	3-1	Genovese, Waddicor, McIlwain	544
Fifth	**Corinthian-Casuals** (Isthmian)	Away	4-2*	Genovese 3, Beech	243
Sixth	**Staveley Works** (Northern Counties East)	Home	3-0	Robson, Allen 2	695
Semi-Final 1st Leg	**Irthlingborough Diamonds** (United Counties)	Away	2-1	Genovese, Waddicor	1,332
2nd Leg	**Irthlingborough Diamonds**	Home	2-0	Waddicor, Allen	1,432

Matches played: 7 goals for: 19 against: 7 * after extra time

Stansted's route from Epping to Wembley

Round	*Opponents*	*Venue*	*Result*	*Scorers*	*Attendance*
Preliminary	**Epping Town** (Isthmian)	Away	2-0	Holt, Doyle	88
First	**Barkingside** (London-Spartan)	Home	4-1	Gillard 2, Holt, Williams L	74
Second	**Basildon United** (Isthmian)	Away	1-0	Williams L	185
Third	**Wivenhoe Town** (Essex Senior)	Home	2-0	Cooper, Holt	146
Fourth	**Heybridge Swifts** (Essex Senior)	Away	2-1*	Callanan, Williams L	326
Fifth	**Bristol Manor Farm** (Western)	Home	2-1	Reeves, Williams L	481
Sixth	**Old Georgians** (Glos. County)	Away	1-1*	Reeves	770
Replay	**Old Georgians**	Home	2-0	Cooper, Holt	711
Semi-Final 1st Leg	**Whickham** (Wearside)	Home	1-1	Doyle	828
2nd Leg	**Whickham**	Away	2-0	Reeves, Gillard	1,102

Matches played: 10 goals for: 19 against: 5 * after extra time

It's the same style of photo we see every year but for a club who had never won more than Vase match in a season before the feeling must have been very special for Stansted. Photo: Eric Marsh

He scored from close range after 64 minutes, to set up a storming finish. But the Lincolnshire side could not manage another goal and Stansted skipper Barry Simpson stepped up to accept the Vase from Nat Lofthouse. Stansted and their boss Dave Edwards had deserved their success for their better organisation and team work, and who can begrudge a side success, having never previously got past the second round of the competition?

The crowd was the lowest ever for a Vase final, but still compared favourably with Football League attendances on the day, being bettered by only a couple in the Third and Fourth Divisions.

The predictable celebrations in the Stansted dressing room produced an unusual sight . . . England star Glenn Hoddle taking a back seat!

His uncle, Dave Hoddle, is Stansted's assistant manager, and the Tottenham star lives near their ground and has played alongside several of their players in years gone by. Even his presence to add his congratulations afterwards could not deflect the glory from the Hargrave Park outfit.

Coe saves at the feet of Genovese. Photo: Leo Hoenig

Tommy Robson stretches to control a pass in mid field while Stansted's Robbie Doyle 'flies' round to cover.
Photo: Bob Thomas

It's the second Stansted goal coming up as Paul Gillard supported by Reeves pulls away from the challenge.
Photo: Bob Thomas

Stamford are back in the game and it's Russ Allen (9) scoring through a crowded goalmouth. Photo: Mike Joss

RESULTS OF PREVIOUS FINALS

1975 (*Attendance:* 9,500)
Epsom & Ewell 1 (Wales) **Hoddesdon Town 2** (Sedgwick 2) Referee: R. Toseland
Epsom & Ewell: Page, Bennett, Webb, Wales, Worby, Jones, O'Connell, Walker, Tuite, Eales, Lee.
Hoddesdon Town: Galvin, Green, Hickey, Maybury, Stevenson, Wilson, Bishop, Picking, Sedgwick, Nathan, Schofield.

1976 (*Attendance:* 11,858)
Billericay Town 1 (Aslett) **Stamford 0** *aet* Referee: Alan Robinson
Billericay Town: Griffiths, Foreman, Pullin, Payne, Bone, Coughlan, Geddes, Aslett, Clayden, Scott, Smith.
Stamford: Johnson, Kwiatkowski, Marchant, Crawford, Downs, Hird, Barnes, Walpole, Smith, Russell, Broadhurst.

1977 (*Attendance:* 14,000)
Billericay Town 1 (Clayden) **Sheffield 1** (Coughlan og) *aet* Referee: J. Worrall
Billericay Town: Griffiths, Payne, Bone, Coughlan, Pullin, Scott, Wakefield, Aslett, Clayden, Woodhouse, McQueen. Sub: Whettell.
Sheffield: Wing, Gilbody, Lodge, Hardisty, Watts, Skelton, Kay, Travis, Pugh, Thornhill, Haines. Sub: Strutt.

Replay at Nottingham Forest (*Attendance:* 3,482)
Billericay Town 2 (Aslett, Woodhouse) **Sheffield 1** (Thornhill) Referee: T. Morris
Billericay Town: Griffiths, Payne, Pullin, Whettell, Bone, McQueen, Woodhouse, Aslett, Clayden, Scott, Wakefield.
Sheffield: Wing, Gilbody, Lodge, Strutt, Watts, Skelton, Kay, Travis, Pugh, Thornhill, Haines.

1978 (*Attendance:* 16,391)
Barton Rovers 1 (Smith) **Blue Star 2** (Dunn, Crumplin) Referee: C. Seel
Barton Rovers: Blackwell, Stephens, Crossley, Evans, Harris, Dollimore, Dunn, Harnaman, Fossey, Turner, Smith. Sub: Cox.
Blue Star: Halbert, Feenan, Thompson, Davidson, S. Dixon, Beynon, Storey, P. Dixon, Crumplin, Callaghan, Dunn. Sub: Diamond.

1979 (*Attendance:* 17,500)
Almondsbury Greenway 1 (Price) **Billericay Town 4** (Young 3, Clayden) Referee: N. Midgley
Almondsbury Greenway: Hamilton, Bowers, Scarrett, Sullivan, Tudor, Wookey, Bowers, Shehean, Kerr, Butt, Price. Sub: Kilbraine.
Billericay Town: Norris, Blackaller, Bingham, Whettell, Bone, Reeves, Pullin, Scott, Clayden, Young, Groom. Sub: Carrigan.

1980 (*Attendance:* 11,500)
Guisborough Town 0 **Stamford 2** (Alexander, McGowan) Referee: R. Lewis
Guisborough Town: Cutter, Scott, Thornton, Angus, Maltby, Percy, Skelton, Coleman, McElvaney, Sills, Dilworth. Sub: Harrison.
Stamford: Johnson, Kwiatkowski, Ladd, McGowan, I. Bliszczak, Mackin, Broadhurst, Hall, Czarnecki, Potter, Alexander. Sub: S. Bliszczak.

1981 (*Attendance:* 12,000)
Willenhall Town 2 (Smith, Stringer) **Whickham 3** (Scott, Williamson, Peck og) *aet* Referee: K. Walmsley
Willenhall Town: Newton, White, Dams, Woodall, Heath, Fox, Peck, Price, Matthews, Smith, Stringer. Sub: Trevor.
Whickham: Thompson, Scott, Knox, Williamson, Cook, Ward, Carroll, Diamond, Cawthra, Robertson, Turnbull. Sub: Allon.

1982 (*Attendance:* 12,500)
Forest Green Rovers 3 (Leitch 2, Norman) **Rainworth Miners' Welfare 0** Referee: B. Daniels
Forest Green Rovers: Moss, Norman, Day, Turner, Higgins, Jenkins, Burns, Guest, Millard, Leitch, Doughty. Sub: Dangerfield.
Rainworth Miners' Welfare: Watson, Hallam, Hodgson, Slater, Sterland, Oliver, Knowles, Raine, Radzki, Reah, Comerford. Sub: Robinson.

1983 (*Attendance:* 13,700)
Halesowen Town 0 **VS Rugby 1** (Crawley) Referee: T. Bune
Halesowen Town: Coldicott, Penn, Edmonds, Lacey, Randle, Shilvock, Hazlewood, Moss, Woodhouse, Joinson E, Joinson L. Sub: Smith.
VS Rugby: Burton, McGinty, Harrison, Preston, Knox, Evans, Ingram, Setchell, Owen, Beecham, Crawley. Sub: Haskins.

Billericay Town's first goal at Wembley and with it Geoff Aslett gave his side a 1-0 extra time victory over Stamford.

F.A. VASE CLUB RECORDS

	74-75	75-76	76-77	77-78	78-79	79-80	80-81	81-82	82-83	83-84	Total
Stamford	S-F	F	3	3	2	W	4	2	3	F	50
Barton R.		Q-F	S-F	F	Q-F	2	2	S-F	3	2	43
*Billericay T..	2	W	W	5	W	Q-F					43
Friar Lane O.B.	S-F	S-F	4	5	5	4	4	2	3	2	43
Blue Star		2	5	W	3	4	3	S-F	5	3	42
Irthlingborough D.				Q-F	5	Q-F	S-F	Q-F	4	S-F	41
Burnham		4	4	Q-F	3	4	4	2	S-F	2	36
Hungerford T.	1	5	4	S-F	2	S-F	5	2	2	1	36
Leyton Wingate	Q-F	2	2	2	5	5	2	4	2	Q-F	36
Molesey	5	5	4	2	4	5	2	Q-F	3		36
Almondsbury Gr.			5	S-F	F	4	4	3	2	2	35
*Windsor & Eton	1	3	1	1	4	Q-F	S-F	4	5		32
Buckingham T.		1	5	4	2	3	2	5	4	5	31
*Farnborough T.	Q-F	S-F	S-F	5	Q-F						31
Lincoln U.	Q-F	4	2	3	4	2	3	2	2	3	31
Whickham					S-F	3	W	2	2	S-F	31
Hallam		4	4	3	2	3	5	4	3	2	30
*Willenhall T.				3	Q-F	5	F	Q-F	2		30
Basildon U.	3	4	2	1	2	3	Q-F	2	3	2	28
Halesowen T.		1	1	4	3	2	3	3	F	3	28
*Forest Green R.	3	1	1	3	2	2	—	W	Q-F		28
Alma Swanley			4	4	3	4	Q-F	2	2	2	27
Kempston R.	5	1	3	4	2	3	5	2	2	—	27
Leeds Ashley Road	3	5	4	3	3	2	3	2	2		27
Newbury T.	1	1	—	4	3	5	3	3	3	4	27
Cray W.	1	1	3	2	1	Q-F	5	2	3	2	26
Frecheville C.A.	1	1	—	Q-F	2	4	2	4	4	2	26
Guiseley		2	3	1	1	4	Q-F	2	2	5	26
Wigston Fields			Q-F	2	2	5	4	2	2	2	25
Eastbourne U.	1	1	3	5	Q-F	2	2	3	1	—	24
Grays A.				4	3	4	2	4	3	4	24
Hinckley A.	1	1	4	4	4	2	2	3	1	2	24
Sheffield	4	3	F	2	3	2	1	—	—	1	24
Winterton R.			Q-F	4	5	2	2	2	2	1	24
Prescot Cables	1	5	3	5	4	3	2				23
*Shepshed Ch.				—	S-F	4	2	2	Q-F	2	23
Guisborough T.					—	F	3	5	4	2	22
Haringey Bor.	1	2	2	Q-F	4	2	2	2	1	—	22
Hoddesdon T.	W	1	3	2	2	1	1	—	1	1	22
Tring T.	3	4	5	2	3	2	1		1	1	22
VS Rugby	2	2	1	1	—	1	—	1	W	4	22
Devizes T.			2			3	Q-F	3	4	3	21
Gosport Bor.	3	4	Q-F	3	5						21
Irlam T.	4	1	2	2	2	1	1	5	1	2	21
Malvern T.	4	3	4	2	2	1	2	1	—	2	21
Ossett A.			2	2	3	2	3	4	3	2	21
Skegness T.				2	4	3	3	5	2	2	21
Whyteleafe	2	1	1	2	1	2	5	3	2	2	21
Blakenall	4	2	5	3	2	1	1	2	—	—	20
Bracknell T.	3	5	2		—	1	—	1	5	3	20
Eastbourne T.	4	5	3	3	2	1	—	2	—	—	20
Epping T.	1	3	5	3	3	2	1	—	2	—	20
Hemel Hempstead	1	3	3	—	—	3	—	5	2	3	20
Marlow	5	2	1	—	—	1	3	3	3	2	20
Rainham T.	2	2	—	5	2	3	2	3	1	—	20
Rushden T.			3	3	3	3	3	2	2	1	20
Brockenhurst	5	4	2	1	—	—	—	4	1	2	19
Congleton T.			4	3	2	3	4	2	1	—	19
East Ham U.			Q-F	2	3	4	2	2	—	—	19
Heybridge Swifts	2	2	—	3	1	1	1	1	4	4	19
Newport (IOW)			2	2	2	4	2	2	1	4	19
Tunbridge Wells	4	4	2	1	4	—	—	1	—	3	19

W=10 F=8 S-F=7 Q-F=6

* Now competing in FA Trophy

The three Stansted goalscorers: Ray Holt, John Reading and Paul Gillard. Photo: Eric Marsh

FA CUP REVIEW

FA CHALLENGE CUP

Committee: L Smart, Chairman; E A Brown, Vice-Chairman; H W Alcock; W T Annable; R Daniel; W S G Needham; G H C Needler; C H Norsworthy; Dr J O'Hara; F J Peart; A L Smith; Sir Arthur South.

Telford United's Year

The past season was not a vintage one for non-League clubs in the FA Challenge Cup, although the performance of Telford United, the FA Trophy holders, in beating three League clubs before just losing to Derby County at the Baseball Ground, must be one of the most impressive season's results ever achieved. Their goal tally of 13-6 speaks for itself.

Harrow Borough received some consolation for their Trophy near-miss in season 1982-83 by reaching the First Round for the first time and then they managed to grab a 1-0 away win at Yeovil, who were playing their 81st tie in the competition proper.

One of the disturbing factors creeping in to ruin little clubs' big days is the bullying attitudes of the supporters of League clubs when visiting non-League clubs. Cup ties tend to attract all sorts of drop-outs who attend just to cause trouble, and the publicity given by the media to the marauding England supporters abroad did no favours to the clubs staging First Round FA Cup ties in the same week.

One sad example of this was seen at Yeovil, where fifty louts, not seen on the ground before, spent the whole match attempting to get to the end allocated by the police to Harrow supporters. They were not watching the match. The police could have done more to stamp out the trouble perhaps, as the ringleaders were very obvious. Although the game was not affected and the visiting supporters not actually molested, all the visitors, including directors and players, had to be bundled into their coaches immediately after the game, and the traditional enjoyment of the home club's hospitality in the clubhouse bars and boardroom had to be curtailed. The non-League game is based on comradeship and a spirit of friendliness between clubs. This was Harrow's first match in the Competition Proper and although they must have enjoyed the result there was nothing else that either side could have appreciated about the day.

At Champion Hill, where Corinthian-Casuals were entertaining Bristol City, a moronic few from the West Country were welcomed by a collection of straying Millwall fans on the terraces. Chelsea supporters seeking trouble also looked in at Harrow Borough when Newport visited and, of course, last season Wokingham and Slough had to patch up their grounds after the visits of Cardiff City and Millwall.

These foul-mouthed little thugs must not be allowed to ruin Football at semi-professional level, where until now real Football lovers have enjoyed the game in a relaxed and happy atmosphere. I know that we are faced with a national disease but we hope that clubs can put pressure on local police and magistrates to punish offenders so heavily that this behaviour will be eliminated at non-League grounds immediately.

'RESULT OF THE ROUND'

Preliminary Round	St Albans City	v	Banstead Athletic	10-0
First Qualifying Round	Halesowen	v	Kings Lynn	6-0
Second Qualifying Round	Hyde United	v	Runcorn	3-0
Third Qualifying Round	Corinthian-Casuals	v	Bognor Regis	3-1
Fourth Qualifying Round	Blyth Spartans	v	Hyde United	2-4 after 1-1
First Round	Halifax Town	v	Whitby Town	2-3
Second Round	Telford United	v	Northampton Town	3-2 after 1-1

Telford United continued to produce two more excellent results when beating Rochdale 4-1 away in the Third Round and narrowly losing 2-3 away to Derby County in the Fourth.

BEST ATTENDANCES

Preliminary Round	Hednesford Town	v	Brigg Town	506
First Qualifying Round	Halesowen	v	Kings Lynn	773
Second Qualifying Round	Oldbury United	v	Halesowen	856
Third Qualifying Round	Merthyr Tydfil	v	Gloucester City	1029
Fourth Qualifying Round	Burton Albion	v	Walthamstowe Avenue	2166
First Round (Best Non-League)	Hyde United	v	Burnley	7701
Second Round	Bournemouth	v	Windsor & Eton	6006

Telford United and Maidstone United could hardly have been drawn away to League clubs with much less potential support and indeed only 3,509 attended the Kent club's visit to Darlington and 4,889 watched Telford's great win at Rochdale.

Although Telford seemed to have little luck on the night they met Derby County in the Fourth Round they probably drew a larger attendance by having their tie postponed to a midweek evening fixture and their share of the receipts from the 21,488 crowd must have been most welcome.

Preliminary Round

Summer Start for Challenge Cup

When the FA Cup first features on the Football calendar, summer is very much still with us. It is a little depressing to be out of the major cup competition before some players have returned from holiday and perhaps only a couple of league fixtures have been completed, but it is unfortunately a harsh fact of life.

Last season such well-known teams as Bromsgrove Rovers, Taunton Town, Metropolitan Police, Willenhall Town and Whitley Bay all disappeared on 3 September.

Results which must have given a lot of pleasure were relegated Durham City's 3-1 victory over Ashington, Lye Town's 1-0 defeat of Willenhall, RS Southampton's 4-1 win in their first-ever FA Cup tie against Oxford City, and Chard Town's 2-1 home success against Taunton.

However the result of the round was surely achieved by St Albans City (recently relegated) who registered a 10-0 victory over a normally quite sound Athenian League side, Banstead Athletic.

Preliminary Round	*Score*	*Att*	*Rcpts*
Peterlee Newtown v Netherfield	3-0	56	£23
Fleetwood Town v Blue Star	2-1	207	£102
Easington Colliery v Whitley Bay	2-0	112	£50
Chester-le-Street v Shildon	2-0	128	£57
Guisborough T v Ferryhill Ath	2-1	78	£42
Gretna v Consett	3-1	90	£37
Durham City v Ashington	3-1	87	£40
Ryhope CA v Harrogate Town	1-3	94	£40
Accrington Stanley v Crook Town	3-1	255	£170
Seaham CW Red Str v Brid'ton Trin	7-0	100	£143
Colwyn Bay v Emley	2-3	219	£74
Chadderton v Denaby United	1-0	120	£32
Droylsden v Prestwich Heys	1-2	147	£91
Radcliffe Borough v Ossett Albion	2-1	140	£75
Formby v North Ferriby United	2-1	100	£35
Prescot Cables v Lytham	0-0	88	£42
Warrington Town v Stalybridge Celtic	0-3	103	£46
Alfreton Town v Ashton United	0-1	129	£63
Congleton Town v Caernarfon Town	1-0	129	£90
Wren Rovers v Appleby Frodingham	3-2 ★	51	£27
Belper Town v Bilston	3-3	127	£62
Brigg Town v Hednesford Town	0-0	91	£29
Boston v Gresley Rovers	1-3	92	£62
Winterton Rangers v Friar Lane OB	1-0	70	£24
Highgate United v Bridgnorth Town	1-2	58	£32
Eastwood Hanley v Desborough Town	1-0	90	£26
Lye Town v Willenhall Town	1-0	220	£97
Skegness Town v Tividale	2-4	100	£39
Blakenall v Buckingham Town	0-1	70	£41
Racing Club Warwick v Banbury U	3-1	66	£27
Wigston Fields v Coventry Sporting	3-1	—	—
Bourne T v Chipping Norton T	4-2	147	£75
March Town U v Bromsgrove Rvrs	3-2	—	—
Boldmere St Michaels v Dudley Town	0-2	67	£34
Ely City v Armitage	3-2	64	£38
Rothwell Town v Newmarket Town	2-0	72	£29
Soham T Rgrs v Harwich & P'kston	1-0	54	£37
Bury Town v Tiptree United	3-3	102	£46
Ampthill Town v Rushden Town	2-1	67	£49
Stevenage Boro v Milton Keynes Cty	2-0	303	£197
Lowestoft T v Letchworth Gdn C	2-0	147	£89
Stowmarket Town v Cheshunt	1-0	118	£51
Wootton Blue Cross v Basildon U	1-1	134	£42
Clapton v Cray Wanderers	2-3	111	£68
Dorking v Berkhamsted Town	1-0	90	£37
Kingsbury T v A'stone & W'brg T	0-1	—	—
Aylesbury United v Harefield United	2-0	205	£151
Molesey v Erith & Belvedere	0-2	60	£38
Burnham v Bracknell Town (at Bracknell Town FC)	2-0	140	£55
Chalfont St Peter v Finchley	2-1	42	£22
Royston Town v Epping Town	4-1	96	£49
St Albans City v Banstead Athletic	10-0	186	£150
Hornchurch v Crawley Town	1-0	83	£61
Metro Police v Horsham YMCA	0-1	59	£36
Haringey Borough v Canterbury City	1-4	30	£17
Horsham v Burgess Hill Town	0-0	78	£33
Three Bridges v Hemel Hempstead	3-2	110	£50
Ringmer v Sittingbourne (at Sittingbourne FC)	0-3	113	£54
Hoddesdon Town v Merstham (at Ware FC)	1-0	50	£24
Hailsham T v Woking (at Woking FC)	2-1	150	£112
Beckenham Town v Ashford Town	1-3	110	£41
Eastbourne United v Arundel	1-0	63	£30
Lancing v Faversham Town	3-1	98	£43
Lewes v Tunbridge Wells	2-2	110	£82
Chertsey T v Pc'hvn & Telscombe	0-1	85	£43
Whitehawk v Horndean	3-0	102	£31
Walton & Hersham v Fleet Town	1-1	115	£69
Tonbridge AFC v Marlow	3-0	235	£171
Wick v Newport IOW	2-1	32	£19
Salisbury v Flackwell Heath	1-0	180	£133
Romsey Town v Chippenham Town	1-1	67	£32
Newbury Town v Devizes Town	4-2	125	£88
RS Southampton v Oxford City	4-1	89	£67
Llanelli v Clevedon Town	3-0	222	£146
Brockenhurst v Clandown	1-1	117	£40
Chard Town v Taunton Town	2-1	147	£74
Mangotsfield United v Ton Pentre	3-1	110	£60
Barry Town v Calne Town	4-1	130	£40
Bristol Manor Farm v Glastonbury	0-1	31	£22
Paulton Rovers v Wellington Town	2-1	44	£18
Haverfordwest C v Weston SM	1-0	150	£30
Falmouth Town v Bridgwater Town	0-1	229	£99
Saltash United v Barnstaple Town	3-1	200	£90

Replays			
Lytham v Prescot Cables	0-3	22	£8
Bilston v Belper Town	1-0	139	£58
Hednesford Town v Brigg Town	3-0	506	£269
Tiptree United v Bury Town	0-1	116	£63
Basildon United v Wootton Blue Cross	2-0	256	£118
Burgess Hill T v Horsham (at Horsham FC)	0-2	119	£52
Tunbridge Wells v Lewes	0-3	185	£102
Fleet Town v Walton & Hersham	0-4	130	£41
Chippenham Town v Romsey Town	0-1 ★	154	£76
Clandown v Brockenhurst	3-0	100	£29

First Qualifying Round
Harrow Borough Score Nine

The 144 cup ties in this round comprise the busiest FA Cup day of the season. Many fancied clubs suffer from 'giant-killing' feats which only hit the headlines in the local papers. Such results as: Yorkshire Amateur 4 Spennymoor United 1; Chester-le-Street 1 Barrow 0; Nuneaton Borough 1 Oldbury United 2; Halesowen Town 6 Kings Lynn 0; Clandown 4 Trowbridge Town 2; and Basildon United 1 Leytonstone/Ilford 0 reflect surprises which go unnoticed by the national papers.

High scores were achieved by Harrow Borough, who scored 9 against Ware; Stalybridge Celtic with 8 against Formby; and Hampton, with 7 at Royston Town, but the result of the round must be that six-goal thrashing of powerful Southern League pacemakers Kings Lynn by Halesowen.

	Score	*Att*	*Rcpts*
Easington Coll v Peterlee Newton	2-1	263	£121
Horden CW v W Auckland T	5-1	152	£68
Chester-le-Street v Barrow	1-0	473	£161
Fleetwood T v Tow Law T	1-2	475	£169
Brandon U v Guisborough T	0-0	133	£60
Morecambe v Guiseley	1-0	303	£214
Evenwood T v North Shields	0-3	58	£28
Gretna v Annfield Plain	1-0	115	£62
Eppleton CW v Durham City	0-2	106	£47
Billingham S v Lancaster C	0-1 ★	63	£21
Yorkshire A v Spennymoor U	4-1	149	£63
Harrowgate T v Whitby T	2-4	350	£129
Willington v Accrington Stanley	1-1	58	£33
Bishop Auckland v Thackley	2-2	303	£129
Clitheroe v South Bank	0-0	201	£153
Seaham CW Red Star v Gateshead	1-3	400	—
Nantwich T v Emley	1-1	148	£72
Chorley v Burscough	2-0	281	£245
Bootle v Bangor City	0-1	150	£57
Chadderton v South Liverpool	1-4	300	£94

St Helens T v Prestwich Heys	0-1	60	£29
Buxton v Curzon Ashton	2-1	273	£214
Farsley Celtic v Horwich RMI	1-4	153	£57
Radcliffe Borough v Southport	1-3	429	£221
Stalybridge Celtic v Formby	8-1	263	£156
Hyde U v Darwen	3-0	374	£304
Ashton U v Runcorn	0-1	362	£277
Prescot Cables v Rhyl	0-5	104	£84
Leyland Motors v Congleton T	1-3	132	£50
Marine v Heanor T	3-2	175	£103
Tamworth v Macclesfield T	1-6	237	£199
Wren R v Oswestry T	0-2	143	£42
Arnold v Bilston	1-2	201	£67
Witton A v Glossop	1-1	360	£256
Leek T v Goole T	1-1	141	£78
Hednesford T v Frickley Athletic	1-2	710	£364
Coleshill T v Gresley Rovers	1-3	89	£53
Matlock T v Winsford U	2-2	460	£287
Hinckley A v Shepshed Charterhouse	0-1	528	£330
Winterton Rangers v Eastwood T	0-3	82	£29
Sutton T v Bridgenorth T	0-2	131	£67
Gainsborough Trinity v Ilkeston T	6-0	288	£207
Rushall Olympic v Grantham	1-1	151	£61
Eastwood Hanley v Leicester U	0-2	80	£33
Long Eaton U v Lye T	1-1	75	£26
Worksop T v Wisbech T	1-2	359	£280
Mile Oak Rovers & Youth v Corby T	0-1	118	£47
Tividale v AP Leamington	0-5	120	£61
Wigston Fields v Buckingham T	1-4	100	£50
Sutton Coldfield T v Spalding U	2-1	239	£175
Bourne T v Shifnal T	1-4	233	£121
Racing Club Warwick v Alvechurch	2-2	120	£41
Walsall Borough v March Town U	1-2	70	£24
Stourbridge v Stamford	2-1	201	£137
Chatteris T v Wellingborough T	0-2	130	£53
Dudley T v Irthlingb'rgh Diamonds	3-1	145	£79
Wednesfield Social v Ely City	4-0	91	£35
Nuneaton Borough v Oldbury U	1-2	716	£741
Halesowen T v Kings Lynn	6-0	773	£556
Rothwell T v Burton Albion	1-5	196	£90
Heybridge Swifts v Soham Town R	1-0	143	£89
Chelmsford Cty v Gorleston	5-1	557	£467
Great Yarmouth T v Holbeach U	3-1	195	£109
Bury Town v VS Rugby	0-2	177	£81
Thame U v Ampthill T	2-1	64	£31
Bedworth United v Dunstable	3-2	106	£88
Barton Rovers v Kidderminster Har	0-1	156	£92
Stevenage Boro v Moor Green	0-0	291	£166
Haverhill Rovers v Lowestoft Town	0-1	113	£51
Billericay T v Thetford T	3-0	249	£152
Sudbury T v Walthamstowe Avenue	1-1	283	£130
Felixstowe T v Rainham T	3-1	50	£20
Saffron Walden T v Stowmarket T	3-0	204	£100
Woodford Town v Aveley	0-2	—	—
Cambridge City v Wealdstone	1-2	295	£136
Basildon United v Leytonstone/Ilford	1-0	273	£124
Addlest'ne & W'brg T v Cray W	3-1	118	£93
Harrow Borough v Ware	9-0	247	£118
Aylesbury United v Boreham Wood	2-0	229	£163
Dorking v Hendon	1-1	250	£133
Hillingdon v Erith & Belvedere	2-1	107	£86
Hayes v Wembley	1-3	200	£148
Tilbury v Chesham United	0-1	105	£86
Burnham v Hitchin Town	1-2	235	£84
Uxbridge v Chalfont St Peter	4-2	72	£27
Feltham v Whyteleafe	0-1	20	£13
Hounslow v Slough Town	0-3	410	£214
Royston Town v Hampton	1-7	120	£62
Leyton-Wingate v St Albans City	1-2	175	£115
Staines Town v Grays Athletic	1-0	122	£89
Edgeware v Windsor & Eton	0-5	167	£70
Hornchurch v Tring Town	3-2	92	£68
Hertford Town v Horsham YMCA	1-1	—	—
Corinthian-Casuals v Camberley T	2-0	47	£28
Southall v Carshalton Athletic	3-3	110	£53
Canterbury City v Bognor Regis T	0-3	124	£100
Sittingbourne v Horsham	1-1	153	£63
Chatham Town v Epsom & Ewell	1-2	130	£106
Hoddesdon Town v Dartford	0-4	201	£137
Three Bridges v Croydon	5-1	200	£125
Eastbourne Town v Hailsham Town	0-1	190	£72
Bromley v Horley Town	3-1	224	£156
Herne Bay v Gravesend & Northfleet	1-3	220	£140
Ashford Town v Deal Town	5-0	210	£130
Redhill v Eastbourne United	1-1	152	£104
Dulwich Hamlet v Ramsgate	5-0	183	£130
Haywards Heath v Folkestone	2-6	171	£149
Lancing v Hastings United	2-2	124	£61
Dover Athletic v Lewes	1-4	173	£125
Egham Town v Sheppy United	2-1	80	£26
Littlehampton Town v Leatherhead	0-2	215	£131
Peaceh'vn & Telscombe v Fisher A	0-3	84	£45
Whitstable Town v Whitehawk	1-2	63	£32
Thanet United v Pagham	1-1	206	£130
Hastings T v Tooting & Mitcham U	3-4	243	£198
Walton & Hersham v Welling U	1-0	208	£125
Chichester City v Tonbridge AFC	1-2	141	£64
Kingstonian v Steyning Town	2-0	150	£112
Southwick v Worthing	1-2	623	£300
Wick v Farnborough Town	1-2	62	£36
Sholing Sports v Salisbury	2-1	242	£134
Dorchester Town v Eastleigh	0-0	165	£111
Abingdon Town v Wokingham Town	0-3	145	£59
Romsey Town v Gosport Borough	0-2	147	£59
Hungerford Town v Newbury Town	2-1	287	£171
Fareham Town v Maidenhead United	1-1	187	£154
Andover v AFC Totton	1-3	177	£119
RS Southampton v Waterlooville	0-0	116	£83
Basingstoke Town v Llanelli	2-1	201	£140
Witney Town v Moreton Town	2-1	234	£137
Forest Green Rovers v Wimborne T	6-0	255	£168
Clandown v Trowbridge Town	4-2	280	£96
Barry Town v Chard Town	2-0	195	£75
Bridgend Town v Redditch United	1-0	46	£15
Glastonbury v Cheltenham Town	0-0	153	£58
Mangotsfield U v Melksham T	4-0	110	£57
Welton Rovers v Paulton Rovers	2-0	70	£34
Bath City v Shepton Mallet Town	4-0	397	£365
Cinderford Town v Merthyr Tydfil	1-2	322	£172
Haverfordwest C'ty v Gloucester City	1-2	115	£82
St Blazey v Bridgwater Town	3-1	155	£61
Frome Town v Torrington	1-1	228	£118
Tiverton Town v Bideford	1-6	102	£44
Saltash United v Poole Town	0-1	230	£126

Replays

Guisborough T v Brandon United	1-2	148	£90
Accrington Stanley v Willington	3-0	310	£233
Thackley v Bishop Auckland	1-4	456	£163
South Bank v Clitheroe	0-0	56	£23
Emley v Nantwich Town	6-2	334	£148
Glossop v Witton Albion	2-0	280	£101
Goole Town v Leek Town	4-0	266	£165
Winsford United v Matlock Town	2-1	130	£104
Grantham v Rushall Olympic	3-0	505	£352
Lye Town v Long Eaton United	4-3	113	£55
Alvechurch v Racing Club Warwick	5-1	232	£141
Moor Green v Stevenage Borough	1-0 ★	240	£132
Walthamstow Avenue v Sudbury T	2-0	188	£137
Hendon v Dorking	4-1	206	£137
Horsham YMCA v Hertford Town	2-2	92	£32
Carshalton Athletic v Southall	3-4	140	£128
Horsham v Sittingbourne	1-2	160	£74
Eastbourne United v Redhill	2-1	101	£48
Hastings United v Lancing	2-0	369	£229
Pagham v Thanet United	0-1	51	£35
Eastleigh v Dorchester Town	0-2 ★	155	£76
Maidenhead United v Fareham Town	0-1	220	£180
Waterlooville v RS Southampton	2-1	257	£142
Cheltenham Town v Glastonbury	0-3	241	£286
Torrington v Frome Town	0-3	291	£189

Second Replays

Clitheroe v South Bank	1-0	323	£247
Hertford Town v Horsham YMCA	2-0	122	£82

Someone isn't keeping his eye on-the-ball! Hectic goalmouth action from the Haverford West v Weston-super-Mare Preliminary Road cup tie. The home side won 1-0. Photo: Mike Joss.

Following an appearance on TVS the previous night, Brockenhurst goalkeeper gets down well to a Clandown attack. Clandown forced a 1-1 draw and went on to win the replay 3-0 and then defeat Trowbridge Town of the Alliance 4-2 in the next round. Photo: Mike Joss.

Slough Town's Tony Doherty (No 5) and Joe Maloney clear this Hampton attack in their 3rd Qualifying Round cup tie. Photo: Slough & Eton Observer.

SECOND QUALIFYING ROUND

Runcorn Defeated

It is interesting to note that attendances begin to take on a more consistent look in this round and only two Isthmian Second Division clubs disappointed, with very small crowds at Corinthian-Casuals (who are tenants at the Molesey ground) and more surprisingly at Uxbridge, who entertained neighbours Hampton. Leading the way were Oldbury United, who rewarded their supporters with a 2-0 win over Halesowen Town in front of 856, and Hyde United who attracted 726 to see them defeat Runcorn 3-0. This, indeed, qualifies as the result of the round as their Alliance opponents were challenging at the top of the League as usual.

	Score	Att	Rcpts
Horden CW v Chester-le-Street	6-1	329	£165
Easington Colliery v Tow Law Town	0-0	152	£66
Morecambe v North Shields	2-2	308	£212
Brandon United v Gretna	1-0	120	£50
Lancaster City v Yorkshire Amateur	2-2	178	£77
Durham City v Whitby Town	1-3	192	£98
Bishop Auckland v Clitheroe	1-0	255	£141
Accrington Stanley v Gateshead	1-1	420	£297
Chorley v Bangor City	2-4	324	£296
Emley v South Liverpool	1-3	380	£164
Buxton v Horwich RMI	0-1	288	£226
Prestwich Heys v Southport	0-1	300	£203
Hyde United v Runcorn	3-0	726	£595
Stalybridge Celtic v Rhyl	2-0	391	£236
Marine v Macclesfield Town	0-3	460	£246
Congleton Town v Oswestry Town	3-0	179	£123
Glossop v Goole Town	4-0	300	£149
Bilston v Frickley Athletic	1-1	206	£80
Winsford U v Shepshed Charterhouse	3-1	398	£256
Gresley Rovers v Eastwood Town	0-1	206	£102
Gainsborough Trinity v Grantham	2-0	601	£415
Bridgnorth Town v Leicester United	2-1	135	£85
Wisbech Town v Corby Town	2-2	511	£260
Lye Town v AP Leamington	4-4	244	£133
Sutton Coldfield Town v Shifnal Town	5-4	252	£191
Buckingham Town v Alvechurch	2-1	174	£79
Stourbridge v Wellingborough Town	2-3	216	£150
March Town United v Dudley Town	3-2	130	£60
Oldbury United v Halesowen Town	2-0	856	£633
Wednesfield Social v Burton Albion	1-2	326	£142
Chelmsford City v Great Yarmouth T	4-2	640	£528
Heybridge Swifts v VS Rugby	2-2	248	£149
Bedworth U v Kidderminster Harriers	2-1	233	£197
Thame United v Moor Green	4-4	121	£69
Billericay Town v Walthamstow Avenue	2-2	403	£235
Lowestoft Town v Felixstowe Town	3-0	195	£111
Aveley v Wealdstone	1-1	266	£290
Saffron Walden Town v Basildon United	2-4	297	£171
Harrow Borough v Aylesbury United	0-0	340	£169
Addlestone & Weybridge T v Hendon	2-1	230	£157
Wembley v Chesham United	0-0	134	£95
Hillingdon v Hitchin Town	0-1	167	£137
Whyteleafe v Slough Town	0-5	253	£101
Uxbridge v Hampton	0-1	75	£33
Staines Town v Windsor & Eton	2-2	271	£206
St Albans City v Hornchurch	3-0	217	£180
Corinthian-Casuals v Southall (at Leatherhead)	3-2	52	£37
Hertford Town v Bognor Regis Town	1-1	144	£112
Epsom & Ewell v Dartford	1-2	308	£205
Sittingbourne v Three Bridges	3-0	220	£90
Bromley v Gravesend & Northfleet	0-4	403	£269
Hailsham Town v Ashford Town	1-3	210	£78
Dulwich Hamlet v Folkestone	1-2	382	£293
Eastbourne United v Hastings United	0-0	394	£310
Egham Town v Leatherhead	1-5	160	£54
Lewes v Fisher Athletic	0-2	258	£168
Thanet United v Tooting & Mitcham U	0-7	285	£191
Whitehawk v Walton & Hersham	4-1	221	£89
Kingstonian v Worthing	3-2	205	£146
Tonbridge AFC v Farnborough Town	1-2	389	£285
Dorchester Town v Wokingham Town	0-3	150	£117
Sholing Sports v Gosport Borough	0-0	254	£145
Fareham Town v AFC Totton	0-3	156	£143
Hungerford Town v Waterlooville	3-3	170	£99
Witney Town v Forest Green Rovers	2-2	269	£157
Basingstoke Town v Clandown	1-1	245	£174
Bridgend Town v Cheltenham Town	0-2	120	£43
Barry Town v Mangotsfield United	4-2	180	£77
Bath City v Merthyr Tydfil	0-1	689	£506
Welton Rovers v Gloucester City	1-4	151	£79
Frome Town v Bideford	0-0	264	£140
St Blazey v Poole Town	0-3	216	£92

REPLAYS

Tow Law Town v Easington Colliery	1-1	174	£59
North Shields v Morecame	4-2*	452	£358
Yorkshire Amateur v Lancaster City	0-2	139	£62
Gateshead v Accrington Stanley	1-2	434	£443
Frickley Athletic v Bilston	2-0	410	£421
Corby Town v Wisbech Town	3-2*	506	£448
AP Leamington v Lye Town	4-0	516	£344
VS Rugby v Heybridge Swifts	2-0	622	£468
Moor Green v Thame United	4-2	349	£183
Walthamstow Avenue v Billericay Town	0-0	347	£257
Wealdstone v Aveley	2-0	506	£597
Aylesbury United v Harrow Borough	1-2	443	£332
Chesham United v Wembley	3-2*	195	£133
Windsor & Eton v Staines Town	2-0	299	£231
Bognor Regis Town v Hertford Town	2-0	410	£296
Hastings United v Eastbourne United	1-0	408	£307
Gosport Borough v Sholing Sports	4-0	310	£281
Waterlooville v Hungerford Town	3-0	276	£171
Forest Green Rovers v Witney Town	1-2	398	£262
Clandown v Basingstoke Town	0-2	230	£78
Bideford v Frome Town	0-2	398	£204

SECOND REPLAYS

Easington Colliery v Tow Law Town	0-1	224	£102
Walthamstow Avenue v Billericay Town	2-1	363	£316

THIRD QUALIFYING ROUND

Top 'Gate' in Wales

This round sees the time when victorious clubs sense they could be in for a Cup run. The winners are in the last of the area group ties and two victories will see them in the bag with Third and Fourth Division League clubs. Most matches are keenly fought out and gates improve again. Over 1,000 saw Merthyr Tydfil defeat Gloucester City and 936 watched Hyde United beat arch rivals Stalybridge Celtic 2-0. Most games went to form but the result of the round was achieved by Corinthian-Casuals who beat Bognor Regis Town (two divisions above them) 3-1 in front of a crowd which was two and a half times larger than their previous home Cup attendance!

	Score	Att	Rcpts
Horden CW v Easington Colliery	3-2	405	£212
North Shields v Brandon United	2-0	409	£321
Lancaster City v Whitby Town	2-2	283	£142
Bishop Auckland v Accrington Stanley	4-1	280	£206
Bangor City v South Liverpool	1-0	690	£428
Horwich RMI v Southport	2-1	428	£293
Hyde United v Stalybridge Celtic	2-0	936	£764
Macclesfield Town v Congleton Town	6-0	757	£496
Glossop v Frickley Athletic	2-3	500	£252
Winsford United v Eastwood Town	0-1	227	£142
Gainsborough Trinity v Bridgnorth T	1-1	371	£255
Corby Town v AP Leamington	2-2	368	£327
Sutton Coldfield T v Buckingham T	2-1	220	£169
Wellingborough T v March Town U	1-0	174	£120
Oldbury United v Burton Albion	0-3	253	£223
Chelmsford City v VS Rugby	2-2	745	£621
Bedworth United v Moor Green (first match abandoned after 20 mins — 0-0)	2-1	457	£392
Walthamstow Avenue v Lowestoft T	0-0	251	£175
Wealdstone v Basildon United	3-1	485	£552
Harrow B v Addlestone & Weybridge T	1-0	218	£133
Chesham United v Hitchin Town	0-2	200	£144
Slough Town v Hampton	3-2	381	£302
Windsor & Eton v St Albans City	4-1	232	£183
Corinthian-Casuals v Bognor Regis T	3-1	137	£78
Dartford v Sittingbourne	2-2	644	£583
Gravesend & Northfleet v Ashford T	1-1	620	£411
Folkestone v Hastings United	2-0	824	£617
Leatherhead v Fisher Athletic	0-4	205	£152
Tooting & Mitcham U v Whitehawk	3-0	333	£314
Kingstonian v Farnborough Town	2-4	158	£126
Wokingham Town v Gosport Borough	2-1	259	£202
AFC Totton v Waterlooville (first match abandoned after 65 mins — 1-0)	1-1	546	£304
Witney Town v Basingstoke Town	2-2	173	£106

England's Colin Williams (hidden) scores Telford United's third goal in their 3-0 defeat of Stockport County.
Photo: Mike Joss.

York City's Derek Hood clears a home corner at Macclesfield where this First Round tie ended in a 0-0 draw. York won the replay 2-0.

Poole score a consolation goal in their 1-3 First Round replay defeat at Newport County.
Photo: Mike Joss.

Bruce Urquart hammers in a shot for Bangor City during their home 1-1 second round draw with Blackpool. Photo: Mike Joss.

Cheltenham Town v Barry Town	3-1	479	£304
Merthyr Tydfil v Gloucester City	3-2	1029	£714
Frome Town v Poole Town	2-3	317	£178

REPLAYS

Whitby Town v Lancaster City	7-3	1018	£517
Bridgnorth T v Gainsborough Trinity	1-4	455	£376
AP Leamington v Corby Town	3-0	564	£391
VS Rugby v Chelmsford City	1-2*	914	£646
Lowestoft Town v Walthamstow Avenue	0-2	785	£521
Sittingbourne v Dartford	1-4	599	£250
Ashford T v Gravesend & Northfleet	3-2*	517	£387
Waterlooville v AFC Totton	3-0	525	£324
Basingstoke Town v Witney Town	2-1*	408	£235

FOURTH QUALIFYING ROUND

One Step from 'The Big Time'

In this round the 36 area winners are joined by 20 senior non-League clubs whose past form has earned them exemption from earlier rounds. The reward for success in this round is a possible financial boost with a pairing against a League club. This round is one of the most exciting of the competition.

Last season 12 of the 28 ties were drawn and the pressure was on. Old First Round regulars were there again. Yeovil Town won a replay at Minehead, Worcester City beat Basingstoke at the second attempt, Maidstone United beat Sutton United also after two games, and Dagenham beat Folkestone in another replay.

Barnet, Wealdstone and Boston United were also familiar qualifiers and little Penrith kept their good reputation in the competition. Newcomers to the First Round were Harrow Borough, who won a tremendous replay against the extremely powerful Fisher Athletic side, 4-2 at home. Surprise winners were Corinthian-Casuals against Merthyr Tydfil and Farnborough Town, who drew at Weymouth before winning 3-2 at home.

Fourteen ties attracted over 1,000 spectators, with Folkestone leading the way with 1,309 to see them draw with Dagenham, and in the replays two ties were watched by over 2,000 and another four reached the 1,000 mark. Indeed the two matches which made up the result of the round, in which Hyde United won at Blyth Spartans 4-2 after a 1-1 home draw, were watched by 1,236 and 2,127 — very satisfying figures.

	Score	Att	Rcpts
Frickley Athletic v North Shields	1-0	958	£988
Horwich RMI v Macclesfield Town	0-0	866	£611
Whitby Town v Bishop Auckland	4-2	1115	£563
Penrith v Horden CW	3-0	281	£216
Bangor City v Scarborough	2-1	1030	£919
Workington v Mossley	0-0	380	£288
Hyde United v Blyth Spartans	1-1	1236	£1014
AP Leamington v Wellingborough T	3-0	640	£446
Walthamstow Avenue v Burton Albion	0-0	422	£310
Kettering T v Sutton Coldfield Town	3-2	1180	£1426
Hitchin Town v Gainsborough Trinity	0-1	817	£628
Boston United v Stafford Rangers	3-1	1349	£1316
Chelmsford City v Bedworth United	2-1	1194	£989
Eastwood Town v Wycombe Wanderers	2-2	800	£475
Fisher Athletic v Harrow Borough	1-1	1012	£690
Folkestone v Dagenham	1-1	1309	£988
Wealdstone v Bishops Stortford	1-0	1168	£1361
Harlow Town v Barnet	1-1	488	£400
Barking v Ashford Town	3-0	342	£232
Dartford v Tooting & Mitcham United	2-0	1257	£1128
Maidstone United v Sutton United	1-1	1204	£1512
Weymouth v Farnborough Town	1-1	985	£877
Windsor & Eton v Cheltenham Town	1-0	559	£442
Basingstoke Town v Worcester City	1-1	1026	£666
Yeovil Town v Minehead	2-2	1069	£911
Poole Town v Slough Town	3-0	1109	£1066
Waterlooville v Wokingham Town	3-2	728	£465
Corinthian-Casuals v Merthyr Tydfil	1-0	520	£479

REPLAYS

Macclesfield Town v Horwich RMI	4-3	1021	£731
Mossley v Workington	1-0	519	£348
Blyth Spartans v Hyde United	2-4	2127	£1548
Burton Albion v Walthamstow Avenue	3-1	2166	£1526
Wycombe Wanderers v Eastwood Town	2-1	1023	£705
Harrow Borough v Fisher Athletic	4-2	826	£542
Dagenham v Folkestone	3-0	743	£693
Barnet v Harlow Town	5-1	889	£768
Sutton United v Maidstone United	1-3	1188	£1219
Farnborough Town v Weymouth	3-2	960	£738
Worcester City v Basingstoke Town	3-1	1919	£1666
Minehead v Yeovil Town	2-4*	716	£579

FIRST ROUND

Headlines for Telford United and Whitby Town

Thirty-two non-League clubs competed in the First Round of the FA Cup. They were made up of: 14 from the Alliance Premier League, 6 from the Servowarm Isthmian League, 5 each from the Northern Premier League and Southern League and one each from the Drybrough's Northern League and the North West Counties League (these included Telford United, Northwich Victoria, Enfield and Altrincham, who were exempt until this round).

Non-League clubs to knock out League opposition at the first attempt were Whitby Town, 3-2 winners at Halifax Town, and Telford United, 3-0 winners at home to Stockport County. Worcester City drew at Aldershot 1-1 before attracting over 5,000 to see them win the replay 2-1 and Maidstone United beat Exeter City by the same score having drawn 1-1 at St James' Park.

Little Waterlooville Town, having already played six ties, took Northampton Town to two replays before the League club got through and other plucky performances were produced by Hyde United, 0-2 at home to the stars of

Burnley; Penrith, 0-2 at home to high-riding Hull City; Macclesfield, who drew 0-0 at home to York City before losing 0-2 in the replay; Barnet, who also held Bristol Rovers at home before losing at Eastville; Dartford, who only succumbed 1-2 at Millwall; and A.P. Leamington who just lost 0-1 at home to Gillingham. Dagenham and Poole Town also held Brentford and Newport County at home respectively before going out in replays.

However, the club who captured the imagination of the media was Corinthian-Casuals, who, having celebrated their centenary year, qualified to entertain Bristol City at home, and after a 0-0 draw put up a gallant performance in losing 0-4 at Ashton Gate. Incidently, of the five Isthmian clubs in this round only two came from the Premier Division and Casuals became the fourth Second Division club to reach the Competition Proper in the last five years, following Windsor & Eton, Barton Rovers and Hungerford Town.

Amongst some excellent results, the result of the round belonged to Whitby Town, who scored three away against League opposition at Halifax.

	Score	Att	Rcpts
Boston United v Bury	0-3	2624	£4459
Hyde United v Burnley	0-2	7701	£13583
Rotherham U v Hartlepool U	0-0	3325	£5784
Halifax Town v **Whitby Town**	2-3	2588	£3703
Frickley Athletic v **Altrincham**	0-1	2267	£2313
Tranmere Rovers v Bolton W	2-2	5497	£7298
Rochdale v Crewe Alexandra	1-0	2496	£3602
Penrith v Hull City	0-2	1962	£3142
Northwich Victoria v **Bangor C**	1-1	2135	£2008
Darlington v **Mossley**	5-0	1863	£2487
Gainsborough T v Blackpool	0-2	2728	£4355
Bradford City v Wigan Athletic	0-0	4599	£9117
Telford United v Stockport County	3-0	2470	£2542
Wrexham v Sheffield United	1-5	2842	£4389
Chester City v Chesterfield	1-2	1774	£2381
Scunthorpe U v Preston North End	1-0	3484	£5666
Macclesfield Town v York City	0-0	3407	£3441
Mansfield Town v Doncaster Rovers	3-0	5097	£6837
Port Vale v Lincoln City	1-2	3647	£5090
Southend United v Plymouth Argyle	0-0	3882	£6808
Oxford U v Peterborough U	2-0	6342	£10970
AFC Bournemouth v Walsall	4-0	4298	£7305
Chelmsford C v **Wycombe W**	0-0	2277	£1973
Barnet v Bristol Rovers	0-0	2235	£4326
Exeter City v **Maidstone United**	1-1	3615	£6267
Aldershot v **Worcester City**	1-1	3553	£5824
Burton Albion v **Windsor & Eton**	1-2	2818	£1934
Corinthian-Casuals v Bristol City	0-0	2236	£5235
Poole Town v Newport County	0-0	4521	£5946
Kettering Town v Swindon Town	0-7	2834	£3375
Millwall v **Dartford**	2-1	4933	£10619
Barking v **Farnborough Town**	2-1	416	£448
Reading v Hereford United	2-0	4373	£7611
Wimbledon v Orient	2-1	3904	£7686
Torquay United v Colchester United	1-2	2126	£3082
Wealdstone v **Enfield**	1-1	1657	£1985
Dagenham v Brentford	2-2	2146	£2894
Northampton Town v **Waterlooville**	1-1	2627	£4563
AP Leamington v Gillingham	0-1	2223	£3129
Yeovil Town v **Harrow Borough**	0-1	1457	£1184

REPLAYS

Hartlepool U v Rotherham U	0-1	2635	£3298
Bolton W v Tranmere Rovers	4-1	6305	£10468
Bangor City v **Northwich Victoria**	1-0	2298	£1989
Wigan Athletic v Bradford City	4-2	4741	£7276
York City v **Macclesfield Town**	2-0	4963	£6121
Plymouth Argyle v Southend United	2-0	5570	£9111
Wycombe W v **Chelmsford C**	1-2	1937	£1423
Bristol Rovers v **Barnet**	3-1	5338	£8901
Maidstone United v Exeter City	2-1	4381	£6829
Worcester City v Aldershot	2-1	5353	£8485
Bristol City v **Corinthian-Casuals**	4-0	5349	£7295
Newport County v **Poole Town**	3-1	3090	£4176
Enfield v **Wealdstone**	2-2	1286	£1313
Brentford v **Dagenham**	2-1	3936	£7573
Waterlooville v Northampton Town	1-1	2982	£4070

SECOND REPLAYS

Wealdstone v **Enfield**	2-0	1609	£2034
Northampton Town v **Waterlooville**	2-0	3534	£6261

SECOND ROUND

Windsor & Eton v Manchester United – Not Quite!

With Alliance 'giants' Maidstone United and Worcester City meeting, at least one APL club was guaranteed a place in the draw with the 'big boys', and desperate fights were put up by Altrincham and Bangor City before losing to Darlington and Blackpool respectively.

Narrow defeats were suffered by Whitby Town at Wigan and Barking at Plymouth Argyle, while Harrow Borough, in the Competition Proper for the first time, followed their First Round victory at Yeovil with an entertaining but unproductive home tie with Newport County. Wealdstone and Chelmsford City enjoyed their visits to League clubs but not the scorelines, while Windsor & Eton, because of their delayed tie against Bournemouth at Stag Meadow, knew they would face Manchester United should they overcome 'The Cherries'. This was not to be, however, despite a brave 0-0 draw at home. Bournemouth's manager, having created the shock of the next round by beating United, was quoted as saying that his team had been caused more problems by little Windsor in the previous round. Congratulations were in order for the Royalists' manager Geoff Chapple and coach Alf Coulton.

The result of the round must go to Telford United, who drew at Northampton Town and then scored three goals at home to win by the odd goal in a thriller.

The 11 Non-League clubs in this round comprised 6 from the Alliance Premier League, 3 from the Servowarm Isthmian League and one each from the Southern League and the Drybrough's Northern League.

	Score	Att	Rcpts
Rotherham United v Hull City	2-1	6885	£12833
York City v Rochdale	0-2	5203	£6394

David Pearce scores for Harrow Borough in the Second Round against Newport County but his side loses 1-3. Photo: Eric Marsh

With the winners due to play Manchester United, both teams had every incentive to do well. Here Bournemouth's goalkeeper Ian Leigh dives at the feet of Windsor & Eton's Chris Yates during the 0-0 draw at Stag Meadow. Bournemouth won the replay 2-0 and, of course, went on to beat United 2-0. Photo: Eric Marsh.

Dave Mather (far left) scores Telford United's second goal in their 3-0 victory over Stockport County. Photo: Mike Joss.

Darlington v **Altrincham**	0-0	2364	£3539
Bangor City v Blackpool	1-1	3579	£6405
Bolton Wanderers v Mansfield T	2-0	6934	£11550
Lincoln City v Sheffield United	0-0	8188	£14366
Wigan Athletic v **Whitby Town**	1-0	4820	£6445
Scunthorpe United v Bury	2-0	3246	£5424
Chesterfield v Burnley	2-2	5788	£9475
Harrow Borough v Newport C	1-3	1574	£2233
Colchester United v **Wealdstone**	4-0	2693	£4000
Gillingham v **Chelmsford City**	6-1	4908	£8598
Maidstone U v **Worcester C**	3-2	2868	£4857
Windsor & Eton v AFC Brn'mth	0-0	3451	£5695
Millwall v Swindon Town	2-3	4597	£9993
Brentford v Wimbledon	3-2	5666	£10995
Reading v Oxford United	1-1	10946	£19457
Bristol Rovers v Bristol City	1-2	14396	£28098
Plymouth Argyle v **Barking**	2-1	4754	£7794
Northampton Town v **Telford U**	1-1	3903	£6322

REPLAYS

Altrincham v Darlington	0-2	2142	£3008
Blackpool v **Bangor City**	2-1	5013	£7374
Sheffield U v Lincoln City	1-0	12547	£22794
Burnley v Chesterfield	3-2	8286	£14098
AFC Brn'mth v **Windsor & Eton**	2-0	6006	£10558
Oxford United v Reading	3-0	7570	£13440
Telford United v Northampton T	3-2	3320	£3557

THIRD ROUND

Telford Through Again

Darlington (1) 4 (Davies, Walsh, Cartwright, McLean)
Maidstone United (1) 1 (Lazarus) **Attendance:** 3,509
Darlington: Barber, Craggs, Johnson, Gilbert, Smith, Barton, Cartwright, Davies, Todd, Walsh, McLean.
Maidstone United: Richardson, Thompson, Moore (sub Maddock), Crowe, Newson, Donn, Lazarus, Stewart, Dingwall, Bartley, Hughes.

Rochdale (1) 1 (Allatt) **Attendance:** 4,889
Telford United (1) 4 (Edwards, Bailey, Hogan, Williams)
Rochdale: Conroy, Greenhoff B, Chapman, Thompson S, Higgins, Williams (sub Oates), Thompson D, Hamilton, Allatt, O'Connor.
Telford United: Charlton, Lewis, Turner, Joseph, Bailey, Eaton, Barnett, Williams, Edwards, Hogan, Alcock (sub Mather).

FOURTH ROUND

Telford Lose at Last at Derby

Derby County (1) 3 (Davison 3) **Attendance:** 21,488
Telford United (1) 2 (Eaton, Bailey)
Derby County: Cherry, Barton, Buckley, Gemmill, Watson, Powell, Futcher, Davison, Wilson, Plummer, Robertson.
Telford United: Charlton, Lewis, Turner, Joseph, Bailey, Eaton, Barnett, Williams, Edwards, Hogan, Alcock (sub Mather).

F.A. Challenge Cup

The Giantkillers

This special table shows the top twenty non-League clubs playing in semi-professional football today who have the best records in the FA Cup. Clubs who have since joined the Football (Canon) League such as Peterborough United, Hereford United, Wimbledon and Wigan Athletic all had impressive records as non-League clubs, as did Bedford Town, Guildford City and Romford (before they disbanded). Gateshead too, who were originally South Shields and have had a couple of constitutional changes, if all their results are put together have amassed a good FA Cup record.

It is difficult to decide the fairest way of judging these records. We could have decided the order on seasons in the Competition Proper, or on a percentage of good results (which would give Altrincham top place). We have decided to use as a criterion the number of Cup ties played in the Competition Proper.

Incidentally, full results of *all* non-League clubs who have reached the First Round Proper since 1925-26 (the year the present qualifying system was introduced) are to be found in Bob Barton's superb 'Non-League, A History of League and Cup Football', details of which can be found in the non-League football publicity feature in this book.

Who's that with John Davison and John King? A very young Sammy Lee takes on the Altrincham stars when the famous Alliance cup fighters travelled to Anfield for a Third Round cup tie in 1981. Liverpool won 4-1 and Graham Heathcote had the thrill of beating Ray Clemence from the spot. Photo: Bob Thomas.

NON-LEAGUE CLUB'S RECORDS IN THE FA CUP COMPETITION PROPER

Club	First Round	Second Round	Third Round	Fourth Round	Fifth Round Ties	League Clubs Beaten	P	W	D	L	F	A
1. Yeovil Town (Seasons in Competition Proper: 36)	18	9	8	—	1	C. Palace (2), Southend (2), Bury, Exeter C, Sunderland, Walsall, Brentford, Bournemouth, Brighton & H, Gillingham	81	29	15	36	109	136
2. Blyth Spartans (Seasons in Competition Proper: 25)	14	9	1	—	1	Crewe Alex, Chesterfield, Stockport Co, Hartlepool U, Stoke City	59	15	19	25	77	118
3. Scarborough (Seasons in Competition Proper: 31)	19	8	4	—	—	Crewe Alex (2), PNE, Rochdale, Oldham Ath, Bradford C, Lincoln C, York City, Darlington	58	16	11	31	78	128
4. Weymouth (Seasons in Competition Proper: 28)	19	7	2	1	—	Aldershot, Cardiff C, Newport Co, Shrewsbury	58	14	16	28	67	123
5. Kettering T (Seasons in Competition Proper: 29)	20	7	2	—	—	Oxford U, Millwall, Swansea, Swindon T	56	11	17	29	72	113
6. Boston United (Seasons in Competition Proper: 27)	18	6	4	—	—	Bradford, Crewe A, Derby Co, Hartlepool, Mansfield, Southport	47	13	7	27	67	102

League Clubs who defeated Yeovil Town
Arsenal, Aldershot, Bournemouth, Bristol City, Brentford, Bury, Brighton, Chester, Colchester U (2), Chesterfield, Shrewsbury T, Fulham (2), Liverpool, Manchester Utd (2), Millwall, Norwich (2), Notts Co, Plymouth (2), Swindon T, Sheff Wed, Southend U. Walsall

League Clubs who defeated Blyth Spartans
Accrington (2), Bournemouth, Carlisle U, Chester, Doncaster, Grimsby T, Hull C, Hartlepool, Mansfield (2), PNE, Reading, Stockport C, Walsall, Wrexham (3), Torquay U, York C

League Clubs who defeated Scarborough
Bradford PA, Bradford City (2), Brighton (2), Burnley, Crewe Alex, C. Palace, Doncaster R (2), Gateshead, Grimsby T, Darlington (2), Halifax T, Hartlepool, Luton T, Mansfield T, Port Vale, Southend, Southport, Tranmere R, Workington,, York City (2)

League Clubs who defeated Weymouth
Aldershot, Bournemouth, Bristol R (2), Cambridge U (2), Gillingham, Orient (2), Northampton T (2), Coventry C, Man Utd, Newport C, Peterborough, PNE, Southend (2), Swindon T, Swansea, Torquay U, Southampton, Colchester U

League Clubs who defeated Kettering Town
Bristol R (2), Coventry C, Charlton A, C. Palace (2), Blackpool, Colchester U, Grimsby T, Oxford U, Northampton, Millwall, Newport C, Orient, QPR, Reading (2), Swansea, Walsall (2)

League Clubs who have defeated Boston United
Bradford PA, Barnsley, Chester, Crewe A, Darlington (2), Derby Co, Orient, Portsmouth, Oldham A, Northampton, Lincoln C, Chesterfield, Sheff U, Scunthorpe U, Sunderland, Tottenham H, Tranmere R, Rotherham U, York City

NON-LEAGUE CLUB'S RECORDS IN THE FA CUP COMPETITION PROPER

	First Round	Second Round	Third Round	Fourth Round	Fifth Round Ties	League Clubs Beaten	Record P	W	D	L	F	A
7. Barnet (Seasons in Competition Proper: 25)	17	4	4	–	–	Newport County	47	12	10	25	64	105
	League Clubs who have defeated Barnet Brentford, Brighton (2), Colchester U, Exeter C, Peterborough, PNE, Southampton, Southend U, QPR (3), Torquay U (2)											
8. Enfield (Seasons in Competition Proper: 20)	10	7	2	1	–	Wimbledon (2), Northampton, Hereford U, Port Vale	45	14	11	20	71	80
	League Clubs who have defeated Enfield Bournemouth, Barnsley, Bristol C, Brighton, Cardiff C (2), Cambridge U, Crystal P, Peterborough (2), Newport C, Reading, Swansea, Swindon, Watford											
Altrincham (Seasons in Competition Proper: 17)	7	4	6	–	–	Rochdale (2), Crewe A, Hartlepool, Scunthrope U (2), Sheffield U, Rotheram U, York City	43	16	11	17	56	61
	League Clubs who have defeated Altrincham Barrow, Burnley, Blackburn R, Crewe A, Darlington, Everton, Huddersfield, Halifax T, Liverpool, Notts Co, Orient, Rotherham U, Tottenham H, Wolverhampton W, Wrexham											
10. Wycombe Wanderers (Seasons in Competition Proper: 22)	15	6	1	–	–	Newport Co, Bournemouth	43	8	13	22	46	70
	League Clubs who have defeated Wycombe Wanderers Bournemouth, Bristol R, Cardiff C, Gillingham, Newport Co, Northampton, Middlesbrough, Peterborough U, Reading, Watford											
11. Bath City (Seasons in Competition Proper: 19)	8	7	4	–	–	C. Palace, Exeter C, Newport C, Notts C, Millwall, Southend	41	16	5	20	61	71
	League Clubs who have defeated Bath City Bolton W, Brentford, Brighton (2), Bournemouth, Colchester U, Charlton A, Coventry C, Grimsby T, Norwich C, QPR, Plymouth A, Swindon T, Walsall											
12. Walthamstow Avenue (Seasons in Competition Proper: 19)	10	8	–	1	–	Northampton, Watford, Stockport Co, QPR	41	12	10	19	73	93
	League Clubs who have defeated Walthamstowe Avenue Bournemouth (3), Brighton, Coventry C, C. Palace, Darlington, Exeter C, Oldham A, Man Utd, Mansfield, Northampton, Ipswich T, Southend U, Stockport Co, QPR (2), Watford											
13. Chelmsford City (Seasons in Competition Proper: 22)	14	6	1	1	–	Darlington, Southampton, Oxford U.	41	11	7	23	56	82
	League Clubs who have defeated Chelmsford Aldershot, Birmingham, Brentford, Colchester, C. Palace, Charlton A, Ipswich T (2), Mansfield T, Northampton, Notts Co, Port Vale, Shrewsbury T, Torquay U, Watford											

NON-LEAGUE CLUB'S RECORDS IN THE FA CUP COMPETITION PROPER

Club	First Round	Second Round	Third Round	Fourth Round	Fifth Round Ties	League Clubs Beaten	P	W	D	L	F	A
14. Bishop Auckland (Seasons in Competition Proper: 17)	8	8	—	1	—	C. Palace, Ipswich T, Tranmere R	36	11	8	17	63	79
15. Telford United (Seasons in Competition Proper: 22)	17	4	—	1	—	Darlington, Wigan Ath, Stockport Co, Northampton T, Rochdale	37	7	7	23	44	83
16. Dartford (Seasons in Competition Proper: 21)	13	6	2	—	—	Aldershot, Cardiff City, Exeter City	36	10	5	21	55	79
17. Rhyl (Seasons in Competition Proper: 21)	15	3	2	1	—	Halifax T, Hartlepool, Notts Co, Stoke C, Wigan Ath, Barnsley	36	10	5	21	39	85
18. Margate (now Thanet Utd) Seasons in Competition Proper: 18)	10	6	2	—	—	Gillingham, Bournemouth, C. Palace, QPR, Swansea	35	11	6	18	62	89
19. Gainsborough Trinity (Seasons in Competition Proper: 20)	10	10	—	—	—	Crewe A (2), Port Vale, Gateshead, Mansfield T	35	11	5	19	47	64
20. Folkestone Town (Seasons in Competition Proper: 17)	11	4	2	—	—	Newport Co, Gillingham, Norwich C	32	8	7	17	44	70

League Clubs who have defeated Bishop Auckland
Bury, Chester, Coventry C, Carlisle U, Halifax T, Tranmere R, PNE, Rochdale, Scunthorpe U, Stockport Co, York City (3)

League Clubs who have defeated Telford United
Accrington S, Aldershot, Bristol C, Bristol R (2), Chester, Doncaster R, Gillingham, Norwich C, Mansfield T (2), Port Vale, Swansea, Southend U, Stockport Co, Walsall, Watford, Tranmere R.

League Clubs who have defeated Dartford
Aldershot, Bristol C (2), Bristol R, Bournemouth, Crystal Palace, Darlington, Derby Co, Orient, Port Vale, Plymouth A, Reading, Swindon T

League Clubs who have defeated Rhyl
Barnsley, Bradford City, Bristol C, Carlisle U, Chesterfield (2), Darlington, Bradford PA, Grimsby T, Hartlepools, Hull C, Oldham A, Norwich C, New Brighton, Rochdale, Swansea.

League Clubs who have defeated Margate
Aldershot, Blackpool, Bournemouth, Brentford, C. Palace (2), Gateshead, Millwall (2), Northampton (2), Notts Co, Peterborough, Torquay U, Walsall, Tottenham H

League Clubs who have defeated Gainsborough Trinity
Aldershot, Chesterfield (2), Colchester U, Darlington, Doncaster R (3), Lincoln C, Mansfield T, Newport Co, Plymouth A, Port Vale, Southport, Walsall, Watford.

League Clubs who have defeated Folkestone Town
Brentford, Brighton (2), Bristol R, Crewe A, Exeter C (2), Luton T, Orient (2), Oxford U (2), Huddersfield T, Swansea

The nearest Bishop Auckland came to scoring in the FA 2nd Round Cup tie with Preston North End when Tony Boylan challenged Preston keeper Roy Tunks for this high ball. Tunks dropped the cross but fell on the ball before Boylan could recover. Photo: Galden Photographers

Once again our club section attempts to feature all clubs who compete in the FA Challenge Trophy and FA Challenge Vase competitions. After the Gola League, which of course is 'national', the sections split into four geographical areas, three of which make up parts of the 'pyramid' structure. Firstly the Isthmian League and it's feeder leagues, then the Southern League and the Northern Premier League with theirs. Lastly come the North East competitions which do not participate within the new structure. Within these sections it is hoped to explain the progress that clubs can make through their respective competitions. Every effort has been made to contact clubs who did not send in their details, so hopefully this year's club coverage should be the most comprehensive so far.

We have encouraged clubs to give the name of their programme editor this year as this may help them collate information for their publications and new features also include lists of players who scored hat tricks and penalties last season. Players marked with a* in their appearances lists are those who were 'ever present' during the season.

CLUBS COMPETING IN DIFFERENT LEAGUES 1984/85

League	New Clubs	Departing Clubs	Leagues from which clubs are coming or going
Gola League (ex Alliance)	Barrow		
	Dartford		Southern League
		Bangor City	Northern Premier League
		Trowbridge Town	Southern League
Athenian League		Banstead Athletic	Isthmian Div 2 (South)
		Berkhamsted Town	Isthmian Div 2 (North)
		Burnham	London Spartan
		Camberley Town	Isthmian Div 2 (South)
		Chalfont St Peter	Isthmian Div 2 (North)
		Chertsey Town	Isthmian Div 2 (South)
		Edgware	London Spartan
		Fleet Town	Combined Counties
		Harefield United	Isthmian Div 2 (North)
		Haringey Borough	Isthmian Div 2 (North)
		Harwich & Parkeston	Eastern Counties
		Hoddesdon	South Midlands
		Horley Town	Combined Counties
		Kingsbury Town	Isthmian Div 2 (North)
		Marlow	Isthmian Div 2 (North)
		Redhill	London Spartan
		Ruislip Manor	Isthmian Div 2 (South)
		Thatcham Town	London Spartan
		Whyteleafe	Isthmian Div 2 (South)
		Wolverton Town	Isthmian Div 2 (North)
Central Midlands	Carriage & Waggon		East Midlands
	Stanton		East Midlands
	Slack & Parr		East Midlands
	Sutton Trinity		Northern Counties (East)
Combined Counties	Fleet Town		Athenian
	Horley Town		Athenian
	Malden Vale		London Spartan
	Merstham		London Spartan
	Southwick		Sussex County
	Farley Rovers		Surrey Premier
		Yateley Town	
		Alton Town	Hampshire
Eastern Counties	Harwich & Parkeston		Athenian
		Saffron Walden T	Isthmian
Essex Senior		Heybridge Swifts	Isthmian
Gloucestershire	Cinderford Town		Midland Combination
	Ellwood		
		Sharpness	Hellenic
Hampshire		Petersfield Utd	Isthmian
		Aldershot Services	
		Enham Alamein	
		B.T.C. Southampton	
	A.C. Delco		Southampton
	Basing Rovers		Northants
	Alton Town		Combined Counties
	West Wight		Island League (I.O.W.)
Hellenic	Hounslow		Southern
	Sharpness		Gloucestershire
		Northwood	London Spartan

CLUBS COMPETING IN DIFFERENT LEAGUES 1984/85

League	New Clubs	Departing Clubs	Leagues from which clubs are coming or going
Isthmian League			
Banstead Athletic	Athenian	Kingsbury Town	Athenian
Berkhamsted Town	Athenian	Marlow	Athenian
Bracknell Town	London Spartan	Petersfield United	Hampshire
Camberley Town	Athenian	Royston Town	South Midlands
Chalfont St. Peter	Athenian	Ruislip Manor	Athenian
Flackwell Heath	Athenian	Saffron Walden Town	Eastern Counties
Harefield United	Athenian	Stevenage Borough	United Counties
Haringey Borough	Athenian	Whyteleafe	Athenian
Heybridge Swifts	Essex Senior	Wolverton Town	Athenian
Kent	Greenwich Borough		London Spartan
	Metropolitan Police (area 4)	Sheppey United	Southern
London Spartan	Burnham		Athenian
	Edgware		Athenian
	Northwood		Hellenic
	Redhill		Athenian
	Thatcham		Athenian
		Greenwich Borough	Kent
		Malden Vale	Combined Counties
		Bracknell Town	Isthmian Div 2 (South)
		Merstham	Combined Counties
		Highfield	
		Ambrose Fleming	
Mid-Cheshire		Rolls Royce	
Midland Combination		Chipping Norton T	Oxfordshire
		Cinderford Town	Gloucestershire
Northern Alliance	Gosforth St. Nicholas		Northern Combination
	Prudhoe East End		Northern Combination
Northern Counties (East)		Scarborough Reserves	
		Brook Sports	
		Sutton Trinity	Central Midlands
		Retford Rail	
Northern Premier League	Bangor City		Gola League
		Barrow	Gola League
North West Counties	Kirkby Town		
	Colwyn Bay		Welsh (North)
		Vulcan Newton	
		Prescot B.I.	
Peterborough & District		Mirrlees Blackstone	United Counties
Southern League	Trowbridge Town		Gola League
	Hednesford Town		West Midlands
	Sheppey United		Kent
		Dartford	Gola League
		Hounslow	Hellenic
		Tamworth	West Midlands
South Midlands	Hoddesdon Town		Athenian
		Stotfold	United Counties
		Royston Town	Isthmian Div 2 (North)
South Western	Falmouth Town		Cornwall Combination
	Western Mill Oak V		
		Torrington	Western
		Plymouth Command	
Sussex County	Cooksbridge		
	Ilfield		
	Oakwood		
	Saltdean United		
		Southwick	Combined Counties
		Lower Bevendon	
Teesside		Newton Aycliffe	Wearside
United Counties	Stotfold		South Midlands
	Mirrlees Blackstone		Peterborough & District
		Stevenage Borough	Isthmian
Wearside	Newton Aycliffe		Teesside
Welsh (North)		Colwyn Bay	North West Counties
Western League	Ilfracombe Town		
	Torrington		South Western
	Westbury United		Wiltshire
West Midlands	Tamworth		Southern
		Hednesford Town	Southern
Wiltshire		Westbury United	Western
		Highworth Town	

THE GOLA LEAGUE

PREVIOUSLY THE ALLIANCE PREMIER FOOTBALL LEAGUE

Chairman: J C Thompson
Secretary: P D Hunter, 24 Barnehurst Rd, Bexleyheath, Kent
Tel: 0322 22616 (business) 0322 521116 (home)

The Gola League

On the playing side we again had a very successful season; in fact it generally ran parallel to last season. For the third year in succession we had two of our teams at Wembley in the F.A. Trophy Final, Northwich Victoria for the second time in two seasons and Bangor City. After a 1-1 draw at Wembley, Northwich won the replay at Stoke by 2 goals to one. Our congratulations go to Northwich and commiserations to Bangor whose exploits in the F.A. Cup, The Welsh Cup and the F.A. Trophy proved their undoing.

Once again fourteen of our clubs went into the draw for the first round of the F.A. Cup, with six reaching the second round. Telford United and Maidstone went into the third round draw, but were not fortunate to draw attractive opposition. Maidstone went out at Darlington, but Telford went one better by defeating Rochdale away. In the fourth round Telford were drawn away to Derby County where they lost, but only after giving a creditable display of football.

At the start of the season, Enfield defeated Runcorn to win the League Championship Shield.

The League Championship was won by Maidstone United who went one better than the previous season. They pipped Nuneaton Borough by one point on the last day of the season, after Nuneaton had led the rest of the league since late January. Both clubs shrugged off early challenges from Runcorn and Wealdstone, and in the later stages from Altrincham.

At the other end of the table Bangor City and Trowbridge Town who occupied the last two places in the league were relegated to the Northern Premier League and Southern Leagues respectively.

Next season we welcome back Barrow who return after one season as Champions of the Northern Premier League, and Dartford as Champions of the Southern League.

The Bob Lord Trophy was a North v South affair, Scarborough v Barnet. Scarborough won the Trophy 2-1 on aggregate.

The league intend to maintain the new points system introduced last season. All agree that the incentive of obtaining three points for a win away from home has been successful.

The two substitutes experiment will also continue.

There is no doubt that the most significant off the field activity has been the signing of the Sponsorship agreement with The Gola Company. The overall sponsorship is based on the incentive to score more goals. Clubs who score goals will reap rich rewards.

We were very pleased to accept the invitation of The Football League to join their new system of the promotion of officials to their Referees list. Three leagues, The Gola League, The Central League and The Football Combination, will each share a "Panel" of selected Referees and Linesmen. Future Football League Referees will only be selected on their performances on the three "Panel" Leagues. The new system will operate in season 1984/85.

We were naturally very disappointed that Maidstone United did not get elected to The Football League. However, their efforts over the past two seasons, and Altrincham's before them, has at last opened the way for discussions with the Associate member clubs of The Football League in respect of a possible future promotion and relegation system. If this can be achieved, then the "Pyramid" of Semi-Professional Football can claim to have reached it's goal.

Peter Hunter

LEAGUE STATISTICS SEASON 1983/84

Largest Home wins

Barnet	10	v	Trowbridge Town	1	13.9.83 Bob Lord
Frickley Ath.	7	v	Boston United	1	26.12.83
Yeovil Town	6	v	Weymouth	3	2.1.84
Dagenham	6	v	Trowbridge Town	2	26.4.84
Weymouth	6	v	Scarborough	1	5.5.84
Maidstone United	6	v	Telford United	0	5.5.84
Wealdstone	6	v	Trowbridge Town	0	13.2.84

Largest Away win

Frickley Ath.	2	v	Wealdstone	5	17.4.84

Highest Aggregate scores

Barnet	10	v	Trowbridge Town	1	13.9.83 Bob Lord
Gateshead	5	v	Boston United	5	7.1.84
Worcester City	4	v	Kidderminster H	4	12.9.83 Bob Lord
Yeovil Town	6	v	Weymouth	3	2.1.84
Frickley Ath.	7	v	Boston United	1	26.12.83
Kidderminster H	4	v	Barnet	4	28.4.84
Runcorn	4	v	Yeovil Town	4	17.3.84
Scarborough	4	v	Worcester City	4	25.2.84

No of clubs competing	20	20	22	22	22
Season	79/80	80/81	81/82	82/83	83/84
1 Altrincham	1	1	11	12	3
2 AP Leamington	18	16	22	–	–
3 Bangor C	9	20	–	13	21
4 Barnet	17	17	18	15	9
5 Barrow	14	9	8	21	–
6 Bath C	16	6	12	10	6
7 Boston U	4	8	10	5	17
8 Dagenham	–	–	5	14	18
9 Dartford	–	–	21	–	–
10 Enfield	–	–	2	1	14
11 Frickley Ath	–	10	15	16	12
12 Gateshead	–	–	–	–	16
13 Gravesend & N	5	15	20	–	–
14 Kettering T	7	2	19	19	19
15 Kidderminster H	–	–	–	–	10
16 Maidstone U	6	7	16	2	1
17 Northwich Vic	8	4	6	8	7
18 Nuneaton Boro	10	18	–	11	2
19 Redditch U	20	–	–	–	–
20 Runcorn	–	–	1	4	5
21 Scarborough	11	3	7	9	13
22 Stafford R	19	11	14	22	–
23 Telford U	13	13	3	6	11
24 Trowbridge T	–	–	17	18	22
25 Wealdstone	15	19	–	3	4
26 Weymouth	2	5	9	7	15
27 Worcester C	3	12	4	17	8
28 Yeovil T	12	14	13	20	20

ALLIANCE PREMIER LEAGUE 1979-84

	P	W	D	L	F A	Pts*	%	Best Position	Seasons
1 Runcorn	126	70	30	26	209-135	170	67.4	1st	81-84
2 Enfield	126	65	26	35	249-154	156	61.9	1st	81-84
3 Altrincham	202	99	48	55	343-227	246	60.8	1st(2)	79-84
4 Maidstone U	202	91	56	55	327-217	238	58.9	1st	79-84
5 Northwich Vic	202	87	54	61	281-234	228	56.4	4th	79-84
6 Weymouth	202	92	43	67	300-237	227	56.1	2nd	79-84
7 Scarborough	202	79	67	56	284-231	225	55.6	3rd	79-84
8 Boston U	202	82	57	63	319-295	221	54.7	4th	79-84
9 Wealdstone	160	61	53	46	234-187	175	54.6	3rd	79-81,82-84
10 Telford U	202	86	47	69	288-276	219	54.2	3rd	79-84
11 Nuneaton Bor	160	62	46	52	234-198	170	53.1	2nd	79-81,82-84
12 Worcester C	202	81	49	72	292-292	211	52.2	3rd	79-84
13 Bath C	202	75	53	74	262-261	203	50.2	6th(2)	79-84
14 Kidderminster H	42	14	14	14	54-61	42	50.0	10th	83-84
15 Dagenham	126	45	35	46	186-195	125	49.6	5th	81-82
16 Frickley Ath	164	58	41	65	242-255	157	47.8	10th	80-84
17 Kettering T	202	68	51	83	307-329	187	46.2	2nd	79-84
18 Barrow	160	55	37	68	202-228	147	45.9	8th	79-83
19 Gravesend & N	118	40	28	50	148-168	108	45.7	5th	79-82
20 Gateshead	42	12	13	17	59-73	37	44.0	16th	83-84
21 Barnet	202	63	44	95	217-300	170	42.0	9th	79-84
Yeovil T	202	64	42	96	280-357	170	42.0	12th	79-84
23 Bangor C	160	44	45	71	201-273	133	41.5	9th	79-81,82-84
24 Stafford R	160	34	55	71	185-235	123	38.4	11th	79-83
25 Dartford	42	10	9	23	49-67	29	34.5	21st	81-82
26 Trowbridge T	126	29	25	72	127-239	83	32.9	17th	81-84
27 AP Leamington	118	21	32	65	119-234	74	31.3	16th	79-82
28 Redditch U	38	5	8	25	26-69	18	23.6	20th	79-80

* 2pts for a win
 1pt for a draw

1983-84

	P	Home W	Home D	Home L	Home F	Home A	Away W	Away D	Away L	Away F	Away A	Pts
Maidstone United	42	12	8	1	40	15	11	5	5	31	19	70
Nuneaton Boro.	42	14	6	1	44	17	10	5	6	24	19	69
Altrincham	42	13	3	5	40	20	10	6	5	24	19	65
Wealdstone	42	15	4	2	48	14	6	10	5	27	22	62
Runcorn	42	11	8	2	34	18	9	5	7	27	27	62
Bath City	42	10	7	4	33	17	7	5	9	27	31	53
Northwich Vic.	42	11	8	2	35	18	5	6	10	19	29	51
Worcester C.	42	9	7	5	36	22	6	6	9	28	33	49
Barnet	42	9	3	9	27	28	7	7	7	28	30	49
Kidderminster H.	42	7	9	5	32	30	7	5	9	22	31	49
Telford United	42	13	3	5	32	19	4	8	9	18	39	49
Frickley Athletic	42	13	3	5	49	25	4	7	10	19	31	48
Scarborough	42	10	10	1	32	16	4	6	11	20	39	48
Enfield	42	8	3	10	27	27	6	6	9	34	31	43
Weymouth	42	5	4	12	28	33	8	4	9	26	32	42
Gateshead	42	7	9	5	35	30	5	4	12	24	43	42
Boston United	42	10	6	5	39	30	3	6	12	27	50	41
Dagenham	42	10	3	8	34	26	4	5	12	23	43	40
Kettering Town	42	8	3	10	31	31	4	6	11	22	36	37
Yeovil Town	42	9	5	7	34	28	3	3	15	21	49	35
Bangor City	42	7	4	10	35	32	3	2	16	19	50	29
Trowbridge Town	42	3	4	14	15	34	2	3	16	18	53	19

Three points for an away win, two points for a home win.
Barrow replace Bangor City
Dartford replace Trowbridge Town
No Servowarm Isthmian League Club wished to replace Yeovil Town

Bob Lord Trophy
1st leg Scarborough 2 Barnet 0
2nd leg Barnet 1 Scarborough 0
Scarborough won 2—1
A.P.L. Charity Shield (to be played at the start of the 1984/85 season)
Maidstone United v Scarborough

SEASON 1983/84

MANAGER OF THE YEAR — BILL WILLIAMS

The Real Mackenzie Whisky **MANAGER OF THE MONTH AWARDS**

1983

August	John Williams	Runcorn
September	Brian Hall	Wealdstone
October	Sean Marshall	Frickley Ath.
November	John Cottam	Scarborough
December	Stan Storton	Telford United

1984

January	Bob Jones	Bath City
February	Ted Hardy	Dagenham
March	Bill Williams	Maidstone United
April	John King	Northwich Victoria

Since the start of the Mackenzie Whisky sponsorship in 1979/80 season, the total awards to individual managers is:—

Stuart Morgan	Weymouth (Bournemouth)	5
Eddie McCluskey	Enfield	4
Tony Sanders	ex-Altrincham	3
Ted Hardy	Dagenham	3
John Williams	Runcorn	3
Stan Storton	Telford United	3

ALLIANCE PREMIER LEAGUE

RESULTS 1983/84

	Altrincham	Bangor City	Barnet	Bath City	Boston United	Dagenham	Enfield	Frickley Ath.	Gateshead	Kettering Town	Kidderminster H.	Maidstone United	Northwich Vict.	Nuneaton Borough	Runcorn	Scarborough	Telford United	Trowbridge Town	Wealdstone	Weymouth	Worcester City	Yeovil Town
Altrincham		2-1	3-2	2-0	3-0	4-0	1-3	1-0	5-0	1-1	0-1	1-0	1-1	0-1	1-3	2-0	1-1	4-0	1-0	2-1	3-4	2-1
Bangor City	1-3		0-1	1-0	0-0	2-4	2-1	4-1	3-3	3-1	1-2	0-2	0-1	1-2	2-3	1-1	4-0	4-0	0-0	1-3	2-4	3-0
Barnet	1-2	3-1		1-2	1-2	3-1	2-1	3-2	0-1	0-3	0-2	0-4	2-1	1-2	2-0	0-1	0-0	2-1	1-1	1-1	2-0	2-0
Bath City	0-0	5-1	0-1		4-2	0-1	3-2	1-0	1-1	1-1	3-0	1-2	2-0	0-1	1-1	4-1	1-1	2-1	0-0	1-0	0-0	3-1
Boston United	2-2	3-2	0-0	0-0		3-0	3-2	2-2	0-4	3-1	2-3	1-0	3-1	3-0	1-2	1-1	2-3	2-0	2-2	4-3	0-1	3-2
Dagenham	0-2	3-1	3-1	3-1	2-0		1-4	1-1	1-2	2-0	0-0	0-1	3-1	4-2	0-2	1-1	1-2	6-2	1-0	1-2	0-1	1-0
Enfield	0-1	3-1	0-1	2-0	1-0	3-0		3-3	0-3	2-2	0-1	0-3	1-2	0-1	0-1	2-1	3-1	2-1	0-2	0-1	2-2	3-0
Frickley Athletic	3-1	2-0	3-1	1-2	7-1	4-0	1-1		4-1	1-1	0-2	2-0	4-1	1-3	2-1	2-1	1-1	2-0	2-5	1-2	3-1	3-0
Gateshead	0-1	2-1	2-3	3-1	5-5	1-1	1-1	2-0		1-2	1-0	0-2	1-3	1-1	1-1	1-1	2-1	2-2	1-1	3-0	1-1	4-2
Kettering Town	1-1	1-3	0-1	0-0	2-1	2-2	1-0	0-1	3-0		4-2	0-2	1-0	3-4	1-0	2-3	4-1	3-2	1-2	0-2	0-1	2-3
Kidderminster H.	0-2	2-1	4-4	1-1	1-1	4-2	1-1	1-1	1-0	3-1		0-0	2-2	3-3	0-2	1-3	1-0	1-1	3-1	0-1	2-1	1-2
Maidstone United	1-0	2-0	1-1	1-1	2-2	2-0	1-1	3-1	1-0	1-0	3-1		0-1	1-0	1-1	1-1	6-0	4-1	2-1	2-2	1-1	4-0
Northwich Vict.	1-1	2-1	0-0	3-2	3-1	3-1	3-1	1-1	3-1	4-0	4-2	1-1		1-1	0-1	3-1	0-0	0-2	1-1	1-0	1-0	0-0
Nuneaton Borough	0-1	3-0	2-2	5-2	4-0	1-1	4-0	1-0	3-2	1-0	2-1	2-2	1-0		2-2	3-0	1-1	2-1	1-1	3-0	1-0	2-1
Runcorn	0-0	0-2	2-0	2-1	3-1	1-0	0-0	2-1	4-2	4-1	1-1	0-0	0-0	0-1		2-0	0-0	2-0	4-2	1-1	2-1	4-4
Scarborough	3-1	3-0	1-0	0-0	2-0	0-0	0-4	3-1	1-1	0-0	2-0	1-1	1-1	1-0	2-1		3-0	0-0	1-1	1-1	4-4	3-0
Telford United	2-1	2-1	0-0	3-2	3-2	3-1	0-3	0-1	4-0	1-0	3-0	3-1	0-2	1-0	1-1	1-0		1-0	0-1	0-1	2-0	2-2
Trowbridge Town	0-0	1-2	0-4	1-2	0-2	1-4	0-0	0-1	0-2	1-2	1-2	1-2	1-1	0-2	0-1	1-0	2-2		1-2	1-2	2-1	1-0
Wealdstone	3-1	5-0	3-0	0-3	1-1	1-0	2-1	0-0	4-0	4-2	2-0	1-2	1-0	0-0	4-2	1-1	4-0	6-0		2-0	3-1	1-0
Weymouth	0-1	5-0	2-2	0-1	0-2	3-1	1-3	0-2	2-0	1-1	0-0	1-3	1-1	0-1	3-1	6-1	2-3	0-1	0-4		0-2	1-3
Worcester City	0-1	0-0	2-0	2-4	2-2	2-2	1-3	0-0	3-1	0-3	1-1	3-0	2-0	1-1	3-0	3-0	0-1	5-2	1-1	1-0		4-0
Yeovil Town	1-2	1-1	2-4	0-2	4-2	0-2	3-2	3-0	0-0	2-0	1-1	1-3	2-0	1-0	0-1	1-2	1-0	3-1	0-0	6-3	2-2	

Leading Goalscorers

	League	B.L.T.	A.P.L. Total	F.A.C.	F.A.T.	Grand Total
Paul Culpin (Nuneaton Boro.)	41	—	41	1	2	44
Mark Graves (Wealdstone)	30	1	31	5	—	36
John Bartley (Maidstone United)	27	2	29	3	3	35
Steve Mahoney (Barnet)	19	9	28	2	2	32
Paul Moss (Worcester C.)	17	3	20	7	—	27
Mark Carter (Bangor City)	17	—	17	2	7	26
Stuart Atkins (Barnet)	14	4	18	1	4	23
Mick Doherty (Yeovil Town)	14	4	18	—	5	23
Gary Hooley (Frickley Ath.)	17+	2	19	3	—	22
Graham Reed (Frickley Ath.)	17	—	17	2	3	22
Paul Wilson (Frickley Ath.)	14	3	17	2	3	22
John Powell (Kidderminster H.)	15	3	18	—	2	20
Frank Murphy (Nuneaton Boro.)	16	2	18	1	—	19×
Dave Hoffbauer (Kettering T.)	15	2	17	—	1	18
Gerry Pearson (Weymouth)	18®	—	18	—	—	18
Colin Williams (Telford United)	11	3	14	3	1	18
Noel Ashford (Enfield)	15*	2	17	—	—	17
Graham Bennett (Altrincham)	17	—	17	—	—	17
Chris Cook (Boston United)	15	—	15	2	—	17
Colin Chesters (Northwich Vic.)	11	—	11	—	5	16
Paul Reid (Northwich Vic.)	12	1	13	1	2	16
Bob Topping (Gateshead)	13	3	16	—	—	16
Bruce Urquhart (Bangor City)	8	1	9	6	1	16

+Includes one goal for Altrincham
×Includes fourteen goals for Kettering.
® Includes two goals for Bath City.
*Includes one goal in Champ. Match.

THE BOB LORD CHALLENGE TROPHY

SEASON 1983/84

1st Round

Barnet 10 1
v
Trowbridge Town 1 0

Kettering Town 4 1
v
Nuneaton Borough 2 1

Dagenham 0 0
v
Yeovil Town 0 1

Worcester City 5 1
v
Kidderminster H 4 3

Bangor City 2 1
v
Gateshead 1 3

Altrincham 3 0
v
Frickley Ath. 1 4

2nd Round

Barnet 2 3
v
Wealdstone 3 1

Maidstone United 1 2
v
Enfield 1 4

Runcorn 4 1
v
Kettering Town 0 1

Northwich Vic. 1 3
v
Telford United 1 4

Yeovil Town 2 1
v
Bath City 0 1

Kidderminster 2 2
v
Weymouth 0 1

Frickley Ath. 2 3
v
Gateshead 4 0

Boston United 0 0
v
Scarborough 1 1

3rd Round

Barnet 1 1
v
Enfield 1 3

Runcorn 3 0
v
Telford United 0 4

Yeovil Town 2 3
v
Kidderminster 1 1

Frickley Ath. 0 1
v
Scarborough 1 3

Semi-finals

Barnet 5 3
1st leg att. 692
v
2nd leg att. 731
Telford United 0 2

Yeovil Town 0 2
1st leg att. 766
v
2nd leg att. 704
Scarborough 2 5

Final

Barnet 0 1
2nd leg att. 1260
1st leg att. 879
Scarborough 2 0

Winners for 1983/84 season
SCARBOROUGH F.C. 2-1 on aggregate.

ALLIANCE PREMIER LEAGUE — 1983/84
FIRST TEAM MATCH STATISTICS

TEAM	LEADING GOALSCORERS	HAT TRICKS	PENALTIES SCORED	MOST APPEARANCES
Altrincham	Graham Bennett 18, John Davison 9, Jeff Johnson 9.	—	John Davison 6, Graham Heathcote, Jeff King	John Davison 48, Ronnie Ellis 44 & 1s, David Constantine 43
Barnet	Steve Mahoney 41, Stuart Atkins 32, Nicky Evans 18.	Steve Ragan, Stuart Atkins	Nicky Evans, Ian Ferguson.	Gary Phillips 69, Bill Baldry 67, Eddie Stein 66.
Barrow	Barry Diamond 41, Colin Cowperthwaite 24, Frank Gamble 21.	Barry Diamond 2.	Barry Diamond 10.	Barry Diamond 57, Steve Brooks 57, Frank Gamble 57. (all ever present)
Bath City	Gary Smith 15, Dave Singleton 12, R. Chandler 6.	Gary Smith, Dave Singleton.	—	D. Moss*, A. Ricketts*, P. Aitken.
Boston United	Chris Cook 18, Jim Lumby 15, Bob Lee 11.	—	Jim Lumby 4.	Kevin Blackwell 47, Gary Mallender 45, Paul Casey 43.
Dagenham	Joe McCombe 16, Joe Dunwell 13, Steve Scott 10, Jon Stille 10.	—	Jon Sille, Steve Page.	Joe Dunwell 64, Alan Campbell 54, Steve Scott 51.
Dartford	Tony Burman 25, Terry Sullivan 16, Joe Simmonds 15.	—	Joe Simmonds 10, George Borg 2, Bobby Arber 2.	Joe Jaques 57, Tony Paphlett 57, Tony Evaman 55.
Enfield				
Frickley Athletic	Gary Hooley 22, Graham Reed 22, Paul Wilson 22.	—	Graham Reed 5, Gary Hooley.	Harry Dunn*, Barry Gill, Paul Wilson
Gateshead	Bob Topping 16, Peter Davies 10, Keith McNall 7.	Bob Topping 2, Keith McNall.	Kevin Pugh 3.	Steve Higgins 44*, Kevin Pugh 40, Kenny Dodds 39.
Kettering Town	David Hofbauer 17, Frank Murphy 13, Peter Denyer 4.	—	—	E. Humphries 45, P. Denyer 45, E. McGoldrick 45.
Kidderminster Harriers	John Powell 29, Paul Davies 16, Elwyn Roberts 10.	John Powell 2.	Martin Woodall 4, John Powell 3, Fraser Wood.	Martin Gavin 61, John Powell 61, Chris Jones 58, Fraser Wood 57.
Maidstone United	John Bartley 37, Clive Green 12, Micky Dingwall 9.	John Bartley.	John Bartley 2, John Watson 2.	John Bartley 53, Derek Richardson 53, Brian Thompson 53.
Northwich Victoria	Paul Reid 28, Colin Chesters 24, Graham Abel 9.	Paul Reid 2, Colin Chesters.	Paul Bennett 4, Colin Chesters 2, Tony Murray.	Dave Ryan 67, Kenny Jones 66, Paul Bennett 65.
Nuneaton Borough	Paul Culpin 54, Trevor Morley 12, Paul Richardson 8.	Paul Culpin 5, Frank Murphy, Paul Richardson.	Paul Culpin 8.	Andy Poole 61, Wille Gibson 60, Paul Culpin 58.
Runcorn	Alan Crompton 17, Ossie Smith 15, John Rogers 7.	—	Alan Crompton 6, Brian Kettle 4, Steve Joel.	Brian Kettle 56*, Ossie Smith 55, Alan Crompton 55, Elfyn Edwards 55.
Scarborough	John Hanson 17, Mitch Cook 12, Trenton Wiggan 12.	—	Mitch Cook.	Graeme Crawford 55*, Richard Dawson 53, Bryan Magee 52.
Telford United	Colin Williams 19, Dean Edwards 17, David Mather 15.	Colin Williams 2.	—	Kevin Charlton 56, Tony Turner 55 & 2s, David Bennett 55 & 2s.
Wealdstone	Nigel Johnson 13, Brian Greenaway 11, Paul Bennett 11, Alan Cordice 11.	Mark Graves 3, Brian Greenaway.	Mark Graves 6, Dennis Byatt 2.	Bob Iles, Dennis Byatt, Mark Graves.
Weymouth	Gerry Pearson 17, Dave Platt 6, Shaun Penny 5, Anniello Iannone 5.	—	Gerry Pearson 6.	Paul Arnold 47, Gerry Pearson 44, Annielo Iannone 44, Peter Morrell 44.
Worcester City				
Yeovil Town	Mick Doherty 25, Jeremy Brown 12, Trevor Finnigan 11.	—	Jeremy Brown 3, Andy Bell 2.	Trevor Finnigan 56, Gary Borthwick 54, Dave Linney 49.

* Denotes ever present.

ALLIANCE LEAGUE
FINAL LEAGUE TABLE FOR THE 1979/80 SEASON

		Home					Away					
	P	W	D	L	F	A	W	D	L	F	A	Pts
Altrincham	38	16	3	0	45	9	8	5	6	34	26	56
Weymouth	38	13	3	3	40	14	9	7	3	33	23	54
Worcester City	38	12	6	1	29	15	7	5	7	24	21	49
Boston United	38	11	7	1	40	20	5	6	8	12	23	45
Gravesend & Northfl't	38	12	4	3	36	18	5	6	8	13	26	44
Maidstone United	38	9	5	5	29	26	6	8	5	26	24	43
Kettering Town	38	9	5	5	29	26	6	8	5	26	24	43
Northwich Victoria	38	11	5	3	31	14	5	5	9	19	24	42
Bangor City	38	9	6	4	21	18	5	8	6	20	28	42
Nuneaton Borough	38	12	5	2	41	16	1	8	10	17	28	39
Scarborough	38	8	8	3	32	14	4	7	8	15	24	39
Yeovil Town	38	8	6	5	26	17	5	4	10	20	32	36
Telford United	38	9	3	7	31	27	4	5	10	21	33	34
Barrow	38	10	3	6	27	18	4	3	12	20	37	34
Wealdstone	38	5	9	5	26	25	4	6	9	16	29	33
Bath City	38	7	9	3	26	21	3	3	13	17	48	32
Barnet	38	7	6	6	18	18	3	4	12	14	30	30
A P Leamington	38	5	5	9	16	27	2	6	11	16	36	25
Stafford Rangers	38	4	7	8	20	21	2	3	14	21	36	22
Redditch United	38	4	5	10	18	29	1	3	15	8	40	18

1980-81

		Home					Away					
	P	W	D	L	F	A	W	D	L	F	A	Pts
Altrincham	38	14	2	3	40	21	9	6	4	32	20	54
Kettering Town	38	13	4	2	38	12	8	5	6	28	25	51
Scarborough	38	10	7	2	25	11	7	6	6	24	18	47
Northwich Victoria	38	12	4	3	32	13	5	7	7	21	27	45
Weymouth	38	11	4	4	30	18	8	2	9	24	22	44
Bath City	38	9	6	4	23	8	7	4	8	28	24	42
Maidstone United	38	12	4	3	42	18	4	5	10	22	35	41
Boston United	38	10	4	5	39	30	6	5	8	24	28	41
Barrow	38	11	3	5	27	18	4	5	10	23	31	38
Frickley Athletic	38	10	4	5	36	22	5	4	10	25	40	38
Stafford Rangers	38	10	4	5	34	22	1	11	7	22	34	37
Worcester City	38	10	4	5	33	25	4	3	12	14	29	35
Telford United	38	7	6	6	26	25	6	3	10	21	34	35
Yeovil Town	38	9	2	8	37	30	5	4	10	23	34	34
Gravesend & Northfleet	38	8	5	6	26	21	5	3	11	22	34	34
AP Leamington	38	6	7	6	29	26	4	4	11	18	40	31
Barnet	38	8	5	6	27	26	4	2	13	12	38	31
Nuneaton Borough	38	6	5	8	27	31	4	4	11	22	34	29
Wealdstone	38	6	8	5	27	19	3	3	13	10	37	29
Bangor City	38	5	6	8	25	34	1	6	12	10	34	24

1981-82

		Home					Away					
	P	W	D	L	F	A	W	D	L	F	A	Pts
Runcorn	42	17	2	2	48	17	11	7	3	27	20	93
Enfield	42	14	4	3	55	22	12	4	5	38	26	86
Telford United	42	13	4	4	38	20	10	4	7	32	31	77
Worcester City	42	12	4	5	38	23	9	4	8	32	37	71
Dagenham	42	10	6	5	34	35	9	6	6	35	26	69
Northwich Victoria	42	12	6	3	35	17	8	3	10	21	29	69
Scarborough	42	11	6	4	34	19	8	5	8	31	32	68
Barrow	42	15	4	2	45	17	3	7	11	14	33	65
Weymouth	42	11	4	6	33	21	7	5	9	23	26	63
Boston United	42	14	4	3	46	23	3	7	11	15	34	62
Altrincham	42	10	6	5	39	22	4	7	10	27	34	55
Bath City	42	7	7	7	30	26	8	3	10	20	31	55
Yeovil Town	42	10	4	7	33	27	4	7	10	23	41	53
Stafford Rangers	42	7	8	6	22	19	5	8	8	26	28	52
Frickely Athletic	42	11	4	6	35	23	3	6	12	12	37	52
Maidstone United	42	8	6	7	33	22	3	9	9	22	37	48
Trowbridge	42	8	7	6	26	33	4	4	13	12	31	47
Barnet	42	5	8	8	17	20	4	6	11	19	32	41
Kettering Town	42	6	7	8	35	32	3	6	12	29	44	40
Gravesend & Northfleet	42	7	6	8	34	31	3	4	14	17	38	40
Dartford	42	7	5	9	23	25	3	4	14	26	42	39
AP Leamington	42	1	7	13	20	44	3	3	15	20	61	22

1982-83

	P	Home W	Home D	Home L	Home F	Home A	Away W	Away D	Away L	Away F	Away A	Pts
Enfield	42	16	3	2	57	21	9	6	6	38	27	84
Maidstone United	42	17	1	3	55	13	8	7	6	28	21	83
Wealdstone	42	13	5	3	45	17	9	8	4	35	24	79
Runcorn	42	15	5	1	50	21	7	3	11	23	32	72
Boston United	42	14	5	2	46	25	6	7	8	31	32	72
Telford United	42	16	3	2	46	17	4	8	9	23	31	71
Weymouth	42	13	6	2	37	14	7	4	10	26	34	70
Northwich Victoria	42	15	5	1	48	22	3	5	13	20	41	64
Scarborough	42	10	6	5	39	23	7	6	8	32	35	63
Bath City	42	12	3	6	41	25	5	6	10	17	30	60
Nuneaton Borough	42	11	6	4	36	20	4	7	10	21	40	58
Altrincham	42	13	5	3	40	17	2	5	14	22	39	55
Bangor City	42	8	9	4	33	29	6	4	11	38	48	55
Dagenham	42	5	9	7	30	26	7	6	8	30	39	51
Barnet	42	9	3	9	37	39	7	0	14	18	39	51
Frickley Athletic	42	11	6	4	41	25	1	7	13	25	52	49
Worcester City	42	10	7	4	43	33	2	3	16	15	54	46
Trowbridge	42	9	5	7	31	30	3	2	16	25	58	43
Kettering Town	42	9	5	7	45	37	2	2	17	24	62	40
Yeovil Town	42	10	4	7	37	36	1	3	17	26	63	40
Barrow	42	7	4	10	26	35	1	8	12	20	39	36
Stafford Rangers	42	4	8	9	22	30	1	6	14	18	45	29

3pts for a win.
Kidderminster Harriers replace Stafford Rangers.
Gateshead replace Barrow.
No Servowarm Isthmian League club wished to replace Yeovil Town.

Bob Lord Trophy:
1st Leg: Runcorn 1 Scarborough 1.
2nd Leg: Scarborough 2 Runcorn 2.
Runcorn win on away goals.
APL Challenge Shield:
Enfield 4 Runcorn 1.

ALLIANCE GOALSCORERS 1979-84

Keeping records of goalscorers is difficult even at Football League level. There are often arguments over 'own goals' or who got the last touch before the ball crossed the line.

In this feature we have tried to collate the goalscoring feats of the leading Alliance strikers since the league was formed in 1979-80. Season's figures for these stars often include goals scored in all Cup competitions but the figures below are those made up of Alliance Premier League and Bob Lord Trophy goals. I have appreciated the help of Peter Hunter, the League Secretary but if anyone feels we have missed anyone out please let me know.

	1979-80	1980-81	1981-82	1982-83	1983-84	Total
Colin Williams	Telford U 2 Northwich V 3	Northwich V 26	Scarborough 27	Scarborough 0 Telford U 14	Telford U 18	90
Anniello Ianonne	Weymouth 22	Weymouth 12	Weymouth 23	Weymouth 21	Weymouth 5	83
Stuart Atkins		Kettering 12	Kettering 19	Barnet 26	Barnet 23	80
Dave Mather	Bangor C 7 Telford U 9	Telford U 13	Telford U 24	Telford U 10	Telford U 15	78
John Bartley				Maidstone U 41	Maidstone U 29	70
Clive Green	Yeovil T 11	Yeovil T 16	Yeovil T 10 Maidstone U 12	Maidstone U 7	Maidstone 12	68
Nicky Evans	Kettering 12	Kettering 25	Kettering 12	Kettering 6	Barnet 11	66
John Rogers	Altrincham 24	Altrincham 21	Altrincham 11	Altrincham 1	Runcorn 7	64
Mark Graves				Wealdstone 23	Wealdstone 38	61
Colin Cowperthwaite	Barrow 12	Barrow 15	Barrow 17	Barrow 15		59
Noel Ashford			Enfield 19	Enfield 21	Enfield 17	57
Paul Culfin				Nuneaton B 13	Nuneaton B 41	54
Ossie Smith			Runcorn 20	Runcorn 13	Runcorn 15	48
Nicky Ironton			Enfield 20	Enfield 15	Enfield 5 Maidstone 1	41
Steve Turner	Barnet 10		Enfield 7	Enfield 19		36
Steve Joel			Runcorn 16	Runcorn 11	Runcorn 7	33

Players such as Noel Ashford, Ossie Smith and the other prolific goalscorers who played for Enfield and Runcorn scored many of their goals before their clubs joined the Alliance.

AGGREGATE ATTENDANCES

	1979-80	80-81	81-82	82-83	83-84
Altrincham	36,947	33,676	24,791	21,811	22,252
Bangor City	15,022	8,948	–	15,210	11,336
Barnet	14,277	13,193	15,879	13,773	14,758
Barrow	16,581	12,708	15,233	11,463	–
Bath City	18,149	17,057	18,348	15,506	13,343
Boston United	32,270	21,990	23,028	26,543	21,103
Dagenham	–	–	19,045	13,614	12,053
Dartford	–	–	15,221	–	–
Enfield	–	–	16,142	17,670	12,047
Frickley Athletic	–	10,411	9,784	9,331	8,940
Gateshead	–	–	–	–	6,062
Gravesend & N	19,408	18,039	19,184	–	–
Kettering T	36,837	31,791	26,103	21,629	21,347
Kidderminster H	–	–	–	–	12,707
Maidstone Utd	17,388	16,115	17,078	30,242	22,260
Northwich Vic	27,823	20,663	19,346	21,384	22,721
Nuneaton Boro	24,858	18,743	–	19,342	22,187
A. P. Leamington	9,598	8,361	7,148	–	–
Redditch	6,790	–	–	–	–
Runcorn	–	–	22,266	15,092	12,986
Scarborough	42,242	31,791	38,360	22,709	19,357
Telford Utd	18,181	13,595	24,762	22,739	22,584
Trowbridge Town	–	–	13,150	14,604	12,011
Stafford R	21,927	21,773	19,607	17,049	–
Wealdstone	12,393	12,282	–	17,387	14,015
Weymouth	25,321	19,602	15,380	16,964	15,919
Worcester C	36,864	26,718	25,930	23,562	25,216
Yeovil Town	30,049	25,686	24,057	23,927	23,421

ALLIANCE PREMIER LEAGUE AVERAGE HOME ATTENDANCES

	1979-80	1980-81	1981-82	1982-83	1983-84	Overall Average
Altrincham	1,945(2)	1,772(1)	1,181(4)	1,039(8)	1,060(6)	1,399(2)
Bangor City	791(16)	471(19)		724(16)	540(20)	632(22)
Barnet	752(17)	694(15)	756(16)	656(19)	703(12)	712(18)
Barrow	873(15)	669(16)	725(18=)	546(21)		703(20)
Bath City	956(13)	898(12)	874(13)	738(15)	635(14)	820(14)
Boston U	1,699(5)	1,157(6)	1,097(7)	1,264(3)	1,005(9)	1,244(6)
Dagenham			907(12)	648(20)	575(17)	710(19)
Dartford			725(18=)			725(17)
Enfield			769(15)	841(9×11)	574(18)	728(16)
Frickley Ath		548(18)	466(21)	444(22)	426(21)	471(25)
Gateshead					289(22)	289(28)
Gravesend	1,022(11)	949(11)	914(11)			955(12)
Kettering T	1,939(4)	1,673(2)	1,244(2)	1,030(9)	1,017(8)	1,381(4)
Kidderminster H					605(16)	605(24)
A.P. Leamington	506(19)	440(20)	340(22)			429(26)
Maidstone U	916(14)	848(13)	813(14)	1,440(1)	1,060(5)	1,016(9)
Northwich V	1,465(7)	1,088(8)	921(10)	1,415(2)	1,082(3)	1,194(7)
Nuneaton B	1,309(9)	986(10)		921(10)	1,057(7)	1,068(8)
Redditch U	358(20)					358(27)
Runcorn			1,060(8)	719(17)	618(15)	799(15)
Scarborough	2,224(1)	1,663(3)	1,827(1)	1,081(7)	922(10)	1,543(1)
Telford U	957(12)	716(14)	1,179(5)	1,083(6)	1,075(4)	1,002(11)
Trowbridge T			626(20)	695(18)	572(19)	631(23)
Stafford R	1,155(10)	1,146(7)	934(9)	812(13)		1,012(10)
Wealdstone	653(18)	646(15)		828(12)	667(13)	699(21)
Weymouth	1,333(8)	1,032(9)	732(17)	808(14)	758(11)	933(13)
Worcester C	1,941(3)	1,406(4)	1,235(3)	1,122(5)	1,201(1)	1,381(3)
Yeovil T	1,582(6)	1,352(2)	1,167(6)	1,139(4)	1,115(2)	1,271(5)

BEST ATTENDANCES EACH SEASON

	1979-80	1980-81	1981-82	1982-83	1983-84
Altrincham	2,670 v Worcester C	2,864 v Yeovil T	1,472 v Enfield	1,712 v Runcorn	1,488 v Runcorn
Bangor City	1,500 v Altrincham	880 v Altrincham	—	1,256 v Northwich	722 v Altrincham
Barnet	1,028 v Scarborough	969 v Wealdstone	1,404 v Enfield	1,702 v Enfield	1,499 v Enfield
Barrow	2,027 v Yeovil T	1,361 v Altrincham	1,212 v Runcorn	757 v Stafford	—
Bath City	1,840 v Yeovil T	—	2,015 v Trowbridge	1,804 v Trowbridge	1,139 v Trowbridge
Boston U	2,284 v Altrincham	—	1,456 v Kettering	1,612 v Enfield	1,357 v Runcorn
Dagenham	—	—	1,227 v Yeovil	1,243 v Enfield	928 v Enfield
Dartford	—	—	1,182 v Gravesend	—	—
Enfield	—	—	1,376 v Runcorn	1,377 v Barnet	1,096 v Barnet
Frickley A	—	789 v Altrincham	760 v Altrincham	656 v Boston U	683 v Nuneaton B
Gateshead	—	—	—	—	710 v Wealdstone
Gravesend	1,438 v Altrincham	1,518 v Maidstone	2,051 v Dartford	—	—
Kettering T	2,867 v Altrincham	2,608 v Boston U	1,623 v Bath C	1,598 v Enfield	1,390 v Scarborough
Kidderminster	—	—	—	—	872 v Runcorn
A.P. Leamington	968 v Northwich V	650 v Worcester C	544 v Worcester C	—	—
Maidstone U	1,706 v Gravesend	1,151 v Gravesend	1,125 v Dartford	2,452 v Wealdstone	2,502 v Telford U
Northwich V	2,394 v Altrincham	2,530 v Altrincham	1,674 v Runcorn	1,018 v Telford U	1,641 v Altrincham
Nuneaton B	1,970 v Kettering T	1,506 v Stafford R	—	1,640 v Stafford R	1,057 v Maidstone
Redditch U	936 v Worcester C	—	—	—	—
Runcorn	—	—	1,682 v Enfield	1,220 v Northwich	826 v Telford U
Scarborough	3,120 v Kettering T	2,225 v Kettering T	2,920 v Enfield	1,772 v Boston U	1,500 v Kettering
Telford U	1,506 v Northwich V	955 v Worcester	1,825 v Runcorn	1,370 v Enfield	1,336 v Kettering
Trowbridge	—	—	1,056 v Bath C	1,439 v Bath C	1,967 v Bath C
Stafford R	2.104 v Kettering	1,599 v Kettering	1,359 v Dartford	—	—
Wealdstone	976 v Nuneaton	1,080 v Barnet	—	1,725 v Enfield	865 v Enfield
Weymouth	2,818 v Yeovil T	2,113 v Yeovil T	1,614 v Yeovil T	1,656 v Yeovil T	1,452 v Yeovil T
Worcester C	2,405 v Weymouth	2,254 v Bath	1,763 v Runcorn	1,704 v Altrincham	2,165 v Kidderminster
Yeovil T	4,872 v Weymouth	2,457 v Weymouth	2,276 v Weymouth	2,299 v Weymouth	1,597 v Runcorn

GOLA LEAGUE PLAYERS

(These records were taken at the end of 1983-84 season)

ALTRINCHAM
Goalkeepers
Trevor Dance: Stafford Rangers, Port Vale (84)
Ian Senior: Manchester City, Ashton United, Horwich RMI

Defenders
Paul Cuddy: Chorley, Bolton Wanderers, Huddersfield Town, Rochdale (1)
David Constantine: Cury (70-2), Hyde United
Paul Beesley: Local
Dave Serella: Blackpool (55-4), Walsall (305-13), Nottingham Forest (78)
John Davison: Bangor City, Altrincham, Burnley
Phil Gardner: Everton

Midfield
Jeff King: Stafford Rangers, Chesterfield (5), Sheffield United (40-5), Sheffield Wednesday (68-7), Walsall (59-6), Derby County (19), Albion Rovers
Phil Derbyshire: Mossley, Avro FC, Stalybridge Celtic
Jeff Johnson: Hyde United, Stockport County (8)
Ronnie Ellis: Runcorn, Winsford United, Burscough, Runcorn, Dunlops
Graham Heathcote: Northwich Victoria, Altrincham

Forwards
Leo Skeete: Runcorn, Mossley, Rochdale (40-14), Burscough, Ellesmere Port
Graham Bennett: Bangor City, Bridgend Town, Barry Town
John Donnelly: South Liverpool, Burscough
Don Page: Local
John Brady: Southport, Burscough

BARNET
Goalkeepers
Gary Phillips: WBA, Brighton

Defenders
Chris Kinnear: Maidstone United, Wealdstone, West Ham United
Bill Baldry: St Albans City, Bishop's Stortford, Hitchin Town, Bedford Town, Cambridge United (27-2), Luton Town
Colin Hardman: Wealdstone, Barnet, Goole Town, Stafford Rangers, Stockport County (9-1)
Mike Pittaway: Arsenal
Kevin Millett: Hillingdon, Dunstable, Seattle Sounders (USA), Luton Town
John Morris: Wealdstone, Harrow Borough

Midfield
Eddie Stein: Dagenham, Harrow Borough, Edgware
Peter Brown: Tring Town, Aylesbury United, Wimbledon (55-3), Chelsea
John Margerrison: Wealdstone, Boreham Wood, Kansas City (USA), Orient (80-6), Fulham (71-9), Tottenham Hotspur
John Docker: Notts County, Glasgow Rangers
Lawrence Ashworth: Leytonstone & Ilford, Bromley, Clapton

Forwards
Stuart Atkins: Kettering Town, Dunstable, Wycombe Wanderers, Chesham United
Steve Mahoney: Hitchin Town, Hertford Town, Stevenage Athletic
Ian Ferguson: Baldock Town, Wimbledon, Brentford
Nicky Evans: Kettering Town, Peterborough United, QPR
Steve Ragan: Maidstone United, Dagenham, Barnet, Hillingdon, Barnet, Tottenham Hotspur

BARROW
Goalkeepers
Peter McDonnell: Hong Kong Rangers, Oldham Athletic (137), Liverpool, Bury (1)
Kevin Brockbank: Local

Defenders
Dave Large: Local
Jon Balm: Everton
Steve Brooks: Hartlepool (63-2), Southport (65-3), Marine
Andy Forbes: Local
Kenny Gordon: Local
Barry Knowles: Runcorn, Southport, Chorley
Glen Skivington: Southend United (15-2), Derby County (54-3), Barrow

Midfield
Vic Halom: Fredrikstad (Nor), Barrow, Rotherham United (20-2), Oldham Athletic (123-43), Sunderland (113-35), Luton Town (59-17), Fulham (71-22), Orient (53-12), Charlton Athletic (12)
Nigel Keen: Manchester United
Dave Woodburn: Local
Keith Kennedy: Mansfield Town (35), Bury (405-4), Newcastle United (1)
Royston Taylor: Blackburn Rovers (3-1), Sunderland (3)
Kevin Mahon: Netherfield, Barrow

Forwards
Barry Diamond: Workington, Barrow
Colin Cowperthwaite: Netherfield, Milnthorpe
Frank Gamble: Derby County (8-2), Burscough
Bruce Cleland: Motherwell, Albion Rovers

Non-contract
George Telfer: Altrincham, Scunthorpe United (7-2), Everton (128-29)
Mick Horswill: Happy Valley (Hong Kong), Hull City (84-6), Plymouth Argyle (102-3), Manchester City (14), Sunderland (69-3)

BATH CITY
Goalkeepers
David Mogg: Bristol City, Atvidaberg (Swe), Bristol City
Gordon Bell: Local

Defenders
Jeff Sherwood: Bristol Rovers (18), Bath City, Taunton Town
Tony Ricketts: Clandown
Dave Palmer: Bristol Rovers (1)
Mike England: Bristol Rovers (1)
Graham Day: Forest Green Rovers, Portland Timbers (USA), Bristol Rovers (130-1)

Midfield
Gary Smith: Bristol City (14)
Peter Aitken: Hong Kong Rangers, York City (18-2), Bristol City (41-1), Bristol Rovers (234-3)
Phil Barton: Blackburn Rovers
Wayne Hughes: Cardiff City (46-1), Tulsa Roughnecks (USA), WBA (6-2)
Peter Hayes: Bristol City
Steve Grapes: Torquay United (31), Cardiff City (147-6), Norwich City (41-3)

Forwards
Keith Brown: Bristol Rovers (7)
Ricky Chandler: Bristol City (61-13)
Dave Payne: Local
Dave Singleton: Weymouth, Taunton Town

BOSTON UNITED
Goalkeepers
Kevin Blackwell: Barnet, Barton Rovers, Bedford Town
Wayne Holland: Local
John McPherson: Holbeach United, King's Lynn, Boston FC

Defenders
Paul Casey: Sheffield United (25-1)
Richard Hearmon: Local
Arthur Mann: Kettering United, Boston United, Mansfield Town (116-3), Shrewsbury Town (8-1), Notts County (253-21), Manchester City (35), Hearts
Gerard Creane: Yaro (Fin), Stafford Rangers, Tsun Wan (Hong Kong), Lincoln City (7)
Kevin Bird: Huddersfield Town (30), Mansfield Town (348-53), Doncaster Rovers
Trevor Parr: Gainsborough Trinity, Boston United, Huddersfield Town, Bradford City, Birmingham City
Phil Jones: Sheffield United (28-1)
Ian Wood: Aldershot (17-1), Mansfield Town (169-11)

Midfield
Gary Simpson: Stoke City
Gary Mallender: Barnsley (2)
Steve Hirst: Ilkeston Town, Long Eaton United
Kevin Scrupps: Boston FC
***Charlie Bell:** Stafford Rangers, Scarborough, Mansfield Town (93-15), Middlesbrough (10-1)
Micky Laverick: York City (41-6), Huddersfield Town (74-9), Southend United (110-18), Mansfield Town (89-13)

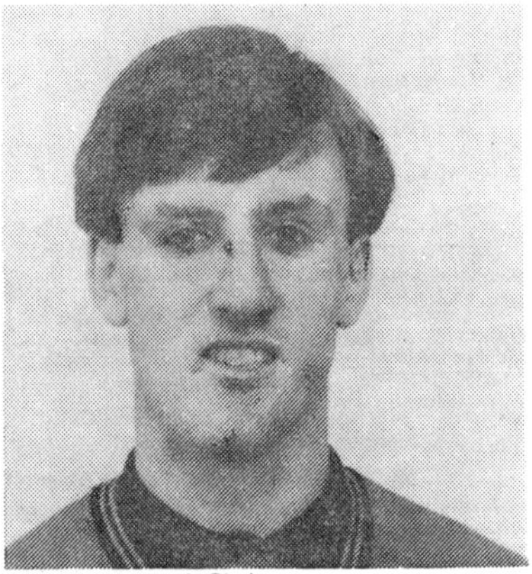

David Mogg (Bath City).

Forwards
Bob Lee: Darlington (8), Southampton, Carlisle United (55-12), Bristol Rovers (23-2), Sunderland (109-32), Leicester City (63-17)
Jim Lumby: Mansfield Town (51-18), Tranmere Rovers (46-21), Carlisle United (27-7), Scunthorpe United (55-28), Brigg Town, Gainsborough Trinity, Boston United, Grimsby Town (31-12)
Stuart Hibberd: Lincoln City (44-3)
Chris Cook: Local
Mark Richardson: Eastwood Town, Derby County
Dave Gilbert: Scunthorpe United (1), Lincoln City (30-1)

* *Has subsequently joined the Nottinghamshire Police Force and left the club.*

DAGENHAM
Goalkeepers
Lloyd Scott: Blackpool (2), Orient, Watford
Terry Moore: Bishop's Stortford, Enfield, Walthamstow Avenue, Ilford, Bishop's Stortford, Hitchin Town, Clapton

Defenders
Alan Campbell: Barnet, Hendon, Finchley
Derek Wells: Hastings United, Leytonstore & Ilford, Walthamstow Avenue, Leatherhead, Fulham

John Tone (Dartford). Photo: Tommy Hindley

John Knapman: Bishop's Stortford, Enfield, Walthamstow Avenue, Bromley, Torquay United
Terry Scales: Brentford (212-5), West Ham United
Roger Wade: Enfield, Leytonstone & Ilford, Tottenham Hotspur
Phil Boyce: Leytonstone & Ilford, Clapton, West Ham United

Midfield
Steve Oliver: Enfield, Barnet, Barking, Tottenham Hotspur
Peter Smith: Barking, Orient (14)
Jon Sille: St Albans City, Kingstonian, Hertford Town
Steve Scott: Leytonestone & Ilford, Cheshunt
Joe Dunwell: Chelmsford City, Tilbury
Steve Page: Barking, Dagenham
Paul Boyce: Local

Forwards
John McCombe: Billericay Town, Sutton United, Enfield, Rayleigh Town
Les Whitton: Croydon, Oxford City, Woodford Town
Lincoln Manderson: Leyton County
Danny Greaves: Weymouth, Chelmsford City, Southend United (50-14), Tottenham Hotspur
Chris Maycock: Local

DARTFORD
Goalkeepers
Dave Mallett: Enfield, Leytonstone & Ilford, Orient
John Holmes: Leytonstone & Ilford

Defenders
Bobby Arber: Dagenham, Atlanta Chiefs (USA), Orient
John Tone: Enfield, Clapton
Terry Pamphlett: Cray Wanderers
Dave Jacques: Leytonstone & Ilford
George Borg: Wycombe Wanderers, Carolina Lighning (USA), Dulwich Hamlet, Leytonstone & Ilford, Millwall
Tony Gibson: Dagenham, Enfield, Ilford, Bishop's Stortford, Enfield

Midfield
Steve Robinson: Local
Bobby Making: Dagenham, Barking
Joe Simmonds: Bishop's Stortford, Bigog Copenhagen (Den), Tottenham Hotspur
Martin Coates: Dulwich Hamlet
Fran Cowley: Tooting & Mitcham United, Wimbledon (8), Derby County, Sutton United, Chelsea
Andy Hessenthaler: Local
Dave Smith: Local

Forwards
Lee Holmes: Enfield, Brentford (28-6), Haringey Borough, Edmonton, West Ham United
Terry Sullivan: Bishop's Stortford
Tony Burman: Charlton Athletic (19-3), QPR

Paul Powell: Leytonstone & Ilford
Paul Lazarus: Maidstone United, TPS Turun (Fin), Dagenham, TPS Turun (Fin), Wimbledon (18-6), Charlton Athletic (2-1)
Steve Browne: Maidstone United, Charlton Athletic (1)

ENFIELD
Goalkeepers
Paul Cotter: Dagenham, Watford

Defenders
Trevor Savage: Local
Keith Barrett: Barking, Tottenham Hotspur
Robert Turpin: Local
Dave Waite: Barking, Dover Athletic
Keith Hayzelden: Leytonstore & Ilford
Paul Haverson: Kettering Town, Wimbledon (28-2), QPR
John Cooper: Croydon, Sutton United, Woking, Leatherhead, Fulham

Midfield
Paul Taylor: Barking
Dave Hatchett: Local
Noel Ashford: Fulham, Barking
Steve Cox: Local

Forwards
Steve King: Leytonstone & Ilford
Dave Flint: Local
Ian Whittingham: Local

FRICKLEY ATHLETIC
Goalkeepers
Stuart Hinchcliffe: Mossley, Spalding United, Orient, Goole Town, Sutton Town, Frickley Athletic
Tommy Meehan: Worksop Town, Sheffield United

Defenders
Steve Daniels: Doncaster Rovers (1)
Harry Dunn: Scarborough
Mally Wright: Scarborough, Leeds Ashley Road
Sean Marshall: Scarborough
Dave McDonnell: Pontefract Colleries

Midfield
Barry Gill: Scarborough, Barnsley
Peter Howey: Scarborough, Frickley Athletic, Newport County, Leeds United, Huddersfield Town (22-3)
John Overton: Gillingham (178-10), Aston Villa (3)
Russell Wilcox: Cambridge United, Doncaster Rovers (1)
Malcolm Smith: Scarborough, York City, Scarborough

Forwards
Ian Smith: Scarborough, Mossley
Gary Hooley: Altrincham, Frickley Athletic, Guiseley
Paul Wilson: Denaby United
Graham Reed: Barnsley (3)
Phil Campbell: Scarborough

GATESHEAD
Goalkeepers
Kenny Dodds: Aldershot, Sunderland, Chelsea
Brendan Carr: Local

Defenders
Steve Higgins: Local
Dave Mitchinson: Blyth Spartans, Gateshead, Whitley Bay
Dave Parnaby: Durham City, Whitby Town, Willington
Lawrence Pearson: Local
Lance Jobling: Hebburn Reyrolles

Midfield
Terry Hibbitt: Newcastle United (90-5), Birmingham City (110-11), Newcastle United (138-7), Leeds United (47-9)
Kevin Pugh: Darlington (7), Gateshead, Newcastle United (1)
Justin Robson: Newcastle United
Keith McNall: Crook Town
John Grady: Ferryhil Athletic

Forwards
Bob Topping: Whitley Bay
John Tweedy: Tow Law Town, Hartlepool, Middlesbrough
Geoff Langley: Bolton Wanderers (6)
Martin Henderson: Durham City, Crook Town
Peter Davies: Whitley Bay, Blyth Spartans, Carlisle United, North Shields
Ian Donaldson: North Shields, Ashington

KETTERING TOWN
Goalkeepers
Steve Humphries: Leicester City, Doncaster Rovers (13), Leicester City
Nicky Goodwin: Graham Street Prims

Defenders
Jem Palmer: Desborough Town
Phil Sandercock: Weymouth, Barnet, Wellingborough Town, Nuneaton Borough, Northampton Town (69-3), Huddersfield Town (81-1), Torquay United (205-13)
Iori Jenkins: Desborough Town, Kettering Town, Brentford (15), Chelsea
Glyn Creaser: Wolverton Town
Glyn Chamberlain: Halifax Town (35), Chesterfield (18), Burnley
Neil Crabb: Local

Midfield
Peter Denyer: Northampton Town (167-33), Portsmouth (145-17)
Willie Kelly: Local
Dougie Keast: Shepshed Charterhouse, Bailleston, Celtic
Eddie McGoldrick: Peterborough United, Kettering Town

Paul Culpin, Nuneaton Borough's record breaking goalscorer, seen here in a match against Barrow in February '83. Photo: Ted Cottrell

Eddie McGoldrick (Kettering Town).

Forwards
Richard Dawson: Gainsborough Trinity, Scarborough, Chesterfield (12-1), Doncaster Rovers (43-14), Rotherham (24-3)
Shaun Diver: Cottingham
Simon Brown: Local
Dave Hofbauer: Corby Town

KIDDERMINSTER HARRIERS
Goalkeepers
Tim Garner: AP Leamington, Nuneaton Borough

John Bartley (Maidstone United).
Photo: Roger Price

Defenders
Martin Woodall: AP Leamington, Willenhall Town, Cheltenham Town, Willenhall Town, Tipton Town, Oldswinford, Wallsall, WBA
Chris Jones: Stourbridge, Bilston, Telford United
John Horne: Walsall (16-1), Aston Villa
John Martin: Telford United, Bromsgrove Rovers
***Fraser Wood:** Stafford Rangers, Tipton Town
***Archie Richards:** Weymouth, Telford United, Kettering Town, Stafford Rangers, Kidderminster Harriers

Midfield
Steve Bowater: Alvechurch, Worcester City, Walsall, Wolves
Andy McGowan: Corby Town, Stamford, Rushden Town, Northampton Town (105-15), Corby Town
Martin Gavin: Telford United, Bromsgrove Rovers, Bilston, Bristol City
John Powell: Corby Town, Nottingham Forest

Forwards
Mick Tuohy: Worcester City, Southend United (21-4), Redditch United, Walsall
Herman Wilson: AP Leamington, Solihull Borough, Sutton Coldfield Town, Dudley Town
Mark Rosegeen: AP Leamington
Elwyn Roberts: Corby Town, Barnet, Canberra City (Aus), Bedford Town, Corby Town, Nottingham Forest
Paul Davies: Herakles (Holl), Trowbridge Town, Cardiff City (2)
** Subsequently released in the close season*

MAIDSTONE UNITED
Goalkeepers
Derek Richardson: Coventry City, Sheffield United (42), QPR (31), Chelsea
Colin Lewington: Chelmsford City, Bromley, Gravesend, Erith & Belvedere

Defenders
Jon Moore: AFC Bournemouth (36-2), Millwall (119-5), Bristol Rovers
Andy Rollings: Brentford, Portsmouth (34-1), Swindon Town (16-2), Brighton (182-11), Norwich City (4)
Mark Newson: Charlton Athletic
Micky Crowe: Hastings United, Gravesend, Glentworth, Dartford, Faversham
Brian Thompson: Mansfield Town (9), Yeovil Town, Sunderland
Paul Yates: Basildon United, Windsor & Eton

Midfield
Malcolm Stewart: Dagenham, Hoddesdon Town
Billy Hughes: Wimbledon (2), Crystal Palace (7), Gillingham (126-8)
Kevin Maddocks: Basildon United
Nigel Donn: Orient (27-2), Gillingham (6)
Nicky Ironton: Enfield, Barking, QPR
Peter Taylor: Exeter City (6), Maidstone United, Orient (62-11), Tottenham Hotspur (140-33), Crystal Palace (144-38), Southend United (78-13), ENGLAND

Forwards
John Bartley: Kuipio ELO (Fin), Millwall (40-8), Welling United
Clive Green: Yeovil Town, Portsmouth, Southampton
Micky Dingwall: Leytonstone & Ilford, Barking
Terry Robbins: Tottenham Hotspur

NORTHWICH VICTORIA
Goalkeepers
David Ryan: Southport (23), Manchester United

Defenders
Dave Fretwell: Wigan Athletic (112), Carolina Lightning (USA), Bradford City (253-5)
Tony Murphy: Bangor City, Runcorn
Jeff Forshaw: Stalybridge Celtic, Winsford United, Portmadog
Ken Jones: Ellesmere Port Town, WBA
***Dave Bradley:** Bury (8), Doncaster Rovers (67-5), Manchester United

Midfield
Paul Bennett: Port Vale (30-1)
Mark Dean: Local
Phil Wilson: Mossley, Runcorn, Tranmere Rovers, Blackburn Rovers
Phil Power: Local
***Kevin Hynett:** Local
Graham Abel: Runcorn

Forwards
Colin Chesters: Crewe Alexandra (61-6), Derby County (9-1)
Paul Reid: Nantwich Town
Mark Clynch: Local
John Anderson: Chester, Everton, Stalybridge Celtic

** Bradley has subsequently joined Dunedin City (NZ) as player-coach.*
** Hynett has subsequently joined Stop Out Wellington (NZ).*

NUNEATON BOROUGH
Goalkeepers
Andy Poole: Gillingham, Port Vale (2), Wolves, Northampton Town (157), Mansfield Town

Defenders
Richard Dixey: Scarborough, Kettering Town, Burnley
Everton Carr: Rochdale (9), Halifax Town (43), Leicester City (14)
Willie Gibson: Leicester City (28)
John Glover: Bedford Town, Dulwich Hamlet
Micky Burke: Local
John Winters: Peterborough United (69-3)
Richard Hill: Leicester City

Midfield
Derek Duggan: Kettering Town, Birmingham City
Tim Smithers: Oxford United (119-7), Nuneaton Borough
Paul Richardson: Eastwood Town, Nottingham Forest
Bobby Parker: Local
Lee Sullivan: Local

Forwards
Frank Murphy: Kettering Town, Desborough Town, Corby Town
Paul Culpin: Leicester City
Trevor Morley: Corby Town, Derby County
Stewart Hamill: Kettering Town, Leicester City (10-2), Pollok

RUNCORN
Goalkeepers
Brian Parker: Yeovil Town, Arsenal, Crewe Alexandra (26)

Defenders
Brian Kettle: Burscough, Wigan Athletic (14-1), Houston Hurricane (USA), Liverpool (3)
Mick Roberts: Winsford United, Mossley, Oldham Athletic
Elfyn Edwards: Tranmere Rovers (62-1), Wrexham
Bobby Fraser: Winsford United, Portmadog, Holyhead, Marine, Skelmersdale United, Tranmere Rovers, Liverpool
Mick Hardman: Warrington Town, Runcorn, Warrington Town

Midfield
Ossie Smith: Altrincham, Manchester United
Mark Jones: Local
John Imrie: Buxton, Bury, Barnsley
John Butler: Blackpool (8)
Alan Crompton: Wigan Athletic (13), Blackburn Rovers (4), Sunderland

Forwards
John Rogers: Barrow, Altrincham, Wigan Athletic, Altrincham, Port Vale (26-1), Portland Timbers (USA), Wigan Athletic
John Stringer: Barnton
Tony Clarke: Local
Peter McCrae: Oldham Athletic

SCARBOROUGH
Goalkeepers
Graeme Crawford: Rochdale (70), York City (17), Scunthorpe United (104), York City (235), Sheffield United (2), East Stirling

Defenders
Richard Dawson: York City (45)
Bryan Magee: Horden Colliery Welfare
John Cottam: Chester (120-1), Chesterfield (120-7), Nottingham Forest (95-4)
Graham Hartley: Local
Kenny Dennis: Peterborough United

Midfield
Neil Thompson: Hull City (31), Nottingham Forest
Neil Sellers: Goole Town, Bridlington Town, Hull City
Mitch Cook: Local
Brendan Phillips: Nuneaton Borough, Boston United, Mansfield Town (17), Boston United, Kettering Town, Nuneaton Borough, Burton Albion, Peterborough United (1), Leicester City
David Bowman: Local

Forwards
John Hanson: Bradford City (1)
Trenton Wiggan: Gainsborough Trinity, Sheffield United (24-3)
Tim Jamieson: Bridlington Trinity, Winterton Rangers, Bridlington Town
Mark Cox: Shepshed Charterhouse, Boston United, Boston FC, Doncaster Rovers (15), Lincoln City (5)
Pat Olney: Bangor City, Preston NE, Manchester United

TELFORD UNITED
Goalkeepers
Kevin Charlton: Bangor City, Hereford United (52), AFC Bournemouth (21), Wolves

Defenders
Steve Eaton: Northwich Victoria, Tranmere Rovers (1)
Antone Joseph: Weymouth, Cardiff City
Malcolm Bailey: Altrincham, Runcorn, Northwich Victoria, Port Vale
Kevin Lewis: Crewe Alexandra (122-2), Stoke City (15), Manchester United
Tony Turner: Nuneaton Borough, Hednesford Town, Stop Out Wellington (NZ), Hednesford Town
Nicky Day: Local
Tim Rutter: Runcorn

Midfield
Dave Barnett: Stafford Rangers, Bangor City, Oldham Athletic
Paul Mayman: Northwich Victoria, Nantwich Town, Crewe Alexandra (43-3)
Eddie Hogan: Nuneaton Borough, Telford United, Redditch United, Derby County
Paul Jackson: Local

Forwards
Dean Edwards: Worcester City, Port Vale, Oulun Palloseura (Fin), Shrewsbury Town (13-1)
Colin Williams: Scarborough, Northwich Victoria, Telford United, Northwich Victoria, Droylsden, Oldham Athletic
John Alcock: Eastwood Hanley
Dave Mather: Bangor City, South Liverpool, Stalybridge Celtic

WEALDSTONE
Goalkeepers
Bob Iles: Chelsea (14), Weymouth

Defenders
Mark Morris: Local
Paul Bowgett: Wimbledon (41), Tottenham Hotspur, Letchworth Garden City
Dennis Byatt: Northampton Town (47-3), Peterborough United (3), Fulham
Steve Perkins: Wimbledon (52), QPR (2), Chelsea
Gary Donnellan: Reading (44-5), Watford, Chelsea

Midfield
Fred Barwick: Tottenham Hotspur
David Price: Orient (10), Crystal Palace (27-2), Arsenal (126-16)
Robin Wainwright: Hillingdon, Dunstable, Northampton Town (32-5), Millwall (4), Luton Town (16-3)
Chris Dibble: Wimbledon (8), Millwall (63-5)
Nigel Johnson: Luton Town

Gerry Pearson (Weymouth). Photo: Focus Press

Gary Borthwick (Yeovil Town).

Forwards
Alan Cordice: Norwich City, Chesham United
Neil Cordice: Northampton Town (8-1), Wycombe Wanderers
Brian Greenaway: Fulham (85-8)
Mark Graves: Plymouth Argyle (33-3)

WEYMOUTH
Goalkeepers
John Turner: Torquay United (5), Chesterfield (149), Torquay United (90), Reading (36), Derby County

Defenders
Paul Arnold: Southampton
Paul Morrell: Poole Town
Richie Bourne: Torquay United (68-7), Bath City, Colchester United (4), Ramsgate
Brian Lawrence: AFC Bournemouth
Steve Falcus: Portesham
Alan Slough: Torquay United, Millwall (14), Peterborough United (105-10), Fulham (154-13), Luton Town (275-28)

Midfield
Anniello Iannone: Dunstable
Geoff Joy: Bridport
Gerry Pearson: Bideford, Barnstaple Town, Sheffield United
Dave McManus: Dorchester Town
Hedley Steele: Dorchester Town, Exeter City
Brian Benjafield: Poole Town, Oxford City, AFC Bournemouth (2)
Wayne Bray: Bristol City (32-2)

Forwards
David Platt: Yeovil Town, Grantham, Leicester City
Shaun Penny: Dorchester Town, Bath City, KTP Kotkan (Fin), Bristol Rovers (60-13), Bristol City
Ashley Doidge: Local
Tony Agana: Welling United
Andy Bell: Yeovil Town, Exeter City (3)

WORCESTER CITY
Goalkeepers
Paul Hayward: Paget Rangers
Phil Parkes: Stourbridge, Toronto Blizzards (USA), Oklahoma City (USA), Worcester City, Chicago Stings(USA), Vancouver Whitecaps (USA), Wolves (313)

Defenders
Graham Selby: Bromsgrove Rovers
Wayne Stokes: Aylesbury United, Gillingham (2), Coventry City
Colin Caddick: Walsall
Malcolm Phelps: Nuneaton Borough, Alvechurch
John McGrath: Shrewsbury Town

Midfield
David Hughes: Lincoln City, Scunthorpe United (21), Lincoln City (62-1), Aston Cilla (4-1)
Barry Lowe: Nuneaton Borough, Worcester City, Weymouth, Stafford Rangers
Duncan Gardner: Nuneaton Borough, Telford United, AP Leamington, Racing Club Warwick, Pottertons
Steve Crompton: Hereford United (34-6), Wolves

Forwards
Paul Moss: Scunthorpe United (42-7), Hull City (54-7), Wolves
Gary Wright: Alvechurch, Worcester City, Moor Green
Graham Jones: Kidderminster Harriers, Stourbridge, Dudley Town, Wallsall
Bobby Evans: Tividale, Stourbridge, Shifnal Town

YEOVIL TOWN
Goalkeepers
Grant Northover: Taunton Town
Kevin Roberts: Weymouth, Swindon Town (1), Welton Rovers

Defenders
Malcolm Gold: Salisbury
Stuart Gibson: Oxford United, Birmingham City
Billy Elliott: Weymouth, AFC Bournemouth (11-1), Plymouth Argyle
David Linney: Oxford United (34), Birmingham City (1)
Paul Charles: Local
Ricky Horton: Local
Nigel Jarvis: Blackburn Rovers, Plymouth Argyle
Jess Payne: Torquay United (25-1), Leicester City

Midfield
Gary Borthwick: Weymouth, Yeovil Town, AFC Bournemouth (74-4), Barnet, Aylesbury United, Southend United, Portsmouth
Trevor Finnigan: Weymouth, Yeovil Town, AFC Bournemouth (25-5), Blackpool (17-3), Runcorn, Everton, Port Vale
Simon White: Local
Paul McLaughlin: Clandown
Phil James: Keinton Mandeville

Forwards
Mick Doherty: Slough Town, Reading (26-5), Basingstoke Town, Hounslow, Harrow Borough, Wigan Athletic, Southampton
Jamie Ward: Glastonbury
Angelo Paparella: Local
Jeremy Brown: Newport County (3), Birmingham City
Andy Morris: Oxford United

EX-ALLIANCE PREMIER LEAGUE FOOTBALL LEAGUE XI

Jim Arnold
(Stafford R, Blackburn R, Everton)

Kirk Stephens
(Nuneaton B, Luton T)

Malcolm Shotton
(Nuneaton B, Oxford U)

Trevor Peake
(Nuneaton B, Lincoln C, Coventry C)

Stuart Pearce
(Wealdstone, Coventry C)

Mark Ward
(Northwich V, Oldham A)

Billy Ayre
(Scarborough, Hartlepool U, Halifax T, Mansfield T)

Paul Sugrue
(Nuneaton B, Manchester C, Middlesbrough)

Mick Vinter
(Boston U, Notts Co, Wrexham, Oxford U)

Colin Barnes
(Barnet, Torquay U)

Keith Bertschin
(Barnet, Ipswich T, B'ham C, Norwich C, England U21)

Over 30 ex Alliance players were in the Football League last season but this total included very few midfield players and I should imagine Nuneaton Borough would like to field a few of their 'old boys' who have done so well.

This effort against Wealdstone at Moss Lane in the last league game of the season brought Altrincham striker Graham Bennett's goal tally to 18, a total which ensured him of being top scorer for the second successive year.
Photo: John Rooney, Robins Review.

Scarborough's Dave Bowman leaps for a fine header against Barnet. Photo: S. Penny

Steve Joel (Runcorn). Photo: Glen Cameron

Eddie Stein (Barnet).

Altrincham *Back Row (L-R): Kevan Hawkins, Stan Allan (trainer), Phil Derbyshire, Ian Senior, Trevor Dance, Leo Skeete, Jeff King. Middle Row: John King (manager), Peter Conning, Paul Cuddy, Don Page, John Donnelly, Graham Bennett, Jeff Johnson, George Rooney (assistant manager). Front Row: John Brady, John Davison, Ronnie Ellis, Graham Heathcote, David Constantine, Phil Gardner.* Photo: John Rooney

ALTRINCHAM

President: L. P. Pollitt
Chairman: Noel White F.S.C.A.
Manager: John King
Assistant Manager: George Rooney
Physiotherapist:

Secretary: David Baldwin
Address & Tel No: Moss Lane, Altrincham, Cheshire WA15 8AP. 061-928 1045 (Ground)
Commercial Manager: Derek Kennerley
Address & Tel No: 061-928 6905

Press Officer & Tel No: Paul Brady. Tel. 061-928 1705, 061-928 8103
Address & Tel No of ground: Moss Lane, Altrincham, Cheshire WA15 8AP. Tel. 061-928 1045 **Club shop:** Yes
Simple ground directions: ½ mile from Altrincham town centre along Moss Lane
No of seats: 1,000 **Covered accommodation:** 5,000 **Capacity:** 10,000 **Floodlights:** Yes
Year formed: 1903 **Nickname:** The Robins **Club sponsor:** Quicks for Ford
Previous names: None
Club colours: Red & White stripes/Black/Red
Previous grounds: None
Change colours: All Yellow
Day for midweek home matches: Monday
Record attendance: 35,530 v Everton F.A. Cup 3rd Round replay **Year:** 1975
Best performance in: F.A. Cup: 1965-6 v Wolves, 1974-5 v Everton, 1978-9 v Spurs, 1979-80 v Orient, 1980-1 v Liverpool, 1981-2 v Burnley, 3rd Round
F.A. Trophy: Winners 1977-8 v Leatherhead, Finalists 1981-2 v Enfield

Previous Leagues: Manchester, Cheshire, Northern Premier

Clubhouse details: Run as a nightclub/bistro only, not owned by club
Present players with Football League experience: David Constantine (Bury), Paul Cuddy (Rochdale), Jeff Johnson (Stockport Co), Trevor Dance (Port Vale), Jeff King (Port Vale)
Past players who progressed into the Football League: Nelson Stiffle (WBA), Steve Johnson (Bury), Frank Carrodus (Manchester City), Graham Barrow (Wigan Ath)
Record transfer fee paid: To Runcorn for Barry Whitbread
Record transfer fee received: From Wigan Athletic for Graham Barrow
Programme details: 24 pages, 30p (avail on subscription)
Club metal badges: Yes
Local newspapers & Tel No: Altrincham & Sale Guardian 061-928 3737, Sale & Altrincham Messenger 061-477 5636, Manchester Evening News 061-832 7200

Major Honours: Alliance Premier League (2), F.A. Trophy & Runners-up, Alliance Premier League Cup, Alliance Premier League Shield, Northern Premier League Cup, Cheshire League (2), Cheshire League Cup (3), Cheshire Senior Cup (4)

Club Captain (1983-84): Graham Heathcote
Player of the Year (1983-84): David Constantine
Programme Editor: Paul V. Brady

Barnet *Back Row (L-R): C. Kinnear, G. Craig, P. Brown, G. Ogbourne (Kit Manager), J. Margerrison, B. Pittaway, B. Baldry, B. Fry (Manager), G. Phillips, S. Ragan, E. Stein, C. Hewitt (Trainer), L. Ashworth, N. Evans, T. Bennett. Front Row: M. Pittaway, S. Atkins, C. Hardman, R. Livermore, J. Skinner, T. Hill (Chairman), L. Lansbury, A. Shaw, J. Docker, K. Millett (Captain), S. Mahoney.*

BARNET

President: C. Whitta
Chairman: Tom Hill
Manager: Barry Fry
Coach: Barry Fry
Physiotherapist: Chris Hewitt
Secretary: Barry Fry
Address & Tel No: 0582 64634
Commercial Manager: John Hartburn
Address & Tel No:
Press Officer & Tel No: Barry Fry, Trudy Archer (01-449 4173)
Address & Tel No of ground: Underhill, Barnet, Herts. Tel. 01-449 4173
Club shop: Yes
Simple ground directions: At the foot of Barnet Hill on London side A1000
No of seats: 884 **Covered accommodation:** 5,500 **Capacity:** 10,000 **Floodlights:** Yes
Year formed: 1888 **Nickname:** The Bees **Club sponsors:** David Godwin Plumbing Supplies
Previous names: None
Previous grounds: None
Club colours: Amber/Black
Change colours: All Red
Day for midweek home matches: Tuesday
Record attendance: 14,000 v Wycombe W. F.A. Am. Cup **Year:** 1949
Best performance in: F.A. Cup: 1972-3, 1981-2 v Brighton 3rd Round Replay
F.A. Trophy: 1971-2 Finalists
Previous Leagues: Athenian, Southern
Clubhouse details: Social club
Present players with Football League experience: P. Sandercock, B. Pittaway, D. Westwood, M. Chivers
Past players who progressed into the Football League: Colin Powell, Gary Borthwick, Graham Pearce, Russell Townsend, Colin Barnes
Record transfer fee paid: £4,000 Stuart Atkins (Kettering)
Record transfer fee received: £30,000 Russell Townsend (Northampton), £20,000+ Graham Pearce (Brighton)
Programme details: 24 pages, 30p
Programme Editor: Tony Holmes
Club metal badges: Yes
Local newspapers & Tel No: Barnet Press 01-441 3003, Hendon Times 01-952 5217, Local Adviser 01-449 5577
Local Radio stations: Capital, L.B.C.
Major Honours: F.A. Amateur Cup & Finalists (2), F.A. Trophy Finalists, Athenian League (7), Southern League Div1 South, Southern League Cup
Club Captain (1983-84): Kevin Millett
Player of the Year (1983-84): Gary Phillips

Barrow AFC *Back Row (L-R) Colin Cowperthwaite, Ken Gordon, Bruce Cleland, Peter McDonnell, Kevin Brockbank, Steve Brooks, John Balm, Mick Richmond. Front Row: David Large, Nigel Keen, Keith Kennedy, Kevin Mahon, Barry Diamond, Royston Taylor, Frank Gamble.*

BARROW

Chairman: W. A. McCullough
Manager:
Coach:
Physiotherapist: T. Rhodes
Secretary: P. Cowing
Address & Tel No: Barrow 55309
Commercial Manager: None
Address & Tel No: 23061
Press Officer & Tel No: Ann Barker, 0229 36767
Address & Tel No of ground: Holker Street, Barrow-in-Furness, Cumbria. Tel 0229 20346
Club shop: Yes
Simple ground directions: M6 to Barrow – A590 into Barrow-in-Furness. Turn right, fourth set of lights (Station ½ mile)
No of seats: 1,250 **Covered accommodation:** All **Capacity:** 9,000 **Floodlights:** Yes
Year formed: 1901 **Nickname:** Bluebirds **Club sponsors:** None
Previous names: None
Previous grounds: None
Club colours: Blue/White/White
Change colours: All Red
Day for midweek home matches: Tuesdays
Record attendance: 16,840 F.A. Cup v Swansea Town **Year:** 1954
Best performance in: F.A. Cup: 1954 v Swansea Town, 1959 v Wolves, 3rd Round
F.A. Trophy: 1980 Quarter Final
Previous Leagues: Football League, Northern Premier
Clubhouse details: Bluebird Club, Holker Street. Modern club, holds 250
Present players with Football League experience: R. Taylor (Blackburn, Preston), N. Keen (Manchester Utd), S. Brooks (Hartlepool), P. McDonnell (Oldham, Liverpool), G. Skivington (Derby Co, Southend), F. Gamble (Derby Co), B. Cleland (Motherwell), K. Kennedy (Bury, Mansfield)
Past players who progressed into the Football League: Glenn Skivington, N. McDonald
Record transfer fee paid: None
Record transfer fee received: Over £20,000 from Derby County
Programme details: Price 20p
Club metal badges: Yes
Major Honours: Lancashire Junior Cup & Finalists
NPL Champions 1983-4
Club Captain (1983-84): S. Brooks
Local newspapers & Tel No: Barrow Evening Mail 0229 21835
BBC Radio Furness 837khz mw, 96.1 VHF
Programme Editor: Anne Barker
Player of the Year (1983-84): F. Gamble

Bath City *Back Row (L-R): Tony Ricketts, Barry Thomson, David Singleton, Dave Mogg, Gordon Bell, Graham Day, Keith Brown, Mike England, Mike Lyons. Centre Row (L-R): Shaun Penny, Brian Wade, Peter Hayes, Bobby Jones, Phil Barton, Steve Grapes, David Palmer. Front Row (L-R): Ricky Chandler, Dave Roberts, Jimmy Gough.* Photo: Wessex Newspapers

BATH CITY

President: R. G. Williams F.R.S.A.
Chairman: T. P. Richards
Manager: Bobby Jones
Coach: Colin Taverner
Physiotherapist: Mike Lyons
Secretary: Ann Cunningham
Address & Tel No: Twerton Park, Bath. Tel 0225 23087
Commercial Manager: Graham Bowen
Address & Tel No: c/o Club
Press Officer & Tel No: Steve Bransgrove
Address & Tel No of ground: Twerton Park, Bath. Tel Bath 23087 **Club shop:** Yes
Simple ground directions: Situated just off the main A36. Lower Bristol Road approx 1¾ miles from the City centre
No of seats: 1,000 **Covered accommodation:** 5,000 **Capacity:** 20,000 **Floodlights:** Yes
Year formed: 1889 **Nickname:** City **Club sponsors:** Hinton Garage
Previous names: None
Previous grounds: None
Club colours: White/Black
Change colours: Red/White
Day for midweek home matches: Tuesday
Record attendance: 18,020 v Brighton, F.A. Cup **Year:** 1960
Previous Leagues: Southern
Best performance in: **F.A. Cup:** 1963-4 v Bolton Wanderers 3rd Round Replay
F.A. Trophy: 1979-80 3rd Round
Clubhouse details: 'Sportsman' 11 a.m.-2.30 p.m. and 6.30 p.m.-10.30 p.m. Presidents Club 7.30 p.m.-10.30 p.m.
Present players with Football League experience: Keith Brown, Dave Palmer (Bristol Rovers), Colin Taverner (Hereford Utd)
Past players who progressed into the Football League: Alan Skirton (Arsenal), Tony Book (Plymouth, Man. City), Ken Allen (Bournemouth), Peter Rogers, Martin Rogers (Exeter), Richard Bourne (Torquay), Dave Wiffil (Man. City), Jeff Sherwood (Bristol R.), G. Withey (Bristol R.).
Record transfer fee paid: £7,000 to Minehead for Brian Durbin
Record transfer fee received: £50,000 Dave Wiffil (Manchester City)
Programme details: 8 pages, 25p
Programme Editor: Steve V. Bransgrove
Local newspapers & Tel No: Bath Evening Chronicle 63051
Club metal badges: No
Major Honours: Southern League (2), League Cup, Somerset Premier Cup (10), Anglo-Italian Cup Finalists
Club Captain (1983-84): Tony Ricketts **Player of the Year (1983-84):** David Mogg

Boston United *Back Row (L-R): Nigel Carter, Wayne Holland, Derrick Nuttell, Kevin Blackwell, Phil Jones, Stuart Hibberd, Trevor Parr, Mick Lyon (now with Stamford), Richard Harben, Front Row (L-R): Stephen Hirst, David Gilbert, Chris Cook, Ian Wood, Gary Simpson, Paul Casey, Gary Mallender, Jim Lumby.*

BOSTON UNITED

Chairman: P. Malkinson
Manager: Arthur Mann
Coach:
Physiotherapist: Dr L. D. Taffinder
Secretary: John Blackwell
Address & Tel No: 14-16 Spain Place, Boston. 0205 65652 (H), 0205 64406 (B)
Commercial Manager: John Blackwell
Address & Tel No: As above
Press Officer & Tel No: None
Address & Tel No of ground: York Street Ground, Boston. 0205 65524/5. Match days only **Club shop:** Yes
Simple ground directions: Two minutes walk from town centre
No of seats: 2,000 **Covered accommodation:** All **Capacity:** 15,000 **Floodlights:** Yes, Mercury Malide
Year formed: 1935 **Nickname:** Pilgrims **Club sponsors:** "Low Fields"
Previous names: Boston Town, Boston Swifts
Club colours: Amber/Black
Previous grounds: None
Change colours: Sky Blue/Claret/White
Day for midweek home matches: Wednesday
Previous Leagues: Central Alliance, Midland Count,, United Counties, West Midlands, Northern Prem.
Record attendance: 10,086 v Corby Town **Year:** Unknown
Best performance in: F.A. Cup: 1955-6 v Tottenham, 1973-4 v Derby Co. 3rd Round
F.A. Trophy: 1979-80 losing Semi-Finalists
Clubhouse details: Open every day except Tuesday. 7-11 p.m. Friday, Saturday 11-3 p.m. Sunday 12-2 p.m. Live entertainment, darts, dominoes. Tel: 0205 62967.
Present players with Football League experience: M. Laverick, J. Lumby, D. Gilbert, P. Casey, A Mann, G. Creane, B. Lee.
Past players who progressed into the Football League: J. Smith (Colchester, Blackburn, Birmingham), S. Thompson (Lincoln City), B. Phillips (Mansfield Town), G. Simmonite (Blackpool)
Record transfer fee paid: £10,000 Brendan Phillips (Mansfield Town)
Record transfer fee received: £15,000 B. Phillips (Mansfield), S. Thompson (Lincoln), G. Simmonite (Blackpool)
Programme details: 20 pages, 30p, photographs
Programme Editors: Nick Thompson and John Blackwell
Club metal badges: Yes + embroidered ones
Local newspapers & Tel No: Lincolnshire Standard 0205 65001, Boston Target, 0205 50220, Boston Choice, Lincs Echo 0522 26101, Local Radio stations: Radio Lincoln, Hereward Radio
Major Honours: United Counties League, West Midland League (2), N.P.L. (4) & Runners-up, N.P.L. Cup (2) & Runners-up, N.P.L. Shield (3), N.P.L. Champs v S.L. Champs (2) & Runners-up
Club Captain: Ian Wood
Player of the Year (1982-83): Paul Casey

Dagenham *Back Row (L-R): Brian Morris (physio), Jon Sille, Joe Dunwell, Derek Wells, Steve Page, Lloyd Scott, Steve Oliver, Terry Scales, Dave Silman (now left), Alan Campbell, Ronny Duke (coach), Ted Hardy (manager). Front Row (L-R): Danny Greaves (now left), John Knapman, Roger Wade, John McCombe, Chris Maycock, Peter Smith, Les Whitton, Steve Scott.*

DAGENHAM

President: Vic Sparrow
Chairman: Vic Sparrow
Manager: Ted Hardy
Coach: Ronnie Duke
Physiotherapist:
Secretary: Eric Ryan
Address & Tel No: 11 Dagenham Avenue, Dagenham, Essex. (H) 01-593 4764
Commercial Secretary: Mrs E. Coney
Tel No: 01-593 3864
Press Officer & Tel No: W. C. A. Bridges. Hornchurch 58879
Address & Tel No of ground: Victoria Road Ground, Dagenham, Essex. RM10 7XL. 01-592 1549 (Reception), 01-592 7194 (Offices)
Club shop: Yes, Manager Fred Hawthorn
Simple ground directions: On A1112 between A12 and A13. By Rail, LTE District Line to Dagenham East. Turn left out of station. Victoria Road is the fifth turning on the left.
No of seats: 507 **Covered accommodation:** 5,000 **Capacity:** 9,000 **Floodlights:** Yes
Year formed: 1949 **Nickname:** The Daggers **Club sponsors:** Dagenham Motors
Previous names: None
Club colours: All Red
Previous ground: The Arena, Old Dagenham Park
Change colours: All Yellow
Day for midweek home matches: Monday
Record attendance: 7,100 v Reading F.A. Cup **Year:** 1968
Best performance in: F.A. Cup: 1967-8 2nd Round Replay v Reading
F.A. Trophy: 1979-80 Winners
Previous Leagues: Metropolitan, Delphian, Corinthian, Athenian, Isthmian
Clubhouse details: Four bars, two halls, offices etc. Various entertainment throughout the year. Open every day, normal 'pub' hours.
Present players with Football League experience: T. Scales (Brentford), L. Scott (Blackpool)
Past players who progressed into the Football League: M. Lazarus (Orient, QPR etc), J. Compton (Chelsea, Ipswich), A. Marshall (Colchester), E. May (Southend, Wrexham, Swansea), M. Newman (West Ham).
Record transfer fee paid: To Harrow Borough for Eddie Stein
Record transfer fee received: For George Duck and Steve Jones (Exchange)
Programme details: 25p
Programme Editor: Fred Hawthorn
Club metal badges: Yes, 95p
Local newspapers & Tel No: Post 01-593 8100, Advertiser 0708 66044.
Local Radio stations: LBC, Capital Radio, Essex
Major Honours: F.A. Challenge Trophy & Runners-up, F.A. Amateur Cup Runners-up (2), London Senior Cup & Runners-up (2), Essex Senior Cup (6) & Runners-up (3), Isthmian League Premier Division Runners-up (2)
Club Captain (1983-84): Joe Dunwell,
Player of the Year (1983-84): Alan Campbell

Dartford *Back Row (L-R): John Still (manager), Jim Detnam (coach), Francis Cowley, Steve Robinson, Tony Pamphlett, Dave Mallett, John Holmes, Martin Coates, George Borg, Joe Simmonds, Steve Brown, Bobby Arber, Paul Powell, George Dudley (assistant manager/coach). Front Row (L-R): Paul Lazarus, David Smith, Bobby Makin, David Jacques, Tony Burman, Terry Sullivan. Trophy: Southern League Premier Division Championship Shield.* Photo: Kentish Times Newspaper

DARTFORD

Chairman: B. Alford
Manager: John Still
Coaches: George Dudley/Jim Detnam
Physiotherapist: J. Payne
Press Officer & Tel No: Mike Brett-Smith, 0322 77243 (H), 0322 21266 (B)

Secretary: D. A. Hargreaves
Address & Tel No: 19 Station Approach, Chelsfield, Orpington, Kent. Farnborough 58818
Commercial Manager: Mrs K. Tree, c/o D.F.C.
Address & Tel No: Watling St, Dartford (73639)

Address & Tel No of ground: Watling Street, Stone, Dartford, Kent (D. 73639) **Club shop:** Yes, open match days
Simple ground directions: From Town Centre/Railway Station, proceed up East Hill, take 3rd right into Watling St. Via Dartford Tunnel/A2 Dartford turn off - floodlights are visible from roundabout (Princes Hotel)
From Kent Coast A2/M2 - take turn off for Greenhithe/Stone, left at r'bout, right at traffic lights into Watling St.
No of seats: 898 **Covered accommodation capacity:** 3,000 **Floodlights:** Yes
Year formed: 1890 **Nickname:** The Darts **Club sponsors:** S.A.R. Builders Supplies
Previous names: None
Previous grounds: Lowfield Street
Club colours: White/Black/Black
Change colours: Red/Black/Black or All Yellow
Day for midweek home matches: Tuesday
Record attendance: 11,004 v Leyton Orient, F.A. Cup 1st Rnd Proper **Year:** 1948/49
Best performance in: **F.A. Cup:** 1935/36 v Derby C (A) lost 2-3, after defeating Cardiff City (A) 3-0, 3rd Round
F.A. Trophy: 1973/74 Finalists, 1980/81 Semi-Finalists
Previous Leagues: Kent, Southern
Clubhouse details: 'Dart Inn' large clubroom open matchdays and all evenings except Wednesday
Present players with Football League experience: Tony Burman (Charlton Athletic), Bobby Arber (Arsenal, Orient), Francis Cowley (Chelsea, Derby Co, Wimbledon), Paul Powell (Colchester U)
Past players who progressed into the Football League: Derek Hales joined Luton in 1972; Riley Cullum & Fred Alexander joint £6,000 to Charlton, 1936, Idris Hopkins (Brentford, Wales), Fred Dell (West Ham U), Trevor Morgan (Bournemouth)
Record transfer fee paid: £2,500, Glen Coupland from Maidstone 1979/80
Record transfer fee received: £4,000, G. Julians to Maidstone
Programme details: 24 pages, 20p; 24 page h/book for 1983-4 75p
Club metal badges: Yes
Local newspapers & Tel No: Dartford & Swanley Chronicle, Dart. 23004; Dartford & Gravesend Reporter, Graves. 60441; Evening Post, Maid. 77880
Major Honours: Southern League Premier Div (2), Southern League (2), Southern League Southern Section, Southern League Cup & Runners-up, F.A. Trophy Runners-up & Semi-Finalists, Kent Senior Cup (7), Kent Senior Shield (4), Winners Inter-League Challenge Match 1974 vs Boston United 5-3 on aggregate
Club Captain (1983-84): Bobby Makin
Player of the Year (1983-84): Terry Sullivan
Programme Editor: Mike Brett-Smith

Enfield *Back Row (L-R): Dave Jones (trainer), Noel Ashford, Terry Graves, Dave Flint, Keith Barrett, Robert Turpin, Paul Cotter, Dave Waite, Trevor Savage, Nick Ironton, Steve Oliver.*
Front Row (L-R): Paul Taylor, Mark Warburton, John Tone, Keith Hayzelden, Steve King, Dave Mallett, Lee Holmes, Paul Haverson.

ENFIELD

Chairman: Tom Unwin
Manager: Eddie McCluskey
Coach: Ian Wolstenholme
Physiotherapist: N. Baxter
Secretary: A. Diment
Address & Tel No: 30 Apple Grove, Enfield
Commercial Manager: None
Address & Tel No:
Press Officer & Tel No: John Jefferson (01-363 6273)
Address & Tel No of ground: The Stadium, Southbury Road, Enfield, Middx. 01-363 2858 **Club shop:** Yes
Simple ground directions: Train to Enfield Town (any bus passes ground). Train to Southbury 5 minutes walk
No of seats: 850 **Covered accommodation:** All 4 sides **Capacity:** 7,500 **Floodlights:** Yes
Year formed: 1900 **Nickname:** None **Club sponsors:** Sampson Coaches
Previous names: None
Club colours: All White/Blue trim
Previous grounds: Cherry Orchard Lane
Change colours: All Yellow
Day for midweek home matches: Tuesday
Record attendance: 35,000 v Barnsley F.A. Cup 4th Round at Spurs **Year:** 1981
Best performance in: **F.A. Cup:** 1980-1 4th Round replay
F.A. Trophy: 1981-2 Winners
Previous Leagues: Athenian, Isthmian
Clubhouse details: Club bar open every lunchtime and evening, snacks available. Starlight night club, cabaret, dine and dance as per programme. Tel. 363 3127 or 363 2858
Present players with Football League experience: John Cooper
Past players who progressed into the Football League: Peter Feeley (Chelsea), Terry Hurlock (Brentford)
Record transfer fee paid: None
Record transfer fee received: None
Programme details: 16 pages, 25p
Club metal badges: Yes
Local newspapers & Tel No: Enfield Gazette 01-367 2345
Enfield Independent, Enfield Advertiser
Major Honours: F.A. Trophy, F.A. Amateur Cup, Isthmian League, Athenian League, Middlesex Senior Cup, London Senior Cup, Alliance Champions, Alliance Charity Shield
Club Captain (1983-84): Dave Waite
Player of the Year (1983-84): Steve King
Programme Editor: Ken Brazier

Frickley Athletic *Standing (L-R): John Buckley (trainer), Peter Howey, John Overton, Mally Wright, Gary Hooley, Tommy Meehan, Graham Reed, Mally Smith, Harry Dunn, Barry Gill, Phil Campbell. Seated (L-R): Russ Wilcox, Steve Daniels, Sean Marshall (manager), Paul Wilson, Steve Miles.*

FRICKLEY ATHLETIC

Chairman: M. Twiby
Vice Manager: J. Barber
Manager: S. Marshall (Sean)
Physiotherapist: J. Buckley
Secretary: R. L. Bates
Address & Tel No: South Elmsall 44575
Commercial Manager: None
Address & Tel No:
Press Officer & Tel No: P. R. Naylor (0977) 611058
Address & Tel No of ground: Westfield Lane, South Elmsall, Pontefract, West Yorks. South Elmsall (0977) 42460 & 44453
Simple ground directions: A638 from A1 to South Elmsall, Westfield Lane. Turn left opposite Westfield Hotel down Oxford Street
Club shop: Yes
No of seats: 900 **Covered accommodation:** 2,000 **Capacity:** 10,000 **Floodlights:** Yes
Year formed: 1910 **Nickname:** The Blues **Club sponsors:** Car Care
Previous names: Frickley Colliery
Club colours: Blue/White
Previous grounds: None
Change colours: All Yellow
Day for midweek home matches: Tuesday
Record attendance: 7,000 F.A. Cup 1st Round v Rotherham U. **Year:** 1971
Best performance in: **F.A. Cup:** 1970-1 1st Round
F.A. Trophy: 1983-4 3rd Round
Previous Leagues: Sheffield County, Midland, Cheshire, Northern Premier
Clubhouse details: Social Club outside the ground
Present players with Football League experience: Barry Gill, Sean Marshall, Ian Smith, Tommy Meehan, Russ Wilcox, Graham Reed, Mally Wright, Phil Campbell, Peter Howey, Stevie Daniels, John Overton, Harry Dunn
Past players who progressed into the Football League: Derek Downing
Record transfer fee paid: £1,500, Dave Smith
Record transfer fee received: £7,000 Peter Howey (Scarborough)
Programme details: 20 pages, 20p
Local newspapers & Tel No: South Yorkshire Times
Programme Editor: R. L. Bates (Sec)
Club metal badges: Yes
Major Honours: Midland League Cup, Sheffield Senior Challenge Cup (2)
Club Captain (1983-4): Barry Gill
Player of the Year (1983-84): Paul Wilson

Gateshead *Back Row (L-R): I. Donaldson, P. Davies, W. McLeod, L. Jobling, D. Mitchinson, G. Brown (Co Sec), D.Mitchell (director). Centre Row (L-R): J. Tudor (coach),, R. Lewin (youth development officer), D. Parnaby, J. Robson, J. Grady, K. Dodds, S. Higgins, G. Hindson, G. Ramshaw (assistant manager), E. Hall (director). Front Row (L-R): C. Dixon, J. Langley, J. Tweedy, R. Wilkie (chairman/manager), E. Hill (ex-chairman), K. Pugh, T. Robinson, M. Henderson.*

GATESHEAD

President: J. C. Thomas
Chairman:
Manager: Ray Wilkie
Asst Manager: George Ramshaw
Physiotherapist: Geoff Carr
Press Officer & Tel No: None
Secretary: B. F. Wright
Address & Tel No: 14 Burnthouse Lane, Whickham, Newcastle upon Tyne NE16 5AT. 091 4887795
Commercial Manager: E. J. Hall
Address & Tel No: 0632 776464
Address & Tel No of ground: International Stadium, Park Road, Gateshead. Tel. 0632 783883 **Club shop:** Yes
Simple ground directions: A6115 from Town Centre (South Shields/Sunderland) 1 mile. Ground left at traffic lights
No of seats: 7,300 **Covered accommodation:** 3,300 **Capacity:** 14,000 **Floodlights:** Yes
Year formed: 1977 **Nickname:** None **Club sponsors:** None
Previous names: None
Previous grounds: None
Club colours: Red with Blue & White stripe, White shorts
Change colours: Sky Blue shirts, Navy shorts
Day for midweek home matches: Monday
Previous Leagues: Northern Premier
Record attendance: 3,095 v Nottingham Forest (Bob McLeod Testimonial) **Year:** 1983
Best performance in: F.A. Cup: 1980-1 1st Round Proper
F.A. Trophy: 1980-1 1st Round Proper
Clubhouse details: Under construction
Present players with Football League experience: R. McLeod (Hartlep'l), T. Hibbitt (Leeds Utd, Newcastle, Birmingham City), G. Hindson (Newcastle, Luton), K. Pugh (Newcastle), J. Tudor (Coventry, Sheffield Utd, Newcastle, Stoke City), J. Pearson (St. Johnstone, Everton, Newcastle)
Past players who progressed into the Football League: O. Williams (Southampton, Stockport Co), J. McGinley (Sunderland)
Record transfer fee paid: £1,000 for J. McGinley from Sunderland
Record transfer fee received: £3,000 from Sunderland for J. McGinley
Programme details: 32 pages, 25p
Club metal badges: Yes
Senior Honours: Champions NPL
Local newspapers & Tel No: Evening Chronicle 0632 327500, The Journal 0632 327500, Northern Echo, Gateshead Post 0632 773245
Club Captain (1983-84): David Parnaby
Player of the Year (1983-84): David Parnaby
Programme Editor: G. Brown

KINGSBURY TOWN

President:
Chairman: M. Hart
Manager: W. Meadows
Coach: A. Randall
Secretary: D. W. Thomas
Address & Tel No: 01-205 2592
Physiotherapist: Judy Montieth
Address & Tel No of ground: Silver Jubilee Park, Townsend Lane, Kingsbury, London NW9 (01-205 1645)
Simple ground directions: Kingsbury (LT) then 183 bus to Kingsbury Green, right into Townsend Lane
No of seats: 100 **Covered accommodation:** 150 **Capacity:** 4,000 **Floodlights:** Yes
Year formed: 1923 **Nickname:** Town **Club sponsors:** All White Double Glazing
Club colours: Yellow/Red
Change colours: All Blue
Previous Leagues: Partheon, London Spartan
Programme: Yes
Clubhouse details: Open every afternoon, evening and weekends
Best Year in F.A. Vase: 1974-75 4th Round
Local Newspapers:

Kettering Town 1983-84 *Back Row (L-R): Les Bradd, David Needham (player-manager), Jeff Palmer, Steve Humphries, Pete Denyer, Eddie McGoldrick, Dave Pownall. Front Row: Arthur Mann (now with Boston), Frank Murphy, Derek Duggan, Don Masson (no longer with club), Paul Bartlett, David Beavon.*

KETTERING TOWN

Chairman: J. T. Murphy
Manager: Dave Needham
Coach/Asst. Manager: Peter Denyer
Physiotherapist: Malcolm Watts
Secretary: R. Abraham
Address & Tel No: 68 Cornwall Road, Kettering (K. 522159)
Commercial Manager: D. Prouse
Address & Tel No: c/o Club
Press Officer & Tel No: M. Tompkins
Address & Tel No of ground: Rockingham Road, Kettering. Tel 83028
Club shop: Yes
Simple ground directions: On A6003 Kettering to Oakham road
No of seats: 2,200 **Covered accommodation:** 7,000 **Capacity:** 14,000 **Floodlights:** Yes
Year formed: 1876 **Nickname:** Poppies **Club sponsors:** None
Previous names: None
Previous grounds: None
Club colours: All Red
Change colours: All Yellow
Day for midweek home matches: Wednesday
Record attendance: 11,526 **Year:** 1947
Best performance in: **F.A. Cup:** 1968-9 1976-7 3rd Round
F.A. Trophy: 1978-79 Beaten Finalists
Previous Leagues: Midland, Southern, Northampton, Central Alliance, Birmingham
Clubhouse details: New small clubhouse at the ground
Present players with Football League experience: D. Duggan, T. Goode (Birmingham C), G. Banton (Fulham), G. Chamberlain (Burnley, Chesterfield, Halifax), R. Haverson (QPR, Wimbledon), P. Denyer, P. Sandercock (Northampton), R. Dawson (Chesterfield), I. Jenkins (Brentford), D. Needham (Notts County)
Past players who progressed into the Football League: B. Kellock (Peterborough), G. Wood (Notts C), D. Longhurst (Notts F), S. Endersby (Ipswich T), S. Fallon (Cambridge U), J. Sellers (Manchester U), A. Rodgers (Plymouth A), M. Forster (Northampton), J. Brown (Chesterfield), S. Conroy (Rochdale)
Record transfer fee paid: To Nuneaton Borough for Brendan Phillips
Record transfer fee received: From Boston United for Brendan Phillips
Programme details: 16 pages, 30p
Programme Editor: Steve Whitney
Local newspaper & Tel No: Evening Telegraph Kettering 81111
Club metal badges: Yes
Major Honours: Trophy Finalists, Southern League, Southern League Cup, County Cup, S.L. Merit Cup
Club Captain (1983-84): J. Palmer **Player of the Year (1983-84):** G. Chamberlain

Kidderminster Harriers *Back Row (L-R): G. Livesey (assistant manager), A. Richards, F. Wood, S. Bowater, A. Dulleston, C. Jones, P. Davies, G. Jones, M. Woodall, C. Pearson (trainer). Front Row (L-R): M. Gavin, J. Horne, G. Allner (manager), J. Powell, A. McGowan*

KIDDERMINSTER HARRIERS

Chairman: David Reynolds
Manager: Graham Allwer
Assistant Manager: Gordon Livsey
Physiotherapist: Cal Pearson
Secretary: Ray Mercer
Address & Tel No: Kidderminster 66111 (B) 67450 (H)
Commercial Manager:
Address & Tel No: Kidderminster 3931
Press Officer & Tel No: Ray Mercer
Address & Tel No of ground: Aggborough, Hoo Road, Kidderminster 3931 **Club shop:** Yes
Simple ground directions: From M5 Nth/Mid A456 (Halesowen). From Sth/Wst Kidderminster turn-off (Worcester)
No of seats: 500 **Covered accommodation:** 4,000 **Capacity:** 10,000 **Floodlights:** Yes
Year formed: 1886 **Nickname:** The Harriers **Club sponsors:** Fair Discount
Previous names: None
Previous grounds: None
Club colours: Red shirts, Red shorts
Change colours: White shirts/shorts
Day for midweek home matches: Monday
Record attendance: 9,155 v Hereford United **Year:** 1948
Best performance in: F.A. Cup: 1935 v Workington 2nd Round
F.A. Trophy: 1981-2 v Wycombe W Quarter-Final
Previous Leagues: Birmingham, West Midland, Birmingham Comb, Southern, Worcestershire Comb
Clubhouse details: Open 7 days a week. Adjoins football ground. All star cabaret, ballroom dancing, disco, bingo, snooker, darts, etc.
Present players with Football League experience: John Horne (Walsall), Martin Galvin (Bristol C), John Powell (Nottingham F), Andy McGowan (Northampton T), Paul Davies (Cardiff C), Mick Tuohy (Walsall, Southend U)
Past players who progressed into the Football League: Gerry Hitchins (Aston Villa, Cardiff, Inter Milan, England), K. Keelan (Norwich), Trevor Meredith (Burnley), Tony Cunningham (Barnsley), Paul McGhee (QPR, Preston, Eire)
Record transfer fee paid: Mick Williams £3,000 from Redditch; Mick Tuohy £3,000 from Worcester C
Record transfer fee received: Peter Wassell £3,000, Gerry Hitchens £2,000
Programme details: 20 pages, 25p
Club metal badges: Yes
Local newspapers & Tel No: Kidderminster Times/ Shuttle (K. 3606), Kidderminster Trader (K. 753377), Kidderminster Source (K. 69951), Worcester Evening News, Express & Star, Birmingham Evening Mail
Senior Honours: Worcs Senior Cup (14), Birmingham Senior Cup (7), Staffs Senior Cup (3), West Midland League Champions (3) & League Cup (4), Birmingham League Champions (3) & League Cup (3), Southern League Cup

Club Captain (1983-84): Andy McGowan
Player of the Year (1983-84): Chris Jones
Programme Editor: Chris Scotford/Karl Davies

Maidstone United *Back Row (L-R): Bill Williams (manager), Frank Brooks (trainer), Micky Dingwall, Micky Crowe, Adrian Lemoine, Kevin Maddocks, Colin Lewington, Derek Richardson, Clive Green, Billy Hughes, Jon Moore, Andy Rollings, Mick Mercer (secretary), Jim Thompson (chairman). Front Row (L-R): Paul Lazarus, Nigel Donn, Malcolm Stewart, Brian Thompson, Mark Newson, John Watson, John Bartley, Peter Taylor, Nicky Ironton, Terry Robbins.*

MAIDSTONE UNITED

President:
Chairman: J. C. Thompson
Manager: Bill Williams
Coach:
Medical Officer: Dr. M. A. Brook
Press Officer & Tel No: M. K. Mercer (54403)

Secretary: M. K. Mercer
Address & Tel No: As stadium. 54403 (B)

Commercial Manager: Bill Williams
Address & Tel No: c/o Club (674221)

Address & Tel No of ground: The Stadium, London Road, Maidstone, Kent ME16 0DT. Tel 54403 **Club shop:** Yes
Simple ground directions: M20 to junction (Maidstone West), London Road to Maidstone Ground on left – 1 mile from town centre
No of seats: 700 **Covered accommodation:** 2,000 **Capacity:** 15,000 **Floodlights:** Yes
Year formed: 1897 **Nickname:** Stones **Club sponsors:** Britelite
Previous names: Maidstone Invicta **Club colours:** Amber/Black
Previous grounds: None **Change colours:** All White
Day for midweek home matches: Wednesday
Record attendance: 10,591 v Charlton F.A. Cup 3rd Round replay **Year:** 1979
Best performance in: F.A. Cup: 1979 v Charlton 3rd Round
1984 v Darlington 3rd Round
F.A. Trophy: 1979 v Kettering 3rd Round proper
1983 v Boston Utd 3rd Round proper

Previous Leagues: East Kent, Thames & Medway Comb., Kent, Corinthian, Athenian, Isthmian, Southern

Clubhouse details: Open every night. Greyhound racing and other entertainments. Catering available.
Present players with Football League experience: Brian Thompson, Derek Richardson, John Bartley, Jon Moore, Clive Green, Billy Hughes, Andy Rollings, Peter Taylor, Nigel Donn
Past players who progressed into the Football League: David Sadler, John Ryan, Neil Ayrton, Tony Weston
Record transfer fee paid: £8,000 to Yeovil for Clive Green
Record transfer fee received: £6,000 from Weymouth for Neil Merrick
Programme details: 16 pages, 30p
Club metal badges: Yes
Local newspapers & Tel No: Kent Messenger Maidstone 77880. Adscene Maidstone 679047
Major Honours: Southern League Div 1 South, Kent Senior Cup (13), East Kent League (2), Kent League (2), Winners Alliance Premier

Club Captain (1983-84): Brian Thompson
Player of the Year (1983-84): Mark Newson
Programme Editor: Mick Mercer

Northwich Victoria *Back Row (L-R): John Anderson, Graham Abel, Dave Ryan, Jeff Forshaw, Dave Fretwell. Middle Row (L-R): George Connolly (dressing room attendant), Phil Gee (reserve team manager), Mark Dean, Tony Murphy, Paul Bennett, Stuart Clynch, John King (manager), Ron Reddy (physio). Front Row (L-R): Phil Power, Phil Wilson, Ken Jones (captain), Colin Chesters, Paul Reid.* Photo: Pat Campion

NORTHWICH VICTORIA

President: Mr. J. Horton
Chairman: J. Burton
Manager: John King
Coach:
Physiotherapist: Ron Reddy
Secretary: A. Tams
Address & Tel No: 70 Darwin Street, Northwich, Cheshire 76701 (H), 41450 (Ground)
Commercial Manager: A. Tams
Address & Tel No: c/o Club
Press Officer & Tel No: A. Tams. Tel. Northwich 41450
Address & Tel No of ground: The Drill Field, Northwich, Cheshire CW9 5IN. Tel (0606) 41450 **Club shop:** Yes
Simple ground directions: Leave the M6 at junction 19. Turn right. After approx. 4 miles at second roundabout. Ground on right immediately before traffic lights (¾-mile). Alongside bus station
No of seats: 660 **Covered accommodation:** 3,500 **Capacity:** 10,000 **Floodlights:** Yes
Year formed: 1874 **Nickname:** The Vics **Club sponsors:** Roberts' Bakery/Northwich Glass
Previous names: None
Previous grounds: None
Club colours: Green/White/Green
Change colours: Claret/Blue
Day for midweek home matches: Monday
Record attendance: 28,635 v Oldham Athletic at Maine Road **Year:** 1977
Best performance in: **F.A. Cup:** 1976-77 4th Round Proper
F.A. Trophy: 1983-84 Winners
Previous Leagues: Football League Div II, Manchester, Cheshire, Northern Premier
Clubhouse details: Being sold
Present players with Football League experience: Dave Ryan (Southport), Dave Fretwell (Wigan), John Anderson (Chester), Dave Bradley (Doncaster, Bury), Paul Bennett (Port Vale), Colin Chesters (Derby, Crewe)
Past players who progressed into the Football League: Frank Corrigan (Wigan), Jim Walker (Chester), Billy Meredith (Manchester City), Mark Ward (Oldham)
Record transfer fee paid: £5,000 for Colin Williams from Telford
Record transfer fee received: £12,000 for Mark Ward (Oldham A)
Programme details: 24 pages, 25p
Club metal badges: Yes
Local newspapers & Tel No: Northwich Guardian 0606 3333, Northwich Chronicle 0606 2272
Major Honours: Cheshire F.A. Senior Cup (15), Manchester League, Cheshire League, N.P.L. Cup, N.P.L. Runners-up, N.P.L. Cup Runners-up, Staffordshire Senior Cup (2), Alliance Premier League Cup, Alliance Premier League Shield,, F.A. Trophy Finalists, F.A. Trophy Winners 1983-84
Club Captain (1983-84): Ken Jones
Player of the Year (1983-84): Dave Ryan
Programme Editor: John Hayes

Nuneaton Borough *Back Row (L-R): G. Carr (manager), J. Glover, G. Dale, A. Poole, S. Hamill, T. Morley, D. Penn, M. Burke, P.Culpin, D. Looms (trainer). Front Row (L-R): E. Carr, P. Richardson, R. Parker, R. Dixey (captain), W. Gibson, P. Brown.* Photo: W.N.Mather

NUNEATON BOROUGH

President: A. Scattergold
Chairman: Noel Kelly
Manager: Graham Carr
Physiotherapist: D. Looms
Press Officer & Tel No: Secretary
Secretary: Dr. John Evans
Address & Tel No: Nuneaton 348416 (H) 0203 617231 (B)
Commercial Manager: Mrs L. Wicks
Address & Tel No: Nuneaton 385738
Address & Tel No of ground: Manor Park, Beaumont Road, Nuneaton **Club shop:** Yes
Simple ground directions: Manor Park is at the northern end of Queens Road, the main street in the town centre
No of seats: 450 **Covered accommodation:** 5,000 **Capacity:** 22,000 **Floodlights:** Yes
Year formed: 1937 **Nickname:** The Boro **Club sponsors:** None
Previous names: None
Previous grounds: None
Club colours: Blue/White stripes/Blue
Change colours: Yellow/Green
Day for midweek home matches: Monday
Record attendance: 22,114 v Rotherham United F.A. Cup 3rd Round **Year:** 1967
Best performance in: F.A. Cup: 1949-50, 1966-7 Third Round
F.A. Trophy: 1976-7, 1979-80 Quarter Finals
Clubhouse details: Open match days, evenings, Sunday lunchtime (Nuneaton 383152)
Previous Leagues: Central Amateur, Birmingham Comb, Birmingham, Southern, Alliance Premier
Present players with Football League experience: Jon Sammels (Arsenal, Leicester)
Past players who progressed into the Football League: Sugrue, Peake, Smithers, Shotton, Stevens
Record transfer fee paid: £9,500 for Richard Dixey to Scarborough
Record transfer fee received: £20,000 from Manchester City for Paul Sugrue
Programme details: 20 pages, 20p
Club metal badges: Yes
Local newspapers & Tel No: Nuneaton Evening Tribune (Nun 382251), Coventry Evening Telegraph (Cov 25588), Nuneaton Observer (Nun 383636)
Senior Honours: Birmingham League (North), Birmingham League Div1, Southern League Inter-Zone, Southern League Midlands, Birmingham Senior Cup

Runcorn *Back Row (L-R): R. Fraser, B. Parker, T. Goodwin, J. Rogers, M. Hardman, R. McBride, P. Simpson, E. Edwards, C. Roberts, S. Joel, T. Murphy. Front Row: M. Fagan, B. Kettle, J. Stringer, J. Williams, O. Smith, J. Butler, J. Imrie, M. Roberts.*

RUNCORN

President: H. Braverman
Chairman: A. A. Littler
Manager: J. D. Williams
Assist. Manager: T. Murphy
Physiotherapist: None
Secretary: P. Redican
Address & Tel No: 22 Riley Drive, Runcorn. Tel. 09285 76454 (H)
Commercial Manager: J. Lloyd
Address & Tel No: 09285-73977
Press Officer & Tel No: J. Corcoran (09285 72382)
Address & Tel No of ground: Canal Street, Runcorn. Tel. 09285 72237. Clubhouse: 75858 **Club shop:** Yes
Simple ground directions: From M56 follow signs for Runcorn Old Town. From M62 follow signs for Runcorn & Widnes Bridge, then Runcorn Old Town.
No of seats: 400 **Covered accommodation:** 2,000 **Capacity:** 7,000 **Floodlights:** Yes
Year formed: 1918 **Nickname:** Linnets **Club sponsors:** Runcorn World
Previous names: None
Previous grounds: None
Club colours: Green/Yellow/Green
Change colours: Blue/White
Day for midweek home matches: Tuesdays
Record attendance: 10,111 v Preston North End **Year:** 1939
Best performance in: **F.A. Cup:** 1939 v Preston North End 3rd Round
F.A. Trophy: 1976-7, 1977-8, 1978-9 Semi-Finals
Previous Leagues: Cheshire County, Northern Premier
Clubhouse details: Next to ground, open every day. Functions by arrangement 09285 75858
Present players with Football League experience: A. Crompton (Wigan), B. Parker (Arsenal), B. Kettle (Liverpool), J. Butler (Blackpool)
Past players who progressed into the Football League: J. Cumbes (Aston Villa)
Record transfer fee paid: Not disclosed
Record transfer fee received: Not disclosed
Programme details: 24 pages, 20p
Programme Editors: Jim Corcoran, David Bettley
Club metal badges: Yes
Local newspapers & Tel No: Runcorn Weekly News 09285 717979, Runcorn World 050-423-3303
Major Honours: Cheshire League (3), Cheshire Senior Cup (7), Cheshire Bowl, Northern Premier League (2), Northern Premier League Cup (3), Northern Premier League Shield (2), Alliance Premier League, Bob Lord Trophy, Jim Thompson League Championship Shield
Club Captain (1983-84); Ossie Smith
Player of the Year (1983-84): Bobby Fraser

Scarborough *Back Row (L-R): John Cottam (player-manager), Mitch Cook, Richard Dawson, Graeme Crawford, Brian Magee (captain), Graham Hartley, Neil Thompson. Front Row (L-R): Neil Sellers, John Hanson, Trenton Wiggan, Pat Olney, Charlie Bell, Brendan Phillips.*

SCARBOROUGH

President: David Jenkinson
Chairman: Tony Burnard
Player/Manager: John Cottam
Trainer: Geoff Bowman
Doctor: Dr. A F. Chico
Secretary: W. Hunter
Address & Tel No: 24 Red Scar Drive, Scarborough. 0723 365523
Commercial Manager: Shirley Nettleton, The Boro Shop
Address & Tel No: 97 Victoria Rd, Scarboro'. 0723 369211
Press Officer & Tel No: John Fawcett. Scarborough 372351 (B), Scarborough 367413 (H)
Address & Tel No of ground: Athletic Ground, Seamer Road, Scarborough. 0723 375094 **Club shop:** Yes
Simple ground directions: A64 main trunk road from York. ¼-mile on left past Plaxtons coach factory
No of seats: 864 **Covered accommodation:** 4,000 **Capacity:** 10,000 **Floodlights:** Yes
Year formed: 1879 **Nickname:** The Boro **Club sponsors:** Crystal of Scarborough
Previous names: None
Previous grounds: None
Club colours: All Red
Change colours: White/Black
Day for midweek home matches: Wednesday
Record attendance: 11,124 v Luton Town **Year:** 1938
Best performance in: F.A. Cup: 1938, 1976, 1978 3rd Round
F.A. Trophy: 1973, 1976, 1977 Winners. 1975 Runners-up
Previous Leagues: Northern, Yorkshire, North Eastern, Midland, Northern Premier
Clubhouse details: Fully licensed bar, concert room, dance floor
Present players with Football League experience: G. Crawford (York C), R. Dawson (York C), N. Thompson (Hull C), B. Phillips (Mansfield T), J. Hanson (Bradford C), T. Wiggan (Sheffield U), P. Olney (Manchester U)
Past players who progressed into the Football League: W. Ayre (Hartlepool), S. Deere (Scunthorpe), C. Appleton (Leicester), K. Ellis (Darlington)
Record transfer fee paid: £12,000 for John Watson
Record transfer fee received: £10,000 from Nuneaton for R. Dixey
Programme details: 20 pages, 25p
Programme Editor: Keith Crowe
Club metal badges: Yes
Local newspapers & Tel No: Scarborough Evening News 0723 363636. The Mercury
Major Honours: F.A. Trophy (3) & Runners-up, Bob Lord Trophy, Northern Premier League Runners-up, Northern Premier League Cup, Vaux Floodlight League (2), Yorkshire League Cup, North Eastern League, North Eastern League Cup, Midland League North Riding Senior Cup (15)
Club Captain (1983-84): Bryan Magee
Player of the Year (1983-84): Bryan Magee

Telford United *Back Row (L-R): Tim Rutter, Dean Edwards, Colin Williams, Kevin Charlton, Paul Jackson, Paul Mayman, Steve Eaton, Antone Joseph. Front Row (L-R): John Alcock, David Barnett, Kevin Lewis, Tony Turner, David Mather, Eddie Hogan.*

TELFORD UNITED

Chairman: G. E. Smith
Manager: Stan Storton
Coach: Brian Daintith
Physiotherapist: S. Day
Press Officer: Secretary
Secretary: M. J. Ferriday
Address & Tel No: 199 Trench Road, Telford TF2 7DX. (0952) 605193
Commercial Manager: D. Harris
Club shop: Yes
Address & Tel No of ground: Buck's Head Ground, Watling Street, Wellington, Telford, Shropshire. (0952) 3838
Simple ground directions: Situated on the B5061 (formerly main A5) in the Wellington district of north Telford. Leave M54 at Junction 6
No of seats: 1,200 **Covered accommodation:** 3,000 **Capacity:** 10,000 **Floodlights:** Yes
Year formed: 1877 **Nickname:** Lillywhites **Club sponsors:** Maxell
Previous names: Wellington Town (until 1969)
Club colours: White with Blue/Red trim/Blue/White
Previous grounds: None
Change colours: All Red
Day for midweek home matches: Tuesday
Record attendance: 13,000 v Shrewsbury Town **Year:** 1935
Best performance in: **F.A. Cup:** 4th Round, 1983-4
F.A. Trophy: 1970-1, 1982-3 Winners; 1969-70 Runners-up
Previous Leagues: Birmingham, Cheshire, Southern
Clubhouse details: Match days and selected other hours
Present players with Football League experience: Kevin Charlton, Paul Mayman, Kevin Lewis, Dean Edwards
Past players who progressed into the Football League: Graham French (Luton), Alan Walker (Lincoln)
Record transfer fee paid: £10,000 for Paul Mayman to Northwich Victoria
Record transfer fee received: Alan Walker (£20,000 to Lincoln)
Programme details: 24 pages, 30p
Programme Editor: B. G. Bagnall
Club metal badges: Yes
Local newspapers & Tel No: Shropshire Star 0952 44377. Telford Journal 0952 56262
Major Honours: F.A. Challenge Trophy & Runners-up, Southern League Cup, Welsh Cup (3), Birmingham League (3), Birmingham League Cup, Cheshire League (3) & Runners-up (2), Birmingham Senior Cup, Walsall Senior Cup, Shropshire Senior Cup (30)
Club Captain (1983-84): Kevin Lewis
Player of the Year (1983-84): Steve Eaton

Wealdstone *Back Row (L-R): Peter Braxton (secretary), Dr Len Goodchild (medical officer), R. Iles, Arnie Reed (physio), Tony Carnana (scout). Centre Row: D. Price, A. Cordice, N. Johnson, N. Cordice, S. McCargo. Front Row: B. Greenaway, M. Graves, P. Bowgett (captain), B. Hall (manager), D. Byatt, S. Perkins, G. Donnellan. Insets: R. Wainwright and C. Dibble*

WEALDSTONE

President: G. D. Morritt
Chairman: D. G. Morritt
Team Manager: Brian Hall
Coach:
Physiotherapist: Arnold Reed
Club Doctor: Dr Len Goodchild
Press Officer & Tel No: E. C. Pope, 01-427 4064

Secretary: Peter Braxton
Address & Tel No: Wealdstone FC, Station Road, Harrow 01-427 4064
Commercial Enquiries Barbara Vane
Address & Tel No: 01-427 4064

Address & Tel No of ground: Lower Mead Stadium, Station Road, Harrow, Middlesex HA1 2TU. (Office: 01-427 4064; Club: 01-427 2840)
Club shop: Yes
Simple ground directions: Station Road (Town Centre), rear of EMI (ABC) Cinema, entrance by car park sign. A409 route from Junction 5 on M1; A312 via Hayes from M3 and M4
No of seats: 800 **Covered accommodation:** 6,500 **Capacity:** 15,000 **Floodlights:** Yes
Year formed: 1900 **Nickname:** Royal Stones **Club sponsors:** Morritt Homes
Previous names: None
Previous grounds: College Farm Ground, Belmont Road, Wealdstone
Club colours: Royal Blue & Yellow
Change colours: All Red
Day for midweek home matches: Tuesday
Record attendance: 13,504 v Leytonstone, F.A. Amateur Cup **Year:** 1949
Best performance in: F.A. Cup: 1977/8 v QPR 3rd Round
F.A. Trophy: 1973/4 v South Shields, Quarter-finals
Previous Leagues: Spartan, Athenian, Isthmian, Southern
Clubhouse details: Three bars plus Directors Bar and Vice Presidents Bar, dance hall and restaurant
Present players with Football League experience: R. Iles, S. Perkins, D. Byatt, P. Bowgett, B. Wainwright, N. Cordice, B. Greenaway, D. Price, N. Johnson, A. Cordice, G. Donellan, M. Graves, F. Barwick, C. Dibble
Past players who progressed into the Football League: Charlie Sells, Colin Franks, Tommy McGee, Bobby Ryan, Eddie Smith, Phil White, Francis Joseph, Stuart Pearce
Record transfer fee paid: £5,000 to Trowbridge (joint fee) for Terry and Derek Evans, Summer 1974
Record transfer fee received: £25,000 from Coventry City for Stuart Pearce, November 1983
Programme details: 24 pages, 30p
Club metal badges: Yes
Local newspapers & Tel No: Harrow Observer 01-427 4404
Major Honours: Amateur Cup Winners, Southern League (Div 1 Sth) Champions, Sthn League (Sthn Div) Champions, Sthn Lge Championship Shield Winners, Sthn Lge Cup Winners, Sthn Lge Challenge Cup Winners, Athenian Lge Champions

Club Captain (1983-84): Paul Bowgett
Player of the Year (1983-84): Bob Iles
Programme Editor: E. C. Pope

Weymouth *Back Row (L-R): Ashley Doidge, Anniello Iannone, John Turner, Richard Bourne, Peter Morrell, Hedley Steele, Tony Agana, Wayne Bray. Front Row (L-R): Andy Townsend, Paul Arnold, Shaun Penny, David McManus, Gerry Pearson*

WEYMOUTH

Chairman: A. Scource
Manager: Brian Godfrey
Coach: J. Clarke
Physiotherapist: R. Lucas
Secretary: C. Steadman
Address & Tel No: 0305 785558
Commercial Manager: R. Russell
Address & Tel No: 0305 784133
Press Officer & Tel No: A. Scource. Weymouth 785558
Address & Tel No of ground: Recreation Ground, Newstead Road, Weymouth, Dorset **Club shop:** Yes
Simple ground directions: Through main town St. Thomas Street (one way) over town bridge turn right, ground straight in front.
No of seats: 520 **Covered accommodation:** 6,500 **Capacity:** 10,000 **Floodlights:** Yes
Year formed: 1890 **Nickname:** The Terras **Club sponsors:** None
Previous names: None
Previous grounds: None
Club colours: Claret & Sky Blue/Sky Blue/Sky Blue
Change colours: All Yellow
Day for midweek home matches: Wednesday
Record attendance: 12,512 v Yeovil **Year:** 1948
Best performance in: F.A. Cup: 1961-2 v Preston North End 4th Round
F.A. Trophy: 1973-4, 1976-7, 1979-80 Quarter-Final
Previous Leagues: Western, Southern
Clubhouse details: Public house and club adjoining the ground — no longer run by the Club. Open during all games
Present players with Football League experience: R. Bourne, P. Arnold, B. Benjafield, H. Steele, J. Turner, B. Godfrey
Past players who progressed into the Football League: R. Pickett, R. Fogg, A. Smith, B. Hutchinson, T. Spratt, T. Gulliver, R. Hall, R. Iles, G. Roberts, M. Cave, D. Fry, A. Beer, B. Carter, N. Townsend, W. Holt, P. Leggett, S. Northover
Record transfer fee paid: £6,000 for G. Roberts from Dorchester Town 1979-80
Record transfer fee received: £70,000 for G. Roberts from Tottenham Hotspur 1979-80
Programme details: 16 pages, 30p
Club metal badges: Yes
Local newspapers & Tel No: Dorset Evening Echo 0305 784804. Western Gazette
Major Honours: Southern Premier League (2) & Runners-up (3), Western League (5) & Runners-up (3), Southern League Cup (1) & Runners-up (4), Alliance Premier League Runners-up, Bob Lord Trophy (Alliance League Cup)
Club Captain (1983-84): Paul Arnold
Player of the Year (1983-84): Anniello Iannone
Programme Editor: Peter Ebrill

Ace goalscorer Paul Moss lines up with Worcester City at Aldershot before their First Round cup tie. After a 1-1 draw the Alliance club won 2-1. Photo: Eric Marsh.

WORCESTER CITY

Chairman: G. Turner
Manager: Bobby Shinton
Coach: Brian. Forsbrook
Physiotherapist: Pat Williams
Press Officer: Secretary
Secretary: Graham Russell
Address & Tel No: 'MVS Huslie', 7 Lucerne Close, Worcester WR3 7NA. Worcester (0905) 53863 (H), Bromyard (0885) 83653 (B)
Commercial Manager: Secretary
Address & Tel No of ground: St. George's Lane, Worcester. Worc 23003 (Social Club Worc 25427) **Club shop:** Yes
Simple ground directions: From M5 junction 5 follow A38 through Droitwich into Worcester. Ground is 500 yards from first set of traffic lights on left. From M5 junction 7, follow A44 into Worcester, go past racecourse, follow A38 Bromsgrove. Ground on left.
No of seats: 2,500 **Covered accommodation:** 5,000 **Capacity:** 15,000 **Floodlights:** Yes
Year formed: 1908 **Nickname:** The City **Club sponsors:** Laugherne Garage
Previous names: None
Previous grounds: None
Club colours: Blue/White shirts
Change colours: Red shirts, White shorts
Day for midweek home matches: Monday
Previous Leagues: Southern
Record attendance: 17,042 v Sheffield Utd, F.A. Cup **Year:** 1958-9
Best performance in: F.A. Cup: 1958-9 4th Round. After beating Liverpool 2-1 at home lost 2-0 to Sheffield Utd. (home)
F.A. Trophy: 1969-70, 1973-4, 1981-2 Quarter-Finals
Clubhouse details: Improvements being made to the social club and dressing rooms at a cost of around £75,000
Present players with Football League experience: Steve Crompton (Hereford), David Hughes (Aston Villa, Scunthorpe, Lincoln), Paul Moss (Wolves, Hull, Scunthorpe), Bobby Shinton
Past players who progressed into the Football League: John Barton (Everton, now Derby), Jimmy Williams (Walsall), Neil Merrick (Bournemouth), John Fairbrother (Peterborough), Keith Ball (Walsall)
Record transfer fee paid: £8,500, Jimmy Williams from Walsall
Record transfer fee received: £27,000, John Barton to Everton
Programme details: Under review
Club metal badges: Yes
Local newspapers & Tel No: Worcester Evening News (Worcester 423434)
Major Honours: Southern League, Southern League Cup, Worcestershire Cup
Club Captain (1983-84): David Hughes
Player of the Year (1983-84): John McGrath

Yeovil Town *Back Row (L-R): M. O'Donnell (trainer), Philip James, Grant Northover, Trevor Finnigan, Billy Elliott, Andrew Bell, Jes Payne. Front Row (L-R): Jeremy Brown, David Linney, Malcolm Gold, Gary Borthwick, Tim Benjamin, Richie Horton*

YEOVIL TOWN

Chairman: G. A. Lock
Manager: Ian MacPharlane
Coach:
Physiotherapist: D. Hunt
Secretary: Mrs. V. O. Masters
Address & Tel No: 26183 (H)
Commercial Manager: Alan Skirton
Address & Tel No: Yeovil 23662
Press Officer & Tel No: Bryan Moore (0935) 76685
Address & Tel No of ground: Huish, Yeovil, Somerset (Yeovil 23662)
Club shop: Yes
Simple ground directions: 400 yards from town centre
No of seats: 2,352 **Covered accommodation:** 9,000 **Capacity:** 15,000 **Floodlights:** Yes
Year formed: 1923 **Nickname:** The Glovers
Club sponsors: None
Previous names: None
Previous grounds: None
Club colours: Green/White
Change colours: All Yellow
Day for midweek home matches: Wednesday
Record attendance: 17,501 **Year:** 1949
Previous Leagues: Southern
Best performance in: **F.A. Cup:** 1948-9 5th Round
F.A. Trophy: 1970-1, 1971-2 Semi-Final
Clubhouse details: Open every lunchtime and evening. Also after all games
Present players with Football League experience: All
Past players who progressed into the Football League: See transfer pages
Record transfer fee paid: £5,000
Record transfer fee received: £8,000
Programme details: 28 pages, 30p
Local newspapers & Tel No: Western Gazette (74551), Western Daily Press, Evening Post
Club metal badges: Yes
Major Honours: Southern League (3), Southern League Cup (4), F.A. Cup - Third Round (9)
Club Captain (1983-84): Gary Borthwick
Player of the Year (1983-84): Dave Linney
Programme Editor: Bryan Moore

SERVOWARM ISTHMIAN FOOTBALL LEAGUE

President: B. D. East, BSc *Chairman:* A. C. F. Turvey, MInstM
Secretary: N. R. Robinson, 226 Rye Lane, Peckham, London SE15 4NL
Tel: H. 01-653 3903; B. 01-639 5726

HARROW BOROUGH ALL THE WAY

If success is measured in terms of representation in the finals of the national cups, then the League did not have a particularly successful season, with Leyton-Wingate being the last club to be knocked out in the FA Vase in the sixth round, and in the Trophy Dulwich Hamlet were the League's last representatives and they lost to Northwich Victoria in a second replay in the third round. There was some solace in the FA Challenge Cup where Barking, Harrow Borough and Windsor & Eton all survived through to the second round proper, with Windsor & Eton going into the third round draw by virtue of forcing a replay against AFC Bournemouth.

In the League competition, Harrow Borough seemed to be a nose in front of all their challengers throughout the season, but never so far that they could ever relax. The runners up were Worthing, who started the season so well by getting maximum points from their first nine* matches. During the season the League maintained records of leading goal scorers for the first time, and the winner by a clear 12 goals in League and Hitachi Cup matches was Mick Edmunds from Worthing, who scored a total of 45 goals.

In Division 1 a closely fought contest resulted in Windsor & Eton gaining the champions trophy and Epsom & Ewell were their runners up. Even though these clubs had qualified for promotion on the playing field they were not assured of promotion until 31st May, which was the date set by the Management Committee for all clubs to have the appropriate ground grading for the respective divisions. In Epsom's case, it really was a matter of the eleventh hour, as their grading was only confirmed in the late afternoon of 31st May. Unfortunately, in the Premier Division Staines Town were not so lucky and as they had not achieved the necessary 'B' grading were regretfully relegated from the Premier Division to Division 1 in place of Tooting & Mitcham, who had finished in 21st place. It was sad to see a team of Staines' stature being relegated in this way, and it is to be hoped that they will carry out sufficient work to obtain their grading and immediately come back into the Premier Division through their playing prowess.

In Division 2 the worthy champions were Basildon United, who were amongst the leaders for the greater part of the season, and in fact 17 points separated Basildon from the fourth placed club. The runners up, who were also promoted with Basildon, were St. Albans City, who, having been relegated the previous season, have made an immediate return to Division 1, following in the steps of Clapton who achieved the similar feat in 1982/83. Relegated from Division 1 were Cheshunt and Feltham, who now go into a regionalised Division 2.

Throughout the season the Grounds Sub-Committee worked very hard inspecting, checking and grading more than 30 clubs who applied to join the League for season 1984/5 and eventually 19 clubs were recommended to the AGM and were duly elected. They have been joined with the existing 22 Division 2 members to form two regionalised divisions, North and South, and it is to be hoped that football in general will benefit from this step towards cutting the travelling time and expenses for member clubs.

In the Hitachi Cup there was a repeat of the 1982/3 final between Sutton United and Wycombe Wanderers, with there being a draw at Loakes Park, Wycombe in the first leg and Sutton United winning the second leg at home to take the trophy for the second year running.

In the Youth Cup, which is also sponsored by our major sponsors, Servowarm, the final was between Chesham United and Farnborough Town, and was staged at The Beveree, the ground of Hampton FC. A most enjoyable game was watched by a disappointing crowd, but Chesham United were worthy winners on the day.

Last, but by no means least, the Harrow Borough players, Andy Pope and David Howell, were selected to play for England in the Four Nation's Tournament in Italy and this was certainly a bright note on which to end the season.

N. R. ROBINSON

League Chairman Alan Turvey and Secretary Nick Robinson present Harry Manoe, Harrow Borough's captain and Player of the Year and manager Mike Tomkys with the Championship Trophy. Photo: Steve Burton

Servowarm Isthmian League — Dylon Charity Shield

1978-79 Enfield (Champions) 2, Dagenham (Cup Winners) 1
1979-80 Barking (Champions) 1, Enfield (Cup Winners) 0
1980-81 Enfield (Double Winners) 2, Sutton United (Cup Finalists) 1
1981-82 Wycombe Wanderers (Third*) 4, Slough Town (Champions) 1
1982-83 Leytonstone-Ilford (Double Winners) 3, Sutton United (League Runners Up) 2
1983-84 Wycombe Wanderers (Champions) v Sutton United (Cup Winners)
1984-85 Harrow Borough (Champions) v Sutton United (Cup Winners)
*Slough Town achieved 'the double' and Enfield (second) joined The Alliance.

Servowarm Isthmian League XI 1, Hendon (75th Anniversary) 3
(Joyce)

Pape (Harrow Borough), Metz (Harrow Borough), Mackay (Sutton United), McCayna (Leytonstone-Ilford), Rains (Sutton United), Lewington (Carshalton Athletic), Alexander (Oxford City), Harrison (Hayes), Joyce (Sutton United), Tate (Oxford City), Dell (Wycombe W).
Substitutes: Collyer (Sutton United) for Pape and Mariner (Bognor Regis) for Mackay.

Club President Sir Stanley Rous presents Casuals skipper Peter Bateman with the match ball before their Vase tie with Stamford. Photo: Eric Marsh

Premier Division

	P	W	D	L	F	A	Pts
Harrow Borough	42	25	13	4	73	42	88
Worthing	42	20	11	11	89	72	71
Slough Town	42	20	9	13	73	56	69
Sutton United	42	18	12	12	67	45	66
Hayes	42	17	13	12	56	41	64
Hitchin Town	42	16	15	11	58	57	63
Wycombe Wanderers	42	16	14	12	63	52	62
Wokingham Town	42	18	10	14	78	55	61*
Hendon	42	17	10	15	62	51	61
Dulwich Hamlet	42	16	11	15	61	64	59
Bishop's Stortford	42	15	13	14	56	57	58
Harlow Town	42	15	11	16	64	70	56
Bognor Regis Town	42	14	13	15	62	69	55
Staines Town	42	15	9	18	63	72	54
Billericay Town	42	15	8	19	53	73	53
Barking	42	13	13	16	60	64	52
Croydon	42	14	10	18	52	58	52
Walthamstow Avenue	42	13	10	19	53	67	49
Leytonstone-Ilford	42	13	9	20	54	67	48
Carshalton Athletic	42	11	10	21	59	72	43
Tooting & Mitcham	42	10	13	19	50	63	43
Bromley	42	7	11	24	33	72	32

*3 points deducted.

HUNTING GATE HOMES
MANAGER OF THE MONTH AWARD 1983/84 SEASON

AUGUST		
Premier Division	Barry Lloyd	Worthing
Division I	Geoff Chappell	Windsor & Eton
Division II	Phil Illman	Dorking
SEPTEMBER		
Premier Division	Jack Pearce	Bognor Regis T
Division I	Alan Dafforn	Wembley
Division II	Fred Saxton	Grays Athletic
OCTOBER		
Premier Division	Barrie Williams	Sutton United
Division I	Terry Dyson	Boreham Wood
Division II	Keith Monk	Epping Town
NOVEMBER		
Premier Division	Eddie Presland	Dulwich Hamlet
Division I	Geoff Chappell	Windsor & Eton
Division II	Tony Horsfall	Hemel Hempstead
DECEMBER		
Premier Division	Mike Tomkys	Harrow Borough
Division I	Terry Dyson	Boreham Wood
Division II	John Mitchell	St Albans City
JANUARY		
Premier Division	Roy Merryweather	Wokingham Town
Division I	Terry Dyson	Boreham Wood
Division II	Jimmy Kelman	Hungerford Town
FEBRUARY		
Premier Division	Iaian MacLean	Staines Town
Division I	Nick Leach	Leatherhead
Division II	John Bowers	Tring Town
MARCH		
Premier Division	Mike Tomkys	Harrow Borough
Division I	Brian Caterer	Maidenhead U
Division II	Ron Hanley	Basildon United
APRIL		
Premier Division	Tom Walley	Barking
Division I	Adrian Hill	Epsom & Ewell
Division II	John Mitchell	St Albans City

SERVOWARM ISTHMIAN FOOTBALL LEAGUE PREMIER DIVISION SEASON 1983/84

	Barking	Billericay T	B. Stortford	Bognor R	Bromley	Carshalton	Croydon	Dulwich H	Harlow T	Harrow B	Hayes	Hendon	Hitchin T	Leytonstone	Slough T	Staines T	Sutton U	Tooting & M	Walthamstow Av	Wokingham T	Worthing	Wycombe Wand.
Barking		2-0	1-1	0-1	3-0	2-4	0-2	2-3	1-0	3-2	0-1	1-3	0-2	1-2	1-0	0-0	1-1	1-1	3-1	2-1	2-0	0-0
Billericay T	1-0		3-2	3-0	1-1	1-1	1-0	2-3	1-1	4-1	1-2	0-1	0-0	3-2	0-3	2-4	1-0	3-0	2-1	0-2	2-2	1-2
B. Stortford	2-2	1-3		1-2	2-1	2-1	2-1	1-0	4-2	1-2	0-3	1-2	2-1	0-0	2-1	2-0	2-0	1-0	1-1	0-3	3-4	2-0
Bognor R	1-2	3-0	0-2		1-0	2-0	1-0	3-1	2-0	1-1	1-1	1-1	3-2	1-1	2-2	1-1	2-1	1-2	1-0	1-4	0-3	1-2
Bromley	1-2	0-2	1-1	1-1		0-0	0-1	1-0	3-3	0-1	0-0	1-0	0-0	0-1	3-3	1-0	0-3	0-2	1-3	1-0	0-5	0-2
Carshalton	1-2	0-1	0-2	3-2	3-2		0-0	1-1	3-2	1-1	0-3	0-1	1-0	1-2	1-2	4-0	0-0	1-2	1-3	1-2	3-4	3-2
Croydon	3-2	3-3	0-1	3-0	2-0	3-2		2-0	1-2	0-3	2-2	3-1	1-2	1-0	2-2	1-1	0-3	2-1	4-0	2-2	2-4	0-1
Dulwich H	4-3	1-1	2-0	0-0	1-2	2-2	2-0		2-0	0-1	1-0	1-2	1-2	2-0	4-6	0-2	2-0	0-3	5-2	1-1	1-1	1-1
Harlow T	0-0	3-0	1-2	4-2	2-1	2-1	2-0	0-1		0-0	2-3	0-1	1-1	1-2	3-2	2-1	0-0	2-2	0-1	3-2	3-2	3-5
Harrow B	2-2	3-1	1-1	2-2	2-0	1-2	1-0	3-3	5-1		2-0	1-0	2-1	1-0	1-0	2-1	0-0	3-2	2-0	2-2	2-1	1-1
Hayes	3-4	4-0	2-2	1-0	0-0	1-0	1-1	0-0	0-1	1-2		1-0	2-0	2-3	2-1	2-2	0-1	2-0	2-0	2-1	1-1	2-0
Hendon T	2-2	0-0	0-0	5-2	0-1	0-1	0-0	3-0	2-2	3-3	1-1		1-2	4-0	0-1	3-0	1-3	1-0	1-2	0-2	3-0	2-1
Hitchin T	2-1	1-0	2-2	1-1	2-1	3-2	1-1	0-0	0-2	1-3	1-1	1-0		1-0	1-1	2-1	2-2	3-1	1-0	4-3	2-1	0-0
Leytonstone	2-2	3-5	2-0	2-4	3-0	1-4	1-2	0-2	1-1	0-2	1-2	2-2	1-1		0-2	0-2	1-2	0-0	5-1	1-0	2-2	1-2
Slough T	1-1	2-0	1-1	3-2	0-0	2-1	5-1	2-4	2-2	0-2	1-0	3-1	5-1	2-1		1-2	1-0	1-0	2-0	0-1	2-4	3-0
Staines T	1-1	0-1	2-1	3-2	0-3	3-0	4-1	4-5	3-4	0-1	2-1	0-0	2-1	0-2	2-3		1-1	3-1	2-1	0-4	2-4	1-1
Sutton U	2-1	3-0	3-2	1-1	3-0	2-0	0-1	1-2	3-1	0-1	1-2	5-1	3-3	1-1	2-0	1-2		4-1	3-4	2-0	2-1	2-1
Tooting & M	1-1	3-0	0-0	0-0	0-5	4-5	0-2	1-1	0-1	2-1	1-0	0-2	3-3	4-0	3-0	1-1	1-2		1-2	1-2	0-2	0-0
Walthamstow Av	0-2	0-1	1-0	5-2	1-1	1-1	1-0	1-2	2-1	2-2	2-1	2-2	2-2	2-1	0-2	1-2	0-0	0-0		2-2	4-0	0-2
Wokingham T	3-2	5-1	3-1	2-3	5-1	2-2	0-2	3-0	1-1	1-2	2-1	3-0	2-0	0-2	0-0	3-2	1-1	2-3	0-0		4-1	2-2
Worthing	4-0	4-2	1-1	1-2	2-0	2-2	1-1	2-0	4-1	2-2	0-0	1-2	2-1	3-2	2-1	5-2	2-1	1-1	3-2	2-0		2-2
Wycombe Wand.	3-2	4-0	2-2	2-2	1-0	2-0	2-0	3-0	1-2	0-1	1-1	1-2	0-2	2-2	1-2	0-2	2-2	2-2	1-0	1-0	5-1	

Preliminary Round

Grays Ath..............2
Newbury T.............0

Horsham................1
Finchley.................2

THE HITACHI CUP 1983/84

First Round

Walton & H............0
Grays Ath...............1

Leyton Wingate.......2
Hertford T..............0

Feltham...................1
Hayes......................2

Wycombe W..........6
Letchworth GC.......0

Hampton.................2
Epping T.................1

Molesey...................0
Staines T.................1

Wokingham T.........6
Rainham T..............1

Windsor & Eton......2
Maidenhead U........1

Hendon...................4
Dorking...................3

Dulwich H...........0:5
Egham T.............0:2

Oxford City............2
Carshalton Ath........1

Barking...................2
Tring T...................1

Tooting & M...........3
Epsom & Ewell.......1

Harlow T................3
Billericay T.............2

Bognor Regis..........2
Walthamstow Av.....0

Lewes.....................2
Kingstonian............3

Clapton..................4
Uxbridge................3

Tilbury....................0
Slough T................4

Basildon U..............6
Ware.......................0

Boreham Wood.......2
Chesham U.............0

Harrow Borough.....3
St Albans City.........1

Barton Rov.............1
Bromley..................2

Sutton U................3
Southall..................1

Worthing................3
Leytonstone/Ilford...1

Finchley.................1
Aveley....................2

Leatherhead............6
Hungerford T.........1

Wembley................3
Hornchurch............2

Farnborough T.......2
Corinthian Cas........3

Hitchin T...............1
Bishops Stortford....2

Croydon.................2
Cheshunt................3

Woking................0:0
Metropolitan P.....0:2

Eastbourne U..........3
Hemel Hempstead...1

Second Round

Grays Ath..............2
Leyton W..............0

Hayes.....................0
Wycombe W..........1

Hampton................0
Staines T................2

Wokingham T.........2
Windsor & Eton......1

Hendon...............2:0
Dulwich H...........2:1

Oxford City............5
Barking...................1

Tooting & M...........4
Harlow T................3

Bognor Regis..........7
Kingstonian............0

Clapton..................1
Slough T................0

Basildon U.............1
Boreham Wood.......0

Harrow Borough.....1
Bromley..................2

Sutton U................4
Worthing................0

Aveley....................1
Leatherhead............0

Wembley................1
C. Casuals..............0

Bishops S............0:5
Cheshunt............0:0

Metropolitan P........4
Eastbourne U..........0

Third Round

Grays Ath..............0
Wycombe W..........1

Staines T................1
Wokingham T.........2

Dulwich Ham.........2
Oxford City............4

Tooting & M...........2
Bognor Regis T.......1

Clapton..................2
Basildon U.............3

Bromley..................1
Sutton U................2

Aveley....................0
Wembley................2

Bishops S................3
Met Pol..................1

Fourth Round

Wycombe W..........1
Wokingham............0

Oxford C................2
Tooting & M...........1

Basildon U.............1
Sutton U................2

Wembley................1
Bishops S................0

Semi Finals

Wycombe W..........1
Oxford C................0

Sutton U................4
Wembley................1

FINAL

WYCOMBE WANDERERS 1 0   SUTTON UNITED 1 2

Goalscoring Awards

Wins by 4 or more clear goals

Premier Division	£100 per win
Wokingham Town	3
Hendon	2
Slough Town	2
Worthing	2
Wycombe Wanderers	2
Bromley	1
Carshalton Athletic	1
Croydon	1
Harrow Borough	1
Hayes	1
Leytonstone-Ilford	1
Sutton United	1
Tooting & Mitcham United	1
Walthamstow Avenue	1
Total	20

Division One	£75 per win
Metropolitan Police	4
Boreham Wood	3
Farnborough Town	3
Oxford City	3
Wembley	3
Windsor & Eton	3
Cheshunt	2
Hampton	2
Woking	2
Aveley	1
Epsom & Ewell	1
Leatherhead	1
Maidenhead United	1
Walton & Hersham	1
Total	30

Division Two	£50 per win
Basildon United	5
Uxbridge	4
Hungerford Town	4
Leyton-Wingate	3
St Albans City	3
Corinthian Casuals	2
Dorking	2
Hemel Hempstead	2
Southall	2
Tring Town	2
Eastbourne United	1
Egham Town	1
Epping Town	1
Grays Athletic	1
Letchworth Garden City	1
Molesey	1
Newbury Town	1
Ware	1
Total	37

DIVISION 1	Aveley	Boreham W	Chesham	Cheshunt	Clapton	Epsom & Ewell	F. Boro Town	Feltham	Hampton	Hertford T	Hornchurch	Kegstonian	Leatherhead	Lewes	Maidenhead Utd	Metropolitan P	Oxford City	Tilbury	Walton & Hersham	Wembley	Windsor & Eton	Woking
Aveley		0-2	3-1	4-0	1-2	2-1	3-1	1-0	2-0	2-2	1-0	2-1	0-0	0-0	2-0	1-1	3-0	1-1	1-4	1-2	0-2	2-5
Boreham W	1-0		0-1	0-0	2-0	3-1	2-1	5-0	4-2	2-0	5-2	3-0	0-4	1-2	4-0	0-0	0-1	2-0	1-1	1-0	4-0	5-0
Chesham	2-0	2-2		4-0	4-1	2-4	1-1	3-0	2-1	2-2	3-0	1-0	3-1	0-2	3-0	2-0	3-0	1-1	1-0	1-1	3-1	1-2
Cheshunt	3-0	3-2	1-3		1-1	0-2	2-0	3-0	1-1	2-3	1-1	0-0	0-3	1-0	1-0	4-0	1-1	2-0	1-0	0-1	1-3	5-0
Clapton	0-3	2-3	2-0	1-3		0-0	0-1	4-1	0-0	1-2	1-0	1-1	2-1	1-0	1-3	0-2	1-0	4-1	3-1	0-0	0-4	3-1
Epsom & Ewell	3-2	2-1	3-1	3-1	2-1		2-2	1-2	0-0	2-0	2-1	3-2	2-0	1-1	2-1	0-3	3-2	1-1	2-0	2-1	4-0	2-1
F. Boro Town	2-1	1-1	1-2	1-0	0-1	1-2		6-0	3-0	5-1	5-1	2-2	1-8	3-2	3-2	4-0	1-1	2-0	3-2	0-2	1-3	4-0
Feltham	0-0	3-1	1-2	1-0	1-1	0-5	0-2		0-5	1-2	1-2	0-0	1-0	3-3	1-0	1-5	0-5	1-2	2-0	0-1	0-5	2-0
Hampton	0-0	0-2	0-1	3-0	4-1	0-0	0-0	3-0		4-0	4-1	0-1	2-3	1-1	1-1	4-2	3-0	1-1	3-0	1-5	1-1	2-1
Hertford T	1-0	3-1	1-0	0-0	3-0	0-3	2-1	4-0	0-2		3-0	1-3	2-2	1-2	0-1	1-2	2-1	0-0	1-1	1-1	0-1	0-7
Hornchurch	1-3	1-0	1-1	2-0	2-1	0-0	1-1	2-1	0-1	0-1		1-1	0-0	1-3	1-0	3-2	1-3	1-2	4-0	0-0	1-0	1-3
Kegstonian	3-2	1-2	2-2	2-1	2-2	1-0	1-4	2-1	0-0	0-2	0-1		2-4	1-1	0-2	0-5	2-0	0-1	1-3	0-4	1-2	1-2
Leatherhead	0-0	2-1	3-1	0-0	1-1	2-1	0-2	6-0	1-2	0-2	2-3	0-1		2-2	2-2	0-1	1-7	6-2	6-0	0-2	1-0	1-1
Lewes	0-1	1-0	3-1	0-1	1-4	2-3	2-2	1-0	2-4	1-1	1-0	3-2	1-0		1-2	2-1	1-0	0-0	1-1	1-4	0-7	3-1
Maidenhead Utd	2-0	3-0	3-1	4-1	2-1	2-0	0-1	4-1	1-2	5-1	3-0	0-2	1-0	0-0		3-1	1-0	4-1	1-0	3-0	1-1	3-3
Metropolitan P	2-1	0-1	1-0	4-1	1-1	3-0	1-2	3-2	4-0	5-3	2-1	0-2	0-1	3-0	0-0		1-2	5-2	0-5	1-1	4-1	2-1
Oxford City	0-0	1-1	0-0	2-0	1-1	1-1	3-3	3-1	3-0	0-1	0-1	3-1	0-1	3-0	0-1	1-4		4-0	2-1	0-1	1-2	3-1
Tilbury	0-1	1-0	1-0	3-1	2-1	0-1	1-1	2-0	1-3	0-0	4-2	2-1	2-1	2-0	0-1	2-0	6-1		3-1	0-5	3-2	0-0
Walton & Hersham	0-0	0-3	4-1	2-1	1-1	3-2	3-0	3-1	0-3	3-2	0-0	2-0	0-0	2-1	1-3	1-7	0-0	2-0		0-1	2-0	0-3
Wembley	4-0	2-3	0-1	1-0	3-0	1-1	2-2	2-0	1-1	5-2	1-2	0-1	1-0	0-0	0-0	1-0	1-2	0-0	3-1		1-0	2-0
Windsor & Eton	3-0	0-0	2-0	4-1	4-0	4-2	1-0	4-1	3-0	2-1	1-1	3-1	4-0	3-2	1-1	2-0	3-0	3-3	0-0	2-1		2-0
Woking	1-3	0-3	5-2	2-1	2-1	1-2	2-2	3-1	0-1	3-2	0-0	0-2	1-2	1-0	2-1	5-1	1-0	0-1	2-2	2-1	1-1	

DIVISION 2	Barton Rov	Basildon U	C. Casuals	Dorking T	Eastbourne Utd	Egham Town	Epping Town	Finchley	Grays Ath	Hemel H	Horsham	Hungerford T	Letchworth	Leyton Wingate	Molesey	Newbury Tn	Rainham Tn	St Albans C	Southall	Tring Town	Uxbridge	Ware
Barton Rov		2-4	0-0	3-1	4-2	0-1	1-1	1-0	2-3	2-1	2-1	1-0	0-1	0-0	1-1	1-0	2-0	2-6	2-3	1-1	0-2	2-2
Basildon U	3-1		4-0	2-0	2-0	5-0	0-1	3-0	1-0	1-0	2-0	3-2	1-0	2-0	0-0	0-2	2-0	1-0	1-1	1-3	1-0	4-0
C. Casuals	3-0	0-0		2-1	2-0	1-1	1-2	2-0	0-4	0-0	4-0	0-2	2-0	1-2	1-2	3-1	3-1	2-2	2-0	1-0	1-0	4-0
Dorking T	1-0	0-2	2-2		1-0	2-1	1-2	2-0	1-1	2-4	5-0	1-0	0-1	0-2	4-0	2-1	1-2	1-0	2-3	1-0	3-3	2-0
Eastbourne Utd	0-2	1-2	0-1	0-5		1-1	0-1	3-2	0-1	1-2	2-1	0-1	2-1	0-4	2-3	0-1	3-2	1-3	2-1	0-1	0-0	5-0
Egham Town	1-2	0-0	1-1	1-1	2-0		1-1	2-1	1-3	3-4	3-0	0-1	2-3	2-1	3-1	3-1	2-1	1-2	0-0	2-2	2-0	2-0
Epping Town	1-0	0-4	1-1	1-2	2-1	1-2		1-0	3-3	2-2	3-3	1-1	2-2	2-1	1-0	1-3	10-0	0-1	0-2	1-2	0-1	3-0
Finchley	0-3	0-3	0-2	0-2	2-1	0-2	0-0		1-0	0-2	0-1	0-2	0-0	1-4	2-2	2-2	2-0	1-1	0-1	0-2	1-0	2-2
Grays Ath	5-1	0-1	3-1	0-2	2-1	2-1	1-1	4-1		3-2	1-0	2-2	1-3	2-7	3-3	3-2	0-0	0-1	1-2	0-1	0-1	3-0
Hemel H	0-3	0-2	2-3	2-0	0-1	1-1	2-2	3-1	0-1		0-0	4-5	0-1	3-0	1-0	1-2	3-1	1-2	0-2	2-3	2-2	1-2
Horsham	1-2	1-7	3-4	1-4	1-1	1-2	0-1	1-2	2-5	0-4		0-3	0-2	1-2	0-1	2-1	2-0	0-1	2-0	0-5	0-2	1-0
Hungerford T	1-0	1-2	1-1	2-1	5-0	0-1	1-2	1-1	2-1	4-1	4-1		9-0	1-2	2-2	3-1	9-1	1-1	0-1	1-1	2-2	5-2
Letchworth	2-0	0-5	0-3	1-2	5-1	1-1	1-2	1-0	1-0	0-0	3-0	0-2		0-1	1-1	1-0	0-1	0-3	5-4	0-1	1-1	5-2
Leyton Wingate	4-0	1-1	0-1	4-0	4-0	2-0	2-1	3-0	1-1	4-1	2-0	1-2	3-0		3-1	3-1	6-1	1-2	3-2	1-0	3-1	4-1
Molesey	1-1	0-0	1-4	1-2	4-1	1-0	0-0	1-1	2-2	2-1	3-6	1-5	2-0	1-2		2-1	3-2	1-2	0-2	2-1	0-1	1-3
Newbury Tn	1-0	1-3	0-2	0-2	1-0	0-0	2-1	1-1	3-1	2-1	4-2	0-3	1-1	1-5	2-2		5-1	2-3	4-2	1-2	1-2	3-1
Rainham Tn	0-2	0-3	1-5	1-4	3-2	0-1	2-2	3-2	0-1	1-1	2-0	1-1	1-0	0-4	1-3	1-3		0-4	0-2	1-4	0-1	1-1
St Albans C	1-1	3-2	2-2	2-0	6-1	2-2	2-1	2-0	3-4	4-1	5-0	2-2	3-2	2-0	1-1	4-1	1-0		3-1	3-0	2-2	5-1
Southall	2-1	2-3	3-1	4-0	6-0	3-3	0-0	2-1	0-1	1-1	2-4	3-0	3-1	3-0	0-2	5-1	2-1	1-2		3-3	1-1	3-1
Tring Town	5-4	0-0	1-2	1-2	2-0	1-1	1-1	3-1	0-2	2-0	5-0	1-1	3-0	1-1	3-0	5-1	7-1	4-1	3-1		1-1	2-1
Uxbridge	2-0	5-1	0-0	1-0	2-1	0-0	0-1	5-0	0-0	1-2	1-0	1-1	1-0	2-3	0-0	1-0	4-0	2-3	0-0	1-1		5-2
Ware	0-2	0-4	3-4	1-1	7-0	0-4	1-1	2-0	1-2	0-5	2-2	1-3	0-2	0-1	0-5	3-0	1-3	1-2	3-1	1-5	0-4	

Division 1

	P	W	D	L	F	A	Pts
Windsor & Eaton	42	26	7	9	89	44	85
Epsom & Ewell	42	23	9	10	73	51	78
Wembley	42	21	11	10	65	32	74
Maidenhead United	42	22	8	12	67	42	74
Boreham Wood	42	22	7	13	74	43	73
Farnborough Town	42	18	12	12	78	60	66
Hampton	42	18	12	12	65	49	66
Metropolitan Police	42	20	5	17	79	64	65
Chesham United	42	18	8	16	64	57	62
Tilbury	42	17	10	15	54	64	61
Leatherhead	42	15	10	17	67	56	55
Aveley	42	15	10	17	49	53	55
Woking	42	16	7	19	66	73	55
Hertford Town	42	15	9	18	56	73	54
Oxford City	42	14	9	19	57	56	51
Lewes	42	13	12	17	49	65	51
Walton & Hersham	42	13	10	19	52	70	49
Hornchurch	42	13	10	19	43	63	49
Kingstonian	42	13	9	20	47	67	48
Clapton	42	12	11	19	49	67	47
Cheshunt	42	12	8	22	45	64	44
Feltham	42	7	4	31	31	106	25

Division 2

	P	W	D	L	F	A	Pts
Basildon United	42	30	7	5	88	27	97
St Albans City	42	29	9	4	100	46	96
Leyton Wingate	42	29	4	9	97	41	91
Tring Town	42	23	11	8	89	44	80
Corinthian Casuals	42	23	11	8	75	47	80
Hungerford Town	42	21	12	9	94	47	75
Uxbridge	42	18	15	9	61	36	69
Grays Athletic	42	20	9	13	72	57	69
Dorking	42	21	5	16	66	54	68
Southall	42	20	8	14	79	60	65*
Egham Town	42	16	15	11	59	49	63
Epping Town	42	15	16	11	61	50	61
Molesey	42	13	14	15	59	68	53
Barton Rovers	42	15	8	19	54	64	53
Letchworth Garden C	42	15	7	20	48	66	52
Newbury Town	42	14	5	23	60	82	47
Hemel Hempstead	42	12	9	21	63	69	45
Rainham Town	42	7	5	30	38	114	26
Finchley	42	5	9	28	28	78	24
Eastbourne United	42	7	3	32	36	98	24
Ware	42	6	6	30	48	114	24
Horsham	42	7	4	31	40	104	24+

* 3 points deducted. + 2 points deducted.

Windsor & Eton *Back Row (L-R): B. Lowe (physio), J. Chapman, C. Yates, D. Langley, K. Mitchell, T. Baron, C. Smith. Front Row (L-R): K. Hill, L. Craker, R. King (capt), J. Mitchell, G. Huxley, G. Woodcraft.*

Basildon United celebrate their Division Two championship success with manager Ron Hanlon.
Photo: Steve Lindrels

SERVOWARM ISTHMIAN LEAGUE CLUBS
FIRST TEAM MATCH STATISTICS 1983-84

	Leading Goalscorers	Hat Tricks	Penalties	Most Appearances
Barking	Nicky Crown 17 Bobby Tappin 8 Paul Shirt 6		John McFarlane Paul Watts	Nicky Crown 54* David Root 51 Kevin Cooper 50
Billericay Town	Danny Westwood 14 Tony James 8 Graham Stewart 8 Clair Darmudas 6		Danny Westwood (2)	Mark McCutcheon 50 T. James 45 G. Stewart 45 Danny Westwood 43
Bognor Regis Town	Kevin Clements 25 David Poole 13 Toby Anderton 10	Kevin Clements	Dallas Whyte (3)	David Poole 58* Vijay Korgaok 57 Mike Pullen 57
Bromley	Steve Tomlin 11 Terry Young 5 Lennie Dennis 5 Neil Collins 5	Steve Tomlin v Tooting (A)	Keith Walden (2)	Micky Brookman 49 Mark Penfold 44 Graham Taylor 41
Carlshalton Athletic	Tommy Tuite 24 Chris Lewington 9 Trevor Dark 8 John Raffington 8	Tommy Tuite v Southall (A) FA Cup	John Raffington (3) Trevor Dark	Tommy Tuite 50 Chris Lewington 49 John Raffington 46
Croydon	Alec Jackson 12 Ian Simpson 11 Les Whitton 9 Marc Flemington 9	Les Whitton v Billericay	Les Whitton (2) Marc Flemington	Mark Denton 51* Stuart Hemsley 47 Alec Jackson 47
Dulwich Hamlet	Karl Richards 21 Neil Norman 10 John Palmer 10 Derek Williams 10	Karl Richards (2) 4 v W'stowA, v Slough John Palmer v Kingstonian (LSC) Derek Williams v Staines T	Peter Kingston (5) Duncan Bassett	Paul Edwards 58 Bobby Knock 57 Peter Kingston 56 Richard Langley 56
Harlow Town	Lawrence Holmes 18 Owen Griffiths 11 Marc Das 8	Owen Griffiths v Bromley Mickey Mann v Billericay	Bobby Harding Andy Walker	Owen Griffiths 48 Kevin Ahern 48 Leo Cusenza 47
Harrow Borough	George Duck 34 David Pearce 30 Clevere Ford 14	George Duck (2) David Pearce	Steve Emmanuel (5)	Steve Emmanuel 63 Mike Garrini 60 David Pearce 59
Hayes	Peter Kemp 13 Byron Walton 13 Mick Keily 11		Keith James (4) Davies, Tilley Harrison	Glen Hayward * Byron Walton Paul Hyde Micky Scott
Hendon	Gary Allen 10 Steve Wilkins 10 Barry Henley 9 Mick Mancini 9	Barry Henley	Steve Wilkins (4) Steve Hudson	Andy O'Brien 55 Clive Kemplen 54 Dermot Drummy 49
Hitchin Town	Mick Every 24 Trevor Parker 13 Alan West 12 Steve Fountain 12		Steve Fountain (11) Trevor Parker	Alan West 65 Neil Madden 63 Ian Kavanagh 62
Leystonstone-Ilford	Terry Harris 16 Steve Edkins 12 Martin McCayna 9		Terry Harris (2)	Tom Horan 54 Frank Coles 54 Phil Stacey 53
Slough Town	Rowan Dodds 17 Keith White 17 Mick Doherty 16 Henry Pacquette 10	Keith White v Dulwich H (A) Rowan Dodds v Wycombe W (H)	Keith White (4) Micky Doherty (2) Howard Kennedy Rowan Dodds	Keith White 49 Eddie Hutchinson 48 Peter Skerritt 42
Sutton United	Micky Joyce 21 Steve Galloway 18 Mark Golley 14	Micky Joyce v Boreham Wood (A) (LSC)	Mark Golley (3)	Dave Collyer 55 Micky Stephens 54 Ricky Kidd 53
Staines Town	Declan Link 24 Simon Read 20 Steve Flack 7 Paul Rumley 7		Declan Link (3)	Declan Link 52* Gary Powell 50 Simon Reed 50
Tooting & Mitcham	Butch Dunn 15 Carlton Fairweather 10 Richard Wilson 8	Dunn, Wilson Fairweather S. Alexander	T. Sampson (4) Dunn, Wilson Pittaway	N. Sullivan 54 D. Godwin 50 P. Ranson 43
Walthamstow Avenue	Devon Gayle 13 Alan Hunter 11 Darren Dennis 8	Norman Milne	Devon Gayle (4)	John Kane 53 Kevin Dare 51 Lee Hunter 51

Wokingham Town	Steve Butler 26 Jimmy Brown 21 Neal Stanley 14	Steve Butler (3)		Kirk Corbin Des McMahon Neal Stanley
Worthing	Mick Edmonds 52 Mike Cornwell 11 Geoff Raynsford 10	Mick Edmonds (4) Tony Verrey	Mick Edmonds 22	Kevin Foreman 52 Mick Edmonds 51 Paul Lelliott 51
Wycombe Wanderers	Terry Glynn 24 Steve Long 11 Ken Wilson 9		George Borg (6) Bob Dell (2) Jim Jacobs (2)	Trevor How 65 Terry Glynn 60 Jimmy Jacobs 59
Bishop's Stortford	Ben Robb 13 Tony Mercer 11 Billy Jennings 11	Ben Robb	John Jacobs (2) (goalkeeper)	Roger Avery 48 Ray Wickenden 47 Ian Smith 45

*Ever present

ISTHMIAN LEAGUE CLUBS FIRST TEAM MATCH STATISTICS 1983-84

	Leading Goalscorers	**Hat Tricks**	**Penalties**	**Most Appearances**
Aveley	Tony Flynn 17 Tony O'Brien 13 Phil Wyles 9		Tony Flynn (2) John Kerslake	Tony O'Brien 49 Keith Day 47 Tony Flynn 47
Boreham Wood	Sean Baker 27 Steve Wallace 23 Steve O'Neill 9	Sean Baker (2) v Lowestoft (A), Windsor (H) Steve Wallace v Woking (H)	Sean Baker (5)	Steve Foody 55* Steve O'Neill 53 Steve Wallace 52 Steve Waller 52
Chesham United	'Eggy' James 12 Godfrey Cordice 10 Paul Currie 9 Chris Martin 9	Paul Currie v Clapton	Paul Currie (3) Chris Martin	Pat Morrissey 53 Paul Currie 53 Dave Lewis 53
Clapton	Nigel McNeil 26 Jon Bolle 16 Robert Waterfall 12	Jon Bolle	Robert Waterfall (8)	Gary Seymour 61 Roy Drake 59 Robert Waterfall 57
Epsom & Ewell	Steve Hill 38 Steve Milton 10 Alan Morton 8	Steve Hill (2) v Windsor (H), Croydon (SSC)	Alan Morton (3) John Russell (2) Miles, Hill	Mick Stratford 56 Tony Borman 51 Steve Hill 50
Farnborough Town	Keith Morris 26 Brian Broome 20 Mark Turkington 17	Keith Norris v Brockenhurst Richard Parkin v Bass (Alton)	Richard Walden (5) Mark Turkington	Richard Walden 56 Brian Broome 54 Tony Carter 53
Feltham	Garing Ewing 10 Paul Clarke 6 Jeff Hunn 5 Billy Edwards 5		Micky Bennett (4)*	Kevin McDonagh 36 Paul Clarke 32 Malcolm Dickenson 29
Hampton	Steve Russell 32 Mick Heselden 25 Peter Shodeinde	Steve Russell (3) 4 v Feltham (A) 3 v Feltham (H) 3 v Royston T (FAC)	Richard Smith (1)	Steve Rogers 58 Richard Smith 58 T. Hollands 53 S. Smith 53
Hertford Town	Martin Sperrin 24 Nick O'Donoghue 20 Micky Dale 12		Nick O'Donoghue (9)	Martin Sperrin 60 Eddie Scales 59 Lennie Merrifield 56
Hornchurch	Kurt Davison 10 Graham Wilsmore 6 David Hughes 4 Leroy Rhodes 4		John Roche	Graham Wilsmore 45 Steve Hopkins 44 Nicky Bissett 43
Kingstonian	John Martin 21 Gary Cooke 13 Chris Kelly 9 David Byrne 9		Ian Armstrong (2)	Graham Yates 56 Ian Armstrong 52 John Martin 51 + 5s
Leatherhead	Brian Perkins 18 Pieter Shodeinde 17 Dave Worth 12			Phil Smith Wayne Falldon Peter Caswell
Lewes	Mick Dorrell 20 Peter Schulz 14 Terry Parris 13		Terry Parris (3)	Ricky West 56 Grant Horscroft 56 Terry Parris 55
Maidenhead United	Mark Franks 23 Lance Cadogan 16 Mark Davis 12	Mark Franks	S. Palfrey, G. Huxley, G. Attrell, R. Mason, A. Brown	Mark Franks 51 + 1s Mark Davis 47 + 1s Richard North 46 + 1s
Metropolitan Police	Mario Russo 40 Nick Matthew 10 Alan Bell 9	Mario Russo (2)		Graham Taylor* Colin Rose Barry Salmon

Oxford City	Colin Tate 34 Bruce McCrae 31 John Doyle 9	Bruce McCrae (2) Colin Tate	Paul Lee Colin Tate	Dave Alexander 55 Dave Burgess 55 Martin Allen 54
Walton & Hersham	Billy Salkeld 16 Gursel Gulfer 15 Peter Fitzgerald 7	Peter Fitzgerald		Gursel Gulfer 59* Ian Stillwell 57 Billy Sakeld 55
Wembley	Richard Cadette 22 Steve Jackson 17 Andy McGonigle 16	Tony Waugh Don Lucas	Ian Whitehead (9) Steve Jackson	Fred Smart 70* 'Spud' Murphy 70* Ian Whitehead 69 Steve Lucas 69
Windsor & Eton	Dave Lansley 27 Chris Yates 26 Trevor Baron 14	Dave Lansley	John Mitchell (3) Chris Yates (2)	Kevin Mitchell 61* Gary Woodcraft 61* Trevor Baron 57

ISTHMIAN LEAGUE
FIRST TEAM MATCH STATISTICS 1983-84

	Leading Goalscorers	**Hat Tricks**	**Penalties**	**Most Appearances**
Barton Rovers	'Chippy' Mead 10 Alan Holt 10 Robbie O'Keefe 9		Alan Dunn (3) N. Mahwinney R. O'Keefe	Robbie O'Keefe 50 Bill Goodyear 49 Alan Holt 42
Basildon United	Colin Russell 27 Alan Hull 23 Vince Cotter 20	Colin Russell (2) Bobby Tappin Alan Hull	Colin Russell (10) Dave Card (2)	Stuart Carmichael 61 Colin Russell 59 Barry Wilson 59
Dorking	Andy Bushnell 37 (club record) Paul Mills 14 Rob Dilger 12	Roy Elcome v Faversham T (FA Vase)	Andy Bushnell (3)	Rob Dilger 58* Paul Otway 58* Andy Bushnell 55
Eastbourne United	Greg Osborne 7 Tim Williams 6 Marcus Cooke 5		Phil Comber (4)	P. Coomber 45 J. Adams 36 K. Fitzpatrick 33
Egham Town	Dave Woodley 13 Dave Osgood 10 Phil Unwin 10 Steve Cordery 10		Dave Osgood (3) Tony O'Connor (2)	Steve Cordery 52 Dobby Dennison 51 Keith Bristow 50
Epping Town	Steve Archer 17 Hugh Burbidge 14 Colin Lenihan 12	Steve Archer v Rainham Hugh Burbidge v Wivenhoe (EST)	Brian Taylor (8) Graham Butterworth	John Meadows 55 Dave Barker 55 Stuart Todd 55
Grays Athletic	Michael Welch 24 John Brennan 14 Trevor Bryson 8	Michael Welch		Steve Jones Phil Sammons John Brennan
Hemel Hempstead	H. Boycott-Brown 15 Mark Dewick 14 Mark Goodson 7 P. Saunders 9	Mark Dewick		Steve Hoar 48 Mark Treadwell 46 Peter Saunders 45 Steve Wilson 45
Hungerford Town	Ian Farr 31 Shane Chandler 20 C. Gwynn 9 D. Bailey 9 K. Bright 9	Farr 4 v Rainham Chandler 4 v Ware Farr 3 v Letchworth Pentland 3 v H. Hempstead (A) Bailey 3 v Rainham	Ian Farr (6)	Shane Chandler 47 Mark Whiffin 46 Simon Pentland 46
Letchworth G.C.	Steve Harris 10 Peter Robinson 5 Martin Beech 5		Vic Pain (3) Martin Bradshaw	Paul Stephens 52* Carl Reyes 49 Steve Harries 47
Leyton Wingate	Steve Godwin 28 Steve Lane 21 Tony Warwick 18	Eligah Bee	Steve Godwin (4)	Andy Mavin 59* Steve Lane 58 Eddie Jones 54
Molesey	John Reader 21 Dave Hanks 11 Frank Hanafin 9		Gary McDonald	Simon Fuller 50 Mick Earley 46 Dave Tippets 46
Newbury Town	Nevada Philips 22 John Griffiths 8 Adrian Cooper 6			
Rainham Town	Allan Roots 12 Steve Kirby 8 Mike Jallow 5		Allan Roots (2) Steve Kirby John Coates	Mike Handleaar 43 Colin Boxall 31 Terry Beck 31
St Albans City	Paul Mayles 36 Laurie Ryan 20 Robin Smale 17	Four	Paul Mayles (10) Terry Benning (4) George Cooper (2) Steve Paterson (2)	Mark Pearson 53* John Watt 51 Steve Oliver 49

Southall	Colin Dennison 25 John Regan 22 Paul Sweales 13	Colin Dennison	Paul Sweales (5) Reg Leather (4)	Ken Lavender 54 John Regan 52 Reg Leather 51
Tring Town	Gary Harthill 27 Graham Coles 17 Joe Maguire 14	G. Coles (4 goals) K. Davies (4 goals) J. Maguire		Stewart Williams 49 Phil Gleadell 49 Alan Paradise 48
Uxbridge	Phil Duff 24 Roy Marshall 9 Chris Dixon 9	Steve Williamson	Roy Marshall (4) Gordon Stewart	Fred Cummins 54 Phil Duff 54 Steve Church 50
Ware	Gary Hayes 16 Peter Twigg 8 Kevin Prosser 8	Kevin Prosser	Gary Hayes 3 Gary Riddle	Richard Turvell 44 Gary Riddle 42 Keith Clemo 34

ISTHMIAN LEAGUE
FIRST TEAM MATCH STATISTICS 1983-84

	Leading Goalscorers	Hat Tricks	Penalties	Most Appearances
Berkhampstead Town	Steve Hayward 23 Steve Woolfrey 13 Paul Hughes 7	S. Hayward 4 v Marlow 3 v Kingsbury	Steve Hayward (7)	Steve Hayward 51* Ray Jeffrey 49 Terry Hows 45
Camberley	Mark Gibbons 5 Ian Setterington 4 Tony Calver 4		N. Shurben (3) K. Ellis (2)	Vernon Pratt 44 Mark Gibbons 42 Tony Calver 42
Chalfont St Peter	Andy Boucher 18 Steve Smith 17 Colin Davies 10	A. Boucher v Ford U Steve Patterson v Thatcham	Seamus Byrne (3) Alan Rooney	Andy Boucher 50* Colin Davies 50* Seamus Byrne 49
Chertsey Town	Ross Mason 11 Steve Wyatt 6 Jezz Griffin 5			Bob Randall 44 Dennis Rogerson 42 Trevor Souter 41
Marlow	Joel Arnett 23 Martin Hunt 11 Paul Dodd 8	Joel Arnett	Neil Wiles Martin Hunt Russell Turner Paul Dodd	Martin Hunt 45 Joel Arnett 44 Mick Farmar 40
Wolverton Town	John Buchanan 12 Gordon Higgins 12 Paul Large 8	Gordon Higgins (2)	Phil Barker	Glyn Creaser 39 Phil Barker 37 Kenny Gregory 37
Banstead	Nicky Cripps 22 Joe McElligott 10 Ged Murphy 8	Nicky Cripps (2) 3 v Fleet 3 v Chalfont St Peter		Steve Black 38 Nicky Cripps 35 Jimmy Bates 34
Ruislip Manor	Paul Rushbrook 13 Steve Long 13 Andrew Skyers 10	Steve Long (all pens) Paul Rushbrook	Steve Long (5)	Steve Long 43 Gary Sutton 36 Richard Burnell 35 Paul Rushbrook 35
Petersfield	Owen McCartney 18 Lennie Phillips 16 Kim Manns 13		Kim Manns (6)	Peter Cottan 46 Kim Manns 44 Micky Gee 43

EX-ISTHMIAN LEAGUE FOOTBALL LEAGUE XI

Paul Barron
(Slough T, Plymouth A, Arsenal, C Palace, WBA)

John Lacy
(Kingstonian, Fulham, Tottenham H)

Eric Young
(Slough T, Brighton)

Steve Hetzke
(Hungerford T, Reading, Blackpool)

Kenny Swain
(Wycombe W, Chelsea, Aston Villa, Nott'm F)

Rachid Harkouk
(Feltham, C Palace, Notts Co)

Terry Hurlock
(Leytonstone, Brentford)

Alan Devonshire
(Southall, West Ham U, England)

Imre Varadi
(Letchworth GC, Sheffield U, Newcastle U, Sheffield W)

Cyrille Regis
(Hayes, WBA, England)

David Crown
(Walthamstow A, Brentford, Portsmouth, Reading)

With just under thirty of their old boys playing with Football League clubs last season it is interesting to note that in this 'eleven' only Slough Town supplied more than one player.

ISTHMIAN LEAGUE — PREMIER DIVISION

	No of clubs competing	22	22	22	22	22	22	22	22	22	22	22
	Season	73/74	74/75	75/76	76/77	77/78	78/79	79/80	80/81	81/82	82/83	83/84
1	Barking	14	17	15	13	10	1	7	18	12	14	16
2	Billericay T							—	—	17	10	15
3	Bishop's Stortford	3	11	12	20	22	—	—	—	15	13	11
4	Bognor Regis T									—	8	13
5	Boreham Wood		—	—	—	15	15	15	21	22	—	—
6	Bromley	19	22	—	—	—	—	—	10	19	15	22
7	Carshalton Ath	—	—	—	—	11	17	19	17	16	16	20
8	Clapton	20	20	22	—	—	—	—	—	—	—	—
9	Corinthian Casuals	22	—	—	—	—	—	—	—	—	—	—
10	Croydon		—	—	15	8	8	20	14	11	11	17
11	Dagenham	—	3	3	3	2	2	5	8			
12	Dulwich Hamlet	4	5	5	21	—	4	3	15	14	6	10
13	Enfield	17	2	1	1	1	3	1	2			
14	Harlow T	—	—	—	—	—	—	11	19	21	—	12
15	Harrow Bor			—	—	—	—	8	9	6	3	1
16	Hayes	10	16	17	18	12	18	17	7	10	4	5
17	Hendon	2	13	6	4	13	9	13	6	13	12	9
18	Hitchin T	13	12	16	9	5	16	12	13	18	20	6
19	Ilford	9	7	4	22	—	—					
20	Kingstonian	15	19	18	17	19	22	—	—	—	—	—
21	Leatherhead	5	6	8	10	7	10	18	16	9	22	—
22	Leytonstone	8	18	20	12	20	21					
23	Leytonstone/Ilford							—	4	1	2	19
24	Oxford C	11	8	21	—	—	19	21	—	—	—	—
25	St Albans C	21	—	—	—	—	—	—	—	—	—	—
26	Slough T	—	9	10	8	16	5	14	1	8	7	3
27	Southall	—	—	19	14	21	—	—	—	—	—	—
28	Staines T	—	—	9	11	17	20	16	11	4	19	14
29	Sutton U	12	10	11	16	6	11	4	5	2	5	4
30	Tilbury	—	—	—	5	18	14	22	—	—	—	—
31	Tooting & Mitcham U	16	4	7	6	4	12	6	12	7	9	21
32	Walthamstow Ave	18	14	13	7	9	13	2	20	5	18	18
33	Walton & Hersham	6	21	—	—	—	—	—	—	—	—	—
34	Woking	7	15	14	19	14	7	9	22	20	21	—
35	Wokingham T	—	—	—	—	—	—	—	—	—	17	8
36	Worthing					—	—	—	—	—	—	2
37	Wycombe W	1	1	2	2	3	6	10	3	3	1	7

Season 1983-84
Leading Goalscorers List
(League and Hitachi Cup)

45	M. Edmunds	Worthing	43 + 2
33	P. Mayles	St Albans City	33
32	M. Russo	Metropolitan Police	30 + 2
28	S. Hill	Epsom & Ewell	28
27	C. Tate	Wycombe Wanderers (17 + 7 with Oxford C)	20 + 7
26	I. Farr	Hungerford Town	26
25	A. Bushnell	Dorking	23 + 2
24	D. Link	Staines Town	24
22	M. Franks	Maidenhead United	22
	G. Duck	Harrow Borough	19 + 3
21	S. Butler	Wokingham Town	19 + 2
20	S. Russell	Hampton	19 + 1
	M. Cox	Woking	20
	G. Harthill	Tring Town	19 + 1
	A. Shodeinde	Leatherhead (9 with Hampton)	20
19	S. Goodwin	Leyton Wingate	19
	S. Baker	Boreham Wood	19
	L. Holmes	Harrow Borough (17 with Harlow T)	19
	S. Read	Staines Town	19
	S. Wallace	Boreham Wood	19
	D. Lambley	Windsor & Eton	18 + 1
	C. Russell	Basildon United	15 + 4
	N. Phillips	Newbury Town	19
18	N. McNeill	Clapton	14 + 4
	D. Pearce	Harrow Borough	18
	T. Glynn	Wycombe Wanderers	15 + 3
	S. Chandler	Hungerford Town	18
	J. Reader	Molesey	18
	G. Coles	Tring Town	18
17	C. Richards	Dulwich Hamlet	16 + 1
	R. Dodds	Slough Town	17
	D. McGrae	Oxford City	15 + 2
	A. Rogers	Tilbury	17
	J. Reagan	Southall	17
16	T. Tuite	Carshalton Athletic	16
	A. Flynn	Aveley	15 + 1
	D. Merron	Corinthian Casuals	15 + 1
	R. Smaile	St Albans City	15 + 1
	G. Hayes	Ware	16
15	M. Joyce	Sutton United	11 + 4
	A. Hull	Basildon United	13 + 2
	V. Cotter	Basildon United	13 + 2
	C. Dennison	Southall	15
	T. Harris	Leytonstone-Ilford	14 + 1
	M. Turkington	Farnborough Town	14 + 1
14	K. Clements	Bognor Regis Town	12 + 2
	K. White	Slough Town	13 + 1
	J. Brown	Wokingham Town	14
	M. Sperrin	Hertford Town	14
	J. Martin	Kingstonian	14
	R. Cadette	Wembley	12 + 2

SERVOWARM ISTHMIAN LEAGUE PLAYERS 1984

(Football League appearances in brackets)

BARKING
Goalkeeper
David Root: Launceston Town.

Defenders
Paul Watts: Local
Dave Burkett: Local
Mark Wright: Dagenham, Enfield, Millwall, Chelsea, Charlton
Eddie Ashdown: Local
Andy Groom: Local
Kevin Cooper: Dagenham, Coventry.

Midfield
Martin Hinshelwood: Kingstonian, Crystal Palace (69-4)
Steve Trice: Tilbury, Leicester City
Paul Shirt: Local
John Harrison: Walthamstow Av, Hayes, Dartford, Charlton Athletic (5-2)
Paul Armstrong: Hornchurch, Hillingdon Borough, Arsenal.

Forwards
Nicky Crown: Epping Town, Grays Athletic
Jimmy Hallybone: Dagenham, Halifax Town (18), Dagenham, Orient (11)
Kevin Barnes: Local
Gary Rolph: Billericay T, Woking, Brentford (12-1)
Nicky Phillips: Coventry C (5).

BILLERICAY TOWN
Goalkeeper
Mark McCutcheon: Leyton-Wingate, Tottenham Hotspur.

Defenders
Paul Blackaller: Brentwood, Bishop's Stortford, Barnet
Tony Cross: Local
Ian Templeton: Colchester United, Ipswich Town
Derek Pedder: Hornchurch, Dagenham
Alan Day: East Thurrock United
Steve Jones: Dagenham, Charlton Athletic, Arsenal
Paul Kerchell: Basildon United
John Pullin: Local.

Midfield
Russell Kean: Barking, Fisher Athletic, Dagenham, Billericay Town, Tilbury, Walthamstow Avenue, Chelsea
Mark Foster: Local
Eddie Nash: Canvey Island, Epping Town
Graham Stewart: Hornchurch, Leytonstone & Ilford, Hendon
Nicky Potts: Local
Paul Wilson: West Ham United.

Forwards
Danny Westwood: Barnet, Gillingham (211-74), QPR (1-1), Billericay Town
Steve Leatt: Local
Tony James: Dulwich Hamlet, Clapton
Clair Darmudas: Chelmsford City, Billericay Town, Chelmsford City, Brighton.

BISHOP'S STORTFORD
Goalkeeper
Alex Welsh: Dunstable, Milton Keynes City, Enfield, Luton Town, Lincoln City, Middlesbrough.

Defenders
Phil Hopkins: Walthamstow Avenue, Chelmsford City
Colin Hull: Watford
Steve Baines: Local
Keith Elley: Dagenham, Enfield, Leytonstone & Ilford, Enfield, Tottenham Hotspur, West Ham United
Ray Wickenden: Harlow Town.

Midfield
Mel Brown: Cambridge United
Ian Smith: Scarborough, Rotherham United, Tottenham Hotspur
Dale Brooks: Ipswich Town
Roger Avery: Cambridge United (1)
Andy Lawrence: Local.

Forwards
Billy Jennings: Luton Town (2-1), Orient (67-21), West Ham United (99-33), Watford (92-33)
Miguel Luque: Harlow Town
Tony Mercer: Clapton, Orient, Crystal Palace, Coventry City
Colin Cardines: Letchworth Garden City
Ben Robb: Walthamstow Avenue.

BOGNOR REGIS TOWN
Goalkeeper
Vijay Korgaokar: Waterlooville, Bognor Regis Town.

Defenders
Steve Parslow: Local
Mark Bird: Local
Dallas Whyte: Waterlooville, Bognor Regis Town
Graham Marriner: Gravesend, Portsmouth
Mick Pullen: Local.

Midfield
Neil Hider: Dorchester Town, Portsmouth
Trevor Cox: Worthing
Steve Chappell: Local
Wayne Orton: Brighton, Littlehampton Town
David Poole: Southampton, Bognor Regis Town
Paul Pullen: Local.

Forwards
Geoff Cooper: Local
Nick Manley: Local
Kevin Clements: Portsmouth
Malcolm Ball: Pagham, Bognor Regis Town
Toby Anderton: Local

Bishop's Stortford top scorer Ben Robb scores against Harlow.

Steve Milton scores Epsom & Ewell's last goal in Division One against Feltham, before they move up to the Premier Division. Photo: Peter Burrin

CARSHALTON ATHLETIC
Goalkeeper
Richard Teale: Staines Town, Slough Town, Wimbledon (15), Fulham (5), QPR (1), Slough Town, Walton & Hersham
Frank Parsons: Slough Town, Woking, Staines Town, AFC Bournemouth, Reading, Cardiff City, Crystal Palace.

Defenders
John Raffington: Croydon
Vic Akers: Slough Town, Hayes, Dartford, Watford, Cambridge United, Tonbridge AFC, Bexley, Tooting & Mitcham United, Fulham
Dave Yerby: Hendon, Slough Town, Tooting & Mitcham United, Slough Town, Hayes, Woking
Tony Tagg: Wimbledon (14), Millwall (133-9), QPR (4)
Tony Maurice: Millwall
Colin Brooks: Kingstonian, Leatherhead, Hitchin Town
Kenny Deacon: Local
Darren Miles: Local.

Midfield
Chris Lewington: Dulwich Hamlet
Gavin Fraser: Sutton United, Wycombe Wanderers
Andy Coghill: Thanet United, Folkestone Town, Gravesend
Micky O'Sullivan: Slough Town, Enfield, Slough Town
Derek Casey: Staines Town, Tooting & Mitcham United, Kingstonian, Leatherhead, Fulham
Paul Dale: Local.

Forwards
Tommy Tuite: Epsom & Ewell, Wimbledon
Trevor Dark: Hendon, Birmingham City (5-1)
Paul Carrell: Local
Gary Gilbert: Harrow Borough, Hayes, Enfield, Luton Town
Gary Mitchell: Local.

CROYDON
Goalkeeper
Steve Dungey: Farleigh Rovers
Terry Fell: Beckenham Town.

Defenders
Mark Denton: Dulwich Hamlet, Chelsea
Tony Jasper: Local
Brian Gayle: Wimbledon
Paul Gbogidi: Local
Stuart Hemsley: Local
Graham Wadley: Wimbledon.

Midfield
Kevin Whitney: Beckenham Town
Ian Paterson: Local
Ian Simpson: Local
Tony Welsh: Local
Phil Smith: Canterbury City
Steve Pattullo: Local.

Forwards
Alec Jackson: Dulwich Hamlet, Chelsea
John McDaid: Local
Tony Paul: Crystal Palace (1)
Marc Flemington: Redhill
Ronnie Hesling: Charlton Athletic
Alan Medcraft: Local
Gary Flemington: Sutton United, Redhill.

DULWICH HAMLET
Goalkeeper
Bobby Knock: Croydon, Wimbledon, Chelsea
David Morgan: Leatherhead, Dulwich Hamlet, Merstham, Whyteleafe, Croydon.

Defenders
Martin Lewis: Croydon, Dulwich Hamlet, Wimbledon
Paul Edwards: Bromley
Alan Roughan: Cheshunt, Hendon, Dulwich Hamlet, Kingstonian
Martin Morgan: Carshalton Athletic, Dulwich Hamlet
Richard Langley: Gillingham
Chris Page: Carshalton Athletic
Tony Baldwin: Dagenham, Tonbridge, Gillingham.

Midfield
Peter Kingston: Carshalton Athletic, Fisher Athletic
Neil Norman: Local
Andy Edwards: Thanet United, Crawley Town, Bromley
Pat Carolan: Carshalton Athletic
Gary Hewitt: Erith & Belvedere, Gateway
Billy Fogarty: Bromley, Canterbury City, Hastings United, Dartford, Dover, Charlton Athletic, Gillingham (28)
Gary Foley: Dagenham, Brentwood.

Forwards
Karl Richards: Local
Paul Hanifan: Kingstonian
Derek Williams: Carshalton Athletic, Tooting & Mitcham United, Tilbury, Sutton United, Brentford
John Palmer: Local
Duncan Bassett: Hampton, Welling United, Tilbury, Maidstone United.

EPSOM AND EWELL
Goalkeeper
Andy Abel: Addlestone
Steve Chapman: Dorking, Hampton, Walton & Hersham, Croydon, Colchester United, Crystal Palace.

Defenders
Steve Delaney: Malden Vale, Epsom & Ewell, Croydon, Carshalton Athletic, Redhill
John Russell: Dorking, Hounslow, Croydon
Chris Hiscock: Beckenham Town
Andy Stewart: Fulham
Robert Winterhalter: Croydon, Sutton United
Russell Harmsworth: Croydon, Redhill, Wimbledon

Barry Walker: Croydon
Robin Lewis: Hampton, Leatherhead, Epsom & Ewell, Wimbledon
Reg Gaston: Bromley, Croydon, Bromley, Croydon.

Midfield
Micky Stratford: Sutton United, Epsom & Ewell, Kingstonian, Woking
Tony Boorman: Crockenhill
Malcolm Spratt: Welling United
Colin Miles: Carshalton Athletic
Ray Woods: Sutton United
Richard Smith: Local.

Forwards
Murray Jones: Welling United, Southend United
Mark Jonas: Dulwich Hamlet, Sutton United
Steve Milton: West Ham United
Alan Morton: Farnborough Town, Walton & Hersham, Wokingham Town, Kingstonian, Woking, Ashford Town, Maidstone United, Stockport County, Crystal Palace, Fulham, Woking
Paul Harding: Sutton United, Whyteleafe
Steve Hill: Hampton, Molesey, Sutton United, Woking.

HARLOW TOWN
Goalkeeper
Julian Drake: Local.

Defenders
Alan Carrington: Enfield, Hayes, Walthamstow Avenue, Cambridge United
Leo Cusenza: Colchester United
Nicky Edkins: Basildon United, Billericay Town, Basildon United
Kevin Ahern: Witham Town
Ray Pask: Local.

Midfield
Owen Griffiths: Local
Micky Taylor: Stansted, Harlow Town
Andy Campbell: Epping Town
Micky Mann: Orient, QPR
Richard Head: Local.

Forwards
Bobby Harding: Enfield, Ilford, Arsenal
Mark Das: Local
Terry Milbourne: Local
Andy Walker: Local.

HARROW BOROUGH
Goalkeeper
Les Currell: Wealdstone, Harrow Borough
Andy Pape: Feltham, Charlton Athletic, Crystal Palace, Ikast (Den), QPR (1)
Nicky Penn: Walthamstow Avenue, Chelmsford City, Gravesend, Chelmsford.

Defenders
Harry Manoe: Ruislip Manor, Southall, Hayes
Ray Metz: Barnet
Derek Harris: Maidenhead United, Wycombe Wanderers, Southall
Gary Fowles: Ruislip Manor, Wembley, Boreham Wood, Wycombe Wanderers, Harrow Borough
Mark Brady: Local
David Howell: Hounslow, Boreham Wood
Colin Payne: Local.

Midfield
Mike Garrini: Boreham Wood, Aylesbury United, Hendon, Tring Town
Steve Emmanuel: Staines Town
Peter Caines: Wembley, Staines Town, Harrow Borough, Kingstonian
Paul Morris: Local
Clevere Forde: Wealdstone, Plymouth Argyle (5), Hounslow
Charlie Flaherty: Local.

Forwards
George Duck: Dagenham, Wealdstone, Southend United
Lawrence Holmes: Harlow Town, Edgware
David Pearce: Wealdstone, Millwall
Ronnie Nelson: Feltham, Wembley
Derek Doyle: Hayes, Bishop's Stortford, Southall.

Two Harrow Borough Championship heroes (above) Captain and player of the year Harry Manoe whose spirited play and excellent leadership epitomises the club itself and (below) George Duck heads home the goal that clinches the Championship. George has now scored 101 goals for Borough in 167 games.
Photos: Stan Allen and Steve Burton

HAYES
Goalkeeper
Paul Hyde: Hillingdon Borough
Alan Cox: Carshalton Athletic, Hayes, Millwall.

Defenders
Mick McGovern: Harrow Borough, Hillingdon Borough, Swindon Town, QPR
Lee Cameron: Southall
Mark Harrison: Local
Steve Hardwick: Slough Town, Wycombe Wanderers
Jimmy Blackman: Local
Robbie Johnson: Brentford (2), Arsenal.

Midfield
Jimmy Richardson: Aylesbury United, Addlestone, Wokingham Town, Napier City (NZ), Aldershot (120-6), Fulham (70-6), Brentford (85-7), Millwall (1)
Glen Hayward: Brentford, Hounslow
Steve Parsons: Orient (36-6), Wimbledon (94-19), Walton & Hersham
Roy Davies: Wealdstone, Hayes, Woking, Wimbledon (9), Torquay United (70-6), Reading (37-2), Slough Town
Micky Scott: Local
Keith James: Staines Town, Woking, Hayes, Walthamstow Avenue, Slough Town.

Forwards
Micky Kiely: Slough Town
Larry Bascoe: Local
Byron Walton: Aylesbury United, Millwall
Graham Drake: Kingstonian, Feltham
Mark Cobb: Hampton
Peter Kemp: Staines Town, Sutton United, Maidstone United, Folkestone Town, Dover.

HENDON
Goalkeeper
Clive Kemplen: Enfield.

Defenders
Robbie Holland: Harrow Borough
Gary Hand: Harrow Borough, Wycombe Wanderers, Hendon, Enfield, Hendon, Wealdstone, Watford
Andy O'Brien: Local
Andy Waddock: Wealdstone
Billy Macmillan: Local
Richard Bradford: Bishop's Stortford, Walthamstow Avenue, Sutton United, Kingstonian.

Midfield
Peter Stapleton: Local
Steve Wilkins: Chesham United, Hayes, Chelsea
Adrian Smith: Harrow Borough
Stewart Mitchell: Hampton, Hayes, Gateshead
Dermot Drummy: Arsenal (5)
Alan Anderson: Local
Mick Donnelly: Azzuri (Australia).

Forwards
Gary Allen: Boreham Wood, Dulwich Hamlet, Carshalton Athletic, Birmingham City
Steve Kirkby: Local
Steve Hudson: Wembley, Boreham Wood, Tottenham Hotspur
Barry Henley: Local
Steve Smith: Harrow Borough

HITCHIN TOWN
Goalkeeper
Tony Luff: Bedford Town
Steve Young: Local.

Defenders
John Woodward: Hendon, Hitchin Town, Luton Town
Steve Gear: Arlesey Town, Barton Rovers, Letchworth Garden City, Hitchin
Steve Fountain: Barton Rovers, Letchworth Garden City, Milton Keynes City, Kempston Rovers, Bedford Town, Charlton Athletic
Ian McDonald: Cambridge United
Ian Kavanagh: Bedford Town
Neil Kirkpatrick: Local.

Midfield
Alan West: Millwall (58-4), Minnesota Kicks (USA), Luton Town (285-16), Burnley (44-3)
Neil Madden: Luton Town (1)
Micky Nunn: Westmills
Alan Cosby: Hendon, Luton Town
Mike Green: Local
Steve Miller: Local.

Forwards
Trevor Parker: Letchworth Garden City
Mick Every: Cambridge City
Tony Wilkinson: Local
Paul Giggle: Pirton, Baldock Town, Hitchin Town, Letchworth Garden City, Hitchin Town, Limbury BC
Peter Harvey: Cambridge United
Clive Bloomfield: Local.

LEYTONSTONE AND ILFORD
Goalkeeper
Ricky Frost: Local
Mark O'Leary: Local.

Defenders
Terry McCarthy: AFC Bournemouth
Phil Stacey: Walthamstow Avenue, Bishop's Stortford
Ken Francis: Local
Paul Baxter: Crystal Palace (1), Tottenham Hotspur
Steve Fearey: Walthamstow Avenue
Tommy Horan: Dagenham, West Ham United
Martin McCayna: Aveley, Southend United.

Midfield
John Lumsden: Stoke City (6), East Fife
Jamie McCayna: Local
Frank Coles: Charlton Athletic
John Bantick: Walthamstow Avenue
Ronnie Howell: Walthamstow Avenue, Barnet, Dagenham, Enfield, Leytonstone & Ilford, Tooting & Mitcham, Swindon Town, Kettering Town, Cambridge United, Millwall.

Forwards
Terry Harris: Enfield, Sutton United, Dagenham
Steve Edkins: Local
Chris Draper: Bromley, Walthamstow Avenue
John Berry: Local
Dave Clarke: Frenford.

Slough Town's Rowan Dodds scores his 50th first team goal, against Croydon.
Photo: Slough & Eton Observer

SLOUGH TOWN
Goalkeeper
Peter Ratkley: Local
Paul Mitchell: Eton Town.
Defenders
Eddie Hutchinson: Brentford, QPR, Chelsea
Peter Skerritt: Local
Francis Araguez: Local
Mark Scriaraffa: Local
Dave O'Flaherty: Local
Steve Norman: Wycombe Wanderers, Molesey, Slough Town.
Midfield
Keith White: Burnham
Gary Attrell: Britwell Hawks
Dave Russell: Marlow, Maidenhead United, Marlow, Burnham, Slough Town
Howard Kennedy: Wycombe Wanderers
Derek Sweetman: Local.
Forwards
Rowan Dodds: Local
Dylan Evans: Hillingdon, Wealdstone, Aylesbury United, Wycombe Wanderers, Cheltenham Town
Devon Petty: Hillingdon, Slough Town, Molesey, Slough Town, Southampton
Tony Gibson: Local.

STAINES TOWN
Goalkeeper
Paul Allies: Chesham United, Staines Town, Epsom & Ewell, Tottenham Hotspur
Peter Lara: Local.
Defenders
Jamie Williamson: Local
Steve Livey: Addlestone
Kevin Fidler: Ashford Town
Dave Jordan: Local
Kevin Tilley: Hayes, Aylesbury United, Maidstone United, Wimbledon (13), QPR
Kevin Collins: Slough Town, Wimbledon.
Midfield
Chris Wheatley: Brentford
Gary Powell: Local
Peter Rumley: Kingstonian, Staines Town
Gary Jones: Local.
Forwards
Declan Link: QPR
Keith Weaver: Walton & Hersham
Simon Read: Local
Keith Seager: Walton & Hersham, Egham Town, Kingstonian.

SUTTON UNITED
Goalkeeper
Dave Collyer: Staines Town, Kingstonian, Slough Town, Dagenham, Woking
Clive Offer: Leatherhead, Sutton United.
Defenders
Roger Mackay: Hendon, Hayes, Staines Town, Slough Town
John Roles: Portsmouth, Southampton
Tony Rains: Fulham, Sutton United
Mark Golley: Crystal Palace
Andy Sunnocks: Croydon
Paul Estall: Leatherhead
Steve Bangs: Carshalton Athletic, Sutton United.
Midfield
Micky Stephens: Local
Lee Batt: Millwall, West Ham United
John Rains: Bromley, Fulham
Steve Tutt: Local
Nigel Golley: Local
Paul Rogers: Local
Ricky Kidd: Dagenham, Sutton United, Redhill.
Forwards
Paul McKinnon: Tollesbury (Swe), Ryoden Sports (Hong Kong), Malmo (Swe), Sutton United, Woking, Chelsea
Steve Galloway: Bromley, Dulwich Hamlet
Ray Sunnocks: Croydon
Micky Joyce: Local
Paul Thornton: Local

Dave Collyer (Sutton United) who has retired after a distinguished career in which his quality goalkeeping has been matched by his excellent sportsmanship.

TOOTING AND MITCHAM UNITED

GOALKEEPERS	
Nicky Sullivan	Woking, Arsenal
DEFENDERS	
Danny Godwin	Dulwich Hamlet, Wimbledon, Chelsea
Peter Ranson	Leatherhead, Tonbridge, Crawley Town, Horsham, Crystal Palace
Warren Farrow	Local
Bob Pittaway	Barnet, Tooting & Mitchem United, Dartford, Chelmsford City, Millwall, Charlton Athletic
Steve Ward	Local
Dave Cracknell	Local
Billy Edwards	Leatherhead, Tooting & Mitcham United, Bromley, Maidstone United, Wimbledon (21-2), Walton & Hersham, Tottenham Hotspur
MIDFIELD	
Micky Sorensen	Woking, Tooting & Mitcham United, Hitchin Town, Sutton United, Wimbledon, Chelsea
Gary Waterman	Wimbledon, Dulwich Hamlet
Alan Budden	Crawley Town, Dartford, Maidstone United, Faversham Town
Neil Ayrton	Hastings United, Maidstone United, Portsmouth (2), Maidstone United
Dave Juneman	Southall, Croydon
Manny Lomotey	Local
FORWARDS	
Butch Dunn	Bromley, Fisher Athletic
Carlton Fairweather	Bromley, Dulwich Hamlet
Ashton Stirling	Hastings United, Maidstone United
Stan Alexander	Hendon, Lynn Oslo (Nor), Harlow Town, Barnet, Barking, Tilbury
Richard Wilson	Hango Idrottsclub (Den), Dagenham, Dartford, Barking, Charlton Athletic (17-1), Chelsea
Jon Warden	Croydon
Keith Hider	Carshalton Athletic

WALTHAMSTOW AVENUE
Goalkeeper
Lee Hunter: West Ham United

Wokingham Town's top scorer Steve Butler, who also had a great season for the Army, in action against Hayes. Photo: Steve Peters

Defenders
Dickie Empson: Boreham Wood
Billy Harrigan: Bishop's Stortford, Cambridge United
John Kane: Orient
Peter Hickey: Hornchurch, West Ham United
Kevin Dare: Crystal Palace (6)
Mark Warburton: Enfield, Leicester City
Dave Silman: Brentford (1), Wolves
Paul Bergonzi: Local

Midfield
John Borland: Leytonstone & Ilford, Enfield, Dagenham, Queen's Park
Ali Sylvester: Wealdstone, Hendon, Cheshunt, Hendon
Brian Kelly: Woodford Town, Walthamstow Avenue
Tony Reilly: Crystal Palace
Alan Hunter: Harlow Town

Forwards
Kimm Connett: Tooting & Mitcham United, Dulwich Hamlet, Charlton Athletic, Dulwich Hamlet
Henry Clark: Dartford, Leytonstone & Ilford
Devon Gayle: Hendon, Cheshunt, Hendon
Darren Dennis: Dulwich Hamlet, Dagenham
Norman Milne: Leytonstone & Ilford, Enfield, Sutton United, Hendon, Billericay Town

WINDSOR AND ETON
Goalkeeper
Kevin Mitchell: Slough Town, Leatherhead, Woking, Windsor & Eton, Egham Town

Defenders
Gary Woodcraft: Reading
Kevin Osnowski: Local
Trevor Baron: Alton Town, Marlow, Burnham, Chertsey
John Mitchell: Woking, Windsor & Eton, Hayes, Windsor & Eton, Egham Town
Gary Edwards: Woking, Windsor & Eton, Harefield United, Southall
Colin Smith: Woking, Windsor & Eton, Uxbridge

Midfield
Bob King: Woking, Windsor & Eton, Alton Town, Farnham Town
Hans Van Den Berg: Molesey, Addlestone, Egham Town, Walton & Hersham, Addlestone, Slough Town
Kevin Hill: Slough Town, Woking, Windsor & Eton, Arcadia Shepherds (SA), Wealdstone, Amersham Town
Laurie Craker: Chesham United, Staines Town, Hayes, Dartford, Watford (66-4), Chelsea
Jeff Chapman: Woking, Windsor & Eton, Slough Town, Egham Town, Hayes
Floyd Dennis: Local

Former Sutton United Trophy finalist Mike Cornwell, who played at Wembley despite the worry of a pending brain tumour operation, has made a complete recovery and finished second highest scorer for Worthing as the Sussex club achieved the Isthmian League runners up position.
Photo: Worthing Gazette and Herald

Forwards
Ross McCulloch: Woking, Windsor & Eton, Alton Town, Fleet Town, Basingstoke Town
Dave Lansley: Local
Steve Giddings: Hampton, Chertsey, Woking, Camberley Town
Gary Huxley: Chesham United, Staines Town, Hayes, Dartford, Aylesbury United, Weymouth, Hillingdon, Brentford
Chris Yates: Farnham Town, Alton Town

WOKINGHAM TOWN
Goalkeeper
Doug Hatcher: Aldershot, Wokingham Town, Wimbledon, Fulham
Steve Aldham: Local

Defenders
Tommy Ryan: Hounslow, Hillingdon Borough, Reading
Kirk Corbin: Cambridge United (3), Wokingham Town
David Cox: Local
Sean Price: Newbury Town, Wycombe Wanderers, Reading
Bobby Purser: Local
John Wilks: Hayes, Slough Town, QPR

Midfield
Bobby Saunders: Farnborough Town, Camberley Town
Des McMahon: Reading (2), Wokingham Town, Hungerford Town, Hackley
Derek Cottrell: Woking, Wycombe Wanderers
Roger Steer: Addlestone, Camberley Town, Woking, Reading, Chelsea
Richard Berkij: Local

Forwards
Jimmy Brown: Hillingdon Borough, Wokingham Town
Neal Stanley: Local
Steve Butler: Windsor & Eton
Jimmy Sweetzer: Leatherhead, Dartford, Wealdstone, Millwall, Oxford United (11-2)
Terry Brown: Hayes, Sutton United, Slough Town

WORTHING
Goalkeeper
Alan Dovey: Southwick, Brighton, Chelsea

Defenders
Gary Elphick: Eastbourne United, Lewes, Orient, Stoke City, Lewes
Russell Cox: Steyning Town, Bognor Regis Town, Leatherhead, Brighton
Mark Nye: Brighton, Worthing
Tony Vessey: Steyning Town, Vasalund (Swe), Brighton (1)
Geoff Raynsford: Lewes, Horsham, Worthing
Martin Cox: Brighton

Midfield
Jimmy Quigg: Steyning Town, Littlehampton Town, Worthing
Paul Lelliott: Local
Micky Cornwell: Sutton United, Horsham, Eastbourne United
Trevor Dove: Burgess Hill, Lewes, Haywards Heath

Forwards
Mick Edmonds: Southwick
Pip Parris: Lewes, West Ham United
Kevin Foreman: Eastbourne United, Horsham, Dover, Worthing
Russell Barnard: Local

WYCOMBE WANDERERS
Goalkeeper
Gary Lester: Chalfont St Peter
Chris Way: Local

Defenders
Jim Jacobs: Northampton Town, Wycombe Wanderers
Graham Pearce: Local
Trevor How: Aylesbury United, Watford (91-2)
Andy Harman: Local
Anton Vircavs: Pressed Steel
Mark Hill: Brentford (56-3), QPR
Robin Turner: Local

Midfield
Kevin Edwards: QPR
Bob Dell: Local
Richard Mikurenda: Local
Paul West: Flackwell Heath
Terry Glynn: Enfield, Leytonstone & Ilford, Brentford, Orient (2)

Forwards
Ken Wilson: Hounslow, Walton & Hersham
Steve Perrin: Northampton Town (22-5), Hillingdon, Portsmouth (28-3), Plymouth Argyle (35-6), Crystal Palace (48-11), Wycombe Wanderers
Steve Thorne: Marlow
Roger Moore: Local
Henry Pacquette: Slough Town, Wembley, Boreham Wood, Hendon, Harrow Borough
Steve Long: Loughborough College, Burton Albion

CONSTITUTION FOR THE LEAGUE FOR SEASON 1984/85

Premier Division
Barking
Billericay Town
Bishops Stortford
Bognor Regis Town
Carshalton Athletic
Croydon
Dulwich Hamlet
Epsom & Ewell
Harlow Town
Harrow Borough
Hayes
Hendon
Hitchin Town
Leytonstone/Ilford
Slough Town
Sutton United
Tooting & Mitcham U
Walthamstow Avenue
Windsor & Eton
Wokingham Town
Worthing
Wycombe Wanderers

Division 1
Aveley
Basildon United
Boreham Wood
Bromley
Chesham United
Clapton
Farnborough Town
Hampton
Hertford Town
Hornchurch
Kingstonian
Leatherhead
Lewes
Maidenhead United
Metropolitan Police
Oxford City
St Albans City
Staines Town
Tilbury
Walton & Hersham
Wembley
Woking

Division 2 North
Barton Rovers
Berkhamsted Town
Chalfont St Peter
Cheshunt
Epping Town
Finchley
Flackwell Heath
Harefield United
Haringey Borough
Hemel Hempstead
Heybridge Swifts
Kingsbury Town
Letchworth Gdn City
Leyton Wingate
Marlow
Royston Town
Saffron Walden Town
Stevenage Borough
Tring Town
Ware
Wolverton Town

Division 2 South
Banstead Athletic
Bracknell Town
Camberley
Chertsey Town
Corinthian Casuals
Dorking
Eastbourne United
Egham Town
Feltham
Grays Athletic
Horsham
Hungerford Town
Molesey
Newbury Town
Petersfield United
Rainham Town
Ruislip Manor
Southall
Uxbridge
Whyteleafe

SERVOWARM ISTHMIAN LEAGUE

PREMIER DIVISION

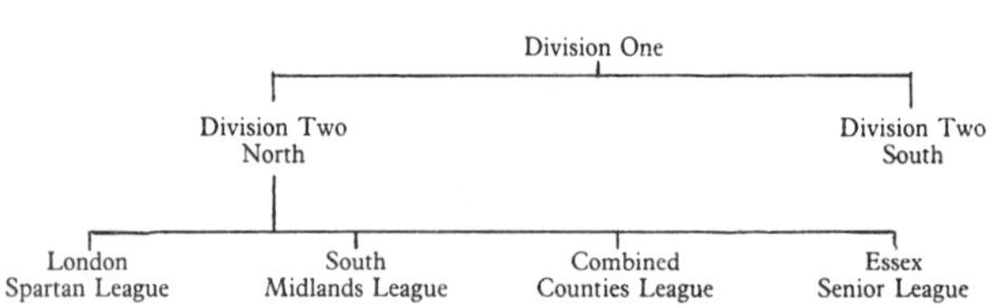

The four champion clubs seeking election to the regional Isthmian Division Two's would be allocated places depending on their geographical location providing they received more votes than the four clubs seeking re-election.

Harrow Borough *Back Row (L-R): A. McDade (physio), G. Fowles, D. Pearce, D. Harris, L. Currell, A. Pape, D. Howell, R. Morris, H. Manoe, G. Duck, B. Laing (coach). Front Row (L-R): L. Holmes, S. Jones, R. Metz, D. Doyle, M. Tomkys (manager), C. Flaherty, S. Emmanuel, C. Forde, R. Nelson.*
Photo: Harrow Observer

HARROW BOROUGH

Chairman: P. K. Rogers
Manager: Mike Tomkys
Coach: Brian Laing
Physiotherapist: Andy McDade
Press Officer & Tel No: Peter Cass (01-866 8029)
Secretary: B. Rogers
Address & Tel No: 01-422 8606
Commercial Manager: None
Address & Tel No:
Club Historian: Tony Booth (01-790 6532)
Address & Tel No of ground: Earlsmead, Carlyon Avenue, South Harrow, Middx. HA2 8SS. 01-422 5989-Foyer, 01-422 5221-Manager
Club shop: Yes
Simple ground directions: LTE stations Northolt (Central Line), South Harrow (Piccadilly Line) then H1 or 114 bus
No of seats: 150 **Covered accommodation:** 2 sides **Capacity:** 4,000 **Floodlights:** Yes
Year formed: 1933 **Nickname:** The Boro **Club sponsors:** Whitbread Ltd/Scottish & Newcastle Ltd
Previous names: Harrow Town, Roxonian
Club colours: All Red
Previous grounds: Northolt Rd
Change colours: All Blue All Yellow
Day for midweek home matches: Tuesday
Record attendance: 3,000+ F.A. Cup, v Wealdstone **Year:** 1946
Best performance in: **F.A. Cup:** 1983-4 2nd Round Proper
F.A. Trophy: 1982-3, Semi-finalist
Previous Leagues: Harrow & Dist, Spartan, West Middx Comb, Middx Senior, Delphian, Athenian
Clubhouse details: Open seven days a week normal daily licensing hours. Four bars, ballroom, games room, varied entertainment. Venue for major sporting occasions.
Present players with Football League experience: George Duck (Southend Utd), Clevere Forde (Plymouth Argyle), Ray Knowles (Wimbledon), David Pearce (Millwall)
Past players who progressed into the Football League: Terry Eden (Raith R), Denis Russell (Arsenal), Ron Shaw (Torquay), Micky Bottans (QPR), Mal Lucas (Leyton Orient, Wales), Dave Bassett (Wimbledon), David Kemp (Crystal Palace), Gary Borthwich (Bournemouth), Chris Hutchings (Chelsea), Mick Doherty (Reading)
Record transfer fee paid: To Dagenham for George Duck and Steve Jones
Record transfer fee received: £10,000, Chris Hutchings (Chelsea)
Programme details: 16 pages, 20p
Local newspapers & Tel No: Harrow Observer 01-427 4404
Programme Editor: Peter Cass
Club metal badges: Yes
Senior Honours: Harrow & District League Runners-up, Spartan League Div. 2 (West) and Runners-up, Spartan League Prem Div Runners-up, Athenian League Div. 2 Runners-up, Isthmian League Div. 1 Runners-up, Middlesex Senior Cup, Middlesex Charity Cup, Isthmian League Champions
Club Captain (1983-4): Harry Manoe **Player of the Year (1983-4):** Harry Manoe

Worthing FC *Back Row (L-R): Sam Harper (Trainer), Tony Vessey, Mike Cornwell, Geoff Raynsford (Captain), Alan Dovey, Res. goalkeeper, Russell Barnard, Bruce Aitken, Trevor Dove, Keith Rowley (Assistant Manager), Barry Lloyd (Manager). Front Row (L-R): Paul Lelliott, Danny Deans, Kevin Foreman, Jimmy Quigg, Russell Cox, Martin Cox, Mark Nye. Missing from picture: Mick Edmonds.*

WORTHING

President: E. T. Ryan
Chairman: M. L. Hollis
Manager: Barry Lloyd
Coach: Barry Lloyd
Physiotherapist: Derek Palmer
Press Officer & Tel No: As Secretary

Secretary: S. A. Rooke
Address & Tel No: 168 Tarring Rd, Worthing. Worthing 201322 (H) Brighton 680231 (B)
Commercial Manager: Barry Lloyd
Address & Tel No: c/o club headquarters

Address & Tel No of ground: Woodside Road, Worthing, West Sussex BN14 7HQ. Tel Worthing 39575 (office), Worthing 39417 (clubhouse)
Club shop: Yes
Simple ground directions: A24 into Worthing, ground 5 mins walk from Worthing Central BR S.R. Station
No of seats: 700 **Covered accommodation:** 800 **Capacity:** 6,000 **Floodlights:** Yes
Year formed: 1886 **Nickname:** The Rebels **Club sponsors:** Anglia Building Society
Previous names: None **Club colours:** All Red, White/Blue trim
Previous grounds: None **Change colours:** White/Blue/White
Day for midweek home matches: Wednesdays
Record attendance: 5,000 F.A. Amateur Cup Quarter-Final **Year:** 1907-8
Best performance in: **F.A. Cup:** 1982-83 2nd Round
F.A. Trophy: 1978-9 2nd Qual Round
Previous Leagues: Sussex County, Corinthian, Athenian
Clubhouse details: Open every evening, various functions including Old Tyme Ballroom Dancing, Discos, Darts for members
Present players with Football League experience: Alan Dovey (Chelsea, Brighton), Barry Lloyd (Chelsea, Fulham, Hereford, Brentford)
Past players who progressed into the Football League: None
Record transfer fee paid: None
Record transfer fee received: None
Programme details: 24 pages, 25p
Programme Editor: S. Rooke
Club metal badges: Yes
Local newspapers & Tel No: Worthing Gazette, West Sussex Gazette, Evening Argus
Senior Honours: Servowarm Isthmian League, Premier Div Runners-up, Div1 Champions, Berger Isthmian League Div2, Sussex Senior Cup (20), Sussex County League, Sussex Rur Cup •
Club Captain (1983-84): Geoff Raynsford **Player of the Year (1983-84):** Geoff Raynsford/Mick Edmonds (joint)

Slough Town *Back Row (L-R): Gary Attrell, Joe Mahoney, Eddie Hutchinson, Frank Parsons, Steve Norman, Henry Pacquette, Dylan Evans. Front Row (L-R): Vaughan Powell, Mick Doherty, Tony Doherty, Keith White, Francis Araguez.* Photo: Slough Express

SLOUGH TOWN

Chairman: G. W. Greig
Vice Chairman: R. E. Goodhram
Manager: Terry Reardon
Ass. Manager: Howard Kennedy
Coach:
Physiotherapist: Dick Errington
Secretary: R. White 0753
Address & Tel No: Slough 27036 (H)

Commercial Manager: R. Bampton
Address & Tel No: Slough 33897
Press Officer & Tel No: J. Tebbit (Slough 27036)
Address & Tel No of ground: Wexham Park Stadium, Wexham Road, Slough, Berks. Slough 23358/9 **Club shop:** Yes
Simple ground directions: A412 off A4 (Slough by-pass), turn left into Broadway Road, continue for the complete length, turn right into Wexham Road, stadium approx. 1 mile on left
No of seats: 395 **Covered accommodation:** 900 **Capacity:** 8,000 **Floodlights:** Yes
Year formed: 1888 **Nickname:** The Rebels **Club sponsors:** Norman Reeves (Slough) Motors
Previous names: Slough, Slough United **Club colours:** Amber shirts, Blue shorts, Blue/Amber socks
Day for midweek home matches: Tuesday **Change colours:** White shirts, Blue shorts/socks
Previous Grounds: Dolphin (1888-1940), Slough Cricket Club (1940-42), York Road (1942-43), Stadium Centre (1943-46), Dolphin (1946-74)
Record attendance: 10,000 v Pegasus, Amateur Cup (at Dolphin) **Year:** 1953
10,000 v Skelmersdale, Amateur Cup (at Dolphin) **Year:** 1968
5,000 v Millwall, FA Cup (at Wexham Park) **Year:** 1982
Best performance in: **F.A. Cup:** 1970-1 v Barnet 0-1, 1978-9 v Yeovil 0-1, 2nd Round
F.A. Trophy: 1976-7 v Dagenham, 0-3/2-3, Semi-Final
Previous Leagues: Southern Alliance, Berks & Bucks, Gt Western Suburban, Spartan, Herts & Middx Corinthian, Athenian
Clubhouse details: Lounge, games and TV room and main hall (seat 350 for meals). Regular entertainment, food available.
Present players with Football League experience: P. Rackley (Reading), E. Hutchinson (Chelsea, QPR, Millwall, Brentford)
Past players who progressed into the Football League: Paul Barron, David Kemp, Roy Davies, Micky Droy
Record transfer fee paid: £3,000 to Woking for Frank Parsons
Record transfer fee received: £22,000 from Brighton for Eric Young
Programme details: 40 pages, 25p
Club metal badges: Yes
Local newspapers & Tel No: Slough & Eton Observer; Slough, Windsor & Eton Express; Midweek Post; Slough Leader; Reading Evening Post
Senior Honours: Isthmian Champions, Isthmian Div 1, Isthmian League Cup (2), Athenian League (4), Athenian League Cup (2), Corinthian League, Berks & Bucks Cup (9), Amateur Cup Finalists

Alan Hull scores Basildon United's first goal of their championship season with a firm close range header at Newbury. Photo: Newbury Weekly News.

The lights went out, literally, on Gravesend's FA Trophy ambitions at Worthing. A blown fuse at half time meant a stoppage before the second half could be started and two goals by the Isthmian club in this period put them through. Photo: David Hills

A brilliant save miraculously foils Hungerford Town's star goalscorer Ian Farr. Pearson of St Albans saves with his feet from point blank range. Photo: Newbury Weekly News.

Barking *Back Row (L-R): Roy Clark (secretary), Ernie Walley (manager), Kevin Cooper, Nicky Phillips, Paul Shirt, David Root, Kevin Barnes, Andy Groom, Martin Hinshelwood, David Patience (assistant manager). Front Row (L-R): John McFarlane, Nicky Crown, Jimmy Hallybone, John Harrison, Paul Watts.* Photo: Gordon Barker

BARKING

President: J. Poneskis
Chairman: P. Thompson
Secretary: John Wilson
Address & Tel No: 01-590 7668 (H) 01-472 1430 x3587 (B)

Manager: Ernie Walley
Assist. Manager: David Patience
Physiotherapist: Brian Bromfield
Commercial Manager:
Address & Tel No:
Press Officer & Tel No: Ron Murrant, 01-471 6233 (H), 01-626 1567 x3171 (B)
Address & Tel No of ground: Mayebrook Park, Lodge Ave., Dagenham, Essex. 01-595 6511/592 7841 **Club shop:** No
Simple ground directions: Underground Barking Station then 162 or 5 bus.
No of seats: 210 **Covered accommodation:** 560 **Capacity:** 4,200 **Floodlights:** Yes
Year formed: 1880 **Nickname:** The Blues **Club sponsors:** None
Previous names: Barking Woodville, Barking Town
Club colours: All Blue
Previous grounds: Vicarage Field
Change colours: All Yellow
Day for midweek home matches: Tuesday
Record attendance: 1,972 v Aldershot F.A. Cup 2nd Round **Year:** 1978
Best performance in: F.A. Cup: 2nd Round 1978-9, 1979-80, 1981-2 and 1983-4
F.A. Trophy: 2nd Round 1979-80
Previous League: South Essex, London, Athenian
Clubhouse details: Dressing rooms with showers, members bar, main hall with bar, car park for 250 cars.
Present players with Football League experience: Martin Hinshelwood (Crystal Palace), Nicky Phillips (Coventry), Jimmy Hallybone (Orient), John McFarlane (Coventry), Kevin Cooper (Coventry)
Past players who progressed into the Football League: Abrahams (Charlton), Kevin Hitchcock (Nottm Forest)
Record transfer fee received: For Kevin Hitchcock (1983) (Nottm Forest) **Paid:** None
Programme details: 20 pages, 20p
Programme Editor: Mike Roberts
Club metal badges: No
Local newspapers & Tel No: Barking & Dagenham Independent 01-597 2613, Barking and Dagenham Advertiser 01-472 1421, Barking & Dagenham Post
Senior Honours: South Essex, London Lge, Athenian Lge, Essex Senior (5), London Senior (4), Dylon Shield, Isthmian Lge Winners
Club Captain (1983-4): Nicky Phillips
Player of the Year (1983-4): David Root

Billericay Town *Back Row (L-R): Roy Battram (coach), Brian King (physio), Paul Gilbert, Graham Stewart, Freddie Clayden, Tony Cross, Mark McCutcheon, Simon Doran, Eddie Nash, Dave Emerick (manager). Front Row: Graham Franklin (not with club), Dave Brown, John Pullin, Paul Kerchell, John McCombe, Tony James, Danny Westwood.* Photo: Steve Lindsell

BILLERICAY TOWN

President: L. Wernick
Chairman: G. F. Hackwell
Manager: Dave Emerick
Coach: Bill Wooten
Physiotherapist::

Secretary: B. King
Address & Tel No: 250 Gloucester Avenue, Chelmsford, Essex CM2 9LB. Tel. Chelmsford 260231 (H), Chelmsford 56281 ext. 40 (B)
Commercial Manager: Harold Rumsey
Address & Tel No: Shoebury (037-08) 4454

Press Officer & Tel No: Len Dewson (Billericay 22375) **Club shop:** Yes
Address & Tel No of ground: New Lodge, Blunts Wall Rd, off Tye Common Rd, Billericay, Essex. Tel: (027 74) 52188
Simple ground directions: From Shenfield (A129) turn right at first traffic lights, then first road on right. From Basildon (A129) proceed over first traffic lights in the town, then left at 2nd traffic lights and first road on the right
No of seats: 250 **Covered accommodation:** 250 **Capacity:** 3,500 **Floodlights:** Yes
Year formed: 1890 **Nickname:** Town **Club sponsors:** None
Previous names: None
Previous grounds: Archer Hall, Laindon Road
Club colours: Blue shirts/socks, White shorts/trim
Change colours: Red shirts/socks, White shorts
Day for midweek home matches: Tuesday
Record attendance: 3,641 v West Ham Utd, inaugural floodlit match **Year:** 1977
Best performance in: **F.A. Cup:** 1977-8 v Hendon 4th Qual. Rnd, lost 2-3
F.A. Trophy/Vase: F.A. Vase winners. F.A. Trophy 3rd Q.
Previous Leagues: Romford & District, Mid Essex, Essex Olympian, Essex Senior, Athenian
Clubhouse details: Open each evening (except Monday) and Saturday & Sunday lunchtimes. Discos, live entertainment, bar snacks, etc. Steward: Jack Bartlett. Alcoves on ground floor. Glass fronted viewing gallery first floor.
Present players with Football League experience: Danny Westwood (QPR, Gillingham)
Past players who progressed into the Football League: Danny Westwood (QPR, Gillingham)
Record transfer fee paid: Not disclosed
Record transfer fee received: Not disclosed
Programme details: 24 pages, 25p
Programme editor: Len Dewson
Club metal badges: Yes, 65p each
Local Newspapers & Tel No: Billericay Gazette, Chelmsford 62421; Billericay Recorder, Basildon 22651; Evening Echo, Basildon 22791
Senior Honours: F.A. Vase (3), Essex Senior League (3), Cup (4), Athenian (2), Isthmian Div 2, Runners-up Div 1, Rothmans Football Yearbook Award, Essex Senior Cup, Essex Senior Trophy (2)
Club Captain (1983-84): Paul Blackaller **Player of the Year (1983-84):** Mark McCutcheon

Wokingham Town's John Wilks sails in to clear ahead of Bishop Stortford's ex-West Ham United star, Billy Jennings. Photo: Eric Marsh.

BISHOP'S STORTFORD

Chairman: E. A. Bentley
Manager: Trevor Harvey
Coach: John Radford
Physiotherapist: Dusty Miller

Secretary: James L. M. Gill
Address & Tel No: 71 Warwick Road, Bishops Stortford. Tel. 0279 53569 (H)
Commercial Manager: E. A. Bentley
Address & Tel No: 0279 54237 (B)

Press Officer & Tel No: John McCree. Harlow 28453 (H)
Address & Tel No of ground: George Wilson Stadium, Rhodes Avenue. 0279 54140 **Club shop:** Yes
Simple ground directions: M11 to Junction 8, A120 to Bishop's Stortford. From station, 800 yds
No of seats: 228 **Covered accommodation:** 1,500 **Capacity:** 6,000 **Floodlights:** Yes
Year formed: 1874 **Nickname:** 'Blues' or 'Bishops' **Club sponsors:** None
Previous names: None
Previous grounds: None
Club colours: Blue/White stripes, White shorts
Change colours: All Yellow
Day for midweek home matches: Tuesday
Record attendance: 6,000 v Peterborough FA Cup 2nd Round **Year:** 1972
6,000 v Middlesbrough FA Cup 3rd Round **Year:** 1983
Best performance in: **F.A. Cup:** 1983 v Middslesbrough, 3rd Round replay
F.A. Trophy: Winners 1981
Previous Leagues: Herts County, Delphian, Athenian
Clubhouse details: Open match days, training nights or private functions. Two bars, three tea bars.
Present players with Football League experience: J. Radford (Arsenal), I. Smith (Spurs)
Past players who progressed into the Football League: P. Phillips, M. Brown, R. Avery (Camb U)
Record transfer fee paid/received: Club does not disclose any fees
Programme details: 12 pages, 20p
Programme Editor: John McCree
Club metal badges: Yes
Local newspapers & Tel No: Herts & Essex Observer Bishop Stortford Gazette/Citizen
Senior Honours: F.A. Trophy, F.A. Amateur Cup, London Senior Cup, Herts Senior Cup (8), Isthmian League Div 1, East Anglian Cup, Herts Charity Cup (2)
Club Captain (1983-84): Keith Elley **Player of the Year (1983-84)** Ray Wickenden

Graham Stewart heads for goal as Billericay Town colleagues Danny Westwood and Alan Day (No. 7) stand by for the rebound in the Tooting and Mitcham goal area.
Photo: Evening Echo.

'Spot the Ball'. Hectic action in the Harlow v Bishops Stortford 'local derby'.
Photo: Herts & Essex Observer.

Harlow keeper Drake saves bravely at the feet of Croydon's young striker Marc Flemington.
Photo: David Fook.

BOGNOR REGIS TOWN

President: R. F. Butlin
Chairman: S. J. Rowlands
Manager: Jack Pearce
Coach: D. Probee
Physiotherapist: S. Robinson
Press Officer & Tel No: N. Nash (B.R. 863676)
Secretary: B. Best
Address & Tel No: 1 Halnaker Gardens, Aldwick, Bognor Pagham 66151 (H) Chichester 786258 (B)
Commercial Manager: Jack Pearce
Address & Tel No: c/o Club or 0243 816803 (H)
Address & Tel No of ground: Nyewood Lane, Bognor Regis, West Sussex PO21 2TY. B.R. 822325 **Club shop:** Yes
Simple ground directions: Follow sea front westwards from Pier, pass Aldwick shopping centre, left into Nyewood Lane
No of seats: 200 **Covered accommodation:** 3,000 **Capacity:** 6,000 **Floodlights:** Yes
Year formed: 1883 **Nickname:** The Rocks **Club sponsors:** Hamilton Lines (office furniture)
Previous names: None
Previous grounds: None
Club colours: White/Green/White
Change colours: All Yellow
Day for midweek home matches: Monday
Record attendance: 3,200 F.A. Amateur Cup **Year:** 1948
Best performance in: F.A. Cup: 1972-3 1st Round
F.A. Trophy: 1980-1 1st Round Proper
Previous Leagues: West Sussex, Sussex County, Southern
Clubhouse details: Members bar (normal opening hours) discos, bingo. Available for private hire.
Present players with Football League experience: None
Past players who progressed into the Football League: Ernie Randall (Chelsea), Andy Woon (Brentford)
Record transfer fee paid: None
Record transfer fee received: None
Programme details: 16 pages, 20p
Programme Editor: Danny Griffiths
Club metal badges: Yes
Local newspapers & Tel No: Bognor Regis Post 865241, Bognor Observer 864267, Brighton Argus 606799, Portsmouth News 64488
Senior Honours: Sussex Senior Cup (7), Southern League Runners-up, Southern League Merit Cup, Southern League Cup Finalists, Berger Isthmian League Div 1 Runners-up
Club Captain (1983-84): Michael Pullen **Player of the Year (1983-84):** David Poole

CARSHALTON ATHLETIC

President: Bill Cooper
Chairman: Wally Stephenson
Manager: Billy Smith
Coach: Carlo Nastri
Physiotherapist: Charlie Millard
Secretary: Bill Plumridge
Address & Tel No: 41 Colston Avenue, Carshalton, Surrey 01-642 7311
Commercial Manager: None
Address & Tel No:
Press Officer & Tel No: John Langridge 01-669 9762
Address & Tel No of ground: War Memorial Sports Ground, Colston Avenue, Carshalton, Surrey. 01-642 8658 (Boardroom), 01-642 8425 (Clubhouse).
Simple ground directions: B.R. (Southern Region) to Carshalton Station, turn right from station approach, Colston Avenue first left, ground entrance 150 yards on right. L.T. 157 bus to Wrythe Green, adjacent to Wrythe Lane ground entrance.
Club shop: Yes
No of seats: 250 **Covered accommodation:** 5,000 **Capacity:** 8,000 **Floodlights:** Yes
Year formed: 1905 **Nickname:** Robins **Club sponsors:** None.
Previous names: Club formed by merger of Mill Lane Mission and Carshalton St. Andrews in 1905.
Club colours: Maroon shirts, White shorts (maroon stripe), Maroon stockings.
Previous grounds: None
Change colours: White shirts (maroon trim), White shorts, White stockings.
Day for midweek home matches: Tuesdays
Record attendance: 8,000 v Tooting and Mitcham **Year:** 1951
Best performance in: F.A. Cup: 1982/3 2nd Round Proper v. Torquay United (A) 1-4.
F.A. Trophy: 1980/1 3rd Round Proper v. Mossley (H) 0-3.
Previous League: London, Surrey Senior, Corinthian, Athenian
Clubhouse details: Club open every evening, Sat., Sun. lunchtimes. Licensed bar, snacks available match days. Gaming machines, computer games, darts, pool. Live music Sat., Sun. evenings, men's darts Mon., Wed., Fri., lady's darts Thur.
Present players with Football League experience: Vic Akers (Cambridge United, Watford), Trevor Dark (Birmingham City), Tony Tagg (Q.P.R., Millwall, Wimbledon).
Past players who progressed into the Football League: Ernie Taylor (Newcastle United, Blackpool, Manchester United), Billy Darragon (Q.P.R.), Alan Eagles (Leyton Orient), Frank George (Leyton Orient), Roy Lunnis (Crystal Palace), Jock McDonald (Notts. County), Derek Razzell (Q.P.R.), Terry Stacey (Plymouth Argyle), Ron Walker (Watford), Nobby Warren (Exeter City), Tommy Williams (Colchester United)
Record transfer fee paid: £1,500 to Tooting & Mitcham United for Desmond Dennis
Record transfer fee received: £3,500 from Dulwich Hamlet for Gary Allen
Programme details: 12 pages, 25p
Club metal badges: £1.00 + postage from club shop.
Programme Editor: John Langridge.
Local newspapers & Tel: No: Wallington & Carshalton Advertiser 01-643 6953, Wallington & Carshalton Times 01-643 4351
Senior Honours: Isthmian League Div 2 Runners-up, Corinthian League Champions (2), Surrey Senior League Runners-up (2), Surrey Senior Shield & Finalists (2), Surrey Senior Cup Finalists

CROYDON

President: C. R. Waters
Chairman: J. H. Milsted
Manager: To be advised
Coach: D. Gill
Physiotherapist: D. Roythorne
Press Officer & Tel No: G. A. Brown (01-656 1022)
Secretary: E. Dukelow
Address & Tel No: Horsham (0403) 56745
Commercial Manager: D. Milsted
Address & Tel No: 01-656 5792
Club shop: Yes
Address & Tel No of ground: Croydon Sports Arena, Albert Road, South Norwood, London SE25 (01-654 5524)
Simple ground directions: By train to East Croydon or Norwood Junction stations. Buses 12A or 197 from stations to Belmont or Dundee Road. Walk down Belmont or Dundee Road, ground at bottom.
No of seats: 450 **Covered accommodation:** 450 **Capacity:** 15,000 **Floodlights:** Yes
Year formed: 1953 **Nickname:** The Blues **Club sponsors:** None
Previous names: Croydon Amateurs
Club colours: Light Blue strip with Dark Blue trim
Previous grounds: None
Change colours: All Red
Day for midweek home matches: Mondays, Wednesdays
Record attendance: 9,815 v Millwall F.A. Cup 2nd Round (at C. Palace) **Year:** 1979-80
Best performance in: **F.A. Cup:** 1979-80 2nd Rnd v Millwall, 1-1; replay 2-3 a.e.t.
F.A. Trophy: 1981-82, 1982-83 2nd Round Proper
Previous Leagues: Surrey Senior, Spartan, Athenian
Clubhouse details: 250 people, licensed bar, snacks available, dancing, discos, bingo, private functions, lounge bar. Club available for private hire – open lunchtimes and every night. (01-654 8555)
Present players with Football League experience: Alec Jackson (Chelsea), Tony Paul
Past players who progressed into the Football League: Peter Bonetti
Record transfer fee paid: Steve Brown
Record transfer fee received: Steve Brown
Programme details: 20 pages, 25p
Local newspapers & Tel No: Croydon Advertiser 01-668 4111
Club metal badges: Yes
Senior Honours: Surrey Senior Cup

DULWICH HAMLET

Chairman: A. G. Bretten
Manager: Eddie Presland
Coach: Stuart Scott
Physiotherapist: G. Brittain
Secretary: R. Searle
Address & Tel No: 42 Friern Road, Dulwich, SE22 0AX 01-693 2304 (H) 01-733 4444 (B)
Commercial Manager: None
Press Officer & Tel No: J. Lawrence (01-733 6385)
Address & Tel No of ground: Champion Hill Ground, Dog Kennel Hill, London SE22. 01-274 5187 **Club shop:** Yes
Simple ground directions: East Dulwich, Denmark Hill then 10 minute walk. Herne Hill then 37 bus stops near ground. Also 184 from Elephant & Castle and 185 from Victoria.
No of seats: 1,500 **Covered accommodation:** 10,000 **Capacity:** 16,000 **Floodlights:** Yes
Year formed: 1893 **Nickname:** The Hamlet **Club sponsors:** None
Previous names: None
Club colours: Pink/Blue
Previous grounds: Woodwarde Rd, College Farm, Sunray Avenue.
Change colours: Yellow/Green
Day for midweek home matches: Tuesdays
Record attendance: 20,744 Kingstonian v Stockton, F.A. Amateur Cup Final **Year:** 1933
Best performance in: **F.A. Cup:** 3 times to 1st Round Proper (last occasion 1948-9)
F.A. Trophy: 1979-80 Quarter-Final
Previous Leagues: Camberwell, Southern Suburban
Clubhouse details: Two bars on match days and for functions. Restaurant for hire.
Present players with Football League experience: None
Past players who progressed into the Football League: W. Bellamy (Tottenham), A. Solly (Arsenal), J. Moseley (Millwall), E. Toser (Millwall), G. Pearce (Plymouth), R. Crisp (Watford), J. Ryan (Charlton), E. Nwajiobi (Luton Town).
Record transfer fee paid: T. Eames, G. Allen
Record transfer fee received: E. Nwajiobi
Programme details: 20 pages, 25p
Local newspapers & Tel No: South London Press 01-769 4444, S.E. London & Kentish Mercury 01-692 1122
Club metal badges: Yes
Senior Honours: Isthmian League (4) Div 1, F.A. Amateur Cup (4), London Senior Cup (4), Surrey Senior Cup (16)

EPSOM & EWELL

President: V. Barrett
Chairman: I. F. Grant **Manager:** Adrian Hill
Coach: Mick Stratford
Physiotherapist: Dennis Kenney
Secretary: D. M. Wilson
Address & Tel No: 01-330 0011
Fund Raising Manager: I. Smith
Address & Tel No: 01-393 7588
Press Officer & Tel No: Stella Lamont, Burgh Heath 56245
Address & Tel No of ground: West Street, Ewell, Surrey. 01-393 7077 **Club shop:** Yes
Simple ground directions: Southern Rail to Ewell West station
No of seats: 250 **Covered accommodation:** 250 **Capacity:** 4,750 **Floodlights:** Yes
Year formed: 1917 **Nickname:** E's **Club sponsors:** Durst U.K. Ltd.
Previous names: Epsom Town, Epsom
Club colours: All Royal Blue
Previous grounds: Horton Lane
Change colours: All Yellow
Day for midweek home matches: Tuesday
Record attendance: 1,604 Semi-Final F.A. Vase v Stamford **Year:** 1975
Best performance in: **F.A. Cup:** 1933-4 1st Round v Clapton Orient (A) 2-4
F.A. Vase: 1975 Final
Previous Leagues: London League, Surrey Senior, South Suburban, Corinthian, Athenian
Clubhouse details: New Clubhouse. Open Mon-Sat lunchtimes and evenings, Sunday lunchtimes
Present players with Football League experience: Alan Morton (ex-Fulham, C. Palace, Stockport)
Past players who progressed into the Football League: Trevor Lee (Millwall, Colchester, Bournemouth & Cardiff), Phil Walker (Millwall, Charlton), Mick Leonard (Halifax, Notts Co.), John Leedham (Millwall)
Programme details: 20 pages, 20p
Programme Editors: Stella Lamont, Dave Wilson
Local newspapers & Tel No: Epsom & Ewell Advertiser 01-668 4111, E&E Herald, Surrey Comet
Club metal badges: Yes
Senior Honours: F.A. Challenge Vase Finalists, Surrey Senior Cup/Runners-up (2), Athenian League Cup, Berger Isthmian League Div 2, Serv. Isth Lge Div 1 Runners-up
Club Captain (1983-4): Mick Stratford
Player of the Year (1983-4): Steve Hill

Epsom & Ewell *Back Row (L-R): Adrian Hill (manager), John Russell, Murray Jones, Andy Abel, Alan Morton, Steve Delaney, Dennis Kenney (physio). Middle Row (L-R): Malcolm Spratt, Steve Milton, Mick Stratford, Russel Harmsworth, Andy Stewart. Front Row (L-R): Chris Hiscock, Tony Boorman. Missing through injury: Steve Hill, Robin Lewis, Gary Kent.* Photo: Epsom and Ewell Advertiser

HARLOW TOWN

President: To be named
Chairman: To be named
Manager: G. Walters
Coach: None
Physiotherapist: K. Cain
Secretary: S. Ray
Address & Tel No: 57 Sakins Croft, Harlow. Harlow 419610 (H), 01-622 4468 (B)
Commercial Manager: To be named
Address & Tel No:
Press Officer & Tel No: Phil Tuson (Harlow 26222 (B), 416743 (H)
Address & Tel No of ground: The Sportcentre, Hammarsgold Road, Harlow
Club shop: No
Simple ground directions: BR to Harlow Town station ground 2 minutes walk
No of seats: 450 **Covered accommodation:** 450 **Capacity:** 15,000 **Floodlights:** Yes
Year formed: 1879 **Nickname:** The Owls **Club sponsors:** None
Previous names: None
Club colours: All Red
Previous grounds: Mulberry Green
Change colours: All Yellow
Day for midweek home matches: Tuesday
Previous Leagues: Athenian, Spartan
Record attendance: 12,000 **Year:** 1971
Best performance in: F.A. Cup: 1979-80 4th Round
F.A. Trophy: 1980-1 2nd Round
Clubhouse details: Large club, darts, pool tables, electronic games, many functions. Evening opening 6-10.30pm and all match days
Present players with Football League experience: None
Past players who progressed into the Football League: Jeff Wood (Charlton), Neil Prosser (Bournemouth)
Record transfer fee paid: Not disclosed
Record transfer fee received: Not disclosed
Programme details: 14 pages, 20p
Local newspapers & Tel No: Harlow Gazette 39970, Harlow Observer, Harlow Star
Club metal badges: Yes
Senior Honours: Spartan League Cup Winners, London League Cup Winners, Athenian League Div I Champions (1971-72), Isthmian League Div I Champions (1978-79) (Div Runners-up 1982-83), Essex Senior Cup Winners (1978-79)

Hendon *Back Row (L-R): S. Wilkins, G. Allen, P. Stapleton, R. Bradford, C. Kemplen, A. O'Brien, A. Smith, R. Holland. Front Row (L-R): D. Drummy, S. Mitchell, A. Waddock, G. Hand, S. Hudson*

HAYES

Chairman: N. H. Sparkes
Manager: George Goode
Coach: Peter Suddaby
Physiotherapist: Cliff Cobb
Secretary: J. Price
Address & Tel No: 10 Minterne Waye, Hayes, Middx. 01-848 0743
Commercial Manager: None
Press Officer & Tel No: Trevor Griffiths (Ruislip 72771)
Club shop: Yes
Address & Tel No of ground: Church Road, Hayes, Middx. 01-573 4598-Ground, 01-573 0933-Clubhouse
Simple ground directions: 1 mile Hayes town centre. From M4 and A4020 (Uxbridge Rd) also buses pass ground
No of seats: 450 **Covered accommodation capacity:** 2,000 **Floodlights:** Yes
Year formed: 1909 **Nickname:** The Missioners **Club sponsors:** None
Previous names: Botwell Mission
Previous grounds: None
Club colours: Gold/Gold/Red
Change colours: All White
Day for midweek home matches: Tuesday
Record attendance: 16,000 v Bromley Amateur Cup **Year:** 1952
Best performance in: **F.A. Cup:** 1972-3 v Reading 2nd Round, 0-0 and 0-1
F.A. Trophy: 1978-9 Quarter-Final
Previous Leagues: Great Western, Suburban, Spartan, Athenian
Clubhouse details: Open every evening and Saturday and Sunday lunchtimes, snacks, dance hall, bar and kitchen facilities, large car park, full-time steward
Present players with Football League experience: Mick McGovern (QPR and Swindon), Peter Suddaby (Blackpool), Robbie Johnson (Brentford, Arsenal), Steve Parsons (Orient, Wimbledon)
Past players who progressed into the Football League: Les Smith (Aston Villa, England), Tony Alleman (Switzerland), Cyrille Regis (WBA, England)
Record transfer fee paid: £3,000 to Kingstonian for G. Drake
Record transfer fee received: £10,000 from WBA for Cyrille Regis
Programme details: 20 pages, 16p
Programme Editor: Kevin Watts
Local newspapers & Tel No: Hayes Gazette 89 37161
Club metal badges: Yes
Senior Honours: Past winners of Athenian, Great Western Suburban, Spartan Leagues. Amateur Cup finalists 1930-1, semi-finalists 1956-7. London Senior Cup (2), Middlesex Senior Cup (8), Middlesex Charity Cup (14), London Charity Cup (1), London Challenge Cup Finalists (1), Hitachi Cup Finalists (1)
Club Captain (1983-4): Mick McGovern
Player of the Year (1983-4): Glen Hayward

HENDON

President: M. Hyams and R. Butlin (Joint)
Chairman: C. Geary
Manager: Roy Ruffell
Coach: Jimmy Quail
Physiotherapist: Tony Jones
Secretary: D. Barrett
Address & Tel No: Weybridge 45213
Commercial Manager: Contact Bar Manager
Address & Tel No: 01-455 9185
Press Officer & Tel No: Secretary
Address & Tel No of ground: Claremont Road, Cricklewood, London NW2 1AE. 01-455 9185
Club shop: Yes
Simple ground directions: Golders Green Station then 226 bus to Claremont Road. Brent Cross Station then walk. Coming from East 1st left after Brent Cross flyover on North Circular
No of seats: 500 **Covered accommodation:** 5,500 **Capacity:** 8,500 **Floodlights:** Yes
Year formed: 1908 **Nickname:** The Dons or Greens **Club sponsors:** Wm. Younger Brewery
Previous names: Hampstead Town, Golders Green
Previous grounds: Record Lane, Cricklewood Lane
Club colours: Green shirts/socks, White shorts
Change colours: Sky Blue/White/Blue
Day for midweek home matches: Tuesday
Record attendance: 8,000 F.A. Cup **Year:** 1953-4
Best performance in: **F.A. Cup:** 1972-3 v Newcastle 3rd Rnd lost replay at Watford
F.A. Trophy: 1976-7, 1977-8 3rd Round
Previous Leagues: Finchley District, Middlesex, Athenian
Clubhouse details: Two bars open during normal licensing hours and match days. Bingo in hall on Wednesdays, Fridays and Sundays. Whist Drives Mondays. Entertainment on selected Saturday evenings
Present players with Football League experience: Dermot Drummy
Past players who progressed into the Football League:
Record transfer fee paid: £1,500 to Edgware for P. Shodeinde
Record transfer fee received: £1,500 from Woking for Tony Field
Programme details: 16 pages, 25p
Local newspapers & Tel No: Hendon Times 01-203 0411, Hampstead & Highgate Express, Kilburn Times
Club metal badges: Yes
Senior Honours: European Amateur Champs, F.A. Amateur Cup (3) Runners-up (2), Isthmian League (2) Runners-up (3), Isthmian League Cup, Athenian League (3), Middlesex Senior Cup (9)
Club Captain (1983/84): Richard Bradford
Player Of The Year (1983/84): Dermot Drummy

HITCHIN TOWN

President: B. Parker
Chairman: D. Morgan
Manager: Maurice Howkins
Player Manager: Alan West
General Manager: Maurice Howkins
Physiotherapist: Mick Walker
Secretary: C. Buck
Address & Tel No: 19 Baliol Road, Hitchin SG5 1TT Hitchin 59152 (H & B)
Commercial Manager: Gerald Lincoln
Tel No: 56979 or 56959 (B)

Press Officer & Tel No: None
Address & Tel No of ground: Top Field, Fishponds Road, Hitchin, Herts. Hitchin 34483/59028 **Club shop:** Yes
Simple ground directions: Approx 1 mile from Town Centre on Bedford Road. Hitchin Station (1 mile).
No of seats: 600 **Covered accommodation:** 600 **Capacity:** 6,000 **Floodlights:** Yes
Year formed: 1865 **Nickname:** Canaries **Club sponsors:** Hunting Gate Homes, N&P Windows, Wallspan Bedroom Furniture, William Cory Ltd, Tony Huckle Greengrocer, Jackson Brady.
Previous names: None
Previous grounds: None
Club colours: Yellow/Royal Blue/Royal Blue
Day for midweek home matches: Tuesday
Change colours: White with Royal Blue trim
Record attendance: 7,878 v Wycombe, Amateur Cup **Year:** 1956
Previous Leagues: Spartan, Athenian
Best performance in: F.A. Cup: 1973-4, 1976-7 (2 replays) 2nd Round
F.A. Trophy: 1976-7,1980-1 3rd Round
Clubhouse details: Lounge, kitchen, 2 bars open every night, midday lunches
Present players with Football League experience: Alan Cosby, Alan West, Neil Madden
Past players who progressed into the Football League: Reg Smith, C. J. Walker, W. R. Odell, S. R. Foss, R. Stevens, G. Goodyear, T. Clark, L. Garwood, P. Burridge, R. Kitchener, D. Bumpstead, M. Dixon, D. Pacey, D. Hills, G. Lay, R. Morton, D. Castle, K. Goodeve, B. Robinson
Record transfer fee paid: £1,000
Record transfer fee received: £3,500, Steve Mahoney to Barnet
Programme details: 20 pages, 25p
Programme Editor: C. Buck
Club metal badges: Yes
Local newspapers & Tel No: Hitchin Comet 31666, Hitchin Gazette 59651
Senior Honours: F.A. Amateur Cup S-Finalists (2), Herts Senior Cup (18), London Senior Cup & Runners-up, Isthmian League Runners-up, Athenian League Runners-Up, Spartan League
Club Captain (83/84): Steve Gear **Player Of The Year (83/84):** Steve Fountain (Players); Steve Gear (Supporters)

Hitchin Town *Back Row (L-R): C.B.C. Buck (Secretary), D. Renney (Trainer), N. Madden, J. Woodward, A. West (Player/Manager), I. Kavanagh, A Luff, S. Fountain, N. Miller, T. Parker, M. Howkins (General Manager). Front Row (L-R): N. Kirkpatrick, M. Nunn, S. Gear (Captain), M. Every, A. Cosby, P. Giggle, A. Wilkinson.*

LEYTONSTONE/ILFORD

President: H. Hammond, J.P.
Chairman: D. Andrews
Manager: Tom Fearey
Player/Coach: Ron Howell
Physiotherapist:
Secretary: D. Almond
Address & Tel No: 01-524 2689 (H) 600 9000 x2122 (B)
Commercial Manager: Len Llewllyn
Address & Tel No: 02775 3262
Press Officer & Tel No: M. Bailey (01-551 2588)
Address & Tel No of ground: Granleigh Road, Leytonstone, London E11. 01-539 6117 **Club shop:** Yes
Simple ground directions: Aside Leytonstone High Rd. BR station 2 mins, buses 10, 262, Leytonstone LT stn 10 mins
No of seats: 350 **Covered accommodation:** 4,000 **Capacity:** 9,000 **Floodlights:** Yes
Year amalgamated: 1979 **Nickname:** The Fords or The Stones **Club sponsors:** None
Previous names: Ilford (separate clubs until 1979) **Club colours:** Red shirts, Blue shorts, White trim
Previous grounds: See 'Did You Know' **Change colours:** All Blue
Day for midweek home matches: Tuesday
Previous Leagues: Southern, London, South Essex
Record attendance: 9,740 F.A. Cup 2nd Round v Newport Co **Year:** 1949
Best performance in: F.A. Cup: 1979-80 v Harlow, 1981-2 v Aldershot 1st Round
F.A. Trophy: 1980-1 v Altrincham 3rd Round Proper. Lost 0-1
Clubhouse details: The Cedars Club is open every evening plus Sunday lunchtime and matchdays. 5.30-10.30pm weekdays. 01-539 0359
Present players with Football League experience: Paul Baxter (Crystal Palace), Keith Tonge (Brentford)
Past players who progressed into the Football League: Terry Hurlock (Brentford), Trevor Morgan (Bournemouth)
Record transfer fee paid: Micky Dingwall (undisclosed) from Barking
Record transfer fee received: Terry Hurlock (undisclosed) to Brentford
Programme details: 12 pages, 20p
Programme Editor: Len Llewellyn
Club metal badges: Yes (£1)
Local newspapers & Tel No: Walthamstow Guardian, 01-531 4141; Stratford & Newham Express, 01-534 1639; Ilford Recorder, 01-478 4444; Barking & Dagenham Post, 01-517 0011
Senior Honours: Isthmian League, Hitachi Cup, London Senior Cup, Essex Senior Cup, Isthmian Div 1
Club Captain (83/84): Tom Horan

SUTTON UNITED

President: Andrew Letts
Chairman: Peter Molloy
Manager: Barrie Williams
Assist. Managers: Larry Pritchard and Ken Ireland
Physiotherapist: Danny Keenan
Secretary: Ralph Carr
Address & Tel No: 8 Shelley Close, Banstead, Surrey Burgh Heath 58103 (H)
Commercial Manager: Barry Aplin
Address & Tel No: Burgh Heath 53939
Press Officer & Tel No: Simon Clennell. Tel Redhill 67765 (H) 01-730 3453 Ext. 2107 (B)
Address & Tel No of ground: Borough Sports Ground, Gander Green Lane, Sutton, Surrey. 01-644 4440
Club shop: Yes, Tony Dolbear, 17 Hilbert Rd, Cheam
Simple ground directions: Gander Green Lane crosses the Sutton by-pass (A217) about one mile south of Rose Hill roundabout. Heading from London, turn left at traffic lights by 'Gander' pub. Rail: West Sutton station.
No of seats: 1,100 **Covered accommodation:** Stands on two sides **Capacity:** 14,000 **Floodlights:** Yes
Year formed: 1898 **Nickname:** U's **Club sponsors:** Business Press International
Previous names: Sutton Association FC and Sutton Guild Rovers FC merged in 1898
Club colours: Amber/Chocolate trim
Change colours: White with Chocolate trim
Previous grounds: Manor Lane, 1898-1911
Day for midweek home matches: Tuesday
Record attendance: 14,000 v Leeds Utd, F.A. Cup 4th Round **Year:** 1970
Best performance in: F.A. Cup: 1969-70 4th Round
F.A. Trophy: 1980-81 Finalists
Previous Leagues: Herald, Surrey Junior, Southern Suburban, Athenian
Clubhouse details: Three bars plus conference/meeting rooms, open lunchtimes and evenings, 7 days a week. Available for private hire. Steward: John Turner, 01-644 4440
Present players with Football League experience: None
Past players who progressed into the Football League: Charlie Vaughan (Charlton), Billy Robinson (C. Palace), Tony Barton (Fulham), Mike Pentecost (Fulham), John Faulkner (Leeds), Micky Fillery (Chelsea)
Record transfer fee paid: Paul McKinnon (Malmo)
Record transfer fee received: Paul McKinnon to Malmo, Sweden
Programme details: 28 pages, 25p
Programme Editor: Simon Clennell
Club metal badges: Yes, 50p each plus post from Club Shop
Local newspapers & Tel No: Sutton Herald 01-643 4351, Sutton & Cheam Advertiser 01-668 4111, Sutton Borough Guardian 01-643 0588
Senior Honours: F.A. Amateur Cup Finalists (2), Anglo-Italian Tournament Winners & Runners-up (2), F.A. Trophy Finalists, Isthmian League Champions & Runners-up (3), Athenian League Champions (3) & Runners-up, London Senior Cup Winners (2), Surrey Senior Cup Winners (7) & Runners-up (8), Hitachi Cup Winners (2) and Runners-up
Club Captain (1983-4): John Rains **Player of the Year (1983-4):** Tony Rains, Ray Sunnocks (Joint)

TOOTING & MITCHAM UNITED

President:
Chairman: J. Payne
Manager/s: D. Juneman & W. Edwards
Physiotherapist: D. Gibson
Secretary: A. T. Gaitt
Address & Tel No: 196 Hamilton Avenue, North Cheam, Surrey SM3 9DT. 01-641 2374 (H)
General Manager Address & Tel No: 01-622 4828
Press Officer & Tel No: F. Jannaway (01-648 7240)
Address & Tel No of ground: Sandy Lane, Mitcham, Surrey. 01-648 3248 **Club shop:** Yes
Simple ground directions: Turning off Streatham Road, Mitcham near "The Swan"
No of seats: 1,990 **Covered accommodation:** 1,990 seated **Capacity:** 8,000 **Floodlights:** Yes
Year formed: 1932 amalgamation **Nickname:** Tooting Terrors **Club sponsors:** None
Previous names: Tooting Town & Mitcham Wanderers
Club colours: Black/White
Previous grounds: None
Change colours: All Pale Blue
Day for midweek home matches: Tuesday
Record attendance: 15,000 v Wimbledon **Year:** 1951
Best performance in: F.A. Cup: 1975-6 v Bradford City 4th Round
F.A. Trophy: 1975-6 4th Round
Previous Leagues: London, Athenian
Clubhouse details: Mon-Thurs 6.30-10.30pm, Fri-Sat 6.30-11.00pm, Sat afternoon 1.00-6.30pm, Sun 12-2.00pm and 7.00-10.30pm
Present players with Football League experience: None
Past players who progressed into the Football League: A. Stepney, D. Bumpstead, V. Akers, H. Smith, P. Hasty
Record transfer fee paid: R. Knowles (Wimbledon)
Record transfer fee received: H. Smith (Luton Town)
Programme details: 16 pages, 25p
Programme Editor: A. T. Gaitt (Secretary)
Local newspapers & Tel No: Mitcham News 01-672 1077
Club metal badges: No
Senior Honours: Isthmian League (2), Athenian League (2), Surrey Senior Cup (8), London Senior Cup (4)
Player of the Year (1983-84): A. Budden

WALTHAMSTOW AVENUE

President: V. Ercolani
Chairman: J. Thompson
Manager: Laurie Wilkinson
Coach: Brian Kelly
Physiotherapist: Ken Davey
Press Officer & Tel No: As Secretary

Secretary: N. R. J. Moss
Address & Tel No: 01-531 0468 (H & B)

Commercial Manager: None
Address & Tel No:

Club shop: Yes
Address & Tel No of ground: Green Pond Road, Higham Hill Road, Walthamstow, E17. 01-527 1130/2795
Simple ground directions: Victoria Line Underground to Blackhorse Road, 123 bus to Lord Palmerston
No of seats: 940 **Covered accommodation:** 6,000 **Capacity:** 10,000 **Floodlights:** Yes
Year formed: 1900 **Nickname:** The Avenue **Club sponsors:** Adisand
Previous names: None
Previous grounds: None
Club colours: Light/Dark Blue hoops
Change colours: Red/White
Day for midweek home matches: Tuesday
Record attendance: 12,500 v Stockport Co, F.A. Cup **Year:** 1939
Best performance in: **F.A. Cup:** 5th Round v Everton
F.A. Trophy: 1976-7 3rd Round Replay

Previous Leagues:
Spartan,
Athenian

Clubhouse details: Club open seven days each week. Refreshment bar. Various sporting sections:- darts, pool, crib, angling, pigeons etc.
Present players with Football League experience: Kevin Dare (C. Palace)
Past players who progressed into the Football League: Jim Lewis (Chelsea), Derek Saunders (Chelsea), Dave Crown (Brentford)
Record transfer fee paid: None
Record transfer fee received: £13,000, D. Crown (Brentford)
Programme details: 16 pages, 25p
Programme Editor: Norman Moss
Club metal badges: Yes
Local newspapers & Tel No: Guardian/Gazette 01-531 4141
Senior Honours: F.A. Amateur Cup (2), Essex Senior Cup, London Senior Cup, Isthmian League
Club Captain (1983-84); John Borland

WINDSOR & ETON

President: Sir David Hill-Wood
Chairman: M. G. Holland
Manager: G. Chapple
Coach: A. Coulton
Physiotherapist: B. Lowe
Press Officer & Tel No: None

Secretary: A. R. Drummie
Address & Tel No: Windsor 66952 (H)
Staines 56456 (Emergency)
Commercial Manager: None
Address & Tel No:

Address & Tel No of ground: Stag Meadow, St Leonards Road, Windsor. Tel: 60656 **Club shop:** Yes
Simple ground directions:
No of seats: 350 **Covered accommodation:** 300 **Capacity:** 5,000 **Floodlights:** Yes
Year formed: 1902 **Nickname:** Royalists **Club sponsors:** Select Carpets
Previous names: Windsor, Windsor Home Park, Windsor Phoenix
Previous grounds: Balloon Meadow, Windsor
Club colours: Red/Green
Change colours: White/Black/White
Day for midweek home matches: Tuesday
Record attendance: **Year:**
Best performance in: **F.A. Cup:** 1983-84 2nd Round
F.A. Vase: 1980-1 Semi-finalists
F.A. Trophy: 1983-84 2nd Round

Previous Leagues:
G.W. Comb, Spartan,
Metrop'tan, Athenian,
Corinthian, Delphian

Clubhouse details: Lounge Bar, club room, kitchen facilities and usual offices
Present players with Football League experience: None
Past players who progressed into the Football League: Vic Woodley (Chelsea & England), Billy Coward (QPR, Walsall), Ken Groves (Preston North End), Jack Dare (Southampton, Exeter City)
Record transfer fee paid: None
Record transfer fee received: £2,000
Programme details: 12 pages, 20p
Programme Editor: G. Johnsey
Club metal badges: Yes
Local newspapers & Tel No: Windsor & Eton Express
Windsor Observer
Senior Honours: Athenian League (2), Athenian Cup, Athenian League Runners-up, Isthmian League Div 1 Winners, Div 2 Runners-up, County Cup Winners (5 times running — a record)
Club Captain (1983-84): Bob King
Player of the Year (1983-84): Kevin Mitchell

Wokingham 1XI squad 1983/4 season *Back Row (L-R): J. Wilks, D. Cottrell, M. Hurdwell, R. Evans, S. Aldham, B. Saunders, B. Purser, T. Ryan, S. Price, T. Brown, R. Merryweather (manager). Front Row (L-R): J. Brown, R. Steer, D. Cox, K. Corbin, D. McMahon, N. Stanley, R. Thorpe (trainer).*

WOKINGHAM TOWN

President: D. Langley
Chairman: G. P. Gale
Manager: R. A. B. Merryweather
Coach: Ernie Howe
Physiotherapists: R. Thorpe/J. Lange
Secretary: J. White
Address & Tel No: 36 Malvern Close, Woodley, Reading
Reading 692661 (H) Wokingham 780253 (B)
Commercial Manager: R. Merryweather
Address & Tel No: Wokingham 780253
Press Officer & Tel No: As Commercial Manager
Address & Tel No of ground: Finchampstead Road, Wokingham, Berks. Wokingham 780253 **Club shop:** Yes
Simple ground directions: Half-mile from the railway station and town centre on Finchampstead Road
No of seats: 250 **Covered accommodation:** 1,500 **Capacity:** 4,500 **Floodlights:** Yes
Year formed: 1875 **Nickname:** The Town **Club sponsors:** Bearwood Glass (UK) Ltd
Previous names: None
Previous grounds: None
Club colours: Amber shirts/socks, Black trim/shorts,
Change colours: Red shirts, White shorts
Day for midweek home matches: Tuesday
Record attendance: 3,473 v Norton Woodseats F.A. Amateur Cup **Year:** 1957-8
Best performance in: F.A. Cup: 1982/83 v Cardiff City 1st Round Proper
F.A. Trophy: 1979-80 v Leatherhead 1st Round Proper
Previous Leagues: Corinthian, Athenian
Clubhouse details: Open for business lunches. Available for private hire. Whippet racing June-October
Present players with Football League experience: Kirk Corbin (Cambridge Utd), Tommy Ryan (Reading)
Past players who progressed into the Football League: Kirk Corbin (Cambridge Utd), Phil Alexander (Norwich C)
Record transfer fee paid: £1,500 Derek Cottrell from Woking
Record transfer fee received: £2,000 Phil Alexander (Norwich C)
Programme details: 32 pages, 15p
Club metal badges: Yes
Local newspapers & Tel No: Wokingham Times 782000, Reading Evening Post 55833, Wokingham & Bracknell News Bracknell 20363
Senior Honours: Berks & Bucks Senior Cup, Berger Isthmian League Div 1
Club Captain: Derek Cottrell **Player of the Year:** Bob Purser

Wycombe Wanderers *Back Row (L-R): Mike Keen (Manager), Alan Davies (Asst. Manager), Terry Glynn, Steve Perrin, Anton Vircavs, Gary Lester, Andy Harman, Mark Hill, Trevor How, Dave Springell (Physio), Front Row: Paul West, Bob Dell, Jim Jacobs, Steve Thorne, Ken Wilson.*

WYCOMBE WANDERERS

President: M. E. Seymour, MPS
Chairman: B. R. Lee
Manager: Paul Bence
Coach: Alan Gane
Physiotherapist: David Springell
Secretary: J. Goldsworthy
Address & Tel No: 35 West Drive, High Wycombe, Bucks. Tel. 0494 38042
Commercial Manager: Paul Birdseye
Address & Tel No: 0494 26567
Press Officer & Tel No: Philip Ball (Bourne End 23165)
Address & Tel No of ground: Loakes Park, High Wycombe, Bucks. Tel. 0494 26567 **Club shop:** Yes
Information Line (for match day news and results) High Wycombe 446763
Simple ground directions: One mile from High Wycombe railway station, adjacent to Wycombe Hospital
No of seats: 1,000 **Covered accommodation:** 4,000 **Capacity:** 12,000 **Floodlights:** Yes
Year formed: 1884 **Nickname:** Blues **Club sponsors:** Norman Reeves (High Wycombe)
Previous names: None
Club colours: Light and Dark Blue
Previous grounds: The Rye, Spring Meadow, Daws Hill Park
Change colours: All Yellow
Day for midweek home matches: Tuesday
Record attendance: 16,000 v St. Albans, FA Amateur Cup 4th Round **Year:** 1950
Best performance in: F.A. Cup: 1974-5 3rd Round v Middlesbrough
F.A. Trophy: 1981-2 Semi-Final v Altrincham
Previous Leagues: Southern, Great Western Suburban, Spartan, Isthmian
Clubhouse details: Match days. Steward: Bob Hart, Princes Risborough 3022
Present players with Football League experience: Trevor How (Watford)
Past players who progressed into the Football League: P. Suddaby, V. Busby, K. Swain, S. Perrin, I. Pearson, J. Delaney, M. Mellows, S. Perrin, M. Hill
Record transfer fee paid: £2,000, George Borg, 1980
Record transfer fee received: £10,000, Ian Pearson, Millwall
Programme details: 12 pages, 20p
Programme Editor: Philip Ball
Club metal badges: Yes
Local newspapers & Tel No: Bucks Free Press 0494 21212
Senior Honours: Isthmian League (7), F.A. Amateur Cup Winners & Runners-up, Berks & Bucks Senior Cup (21)
Club Captain (1983-84): Steve Perrin **Player of the Year (1983-84):** Trevor How

AVELEY

President: K. Clay
Chairman: A. Wallace
Manager: R. Kean
Coach:
Physiotherapist: P. Hunter
Secretary: R. Scarborough
Address & Tel No: 43 Martin Road, Aveley. Purfleet 2453
Commercial Manager: None
Address & Tel No:
Press Officer & Tel No: Mrs E. Scarborough. Purfleet 2453
Address & Tel No of ground: Mill Field, Mill Road, Aveley, Essex **Club shop:** No
Simple ground directions: ¼ mile off A13. Rainham Station and 375 Bus
No of seats: 500 **Covered accommodation:** 500 **Capacity:** 10,000 **Floodlights:** Yes
Year formed: 1927 **Nickname:** The Blues **Club sponsors:** None
Previous names: None
Club colours: Royal Blue, White
Previous grounds: None
Change colours: Red, White
Day for midweek home matches: Tuesday
Record attendance: 4,800 v Slough **Year:** 1972
Best performance in: F.A. Cup: 1970-1 1st Round
F.A. Trophy: 1974-5 3rd Qualifying Round
Previous Leagues: London Delphian, Athenian
Clubhouse details: Keep fit, darts, bingo and dancing
Record transfer fee received: None
Programme details: 12 pages, 20p
Local newspapers & Tel No: Thurrock Gazette
Programme Editor: Elaine Scarborough
Club metal badges: Yes
Senior Honours: London League Premier, Athenian League Div2
Club Captain (1983-84): John Kerslake **Player of the Year (1983-84):** Keith Day

BASILDON UNITED

President: Michael Roffey
Chairman: Ron Hill
Manager: Ron Hanley
Coaches: Peter Heathcote, Bill L'ePage
Physiotherapist: Roger Marshall
Secretary: Terry Woolton
Address & Tel No: 03744 61558 (H) 0268 3040 x421 (B)
Commercial Manager: None
Address & Tel No:
Press Officer & Tel No: As Secretary
Address & Tel No of ground: Basildon Stadium, Gardiners Close, Gardiners Lane, Basildon, Essex. Basildon 20268 (Clubhouse) 282175 (Boardroom) **Club shop:** Yes
Simple ground directions:
No of seats: 350 **Covered accommodation:** 3 stands **Capacity:** 4,000 **Floodlights:** Yes
Year formed: 1963 **Nickname:** The'Bee's **Club sponsors:** None
Previous names: Armada FC
Club colours: Amber-Black stripes/Black/Amber
Previous grounds: None
Change colours: Blue-White stripes/Blue/Blue
Day for midweek home matches: Tuesdays
Record attendance: 4,000 v West Ham **Year:** 1963
Best performance in: F.A. Cup: None
F.A. Vase: 1980-1 5th Round
Previous Leagues: Athenian, Essex Senior
Clubhouse details: Open every day, lunchtime and evening
Present players with Football League experience: Graham Franklyn (Norway & English F.L.), Alan Hull, Jeff Hull
Past players who progressed into the Football League: Jeff Hull (Colchester)
Programme details: 16 pages, 20p
Programme Editors: John Powles, Robin Marshal
Local newspapers & Tel No: Southend Evening Echo, Basildon Radio & Essex Radio
Club metal badges: Yes
Senior Honours: Essex Senior League (4), Essex Senior Trophy, Essex Elizabethan Trophy, Essex Senior League Cup & Reserve Cup, Isthmian League Div 2 Champions 1983-4

BOREHAM WOOD

President: H. E. S. Payne
Chairman: W. F. O'Neill
Manager: Terry Dyson
Coach: Les Baker
Physiotherapist: Joe Parish
Secretary: J. L. Nixon
Address & Tel No: 114 Brook Road, Boreham Wood 01-953 7765
Commercial Manager: None
Address & Tel No:
Press Officer & Tel No: John Gill 01-998 6446 (H)
Address & Tel No of ground: Broughinge Road, Boreham Wood, Herts. 01-953 9883 Boardroom, 5097 Club
Simple ground directions: Elstree & Boreham Wood station. Buses 292 & 107
No of seats: 250 **Covered accommodation:** 1,500 **Capacity:** 2,500 **Floodlights:** Yes
Year formed: 1948 **Nickname:** The Wood **Club sponsors:** None
Previous names: None
Club colours: All White with Red/Black trim
Previous grounds: Eldon Avenue
Change colours: Red/White
Day for midweek home matches: Tuesday
Record attendance: 2,500 v St Albans, Amateur Cup **Year:** 1970-71
Best performance in: F.A. Cup: 1973-4, 1977-8 1st Round Proper
F.A. Trophy: 1979-80 3rd Qualifying Round
Previous Leagues: Mid Herts, Parthenon, Spartan, Athenian
Clubhouse details: Facilities for 250 people. Bingo, discos, dancing, darts matches, club available for private hire. Open market every Thursday 9.00am-4.00pm
Present players with Football League experience: Russell Townsend (Arsenal, Northampton Town)
Past players who progressed into the Football League: Colin Franks
Programme details: 20 pages, 20p
Programme Editor: John Gill
Club metal badges: No
Local newspapers & Tel No: Borehamwood Post Barnet & District Local Advertiser, Herts Advertiser Barnet Press
Senior Honours: Isthmian League Div 1, Athenian League Premier Div, Athenian League Div 1 Runners-up, Athenian League Div 2, Herts Senior Cup, Herts Charity Cup
Club Captain (1983-4): Les McCormack **Player of the Season (1983-4):** Steve Wallace

Bromley *Back Row (L-R): Gus Johnson (medical attendant), Dave Cook (manager), Colin Powell, Alan Mignot, John Vincent, Alan Seamons, Geoff Fuller, Brian Frampton, Graham Taylor, Keith Waldon (youth and reserve team manager). Front Row (L-R): Conrad Kane, Andy Smith, Steve Dixson, Mark Penfold, Terry Young, Trevor Ford.*
Photo: Bromley Advertiser

BROMLEY

President:
Chairman: G. T. Ransom
Manager: Dave Cook
Ass. Manager: Trevor Ford
Coaches: Keith Waldon, Colin Powell
Secretary: J. M. Cooper
Address & Tel No: 01-857 3961 (H) 01-659 6918 (B)
Commercial Manager: (Lottery) K. Cafferty
Address & Tel No:
Physiotherapist: Peter Mickleburgh MSF MSSCH
Press Officer & Tel No: J. Fiorini. 01-460 9013 (H) 01-736 3435 (B)
Address & Tel No of ground: Hayes Lane, Bromley, Kent. 01-460 5291
Club shop: Yes
Simple ground directions: Bromley South and 119 or 146 goes past the ground.
No of seats: 2,000
Covered accommodation capacity: 3,000
Floodlights: Yes
Year formed: 1892
Nickname: Lillywhites
Club sponsors: Cocoa Sports
Previous names: None
Club colours: White shirts, Black shorts
Previous grounds: Glebe Road
Change colours: Red shirts, Black shorts
Day for midweek home matches: Tuesdays
Record attendance: 12,000 v Nigerian XI **Year:** 1950
Best performance in: **F.A. Cup:** 1976-7 1st Round
F.A. Trophy: 1982-83 1st Round
Previous Leagues: Athenian, London, Kent Spartan
Clubhouse details: Open on match days and for functions.
Present players with Football League experience: Colin Powell, Mark Penfold (Charlton Athletic)
Past players who progressed into the Football League: Roy Merryfield (Chelsea), Stan Charlton (Arsenal), Ron Heckman (Leyton Orient, Crystal Palace), John Gregory (West Ham, Scunthorpe), Bill Lloyd (Millwall), Brian Kinsey (Charlton), Harold Hobbis (Pre-war Charlton & England)
Record transfer fee paid: Not disclosed
Record transfer fee received: Not disclosed
Programme details: 20 pages, 20p
Club metal badges: Yes
Local newspapers & Tel No: Bromley Times 01-300 1234, Bromley Advertiser 01-668 4111
Senior Honours: F.A. Amateur Cup (3), London Senior Cup (3), Isthmian League Champions (4), Kent Senior Cup Winners (2), Kent Amateur Cup (11), Athenian League Champions (3), London League (2), Spartan League

Boreham Wood *Back Row (L-R): Les Baker (assistant manager), Russell Townsend, Steve Robinson, Mick Freeman, Mick O'Shea, Andy Goodchild, Steve Waller, Steve O'Neill, Steve Foody, Terry Dyson (manager). Front Row (L-R): Steve Wallace, Les McCormack (captain), Leroy Rhodes, Sean Baker, Desmond Dennis.*
Photo: Boreham Wood Post

CHESHAM UNITED

Chairman: L. Mangan
President: Jack Smethurst
Player/Manager: Pat Morrissey
Coach: Brian Greenhagh
Physiotherapist: Brian Lay
Press Officer & Tel No: N. C. Vince

Secretary: N. C. Vince
Address & Tel No: Aldbury Common 373
Commercial Manager: L. Vockins
Address & Tel No: 36 Cheyne Walk, Chesham. 771667

Address & Tel No of ground: The Meadow, Amersham Rd, Chesham, Bucks. Chesham 782456/783964 **Club shop:** Yes
Simple ground directions: Off A416, foot of Amersham Hill. 10 mins walk from Chesham station (Metropolitan Line)
No of seats: 200 **Covered accommodation:** both sides **Capacity:** 5,000 **Floodlights:** Yes
Year formed: 1917 **Nickname:** United **Club sponsors:** Chesham Service Stn
Previous names: Chesham Town
Club colours: Claret & Blue/White/Blue
Previous grounds: None
Change colours: All White
Day for midweek home matches: Wednesday
Record attendance: 5,000 v Cambridge United F.A. Cup 3rd Round **Year:** 5th Jan 1930
Best performance in: **F.A. Cup:** 1979-80 3rd Round Proper
F.A. Trophy: 1981-2 1st Round Proper

Previous Leagues: Spartan, Corinthian, Athenian

Clubhouse details: Open each night and lunchtimes, bar, snacks. Also available for private hire
Present players with Football League experience: Pat Morrissey
Past players who progressed into the Football League: Stewart Scullion (Charlton Athletic, Watford, Sheffield United), Bill Shipwright (Watford), Kerry Dixon (Chelsea)
Record transfer fee paid: None
Record transfer fee received: £652
Programme details: 28 pages, 25p
Programme Editor: Nick Vince
Local newspapers & Tel No: Bucks Examiner Chesham 4591. Bucks Advertiser
Club metal badges: Yes
Senior Honours: Berks & Bucks Senior Cup (9), Spartan League Div1 (3) Prem Div, F.A. Amateur Cup Finalists
Club Captain (1983-84): Paul Currie
Player of the Year (1983-84): Pat Morrissey

Chesham United *Standing (L-R): Brian Greenhough (Coach), Paul Currie (Captain), John Franks, Eggy James, Dave Carlisle, Mick Martin, Dave Lewis, Mark Bensted, Brian Lay (Physio). Front Row (L-R): Chris Martin, Dave Lay, Nigel Carter, Matt Strange, Patt Morrissey (Player Manager).*

The first Division Two Manager of the Month award last season went to Dorking's Phil Illman who had built a new young side and started the season in brilliant form. Here, Dennis Frost of Huntingate Homes Ltd presents Phil with a bottle of champagne and a football.

Photo: Eric Marsh

CLAPTON

Chairman: M. E. Fogg
Manager: Ted Marjoram
Coach:
Physiotherapists: George Barwick, Ron Cleaver
Secretary: Martin McShea
Address & Tel No: 208 Portway, Stratford, London E15 3QY. 01-472 5696 (H), 01-472 3844 (B)
Commercial Manager:
Address & Tel No:
Press Officer & Tel No: Hon Secretary **Club shop:** Yes
Address & Tel No of ground: Spotted Dog Ground, Upton Lane, Forest Gate, London E7. 01-472 1655
Simple ground directions: Nearest station, Forest Gate (Eastern region BR), bus route 278 (passes ground).
No of seats: 378 **Covered accommodation:** Two stands **Capacity:** 5,500 **Floodlights:** Yes
Year formed: 1878 **Nickname:** The Tons **Club sponsors:** None
Previous names: Downs F.C. 1877-78
Club colours: Red/White stripes, Black shorts
Previous grounds: Hackney Downs
Change colours: All Yellow
Day for midweek home matches: Tuesday
Record attendance: 12,000 **Year:** 1898-9
Best performance in: F.A. Cup: 1925-26 3rd Round Proper
F.A. Trophy: 1980-1 2nd Qualifying Round
Previous Leagues: Southern League (founder member)
Clubhouse details: Open Mon-Thurs evenings, Saturday afternoon and evening, Sunday lunchtime.
Present players with Football League experience: Bryn Key (Crystal Palace), Colin Mackleworth (West Ham Utd), Gary Seward (Blackpool)
Past players who progressed into the Football League: Harry Earle (Notts County), Stanley Earle (West Ham Utd), W. V. T. Gibbins (West Ham Utd), Bill Bryant (Millwall), George Male (Arsenal)
Programme details: 8 pages, 10p
Programme Editor: Ray Stilwell (01-472 3465)
Local newspapers & Tel No: Newham Recorder 01-478 4444
Club metal badges:
Senior Honours: F.A. Amateur Cup (5), Isthmian League, London Senior Cup, Essex Senior Cup, Middlesex Senior Cup, London Charity Cup, Isthmian League Div 2, Essex Thames-Side Trophy
Club Captain (1983-84): Bryn Key **Player of the Year (1983-84):** Gary Seymour

FARNBOROUGH TOWN

Chairman: Ron Wallace
Manager: Ted Pearce
Trainer: Jim Pierson
Physiotherapist: Dennis Rose
Secretary: Garry Ward
Address & Tel No: 25 Teal Crescent, Kempshott, Basingstoke, Hants. Yately 876841
Commercial Manager: None
Press Officer & Tel No: John Robinson. Camberley 34007
Address & Tel No of ground: John Roberts Ground, Cherrywood Road, Farnborough, Hants. Farnborough 541469 (Boardroom), 545553 (Club) **Club shop:** Yes
Simple ground directions: From station, north along A325 third left, second right, ground is approx 300 yards on right
No of seats: 310 **Covered accommodation:** 400 **Capacity:** 4,000 **Floodlights:** Yes
Year formed: 1967 **Nickname:** The Boro' **Club sponsors:** None
Previous names: None
Club colours: Yellow shirts, Blue shorts
Previous grounds: Queens Road
Change colours: All Red
Day for midweek home matches: Tuesdays
Record attendance: 3,000 v Billericay Town Semi-Final FA Vase **Year:** 1977
Best performance in: F.A. Cup: 1980-1 v Yeovil & 1983-4 v Barking 1st Round Proper
F.A. Trophy: 1980-1, 1981-2, 1983-4 1st Qualifying Round
F.A. Vase: 1975-6, 1976-7 Semi-Final
Previous Leagues: Surrey Senior, Spartan, Athenian
Clubhouse details: Large bar open every night and lunchtimes Sat and Sundays. Frequent entertainment and disco's
Present players with Football League experience: R. Walden (Aldershot, Sheffield Wed. and Newport County)
Past players who progressed into the Football League: None
Programme details: 40-48 pages, 25p
Local newspapers & Tel No: Farnborough News, 0252 28221
Programme Editors: Mike Keith and Keith Wickham **Club metal badges:** Yes
Senior Honours: Isthmian League Div 2, Athenian League Div 2, Spartan League (4), Spartan League Cup (2), Hampshire Senior Cup (3), F.A. Vase Semi-Finalists (2)
Club captain 83-84: Richard Walden **Player of the Year (83-84):** Keith Morris

Farnborough Town *Back Row (L-R): John Cooper (assistant), Mark Turkington, Dave Steele, Steve Atkins, Tom Hammond, Alex MacFarlane, Kevin Dupree, Tommy Jones, Tony Carter, Richard Berkij, Dennis Rose (trainer/physio). Front Row (L-R): Gordon Wood (assistant manager), Chris Hodge, Brian Broome, Richard Walden (captain), Ted Pearce (manager), Hugh Richardson, Richard Parkin, Keith Morris, Lionel Dodson (reserve team manager).* Photo: Aldershot News

HAMPTON

President: Alan Simpson
Chairman: Bert Lusty
Manager: Roger Charland
Coach:
Physiotherapist:
Press Officer & Tel No:
General Secretary: Adrian Mann
Address & Tel No: 01-568 7358
Commercial Manager:
Address & Tel No:
Address & Tel No of ground: 'Beveree', Station Road, Hampton, Middx. 01-979 2456 **Club shop:** Yes
Simple ground directions: Seven minutes walk from Hampton BR Southern Region
No of seats: 187 **Covered accommodation:** 2,000 **Capacity:** 3,500 **Floodlights:** Yes
Year formed: 1920 **Nickname:** 'Beavers' **Club sponsors:** Normond Instruments
Previous names: None
Previous grounds: None
Club colours: White/Black/Black
Change colours: Sky Blue shirts and shorts
Day for midweek home matches: Tuesday
Record attendance: Unknown **Year:**
Best performance in: F.A. Cup: 1977-78 4th Qualifying Round v Barnet, 1-2
F.A. Trophy: 1983-84 1st Round Proper v Maidstone U, 0-2
Previous Leagues: Kingston District, S.W. Middx, Surrey Senior, Spartan, Athenian, Isthmian
Clubhouse details: Open six nights a week and Sunday lunchtimes during the season, snack bar on match days
Present players with Football League experience: None
Past players who progressed into the Football League: Andy Rogers (Southampton)
Record transfer fee paid: £400 to Hendon for Peter Shodeinde (November 1981)
Record transfer fee received: £400 from Leatherhead for Peter Shodeinde (December 1983)
Programme details: 30 pages, 20p
Programme Editor: Adrian Mann
Local newspapers & Tel No: Surrey Comet, Middlesex Chronicle, Richmond-Twickenham Times
Club metal badges: No
Senior Honours: Surrey Senior Cup, Spartan League (4), Spartan League Cup (4), Middlesex Charity Cup, Southern Combination Cup (3)
Club Captain (1983-84): Steve Rogers **Player of the Year (1983-84):** Steve Rogers

Hampton *Back Row (L-R): Mick Heselden, Simon Constable (now Dorking), Peter Shodeinde (now Leatherhead), Chris Vagg, Paul Riley (now Molesey), Richard Smith, Gary Maynard (no longer with club), Tim Hollands, Steve Russell. Front Row (L-R): John Reader (now Molesey), Brian Lake, Steve Rogers, Clive Marich (now Dorking), Sean O'Connell.* Photo: Surrey Comet

HERTFORD TOWN

President:
Chairman: Colin Vango
Manager: Tommy Barnett
Coach: Dave Lawrence
Physiotherapist: Don Prior
Secretary: Martin Rose
Address & Tel No: 12 The Green, Ware, Herts SG12 0QN. Ware 4448 (H)
Commercial Manager: Martin Rose
Address & Tel No: As above
Press Officer & Tel No: Martin Rose (Ware 4448)
Address & Tel No of ground: Hertingfordbury Park, West Street, Hertford. Hertford 53716 **Club shop:** No
Simple ground directions: By train: Moorgate—Hertford North; Liverpool Street—Hertford East, both 15 mins walk. Green Line: 734/735 to town centre, 10 mins walk.
No of seats: 200 **Covered accommodation:** 1,500 **Capacity:** 6,500 **Floodlights:** Yes
Year formed: 1908 **Nickname:** The Blues **Club sponsors:** Hartham Breakers
Previous names: None
Previous grounds: None
Club colours: Royal Blue
Change colours: Red
Day for midweek home matches: Tuesday
Record attendance: 3,000 v Boston United (East Anglian Cup Final) **Year:** 1963
Best performance in: F.A. Cup: 1973-4 4th Qualifying Round
F.A. Trophy: 1979-80 2nd Round
Previous Leagues: Spartan, Delphian, Athenian, Eastern Counties
Clubhouse details: Open each evening and Sunday lunchtime
Present players with Football League experience: None
Past players who progressed into the Football League: G. Mazzon (Aldershot)
Record transfer fee paid: None
Record transfer fee received: None
Programme details: 20 pages, 20p
Programme Editor: Steven Hedley
Local newspapers & Tel No: Hertfordshire Mercury Hertford 56401
Club metal badges: No
Senior Honours: Herts Charity Cup, Herts Senior Cup, Eastern Counties Cup, East Anglian Cup, Milthras Cup
Club Captain (1983-84): Dave Cooper **Player of the Year (1983-84):** Lennie Merrifield

HORNCHURCH

President: E. A. Prior
Chairman: J. A. Bradshaw
Manager: P. Delea
Coach: A. Butcher
Physiotherapist: B. Davie
Secretary: E. W. Harris
Address & Tel No: 13 Claremont Gardens, Upminster, Essex. Upminster 27891 (H)
Commercial Manager:
Address & Tel No:
Press Officer & Tel No: B. Davie, Hornchurch 45107
Address & Tel No of ground: The Stadium, Bridge Avenue, Upminster, Essex. Upminster 20080 **Club shop:** Yes
Simple ground directions: Fenchurch St to Upminster (BR), 10 mins Upminster station. LT to Upminster Bridge (District Line). Turn right outside station, ground 5 mins away, 2nd turning right — Bridge Avenue
No of seats: 300 **Covered accommodation:** Yes **Capacity:** 4,100 **Floodlights:** Yes
Year formed: 1923 **Nickname:** Urchins **Club sponsors:** Abbey Life
Previous names: Upminster FC; Hornchurch & Upminster FC
Previous grounds: None
Club colours: White/Red trim, Red shorts/socks
Day for midweek home matches: Tuesday
Change colours: Green/Yellow stripes, Green shorts
Record attendance: 2,754 v Chelmsford 2nd Qual. Rnd F.A. Cup **Year:** 1966
Best performance in: **F.A. Cup:** 1966-7 2nd Qual. Rnd
F.A. Trophy: 1966-7 2nd Qual Rnd **F.A. Vase:** 1974-5 5th Rnd
Clubhouse details: Each evening 7.30pm. Disco Saturdays
Present players with Football League experience: None
Past players who progressed into the Football League: D. Armstrong (Millwall), I. Lee (Charlton)
Record transfer fee paid: None
Record transfer fee received: None
Programme details: 10 pages, 15p
Local newspapers & Tel No: Romford Recorder 66044
Programme Editor: Clive Tickner
Club metal badges: Yes
Club Captain (1983-4): Graham Wilsmore

Hornchurch *Back Row (L-R): A. Jacobs, L. Murcott, G. Wilsmore, G. Harrold, S. Hopkins, N. Bissett. Front Row (L-R): K. Davidson, J. Roche, H. Higgins, C. Norman, M. Cleaver, L. Tomkins.*

KINGSTONIAN

President: E. A. Croker
Chairman: F. R. Jones
Manager: Billy Miller
Coach: Chris Kelly
Physiotherapist: John Chick
Secretary: Mrs M. W. Rowat
Address & Tel No: 11 Eastbury Road, Kingston upon Thames. 01-546 5538
Commercial Manager:
Address & Tel No:
Press Officer & Tel No: Derek Guppy (Bagshot 73737)
Address & Tel No of ground: Richmond Road, Kingston upon Thames, Surrey. 01-546 4116 **Club shop:** Yes
Simple ground directions: On main A307 Kingston-Richmond Road, about one mile from town centre
No of seats: 1,200 **Covered accommodation:** 2,500 **Capacity:** 6,500 **Floodlights:** Yes
Year formed: 1885 **Nickname:** The K's **Club sponsors:** None
Previous names: Kingston and Surbiton YMCA, Saxons, Kingston Wanderers, Kingston-on-Thames, Old Kingstonians
Club colours: Red shirts, White shorts
Previous grounds: Richmond Road since 1919
Change colours: Light Blue shirts, Dark Blue shorts
Day for midweek home matches: Tuesday
Record attendance: Not known **Year:**
Best performance in: **F.A. Cup:** 1926, 1930, 1932, 1933 First Round Proper
F.A. Trophy: 1977-8 3rd Qualifying Round
Previous Leagues: Kingston and District, West Surrey, Southern Suburban, Athenian
Clubhouse details: Open every evening and Sunday lunchtime. Large hall for dances, dinners, meetings, socials, etc.
Present players with Football League experience: Chris Kelly (Millwall), Terry Eames (Wimbledon)
Past players who progressed into the Football League: Giles Stille (Brighton), John Lacy (Tottenham Hotspur)
Record transfer fee paid: Alan Morton, Dave Alexander (Woking), Jester Williams (Staines Town)
Record transfer fee received: Giles Stille (Brighton)
Programme details: Available on subscription, 24 pages, 25p
Programme Editor: John Trevor (Chertsey 61790)
Local newspapers & Tel No: Surrey Comet 01-546 2261, Kingston Informer 01-546 2522
Club metal badges: Yes, 65p plus postage
Senior Honours: F.A. Amateur Cup Winners, Finalists; Isthmian League (2), Runners-up (2); Hitachi Cup Finalists; London Senior Cup (2), Finalists (5); Surrey Senior Cup (11), Finalists (5)
Club Captain (1983-84): Ian Armstrong
Player of the Year (1983-84): Micky Preston

LEATHERHEAD

President: W. Stuart Surridge
Chairman: Brian Reynolds
Manager: Micky Leach
Physiotherapist: J. Deary, MBE
Secretary: Jeff Morrell
Address & Tel No: 4 Windsor Court, Anlaby Road, Teddington, Surrey TW11 0PH. Tel: 01-977 5676
Commercial Manager: Secretary
Press Officer & Tel No: Tim Edwards (Guildford 502870) **Club shop:** Yes
Address & Tel No of ground: Fetcham Grove, Guildford Road, Leatherhead, Surrey. Tel. Leatherhead (0272) 377636
Simple ground directions: Fetcham Gr, Leath'hd off Guildford Rd (A246), SW town, follow signs Leath'hd leisure centre
No of seats: 406 **Covered accommodation:** 2,000 **Capacity:** 7,500 **Floodlights:** Yes
Year formed: 1946 **Nickname:** The Tanners **Club sponsors:** None
Previous names: Leatherhead Rose, Leatherhead United
Club colours: Green shirts, Black shorts
Previous grounds: None
Change colours: All Royal Blue
Day for midweek home matches: Tuesday
Record attendance: 32,000 v Leicester City FA Cup 4th Round **Year:** 1975
Best performance in: **F.A. Cup:** 1974-5 v Leicester 4th Rnd, lost 2-3 (h) at Filbert St
F.A. Trophy: 1977-8 v Altrincham Final, lost 1-3
Previous Leagues: Surrey Senior, Metropolitan, Delphian, Corinthian, Athenian
Clubhouse details: Two bars and a 6-a-side hard court available for hire 7 days a week. Bars for darts and disco functions. Times as for pub hours. Steward: Richard Samuels, Leatherhead 72634
Present players with Football League experience: P. Caswell (C. Palace, Crewe), Jimmy Richardson (Wimbledon, Partick T), Micky Belfield (Wimbledon), Mickey Leach (QPR)
Past players who progressed into the Football League: C. Kelly (Millwall), B. Friend (Fulham), L. Harwood (P. Vale), W. Smith (Wimbledon)
Record transfer fee paid: £1,500 for Billy Salkeld from Croydon **Club metal badges:** Yes (£1)
Record transfer fee received: £1,500 from Croydon for Billy Salkeld
Programme details: 20 pages, 20p
Programme Editor: Tim Edwards
Local newspapers & Tel No: Surrey Advertiser, Guildford 71234; Leatherhead Advertiser, Dorking 86661
Senior Honours: Surrey Senior League (4), Corinthian League, Athenian League, Surrey Senior Cup
Club Captain (1983-84): Jimmy Richardson **Player(s) of the Year (1983-84):** Phil Smith, Peter Shodeinde

LEWES

President: C. Elphick
Chairman: G. J. Fowlie
Manager: (Team) B. Jones; (General) D. Southouse
Coaches: H. Wood, R. Smith, P. Swaysland
Secretary: M. J. Webster
Address & Tel No: 2 Station Road, Seaford, Sussex 0323 891890 (H & B)
Commercial Manager:
Press Officer & Tel No: S. Pitman (0273 683385)
Address & Tel No of ground: The Dripping Pan, Lewes. Lewes 2100. Boardroom, Lewes 2574 **Club shop:** Yes
Simple ground directions: Next to Lewes railway station
No of seats: 400 **Covered accommodation:** Yes **Capacity:** 5,000 **Floodlights:** Yes
Year formed: 1885 **Nickname:** The Rooks **Club sponsors:** None
Club colours: Red/Black **Change colours:** Yellow/Black
Day for midweek home matches: Tuesday
Record attendance: 2,500 v Newhaven **Year:** 1947
Best performance in: **F.A. Cup:** 1976-7 4th Qualifying Round
F.A. Trophy: 1982-83 1st Round Proper
Previous Leagues: Sussex County, Athenian
Player of the Year (1983-84): Ricky West
Clubhouse details: Lounge bar open match days
Present players with Football League experience: M. French (Rochdale) **Club Captain (1983-84):** Steve Eke
Past players who progressed into the Football League: G. Elphick (Stoke), G. Geard (Brighton), S. Ford (Stoke)
Record transfer fee received: £2,000 S. Ford to Stoke City
Programme details: 28 pages, 20p
Programme Editor: Sid Pittman
Club metal badges: Yes
Local newspapers & Tel No: Evening Argus, Brighton 606799; Sussex Express, Lewes 6363; Kent & Sussex Courier, Tun Wells 26262
Senior Honours: Sussex Senior Cup Winners (2), Athenian League Div 1 and 2 Winners, Berger Isthmian League Div 2 Runners-up, Gilbert Rice Floodlight Cup Winners

MAIDENHEAD UNITED

President: C. L. West
Chairman: R. C. Cross
Manager: Brian Caterer
Coach: Colin Lippiatt
Press Officer & Tel No: R. West
Secretary: K. Sharp
Address & Tel No: 122 Alwyn Rd, Maidenhead Maidenhead 23258
Commercial Manager: B. Knights
Address & Tel No: High Wycombe 41849 (H)
Address & Tel No of ground: York Road, Maidenhead, Berks. Maidenhead 24739 **Club shop:** Yes
Simple ground directions: 200 yards from Maidenhead railway station (BR Western region)
No of seats: 400 **Covered accommodation:** 3,000 **Capacity:** 7,000 **Floodlights:** Yes
Year formed: 1869 **Nickname:** The Magpies **Club sponsors:** Queensgate Developments Ltd
Previous names: Maidenhead F.C.
Club colours: White shirts, Black shorts
Previous grounds: None
Change colours: Yellow shirts, Blue shorts
Day for midweek home matches: Tuesday
Record attendance: 7,901 v Southall F.A. Amateur Cup Quarter-Final **Year:** 1935-6
Best performance in: **F.A. Cup:** 1872-3 v Oxford University Semi-Final
F.A. Trophy: 1978-9 v Minehead 3rd Qualifying Round
Previous Leagues: Southern, W. Berks, Gt Western Surburban, Spartan, Gt Western Comb, Corinthian, Athenian
Clubhouse details: Open most nights for darts, discos etc
Past players who progressed into the Football League: P. Priddy, D. Kemp, R. Davies, A. Cordice, Laurie Sanchez, E. Kelsey, J. Palethorpe
Record transfer fee received: £5,000 from Norwich for Alan Cordice
Programme details: 12 pages, 20p
Programme Editor: Jon Swan
Club metal badges: Yes (2 designs)
Local newspapers & Tel No: Maidenhead Advertiser, Maidenhead 20451; Evening Post, Reading 55833
Senior Honours: Berks & Bucks Senior Cup (15), Spartan League (3), Corinthian League (2), Mithras Cup
Club Captain (1983-84): Steve Palfrey **Player of the Year (1983-84):** Mark Franks

METROPOLITAN POLICE

President: Sir Kenneth Newman
Chairman: J. M. Sewell QPM
Manager: Vic Rouse
Coach: Brian Dennis
Physiotherapist: Ian Falconer
Press Officer & Tel No: G. Davis 01-399 7374
Secretary: D. J. F. Alldridge MBE
Address & Tel No: 'Woodbeck', 3 Elmshorn, Epsom Downs, Surrey. Burgh Heath 50527 (H), 01-230 2736 or 3518 (B)
Commercial Manager: None
Address & Tel No:
Address & Tel No of ground: Police Sports Ground, Imber Court, East Molesey, Surrey. 01-398 1267 **Club shop:** No
Simple ground directions: A3 then A307 to Scilly Isles roundabout, right into Hampton Court Way, left at roundabout into Embercourt Road and ground faces in 200 yds
No of seats: 600 **Covered accommodation:** 1,000 **Capacity:** 5,000 **Floodlights:** Yes
Year formed: 1919 **Nickname:** The Blues **Club sponsors:** None
Previous names: None
Previous grounds: None
Club colours: All Blue
Change colours: Red or Yellow
Day for midweek home matches: Tuesday
Record attendance: 4,500 v Kingstonian F.A. Cup **Year:** 1934
Best performance in: **F.A. Cup:** 1932 v Northampton 1st Round
F.A. Trophy: 1980 v Aylesbury Utd 3rd Qualifying Round
Previous Leagues: Spartan, Metropolitan, Southern
Clubhouse details: Cafeteria, dining and dance hall with four bars
Present players with Football League experience: Jim Crinigan (Wrexham), Charlie Young (Aston Villa, Gillingham), Ray McIntosh (Glasgow Rangers)
Past players who progressed into the Football League: None
Record transfer fee paid: None
Record transfer fee received: None
Programme details: 8 pages, 10p
Programme Editor: Cyril Davis
Local newspapers & Tel No: Surrey Comet
Club metal badges: No
Senior Honours: Spartan League (8), Middlesex Senior Cup, Surrey Senior Cup, Metropolitan League Cup
Club Captain (1983-84): Colin Rose **Player of the Year (1983-84):** Colin Rose

OXFORD CITY

President: P. J. Tompkins
Chairman: A. E. Rosser
Managing Director: L. T. Goodchild
Manager: John Maskell
Coach: Ian Rundle
Physiotherapist: Andy Glass
Secretary: J. Shepperd
Address & Tel No: 20 Howe Close, Wheatley, Oxford. Wheatley 2181 (H) 0865 726222 (B)
Commercial Manager: B. Breen
Address & Tel No: 0865 726914
Press Officer & Tel No: Club Office 726222, R. Collett
Address & Tel No of ground: White House Ground, White House Road, Oxford. 0865 726222-3 (Office), 248391 (Boardroom), 246308 (Press Box) **Club shop:** Yes
Simple ground directions: One mile south of city centre off Abingdon Road, behind The Folly public house
No of seats: 800 **Covered accommodation:** 500 **Capacity:** 9,000 **Floodlights:** Yes
Year formed: 1882 **Nickname:** The City **Club sponsors:** Oxford Journal
Previous names: None
Previous grounds: None
Club colours: Blue shirts, White shorts/socks
Change colours: Red shirts, White shorts/socks
Day for midweek home matches: Tuesday
Record attendance: 9,500 v Leytonstone Amateur Cup **Year:** 1950 **Previous Leagues:** None
Best performance in: **F.A. Cup:** 1970-1 v Swansea City 2nd Round
F.A. Trophy: 1978-9, 1979-80 3rd Qualifying Round
Clubhouse details: Open normal times daily (242439). Folly Restaurant. Folly Pub and O'Haras cocktail bar: open normal hours
Present players with Football League experience: J. Dolyle, P. Lee
Past players who progressed into the Football League: C. Holton, K. Savin, F. Willcox, R. Adams, A. Jefferies, A. Blakeman, D. Gordon, V. Mobley, J. Varney, P. James, P. Lee, H. Poole, G. Parker
Record transfer fee paid: £3,000 for S. Adams from Woking
Record transfer fee received: £2,000 for P. Dallaway to Witney
Programme details: 24 pages, 20p
Programme Editor: Rodney Collett
Local newspapers & Tel No: Oxford Mail & Times 244988, Oxford Journal 880505
Club metal badges: Yes
Senior Honours: F.A. Amateur Cup Winners; Finalists (2)
Club Captain (1983-84): Gary Goodwin **Player of the Year:** Dale Thorne

Oxford City *Back Row (L-R): Dale Dennis, Dave Alexander, Eddie Innes, Dave Burgess, Mark Teasdale, Neil Munt, John Doyle. Front Row (L-R): Martin Allen, Dale Thorne, Gary Goodwin, Bruce McCrae, Paul Lee.*

ST. ALBANS CITY

President: Ken Hill
Chairman: Mike Watson-Challis
Manager: J. Mitchell
Coach:
Physiotherapist: B. Pyke
Secretary: R. T. Mann
Address & Tel No: 0727 50886
Commercial Manager: Bob Murphy
Address & Tel No:
Press Officer & Tel No: As Secretary
Address & Tel No of ground: Clarence Park, St. Albans. St. Albans 64296
Club shop: Yes
Simple ground directions: 200 yards from St Albans City station
No of seats: 1,000 **Covered accommodation:** Both sides **Capacity:** 8,000 **Floodlights:** Yes
Year formed: 1908 **Nickname:** The Saints/City **Club sponsors:** Blue Arrow Group
Previous names: None
Club colours: All Yellow
Previous grounds: None
Change colours: All Blue
Day for midweek home matches: Tuesday
Previous Leagues: Herts County, Spartan, Athenian
Record attendance: 9,745 v Southall, F.A. Amtr Cup 3rd Rnd Rply **Year:** 1925-26
Best performance in: **F.A. Cup:** 1968-9, 1980-1 2nd Rnd Replay v Walsall, Torquay
F.A. Trophy: 1981-2 2nd Rnd
Clubhouse details: Bar and Boardroom for 200
Present players with Football League experience: None
Past players who progressed into the Football League: John Mitchell
Record transfer fee paid: None
Record transfer fee received: £500 J. Mitchell (Fulham), J. Mawhinney (Letchworth)
Programme details: 16 pages, 20p
Programme Editors: Terry Edwards, Ray Stanton
Local newspapers & Tel No: Herts Advertiser, St Albans 66166
Senior Honours: Isthmian League (3), Spartan League, Athenian League (2), London Senior Cup, Herts County League, A.F.A. Cup, Herts Senior Cup (12), Herts Charity Cup (22), F.A. Amateur Cup Semi-Finalists (4)
Club Captain (1983-84): John Watt
Player of the Year (1983-84): Mark Pearson

St. Albans City *Back Row (L-R): L. Ryan, N. Dudman, M. Riddell, M. Pearson, R. Smale, S. Patterson, J. Mitchell (Manager). Front Row (L-R): P. Wood, P. Mayles, G. Keen, J. Watt, G. Cooper, S. Oliver. Inset, Left: R. Tucker, Right: J. Smith.*

Staines Town *Back Row (L-R): Peter Judd (physio), Dencell Green, Steve Flack, Peter Kemp, Jamie Williamson, Kevin Fidler, Declan Link, Mike Nicks, Henry Tumbridge (treasurer). Front Row (L-R): Steve Livey, Kevin Collins, Paul Allies, Gary Powell, Simon Read (captain), Paul Rumley, Bob Mapleson (now left).*
Photo: Middlesex Chronicle

STAINES TOWN

President: A. Brown
Chairman: A. Boon
Manager: Iain Maclean
Ass. Manager: Bruce Butler
Physiotherapist: Peter Judd
Secretary: J. D. Horne
Address & Tel No: 01-898 3581 (H & B)
Commercial Manager:
Address & Tel No:
Press Officer & Tel No: Steve Parsons (Staines 50420), Colin Simpson (Staines 63910)
Club shop: No
Address & Tel No of ground: Wheatsheaf Lane, Staines, Middx. Staines 55988
Simple ground directions: From Staines (B.R.) turn right along Gresham Rd to 'T' junction, left into Laleham Rd (B376), Wheatsheaf Lane one mile on right, ground 100 yards on left. Bus: No 218.
Capacity: 3,000 **Floodlights:** Yes
No of seats: 300 **Covered accommodation:** 1,000
Club sponsors: Driver & Boon Ltd
Year formed: 1892 **Nickname:** The Swans
Previous names: Staines Albany, Staines Lagonda, Staines Vale
Club colours: Old Gold shirts, Blue shorts/Old Goldsocks
Previous grounds: Staines Lammas, Hammonds Farm, Linoleum Sports Ground, Staines Moor, The Angler's Rest, Goring's Meadow, Shepperton Rd.
Change colours: Light Blue/White
Day for midweek home matches: Tuesday
Record attendance: 2,750 v Banco de Roma Barassi Cup **Year:** 1975
Best performance in: **F.A. Cup:** 3rd Qual. Round Replay 1973-74
F.A. Trophy: 2nd Round proper 2nd Replay 1976-7
Previous Leagues: West London Alliance, West London, West Middlesex, Great Western Suburban, Munitions Works, London Works, Spartan, Middlesex Senior (Parthenon), Hellenic, Athenian
Clubhouse details: Fully furnished clubhouse and function hall 7-11pm
Present players with Football League experience: None
Past players who progressed into the Football League: John Love (Crystal Palace), Peter Shaw (Charlton Athletic)
Record transfer fee paid: £1,750 to Slough for Richard Teale
Record transfer fee received: £10,000 for Peter Shaw to Charlton Athletic
Local newspapers & Tel No: Staines & Egham News, Middlesex Chronicle
Programme details: 16 pages, 20p
Programme Editors Steven Parsons & Colin Simpson
Club metal badges: No
Senior Honours: Athenian League Div 2, Isthmian League Div 2, Middlesex Senior Cup (3), Barassi Cup, London Senior Cup Finalists (2), Athenian League Div 1 Runners-up, Hellenic League, Runners-up
Club Captain (83-84) Simon Read **Player of the Year** (83-84) Simon Read

TILBURY

President: J. Spindley
Chairman: A. D. Raven
Manager: T. Matthews
Coach: B. Reid
Physiotherapist: John Smith
Secretary: J. B. Wilson
Address & Tel No: Tilbury (03752) 71406 (H)
Commercial Manager: F. Morgan
Address & Tel No: Tilbury 75630
Press Officer & Tel No: L. Brown (Grays Thurrock (0375) 71801)
Club shop: Yes
Address & Tel No of ground: St. Chads Road, Tilbury, Essex. Tilbury 3093
Simple ground directions: 15 mins walk from Tilbury Town station (BR Eastern Region). Buses 370, 377, 378
Capacity: 9,750 **Floodlights:** Yes
No of seats: 200 **Covered accommodation:** 2,000
Club sponsors: MOR Line
Year formed: 1900 **Nickname:** The Dockers
Club colours: White shirts, Black shorts/socks
Previous names: None
Change colours: Red or White shirts, Black or White shorts
Previous grounds: Field next to present site
Previous Leagues: Kent, London, Corinthian, Delphian Athenian
Day for midweek home matches: Tuesday
Record attendance: 5,500 v Gorleston F.A. Cup **Year:** 1955
Best performance in: **F.A. Cup:** 1977-8 v Stoke City 3rd Round
F.A. Trophy: 1982-83 v Dartford 3rd Round
Clubhouse details: Open every lunchtime and evening. Pool, darts, bingo, disco's and live bands
Present players with Football League experience: None
Past players who progressed into the Football League: None
Local newspapers & Tel No: Thurrock Gazette, Grays Thurrock 72293
Programme details: 16 pages, 20p
Club metal badges: No
Senior Honours: Essex Senior Cup (4), London League (4), London League Cup (2), Mithras Cup, Isthmian League Cup, Essex Professional Cup

Tilbury *Standing (L-R): Terry Matthews (manager, John Smith (physio), Kim Russell, Tony Rogers, Mark Armstrong, Lee Murcott, Graham Dockrill, Ian North, Chris Bushell (assistant physio), Brian Reed (assistant manager). Front row (L-R): Nicky Smith, Colin Sowerby, Steve Hibbert, Gerry Sullivan, Aidrian Woodstock, Tommy Campbell.*
Photo: Peter Burrin

WALTON & HERSHAM

President:
Chairman: R. Nourse
Manager: W. Salkeld
Asst. Manager:
Physiotherapist: B. Mullett
Press Officer & Tel No: C. Florence
Secretary: G. Pouncey
Address & Tel No: 8 Heathlands, Queens Road, Weybridge, Surrey. Weybridge 53946 (H) 45522 (B)
Commercial Manager:
Address & Tel No:
Address & Tel No of ground: Stompond Lane Sports Grnd, Hersham Rd, Walton-on-Thames, Surrey. Walton 29167
Simple ground directions: Buses 218, 264 or 10 min walk from station (BR Southern Region)
No of seats: 500 **Covered accommodation:** 2,500 **Capacity:** 6,500 **Club shop:** Yes
Year formed: 1896 **Nickname:** The Swans **Floodlights:** Yes
Previous names: None **Club sponsors:** Tony Brooks
Previous grounds: None **Club colours:** Red shirts, Red shorts
Day for midweek home matches: Tuesday **Change colours:** Yellow shirts, Blue shorts
Record attendance: 6,500 v Brighton F.A. Cup **Year:** 1973-74
Best performance in: F.A. Cup: 1972-73, 1973-74 2nd Round
F.A. Trophy: 1983-84 3rd Qualifying Round
Previous Leagues: Surrey Senior, Corinthian, Athenian
Clubhouse details: Open most nights, bar, TV, bingo, darts and pool. Refreshments bar open on match days
Present players with Football League experience: D. Malley, A. Gane
Past players who progressed into the Football League: A. McCulloch (QPR), R. Teale (QPR), S. Parsons (Wimb'don)
Record transfer fee paid: M. Clarke
Record transfer fee received: None
Programme details: 18 pages, 20p
Programme Editor: Chris Florence
Local newspapers & Tel No: Surrey Herald Chertsey 61111
Club metal badges: Yes
Senior Honours: F.A. Amateur Cup, Isthmian League Runners-up, Barassi Cup, Surrey Senior Cup (7), Athenian League, Corinthian League (3)
Club Captain (1983-84): Dennis Malley

WEMBLEY

President: J. E. Bryan BEM
Chairman: E. G. Stringer
Manager: Alan Dafforn
Coach: Ernie Ford
Physiotherapist: Alan King
Secretary: Roy Calmels
Address & Tel No: 01-902 4646
Treasurer: Cyril Farmer
Address & Tel No: 01-902 4821
Press/Publicity Officer & Tel No: Pete Burrin. 01-328 0414 (H), 01-928 2345 ext 675 (B)
Address & Tel No of ground: Vale Farm, Watford Road, Sudbury, Middlesex. 01-904 8169
Simple ground directions: Sudbury Town or North Wembley Underground
No of seats: 250 **Covered accommodation:** 1,000 **Capacity:** 3,000 **Floodlights:** Yes
Year formed: 1946 **Nickname:** The Lions
Previous names: None **Club sponsors:** Sports Programmes
Previous grounds: None **Club colours:** Red/White/Black
Day for midweek home matches: Tuesday **Change colours:** All White
Record attendance: 2,000 v Hendon, M.G.Cup **Year:** 1959-60
Best performance in: F.A. Cup: 1980-1 1st Round
F.A. Trophy: 1978-9 1st Round
Previous Leagues: Middlesex, Spartan, Delphian, Corinthian, Athenian
Clubhouse details: Open nightly, large bar, usual club facilities
Present players with Football League experience: None
Past players who progressed into the Football League: G. Roberts, K. Coote (Brentford), K. Cassels (Watford), C. Johnson (Fulham), M. O'Donaguoe (Southampton), A. McGonigle (Olympiakos)
Record transfer fee paid: None
Record transfer fee received: £10,000 from Brentford for Gary Roberts
Programme details: 32 pages, 20p (voted 2nd best Isthmian League) **Local newspapers & Tel No:** Wembley & Harrow Observer
Programme Editor: Peter Burrin
Senior Honours: Middlesex Senior Cup (1983-4), Middx Charity Cup Winners (1982-3)
Club Captain (1983-4): 'Spud' Murphy **Player of the Year (1983-4):** Steve Lucas

Wembley *Back Row (L-R): Alan Witham (reserve manager), Ernie Ford (assistant manager), Paul Shields, Fred Smart, Peter Ampofo, Don Lucas, Barry Henley, Steve Lucas, Chris Farley, Ian Whitehead, Alan Dafforn (manager), Alan King (physio). Front Row (L-R): Richard Cadette, Declan O'Doherty, Tony Waugh, Dave Head, Spud Murphy (captain), Andy McGonigle, Tony Simpson, Micky Schools, Steve Jackson. In Front: Middlesex Senior Cup Winners 1983/84.* Photo: Peter Burrin

WOKING

President: L. A. Gosden MBE
Chairman: T. H. Spong
Manager:
Coach: Bill Dodgin, Jr
Physiotherapist: B. Kimber
Secretary: P. J. Ledger JP
Address & Tel No: Woking FC, Kingfield. Woking 72470
Commercial Manager: None
Address & Tel No:
Press Officer & Tel No: Geoff Elliss
Address & Tel No of ground: Kingfield Sports Ground, Woking, Surrey (Woking 72470/60855) **Club shop:** Yes
Simple ground directions: 1 mile from Woking Station, down Guildford Road
No of seats: 750 **Covered accommodation:** 600 **Capacity:** 6,000 **Floodlights:** Yes
Year formed: 1889 **Nickname:** Cardinals **Club sponsors:** Several
Previous names: None
Previous grounds: Six other grounds
Club colours: Red & White/Red/Red
Change colours: White shirts, Blue shorts
Day for midweek home matches: Tuesday
Record attendance: 7,762 v Finchley F.A. Cup 4th Round **Year:** 1958
Previous League: West Surrey
Best performance in: **F.A. Cup:** 1978-9 2nd Round
F.A. Trophy: 1979-80 Semi-Final
Clubhouse details: Members bar and separate hall for functions
Present players with Football League experience: M. Hepworth (Sunderland)
Past players who progressed into the Football League: C. Mortimore, J. Mortimore (Chelsea)
Record transfer fee paid: £3,000 Reg Leather (Hillingdon)
Record transfer fee received: £2,500 Tony Field (Dulwich H)
Programme details: 16 pages, 15p
Programme Editor: Geoff Ellis
Local newspapers & Tel No: Woking News & Mail, Woking 61581. Woking Herald
Club metal badges: Yes
Senior Honours: F.A. Amateur Cup, Surrey Senior Cup (5), Surrey Senior Shield (9), Surrey Invitation Cup, Guernsey Victory Cup (2), London Senior Cup Runners-up
Club Captain(s) (1983-84): Paul Holder & M. Hepworth

Walton & Hersham *Standing (L-R): Nick Swindley (Asst Manager), Les Hopgood, Sean Dixon, Steve McCann, Ian Stillwell, Billy Salkeld (Manager), Jeff Hunn, Robert Bray, Mickey Lee. Kneeling (L-R): Gerry Robinson, Gursel Gulfer, Dennis Malley (Capt), John Cahillane, Chris Hills.*

BARTON ROVERS

President: T. Bailey
Chairman: F. Osborne
Manager: D. Bevis
Coach: T. Lamb
Physiotherapist: R. Cullis
Secretary: V. E. Evans
Address & Tel No: 31 Sharpenhoe Road, Barton-le-Clay, Beds. Luton 882866 (H) Luton 882345 (B)
Commercial Manager: None
Address & Tel No:
Press Officer & Tel No: A. Rowley, Luton 882301 **Club shop** Yes
Address & Tel No of ground: Sharpenhoe Road, Barton-le-Clay, Beds. Club – Luton 881075, Boardroom – Luton 882607
Simple ground directions: M1 junction 12, turn right, 2nd right through Harlington & Sharpenhoe, ground on right
No of seats: 120 **Covered accommodation:** 1,000 **Capacity:** 4,000 **Floodlights:** Yes
Year formed: 1898 **Nickname:** 'Rovers' **Club sponsors:** Wallspan Bedrooms Ltd
Previous names: None
Previous grounds: Hexton Road, Barton
Club colours: White/Navy Blue/White
Change colours: Red shirts, White shorts, Red socks
Day for midweek home matches: Tuesday
Record attendance: 1,900 v Nuneaton Boro' **Year:** 1976
Best performance in: F.A. Cup: 1981 1st Rnd v Torquay (A) lost 2-0
F.A. Vase: 1978 Final v Blue Star, lost 2-1
Previous Leagues: Luton & District, South Midlands
Clubhouse details: Two Bars, open match days and every evening. Light meals available at weekends, snacks always
Present players with Football League experience: D. Bevis (Luton)
Past players who progressed into the Football League: None
Record transfer fee paid: None
Record transfer fee received: None
Programme details: 20 pages, 20p
Programme Editor: Owen Clark
Local newspapers & Tel No: Luton News, Luton 21222; Herald, Luton 415061
Club metal badges: Yes
Senior Honours: Bedfordshire Senior Cup (4)
Club Captain (1983-84): Bill Goodyear
Player of the Year (1983-84): Bill Goodyear

BERKHAMSTED TOWN

Chairman: E. Hext
Manager: C. Stevens
Coach: D. Jones
Physiotherapist: C. Hewitt
Secretary: S. G. Hastie
Tel No: Berkhamsted 5393
Commercial Manager: A. Dumpleton
Press Officer: R. Sear
Address & Tel No of ground: Sports Ground, Lower Kings Road, Berkhamsted, Herts. Berkhamsted (2815)
Simple ground directions: Adjoins Berkhamsted Station. A41 to Berkhamsted town centre, traffic lights, turn into Lower Kings Road
No of seats: 65 **Covered accommodation:** 300 **Capacity:** 2,000 **Floodlights:** Yes
Year formed: 1895 **Nickname:** Lillywhites **Club sponsors:** G.F. Kite
Day for midweek home matches: Tuesday
Club colours: White shirts, Black shorts **Change colours:** Red
Previous Leagues: London Spartan, Spartan, Athenian, Delphian, Herts County, West Herts
Clubhouse details: Open daily. Activities include discos, darts, dominoes, pool, pigeon racing
Past players who progressed into the Football League: Maurice Cook (Watford, Fulham)
Best Year in F.A. Vase: 1974-75, 1978-79, 1981-82 2nd Round
Programme: Yes **Club metal badges:** Yes
Programme Editor: Bob Sear
Local Newspapers: Berkhamsted Gazette, Berkhamsted Mail
Senior Honours: Herts Senior Cup 1952-53, London Spartan League Premier Division 1979-80, Spartan League Division II 1926-27, Herts Charity Shield 1950-51 (joint), 1973-74, 1979-80
Club Captain (1983-84): Terry Hows

CHALFONT ST. PETER

President: D. N. Pembroke
Chairman: Ted Brown
Manager: N. C. Beach
Physiotherapist: C. Daily
Secretary: C. E. R. Franks
Address & Tel No: Gerrards X 884514
Address & Tel No of ground: The Playing Fields, Amersham Road, Chalfont St Peter, Bucks (Gerrards Cross 885797)
Simple ground directions: Take A413 from Uxbridge (London) to Chalfont. Turn left at second major roundabout
No of seats: 220 **Covered accommodation:** 200 **Capacity:** 4,000 **Floodlights:** Yes
Year formed: 1926 **Nickname:** The Saints **Club sponsors:** Highlight Windows & Mark Scott Construction
Club colours: White/Green/White **Change colours:** Red/White/Red
Previous Leagues: Great Western Combination, Spartan, Athenian **Programme:** Yes
Clubhouse details: Open every evening, Saturday afternoons and Sunday lunchtime.
Best Year in F.A. Vase: 1975-76 1976-77 1977-78 3rd Round
Local Newspapers: Bucks Advertiser (Gerrards Cross 888333), Bucks Examiner, Bucks Free Press & Midweek
Club Captain (1983-84): Colin Davies **Player of the Year (1983-84):** Andy Boucher

Wembley's Richard Cadette (left) challenges Hayes defender Robbie Johnson in the heart of the home sides defence. Wembley won 3-1 in this First Qualifying Round match.

Photo: Peter Burrin.

Berkhamsted Town *Back Row (L-R): Cliff Stevens, Mark Fussell, John Proctor, Jim Sweeney, Colin Howe, Paul Hughes, Steve Woolfrey, Ray Jeffries. Front Row: Steve Hayward, Roy Jackson, Clive Wright, Paul Bettis, David Bateman.*

Photo: Berkhamsted Gazette.

Chalfont St Peter *Back Row (L-R): N. Beach (Manager), A. Childs (Asst Man), T. Elderfield, S. Pattison, P. Mitchell, R. Ward, T. Gilbert, R. Donovan, C. Daily (Physio), V. Mazurek. Front Row (L-R): S. Mowle, S Byrne, C. Davies, A. Boucher, A. Rooney, S. Smith.*

CHESHUNT

President: Roy Bailey
Chairman: J. Rea
Manager: John Drabwell
Asst. Manager: Dave Woods
Physiotherapist:
Press Officer & Tel No: Roger Carter (01-802 5860)

Secretary: Stan Bailey
Address & Tel No: 01-739 4105

General Manager: B. Pratt
Address & Tel No: Waltham Cross 20239

Address & Tel No of ground: The Stadium, Theobalds Lane, Cheshunt, Herts (Waltham Cross 26752) **Club shop:**
Simple ground directions: Ground on right, four miles after Enfield on London-Cambridge Road (A11) or one mile from M25 orbital motorway
No of seats: 300 **Covered accommodation:** 400 **Capacity:** 4,000 **Floodlights:** Yes
Year formed: 1946 **Nickname:** None **Club sponsors:**
Previous names: None
Previous grounds: None
Club colours: Yellow/Yellow/Blue
Change colours: Blue
Day for midweek home matches: Tuesday
Record attendance: **Year:**
Best performance in: **F.A. Cup:** 4th Q Rd (4)
F.A. Vase: 1981-2 Quarter Final
Previous Leagues: London, Delphian, Athenian, Spartan
Clubhouse details: Two bars open nightly
Present players with Football League experience: None
Past players who progressed into the Football League: None
Record transfer fee paid: None
Record transfer fee received: None
Programme details: 12 pages, 20p
Programme Editor: Roger Carter
Local newspapers & Tel No: Cheshunt-Waltham Telegraph, Enfield Advertiser
Club metal badges:
Senior Honours:
Club Captain (1983-84): Brian Reeves
Player of the Year (1983-84): Paul Read

Epping Town *Back Row (L-R): Hugh Burbridge, Keith Monk (manager), Roy Edwards, Brian Taylor, Kevin Barry, Gary Lloyd, Graham Butterworth, John Spring, Graham Futter (physio), Norman Mitchell, John Preece (kit man). Front Row (L-R): Steve Archer, Paul Austin, Stuart Todd, John Meadows, Dave Barker, Colin Lenihan, Pat Hickey (assistant manager).* Photo: Gazette Sport

EPPING TOWN

President:
Chairman: B. Euston
Manager: Keith Monk
Coach: As Manager
Physiotherapist: G. Futter
Press Officer & Tel No: As Secretary

Secretary: G. Auger
Address & Tel No: 01-211 5606 (B)

Commercial Manager: (Vacant)
Address & Tel No:

Address & Tel No of ground: Stonards Hill, Fairfield Road, Epping, Essex **Club shop:** No
Simple ground directions: From London B1393 (former A11) to Epping through High Street to top of hill, turn sharp right into Tidys Lane, entrance at far end.
No of seats: 250 **Covered accommodation:** 600 **Capacity:** 3,750 **Floodlights:** Yes
Year formed: 1888 **Nickname:** The Town **Club sponsors:** Comet Roofing, Avant Garde Hair Studios, 'Cock & Magpie'
Previous names: None
Previous grounds: Bury Lane
Club colours: White shirts, Black shorts
Change colours: All red or All Blue
Day for midweek home matches: Tuesday
Record attendance: 1,800 v Chelmsford City F.A. Cup **Year:** 1973
Best performance in: **F.A. Cup:** 1973-4 4th Qualifying Round
F.A. Trophy: 1976-7 5th Round
Previous Leagues: Spartan, Parthenon, London, Greater London, Metropolitan, Metro. London, Athenian
Clubhouse details: Open every night except Sundays. Darts, pool, cards. Available for hire
Present players with Football League experience: Garry Steel (Southend U)
Past players who progressed into the Football League: None
Programme details: 12 pages, 20p
Programme Editor: Graeme Auger
Local newspapers & Tel No: West Essex Gazette (Harlow 39970)
Club metal badges: No
Senior Honours: Spartan League Cup, London League, Greater London League, Metropolitan League (2) & League Cup, Athenian League Div 2
Club Captain (1983-84): Kevin Barry
Player of the Year (1983-84): John Meadows

FINCHLEY

President: Rt Hon Margaret Thatcher, MP
Chairman: J. Raymond
Manager: Jeff Voyce
Coach: Ted Goldney
Physiotherapist:
Press Officer & Tel No:
Secretary: J. Jones
Address & Tel No: 01-445 1918
Match Secretary: A. S. Layson
Address & Tel No: 01-449 4707
Commercial Manager: V. Jolly
Address & Tel No of ground: Summers Lane, North Finchley, London N12. 01-445 1400 **Club shop:**
Simple ground directions: Via East Finchley (Northern Line) thence by bus to Summers Lane
No of seats: 650 **Covered accommodation:** 2,000 **Capacity:** 8,650 **Floodlights:** Yes
Year formed: 1874 **Nickname:** Finches **Club sponsors:** None
Previous names: None
Previous grounds:
Club colours: White/Blue/White
Change colours: All Yellow
Day for midweek home matches:
Record attendance: 10,000 v Bishop Auckland **Year:**
Best performance in: F.A. Cup: 3rd Round
F.A. Trophy:
Previous Leagues: North London, Spartan, London Athenian,
Clubhouse details: Two bars, open evenings, Sunday am.
Programme details:
Local newspapers & Tel No:
Senior Honours: Third Round Proper F.A. Cup v Shrewsbury, 1st Round Proper (4), semi-final Amateur Cup, 4th Round Amateur Cup (5), Champions: Athenian League , London Senior Cup (3), Middlesex Senior Cup (4)

FLACKWELL HEATH

President: K. Wootten
Chairman: W. H. Dean
Manager: David Saunders
Secretary: C. H. Robinson
Address & Tel No: 5 Chapman Lane, Flackwell Heath, Bucks. Bourne End 26204
Address & Tel No of ground: Wilks Park, Flackwell Heath, Bucks. Bourne End 23892
Simple ground directions: M40 to A404 take first right to Daws Hill Lane at foot of Marlow Hill. M4 to Marlow By Pass onto A404 and as above
No of seats: 150 **Covered accommodation:** 150 **Capacity:** 3,000 New stand planned **Floodlights:** Yes
Year formed: 1907 **Nickname:** Heathens **Club sponsors:** None
Club colours: Red/White **Change colours:** Yellow/Black
Previous Leagues: Wycombe & District, Hellenic, Athenian
Best Year in F.A. Vase: 2nd Round, 1981-82
Local Newspapers: Bucks Free Press, Bucks Herald, Evening Mail
Major Honours: Berks & Bucks Intermediate Cup (3)

HAREFIELD UNITED

President: G. Preston Jr.
Chairman: L. Wiggins
Manager: Derek Carpenter
Secretary: D. Collier
Address & Tel No:
Address & Tel No of ground: Preston Park, Breakspear Road North, Harefield (Harefield 3474)
Simple ground directions: B.R. (SR) to Denham or Metropolitan or Piccadilly line to Uxbridge, Bus 347
No of seats: 200 **Covered accommodation:** 200 **Capacity:** 4,000 **Floodlights:** Yes
Year formed: 1868 **Nickname:** Hares **Club sponsors:** None
Club colours: Red/Black **Change colours:** All Yellow with Green trim
Previous Leagues: Uxbridge & District, Parthenon, Middlesex, Spartan
Clubhouse details: Two bars, disco and live entertainment
Best Year in F.A. Vase: 3rd Round, 1980-81
Local Newspaper: Middlesex Advertiser

HARINGEY BOROUGH

President: G. Walker (of L.F.A.)
Chairman: M. Jaynoy
Managers: R. Reader & L. Tilley
Coach:
Secretary: J. T. Gates
Address & Tel No: Club, 01-888 4586
Press Officer: J. T. Gates
Address & Tel No of ground: Coles Playing Fields, White Hart Lane, Wood Green, London N17 (01-888 4586)
Simple ground directions: Wood Green (Piccadilly Line), BR(ER) to White Hart Lane
No of seats: 220 **Covered accommodation:** Yes **Capacity:** 2,500 **Floodlights:** Yes
Year formed: 1907 **Nickname:** Borough **Club sponsors:** Yes
Club colours: Amber & Black **Change colours:** Green & White
Previous Leagues: Isthmian, Delphian **Programme:** Yes
Clubhouse details: Bar and social club
Best Year in F.A. Vase: 1974-75 Quarter-Final
Local Newspapers: Tottenham & Wood Green Weekly Herald (01-808 6333)

HEMEL HEMPSTEAD

President: R. Doyle Esq
Chairman: S. Miller Esq
Manager: A. Horsfall
Coach: H. Cowley
Physiotherapist: R. Foster
Secretary: W. J. McGrae
Address & Tel No: 209 Fletcher Way, Hemel Hempstead, Herts. Hemel Hempstead 51503 (H & B)
Commercial Manager: D. R. Howells
Address & Tel No: Hemel Hempstead 58554
Vice Chairman &Press Officer & Tel No: D. R. Howells, Hemel Hempstead 58554
Address & Tel No of ground: Vauxhall Road, Adeyfield, Hemel Hempstead, Herts. Hemel Hempstead 42081
Simple ground directions: BR to Hemel Hempstead station. Bus to Vauxhall Road **Club shop:** Yes
No of seats: 100 **Covered accommodation:** 300 **Capacity:** 3,000 **Floodlights:** Yes
Year formed: 1885 **Nickname:** Hemel **Club sponsors:** None
Previous names: Apsley F.C.
Club colours: Red/Navy/Red socks
Previous grounds: Crabtree Lane
Change colours: All Sky Blue
Day for midweek home matches: Tuesday
Previous Leagues: Delphian, Athenian
Record attendance: v Tooting & Mitcham **Year:** 1963
Best performance in: F.A. Cup: 1963 1st Round
F.A. Vase: 1981-2 5th Round
Clubhouse details: Approx 650 members. Saloon Bar, Entertainment Room and large Bar
Present players with Football League experience: None
Past players who progressed into the Football League: Steve Bateman (Youth Player) (Everton)
Record transfer fee paid: None
Record transfer fee received: None
Programme details: 16 pages, 20p
Local newspapers & Tel No: Hemel Gazette, Hemel Mail
Programme Editor: Roy Howells
Club metal badges: No
Senior Honours: Herts Senior Cup Winners 1906-1908-1909-1925-26
Club Captain (1983-4): Mick Vipond

KINGSBURY TOWN

President:
Chairman: M. Hart
Manager: W. Meadows
Coach: A. Randall
Secretary: D. W. Thomas
Address & Tel No: 01-205 2592
Physiotherapist: Judy Montieth
Address & Tel No of ground: Silver Jubilee Park, Townsend Lane, Kingsbury, London NW9 (01-205 1645)
Simple ground directions: Kingsbury (LT) then 183 bus to Kingsbury Green, right into Townsend Lane
No of seats: 100 **Covered accommodation:** 150 **Capacity:** 4,000 **Floodlights:** Yes
Year formed: 1923 **Nickname:** Town **Club sponsors:** All White Double Glazing
Club colours: Yellow/Red
Change colours: All Blue
Previous Leagues: Partheon, London Spartan
Programme: Yes
Clubhouse details: Open every afternoon, evening and weekends
Best Year in F.A. Vase: 1974-75 4th Round
Local Newspapers:

HEYBRIDGE SWIFTS

Chairman: C. Gill
Manager: J. Sullivan
Coach:
Physiotherapist:
Secretary: D. Fenn
Address & Tel No: 31 Saxon Way, Maldon, Essex (Maldon 54798)
Address & Tel No of ground: Scraley Road, Heybridge, Maldon, Essex. (Maldon 52978)
Simple ground directions: Leave Maldon on main road to Colchester, then on outskirts follow sign to Tolleshunt D'Arcy which leads to ground
No of seats: **Covered accommodation:** **Capacity:** **Floodlights:** Yes
Year formed: **Nickname:** **Club sponsors:**
Club colours: Black & White stripes/Black/White
Change colours: Red/White/Red
Previous Leagues: Essex & Suffolk Border
Clubhouse details:
Programme: 14 pages, 10p
Best Year in F.A. Vase:
Local Newspapers:

LETCHWORTH GARDEN CITY

President: None
Chairman: Ken Fenemore
Manager: Bob Taylor
Coach: Derrick Mardle
Physiotherapist: Doug Page
Press Officer & Tel No: None
Secretary: Jane B. Bygrave
Address & Tel No: 7 Bowershott, Letchworth, Herts Letchworth 5139
Commercial Manager: None
Address & Tel No:
Address & Tel No of ground: Baldock Road, Letchworth, Herts. Letchworth 4691 **Club shop:** No
Simple ground directions: Letchworth exit off A1, to A505, turn right, ground on right 150yds in Baldock direction
No of seats: 250 **Covered accommodation:** 550 **Capacity:** 3,000 **Floodlights:** Yes
Year formed: 1906 **Nickname:** Bluebirds **Club sponsors:** Javelin Holdings
Previous names: Letchworth Town
Club colours: Blue & White
Previous grounds: None
Change colours: White
Day for midweek home matches: Tuesday
Record attendance: 2,000
Previous League: Athenian
Best performance in: F.A. Cup: Unknown
F.A. Vase: 1882-83 3rd Round v Great Yarmouth, 2-5
Clubhouse details: Capacity 200. Two bars, stage and dressing rooms
Present players with Football League experience: None
Past players who progressed into the Football League: Imré Varadi
Record transfer fee paid: £1,500 for G. Cooper from Herakles, Holland
Record transfer fee received: £1,000 each for I. Adcroft (Hitchin) and P. Bowgett (Tottenham)
Programme details: 12 pages, 15p
Local newspapers & Tel No: Comet & Gazette
Programme Editor: Ken Fenemore
Club metal badges: No
Senior Honours: None
Club Captain (1983-84): Chris Hulett
Player of the Year (1983-84): Carl Reyes

Letchworth Garden City *Back Row (L-R): R. Taylor (manager), M. Beech, M. Roche, C. Hulett, P. Gallagher, P. Stephens, G. Day, D. Mardle (assistant manager). Front Row: D. Page (physio), M. Bradshaw, D. Brown, C. Belton, C. Reyes, M. Vooght, S. Harris.*

Leyton-Wingate *Back Row (standing, L-R): L. Reed (coach), E. Joliffe (physio), D. Trainor, C. Tucker, G. Wakeling (manager), S. Goodwin, S. Lane, K. Harris (assistant manager), O. Parkinson, A. Mavin, J. Maloney, G. Mackenzie, E. Tippett. Front Row (L-R): P. Thomas, E. Bee, E. Jones (captain), T. Warwick, D. Rhoden, D. Sharp.*

LEYTON-WINGATE F.C.

Amalgamation of Leyton F.C. (1868) and Wingate F.C. (1946)

Chairman: G. Gross
Manager: G. Wakeling
Coach: Les Reed
Physiotherapist: Andy Taylor
Secretary: Derek Dignum
Address & Tel No: 01-790 4480 (Home)
Commercial Manager: Alan Jackson (01-407 8597)
Press Officer & Tel No: R. Borchard (01-904 5655)
Address & Tel No of ground: Wingate-Leyton Stadium, 282 Lea Bridge Road, Leyton, London E10 7LD (01-539 5405)
Simple ground directions: Leyton (Cent Line), Lea Bridge (BR) or Blackhorse Road (Vic Line) then bus 48, 55, 58 or 230 to Lea Bridge Road
No of seats: 150 **Covered accommodation:** Yes **Capacity:** 3,000 **Floodlights:** Yes
Year formed: Leyton 1868, Wingate 1946, Leyton-Wingate 1975-6 **Nickname:** None **Club sponsors:** O.T.V.
Previous names: Matlock Swifts, Leyton
Club colours: Blue/White/Blue
Previous grounds: Orient FC Ground, Brisbane Road
Change colours: White/Blue/White
Day for midweek home matches: Tuesday
Best performance in: F.A. Cup: 2nd Round 1952
F.A. Vase: 6th Round
Previous Leagues: London, Athenian
Clubhouse details: Open each day of the week
Programme details: 16 pages, 15p
Local newspapers & Tel No: Waltham Forest Guardian
Programme Editor: George Gross (01-850 9082)
Club metal badges: Yes
Senior Honours (since Amalgamation Leyton-Wingate): Athenian League (3), Essex Thameside Trophy, Essex & Herts Border Combination, E & H Border Comb Cup
Club Captain (1983-4): Eddie Jones
Player of the Year (1983-4): Steve Hamberger

MARLOW

Chairman: G. Thomson
Manager: S. Melledew
Coach: M. Hunt
Secretary: P. C. Burdell
Address & Tel No: Marlow 3722
Physiotherapist:
Address & Tel No of ground: Alfred Davis Memorial Ground, Oak Tree Road, Marlow, Bucks (06284 3970)
Simple ground directions: Enter town from by-pass — Esso Service Station on right — turn right into Maple Rise, Oak Tree Road opposite
No of seats: 300 **Covered accommodation:** 300 **Capacity:** 8,000 **Floodlights:** Yes
Year formed: 1870 **Nickname:** The Blues **Club sponsors:** Fineweave Carpets
Club colours: Royal Blue, White trim
Change colours: Orange shirts, Black shorts
Previous Leagues: Southern, Spartan, Athenian
Programme: Yes
Clubhouse details: Open most evenings. Bar with refreshments
Best Year in F.A. Vase: 1974-75 5th Round
Programme Editor: Paul Burdell
Local Newspapers: Bucks Free Press, Evening Post, Maidenhead Advertiser
Club Captain (1983-84): Martin Hunt
Player of the Year (1983-84): Robin Collins

ROYSTON TOWN

Chairman: F. Bradley
Manager: John Bailey
Player/Coach: David Donaldson
Physiotherapist: Paul Scott
Press Officer: As Secretary
Secretary: T. Glasscock
Address & Tel No: 9 Honey Way, Royston Herts. Royston (0763) 44580 (H), 71611 ext 281 (B)
Commercial Manager: A. Barlow
Address & Tel No of ground: Garden Walk, Royston, Herts.
Simple ground directions: From Baldock take A595, to Town Hall roundabout, then A10 to Cambridge, first turn on right is Garden Walk; ground 100 metres on left
No of seats: 40 **Covered accommodation:** 300 **Capacity:** 4,000 **Floodlights:** Yes
Year formed: 1875 **Nickname:** The Crows **Club sponsors:** Comac Computers & Computer Search
Club colours: White/Black
Change colours: Red/White
Players with Football League experience: Dave Donaldson, Tommy O'Neil
Previous Leagues: Herts County, South Midlands
Programme:
Clubhouse details: Open every evening, large clubroom for darts and pool
Major Honours: Herts County Premier, Div.1 (2), S Mid Div. 1
Local Newspapers: Royston Chronicle, Cambridge Evening News

SAFFRON WALDEN TOWN

President: D. Bailey
Chairman: H. Clayden
Manager: John Ryan
Coach: Robin Mills
Physiotherapist: Peter White
Secretary: David Simper
Address & Tel No: 5 Dawson Close, Saffron Walden 0799 22161 (H)
Commercial Manager: John Penny
Press Officer & Tel No: Secretary
Address & Tel No of ground: Caton's Lane, Saffron Walden. (0799 22789) **Club shop:** Yes
Simple ground directions: Ground 250 yards north of common on the B1052
No of seats: 300 **Covered accommodation:** 500 **Capacity:** 1,200 **Floodlights:** Yes
Year formed: 1872 **Nickname:** The Bloods **Club sponsors:** P. Clayden Construction
Club colours: Red & Black
Change colours: White/Red & Black trim
Previous Names: None
Previous Grounds: Saffron Walden Common
Previous Leagues: Essex Senior, Herts County, Spartan
Record Attendance: 1,200 **Year:**
Clubhouse Details: Hall and lounge, both have bars. Open most evenings
Senior Honours: Essex Senior League, Spartan League Div 2, Essex Counties League, Essex Senior Trophy (2)

STEVENAGE BOROUGH F.C.

Chairman: George Clarke
Managers: Frank Cornwell, Paul Peterson
Coach:
Physiotherapist: Alan English
Secretary: Keith Berners
Address & Tel No: Stevenage 724137 (H)
Commercial Manager: None
Address & Tel No:
Press Officer & Tel No: Mark Venables, Stevenage 729906 (H), Letchworth 73508 (B)
Address & Tel No of ground: Stevenage Stadium, Broadhall Way, Stevenage, Herts. 67059 **Club shop:** Yes
Simple ground directions: A602 to Hertford, 1 mile from town centre
No of seats: 500 **Covered accommodation:** Yes **Capacity:** 7,500 **Floodlights:** Yes
Year formed: 1976 **Nickname:** Boro **Club sponsors:** Cadwell Coachworks
Previous names: None
Previous grounds: None
Club colours: Red/White
Change colours: Sky Blue
Day for midweek home matches: Tuesday
Record attendance: 3,000 v All Star XI **Year:** 1981
Previous League: None
Clubhouse details: Portakabin system at present waiting planning permission to build new clubhouse
Programme details: 15 pages, 15p
Club metal badges: Yes
Local newspapers & Tel No: Stevenage Gazette, Stevenage Comet
Senior Honours: UCL Div I winners, Div I KO Cup winners

Flackwell Heath defenders, Simon Bowyer (5), Steve Hunt (4), and Steve Toll close in as Colin Upton fires in a shot for Thatcham. Photo: Newbury Weekly News.

The Ware defence is beaten as Jimmy Rowland scores Newbury Town's first goal. The two sides met at Newbury. Photo: Newbury Weekly News.

TRING TOWN

President: Mr Dorian Williams OBE
Chairman:
Manager: Doug Parkin
Coach: Roy Butler
Physiotherapist: K. Jackson
Press Officer & Tel No: R. Pearson, Garston. 671939
Secretary:
Address & Tel No:
Commercial Manager: None
Address & Tel No:
Address & Tel No of ground: Pendley Sports Centre, Cow Lane, Tring. 3075 **Club shop:** No
Simple ground directions: One mile centre of Tring on A41, turn right just after start M41(M)
No of seats: 200 **Covered accommodation:** Yes, Stand **Capacity:** 4,000 **Floodlights:** Yes
Year formed: 1904 **Nickname:** 'T's **Club sponsors:** VPVC Windows
Previous names: None
Previous grounds: None
Club colours: White/Red/Red
Change colours: All Blue
Day for midweek home matches: Wednesday
Record attendance: 3,000 v West Ham **Year:**
Best performance in: **F.A. Cup:** 1981-2 3rd Qualifying Round
F.A. Vase: 1976-7 4th Round
Previous Leagues: Gt Western Comb, Spartan, Athenian
Clubhouse details: Open every evening except Monday
Programme details: 16 pages, 20p
Club metal badges: Yes
Local newspapers & Tel No: Aylesbury Plus, Bucks Herald, Tring Gazette, Chiltern Radio
Senior Honours: Spartan League, Athenian League Div 2 Runners-up, Herts Senior Cup Finalists
Player of the Year (1983-84): Phil Gleadell

WARE

President:
Chairman: C. T. Hudson
Manager: Arthur Hayes
Coach: Ralph Coates
Physiotherapist: Roy Mautterer
Press Officer & Tel No: C. T. Hudson. Hertford 51862
Secretary: C. J. Dance
Address & Tel No: 18 Salwey Crescent, Broxbourne Herts EN 10 7NJ. Hoddesdon 461177 (H)
Commercial Manager:
Address & Tel No:
Address & Tel No of ground: Buryfield, Park Road, Ware, Herts. Ware 3247 **Club shop:** Yes
Simple ground directions: A10 off at junction with A602 & B1001, signposted behind Rank Radio factory
No of seats: 250 **Covered accommodation:** 500 **Capacity:** 4,500 **Floodlights:** Yes
Year formed: 1892 **Nickname:** The Blues **Club sponsors:** None
Previous names: None
Previous grounds: None
Club colours: Blue & White/Royal Blue/Red
Change colours: Amber/Black shirts, Black shorts, Amber socks
Day for midweek home matches: Tuesday
Record attendance: 2,500 v Arsenal XI **Year:** 1974
Best performance in: **F.A. Cup:** 1968-9 v Luton Town 1st Round Proper
F.A. Trophy: 1979-80 3rd Qualifying Round
Previous Leagues: Herts County, Spartan, Delphian, Athenian
Clubhouse details: Fully licensed, open most nights
Present players with Football League experience: Ralph Coates
Past players who progressed into the Football League: Derek Saunders (Chelsea), Ken Humphrey (QPR)
Record transfer fee paid: None
Record transfer fee received: None
Programme details: 12 pages, 15p
Programme Editor: C. T. Hudson
Club metal badges: No
Local newspapers & Tel No: Herfordshire Mercury Hertford 56401
Senior Honours: Herts Senior Cup (5), Herts Charity Shield (4), Spartan League, Spartan League Div 1
Club Captain (1983-84): Ralph Coates **Player of the Year (1983-84):** Peter Twigg

WOLVERTON TOWN FC

President: Mr. Roche
Chairman: T. Blake
Manager: Ray Richards
Secretary: R. F. Swann
Address & Tel No: 36 Bedford Street, Wolverton MK12 5HR (0908 313374)
Address & Tel No of ground: The Park, Old Wolverton Road, Wolverton (Milton Keynes 312264)
Simple ground directions: M1 turn off at junction 14, ground adjacent to station.
No of seats: 600 **Covered accommodation:** 600 **Capacity:** 3,000 **Floodlights:** Yes
Year formed: 1887 **Nickname:** Wolves
Club sponsors: Stacey Bushes Self-Serve, Knights European Foods
Club colours: Gold/Black **Change colours:** All pale Blue
Previous Leagues: United Counties, London Spartan, Athenian **Programme Editor:** Peter Mumford
Best Year in F.A. Vase: 1974-75, 1975-76, 1976-77, 1977-78 3rd Round
Local Newspaper: Milton Keynes Gazette, Milton Keynes Citizen
Club Captain (1983-84): Phil Barker **Player of the Year (1983-84):** Mark Caswell

Hectic action in the Ware defence as Tring put on the pressure.

After a disastrous start Ware did extremely well to catch up with the pack and only finished in the bottom two on goal difference. Much of the credit for this revival went to ex-England player Ralph Coates (seen dictating play against Hungerford).

Photo: Newbury Weekly News.

Wolverton's distinctive grandstand acts as an impressive backcloth to some goalmouth action during the visit of Ruislip Manor. Photo: Mike Joss.

BANSTEAD ATHLETIC

Chairman: Malcolm Baker
Manager: Colin Turner
Coach: Ted Yorke
Physiotherapist: Ken Jones
Secretary: G. A. Taylor
Address & Tel No: 116 Kingston Avenue, North Cheam, Surrey. 01-641 2957 (H)
Press Officer: Eric Winser
Address & Tel No of ground: Merland Rise, Tadworth, Surrey (Burgh Heath 50982)
Simple ground directions: Follow signs to Tattenham Corner (Epsom Racecourse) then to Banstead Swimming Pool, Ground is next to Swimming Pool
No of seats: 250 **Covered accommodation:** 250 **Capacity:** 4,000 **Floodlights:** Yes
Year formed: 1944 **Nickname:** The "A's" **Club sponsors:** None
Previous Leagues: Surrey Senior, Spartan, London Spartan, Athenian
Clubhouse details: Bar, dance hall, boardroom and kitchen
Best Year in F.A. Vase: 1974-75 3rd Round
Programme: 20-24 pages, 15p (Voted Athenian best programme)
Programme Editor: Malcolm Baker (Chairman)
Club colours: Amber/Black/Black
Change colours: All Red
Local Newspapers: Banstead Advertiser (01-643 4351)
Major Honours: Surrey Senior League (6), Banstead Herald League Cup (2), Surrey Senior League Cup (1), League Charity Cup (3), Surrey County Shield
Club Captain (1983-84): Steve Black **Player of the Year (1983-84):** Jimmy Bates

BRACKNELL TOWN

Chairman: A. Potter
Manager: S. McClurg
Coach:
Physiotherapist:
Secretary: Mrs J. Bradley
Address & Tel No: 7 Furzemoors, Bracknell, Berks RG12 4HT. (Bracknell 427304)
Address & Tel No of ground: Larges Lane, Bracknell, Berks. (Bracknell 423255)
Simple ground directions: Come off A329 at Met. Office roundabout, turn left at tyre company ground, about 100 yds on right
No of seats: 'A' stand 90, 'B' stand 100 **Covered accommodation:** **Capacity:** **Floodlights:** Yes
Year formed: 1896 **Nickname:** **Club sponsors:**
Club colours: Red, White trim/Red/Red, White trim **Change colours:** White/Red/Black, White trim
Previous Leagues: Surrey Senior, London Spartan
Clubhouse details: Yes **Programme:** Yes (new this season)
Best Year in F.A. Vase:
Local Newspapers:

CAMBERLEY TOWN

President: Ian Over
Chairman: Rick Wakeman
Team Manager: Bob Hatt
Secretary: Roy Calver
Address & Tel No: 4 Lincoln Close, Camberley, Surrey, Surrey GU15 1EN. (Camberley 21287)
Ground Address & Tel. No: Krooner Park, Krooner Road, off Frimley Road, Camberley, Surrey (Camberley 65392)
Simple Ground Directions: Halfway between A30 and Frimley on A321 or M3 (exit 4) bear left and follow A321 to shops Krooner Road on left past mini roundabout
No of seats: 250 **Covered accommodation:** 250 seats **Capacity:** 3,500 **Floodlights:** Yes
Year formed: 1896 **Nickname:** 'Town' **Club sponsors:** T.B.A.
Club colours: Red/White **Change colours:** Blue/White
Previous Leagues: Surrey Senior, Spartan, Athenian, Isthmian
Clubhouse details: Large bar open most evenings **Programme:** Yes
Best Year in F.A. Vase: 1978-79 4th Round
Local Newspapers: Camberley News **Club Captain (1983-84):** N. Shurben

The St Albans defence in action again here but this time George Cooper has just bundled over Newbury Town's David Ingram and Steve Foster appeals for, and gets, a penalty awarded.
Photo: Newbury Weekly News.

Ruislip Manor (light shirts) entertain Camberley and win 2-0. Camberley's No. 8 seems to be lifting his foot a little high but the referee doesn't seem to be worried. Photo: Mike Joss

CHERTSEY TOWN

Chairman: Tony Gibbon
Manager: Derek Belsey
Coach:
Secretary: Chris Gay
Address & Tel No: 23 Richmond Close, Frimley, Camberley, Surrey. (Camberley 20745)
Physiotherapist: Don Hanks
Address & Tel No of ground: Alwyns Lane, Chertsey, Surrey (Chertsey 61774)
Simple ground directions: BR(SR) to Chertsey, 10 minute walk, or Buses 459 from Feltham, 436 or 462 from Staines
No of seats: 200 **Covered accommodation:** 500 **Capacity:** 3,000 **Floodlights:** Yes
Year formed: 1898 **Nickname:** Curfews **Club sponsors:** Window World
Club colours: Blue & White **Change colours:** Red & Black
Previous Leagues: Surrey Junior, Surrey Senior, Metropolitan, Greater London, Spartan, London Spartan, Athenian
Clubhouse details: Open match days and most evenings **Programme:** Yes
Best Year in F.A. Vase: 1974-75 4th Round **Programme Editor:** Peter West
Local Newspapers: Chertsey & Addlestone Herald (Surrey Herald Series)
Club Captain (1983-84): Peter Inskip **Player of the Year (1983-84):** Trevor Souter

Included in the Corinthian Casuals centenary celebrations was a match at Hampden against the amateurs of Queens Park. Photo: Leo Hoenig

CORINTHIAN CASUALS

President: Sir M. F. Coop
Chairman: G. D. Harvey
Manager: Johnny Johnson
Coach:
Physiotherapist:
Secretary: Terry Stephens
Address & Tel No: 27 Christchurch Close, Colliers Wood, London SW19 2NZ. 01-542 8905 (H): Staines 57608 (B)
Commercial Manager:
Address & Tel No: Staines 57608
Address & Tel No of ground: Negotiating for new ground
Club shop:
Simple ground directions:
No of seats: **Covered accommodation:** **Capacity:** **Floodlights:**
Year formed: 1882/1883; (merged 1939)
Nickname: Casuals
Club sponsors: None
Previous names: Corinthians & Casuals
Club colours: White/Navy Blue
Previous grounds: several: Oval, Kingston, Dulwich, etc
Change colours: Chocolate & Pink
Day for midweek home matches: Tuesday
Previous Leagues: Southern Amateur
Record attendance: FA Amateur Cup **Year:** 1956
Best performance in: **F.A. Cup:** 1965-66, 1983-84 1st Round
F.A. Vase: 1983-84 5th Round
Clubhouse details:
Present players with Football League experience: None
Past players who progressed into the Football League: Peter Phillips (Luton Town)
Record transfer fee paid: None
Record transfer fee received: None
Programme details: 4/8 pages, 15p
Local newspapers & Tel No:
Club metal badges: Yes
Senior Honours: FA Amateur Cup winners and finalists

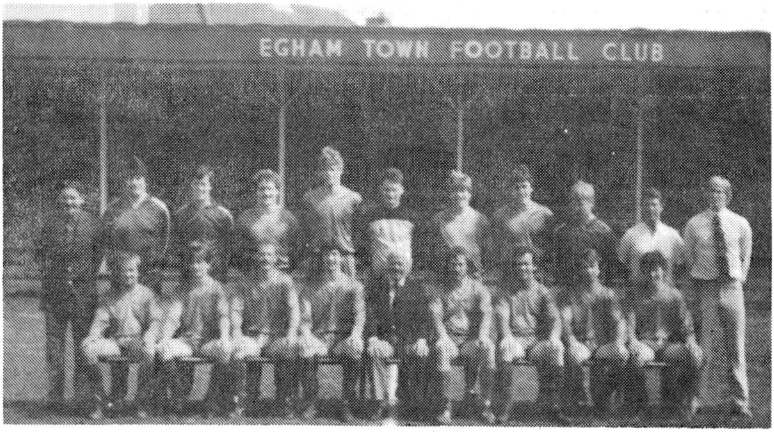

DORKING

President:
Chairman: Terry Connors
General Manager: Phil Illman
Player/Coach: Martyn Spong
Physiotherapist: Gordon Bosworth
General Secretary: Shirley Carpenter (Mrs)
Address & Tel No: Dorking 883927 (B)
Football Secretary: Roger Young
Address & Tel No: Dorking 882284 x63 (Home)
Press Officer & Tel No: Dick Richards, Ashtead 77013
Address & Tel No of ground: Meadowbank Ground, Mill Lane, Dorking. Tel No 884112
Club shop: No
Simple ground directions: Mill Lane opposite White Horse Hotel in Dorking town centre. Fork right in Mill Lane which leads direct to ground
No of seats: 100 **Covered accommodation:** 100 **Capacity:** 3,000 **Floodlights:** Yes
Year formed: 1977
Nickname: 'The Chicks'
Club sponsors: None
Previous names: Dorking Town F.C.
Club colours: Green/White/Red
Previous grounds: None
Change colours: Red/Blue striped shirts, red or green shorts/socks
Day for midweek home matches: Tuesday
Record attendance: 800 v Haugar (Norway) **Year:** 1980
Previous Leagues: Surrey Senior, Athenian
Best performance in: **F.A. Cup:** 1978-9 2nd Qualifying Round
F.A. Vase: 1983-4, 3rd Round
Clubhouse details: Small Clubroom (to be extended this summer). Open every evening & Sunday morning
Record transfer fee paid: £400 to Dartford for Charlie Pooley
Record transfer fee received: None
Programme details: 16 pages, 15p
Local newspapers & Tel No: Dorking Advertiser, Surrey Advertiser
Programme Editors: Roger Young & Shirley Carpenter
Club metal badges: No
Senior Honours: None
Club Captain (1983-4): Kevin Wellstead & Jimmy Davies
Player of the Year (1983-4): Ronnie McNamara

EASTBOURNE UNITED

President: C. Philcox
Chairman: M. Dow
Manager: Brian Donnelly
Coach: Doug Thomas
Physiotherapist: J. Maguire
Press Officer & Tel No: Derek York. Polegate 4136
Secretary: D. York
Address & Tel No: Eastbourne 30634 (H)
Commercial Manager: None
Address & Tel No:
Club shop: Yes
Address & Tel No of ground: The Oval, Channel View Road, Eastbourne, Sussex, BN23 7JP. 0323 26989
Simple ground directions: A22 to seafront, turn East to Princes Park on left at Channel View Rd
No of seats: 250 **Covered accommodation:** 1,000 **Capacity:** 7,000 **Floodlights:** Yes
Year formed: 1894 **Nickname:** The 'Us' **Club sponsors:** Kings Country Club and M&B Motors
Previous names: None
Previous grounds: None
Club colours: White shirts, Black shorts/socks
Change colours: Red shirts, White shorts/socks
Day for midweek home matches: Tuesday
Record attendance: 2,000 v Millwall **Year:** 1980
Best performance in: **F.A. Cup:** 1978-9 3rd Qualifying Round
F.A. Vase: 1978-9 Quarter Finals
Previous Leagues: Athenian, Metropolitan, Sussex County
Clubhouse details: Large Bar open most days
Present players with Football League experience: None
Past players who progressed into the Football League: T. Funnell, B. Salvage, G. French
Record transfer fee paid: None
Record transfer fee received: £3,000
Programme details: 20 pages, 20p
Programme Editor: Derek York
Local newspapers & Tel No: Eastbourne Gazette & Herald
Club Captain (1983-84): Phil Comber
Player of the Year (1983-84): John Adams

EGHAM TOWN

President: J. H. S. Ward
Chairman: A. L. Doye
Manager: Dave Brown
Coach: Tony Clerkin
Physiotherapist: Gary Anderson
Press Officer & Tel No: Neil Morrell
Secretary: S. F. Payne
Address & Tel No: 14 Brookside, Uxbridge 0895 36709 (H), 01-573 3888/3062 (B)
Commercial Manager: Neil Morrell
Address & Tel No: 0753 823822
Address & Tel No of ground: Tempest Road, Egham, Surrey. Egham 35226 **Club shop:** No
Simple ground directions:
No of seats: 250 **Covered accommodation:** 150 **Capacity:** 5,000 **Floodlights:** Yes
Year formed: 1963 **Nickname:** 'Town' **Club sponsors:** None
Previous names: None
Previous grounds: None
Club colours: Blue & Gold
Change colours: All White
Day for midweek home matches: Tuesday
Record attendance: 3,500 v C. Palace **Year:** 1981
Best performance in: **F.A. Cup:**
F.A. Trophy:
Previous Leagues: Surrey Senior, Spartan, Athenian
Clubhouse details: Main Hall & Bar, Lounge Bar, Games Room and Boardroom
Present players with Football League experience: None
Past players who progressed into the Football League: None
Record transfer fee paid: None
Record transfer fee received: None
Programme details: 4 pages, 10p
Programme Editor: Neil Morrell
Local newspapers & Tel No: Staines & Egham News
Senior Honours: Spartan League, Athenian League
Club Captain (1983-84): Wayne Clift
Player of the Year (1983-84): Keith Bristow

FELTHAM

President: E. J. Pauling MBE JP
Chairman: John Lally
Manager: Ian Wenlock
Coach: Ian Wenlock
Physiotherapist:
General Secretary: J. E. Pauling
Address & Tel No: 31, St. Georges Road, Hanworth, Feltham, Middx 01-898 0515 (H), 01-560 2131 x4374 (B)
Commercial Manager: J. Pauling
Address & Tel No:
Press Officer & Tel No: Martin Simpson. Ashford (Middx) 46059
Address & Tel No of ground: Feltham Arena, Shakespeare Avenue, Feltham, Middx. 01-890 6119 (Ground), 01-890 6241 (Club), 01-890 0490 (Boardroom)
Club shop: Yes
Simple ground directions: From Feltham (S.R.) five minutes walk through Glebelands Park
No of seats: 1,600 **Covered accommodation:** 2,500 **Capacity:** 12,000 **Floodlights:** Yes
Year formed: 1946 **Nickname:** The Blues **Club sponsors:** None
Previous names: Tudor Park
Previous grounds: None as Feltham
Club colours: Blue/White
Change colours: All Red
Day for midweek home matches: Wednesday
Record attendance: 1,938 v Hampton, Middx Senior Cup **Year:** 1972-3
Best performance in: **F.A. Cup:** 1977-8, 1982-3 3rd Qual. Round
F.A. Vase: 1982-3 1st Qual. Round
Previous Leagues: Surrey Senior, Spartan, Athenian
Clubhouse details: Two bars, dance floor for 120 people. Open every night. Live ents. Tues, Thur, Fri, Sat and Sunday
Present players with Football League experience: None
Past players who progressed into the Football League: Rachid Harkouk (Notts County), Andy Pape (QPR)
Record transfer fee received: Not disclosed
Programme details: 12 pages, 15p
Programme Editor: Martin Simpson
Local newspapers & Tel No: The Informer 01-546 2522, Middlesex Chronicle 01-572 0016
Senior Honours: Surrey Senior League Charity Cup (2), Surrey Senior League Cup, Berger Isthmian League Div 2
Club Captain (1983-84): Kevin McDonagh
Player of the Year (1983-84): Paul Clarke

GRAYS ATHLETIC

Patron: R. J. Billings
President: B. S. Coker
Chairman: Jim Myers
Managers: Jeff & Fred Saxton
General Manager: Gordon D. Norman
243B Wingletye Lane, Hornchurch (Horn. 51733)
Secretary: J. G. Saxton
Address & Tel No: 2 Cotswold Gardens, Newbury Park, Ilford, Essex. 01-554 3920 (H)
Commercial Manager: G. R. Jarvis
Address & Tel No: 8 Pargetters Hyam, Huckley, Essex. 0702 546366 (B)
Address & Tel No of ground: The Recreation Ground, Bridge Road, Grays, Essex (Grays Thurrock 73424)
Simple ground directions: A13 to Southend, right at first traffic lights, past Dartford Tunnel to Grays Town. Ground to east of town. Rail: BR(ER) from Fenchurch St to Grays Station (5 mins walk)
No of seats: 200 **Covered accommodation:** 3,000 **Capacity:** 6,000 **Floodlights:** Yes
Year formed: 1890 **Nickname:** The Blues **Club sponsors:** The Boys from Rathbone Street
Record attendance: 9,500 v Chelmsford City **Year:** 1959
Club colours: Sky Blue/Royal Blue/Sky Blue **Change colours:** White/Blue/Black
Previous Leagues: Essex Senior, Corinthian, Athenian **Programme:** 8 pages, 20p
Clubhouse details: Open normal licensing hours. Discos, darts, bar billiards, dances etc
Best Year in F.A. Vase: 1977-78 1979-80 1981-82 4th Round
Programme Editor: Graham Deats **Local Newspaper:** Thurrock Gazette (Grays Thurrock 72293)
Club Captain (1983-84): Phil Wettell **Player of the Year (1983-84):** Michael Welch

HORSHAM

President: G. G. Holtom
Chairman: J. Isaacs
Manager: Ray McCarthy
Coach: G. Russell
Physiotherapist: Coach
Secretary: Frank King
Address & Tel No: c/o Club, 0403 64647
Vice Chairman & Commercial Manager: E. Streeter
Address & Tel No: 0403 62806 (H)
Press Officer & Tel No: J. Bramley **Treasurer:** J. Barrett
Address & Tel No of ground: Queen Street, Horsham, West Sussex. Horsham 52310 **Club shop:** Yes
Simple ground directions: From Horsham station turn left, take left fork, turn left at lights, proceed under railway bridge, ground 120 yds on right
No of seats: 300 **Covered accommodation:** 3 sides of ground **Capacity:** 2,000 **Floodlights:** Yes
Year formed: 1885 **Nickname:** The Hornets **Club sponsors:** Arco (Waterford Road, Horsham)
Previous names: None **Club colours:** Amber/Green/Amber
Previous grounds: None **Change colours:** White
Day for midweek home matches: Wednesday
Previous Leagues: Corinthian, Sussex County, Metropolitan, West Sussex, Athenian
Record attendance: 9,000 v Swindon, F.A. Cup **Year:** 1966
Best performance in: **F.A. Cup:** 1966 1st Round Proper
F.A. Vase: Unknown
Clubhouse details: 'Hornets Nest' Members Club. Open most evenings
Present players with Football League experience: Marvin Hinton (Chelsea)
Past players who progressed into the Football League: None
Record transfer fee paid: None
Record transfer fee received: None **Programme Editor:** John Bramley
Programme details: 24 pages, 20p **Local newspapers & Tel No:** West Sussex County Times
Club metal badges: No
Senior Honours: Sussex Senior Cup (7), Athenian League, Floodlight League
Club Captain (1983-84): Terry King

Hungerford Town *Back Row (L-R): Tim North, Robin Gosnell, Martin Turner, Mark Whiffin, Simon Pentland, Dean Bailey, Paul Duffy. Front Row (L-R): Chris Gwynn, Kevin Bright, Roy Clark, Ian Farr, Shane Chandler.*

HUNGERFORD TOWN

President: E. Barrett
Chairman: R. Tarry
Manager: J. Kelman
Coach: J. Kelman
Physiotherapist: P. Bailey
Press Officer & Tel No: Malcolm Howe, Newbury 46464
Secretary: Keith Lovitt
Address & Tel No: 42 Pear Tree Lane, Newbury, Berks RG13 2LX. New. 42441 (H), New. 45321 x301 (B)
Commercial Manager: Nick Savage
Address & Tel No: "Porthkerry", St. James Close, Littleworth, Norton, Worcs. 0905 821167
Address & Tel No of ground: Town Ground, Bulpit Lane, Hungerford. Tel. H. 82939 **Club shop:** Yes
Simple ground directions: M4 exit 14, to A4, turn right, left at Bear Hotel, through town up High St, left to ground and swimming pool
No of seats: 100 **Covered accommodation:** 500 **Capacity:** 3,000 **Floodlights:** Yes
Year formed: 1886 **Nickname:** Crusaders **Club sponsors:** Hungerford Cab Hire
Previous names: None **Previous grounds:** None **Club colours:** All White **Change colours:** All Red
Day for midweek home matches: Tuesdays
Record attendance: 1,541 v Barton Rovers, F.A. Vase Semi-Final **Year:** 1978
Best performance in: F.A. Cup: 1979-80 1st Round Proper
F.A. Vase: 1977-8, 1979-80 Semi-final
Previous Leagues: Newbury & District, Swindon, Hellenic
Clubhouse details: Three bars, stage, video club. Open 7 days week. Lunchtimes, weekends, refreshments available, hot and cold food. Associated darts section
Present players with Football League experience: Ian Farr (Swindon T)
Past players who progressed into the Football League: Steve Hetzke (Reading), Des McMahon (Reading), Brian Mundee (Bournemouth)
Record transfer fee paid: £4,000, Joe Scott, Yeovil Town
Record transfer fee received: £3,800, Joe Scott, Barnstaple Town
Programme details: 8 pages, 10p
Programme Editor: Diane Kelman
Local newspapers & Tel No: Newbury Weekly News, Reading Evening Post, Swindon Post
Club metal badges: Yes
Senior Honours: Berks & Bucks Senior Cup & Finalists (3), One of Four British Reps in Anglo/Italian 1980/1
Club Captain (1983-84): Martin Turner **Player of the Year (1983-84):** Simon Pentland

MOLESEY

President: K. F. Alderton
Chairman: Graham Pearce
Manager: Arthur Evans
Coach: None
Physiotherapist: Bob Lumsden
Secretary: Kevin Wilkins
Address & Tel No: 15 Berkeley Drive, West Molesey, Surrey. 01-979 4073
Commercial Manager: None
Address & Tel No:
Press Officer & Tel No: Peter Bowers (01-330 1306)
Address & Tel No of ground: Walton Road, West Molesey, Surrey (01-979 4823) **Club shop:** No
Simple ground directions: From Hampton Court take Esher Road, turn right to West Molesey, ground 1 mile on left
No of seats: 400 **Covered accommodation:** 500 **Capacity:** 4,000 **Floodlights:** Yes
Year formed: 1953 **Nickname:** The Moles or Whites **Club sponsors:** None
Previous names: Molesey St. Pauls United **Club colours:** White/Black/Black
Previous grounds: None **Change colours:** Blue/Sky Blue/Sky Blue
Day for midweek home matches: Wednesday
Record attendance: 1,100 v Billericay T. **Year:** 1979-80
Best performance in: F.A. Cup: 1975-6 3rd Qualifying Round
F.A. Vase: 1981-2 Quarter Final v Rainworth M.W.
Previous Leagues: Surrey, Spartan Athenian
Clubhouse details: Open every night. Two bars, Saturday disco, live artists on occasional Saturday nights, bar nights, darts, eight ball pool, bingo. Steward: T. Kavanagh
Present players with Football League experience: None
Past players who progressed into the Football League: Cyrille Regis (W.B.A. via Hayes)
Programme details: 12 pages, 20p
Programme Editor: Graham Pearce
Local newspapers & Tel No: Surrey Herald, Surrey Comet, Molesey News and Mail
Club Metal Badges: No
Senior Honours: Surrey Senior League Charity Cup, Surrey Senior League, Spartan League Runners-up, Senior Challenge Cup Runners-up, Spartan League Challenge Cup & Runners-up, Surrey Senior Shield Runners-up
Club Captain (1983-4): Tony Coombe **Player of the Year (1983-4):** Gary McDonald

Newbury Town *Back Row (L-R): John Griffith, Dave Crowdy, Steve Foster, Sandy Davidson, Charlie Penny, Mick Denny, Adriam Cooper. Front Row: Jimmy Rowland, Alan Prior, Tony Ingram, David Ingram, Nevada Phillips.*

NEWBURY TOWN

President:
Chairman: D. Raynor
Manager: John Murray
Coach: Sav Ramayon
Secretary: N. D. Whiting
Address & Tel No: 103 Digby Road, Newbury, Berks 0635 47976
Address & Tel No of ground: Faraday Road, Newbury (Newbury 40048)
Simple ground directions: Turn off A4, through Industrial Estate, 100 yards from Robin Hood roundabout on Ring Road
No of seats: 100 **Covered accommodation:** 200 **Capacity:** 2,500 **Floodlights:** Yes
Year formed: 1887 **Nickname:** Town **Club sponsors:** Bayer (UK) Ltd
Previous names: None
Previous grounds: None
Club colours: Gold & Black
Change colours: Green & Black
Day for midweek home matches:
Best performance in: F.A. Cup: 1980-81 3rd Qual Round
F.A. Vase: 1979-80 5th Round
Previous Leagues: Great Western, Suburban, Hampshire, Reading & District, Metropolitan, Hellenic, Athenian
Clubhouse details: Two bars with large dance hall and well equipped kitchen
Present players with Football League experience: John Murray (Burnley, Bury, Blackpool, Reading, Brentford)
Past players who progressed into the Football League: D. McCartney (WBA)
Record transfer fee paid: None
Record transfer fee received: None
Programme details: 20 pages, 20p
Club metal badges: No
Local newspapers & Tel No: Newbury Weekley News Reading Post
Senior Honours: Berks & Bucks Senior Cup 1898, Hellenic League (2), Hellenic League Cup (2), Athenian League

PETERSFIELD UNITED

President: H. J. Wicks
Chairman: J. D. Stimpson
Managers: M. Wallis, J. Woollett (joint)
Coach: J. O'Kane
Secretary: B. S. Hall
Address & Tel No: 14 Norevil Road, Petersfield, Hants GU32 3BA. Petersfield 68211 (B)
Address & Tel No of ground: Love Lane, Petersfield. Petersfield 62177
Simple ground directions: 10 minutes' walk from railway station heading towards London
No of seats: 150 **Covered accommodation:** stand **Capacity:** 2,500 **Floodlights:** Yes
Year formed: 1946 **Nickname:** United **Club sponsors:** Royal Oak
Club colours: Red & Black stripes, Black shorts & socks **Change colours:** White shirts, Red shorts & socks
Previous names: None **Previous grounds:** None
Record attendance: 800 v Portsmouth (friendly), 1983
Previous Leagues: Hampshire League, Portsmouth Premier League
Clubhouse details: Bar, boardroom, showers, dressing rooms **Programme:** 8 pages, 10p
Major Honours: Hants League Div 2 championship 1982, Aldershot Senior Cup winners 1982, 1983

RAINHAM TOWN

President: H. G. Stoneham
Chairman: G. Burrell
Manager: Mike Acland
Coach: Tony Brooking
Physiotherapist: Mrs J. Kershaw
Secretary: T. M. King
Address & Tel No: Rainham 57596 (H) 01-283 8989 x63123 (B)
Commercial Manager: None
Address & Tel No:
Press Officer & Tel No: As Secretary
Address & Tel No of ground: Deri Park, Wennington Road, Rainham, Essex. Rainham 53280/54778 **Club shop:** No
Simple ground directions: Along A13 turn into B1335 past Rainham station, 400 yds on right
No of seats: 600 **Covered accommodation:** 1,500 **Capacity:** 4,000 **Floodlights:** Yes
Year formed: 1945 **Nickname:** The Reds **Club sponsors:** None
Previous names: None
Club colours: All Red
Previous grounds: Rainham Working Men's Club
Change colours: Black & White
Day for midweek home matches: Tuesday
Record attendance: 2,300 v Finchley **Year:** 1950
Best performance in: F.A. Cup: 1974-5 2nd Qualifying Round
F.A. Vase: 1977-8 5th Round
Previous Leagues: South Essex, London, Delphian, Metropolitan, Athenian
Clubhouse details: Open 7 days. Food and Snacks available
Programme details: 6 pages, 10p
Club metal badges: Yes
Programme Editor: T. King
Local newspapers & Tel No: Romford Recorder 66044
Senior Honours: None
Club Captain (1983-4): Colin Boxall
Player of the Year (1983-4): Colin Boxall

RUISLIP MANOR

Chairman: C. Gregory
Manager: Ray Farrell
Coach: Roger Goodhind
Secretary: Ray Farrell
Address & Tel No: 9 Harcourt Road, Dorney Reach, Nr. Maidenhead, Berks. Maidenhead 24069
Address & Tel No of ground: Grosvenor Vale, Ruislip, Middlesex (Ruislip 37487)
Simple ground directions: Ruislip Manor Station, turn left, first right into Shenley Avenue then third left Cranley Drive to ground
No of seats: 250 **Covered accommodation:** 500 **Capacity:** 6,000 **Floodlights:** Yes
Year formed: 1938 **Nickname:** Manor **Club sponsors:** Rational
Club colours: Yellow/Black/Yellow
Change colours: All White
Previous Leagues: Middlesex Senior, London, Spartan, Athenian
Programme: Yes
Programme Editor: M. Howard
Clubhouse details: Open every evening and lunchtime. Refreshments available
Best Year in F.A. Vase: 1977-78 1980-81 1981-82 3rd Round
Local Newspapers: Ruislip Northwood Gazette
Club Captain (1983-84): Richard Burnell

SOUTHALL

President: R. F. Fowler
Chairman: None
Manager: M. Byrne
Coach: G. Bartlett
Physiotherapist: None
Secretary: A. J. Bevis
Address & Tel No: 01-866 1063 (H)
Commercial Manager: None
Address & Tel No:
Press Officer & Tel No: A. Evans (01-864 9963)
Address & Tel No of ground: Western Road, Southall. 01-574 1084 **Club shop:** No
Simple ground directions: Turn left out of Southall station, 3rd right Western Road
No of seats: 150 **Covered accommodation:** 400 **Capacity:** 12,000 **Floodlights:** Yes
Year formed: 1871 **Nickname:** The Hall **Club sponsors:** Ealing Sports
Previous names: None
Club colours: Red/White stripes, Red shorts/socks
Previous grounds: None
Change colours: All White
Day for midweek home matches: Tuesday
Record attendance: 20,000 **Year:** 1935-36
Best performance in: F.A. Cup: 1935-6 3rd Round Proper
F.A. Vase: 1981-2
Previous Leagues: Southern, London, Great Western Suburban, Athenian
Clubhouse details: Open every night and Sunday lunchtime
Present players with Football League experience: None
Past players who progressed into the Football League: Alan Devonshire (West Ham), Gordon Hill (Millwall, Manchester Utd), Chris Hutchings (Chelsea, Brighton)
Record transfer fee paid: None
Record transfer fee received: £5,000 for Alan Devonshire
Programme details: 20 pages, 15p
Local newspapers & Tel No: Ealing Gazette, Middlesex Chronicle
Programme Editor: Alan Evans
Club metal badges: Yes, 75p
Senior Honours: Athenian League Champions, Amateur Cup Finalists
Club Captain (1983-84): Reg Leather
Player of the Year (1983-84): Ken Lavender

UXBRIDGE

President: T. H. Try
Chairman: T. H. Barnard
Manager: R. Clack
Coach: P. Marshall
Physiotherapist: E. Kempster
Secretary: D. L. Tucker
Address & Tel No: 0895 832921 (H) 01-626 4588 (B)
Commercial Manager: None
Address & Tel No:
Press Officer & Tel No: J. Wormald (01-573 3392)
Address & Tel No of ground: Honeycroft, Horton Road, West Drayton, Middx. 0895 443557 **Club shop:** Yes
Simple ground directions: From West Drayton (BR) Station turn right, then first right into Horton Road, Ground 1 mile on left
No of seats: 180 **Covered accommodation:** 180 **Capacity:** 5,000 **Floodlights:** Yes
Year formed: 1871 **Nickname:** Reds **Club sponsors:** None
Previous names: None
Club colours: Red/White/Red
Previous grounds: Cleveland Rd, Uxbridge
Change colours: Sky Blue
Day for midweek home matches: Tuesday
Previous Leagues: Athenian
Record attendance: 1,000 v Arsenal, Floodlight opening **Year:** 1981
Best performance in: F.A. Cup: 1873-74 2nd Round
F.A. Vase: 1983-84 4th Round
Clubhouse details: Large clubhouse with bar and dance hall. Open every evening except Monday
Present players with Football League experience: None
Past players who progressed into the Football League: Colin Franks
Record transfer fee paid: None
Record transfer fee received: None
Programme details: 12 pages,
Local newspapers & Tel No: Middlesex Advertiser 0895 37161
Programme Editor: Gary Trimby
Club metal badges: Yes
Senior Honours: Middlesex Senior Charity Cup
Club Captain (1983-84): Roger Nicholls
Player of the Year (1983-84): Roy Marshall

Uxbridge *Back Row (L-R): Peter Marshall (Coach), Jon Flanagan, Clifford Williamson, Andy Everley, Fred Cummings, Roger Nicholls, Roy Marshall, Gordon Stewart, Ron Clack (Manager). Front Row (L-R): Peter Hewitt, Steve Williamson, Steven Church, Mark Nicholls (Mascot), Chris Dixon, Phil Duff, Ernie Kempster (Trainer).* Photo: Uxbridge Gazette Series

WHYTELEAFE

President:
Chairman: Fred Ovenden
Manager: Roy Burton
Secretary: K. Rawson
Address & Tel No: 22 Foxon Lane Gardens, Caterham, Surrey. Caterham 47390
Address & Tel No of ground: Church Road, Whyteleafe, Surrey (01-660 5490)
Simple ground directions: BR(SR) to Whyteleafe. By road on A22 to Whyteleafe, then up Whyteleafe Hill, Church Road 200 yds on left
No of seats: 200 **Covered accommodation:** 200 **Capacity:** 5,000 **Floodlights:** Yes
Year formed: 1946 **Nickname:** Leafe **Club sponsors:** BP Automobiles
Club colours: White shirts, Green shorts
Change colours: Yellow shirts, Black shorts
Previous Leagues: Surrey Senior, London Spartan
Programme: Yes
Clubhouse details: Open every lunchtime and evening
Best Year in F.A. Vase: 1981-82 5th Round
Local Newspapers:

ATHENIAN LEAGUE

Chairman: F. E. Bell

Secretary: B. W. Hitchings, 18 Tany's Dell, Harlow, Essex CM20 2LJ

'REDS' WIN FIRST CHAMPIONSHIP FOR SIXTY YEARS

Redhill pipped Chalfont St. Peter by two points to clinch their first league title for sixty years. The 'Reds' needed a win in their last match at Marlow which they won 1-0 with a second half goal from Brian Medlicott. It was also Redhill's last season on their present Memorial Sports Ground before moving to a new site at Kiln Brow. Chalfont St. Peter's chances of becoming Champions slipped when they could only manage a 1-1 draw against Harwich & Parkeston; early leaders Burnham finished a respectable third.

It is third time lucky for Harefield United who won the League Challenge cup, the 'Hares', beaten semi-finalists the previous two years beat Wolverton Town 3-1 aet at Berkhamsted.

Athenian clubs did not have much cup success in F.A. Competitions, although Whyteleafe and Chalfont St. Peter reached the Semi-Finals of the Surrey Senior and Berks & Bucks Senior Cups respectively. Three Burnham players were selected to play for the F.A.XI against the Amateur Football Alliance, but the match was postponed.

The majority of clubs in the league will be joining the Servowarm Isthmian League with the remainder probably feeding into the Combined Counties, Essex Senior, London Spartan and South Midlands Leagues. One exception, Harwich & Parkeston, have opted to join the Eastern Counties League.

Contrary to various reports in the national press the Athenian League is not winding up but simply going into hibernation for a year. The officers will continue to meet and will be watching any further developments that may occur in the near future.

As mentioned earlier, the 1983/4 season was Redhill's last on their ground and to mark the occasion the club's final fixture was against an Athenian League side. The Athenian League won 2-1 with Tony Algar scoring the winning goal.

Mike Wilson
Hon. Press Secretary

Thatcham's Simon Eighteen rides a tackle from Gary Collier of Flackwell Heath.
Photo: Newbury Weekly News

ATHENIAN LEAGUE TABLE
1983-84

	P	W	D	L	F	A	Pts
Redhill	40	28	9	3	73	28	93
Chalfont St. Peter	40	27	10	3	88	32	91
Burnham	40	27	7	6	80	29	88
Whyteleafe	40	24	8	8	63	32	80
Flackwell Heath	40	21	7	12	57	37	70
Harefield United	40	20	8	12	62	47	68
Banstead Athletic	40	19	10	11	63	48	67
Marlow	40	17	7	16	65	63	58
Hoddesdon Town	40	15	13	12	53	52	58
Ruislip Manor	40	16	9	15	59	44	57
Kingsbury Town	40	15	12	13	58	52	57
Wolverton Town	40	12	12	16	59	65	48
Edgware	40	13	8	19	47	51	47
Harwich & Parkeston	40	13	9	18	54	66	45*
Chertsey Town	40	12	6	22	41	63	42
Berkhamsted Town	40	10	11	19	50	63	41
Thatcham Town	40	8	14	18	65	79	35*
Horley Town	40	9	6	25	34	83	33
Haringey Borough	40	8	8	24	44	80	32
Fleet Town	40	6	8	26	31	82	26
Camberley Town	40	4	10	26	35	85	22

* Denotes 3 points deducted.

Top Goalscorers	Goals
J. Arnett (Marlow)	28
S. Hayward (Berkhamsted Town)	24
J. Ling (Burnham)	22
D. Taylor (Harefield United)	22
N. Cripps (Banstead Athletic)	20
D. Smith (Chalfont St. Peter)	20
R. Knowles (Burnham)	18
T. Elmes (Redhill)	18
C. Upton (Thatcham Town)	18
C. Chard (Thatcham Town)	18

Representative Match
Redhill (1) 1 v Athenian League (0) 2
Elmes Arnold, Algar
Att: 500

Redhill: D. Jackson, B. Medlicott, T. Dark, R. Purvis, D. Vaughan, J. Cooper, P. Dearman, S. Wright, T. Elmes, A. Hodge, P. Butler Subs: K. Stevens, J. Chandler, L. Dolding.

Athenian League: M. Borrelli (Whyteleafe), B. Hunt (Horley T), T. Souter (Chertsey T), J. Clifton (Whyteleafe), L. Richardson (Whyteleafe), D. Rose (Whyteleafe), B. Paterson (Whyteleafe), G. Arnold (Harwich & P), S. Haywood (Berkhamsted T), M. Doctrove (Horley T), P. Goodwin (Whyteleafe) Subs: B. Hanks (Harwich & P), T. Algar (Whyteleafe) Manager: Roy Burton (Whyteleafe)

Athenian League Honours List
League Champions: Redhill
Runners-Up: Chalfont St. Peter
League Challenge Cup Winners: Harefield United
Runners-Up (Memorial Shield Winners): Wolverton Town
FA Challenge Cup: Whyteleaf reached the 2nd Qualifying Round.
FA Challenge Vase: Harefield United reached the 3rd Round
Biggest home win in league: Chalfont St. Peter 7, Chertsey Town 0. Thatcham Town 7, Horley Town 0.
Biggest away win in league: Marlow 0, Ruislip Manor 5.
Biggest score on aggregate: Redhill 5, Marlow 4. Wolverton Town 3, Harefield United 6.

ATHENIAN LEAGUE RESULTS 1983-84

	Banstead Ath	Berkhamsted T	Burnham	Camberley T	Chalfont St Ptr	Chertsey T	Edgware	Flackwell Hth	Fleet T	Harefield U	Haringey Brgh	Harwich & Pkstn	Hoddesdon T	Horley T	Kingsbury T	Marlow	Redhill	Ruislip Manor	Thatcham Town	Whyteleafe	Wolverton T
Banstead Ath	—	2-1	0-3	3-0	6-0	1-0	3-0	2-2	3-0	0-2	3-1	2-2	2-0	2-1	1-0	0-2	1-0	2-1	2-1	1-1	0-1
Berkhamsted T	0-2	—	0-4	1-2	0-3	0-1	0-0	1-3	3-1	0-2	1-0	0-2	0-0	5-0	5-2	5-2	0-2	1-0	0-0	1-1	1-1
Burnham	3-1	2-0	—	4-0	1-1	2-0	1-0	2-3	7-1	3-1	2-0	2-0	0-0	3-0	1-1	1-3	1-1	1-0	1-0	2-1	3-0
Camberley T	1-1	3-3	0-1	—	0-4	1-0	0-1	0-1	2-2	1-2	1-3	0-1	1-1	0-1	1-2	1-2	1-1	1-1	3-5	1-2	2-3
Chalfont St Ptr	4-0	3-0	1-0	3-0	—	7-0	2-1	0-1	3-2	2-1	2-2	1-1	3-3	3-0	2-0	2-0	3-0	2-0	4-1	1-1	2-2
Chertsey T	2-2	2-1	0-3	1-0	0-2	—	3-1	1-1	1-1	0-1	3-2	4-1	1-4	1-0	0-1	0-3	0-1	1-2	0-2	1-0	3-3
Edgware	2-3	1-1	0-2	5-0	0-2	0-2	—	1-0	2-2	0-2	0-0	2-0	1-1	2-0	1-0	0-2	1-3	2-1	2-2	0-3	2-0
Flackwell Hth	3-0	0-0	2-3	4-1	3-0	2-0	2-1	—	2-0	0-2	2-0	2-1	2-1	3-1	1-3	1-3	0-2	0-1	1-1	0-0	1-2
Fleet T	1-4	0-0	2-0	0-0	0-3	0-1	0-4	0-1	—	0-2	1-2	1-2	1-1	0-1	1-1	0-1	1-2	0-2	0-3	0-3	1-0
Harefield U	2-2	1-0	1-2	2-0	1-4	1-0	0-4	0-1	2-0	—	2-0	0-0	1-2	3-0	4-3	2-1	0-0	0-2	2-2	0-1	0-1
Haringey Brgh	1-3	1-2	0-4	2-2	1-1	0-4	0-3	0-4	2-3	2-3	—	0-2	2-2	3-0	2-0	1-1	1-2	3-1	2-0	0-2	2-1
Harwich & Pkstn	0-1	2-2	1-1	2-0	0-3	2-1	0-3	3-1	5-0	2-2	0-2	—	1-2	3-0	1-1	1-2	1-2	1-5	4-3	1-2	1-0
Hoddesdon T	2-1	1-2	0-3	0-1	1-2	3-1	1-1	0-0	0-1	1-2	2-1	1-3	—	1-0	0-0	1-0	0-3	4-3	1-1	1-1	1-3
Horley T	0-0	1-4	2-0	0-0	0-3	0-2	2-0	1-3	4-3	1-1	1-1	5-1	0-1	—	0-2	1-0	1-2	2-1	2-3	1-3	2-0
Kingsbury T	2-0	2-2	1-0	3-2	1-1	1-1	2-0	1-0	1-2	0-0	4-2	0-3	1-3	6-1	—	1-1	1-3	1-0	2-1	0-1	3-1
Marlow	3-2	1-0	2-4	2-2	1-2	1-1	1-2	1-2	4-0	0-4	3-0	2-1	0-1	4-1	1-4	—	0-1	0-5	5-3	0-1	1-1
Redhill	1-1	2-0	0-0	3-1	1-1	2-0	1-0	1-0	2-0	2-1	2-0	5-1	0-1	3-0	2-2	5-4	—	1-1	1-1	2-0	4-0
Ruislip Manor	1-0	3-1	1-1	2-0	0-1	3-1	3-0	1-0	3-1	0-1	1-0	0-0	2-0	1-1	0-0	2-3	1-2	—	0-1	2-1	3-3
Thatcham Town	1-1	1-2	2-4	2-3	0-2	3-1	1-1	0-2	1-2	1-1	2-2	2-2	2-4	7-0	2-1	1-1	1-3	1-1	—	2-4	2-2
Whyteleafe	0-2	3-2	0-1	4-0	1-1	1-0	1-0	0-1	1-0	4-2	4-0	2-0	2-2	2-0	1-0	1-1	0-2	2-1	4-1	—	1-0
Wolverton T	1-1	4-3	1-2	5-1	0-2	2-1	2-1	0-0	1-1	3-6	4-1	2-0	1-3	1-1	2-2	0-1	0-1	2-2	4-0	0-1	—

Steve Smith scores Chalfont St Peter's first goal in their 4-1 defeat of Thatcham.
Photo: Mike Joss.

ATHENIAN LEAGUE CHALLENGE CUP

1st Round

Banstead Athletic	1	Camberley T	0
Wolverton T	2	Horley T	0
Whyteleafe	1	Edgeware	0 aet
Thatcham T	3	Flackwell Heath	2 aet
Redhill	2	Hoddesdon T	1

2nd Round

Harwich & Pkstn	0	Ruislip Manor	1
Thatcham T	0	Banstead Ath	0 aet
Chalfont St P	1	Harefield U	2
Berkhamsted T	2	Fleet T	1
Whyteleafe	0	Chertsey T	1
Burnham	2	Redhill	0
Haringey Borough	1	Marlow	3
Wolverton T	2	Kingsbury T	0

2nd Round Replay

Banstead Ath	1	Thatcham T	5

3rd Round

Berkhamsted T	0	Ruislip Manor	1
Thatcham T	2	Harefield U	2 aet
Chertsey T	0	Burnham	3
Wolverton T	3	Marlow	0

3rd Round Replay

Harefield U	3	Thatcham T	1 aet

Semi-Finals

Ruislip Manor	2	Harefield U	3 aet
Wolverton T	2	Burnham	1

Final
(at Berkhamsted Town FC)

Harefield U	3	Wolverton T	1 aet
Taylor (2), Walker (pen)		Hollis	

Half-time: 0-0
Att: 305

Team Line-Ups

Harefield United: I'Anson, Roper, Leavy, Bateman, Goodliffe, Bignell, Walker, Barr, Kelly, Taylor, Dunn. Sub: Charlton.

Wolverton Town: Knight, Hollis, Browne, Caswell, Creaser, Brown, Barker, Glean, Large, Smith, Richards. Sub: Heath.

The Memorial Shield
(Presented to the Runners-Up of the Challenge Cup)
1983/84: Wolverton Town

Previous Winners

1969/70	Redhill
1970/71	Redhill
1971/72	Slough Town
1972/73	Slough Town
1973/74	Erith & Belvedere
1974/75	Cheshunt
1975/76	Cheshunt
1976/77	Chalfont St Peter
1977/78	Billericay Town
1978/79	Alton Town
1979/80	Windsor & Eton
1980/81	Banstead Athletic
1981/82	Banstead Athletic
1982/83	Chalfont St Peter

Previous Runners-Up
(Memorial Shield Winners)

1969/70	Walton & Hersham
1970/71	Dagenham
1971/72	Dagenham
1972/73	Worthing
1973/74	Redhill
1974/75	Redhill
1975/76	Eastbourne Town
1976/77	Epsom & Ewell
1977/78	Grays Athletic
1978/79	Windsor & Eton
1979/80	Grays Athletic
1980/81	Windsor & Eton
1981/82	Uxbridge
1982/83	Banstead Athletic

ATHENIAN LEAGUE
Past Champions

Max Pts	*Season*	*1st*	*2nd*	*3rd*	*4th*
32	1912/13	25 Catford Southend	21*Barnet	21 Tufnell Park	20 Finchley
44	1913/14	33 Tufnell Park	32 Luton Clarence	29 Grays A	25 Metrogas
44	1919/20	37 Luton Clarence	29 Metrogas	26*Barnet	26 Hendon
44	1920/21	33 St Albans C	31 Wimbledon	28 Hendon	26 Metrogas
52	1921/22	41 St Albans C	36 Metrogas	31 Summerstown	29 Hendon
48	1922/23	40 Bromley	34 St Albans C	32 Southall	29*Kingstonian
48	1923/24	36 Kingstonian	33 Redhill	31 Southall	28 Barnet
52	1924/25	41 Redhill	35 Barking	34 Kingstonian	33 Southall
52	1925/26	44 Kingstonian	38 Redhill	36 Barking	31 Hendon
52	1926/27	39 Southall	34 Kingstonian	33 Barking	30 Enfield
52	1927/28	43 Sutton U	41 Redhill	36 Barking	35 Leyton
52	1928/29	43 Leyton	35 Hendon	33 Sutton U	29*Southall
52	1929/30	41 Walthamstow Ave	37*Barnet	37 Leyton	31 Barking
52	1930/31	46 Barnet	34*Walthamstow Ave	34 Leyton	29*Enfield
52	1931/32	39 Barnet	36 Hayes	34 Leyton	32*Hendon
52	1932/33	38 Walthamstow Ave	36 Hendon	34*Barnet	34 Barking
52	1933/34	41 Walthamstow Ave	36 Romford	34 Hendon	29 Enfield
52	1934/35	35 Barking	33*Enfield	33 Leyton	31 Walthamstow Ave
52	1935/36	38 Romford	37 Bromley	36 Walthamstow Ave	32 Enfield
52	1936/37	49 Romford	39 Walthamstow Ave	37 Wealdstone	27*Sutton U
52	1937/38	42 Walthamstow Ave	33 Barnet	31 Romford	29 Wealdstone
52	1938/39	42 Walthamstow Ave	37 Romford	35 Wealdstone	34 Hayes
52	1945/46	40 Sutton U	39 Leyton	36*Tooting & Mitch.U	36 Hayes
52	1946/47	34*Barnet	34 Sutton U	30*Bromley	30*Wealdstone
52	1947/48	38 Barnet	33 Hendon	30 Bromley	28 Tooting & Mitch.U
52	1948/49	41 Bromley	37 Hendon	34 Tooting & Mitch.U	29 Wealdstone
52	1949/50	39 Tooting & Mitch.U	34 Hayes	33*Bromley	33 Barking
60	1950/51	49 Bromley	45 Walton & Hersham	44 Hayes	36 Hendon
60	1951/52	50 Wealdstone	48 Hendon	38*Bromley	38 Sutton U
52	1952/53	42 Hendon	37 Wealdstone	36 Southall	28*Tooting & Mitch.U
52	1953/54	38 Finchley	35 Hitchin T	33 Southall	29*Tooting & Mitch.U
52	1954/55	38 Tooting & Mitch.U	37 Southall	33 Enfield	30 Sutton U
56	1955/56	41 Hendon	38 Hounslow	37 Enfield	36 Tooting & Mitch.U
56	1956/57	40*Hayes	40 Finchley	38 Hounslow	34 Hendon
60	1957/58	43 Sutton U	42 Maidstone U	37*Hendon	37 Barnet
60	1958/59	44*Barnet	44 Wealdstone	38 Maidstone U	36 Hendon
60	1959/60	46 Hounslow	43 Barnet	35*Enfield	35*Wealdstone
60	1960/61	42 Hendon	41 Wealdstone	39 Barnet	37 Sutton U
60	1961/62	52 Enfield	49 Barnet	37 Wealdstone	36 Hayes
60	1962/63	54 Enfield	47 Barnet	42 Wealdstone	36 Sutton U
52	1963/64	38 Barnet	34*Finchley	34 Carshalton A	30 Hayes
60	1964/65	50 Barnet	41 Leyton	39 Finchley	38 Worthing
60	1965/66	48*Leyton	48 Finchley	45 Maidenhead U	37 Leatherhead
60	1966/67	43*Leyton	43 Bishop's Stortford	38 Finchley	37 Leatherhead
60	1967/68	51 Slough T	44 Dagenham	39 Bishop's Stortford	35 Hayes
60	1968/69	52 Walton & Hersham	48 Slough T	39 Southall	38 Leatherhead
60	1969/70	45 Bishop's Stortford	40 Walton & Hersham	39*Dagenham	39*Slough T
60	1970/71	51 Dagenham	47 Walton & Hersham	41 Slough T	39 Cheshunt
60	1971/72	48 Slough T	43 Dagenham	40 Leatherhead	39 Tilbury
60	1972/73	48 Slough T	43*Dagenham	43 Tilbury	41 Harlow T
68	1973/74	56 Boreham Wood	47 Cheshunt	46 Ruislip Manor	40 Ware
68	1974/75	49 Letchworth G.C.	48 Wembley	47 Grays A	42 Cheshunt
60	1975/76	41 Cheshunt	39 Egham T	37 Addlestone & Wey T	36 Grays A
68	1976/77	50 Leyton-Wingate	49 Letchworth G.C.	48 Addlestone & Wey T	44*Lewes
68	1977/78	53 Billericay T	50 Leyton-Wingate	48*Grays A	48 Burnham
72	1978/79	57 Billericay T	54 Burnham	49 Edgware	48 Windsor & Eton
76	1979/80	58 Windsor & Eton	56 Burnham	52 Leyton-Wingate	48 Dorking
76	1980/81	60 Windsor & Eton	59 Basildon U	56 Banstead A	53 Grays A
72	1981/82	64 Leyton-Wingate	50 Edgware	49 Uxbridge	45 Burnham
76	1982/83	59 Newbury Town	53 Grays Athletic	53 Redhill	50 Marlow

* goal average/difference

Very sadly the Athenian League will not be operating this season and as one who thoroughly enjoyed Athenian football with Redhill, Epsom, Ewell and Harrow Borough, Southern non-league football will not be the same. Perhaps the famous old competition will make a 'comeback'! T.W.

Combined Counties Football League

President: N. E. McLellan
Chairman: W. E. J. Lale
General Secretary: J. J. Whitefoot

Promotion and Relegation for Combined Counties

The season has been a continuation of the steady growth and development of the League since its formation in 1978. Inclusion in the newly created Isthmian Football League Pyramid System, in partnership with the Essex Senior, London Spartan and South Midland Football Leagues, has stimulated interest from many clubs whose ultimate ambition is to gain entry to the Isthmian League. Enquiries have been received from such clubs who are members of the Athenian, Sussex County and Hampshire County Leagues.

The planned improvement to the overall standard of facilities for clubs already in membership caused the withdrawal of Yateley Town FC, together with a severe examination of those used by Guildford & Worplesdon FC. The latter have been given a further year to obtain the use of new ground and facilities which have been promised for some years.

New clubs which have now been accepted into membership for the coming season are Fleet Town and Horley Town from the Athenian League, Southwick FC from the Sussex County League, together with Malden Vale and Merstham FCs from the London Spartan Football League. The latter two clubs moved laterally in an attempt to reduce the economic burden of excessive travelling which is caused by the majority of clubs in the Spartan now being based north of the Thames. After discussion by the Isthmian Joint Liaison Committee both were granted permission to move.

The implementation of a promotion/relegation 'pyramid' with the Surrey County Football Association, which was agreed during 1983, saw the relegation of Chessington United to the Surrey Country Premier League and the promotion of Farley Rovers to this League.

The League Championship was keenly competed for throughout the season mainly between Ash United, Chobham, Godalming Town and Malden Town FCs. Godalming Town eventually ran out winners with Malden Town finishing as runners-up. The Reserve Section, Divisions I & II, winners were Ash United and Hartley Wintney FCs respectively.

In the Challenge Cup Competitions Guildford & Worplesdon FC won the Premier Cup (the Concours Motors Trophy) by beating Farnham Town FC by the solitary goal in a dour final held at Woking FC. The Reserve Section Cup was won by Farnham Town FC who defeated Malden Town FC in the final played at Alton Town FC.

A new competition was introduced for the Reserve Section — The Challenge Shield — to supplement a shortened League programme caused by the creation of two divisions. The whole Section was drawn into four divisions with the divisional winners taking part in an elimination stage. This was eventually won by Farnham Town FC who defeated Ash United FC in the final played at Chobham FC.

Goldalming Town: League Champions

COMBINED COUNTIES LEAGUE
PREMIER DIVISION
SEASON 1983/84

	Alton Town	Ash United	British Aerospace (Weybridge)	Chessington United	Chobham	Cobham	Cove	Cranleigh	Farnham Town	Frimley Green	Godalming Town	Guildford & Worplesdon	Hartley Wintney	Malden Town	Virginia Water	Westfield	Yateley Town
Alton Town		0-0	1-3	1-1	1-2	0-2	1-0	6-3	1-2	1-0	0-4	3-3	1-2	2-5	1-4	3-2	3-0
Ash United	4-0		2-2	2-3	0-0	3-0	3-1	3-0	1-1	2-2	2-3	1-0	2-1	0-1	3-0	1-0	1-0
British Aerospace (Weybridge)	3-3	2-3		2-1	0-1	3-0	2-1	0-1	0-0	0-4	0-1	2-4	4-5	2-2	1-2	2-3	2-2
Chessington United	1-3	2-2	0-1		1-3	0-1	1-0	0-1	2-2	0-1	0-0	1-3	1-0	1-2	0-0	1-1	0-2
Chobham	5-1	1-2	1-0	1-1		1-2	4-0	1-0	0-1	2-0	3-2	0-2	1-0	0-3	1-1	2-1	1-0
Cobham	1-0	1-2	0-3	1-1	0-1		3-1	1-0	2-3	0-1	1-1	1-0	1-1	1-3	1-2	3-2	1-1
Cove	3-2	1-0	1-0	3-2	1-1	0-1		0-0	1-3	2-1	1-1	4-1	1-3	2-4	2-0	2-2	1-0
Cranleigh	3-2	0-1	1-2	3-1	2-3	1-2	1-1		1-1	0-0	0-1	1-1	4-1	0-3	1-2	0-3	1-2
Farnham Town	1-1	1-1	3-1	1-0	2-1	5-0	3-3	1-3		1-0	0-1	4-4	1-1	3-5	0-1	1-1	0-2
Frimley Green	0-2	2-0	1-0	1-2	0-2	1-1	4-1	6-1	3-3		3-2	1-1	0-1	1-2	1-0	0-1	2-1
Godalming Town	3-0	5-1	1-1	3-1	1-2	1-0	3-0	2-0	3-0	3-1		1-2	1-0	0-1	2-1	1-0	2-3
Guildford & Worplesdon	1-2	0-0	5-2	3-1	0-0	1-1	1-1	1-3	2-1	5-2	0-2		1-1	2-2	3-1	1-1	4-0
Hartley Wintney	3-1	1-3	1-2	4-2	3-0	2-0	1-0	3-0	0-1	2-0	0-1	2-1		1-4	2-1	2-1	0-0
Malden Town	5-2	2-2	1-3	5-1	0-1	7-0	0-0	1-1	0-0	0-2	0-1	3-1	4-1		2-0	4-0	3-0
Virginia Water	3-2	0-3	0-1	0-0	0-0	0-0	0-2	3-0	1-1	1-0	1-4	1-0	0-0	1-5		2-0	2-0
Westfield	3-2	0-3	3-2	4-0	2-0	0-1	2-1	3-0	1-1	3-0	0-1	4-0	1-3	2-2	3-1		1-2
Yateley Town	3-2	0-2	1-3	1-1	2-1	1-1	0-0	1-2	2-2	3-2	0-2	2-3	1-3	1-0	0-3	1-3	

The Guildford & Worplesdon captain receives The Concours Motors Trophy for the League Cup Competition from the League Secretary John Whitefoot.

COMBINED COUNTIES LEAGUE

PREMIER DIVISION

	P	W	D	L	F	A	Pts
Godalming Town	32	22	4	6	59	24	70
Malden Town	32	20	7	5	81	34	67
Ash United	32	17	9	6	55	32	60
Chobham	32	17	6	9	42	31	57
Hartley Wintney†	32	16	5	11	50	41	55
Westfield	32	13	6	13	53	45	45
Guildford & W	32	11	11	10	56	51	44
Farnham Town*	32	10	15	7	49	45	44
Virginia Water	32	12	7	13	34	41	43
Cobham	32	11	8	13	30	48	41
BAe (Weybridge)	32	11	6	15	51	55	39
Frimley Green	32	11	5	16	42	45	38
Cove	32	9	9	14	37	50	36
Yateley Town	32	9	7	16	34	54	34
Cranleigh	32	8	6	18	34	58	30
Alton Town	32	8	5	19	50	75	29
Chessington United	32	4	10	18	29	57	22

† — points awarded
* — points deducted; ineligible player

HIGHEST LEAGUE SCORES

PREMIER DIVISION

Home: Ash United 9, Clarion 0 — 1.9.1979
Ash United 9, Godalming Town 0 — 2.5.1981
Away: Yateley 0, Ash United 11 — 5.4.1980

RESERVE DIVISION 1

Home: Malden Town 10, Yateley 0 — 22.1.1983
Away: Lingfield 0, Malden Vale 10 — 12.5.1983

RESERVE DIVISION 2

Home: Yateley Town 16, Alton Town 0 — 24.12.1983
Away: Alton Town 0, Cove 9 — 17.09.1983

ASH UNITED (1911)

Chairman: Robin Lunn **Manager:** Chick Botley
Secretary: Mrs Dawn Reynolds, 'Owls', 8 Lime Crescent, Ash, Aldershot, Hampshire GU12 6NF. Tel: Aldershot 24711
Ground Address & Tel No: Youngs Drive, off Shawfield road, Ash. 0252 20385
Directions to Ground: Turn off at Greyhound PH roundabout from A323 Aldershot to Guildford road into Shawfield Road, ½ mile on left hand side
Previous Leagues: Surrey Senior, Aldershot Senior **Colours:** Green **Change colours:** Blue
Programmes: 32 pages, 25p **Clubhouse:** Two bars, open every lunchtime and evenings **Floodlights:** No **Seating:** No

CHOBHAM (1905)

Chairman: Mr Bosgood **Manager:** H. Newell
Secretary: Mrs D. Walley, 8 Brooks Green, Chertsey Road, Chobham, Surrey GU24 8PN. Tel: Chobham 8039
Ground Address & Tel No: Recreation Ground, Station Road, Chobham. Chobham 7876
Directions to Ground: British Rail service from Waterloo to Woking, then Alder Valley Service 255, 256
Previous Leagues: Surrey Senior, London Spartan
Colours: Light & Dark Blue stripes **Change colours:** White shirts, Black shorts
Programmes: **Clubhouse:** **Floodlights:** **Seating:**

COBHAM (1892)

Chairman: B. Harlow **Manager:** J. Hounseil
Secretary: Reg Osborn, 39 Manor Drive, Surbiton, Surrey. 01-399 1511 (H),1 01-399 8892 (B)
Ground Address & Tel No: Leg O'Mutton Field, off Downsend Bridge Road, Cobham, Surrey. Cobham 5959 or 7295
Directions to Ground: Off A3 into Between Streets, turn right into Downside Bridge Road, then turn right onto Council recreation space, ground is at back
Previous Leagues: **Colours:** Red & White stripe/White with Red trim/Red **Change colours:** All Navy
Programmes: 12 pages, 25p **Clubhouse:** Yes **Floodlights:** No **Seating:** No

COVE (1897)

Chairman: R. J. Clarke **Manager:** N. Patient
Secretary: G. R. Brown, 126 Prospect Road, Cove, Farnborough, Hants. Tel: Farnborough 541152
Ground Address & Tel No: Oak Farm Fields, off Romayne Close, Cove, Farnborough. 543615
Directions to Ground: British Rail service from Waterloo via Woking to Farnborough Main station, ground 1 mile
Previous Leagues: Surrey Senior, Hampshire County
Colours: Amber shirts, Black shorts **Change colours:** Blue shirts, White shorts
Programmes: No **Clubhouse:** Yes **Floodlights:** No **Seating:** No

CRANLEIGH (1893)

Chairman: P. Ford **Manager:** B. Newman
Secretary: P. Auzins, 81 Glebe Road, Cranleigh, Surrey. Tel: Cranleigh 275969
Ground Address & Tel No: Snoxhall Playing Fields, Knowle Lane, Cranleigh, Surrey. 275292
Directions to Ground: British Rail service from Guildford then bus 273, 283 or 295
Previous Leagues: Surrey Senior, West Sussex **Colours:** All Royal Blue **Change colours:** White shirts, Black shorts
Programmes: 8 pages, 10p **Clubhouse:** Yes **Floodlights:** No **Seating:** No

FARLEIGH ROVERS (1922)

Chairman: R. B. Peters **Manager:** M. McCue
Secretary: M. McCue, 8 Forge Croft, Edenbridge, Kent. Tel: 0732 863645
Ground Address & Tel No: Parsonage Field, Harrow Road, Warlingham, Surrey. Upper Warlingham 6483
Directions to Ground: From Warlingham Green continue through Warlingham in the direction of Limpsfield on the B269 for about ½ mile, turn left down Chelsham Road. Bus garage on left. Take left fork at Bull Common, continue to small crossroads, turn left down Harrow road, Ground 200 yds on left
Previous Leagues: Surrey Premier **Colours:** Red/Black/Black **Change colours:** White/White/Red
Programmes: 4 pages, 20p **Clubhouse:** Yes **Floodlights:** No **Seating:** No

FARNHAM TOWN (1921)

Chairman: J. Butters **Manager:** D. Colston
Secretary: J. H. Winslade, 11 Stoke Hills, Farnham, Surrey GU9 7TE. Tel: Farnham 725133
Ground Address & Tel No: Memorial Ground, West Street, Farnham, Surrey. Farnham 715305
Directions to Ground: Farnham (SR) then 10 minute walk approx via Town Centre. By Road: From Guildford A31/ Farnborough A325 onto Farnham bypass roundabouts, follow signs Town Centre into East Street, left into one-way system South Street, Union Road, Downing Street then left into West Street. Memorial Ground ½ mile approx on left hand side next to Crosby Boors Ltd
Previous Leagues: Surrey Intermediate, Surrey County Senior, Spartan
Colours: Blue & Claret/Maroon/Light Blue **Change colours:** All Yellow
Programmes: No **Clubhouse:** Yes **Floodlights:** No **Seating:** No

FLEET TOWN (1896)

Chairman: J. R. Smith **Manager:** E. O'Riordan
Secretary: P. D. Putman, 15 Hawkwell, Church Crookham, Aldershot, Hants GU13 0XF. Tel: Fleet 3454
Ground Address & Tel No: Calthorpe Park, Crookham Road, Fleet
Directions to Ground: From Fleet town centre at crossroads, Crookham Road, 200 yards right turn
Previous Leagues: Hampshire, Athenian **Colours:** Light Blue/Dark Blue/Dark Blue **Change colours:** Old Gold
Programmes: 10 pages, 15p **Clubhouse:** Yes **Floodlights:** Yes **Seating:** 100

FRIMLEY GREEN (1919)

Chairman: **Manager:** A. Cherry
Secretary: E. B. Stephens, 14 Diamond Ridge, Camberley, Surrey. Tel: 0276 24540
Ground Address & Tel No: Frimley Green Recreation Ground
Directions to Ground: A321 Guildford to Camberley (2 miles from M3)
Previous Leagues: Surrey Senior, London Spartan
Colours: Light & Dark Blue stripes/Light Blue shorts **Change colours:** Red & White shirts/Black shorts
Programmes: 2 pages, 20p **Clubhouse:** Yes **Floodlights:** No **Seating:** No

GODALMING TOWN (1971) **Chairman:** M. Palmer **Manager:** R. Newman

Secretary: A. J. Hankers, The Nook, Kings Road, Farncombe, Surrey. Tel: 04868 23891
Ground Address & Tel No: Wey Court, Mead Row, Godalming. 04868 7520
Directions to Ground: 1 mile from Godalming Town centre on A3100 Godalming to Guildford road. Nearest Station Farncombe (5 min walk)
Previous Leagues: Surrey Intermediate **Colours:** Green shirts/White shorts **Change colours:** White shirts/Black shorts
Programmes: 12 pages, 10p **Clubhouse:** Yes **Floodlights:** No **Seating:** No

GUILDFORD & WORPLESDON (1978)

Chairman: T. Thompson **Manager:** J. Hollis
Secretary: Mrs J. Phillips, 135 Manor Road, Guildford, Surrey. Tel: Guildford 571372
Ground Address & Tel No: Memorial Ground, Bagshot Road, Worplesdon
Directions to Ground: A320 Bagshot road out of Guildford. Ground on left just past Worplesdon Place Hotel
Previous Leagues: Surrey Senior **Colours:** Red & White shirts/Black shorts **Change colours:** Yellow shirts/Green shorts
Programmes: 10 pages, 20p **Clubhouse:** Yes **Floodlights:** No **Seating:** No

HARTLEY WINTNEY (1897) **Chairman:** W. Mitchell **Manager:** Ian Bedford

Secretary: D. Willoughby, 29 Carters Way, Wisborough Green, Billingshurst, Sussex. Tel: 0403-700 691
Ground Address & Tel No: Memorial Ground, Green Lane, Hartley Witney, Hants. 025-126 3586
Directions to Ground: From A30 turn in village towards Fleet, then immediately right into Green Lane, Ground 400m on right. Railway Station Winchfield
Previous Leagues: Basingstoke & District, Aldershot & District
Colours: Tangerine & Black shirts/Black shorts **Change colours:** White shirts/Royal Blue shorts
Programmes: 16 pages, 20p **Clubhouse:** Yes **Floodlights:** No **Seating:** No

HORLEY TOWN (1898) **Chairman:** T. Purvis **Manager:** M. Rosser

Secretary: S. K. Osborne, Bridleway, 57 Silverlea Gardens, Horley, Surrey RH6 9BA. Tel: 0294 2986
Ground Address & Tel No: The Defence, Smallfield Road, Horley, Surrey. 02934 6075
Directions to Ground: British Rail to Horley, then bus 424
Previous Leagues: Surrey Senior, London Spartan, Athenian
Colours: Red & Blue striped shirts/Blue shorts **Change colours:** All Yellow
Programmes: 10 pages, 20p **Clubhouse:** Yes **Floodlights:** Yes **Seating:** Yes

MALDEN TOWN (1936) **Chairman:** W. Lewis **Manager:** N. Harris

Secretary: A. H. Dibble, 25 Woodcote Hurst, Epsom, Surrey. Tel: Epsom 20652
Ground Address & Tel No: Manor Park, Malden Road, Malden, Surrey
Directions to Ground: British Rail to either Worcester Park or Motspur Park
Previous Leagues: Surrey Senior **Colours:** Red shirts/White shorts **Change colours:** All White
Programmes: Yes **Clubhouse:** Yes **Floodlights:** No **Seating:** Yes

MALDEN VALE (1967) **Chairman:** M. I. Webb **Manager:** R. Kingdon

Secretary: S. A. Pearce, 4 Raleigh Drive, Tolworth, Surrey. Tel: 01-337 4302
Ground Address & Tel No: Grand Drive, Raynes Park, London SW20. 01-542 2193
Directions to Ground: Five minutes walk from Raynes Park Station (BRSR)
Previous Leagues: Surrey Senior, London Spartan **Colours:** Navy Blue shirts/White shorts **Change colours:** All White
Programmes: 12 pages, 40p **Clubhouse:** Yes **Floodlights:** No **Seating:** No

MERSTHAM (1892) **Chairman:** S. Baker **Manager:** C. Humphries

Secretary: F. Fox, 153 Albury Road, Merstham, Redhill, Surrey RH1 3LW. Tel: Merstham 3279
Ground Address & Tel No: Merstham Recreation Ground. Merstham 4046
Directions to Ground: A23 to Merstham via Bletchingley Road to Weldon Way
Previous Leagues: Surrey Senior, London Spartan **Colours:** Amber & Black **Change colours:** Black & White
Programmes: Yes **Clubhouse:** Yes **Floodlights:** No **Seating:** Yes

SOUTHWICK (1882) **Chairman:** W. Earl **Manager:** A. Pook

Secretary: M. Grinstead, 27 Greenways Crescent, Shoreham-by-Sea, Sussex BN4 6HR. Tel: 079-17 4937
Ground Address & Tel No: Old Barn Way, Southwick. Brighton 591744
Directions to Ground: A27 into Southwick, south into Hadrian Avenue, at end turn left into Manor Hall Road,Old Barn Way is second on right
Previous Leagues: Sussex County **Colours:** Red shirts/Black shorts **Change colours:** White shirts/Black shorts
Programmes: 20 pages, 10p **Clubhouse:** Yes **Floodlights:** Yes **Seating:** Yes

VIRGINIA WATER (1921) **Chairman:** R. Gisher **Manager:** M. Gowan

Secretary: C. White, 65 Simplemarsh Road, Addlestone, Surrey. Tel Weybridge 41094
Ground Address & Tel No: The Timbers, Crown Road, Virginia Water. Wentworth 3811
Directions to Ground: British Rail to Virginia Water. A30 to Virginia Water
Previous Leagues: Woking & District, Surrey Senior, London Spartan
Colours: Red & Green shirts/Red shorts **Change colours:** All Maroon
Programmes: No **Clubhouse:** Yes **Floodlights:** No **Seating:** No

WESTFIELD (1953) **Chairman:** L. Brewin **Manager:** B. Hennessey

Secretary: R. Hill, 16 Westfield Avenue, Woking, Surrey. Tel: Woking 67144
Ground Address & Tel No: Woking Park, Kingfield, Woking
Directions to Ground: On Guildford side of Woking, in Old Woking opposite Woking FC Ground
Previous Leagues: Woking & District, Surrey Senior **Colours:** All Royal Blue **Change colours:** Yellow and Blue
Programmes: No **Clubhouse:** Yes **Floodlights:** No **Seating:** No

ESSEX SENIOR FOOTBALL LEAGUE

President: A. Stratheam. Chairman: F. S. Wiseman.

IN A SEASON when several revolutionary decisions were taken and a threat to its existence was beaten off, the Essex Senior League emerged stronger and healthier than ever.

The 13th season — certainly not the unluckiest — was dominated by two clubs, Heybridge Swifts and Stansted, who between then mopped up seven pieces of silverware, domestic, national and geographical.

Heybridge romped away with their third successive championship, a fitting climax before they departed to join the newly-established zonal second division of the Isthmian League. Heybridge, one of the Senior League's founder members, might have completed a clean sweep of the League's trophies but for an administrative slip-up which ended their hopes in the League Cup.

They were excluded after winning through the semi-finals, their opponents, Brentwood, going through to play Stansted in the final which the latter won 1-0. Otherwise it was Heybridge all the way, taking the title by a clear 13 points over runners-up, Bowers United, a record margin.

Their 27 victories from 32 matches was also a record for the League while their reserves completed the Reserve Section league and cup double without losing a match — 30 games unbeaten.

Stansted confirmed themselves as the cup kings. The pinnacle of their long list of successes came on April 28 at Wembley Stadium when, as underdogs, they carried off the FA Vase in style, beating previous winners Stamford 3-2 in a see-saw tussle.

After their Wembley celebrations had subsided, Stansted went on to collect the Senior League Cup, the East Anglian Cup (beating Sudbury) and the Courage Eastern Floodlight Competition (winning a two-legged final against Basildon).

Their pre-occupation and considerable success mean't that Stansted amassed a backlog of league games which, at one time, still gave them a chance of depriving Heybridge of the title. But despite the efforts of their manager Dave Edwards and his gallant crew the task proved too much and they eventually finished fourth with one match — against Sawbridge — left unplayed.

The League's other silverware, the Harry Fisher Memorial Cup for clubs eliminated from the preliminary and first rounds of the League Cup, was won by Wivenhoe while Canvey Island's vastly improved disciplinary record earned them the Sportsmanship Shield for the first time. In fact, on-the-field conduct during the past season showed a continued improvement much to the delight of League officials.

On the representative front, the Essex Senior League travelled to play the Sussex County League in return for Sussex's visit to Chelmsford two seasons earlier. The latest match took place at Burgess Hill FC and resulted in the home side winning 1-0.

A link was also forged with the Herts County League at intermediate level when a match at Stansted saw Herts win 1-0 against a Senior League Reserve Section line-up.

Players from Heybridge and Stansted also represented the FA in a match at Dagenham against London University.

During the season clubs agreed plans for the Senior League to join with the London Spartan, South Midland and Combined Counties Leagues to form the feeder leagues in the Isthmian League pyramid. But a threat that the proposed expansion of the Eastern Counties League would descimate the Senior League was successfully avoided, the clubs involved deciding to stay.

However, the departure of Heybridge leaves the Senior League with one less side (16) in the Senior Section for this season but the Reserve Section will again operate with 14 after the addition of Loughton Athletic to the ranks.

Two other clubs, East Thurrock United and Eton Manor, expect to move to new grounds this season.

SENIOR SECTION RESULT CHART 1983-1984

	Bowers	Brentwood	Brightlingsea	Canvey Is	Chelmsford	Coggeshall	East Ham	East Thurrock	Eton Manor	Ford	Halstead	Heybridge	Maldon	Sawbridgeworth	Stansted	Witham	Wivenhoe
Bowers		1-1	0-0	2-0	2-1	5-0	2-2	2-0	3-0	2-3	3-0	2-2	2-0	2-1	2-0	0-3	0-0
Brentwood	1-1		2-1	2-1	3-5	2-0	0-1	0-1	2-1	3-0	1-1	0-3	1-2	1-4	3-0	0-2	2-2
Brightlingsea	0-7	1-1		2-2	1-1	2-2	1-1	1-4	1-1	1-2	0-0	0-2	3-1	1-2	3-3	1-1	3-0
Canvey Is	1-0	1-2	1-4		2-0	11-0	1-0	1-2	6-1	0-1	0-0	0-3	0-1	2-2	1-0	2-5	2-3
Chelmsford	1-3	3-0	0-0	4-0		6-0	3-2	2-0	1-1	6-1	3-2	1-3	4-0	2-0	0-1	1-0	3-4
Coggeshall	0-2	0-4	0-7	1-1	3-2		1-1	0-1	0-0	0-5	2-2	1-2	1-5	1-5	1-15	0-4	0-3
East Ham	1-3	1-3	2-1	1-3	2-3	4-1		1-1	2-2	3-1	2-2	0-1	2-0	0-3	0-2	0-2	2-1
East Thurrock	0-1	0-3	1-0	0-1	1-0	3-0	0-3		1-0	2-0	1-0	0-1	0-1	2-1	1-1	0-0	1-3
Eton Manor	1-1	0-0	6-1	1-1	1-2	4-1	2-2	9-0		1-0	3-4	2-3	3-0	1-0	0-2	2-0	1-1
Ford	1-0	1-2	2-1	2-2	0-1	2-0	1-1	1-1	2-4		2-0	2-2	3-2	0-1	1-4	1-2	2-1
Halstead	0-0	1-0	2-2	0-1	1-1	1-1	1-0	2-2	1-3	0-3		1-4	5-3	3-3	1-3	1-1	1-1
Heybridge	1-0	2-0	3-0	2-0	1-0	1-0	5-1	1-0	3-1	2-1	1-2		3-2	1-0	2-0	0-2	4-1
Maldon	0-1	1-3	3-3	0-0	0-2	5-0	3-0	2-0	0-2	0-1	1-0	0-0		0-2	2-0	3-1	0-3
Sawbridgeworth	2-3	1-4	6-0	1-2	0-2	3-1	3-2	0-0	3-2	3-2	2-0	0-1	3-0		0-2	1-2	0-0
Stansted	1-1	4-0	2-0	1-2	1-0	4-2	0-0	1-0	2-0	1-2	2-0	0-2	3-0	NP		0-2	3-1
Witham	2-2	1-1	3-0	1-1	1-2	4-0	2-0	4-0	1-0	5-2	4-0	1-2	0-2	0-3	0-3		3-2
Wivenhoe	0-1	2-3	0-0	0-0	1-0	0-0	6-2	2-0	1-1	2-2	1-0	1-2	2-1	1-1	0-1	0-2	

NP — not played

ESSEX SENIOR FOOTBALL LEAGUE

SEASON 1983/84 HONOURS

Senior Section Champions........... **Heybridge Swifts**
Runners Up.............. Bowers United

Senior Section Cup Winners.................. **Stansted**
Runners Up.................. Brentwood

Harry Fisher Memorial Cup Winners.... **Wivenhoe Town**
Runners Up..... E. Thurrock Utd

Reserve Section Champions........... **Heybridge Swifts**
Runners Up .... Bowers United

Reserve Section Cup Winners .... **Heybridge Swifts**
Runners Up................ Brentwood

Sportsmanship Trophy................ **Canvey Island**

LEADING GOALSCORERS

Senior Section

(League, Challenge Cup and Harry Fisher Cup)

28—D. Copney (Eton Manor)
20—J. Lamb (Heybridge — 1 for Wivenhoe)
18—Liddle (Sawbridgeworth)
16—Newbury (Maldon), Selwyn (Witham)
14—Doyle (Stansted), Wakefield (Bowers)
13—Holt (Stansted), Lawrence (Heybridge — 8 for Ford)
12—Farrow (Canvey Is), Ridgwell (Chelmsford), Stapleton (Sawbridgeworth), Thrift (Chemlsford)
11—Bingham (Bowers), Hollands (Witham), Legge (Heybridge)
10—Foley (Canvey Is), Fox (Heybridge), Gildea (Brentwood), Pratten (Witham)
9—Cutmore (Halstead), Heale (Canvey Is), Johnson (Bowers), Reeves (Stansted), Waters (Wivenhoe).

Reserve Section

(League and League Cup)

30—Bannister (Heybridge)
21—Martin (Bowers)
20—Avis (Heybridge)
19—Sams (Eton Manor)
15—Hook (East Thurrock)
10—Bousfield (Brightlingsea), Jones (Heybridge)
9—Skingle (Stansted)

SENIOR SECTION

	P	W	D	L	F	A	Pts
Heybridge	32	27	3	2	65	21	57
Bowers	32	17	10	5	56	25	44
Witham	32	18	6	8	61	32	42
Stansted	31	18	4	9	62	29	40
Chelmsford	32	17	4	11	62	37	38
Brentwood	32	14	7	11	50	45	35
Sawbridgeworth	31	14	5	12	56	40	33
Canvey Island	32	11	9	12	48	44	31
Wivenhoe	32	10	11	11	45	43	31
Ford	32	13	5	14	49	55	31
Eton Manor	32	10	10	12	56	47	30
East Thurrock	32	11	6	15	25	44	28
Maldon	32	11	3	18	40	53	25
East Ham	32	7	9	16	41	60	23
Halstead	32	5	13	14	34	56	23
Brightlingsea	32	4	14	14	41	63	22
Coggeshall	32	1	7	24	19	116	9

LEAGUE CUP RESULTS

PRELIMINARY ROUND

Wivenhoe	2	Bowers	0

FIRST ROUND

Maldon	1	Canvey Island	2
East Ham	4	Halstead	2 (aet)
Coggeshall	0	Heybridge	3
Sawbridgeworth	1	Brentwood	1 (aet)
	replay: 1-2		
Ford	2	Eton Manor	1
Witham	2	Brightlingsea	1
Stansted	3	East Thurrock	1
Wivenhoe	0	Chelmsford	1

SECOND ROUND

Heybridge	3	Canvey Island	0
Chelmsford	0	Ford	1
Brentwood	1	East Ham	1 (aet)
	reply: 3-0		
Stansted	4	Witham	1

SEMI-FINALS

Ford	0	Stansted	1
	2nd leg: 1-1; agg: 1-2		
Brentwood	0	Heybridge	1
	2nd leg: 0-1; agg: 0-2		

(Heybridge excluded for fielding ineligible player)

FINAL

Brentwood	0	Stansted	1

BOWERS UNITED (1946)

Chairman: C. Wiggins **Manager:** R. Hobbs
Secretary: R. Short, Floriana, High Road, Langdon Hills, Basildon Essex. Tel: 413411
Ground Address & Tel No: Crown Avenue, off Kenneth Road, off Rectory Road, Pitsea, Basildon, Essex. Tel: 555583
Directions to Ground: Turn into Rectory Road from Pitsea Broadway, then turn into Kenneth Road, right turn at top into Crown Avenue
Previous Leagues: Thurrock Thameside Combination, Olympian, Essex
Colours: Red & Black **Change colours:** Yellow & Blue
Programmes: 4 pages, free **Clubhouse:** Yes **Floodlights:** No **Seating:** Yes

BRIGHTLINGSEA UNITED (1902)

Chairman: J. Couzens **Manager:** A. Dennis
Secretary: H. Beere, 121 Chapel Road, Brightlingsea, Essex
Ground Address & Tel No: North Road. Tel: 4199
Directions to Ground: Main Church Road from Thorrington Cross, bear left into Spring Road then first left
Previous Leagues: Essex & Suffolk Border **Colours:** Red/White/Red **Change colours:** Blue/White/Blue
Programmes: 16 pages, 10p **Clubhouse:** Yes **Floodlights:** No **Seating:** No

CANVEY ISLAND (1926)

Chairman: Paul Norton-Ashley **Manager:** Ben Embery
Secretary: John Wellmen, 127 Church Parade, Canvey Island, Essex. Tel: 0268 697657
Ground Address & Tel No: Park Lane, Canvey Island, Essex. Tel: 0268 682991
Directions to Ground: Take A130 from A13 or A12 (A127) from London or A130 from Chelmsford. Take High Street from Town Centre to old Bus Station. Park Lane is first turning past the garage. By train: to Byfleet (Fenchurch St. Line). Bus 3 or 151 to stop after Admiral Jellicoe (public house)
Previous Leagues: Greater London, Metropolitan, Parthenon, Thurrock & Thameside Combination, South East Essex
Colours: Yellow with Blue pinstripes/Blue/Blue **Change colours:** Red/Black/Red
Programmes: 20 pages, 10p **Clubhouse:** Yes **Floodlights:** No **Seating:** No

EAST HAM UNITED (1933)

Chairman: P. Horner **Manager:** Reuben Gane
Secretary: R. Gane **Address & Tel No:** 108 Beccles Drive, Barking, Essex.
Ground Address & Tel No: Manorway Ground, East Ham Manor Way, Newham, London E6
Directions to Ground: Tube to East Ham Station or bus 101 from East Ham or North Woolwich
Previous Leagues: Spartan, London, Metropolitan
Colours: Emerald Green/White/Gold **Change colours:** Gold/Green/White
Programmes: 10 pages, 10p **Clubhouse:** Bar, tea bar
Floodlights: To be re-vamped for League strength 1984-85 **Seating:** Yes

EAST THURROCK UNITED (1969)

Chairman: A. L. Firman **Manager:** Roger Bond
Secretary: T. J. Keating, 3 Laburnum Drive, Corringham, Essex SS17 7QE. Tel: Stanford-le-Hope 675399
Ground Address & Tel No: Rookery Hill, Corringham, Essex
Directions to Ground: Leave M25 at Junction with A13, travel towards Southend, leave A13 onto A1014, Ground situated on left, two miles from A13. (Dual carriageway from Ground entrance to M25)
Previous Leagues: London Metropolitan, London Spartan **Colours:** Amber/Black/Black **Change colours:** All Red
Programmes: 8 pages (4 adverts, 4 editorial) **Clubhouse:** Yes
Floodlights: under construction (for end 1984-85 season) **Seating:** (as floodlights)

FORD UNITED (1934)

Chairman: L. H. R. Constable **Manager:** Don Wiltshire
Secretary: Ken Dobson, 16 Tenby Court, Tenby Road, Walthamstow, London E17. 01-521 9285 (H)
Ground Address & Tel No: Ford Sports & Social Club, Rush Green Road, Romford, Essex. Romford 45678
Directions to Ground: Club is on the A124
Previous Leagues: Greater London **Colours:** Royal Blue & White **Change colours:** Red/Red/White
Programmes: 16 pages, 10p **Clubhouse:** Yes **Floodlights:** No **Seating:** 700

HALSTEAD TOWN (1879)

Chairman: L. Cook **Manager:** B. Archer
Secretary: Mrs C. White, 44 Beridge Road, Halstead, Essex CO9 1LB. Tel: Hal. 475037
Ground Address & Tel No: Rosemary Lane, Halstead, Essex. 472082
Directions to Ground: From London via Chelmsford, Braintree then A131 to Halstead, Ground off High Street From Colchester, A604 to Halstead, down High Street, second right
Previous Leagues: Essex & Suffolk Border
Colours: Blue/White/Blue **Change colours:** White/Black/Black with Red turnover
Programmes: 8 pages, inclusive with admission **Clubhouse:** Yes **Floodlights:** No **Seating:** 500

SAWBRIDGEWORTH TOWN (1890)

Chairman: Ian Rankin **Manager:** Barry Hervey
Secretary: David Pask, 16 Gilders, Sawbridgeworth, Herts CM21 0EF. Tel: Bishops Stortford (0279)723541
Ground Address & Tel No: Crofters End, West Road, Sawbridgeworth. Tel: Bishops Stortford (0279) 722039
Directions to Ground: BR Eastern Region, Liverpool Street-Cambridge line, Sawbridgeworth Station ¾mile via Station Road – West Road
Previous Leagues: Essex Olympian **Colours:** All Red **Change colours:** All Sky
Programmes: 10 pages, inclusive with admission **Clubhouse:** Yes **Floodlights:** No **Seating:** 20, in clubhouse

STANSTED

President: M. C. Elliott
Chairman: J. Field
Manager: D. Edwards
Coach: D. Huddle
Physiotherapist: P. Fox
Secretary: P. A. G. Heal
Address & Tel No: 28 Mountfitchet Road, Stansted, Essex CM24 8NW. 0279 812053
Press Officer & Tel No:
Address & Tel No of ground: Hargrave Sports Ground, Cambridge Road, Stansted, Essex
Simple ground directions: M11 to Bishop's Stortford, then A1183 (old A11) toward Cambridge, on left hand side of Cambridge Road, 100 yards beyond Bell & Feathers Inn
No of seats: 200 **Covered accommodation:** **Capacity:** 1,500 **Floodlights:**
Year formed: 1892 **Nickname:** **Club sponsors:**
Club colours: Blue/White/Blue **Change colours:** All White
Previous Names: **Previous Grounds:** Green's Meadow, Chapel Hill, Stansted
Record attendance:
Previous Leagues: Stansted & District, East Herts, Herts County, Spartan **Programme:** 6 pages, 15p
Senior Honours: F.A. Challenge Vase 1983-84, East Anglian Cup 1983-84, Courage Eastern Flootlight Competition 1983-84, Essex Senior League Challenge Cup 1983-84

WIVENHOE TOWN (1927)

Chairman: Dave Whymark **Manager:** Mick Packer (ex Colchester & Watford)
Secretary: Eddie Goldsmith, 31 Holly Way, Elmstead Market. Tel: Wiv. 4170
Ground Address & Tel No: Broad Lane, Wivenhow. 5380
Directions to Ground: Coming out of Colchester heading towards Clacton, take first turning on right towards Wivenhoe and ground is clearly visible on left turning left towards Clacton on B1027
Previous Leagues: Essex & Suffolk Border, Colchester & East Essex
Colours: White and Blue stripes/Black/Black **Change colours:** Maroon & Light Blue
Record attendance: 1,300 Wivenhoe v Bobby Charlton XI, 1983-84 **Club sponsors:** Wivenhoe Port
Programmes: 16 pages, 10p **Clubhouse:** Yes **Floodlights:** Yes **Midweek games:** Wednesday **Seating:** being erected
Senior Honours: Essex Senior League Runners-up (2), Worthington Evans Cup Winners & Runners-up, Coggleshall Brotherhood Cup Winners, Essex & Suffolk Border League Winners, Harry Fisher Memorial Cup Winners, F.A. Vase 5th Round 1982-83, 3rd Round 1981-82, 1983-84

WITHAM TOWN (1948)

Chairman: S. Kelly **Manager:** A. Wenborn
Secretary: A. Dowdall, 19 Cross Road, Witham, Essex CM8 2NA. Tel: 515945
Ground Address & Tel No: Spa Road, Witham. 511198
Directions to Ground: From Chelmsford, turn off A12 to Witham, first left past fire station into Spinks Lane, follow road to junction, turn right, follow road under railway bridge, first left, approx 100 yards from bridge
Previous Leagues: Mid-Essex, South-East Essex, Essex & Suffolk Border
Colours: Red/Black/Black **Change colours:** All Blue
Programmes: 8 pages, 10p **Clubhouse:** Yes **Floodlights:** No **Seating:** No

Collier Row FC

LONDON SPARTAN FOOTBALL LEAGUE

Chairman: B. Stallard, Esq. LFA

Hon Secretary: D. Cordell, 44 Greenleas, Waltham Abbey, Essex. Tel: Lea Valley 712428

LONDON SPARTAN FOOTBALL LEAGUE 1983/84

The honours of the season were fairly well spread among the clubs with Collier Row becoming League Champions but losing out to Malden Vale in the League Cup after extra time. Hanwell Town won the second division at their first attempt whilst Barkingside won the Harry Sunderland Shield. Crown and Manor reached the 4th round of the FA Vase, Brimsdown Rovers were losing finalists in the Middlesex Premier Cup.

Southgate Athletic won the Intermediate Division of the League but like Collier Row lost out to Old Roan in the Intermediate Cup Final. Leyton County were finalists in the Essex Intermediate Cup whilst Thamesmead were finalists in both the London and the Kent Junior Finals.

After some three years of uncertainties the long awaited Isthmian Pyramid came into being and it is now hoped that there will be a period of stability within the Leagues in the South and South East.

Clubs in membership are being given advice and encouragement in improving their ground facilities so that they can obtain their gradings and thereby obtain promotion to the Isthmian League.

The Grounds Committee will also help the members of the Leagues Intermediate Division in their quest for Senior Status. The members of Intermediate Clubs who have moved up to Senior Status in the last ten years is considerable but there is still room for more.

The end of the season saw many changes in the constitution of the League following the disbandment of the Athenian League and the enlargement of the Isthmian League.

Bracknell Town moved up to the Isthmian whilst Burnham, Edgware Town, Thatcham Town and Redhill joined from the Athenian. Redhill were the Athenian Champions, Greenwich Borough joined the Kent League whilst Northwood moved to the League from the Hellenic. Malden Vale and Merstham remained in the Isthmian Pyramid but joined the Combined Counties League. Three Clubs joined the Premier Division from the Senior Division, namely Hanwell Town, Danson and Pennant. The strength of the Premier Division is probably stronger than for many seasons and the Grounds Committee are hoping that the Senior Division can be strengthened by the beginning of Season 1985/6 to give the League a more balanced look.

The League commences its 89th season with optimism. B.S.

Premier Division

	P	W	D	L	F	A	Pts
Collier Row	28	21	4	3	66	26	46
Malden Vale	28	21	1	6	80	25	43
Brimsdown Rovers	28	18	7	3	63	22	43
Bracknell Town	28	17	3	8	69	43	37
Waltham Abbey	28	14	8	6	52	26	36
Beaconsfield United	28	12	9	7	39	29	33
Beckton United	28	14	4	10	46	36	32
Greenwich B	28	14	2	12	58	50	30
Swanley Town	28	12	5	11	45	37	29
Merstham	28	9	9	10	42	45	27
Amersham Town	28	4	10	14	31	66	18
BROB Barnet	28	5	6	17	34	66	16
Highfield	28	4	4	20	34	77	12
Chingford	28	5	2	21	29	78	12
Ambrose Fleming	28	2	2	24	16	78	6

Senior Division

	P	W	D	L	F	A	Pts
Hanwell Town	20	15	3	2	50	11	33
Crown and Manor	20	10	7	3	50	20	27
Danson	20	12	3	5	32	28	27
Pennant	20	10	5	5	48	28	25
Penhill Standard	20	10	4	6	35	24	24
Barkingside	20	7	9	4	33	22	23
Thames Poly	20	5	5	10	29	47	15
Wandsworth	20	5	4	11	25	45	14
Royal Arsenal Sports	20	4	5	11	25	44	13
Ulysses	20	3	5	12	19	39	11
Brent	20	3	2	15	15	53	8

LONDON SPARTAN FOOTBALL LEAGUE
RESULTS FOR SEASON 1983/84

PREMIER DIVISION	Ambrose Fleming	Amersham	Beaconsfield	Beckton United	Bracknell	Brimsdown	Brob Barnet	Chingford	Collier Row	Greenwich	Highfield	Malden Vale	Merstham	Swanley	Waltham Abbey
Ambrose Fleming	—	1-1	0-3	0-1	1-3	0-3	0-3	0-5	0-1	0-2	1-6	0-5	3-0	0-6	0-1
Amersham	3-2	—	0-2	1-1	1-1	0-3	4-3	1-0	1-4	4-6	3-2	0-2	0-0	1-1	1-5
Beaconsfield	4-1	1-1	—	0-0	1-3	1-1	5-1	2-1	1-0	1-3	1-0	0-4	0-1	1-0	1-1
Beckton United	3-0	3-1	3-0	—	3-1	1-2	1-1	2-0	0-1	3-0	4-0	1-2	2-1	2-3	2-2
Bracknell	5-2	6-1	0-4	1-0	—	3-0	2-2	7-0	0-2	5-1	4-0	2-1	2-1	3-2	1-4
Brimsdown	2-0	4-1	0-0	2-1	3-1	—	5-0	2-1	1-1	5-1	2-0	2-0	4-1	1-1	2-1
Brob Barnet	2-0	1-1	0-0	1-2	1-1	0-4	—	2-2	1-2	1-4	4-2	0-1	1-2	0-3	0-3
Chingford	2-1	3-0	0-4	1-3	0-4	1-6	1-4	—	2-3	4-3	0-3	0-3	0-2	0-1	0-0
Collier Row	4-1	1-1	2-1	1-0	3-0	2-1	3-1	4-0	—	1-2	10-0	1-0	1-1	1-0	1-1
Greenwich Boro	4-1	2-1	0-1	2-3	4-1	0-0	4-0	2-1	0-2	—	3-2	4-2	1-2	0-2	2-3
Highfield	0-2	3-3	0-1	0-1	0-4	2-2	1-3	1-3	1-3	1-0	—	1-6	2-2	1-5	2-2
Malden Vale	1-0	2-0	3-0	6-0	4-3	1-1	3-0	6-?	7-1	2-4	3-2	—	2-0	2-0	0-1
Merstham	3-0	0-0	2-2	4-2	1-3	0-3	3-1	3-0	2-4	1-1	0-1	1-4	—	1-0	4-2
Swanley Town	1-1	1-0	2-0	1-2	0-1	1-2	6-1	2-1	0-4	0-3	3-1	0-5	3-3	—	1-0
Waltham Abbey	4-0	6-0	1-1	2-0	1-2	1-0	1-0	6-0	1-3	1-8	2-0	0-3	0-0	0-0	—

LONDON SPARTAN LEAGUE
SENIOR CUP

FIRST ROUND		SECOND ROUND		THIRD ROUND		SEMI FINAL		FINAL	
Bracknell	3	Bracknell	3						
Brob Barnet	0			Bracknell	3				
Barkingside	2	Barkingside	2						
Pennant	1					Malden Vale	2	Malden Vale	2
Ambrose Fleming	bye	Ambrose Fleming	0	Malden Vale	7*				
Thames Poly	1							(at Bracknell)	
Malden Vale	6	Malden Vale	2						
				Wandsworth	1				
Chingford	2					Merstham	0		
Highfield	3	Highfield	2						
								Collier Row	1*
Wandsworth	1	Wandsworth	5						
Amersham	0			Merstham	3				
Ulysses	bye	Ulysses	1						
Merstham	bye	Merstham	2	Brimsdown	2	Brimsdown	0		
								* After extra time.	
Danson	bye	Danson	1						
				Beaconsfield	1				
Brent	1	Brimsdown	3*						
Brimsdown	8					Collier Row	1		
Greenwich	0	Swanley	1*						
Swanley	3			Waltham Abbey	1				
Beaconsfield	3	Beaconsfield	1*						
Beckton	0	(won on penalties)							
Pewhill	1								
Rasra	3	Rasra	1	Collier Row	2*				
Waltham Abbey	bye	Waltham Abbey	2						
Crown Manor	bye	Crown Manor	2						
Collier Row	bye	Collier Row	3						

AMERSHAM TOWN F.C. ( )

Chairman: S. Rawes **Manager:** P. Terp
Secretary: D. C. Dumbarton, 11 Walton Way, Aylesbury, Bucks HP21 7JJ. Tel: Aylesbury 81623
Ground Address & Tel No: Spratley's Meadow, School Lane, Old Amersham, Bucks. 7428
Directions to Ground: Off A413
Previous Leagues: Hellenic **Colours:** White/Black/White **Change colours:** Tangerine or Red
Programmes: Starting this season, price and contents not available **Clubhouse:** Yes **Floodlights:** Yes **Seating:** Yes

BEACONSFIELD UNITED F.C.

Chairman: David Pierly
Manager: Terry Long
Coach: Peter Edmonds
Physiotherapist:
Secretary: David Lane
Address & Tel No: 28 Baring Road, Beaconsfield, Bucks Beaconsfield 71424
Press Officer/President: Martin Speirs
Address & Tel No of ground: Holloway Park, Slough Road, Beaconsfield. Beaconsfield 6868
Simple ground directions: M40 to junction 2, first exit left at roundabout, ground immediately on right
No of seats: None **Covered accommodation:** Yes **Capacity:** 100 **Floodlights:** No
Year formed: 1921 **Nickname:** Rams **Club sponsors:** None
Club colours: Royal Blue/White/Royal Blue **Change colours:** White/Blue/White
Record attendance: 300 **Previous Leagues:** Wycombe & District
Clubhouse details: Bar, lounge, hall **Programme details:** 4 pages, with admission
Major Honours: 1982-83: 1st XI Winners Spartan League Senior Div., Res XI Runners Up Spartan League Div. 2, A XI Winners Wycombe & District Junior Cup, B XI Winners Wycombe & District Div. 4

BRIMSDOWN ROVERS (1946)

Chairman: G. Dodd **Manager:** P. Anglis
Secretary: J. Bowman, 30 Marryat Road, Enfield, Middx EN1 4RF.
Ground Address & Tel No:
Directions to Ground: Railway from London Liverpool Street to Brimsdown then 3 minutes walk to Ground. Bus from Enfield stops outside Ground
Previous Leagues: Northern Suburban Intermediate
Colours: Black & White vertical stripes **Change colours:** All Yellow
Programmes: 16 pages, 25p **Clubhouse:** Yes **Floodlights:** No **Seating:** No

BURNHAM

President: Dr Maxwell Summers, DSO, OBE
Chairman: M. Higton
Manager: Mick Jones
Secretary: Dave Eavis
Address & Tel No: 27 Taplow Road, Taplow, Maidenhead, Berks SL6 0JN Burnham 62934
Address & Tel No of ground: Wymers Wood Road, Burnham, Bucks (Burnham 2697/2467)
Simple ground directions: Two miles from M4 (exit 7) and 5 miles from M40 (exit 2), ½-mile north-west of village centre
No of seats: 200 **Covered accommodation:** 200 **Capacity:** 3,000 **Floodlights:** Yes
Year formed: 1878 **Nickname:** The Blues **Club sponsors:** A.C. Frost & Co
Club colours: Blue & White Quarters/Black/Blue **Change colours:** Amber/Black/Black
Previous Leagues: Great Western Comb., Wycombe Comb., Reading Comb., Hellenic, Athenian
Clubhouse details: Two storeyed building with glass-fronted bar on first floor. Two bars, kitchen, live entertainment
Best Year in F.A. Vase: 1982-83 Semi-Final
Programme: Yes **Programme Editor:** Michael Boxall
Local Newspapers: Slough Observer, Bucks Free Press, Windsor, Slough & Eton Express, Maidenhead Advertiser
Club Captain (1983-84): Jackie Graham **Player of the Year (1983-84):** Jackie Graham

COLLIER ROW F.C.

Chairman: R. Walker
Manager: A. Marson
Coach: L. Ellis
Physiotherapist: C. Lunn
Secretary: P. Sammons
Address & Tel No: 4 Riversdale Road, Romford, Essex Romford 68845
Commercial Manager: Mrs M. Taylor
Press Officer: A. Marson
Address & Tel No of ground: Collier Row F.C., Collier Row Road, Collier Row, Romford, Essex. Romford 2276
Simple ground directions: A12 from London, turn left at traffic lights at Moby Dick PH, to next roundabout, take right hand exit, ground 200 yds on right
No of seats: None **Covered accommodation:** Yes **Capacity:** 100 **Floodlights:** Yes
Year formed: 1929 **Nickname:** The Row **Club sponsors:** None
Club colours: All Red **Change colours:** Silver/Black
Record attendance: 450 v West Ham, 1983 **Previous Leagues:** Essex Olympian League
Clubhouse details: Members bar, 120 people max. Functions bar, 150 people max.
Programme details: 8 pages with admission
Major Honours: London Spartan League Senior Division Joint Winners 1982/83

EDGWARE

President: K. Batten
Chairman: R. Elliott
Managers: Mick Smith and Keith Witt
Secretary: T. J. Higgins
Address & Tel No: 34 Francis Road, Harrow, Middx. 01-863 4022
Address & Tel No of ground: White Lion Ground, High Street, Edgware, Middlesex (01-952 6799)
Simple ground directions: Edgware (Northern Line) or buses 32, 251 and 107 which pass ground
No of seats: 450 **Covered accommodation:** 1,200 **Capacity:** 6,000 **Floodlights:** Yes
Year formed: 1939 **Nickname:** Wares **Club sponsors:** None
Club colours: Green/Black **Change colours:** R/Blue/White
Previous Leagues: Delphian, Nemean
Clubhouse details: Open seven days a week lunchtimes and evenings
Best Year in F.A. Vase: 4th Round, 1979-80 **Programme Editor:** T. J. Higgins
Local Newspapers: Edgware and Mill Hill Times
Club Captain (1983-84): Ray Mangan **Player of the Year (1983-84):** Dave Ede

Bracknell Boys Club celebrate their victory over the much fancied Peppard in the Evening Post Reading Senior Cup Final at Elm Park. This season they have changed their name to Englefield Green Sports and will be competing in the London Spartan League. Photo: Reading Evening Post

Brimsdown Rovers FC

Hanwell Town *Back Row (L-R): M. Frolich (Trainer), J. Gadston (Manager), C. James, T. Soutar, J. Morton, D. Fleet, K. Cotton, R. Nairn (Coach). Front Row (L-R): P. Palmer, M. Biggins, R. Williams, I. Taylor, S. Swift, M. Box.*

SOUTH MIDLANDS FOOTBALL LEAGUE

President: A.G. Joyce

Chairman: D. Copp

Hon. Secretary and Treasurer: Clive Moyse, 33 Markham Crescent, Dunstable, Beds LU5 4SS. Tel: Dunstable 64682

SHEFFORD TOWN MAKE HISTORY

For the second successive Season Shefford Town made history by becoming the first side to win the Premier Division championship in the Season after winning Division One. The progress of Shefford over the past few Seasons has been remarkable and a tribute to the Manager Roland Legate and the Club Committee for their full backing. Runners up to Shefford were Pirton who thus failed in their attempt to clinch a third consecutive title. Eaton Bray United were the successful cup side in the League by winning the Challenge Trophy against Shefford after trailing from their first leg at Home; they also became the first winners of the Cove Windows SML Trophy defeating 61 FC (Luton) in the Final. Compensation for 61 FC came in the Beds. Senior Cup Final when the beat fellow South Midlands Leaguers Stotfold. Stotfold are leaving the League to join the UCL next Season. Also leaving the League will be Royston Town who is spite of having their worst ever Season in the South Midlands League have been accepted into the newly formed regional Division Two of the Isthmian League. As a result of the demise of the Athenian League Hoddesdon Town will be joining the South Midlands next Season and their inclusion will be welcomed.

Division One was won by New Bradwell St. Peter who had a very good Season and finished five points clear of Brache Sparta. Promoted along with these two teams will be Knebworth and Leighton Town.

The League's facility requirements for Premier Divison teams will be fully effective from next Season and the progress being made by many of the current Division One sides with regard to facilities augurs well for the future. The South Midlands League are now a part of the Isthmian 'Pyramid' and are looking forward to taking a full part in this area of Non-League Football.

Joining the League next Season in addition to Hoddesdon Town will be Milton Keynes Borough from the Hellenic League, Ickleford from North Herts. League and MK United who come from the North Bucks. League.

PREMIER DIVISION

	P	W	D	L	F	A	Pts
Shefford Town	28	17	9	2	55	23	43
Pirton	28	19	4	5	58	25	42
Eaton Bray United	28	16	6	6	51	30	38
Stotfold	28	15	6	7	48	31	36
Hatfield Town	28	14	4	10	48	38	32
61 FC (Luton)	28	10	11	7	40	31	31
GS Ashcroft Co-op	28	11	6	11	42	41	28
Shillington	28	9	9	10	31	41	27
Winslow United	28	9	7	12	58	57	25
Waterlows	28	10	4	14	31	47	24
Welwyn Garden City	28	9	5	14	43	46	23
Vauxhall Motors	28	9	5	14	29	41	23
Selby	28	7	8	13	36	53	22
Royston Town	28	6	7	15	33	43	19
Walden Rangers	28	2	3	23	22	78	7

DIVISION ONE

New Bradwell St. Peter	30	23	5	2	63	15	51
Brache Sparta	30	21	4	5	69	20	46
Knebworth	30	17	7	6	75	42	41
Leighton Town	30	16	8	6	71	32	40
Langford	30	15	5	10	49	39	35
Mowlem	30	15	5	10	61	51	35
Cranfield United	30	12	9	9	50	42	33
Totternhoe	30	12	7	11	55	44	31
Harpenden Town	30	11	9	10	45	46	31
Sandy Albion	30	12	6	12	39	45	30
Electrolux	30	9	8	13	43	52	26
Pitstone & Ivinghoe	30	9	7	14	50	54	25
Biggleswade Town	30	8	8	14	39	60	24
Welwyn Garden United	30	4	7	19	37	78	15
Henlow	30	5	3	22	20	73	13
Biggleswade United	30	1	2	27	16	89	4

Eaton Bray's fine 2-0 win at the ground of League Champions Shefford Town enabled them to win the League Cup 3-2 on aggregate. Photo: David Shute

SOUTH MIDLANDS FOOTBALL LEAGUE 1983-84 PREMIER DIVISION

	Ashcroft Co-op	Eaton Bray Utd	Hatfield Town	Pirton	Royston Town	Selby	Shefford Town	Shillington	Stotfold	Vauxhall Motors	Walden Rangers	Waterlows	Welwyn Gdn City	Winslow Utd	61 FC (Luton)
Ashcroft Co-op		1-1	1-3	1-2	1-0	2-0	1-1	2-2	0-1	0-1	3-0	3-0	0-2	2-5	3-0
Eaton Bray Utd	2-1		5-0	0-2	0-1	2-2	2-2	1-0	2-1	1-0	4-2	1-2	3-1	2-0	0-0
Hatfield Town	3-2	0-3		1-1	3-0	0-0	0-1	1-2	2-0	1-2	5-0	1-0	1-2	2-1	2-0
Pirton	4-0	1-3	3-1		2-0	3-0	3-2	2-0	2-3	1-1	3-0	3-1	2-1	0-3	0-0
Royston Town	4-2	0-2	1-4	1-1		0-0	0-2	0-1	0-1	3-1	8-1	3-0	1-2	2-3	1-3
Selby	2-3	7-3	0-2	0-2	1-1		0-1	3-0	2-0	0-1	1-1	0-1	1-6	2-5	2-1
Shefford Town	1-1	2-1	1-1	1-0	1-1	3-0		3-0	3-3	2-0	6-1	2-1	1-0	0-1	4-1
Shillington	0-2	1-1	4-0	0-2	0-0	0-0	1-1		0-5	1-1	2-0	2-2	2-1	1-2	1-2
Stotfold	3-0	0-2	1-2	2-0	1-2	5-1	0-3	1-1		2-1	3-2	1-0	3-1	2-1	0-0
Vauxhall Motors	0-2	0-1	1-0	1-3	3-0	2-4	0-1	2-2	0-2		2-1	0-1	1-1	2-2	1-2
Walden Rangers	0-2	0-2	1-4	1-3	1-0	0-1	2-2	0-1	0-2	2-3		0-1	0-0	6-2	0-6
Waterlows	0-0	1-4	1-3	1-2	2-1	1-4	1-3	0-1	1-1	1-0	1-0		2-0	2-2	4-2
Welwyn Gdn City	1-3	1-0	2-3	0-7	2-2	5-0	0-1	1-2	2-2	0-1	4-0	0-2		2-1	1-1
Winslow Utd	1-2	0-1	2-2	1-3	0-0	3-3	2-4	2-4	1-3	5-2	4-0	5-1	2-5		1-1
61 FC (Luton)	2-2	2-2	2-1	0-1	2-1	0-0	0-0	4-0	0-0	0-1	3-1	3-1	2-0	1-1	

DIVISION ONE

	Biggleswade Town	Biggleswade United	Brache Sparta	Cranfield United	Electrolux	Harpenden Town	Henlow	Knebworth	Langford	Leighton Town	Mowlem	New Bradwell St Peter	Pitstone & Ivinghoe	Sandy Albion	Totternhoe	Welwyn Gdn Utd
Biggleswade Town		2-0	2-7	0-0	1-3	0-0	4-0	0-2	1-0	0-8	1-2	0-2	2-2	2-0	0-0	3-0
Biggleswade United	0-0		0-2	1-3	0-1	1-5	0-3	1-4	0-1	0-5	0-3	0-3	1-3	1-2	1-5	1-3
Brache Sparta	2-1	7-0		0-0	3-0	0-0	4-1	1-1	4-1	1-0	2-0	0-2	3-1	2-0	1-0	2-1
Cranfield United	4-0	2-3	1-0		0-0	2-2	3-0	4-2	2-0	2-2	1-1	1-1	1-3	1-1	4-0	5-2
Electrolux	3-1	3-0	1-2	1-2		3-3	2-1	0-2	0-2	1-1	0-1	1-0	3-3	3-1	2-2	5-1
Harpenden Town	2-1	1-0	0-1	1-2	1-1		5-1	0-0	3-2	3-1	3-4	0-3	0-0	1-1	1-3	2-0
Henlow	0-1	1-1	0-6	0-1	1-0	0-1		2-2	1-2	2-1	0-2	0-2	1-0	1-2	0-2	2-2
Knebworth	2-2	5-0	2-1	4-1	1-0	7-2	4-0		1-4	1-2	3-1	2-1	3-1	1-3	1-3	5-0
Langford	5-3	3-0	0-3	1-1	1-0	0-2	4-0	2-2		2-2	2-1	1-3	1-0	2-0	2-0	4-0
Leighton Town	5-1	3-0	1-0	4-0	3-3	3-1	5-0	2-4	3-0		2-0	1-2	4-1	3-0	2-0	1-1
Mowlem	5-3	2-1	2-5	2-1	3-1	0-1	5-0	2-2	1-1	4-1		3-3	2-0	2-2	2-3	3-0
New Bradwell St Peter	3-2	3-0	1-0	2-0	5-0	3-0	2-1	1-0	1-0	0-0	3-1		1-0	4-0	1-1	0-0
Pitstone & Ivinghoe	2-2	3-2	0-3	2-3	2-2	2-0	2-0	1-2	3-1	1-1	3-1	1-3		1-2	0-4	6-0
Sandy Albion	0-2	2-0	0-2	1-0	2-0	2-2	3-0	3-3	1-2	0-1	0-3	0-3	2-1		4-1	4-1
Totternhoe	0-0	5-1	1-1	3-2	4-0	2-1	1-2	2-3	0-2	1-3	5-0	0-2	2-2	0-1		1-1
Welwyn Gdn Utd	1-2	4-1	1-4	3-1	3-4	1-2	4-0	0-4	1-1	1-1	2-3	0-3	2-4	0-0	2-4	

CHALLENGE TROPHY SEASON 1983-1984

FIRST ROUND

Pitstone & Ivinghoe	0	New Brad St Peter	1
Mowlem	1	Totternhoe	2*
Selby	5	Welwyn Gdn Utd	1
Royston Town	2	Stotfold	1
Biggleswade Town	0	Sandy Albion	2
Welwyn Gdn City	1	Winslow United	5
Ashcroft Co-op	2	Leighton Town	1
Pirton	2	Vauxhall Motors	1
Eaton Bray United	3	Waterlows	0
Knebworth	2	Shefford Town	3*
Shillington	1	Brache Sparta	5*
Hatfield Town	5	Walden Rangers	0
Henlow	1	Harpenden Town	2
Electrolux	3	Biggleswade United	0
Langford	1	61 FC (Luton)	3

*Denotes Extra Time

SECOND ROUND

Ashcroft Co-op	1	Shefford Town	2
Pirton	5	Royston Town	0
Cranfield United	3	Selby	2
Eaton Bray United	4	Electrolux	1*
Harpenden Town	1	Brache Sparta	2
Totternhoe	2	Sandy Albion	1
Hatfield Town	2*:3	New Brad St Peter	2:1
Winslow United	2	61 FC (Luton)	1

THIRD ROUND

Brache Sparta	4	Totternhoe	1
Pirton	1	Hatfield Town	0
Winslow United	0	Eaton Bray United	4
Cranfield United	1	Shefford Town	3

SEMI FINALS

Brache Sparta	1	Eaton Bray United	4
Shefford Town	2	Pirton	1

FINAL

Eaton Bray United	1	Shefford Town	2
Shefford Town	0	Eaton Bray United	2

Eaton Bray won 3-2 on aggregate.

COVE WINDOWS SML TROPHY
SEASON 1983-1984

FIRST ROUND

Eaton Bray United 5, Ashcroft Co-op 2 (agg score)
Royston Town 5, Sandy Albion 0 (agg score)
Shefford Town 1, Shillington 4 (agg score)
Walden Rangers 2, Winslow United 2 (agg score)
(Walden Rangers won 4-3 on penalties)
Waterlows 1, Vauxhall Motors 1 (agg score)
(Waterlows won on Away Goals rule)
Pirton 1, Welwyn Garden City 3 (agg score)
Selby 0, 61 FC (Luton) 8 (agg score)
Stotfold 5, Hatfield Town 3 (agg score)

SECOND ROUND

Stotfold 5, Walden Rangers 1
Welwyn Garden City 1, Waterlows 2
Shillington 0, 61 FC (Luton) 1
Eaton Bray United 5, Royston Town 1

SEMI FINALS

Eaton Bray United 2, Waterlows 0
Stotfold 0, 61 FC (Luton) 2 (aet)

FINAL (at Ashcroft Co-op FC)

Eaton Bray United 3, 61 FC (Luton) 1

Competition sponsored by Cove Windows Ltd., Luton

SOUTH MIDLANDS LEAGUE SEASON 1983-4
LEADING SCORERS

PREMIER DIVISION: G. Bailey (Hatfield Town) 22, K. Lowe (Pirton) 17, B. Marshall (Welwyn Gdn City) 15, M. Watkins (Winslow Utd) 14, P. Robinson (Selby) 14, D. Rowe (Winslow Utd) 14, S. Simon (61 FC (Luton) 14, D. Stone (Stotfold) 12, P. Sweeney (Shefford Town) 11, C. Henry (Shillington) 10.

DIVISION ONE: R. Vale (Langford) 23, D. Griffith (Knebworth) 22, J. Snape (Leighton Town) 21, A. McErlane (Brache Sparta) 20, P. Cumberbatch (Mowlem) 18, Y. Bohkecht (Pitstone & Ivinghoe) 15, L. Lawes (Totternhoe) 15, K. Stapleton (Harpenden Town) 12, M. Howe (New Bradwell St Peter) 12, I. Kane (Knebworth) 12.

Eaton Bray's captain triumphantly lifts the South Midlands League Cup. Photo: Leo Hoenig

The successful Eaton Bray squad which won the South Midlands League Cup. Photo: Mike Joss

ASHCROFT CO-OP (1970) **Chairman:** D. Reilly **Managers:** T. Tomkins & M. Lowndes

Secretary: Terry Gilmore, 37 Stockingstone Road, Luton, Beds LU2 7ND. Tel: Luton 32448
Ground Address & Tel No: Co-op Sports & Social Club, Stockingstone Road, Luton, Beds. Luton 23606
Directions to Ground: A505 from Luton to Round Green Roundabout, first turn left, ground 200 metres on right
Previous Leagues: Luton & South Beds, Wallspan Combination
Colours: White/Navy/Navy **Change colours:** Red & White striped/Black/Red
Programmes: 10 pages, 30p **Clubhouse:** Yes **Floodlights:** No **Seating:** 25-30

BRACHE SPARTA (1960) **Chairman:** R. Standring **Manager:** Barry Fanconi

Secretary: M. R. Franklin, 62 Katherine Drive, Dunstable, Beds LU5 4NU. Tel: 61177
Ground Address & Tel No: Foxdell Sports Ground, Dallow Road, Luton, Beds. 20751
Directions to Ground: On Main A505 Luton to Dunstable, turn into Kingsway, proceed to end of Kingsway, turn right at traffic lights. Entrance to ground at end of Dallow Road, adjacent to Foxdell Junior School
Previous Leagues: Luton & South Beds **Colours:** All White **Change colours:** All Blue
Programmes: 8 pages, 40p **Clubhouse:** Yes **Floodlights:** No **Seating:** Yes

EATON BRAY UNITED (1946) **Chairman:** A. Fieldhouse **Manager:** J. Davis

Secretary: Frank Ashton, 17 Totternhoe Road, Eaton Bray, Dunstable, Beds. Tel: Eaton Bray 220132
Ground Address & Tel No: The Rye, Eaton Bray. Eaton Bray 221443
Directions to Ground: Leave Dunstable on Aylesbury road, turn right towards Totternhoe, follow signs to Eaton Bray
Previous Leagues: Luton & District **Colours:** White/Blue/Red **Change colours:** All Blue
Programmes: 6 pages, 20p **Clubhouse:** Yes **Floodlights:** No **Seating:** Yes

HODDESDON TOWN

Chairman: Elmer Elliott **Secretary:** Dave Smith
Manager: Terry Scales **Address & Tel No:** 01-804 3608
Coach: Bill Major
Address & Tel No of ground: Lowfield, Parkview, Hoddesdon, Herts
Simple ground directions: Broxbourne or Rye House Station, 392 bus to Hoddesdon High Street, 5 minute walk
No of seats: 250 **Covered accommodation:** 250 **Capacity:** 3,000 **Floodlights:** Yes
Year formed: 1879 **Nickname:** Lily Whites **Club sponsors:** Hoddesdon Motor Co
Club colours: White/Black **Change colours:** All Yellow
Previous Leagues: East Herts, Herts County, Spartan, London Spartan, Athenian **Programme:** Yes
Clubhouse details: Open match days, training nights, and other functions
Best Year in F.A. Vase: 1974-75 First Winners
Local Newspapers: Lea Valley Mercury (Waltham Cross 23740)

KNEBWORTH (1901) **Chairman:** M. R. Thody **Manager:** Bob Boyden

Secretary: John Stevens, 12 Olden Mead, Letchworth, Herts. Tel: Letchworth 73735
Ground Address & Tel No: Old Knebworth Lane. Stevenage 313863
Directions to Ground: B197 to Roebuck Motel, Stevenage, Old Knebworth Lane opposite Motel. Ground entrance 150 yards on left
Previous Leagues: Herts County **Colours:** Tangerine/Black **Change colours:** Sky Blue
Programmes: 4 pages, free **Clubhouse:** Yes **Floodlights:** No **Seating:** Yes

LEIGHTON TOWN **Chairman:** Stuart Pollard **Manager:** John Wortley

Secretary: Tony Yates, 93 Stanbridge Road, Leighton Buzzard, Beds LU7 8QA
Ground Address & Tel No: Bell Close, Lake Street, Leighton Buzzard. Leighton Buzzard 373311
Directions to Ground: A5 to Stanbridge signpost, through Stanbridge and Tilsworth into Lake Street. Ground at rear of Camden Motors
Previous Leagues: Spartan, United Counties **Colours:** Red & White stripe/Red/Red **Change colours:** All Blue
Programmes: 4 pages, free **Clubhouse:** Yes **Floodlights:** No **Seating:** Yes

LONG EATON GRANGE (1953) **Chairman:** John Shardlow **Manager:** Bill Fearn

Secretary: William A. Northover, 94 Risley Lane, Breaston, Derbys. Tel: Draycott 2168
Ground Address & Tel No: Grange Park, Long Eaton, Notts. Long Eaton 2024
Directions to Ground: M1 exit 25 take A52 to Nottingham, turn right at first roundabout (Gregory's Roses), travel to second set of traffic lights, turn right (to Long Eaton) and first left for a further 500 yds, turn left opposite Long Eaton Stadium
Previous Leagues: Notts Alliance, East Midlands Regional, Midland Counties, Northern Counties East
Colours: Blue & Red striped/Blue/Black **Change colours:** Yellow/Green/Yellow
Programmes: No **Clubhouse:** No 3 covered stands **Floodlights:** No **Seating:** No

MILTON KEYNES BOROUGH F.C.

Presidents: V. Cheshire, L. Hennesey
Chairman: D. Hamilton

Manager: E. Byrne
Coach:
Physiotherapist: B. Wood

Secretary: A. Bond
Address & Tel No: (H) Milton Keynes 78398
(B) 0908 74811
Commercial Manager: None
Address & Tel No:
Press Officer & Tel No: D. Hamilton, J. O'Hara
Address & Tel No of ground: Denbigh Sports Ground, Mount Farm, Milton Keynes (Milton Keynes 72879)
Simple ground directions: Davenport Vernon Garage, A5 turn towards City Centre, entrance 200yds on left opp Cole Plastics.
No of seats: None **Covered accommodation:** Yes **Capacity:** 150 **Floodlights:** No
Year formed: 1966 **Nickname:** The Borough **Club sponsors:** None
Club colours: All Light Blue **Change colours:** Green & Yellow stripes/Green/Yellow
Previous Names: Belsize F.C. **Previous Grounds:** Manor Fields
Record attendance: 300 v Milton Keynes City, B & B Cup
Previous Leagues: United Counties, Hellenic **Programme:** For special matches
Clubhouse details: Small Bar.
Major Honours: UCL Division 2 Champions 1972-73, K.O. Cup 1971, 1972, 1973, UCL Division 1 Winners 1978-79, Runners-Up 1976-77, 1977-78

NEW BRADWELL ST. PETER

(1902) Chairman: G. Hall **Manager:** M. Burridge
Secretary: D. Ferguson, 178 Church Street, Wolverton, Milton Keynes, MK12 5JS. Tel: 0908 318009
Ground Address & Tel No: Recreation Ground, Bradwell Road, New Bradwell, Milton Keynes. 0908 313835
Directions to Ground: M1, Junction 14, go towards Newport Pagnell, left at 1st roundabout onto H3 - A422 Monks Way, go 6 roundabouts, turn right onto V6 Grafton Street, 1st right then left, ground ½ mile on left
Previous Leagues: North Bucks **Colours:** Claret & Blue/Sky Blue/Sky Blue **Change colours:** White/Black/White
Programmes: 12 pages, 25p **Clubhouse:** Yes **Floodlights:** No **Seating:** Yes

PIRTON

Chairman: Brian Britell **Manager:** Tony Martin
Secretary: Bob Castle, 26 Crab Tree Lane, Pirton, Hitchin, Herts
Ground Address & Tel No: Walnut Tree Road, Pirton, Hitchin. 712531
Directions to Ground: From A6, through Barton and Shillington, from Hitchin, first right off Luton Road (A505)
Previous Leagues: North Herts **Colours:** Yellow/Royal Blue/Royal Blue **Change colours:** All Red
Programmes: 4 pages, free **Clubhouse:** Yes **Floodlights:** No **Seating:** Yes

SELBY

Chairman: **Manager:**
Secretary: Deryck Taylor, 2 Telford Road, London Colney, St. Albans, AL2 1RT. Tel: Bowans Green 24658
Ground Address & Tel No: Toulmin Drive, New Greens Estate, St. Albans. St. Albans 52401
Directions to Ground: From A5 or A6 enter Batchwood Drive, enter Green Lane, first left into Toulmin Drive. Ground at end of Toulmin Drive
Previous Leagues: Mid Herts **Colours:** Red/White/Red **Change colours:** Blue/White/Blue
Programmes: with admission **Clubhouse:** No **Floodlights:** No **Seating:** Yes

SHEFFORD TOWN

(1948) **Chairman:** C. Rockall **Manager:** R. Legate
Secretary: P. Ward, 7 George Street, Shefford, SG17 5BP
Ground Address & Tel No: Ivel Road, Shefford, Beds. Hitchin 813487
Directions to Ground: From Hitchin, turn left into Ivel Road at fire station. From Bedford, first right after traffic lights
Previous Leagues: Parthenon, United Counties **Colours:** Sky Blue **Change colours:** Claret
Programmes: 8 pages, 20p **Clubhouse:** Yes **Floodlights:** No **Seating:** No

SHILLINGTON

(1946) **Chairman:** Stan Burgoine **Manager:** Ron Crawley
Secretary: Aubrey Cole, 32 Greenfields, Shillington, Hitchin, Herts SG5 3NX. Tel: Hitchin 711322
Ground Address & Tel No: Greenfields, Shillington, Hitchin, Herts SG5 3NX. 711757
Directions to Ground: From Bedford or Luton, A6 turn off at Barton. From Hitchin or Bedford, turn off at "Bird in Hand" A600, Henlow Camp (RAF)
Previous Leagues: Luton District **Colours:** White/Black/Black **Change colours:** All Red
Programmes: 6 pages, 30p **Clubhouse:** Yes **Floodlights:** No **Seating:** Yes

61 FC (LUTON)

(1961) **Chairman:** C. Self **Manager:** R. Everitt
Secretary: R. Everitt, 11 Chiltern Gardens, Luton. Tel: 508112
Ground Address & Tel No: Kingsway, Beverley Road, Luton. 582965
Directions to Ground: Situated on A505 approx 1 mile from M1 Junction 11
Previous Leagues: Luton **Colours:** Sky Blue/Royal Blue/Royal Blue **Change colours:** Red, Black & Yellow/Black/Red
Programmes: 8 pages, 10p **Clubhouse:** Open 7 nights, Sat & Sun lunchtime **Floodlights:** No **Seating:** 30

STOTFOLD

President: E. Perrin
Chairman: J. R. Talbot
Manager: B. Lambert
Coach: L. Wood
Physiotherapist: D. Northern
Secretary: W. Clegg
Address & Tel No: 12 Common Road, Stotfold, Hitchin, Herts. 73042
Commercial Manager: Miss J. Longhurst
Press Officer: Miss J. Longhurst
Address & Tel No of ground: Roker Park, The Green, Stotfold, Hitchin, Herts. (Hitchin 730421)
Simple ground directions: A507 from A1: Turn right at traffic lights, right at T-junction; A507 from Bedford: Via Shefford, left at traffic lights, right at T-junction
No of seats: 50 **Covered accommodation:** Yes **Capacity:** 200 **Floodlights:** Yes
Year formed: 1904, reformed 1945 **Nickname:** Canaries **Club sponsors:** Icknield Instruments
Club colours: Amber/Black **Change colours:** Red
Previous names: Stotfold O.B., Stotfold Hornets, Stotfold Athletic
Previous grounds: Hitchin Road Recreation Ground
Previous Leagues: Biggleswade League, North Herts, South Midlands
Clubhouse details: Clubroom, bar, dressing rooms, physio room **Programme:** 10 pages, free
Major Honours: Beds Senior Cup 1964-65, Beds Premier Cup 1980-81, S.M.L. Premier Div 1980-81, S.M.L. Challenge Cup 1981-82, North Beds Charity Cup 1955-56, 1956-57, 1961-62

VAUXHALL MOTORS (1907)

Chairman: I. Burgess **Manager:** J. Symonds
Secretary: S. R. Whitworth, 4 King William Close, Barton-le-Clay, Beds. Tel: Luton 882451 (H), 426203 (B)
Ground Address & Tel No: Brache Estate, Park Street, Luton. Luton 23061
Directions to Ground: Through Luton entering Park Street or M1 Cuttenhoe Road, Park Street entrance
Previous Leagues: Spartan, United Counties
Colours: Gold with Blue trim/Blue/Gold **Change colours:** Blue & White/Blue/Blue
Programmes: 6 pages, 10p **Clubhouse:** Yes **Floodlights:** No **Seating:** Yes

WATERLOWS (1961)

Chairman: D. A. Parrett **Manager:** A. Loasby
Secretary: M. G. Willmore, 68 Elmwood Crescent, Luton LU2 7HY. Tel: Luton 22654
Ground Address & Tel No: High Street North, Dunstable. Dunstable 61549
Directions to Ground: Left hand side of main A5 leaving Dunstable northwards
Previous Leagues: Luton & District, South Beds **Colours:** Red **Change colours:** Blue
Programmes: 8 pages, 30p (includes admission) **Clubhouse:** Yes **Floodlights:** No **Seating:** Yes

WELWYN GARDEN CITY (Reformed 1973)

Chairman: John Newman **Manager:** John Sneddon
Secretary: Dick Dunning, 38 Cowper Road, Welwyn Garden City, Herts AL7 3LS.
Ground Address & Tel No: Herns Lane, Welwyn Garden City. Welwyn Garden 28470
Directions to Ground: From A1, ground east of town off A1000 close to Panshanger Estate and municipal golf course
Previous Leagues: None since reformation
Colours: Claret & Blue/White/Claret **Change colours:** Yellow/Black/Yellow
Programmes: 12 pages, 50p (with admission) **Clubhouse:** Yes **Floodlights:** No **Seating:** Yes

WINSLOW UNITED (1891)

Chairman: C. Spinks **Manager:** Dermot Callaghan
Secretary: R. S. Hamley, 4 Cricketers Row, Winslow, Buckingham MK18 3JT
Ground Address & Tel No: Elmfields Gate. Winslow 3057
Directions to Ground: Ground off High Street, turn right after pelican crossing from Aylesbury, turn left before pelican crossing from Buckingham
Previous Leagues: North Bucks **Colours:** Yellow/Blue/Blue **Change colours:** Red/Black/Black
Programmes: 16 pages, 20p **Clubhouse:** Bar open training nights, after matches **Floodlights:** No **Seating:** 25 in stand

Biggleswade Town *Back Row (L-R): D. Smith (Chairman), Roger Tomlin (Player/Manager), Steve Johnson, Norman Gunn, Gary Tilbrook, Steve Butterworth, Paul Hamshere, M. Bryant (Kit sponsor). Front Row: Dave Lindsay, Micky Uhl, Neil Daniels, Alan Owen, Glyn Warren, Steve Hay.* Photo: George W. Skevington.

The Tottenhoe and Watford sides when they met in August 1983.

Knebworth Back Row (L-R): Bob Boyden (Manager), Joe Colgan, Phil Sandford, Roy Chesterton, Butch Phillips, Ken Halliday, Peter Gormley, Richard Wilman, Duncan Aitchison (Fixt Sect). Front Row: Alex Ward, Alex Matheson, Brian Roberts, Don Griffith, John Ashworth, Alan Cato. Missing from photograph: John Huxtable, Gary Lock, Ian Kane.

HERTS COUNTY LEAGUE

President: D. R. Jenkins
Chairman: C. T. Hudson
Secretary: E. H. Dear, 48 Wilshere Road, Welwyn, Herts AL6 9PX

IT'S COCKFOSTERS ALL THE WAY

Cockfosters won the Premier Division Championship having led the title race from start to finish, winning the championship for the third time in six seasons. Bedmond Social finished as runners-up in not only the league, a best ever position, but also the Aubrey Cup (League Cup). It was third placed Leavesden Hospital who won the Aubrey Cup, defeating Bedmond by one goal to nil after extra time. Most observers regarded it as the best cup final seen for many seasons, with M. McDonagh in the Leavesden goal having an outstanding match.

The club that hosted the Aubrey Cup Final, Bovingdon, won the Division One Championship with a ten point margin to spare. In Division Two Little Heath were victorious in their first season in membership of the league.

Next season sees the implementation of the first stage of the league's facility requirements for the Premier Division and the following season the final stage. This means that by the start of season 1985-86 ALL Premier Division clubs will have to meet requirements suitable for competing in the Football Association Challenge Vase. Starting next season the Hertfordshire Football Association will be introducing a two tier structure for Senior clubs, which means that many of the Herts County League Premier Division clubs will be competing in the newly formed Herts Senior Trophy Competition against neighbouring clubs based in Hertfordshire who play in the South Midlands, Essex Senior and London Spartan leagues. To coincide with the more stringent requirements for the Premier Division the league are hopeful of opening up negotiations to establish themselves in the FA Pyramid within the near future.

This season has been a particularly successful one; not only have the league's facility requirements been unanimously accepted by the clubs, but the league has also run a Representative Team for the first time for many seasons. The team played matches against the Essex Senior League and the Middlesex League and it is hoped the fixture with the Essex Senior League will become an annual event; it is sad that the Middlesex League is disbanding in its current form.

Next season the league is expanding the size of its divisions to sixteen teams in each division and welcomes to the league Wingate FC from Arkley, Johnson Mathey from the Northern Suburban League, Biggleswade United from the South Midlands league, Ashwell and St Ippolyts both from the North Herts League, Kimpton Rovers from the Mid Herts League and E.S. Sports from Borehamwood. Borehamwood Rangers, Offley Social and Watford All Nations are retiring from the league.

We now feel the league is progressing in the right direction and we can look to what promises to be an exciting future with great optimism.

Michael Cooper
Hon Fixtures Secretary

Premier Division

	P	W	D	L	F	A	Pts
Cockfosters	30	21	6	3	66	25	48
Bedmond Social	30	18	8	4	67	36	44
Leavesden Hospital	30	17	7	6	63	36	41
London Colney	30	15	7	8	59	35	37
Sandridge Rovers	30	14	8	8	63	44	36
Wellcome	30	13	8	9	60	55	34
St Margaretsbury	30	10	10	10	45	42	30
Sun Sports	30	10	10	10	33	36	30
Mount Grace OS	30	11	6	13	43	43	28
Rolls Royce Engines	30	10	6	14	31	41	26
Evergreen	30	10	6	14	35	47	26
Tudor Corinthians	30	7	11	12	28	43	25
Whitwell Athletic	30	8	7	15	43	64	23
Leverstock Green	30	7	5	18	41	52	19
Walkern	30	7	5	18	34	75	19
Hadley	30	5	4	21	31	68	14

Division 1

Bovingdon	26	20	5	1	75	17	45
Potters Bar Crsdrs	26	15	5	6	63	33	35
Oxhey Jets	26	15	4	7	56	38	34
Sarratt	26	14	5	7	57	28	33
BAC Stevenage	26	13	7	6	54	36	33
Wormley Rovers	26	13	3	10	45	43	29
Bushey Rangers	26	11	4	11	42	49	26
Offley Social	26	11	3	12	39	44	25
Chipperfield	26	10	3	13	41	42	23
Park Street	26	8	6	12	52	48	22
Cuffley	26	6	9	11	41	59	21
Kings Langley	26	3	10	13	26	52	16
Borehamwood R	26	5	4	17	35	77	14
Watford All Nations	26	3	2	21	29	89	8

HERTS COUNTY LEAGUE

	Premier Division Champions	Aubrey Cup Winners
1964-65	Leggatts Way Old Boys (Now Evergreen)	Leggatts Way Old Boys
1965-66	Kings Langley	Marconi Instruments
1966-67	Kings Langley	Leggatts Way Old Boys
1967-68	Leggatts Way Old Boys	Kings Langley
1968-69	Leggatts Way Old Boys	Marconi Instruments
1969-70	Leggatts Way Old Boys	Leggatts Way Old Boys
1970-71	Leggatts Way Old Boys	Leggatts Way Old Boys
1971-72	Leggatts Way Old Boys	St Margaretsbury
1972-73	Rolls Royce Engines	Rolls Royce Engines
1973-74	Knebworth	Rolls Royce Engines
1974-75	Rolls Royce Engines	Rolls Royce Engines
1975-76	Rolls Royce Engines	Rolls Royce Engines
1976-77	Royston Town	Knebworth
1977-78	Chipperfield	Chipperfield
1978-79	Cockfosters	Cockfosters
1979-80	Leggatts Way Old Boys	Leavesden Hospital
1980-81	Cockfosters	Bedmond Social
1981-82	Sandridge Rovers	London Colney
1982-83	Sandridge Rovers	Leavesden Hospital
1983-84	Cockfosters	Leavesden Hospital

Herts Charity Shield Winners

1945-46	Chipperfield
1961-62	London Colney
1966-67	Kings Langley
1972-73	Leggatts Way Old Boys
1974-75	Rolls Royce Engines
1975-76	Rolls Royce Engines

Best Season in FA Vase
(While in membership of Herts County League)

Evergreen	1975-76	Second Round
Knebworth	–	Preliminary Round
Rolls Royce Engines	1979-80	Second Round
Royston Town	1975-76	First Round
Sun Sports	1978-79	First Round

ESSEX THAMES-SIDE CHALLENGE TROPHY

Chairman: J. J. A. Bays
Secretary: A. P. Oliver, 15 Anstey Close, Eastwood, Leigh-on-Sea,
Essex SS9 5AW (0702 526400)

CLAPTON RETAIN TROPHY IN SUPERB FINAL

Each year records are broken and this competition was no exception when the largest number of clubs yet, seventeen in all, entered in 1983-84. Before the season had officially started our two illustrious Football League clubs, Southend United and Orient, had met at Roots Hall Football Ground, Southend-on-Sea, before a 2000 crowd. The warm summer's evening brought the large shirt-sleeved crowd who were drawn no doubt with the prospect of a good competitive game instead of the usual pre-season fare. They were not disappointed as an exciting tie resulting in a close win for Orient ensued and it is to be hoped that more clubs will consider playing their ties earlier in the good weather, not that this season was disrupted much, as the weather this season was particularly kind. Indeed, only nine games were postponed; the rain mainly selecting Leytonstone/Ilford to wash out on no less than five separate occasions.

The matches this season were again very competitive. The Semi-Finals were decided in early April. Chelmsford City accounted for Leyton-Wingate with a dramatic late goal on a very damp evening by two goals to one and Clapton defeated Aveley by two goals to nil. Thus, the holders, Clapton, were hosts again in the Final. The match unfolded slowly and gradually blossomed into one of the finest Finals we have ever experienced. The score was 0-0 when a penalty for hands midway through the second half was converted by Clapton. Despite intense pressure by Chelmsford this looked the final score as the awards were being prepared for presentation 2 minutes from the end. A mighty roar and Chelmsford were level. The first period of extra time brought two goals for Chelmsford and a 3-1 interval lead. Clapton's cup fighting spirit was not to be denied as they clawed their way back again to lock the Final at 3-3 after extra time. In the history of the competition only two other matches have been decided on penalties, and Clapton had featured in them both. This expertise did not fail them as they ran out winners by 5 penalties to 4. Norman Posner, Vice-Chairman and Referees Secretary, supported by Brian Hitchings and Tony Oliver, Hon Treasurer and Secretary respectively, presented the £6000 Silver Galleon Trophy and plaques.

1983-1984 RESULTS

	First Round		
Epping Town	0	Woodford Town	1
	Second Round		
Rainham Town	0	Aveley	2
Leyton-Wingate	2	Grays Athletic	1
Woodford Town	0	Barkingside	2
Ford United	0	East Thurrock United	4
(Played at Tilbury FC)			
Southend United	0	Orient	2
Hornchurch	1	Chelmsford City	3
Barking	0	Leytonstone/Ilford	2
Tilbury	1	Clapton	3
	Third Round		
East Thurrock United	1	Aveley	2
(Played at Aveley FC)			
Leyton-Wingate	4	Barkingside	1
Clapton	2	Leytonstone/Ilford	1
Chelmsford City	2	Orient	0
	Semi-Finals		
Clapton	2	Aveley	0
Chelmsford City	2	Leyton/Wingate	1
	Final		
Clapton (5 penalties)	3	Chelmsford (4 penalties)	3

After extra time. The score at full time was 1-1.

RESERVE TEAM FOOTBALL

MIDDLESEX BORDER LEAGUE

	P	W	D	L	F	A	Pts
Aylesbury	26	22	1	3	69	23	45
Chesham	26	12	7	7	42	30	31
Burnham	26	10	9	7	39	29	29
Newbury	26	13	3	10	50	45	29
Chalfont St Peter	26	10	8	8	40	30	28
Hemel Hempstead	26	11	6	9	30	33	28
Edgware	26	10	6	10	38	30	26
Maidenhead	26	13	—	13	36	36	26
Marlow	26	10	4	12	37	40	24
Flackwell Heath	26	7	9	10	36	50	23
Bracknell	26	9	4	13	35	50	22
Ruislip Manor	26	7	7	12	36	49	21
Harefield	26	8	4	14	32	42	20
Amersham	26	3	6	17	29	62	12

League Cup: winners Chesham United.
Runners-up: Aylesbury United
A.W.A. Cup winners: Aylesbury United.
Runners-up: Chesham United.

WALLSPAN SOUTHERN COMBINATION LEAGUE

Secretary: K. Thornton, 31 Cam Mead, Bedgrove, Aylesbury, Bucks. HP21 7BZ. Tel: Aylesbury 81489

	P	W	D	L	F	A	Pts
Witney Town	20	14	3	3	53	14	45
St Albans City	20	12	5	3	38	19	41
Hitchin Town	20	10	5	5	36	22	35
Stevenage Borough	20	9	6	5	35	27	33
Oxford City	20	8	3	9	37	34	27
Baldock Town	20	6	7	7	21	28	25
Milton Keynes City	20	6	5	9	24	41	23
Barton Rovers	20	5	6	9	23	31	21
Berkhamsted Town	20	5	6	9	22	34	21
Wolverton Town	20	5	3	12	24	51	18
Letchworth Gdn City	20	4	3	13	22	34	15

League Cup Final: St Albans City 1, Hitchin Town 5

SUBURBAN LEAGUE

NORTH

	P	W	D	L	F	A	Pts
Wycombe Wanderers	34	27	4	3	95	38	58
Harrow Borough	34	25	6	3	97	20	56
Staines Town	34	19	8	7	67	34	46
Hendon	34	18	6	10	78	43	42
Woking	34	17	6	11	47	44	40
Wembley	34	16	7	11	78	46	39
Uxbridge	34	15	9	10	64	41	39
Farnborough Town	34	11	10	13	50	52	32
Egham Town	34	11	10	13	38	51	32
Slough Town	34	10	11	13	75	66	31
Hillingdon	34	11	7	16	61	47	29
Chertsey Town	34	10	8	16	39	79	28
Hounslow	34	10	7	17	51	61	27
Southall	34	9	8	17	43	67	26
Feltham	34	10	6	18	50	93	26
Addlestone & W'bridge	34	8	8	18	48	84	24
Wokingham Town	34	8	4	22	35	57	20
Camberley Town	34	6	5	23	27	117	17

Suburban League Challenge Cup Final
Harrow Borough v Wembley: 2—1

SOUTH

	P	W	D	L	F	A	Pts
Sutton United	34	25	7	2	95	35	57
Walton Casuals	34	19	7	8	52	30	45
Croydon	34	19	6	9	58	34	44
Dulwich Hamlet	34	18	6	10	70	41	42
Walton & Hersham	34	18	5	11	64	46	41
Bromley	34	17	7	10	64	47	41
Epsom & Ewell	34	15	10	9	59	40	40
Hampton	34	14	8	12	46	44	36
Dorking	34	12	8	14	55	63	32
Tooting & Mitcham U	34	12	6	16	54	61	30
Carshalton Athletic	34	11	7	16	44	54	29
Metropolitan Police	34	11	7	16	50	64	29
Whyteleafe	34	11	7	16	34	53	29
Leatherhead	34	11	6	17	45	60	28
Banstead Athletic	34	9	9	16	50	66	27
Kingstonian	34	8	10	16	35	55	26
Redhill	34	5	10	19	47	74	20
Horsham	34	4	8	22	32	87	16

Surrey Premier Cup Final
Worcester Park v Woking: 1—4.

ESSEX & HERTS BORDER COMBINATION

Secretary:
B.H. Daniels, 21 Doddinghurst Road, Brentwood, Essex CM15 9EP (Brentwood 217745)

EASTERN DIVISION

	P	W	D	L	F	A	Pts
Maidstone United	28	24	1	3	85	25	73
Dagenham	28	19	3	6	76	30	60
Grays Athletic	28	16	3	9	48	30	51
Barking	28	14	7	7	52	43	49
Welling United	28	13	7	8	51	37	46
Tilbury	28	12	4	12	46	53	40
Aveley	28	10	7	11	54	58	37
Billericay Town	28	10	5	13	42	44	35
Dartford	28	8	8	12	48	55	32
Basildon United	28	9	5	14	43	53	32
Gravesend & Northfleet	28	9	5	14	59	71	32
Hornchurch	28	8	5	15	46	74	29
Collier Row	28	8	3	17	38	60	27
Ford United	28	8	2	18	44	61	26
Rainham Town	28	7	5	16	41	79	26

WESTERN DIVISION

	P	W	D	L	F	A	Pts
Walthamstow Avenue	24	19	4	1	89	19	61
Leyton-Wingate	24	18	3	3	58	19	57
Kingsbury Town	24	16	3	5	49	28	51
Boreham Wood	24	14	3	7	50	29	45
Enfield	24	12	4	8	49	40	40
Harlow Town	24	11	3	10	46	39	36
Saffron Walden Town	24	6	8	10	36	58	26
Bishop's Stortford	24	6	7	11	26	40	25
Hertford Town	24	7	3	14	23	64	24
Woodford Town	24	7	2	15	27	45	23
Hoddesdon Town	24	5	7	12	30	51	22
Haringey Borough	24	4	7	13	36	55	19
Ware	24	1	6	17	33	65	9

Championship Play-Off:
Maidstone United 2 Walthamstow Avenue 2 aet
(Maidstone won 4-3 on penalties)

Combination Cup Final:
Leyton-Wingate 2 Maidstone United 1

Fred Budden Trophy Final:
Barking 3 Basildon United 0

B & W CHAMPIONS' CUP

Sponsored by B & W Darts & Trophies Limited, Walthamstow, London E17
Secretary: B.W. Hitchings, 18 Tany's Dell, Harlow, Essex CM20 2LJ (Harlow 39757)

Semi-Finals:
St Albans City (WSC) 2 Harrow Borough (SFL) 1
Harrow Borough 2 St Albans City 0 (agg 3-2)

Dagenham (EHBC) 2 Burnham (MBL) 1
Burnham 1 Dagenham 3 (agg 2-5)

Final:
Harrow Borough 3 Dagenham 1
Dagenham 1 Harrow Borough 0 (agg 2-3)

NORTH BERKS LEAGUE

DIVISION ONE

	P	W	D	L	F	A	Pts
Childrey United	26	18	5	3	60	19	41
Harwell	26	20	1	5	57	30	41
Milton United	26	17	6	3	66	23	40
Saxton Rovers	26	13	10	3	51	25	36
Didcot Casuals	26	15	4	7	54	34	34
Berinsfield	26	13	7	6	77	34	33
RAF Abingdon	26	11	5	10	56	37	27
Wootton	26	10	3	13	47	50	23
Buckland	26	7	6	13	37	62	20
Woodcote	26	8	3	15	36	58	19
Faringdon Town	26	7	4	15	34	53	18
Drayton	26	5	3	18	22	81	13
Steventon	26	3	5	18	22	66	11
L. Wittenham	26	2	4	20	22	69	8

DIVISION TWO

	P	W	D	L	F	A	Pts
Sutton Crtny	26	19	6	1	76	25	44
Chieveley	26	17	7	2	73	31	41
Aston Tirrold	26	13	7	6	55	47	33
Botley United	26	14	4	8	62	41	32
Uffington United	26	11	3	12	49	49	25
Harwell Res	26	9	6	11	41	44	24
Shrivenham	26	9	6	11	45	51	24
Great Shefford	26	7	9	10	42	43	23
AWRE Harwell	26	7	9	10	43	67	23
Stanford-Vale	26	9	4	13	43	55	22
Grove Rangers	26	8	5	13	51	67	21
Ardington	26	7	6	13	36	46	20
Marcham	26	7	4	15	39	59	18
Kintbury Res	26	3	8	15	31	61	14

READING COMBINATION LEAGUE

PREMIER DIVISION

	P	W	D	L	F	A	Pts
Reading Garage	22	19	0	3	86	26	38
Phoenix	22	15	5	2	65	26	35
Northcroft	22	16	2	4	58	28	34
Newtown	22	13	5	4	57	24	31
REME	22	14	2	6	83	40	30
Bulmershe	22	11	3	8	62	40	25
Highmoor	22	7	3	12	38	58	17
Theale	22	5	6	11	43	48	16
Stoke Row	22	5	4	13	34	57	14
Weller	22	6	1	15	45	77	13
Univ	22	3	1	18	42	73	7
Buck'bury	22	2	0	20	22	148	4

WYCOMBE & DISTRICT

ERCOL SENIOR LEAGUE

	P	W	D	L	F	A	Pts
Penn & Tylers Green	28	23	4	1	62	17	50
Coopers-Payen	28	22	2	4	84	21	46
Holmer Green	28	17	8	3	70	31	42
Wooburn Athletic	28	15	8	5	52	28	38
Rivets Sports	28	12	7	9	44	36	31
Prestwood	28	10	7	11	42	40	27
Chinnor	28	10	5	13	44	50	25
Haddenham United	28	9	6	13	42	52	24
Broomwade Sports	28	8	6	14	36	51	22
St Johns Hospital	28	8	6	14	36	52	22
Lacey Green	28	8	5	15	44	58	21
Chalfont Wasps	28	7	7	14	26	55	21
Henley Town	28	8	4	16	43	43	20
Hambleden	28	8	4	16	40	54	20
Molins Sports	28	4	3	21	23	77	11

DIVISION 1

	P	W	D	L	F	A	Pts
Marlow United	22	18	2	2	69	30	38
Seer Green	22	15	3	4	62	29	33
Loudwater	22	15	3	4	74	43	33
Risboro RG	22	10	4	8	48	34	24
Chesham YC	22	11	2	9	52	47	24
Chesham STM	22	8	7	7	62	54	23
Wendover	22	8	5	9	52	43	21
Risboro Pk	22	5	8	9	34	50	18
Aston Park	22	5	5	12	46	62	15
St Johns	22	5	4	13	44	70	14
Flackwell	22	4	3	15	34	69	11
Winchmore	22	3	4	15	29	74	10

League Cup Winners:
Coopers-Payen, Wycombe District League

READING AND DISTRICT LEAGUE

PREMIER DIVISION

	P	W	D	L	F	A	Pts
Huntley & Palmer	24	17	1	6	48	27	35
Courage	24	14	7	3	40	20	35
Forest	24	15	4	5	43	24	34
Finch	24	15	3	6	68	31	33
Peppard	24	13	4	7	43	30	30
Wests	24	12	5	7	57	40	29
Thames Vale	24	12	3	9	43	41	27
Rabson	24	5	9	10	36	50	19
Exiles	24	6	5	13	29	41	17
Sonning	24	6	5	13	39	55	17
Woodley	24	6	4	14	33	54	16
Wall'ford	24	5	3	16	34	52	13
Burghfick	24	2	3	19	22	69	7

Abingdon United put Wokingham (stripes) under pressure during their famous County Cup victory over their Isthmian Premier Division opponents. Photo: Leo Hoenig

Dulwich Hamlet *Back Row (L-R): Andy Edwards, Karl Richards, Tony Baldwin, Paul Edwards, Bobby Knock, Martin Lewis. Front Row (L-R): Derek Williams, Richard Langley, Alan Roughan, Peter Kingston, Neil Norman, Pat Carolan.*

London Senior Cup

First Qualifying Round

Alma Swanley v Ruislip Manor 3-1
Ambrose Fleming v Brimsdown Rovers 0-4
Barkingside v East Ham United 2-1
Beckton United v Haringey Borough 2-1
Chingford v Cray Wanderers 4-1
Clapton v Thames Polytechnic 4-1
Corinthian Casuals v Malden Vale 4-0
Edgware v Civil Service 0-1
Finchley v Erith & Belvedere 1-0
Harefield United v Danson (Bexley Borough) 2-0
Highfield v Wandsworth 1-2
Hoddesdon Town v Penhill Standard 1-1, 2-0
Pennant v Eton Manor 3-2
Redhill v Ford United 3-3, 2-1
Royal Arsenal Sports v B.R.O.B. Barnet 3-1
St Albans City v Wembley 1-3

Second Qualifying Round

Alma Swanley v Beckton United 1-2
Barkingside v Cheshunt 2-1
Beckenham Town v Metropolitan Police 1-4
Clapton v Chingford 7-2
Collier Row v Wembley 3-2
Corinthian Casuals v Royal Arsenal Sports 6-1
Civil Service v Brimsdown Rovers 0-4
Finchley v Harefield 1-2
Fisher Athletic v Kingsbury Town 5-0
Hoddesdon Town v Wandsworth 0-2
Pennant v Walton & Hersham 3-0
Southall v Redhill 4-2

Third Qualifying Round

Barkingside v Collier Row 0-0, 1-2
Brimsdown Rovers v Hampton 1-2
Epsom & Ewell v Pennant 2-1
Fisher Athletic v Beckton United 8-0
Harefield United v Corinthian Casuals 1-3
Southall v Woodford Town 1-2
Uxbridge v Clapton 1-2
Wandsworth v Metropolitan Police 1-1, 0-8

First Round Proper

Leytonstone/Ilford v Feltham 2-1
Walthamstow Avenue v Bishop's Stortford 2-1
Collier Row v Staines Town 2-1
Carshalton Athletic v Hayes 1-1, 0-2
Leatherhead v Farnborough Town 3-0
Bromley v Epsom & Ewell 2-1
Fisher Athletic v Hitchin Town 2-3
Boreham Wood v Sutton United 2-4
Leyton-Wingate v Hampton 2-1
Woodford Town v Metropolitan Police 5-1
Welling United v Clapton 1-2
Corinthian Casuals v Kingstonian 0-2
Harrow Borough v Hendon 2-1
Croydon v Dulwich Hamlet 0-1
Tooting & Mitchum v Woking 4-1
Barking v Barnet 2-3

Second Round Proper

Leytonstone-Ilford v Walthamstow Avenue 2-1
Collier Row v Hayes 0-2
Leatherhead v Bromley 4-0
Hitchin Town v Sutton United 1-2
Leyton-Wingate v Woodford Town 2-1
Clapton v Kingstonian 1-1, 0-3
Harrow Borough v Dulwich Hamlet
Tooting & Mitchum Utd v Barnet 3-1*

Third Round

Leytonstone/Ilford v Hayes 1-0
Leyton-Wingate v Kingstonian 1-2
Leatherhead v Sutton United 0-1
Dulwich Hamlet v Tooting & Mitchum 0-1*
*Tooting resigned for playing unregistered player

Semi Finals

Leytonstone/Ilford v Dulwich Hamlet 1-1 aet, 1-3
Kingstonian v Sutton United 3-2 aet

Final

Dulwich Hamlet v Kingstonians 2-2 aet, 3-2

Berks & Bucks Senior Cup

Preliminary Round

Milton Keynes Boro v Milton Keynes C .2-2 aet, 3-3 aet, 1-2
Winslow United v Holmer Green .... 3-2 aet
Wycombe Wanderers v Didcot Town 2-0

First Round

Abingdon United v Abingdon Town .... 3-1 aet
Beaconsfield United v Thatcham Town .... 0-0 aet
Flackwell Heath v Wantage Town 2-1
Hungerford Town v Hazells 2-3
Lambourn Sports v Winslow United 0-7
Maidenhead Town v Chalfont St Peter 0-2
Maidenhead United v Burnham .... 2-1 aet
Marlow v Buckingham Town 1-3
Milton Keynes City v Windsor & Eton 0-3
Newbury Town v Amersham Town 1-0
Newport Pagnell Town v Wallingford Town 3-0
Olney Town v Aylesbury United 1-2
Slough Town v Wolverton Town 2-1
Wycombe Wanderers v Chesham United 3-0
Bracknell Town and Wokingham Town byes

Second Round

Bracknell Town v Wycombe Wanderers 2-1
Buckingham Town v Windsor & Eton 3-1
Flackwell Heath v Wokingham Town 1-4
Hazells v Abingdon United 1-2
Maidenhead United v Beaconsfield United 1-3
Newbury Town v Aylesbury United 2-1
Slough Town v Chalfont St Peter 1-2
Winslow United v Newport Pagnell .... 1-1 aet, 0-2

Third Round

Beaconsfield United v Wokingham Town 0-3
Chalfont St Peter v Bracknell Town 3-0
Newbury Town v Buckingham Town 0-2
Newport Pagnell v Abingdon United 1-3

Semi-Finals

Abingdon United v Wokingham Town 2-0
Buckingham Town v Chalfont St Peter 1-1, 2-0

Final

Buckingham Town v Abingdon United 3-1

Middlesex Senior Cup

First Round

Hounslow v Feltham 1-2
Kingsbury Town v Hillingdon 1-3
Uxbridge Town v Haringey Borough 3-1

Second Round

Enfield v Hillingdon 4-3
Hampton v Uxbridge 0-0,0-3
Harefield United v Hayes 0-1
Harrow Borough v Edgware 3-2
Feltham v Ruislip Manor 1-0
Northwood v Wembley 0-4
Southall v Staines Town 1-0
Wealdstone v Hendon 1-2

Third Round

Harrow Borough v Uxbridge 0-0,0-1
Hendon v Feltham 3-0
Southall v Hayes 1-1,2-3
Wembley v Enfield 1-1,1-0

Semi-Finals

Hendon v Hayes 1-0
Wembley v Uxbridge 1-1,2-0

Cup Final

Hendon v Wembley 1-5

Middlesex Premier Cup

Semi-Final

Brimsdown Rovers v Constantine United 4-0
Rayners Lane v Harrow Borough Reserves 1-0

Final (at Hendon FC)

Brimsdown Rovers v Rayners Lane 0-3

Middlesex Senior Charity Cup

Played in groups

Wembley v Feltham 2-1
Hayes v Feltham 4-1
Wembley v Hayes 3-1

Harefield U v Edgware 1-0
Southall v Edgware 2-1
Harefield v Southall 0-1

Ruislip M v Kingsbury Town 1-3
Ruislip M v Northwood 0-0
Northwood v Kingsbury Town 1-3

	P	W	D	L	F	A	Pts
Wembley	2	2	0	0	5	2	6
Hayes	2	1	0	1	5	4	3
Feltham	2	0	0	2	2	6	0
Southall	2	2	0	0	3	1	6
Harefield Utd	2	1	0	1	1	1	3
Edgware	2	0	0	2	1	3	0
Kingsbury Town	2	2	0	0	6	2	6
Northwood	2	0	1	1	1	3	1
Ruislip Manor	2	0	1	1	1	3	1

Play-Off Group TBA

Wembley v Southall 1-0
Kingsbury Town v Wembley 0-2
Southall v Kingsbury Town 4-1

Cup Final

Wembley v Southall 0-1*

Dave Penny (far left) outjumps the Brimsdown Rovers defence to score Rayners Lane's second goal in their 3-0 Middlesex Premier Cup Final win over the Spartan League side at Hendon FC. Lane's Phil Lynn (striped shirt, centre) looks on.

Kent Senior Trophy

First Round

Alma Swanley v Snowdown Colliery .... 1-0 aet
Brent v Catford Wanderers .... 2-2 aet, 1-7
Charlton Town v Slade Green Athletic 1-4
Crockenhill v Cray Wanderers...................... 3-1
Deal Town v Hythe Town........................ 2-3
Greenwich Borough v Beckenham Town 1-2
Kent Police v Corinthians .... 3-5 aet
Met Police 4 District v Erith & Belvedere 0-1
Penhill Standard v Danson 2-0
Swanley Town v Thames Polytechnic............... 3-0
Tunbridge Wells v Faversham Town 2-0
Whitstable v Darenth Heathside 0-1

Second Round

Bexley/Gateway v Erith & Belvedere................ 0-2
Catford Wanderers v Swanley Town................ 1-4
Corinthians v Ramsgate.......................... 3-1
Crockenhill v Alma Swanley 0-1
Herne Bay v Tunbridge Wells...................... 1-2
Penhill Standard v Beckenham Town 2-4
Royal Arsenal Sports v Hythe Town 0-2
Slade Green Athletic v Darenth Heathside 2-1

Third Round

Alma Swanley v Tunbridge Wells.................. 0-2
Beckenham Town v Hythe Town 2-4
Slade Green v Corinthians........................ 0-2
Swanley Town v Erith & Belvedere................. 1-2

Semi-Finals

Hythe Town v Corinthians 3-4
Erith & Belvedere v Tunbridge Wells 3-1

Final (at Sittingbourne FC)

Corinthians v Erith & Belvedere 3-2

Kent-Chatham Reliance-Senior Cup

First Round

Ashford v Tonbridge............................. 4-1
Canterbury City v Fisher Athletic.................. 0-1
Dover Athletic v Dartford 0-2
Gravesend & Northfleet v Chatham Town 1-0
Sheppey United v Sittingbourne................... 2-1
Thanet United v Bromley 2-1
Welling United v Maidstone United................ 1-4

Second Round

Ashford Town v Gravesend & Northfleet 2-1
Maidstone United v Dartford 2-1
Sheppey United v Fisher Athletic 1-2
Thanet United v Folkestone 1-4

Semi-Finals

Folkestone v Fisher Athletic 2-3
Ashford Town v Maidstone United................. 1-3

Final

Fisher Athletic v Maidstone United 1-0

Herts Charity Cup

First Round
Boreham Wood v Bishop's Stortford 1-0
Cheshunt v St Albans City 3-0
Hitchin Town v Hertford Town 2-0
Tring Town v Letchworth Garden City 2-0

Semi-Finals
Cheshunt v Hitchin Town . . . . . 0-0 aet
Hitchin win 7-6 on pens
Boreham Wood v Tring Town 2-1

Final
Boreham Wood v Hitchin Town 3-2

Herts Charity Shield

First Round
Hatfield Town v Royston Town 0-1
Hemel Hempstead v Berkhamstead Town 2-0
Hoddesdon Town v Baldock Town 2-3
Stevenage Borough v Ware 3-1

Semi-Finals
Baldock Town v Stevenage Borough 1-2
Royston Town v Hemel Hempstead . . . . . 2-3 aet

Final
Stevenage Borough v Hemel Hempstead 0-1

Herts Senior Cup

First Round
Berkhamstead Town v Ware . . . . . 1-1 aet, 2-0
Cheshunt v Highfield 4-1
Hertford Town v BROB Barnet 5-0
Pirton v Royston Town 5-0
Sawbridgeworth Town v Baldock Town 2-3
Selby v Hatfield Town 1-3
Tring Town v Hitchin Town . . . . . 2-3 aet
Welwyn Garden City v Stevenage Borough 3-1

Second Round
Baldock Town v Berkhamstead Town 2-2, 4-2
Barnet v Hatfield Town 3-2
Hertford Town v Hemel Hempstead 1-1, 5-1
Hoddesdon Town v Bishop's Stortford 0-1
Pirton v Boreham Wood 1-2
St Albans City v Cheshunt 2-1
Watford v Letchworth Garden City 2-0
Welwyn Garden City v Hitchin Town 1-2

Third Round
Hitchin Town v Baldock Town 4-1
Barnet v St Albans City 6-2
Bishop's Stortford v Hertford Town 1-2
Boreham Wood v Watford 1-3

Semi-Finals
Watford v Barnet 5-0
Hitchin Town v Hertford Town 1-2

Final
Hertford Town v Watford 0-1

ESSEX SENIOR CUP

First Round
All clubs received byes

Second Round

Barking	v	Billericay Town	1-0
Chelmsford City	v	Woodford Town	6-0
Dagenham	v	Hornchurch	4-0
Harlow Town	v	Tilbury	1-0
Walthamstow Avenue	v	Leytonstone-Ilford	3-2

Third Round

Barking	v	Aveley	4-2
Clapton	v	Chelmsford City	2-1
Dagenham	v	Southend United	1-2
Walthamstow Avenue	v	Harlow Town	0-2

Semi-Finals

Clapton	v	Harlow	1-0
Barking	v	Southend United	0-1

Final

Clapton	v	Southend United	1-0

ESSEX SENIOR CHALLENGE TROPHY

First Round

Basildon United	v	Backton United	2-1	
Brentwood	v	Waltham Abbey	2-0	
Brightlingsea United	v	Leyton-Wingate	0-7	
Chingford	v	Eton Manor	2-1	
Coggeshall Town	v	Heybridge Swifts	1-4	
Collier Row	v	Canvey Island	1-0	
East Thurrock United	v	Maldon Town	1-1	0-1
Grays Athletic	v	Braintree Town	1-0	
Pennant	v	Bowers United	1-3	
Rainham Town	v	Barkingside	2-0	
Saffron Walden Town	v	Halstead Town	3-0	
Stansted	v	Ford United	3-3	1-2
Tiptree United	v	Clacton Town	2-2	6-2
Witham Town	v	East Ham United	3-1	
Wivenhoe Town	v	Epping Town	1-3	

Harwich & Parkeston: bye

Second Round

Basildon United	v	Rainham Town	6-1	
Chingford	v	Tiptree United	1-3	
Collier Row	v	Brentwood	3-1	
Epping Town	v	Witham Town	1-0	
Ford United	v	Leyton-Wingate	1-4	
Grays Athletic	v	Bowers United	4-1	
Harwich & Parkeston	v	Maldon Town	2-2	2-3
Saffron Walden Town	v	Heybridge Swifts	4-2	

Third Round

Basildon United	v	Epping Town	2-0
Collier Row	v	Tiptree United	2-3
Maldon Town	v	Grays Athletic	2-0
Saffron Walden Town	v	Leyton-Wingate	3-1

Semi-Finals

Basildon United	v	Tiptree United	1-0
Maldon Town	v	Saffron Waldon Twn	0-2

Cup Final

Basildon United	v	Saffron Waldon Twn	2-1

Sutton Utd

Surrey Senior Cup

No matches in the First Qualifying Round

Second Qualifying Round

British Aero Weybridge v Reigate Priory 2-0
Camberley Town v Farnham Town 0-3
Carshalton v Old Suttonians 5-3
Chessington United v Kew Association.............. 1-2
Chobham v Shene O. Grammarians 3-1
Cobham v Nat West Bank 0-1
Corinthian-Casuals v Chertsey 3-1
Egham Town v Horley Town 3-0
Godalming Town v Cranleigh..................... 3-0
Frimley Green v Yateley Town 3-1
Malden Town v Guildford & Worplesdon 0-0, 5-3
Malden Vale v Sheerwater 4-1
Lingfield v Virginia Water........................ 1-2
Westfield v Hartley Wintney...................... 1-3
(Replayed match 0-2)
Ulysses v Whyteleafe 0-5
Farleigh Rovers bye

Third Qualifying Round

Chobham v Egham Town 2-1
Farleigh Rovers v Kew Association 2-1
Frimley Casuals v Corinthian-Casuals 2-4
Godalming Town v Virginia Water................. 3-4
Malden Town v Hartley Wintney 0-2
Malden Vale v Carshalton 1-0
Nat West Bank v Farnham Town 3-0
Whyteleafe v British Aerospace Weybridge........... 1-0

Fourth Qualifying Round

Chobham v Nat West Bank 3-0
Farleigh Rovers v Virginia Water 2-0
Malden Vale v Corinthian-Casuals 1-4
Whyteleafe v Hartley Wintney 1-0

Fifth Qualifying Round

Banstead Athletic v Farleigh Rovers 2-1
Dorking v Ash United 3-2
Molesey v Corinthian-Casuals...................... 0-5
Woking v Merstham 3-0
Whyteleafe v Chobham 2-0

First Round

Tooting & Mitcham v Woking...................... 3-0
Walton & Hersham v Sutton United 0-1
Carshalton Athletic v Redhill 3-1
Epsom & Ewell v Addlestone & Weybridge 1-1, 2-1
Metropolitan Police v Banstead Athletic............. 1-2
Corinthian-Casuals v Kingstonian 0-1
Leatherhead v Whyteleafe 0-2
Croydon v Dorking 2-1

Second Round

Banstead Athletic v Epsom & Ewell................. 0-3
Carshalton Athletic v Croydon 0-1
Sutton United v Kingstonian....................... 1-0
Whyteleafe v Tooting & Mitcham Utd 1-0

Semi-Finals

Whyteleafe v Sutton United....................... 0-2
Croydon v Epsom & Ewell......................... 2-2

Final

Epsom & Ewell v Sutton United 0-4

Gary Julians, Gravesend's top goalscorer, leaps to avoid a tackle from Herne Bay defender Andy Bampton.
Photo: David Hills

A memorable moment at VS Rugby as their floodlights are used for the first time, against Heybridge Swifts in the FA Cup.
Photo: John Denton

THE SOUTHERN FOOTBALL LEAGUE

President: G. E. Templeman *Chairman:* D. J. Setterfield
Secretary: D. J. Strudwick, 49 Woodlands Way, Southwater, Horsham, West Sussex RH13 7TF. Tel: 0403 66494

DARTFORD HOLD OFF FISHER ATHLETIC

National and County Cup successes, the steady progress of new Clubs within the Competition, the consistency of some of the more established members and the sheer unpredictability of some other Clubs have been the hallmark of yet another incredibly competitive season in our League.

Despite all this activity, though, the year will always be remembered as the season in which we lost our much loved former Secretary of twenty-six years, Mr Bill Dellow. Bill gave the League unparalleled service and will never be wholly replaced. He is proving a difficult man to follow. On behalf of the League I would like to take this opportunity of thanking the Clubs for their most genuine respect for Bill and for their thoughts of his widow Laura. Laura appreciated your kindness very much indeed and still takes an active interest in the League and wishes to be remembered to you all.

But as Bill and Laura would have wished, football carried on in earnest. The Championship races have all been well contested up to the last day of the season.

After the early runaway leaders of the Premier Division, King's Lynn, began to fade, the race developd into a three Club competition between Dartford, Fisher Athletic and dark horse Chelmsford City. Chelmsford came into the frame late after catching up on their fixture programme which had been delayed because of F.A. Cup progress. Fisher Athletic continued their amazing emergence following their Southern Division Championship win

EX-SOUTHERN LEAGUE FOOTBALL LEAGUE XI

Nigel Spink
(Chelmsford City, Aston Villa, England)

Barry Cowdrill
(Sutton Coldfield, WBA)

Roger Brown
(AP Leamington, Bournemouth, Norwich C, Fulham, Bournemouth)

Ernie Howe
(Hounslow, QPR, Fulham, Portsmouth)

Colin Brazier
(Alvechurch, Wolves, B'ham C, Lincoln, Walsall)

Nigel Spackman
(Andover, Bournemouth, Chelsea)

Richard Kelly
(Alvechurch, Walsall)

Sean O'Driscoll
(Alvechurch, Fulham, Eire)

George Reilly
(Corby T, Northampton T, Cambridge U, Watford)

Gordon Davies
(Merthyr Tydfil, Fulham, Wales)

David Moss
(Witney T, Swindon T, Luton T)

A second front three with less First Division experience but arguably better goal scoring records are:

Alan Smith
(Alvechurch, Leicester C)

Trevor Senior
(Dorchester, Portsmouth, Reading)

Kerry Dixon
(Dunstable T, Reading, Chelsea)

Although there were over forty players in the Football League last season who started their careers in the Southern League only four of these were defenders. However, it's interesting to note that four of the above fourteen quality players joined Football League clubs from Alvechurch.

last year, but it was Dartford who re-affirmed themselves as a Southern League giant after relegation from the Alliance League two seasons ago.

The Midland Championship race looked for the best part of the season to be a two Club contest between Willenhall Town and 'freshmen' Shepsted Charterhouse. Good competition was provided, however, by two more newcomers, Rushden Town and Moor Green. Aylesbury United came with a late run and Dudley Town again proved a difficult side to beat.

The Southern Division Championship was wide open. Five teams were in the hunt throughout the year with R.S. Southampton taking the title after catching up on their fixtures, lost because of good progress in the F.A. Vase. Having reached the fifth round of the Vase they must have had their sights set on Wembley. Sadly it wasn't to be. Even last year's winner V.S. Rugby were surprisingly beaten one round earlier. Crawley Town finished runners-up to R.S. Southampton, but it needed a run of eight wins in the last nine games to clinch the promotion spot.

With A.P. Leamington reaching the Quarter Final stage of the F.A. Trophy and as many as seven Clubs reaching the second round proper the League again showed its improving strength. This was demonstrated even better in the F.A. Cup where five Clubs (three more than last year), Chelmsford City, Poole Town, Dartford, Waterlooville and A.P. Leamington all reached the first round proper. Only one made an immediate exit, three forced draws (Waterlooville twice) and Chelmsford went into round two where they fell to Gillingham. The progress of all Clubs in this competition was extremely good considering that not one of the League's Clubs received an exemption beyond the First Qualifying Round!!

In our own domestic Cup Competition, A.P. Leamington won 3-0, after extra time, in front of a massive crowd at Dartford after being held to a goalless draw at the Windmill. 2,443 people attended the matches and saw what was described as the best ever Southern League Challenge Cup Final. The Management Committee extended their congratulations to both teams for serving up a superb game.

In congratulating all the winners I, of course, commiserate with the not so successful, especially those who finished at the wrong of the table and will be missing from the League next year. In saying that, I welcome the new Clubs from the Feeder Leagues and thank the Leagues themselves for the tremendous co-operation and goodwill achieved through the Joint Liaison Committee. This association with other Leagues at either end of our own League is surely in the best interest of good competition. The top Clubs can progress in a higher League, the relegated Clubs can re-establish themselves in a slightly lower competition.

DENNIS STRUDWICK

A great diving header from Tony Thompson gives Aylesbury United a spectacular goal during their 3-3 draw with Milton Keynes City. Photo: Mike Joss

PREMIER DIVISION 1983/84

	A.P. Leamington	Alvechurch	Bedworth United	Chelmsford City	Cheltenham Town	Corby Town	Dartford	Dorchester Town	Fareham Town	Fisher Athletic	Folkestone	Gloucester City	Gosport Borough	Gravesend & Northf't	Hastings United	King's Lynn	Stourbridge	Sutton Coldfield Town	Welling United	Witney Town
A.P. Leamington	—	3-1	0-0	2-2	4-2	3-1	3-4	2-2	4-2	0-5	1-1	4-1	2-3	3-1	3-1	1-0	2-1	1-1	1-1	4-2
Alvechurch	3-1	—	2-3	2-4	0-2	4-3	0-4	2-2	3-3	0-4	2-1	0-0	5-0	0-1	1-3	2-0	2-0	3-1	2-0	2-1
Bedworth United	2-3	2-0	—	0-0	3-0	2-1	0-1	1-0	1-2	1-1	3-1	0-0	2-2	1-0	4-1	2-0	2-1	0-1	1-3	1-0
Chelmsford City	2-3	2-2	2-0	—	2-1	2-1	1-0	5-0	1-1	1-1	4-2	2-1	1-1	1-2	3-1	0-1	6-1	2-0	2-0	1-0
Cheltenham Town	5-1	2-2	2-2	0-2	—	0-3	3-0	2-1	0-0	1-4	1-1	4-1	4-1	1-1	2-0	2-0	2-0	2-2	3-0	2-1
Corby Town	3-1	2-0	5-2	0-0	1-0	—	1-2	2-0	0-0	2-7	1-1	0-0	0-0	0-0	0-0	0-1	2-0	2-0	2-1	2-4
Dartford	2-0	1-1	0-0	3-0	1-0	2-2	—	2-0	2-1	3-1	4-1	0-2	2-1	4-1	2-1	0-1	3-0	1-0	2-1	4-1
Dorchester Town	4-1	2-2	0-2	2-3	2-0	1-2	0-0	—	4-0	0-1	2-3	1-3	1-0	1-2	1-2	0-3	1-2	0-0	1-3	2-2
Fareham Town	3-4	4-2	2-1	4-1	3-2	3-2	1-2	1-0	—	0-1	4-2	2-0	1-2	2-2	1-2	2-2	0-1	0-3	1-0	2-1
Fisher Athletic	5-0	0-0	2-3	2-1	2-0	2-2	1-1	2-0	6-3	—	1-3	2-0	3-2	3-2	1-0	2-3	0-0	3-2	1-2	1-0
Folkestone	2-1	1-1	2-1	1-3	1-3	1-0	1-0	3-2	1-1	1-1	—	1-3	3-0	1-0	0-0	2-1	1-0	3-0	0-2	1-2
Gloucester City	2-1	1-2	5-2	2-0	0-0	1-1	1-1	3-3	3-3	2-1	0-0	—	3-0	1-0	2-2	1-2	4-0	1-1	1-1	0-4
Gosport Borough	1-1	1-0	3-1	0-4	0-3	0-0	2-2	1-0	0-0	0-2	0-2	1-1	—	0-2	1-1	1-1	0-1	1-1	0-3	0-2
Gravesend & Northf't	1-0	2-0	2-0	1-1	2-0	1-1	1-1	1-0	1-0	1-2	2-0	3-1	0-0	—	2-1	0-1	1-1	1-1	2-0	5-1
Hastings United	2-1	1-3	0-0	2-0	1-2	2-1	2-1	3-2	3-3	3-2	0-3	1-1	3-0	2-0	—	2-0	3-1	2-3	1-1	0-3
King's Lynn	1-1	1-1	2-0	1-0	3-2	0-1	0-0	2-0	1-0	0-3	3-2	1-2	3-2	0-1	1-2	—	1-0	1-1	2-1	0-3
Stourbridge	1-3	1-1	0-3	1-3	3-5	1-2	1-3	1-0	4-6	1-1	1-4	1-2	0-1	0-2	1-1	0-1	—	0-1	0-4	0-0
Sutton Coldfield Town	4-4	0-1	0-2	3-1	1-0	4-1	0-2	1-1	1-2	0-1	4-4	1-1	1-1	1-2	2-1	2-0	1-1	—	0-1	3-1
Welling United	4-3	3-2	1-1	0-1	2-3	5-5	0-4	1-0	2-3	1-1	1-0	1-3	2-2	4-1	1-3	1-2	4-0	2-1	—	1-0
Witney Town	5-1	3-0	8-0	1-1	3-0	1-1	0-1	3-2	3-1	1-2	1-3	1-0	1-1	2-1	2-0	3-0	4-3	1-1	4-1	—

MIDLAND FIRST DIVISION 1983/84

	Aylesbury United	Banbury United	Bridgnorth Town	Bridgwater Town	Bromsgrove Rovers	Coventry Sporting	Dudley Town	Forest Green Rovers	Leicester United	Merthyr Tydfil	Milton Keynes City	Moor Green	Oldbury United	Redditch United	Rushden Town	Shepshed Charterh'se	Tamworth	V.S. Rugby	Wellingborough Town	Willenhall Town
Aylesbury United	—	0-0	4-0	2-0	1-1	2-1	1-1	0-2	1-0	0-0	0-0	2-1	2-2	3-4	1-1	1-0	6-0	1-2	2-1	0-1
Banbury United	1-1	—	0-3	1-1	1-2	0-1	1-1	1-1	0-0	1-2	4-1	0-1	0-2	1-4	1-3	1-1	2-1	3-3	2-1	1-4
Bridgnorth Town	0-2	4-1	—	5-0	1-0	2-3	1-0	2-2	2-1	2-2	7-1	2-1	2-2	4-1	1-1	2-3	4-1	3-2	0-3	0-2
Bridgwater Town	1-3	2-0	0-1	—	0-1	1-0	1-3	5-0	1-4	1-1	1-1	1-3	3-0	2-4	1-1	0-0	1-0	2-2	0-0	1-0
Bromsgrove Rovers	0-0	4-1	1-2	6-0	—	1-0	2-2	2-1	1-2	3-2	6-0	0-2	1-0	2-2	1-1	1-1	5-0	0-2	1-0	0-3
Coventry Sporting	0-1	1-2	2-0	1-2	1-0	—	1-1	0-2	2-1	1-0	1-3	0-1	2-2	1-0	1-0	1-2	2-2	0-2	0-1	3-5
Dudley Town	1-3	4-1	1-0	2-0	1-2	5-1	—	1-0	0-0	1-0	1-1	2-1	1-0	3-0	1-1	2-2	5-1	1-0	1-0	5-2
Forest Green Rovers	2-2	1-1	5-1	2-1	3-2	4-0	1-1	—	1-1	2-0	4-3	1-1	1-0	2-2	1-1	1-2	3-1	4-0	4-1	1-2
Leicester United	2-2	2-1	2-1	4-0	0-0	1-2	1-0	0-1	—	0-2	0-1	2-5	2-1	2-2	0-1	0-2	7-0	0-1	2-1	0-2
Merthyr Tydfil	0-1	3-0	0-0	3-1	1-2	4-0	0-3	3-1	1-1	—	2-0	1-1	4-1	0-2	3-0	0-2	3-0	3-2	6-0	1-1
Milton Keynes City	0-5	2-0	0-4	1-4	0-3	1-2	0-2	2-2	3-4	1-2	—	0-2	0-2	0-2	1-4	0-5	1-5	1-2	0-0	0-5
Moor Green	1-2	1-1	1-0	1-1	2-5	1-1	2-2	3-2	2-2	2-2	2-2	—	1-0	2-0	1-0	2-1	1-0	2-1	5-0	0-2
Oldbury United	1-1	2-0	0-0	3-0	1-2	4-0	1-1	0-0	4-1	0-1	5-0	0-0	—	2-0	2-4	0-3	4-0	0-0	2-5	1-2
Redditch United	0-0	2-1	0-0	5-3	1-1	1-1	4-0	2-1	2-1	0-2	3-0	1-2	2-1	—	2-4	3-2	4-2	1-1	2-1	4-3
Rushden Town	4-3	0-1	1-0	1-0	2-0	1-1	1-1	1-0	2-1	5-0	3-3	2-2	1-1	2-1	—	0-1	8-0	0-1	3-0	0-3
Shepshed Charterh'se	3-2	8-0	3-0	1-0	4-1	3-1	4-1	1-0	4-2	3-2	5-0	3-1	2-3	3-0	0-2	—	5-0	2-0	2-0	0-1
Tamworth	0-0	2-2	0-3	1-0	0-6	2-4	0-4	0-3	1-3	0-2	1-1	0-3	0-0	1-1	0-3	0-3	—	0-3	2-2	1-3
V.S. Rugby	0-0	2-0	1-1	0-1	2-3	2-0	3-3	1-2	3-2	1-2	4-0	1-1	2-2	4-0	1-1	3-1	3-0	—	7-1	0-4
Wellingborough Town	2-3	1-3	2-2	0-1	0-2	1-1	0-5	2-1	1-3	1-3	1-1	1-3	1-1	1-3	2-1	1-1	3-0	2-2	—	4-1
Willenhall Town	0-2	4-1	1-2	2-0	1-3	4-1	4-2	3-3	2-2	2-0	5-0	1-0	4-1	6-0	3-2	3-0	5-1	2-2	2-0	—

A textbook header gives Fisher Athletic's Dennehey a late winner against Chelmsford City on Boxing Day.
Photo: Mike Joss

Willenhall Town *Back Row (L-R): John Jones (player/coach), Gary Matthews, Clive Perrens, Brian Fox, Steve Clay, Paul Knox, Alan Forrester. Front Row (L-R): Andy Hill, Bobby Peck, Paul Stringer, Richie Adams, Richus White, Garry Stevens*

RS Southampton *Back Row (L-R): P. Price (manager), B. Andrews, P. Bennett, P. Young, P. Moore, T. Cleveland, D. Mooney, I. Thakore, T. Jewitt (trainer). Front Row (L-R): K. White, M. Dowding, P. Baxter, P. Earles, D. Young, M. Farmer.* Photo: Southern Newspapers

THE SOUTHERN FOOTBALL LEAGUE

Premier Division

	P	W	D	L	F	A	Pts
Dartford	38	23	9	6	67	32	78
Fisher Athletic	38	22	9	7	80	42	75
Chelmsford City	38	19	9	10	67	45	66
Gravesend & Northfleet	38	18	9	11	50	38	63
Witney Town	38	18	6	14	75	50	60
King's Lynn	38	18	6	14	42	45	60
Folkestone	38	16	9	13	60	56	57
Cheltenham Town	38	16	7	15	63	56	55
Gloucester City	38	13	15	10	55	50	54
Hastings United	38	15	9	14	55	57	54
Bedworth United	38	15	9	14	51	55	54
Welling United	38	15	7	16	61	61	52
A.P. Leamington	38	14	9	15	73	83	51
Corby Town	38	12	14	12	55	54	50
Fareham Town	38	13	11	14	65	70	50
Alvechurch	38	12	12	14	56	63	48
Sutton Coldfield Town	38	10	14	14	49	53	44
Gosport Borough	38	6	15	17	31	64	33
Dorchester Town	38	4	8	26	40	69	20
Stourbridge	38	4	7	27	30	82	19

Leading Goalscorers
(League and League Cup)
Premier Division

P. Shinners (Fisher Athletic) 29
K. Casey (A.P. Leamington) 23
C. Campbell (A.P. Leamington) 22
P. Hutter (Witney Town) 22
D. Leworthy (Fareham Town) 22
F. Bishop (Chelmsford City) 20
M. Bruton (Gloucester City) 20
T. Burman (Dartford) 19
M. Coupe (King's Lynn) 19

Division One
Midland Division

	P	W	D	L	F	A	Pts
Willenhall Town	38	27	4	7	100	44	85
Shepshed Charterhouse	38	25	5	8	88	37	80
Bromsgrove Rovers	38	20	8	10	73	43	68
Dudley Town	38	18	13	7	71	43	67
Aylesbury United	38	17	15	6	62	35	66
Moor Green	38	18	12	8	63	44	66
Rushden Town	38	17	12	9	68	42	63
Merthyr Tydfil	38	18	8	12	63	44	62
Redditch United	38	17	9	12	67	67	60
V.S. Rugby	38	15	12	11	68	51	57
Forest Green Rovers	38	15	12	11	67	51	57
Bridgnorth Town	38	16	9	13	64	52	57
Leicester United	38	12	9	17	58	58	45
Oldbury United	38	10	13	15	53	51	43
Coventry Sporting	38	11	7	20	40	67	40
Bridgwater Town	38	10	8	20	39	65	38
Wellingborough Town	38	7	9	22	43	80	30
Banbury United	38	6	11	21	37	78	29
Milton Keynes City	38	3	9	26	31	110	18
Tamworth	38	2	7	29	25	118	13

Midland Division

D. Beresford (Shepshed Charterhouse) 28
M. Langford (Bromsgrove Rovers) 27
C. Rue (Shepshed Charterhouse) 24
G. Matthews (Willenhall Town) 21
D. Conway (V.S. Rugby) 20
J. Steele (Bridgnorth Town) 20
C. Cotton (Moor Green) 19
S. McIlroy (Rushden Town) 19
M. Stanton (Dudley Town) 19
J. Davie (Aylesbury United) 18

Division One
Southern Division

	P	W	D	L	F	A	Pts
R.S. Southampton	38	26	6	6	83	35	84
Crawley Town	38	22	9	7	68	28	75
Basingstoke Town	38	20	9	9	54	36	69
Tonbridge A.F.C.	38	20	9	9	61	44	69
Addlestone & W'bridge	38	19	11	8	58	34	68
Poole Town	38	20	7	11	68	42	67
Hillingdon	38	18	11	9	43	20	65
Ashford Town	38	19	5	14	65	47	62
Salisbury	38	17	8	13	61	48	59
Cambridge City	38	13	9	16	43	53	48
Canterbury City	38	12	9	17	44	52	45
Waterlooville	38	12	9	17	56	69	45
Dover Athletic	38	12	9	17	51	74	45
Chatham Town	38	11	10	17	46	56	43
Andover	38	12	6	20	35	54	42
Erith & Belvedere	38	11	9	18	43	68	42
Dunstable	38	10	8	20	38	65	38
Thanet United	38	9	8	21	40	65	35
Woodford Town	38	7	8	23	30	69	29
Hounslow	38	4	12	22	30	58	24

Southern Division

B. Gregory (Crawley Town) 34
S. Finnieston (Addlestone & Weybridge) 25
J. Young (Ashford Town) 23
D. Courtney (Poole Town) 19
D. Dowding (R.S. Southampton) 19
P. Earles (R.S. Southampton) 19
C. White (Waterlooville) 18
P. Churchill (Tonbridge A.F.C.) 17
T. Patterson (Salisbury) 16

SOUTHERN FIRST DIVISION	Addlestone & Weybridge	Andover	Ashford Town	Basingstoke Town	Cambridge City	Canterbury City	Chatham Town	Crawley Town	Dover Athletic	Dunstable	Erith & Belvedere	Hillingdon	Hounslow	Poole Town	R.S. Southampton	Salisbury	Thanet United	Tonbridge	Waterlooville	Woodford Town
Addlestone & Weybridge	—	1-1	2-1	1-1	0-0	2-0	4-0	1-1	6-0	1-0	1-0	0-0	2-0	0-0	1-0	2-0	1-1	0-0	3-2	6-1
Andover	1-2	—	1-0	0-2	1-1	0-1	2-1	0-1	1-2	1-4	2-0	0-0	1-0	1-4	0-2	0-2	1-0	2-3	3-1	2-0
Ashford Town	1-2	2-1	—	1-0	3-1	3-1	2-2	0-2	3-0	4-1	3-0	1-2	2-0	3-1	1-2	2-1	2-0	2-2	0-1	2-0
Basingstoke Town	1-0	6-0	0-2	—	1-0	2-0	3-1	0-0	3-2	5-1	1-0	1-0	0-0	2-0	0-3	2-1	3-3	1-4	0-1	3-0
Cambridge City	0-1	1-0	3-4	0-1	—	2-1	3-0	0-3	4-3	2-2	1-2	0-2	1-4	1-0	2-1	0-0	1-0	2-2	1-1	0-1
Canterbury City	3-1	0-0	0-1	0-2	4-1	—	0-1	0-1	1-2	0-0	1-2	1-2	2-1	1-1	1-1	3-2	3-1	2-1	1-1	1-0
Chatham Town	1-3	0-0	0-2	1-0	0-2	1-1	—	0-2	5-2	1-1	3-0	0-2	0-0	2-3	1-2	3-0	2-2	0-0	2-0	2-2
Crawley Town	1-0	5-0	2-2	0-1	2-1	1-1	2-0	—	2-0	1-1	2-2	1-1	2-1	1-3	0-1	2-0	1-0	2-0	4-1	5-0
Dover Athletic	3-1	2-1	1-0	2-2	0-0	1-0	1-1	0-0	—	3-0	2-2	2-0	0-1	3-2	1-3	0-3	2-0	1-1	6-0	0-1
Dunstable	0-2	0-4	0-0	1-0	1-0	0-3	0-3	0-2	2-0	—	4-2	0-0	0-2	1-0	2-1	2-4	1-0	0-0	3-1	2-3
Erith & Belvedere	1-1	2-1	1-1	1-1	0-2	1-0	3-1	0-3	1-0	0-2	—	0-1	3-1	1-3	0-0	1-1	3-4	0-1	1-4	3-1
Hillingdon	2-0	2-0	1-0	0-1	2-0	0-2	2-0	1-0	4-1	2-0	5-0	—	0-0	0-1	1-2	1-1	0-0	0-0	0-0	2-0
Hounslow	1-2	0-1	3-2	0-1	1-1	2-2	0-2	1-3	2-2	0-0	0-1	0-0	—	1-2	0-2	1-1	1-2	3-4	1-1	1-1
Poole Town	1-2	1-2	1-0	3-0	0-1	4-1	2-1	2-1	7-1	4-0	1-1	0-0	1-0	—	2-1	2-1	4-1	0-1	2-3	3-1
R.S. Southampton	2-1	4-2	4-2	4-1	1-1	4-1	2-1	2-0	3-0	2-1	6-1	1-2	4-0	3-3	—	1-0	1-1	2-1	5-0	2-1
Salisbury	2-0	0-0	4-2	0-1	3-1	2-1	1-1	2-2	3-2	3-2	4-1	3-1	2-0	0-1	1-0	—	1-0	4-1	3-4	0-0
Thanet United	1-2	1-0	1-2	1-1	0-2	1-2	1-2	0-6	1-1	2-1	0-2	1-0	3-2	2-1	2-3	1-0	—	1-2	1-2	0-1
Tonbridge	2-1	1-0	2-1	2-2	3-0	3-0	1-2	2-3	1-1	3-2	1-0	1-0	1-0	1-2	0-3	3-1	4-1	—	2-0	2-0
Waterlooville	3-3	0-1	2-4	0-2	1-2	1-1	1-3	2-1	6-0	2-0	1-3	0-2	4-0	0-0	1-1	1-2	1-1	3-2	—	2-3
Woodford Town	0-0	0-2	0-2	1-1	2-3	1-2	2-0	0-1	1-2	2-1	2-2	0-3	0-0	1-1	0-2	1-3	1-3	0-1	0-2	—

Bill Dellow

It was with very great sadness throughout Non-League Football that the death of The Southern League's Senior Executive was announced during last season. Bill had given a lifetime of service to football and was much admired by all who met him. Thankfully we were able to present Bill with a little token of our respect for his wonderful work at Maidstone at the beginning of the season and the help and encouragement he gave me with all the Non-League publications will always be appreciated.

SOUTHERN LEAGUE CHALLENGE CUP 1983-84

First Round (two legs)	Second Round	Third Round	Fourth Round	Semi-Finals (two legs)	Final
AP Leam. . . 3:2 Bedworth. . . . 2:1	**AP Leam. 3**	**AP Leam. 1**			
VS Rugby. . . . 1:3 Sutton C. 1:0	VS Rugby. 1		**AP Leam. 4**		
Bromsgrove. . 3:3 Redditch. 2:1	Bromsgrove. . 1:0	Bromsgrove. . . . 0			
Alvechurch. . . 0:0 Shepshed. . . . 0:4	Shepshed. . . . 1:2			**AP Leam. . . 1:4**	
Bridgwater. . . 1:1 Witney Tn. . . 3:0	Witney Tn. 1	Witney Tn. . . 0:0			
Aylesbury. . . . 3:4 Milton Keyn. 3:1	Aylesbury. 0		Gloucester. 1		
Gloucester. . . 3:1 Forest Gr. . . . 2:1	Gloucester. 1	Gloucester. . . 0:3			
Merthyr Td. . 3:0 Cheltenham. . 0:2	Merthyr Td. . . . 0				**AP Leam. . . 0:3**
Rushden. . . . . 0:0 Kings Lynn. . 1:1	Kings Lynn. . . . 0	Corby Tn. . . . 2:0			
Cambridge. . . 3:1 Corby Tn. . . . 3:3	Corby Tn. 1		Bridgnorth. . . . 2		
Coventry. . . . 1:1 Bridgnorth. . . 2:1	Bridgnorth. . . . 2	Bridgnorth. . . 2:1			
Moor Green. . 3:2 Tamworth. . . 0:0	Moor Green. . . 0			Bridgnorth. . . 1:2	

Leicester... 1:1:2 Wellingbor. 2:0:1	Leicester bye				
		Leicester...... 4			
			Leicester...... 0		
Dudley Tn... 1:2 Oldbury..... 0:0	Dudley Tn.... 0				
		Willenhall..... 0			
Willenhall... 1:1 Stourbridge.. 0:0	Willenhall..... 1				
Thanet...... 0:1 Dover....... 0:0	Thanet Utd bye				
		Thanet Utd.... 0			
			Welling....... 3		
Tonbridge... 1:0 Welling..... 3:2	Welling ... 1:3				
		Welling....... 2			
Folkestone... 2:0 Ashford..... 1:0	Folkestone. 1:3**				
				Welling..... 0:1	
Poole Tn.... 3:1 Fareham..... 2:1	Poole Tn...... 2				
		Poole Tn...... 2			
RS Soton.... 2:2 Waterloo.... 1:1	RS Soton...... 0				
			Poole Tn...... 1		
Salisbury.... 1:2 Gosport..... 2:2	Gosport..... 1:2				
		Gosport....... 0			
Andover..... 2:1 Dorchester... 3:1	Dorchester... 1:1				
					Dartford.... 0:0
Banbury..... 1:2 Dunstable.... 1:4	Dunstable..... 1				
		Hillingdon..... 3			
Hillingdon... 2:2 Basingstoke.. 0:0	Hillingdon..... 3				
			Hillingdon... 1:0		
Crawley..... 3:1 Gravesend... 0:2	Crawley....... 1				
		Crawley Tn.... 1			
Addlestone 3:0:2 Hounslow. 2:1:2*	Hounslow..... 0				
				Dartford.... 2:1	
Fisher....... 4:3 Erith........ 1:0	Fisher Ath..... 4				
		Fisher Ath..... 1			
Canterbury... 0:2 Hastings..... 0:1	Canterbury.... 1				
			Dartford.... 1:2		
Woodford.... 1:1 Chelmsford.. 4:9	Chelmsford.... 0				
		Dartford..... 4			
Chatham.... 1:1 **Dartford.... 1:3**	**Dartford..... 2**				

*Hounslow won on penalties **Welling won on penalties

Another trophy for Fisher Athletic, this time presented by the Mayor of Southwark.

SOUTHERN LEAGUE CLUBS
FIRST TEAM MATCH STATISTICS 1983-84

	Leading Goalscorers	Hat Tricks	Penalties	Most Appearances
AP Leamington	Kim Casey 40 Cliff Campbell 29 Chris Downes 20	Kim Casey (2) Cliff Campbell	Martin Woodall (5) Alan Ottis (3) Kim Casey	Graham Mackenzie 54 Malcolm Kavanagh 54 Kim Casey 51
Alvechurch			Adrian O'Dowd (7)	Andy Taylor Adrian O'Dowd Malcolm Goodman
Chelmsford City	Frank Bishop 36 Glyn Cowlishaw 23 Graham Powell 14			Frank Bishop 67 Graham Powell 63 Willie Carrick 62 Phil Dudley 62 Colin Johnson 62
Cheltenham Town	Ray Baverstock 13 Nick Gazzard 12 Nick Jordan 12		Ray Baverstock (5) Steve Scarrott	Paul Collicutt 46 Stuart Cornes 46 John Murphy 45
Corby Town	Roy Clayton 15 Derek Walker 11 Kevin McGuire 9	Derek Walker	Kevin McGuire (2) Derek Walker (2)	Kevin Johnson 51* Derek Johnson 49 Roy Clayton 48
Fareham Town	Dave Leworthy 26 Kevin Bartlett 26 Ken Todd 16			Ken Todd Paul Grant Peter Tindall
Fisher Athletic	Paul Shinners 50 Ossie Bayram 28 Mark Dennehy 16			Steve Bowtell Bobby Shinners Paul Shinners
Folkestone	Neil Cugley 21 Terry Jolley 21 Frank Ovard 14	Terry Jolley v Haywards Heath (FA Cup)	Terry Jolley (4) Kevin Smart (4) Frank Ovard (3)	Neil Cugley 51 Kenny Hill 51 Terry Jolley 50 Maurice Munden 50
Gloucester City	Mike Bruton 27 Mario Waite 14 David Gwyther 14	Bruton 4 v Bedworth 3 v Fisher A (Trophy)	Bruton (6)	Gerry Sweeney 47 Dave Gwyther 46 Neil Hards 46
Gosport Borough	Ali Unitt 16 John Hawes 12 Richard Reed 4		Gary Juryeff (3)	Tony Mahoney 47* Tony Stares 47* Roger Buckland 46 John Hawes 46
Gravesend & Northfleet	Gary Julians 16 Steve Hermitage 11 Alan Hart 7	Steve Hermitage v Witney	Alan Hart (3) Ray Tumbridge (3)	Gary Julians 46 Ray Tumbridge 46 Willie O'Sullivan 45
Hastings United	Ernie Batten 21 John Daubney 19 Wayne Peacock 9		Chris Hamshare (4) John Daubney (4) Ernie Batten (3)	Nicky Westburgh 52* Malcolm Streeter 48 Tony Noakes 42
Kings Lynn	Martin Coupe 18 Jim Kabia 12 Freddie Easthall 12			Colin Foster 63 Freddie Easthall 63 Colin Foster 61
Stourbridge	Bobby Evans 10 Kevin Truswell 8 David Round 5			Kevin Ash 50* Kevin Truswell 8 David Round 5
Sutton Coldfield T	John Winwood 13 Andy Keeling 10 Bobby Hope 6	Bobby Hope	John Davies (5) Jimmy Brown	Andy Keeling 50 Fred Whitehouse 47 Dave Seddon 38
Welling United	Tony Agana 14 Andy Townsend 12 Terry Warren 10		Colin Ford 6 Andy Townsend Graham Hall	Ian Starkey 54 Stuart White 52 Ray Burgess 51 Nigel Ransom 51

SOUTHERN LEAGUE MIDLAND DIVISION ONE FIRST TEAM MATCH STATISTICS 1983-84

	Leading Goalscorers	Hat Tricks	Penalties	Most Appearances
Aylesbury United	John Davie 22 Mark Heeley 10 Peter Coffill 7 Tommy McGuiness 7	John Davie	John Davie (3) Peter Coffill (2)	Peter Mead 50* Keith Baker 47 Andy Dockery 46
Banbury United	Mark Boyland 12 Kenny Smith 7 John Baker 5		John Baker 5	R. Stockley 37 M. Taylor 30 K. Smith 29
Bridgnorth	Jimmy Steele 26 Neil Rogers 20 Gwynn Parry 10	J. Steele G. Parry N. Rogers	Neil Rogers (4) Delwyn Humphreys (2)	Gwyn Parry 48 Billy Ball 48 Rogers, Frisby, Steele 46
Coventry Sporting	Gez O'Neill 10 Kenny Hoyte 6 Steve Smith 5			Kenny Hoyte 43 Alan Harkus 34 Bob Mundy 34
Dudley Town	Mark Stanton 20 Russell Gordon 17 Andy Reece 9	Mark Stanton John Mitchell		Andy Foore 50 Russell Gordon 49 Mark Stanton 48
Forest Green R	Jeff Meacham Steve Doughty Jimmy Salt	Jeff Meacham	Mike Malpas (5)	Mike Malpass David Moss Jeff Meacham
Hednesford Town	John Branch 24 Mark Unitt 16 Keith Kelly 13	Keith Kelly 3 v Rushall O (A)	David Storey (6)	John Branch 48 Frank McLeod 47 Bob Page 45 Mark Unitt 40 + 12
Merthyr Tydfil	Paul Fisher 14 Ian Love 13 Derek Elliott 9	Phil Fisher	Phil Fisher (5)	Wayne Jones* Chris Holvey
Leicester United	P. Bale 7 J. Massey 5 G. Hammond 3			Ian Marsden 46* Steve Potter 46* John Carrigan 40
Milton Keynes C	Dave Drewe 4 Steve Drewe 4 John Loughran 4 Paul Burnett 4	Dave Drewe v Rushden T (A)	John Loughran Dave Brady Dean Bryden	Dave Howitt 32 Dave Brady 31 Zane Flanagan 25
Moor Green	Chris Cotton 23 Garry Edrop 10 Ray Howell 9	Chris Cotton	Joe Chaney (4) Garry Edrop (3) Cotton, Mitchell	Garry Edrop 47 Ian Pinner 43 Ron Skinner 41
Redditch United	Mark Whitehouse 26 Bobby Trindle 17 Don Wade 10			Graham Milward 37 Mark Chambers 36 Steve Evans 35 Tommy Owens 35
Rushden Town	Steve McIlroy 20 Ian Lindsay 11 D. Bottarill 7 C. Smith 7	Steve McIlroy	Dave Botterill (5)	David Botterill 44 Kevin James 44 Chris Smith 44 Steve McIlroy 44
Shepshed Chaterhouse	Jeff Lissamen 20 Dennis Jenas 17 Mark Cox 13	Mark Cox (2) Doug Keast	Jeff Lissaman (7)	Tim Thacker 51* Dave Wharton 49 Jeff Lissamen 47
VS Rugby	Danny Conway 28 Dave Ingram 16 Ian Crawley 15	Danny Conway v Skegness	John McGinty (7) John Setchell	Colin Burton 54* Danny Conway 53 John McGinty 53
Wellingborough T	Val Simpson 16 Derek Atkinson 8 Gary Smith 6			Tony Bell 44 Val Simpson 44 Dino Cirelli 43
Willenhall	Gary Matthews 28 Brian Beresford 28 Garry Stevens 25	Brian Beresford (2) Gary Matthews Garry Stevens	Brian Beresford (5) Willie Carr Gary Matthews	Garry Stevens 54 Chris Birch 50 Paul Stringer 48

*Ever present

SOUTHERN LEAGUE DIVISION ONE (SOUTHERN)
FIRST TEAM MATCH STATISTICS 1983-84

	Leading Goalscorers	Hat Tricks	Penalties	Most Appearances
Addlestone & Weybridge T	Steve Finnieston 30 Steve Matthews 11 Dave Donaldson 7 Noel Fletcher 7		Steve Finnieston (10)	Steve Finnieston 48* John Cassidy 48* Mark Woods 48* D. Donaldson 47 + 1s
Ashford Town	John Young 42 Ada Carter 14 Tony Reynolds 10	John Young	John Young (9) Hogben (2) Rayner, Carter	John Young 59* Ada Carter 57 Carmen, McRobert, Reynolds 56
Basingstoke	David Eddie 14 Steve Trotter 10 Murray Brodie 9	Dave Eddie v Thanet U	Steve Haysom (6)	Steve Haysom 53* Keith Champ 52 Billy Coombs 51
Canterbury City	Peter Venn 11 Jimmy McVeigh 9 Carl Gilbert 7 Gary Pugh 7		Jimmy McVeigh (4) Tony Bottiglieri	Peter Venn 46* Clay Sheild 44 Jimmy McVeigh 42
Chatham Town	Nigel Pointon 14 Derek Grant 9 Dave O'Hare 6			Nigel Pointon Wayne Finch Steve Brown
Crawley Town	Brian Gregory 45+ Jeff Wood 19 Russell Burtenshaw 8	Brian Gregory (3) Jeff Wood	Brian Gregory (5)	Steve Breach 55 Brian Gregory 55 Cliff Cant 54 R. Burtenshaw 54
Dover Athletic	John Brooks 12 Lennie Lee 6 Mark Harrop 4		Andy Young (4) Mark Harrop Bryan Lloyd	J. Radford * G. White D. Winstrom
Dunstable	Selvin Campbell 9 Trevor Mead 5 Gilchrist, Revell, Mawhinne 4		Les Harriott (2) John Mawinney	Andy Falconer 35 Jim McCarthy 34 Mark Fordham 33
Erith & Belvedere	Steve Barry 17 Junior Crooks 8 Bobby Moyle 7			
Hillingdon	Andy Pierre 15 Robert Rosario 8 Tony Angin 7		Paul Waites (2) Dave Gregory	Jeff Bateman 50* Jeff Fanner 50* Terry Evans 48
Poole Town	Derek Courtney 24 Mark Baber 13 Ashley Coombes 10 Nicky Brindle 10	Derek Courtney	Derek Courtney (5) Brian Chambers (3)	Kevin Mulkern Martin Jones Brian Chambers
RS Southampton	Pat Earles 33 Martin Dowding 29 Dean Mooney 23	Dean Mooney (2) Pat Earles (2)	Martin Dowding (4) Paul Baxter (2)	Phil Moore 64* Paul Baxter 61 Dowding, Earles 60
Salisbury	Tommy Paterson 20 Steve Slade 15 Brian Smith 14	Tommy Paterson v Erith	Lee Frost (4) Kevin Dawtry (3) Smith, Battams	Geoff Battams 58 Barry Cranmer 56 Ricky Haysom 55
Sheppey United	Neville Smith 26 Gary Doe 11 Marrhew Stock 7	Neville Smith (2) Paul Priston	Graham Mitchell (2) Alan Whitehead	Roger Steed 40* Andy Krush 39 David Samwell 33 Graham Mitchell 33
Thanet United	Steve Dudley 12 Karl Lloyd 8 Lennie Lee 7			Terry Norton 49* Wayne Godden 46 Richard Hemmings 40 Steve Dudley 40
Waterlooville	Colin White 23 Calvin Hore 9 Garry Holland 8		Calvin Hore (2) Colin White (2)	Calvin Hore 52* Trevor Gilbert 51 Billy Cole 46

*Ever present

SOUTHERN LEAGUE PREMIER DIVISION PLAYERS 1984

(Football League appearances in brackets)

ALVECHURCH
Goalkeeper
Jeff Allard: Stourbridge, Tividale

Defenders
Alex Travis: Stourbridge, Willenhall Town, Kidderminster Harriers, Alvechurch
Andy Taylor: Northampton Town (17), Aston Villa
Malcolm Goodman: Halifax Town (88-3), Bromsgrove Rovers
Nigel Green: Oldbury United
John Dyer: Cheltenham Town, Kidderminster Harriers, Bromsgrove Rovers, Worcester City, Alvechurch
Trevor Kirby: Kidderminster Harriers

Midfield
John Chambers: Cheltenham Town, Kidderminster Harriers, Worcester City, Bromsgrove Rovers, Stourbridge, Merthyr Tydfil, Southend United, Aston Villa
Adrian O'Dowd: Banbury United, Oxford United (10-1), Aston Villa
Micky Brennan: Worcester City, Kidderminster Harriers, Telford United, Redditch United
Micky Williams: Bromsgrove Rovers, Kidderminster Harriers, Redditch United, Sutton Coldfield Town

Forwards
Paul Waddington: Palloseura (Fin), Kidderminster Harriers, Worcester City, Walsall (19)
Phil Mullen: Kidderminster Harriers, Bromsgrove Rovers, Moor Green, Atherstone United, Cinderford Town
Joe Maffei: Kidderminster Harriers, Oxford United
Steve Round: Trowbridge Town, Walsall (26-4), Kidderminster Harriers

AP LEAMINGTON
Goalkeepers
Mick Lawrence: Solihull Borough, Alvechurch, Redditch United, Bromsgrove Rovers, Ledbury Town, Lye Town, Stourbridge, Worcester City, Stourbridge, Swindon Town
Glyn Conway: Local

Defenders
Ian Britton: Stourbridge, AP Leamington, Tamworth, Telford United, Walsall, Birmingham City
Clive Boxall: Cheltenham Town
Malcolm Kavanagh: Cheltenham Town, Moor Green, Sutton Coldfield Town, Derby County
Kevin Kane: Local
Steve Rigby: Alvechurch
Mark Butler: Local

Midfield
Graham Mackenzie: Cheltenham Town, Wycombe Wanderers
Nigel Shanahan: Local
Alan Ollis: Cheltenham Town, Luton Town, Aston Villa, Everton
Chris Downes: Bedworth United, Coventry Sporting, Lincoln City

Forwards
Kim Casey: Sutton Coldfield Town
Phil Griffin: Bromsgrove Rovers, Northfield Town
Steve Rhodes: Tamworth, Sutton Coldfield Town, Boldmere St Michaels
Cliff Campbell: Bedford Town, Nuneaton Borough, Banbury United

BEDWORTH UNITED
Goalkeeper
Mick Martin: Hinckley Athletic, Leicester City

Defenders
Dennis Taylor: AP Leamington
Steve Jackson: Local
Mark Thomas: Shepshed Charterhouse, Chesterfield, Notts County
Liam Halton: Local
John Peacock: Worcester City, Corby Town, Stafford Rangers, Boston United, Scunthorpe United (190-1)
Ken Trickett: Local
Tom Kilkelly: AP Leamington, Durban City (SA)

Midfield
Tommy Gorman: AP Leamington, Solihull Borough
Gary Bradder: Bermuda FC
Paul Purser: Local
Martin Smith: Coventry Sporting
Stuart Carmichael: Local

Forwards
Les Ebrey: Hinckley Athletic, Coventry Sporting
Mark Neale: Telford United, Nuneaton Borough, Atherstone, Bedworth United
Alan Hoult: Nuneaton Borough, Bristol Rovers, Leicester City
Carlo Rossi: Tamworth, Paget Rangers, Tamworth, Burton Albion, Tamworth, Tividale, Cheltenham Town, Macclesfield Town, Moor Green, Birmingham City

CHELMSFORD CITY
Goalkeeper
Willie Carrick: Hoddesdon Town, Bishop's Stortford, Enfield, Chelmsford City, Luton Town, Manchester United

Defenders
Phil Dudley: Southend United (110-3)
Colin Johnson: Hounslow, Wealdstone, Dartford, Orient
Micky Bright: Orient
John Devine: Billericay Town, Chelmsford City
Mark Whitmore: Southend United
Lee Wooldridge: Witham Town, Colchester United
Mick Kilbey: Local

Chelmsford City's top scorer Frank Bishop fires in a shot against Clapton in a home FA Trophy tie.
Photo: Mike Joss

Celebrations for A P Leamington as Herman Wilson (No 6) has just scored his second and Leamington's third in their 4-2 second leg home win against Bridgnorth in the Southern League Cup Semi-Final.
Photo: Mike Joss

Midfield
Dennis Longhorn: Colchester United (77), Aldershot (64-3), Sheffield United (38-1), Sunderland (43-3), Mansfield Town (105-6), AFC Bournemouth (35-1)
Gary Anderson: Maidstone United, Barking, Northampton Town, Tottenham Hotspur
Mick Tiffin: Local
John Herbert: Local
Bobby Moss: Wealdstone, Barnet, Colchester United, Orient

Forwards
Graham Powell: Tiptree United
Glyn Cowlishaw: Heybridge Swifts, Maidenhead United
Martin Thorpe: Local
Frank Bishop: Dartford, Chelmsford City, Tonbridge, Romford
Ernie Batten: Hastings United, Maidstone United, Folkestone Town, Sheppey United, Crystal Palace
Phil Thrift: Writtle

CHELTENHAM TOWN
Goalkeepers
Chris Ogden: Bath City, Rotherham United (3), Swindon Town (24), Oldham Athletic (128)
Stuart Martyn: Local

Defenders
John Murphy: Harrogate Town, Scarborough, Cheltenham Town, Cinderford Town
Steve Scarrott: Trowbridge Town, Gloucester City, Cheltenham Town, Bath City, Swindon Town
Paul Collicutt: Trowbridge Town, Swindon Town, Cheltenham Town
Stuart Cornes: Hereford United (93-3)

Midfield
Terry Paterson: Gloucester City, Cheltenham Town, Forest Green Rovers, Redditch United
Duncan Berry: Local
Nick Jordan: Moreton Town
Ray Baverstock: Swindon Town (19)
Ian Garthwaite: Local
Mike McFarlane: Banbury United, Nuneaton Borough, Witney Town, Oxford United

Forwards
Nick Gazzard: Bristol Manor Farm, Bristol Rovers
John Evans: Trowbridge Town, Gloucester City, Forest Green Rovers
Steve Slattery: Clanfield
Clive Shatford: Local
Norman Pemberton: Worcester City, Northfield Town

CORBY TOWN
Goalkeeper
Kevin Johnson: Stamford, Spalding United, Peterborough United

Defenders
Ian Ladd: Stamford, Bourne, Portsmouth, Notts County, Peterborough United
John Lane: Wigston Fields, Leicester United, Leicester City
Tony Ferns: Local
Mark Hesk: Grantham, Shepshed Charterhouse, Leicester United, South Liverpool, Chesterfield, Coventry City, Liverpool
Glyn Bradshaw: Leicester United, Notts County
Kevin Byrne: Stewarts & Lloyds, Desborough Town

Midfield
John Flannagan: Bedworth United, Corby Town, Nuneaton Borough, Worcester C., Kettering Town, Atherstone, Banbury United, Tamworth, Boston United, Leicester City
Derek Walker: Nuneaton Borough, Corby Town, Kettering Town
Neil Addy: Local
Gordon Hall: Stamford, Corby Town
Graham Leech: Local

Forwards
Roy Clayton: Nuneaton Borough, Barnet, Kettering Town, Oxford United
Dean Smith: Leicester United, Nuneaton Borough, Houston Hurricane (US), Brentford (54-16), Leicester City (10-1)
Phil McHutchison: Local
Steve Smith: Leicester United, Nuneaton Borough, Leicester United

CRAWLEY TOWN
Goalkeeper
Rick Collier: Carshalton Athletic, Sutton United, Staines Town

Defenders
David Myers: Chatham Town, Dartford, Canterbury City, Tonbridge
Bob Glozier: Hastings United, Gravesend, Maidstone United, Dover, Dartford, Guildford City, Torquay United, West Ham United
Phil Keeping: Chelmsford City, Dartford, Chelmsford City, Southend United
Steve Breach: Thanet United, Dover, Brighton, Arsenal
Jeff Bryant: Tooting & Mitcham United, Gravesend, AFC Bournemouth (16-2), Wimbledon (73-9), Fulham
Derek McMillan: Forfar Athletic

Midfield
Cliff Cant: Carshalton Athletic, Fulham, Arsenal
Russell Burtenshaw: Dagenham, Wimbledon, Southampton
Gary Grabban: Crystal Palace
Peter O'Sullivan: Maidstone United, Aldershot (10), Fulham (46-1), Brighton (435-38), Manchester United
Gary Richards: Local

Forwards
Brian Gregory: Dartford, Dover, Gravesend, Maidstone United, Weymouth, Luton Town, Thanet United, Gillingham
Mike Rose: Sutton United
Jeff Wood: Greenwich Borough

FAREHAM TOWN
Goalkeepers
Paul Grant: Local
Tim Hillier: Chichester City

Defenders
Russell Davies: Andover, Gosport Borough
Andy Bye: Gosport Borough
Steve Watt: Newport IOW, Havant Town
Mark Atkins: Brading Town, Fareham Town, Portsmouth
Keith Avery: BTC Southampton
Paul Marlow: Local
Bruce Kendall: Waterlooville, Portsmouth
Martin Winning: Gosport Borough, Havant Town, Bognor Regis Town, Gosport Borough

Midfield
Peter Tindall: Bognor Regis Town, Salisbury, Yeovil Town, Portsmouth
Kenny Todd: Portsmouth (3-1), Port Vale (44-9), Wolves (5-1)
Malcolm Wilkes: Newport IOW, Fareham Town
Mark Tuck: Newport IOW, Fareham Town
Joe Laidlaw: Mansfield Town (4), Hereford United (62-8), Portsmouth (60-19), Doncaster Rovers (128-27), Carlisle United (151-44), Middlesbrough (111-20)

Forwards
Kevin Bartlett: Portsmouth (3)
Alan Hallett: Havant Town
Gary Wheatcroft: Selsey
Dave Leworthy: Portsmouth (1)
Steve White: Pagham
Steve Hiscock: Local

FISHER ATHLETIC
Goalkeeper
Steve Bowtell: Woking, Dulwich Hamlet, Thanet United, Orient

Defenders
Bobby Shinners: Derby County
Ray Shinners: Croydon, St Lukes, Croydon
David Boulter: Enfield, Crawley Town, Crystal Palace (16)
Dennis Sharp: Local
Billy Parry: Cray Wanderers
Paul Collins: Millwall
Keith Wotherspoon: Dulwich Hamlet, Gravesend
Jeff Sault: Local

Midfield
Dave Sansom: Tooting & Mitcham United, Crystal Palace
Billy Davis: Local
Derek Garcia: QPR
Alan Hodges: Local
Derek Brown: Leytonstone & Ilford, Dartford, Bromley, Alma Swanley, Charlton Athletic, West Ham United
Peter Hawkes: Millwall, Fisher Athletic, Tottenham Hotspur

Forwards
Mark Dennehy: Dagenham, Kuopio ELO (Fin), Millwall
Paul Shinners: Croydon
Ronnie Murrock: Tooting & Mitcham United, Bromley, Beckenham Town
Ossie Bayram: Dulwich Hamlet

FOLKESTONE TOWN
Goalkeeper
Maurice Munden: Charlton Athletic

Defenders
Kevin Smart: Wigan Athletic (49-1), Plymouth Argyle (32)
Michael Dix: Local
Kenny Hill: Maidstone United, Washington Diplomats (USA), Baltimore Comets (USA), Lincoln City (1), Gillingham (125-7)
Billy Plews: Snowdown
Ricky Fusco: Dover, Thanet United, Maidstone United, Ramsgate
Ian Christie: Dover, Coventry City
Adrian Lemoine: Maidstone United

Midfield
Norman Fusco: Maidstone United, Gravesend, Thanet United, Charlton Ath.
Chris Hamshare: Hastings United, Dover, Gillingham
John Lineham: Local
Bobby Wilson: Dover, Charlton Athletic
Steve Bartlett: Local
Dave Wiltshire: Maidstone United, Dover, Aldershot (5), Gillingham (63-5)

Gravesend's popular Kenny Burrett left the club to join Sheppey United after creating a record of 535 appearances for 'Fleet'. Photo: David Hills

Forwards
Pat Hilton: Dover, Folkestone Town, Southport (27-5), Gillingham (26-1), Blackburn Rovers (16-2), WBA, Brighton (20-1), Canterbury City
Neil Cugley: Dover, Dartford, Folkestone Town, Thanet United, Ashford
Andy Allon: Local
Terry Jolley: Gravesend, Dover, Gillingham (21-5), West Ham United
Frank Ovard: Maidstone United, Gillingham (6), Maidstone United, Folkestone Town
Simon Bryant: Local

GLOUCESTER CITY
Goalkeeper
Neil Hards: Plymouth Argyle (9)

Defenders
Dennis McKay: Spencer Works
Paul Hunt: Worcester City, Trowbridge Town, Hereford United (51-4), Swansea City, Coventry City
Dave Dangerfield: Forest Green Rovers, Gloucester City, Cheltenham Town, Charlton Athletic, Swindon Town
Steve Harding: Trowbridge Town, Bristol Rovers (38-1), Bristol City (2)
Keith Tanner: Trowbridge Town, Swindon Town
Dave Bruton: Newport County (88-10), Swansea City (193-19), Bristol City (17)

Gravesend & Northfleet leading scorer, Gary Julians, is seen here scoring at home against Hastings United.
Photo: David Hills

Midfield
Barrie Vassallo: Merthyr Tydfil, Kidderminster Harriers, Bridgend Town, Torquay United (46-4), Plymouth Argyle (13-2), Arsenel
Shane Walker: Phoenix Inferno (USA), Trowbridge Town, Newport County (28-2), Sligo Rovers, Hereford United (17-2), Arsenal
Gerry Sweeney: Forest Green Rovers, York City (12), Bristol City (406-22), Morton, Celtic
Ian John: Merthyr Tydfil, QPR
Mario Waite: Pontllanfraith
Chris O'Reilly: Newport County

Forwards
David Gwyther: Newport County (92-30), Rotherham United (162-45), Halifax Town (104-26), Swansea City (217-59)
Mike Burford: Hereford United
Andy Leitch: Old Georgians, Forest Green Rovers, Yeovil Town, Bath City, Minehead, Weymouth, Swansea City
Mike Mulraney: Local
Mike Bruton: Oxford City, Gloucester City, Newport County (9-1), Gloucester City

GRAVESEND AND NORTHFLEET
Goalkeepers
Paul Burnham: Tonbridge, Maidstone United, Tonbridge, Charlton Athletic
Russ Cochrane: Local

Defenders
Kevin Wallis: Hastings United, Gravesend
Ray Tumbridge: Dartford, Weymouth, Charlton Athletic
Alan Risk: Local
Colin Dalton: Local
Kenny Burrett: Faversham Town
David Jones: Local

Midfield
Alan Hart: Dulwich Hamlet, Millwall, Charlton Athletic
Willie O'Sullivan: Dartford, Charlton Athletic (2)
Trevor Burke: Dartford, Bromley, Crystal Palace
Steve Howe: Local
Ian Carolan: Canterbury City, Tonbridge, Dover, Tonbridge
Steve Brignall: Tonbridge, Hastings United, Arsenal
Geoff Eyers: Dartford, Orient

Forwards
Gary Julians: Welling United, Maidstone United, Dartford, Millwall
Ray Kenny: Thanet United, Tonbridge, Hastings United, Crawley, Sevenoaks
Darren Poppy: Local
John Archbold: Maidstone United
Steve Leahy: Crystal Palace (4)
Gary Aldous: Tonbridge, Gravesend, Sheppey United
Steve Hermitage: Sheppey United
Graham Astbury: Local
Leroy Bess: Tonbridge, Alma Swanley

HASTINGS UNITED
Goalkeepers
Mick Green: Eastbourne United
Tim Flynn: Local

Defenders
Micky Westburgh: Guildford City, Hastings United, West Ham United, Everton
Dermot Slattery: Local
Peter Petkovic: Local
Tony Noakes: Eastbourne United, Bexhill Town
Malcolm Streeter: Gravesend, Hastings United, Deal Town
Mike Harrison: Local

Midfield
Terry Hewitt: Sheppey United
Paul Saxby: Local
Duncan Boon: Eastbourne United
Paul Stirling: Maidstone United
Tommy Bristow-Diamond: Local
Alan Hodd: Local

Forwards
John Daubney: Bromley, Tooting & Mitcham United, Gravesend, Maidstone United, Eastbourne United, Crawley Town, Horsham
Mark Stevens: Local
Wayne Peacock: Maidstone United, Hastings United
Glyn White: Local
David Holmes: Maidstone United

Pat Earles the high scoring R S Southampton striker who joined them from Reading.
Photo: Eric Marsh

Shepshed Charterhouse (white shirts) and Bridgwater couldn't break the stalemate in this 0-0 draw in Somerset. Photo: David Shute

KING'S LYNN
Goalkeeper
Andy Claxton: Local

Defenders
Les McJannet: Mansfield Topwn (74)
John Cockerill: Lincoln United, Grantham, Boston FC
Colin Foster: Grantham, Peterborough United (71-4), Mansfield Town (205-17)
Richard Johnston: Local
Martin Wiles: Wisbech Town, King's Lynn

Midfield
Clive Adams: March Town United, King's Lynn, Wisbech Town, King's Lynn
Freddie Easthall: Kettering Town, King's Lynn, Norwich City
Chris Watts: Wisbech Town, King's Lynn, Norwich City
Paul Bartlett: Kettering Town, Boston United, Derby County (13)
Jim Kabia: Stafford Rangers, Boston United, Chesterfield, Derby County

Forwards
Keith Alexander: Corby Town, Grantham, Spalding United, Stamford, Boston United, Boston FC
Martin Coupe: Huddersfield Town, Nottingham Forest
Mark Howard: Local
Keith Rudd: Gainsborough Trinity, King's Lynn, Corby Town, King's Lynn, Wisbech Town, King's Lynn

ROAD SEA SOUTHAMPTON
Goalkeeper
Phil Moore: Fareham Town, Brading Town

Defenders
Paul Young: Fareham Town, Newport IOW
David Lock: Fareham Town, Basingstoke Town, Salisbury, Poole Town
Mick Farmer: Local
Ian Thakore: Waterlooville, Fareham Town
Tony Cleveland: Fareham Town, Newport IOW
Paul Bennett: Aldershot (113-2), Reading (105-3), Southampton (116-1)

Midfield
Joe Blochel: IFK Arvika (Swe), Southampton
Dale Young: Fareham Town, Waterlooville
Kevin White: Brockenhurst
Martin Dowding: Sholing Sports, Basingstoke Town, Warsash
Paul Baxter: Fareham Town, Basingstoke Town, Poole Town, BAT

Forwards
Dean Mooney: Trowbridge Town, AFC Bournemouth (27-10), Vasalund (Swe), FC Gais (Swe), Haugar (Swe), Walthamstow Avenue, Orient (22-3)
Pat Earles: Reading (274-84), Southampton (14-2)
Dave Pitter: AFC Totton
Steve Slade: AFC Totton
Kevin Dawtry: AFC Bournemouth (27-5), Reading (4), AFC Bournemouth (44-6), Crystal Palace, Southampton (1)
Kevin Maddock: Waterlooville, Fareham Town, Portsmouth

SHEPSHED CHARTERHOUSE
Goalkeepers
Colin King: Mansfield Town, Notts County, Clydebank, Blackpool
Kevin Massey: Local

Defenders
Tim Thacker: Grantham, Notts County
Paul Mitchell: Local
Dave Wharton: Eastwood Town
Mark Kendrick: Leicester City
Nigel Thrower: Eastwood Town, Nottingham Forest

Midfield
Austin Straker: Local
Graham Fearn: Burton Albion, Derby County
Andy Gould: Leicester City
Neil Grewcock: Gillingham (40-4), Leicester City (9-1)
Peter Currie: Leicester City
Simon Mason: Leicester United, Leicester City

Forwards
Colin Rue: Leicester United, Shepshed Charterhouse, Leicester United
Jon Nixon: Grantham, Burton Albion, Halifax Town (19-1), Barnsley (10), Shrewsbury Town (23-3), Peterborough United (110-16), Notts County (179-32)
Dennis Jenas: Nuneaton Borough, Shepshed Charterhouse, Matlock Town, Burton Albion, Grantham
Gilbert Scoular: Leicester United, Bedworth United, Shepshed Charterhouse
Brian Beresford: Willenhall Town, Corby Town, Worcester City, Willenhall Town, Brereton Social, Armitage, Chesterfield, Walsall
Jeff Lissaman: Local

TROWBRIDGE TOWN
Goalkeeper
Steve Smith: Crewe Alexandra (49), Bradford City (127), Birmingham City (3)

Defenders
Trevor Tainton: Torquay United (19-1), Bristol City (487-24)
Steve Ritchie: Yeovil Town, Torquay United (58-2), Aberdeen, Hereford United (102-3), Morton, Birstol City (1)
Duncan Ross: Walsall, Chelsea
Dave Roberts: Bath City, Tsun Wan (Hong Kong), Blackpool, Cardiff City (41-2), Hull City (86-4), Oxford United (161-8), Fulham (22) *(Wales)
Mark Ashton: Salisbury

Midfield
Danny Bartley: Hereford United (73-6), Swansea City (199-8), Bristol City (100-7)
Marcus Bray: Local
Barry Thomson: Bath City, Melksham Town
Gareth Dale: Kidderminster Harriers, Nuneaton Borough, Redditch United
Paul Neate: Local
Dave Mitchell: Local
Martin Thomas: Cardiff City

Forwards
Gary Harris: Cardiff City (4)
Craig Moss: Worcester City, Trowbridge Town, Worcester City, Wolves (4)
Bernie Wright: Kidderminster Harriers, Port Vale (76-23), Bradford City (66-13), Walsall (152-38), Everton (11-1), Walsall (15-2)
Paul Spittle: Oxford United

WELLING UNITED
Goalkeepers
Terry Jessop: Hastings United, Maidstone United
Gary Collins: Hornchurch, Dagenham, Brighton

Defenders
Colin Ford: Gillingham (1)
Nigel Ransom: Local
Kevin Corbett: Local
Ian Starkey: Dartford, Bromley, Maidstone United
Paul Sawyer: Local
Paul Summersby: Local
Willie Winch: Local
Andy Leach: Whitstable Town, Hillingdon

Midfield
Ray Burgess: Local
Stuart White: Gillingham, Charlton Athletic
Graham Hall: Local
Kevin Hall: Local
Adrian Foley: Sutton United, Maidstone United, Dartford
Andy Townsend: Local

Forwards
Terry Warren: Aveley, Tilbury
Gary Abbott: Local
Alf Wright: Local
Rupert Jones: Hampton, Feltham, Kingstonian

WILLENHALL TOWN
Goalkeepers
Brian Lewis: Blakenall
Steve Clay: Tipton Town

Defenders
Richus White: Bilston
Chris Birch: Alvechurch, Hednesford Town
Richard Dams: Wolves
Roy Cross: Nuneaton Borough, Tamworth, Nuneaton Borough, Port Vale, Walsall
Alan Hill: Local
Brian Fox: Hednesford Town, Sutton Coldfield, Darlaston, Coventry City

Midfield
Gary Stevens: Cheltenham Town, Worcester City, Alvechurch, Biston, Darlaston, Willenhall Town
Paul Stringer: Armitage, Chasetown, Lichfield, Walsall
Bobby Peck: Wolves
Ian Wells: Local
Alan Forrester: Dudley Town, Willenhall Town, Wednesfield Social

Forwards
Gary Matthews: Wolves
Clive Perrins: Sutton Coldfield, Alvechurch, Hednesford Town
John Wootton: Moor Green, Sutton Coldfield, Blakenall, Sutton Coldfield
Terry Norton: Local
Frank Sromec: Alsager Town, Northwich Victoria, Telford United, Cross Keys, Hednesford Town

WITNEY TOWN
Goalkeepers
Ian Turner: Walsall (39), Southampton (77), Grimsby Town (26), Huddersfield Town, South Bank
Nick Taylor: Local

Defenders
Malcolm Young: Oxford United
Kent Drackett: Headington Amateurs
Paul Lewis: Local
Jimmy Light: Oxford United (64)
David Cook: Local
Malcolm McIntosh: Oxford United (2), Kettering Town, Oxford United (63)

Midfield
Martin Blackler: Swindon Town (9)
Paul Bryant: Local
Tim Mills: Devizes Town, Vickers
Hugh McGrogan: Banbury United, Carlisle United (2), Oxford United (126-13)
Jason Seacole: Oxford United (120-22)

Forwards
Paul Berry: Oxford United (110-20)
David Groves: Local
Steve Abbley: Cheltenham Town, Swindon Town (23)
Paul Townsend: Local
Peter Hutter: Local
Steve Brooks: Clanfield

VS Rugby keeper Burton makes a spectacular save in a friendly game against a Manchester United XI.

Action in an Alliance League local 'Derby' between Bath City and Trowbridge Town (dark shirts).
Photo: Wessex Newspapers

TROWBRIDGE TOWN

President: D. W. Hurst
Chairman: L. Doel
General Manager: Tony Senter
Manager: Steve Smith
Physiotherapist: S. Peters
Secretary: T. Senter
Address & Tel No: c/o Club (02214) 2076/65086
Commercial Manager: T. Senter
Address & Tel No:
Press Officer & Tel No: General Manager
Address & Tel No of ground: Frome Road, Trowbridge. Tel. Trowbridge 2076
Club shop: Yes
Simple ground directions: Entrance 100 yards from traffic lights in Frome Road
No of seats: 600 **Covered accommodation:** 5,000 **Capacity:** 10,000 **Floodlights:** Yes
Year formed: 1880 **Nickname:** None **Club sponsors:** Patrick U.K.
Previous names: Trowbridge FC
Previous grounds: Old Flower Show Ground
Club colours: Blue with White trim/Blue/Blue
Change colours: All Red
Day for midweek home matches: Tuesday
Previous Leagues: Somerset Senior, Trowbridge & Dist, Wiltshire, Western, Southern, Alliance
Record attendance: 9,009 v Weymouth F.A. Cup, 4th Qual Round **Year:** 1949-50
Best performance in: F.A. Cup: 1947-8 1st Round Replay v Brighton
F.A. Trophy: 1970-1 1st Round Replay v Leytonstone & Ilford
Clubhouse details: Refreshments available before and after matches. Steward: M. Davenport. Trowbridge 2600
Present players with Football League experience: Paul Collicott (Swindon), Bernie Wright (Everton), Trevor Tainton (Bristol C.), Neil Merrick (AFC Bournemouth), John Layton (Hereford), Geoff Chacklin (Swindon)
Past players who progressed into the Football League: Paul Compton (Bournemouth), John Smeulders (Bournemouth)
Record transfer fee paid: £5,000 for John Smeulders
Record transfer fee received: £10,000 for Paul Compton
Programme details: 24 pages, 25p
Programme Editor: T. Senter
Club metal badges: Yes
Local newspapers & Tel No: Wiltshire Times, Trow. 2532; Bath Evening Chronicle, 0225 63052; Western Daily Press; Evening Post, 0272 20080
Major Honours: Wiltshire Senior Cup, Wiltshire Professional Shield, Western League, Western League Professional Cup, Wiltshire League Divs 1 & 2, Bristol Charity Cup, Western Counties Floodlight League Cup, Somerset Senior League, Trowbridge & District League
Club Captain (1983-84):
Player of the Year (1983-84):

Fisher Athletic *Back Row (L-R): Paul Shinners, Dave Sampson, Bobby Shinners, Dennis Shape, Bert Davies, Ronnie Murrock, Steve Bowtell. Front Row (L-R): Alan Hodges, Ossie Bayram, Mark Denney, David Boutler, Derek Brown.*

FISHER ATHLETIC

Chairman: T. McCarthy
Manager: D. Arif
Coaches: D. Mann & R. Abbott
Physiotherapist: D. Cunningham
Secretary: D. Kent
Address & Tel No:
General/Commercial Manager: L. Rowe
Address & Tel No: 237 8379
Press Officer & Tel No: None
Address & Tel No of ground: Surrey Docks Stadium, Salter Road, Surrey Docks, London SE16 **Club shop:** Yes
Simple ground directions: Head for southern entrance of Rotherhithe Tunnel, turn into Brunel Rd, turn right Rotherhithe St, right into Salter Rd, ground on right
No of seats: 400 **Covered accommodation:** Yes **Capacity:** 1,000 **Floodlights:** Yes
Year formed: 1908 **Nickname:** The Club **Club sponsors:** Master Mail
Previous names: None
Previous grounds: Mitcham
Club colours: Black/White stripes, Black shorts/socks
Change colours: Gold/Black stripes, Black shorts/hose
Day for midweek home matches: Tuesday
Record attendance: 1,842 v Dartford **Year:** 1984
Best performance in: F.A. Cup: 1984, 4th Qual Round
F.A. Trophy: 1984, 3rd Round
Previous Leagues: Kent Amateur, London Spartan
Clubhouse details: Bar and Light Refreshments. Open 7 days a week
Present players with Football League experience: S. Bowtell (Orient)
Past players who progressed into the Football League: None
Record transfer fee paid: None
Record transfer fee received: None
Programme details: 16 pages, 20p
Programme Editor: Tony Incenzo
Local newspapers & Tel No: South London Press, Kentish Mercury
Club metal badges: No
Senior Honours: Kent Senior Trophy, Kent Senior Cup, London Spartan Prem Div (2)/Senior Div, Southern League Div 1 (S) Champions 1983, Southern League Premier Div Champions 1984
Club Captain (1983-84): Denis Sharp
Player of the Year (1983-84): Paul Shinners

Chelmsford City *Back Row (L-R): Glyn Cowlishaw, Micky Bright, John Devine, Willie Carrick, Dennis Longhorn, Mark Blackhall, Colin Johnson. Front Row (L-R): Bobby Moss, Graham Powell, Phil Dudley, Gary Anderson, Phil Thrift*

CHELMSFORD CITY 1980 LTD

Chairman: B. T. Reeve
Manager: M. G. Loughton
Coach: D. Reynolds
Physiotherapist: Len Wills
Secretary: V. A. W. Keeble
Address & Tel No: 52 Coggeshall Road, Earls Colne, Essex. Earls Colne 2978 (H) Chelmsford 353052 (B)
Commercial Manager: V. A. W. Keeble
Address & Tel No: Chelmsford 353052
Press Officer & Tel No: None
Address & Tel No of ground: The Stadium, New Writtle Street, Chelmsford, Essex. Tel 353052
Club shop: Yes
Simple ground directions: 5 minutes walk from railway station – by road 5 minutes from A12
No of seats: 1,500 **Covered accommodation:** 12,500 **Capacity:** 16,000
Floodlights: Yes
Year formed: 1980 **Nickname:** City
Club sponsors: None
Previous names: Chelmsford City (1938)
Club colours: White/Claret/White
Previous grounds: None
Change colours: Gold/Black/Gold
Day for midweek home matches: Monday
Previous League: None
Record attendance: 15,557 v Ipswich F.A. Cup **Year:** 1973
Best performance in: **F.A. Cup:** 1938-9 v Birmingham City 4th Round
F.A. Trophy: 1969-70 v Telford Utd Semi-Final
Clubhouse details: Available for private hire. Open evenings and Sunday lunchtime. Special events. Snacks. Disco on Thursday, Club night Friday
Present players with Football League experience: Willie Carrick (Manchester U, Luton T.), Bobby Moss (Colchester), Phil Dudley (Southend)
Past players who progressed into the Football League: Peter Collins (Tottenham), Nigel Spink (Aston Villa, England)
Record transfer fee paid: None
Record transfer fee received: For Nigel Spink
Programme details: 12 pages 20p
Programme Editor: Vic Keeble
Local newspapers & Tel No: Essex Chronicle, Chelms. 62421. Essex & Chelmsford Weekly News, Chelms. 64311
Club metal badges: Yes
Senior Honours: Southern League (3), Southern League Cup (2), Essex Pro Cup (4), Non-League Champs Challenge Cup, Essex Prof Cup (4), Eastern Floodlight Comp (4) Cup (1)
Club Captain (1983-84): Dennis Longhorn
Player of the Year (1983-84): Willie Carrick

ALVECHURCH

Chairman: Don Pedley
Manager: John Chambers
Coach: Geof Green
Trainer: Jimmy Conway
Secretary: Brian Nevett
Address & Tel No: 09057-71718
Commercial Director: Roy Yardley
Address & Tel No: 021-445 2960
Press Officer & Tel No: Roy Yardley (021-445 2960)
Address & Tel No of ground: Lye Meadow, Redditch Road, Alvechurch. 021-445 2929 **Club shop:** No
Simple ground directions: Situated on the Birmingham to Redditch Road, 10 miles Birmingham, 3 miles Redditch
No of seats: 350 **Covered accommodation:** Seated and standing **Capacity:** 7,500 **Floodlights:** Yes
Year formed: 1929 **Nickname:** The Church **Club sponsors:** Dowsett
Previous names: None
Club colours: Amber/Black
Previous grounds: 'The Meadows'
Change colours: All White
Day for midweek home matches: Wednesday
Record attendance: 13,500 v Enfield Amateur Cup **Year:** 1964
Best performance in: **F.A. Cup:** 1973-4 v Bradford 3rd Round
F.A. Trophy: 1980-81 Last 16
Previous Leagues: Midland Combination, West Midland
Clubhouse details: Function room for 200. Separate lounge, open week nights, Sunday lunchtime and match days
Present players with Football League experience: John Chambers (Villa), Malcolm Goodman (Halifax), Adrian O'Dowd (Villa), Andy Taylor (Northampton)

Alvechurch go close following a corner against Kings Lynn. Photo: Mike Joss

A.P. LEAMINGTON

President: D. Wright
Chairman: J. R. Soldan
Manager: Jim Watson
Coach: To be appointed
Physiotherapist: To be appointed
Secretary: D. Gardiner
Tel No: Leamington Spa 30719
Commercial Manager: Bill Branston
Tel No: Leamington Spa 26039
Press Officer: D. Donohue
Address & Tel No of ground: "The Windmill", Tachbrook Road, Leamington Spa, Warwicks (26039) **Club shop:** Yes
Simple ground directions: From South: leave A41 at Bishop's Tachbrook turning, follow signs to Leamington (2 miles)
No of seats: 440 **Covered accommodation:** 1,600 **Capacity:** 6,000 **Floodlights:** Yes
Year formed: 1945 **Nickname:** The Brakes **Club sponsors:** None
Previous names: Lockheed Leamington
Club colours: Gold/Black
Previous grounds: None
Change colours: All White/Royal Blue trim
Day for midweek home matches: Tuesday
Record attendance: 3,200 v Stafford F.A. Cup **Year:** 1975
Best performance in: **F.A. Cup:** 1978 reaching 2nd Round
F.A. Trophy: 1983/84 Quarter-finals
Previous Leagues: Midland, Southern, Alliance Premier
Clubhouse details: Social club open to non-members on match days. Live shows, darts, quiz nights etc. Snacks available
Present players with Football League experience: Mark Hopkins (Newcastle Utd, Sheffield Wed), Carlo Rossi (Birmingham City), Shaun Hemmings (Coventry City)
Past players who progressed into the Football League: Roger Brown (Bournemouth, Norwich, Fulham), Vince O'Keefe (Exeter C., Torquay, Blackburn R.), Errington Kelly (Bristol R, Peterborough), Maurice Muir (Northampton), Mark Buckland (Wolves), Graham Rodger (Wolves)
Record transfer fee paid: Various four-figure deals
Record transfer fee received: For Roger Brown from Bournemouth
Programme details: 20 pages, 15p **Programme Editor:** To be appointed **Club metal badges:** Yes
Local newspapers: Leamington Spa Courier, Coventry Evening Telegraph, Warwickshire Weekly News. Local Radio station: Radio Mercia
Major honours: Birmingham Senior Cup (3), Southern League Cup (2), S.L. Premiership Trophy, Southern League Champions
Club Captain (1982-83): Graham Mackenzie **Player of the Year (1982-83):** Kim Casey

Cheltenham Town *Back Row (L-R): Stuart Cornes, Steve Scarrott, Paul Collicutt, Chris Ogden, Nick Gazzard, John Murphy (player/manager), John Evans, Bert Williams (trainer). Middle Row (L-R): Reg Woodward (general secretary/director), Rod Burge (director), Don Perry (company secretary/director), Keith Rushworth (president), Arthur Hayward (chairman/director), Dave Hudd (director). Front Row (L-R): Nick Jordan, Russell Wilton, Norman Pemberton, Ray Baverstock, Terry Paterson.*

CHELTENHAM TOWN

President: K. Rushworth JP
Chairman: A. W. Hayward
Player/Manager: John Murphy
Physiotherapist: Bert Williams
Press Officer: Andy Brouwer
Secretary: Reg Woodward
Address & Tel No: 23 Enfield Villas, Winchcombe, Glos. GL54 5QH. 0242 602261 (H), 0242 516328 (B)
Commercial Manager: Fran Ward
Address & Tel No: 0242 513397
Address & Tel No of ground: Whaddon Road, Cheltenham, Glos. GL52 5NA. Tel 0242 513397/521974 **Club shop:** Yes
Simple ground directions: Situated NE side of Cheltenham, approx 1 mile from town centre, off A46 (Prestbury Rd)
No of seats: 1,200 **Covered accommodation:** 8,000 **Capacity:** 13,000 **Floodlights:** Yes
Year formed: 1892 **Nickname:** The Robins **Club sponsors:** Independent Insulations
Previous names: None
Previous grounds: None
Club colours: All Red
Change colours: All White
Day for midweek home matches: Wednesday
Record attendance: 8,326 v Reading in F.A. Cup 1st Round **Year:** 1956
Best performance in: F.A. Cup: 1933-4 v Blackpool 3rd Round, lost 3-1
F.A. Trophy: 1978-9 3rd Round proper
Previous League: Birmingham Combination
Clubhouse details: Open 7 nights a week. 3 bars, clubroom, lounge and Robin's Nest function room. Nest and clubroom available for private hire. Open before and after Saturday matches
Present players with Football League experience: Chris Ogden (Oldham, Swindon), Stuart Cornes (Hereford), Ray Baverstock (Swindon)
Past players who progressed into the Football League: James Currier (Bolton W), Jack Wheeler (Birmingham C), Peter Goring (Arsenal), Peter Rushworth (Leicester C), Roy Shiner (Huddersfield T), Tim Ward (Derby C), Ray Bishop (Cardiff C), Jack Haycox (Newport C), Jack Bowles (Stockport C), Roy Hill (Newport C), Ernie Thornley (Bristol C), Reg Watts (Bristol C), Jimmy Heal (Doncaster R), John McIlvenny (Bristol R), Peter Hauser (Chester), Paul Collicutt (Swindon T), Paul Tester (Shrewsbury T)
Record transfer fee paid: £3,000 joint-fee for Gary Fleet and Dave Lewis (Nuneaton Boro' 1979); £2,000 Gary Stevens (Alvechurch 1983)
Record transfer fee received: £1,500 Roy Shiner, (Huddersfield 1951); £10,000 Paul Tester (Shrewsbury 1983)
Programme details: The Robin, 16 pages, 20p
Programme Editor: Andy Brouwer
Club metal badges: Yes
Local newspapers & Tel No: Gloucestershire Echo 0242 526261. Local radio station 'Severn Sound' gives match coverage/live reports from h & a games
Senior Honours: Gloucestershire Senior Cup (North) (24), Southern League Midland Divn Winners 1983
Club Captain (1983-4): Paul Collicutt
Player of the Year (1983-4): Norman Pemberton (Supporters) Stuart Cornes (Players)

BEDWORTH UNITED

President: Alan Robinson
Chairman: H. Jones
Manager: John Peacock
Coach: Ray Gooding
Physiotherapist: John Roberts
Press Officer & Tel No: Secretary
Secretary: Norman Peacock
Address & Tel No: 315172 (H), 312295 (B)
Commercial Manager: G. Wing
Address & Tel No: 0203 314730
Address & Tel No of ground: The Oval, Miners Welfare Park, Bedworth (0203 314302) **Club shop:** Yes
Simple ground directions: On main Coventry to Bedworth Road, near town centre, ½-mile from M6 junction 3
No of seats: 300 **Covered accommodation:** 1,000 **Capacity:** 10,000 **Floodlights:** Yes
Year formed: 1968 **Nickname:** Greenbacks **Club sponsors:** None
Previous names: Bedworth Town
Previous grounds: None
Club colours: Green/White stripes, White shorts
Change colours: Yellow, Green shorts
Day for midweek home matches: Tuesday
Record attendance: 5,127 v Nuneaton B (S. League) **Year:** 1982
Best performance in: F.A. Cup: 1975 3rd Qualifying Round
F.A. Trophy: 1980-1 2nd Round
Previous Leagues: Birmingham Combination, West Midlands
Clubhouse details: Social club. Normal opening times and Saturday, Sunday mid-day
Present players with Football League experience: J. Peacock, R. Gooding
Past players who progressed into the Football League: Ray Train
Record transfer fee paid: £500 for Ian Crawley
Record transfer fee received: N/A
Programme details: 20 pages, 20p
Club metal badges: Yes, 25p
Local newspapers & Tel No: Nuneaton Tribune (Nun. 382251), Bedworth Echo, Coventry Evening Telegraph
Senior Honours: Birmingham Senior Challenge Cup (2), Midland Floodlight Cup

Crawley Town FC *Back Row (L-R): Stan Markham (secretary/general manager), Ricky Fitzgerald, Gary Richards, Jeff Bryant, David Myers, Ricky Collier, Bob Glozier, Phil Keeping, Kenny Wallace, Dave Haining (physio/trainer), John Maggs (team manager). Front Row (L-R): Brian Gregory, Aidan O'Sullivan, Russell Burtenshaw, Steve Breach (captain), Cliff Cant, Jeff Wood*

CRAWLEY TOWN

Chairman: K. N. Symons
Manager: J. W. Maggs
Coach: J. W. Maggs
Physiotherapist: D. Haining
Press Officer & Tel No: Dennis Lovell
Secretary/General Manager: S. H. Markham
Address & Tel No: 105 Winchester Road, Crawley 22371 (H)
Commercial Manager: F. Pitts
Address & Tel No: Crawley 37190
Address & Tel No of ground: 'Town Mead', Ifield Avenue, West Green, Crawley, Sussex. 21800 **Club shop:** Yes
Simple ground directions: Crawley BR S.R. 10 min walk 'thru High Street. Ground next to Fire Station in Ifield Avenue
No of seats: 250 **Covered accommodation:** 1,000 **Capacity:** 5,000 **Floodlights:** Yes
Year formed: 1896 **Nickname:** 'The Reds' **Club sponsors:**
Previous names: None
Previous grounds: None
Club colours: All Red
Change colours: All Blue
Day for midweek home matches: Tuesday
Record attendance: 3,052 v Wimbledon F.A. Cup replay **Year:** 1969
Best performance in: F.A. Cup: 1970-1 v Chelmsford C, 1971-2 v Exeter C 1st Rnd
F.A. Trophy: Never beyond 3rd Qualifying Rnd
Previous Leagues: Sussex County, Metropolitan
Clubhouse details: Daily, except Tuesday, lunchtime; Saturday evening 4.45-6.30pm
Present players with Football League experience: Jeff Bryant (Wimbledon), Bob Glozier (West Ham), Brian Gregory (Luton T)
Past players who progressed into the Football League: None
Record transfer fee paid: None
Record transfer fee received: £2,250 Trevor Smith to Gravesend October 1980
Programme details: 16 pages, 20p
Programme Editor: Dennis Lovell
Local newspapers & Tel No: Crawley Observer, Crawley 29551, Crawley News, Crawley 510148
Club metal badges: No
Senior Honours: Southern League Merit Cup, Sussex Professional Cup
Club Captain (1983-84): Steve Breach

CORBY TOWN

Chairman: Tom Haworth
Manager: John Flannagan
Assistant Manager: Jim Flannagan
Physiotherapist: Donald Johnson
Secretary: John Wiseman
Address & Tel No: 05363 68144 (H)
General Manager: Harry Fallon
Address & Tel No: 82 George Street, Corby. 05363 2757
Press Officer & Tel No: None
Address & Tel No of ground: P.O. Box 7, Occupation Road, Corby, Northants. Corby 3969 **Club shop:** Yes
Simple ground directions: One mile from centre of town, off Rockingham Road
No of seats: 600 **Covered accommodation:** 6,000 **Capacity:** 14,000 **Floodlights:** Yes
Year formed: 1948 **Nickname:** The Steelmen **Club sponsors:** Graham Holmes Plastics (Astraseal)
Previous names: Stewarts & Lloyds
Previous grounds: None
Club colours: White shirts, Black shorts
Change colours: All Yellow
Day for midweek home matches: Monday
Record attendance: 10,239 v Peterborough U. F.A. Cup 3rd Qual. Rnd **Year:** 1953-4
Best performance in: F.A. Cup: 1965-6 3rd Round v Plymouth Argyll
F.A. Trophy: 1969-70, 1975-6 2nd Round
Previous Leagues: United Counties, Midland
Clubhouse details: Open 7 days a week, usual club facilities
Present players with Football League experience: Roy Clayton (Oxford), Ian Ladd (Notts County), Dean Smith (Leicester, Brentford)
Past players who progressed into the Football League: D. Dall (Scunthorpe), P. Bannon (Carlisle), D. McNeil (Wrexham), G. Reilly (Cambridge, Watford), V. Overson (Burnley), Phil Chard (Peterborough), Len Chalmers (Leicester)
Record transfer fee paid: Elwyn Roberts (Barnet) £2,700
Record transfer fee received: Trevor Morley (Nuneaton) £7,700
Programme details: 8 pages, 20p
Programme Editor: John Wiseman
Local newspapers & Tel No: Northamptonshire Evening Telegraph (Kettering 81111)
Club metal badges: No
Senior Honours: United Counties League Championship (2), Southern League Merit Cup
Club Captain (1983-4): Gordon Hall
Player of the Year (1983-4): Kevin Johnson

FAREHAM TOWN

Chairman: R. A. Grant
Manager: R. Reynolds
Coach: D. Edwards
Physiotherapist: G. Buckner
Secretary: K. F. Atkins
Address & Tel No: Gosport (07017) 83049 (H) 23411 (B)
Commercial Manager: R. Long
Address & Tel No: Fareham (0329) 232156
Press Officer & Tel No: M. Willis (0705 472217)
Address & Tel No of ground: Cams Alders, Highfield Avenue, Fareham, Hants. Fareham (0329) 231151 **Club shop:** Yes
Simple ground directions: From Fareham railway station follow A27 towards Southampton, take 2nd turning left into Redlands Lane and then follow signs "Cams Alders Sports Centre"
No of seats: 500 **Covered accommodation:** 500 **Capacity:** 5,500 **Floodlights:** Yes
Year formed: 1947 **Nickname:** The Town **Club sponsors:** None
Previous names: None
Previous grounds: Bath Lane, Fareham
Club colours: Red shirts, White Shorts
Change colours: White/Black/White
Day for midweek home matches: Monday
Record attendance: 2,560 v Wimbledon **Year:** 1965
Best performance in: F.A. Cup: 1979-80 1st Round
F.A. Trophy: 1975-76, 1983-84 1st Round Proper
Previous Leagues: Portsmouth, Hampshire
Clubhouse details: Open each evening except Sunday. Open Saturday lunchtime & from 4.45pm on match day afternoons
Present players with Football League experience: Ken Todd, Kevin Bartlett, Dave Leworthy
Past players who progressed into the Football League: Ray Hiron, John Hold
Record transfer fee paid: £1, 000 P. Baxter (Poole T.)
Record transfer fee received: None
Programme details: 16 pages, 10p
Programme Editor: Ray Grant
Club medal badges: Yes
Local newspapers & Tel No: Portsmouth News, Portsmouth 64488; Southampton Echo, Southampton 34134; Gosport & Fareham Standard
Senior Honours: Hants Senior Cup (3), Hants County League (8), F.A. Sunday Cup, S.W. Counties (Pratten) Cup (2)
Club Captain (1983-84): Peter Tinday
Player of the Year (1983-84): David Leworthy

Folkestone *Back Row (L-R): Alf Bentley (former manager), Jack Pritchard (trainer), Fred Frost (chairman), Robin Thacker (manager), Neil Cugley, Ricky Fusco, John Rigden, Pat Hilton (club coach), Norman Fusco, Terry Jolley, Maurice Munden, Graham Rutherford (secretary), David Setterfield (vice-chairman), Roy Hemingway (director). Front Row (L-R): Stan Gardiner, Kevin Smart, Simon Bryant, Bobby Wilson, Mickey Dix, Kenny Hill.*

FOLKESTONE TOWN

President: W. Armory
Chairman: F. Frost
Manager: R. Thacker
Coach: P. Hilton
Physiotherapist: J. Riddell, M.C.S.P.
Press Officer & Tel No: N. Pilcher (0303) 75718
Secretary: G. Rutherford
Address & Tel No: "Sheridan", Alkham Road, Alkham, Nr. Dover, Kent. (0303) 51374 (B), 0304 823993 (H)
Commercial Manager: A. Marshallsay
Address & Tel No: 51374
Address & Tel No of ground: Cheriton Road, Folkestone, Kent (0303) 51374 **Club shop:** Yes
Simple ground directions: On A20 behind Presto Stores. Midway between Folkestone Central and West stations
No of seats: 900 **Covered accommodation:** On three sides **Capacity:** 8,000 **Floodlights:** Yes
Year formed: 1884 **Nickname:** Town **Club sponsors:** Ron Sports
Previous names: Folkestone & Shepway, Folkestone
Club colours: Black/Amber/Black
Previous grounds: None
Change colours: All Red
Day for midweek home matches: Wednesday
Record attendance: 7,801 v Margate, Kent Senior Cup **Year:** 1958
Previous League: Kent
Best performance in: F.A. Cup: 1932-3, 1965-6 3rd Round
F.A. Trophy: 1979-80 3rd Qualifying Round
Clubhouse details: Black & Amber Club, open every day normal opening hours. Pool, darts, etc.
Present players with Football League experience: Pat Hilton, Frank Ovard, Terry Jolley, Kevin Smart
Past players who progressed into the Football League: P.Hilton, T. Pearce, G. Towse, J. Hill, M. Barham, J. Goss
Record transfer fee paid: £1,500 to Maidstone U. for N. Fusco
Record transfer fee received: £5,000 for F. Ovard to Maidstone
Programme details: 16/20 pages, 20p
Programme Editor: Neil Pilcher
Local newspaper & Tel No: Folkestone Herald & Gazette (0303) 41411
Club metal badges: No
Senior Honours: Kent Senior Shield (7), Kent Senior Cup (5)
Club Captain (1983-4): Norman Fusco
Player of the Year (1983-4): Terry Jolley

Gloucester City *Back Row: Peters, Tandy, D. Bruton, Harding, Watson, Garwood, Butt, Walker, Porter. Front Row: Curtis, Sweeney, Gillies, Mursell (manager), Burford, Tanner, Lewis*

GLOUCESTER CITY AFC (1980)

Chairman: G. K. Hester
Manager: Tony Freely
Coach:
Physiotherapist: None
Press Officer & Tel No: M. Heather (0452 26019)
Secretary: Brian H. Hobbs
Address & Tel No: 8 Chantry Road, Thornbury, Bristol 0454 412201 (H)
Commercial Manager: David Stallworthy
Address & Tel No: 0452 4214001
Address & Tel No of ground: The Stadium, Horton Road, Gloucester 23883/421400 **Club shop:** Yes
Simple ground directions: Gloucester Ring Road to Barnwood Road, towards city centre traffic lights, left into Horton Road, stadium on left
No of seats: 450 **Covered accommodation:** 4,500 **Capacity:** 10,000 **Floodlights:** Yes
Year formed: 1980 **Nickname:** City **Club sponsors:** Westbury Homes
Previous names: Gloucester City (1889)
Club colours: All Yellow
Previous grounds: Longlevens
Change colours: White shirts/socks, White shorts
Day for midweek home matches: Tuesday
Record attendance: 11,000 v Tottenham H. (friendly) won 2-1 **Year:** 1952
Previous League: Birmingham
Best performance in: F.A. Cup: 1948, 49, 50, 1952, 1955 1st Round proper
F.A. Trophy: 1980-81, 1983-84 1st Round proper
Clubhouse details: Open on match days, before and after game
Present players with Football League experience: Neil Hards, Steve Harding, Barrie Vassallo
Past players who progressed into the Football League: Bob Etheridge, Alan Grubb, Gordon Boseley
Record transfer fee paid: £4,000 for Ken Stevens from Hereford
Record transfer fee received: £4,000 for Mike Bruton to Newport
Programme details: 16 pages, 20p
Programme Editor: Richard Goddard
Local newspapers & Tel No: Citizen, (0452) 24442. Local Radio: Severnsound (0452) 423791
Club metal badges: Yes
Senior Honours: Southern League Cup 1955-56
Club Captain (1983-84): Gerry Sweeney
Player of the Year (1983-84): Mario Waite

Gravesend & Northfleet *Back Row (L-R): F. R. Wilmshurst (director), Wallace, T.L.P. Bonnywell, Palfreman, D.F. Holloway (vice chairman), Aldous, D. Lucas (secretary), T.A. Jenner (director). Middle Row (L-R): Julians, Hermitage, Bodle, Burrett, Kent, Bright, Eyers, Risk, Idle, H. Ward (physio). Front Row (L-R): Everest, Brignull, Tony Burns (manager), Ray Tumbridge (captain), L.G.F. Ball (chairman), Wallis, Hart.* Photo: Gravesend & Dartford Recorder

GRAVESEND & NORTHFLEET

Chairman: Lionel G. F. Ball
Manager: Tony Burns
Coach: Mick Ward
Physiotherapist: Mick Ward
Secretary: Daryl Lucas
Address & Tel No: 16 Woodfield Avenue, Gravesend, Kent DA11 7QG. 0474 23778
Commercial Manager:
Address & Tel No:
Press Officer & Tel No:
Club shop: Yes
Address & Tel No of ground: Stonebridge Road, Northfleet, Gravesend, Kent DA11 9BA. Tel. 0474 533796 (Club). 0474 533404 (Social Centre)
Simple ground directions: From A2 trunk road take B262 Northfleet turn-off then B2175 to T junction with A226. Turn left continue to bottom of hill – ground is on right. Ground is 5 minutes walk from Northfleet station (B.R.)
No of seats: 1,200 **Covered accommodation capacity:** 5,000 **Floodlights:** Yes
Year formed: 1946 **Nickname:** The Fleet **Club sponsors:** Batt Cables
Previous names: Northfleet Utd and Gravesend Utd
Club colours: Red/White/Red
Previous grounds: None
Change colours: Blue & Yellow
Day for midweek home matches: Tuesday
Previous League: Southern Alliance Premier
Record attendance: 12,032 v Sunderland F.A. Cup 4th Round **Year:** 1963
Best performance in: F.A. Cup: 1963 v Sunderland 4th Round replay (a)
F.A. Trophy: 1969-70, 1977-8 2nd Round proper
Clubhouse details: Bar open matchdays and Tuesday, Thursday, Friday, Saturday evenings at Fleet Social Centre
Present players with Football League experience: Alan Hart (Millwall, Charlton), Steve Leahy (Crystal Palace), Steve Brignall (Arsenal), Paul Burnham (Charlton), Ray Tumbridge (Charlton, Northampton), Alan Hart (Charlton, Millwall), Jeff Eyers (Orient), Willie O'Sullivan (Charlton)
Past players who progressed into the Football League: Lee Smelt
Record transfer fee paid: £3,500 for Dave Busby from Barrow
Record transfer fee received: £15,000 for Lee Smelt to Nottingham Forest
Programme details: 28 pages, 30p
Programme Editor: Paul Harrison
Club metal badges: Yes
Local newspapers & Tel No: Gravesend & Dartford Reporter 0474 60441, Kent Evening Post 0622 77880
Major Honours: Southern League, Southern League Div1 South & Runners-up, Southern League Cup & Runners-up, Southern League Championship Cup, Kent Senior Cup (3) & Runners-up (2), Kent Floodlight Cup & Runners-up
Club Captain (1983-4): Ray Tumbridge **Player of the Year (1983-4):** Alan Risk

AP Leamington *Back Row (L-R): J. Chapman (Physio), S. Rhodes, J. Watson (manager), I. Britton, S. Rigby, G. Conway, M. Kavanagh, C. Campbell, C. Boxall. Front Row (L-R): K. Kane, H. Wilson, A. Ollis, P. Griffin, G. MacKenzie, K. Casey, C. Downes, K. Couchman.*

HASTINGS UNITED

Chairman: M. S. Piper
Manager: Gerry Boon
Coach: Gerry Boon
Physiotherapist: Chris Emary
Press Officer & Tel No: Tony Cosens, 427867
Secretary: R. A. Cosens
Address & Tel No: 22 Baldslow Road, Hastings. (0424) 427867 (H), (0424) 436868 (B)
Commercial Manager: John Huggett
Address & Tel No: c/o Hastings Stadium, 437187
Address & Tel No of ground: Hastings Stadium, Elphinstone Road, Hastings. (0424) 437187/429743 **Club shop:** Yes
Simple ground directions: From town centre go up Queen's Road, turn right into Elphinstone Road at traffic lights. Ground about 1 mile on right. Signposted from town centre
No of seats: 1,750 **Covered accommodation:** 3,500 **Capacity:** 10,000 **Floodlights:** Yes
Year formed: 1948 **Nickname:** The U's **Club sponsors:** Newtime Foods (name on track suits)
Previous names: None
Previous grounds: None
Club colours: Claret & Blue
Change colours: All Yellow
Day for midweek home matches: Tuesday
Record attendance: 12,760 v Norwich City, F.A. Cup **Year:** 1954-5
Best performance in: F.A. Cup: 1953-4, 1954-5 3rd Round
F.A. Trophy: 1979-80, 1980-1 3rd Round
Previous Leagues: None
Clubhouse details: Social area and squash courts open 7 days a week (as from 1981). Regular entertainment
Present players with Football League experience: None
Past players who progressed into the Football League: Syd Asher (Luton), Jim Ryan (Plymouth)
Programme details: 20 pages, 20p
Programme Editor: Tony Cosens
Local newspapers & Tel No: Hastings Observer 51351 Hastings News 433186
Club metal badges: Yes
Senior Honours: Sussex Senior Cup
Club Captain (1983-4): Peter Petkovic
Player of the Year (1983-4): Nicky Westburgh

KING'S LYNN

President:
Chairman: Mrs F. Farrier
Manager:
Coach: Colin Foster
Physiotherapist: Tom Ryan
Press Officer & Tel No:
Secretary: D. J. Stewart
Address & Tel No:
Commercial Manager: Steve Tyros
Address & Tel No: Gayton (0553 86) 408
Address & Tel No of ground: The Walks Stadium, King's Lynn, Norfolk. 0553 3567 **Club shop:** No
Simple ground directions: Junction of A47 & A17 on South side of Town
No of seats: 1,800 **Covered accommodation:** 8,000 **Capacity:** 15,000 **Floodlights:** Yes
Year formed: 1879 **Nickname:** The Linnets **Club sponsors:** Skoda
Previous names: Lynn Town
Previous grounds: None
Club colours: Yellow shirts/socks, Blue shorts/Yellow
Change colours: Blue shirts, White shorts/socks
Day for midweek home matches: Wednesdays
Record attendance: 13,500 v Exeter City 1st Rnd FA Cup **Year:** 1951
Best performance in: F.A. Cup: 1961-2 v Everton 3rd Round
F.A. Trophy: 1978-9 2nd Round
Previous Leagues: Eastern Counties, Midland League, Southern League
Clubhouse details: Open most evenings. 3 bars, pool, darts, dominoes etc
Present players with Football League experience: Les McJannet, Jim Kabia, Colin Foster
Past players who progressed into the Football League: John Neal
Record transfer fee paid:
Record transfer fee received: £1,000 from Kettering for Freddie Easthall
Programme details: 15 pages, 10p
Club metal badges:
Local newspapers & Tel No: Eastern Daily Press 0553 3401, Lynn News & Advertiser 61188

R.S. SOUTHAMPTON

President: P. Price
Chairman: J. Brett
Manager: P. Price
Coach: P. Bennett
Physiotherapist: T. Jewitt
Secretary: B. D. Jordan
Address & Tel No: Road Sea House, 18 Canute Rd, Southampton SO1 1FJ, 0703 446189 (H) 0703 30656 (B)
Commercial Manager: Ray Long, address as above
Tel No: 0703 30656 (B)
Press Officer & Tel No: Roger Hawkins, Botley 6810 **Club shop:** Yes
Address & Tel No of ground: Road-Sea Park, Long Lane, Marchwood, Southampton SO4 4WR. 0703 869010
Simple ground directions: A35 out of Southampton to Bournemouth, at Totton A326 to Fawley, 2nd left off A326 into Staplewood Lane
No of seats: 300 **Covered accommodation:** 500 **Capacity:** 4,000 **Floodlights:** Yes
Year formed: 1973 **Nickname:** None **Club sponsors:** H. Young Transport Ltd
Previous names: Road-Sea F.C.
Previous grounds: None
Club colours: Red shirts/black trim, Black shorts/socks Red trim
Change colours: All White, Red trim
Day for midweek home matches: Wednesday
Record attendance: 500 **Year:** 1982-3
Best performance in: F.A. Cup: First qual.
F.A. Vase: Fifth round 1983-4
Previous Leagues: City of Southampton Sunday Premier Div
Clubhouse details: Open Match days, and also more evenings during 1984-5 season
Present players with Football League experience: Paul Bennett, Pat Earles and Dean Mooney
Past players who progressed into the Football League: None
Programme details: 12 pages, 20p
Programme Editor: Steve Farmery
Local newspaper & Tel No: Southampton Evening Echo & Sports Echo
Club metal badges: No
Senior Honours: S.W. Counties Pratten Cup, Southern League Southern Division champions 1983-4, S.W. Counties Sutton Vase Winners 1983-4, Russell-Cotes Cup Winners 1983-4
Club Captain (1983-4): Paul Baxter
Player of the Year (1983-4): Mick Farmer

Shephed Charterhouse *Back Row (L-R): Dick Cooper (general manager), Geoff Hickinbottom (assistant physio), Michael Cohen (physio), Graham Fearn, Dave Wharton, Andy Gould, Colin King, Colin Rue, Jeff Lissaman, Ian Storey-Moore (manager), Willie Cook (kit manager), Sam Lakin (assistant physio). Front Row (L-R): Niel Grewcock, Dennis Jenas, Austin Straker (captain), Maurice Clayton (chairman), Tim Thacker, Nigel Thrower, Brian Beresford.* Photo: Leicester Mercury

SHEPSHED CHARTERHOUSE

President:
Chairman: Maurice F. Clayton
Manager: Geoff Blockley
Secretary: Brian Edwards
Address & Tel No: 33 Outwoods Drive, Loughboro' Leics LE11 3LR. (0509) 36561 (B) (0509) 232957, (0604) 67302 (H)
Reserve Team Manager: Arthur Chadburn
Physiotherapist: I. Gheeson
Commercial Manager: David Allen
Address & Tel No: 106 Anson Road, Shepshed, Leics (0509) 502524 (H), (0509) 505050 (B)
Press Officer & Tel No: Maurice Brindley (0509) 67922
Club shop: No
Address & Tel No of ground: The Dovecote, Butthole Lane, Loughborough Road, Shepshed, Leics. (05095) 502684
Simple ground directions: M1 Junction 23, A512 to Ashby, right at traffic lights, right at garage into Forest St, right into Butthole Lane opposite Black Swan P.H.
No of seats: 45 **Covered accommodation:** 1,000 **Capacity:** 5,000 **Floodlights:** Yes
Year formed: 1891 **Nickname:** None **Club sponsors:** Charterhouse Textiles
Previous names: Shepshed Albion
Club colours: White shirts, Black shorts/socks, Red trim
Previous grounds: None
Change colours: All Red
Day for midweek home matches: Monday
Record attendance: 1,672 **Year:** 1982/83
Best performance in: F.A. Cup: 1981-2 1st Round
F.A. Vase: 1978-9 Semi-Finalists
Previous Leagues: Leicestershire Senior, Midland Counties, Northern Counties East
Clubhouse details: On ground. Small and caters for visiting players and officials in the main
Present players with Football League experience: A. Gould (Leicester), C. King (Mansfield, Notts County, Clydebank)
Past players who progressed into the Football League: None
Record transfer fee paid: M. Cox
Record transfer fee received: None
Programme details: 16 pages, 20p
Programme Editor: Cliff Wright
Local newspapers & Tel No: Loughborough Echo, Notts Post, Leicester Mercury
Club metal badges: No
Senior Honours: Northern Counties East League & Cup, Midland Counties League & Cup, Derbyshire Premier League & Cup, Leicestershire Senior League (3) & Cup (4), Leicestershire Challenge Cup, Southern League Mid Div Runners-up
Club Captain (1983-84): Austin Straker **Player of the Year (1983-84):** Tim Thacker

Welling United *Back Row (L-R): Nigel Ransom, Tony Agana (now Weymouth), Murray Jones, Ian Shead, Ian Starkey, Terry Warren, Stuart White. Front Row (L-R): Adrian Foley, Andy Townsend, Kevin Corbett, Kevan Hall, Graham Hall.* Photo: Kentish Times Newspapers

WELLING UNITED

Chairman: P. Websdale
Manager: Graham Hobbins
Coach: Nicky Brigden
Physiotherapist: B. Carnaby
Secretary: Barrie Hobbins
Address & Tel No: c/o Club 01-301 1196 (H or B)
Commercial Manager: c/o Secretary
Address & Tel No: As Secretary
Press Officer & Tel No: c/o Secretary
Address & Tel No of ground: Park View Road, Welling, Kent DA16 1SY (01-301 1196) **Club shop:** Yes
Simple ground directions: Ten minutes walk from Welling or Bexley Heath (BR)
No of seats: 800 **Covered accommodation:** 1,000 **Capacity:** 8,500 **Floodlights:** Yes
Year formed: 1963 **Nickname:** The Wings **Club sponsors:** D. F. Winter Carpets
Previous names: None
Previous grounds: Butterfly Lane, Eltham
Club colours: Red/White/Red
Change colours: Light Blue
Day for midweek home matches: Wednesday
Record attendance: 1,100 v Gravesend, F.A. Cup **Year:** 1978-9
Best performance in: **F.A. Cup:** 1979-80 4th Qualifying Round
F.A. Vase: 1979-80 3rd Round
F.A. Trophy: 2nd Round Proper
Previous Leagues: Spartan, Athenian
Clubhouse details: Lounge with bar, pool table, darts
Present players with Football League experience: None
Past players who progressed into the Football League: Paul Barron (Plymouth, Arsenal, C. Palace, W.B.A.), John Bartley (Millwall), Ian Thompson (Bournemouth)
Record transfer fee paid: £1,000 for Gary Julians
Record transfer fee received: £12,000 for John Bartley (Millwall)
Programme details: 18 pages, 25p
Programme Editor: Andy Legg
Local newspaper & Tel No: Kentish Times (01-309 1234) Kentish Independent (01-854 7704)
Club metal badges: Yes
Senior Honours: London Spartan League Cup, Kent Youth Cup (4)
Club Captain (1983-4): Ray Burgess **Player of the Year (1983-4):** Stuart White

Canterbury City winger Roger Russell stretches to score City's equalizing goal against Erith & Belvedere.
Photo: Kentish Gazette

WILLENHALL TOWN

President:
Chairman: J. Williams
Manager: Ian Cooper
Coach: John Jones
Physiotherapist: None at present
Match Secretary: J. J. Davenport
Address & Tel No: 130 Silverton Way, Wednesfield, Wolverhampton. Willenhall 632505 (H), Wolv. 731271 (B)
Commercial Manager: None at present
Address & Tel No:
Press Officer & Tel No: Secretary
Address & Tel No of ground: Noose Lane, Willenhall. Willenhall 65132 **Club shop:** Yes
Simple ground directions: Main road from Wolverhampton to Walsall goes through Willenhall
No of seats: 220 **Covered accommodation:** Yes **Capacity:** 200 **Floodlights:** Yes
Year formed: 1953 (re-formed) **Nickname:** 'The Reds' **Club sponsors:** Rothley Brass Ltd
Previous names: None
Previous grounds: Memorial Park, Willenhall
Club colours: All Red with White trim
Change colours: White/White or Blue/Blue
Day for midweek home matches: Wednesday
Record attendance: 3,454 v Crewe Alexandra, F.A. Cup 1st Rnd **Year:** 1981
Best performance in: **F.A. Cup:** 1981-82 1st Round
F.A. Trophy: 1st Qual Round
F.A. Vase: 1980-81 Finalist
Previous Leagues: Wolverhampton Amateur, Staffs County (South), W. Midlands (Regional)
Clubhouse details: Lounge, bar, boardroom, Executive lounge
Present players with Football League experience: None
Past players who progressed into the Football League: Sean O'Driscoll (Fulham, Bournemouth), Joe Jackson, Stuart Watkiss (Wolves)
Record transfer fee paid: £2,000
Record transfer fee received: None
Programme details: 32 pages, 20p
Programme Editor: Terry Wilkins
Local newspapers & Tel No: Wolverhampton Express and Star, Walsall Observer
Club metal badges: Yes
Senior Honours: Staffs County (South) League & Cup, West Midlands League Div 1/Premier Div/Premier League Cup, Southern Lge, Midland Div
Club Captain (1983-84): Chris Birch

WITNEY TOWN

President: Mr Gittings
Chairman: A. N. Oakley
Manager: Dick Lucas
Coach: None
Physiotherapist: Trevor Stokes
Secretary: C. F. J. Miles
Address & Tel No: Witney 3592 (H)
Commercial Manager: None
Address & Tel No:
Press Officer & Tel No: Secretary
Address & Tel No of ground: Marriott's Close, Welch Way, Witney, Oxon. Witney 2549/5930 **Club shop:** No
Simple ground directions: Ground is in centre of the town and adjacent to the public car park
No of seats: 150 **Covered accommodation:** 1,500 **Capacity:** 3,500 **Floodlights:** Yes
Year formed: 1885 **Nickname:** None **Club sponsors:** Bucknell & Ballard
Previous names: Witney
Previous grounds: None
Club colours: Yellow/Royal Blue
Change colours: White
Day for midweek home matches: Tuesday
Record attendance: 3,500 v WBA v Nottm Forest. Trevor Stokes benefit match **Year:** 1965
Best performance in: **F.A. Cup:** 1971-72 1st Round
F.A. Trophy: 1978-79 2nd Round
Previous Leagues: Oxfordshire Senior, Hellenic
Clubhouse details: Open every evening (except Christmas Day), also lunchtime on Saturdays, Sundays and Bank Holidays. Four bars including clubroom, lounge and 2 function rooms. Entertainment 5-6 nights each week. Basket meals and snacks. (Steward: J. Drinkwater, mornings/evenings W. 2549)
Present players with Football League experience: J. Light, J. Seacole
Past players who progressed into the Football League: David Moss (Swindon T.)
Record transfer fee paid: £3,000, Peter Dallaway (Oxford C.)
Record transfer fee received: £3,000, John Bailey (Aylesbury T.)
Programme details: 24 pages, 20p
Local newspapers & Tel No: Witney Gazette Witney 4265, Oxford Mail and Oxford Times Oxford 44988
Club medal badges: No
Senior Honours: Southern League Div 1 (North), Oxfordshire Senior Cup (9), Hellenic League (8)

DIVISION ONE (MIDLAND)

AYLESBURY UNITED

President: N. P. Ramsden
Chairman: C. Doherty
Manager: Trevor Gould
Coach:
Physiotherapist: P. Smith
Press Officer & Tel No: G. J. Aldridge (Aylesbury 24759)

Secretary: R. A. Clark
Address & Tel No: 11 The Spiert, Stone, Aylesbury 0296 748319

Address & Tel No of ground: The Stadium, Turnfurlong Lane, Aylesbury, Bucks. Aylesbury 20044 **Club shop:** Yes
Simple ground directions: By A41 from Tring – turn left into Bedgrove, right into Turnfurlong Lane. By A413 from Wendover – turn right into Bedgrove, left into Turnfurlong Lane
No of seats: 500 **Covered accommodation:** Stand and Terrace **Capacity:** 9,500 **Floodlights:** Yes
Year formed: 1897 **Nickname:** The Ducks **Club sponsors:** Aylesbury Plus
Previous names: None
Previous grounds:
Club colours: Green/White shirts, Green shorts/socks
Change colours: All Red
Day for midweek home matches: Tuesday
Record attendance: 7,440 v Watford **Year:** 1951-2
Previous League: Athenian
Best performance in: F.A. Cup: 1951-2 v Watford 1st Round Proper
F.A. Trophy: 1980-1 v Sutton United Quarter-Finals
Clubhouse details: Social club open 7 days per week. Recently extended with 2 bars, including members own lounge
Present players with Football League experience: P. Mead (Northampton), K. Baker (Millwall, Grimsby), Paul Saunders (Northampton), Mark Heeley (Peterborough, Arsenal, Northampton), Peter Coffill (Watford, Torquay, Northampton), Trevor Gould (Coventry C, Northampton)
Past players who progressed into the Football League: R. Mabbut (Bristol Rovers), Phil Barber (C. Palace)
Record transfer fee paid: £2,000 for Steve Brinckman (Barnet)
Record transfer fee received: £7,500 Phil Barber (Crystal Palace)
Programme details: 24 pages, 25p
Programme Editors: Geoff Aldridge, Derek Plater
Club metal badges: Yes
Senior Honours: None
Local newspapers & Tel No: Bucks Herald (0296) 24444, Bucks Advertiser (0296) 82784, Aylesbury Plus (0296) 89363
Club Captain (1983-4): Peter Mead
Player of the Year (1983-4): Andy Dockery

Aylesbury United *Back Row (L-R): Andy Dockery, Phil Barber (now with Crystal Palace), Keith Baker, Wayne Stokes, Paul Saunders, Peter Arch, Peter Coffill. Front Row (L-R): Peter Mead, John Davie, Ralph Perna, Mark Heeley, Paul Hackett.* Photo: Bucks Herald

Bridgnorth Town *Back Row (L-R): M. Comerford, P. Green (physio), G. Parry, N. Rogers, W. Ball, R. Evans, P. Bennett, R. Baker, T. Edwards (trainer). Front Row (L-R): S. Frisby, D. Humphreys, J. Steele, K. Jones (manager), A. Rogers, O. Daley, K. Harris.* Photo: Martin Thorneycroft

Banbury United *Back Row (L-R): Ian Bowyer, Dave Matthews, Mark Taylor, John Thorne, Mark Boyland, Daryl Watson. Front Row: Bob Stockley, Mike McFarlane, Kenny Smith, Phil Lines, Paul Lee, Shaun Bradbury (Mascot — Master Stockley)*

BANBURY UNITED

Chairman: L. M. Townley
Manager: W. Tranter
Coach: (To be appointed)
Physiotherapist: None
Press Officer & Tel No: Norman Matthews, 0869 40347
Secretary: Norman A. S. Matthews
Address & Tel No: Cedar Court, Steeple Aston, Oxford OX5 3SB. 0869 40347 (H), 0295 3354 (Ground)
Commercial Manager: Ronnie Johnson
Address & Tel No: The Stadium, Banbury
Address & Tel No of ground: The Stadium, Off Station Road, Banbury, Oxon. Banbury 3354 **Club shop:** No
Simple ground directions: Right turn before entering station forecourt at eastern end of town
No of seats: 400 **Covered accommodation:** 2,500 **Capacity:** 6,500 **Floodlights:** Yes
Year formed: 1965 (re-formed) **Nickname:** **Club sponsors:** Everstone Cladding Ltd
Previous names: Banbury Spencer
Previous grounds: None
Club colours: Light Blue with Dark Blue shadow stripe
Change colours: Yellow with Red trim
Day for midweek home matches: Tuesday
Record attendance: 7,000 F.A. Cup Qualifying Round v Oxford City **Year:** 1947
Best performance in: F.A. Cup: 1947, 1960, 1973 1st Round Proper Replay v Northampton
F.A. Trophy: 1973-4 3rd Round Proper
Previous Leagues: West Midlands, Birmingham Combination
Clubhouse details: Open match days and at weekends. Mid-weekdays on hire
Present players with Football League experience: None
Past players who progressed into the Football League: O. Kearns (Reading), K. Wilson (Derby County), M. Singleton (Coventry)
Record transfer fee paid: £2,000 P. Emsden (Oxford Utd)
Record transfer fee received: £20,000 K. Wilson (Derby)
Programme details: 14 pages, 25p
Programme Editor: Norman Matthews
Club metal badges: No
Club Captain (1983-84): R. Stockley
Local newspapers & Tel No: Banbury Guardian, Banbury 4321; Oxford Mail, Oxford 44988; Banbury Focus, Banbury 51011; Banbury Cake, Banbury 56111/5
Player of the Year (1983-84): R. Stockley

BRIDGNORTH TOWN

President: W. S. Antony
Chairman: Pat Fellows
Manager: Ken Jones
Coach:
Physiotherapist: Peter Green
Press Officer & Tel No:
Secretary: Gordon Thomas
Address & Tel No: 7 Meadow Close, Bridgnorth Bridgnorth 5178
Commercial Manager: Stan Johnson
Address & Tel No: Bridgnorth 3290
Address & Tel No of ground: Crown Meadow, Innage Lane, Bridgnorth. Tel. 2747 **Club shop:** No
Simple ground directions: High Town, Bridgnorth
No of seats: None **Covered accommodation:** Yes **Capacity:** 2,000 **Floodlights:** Yes
Year formed: 1946 **Nickname:** The Town **Club sponsors:** Tatung UK Ltd
Previous names: None
Previous grounds:
Club colours: Blue/White
Change colours: Red/White
Day for midweek home matches: Tuesday
Record attendance: 1,600 v South Shields, F.A. Vase **Year:** 1975-6
Best performance in: F.A. Cup: 3rd Qualifying Round, 1983-4
F.A. Vase: 6th Round, 1975-6
Previous Leagues: Midland Combination Kidderminster
Clubhouse details: Open 7 days, Members Club
Present players with Football League experience: None
Past players who progressed into the Football League: Roger Davies (Derby C)
Programme details: 6 pages, free
Programme Editor: Gordon Thomas
Local newspapers & Tel No: Bridgnorth Journal 61411, Shropshire Star (Telford 44377)
Senior Honours: Welsh Amateur Cup, Shropshire County Challenge Cup (5), Midland Comb League Div I (2), League Cup
Club Captain (1983-4): Martin Goodall **Player of the Year (1983-4):** Robert Evans

BROMSGROVE ROVERS

President: C. W. Poole
Chairman: Chris Lloyd
Manager: Bobbie Hope
Coach: Doug Griffiths
Physiotherapist: Alec Blankley
Football Secretary: B. A. Hewings
Address & Tel No: 21 Carol Avenue, Bromsgrove, Worcs B61 8RN. Bromsgrove 31182 (H)
Commercial Manager: see Chairman
Address & Tel No:
Press Officer & Tel No: Brian Evans
Company Secretary & Address: E. Million, 41 Birmingham Road, Bromsgrove
Address & Tel No of ground: Victoria Ground, 33 Birmingham Road, Bromsgrove, Worcs. B/G 73028 **Club shop:** Yes
Simple ground directions: A38 twixt Midland Red bus garage/Victoria Rd; B'ngham side town centre, opp. petrol stn
No of seats: 375 **Covered accommodation:** 1,350 **Capacity:** 7,000 **Floodlights:** Yes
Year formed: 1885 **Nickname:** The Greens **Club sponsors:** None
Previous names: None
Club colours: Green/White
Previous grounds: Well Lane
Change colours: White
Day for midweek home matches: Tuesday
Record attendance: 7,563 v Worcs City, Birmingham Senior Cup **Year:** 1957-8
Best performance in: F.A. Cup: 1st Round 4 times
F.A. Trophy: 1975-6 Quarter-Finals
Previous Leagues: Birmingham Comb., West Midland (Regional)
Clubhouse details: Open 7 nights per week and match afternoons. Monday to Saturday. Licensed. Steward: Mr. E. Kimberley. Tel 78260
Present players with Football League experience:
Past players who progressed into the Football League:
Record transfer fee paid: Not available
Record transfer fee received: £10,000 for Steve Smith from Walsall
Programme details: 12 pages, 10p
Programme Editor: Brian Evans
Local newspapers & Tel No: Bromsgrove Messenger 72254. Bromsgrove Advertiser
Club metal badges: No
Senior Honours: None
Club Captain (1983-84): M. O'Connell
Players of the Year (1983-84): M. Lansford (Supporters) Mesic Kalewski (Press)

COVENTRY SPORTING

President: B. Craddock
Chairman: T. Smith
Manager: T. Smith
Coach: Mick Haycock
Physiotherapist: Paul Nicholson
Secretary: R. Griffis
Address & Tel No: 0203 464547
Commercial Manager: John Hollands
Address & Tel No: 464547
Press Officer & Tel No: B. Bannister (0203) 411277
Football Secretary: 103 Eastcotes, Tile Hill, Coventry CV4 9AW. 0203 461664 (H)
Address & Tel No of ground: Kirby Corner Road, Canley, Coventry (464547)
Simple ground directions: Take A45 from Birmingham, at first roundabout in city boundary turn right. Then proceed over traffic lights, turn first right into Kirby Corner Road. ½ mile on left-hand side is ground. Next to Warwick University
No of seats: 100 **Covered accommodation:** Yes **Capacity:** 5,000 **Floodlights:** Yes
Year formed: 1946 **Nickname:** None **Club sponsors:** Henlys
Club colours: All Red
Change colours: All Gold
Previous Names: None
Previous Grounds: None
Record attendance: 8,500 v Peterborough Utd (played at Highfield Rd) **Year:** 1975
Previous Leagues: Central Amateurs, Warwickshire Combination, West Midlands (Regional)
Clubhouse details: Open 7 days a week. Facilities for all types of functions private and public, also nightclub and restaurant
Programme: 20 pages, Free
Programme Editor: Bob Bannister
Local newspapers & Tel No: Coventry Evening Telegraph
Local Radio: 'Mercia Sound'
Club Captain (1983-84): Bob Mundy
Player of the Year (1983-84): Lennie Derby

DUDLEY TOWN

President: None
Chairman: N. D. Jeynes
Manager: Graham Smith
Coach: Lional Martin
Physiotherapist: E. Morden
Secretary: N. D. Jeynes
Address & Tel No: Stourbridge 395741 (H) 021-552 1511 (B)
Commercial Manager: John Edwards
Address & Tel No: Stourbridge 371048 (H)
Press Officer & Tel No: None
Address & Tel No of ground: The Sports Centre, Birmingham Road, Dudley, West Midlands. Dudley 235005 (office). Dudley 53390 (social club)
Club shop: No
Simple ground directions:
No of seats: 1,000 **Covered accommodation:** 1,500 **Capacity:** 30,000 **Floodlights:** Yes
Year formed: 1893 **Nickname:** The Robins **Club sponsors:** None
Previous names: None
Club colours: Red shirts, White shorts
Previous grounds: Shavers End
Change colours: All Yellow
Day for midweek home matches: Tuesday
Record attendance: 7,600 v Worcester City, F.A. Cup **Year:** 1964
Best performance in: F.A. Cup: 1976-7 1st Round Proper
F.A. Trophy: 1977-8 1st Round Proper
Previous Leagues: Birmingham Combination, West Midlands (Regional)
Clubhouse details: Licensed social club. Open evenings, match occasions, Sundays
Present players with Football League experience: None
Past players who progressed into the Football League: Joe Mayo, Ken Price
Record transfer fee received: £1,000 for Ken Price from Southend
Programme details: 10 pages 15p
Programme Editor: John Edwards
Local newspapers & Tel No: Evening Herald, County Express, Express & Star
Club metal badges: Yes
Senior Honours: Birmingham Combination, Maserfield Cup, Worcestershire Senior Cup
Club Captains (1983-4): Benny Brown, John Loveridge
Players of the Year (1983-4): Andy Foote (Supporters) Russell Gordon (Players)

Bridgwater Town will be competing in the Somerset & Avon League in season 1984/85.

FOREST GREEN ROVERS

President: G. C. Mills
Chairman: John Duff
Manager: Steve Millard
Coach:
Physiotherpist: Adrian Brown
Press Officer & Tel No:
Secretary: Graham Collins
Address & Tel No: 59 Etheldene Rd, Cashes Green, Stroud, Glos. 04536 77872 (H) 045382 6661 (B)
Club shop: Yes
Address & Tel No of ground: The Lawn, Nympsfield Road, Forest Green, Nailsworth, Stroud, Glos. 045 383 4860
Simple ground directions: Nailsworth is on A46 (Bath-Stroud) 4 miles south of Stroud. From town centre proceed up Spring Hill for 1 mile, ground is on left-hand side of road.
No of seats: 131 **Covered accommodation:** Grandstand/standing area **Capacity:** 4,500 **Floodlights:** Yes
Year formed: 1890 **Nickname:** The Green **Club sponsors:** Various
Previous names: None
Previous grounds: None
Club colours: Black/White shirts, Black shorts, Red socks
Change colours: All Green
Day for midweek home matches: Tuesday
Record attendance: 2,200 v Wolverhampton Wanderers **Year:** 1981
Best performance in: F.A. Cup: 1979-80 2nd Round Qualifying
F.A. Vase: Winners of F.A. Vase, 1982
Previous Leagues: Stroud & Dursley Dist. Glos. Northern Senior, Glos. County, Hellenic
Clubhouse details: Bar/Lounge. Open every evening, 7-10.30/11pm. Open before/after matches on Saturday afternoons
Present players with Football League experience: G. Day (Bristol R), P. Higgins (Bristol R, Doncaster R), D. Dangerfield (Swindon T)
Past players who progressed into the Football League: None
Record transfer fee paid: None
Record transfer fee received: None
Programme details: 20 pages, 20p
Programme Editor: Martin Morgan
Local newspapers & Tel No: Stroud News & Journal, The Citizen, Western Daily Press
Club metal badges: Yes
Senior Honours: F.A. Vase Winners, Hellenic League Premier Div Winners, Glos. Senior Amateur Cup (4)
Club Captain (1983-4): Bobby Brown

HEDNESFORD TOWN

President: Ron Gray
Chairman: Mick Smith
Manager: Mick Babb
Coach: Bob Wickett
Physiotherapist: Trevor Saunders
Press Officer & Tel No: Steve Smith
Secretary: Paul Westwood
Address & Tel No: Hednesford 77517
Commercial Manager: Philip Talbot
Address & Tel No:
Address & Tel No of ground: Cross Keys Ground, Hill Street, Hednesford, Staffs. Hednesford 2870 **Club shop:**
Simple ground directions: Leave M6 at junction 11. Follow signs to Cannock and then Hednesford
No of seats: 250 **Covered accommodation:** 2,000 **Capacity:** 9,000 **Floodlights:** Yes
Year formed: 1880 **Nickname:** The Pitmen **Club sponsors:** S. Wakeman (Fuels) Ltd
Previous names: The Colliers, The Lilywhites
Previous grounds: The Anglesey Ground (The Tins)
Club colours: White/Black/Black
Change colours: Blue/White/Blue
Day for midweek home matches: Monday
Record attendance: 10,000 v Walsall (League) **Year:** 1922
Best performance in: F.A. Cup: 1919-20 1st Round Proper
F.A. Trophy: 1977-78 3rd Round Proper
Previous Leagues: Walsall & District, Birmingham Comb, Birmingham, West Midlands, Midland
Clubhouse details: Open 7 days and matchday extension
Present players with Football League experience: None
Past players who progressed into the Football League: V. Allatt (Crewe), S. Biggins (Oxford Utd), B. Horton (Hull City) (many others over the years — details in club centenary book)
Record transfer fee paid: £500 to Kidderminster for Andy Allen
Record transfer fee received:
Programme details: 32 pages,
Programme Editors: Terry Brumpton and David Smith
Local newspapers & Tel No: Wolverhampton Express & Star W'ton 22351, Cannock Advertiser Cannock 3663
Club metal badges: Yes
Senior Honours: Staffs Junior Cup, Birmingham Senior Cup, Birmingham Combination, Staffs County League, Rugeley Charity Cup, Staffs Senior Cup, West Midlands League Challenge Cup, West Midlands League Championship
Club Captain (1983-84): Kevin Lane **Team Captain:** Eddie Paton **Player of the Year (1983-84):** Eddie Paton

LEICESTER UNITED

Chairman: George Smith
Manager:
Coach: B. Davies
Physiotherapist:
Secretary: V. R. White
Address & Tel No: 863154 (G), 0533 550276 (H)
Commercial Manager:
Address & Tel No:
Press Officer & Tel No: A. Forman
Address & Tel No of ground: George Street Ground, Coleridge Drive, Enderby, Leicester. 863154 **Club shop:** No
Simple ground directions: 1½ miles from junction 21, M1 and M69. Leave motorway, take B4114 to Narborough, then B582 to Enderby
No of seats: 750 **Covered accommodation:** 2,250 **Capacity:** 9,750 **Floodlights:** Yes
Year formed: 1900 **Nickname:** None **Club sponsors:** None
Previous names: Enderby Town
Club colours: Red/Red/Black
Previous grounds: None
Change colours: All Blue
Day for midweek home matches: Monday
Record attendance: 6,000+ Schoolboy fixture England v Wales **Year:** 1978-9
Best performance in: **F.A. Cup:** 1977-8 1st Round
F.A. Trophy: 1978-9 3rd Round
Previous Leagues: Leicestershire Senior, East Midland Regional
Clubhouse details: Open every evening and Saturday-Sunday lunchtimes. Available for all functions, weddings, etc.
Present players with Football League experience: None
Past players who progressed into the Football League: None
Record transfer fee paid: £1,000
Record transfer fee received: £1,500
Programme details: 10 pages, 20p
Programme Editor: Alan Forman
Local newspapers & Tel No: Leicester Mercury Leicester 20831
Club metal badges: No
Senior Honours: Leicestershire Senior Cup (6), Leicestershire Senior League (3)
Club Captain (1983-4): John Carrigan
Player of the Year (1983-4): Paul Bale

Merthyr Tydfil *Back Row (L-R): Derek Elliott, Chris Holvey, Barrie Vassallo, Wayne Jones, Keith Pontin, Jeff Shaw. Front Row (L-R): Ian Love, Chris Williams, Peter Jones, Jimmy McInch, Phil Fisher, Ieuan John.*

MERTHYR TYDFIL

Chairman: Cyril Stuckey
Manager: Fred Davies
Assistant Manager: Ievan Evans
Physiotherapist:
Secretary: Ken Tucker
Address & Tel No: Merthyr Tydfil 3884
Commercial Manager: Terry Collins
Address & Tel No: Ynysowen 690 052
Press Officer & Tel No:
Address & Tel No of ground: Pendydarren Park, Merthyr Tydfil 71395/71525 **Club shop:** No
Simple ground directions: Situated in the town a few hundred yards from railway station
No of seats: 300 **Covered accommodation:** 3,000 **Capacity:** 8,000 **Floodlights:** Yes
Year formed: 1945 **Nickname:** The Martyrs **Club sponsors:** T.S.B.
Previous names: Merthyr Town
Club colours: Black & White stripes/White/Black
Previous grounds: None
Change colours: Amber shirts, Black shorts
Day for midweek home matches: Wednesday
Record attendance: 21,000 v Reading F.A. Cup **Year:** 1949
Best performance in: **F.A. Cup:** 3 x 2nd Rnd. 1979-80 lost 3-1, home, Chesham U
F.A. Trophy: 1977-8 Quarter-Finals
Previous Leagues: Football League (3rd Div South)
Clubhouse details: Large social club on ground. Open every night
Present players with Football League experience:
Past players who progressed into the Football League: Ray Prait (Exeter), Gordon Davies (Fulham)
Record transfer fee paid:
Record transfer fee received: £12,000 Ray Pratt (Exeter)
Programme details: 6 pages, 10p
Programme Editor: Ken Tucker
Local newspapers & Tel No: Merthyr Express (Celtic Press Ltd, Merthyr 3255). Sports Editor: John Hughes
Club metal badges: Yes
Senior Honours: Southern League (5), Southern League Cup (2), Welsh Cup (2)
Player of the Year (1983-84): Phil Fisher, Wayne Jones (joint)

MILTON KEYNES CITY

Chairman: F. C. W. Dare
Manager: Tom Flanagan
Coach:
Physiotherapist: Peter Leach
Secretary: S. C. Beck
Address & Tel No: 0908 310702 (H) 0908 566222 (B)
Commercial Manager: S. C. Beck
Address & Tel No: As above
Press Officer & Tel No: Mike Warth (052523 486)
Address & Tel No of ground: City Ground, Manor Fields, Bletchley, Milton Keynes MK2 2HX. Tel M.K. 0908 73727
Simple ground directions: On Watling Street (old A5) at Fenny Stratford, Bletchley **Club shop:** Yes
No of seats: 200 **Covered accommodation:** 3,200 **Capacity:** 8,000 **Floodlights:** Yes
Year formed: 1914 **Nickname:** The Gladiators **Club sponsors:** Chalky Whites – Tyres and Exhausts
Previous names: Bletchley Town
Club colours: Tangerine/Black/Tangerine
Previous grounds: Bletchley Park
Change colours: Blue/Navy/White
Day for midweek home matches: Wednesday
Record attendance: 1,997 v Wolverton T & BR. Utd Counties Lge Cup Final **Year:** 1967
Best performance in: **F.A. Cup:** 1964-5, 1965-6 4th Qualifying Round
F.A. Trophy: 1973-4 2nd Round proper
Previous Leagues: North Bucks, S. Midlands, Spartan Hellenic, Metropolitan, Utd Counties
Clubhouse details: Open daily. Licensed bar and hall for club and private functions
Present players with Football League experience: Dave Howitt (Aldershot)
Past players who progressed into the Football League: Barry Lines (Northampton)
Record transfer fee paid: £200 for Ray Brimson from Hitchin Town
Record transfer fee received: Nil
Programme details: 16 pages, 20p
Club metal badges: No
Senior Honours: Berks & Bucks Senior Cup
Club Captain (1983-84): Dave Howitt
Local newspapers & Tel No: Milton Keynes Gazette 0908 74040, Milton Keynes Mirror, Milton Keynes Citizen

Dudley Town *Back Row (L-R): Graham Smith (manager), Danny McCormack, Andy Allen, Steve Pomroy, Andy Foote, Jeff Rumjahn, Benny Brown, Lional Martin (coach), Ernie Morden (physio). Front Row (L-R): Andy Reece, John Loveridge, Russell Gordon, Doug Devlin, Paul Lippett, Mark Stanton.*

MOOR GREEN

President: Geoff Hood
Chairman: John Mowl
Manager: Chris Wright
Coach: Reg Brassington
Physiotherapist: Cyril Bird
Secretary: Brian Smith
Address & Tel No: 021-777 1488
Commercial Manager: David Savage
Address & Tel No: 021-777 1833 (24hrs)
Press Officer & Tel No: Peter Clynes (021-444 7903)
Address & Tel No of ground: The Moorlands, Sherwood Road, Hall Green, Birmingham B28 0EX **Club shop:** Yes
Simple ground directions: A34 Birmingham to Stratford Road, 5 miles city centre, turn into Highfield Road, Sherwood Road is 2nd right
No of seats: 300 **Covered accommodation:** 1,500 **Capacity:** 6,000 **Floodlights:** No, permission sought
Year formed: 1901 **Nickname:** The Moors **Club sponsors:** Midas Exhausts
Previous name: None
Club colours: Dark/Light Blue stripes
Previous grounds: Moor Green Lane, Windermere Road
Change colours: All Yellow
Day for midweek home matches: Tuesday
Record attendance: 5,000 v Romford, FA Amateur Cup **Year:** 1951
Best performance in: **F.A. Cup:** 1979-2, v Stafford Rangers, 1st Round Proper
F.A. Trophy: 2nd Qualifying
Previous Leagues: Central Amateur, Birmingham Comb, West Midland, Midland Comb
Clubhouse details: Open evenings, plus Sat/Sun lunch, two bars, one with dance floor. Many functions
Present players with Football League experience: John Capaldi (Aston Villa, Motherwell)
Past players who progressed into the Football League: Ken Barnes (Manchester C), Howard Williams (Manchester U), Brian Mack (WBA), Steve Cooper (Birmingham C), Herbie Smith (Aston Villa)
Record transfer fee paid: None
Record transfer fee received: None
Programme details: 32 pages, 20p
Programme Editor: Peter Clynes (021-444 7903)
Club metal badges: No
Local newspapers & Tel No: Solihull News, Solihull Times, Birmingham Evening Mail
Senior Honours: Midland Comb League and Cup Double, Birmingham Senior and Junior Cups, Central Amateur (3)
Club Captain (1983-4): Jerry Brosnan **Player of the Year (1983-4):** Garry Edrop

OLDBURY UNITED

President: None
Chairman: S. H. Warren
Manager: D. Robinson
Coach: H. Shepherd
Physiotherapist: P. Anson
Press Officer & Tel No: M. Scott
Secretary: A. W. Grove
Address & Tel No: 021-552 4445
Commercial Manager: None
Address & Tel No:
Club shop: No
Address & Tel No of ground: The 'Cricketts', York Road, Rowley Regis, Warley, West Midlands. 021-559 5564
Simple ground directions: M5 junction 2 onto Halesowen, Blackheath, 1st left at lights then 1st right
No of seats: 40 **Covered accommodation:** 125 **Capacity:** 6,000 **Floodlights:** Yes
Year formed: 1958 **Nickname:** Cricketts **Club sponsors:** None
Previous names: Queens Colts
Club colours: Sky Blue & White stripes/R. Blue/R. Blue
Previous grounds: Oldbury Sports Centre
Change colours: White/Black/White
Day for midweek home matches: Tuesday
Record attendance: 2,200 v Walsall Wood, Walsall Senior Cup Final **Year:** 1982
Best performance in: F.A. Cup: None
F.A. Vase: None
Clubhouse details: Members club and bar facilities
Present players with Football League experience: G. Burgess (Walsall), V. Hodgson (WBA)
Past players who progressed into the Football League: None
Record transfer fee paid: None
Record transfer fee received: None
Programme details: 12 pages, 15p
Club metal badges: No
Senior Honours: Walsall Senior Cup
Programme Editor: M. Scott, H. Burgess
Local newspapers & Tel No: Warley News Telephone Sandell Evening Mail
Club Captain (1983-84): Paul Cooper
Player of the Year (1983-84): Neal Civil

Redditch United *Back Row (L-R): Gordon Cooper, Perry Adams, Mark Crisp, Don Wade, Mick Brookes, Tommy Owens, Alan Potts, Phil Summerill, Ivor Chambers (assistant manager). Front Row (L-R): Jimmy Guinivan, Graham Milward, Graham Smith, Steve Evans, Mark Chambers.* Photo: Marshalls Sports Service

REDDITCH UNITED

President: Bob Thompson
Chairman: R. T. Berry
Team Manager: Gordon Cooper
Assistant Manager: Ivor Chambers
Physiotherapist: Kevan McHugh
Secretary: M. A. Langfield
Address & Tel No: Redditch 26603 (H) 63646 (B)
General Manager: Nobby Clark
Commercial Managers: Dave Roberts, Tom Beard
Address & Tel No:
Press Officer & Tel No: David Cooke (H. Redditch 65813)
Address & Tel No of ground: Valley Stadium, Bromsgrove Road, Redditch 62540
Club shop: Yes — usually by appointment only
Simple ground directions: Ground located near town centre and on the Bromsgrove side of Redditch
No of seats: 600 **Covered accommodation:** 3,000 **Capacity:** 10,000 **Floodlights:** Yes
Year formed: 1948 (re-formed) **Nickname:** Reds **Club sponsors:** J.T. Edwards & Phoenix Building Supplies
Previous names: Redditch Town
Club colours: Red/Red/Black
Previous grounds: Millsbrough Road & HDA
Change colours: Blue
Day for midweek home matches: Tuesday
Record attendance: 5,300 v Bromsgrove **Year:** 1955
Best performance in: F.A. Cup: 1971-2 v Peterborough 1st Round Replay
F.A. Trophy: 1978-9 v Kings Lynn 1st Round
Previous Leagues: West Midland (Regional), Founder member of Alliance Premier
Clubhouse details: Large club room and lounge board room. Room holds 150 people and is open most nights
Present players with Football League experience: None
Past players who progressed into the Football League: Mick Tuohy (Southend, now at Worcester C.)
Record transfer fee paid: £1,500 Eddie Hogan (Burton A)
Record transfer fee received: £7,500 Mick Tuohy (Southend U)
Programme details: 8 pages, 20p
Programme Editor: Dave Cooke
Local newspapers & Tel No: Redditch Indicator 63611 Redditch Advertiser, Birmingham Evening Mail
Club metal badges: 60p
Senior Honours: Birmingham Senior Cup (4) Runners-up (3), Worcs Senior Cup (4) Runners-up (3), Southern League Div 1 (N) Champions
Club Captain (1983-4): Don Wade
Player of the Year (1983-4): Graham Milward

RUSHDEN TOWN

President: A. Rich
Chairman: K. Ambridge
Manager (Gen) A. J. Sabey **(Team)** M. Walpole
Coach: S. Wisman
Physiotherapist: T. Graham
Press Officer & Tel No:

Secretary: D. M. Joyce
Address & Tel No: W'boro 79466 (H)
Northampton 493161 (B)
Commercial Manager: R. Denny
Address & Tel No: 311453

Address & Tel No of ground: Hayden Road, Rushden, Northants. Rushden 53575 **Club shop:** Yes
Simple ground directions: A6 turn left into Newton Road, third left into Cromwell Road, straight into Hayden Road
No of seats: 500 **Covered accommodation:** 1,100 **Capacity:** **Floodlights:** Yes
Year formed: Reformed 1919 **Nickname:** Russians **Club sponsors:** Totectors, A & S Footwear, Graham Holmes Plastics (Astraseal)
Previous names: None
Previous grounds: None
Day for midweek home matches: Tuesday
Record attendance: 5,600 v Kettering Town **Year:** 1950

Club colours: Red/White/Black
Change colours: Sky/Navy

Previous Leagues:
Central Alliance
United Counties

Clubhouse details: 1968 present Clubroom erected. Extended 1973 to include lounge, office, etc.
Present players with Football League experience: Sean Suddards
Programme details: 4 or 8 pages, 10p
Programme Editors: David Joyce, Tony Sabey
Club metal badges: No
Local newspapers & Tel No: Evening Telegraph
Chronicle & Echo
Senior Honours: UC League Premier Div, UC Div I, UCL KO Cup, Northamptonshire FA Senior Cup
Club Captain (1983-4): Sean Suddards

STOURBRIDGE

President: J. H. Guest
Chairman: G. Taylor
Manager: G. Newton
Coach: None
Physiotherapist: 'Tucker' Whitfield

Secretary: H. F. Clark
Address & Tel No: 10 Burnt Oak Drive, Stourbridge, West Midlands DY8 1HL. 0384 392975
Press Officer: H. F. Clark

Address & Tel No of ground: War Memorial Athletic Ground, High Street, Amblecote, Stourbridge, W. Midlands. Tel. 0384 394040 **Club shop:** Yes
Simple ground directions: 200 yards from Stourbridge Ring Road on A491 to Wolverhampton
No of seats: 460 **Covered accommodation:** 2,000 **Capacity:** 6,000 **Floodlights:** Yes
Year formed: 1876
Previous names: None
Previous grounds: None
Day for midweek home matches: Tuesday
Record attendance: 6,000 v Cardiff City Welsh Cup Final **Year:** 1973-4
Best performance in: **F.A. Cup:** 1967-8 v Arnold 4th Qualifying Round
F.A. Trophy: 1970-1 v Yeovil Quarter-Final

Nickname: The Glassboys
Club colours: Red/White/Black
Change colours: White/Black

Previous Leagues:
West Midlands (Regional),
Birmingham,
Birmingham Comb

Clubhouse details: Every night, 8-10.30pm (11pm Fri/Sat). Bingo + live enter. (Sat). Steward: Lol Tibbotts, Stour.
Present players with Football League experience: Willie Carr, Phil Parkes
Past players who progressed into the Football League: P. Freeman, P. Bates, R. Haywood, L. Lawrence, S. Cooper, T. Cunningham, G. Pulley, C. Taylor, A. Rowley
Record transfer fee paid: None
Record transfer fee received: £20,000 for T. Cunningham (Lincoln C)
Programme details: 24 pages, 20p
Club metal badges: Supporters' club badges
Local newspapers: Stourbridge News and County Express, Wolverhampton Express & Star, Dudley Evening Mail
Senior Honours: Birmingham Senior Cup (3), Worcs Senior Cup (9), S.L. Div 1 (North), S.L. Merit Cup
Club Captain: Martin Lander
Player of the Year: Martin Lander

Sutton Coldfield Town *Back Row (L-R): R. Peyton, P. Smith, J. Winwood, K. Richardson, F. Whitehouse, A. Parsons (captain), J. Skidmore, P. Knox. Front Row (L-R): D. Holmes, G. Clegg, J. Brown, A. Keeling, D. Seddon*

SUTTON COLDFIELD TOWN

President:
Chairman: Ron Timmings
Manager: Rhys Davies
Coach: John Hayward
Physiotherapist:
Press Officer & Tel No: Ian Price
Secretary: George Humpherson
Address & Tel No: Tamworth 289817 (H) Tamworth 289999 x57 (B)
Commercial Manager: Ron Timmings
Address & Tel No: 2 Churchill Road, Sutton Coldfield 021-378 0825
Club shop: No
Address & Tel No of ground: Central Grnd, Coles Ln, Sutton Coldfield, W. Midlands B72 1NI. 021-354 2997/355 5475
Simple ground directions: Ten minutes walk from Sutton Coldfield main shopping centre
No of seats: 250 **Covered accommodation:** 200 **Capacity:** 4,500 **Floodlights:** Yes
Year formed: 1879 **Nickname:** None **Club sponsors:** None
Previous names: None
Previous grounds: None
Club colours: Royal Blue shirts/socks, White shorts
Change colours: All White
Day for midweek home matches: Wednesday
Record attendance: 2,000 v Doncaster R, F.A. Cup 1st Rnd Proper **Year:** 1980-81
Best performance in: F.A. Cup: 1980-81 1st Round Proper
F.A. Trophy: 1980-81, 1981-82 3rd Round Qualifying
Previous Leagues: Midland Combination, West Midland (Regional)
Clubhouse details: Brick building consisting of lounge and concert room (licenced)
Present players with Football League experience: Dave Seddon, Graham Clegg
Past players who progressed into the Football League: Paul Cooper, Barry Cowdrill, Noel Blake
Record transfer fee paid: £1,000
Record transfer fee received: £5,000
Programme details: 12 pages, 20p
Programme Editor: Ian Price
Local newspapers & Tel No: Sutton Coldfield News, Birmingham Evening Mail
Senior Honours: Midland Comb Div 1 (2), West Midland (Regional) League Premier Div/Premier Div League Cup (2), Walsall Senior Cup (3)
Club Captain (1983-84): Alan Parsons
Player of the Year (1983-84): Fred Whitehouse

WELLINGBOROUGH TOWN

President: F. Blackwell
Chairman: M. McMamee
Manager: I. Young
Coach: J. Daldy
Physiotherapist: D. Casey
Secretary: M. Walden
Address & Tel No: 5 Fernie Way, Wellingborough 0933 79561 (H) 76711 (B)
Commercial Manager: M. McNamee
Address & Tel No: 0604 811685
Address & Tel No of ground: London Road, Wellingborough. 0933 223536 **Club shop:** No
Simple ground directions: On A45 east of Wellingborough
No of seats: 300 **Covered accommodation:** 300 **Capacity:** 5,000 **Floodlights:** Yes
Year formed: 1867 **Nickname:** Doughboys **Club sponsors:** Saxbys
Previous names: None
Previous grounds: None
Club colours: Blue/White
Change colours: Yellow/Blue
Day for midweek home matches: Wednesday
Record attendance: 4,013 v Kettering, F.A. Cup 2nd Qual Round, Replay **Year:**
Best performance in: F.A. Cup: 1965 v Aldershot 1st Round
F.A. Trophy: 1972 1st Round
Previous Leagues: United Counties, West Midland, Metropolitan
Clubhouse details: Social club on ground with full facilities
Present players with Football League experience: W. Hurrell
Past players who progressed into the Football League: Phil Neal
Programme details: 8 pages, 20p
Programme Editor: M. Walden
Local newspapers & Tel No: Evening Telegraph Kettering 81111, Chronicle & Echo
Senior Honours: Northants Senior Cup
Club Captain (1983-4): Bill Hurrell

Hednesford Town FC *Back Row (L-R): Trevor Saunders (second team physio), Les Youll, Bob Page, Graham Glover, Vic Sharard, Dave Storey, Andy Walsh, Frank McLeod, Mick Babb (manager), Bob Wickett (coach). Front Row (L-R): Reg Pickering (1st team physio), Mark Unitt, Ian Allcock, Kevin Lane, Roger Cope, Archie King, Paul Kent (reserve and youth team manager). Picture with West Midland League Cup and West Midland League Runners-up Trophy.*

VS Rugby FC *Standing Back Row (L-R): Mick Preston (captain), Colin Burton, Stewart Gallagher, Danny Conway, Steve Harrison, Robbie Farmer, Rob McKay, John McGinty, Steve Knox, Steve Harfield. Kneeling in Front: Martin Deffered (supporters club chairman), Dave Ingram — supporters club player of the year 1983-84, Kevin Mills (mascot), John Setchell.*

V.S. RUGBY

President:
Chairman: Roy Gallimore
Managing Director: Michael Vousden
Manager: Jimmy Knox
Coach: Barrie Fergusson
Secretary: Keith Coughlan
Address & Tel No: 3 Evans Road, Rugby, Warw CV22 7HT. (0788) 814746
Commercial Manager: Jimmy Knox
Address & Tel No: 23 Dyson Close, Rugby
Physiotherapist: Barrie Fergusson
Press Officer & Tel No: Doug Hughes, Leamington (0926) 316261
Address & Tel No of ground: Butlin Road, Rugby, Warwickshire CV21 3ST. Rugby (0788) 3692
Simple ground directions: Butlin Road is off Clifton Road, Rugby which is B5414 near to Rugby Golf Club within walking distance of Rugby Midland Station — exactly 1 mile
No of seats: 200 **Covered accommodation:** 250 **Capacity:** 2,000 **Floodlights:** Yes
Year formed: 1956 **Nickname:** The Valley **Club sponsors:** Byfield Builders
Day for midweek home matches: Wednesday **Club colours:** Sky Blue/Navy and White
Previous names: Valley Sports and Valley Sports Rugby **Change colours:** Green and White
Previous Grounds: Thornfield
Record attendance: 1,777 v Great Yarmouth (F.A. Vase Semi-Final) **Year:** 1983
Previous Leagues: Rugby & District Coventry & North Warwickshire, United Counties Football, West Midlands (Reg.)
Clubhouse details: Top class facilities open 7 nights per week plus Saturday lunch and after match and Sunday lunch. Top local groups featured every Saturday evening, disco night on last Friday of month. Darts, pool and skittles teams in local leagues.
Programme details: 34 pages, 20p
Programme Editor: Doug Hughes
Club Captain (1983-84): Mick Preston **Player of the Year (1983-84):** Dave Ingram

DIVISION ONE (SOUTHERN)

ADDLESTONE & WEYBRIDGE TOWN

Chairman: B. Smith
Player/Manager: Dave Donaldson
Assist. Manager: George Talbot
Physiotherapist: Ron Lucas
Secretary: Mrs. J. Woods
Address & Tel No: Weybridge 49044
Commercial Manager: Peter Davies
Address & Tel No: Weybridge 46430
Press Officer & Tel No: J. Richards (Weybridge 40607)
Address & Tel No of ground: Liberty Lane, Addlestone, Weybridge, Surrey. Weybridge 44054 **Club shop:** Yes
Simple ground directions: From junction 11 on M25 follow signs to Addlestone. Go through 1st set of traffic lights but turn right into Liberty Lane at the second ground ½ mile on the left
No of seats: 300 **Covered accommodation:** 1,500 **Capacity:** 3,500 **Floodlights:** Yes
Year formed: 1885 **Nickname:** The Stones **Club sponsors:** Mark One
Previous names: Addlestone F.C.
Previous grounds: Six grounds
Club colours: Red shirts and shorts
Change colours: Yellow shirts and shorts
Day for midweek home matches: Wednesday
Record attendance: 2,027 v Woking **Year:** 1966
Best performance in: **F.A. Cup:** 1980-1, 1st Round Proper v Brentford (2-2, 0-2)
F.A. Trophy: 1979-80, 1980-1, 1981-2 3rd Qualifying Round
F.A. Vase: 1974-5, 1975-6 Quarter Final
Previous Leagues: West Surrey Village Competition, Spartan, Athenian
Clubhouse details: Eves: Mon, Tue & Thur 7.30-10.30pm; Fri, Sat, Wed (match days 7.30-11pm). Lunchtime Sun 12-2pm
Present players with Football League experience: Dave Donaldson (Wimbledon), Steve Finnieston (Chelsea & Sheffield U)
Past players who progressed into the Football League: None
Record transfer fee paid: £1,000 N. Fletcher (Woking)
Record transfer fee received: £1,000 K. Morris (Hayes)
Programme details: 16 pages 20p
Programme Editor: Keith Smith
Local newspapers & Tel No: Surrey Herald, Chertsey 61111; Woking News and Mail, Woking 61581; Molesey News; Walton & Weybridge Informer
Senior Honours: Spartan League Cup, Southern Comb Cup (2), Surrey Senior League, Surrey County Cup, Athenian League Div 2 Runners-up
Club Captain (1983-4): Mark Woods **Player of the year (1983-4):** Steve Matthews

Addlestone & Weybridge *Back Row (L-R): Adie Cowler, Danny Pipe, Micky Noad, Mark Woods, Colin Caulfield, Steve Finnieston, Keith Powlesland, Dave Donaldson (manager), George Talbot (assistant manager). Front Row (L-R): Steve Matthews, Noel Fletcher, John Cassidy, Tommy Hewitt, Paul Stenning.*

ANDOVER

President: J. S. Monro
Chairman: Tony Baker
Manager: Eric Lisle
Coach:
Physiotherapist: Terry Carr
Secretary: Archie Park
Address & Tel No: 32 Balmoral Road, Andover SP10 3HY. 0264 4862 (H), 0264 58611 (B)
Commercial Manager: Secretary
Address & Tel No:
Press Officer & Tel No: Secretary
Address & Tel No of ground: The Walled Meadow, London Road, Andover (3152) **Club shop:** Yes
Simple ground directions: A303 from London, take B3400, follow town centre signs to London Road
No of seats: 350 **Covered accommodation:** 800 **Capacity:** 7,000 **Floodlights:** Yes
Year formed: 1883 **Nickname:** The Lions **Club sponsors:** None
Previous names: Andover Town
Previous grounds: Weyhill Road, Andover
Club colours: Red/Black/White piping
Change colours: Tangerine
Day for midweek home matches: Wednesday
Record attendance: 4,600 v Gillingham F.A. Cup 1st Round **Year:** 1961-2
Best performance in: **F.A. Cup:** 1961-2 v Gillingham 1st Round
F.A. Trophy: 1st Qualifying Round
Previous Leagues: Salisbury District, May, Hampshire, Western
Clubhouse details: Dance hall, bars etc. As public houses (not Sundays)
Present players with Football League experience: I. Thompson (Bournemouth)
Past players who progressed into the Football League: P. Brown (Southpton, Walsall), Spackman (Bournemth)
Record transfer fee paid: £1,200 to Salisbury for Alan Green
Record transfer fee received: £1,750 from Salisbury for Ricky Hays
Programme details: 20 pages, 25p
Programme Editor: David Misledine
Local newspaper & Tel No: Andover Advertiser Andover 62600; Southern Evening Echo
Club metal badges: Yes, 40p
Senior Honours: Western League Runners-up (2), Hampshire League (7), Hants Senior Cup (4), Russell Cotes Cup (8)
Club Captain (1983-84): David Peach **Player of the Year (1983-84):** John Bailey

ASHFORD TOWN

President: J. Skinner MBE
Chairman: Doug Gillard
Manager: Chris Weller
Coach:
Physiotherapist: None
Secretary: Alan G. Lancaster
Address & Tel No: 0233 21325
Commercial Manager: Doug Gillard
Address & Tel No: Charing 2649
Press Officer & Tel No: Doug Gillard (Charing 2649)
Address & Tel No of ground: Essella Park, Essella Road, Ashford, Kent (0233 20528) **Club shop:** Yes
Simple ground directions: Leave inner ring road at the Folkestone junction. After ½-mile turn right and sharp left at Fina filling station
No of seats: 300 **Covered accommodation:** 2,000 **Capacity:** 7,000 **Floodlights:** Yes
Year formed: 1930 **Nickname:** Nuts & Bolts **Club sponsors:** None
Previous names: None **Club colours:** All Green
Previous grounds: None **Change colours:** All Yellow
Day for midweek home matches: Tuesday **Previous League:** Kent
Record attendance: 6,525 v Crystal Palace F.A. Cup 1st Round **Year:** 1959
Best performance in: F.A. Cup: 1961-2 v QPR (h) lost 3-0, 1966-7 v Swindon (a) lost 5-0 2nd Rnd
F.A. Trophy: 1972-3 v Scarborough at Peterborough, Semi-Final, lost 1-0
Clubhouse details: Small single room clubroom with bar open match days only
Present players with Football League experience: None
Past players who progressed into the Football League: Tony Godden (WBA)
Record transfer fee paid: None
Record transfer fee received: £2,500 for Alan Morton from Maidstone U
Programme details: 6 pages, 10p
Programme Editor: Allan Wilson
Local newspapers & Tel No: Kentish Express (0233 23232); Ashford Advertiser
Club metal badges: No
Senior Honours: Kent Senior Cup (2)
Club Captain (1983-4): John Barron

Ashford Town *Back Row (L-R): Tony MacDonald, John Young, Peter Carman, Liam Walsh, Peter McRobert. Middle Row (L-R): Chris Weller, Peter Lamb, Kevin Raymer, Dean Burden, John Borrow, Les Ireland, George Sergeant. Front Row (L-R): Ade Carter, Tony Reynolds, John Barton, Dave Arter.*

BASINGSTOKE TOWN

President: C. Foyle
Chairman: D. Letts
Manager: Colin Stoker
Coach:
Trainer: Bryan Wilkinson
Secretary: Bryan Banning
Address & Tel No: 7 Whitehouse Close, Basingstoke, Hants 0256 64164
Commercial Manager: Refer to Club
Address & Tel No: As Club
Press Officer & Tel No: As Secretary
Address & Tel No of ground: Camrose Ground, Western Way, Basingstoke (64353) **Club shop:** Yes
Simple ground directions: 2 miles from Rail and Bus Station. Exit 6 off M3. Near A30 road
No of seats: 830 **Covered accommodation:** 1,000 **Capacity:** 6,000 **Floodlights:** Yes
Year formed: 1886 **Nickname:** Stoke **Club sponsors:** Basingstoke Press Ltd
Previous names: None **Club colours:** Blue/Yellow trim
Previous grounds: Castle Field **Change colours:** Yellow/Blue trim
Day for midweek home matches: Wednesday **Previous League:** Hampshire
Record attendance: 4,000 v Northampton F.A. Cup, 1-5 **Year:** 1971-2
Best performance in: F.A. Cup: 1971-2 v Northampton 1st Round
F.A. Trophy: 1975-6 1st Round Proper
Clubhouse details: Club opened 11 years. Open every evening. Entertainment every weekend
Present players with Football League experience: Murray Brodie
Past players who progressed into the Football League: Tony Godfrey (Southampton), Mick Doherty (Reading)
Record transfer fee paid: £500 for Alan Tyler (Guildford)
Record transfer fee received: £2,000 for Mick Doherty (Reading)
Programme details: 20 pages, 20p
Programme Editor: David Knight
Local newspaper & Tel No: Basingstoke Gazette 61131
Club metal badges: Not at present
Senior Honours: Hants Senior Cup
Club Captain (1983-84): Steve Haysom
Player of the Year (1983-84): Keith Champ

CAMBRIDGE CITY

Chairman: D. Few
Manager: W. E. Leivers
Asst Manager: P. Martin
Coach:
Physiotherapist: Secretary
Secretary: P. Woolston
Address & Tel No: 9 Armitage Way, Cambridge CB4 2UE. 314632 (H), 357973 (Club)
Commercial Manager: J. Mills
Address & Tel No:
Press Officer & Tel No: As Secretary
Address & Tel No of ground: City Ground, Milton Road, Cambridge CB4 1UY. Cambridge 357973 **Club shop:** Yes
Simple ground directions: 50 yards on left from the beginning of A10, Cambridge to Ely Road
No of seats: 1,000 **Covered accommodation:** 8,000 **Capacity:** 16,000 **Floodlights:** Yes
Year formed: 1908 **Nickname:** City Devils **Club sponsors:** Landbeach Marina Park
Previous names: Cambridge Town
Club colours: Cambridge Blue
Previous grounds: None
Change colours: White shirts, Black shorts
Day for midweek home matches: Wednesday
Record attendance: 22,000 v Walthamstow Avenue **Year:** 1950
Best performance in: F.A. Cup: 1965 1st Round proper
F.A. Trophy: 1978 1st Round proper
Previous Leagues: Southern Amateur, Spartan, Athenian
Clubhouse details: Open every night. Bingo, dances, darts, pool stag nights
Present players with Football League experience: Keith Pointer, Jon O'Donnell
Past players who progressed into the Football League: Tommy Carroll (Ipswich)
Record transfer fee paid: £500 Dave Hickson
Record transfer fee received: £1,500 Tommy Carrol to Ipswich
Programme details: 12 pages, 20p
Local newspaper & Tel No: Cambridge Evening News 358877
Programme Editor: Paul Martin
Senior Honours: County Cup
Club Captain (1983-84): Phil Hubbard
Player of the Year (1983-84): Phil Hubbard

Basingstoke *Back Row (L-R): B. Schmidt, J. Adams, T. Clegg, I. Gosling, T. Jones, I. Terry, K. Champ, B. Budd, S. Haysom, S. Trotter, C. Stoker (manager). Middle Row (L-R): B. Combs, S. Frangou, M. Murphy, M. Brodie, T. Davies, D. Pearce, G. Yates, B. Snow, A. Green. Front Row (L-R): I. Spreadborough, P. Heather, P. Upton, J. Gregory, M. Brown, B. Winter, D. Maguire.*
Photo: Basingstoke Gazette

CANTERBURY CITY

President: F. Wood
Chairman: K. Longley
Manager: Alf Bentley
Coach:
Physiotherapist: None
Secretary: V. H. Heslop
Address & Tel No: 119 Tennyson Avenue, Canterbury, Kent CT1 1ER. 68555 (H)
Commercial Manager: D. Owen
Address & Tel No: 455880
Press Officer & Tel No: Keith Smith (456116)
Address & Tel No of ground: Kingsmead Stadium, Kingsmead Road, Canterbury, Kent. 464732 **Club shop:** Yes
Simple ground directions: A28 sign posted
No of seats: 600 **Covered accommodation:** 1,500 **Capacity:** 10,000 **Floodlights:** Yes
Year formed: 1947 **Nickname:** The 'City' **Club sponsors:** Three Way School of Motoring
Previous names: Canterbury Waverley
Club colours: Green shirts, Black shorts, Green socks
Previous grounds: Bretts Corner
Change colours: All Blue
Day for midweek home matches: Tuesday
Record attendance: 3,001 v Torquay F.A. Cup 1st Round **Year:** 1964
Best performance in: F.A. Cup: 1964 v Torquay, 1968 v Swindon 1st Round
F.A. Trophy: 1974-5 2nd Round v Dagenham
Previous Leagues: Kent, Metropolitan
Clubhouse details: Bar open matchdays
Present players with Football League experience: Graham Knight (Gillingham), Jimmy McVeigh (Wolves), Tony Bottiglieri (Gillingham), Gary Pugh (AFC Bournemouth)
Past players who progressed into the Football League: Pat Hilton (Brighton), Tommy Horsfall (Cambridge), Terry Norton (Brighton), Mark Weatherly (Gillingham), Dave Wiltshire (Gillingham)
Record transfer fee paid: £1,000 for Graham Knight (Maidstone U.)
Record transfer fee received: £2,000 for David Wiltshire (Gillingham)
Programme details: 16 pages
Local newspapers & Tel No: Kentish Gazette (68181)
Programme Editor: Keith Smith
Senior Honours: Kent League Cup, Kent Messenger Trophy, Kent Senior Cup, Kent Senior Trophy
Club Captain (1983-84): Jimmy McVeigh
Player of the Year (1983-84): Tommy Warrilow

CHATHAM TOWN

Chairman: B. A. Troke
Manager: B. J. Watling
Coach: J. Whiteley
Physiotherapist: J. Whiteley
Secretary: H. A. Salkind
Address & Tel No: 17 Crestway, Chatham, Kent. Medway 49834
Commercial Manager:
Press Officer & Tel No: R. S. Salkind. Medway 50920
Address & Tel No of ground: Maidstone Road Ground, Maidstone Road, Chatham, Kent. (Medway) 43678
Simple ground directions: M2 — A229 Chatham turn off, follow signs to Chatham. Ground approx 1½ miles on right opposite garage
No of seats: 600 **Covered accommodation:** 1,000 **Capacity:** 5,000 **Floodlights:** Yes
Year formed: 1882 **Nickname:** Chats **Club sponsors:** None
Previous names:
Club colours: All Red
Previous grounds: None
Change colours: All White
Day for midweek home matches: Tuesday
Record attendance: 5,500 **Year:** 1980
Best performance in: **F.A. Cup:** 1889 beat Nottm Forest 2-0, Quarter Final
F.A. Trophy: 1970-1 last 16
Previous League: Aetolian, Southern, Kent
Clubhouse details: Open Tuesday, Thursday evenings, Saturday, match days, Sunday lunchtime
Present players with Football League experience: D. Richardson, J. Hutton, D. Grant, S. Brown
Past players who progressed into the Football League:
Programme details:
Local newspaper & Tel No: Chatham News
Programme Editor: C. Coward
Senior Honours: Kent League Champions (4) Runners-up (3), Kent League Cup Winners (2) Runners-up (3)
Club Captain (1983-84): Steve Brown **Player of the Year (1983-84):** Nigel Pointon

DORCHESTER TOWN

Chairman: P. Aiken
Manager: Keith Miller
Coach:
Physiotherapist: Bill Hall
Secretary: A. E. Miller
Address & Tel No: 29 Shaston Crescent, Dorchester. 03056 64843 (H) 03056 6236 (B)
Commercial Manager: None
Press Officer & Tel No: S. Legge
Address & Tel No of ground: The Avenue Ground, Dorchester, Dorset. Dorchester 62451 **Club shop:** Yes
Simple ground directions: Half mile from centre on Weymouth Road
No of seats: 280 **Covered accommodation:** 3,000 **Capacity:** 6,000 **Floodlights:** Yes
Year formed: 1880 **Nickname:** The Magpies **Club sponsors:** Old's Motor Group
Previous names: None
Club colours: Black/White striped shirts/Black
Previous grounds: None
Change colours: All Red
Day for midweek home matches: Tuesday
Record attendance: 5,000 v Bournemouth, F.A. Cup **Year:** 1981
Previous League: Western
Best performance in: **F.A. Cup:** 1954-55, 1957-58, 1981-82 2nd Round Proper
F.A. Trophy: 1971-2 3rd Round
Clubhouse details: Magpie social club and vice-presidents club within the ground. Open every evening
Present players with Football League experience: K. Miller (West Ham, Bournemouth), Kevin Dove (Northampton), Derek Showers (Bournemouth, Cardiff City)
Past players who progressed into the Football League: T. Senior (Portsmouth), D. West (Liverpool)
Record transfer fee paid: £1,500 to Yeovil for Kevin Leigh
Record transfer fee received: £35,000 from Portsmouth for Trevor Senior
Programme details: 24 pages, free with admission
Club metal badges: Yes
Local newspapers & Tel No: Dorset Evening Echo, Western Gazette, Western Daily Press
Senior Honours: Southern League Div 1 (South), Mark Frowde Cup (last 3 years)

DOVER ATHLETIC

Chairman: J. Husk
Manager: Alan Jones
Coach: B. Hutchinson
Physiotherapist:
Secretary: M. J. Taylor
Address & Tel No: 5 Owen Square, Walmer, Deal, Kent. Deal 374557 (H), 373256 (B), Dover 202623 (B)
Commercial Manager: Secretary
Press Officer & Tel No: Secretary
Address & Tel No:
Address & Tel No of ground: Lewisham Road, River Dover. Kearsney 822306 **Club shop:** Yes
Simple ground directions: Main A2 from Canterbury to Hammonds Roundabout, follow directions to town centre, left first T junction, right at traffic lights
No of seats: 855 **Covered accommodation:** 4,000 **Capacity:** 9,000 **Floodlights:** Yes
Year formed: 1983 **Nickname:** Lillywhites **Club sponsors:** Sealink
Previous names: Dover United, Dover
Club colours: Black/white striped shirts, Black shorts, Red socks
Previous grounds: None
Day for midweek home matches: Wednesday
Change colours: All Red
Record attendance: 6,900 v Folkestone, FA Cup **Year:** 1951-2
Previous League: Kent
Best performance in: **F.A. Cup:** 1975-6 lost to Southend 2nd Round
F.A. Trophy: 1970-1 last 16
Clubhouse details: Social club with bars, open each match day and every Thursday, Friday and Saturday evenings. Cabaret on Saturdays, light refreshments. **Steward:** Mr. K. Hughes
Present players with Football League experience: None
Past players who progressed into the Football League: P. Broadbent (Wolves), A. Knight (Brighton), T. Horsfall (Southend), G. Pugh (Bournemouth)
Record transfer fee paid: T. Jolley from Gillingham £4,000
Record transfer fee received: A. Knight to Brighton £12,000
Programme details: 16 pages, 10p
Club metal badges: Yes
Local newspaper & Tel No: Dover Express (Dover 201660)
Senior Honours: Kent Senior Cup (7), Kent Senior Shield, Southern League Div 1 (as Dover F.C.)

DUNSTABLE

Chairman: P. Culley
Managers: To be appointed
Coach:
Physiotherapist: C. Jones
Secretary: H. Stew
Address & Tel No: 0582 63755
Commercial Manager: None
Address & Tel No:
Press Officer & Tel No: John Crumley (0582 67638). Clubroom 63800 **Club shop:** Yes
Address & Tel No of ground: Creasey Park, Brewers Hill Rd, Dunstable, Beds. Dun. 606691 (Boardroom), 63800 (Club)
Simple ground directions: Brewers Hill Road runs west from A505 at the north end of Dunstable at large traffic island
No of seats: 500 **Covered accommodation:** 750 **Capacity:** 10,000 **Floodlights:** Yes
Year formed: 1895 **Nickname:** The Blues **Club sponsors:** None
Previous names: Dunstable Town
Previous grounds: Kingsway, Dunstable
Club colours: Royal Blue
Change colours: All Red
Day for midweek home matches: Wednesday
Record attendance: 6,000 **Year:** 1974
Best performance in: **F.A. Cup:** 1956 1st Round
F.A. Trophy: 1971-2, 1975-6 3rd Qualifying Round
Previous Leagues: Metropolitan, Hellenic, United Counties
Clubhouse details: Large clubroom and bar, small room and bar, restaurant, full catering service
Present players with Football League experience: G. Banton (Plymouth, Fulham)
Past players who progressed into the Football League: K. Dixon
Record transfer fee paid: £1,500 — S. Atkins (from Wycombe, 1979)
Record transfer fee received: £20,000 from Reading for Kerry Dixon
Programme details: (including adverts) 20 pages, 20p
Programme Editor: John Crumley (0582-67638)
Local newspapers & Tel No: Dunstable Gazette, Leader, Herald, Chronicle, Echo
Senior Honours: Beds. Senior Cup (3 times), Beds Premier Cup (2 times)
Club Captain (1983-4): Jim McCarthy **Player of the year (1983-4):** Mark Fordham

ERITH & BELVEDERE

President: A. D. Clarke
Chairman: G. Cornes
Manager: P. Peters
Coach: P. Peters
Physiotherapist: R. Bates
Secretary: L. G. Meakins
Address & Tel No: 0322 29406
Commercial Manager: J. Freeman
Address & Tel No: 01-300 1280
Press Officer & Tel No: R. Fysh (Erith 33762)
Address & Tel No of ground: Park View, Lower Road, Belvedere, Kent. 01-311 4444 **Club shop:** No
Simple ground directions: Adjoining Belvedere SR Station
No of seats: 800 **Covered accommodation:** 3,000 **Capacity:** 8,000 **Floodlights:** Yes
Year formed: 1922 **Nickname:** Deres **Club sponsors:** None
Previous names: None
Previous grounds: None
Club colours: Blue/White
Change colours: White
Day for midweek home matches: Tuesday
Record attendance: 8,000 v Coventry, F.A. Cup **Year:** 1932
Best performance in: **F.A. Cup:** 1933 1st Round
F.A. Vase: 1981 2nd Round
Previous Leagues: Kent, Corinthian, Athenian
Clubhouse details: Large Licensed Social Bar and separate Tea Bar
Present players with Football League experience: None
Past players who progressed into the Football League: None
Record transfer fee received: None
Programme details: 16 pages, 20p
Club metal badges: No
Programme Editor: Ray Fysh
Local newspapers & Tel No: Kentish Times, Kentish Independent
Senior Honours: London Senior Cup, F.A. Amateur Finalists (2), Kent League, Kent Senior Cup, Kent League Cup Finalists, Kent Amateur Cup, Finalists Kent Senior Trophy
Club Captain (1983-84): Geoff Cornes **Player of the Year (1983-84):** Neil Lawrence

Gosport Borough *Back Row (L-R): Steve Ingman, Tony Mahony, Tony Stares, Paul Reay, Gary Juryeff. Middle Row (L-R): Stan Marlow (assistant manager), Richard Reed, Ali Unitt, Andy Lowman, Roger Buckland, David Lappage, John Hawes, Tony Callahan, Graham Wake, Peter Edgar (joint manager). Front Row (L-R): M. Richardson (life president), W.J. Adams (honorary secretary & life president), F.G. Schomberg (president), Mayor of Gosport, P.A. Wall (chairman), A.E. Cooper (vice chairman), P. Campbell (publicity officer).*

GOSPORT BOROUGH

President: F. G. Schomberg
Chairman: P. A. Wall
Manager: A. J. Brickwood/P. Edgar (joint)
Coach: P. Mullice
Physiotherapist: K. E. Pyke
Secretary: W. J. Adams
Address & Tel No: "Clapper Oaks", 13 Bentham Road, Alverstoke, Gosport 581604 (H)
Commercial Manager: As Secretary
Address & Tel No:
Press Officer & Tel No: Paul Campbell (Gosport 528579)
Address & Tel No of ground: Privett Park, Privett Road, Gosport 583986 **Club shop:** Yes
Simple ground directions: A32 from Fareham for approx 3 miles. Follow signs from Fort Brockhurst to Privett Park.
No of seats: 600 **Covered accommodation:** 600 **Capacity:** 5,000 **Floodlights:** Yes
Year formed: 1944 **Nickname:** The Borough **Club sponsors:** M. D. Weston & Co (Builders)
Previous names: Gosport Borough Athletic
Club colours: Yellow/Blue/Yellow
Previous grounds: None
Change colours: All White
Day for midweek home matches: Tuesday
Previous League: Hampshire
Record attendance: 4,770 v Pegasus F.A. Amateur Cup 1st Round **Year:** 1950-1
Best performance in: **F.A. Cup:** 1980-1 v Windsor & Eton 0-2 (a), 4th Qual Round
F.A. Vase: 1976-7 v Barton R 1-1, 1-3 (a) 6th Round
F.A. Trophy: 1980-1 v Aylesbury 0-1 (a) 3rd Qual Round
Clubhouse details: Bar facilities available to club members and visitors on match days. Open most evenings Mon-Sat
Present players with Football League experience: None
Past players who progressed into the Football League: Peter Harris (Portsmouth), Jimmy Scoular (Portsmouth, Newcastle), Albert Mundy (Portsmouth), Ronnie Blackman (Reading), Gary Juryeff (Portsmouth)
Record transfer fee received: £5,000
Programme details: 8 pages, 10p
Club metal badges: No
Programme Editor: Paul Campbell
Senior Honours: Hampshire League (3)
Local newspaper & Tel No: Portsmouth Evening News Gosport 587621
Club Captain (1983-4): Tony Mahoney
Player of the Year (1983-4): Ali Unitt

HILLINGDON

Chairman: Bernard Thistle
Manager: Alan Humphries
Coach:
Physiotherapist: Roy Clark
Match Secretary: Mike Stapleton
Address & Tel No: 01-848 9060 (H), 01-561 8049 (B)
Press Officer & Tel No: Alan Humphries (West Drayton 45292)
Address & Tel No of ground: Leas Stadium, Falling Lane, Yiewsley, W. Drayton, Middx. 42948/45292 **Club shop:** Yes
Simple ground directions: Five minutes walk from town centre, nearest station, West Drayton (B.R.)
No of seats: 1,000 **Covered accommodation:** 9,000 **Capacity:** 13,000 **Floodlights:** Yes
Year formed: 1872 **Nickname:** The Blues **Club sponsors:** None
Previous names: Yiewsley Town
Club colours: Light Blue/Dark Blue
Previous grounds: Evelyns
Change colours: All White
Day for midweek home matches: Tuesday
Previous Leagues: Corinthian, Delphian
Record attendance: 9,033 v Luton F.A. Cup **Year:** 1969
Best performance in: **F.A. Cup:** 1969-70 lost to Sutton Utd 3rd Round replay
F.A. Trophy: 1970-1 lost to Telford Utd Final
Clubhouse details: Open 7 days a week, lunchtimes and evenings. Thursday, Friday and Sunday evenings – bingo. Saturday evening – dances, darts and pool also available
Present players with Football League experience: Chris Ampofo, Jimmy Sweetzer, Eddie Reeve, Paul Waites, Vince Durcan
Past players who progressed into the Football League: Various, mostly recently Robert Rosario (Norwich City)
Record transfer fee paid: £2,000
Record transfer fee received: £7,000
Programme details: 12 pages, 20p
Programme Editor: Graham Wiseman
Senior Honours: Middlesex Charity Cup
Local newspapers & Tel No: Middlesex Advertiser & Gazette (Ux. 37161)

POOLE TOWN

President: F. Rowe
Chairman: G. K. Dexter
Manager: Roger Bazeley
Coach: Brian Chambers
Physiotherapist: K. Sturgess
Secretary: David Gill
Address & Tel No: Poole Town F.C., The Stadium, Wimborne Road, Poole. Poole 674747
Commercial Manager: G. K. Dexter
Address & Tel No: c/o Club
Press Officer & Tel No: G. K. Dexter, c/o Club
Address & Tel No of ground: The Stadium, Wimborne Road, Poole, Dorset BH15 2BP. Poole 674747 **Club shop:** Yes
Simple ground directions: Centre of Poole. Stadium behind fire station & Barclays International, adjacent to BR station
No of seats: 750 **Covered accommodation:** 1,500 **Capacity:** 11,500 **Floodlights:** Yes
Year formed: 1880 **Nickname:** The Dolphins **Club sponsors:** Deansport
Previous names: None
Previous grounds:
Club colours: Yellow shirts, Blue shorts, Yellow socks
Change colours: Blue shirts, White shorts/socks
Day for midweek home matches: Monday
Record attendance: 11,155 v Watford F.A. Cup **Year:** 1962-3
Previous Leagues: Western
Best performance in: F.A. Cup: Newport County (year not known)
F.A. Trophy: 1969-70, 1970-1, 1974-5 1st Round proper
Clubhouse details: Open every evening and lunchtime. Occasional entertainment in evenings
Present players with Football League experience: B. Chambers, K. Allen, N. Merrick
Past players who progressed into the Football League: B Iles (Chelsea), P Ferns, jnr (Bournem'th), D Lyon (S'thport)
Record transfer fee paid: £1,500 Derek Courtney
Record transfer fee received: £3,000 Paul Morell to Bath City
Programme details: usually 16 pages, 20p
Programme Editor: Chris Reeves
Club metal badges: Yes
Local newspapers & Tel No: Evening Echo, Bournemouth 0202 24601; Local Radio: 2CR, Southcote Rd, B'mouth
Senior Honours: Western League, Western Counties Cup (2), Anglo-Italian Tournament Runners-up
Club Captain (1983-4): Neil Merrick **Player of the Year (1983-4):** Neil Merrick

SALISBURY

President: J. Benson
Chairman: Ray McEnhill
Manager: G. Butler
Coach:
Physiotherapist: D. Barnes
Secretary: Derek F. Sharp
Address & Tel No: Salisbury 27248
Commercial Manager: G. Butler
Address & Tel No: Salisbury 26454
Press Officer & Tel No: Jon Hancock
Address & Tel No of ground: Victoria Park, Castle Road, Salisbury (Salisbury 336689) **Club shop:** Yes
Simple ground directions: On A345 north of city centre road to Amesbury/Stonehenge 800 yards from inner ring road
No of seats: 300 **Covered accommodation:** 1,000 (incl stand) **Capacity:** 8,000 **Floodlights:** Yes
Year formed: 1947 **Nickname:** None **Club sponsors:** Churchfields Dairies
Previous names: None
Previous grounds: None
Club colours: White/Black
Change colours: Red/White
Day for midweek home matches: Tuesday
Record attendance: 8,900 v Weymouth, Western League **Year:** 1948
Previous League: Western
Best performance in: F.A. Cup: 1959-60 2nd Round
F.A. Trophy: 3rd Qualifying Round on 4 occasions
Clubhouse details: Open 7 nights a week, Saturday and Sunday lunchtime. Lounge bar and dance room also used for bingo and other social functions. Week-end entertainment
Present players with Football League experience: Geoff Butler, Lee Frost, Brian Smith, Tommy Paterson, Kevin Dawtry
Past players who progressed into the Football League: Ian Thompson
Record transfer fee paid: £1,750 for Richard Haysom
Record transfer fee received: £16,000 for Thompson from AFC Bournemouth
Programme details: 16 pages (own production), 20p
Programme Editor: Jon Hancock
Club metal badges: Yes
Local newspapers & Tel No: Salisbury Journal (336933) Southern Daily Echo (334293)
Senior Honours: Wiltshire County Shield, Hants Senior Cup
Club Captain (1983-84): Lee Frost

SHEPPEY UNITED

President: None
Chairman: V. E. Ward
Manager: Dave Perkins
Coach: A. Woolford
Physiotherapist: None
Secretary: G. E. Carpenter
Address & Tel No: 53 Cecil Avenue, Sheerness, Kent ME12 1DX. 0795 662013
Commercial Manager: W. Vellin
Address & Tel No: 0795 662301
Address & Tel No of ground: Botany Road, St. George's Avenue, Sheerness, Kent. 0795 665299
Simple ground directions: 200 yards from main shopping area of Sheerness
No of seats: 400 **Covered accommodation:** 2,000 **Capacity:** 7,000 **Floodlights:** Yes
Year formed: 1889 **Nickname:** Islanders **Club sponsors:** None
Club colours: Red and White shirts, Black shorts **Change colours:** All Light Blue
Previous Names: Sheppey Athletic **Previous Grounds:** None
Record attendance: 3,000 v Sittingbourne **Year:** 1922
Best performance in: F.A. Cup: 1975-76 v Canterbury, 2nd Qual Round
F.A. Trophy: 1969-70 v Dover, 3rd Qual Round
Previous Leagues: Metropolitan, Greater London, Aetolian
Clubhouse details: Open Match day only
Programme details: 6 pages, 10p
Club metal badges: No
Programme Editor: Peter Fagg
Club Honours: Kent Amateur Cup Winners 1946, 1952; Kent Senior Shield Winners 1978; Kent League Champions 1973, 1975, 1979; Kent League Div I Winners 1976, 1979
Club Captain (1983-84): Andy Woolford **Player of the Year (1983-84):** David Samwell

THANET UNITED

President: R. W. Griffiths
Chairman: D. Lazell
Manager: J. Wickens
Coach: P. Winfield
Physiotherapist: D. Garrod
Secretary: R. J. Hopper
Address & Tel No: 71 High Street, Garlinge, Nr Margate, Kent.
Commercial Manager:
Lottery Officer: G. Launder (0843) 34838
Press Officer & Tel No: D. Scott, 21969 **Club shop:** Yes
Address & Tel No of ground: Hartsdown Park, Hartsdown Road, Margate, Kent. Thanet (0843) 21769
Simple ground directions: Hartsdown Park is five minutes walk from Margate station (Southern Region). Turn right at roundabout, under bridge, left into Tivoli Road. Ground on right beyond golf course
No of seats: 650 approx. **Covered accommodation:** All **Capacity:** 8,500 **Floodlights:** Yes
Year formed: Reformed 1929, 1981 **Nickname:** The 'Gate or the Islanders **Club sponsors:** Various.
Previous names: Margate
Club colours: White/Blue/Red
Previous grounds: Dreamland, Northdown Park
Change colours: Red/White/White or Blue
Day for midweek home matches: Tuesday
Previous League: Kent
Record attendance: 8,500 v Tottenham, F.A. Cup 3rd Round **Year:** Jan 1973
Best performance in: F.A. Cup: 1936-7 3rd Rnd v Blackpool (a), 1972-3 v Spurs (h)
F.A. Trophy: 1978-9 3rd Round Replay v Runcorn (h)
Clubhouse details: Social club open on match days, snacks available by special arrangement with social club committee
Present players with Football League experience: T. Norton (Brighton)
Past players who progressed into the Football League: D. Carr (Luton, Lincoln), T. Jenkins (Reading, Southampton, Swindon), R. Flannigan (Reading), B. Gregory (Luton), J. O'Mara (Aldershot), L. Smelt (Gravesend, N. Forest)
Record transfer fee paid: £3,750, Neil Cugley, March 1978
Record transfer fee received: £2,500
Programme details: 16 pages, 20p
Programme Editor: R. J. Hopper
Local newspapers & Tel No: Isle of Thanet Gazette/ Thanet Times, Thanet (0843) 21313; Thanet Extra
Club metal badges: Not yet
Senior Honours: Southern League (2); Southern League Div 1 (2); Southern League Cup, Finalists (2); Southern League Merit Cup (2); Kent Senior Cup (3); Kent Floodlit Cup (3)
Club Captain (1983-84): Terry Norton **Player of the Year (1983-84):** Steve Dudley

TONBRIDGE A.F.C.

Chairman: W. Wheeler
Manager: John Keirs
Coach: John Keirs
Physiotherapist: Clifford Gower
Secretary: Mrs. P. A. Westguard
Address & Tel No: 7 Baltic Road, Tonbridge, Kent. Ton. 358492 (H), Ton. 352417 (B)
Commercial Manager: None
Press Officer & Tel No: Kevan Martin. 0622 51511 (H), 01-222 0721 (B)
Address & Tel No of ground: Longmead Stadium, Darenth Avenue, Tonbridge, Kent (Ton. 352417) **Club shop:** Yes
Simple ground directions: From Tonbridge station through High Street, up Shipbourne Road to Pinnacles pub, Darenth Avenue immediately left, then straight on down for Longmead Stadium, approx 2 miles walk
No of seats: None **Covered accommodation:** Standing one side **Capacity:** 5,000 **Floodlights:** Yes
Year formed: 1948, New company 1976 **Nickname:** The Angels **Club sponsors:** Cannon Lane Timbers
Previous names: Tonbridge F.C.
Club colours: Blue/Navy Blue
Previous grounds: The Angel until 1950
Change colours: Yellow/White
Day for midweek home matches: Tuesday
Previous League: None
Record attendance: 8,236 v Aldershot, F.A. Cup 1st Round **Year:** 1951
Best performance in: F.A. Cup: 1951-2, 1952-3, 1967-8, 1972-3 1st Round proper
F.A. Trophy: 1970-1, 1971-2 1st Round proper
Clubhouse details: Licensed bar, tea bar. Open match days, Tuesday and Thursday evenings, Sunday lunchtimes
Present players with Football League experience: J. Keirs (Charlton), Tony Booth (Charlton)
Past players who progressed into the Football League: R Saunders, M MacDonald, T Burns, I Seymour, G Moseley
Record transfer fee paid: None
Record transfer fee received: None
Programme details: 8 pages, 15p
Programme Editor: Kevan Martin
Club metal badges: Yes
Local newspapers & Tel No: Kent & Sussex Courier (T.W. 26262), Kent Messenger (Maid. 77880) News Review (T.W. 46577)
Senior Honours: Southern League Cup Runners-up (2), Kent Senior Cup (2) Runners-up (2), Kent Senior Shield (4)
Club Captain (1983-84): Phil Stonebridge **Player of the Year (1983-84):** Mark Gillham

WATERLOOVILLE

Chairman: F. P. Faulkner
Manager: Ernie Bradwell
Coach:
Physiotherapist: Len Slaughter, S.R.P., Mc.S.P.
Press Officer & Tel No: R. Stainton
Secretary: M. Richards
Address & Tel No: 0705 388119 (H)
Commercial Manager: R. Stainton
Address & Tel No: Waterlooville 55333
Address & Tel No of ground: Jubilee Park, Aston Road, Waterlooville (3867) **Club shop:** Yes
Simple ground directions: Town by-pass road, take righthand turning at roundabout, first turning right Aston Road
No of seats: 560 **Covered accommodation:** 1,000 **Capacity:** 6,000 **Floodlights:** Yes
Year formed: 1910 **Nickname:** Ville **Club sponsors:** H. Standley & Sons (Portsmouth) Ltd, Toyota dealer
Previous names: None
Previous grounds: Waterlooville Rec.
Club colours: All White
Change colours: All Yellow
Day for midweek home matches: Monday
Record attendance: 4,500 v Wycombe Wanderers F.A. Cup **Year:** 1976-7
Best performance in: **F.A. Cup:** 1983-84, 1st Round 2nd Replay
F.A. Trophy: 1976-77 2nd Round
Previous Leagues: Waterlooville District, Portsmouth, Hampshire County
Clubhouse details: Open every night and lunchtime. Three bars, cabaret room, disco room, function room, 6 squash courts, sports hall (3 badminton courts, basketball, indoor cricket, etc.)
Present players with Football League experience: Mick Mellows (Portsmouth), Manny Andruszewski (Southampton), Lee Harwood (Port Vale)
Past players who progressed into the Football League: None
Record transfer fee paid: £50
Record transfer fee received: None
Programme details: 16 pages, 20p
Local newspaper & Tel No: News (Portsmouth 64488)
Programme Editor: Andy Stonebridge
Senior Honours: Hampshire Senior Cup (2), Southern league Div I
Club Captain (1983-84): Calvin Hore
Player of the Year (1983-84): Calvin Hore

WOODFORD TOWN

President: Bobby Moore, OBE
Chairman: Wm. Larkin
Manager: M. Newman
Coach: A. Shaw
Physiotherapist:
Secretary: V. Hammerton
Address & Tel No: 0279 52821 (H) 01-534 3983 (B)
Commercial Manager: Secretary
Address & Tel No:
Press Officer & Tel No: K. Drury. Romford 68710
Address & Tel No of ground: Snakes Lane East, Woodford Green, Essex. Tel: 01-504 0831 **Club shop:** Yes
Simple ground directions: Woodford Station (Central line). From station turn into Snakes Lane East, follow road, direct to ground, about 8 mins
No of seats: 400 **Covered accommodation:** 500 **Capacity:** 3,500 **Floodlights:** Yes
Year formed: 1937 **Nickname:** The Town **Club sponsors:** MOR Shipping
Previous names: None
Previous grounds: Woodford Wells
Club colours: White shirts, Black shorts
Change colours: Red and White
Day for midweek home matches: Tuesday
Record attendance: v Colchester United, FA Cup **Year:** 1952
Best performance in: **F.A. Cup:** 1951-2, 1958-9 4th Qualifying Round
F.A. Vase: 1981-2 3rd Round
Previous Leagues: Athenian, Essex Senior, Southern, Delphian, Metropolitan
Clubhouse details: Woody's Club, luxuriously appointed
Present players with Football League experience: M. Taylor (Charlton Ath)
Past players who progressed into the Football League: C. Flatt (Orient, Southend)
Record transfer fee paid: None
Record transfer fee received: £10,000 from Norwich City for Peter Fishenden
Programme details: 12 pages, included in admission
Local newspapers & Tel No: Recorder & Guardian 478 4444/531 4140
Club metal badges: No
Senior Honours: None
Club Captain (1983-84): David Gregory
Player of the Year (1983-84): David Gregory

SOUTHERN PREMIER DIVISION

DIVISION ONE (MIDLANDS)				DIVISION ONE (SOUTHERN)				
W Midland (Regional) League	**Midland** Combination	**United** Counties League	**Eastern** Counties League	**Hellenic** League	**Kent** League	**Sussex** League	**Hampshire** League	**Western** League

Clubs from the nine feeder leagues who are recommended by their League Management committees for Southern League membership, may be elected if they receive more votes than the clubs seeking re-election at the foot of the two Divisions One. i.e. At the end of last season Hednesford Town (West Midland (Regional) League) swapped places with Tamworth (Division One (Midland)) and Sheppey United (Kent League) took the place of Hounslow in Division One (Southern). The Middlesex club were accepted by the Hellenic League which suited them best geographically.

WEST MIDLANDS (REGIONAL) LEAGUE

President: R. H. Juggins

Secretary: K. H. Goodfellow
43 Yardley Green Road, Bordesley Green, Birmingham B9 5PU. Tel: 021-772 0375

HALESOWEN WIN 32 LEAGUE GAMES

The past year has been perhaps in many respects one of the best years the League has enjoyed for some time. The particularly mild weather during the winter months has meant that fixture programmes have been carried out with minimum disruption. Halesowen Town FC have once again had a very successful season in the League, winning 32 out of their 38 games clinching the League title quite early on in the season as compared with last season.

In the Premier Division League Cup it took three matches for an eventual winner to be declared and then Hednesford Town FC had a resounding victory over Shifnal Town FC, winning 5-nil. Hednesford Town FC were also League runners-up and have now moved to the Southern League, being replaced by Tamworth FC.

It would appear in Division One for the last three seasons the team who win the League also win the League Cup, and once again Tipton Town FC won the League, playing 30 games with 47 points, while Gornal Athletic FC were runners-up. Tipton Town FC also defeated Cheltenham Town FC Reserves to take the League Cup.

Congratulations must go to Tipton Town FC on being promoted to the Premier Division, replacing Cradley Town FC who have been relegated to the First Division, while Cheltenham Town FC Reserves, Hednesford Town FC Reserves, and Willenhall Town FC Reserves have all resigned from Division One.

Promoted to the First Division are Halesowen FC Reserves, who won the Second Division title, Westfields FC who were runners-up, Newport Town FC, Pelsall Villa FC and Wolverhampton Casuals FC, bringing the strength of the Division up to 18 clubs. While in the Second Division League Cup Pelsall Villa FC went down 1-0 to Westfields FC.

The following new clubs were accepted into Division Two: Broseley Athletic FC, Bloxwich Town FC, Ettingshall HT FC, Halesowen Harriers FC, Jamaica City FC, Minworth FC and Stuarts Athletic FC.

During the past season ground inspections have been carried out at every club in the League and also to the new applicants and a grading will be made to all clubs during next season. It is essential to maintain the status of the League in view of the fact that the League has been selected as one of the appointed leagues within the new Referees System, for which we are very proud.

In "outside" Cup competitions it was very encouraging to note that in the Walsall Senior Cup all the last eight teams were West Midlands (Regional) League teams, with Atherstone United defeating Tividale FC 4-0 in the Final and Halesowen Town FC defeating Dudley Town FC in the Birmingham Senior Cup 1-0 after extra time.

K. GOODFELLOW

Roy Priest scores the winning goal for Wolverhampton United at Rushall Olympic. Photo: Leo Hoenig

West Midlands (Regional) League

Premier Division

	P	W	D	L	F	A	Pts
Halesowen Town	38	32	3	3	112	36	67
Hednesford Town	38	23	10	5	70	34	56
Atherstone United	38	17	11	10	63	44	45
Gresley Rovers	38	17	9	12	68	61	43
Lye Town	38	15	12	11	55	45	42
Wolverhampton U	38	17	7	14	53	55	41
Oldswinford	38	15	11	12	61	64	41
Armitage	38	17	5	16	67	61	39
Shifnal Town	38	13	12	13	59	56	38
Wednesfield Social	38	15	8	15	52	58	38
Tividale	38	12	12	14	53	48	36
Malvern Town	38	14	7	17	64	61	35
Rushall Olympic	38	11	11	16	55	59	33
Hinckley Athletic	38	12	9	17	51	61	33
GKN Sankey	38	13	7	18	54	74	33
Brereton Social	38	10	12	16	46	62	32
Bilston Town	38	10	11	17	44	58	31
Blakenall	38	11	7	20	39	59	29
Chasetown	38	9	8	21	39	81	26
Bradley Town	38	9	4	25	44	72	22

League Cup:
Hednesford Town 1 Shifnal Town 1 aet.
1st Replay: 0-0 aet.
2nd Replay: 5-0.

Division 1

	P	W	D	L	F	A	Pts
Tipton Town	30	18	11	1	65	28	47
Gornal Athletic	30	18	8	4	60	29	44
Northpark United	30	19	5	6	73	23	43
Harrisons	30	19	5	6	60	29	43
Cheltenham T Res	30	13	10	7	51	37	36
Brewood	30	14	7	9	49	36	35
Great Wyrley	30	13	6	11	52	44	32
Darlaston	30	14	3	13	49	40	31
Dudley Town Res	30	9	9	12	31	43	27
Lichfield	30	10	6	14	34	44	26
Willenhall T Res	30	6	10	14	33	58	22
Nuneaton Brgh Res	30	8	6	16	31	60	22
Ludlow Town	30	8	4	18	38	64	20
Hednesford T Res	30	5	9	16	36	58	19
Shirley Town	30	3	11	16	27	63	17
Bilston United	30	3	10	17	26	59	16

League Cup:
Tipton Town 2 Cheltenham Town Res 0.

Leading Goalscorers Season 1983-84

Premier Division

P. Joinson	Halesown Town	31
N. A. Tilley	Gresley Rovers	26
G. Westwood	Armitage	24
M. J. Folland	Rushall Olympic	23
L. Joinson	Halesowen Town	22
R. Sidaway	Lye Town	22
J. Branch	Hednesford Town	21
M. J. Abbots	Brereton Social	20

Division 1

J. G. Muir	Gornal Athletic	27
K. E. Henry	Northpark United	26
F. Rowe	Tipton Town	24
R. Nicholls	Tipton Town	22
S. Ryan	Northpark United	18

Division 2

M. Green	Newport Town	23
J. W. T. France	Donnington Wood	17
R. Stafford	Halesowen Town Res	17
C. Cole	Westfields	17
A. G. Harris	Dales United	14
D. Lee	Stourport Swifts	13

WEST MIDLANDS (REGIONAL) LEAGUE

PREMIER DIVISION — LEAGUE CUP
SEASON 1983/84

FIRST ROUND

Rushall Olympic	v	GKN Sankey	1-0
Halesowen T	v	Malvern T	3-0
Wolverhampton U	v	Atherstone U	1-3
Brereton Social	v	Bilston T	3-1

SECOND ROUND

Blakenall	v	Cradley Town	0-3
Shifnal T	v	Armitage	2-0
Rushall Olympic	v	Wednesfield Soc.	2-3
Halesowen T	v	Lye Town	3-2
Hednesford T	v	Oldswinford	3-2
Hinckley Ath	v	Atherstone U	0-1
Brereton Social	v	Gresley Rvrs	4-4,3-4
Chasetown	v	Tividale	0-1

QUARTER FINALS

Shifnal T	v	Cradley T	2-1
Wednesfield Soc.	v	Halesowen T	3-1
Hednesford T	v	Atherstone U	3-0
Gresley Rovers	v	Tividale	5-0

SEMI-FINALS

Shifnal T	v	Wednesfield Soc.	1-1,2-1
Hednesford T	v	Gresley R	4-0,3-2

FINAL 18.4.84

Hednesford T	v	Shifnal T	AET 1-1
1st Replay 28.4.84			AET 0-0
2nd Replay 14.5.84			5-0

Gresley Rovers *(West Midland League) 1983-84. Back Row (L-R): K. Milner (trainer), John Wain, Terry Mulholland, Geoff Kemm, Richard Bradwell, Ray Skeemer, Kevin Joyce, Richard Walshe, Dave Nish. Front Row: Nigel Tilley, Ian Earley, Jimmy Rose, Tony Parry (capt), Tommy Thompson.*
Photo: Derek Kinsey

DIVISION ONE	Bilston Utd	Brewood	Cheltenham Town Res	Darlaston	Dudley T. Res	Gornal Athletic	Great Wyrley	Harrisons	Hednesford Town Res	Lichfield	Ludlow Town	Northpark Utd	Nuneaton Boro' Res	Shirley Town	Tipton Town	Willenhall Town Res
Bilston Utd	—	2-2	1-1	0-1	2-1	0-3	4-0	1-2	1-1	2-1	0-1	0-5	0-2	1-1	1-1	0-3
Brewood	2-2	—	2-3	1-0	1-1	0-1	1-0	2-1	1-1	3-1	2-0	0-1	3-1	1-1	1-3	7-0
Cheltenham Town Res	0-0	3-0	—	2-1	1-1	2-2	2-3	1-2	2-2	2-0	2-1	1-2	4-1	3-0	1-1	2-2
Darlaston	5-0	1-2	2-0	—	1-2	1-3	0-0	1-1	1-2	3-0	3-2	0-1	3-0	4-0	2-4	1-0
Dudley T. Res	2-0	0-0	1-3	2-1	—	1-5	0-4	0-1	3-1	1-0	2-0	0-2	3-0	1-1	2-2	0-2
Gornal Athletic	4-2	1-2	1-2	2-1	2-0	—	1-0	1-2	1-1	2-1	3-1	0-0	4-0	2-1	1-3	5-1
Great Wyrley	3-1	3-1	2-0	1-2	2-1	2-3	—	3-2	3-0	2-1	0-3	1-5	0-1	2-2	0-2	4-1
Harrisons	3-1	1-0	3-0	3-1	0-2	0-0	2-1	—	1-1	3-0	2-0	0-4	5-0	7-0	2-2	3-0
Hednesford Town Res	3-1	0-3	0-4	6-2	0-1	1-3	2-4	0-0	—	1-3	2-2	1-3	2-3	2-1	2-3	0-0
Lichfield	1-1	1-0	0-1	01	1-1	0-0	2-1	1-0	2-1	—	1-4	1-0	0-0	1-0	1-2	1-1
Ludlow Town	3-0	1-3	0-0	0-2	1-1	1-1	0-4	0-1	0-2	2-4	—	0-6	3-2	1-3	2-3	1-0
Northpark Utd	3-0	2-2	2-3	1-2	5-0	0-1	2-2	2-4	2-1	4-1	7-1	—	0-1	4-0	1-0	2-0
Nuneaton Boro' Res	2-2	1-3	0-3	1-1	2-0	1-4	0-2	1-2	1-0	1-1	1-2	0-3	—	3-1	0-1	1-1
Shirley Town	1-1	1-2	0-0	1-3	1-0	0-0	1-1	1-4	4-1	0-4	0-2	0-0	1-2	—	0-5	2-2
Tipton Town	1-0	3-0	2-2	3-0	0-0	2-2	0-0	2-1	3-0	4-1	2-1	1-1	5-2	2-2	—	4-0
Willenhall Town Res	1-0	0-2	3-1	1-3	2-2	1-2	3-3	1-2	0-0	1-3	5-3	0-3	1-1	2-1	0-0	—

PREMIER DIVISION	Armitage	Atherstone United	Bilston Town	Blakenall	Bereton Social	Chasetown	Cradley Town	GKN Sankey	Gresley Rovers	Halesowen Town	Hednesford Town	Hinckley Athletic	Lye Town	Malvern Town	Oldswinford	Rushall Olympic	Shifnal Town	Tividale	Wednesfield Social	Wolv'ton United
Armitage	—	1-2	1-0	1-2	1-2	5-1	3-1	0-3	3-2	2-1	0-1	2-3	0-2	1-2	2-0	4-1	0-2	1-0	1-0	2-2
Atherstone United	1-1	—	1-0	3-0	4-1	1-1	1-0	3-1	3-3	1-3	1-1	3-1	1-1	0-0	3-1	1-0	1-1	1-3	3-1	2-1
Bilston Town	0-2	1-3	—	2-3	1-0	0-0	1-2	0-2	2-2	0-2	1-3	2-0	0-4	1-0	1-2	1-0	0-0	1-3	1-1	1-3
Blakenall	2-3	0-7	1-2	—	1-0	0-0	1-4	2-1	1-2	0-3	1-1	0-2	1-0	1-1	3-3	0-2	2-2	1-2	1-2	1-1
Bereton Social	1-1	3-2	0-2	1-3	—	1-1	2-2	1-0	0-0	2-6	0-0	4-0	2-1	3-1	3-2	2-2	0-1	0-1	3-2	0-1
Chasetown	2-1	1-0	0-2	0-1	0-0	—	1-2	1-2	3-2	0-6	0-3	2-1	3-3	1-4	3-4	3-1	0-1	1-0	1-1	1-2
Cradley Town	1-2	0-1	2-4	0-4	3-2	4-2	—	4-1	0-1	1-2	1-2	1-2	1-3	0-3	2-2	0-1	1-3	0-1	1-2	0-3
GKN Sankey	1-4	4-1	1-2	1-0	1-1	1-0	0-1	—	2-1	0-4	2-4	0-2	1-1	4-1	1-0	1-1	2-2	2-0	0-0	2-0
Gresley Rovers	1-0	0-3	2-1	2-1	4-0	4-1	3-1	5-2	—	1-0	3-6	3-0	1-1	1-0	3-2	1-1	3-1	2-4	1-1	3-1
Halesowen Town	3-2	1-1	1-1	2-0	4-1	2-0	3-0	8-1	3-2	—	2-1	5-1	1-1	3-2	5-0	3-1	3-2	3-0	6-0	4-0
Hednesford Town	3-1	2-0	1-1	2-0	3-1	0-0	2-1	0-2	2-2	1-2	—	1-0	2-1	3-0	4-1	2-0	0-0	1-0	0-0	1-2
Hinckley Athletic	2-2	0-2	1-1	1-0	2-2	6-0	3-0	3-1	0-0	1-5	0-2	—	1-2	1-1	1-1	0-0	2-2	1-1	2-0	0-1
Lye Town	2-0	1-0	5-4	1-0	1-1	2-3	2-0	2-2	2-0	0-2	2-2	2-1	—	0-0	1-2	0-2	3-0	1-2	0-1	1-0
Malvern Town	0-3	3-1	3-1	2-0	3-2	3-0	0-2	6-£2	2-0	2-3	3-1	5-2	0-0	—	1-2	1-1	0-1	2-2	1-0	5-1
Oldswinford	2-0	1-1	1-1	1-0	1-3	2-0	0-2	2-3	4-2	1-3	0-0	1-0	1-2	2-1	—	1-1	3-1	1-1	3-1	2-2
Rushall Olympic	2-5	2-1	1-1	0-1	0-0	1-0	1-1	5-1	4-0	1-2	2-3	1-2	2-1	4-2	2-2	—	3-2	1-1	2-3	2-3
Shifnal Town	3-3	0-0	2-2	0-2	2-0	0-3	3-2	2-1	2-3	1-2	0-1	2-1	4-0	4-0	1-2	2-1	—	2-2	3-1	3-4
Tividale	3-4	0-0	1-0	1-1	1-1	7-0	0-0	2-1	0-2	1-2	2-3	3-0	1-1	2-1	2-3	2-3	0-0	—	1-2	1-1
Wednesfield Social	4-1	1-2	0-1	0-2	2-0	4-0	3-1	2-1	1-1	4-0	0-5	0-4	1-1	3-2	2-3	1-0	2-2	1-0	—	2-0
Wolv'ton United	1-2	3-2	2-2	1-0	0-1	2-4	2-0	1-1	1-0	1-2	0-1	1-2	0-2	3-1	0-0	3-1	1-0	1-0	2-1	—

Hinckley Athletic *Back Row (L-R): Stuart Martin (trainer), Steve Carr (now Atherstone United), Neil Costello, Lol Chamberlain, John Allen, Martin Haskins, Jimmy Childs, Graham Cross (manager), Keith Mann (coach). Front Row (L-R): Steve Taylor, Tom Hardy, Andy Clark, Warren Lewis, Brian Barraclough, Steve Childs (now Narborough and Littlethorpe).*

WEST MIDLANDS

	Goalscorers		Hat-tricks	Penalties	Appearances	
Atherstone United	Alan Bennetts	9	Phil Summerill	Alan Bennetts 7	Alan Bennetts*	
	Phil Summerill	7			Paul Hayward	
	Tommy Fallon	7			Paul Montgomery	
G.K.N. Sankey	Chris Evans	17	—	Alan Harris 2	Trevor Clarke	37
	Frank Hull	12		Chris Evans	Frank Hull	36
	Paul Evans	10		Paul Evans	Chris Evans	34
Gresley Rovers	Nigel Tilley	29	Nigel Tilley 2	Richard Walshe 6	Tony Parry	53
	Mickey Collins	16		Geoff Kemm 3	Nigel Tilley	50
	Geoff Kemm	10			Tommy Thompson	50
Hinckley Athletic	Andy Clark	14	—	Steve Carr 3	Brian Barraclough	44
	Steve Carr	11			Steve Taylor	44
	Brian Barraclough	8			Warren Lewis	44
	Jimmy Childs	8				
Lichfield	Willie Ashley	9	—	Richard Baker 3	Chris Todd	35
	Gary Dimmack	8			Robert Taylor	33
	Richard Baker	7			Gary Dummack	33
Rushall Olympic	Michael Folland	24	M. Folland	A. Lacy 2	M. Folland	46
	Steve Cant	8		S. Cant 2	N. Atthey	41
	Andrew Lacy	7			S. Peach	41
Shifnal Town	Steve Kelly	24	—	Barry Howells 5	Andrew Robinson	51
	Sammy Pearce	14		Kenny Howells 1	Martin Wright	48
	Mickey Drury	7		Sammy Pearce 1	Jimmy Brown	46
					Trevor Jones	46
Shirley Town	Bob Nimmons	7	—	—	Bob Nimmons	32
	Russ Yeomans	6			Steve Grant	30
	Steve Fitzpatrick	5			Steve Wypler	27
Stourbridge Swifts	David Lee	13	G. Crowther	R. Parenter 4	David Lee	39*
	Gary Crowther	12			Paul Blakeley	37
	Phil Green	10			Phil Green	37
Tamworth	Tony Hadley	6	—	—	Chris Bell	25
	Chris Bell	3			Tommy Wooley	19
	Mark Whitehouse	3			Charlie Newall	17
Westfields	Chris Cole	20	D. Newman	P. Hallett 5	Alan Riches	43
	Doug Newman	15			Kevin Morris	42
	Phil Hallett	10			Mark Tabb	42
West Midlands Police	Billy Shannon	22	Not known	Several	Billy Shannon	46
	Dave Ellis	16			Brian Dorrian	45
	Mark Pigott	13			Dave Ellis	45

ARMITAGE

Chairman:
Manager:
Coach:
Physiotherapist:
Secretary: Ken Conway
Address & Tel No: 08894 5746
Commercial Manager:
Press Officer & Tel No:
Address & Tel No of ground: Kings Bromley Road, Handsacre, Rugeley, Staffs. (0543 491077)
Simple ground directions:
Club colours: All Royal Blue
Change colours: Red and Black
Clubhouse: Yes
Programme: Yes
Floodlights: No

ATHERSTONE UNITED

President:
Chairman: D. Durno
Manager: Ron Bradbury
Coach: P. Turner
Physiotherapist: Brian Kendall
Secretary: Alan Kendall
Address & Tel No: 109 Green Lane, Nuneaton, Warwicks CV10 9EQ. 0203 394492
Commercial Manager:
Press Officer & Tel No: R. Hayes
Address & Tel No of ground: Sheepy Road, Atherstone, Warwicks
Simple ground directions: ½ mile north of town centre on B4416 Tycross - Ashby road. Atherstone is bypassed by main A5 trunk road
No of seats: 500 **Covered accommodation:** 500 **Capacity:** 2,000 **Floodlights:** Yes
Year formed: 1979 **Nickname:** The Adders **Club sponsors:** Crompton & Rathbone Tools
Club colours: Red & White/Black/Black
Change colours: Yellow & Blue/Yellow/Yellow
Previous Names: None
Previous Grounds: None
Record attendance: Not known
Previous Leagues: None
Programme Editor: Brian Wills
Clubhouse details: Adjoining ground, good facilities, bar etc, concert hall
Programme: 8 pages, 10p
Local newspapers & Tel No:
Major Honours: Division 1 West Midland League Champions 1981-82, League Cup Winners 1981-82, Walsall Senior Cup
Club Captain (1983-84): Gary Brown
Player of the Year (1983-84): Paul Montgomery

BLAKENALL F.C.

President: F. Rowley
Chairman: J. R. Bickley
Manager: M. Plimmer
Coach:
Physiotherapist: J. Ruddel
Secretary: F. Hitchcock
Address & Tel No: (0922) 79336
Commercial Manager: None
Address & Tel No:
Press Officer & Tel No: F. Rowley
Address & Tel No of ground: Somerfield Road, Bloxwich. (0922 405835)
Simple ground directions: Half mile from A34 in centre of Bloxwich
No of seats: **Covered accommodation:** 300 **Capacity:** 4,000 **Floodlights:** No, plans passed
Year formed: 1946 **Nickname:** The 'Nall' **Club sponsors:** J.L.S. Heating
Club colours: All White
Change colours: Claret & Blue
Previous Names:
Previous Grounds:
Record attendance:
Previous Leagues: Bloxwich Combination, Staffs County, Midlands Combination
Programme: None
Clubhouse details: Members lounge
Major Honours: Midland Combination 1977, Walsall Senior Cup (6)

BRERETON SOCIAL

Chairman:
Manager: Micky Morris
Coach:
Physiotherapist:
Secretary: George Burton
Address & Tel No: 16 Rudge Road, Brereton, Rugeley, Staffs. 08894 3358
Commercial Manager:
Address & Tel No of ground: Red Lion Ground, Armitage Lane, Brereton, Rugeley, Staffs. 08894 5526
Simple ground directions:
Club colours: Red/White
Change colours: Blue
Programme: No

CHASETOWN

Chairman:
Manager: Bryne Scorey
Coach:
Physiotherapist:
Secretary: Brian Simpson
Address & Tel No: 23 Freeth Road, Brownhills, Walsall, West Midlands. 05433 3889
Commercial Manager:
Address & Tel No of ground: Church Street, Chasetown. 05436 2222
Simple ground directions:
Club colours: Blue with White pinstripes/Blue/Blue
Change colours: Red with Blue & White trim/Red/Red
Programme: 12 pages, 15p
Programme Editor: M. Joiner

GKN SANKEY

Chairman: L. R. Tait
Manager: C. S. M. Walker
Coach: A. Harris
Physiotherapist: P. J. Evenden
Secretary: T. R. Booth
Tel No: Telford 0952 615036
Commercial Manager: None
Press Officer: J. G. Ellis
Address & Tel No of ground: Sankey Stadium, Castle Street, Hadley, Telford. (0952 3411)
No of seats: 500 **Covered accommodation:** Yes **Capacity:** 5,000 **Floodlights:** No
Year formed: 1910
Nickname: Blues
Club colours: All Blue
Change colours: All Yellow
Previous Names: None
Record attendance: 3,500 **Year:** 1957
Previous Leagues: Shropshire County, Cheshire
Clubhouse details: None
Major Honours: Shropshire FA County Cup Winners 1966-67, 1968-69, 1982-83, West Midlands Div II Champions 1981-82
Club Captain: Alan Harris

GRESLEY ROVERS

President: B. Mole
Chairman: B. Spare
Manager: David Nish
Coach: None
Physiotherapist: None
Secretary: S. R Bradwell
Address & Tel No: 56 Fabis Close, Swadlincote, Burton-on-Trent. 215312
Commercial Manager: None
Press Officer: None
Address & Tel No of ground: Moat Street, Church Gresley (Burton 216315)
Simple ground directions: Off A514 or A444 near Swadlincote **No of seats:** 100
Covered accommodation: 250 **Capacity:** 2,000 **Floodlights:** Being installed for 84/85 season
Year formed: 1882 **Nickname:** Moatmen **Club sponsors:** Burton Office Equipment
Club colours: Red
Change colours: Blue and white
Previous Names: None
Previous Grounds: Mushroom Lane, Albert Village
Record attendance: 3,950 v Burton Albion **Year:** 1957
Programme Editors: Brian Spare and Derek Kinsey
Previous Leagues: Birmingham Combination, Midland, Leics Senior, East Midlands **Programme:** Yes
Clubhouse details: Social club on ground open Mon-Thurs evenings and Saturday (match day).
Club captain: Tony Parry
Player of the Year: Tommy Thompson

Tipton United FC Photo: Leo Hoenig

Gresleys Mickey Collins wins an aerial dual with Tividales Goodhead in a West Midland league game at Moat Street, Kevin Hector (left) and Roger Davies also in picture in dark shirts. Photo: Derrick Kinsey

Westfields *The Westfield side that recorded their best ever season. Back Row (L-R): Kevin Merril, Phil Powell, Ian Rees, Alan Richers, Mark Tabb, Doug Newman, Brian Message, Phil Hallett (player/manager). Front Row: Ian Osborne, Mark Williams, Bob Graham (trainer), Andy Morril (general manager/secretary), Jim Greenly (coach), Kevin Davies, Rob Preedy.*

HALESOWEN TOWN F.C.

President: N. Siviter
Chairman: L. Wood
Manager: P. Page
Physiotherapist: B. Whyle
Secretary: H. Rudge
Address & Tel No: 19 Carol Crescent, Halesowen, West Midlands. 021-550 1456
(All correspondence to the Secretary
Address & Tel No of ground: Grove Recreation Ground, Stourbridge Road, Halesowen. 021-550 2179
Simple ground directions: From M5: Leave at Junc. 3, follow sign A456 to 1st roundabout (turn right), at 2nd roundabout (turn left) A458, next roundabout straight on, ground on right approx ½ mile
No of seats: 300 **Covered accommodation:** 800 **Capacity:** 5,000 **Floodlights:** Yes
Year formed: 1873 **Nickname:** The Yeltz **Club sponsors:** Hardanger Properties Ltd
Club colours: Royal Blue/White **Change colours:** Red/Black/White
Previous Names: None **Previous Grounds:** None
Record attendance: 5,000 v Hendon F.A. Cup 1st Round Proper **Year:** 1955
13,700, F.A. Vase Final (Wembley) **Year:** 1983
Previous Leagues: Birmingham Combination prior to 1946, Birmingham League, West Midlands (Regional) League
Club metal badges: Yes **Club shop:** Yes **Programme:** Yes
Clubhouse: Yes. open seven nights + match days (021-550 8907) **Day for midweek matches:** Tuesday
Club honours: Birmingham League Champions 1946-47; Worcs. Senior Cup winners 1951-52, 1961-62; F.A. Cup 1st Rnd Proper 1955-56; W. Midlands League Champions 1982-83, 1983-84; W. Midlands League Cup winners 1982-83; Thorn EMI Floodlighting Competition winners 1982-83; F.A. Vase finalists 1983; Birmingham Senior Cup winners 1984; Staffs Senior Cup runners-up 1984

HINCKLEY ATHLETIC

Chairman: D. W. Loakes
Manager: G. Cross
Coach: K. Mann
Physiotherapist: S. Martin
Secretary: J. Colver
Tel No: (H) Hinckley 30263. (B) Hinckley 636361
Commercial Manager: R. Holtham
Tel No: Hinckley 632402
Press Officer: R. Harris
Address & Tel No of ground: Middlefield Lane, Hinckley (613553)
Simple ground directions: Off A447 through town centre, follow signs to public weighbridge
No of seats: 300 **Covered accommodation:** 1,000 **Capacity:** 5,000 **Floodlights:** Yes
Year formed: 1879 **Nickname:** Robins **Club sponsors:** Various
Club colours: All Red **Change colours:** White/Black/Black
Previous Names: Hinckley, Hinckley Town, Hinckley United
Previous Grounds: Holywell, London Road, Hinckley **Record attendance:** 5,410 v Nuneaton Borough **Year:** 1949
Previous Leagues: Nuneaton Comb, Birmingham Comb, Birmingham League, Southern League
Present players with Football League experience: Graham Cross (Leicester City, Chesterfield, Brighton, R.N.E., Lincoln City), John Allan (Port Vale)
Past players who progressed into the Football League: John Allan (Port Vale)
Clubhouse details: New Social Club with lounge, games room and concert room. Open each evening, Sunday lunch and match days (Hinckley 615012)
Major Honours: Birmingham Comb. champions 1923-4, 1926-7; Leicestershire Senior League champions 1897-98, 1899-1900, 1908-09, 1909-10, 1913-14; Birmingham Senior Cup joint winners 1954-55; Leicestershire Senior Cup winners 1899-1900, 1900-01, 1909 10, 1982-83; Leicestershire Challenge Cup winners 1957-58, 1958-59, 1959-60, 1960-61, 1961-62, 1967-68
Best performance in **F.A. Cup:** 2nd Round Proper 1954-55
F.A. Trophy: 1st Qualifying Round 1969-70, 1972-73, 1973-74
F.A. Vase: 4th Round Proper 1976-77, 1977-78, 1978-79
Programme: 28 to 36 pages, 20p (can be ordered for 20p each from Alan Mason, 11 Newarke St, Leicester LE1 5SS
Programme Editor: Alan Mason **Club shop:** No **Club metal badges:** No
Club captain: Warren Lewis **Player of the Year:** Warren Lewis

LYE TOWN

President: Derick Webb
Chairman: John Humphries
Manager: Roddy Evans
Coach: John Day
Physiotherapist: Harry Hill
Press Officer & Tel No: Secretary
Secretary: W. Homer
Address & Tel No: 64 Britannia Road, Rowley Regis, Warley, West Midlands. 021-559 3368
Commercial Manager: Albert Philpott
Address & Tel No: 12 Rock Street, Upper Gornal, Dudley DY3 2BL. Sedgley 76331
Address & Tel No of ground: Lye Sports Ground, Stourbridge Road, Lye, Stourbridge. Lye 2672
Simple ground directions: Train within 200 yards and Midland Red Buses from B'ham all stop outside ground
No of seats: 250 **Covered accommodation:** 300 **Capacity:** 4,250 **Floodlights:** Yes
Year formed: 1930 **Nickname:** Flyers **Club sponsors:** C.I.P. Ltd, St James Road, Dudley
Club colours: White/Navy Blue/Navy Blue **Change colours:** All Red
Previous Names: None **Previous Grounds:** None
Record attendance: 3,542 v Brierley Hill **Year:** 1952-53
Previous Leagues: Birmingham Youth & Old Boys Assoc, Worcester Combination, Birmingham League
Clubhouse details: Large room, Banks' beers, darts and pool
Programme: 8 pages, 20p **Local newspapers & Tel No:**
Programme Editor: Ian Davies
Major Honours: Worcs Combination Winner 1935-36, League Cup 1976-77, Birmingham Senior Cup Runner-up 1980-81, League Runners-up 1977-78, 1978-79, 1979-80, 1980-81
Club Captain (1983-84): John Day **Player of the Year (1983-84):** John Day

Northpark United Photo: Leo Hoenig

Northpark United clear a high cross during their home game with Darlaston. Photo: Leo Hoenig

Chris Wilson equalises for Rushall Olympic to give them a 2-2 home draw with Wolverhampton United. Photo: Leo Hoenig

MALVERN TOWN

President:
Chairman: R. W. Stallard
Manager: S. Northwood
Coach: B. Kenning
Trainer: K. Wilkinson
Secretary: G. F. Knapper
Address & Tel No: (06845 4861)
Commercial Manager: None
Address & Tel No:
Press Officer & Tel No: None
Address & Tel No of ground: Langland Stadium, Langland Avenue, Malvern, Worcs (06845 4068)
Simple ground directions: Take A4352 off the A449 in Malvern Link for 1 mile, turn left down Madresfield Road, second left Langland Avenue
No of seats: 150 **Covered accommodation:** 300 **Capacity:** 8,000 **Floodlights:** Yes
Year formed: 1947 **Nickname:** None **Club sponsors:** None
Club colours: Claret and blue/White/Blue **Change colours:** Mid Blue/Black/Claret
Previous Names: Barnards Green **Previous Grounds:** None
Record attendance: 1,221 v Worcester City **Year:** 1980
Previous Leagues: Worcester, Worcestershire Combination, Midland Combination **Programme:** Yes
Clubhouse details: Open every night and Saturday and Sunday lunchtimes. Snacks available match days.
Club Captain (1983-84): T. Hall **Player of the Year (1983-84):** S. Essex
Leading Scorer: H. Rawle **Most Appearances:** N. White

OLDSWINFORD

President:
Chairman: H. C. Hackett
Managers: M. Woodhouse & E. Edwards
Coach:
Physiotherapist:
Secretary: D. Dew
Address & Tel No: 148 King William Street, Amblecote, Stourbridge (376902)
Commercial Manager: P. Brittain, Sedgeley 62528
Press Officer & Tel No: Secretary
Address & Tel No of ground: The Dell, Sports Stadium, Bryce Road, Pensnett, Brierley Hill, West Midlands. (0384 77289)
Simple ground directions: 1¼ miles from Brierley Hill town centre on Pensnett Road
No of seats: 300 **Covered accommodation:** 300 **Capacity:** 5,000 **Floodlights:** No
Year formed: 1955 **Nickname:** Swinford **Club sponsors:** Several
Club colours: Royal Blue & Sky Blue **Change colours:** Claret/Yellow/Red
Previous Names: None **Previous Grounds:** Cottage Street, Brierley Hill; South Road, Stourbridge
Record attendance: Not known
Previous Leagues: Staffs County, Kidderminster
Clubhouse details: Open nightly, licensed bar
Programme: 10 pages, 15p **Local newspapers & Tel No:**
Programme Editor: Secretary/Chairman
Major Honours: West Midlands Div 1, West Midlands League Cup Div 1 Winners

RUSHALL OLYMPIC

President: E. Venables
Chairman: B. W. Greenwood
Manager: C. Painter
Coach: None
Physiotherapist: None
Secretary: M. Clayton
Tel No: (H) Walsall 29032. (B) Aldridge 55311
Commercial Manager: None
Press Officer: D. Sedgwick
Address & Tel No of ground: Dale's Lane, off Daw End Lane, Rushall, nr Walsall, West Midlands
Simple ground directions: Daw End Lane off Walsall-Lichfield (A461) main road, ground 500 yards on right
No of seats: 100 **Covered accommodation:** 100 **Capacity:** 5,000 **Floodlights:** No
Year formed: 1896 **Nickname:** The Pics **Club sponsors:** Goodfellows Garage
Club colours: Gold/Black **Change colours:** White/Gold
Previous Names: None **Previous Grounds:** Rushall Recreational
Record attendance: 2,400 v Leeds XI (charity game) **Year:** 1977 **Programme:** Yes
Previous Leagues: Walsall Amateur League, Staffs County League **Programme Editor:** David Sedgwick
Clubhouse details: Excellent bar-lounge, kitchen, adjoining large refreshment facilities
Club captain: Kim While **Player of the Year:** Michael Folland & Simon Reach (joint)

SHIFNAL TOWN

President: J. Doyle
Chairman: R. Turnock, JP
Manager: Peter Houlston
Player/Coach: Roy Cross
Physiotherapist: None
Press Officer: None
Secretary: J. D. Groucott
Address & Tel No: 4 Idsall Crescent, Shifnal, Shropshire TF11 8ES. Telford (0952) 461466
General Manager: G. Davies
Address & Tel No: 30 Drayton Road, Shifnal. Telford (0952) 460326
Address & Tel No of ground: Admirals Park, off Drayton Road, Shifnal, Shropshire. Telford (0952) 460326
Simple ground directions: Take Shifnal Road from A5, 1st left after passing under M54 bridge into Drayton Road, Ground at end of road on right; or from Town Centre head north up main street for A5, take last turning right before motorway into Drayton Road
No of seats: None **Covered accommodation:** 200 **Capacity:** 5,000 **Floodlights:** No
Year formed: 1964 **Nickname:** Town **Club sponsors:** Staffordshire Building Society
Club colours: Red/White/Black **Change colours:** All Green
Previous Names: Shifnal Youth Club, Shifnal Juniors **Previous Grounds:** Idsall Sports Centre, Shifnal
Record attendance: 1,002 v Bridgnorth Town (3rd Round, F.A. Vase **Year:** 1983-84)
Previous Leagues: Wellington and District, Shropshire County, West Midlands (promoted to Premier Div 1979-80)
Clubhouse details: Lounge and Bar, open at weekends and every night during week, also after matches
Programme details: 12 pages, free with admission **Programme Editor:** Dave Adams
Major Honours: West Midland Premier Division Champions 1980-81, 1981-82
Club Captain (1983-84): Jimmy Brown **Player of the Year (1983-84):** Dave Frances (Supporters), Jimmy Brown (Player)

TAMWORTH

Chairman: John Bayliss
Manager: Dave Seedhouse
Ass. Manager: Peter Nicholls
Physiotherapist: None
Secretary: L. Greenfield
Address & Tel No: 5 Mercia Close, Caton Square, Tamworth. (61019).
Address & Tel No of ground: The Lamb Ground, Kettlebrook, Tamworth, Staffs. Tamworth 65798 **Club shop:** Yes
Simple ground directions: From town centre follow one-way road marked 'South' into Kettlebrook Road, ground is on right, opposite Railway Arches
No of seats: 500 **Covered accommodation:** 250 **Capacity:** 5,000 **Floodlights:** Yes
Year formed: 1933 **Nickname:** The Lambs **Club sponsors:** None
Previous names: None **Club colours:** Red/White
Previous grounds: None **Change colours:** Sky Blue
Record attendance: 5,000 v Torquay **Year:** 1969-70
Best performance in: **F.A. Cup:** 1969-70 2nd Round
F.A. Trophy: 1970-1 Quarter-Final
Previous Leagues: Birmingham, Southern, Northern Premier
Clubhouse details: On ground
Present players with Football League experience: None
Past players who progressed into the Football League: P. Weir (Cardiff C), S. Fox (Wrexham, Birmingham C)
Record transfer fee paid: None **Record transfer fee received:** None
Programme details: 8 pages, 15p **Local newspapers:** Tamworth Herald, Tamworth Trader
Senior Honours: Birmingham Senior Cup (3), Staffordshire Senior Cup (2)
Club metal badges: Yes **Player of the Year:** Chris Bell

TIVIDALE

President: P. Archer MP
Chairman: D. McDonald
Manager: I. Cole
Coach: A. Moore
Physiotherapist: G. Bennett
Secretary: A. D. Morson
Address & Tel No: 7 Trafalgar Road, Tividale Dudley 58927
Commercial Manager: None
Press Officer & Tel No: None
Address & Tel No of ground: The Beeches, Packwood Road, Tividale, Warley, West Midlands
Simple ground directions: Dudley Port Station to Burnt Tree, left towards B'ham ground 1 mile on right or M5 to Junction 2 (Oldbury Junction) right towards Wolverhampton ground, approx 2 miles on left
No of seats: 200 **Covered accommodation:** Stand, one side of ground **Capacity:** 3,000 **Floodlights:** No
Year formed: 1957 **Nickname:** None **Club sponsors:** None
Club colours: Sky Blue **Change colours:** Yellow
Previous Names: None **Previous Grounds:** City Road, Tividale
Record attendance: 2,500 (approx) v Telford, F.A. Cup
Previous Leagues: **Programme:**
Clubhouse details: Clubhouse and ground combined
Major Honours: West Midland League Cup Winners (19), West Midland League Division One Winners
Club Captain (1983-84): P. Jackson **Player of the Year (1983-84):** P. Jackson

WEDNESFIELD SOCIAL

President: B. C. Jones
Chairman: L. Horton
Manager: W. Challenor
Coach: B. Clarke
Physiotherapist: None
Secretary: B. W. Collins
Address & Tel No: Wolverhampton 721831
Commercial Manager: Mrs. C. Myatt
Address & Tel No: Bloxwich 75275
Press Officer & Tel No: John Myatt, 75275
Address & Tel No of ground: Cottage Ground, Amos Lane, Wednesfield (Wolverhampton 735506)
Simple ground directions: From High Street Wednesfield:along Lichfield Road into Wood End Road and take second left into Arms Lane.
No of seats: 200 **Covered accommodation:** Yes **Capacity:** 1,000 **Floodlights:** No
Year formed: 1961 **Nickname:** Social **Club sponsors:** None
Club colours: Red/Red/Red and black **Change colours:** Royal Blue
Previous Names: None **Previous Grounds:** None
Record attendance: 490 v Burton Albion, F.A. Cup **Year:** 1983
Programme: 14 pages, 10p (7th in Midlands) **Programme Editor:** John Myatt
Previous Leagues: Wolverhampton and District Amateur
Clubhouse details: None

LICHFIELD F.C.

President: Ken Hughes
Chairman: Ron Walters
Manager: Brian Sawyer
Secretary: Brian Smith
Address & Tel No: 9 Beech Gardens, Lichfield, Staffs. Lichfield 55874
Address of ground: Shortbutts Lane, Lichfield
Simple ground directions: London/Coventry/Warwick road out of Lichfield (via Upper St. John Street), in ½ mile turn right at lights at London Road Garage into Shortbutts Lane. Ground 200 yards on right
Year formed: 1966 **Club colours:** All Royal Blue **Change colours:** All Red
Previous Leagues: Staffs County Premier Div. (South) **Programme:** 4 pages, 15p **Programme Editor:** Brian Smith
Major Honours: Walsall Challenge Cup 1967; Lichfield Charity Cup (3)
Club Captain: Richard Baker **Player of the Year:** Gary Westwood

SHIRLEY TOWN F.C.

President: John France
Chairman: Clive Shipman
Manager: Andy Burman
Coach: Pending
Physiotherapist: Pending
Secretary: John France
Address & Tel No: 105 Coppice Walk, Cheswick Grn, Shirley (021-728 3011)
Commercial Manager: John Jolly
Address & Tel No: 40 Greenhill Way, Shirley B90 3PR (021-745 6644)
Address & Tel No of ground: Tilehouse Lane, Shirley, Solihull (021-744 1560)
Simple ground directions: From Birmingham city centre along A34 to Shirley, turn right along B4025 towards Shirley railway station. Ground approx 1½ miles past on left
No of seats: None **Covered accommodation:** Yes **Capacity:** 100 **Floodlights:** No
Year formed: 1926 **Club sponsors:** J. A. Harrison (Brokers) Ltd
Club colours: All Red **Change colours:** White shirts, Pale Blue shorts, Maroon stockings
Clubhouse details: Bar facilities and food **Programme:** Pending
Player of the Year: Bob Nimmons

STOURPORT SWIFTS

President: R. P. Crowe
Chairman: P. Worton
Manager: R. Leach
Coach: R. Bradley
Physiotherapist: J. Allen
Secretary: J. W. McDonald
Address & Tel No: 65 Princess Way, Stourport-on-Severn, Worcs (2088)
Commercial Manager: As Secretary
Press Officer: Ian Johnson
Address of ground: Walshes Meadow, Stourport, Worcs
Simple ground directions: Rear of Stourport swimming baths, Dunley Road, Stourport
No of seats: None **Covered accommodation:** 200 **Capacity:** 10,000 **Floodlights:** None
Year formed: 1882 **Nickname:** Swifts **Club sponsors:** Black & White Garages
Club colours: Black/Gold **Change colours:** Red & White stripes
Previous names: None **Previous grounds:** None **Programme:** None
Record attendance: Not known **Previous Leagues:** Kidderminster League, Worcester League
Club captain: Paul Blakeley **Player of the Year:** Russell Parmenter

WESTFIELDS F.C.

President: Ken Morris
Chairman: Robert Doddy
Manager: Phil Hallett
Coach: Jim Greenly
Physiotherapist: Peter Isaac
Secretary: Andy Morris
Tel No: 0432 266775
Commercial Manager: Stuart Daviet
Address & Tel No: 61 Cotterell St, Hereford (268114)
Press Officer: Andy Morris
Address & Tel No of ground: Thorn Lighting, Holme Lacy Road, Rotherwas, Hereford
Simple ground directions: Proceed 1 mile south of Hereford, turn left into Holme Lacy Road, proceed 1 mile to Thorn Lighting Rotherwas, ground on right
No of seats: None **Covered accommodation:** 50 **Capacity:** 3,000 **Floodlights:** No
Year formed: 1966 **Nickname:** The Fields **Club sponsors:** Stooke Hill & Co (Estate Agents)
Club colours: Claret/Sky Blue **Change colours:** White **Programme:** Yes
Previous Names: None **Previous Grounds:** Widemarsh Common **Programme Editor:** Andy Morris
Record attendance: 800 **Year:** 1979 v Hereford Utd
Previous Leagues: Herefordshire Sunday, Herefordshire Premier, Worcester & District, West Midland
Clubhouse details: "Thorn Lighting" on ground
Major Honours: West Midland League Cup 1979-80; Worcestershire Junior Cup 1979-80; Presteigne Otway Cup 1980-81; West Midland League Cup winners 1983-84; Kington Challenge Cup winners 1983-84; West Midland League Div 2 runners-up 1983-84
Club captain: Phil Hallett **Player of the Year:** Rob Preedy

HELLENIC LEAGUE

President: C. J. Green Esq (1963)
Chairman: N. A. S. Matthews (1953), Cedar Court, Steeple Aston, Oxford.
Tel: Steeple Aston (0869) 40347
Secretary: D. A. G. Harrison (1959), 107 Thame Road, Haddenham, Aylesbury, Bucks.
Tel: Haddenham (0844) 290590

DOUBLE TRIUMPH FOR ALMONDSBURY GREENWAY

Despite the kind weather that produced an unusually low number of postponements last season, by the end of April only Morris Motors had secured their title. Motors won promotion back to the Premier Division and the Divisional Championship all in one go, at Lambourn, on the last Saturday in April.

Six days in early May at Wantage settled both Premier Division trophies and the relegation issues. It began on Wednesday 2nd May when a 4-0 win by Almondsbury Greenway over Wantage Town clinched the League title for the Almonds, their first Hellenic trophy. On the Saturday it was Wantage's turn to win 4-0 and ensure they have another season in the Premier Division. This win sent Avon (Bradford) down to the First Division at the end of their first season of Hellenic football with Hazells (Aylesbury).

The following Monday the Almonds beat Abingdon Town 3-0 at Wantage to win the Premier Division Cup. For Almondsbury Greenway in only their second season in the Hellenic League this was this remarkable Club's greatest triumph to date. They also maintained the Gloucestershire stranglehold on the Premier Division titles taking over from last season's double winners Moreton Town. This season Moreton again tried to overhaul the Almonds with their games in hand but despite conceeding only ten League goals all season and losing two games less than Almondsbury they were left trailing eight points behind in the Runners-up spot. Thame United after topping the League for some time ran out of games and had to settle for third place. Fourth place Abingdon United reached the League Cup Semi-Final but were unable to overcome Almondsbury to set up an all Abingdon Final. They did reach one Final. This was the Berks & Bucks Senior Cup Final at Marlow. After taking a one goal lead it looked as though they were going to be triumphant as they out played Buckingham Town. It was not to be and defensive mistakes in the second half let in Buckingham who finally ran out 3-1 winners.

Fifth placed Abingdon Town did reach the League Cup Final but found Almondsbury too much of a handful as Steve Price scored the first Cup Final hat trick that can be remembered. The chance of the all Abingdon Final will have to wait until at least 1986 as the two Clubs have drawn each other in the First Round of this season's competition.

In Division One only the Oxford based Morris Motors stopped a Gloucestershire clean sweep of the trophies as Shortwood United claimed both the Cup and Runners-up spot in the League. Shortwood did things the hard way. They dropped points to lowly Clubs when they should have won and edged back into the second promotion place only at the last gasp. In the League Cup Final they fell behind to opponents Kidlington, equalised to put the game into extra time and then went into overdrive as they romped away to win 4-1.

Earlier that week Shortwood had added the top Gloucestershire Cup, the G.F.A. Trophy, to their collection with a 1-0 win over Western League Portway Bristol. Rayners Lane also collected a County Cup making two out of three successful Cup Final appearances for Hellenic Clubs last season. Rayners Lane, who finished 6th in the Premier Division, won the Middlesex Premier Cup with a 3-0 Final win over Brimsdown Rovers.

In the Wirral Programme Club survey Badminton Picksons finished 4th nationally with Didcot Town 11th. Supermarine and Lydney Town were joint third in the Hellenic League section helping to maintain the League's reputation for good quality programmes much sought after by collectors.

Three Clubs are leaving the League for pastures new while we welcome three new Clubs to maintain the standards of the League. Going are:- Northwood to the London Spartan League, Lydney Town to the North Gloucestershire Senior League and Milton Keynes Borough to the South Midlands League. Replacing them are:- Hounslow relegated from the Southern League Southern Division, Sharpness elected as Gloucestershire County League Champions and Highworth Town elected from the Wiltshire County League.

HELLENIC LEAGUE FINAL TABLES — SEASON 1983-84

PREMIER DIVISION

	Pl	Home W	Home D	Home L	Home For	Home Agt	Away W	Away D	Away L	Away For	Away Agt	Pts	G.D.
ALMONDSBURY GREENWAY...	32	14	2	0	34	4	9	2	5	25	15	73	+40
Moreton Town	32	10	5	1	30	3	8	6	2	21	7	65	+41
Thame United	32	10	3	3	27	15	9	2	5	26	15	62	+23
Abingdon United	32	9	5	2	40	12	7	4	5	28	22	57	+34
Abingdon Town	32	7	4	5	27	17	7	5	4	26	21	51	+15
Rayners Lane	32	8	4	4	24	18	5	5	6	14	22	48	−2
Supermarine	32	6	4	6	17	12	5	8	3	23	22	45	+6
Bicester Town	32	8	3	5	23	11	5	3	8	14	21	45	+5
Didcot Town	32	4	5	7	18	31	6	5	5	21	18	40	−10
Wallingford Town	32	6	2	8	26	27	4	7	5	16	18	39	−3
Clanfield	32	3	8	5	25	27	4	8	4	14	16	37	−4
Maidenhead Town & Youth	32	6	6	4	20	17	2	6	8	20	27	36	−4
Northwood	32	5	5	6	20	21	4	2	10	14	32	34	−19
Fairford Town	32	6	6	4	22	20	1	6	9	17	37	33	−18
Wantage Town	32	5	3	8	26	23	3	3	10	17	30	30	−10
Avon Bradford	32	5	6	5	27	24	2	1	13	9	47	28	−35
Hazells (Aylesbury)	32	2	5	9	19	36	1	3	12	11	53	17	−59

DIVISION ONE

	Pl	Home W	Home D	Home L	Home For	Home Agt	Away W	Away D	Away L	Away For	Away Agt	Pts	G.D.
MORRIS MOTORS	34	14	3	0	41	9	9	5	3	30	21	77	+41
Shortwood United	34	12	1	4	44	23	9	4	4	30	16	68	+35
Yate Town	34	9	8	0	44	26	9	3	5	46	27	65	+37
Bishops Cleeve	34	12	2	3	31	16	7	4	6	28	27	63	+16
Pegasus Juniors	34	12	0	5	42	17	7	5	5	29	23	62	+31
Milton Keynes Borough	34	9	7	1	40	22	9	0	8	29	25	61	+22
Pressed Steel	34	11	3	3	51	18	5	3	9	31	26	54	+38
Viking Sports	34	11	2	4	37	18	4	7	6	24	25	54	+18
Kintbury Rangers	34	7	5	5	31	26	7	5	5	35	30	52	+10
Easington Sports	34	13	3	1	37	20	2	4	11	22	48	52	−9
Kidlington	34	7	3	7	40	30	5	5	7	24	28	44	+6
Cirencester Town	34	5	7	5	25	29	6	1	10	17	21	41	−8
AFC Aldermaston	34	6	3	8	21	23	3	5	9	28	40	35	−14
Worrall Hill	34	7	3	7	33	34	2	3	12	31	45	33	−15
Lambourn Sports	34	6	2	9	32	44	2	5	10	15	41	31	−38
Badminton Picksons	34	6	4	7	28	31	1	3	13	20	54	28	−37
Lydney Town	34	1	7	9	16	32	3	1	13	23	43	20	−36
Dowty-Staverton	34	3	1	13	14	54	1	1	15	10	67	14	−97

HELLENIC LEAGUE

PREMIER DIVISION

HOME CLUB / AWAY CLUB	Abingdon Town	Abingdon United	Almondsbury Greenway	Avon (Bradford)	Bicester Town	Clanfield	Didcot Town	Fairford Town	Hazells (Aylesbury)	Maidenhead Town & Y	Moreton Town	Northwood	Rayners Lane	Supermarine	Thame United	Wallingford Town	Wantage Town
Abingdon Town		1-2	2-1	7-0	2-1	0-0	0-1	2-2	4-0	3-1	0-2	1-0	0-2	2-2	0-0	2-0	1-3
Abingdon United	1-1		4-0	5-1	2-1	0-1	2-0	4-0	7-0	1-1	0-0	5-0	1-1	2-2	1-2	2-1	3-1
Almondsbury Greenway	1-0	4-1		1-0	2-0	2-0	1-0	1-0	6-1	1-1	0-0	3-1	3-0	3-0	1-0	1-0	4-0
Avon (Bradford)	2-2	3-1	0-0		0-0	0-0	2-3	3-3	5-1	1-2	1-0	5-1	1-3	1-3	0-3	1-1	2-1
Bicester Town	2-0	1-2	0-2	2-0		0-1	3-0	2-1	4-0	1-0	1-1	0-1	3-0	1-1	1-2	0-0	2-0
Clanfield	1-1	3-2	3-2	0-1	0-2		2-2	2-2	1-1	2-2	1-3	2-2	3-0	2-2	1-2	1-2	1-1
Didcot Town	2-2	0-6	1-2	2-1	0-1	6-1		1-1	0-0	3-2	0-3	2-1	0-0	1-1	0-3	0-5	0-2
Fairford Town	1-2	0-1	0-6	3-0	3-0	1-1	0-2		1-1	2-2	1-1	0-0	1-1	1-0	3-1	3-2	2-0
Hazells (Aylesbury)	3-4	1-1	0-0	2-1	1-1	2-2	1-3	4-2		1-1	0-5	1-2	1-2	1-2	0-4	0-1	1-5
Maidenhead Town & Y	2-4	0-3	0-1	1-1	2-1	1-0	0-0	1-1	1-2		0-0	4-1	3-0	1-1	1-0	1-1	2-1
Moreton Town	1-0	2-0	0-1	6-0	2-0	0-0	0-0	3-1	4-0	1-0		2-0	1-0	0-0	1-1	5-0	0-0
Northwood	1-1	2-2	1-2	1-0	0-1	1-3	3-1	0-1	2-1	1-1	0-2		2-0	2-3	4-3	0-0	0-0
Rayners Lane	0-2	1-1	3-1	3-1	1-1	2-1	0-4	3-1	3-1	2-0	0-1	2-0		1-1	0-2	0-0	3-1
Supermarine	1-2	0-1	0-1	3-0	0-2	0-0	1-1	0-0	3-0	1-0	0-2	2-0	0-1		2-0	1-1	3-1
Thame United	2-0	0-0	1-0	4-0	0-3	0-0	2-1	4-2	4-2	3-2	0-1	2-1	1-1	2-0		0-1	2-1
Wallingford Town	1-4	3-1	0-2	2-3	2-0	1-1	1-3	4-0	2-1	2-5	2-1	0-1	1-1	1-2	0-2		4-0
Wantage Town	0-1	1-4	0-4	5-0	4-0	0-3	0-0	3-0	6-0	2-0	1-1	1-3	1-2	1-3	0-1	1-1	

HELLENIC LEAGUE

DIVISION ONE

HOME CLUB / AWAY CLUB	AFC Aldermaston	Badminton Picksons	Bishops Cleeve	Cirencester Town	Dowty-Staverton	Easington Sports	Kidlington	Kintbury Rangers	Lambourn Sports	Lydney Town	Milton Keynes Boro	Morris Motors	Pegasus Juniors	Pressed Steel	Shortwood United	Viking Sports	Worrall Hill	Yate Town
AFC Aldermaston		3-1	3-1	0-1	3-0	1-1	1-3	1-1	2-0	2-1	0-1	0-2	0-1	1-0	0-2	1-2	1-1	2-5
Badminton Picksons	2-2		2-3	2-1	3-0	6-4	1-4	2-2	1-1	2-1	2-0	0-3	1-5	0-1	0-1	1-1	3-1	0-1
Bishops Cleeve	1-0	3-2		1-0	4-0	4-2	4-1	0-2	3-1	2-1	0-1	2-2	1-1	1-0	1-0	1-0	3-1	0-2
Cirencester Town	2-2	5-2	0-2		2-1	2-0	1-1	2-4	1-1	1-1	0-3	2-2	0-3	0-2	2-1	1-1	2-1	2-2
Dowty-Staverton	2-3	0-3	1-2	0-3		0-3	2-1	2-1	2-0	0-3	2-1	0-1	2-2	1-7	0-2	1-5	0-3	0-11
Easington Sports	1-1	2-1	3-1	3-1	1-0		1-0	4-2	2-0	3-2	2-1	2-0	1-0	2-2	2-2	4-3	3-2	1-2
Kidlington	2-0	3-2	3-2	0-1	6-0	9-0		1-1	0-1	2-3	2-5	2-4	0-2	2-1	1-0	1-2	2-2	4-4
Kintbury Rangers	3-2	1-1	0-2	1-2	4-0	1-1	3-1		3-3	2-1	0-4	1-1	1-2	2-1	1-1	0-1	4-3	4-0
Lambourn Sports	3-5	6-2	1-3	2-0	0-3	2-1	2-3	4-3		0-5	0-1	1-3	3-2	3-2	1-5	1-1	2-2	1-3
Lydney Town	0-0	1-1	1-2	0-3	1-1	3-1	1-1	0-4	1-1		1-2	0-1	1-2	2-2	0-3	2-2	2-5	0-1
Milton Keynes Boro	2-2	4-1	1-0	4-2	5-1	5-3	1-1	3-3	0-0	4-0		1-1	1-1	1-0	0-3	2-2	4-1	2-1
Morris Motors	3-1	5-1	0-0	1-0	5-0	2-0	0-0	5-1	1-0	2-1	5-2		2-0	4-1	1-0	0-0	3-2	2-0
Pegasus Juniors	2-0	2-0	0-2	1-0	7-1	5-0	1-0	1-2	1-2	6-0	1-0	1-3		2-0	2-3	2-0	6-3	2-1
Pressed Steel	3-5	6-0	3-1	1-1	9-0	1-0	0-1	1-3	10-0	3-0	3-0	3-1	3-1		2-2	1-0	2-1	1-1
Shortwood United	2-0	3-3	2-0	1-0	5-1	3-1	1-2	1-2	4-1	5-0	4-1	2-3	2-1	3-1		2-1	3-1	1-5
Viking Sports	5-1	3-0	2-2	0-1	4-0	0-1	2-1	1-0	1-0	3-0	3-1	2-0	2-2	1-4	1-2		3-1	4-2
Worrall Hill	3-2	2-0	3-3	3-1	6-1	2-2	3-3	0-2	3-1	2-1	0-1	1-2	0-1	0-6	1-2	3-1		1-5
Yate Town	4-2	5-0	2-2	1-0	2-1	2-2	4-1	2-2	6-3	4-3	2-1	1-1	3-3	1-1	1-1	2-2	2-1	

Almondsbury Greenway *Back Row (L-R): Steve Brunsdon, Craig Stratford, Mike Tidcombe, Andy Kerr, Geoff Lever, Mike McCormack, Nigel Leeson (Physio), Brian Tufton (Manager), Front Row (L-R): David Wookey, Steve Price, Peter McCall, John Shehean, Phil Rugman, Eion Bailey, Adie Walker.*

Abingdon Town *Back Row (L-R): Paul Holden (Manager), John Lever, Malcolm Pledge, Steven Lymer, Nicky Dollard, David Shorter, Gerald O'Loughlin, Phil Emsden, Steve Morton (Coach), Front Row (L-R): Mike Worgan (Coach), Declan Cuddy, Buzz Fowler, Alan McNab, Paul Bryant, John Merrill.*

Another superb action photo from Newbury Weekly News star photographer Peter Bloodworth. Here he catches Kintbury's Bob Bright flying in to head clear against Shortwood United in an Hellenic League Cup tie in March which Shortwood won 3-0.

Milton Keynes Borough who have now left the Hellenic league

NOTABLE CUP RESULTS BY MEMBER CLUBS

Tuesday 16th August 1983
Oxford Benevolent Cup Final

Witney Town 1 v Moreton Town 2
(Southern League)

Saturday 24th September 1983
Berks & Bucks Senior Cup Preliminary Round

Milton Keynes Boro 2 v Milton Keynes City 2

Tuesday 27th August 1983
Berks & Bucks Senior Cup Prel Round Replay

Milton Keynes City 3 v Milton Keynes Boro 3

Saturday 1st October 1983
Berks & Bucks Senior Cup Prel Round 2nd Replay

Milton Keynes Boro 1 v Milton Keynes City 2
(Southern League)

Saturday 22nd October 1983
Berks & Bucks Senior Cup 1st Round

Hungerford Town 2 v Hazells (Aylesbury) 3
(Isthmian League)

Saturday 25th February 1984
Berks & Bucks Senior Cup Semi-Final

Abingdon United 2 v Wokingham Town 1
(Isthmian League)

HELLENIC LEAGUE

Club	Leading Goalscorers		Hat-Tricks	Penalties	Most Appearances	
Abingdon Town	Paul Lee	14	Paul Lee (2)	—	Trevor Joseph	36
	Stuart Haigh	10			John Merrill	35
	Trevor Joseph	10			Steve Lymer	32
Abingdon United	Sean Sunderland	17	Kenny Uzzell (2)	—	Tommy Moxon	38
	Kenny Uzzell	15	Peter Cullen (2)	—	Sean Sunderland	36
	Pete Cullen	14	(one 3 & one 4)		Jimmy Austin	35
					Bob Pratley	35
Almondsbury Greenway	Steve Price	32	Steve Price (2)	David Wookey (1)	Peter McCall	40
	Andy Kerr	13			David Wookey	39
	Gion Bailey	7			M. McCormack	38
					S. Price	38
					P. Rugman	38
Bicester Town	Saun Cross	23	Terry O'Neill (2)	David Burns (3)	Paul Catling	46
	Terry O'Neill	13		Saun Cross (2)	Liam Herbert	45
	Nick Hunt	11			Stuart Hallam	39
Clanfield	Nigel Hiscock	8	—	Tony Kane (2)	Martin Straddon	34
	Richard Freeman	6		Adrian Cooksley	Gary Ackling	32
	Adrian Cooksley	5			A. Notton	22
					R. Freeman	22
Didcot Town	Tony O'Donovan	17	Tony O'Donovan	John Cullen (4)	Peter Dallaway	36*
	Peter Dallaway	6	(1)	Peter Dallaway	Clive Gilkes	32
	John Cullen	6			Alan Hyatt	32
Fairford	Pat Toomey	15	—	—	Paul Gibbons	34
	Steve Saunders	5			Pat Toomey	34
	Pete May	4			Kevin Prictor	28
Hounslow	Cecil Collins		—	Martin Francis (3)	Stuart Mackenzie	
	Martin Francis			Terry Boyle (2)	Steve Croad	
					Dean Hyatt	
Maidenhead Town & Y	David Di Baltimelli	12	—	Pat Sweeney (6)	David Di Baltimelli	32
	Pat Sweeney	7			Andy Robinson	31
	Ian Shiell	3			Rodney Hing	30
Moreton Town	David James	16	David James (1)	A. Spedding (4)	A. Scarsbrook	42*
	Percy Hickman	10			A. Ogg	38
	Paul Smith	7			B. Humphries	37
Morris Motors	Micky Long	34	Micky Long (3)	Micky Long (5)	Paul Baker	
	Mark Stevens	18			Aidy Blay	
	Danny O'Loughlan	12			Sean Lydon	
Rayners Lane	Dave Penny	17	—	Kevin Kelly (3)	Phil Robson	38
	Val Boyle	9		Val Boyle	Bobby Hanson	37
	Gary Woosley	9			Dave Penny	36
Sharpness	Nick Rock	37	Nick Rock (4)	Nick Rock (4)	S. Billett	45*
	Kevin Willetts	28	Jimmy Rigg (1)	K. Willetts (2)	N. Rock	45*
	Jimmy Rigg	25	Doug Foxwell (1)	R. Breedon	J. Robbie	44
			K. Willetts (2)	P. Bowers	D. Foxwell	44
Shortwood United	Nick Bell	24	Larry Gough	M. Carroll (2)	Andy Ireland	37
	Larry Gough	22	Nick Bell	L. Gough	Peter Grant	36
	Andy Ireland	12		P. Grant	Larry Gough	35
					Nick Bell	35
Supermarine	Terry Brown	14	—	—	Martyn Spackman	
	Bob Moore	5			Glynn Dubber	
	Sean O'Connell	4			Charlie North	
Thame United	John Gilligan	18	—	John Gilligan (3)	Steve Mayhew	32*
	Nigel Lynch	8			John Gilligan	29
	John Watts	7				
Wallingford	Brendon McKevitt	9	D. Romaom (1)	Hughie Cheetham	Charlie Allum	34
	Harold Wilson	6		(2)	Hughie Cheetham	34
	Donley Romain	5			Ian Barrett	31
Wantage Town	Jeff Crame	20	Jeff Crame (1)	—	John Culley	34
	Kevin O'Hanlon	11			Jeff Crame	31
	John Culley	7			Kevin O'Hanlon	18

*Ever present

HELLENIC LEAGUE

Club	Leading Goalscorers		Hat-Tricks	Penalties	Most Appearances	
AFC Aldermaston	Dave Griffiths (Jnr)	15	—	—	Dave Griffiths (Jnr)	38*
	Alan Kersley	10			Ray Weeks	37
	Roy Bird	7			Karl Griffiths	34
Avon (Bradford)	Mick Baggs	7	—	John Amor (1)	Mick Baggs	31
	Ron Thompson	6			Phil Trolley	30
	Andy Bonser	3			Colin Trott	30
					Andy Bonser	30
Badminton Pickson	Steve Matthews	19	Dave Bone v	S. Matthews (3)	Steve Matthews	37*
	Dave Bone	10	Easington	Paul Sims (2)	Paul Gosling	36
	Mark Hatherell	8			Ray Gunning	36
					Dave Bone	36
Bishops Cleeve	Peter Wilson	25	Bob Styman (1)	Tim Bayliffe (5)	Dave Walker	34*
	Bob Styman	12			Bob Styman	26
	Tony Danaher	7			Tim Bayliffe	26
Dowty Staverton	Martin Birt	6	—	—	Stephen Cooper	31
	Robert Brown	5			Martin Birt	29
	Brian James	4			Brian James	28
Easington Sports	D. Brooker	10	—	C. Heath (2)	A. Farr	35
	D. Foreman	8		L. Hastie (2)	D. Brooker	34
	L. Hastie	7			M. Rolph	34
Kidlington	Robert Mason	25	Robert Mason 4 v	Kevin Walton	Nick Griffiths	42
	Kevin Walton	15	Easington Sports	9 out of 9	Kevin Walton	41
	Dave Hunter	11			Robert Mason	40
Kintbury Rangers	Ged Farr	25	Ged Farr (1)	Martyn Stratford	Wayne Bailey	45*
	Kevin Monaghan	17		(3)	Nigel Thorne	45*
	Terry Bailey	8		Chris Mundy (3)	Gerry Smith	44
Lambourn Sports	Geoff Glass	14	—	Tony Woosnam (1)	Dick Brinkworth	29
	Steve Hooper	8			Tony Woosnam	27
	Bill Silto	5			Pat Mooney	27
Pegasus Juniors	George Bowen	28	G. Bowen	L. Braithwaite (2)	Gary Morgan	51*
	Chris Booton	23	L. Silcox	C. Burton	Bryan Bouston	48
	Len Braithwaite	10		N. Chapman	Chris Burton	46
Pressed Steel	Paul Bradbury	19	Four	Pat Kilgariff (2)	Dave Wallcraft	33
	Gary Todd	12			Ricky Pratt	32
	Donny Romain	9			Pat Kilgariff	31
Viking Sports	Terry Cross	12	Frank Healy (1) v	—	Gary Amer	37
	Frank Healy	11	Dowty Staverton		Paul Buckland	37
	Bob Butler	8			Bob Butler	36
Worrall Hill	Cliff Powell	19	Cliff Powell (1)	C. Powell	Alan Lawrence	35
	Tony Price	12	Tony Price (1)	T. Price	T. Price	35
	Trevor Foxwell	6		P. Broadman	Brian Payne	30
	Gary Evans	6		B. Lawrence		
Yate Town	Steve Moore	39	S. Moore (3)	S. Moore (4)	B. Walker	42*
	Bob Walker	26	B. Walker (1)	C. Wilkey (4)	A. Hussey	40
	Kevin Prue	14			S. Moore	40

*Ever present

Fairford Town's winner is scored by May, away to Northwood in the home side's last season in the Hellenic League. Photo: Mike Joss

ABINGDON TOWN

President: R. F. Cox
Chairman: A. R. Bricknell
Manager: P. Holden
Coach: S. Morton
Physiotherapist: Dr R. Casson
Secretary: B. M. Crook
Address & Tel No: 41 Radley Rd., Abingdon, Oxon OX14 3PL. 0235 24461
Commercial Manager: None
Address & Tel No:
Press Officer & Tel No: N. Quail
Address & Tel No of ground: Culham Road, Abingdon. 023521684
Simple ground directions: A415 Abingdon - Dorchester Road, ½ mile from town centre
No of seats: 100 **Covered accommodation:** 200 **Capacity:** 2,000 **Floodlights:** No
Year formed: 1880 **Nickname:** The Town **Club sponsors:** None
Club colours: Yellow & Green
Change colours: Blue
Record attendance: 2,500
Programme: Yes
Previous Leagues: Reading & District
Programme Editor: E. Quail
Clubhouse details: Social Club
Major Honours: Berks & Bucks Senior Cup 1958-59, Hellenic League Winners 1956-57, 1958-59, 1959-60, Cup 1957-58, 1970-71, 1981-82
Club Captain (83-84): Malcolm Pledge **Player of the Year:** John Merrill

ABINGDON UNITED

President: R. H. Barlow
Chairman: A. White
Manager: Nick Brown
Coach: Martin Presscot
Physiotherapist: L. Clarke
Secretary: Terry Hutchinson
Address & Tel No: 0235 23017
Commercial Manager: None
Address & Tel No:
Press Officer & Tel No: Bill Fletcher
Address & Tel No of ground: Northcourt Road, Abingdon. 0235 20255
Simple ground directions: A4183 Abingdon - Oxford. Ground approx 1 mile north of town centre
No of seats: Nil **Covered accommodation:** Nil **Capacity:** 2,000 **Floodlights:** Yes
Year formed: 1946 **Nickname:** **Club sponsors:** Glasurit Beck
Club colours: Yellow shirts, Blue shorts
Change colours: White shirts, Blue shorts
Record attendance: 400+
Programme: Yes
Previous Leagues: North Berks
Programme Editor: William Fletcher
Clubhouse details: Small club house, 2 bars, membership 350
Club Captain (83-84): Neil Taylor **Player of the Year:** Neil Taylor

ALMONDSBURY GREENWAY

President: David H. Lansdown
Chairman: B. R. Tufton
Vice-Chairman: Dr B. J. H. Levers
Manager: B. R. Tufton
Coach: J. Switalski
Physiotherapist: N. Leeson
Treasurer: G. Weatherley
Secretary: K. G. Robbins
Sec. Address & Tel No: 47 Westfield Road Backwell, Bristol BS19 3ND. Flax Bourton (027583) 2323
Commercial Manager: Mark Townsend
Address & Tel No: 17 Nicholettes, Millers Lodge, Warmley, Bristol BS15 5YF. 027588 6529
Press Officer & Tel No: Dr B. G. H. Levers
Address & Tel No of ground: The Field, Gloucester Road, Almondsbury, Bristol. Almondsbury (0454 612240)
Simple ground directions: From M4 West leave at junction 20 to M5 (South West). Leave immediately at junction 16 (A38), turn right onto A38 — ground on right 200 yards. 7 miles north Bristol on A38
No of seats: None **Covered accommodation:** None **Capacity:** 2,000 **Floodlights:** No
Year formed: 1890 (AG 1974) **Nickname:** The Almonds **Club sponsors:** Walford Caravans
Club colours: Blue/White
Change colours: All White
Previous Names: Almondsbury. Greenway Sports
Previous Grounds: None
Record attendance: 900 v Billericay Town FA Vase 1977
Previous Leagues: Bristol Weslyan early 1900s. Bristol Suburban League 1949-1973. Bristol Premier Combination 1968-1975. Gloucestershire County League 1975-1982
Clubhouse details: Open 7 days (evenings, lunchtimes). All sport catered for, refreshments, entertainment, function rooms, hockey, tennis, skittles and cricket
Programme Editor: Mark Townsend **Programme details:** 20 pages, 50p, including admission
Major Honours: Glos County League Champions 1976-77, 1977-78, 1978-79, 1979-80, 1980-81, Runners-Up 1975-76, 1981-82, GFA Challenge Trophy Winners 1978-79, Runners-Up 1980-81, FA Vase Wembley Finalists 1978-79, Semi-finalists 1977-78, Avon Premier Combination Champions 1974-75. (NB Honours relate to Almondsbury Greenway from 1974), Hellenic League Premier Division: Runners-Up 1982-83, Champions 1983-84, Premier Division Challenge Cup: Winners 1983-84.
Club Captain (83-84): John Shehem

BICESTER TOWN

President: G. Titchener Esq.
Chairman: D. Waller
Manager: Trevor Cuss
Coach: As above
Physiotherapist: None
Secretary: C. H. Rawlings
Address & Tel No: Bicester 241085
Commercial Manager; As above
Press Officer & Tel No: As above
Address & Tel No of ground: Sports Ground, Oxford Road, Bicester
Simple ground directions: Outskirts of town on the Oxford Road
No of seats: 250 **Covered accommodation:** 250 **Capacity:** Plenty **Floodlights:** No
Year formed: 1873 **Nickname:** Foxhunters **Club sponsors:** Bicester Roofing Co
Club colours: Red shirts, Black shorts
Change colours: Light Blue stripes
Record attendance: 1,000
Programme Editor: D. Waller
Previous Leagues: Oxon Senior
Programme: None
Clubhouse details: Bar separate from hall (alterations now taking place for a lounge, clubhouse on the ground itself)
Major Honours: Hellenic Champions 1960-61, 1977-78, Reserve Champions same year after winning Hellenic Div 1 1976-77 and gaining promotion
Club Captain (83-84): Paul Carling **Player of the Year:** Andy Leach

CLANFIELD

President: H. Wallis
Chairman: W. R. Goddard
Manager: L. Hill
Coach: L. Hill
Physiotherapist: None
Secretary: J. M. Osborne
Address & Tel No: Witney 71631
Commercial Manager:
Press Officer & Tel No: W. R. Goddard
Address & Tel No of ground: Radcot Road, Clanfield. 036 781 314
Simple ground directions: A4095, 8 miles west of Witney
No of seats: None **Covered accommodation:** 200 **Capacity:** 2,000 **Floodlights:** No
Year formed: 1890 **Nickname:** The Robins **Club sponsors:** None
Club colours: Red/White/Red **Change colours:** Blue/White/Blue
Record attendance: Not known
Previous Leagues: Witney & District **Programme:** None
Clubhouse details: Open every night, Saturday, Sunday lunchtime and after matches
Major Honours: Oxon Junior Shield 1933, Oxon Intermediate Cup 1968, Witney Div 2 1964-65, Witney Div 1 1965-66, Witney Prem 1966-67, Hellenic Div 1 & Cup 1969-70, Hellenic Prem Cup 1973-74
Club Captain (83-84): Gary Ackling **Player of the Year:** Gary Ackling

DIDCOT TOWN

President: John Merrifield
Chairman: Peter Robinson
Manager: John Bailey
Coach: Eddie King
Physiotherapist: Eddie King
Secretary: Norman Bennett
Sec. Address & Tel No: 75 Churchill Road, Didcot, Oxon OX11 7BU. Didcot 813016
Press Officer: K. Coles
Address: 8 Lockinge House, Didcot
Address & Tel No of ground: 58 Station Road, Didcot. 813212
Simple ground directions: Midway down Station Road, Didcot, situated on right, ¼ mile from Railway Station towards town centre
No of seats: None **Covered accommodation:** Yes **Capacity:** 100 **Floodlights:** No
Year formed: 1907 **Nickname:** None **Club sponsors:** Express Dairies
Club colours: Red with White pin stripe **Change colours:** Tangerine & Black
Record attendance: 3,000 v Wycombe Wanderers (Berks & Bucks Cup) **Year:** 1957
Previous Leagues: Metropolitan **Programme:** Yes
Clubhouse details: Daily evenings and Sunday lunchtimes **Programme Editor:** Steve Culliford
Major Honours: Hellenic Premier 1953-54, Premier Cup 1965-66, 1966-67, Hellenic Div 1 1976-77, Div 1 Cup 1976-77
Club Captain (83-84): Bob Humphries **Player of the Year:** Peter Dallaway

FAIRFORD TOWN

President: A. E. Smith
Chairman: M. B. Tanner
Manager: S. Crowley
Coach: None
Physiotherapist: T. Williams
Secretary: M. J. Cook
Secretary Address: "Bow-Wow", Down Ampney, Cirencester, Glos. Tel: (H) Swindon 751240, (B) Cirencester 5995
Commercial Manager: E. Howard
Press Officer & Tel No: As Secretary
Address & Tel No of ground: Cinder Lane, Fairford (Cirencester 712071)
Simple ground directions: Entering Fairford from Lechlade turn left down Cinder Lane opposite petrol filling Station on right.
No of seats: None **Covered accommodation:** 200 **Capacity:** 2,000 **Floodlights:** No
Year formed: 1891 **Nickname:** None **Club sponsors:** Jewson
Club colours: Red Shirts, White Shorts **Change colours:** Blue or Yellow
Previous Names: **Previous Grounds:** None
Record attendance:
Previous Leagues: Cirencester and District. Swindon and District **Programme:**
Clubhouse details: Open every evening and Saturday, Sunday and Bank Holiday Lunchtimes
Major Honours: Gloucester Challenge Trophy Winners 1979-80, Runners-Up 1982-83
Club Captain (83-84): Bob Dorey **Player of the Year:** Paul Gibbons

HOUNSLOW

President: Derek Roberts
Chairman: J. Brewster
Team Manager: D. Jones
General Manager: C. Barnes
Physiotherapist:
Press Officer & Tel No: Barry Sutherns
Secretary: Barry Sutherns
Address & Tel No: 8 Southland Way, Hounslow, Middx. 01-898 8230 (H), 01-890 5181 (B)
Commercial Manager: None
Address & Tel No:
Address & Tel No of ground: Denbigh Road, Hounslow, Middx. 01-570 4983 **Club shop:** Yes
Simple ground directions: By train Hounslow East (Piccadilly), Hounslow B.R. by road, 5 mins from A4 and A315 London Road. Denbigh Road is off Kingsley Road
No of seats: 150 **Covered accommodation:** 1,000 **Capacity:** 6,000 **Floodlights:** Yes
Year formed: 1884 **Nickname:** The Town **Club sponsors:** None
Previous names: Hounslow Town **Club colours:** Red/Black stripes
Previous grounds: None **Change colours:** White/Black
Day for midweek home matches: Monday
Record attendance: Not known **Year:**
Best performance in: F.A. Cup: 1962-3 1st Round Proper
F.A. Trophy: 1979-80 1st Round
Clubhouse details: New clubhouse open every evening and lunchtime
Previous Leagues: Spartan, Corinthian, Athenian Southern
Present players with Football League experience: None
Past players who progressed into the Football League: C. Forde (Plymouth), E. Howe (Fulham), K. Osgood (Spurs), T. Spencer (Brentford)
Record transfer fee paid: None
Record transfer fee received: £4,000 for Clevere Forde from Plymouth Argyle
Programme details: 20 pages, 20p
Programme Editor: Barry Sutherns
Club metal badges: Yes
Senior Honours: F.A. Amateur Cup Finalists
Local newspapers & Tel No: Middlesex Chronicle (01-572 0016), Informer (01-4546 2522)
Club Captain (83-84): Phil Ash **Player of the Year:** Stuart Mackenzie

Aldermaston's Dave Griffiths (dark shirt) duels with a Lambourn player in their club's Hellenic League 'local derby'. Photo: Newbury Weekly News

Aldermaston *Back Row (L-R): Roy Bird, Keith Munt, Steve Thompson, Keith Bruce, Shaun Tull, Karl Griffiths, Alan Kersley, Front Row (L-R): Dave Griffiths (Jun.), Chris Rampton, Dave Beare, Ray Weeks, Ken Jubin.*

MAIDENHEAD TOWN YOUTH

President:
Chairman: G. T. Jenkins
Manager: R. Barber
Asst Manager: T. Ovens
Physiotherapist: J. Dell
Secretary: D. Jenkins
Address & Tel No: 0628 27239
Commercial Manager: F. Lummes
Address & Tel No:
Press Officer & Tel No: F. Lummes
Address & Tel No of ground: Hayes Park, Courthouse Road, Maidenhead. 0628 22340
Simple ground directions: Oxford, Aylesbury, Swindon Thicket roundabout, A40 to Slough, 1 mile turn left, Courthouse Road ground 300 yards on left
No of seats: None **Covered accommodation:** None **Capacity:** N/A **Floodlights:** No
Year formed: 1946 **Nickname:** The Stags **Club sponsors:** Boxall Ltd
Club colours: Dark Blue shirts, White shorts **Change colours:** Yellow
Record attendance: 500+ v Panathinaikos (Greece) Friendly **Year:** 1982
Previous Leagues: **Programme:**
Clubhouse details: Open 6 nights a week (closed Sunday)
Major Honours: Hellenic League Division 1 Champions 1974-75, Norfolkian Cup Winners 1980-81

MORETON TOWN F.C.

President: Lord Dulverton
Chairman: C. Miles
Manager: C. Shephard
Assistant Manager: J. Hook
Coaches: J. Hutchison, M. Hemming
Physiotherapist: M. Pugh
Secretary: Janette Burden
Address & Tel No: (0608) 50875
Commercial Manager: None
Address & Tel No:
Press Officer & Tel No: B. Eldridge
Address & Tel No of ground: London Rd, Moreton in Marsh Glos (0608 50861)
Simple ground directions: On main Worcester Rd, 8 miles Chipping Norton.
No of seats: None **Covered accommodation:** Yes **Capacity:** 3,000 **Floodlights:** Yes
Year formed: Pre 1903 **Nickname:** Lilywhites **Club sponsors:** Cotswold Casement Co
Club colours: White **Change colours:** Red or Blue
Previous Names: None **Previous Grounds:** None
Record attendance:
Previous Leagues: Cheltenham League 1928-70. Cotswold League 1908, 1928. **Programme:** None
Clubhouse details: Open every night, except Mondays, dancing, bingo etc.
Major Honours: Biggart Cup Winners 1969-70, League Champions 1973-74, 1975-76, Glos County Cup Winners 1973-74, League Runners-Up 1974-75, County Cup Winners 1981, League Runners-Up & County Cup Winners 1982, League Champions 1982-83, League Cup Winners 1982-83.
Club Captain (83-84): Graham Fell **Player of the Year:** Brian Humphries

MORRIS MOTORS

President: Freddy Williams
Chairman: Ricky Waitworth
Manager: Alan Holliday
Coach: Biller Trinder
Physiotherapist: Mr Taylor
Secretary: Steve Giles
Address & Tel No: Turner Close, Oxford. (0865) 772626
Commercial Manager: A. Bates
Address & Tel No: 24 Birch Rd, Garsington, Oxon. (08736 481)
Press Officer: D. Hawkes
Address & Tel No of ground: Oxford (0865) 778476 Clubhouse
Simple ground directions: On reaching Oxford take by-pass following directions to Cowley, at Horsepath Rd roundabout turn off and turn right again at Holloway, ground on right hand side
No of seats: 50 **Covered accommodation:** 60 **Capacity:** 1,000 **Floodlights:** No
Year formed: 1922 **Nickname:** Motors **Club sponsors:** To be negotiated
Club colours: Blue (Dark) **Change colours:** White shirts
Previous Names: N/A **Previous Grounds:** N/A
Record attendance: 800 v Oxford City 1979-80 **Programme:** Special games only (50p)
Previous Leagues: Oxfordshire Senior League **Programme Editor:** A. Bates
Clubhouse details: As ground only left at Hollaway, right into Cresecent Road
Major Honours: Oxford Senior Cup Winners, Hellenic Premier League Winners, Hellenic First Division Champions
Club Captain (83-84): Paul Baker **Player of the Year:** Sean Lydon

RAYNERS LANE

President:
Chairman: Tom Lynn
Manager: Don Durkin
Coach: Don Durkin
Physiotherapist:
Secretary: Tony Pratt
Address & Tel No: 0895 33853
Commercial Manager:
Treasurer: Danny Maher
Press Officer & Tel No: Geoff Mills (Ruislip) 32044
Address & Tel No of ground: 51 Rayners Lane, Harrow, Middlesex. 01-866 9659
Simple ground directions: Turn right from Rayners Lane LT Station, take 2nd turning left (Rayners Lane), ground on right
No of seats: None **Covered accommodation:** Yes **Capacity:** 1,000 **Floodlights:** No
Year formed: 1933 **Nickname:** The Lane **Club sponsors:** A & J Bull Ltd
Club colours: Yellow & Green stripes/Green **Change colours:** Maroon
Record attendance: 250 **Programme:** Yes 20 pages, 20p
Programme Editor: Geoff Mills
Previous Leagues: Parthenon, Spartan, Middlesex, Hellenic Div 1
Clubhouse details: 2 bars, entertainment hall, separate dressing rooms
Major Honours: Middlesex League Cup 1971-72, Hellenic Div 1 Cup 1980-81, Champions 1982-83, Middlesex Premier Cup Winners 1983-84
Club Captain (83-84): Dave Mills **Player of the Year:** Dave Penny

Shortwood United Celebrate their superb County Cup success. *Back Row (L-R): Dave Trowell, Paul Trowell, Les White, Larry Gough, Mike Carroll (Manager), Wayne Hams, Paul Shiers, Peter Grant, Andy Ireland, Tony Lewis (Trainer), Front Row: Nick Bell, Mike Davis, John Dangerfield, Keith Hardcastle.*

SHORTWOOD UNITED

President: J. Claridge
Chairman: I. Martin
Manager: M. Carroll
Coach: A. Lewis
Physiotherapist:
Secretary: P. J. Grant
Address & Tel No: Nailsworth 2577
Commercial Manager: R. C. Webb
Address & Tel No: 11 Kings Rd, Rodborough, Stroud, Glos. Stroud 3391
Press Officer: C. F. Webb. Shortwood, Nailsworth, Glos. Nailsworth 3204
Address & Tel No of ground: "Meadow Bank", Shortwood, Nailsworth, Glos. Tel: Nailsworth 3936
Simple ground directions: ¾ mile from Nailsworth, keep left past "Britannia"
No of seats: None **Covered accommodation:** Grandstand standing **Capacity:** 150 **Floodlights:** No
Year formed: 1900 **Nickname:** The Wood **Club sponsors:** Astro Vision & Video Libraries, Stroud & Gloucester, also many other sponsors advt boards etc.
Club colours: Red White stripes
Change colours: White, Blue stripes
Record attendance: 830 F.A. Vase **Year:** 1982
Programme: Free with Ad charge to ground.
Previous Leagues: Gloucester County
Programme Editor: Richard Weber
Clubhouse details: Sports and social club on ground open after matches at 4.00pm
Major Honours: Glos County League 1981-82, Glos F.A. Trophy 1983-84, Hellenic League Division One Cup 1983-84
Club Captain (83-84): M. Carroll
Player of the Year: Andy Ireland

SHARPNESS

President: A. Aldridge
Chairman: D. Thomas
Manager: P. Casey
Coach:
Physiotherapist:
Secretary: J. D. Thomas
Address & Tel No: 69 Oldminster Road, Sharpness, Glos GL13 9UR. Dursely 811397
Commercial Manager: K. Coughlin
Address & Tel No: New Brookend, Nr Sharpness, Glos. Dursely 810657
Press Officer & Tel No:
Address & Tel No of ground: "The Port", The Docks, Sharpness, Glos
Simple ground directions:
No of seats: 250 **Covered accommodation:** Yes **Capacity:** 3,000 **Floodlights:** No
Year formed: 1900 **Nickname:** The Sharks **Club sponsors:** None
Club colours: Red Shirts, White Shorts, Red Socks
Change colours: Blue Shirts, Blue Shorts, Blue Socks
Previous Names: None
Previous Grounds: None
Record attendance: 3,500 v St Austell 1955
Previous Leagues: Gloucestershire Northern League, Gloucestershire County League
Clubhouse details: Bar + skittle alley, open every evening & match days
Programme: 16 pages, 10 pence
Programme Editor: K. Loughlin
Major Honours: Gloucestershire County League Winners 1983-84
Club Captain (83-84): Nick Rock
Player of the Year: Nick Rock

THAME UNITED

President: P. Smith
Chairman: R. Eele
Manager: Brian Wyatt
Coach: Ken Norton
Physiotherapist:
Secretary: Club
Address & Tel No: Windmill Road, Thame. Thame 3017
Commercial Manager:
Address & Tel No:
Press Officer & Tel No: No
Address & Tel No of ground: Windmill Road, Thame. Thame 3017
Simple ground directions: From Oxford centre of town and turn right, Nelson St from Princes Risborough, first turning left town centre
No of seats: 100 **Covered accommodation:** Yes **Capacity:** **Floodlights:** Yes
Year formed: 1883 **Nickname:** Utd **Club sponsors:** Haddenham Carpets, Gibbs Garage
Club colours: Red
Change colours: White
Previous Names: No
Previous Grounds: 2
Record attendance: Hazells, 450 **Year:** 1960-61
Previous Leagues: Oxon Senior League
Programme: 4 pages, 10p
Clubhouse details: Bar, holds 300 people
Programme Editor: R. Eele
Major Honours: Hellenic League 61-62, Hellenic Cup 60-61, Oxon Senior Cup 62-63, Oxon Senior Cup 80-81
Club Captain (83-84): Brian Knight
Player of the Year: Martin Ford

The Chairman of Wallingford Town, Mr Albert Miles (front left), thanks the Managing Director of Polar Homes Ltd, Mr David Blake, for his company's sponsorship.

WALLINGFORD TOWN

President: A. Hume
Chairman: A. Miles
Manager: Alan Brannan
Coach: David Escott
Physiotherapist: W. Revell, BEM
Secretary: David S. Sharp
Address & Tel No: (H) 0491 36796
Commercial Manager: None
Address & Tel No:
Press Officer & Tel No: None
Address & Tel No of ground: The Hithercroft Sports Compley, Wallingford Oxon, Wallingford 35044
Simple ground directions: St Johns Rd and follow signs marked Industrial Estate, Ground 200yds on right.
No of seats: None **Covered accommodation:** Yes **Capacity:** 2,000 **Floodlights:** No
Year formed: 1922 **Nickname:** The Town **Club sponsors:** Jim Pink Motors & Polar Improvements Ltd
Club colours: Red/Black trim
Change colours: Blue/White trim
Previous Names: None
Previous Grounds: The Bull Croft
Record attendance: 490
Programme Editor: Jim Whitehorn
Previous Leagues: Reading and District
Programme: price with admission 8 pages
Clubhouse details: Bar and members Lounge, club house open every night
Major Honours: Hellenic League Premier Division 1969
Club Captain (83-84): Norman Marthens
Player of the Year: John Dreyer

WANTAGE TOWN

President:
Chairman: E. Smart
General Manager: Grahame Nash
Manager: Clive Corrigan
Coach: Clive Corrigan
Physiotherapist: Jim Potter
Secretary: Mr J. K. Thomas
Address & Tel No: Rose Cottage, Main Street, Grove, Wantage, Oxon OX12 7JT. Wantage 68556
Commercial Manager: John Russell
Address & Tel No:
Press Officer & Tel No: Geoff Smith
Address & Tel No of ground: Alfredian Park, Wantage, Oxon. 4781
Simple ground directions: Take Hungerford Road from Wantage, ground on right opposite recreation ground
No of seats: 50 **Covered accommodation:** 300 **Capacity:** 5,000 **Floodlights:** Yes
Year formed: 1892 **Nickname:** None **Club sponsors:** National Bus Co, Normans Cash & Carry, Bear Hotel, Wantage
Club colours: Green/White
Change colours: White
Record attendance: 1,800 **Year:**
Previous Leagues: Swindon & District
Programme Editor: Geoff Smith
Clubhouse details: Bar open evenings, Tuesday, Wednesday, Thursday, Friday, Saturday
Major Honours: Hellenic Division Champions 1981, Premier Runners-Up 1982, Senior Cup Winners 1983
Club Captain (83-84): Bruce Panting

A.F.C. ALDERMASTON

President: K. Norridge M.B.E.
Chairman: Ted Russell
Managers: George Hughes/Peter Kerr
Coach: Dave Griffiths (Sen)
Physiotherapist: Ken Bayford
Secretary: Don Campbell
Address & Tel No: 68 Priors Road, Tadley. Tel: Tadley 4319 (Bus), Tadley 4111 X5372
Commercial Manager:
Address & Tel No:
Press Officer & Tel No: K. Norridge
Address & Tel No of ground: A.W.R.E. Recreational Society Sports Ground. Tel: Tadley (07356) 4111 Ext 344
Simple ground directions: From Reading/Newbury (A4) trunk road, take A340 through Aldermaston Village, 1½ miles to Sports Ground (left 100 m before roundabout)
No of seats: 20 **Covered accommodation:** Yes **Capacity:** 20 **Floodlights:** No
Year formed: 1952 **Nickname:** **Club sponsors:** Toucan Travel
Club colours: Red shirts, Black shorts
Change colours: Yellow shirts, Black shorts
Record attendance: Not known
Programme Editor: John McBryde
Previous Leagues: North Hants
Programme: Every home game
Clubhouse details: Open standard licensing hours + from 4.30 on match days (Saturday)
Club Captain (83-84): D. Griffith (Jnr)
Player of the Year: Ray Weeks

AVON (BRADFORD)

President: B. Carter
Chairman: W. Martin
Manager: T. Quincey
Coach: B. Carter
Physiotherapist: O. Swanbury
Secretary: D. L. Wilson
Address & Tel No: 44 Princes Gardens, Hilperton, Trowbridge, Wilts. (02214) 68832
Commercial Manager: No
Press Officer & Tel No: T. Quincey. (02214) 5656
Address & Tel No of ground: Avon Sports & Social Club, Trowbridge Road, Bradford-on-Avon, Wilts. (022 16) 6649
Simple ground directions: Approx ½ mile from town centre on the Bradford-on-Avon to Trowbridge road
No of seats: None **Covered accommodation:** Small **Capacity:** 2,000 **Floodlights:** No
Year formed: 1920 **Nickname:** The Firm **Club sponsors:** Express Dairies
Club colours: Green/White
Change colours: Yellow
Record attendance: 3,500
Programme Editor: T. Quincey
Previous Leagues: Wiltshire County Div. 1
Programme: Free with admission
Clubhouse details: Large club with skittle alley, pool table, dart boards. Comfortable lounge and kitchen facilities. Fully licensed and open 7 days a week
Major Honours: County Senior Cup Finalists 1977-78
Club Captain (83-84): Kevin Henely
Player of the Year: Phil Tolley

BADMINTON PICKSONS F.C.

President: His Grace the Duke of Beaufort
Chairman: Barry Watkins
Manager: Paul Gosling
Coach:
Secretary: S. Martin
Address & Tel No: 8 Stadium Road, Westbury Park, Bristol. (0272) 43329
Commercial Manager:
Address & Tel No:
Press Officers: John Greenwood/Colin Pick
Address & Tel No of ground: Badminton Sports Field, Badminton. Tel: 493 (match days only)
Simple ground directions: Access via Junction 18 (M4) — take A46 (Stroud), turn right at Crosshands traffic lights. Via A433 and A46, turn left Dunkirk crossroads
No of seats: None **Covered accommodation:** None **Capacity:** **Floodlights:** No
Year formed: Early 1900 **Nickname:** None **Club sponsors:** Picksons Parts Distribution Ltd
Club colours: Blue/White/White
Change colours: Red shirts
Record attendance: Not known
Programme Editor: John Greenwood
Previous Leagues: Stroud & District
Programme: 32-36 pages, 20p
Clubhouse details: Lounge and bar facilities available — adjoining changing rooms
Major Honours: Stroud League: Div 1 Champions 1980-81, Div 2 Champions 1979-80, Div 3 Champions 1982-83, Runners-Up 1978-79, Div 4 Champions 1981-82, Berkeley Hospital Cup Winners 1979-80, 1982-83, Cossham Hospital Cup Winners 1979-80, Stroud Charity Cup Winners 1980-81, G.F.A. Senior Cup 1981-82, G.F.A. Minor Cup 1957-58 & 1981-82
Club Captain (83-84): Gary Jones
Player of the Year: Roy Gumming

BISHOPS CLEEVE

President: Alf Davies
Chairman: Bob Miles
Manager: David Walker
Coach: David Goring
Physiotherapist:
Secretary: Alf Davies
Address & Tel No: Bishops Cleeve 3821
Commercial Manager: David Walker
Address & Tel No:
Press Officer: Doug Munday
Address & Tel No of ground: Stoke Road, Bishops Cleeve, Cheltenham, Glos. Tel: B.C. 6257
Simple ground directions: Centre of Bishops Cleve, turn left, ground 100 yards on right
No of seats: None **Covered accommodation:** None **Capacity:** 2,500 **Floodlights:** No
Year formed: 1895 **Nickname:** None **Club sponsors:** Negotiating
Club colours: Green
Change colours: White
Record attendance: 500 **Year:**
Programme Editor: Doug Munday
Previous Leagues: Cheltenham, Glos Northern Senior
Clubhouse details: On ground, separate dressing rooms and bar
Major Honours: Cheltenham League Div 1 Champions (7), Cheltenham Senior Charities Cup (8), Gloucestershire Northern Senior League, Amateur Cup
Club Captain (83-84): Tim Bayliffe

Kidlington *Back Row (L-R): A Sinnott (Manager), C Crozier, S Sensecall, M Hunt, N Price, K Walton, T Wiffen, D Jones (Physio), Front Row (L-R): D Hunter, R Mason, P Longford, M Hickey, G Cooper, N Griffiths.*

Viking Sports *Back Row (L-R): Al Ricales (Manager), Ray Morris (Coach), Gary Amer, Brian Callaghan, Peter Carter, Ron Dixon, Paul Buckland, Bob Butler, Terry Cross, Eric Neill (Physio), Front Row: Kevan Lawton, Lee Thornton, Trevor Webb, Dave O'Brien, Denis Ryan.*

Pegasus Juniors *Back Row (L-R): Neil Chapman, Chris Burton, Chris Booton, Dave Dixon, Gary Morgan, Russell Pritchard, Alan Wilding, Mick Williams (Trainer), Dave Llewellyn (Manager), Front Row (L-R): Clive Trenchard (Coach), Bryan Bouston, Dave Mills, Bill Fraser, Len Silcox, Lew Braithwaite, Ian Rodgerson.*

CIRENCESTER TOWN F.C.

President: A. Hibberd
Chairman: E. Rutter
Manager: Mick Hughes
Coach: N/A
Physiotherapist:
Secretary: M. A. Hall
Address & Tel No: Winterwell Cottage, Barnsley Road Near Cirencester. 0285 3618
Commercial Manager: Ron Swatton
Press Officer & Tel No:
Address & Tel No of ground: Tetbury Road Ground (Ciren 4783)
Simple ground directions: Follow by-pass towards Bristol. The ground is on left hand side approx ¼ mile from town centre; sign showing turning to ground has been erected
No of seats: None **Covered accommodation:** Yes **Capacity:** 150 **Floodlights:** No
Year formed: 1870 **Nickname:** The Town **Club sponsors:** Gardiner Home Improvement Centre
Club colours: Red and Black Stripes/Black/Black
Change colours: Yellow/Blue/Yellow
Previous Names: None
Previous Grounds: None
Record attendance: 1,800 v Fareham (F.A. Amateur Cup) **Year:** 1968
Previous Leagues: None
Programme:
Clubhouse details: Open 7 nights
Major Honours: GFA Senior Amateur Cup Winners 1980, Hellenic League Division One Champions 1973-74
Club Captain: Clive Scarlett

DOVEY STAVERTON

President: T. B. Davis
Chairman: B. Lacey
Manager: Paul Handley
Coach: Paul Handley
Physiotherapist:
Secretary: P. Willis
Address & Tel No: 7 Kingsley Gardens, St. Marks, Cheltenham. Chelt: 36544
Commercial Manager:
Address & Tel No:
Press Officers:
Address & Tel No of ground: Down Hatherley Lane, Cheltenham Road East, Gloucester. Churchdown 712223. Phone only 12am-2pm Saturday lunchtime or 5pm-11pm Saturday evening.
Simple ground directions: Between Gloucester & Cheltenham on B4063 down Hatherley Lane on edge of Dowry-Rotol factory
No of seats: N/A **Covered accommodation:** N/A **Capacity:** N/A **Floodlights:** N/A
Year formed: 1947 **Nickname:** N/A **Club sponsors:** N/A
Club colours: Royal Blue
Change colours: All White
Previous Names: Rotol A.F.C.
Previous Grounds: N/A
Record attendance: N/A
Programme Editor:
Previous Leagues: Cheltenham & Stroud **Programme:** N/A
Clubhouse details: Opening times 12-2pm & 5pm-11pm Saturdays, address as above, hot & cold snacks available
Major Honours: Cheltenham League Division 1 1952-53, Cheltenham League Senior Charities Cup 1960-61
Club Captain (83-84): Paul Thomas

EASINGTON SPORTS F.C.

President: Vacant
Chairman: Terry Horley
Manager: George Veitch
Coach: Norman Wilkins
Physiotherapist: None
Secretary: F. Maycock
Address & Tel No: Banbury 4854
Commercial Manager: N. Wilkins
Address & Tel No:
Press Officer & Tel No: D. Foreman
Address & Tel No of ground: Addison Rd, Easington Estate Banbury Oxon.
Simple ground directions: From Oxford A423. After passing under flyover on the outskirts take the first turning left into Grange Rd, then third turning right into Addison Rd (a cul-de-sac).
No of seats: Nil **Covered accommodation:** Yes **Capacity:** Approx 80 **Floodlights:** No
Year formed: 1945 **Nickname:** None **Club sponsors:** Friswell Steel Ltd
Club colours: Red & White striped shirts
Change colours: Amber
Previous Names:
Previous Grounds: None
Record attendance: 200 v Witney Town in Oxon Senior Cup semi-final.
Previous Leagues: Banbury Junior LGE. Oxen Sen LGE. Warwick Combination **Programme Editor:** D. Foreman
Clubhouse details: Changing Rooms and showers, Bar facilities and food available.
Major Honours: Oxon Senior Cup Finalists & Winners, Oxon Intermediate League & Cup Winners
Club Captain (83-84): L. MacFie
Player of the Year: Andy Farr

KIDLINGTON

President: H. Blake
Chairman: A. Grose
Manager: A. Sinnott
Coach/Physiotherapist: D. Jones
Secretary: T. Canning
Address & Tel No: Kidlington 71631
Commercial Manager:
Address & Tel No:
Press Officer: A. Sinnot
Address & Tel No of ground: Yarnton Road, Kidlington, Oxford. Kidlington 5628
Simple ground directions: From Kidlington roundabout travel north on A423 towards Kidlington, after 1st traffic lights take 2nd left, turn into Yarnton Road, ground 200 yards on left
No of seats: None **Covered accommodation:** None **Capacity:** **Floodlights:** No
Year formed: 1920 **Nickname:** None **Club sponsors:** DIY Supplies Kidlington, Snips Kidlington, Newman Insulation Witney
Club colours: Yellow/Green shorts
Change colours: Claret/Light Blue shorts
Record attendance: **Year:**
Programme Editor: T. Canning
Previous Leagues: Oxon Senior
Clubhouse details: Clubhouse on ground, open matchdays 4pm (or 4.30pm) to 6.00pm. Visitors to be signed in
Club Captain (83-84): Kevin Walton **Player of the Year:** Kevin Walton

Kintbury *Back Row (L-R): Brian Head, Wayne Bailey, Martin Stratford, Bob Bright, Terry Bailey, Mark Annetts, Front Row (L-R): Kevin Monaghan, Gerrald Smith, Nigel Thorne, Ged Farr, Arnie Andrews, Nigel Llewellyn, Andy Head.*

KINTBURY RANGERS

President: C. H. Walker
Chairman: H. J. Newman
Manager: R. D. Alton
Coach:
Physiotherapist:
Secretary: A. K. Plank
Address & Tel No: 26 Kennet Road, Kintbury, Newbury, Berks RG15 0XW. Kintbury 58460
Commercial Manager:
Address & Tel No:
Press Officer: A. K. Plant
Address & Tel No of ground: Recreation Ground, Inkpen Road, Kintbury
Simple ground directions: Turn off A4 between Newbury/Hungerford, 2nd left into Inkpen Road, 200 yards on right
No of seats: None **Covered accommodation:** None **Capacity:** **Floodlights:** No
Year formed: 1943 **Nickname:** Rangers **Club sponsors:** Dundas Arms
Club colours: Amber shirts, Black shorts
Change colours: Green shirts
Record attendance: **Year:**
Programme: Yes
Previous Leagues: Newbury District, North Berks
Programme Editor: Peter Adamson
Clubhouse details: Open evenings except Monday, Wednesday
Major Honours: North Berks League Winners 1977-78, 1981-82
Club Captain (83-84): Gerry Smith **Player of the Year:** Gerry Smith

LAMBOURN SPORTS F.C.

President: N. L.Fraser
Chairman: A. E. Cripps
Manager: L. Hill
Coach: L. Hill
Physiotherapist: None
Secretary: C. G. Bettison
Address & Tel No: 0488 71834
Commercial Manager: None
Address & Tel No:
Press Officer & Tel No: As Secretary
Address & Tel No of ground: Lambourn Sports Club, Bockhampton Rd, Lambourn, Berks. (0488 71335)
Simple ground directions: From Lambourn Church take Newbury St, then 1st right into Station Rd, then 1st left into Bockhampton Rd, Ground on left.
No of seats: None **Covered accommodation:** 150 **Capacity:** 2,000 **Floodlights:** No
Year formed: 1889 **Nickname:** None **Club sponsors:** None
Club colours: Red/White stripes
Change colours: Lemon
Previous Names:
Previous Grounds: None
Record attendance:
Previous Leagues: Newbury & District League 1911-1951. Swindon & District League 1951 to 1961. North Berks League 1972-1977. Hellenic League 1961-1972 and 1977 to date.
Programme: No (discontinued)
Clubhouse details: 3 bars, refreshments, billiard room, lounge, dance hall etc
Major Honours: Berks & Bucks County Cup 61-62 and 79-80, Hellenic League Division One Champions 1981-82, Runners-up 1961-62, Hellenic League Division One Cup Winners 1961-62, 1979-80.
Club Captain (83-84): Paul Mooney **Player of the Year:** John Weaver

PEGASUS JUNIORS

President: P. Hill
Chairman: R. W. Pasley
Manager/Coach: D. Llewellyn
Secretary: R. J. Perks
Address & Tel No: Hereford 272524
Commercial Manager: None
Address & Tel No:
Physiotherapist: P. Isaacs (Hereford Utd)
Press Officer & Tel No:
Address & Tel No of ground: c/o Hereford United F.C. Edgar St, Hereford (0432 274037)
Simple ground directions: Turn off ring road at Edgar St into Blackfrairs St for entry.
No of seats: 5,000 **Covered accommodation:** Yes **Capacity:** 15,000 **Floodlights:** Yes
Year formed: 1955 **Nickname:** **Club sponsors:** Freezer Fare Hereford
Club colours: All Red **Change colours:** All Yellow
Previous Names: None **Previous Grounds:**
Record attendance: **Programme:** Yes
Previous Leagues: Herefordshire, Worcester. **Programme Editor:** R. V. Perks
Clubhouse details: Full facilities at Hereford United, own clubhouse St Owen's Street, Hereford
Major Honours: HFA County Cup Winners 1981-82, 1982-83, Charity Bowl 1981-82, 1982-83, Youth Cup 1981-82
Club Captains: Chris Burton and Ken Gladwin

PRESSED STEEL

President:
Chairman: M. Freeman
Manager: Phil Emsden
Coach: Colin Maskery
Physiotherapist:
Secretary: B. Barr
Address & Tel No: 7B Farm Close Road, Wheatley, Oxon. Wheatley 2508
Commercial Manager: T. Bishop
Address & Tel No: 51 Delbush Avenue, Sandhills, Oxford. Oxford 61778
Address & Tel No of ground: Roman Way, Cowley, Oxford. Oxford 770163
Simple ground directions: Turn off Oxford Ring Road as signposted for Cowley. Turn off at roundabout to Horspath. Proceed 300 yds., turn right, ground on left.
No of seats: 50 **Covered accommodation:** Yes **Capacity:** Unknown **Floodlights:** No
Year formed: 1929 **Nickname:** The Steelmen **Club sponsors:** M. A. John
Club colours: Blue **Change colours:** Red
Previous Leagues: Oxfordshire Senior
Club Captain (1983-84): Pat Kilgariff **Player of the Year (1983-84):** Dave Wallcraft

SUPERMARINE

President:
Chairman: C. Humphreys
Manager: A. J. Belcher
Coach: D. Firmin
Physiotherapist: Kevin Retter
Secretary: E. Stott
Address & Tel No: 43 Stanier Street, Swindon, SN1 5QU. Swindon 21301
Commercial Manager: None
Address & Tel No:
Press Officer & Tel No: None
Address & Tel No of ground: Supermarine Sports & Social Club, Hunts Copse, Highworth Road, South Marston, Swindon. 0973 824828
Simple ground directions: Highworth Road (A361) north of Swindon, via Stratton St Margaret
No of seats: None **Covered accommodation:** North Stand **Capacity:** Approx 100 **Floodlights:** No
Year formed: 1947 (as Vickers) **Nickname:** None **Club sponsors:** Allen Coin
Club colours: Blue & White **Change colours:** Red & White
Record attendance: Not known
Previous Leagues: Wilts **Programme:** 1st Team match days
Clubhouse details: **Programme Editor:** George Ransom
Major Honours: Wilts Senior Cup Runners-Up 1974-75, Wilts Combination League (Senior) Winners 1975-76, Dr Elliott Cup Winners 1974-75, 1977-78, 1978-79, 1979-80, 1980-81, Farningdon Thursday Memorial Cup Winners 1973-74, 1974-75, 1978-79, Hellenic League Division One Runners-Up 1982-83, Hellenic Reserve Section Cup Winners 1983-84
Club Captain (83-84): Brian Clapham **Player of the Year:** Martin Shackman

VIKING SPORTS F.C.

President: R. Bartlett
Chairman: D. Johnson
Manager: A. E. Riches
Coach: R. Morris
Physiotherapist: Eric Neill
Secretary: J. Bennett
Address & Tel No: 6 Bridge House, Boston Manor Road, Brentford. 01-568 9047 (H), Uxbridge 58266 (B)
Commercial Manager: None
Address & Tel No:
Press Officer & Tel No: H. Rose 01-845 5837
Address & Tel No of ground: Avenue Park, Western Avenue, Greenford, Middlesex (01-578 2706)
Simple ground directions: A40 Eastbound Lane, 300 yards prior to Greenford flyover.
No of seats: None **Covered accommodation:** None **Capacity:** 500 **Floodlights:** No
Year formed: 1945 **Nickname:** Vikings **Club sponsors:** None
Club colours: Tangerine and Black **Change colours:** Sky Blue and Black
Previous Names: None **Previous Grounds:**
Record attendance: **Previous Leagues:** Middlesex League, Nemean League
Programme: 12 pages, 10p **Programme Editor:** Kevin Kelly
Clubhouse details: Bar, boardroom. Club open every night except Sundays and Mondays
Club Captain (1983-84): Trevor Webb **Player of the Year (1983-84):** Denis Ryan

WORRALL HILL F.C.

President:
Chairman: K. Bradley
Manager: T. Foxwell
Coach: T. Foxwell
Physiotherapist: M. Clark
Secretary: B. Wadley
Address & Tel No: (H) 0594 60587 (B) 098964867
Commercial Manager: None
Address & Tel No:
Press Officer & Tel No: K. Bradley, 0594 23499
Address & Tel No of ground: Worrall Hill, Lyd Brook Gloucester. (0594 60532)
Simple ground directions: A40 from Gloucester to Huntley turn left onto A4136 approx 9 miles on main road.
No of seats: **Covered accommodation:** **Capacity:** **Floodlights:** No
Year formed: 1955/56 **Nickname:** None **Club sponsors:** Subark
Club colours: Yellow
Change colours: Blue
Previous Names: None
Previous Grounds:
Record attendance:
Previous Leagues: Gloucestershire County
Programme: 12 pages, 10p
Programme Editor: K. Bradley
Clubhouse details: Incorporated in Community Centre at Worral Hill part of which is Worrall Hill Sports Social Club.
Club Captain (1983-84): Cliff Powell
Player of the Year (1983-84): Cliff Powell

YATE TOWN

President: R. Hewetson
Chairman: R. G. Hawkins
Manager: P. Jackson
Coach: L. Parsons
Physiotherapist: R. Jordan
Secretary: T. Tansley
Address & Tel No: 0454 313607
Commercial Manager: T. Chandler
Address & Tel No: 73 Broad Street, Chipping Sodbury 0454 318974
Press Officer: T. Tansley
Address & Tel No of ground: Lodge Road, Yate. Chipping Sodbury (0454) 312886
Simple ground directions: A432 to Yate, turn into North Road at top of railway bridge, first left past traffic lights
No of seats: None **Covered accommodation:** None **Capacity:** 2,000 **Floodlights:** No
Year formed: 1906 (as Yate Rovers) **Nickname:** Whites **Club sponsors:** No individual sponsor
Club colours: White shirts, Navy shorts
Change colours: Sky Blue shirts, Navy shorts
Record attendance: **Year:**
Programme Editor: Terry Tansley
Previous Leagues: Gloucestershire County
Clubhouse details: On ground, bar facilities, car park
Major Honours: G.F.A. Senior Amateur Cup Winners 1977-78, G.F.A. Challenge Trophy Runners-Up 1978-79
Player of the Year (1983-84): Kevin Price

Rayners Lane *Back Row (L-R): Don Durkin, Dave Russell, Bobby Hanson, Paul Abell, Phil Lynn, Ronnie Marsh, Phil Robson, Dave Frimley, George Giles, Front Row (L-R): Geoff Mills, Barry Nivett, Gary Ryan, Dave Penny, Gary Woolsey, Kevin Kelly, Richard Mitchell. (Missing: Val Boyle, Alan Williams).*

Photo: D. Maher

UNITED COUNTIES FOOTBALL LEAGUE

Chairman: T N Bates

Secretary: G T Ellitson, 2 St Marks Close, Rushden, Northants
(Rushden 313106)

BUCKINGHAM TOWN LEAD ALL THE WAY

I am pleased to be able to write my annual report once again after another successful season for so many Clubs in our League. On the home front Buckingham Town led from the beginning of the season and although faltering a little nearing May they held off the challenge by Baldock and Stamford to be worthy winners of the Premier Division with Baldock town in their first season with us becoming runners up.

Brackley Town also in their first U.C.L. season won Division One followed closely by British Timken Duston and Kempston Rovers. Arlesey Reserves in the 1st Division reserve section took over the championship from Irthlingborough Reserves, holders for the past two seasons, who this time became runners up. The most exciting finish was in the newly formed Reserve Division 2 when the final game at Raunds between Raunds reserves and Cottingham reserves decided the top two positions and although the game ended in a draw Raunds were the winners on goal average.

The cup scene was also very successful for our clubs with Stamford leading the way by reaching Wembley in the FA Vase but although losing the match did the League proud in a very exciting game. Buckingham not only won the Prem/Div One KO Cup but also took home the Bucks Senior Cup and Berks & Bucks Charity Cup.

In Northamptonshire, Cottingham won the Northants Junior Cup and not to be outdone their reserve team triumphed in the Lower Junior Cup. Also Long Buckby in the Northants Senior Cup held Kettering Town at Rockingham Road in the final but unfortunately lost at home in the replay but were worthy runners up. Finally on the Cup scene Arlesey Town beat Barton Rovers to win the Beds Premier Cup.

The coming season will see more clubs joining our League and I would like to welcome Stotfold into the Premier Division, Long Sutton and Mirlees Blackstone into Division One. Into the reserve sections come Stotfold, Thrapston and Corby Gainsborough. Also we are hoping to have at least three more clubs with floodlights in the coming season making fourteen clubs with lights all told.

Finally, we are sorry to lose Stevenage Borough this season but wish them all the best for the future in their new League.

G T ELLITSON
(Hon Gen Sec)

CONSTITUTION OF DIVISIONS

1984/5 SEASON

Premier Division

Ampthill Town, Arlesey Town, Baldock Town, Bourne Town, Brackley Town, Buckingham Town, Desborough Town, Eynesbury Rovers, Holbeach United, Irthlingboro Diamonds, Long Buckby, Newport Pagnell, Potton United, Raunds Town, Rothwell Town, St Neots Town, S&L Corby, Stamford, Stotfold, Wootton Blue Cross.

Division One

British Timken Athletic, British Timken Duston, Burton PW, Corby Gainsborough, Cottingham, Ford Sports, Higham Town, Irchester Eastfield, Kempston Rovers, Long Sutton, Mirrlees Blackstone, Northampton Spencer, Olney Town, ON Chenecks, Sharnbrook, Thrapston Venturas, Towcester Town.

Buckingham Town — League Champions. Photo: Mike Joss

The United Counties Football League
Season 1983-84
Final League Tables

Premier Division

	P	W	D	L	F	A	Pts
Buckingham	36	26	6	4	77	24	58
Baldock	36	21	8	7	75	42	50
Stamford	36	18	11	7	75	42	47
Bourne	36	19	8	9	66	49	46
Potton	36	13	16	7	50	39	42
Stevenage	36	16	9	11	52	46	41
Irthlingborough	36	15	10	11	59	40	40
Long Buckby	36	13	13	10	55	48	39
Wooton	36	13	11	12	56	49	37
Ampthill	36	13	10	13	56	54	36
Arlesey	36	12	12	12	45	56	36
Newport Pagnell	36	11	11	14	40	50	33
Rothwell	36	11	10	15	52	58	32
Raunds	36	10	10	16	56	68	30
Holbeach	36	12	6	18	44	68	30
Eynesbury	36	10	9	17	51	74	29
S & L Corby	36	7	7	22	34	63	21
Desborough	36	5	10	21	32	62	20
St Neots	36	3	11	22	28	74	17

No clubs relegated.

Division 1

Brackley	30	22	6	2	70	21	50
BT Duston	30	19	8	3	62	15	46
Kempston	30	19	6	5	56	26	44
BT Athletic	30	18	7	5	65	28	43
Cottingham	30	14	10	6	57	30	38
N'pton Spencer	30	15	5	10	57	36	35
Thrapston	30	13	9	8	49	39	35
Irchester	30	9	11	10	38	48	29
Higham	30	9	10	11	37	33	28
Burton PW	30	10	5	15	40	56	25
ON Chenecks	30	9	5	16	43	64	23
Towcester	30	8	6	16	33	52	22
Corby Gains	30	8	6	16	33	60	22
Ford Sports	30	3	11	16	36	65	17
Olney	30	4	6	20	23	66	14
Sharnbrook	30	2	5	23	16	76	9

SEASON 1983/84

Name	Ampthill	Arlesey	Baldock	Bourne	Buckingham	Desborough	Eynesbury	Holbeach	Irthlingboro	Long Buckby	Newport Pagnell	Potton	Raunds	Rothwell	St Neots	Stamford	Stevenage	S&L Corby	Wootton
Ampthill		0-1	4-0	4-2	0-3	1-1	1-0	3-0	1-4	2-2	0-0	1-1	1-1	2-1	5-0	0-0	2-1	2-1	1-0
Arlesey	1-3		2-0	1-1	1-2	2-0	3-1	1-0	2-3	1-1	3-0	0-1	1-3	1-1	2-1	1-1	0-3	1-4	2-2
Baldock	4-0	1-2		4-1	0-1	4-0	2-0	2-1	1-0	0-0	2-0	2-1	6-0	1-0	2-0	4-4	3-2	2-2	4-0
Bourne	3-1	1-0	1-3		2-0	2-2	5-0	2-1	0-1	2-3	1-1	2-0	4-1	5-2	2-0	1-0	4-0	3-0	1-0
Buckingham	2-1	0-1	2-1	1-1		4-1	5-1	4-0	0-0	1-1	3-0	1-1	2-1	6-0	1-1	3-2	1-0	3-0	3-1
Desborough	1-4	1-2	0-1	1-2	0-2		3-3	0-1	1-1	3-2	1-0	1-2	0-3	0-1	4-2	0-1	0-2	0-0	1-3
Eynesbury	3-1	2-1	0-0	1-1	1-4	1-1		5-0	4-3	1-3	1-0	1-3	3-3	4-0	2-1	1-3	2-2	0-1	2-1
Holbeach	1-2	2-0	1-1	4-1	0-5	0-0	2-0		2-5	3-2	3-3	3-3	1-0	1-0	4-0	1-2	3-0	1-1	0-2
Irthlingboro	1-1	4-0	2-2	0-1	0-1	3-1	5-2	1-0		5-2	0-1	2-1	0-3	1-0	1-1	1-2	2-0	6-0	1-1
Long Buckby	1-1	5-0	0-2	2-2	1-2	0-0	1-0	1-1	2-0		2-3	3-1	0-0	4-1	0-0	1-1	2-0	1-0	0-3
Newport Pagnell	3-0	2-2	2-3	1-2	0-2	2-1	2-0	2-3	0-2	0-0		0-0	3-1	0-2	1-1	1-1	2-0	2-1	2-1
Potton	0-3	0-0	1-2	0-0	2-2	1-1	0-0	2-0	2-0	2-0	1-1		1-1	3-3	3-0	1-0	1-1	0-0	2-0
Raunds	3-2	2-2	4-4	2-4	0-1	2-1	1-3	0-2	0-0	3-1	5-1	1-3		3-3	2-1	1-3	0-0	3-1	0-1
Rothwell	2-2	1-2	1-0	1-2	0-1	0-0	2-3	4-0	1-1	1-2	2-1	0-0	4-1		0-0	2-4	1-1	2-0	3-1
St Neots	0-0	1-3	2-3	0-2	0-3	0-3	1-1	2-0	0-2	0-1	0-0	0-2	2-1	2-3		0-4	2-4	1-1	1-5
Stamford	2-1	1-1	2-5	3-0	0-2	5-0	5-1	3-0	2-0	2-3	4-2	0-2	2-2	1-1	1-1		3-0	4-0	2-2
Stevenage	1-0	0-0	2-1	1-1	2-1	2-1	3-1	4-0	1-0	4-2	0-1	5-3	4-2	2-1	1-1	0-0		2-1	0-0
S&L Corby	4-2	1-1	0-1	5-1	1-0	1-0	4-0	1-3	0-0	0-3	0-1	1-2	0-1	0-4	2-3	0-3	0-2		1-2
Wootton	4-2	2-2	2-2	3-1	1-3	0-2	1-1	4-0	2-2	1-1	0-0	2-2	1-0	1-2	3-1	1-2	2-0	1-0	

SEASON 1983/84

Name	Brackley	Brit. Tim. Ath.	Brit. Tim. Duston	Burton PW	Corby Gains.	Cottingham	Ford Sports	Higham Town	Irchester	Kempston	Northampton Spencer	O'n Chenecks	Olney	Sharnbrook	Thrapston	Towcester
Brackley		2-1	1-0	4-1	2-1	3-0	1-0	1-0	4-0	1-1	3-2	2-0	2-0	1-0	3-3	2-1
Brit. Tim. Ath.	1-1		1-1	5-0	5-0	1-0	3-2	1-1	1-1	1-2	5-3	2-1	3-0	2-1	1-0	4-0
Brit. Tim. Duston	1-0	0-0		3-2	3-0	1-1	2-0	3-0	6-0	1-0	3-0	4-1	0-0	7-0	3-0	0-1
Burton PW	3-2	2-1	1-4		0-1	1-1	2-1	0-0	1-2	2-0	0-1	3-2	1-2	2-0	0-1	1-3
Corby Gains	0-3	1-2	0-3	2-0		0-4	1-0	0-3	1-0	1-3	0-1	2-2	3-1	5-0	0-4	0-2
Cottingham	0-3	0-1	1-1	2-2	2-2		3-0	3-1	0-0	0-0	1-1	4-1	2-1	5-1	2-0	4-2
Ford Sports	0-6	2-6	1-1	0-2	2-0	1-1		0-0	1-2	0-5	1-4	0-1	1-1	4-1	3-3	3-3
Higham Town	1-4	0-1	2-0	2-2	1-1	0-0	2-0		1-1	1-1	2-0	0-1	4-0	5-0	0-1	2-0
Irchester	1-4	1-1	1-1	2-2	4-3	0-3	3-1	3-0		2-4	2-2	5-0	1-1	1-1	1-1	1-1
Kempston	1-1	2-0	1-2	2-0	1-1	3-2	2-1	2-1	3-0		3-2	5-2	2-0	0-0	2-1	1-0
Northampton Spencer	0-2	1-3	0-1	4-0	6-1	2-0	2-2	3-0	1-0	0-2		0-1	5-0	3-0	2-1	3-1
O'n Chenecks	0-5	1-2	0-3	4-2	1-1	0-1	3-3	0-3	1-2	0-3	1-1		3-1	4-1	1-2	2-0
Olney	1-1	0-3	1-2	1-2	0-1	0-5	1-3	1-0	0-1	0-2	1-1	1-4		2-0	1-4	1-3
Sharnbrook	0-3	0-6	0-2	1-3	0-0	0-5	2-2	1-2	1-0	1-2	0-2	0-1	4-1		0-1	1-1
Thrapston	1-2	1-1	0-0	3-2	3-1	2-4	1-1	2-2	2-0	2-1	0-2	3-3	1-1	2-0		2-0
Towcester	1-1	2-1	0-4	0-1	2-4	0-1	1-1	1-1	0-1	1-0	0-3	3-2	2-3	2-0	0-2	

UNITED COUNTIES PREMIER/DIVISION ONE LEAGUE CUP

PRELIMINARY ROUND

Rothwell v Towcester 3-0
B.T. Duston v Kempston Rovers 1-2
Higham v O.N. Chenecks 3-2

FIRST ROUND

Ford Sports v S&L Corby 0-2
Baldock v Potton 5-1
St Neots v Cottingham 2-0
Thrapston v Ampthill 2-6
Northampton Spencer v Eynesbury 2-2,1-4
Sharnbrook v Corby Gains 0-1
Desborough T v Wootton B.C. 3-0
Raunds v Irthlingborough D 4-2
Arlesey T v Holbeach 1-1,1-3
Buckingham Town v Kempstopn R 2-0
Burton P.W. v British Timken A 2-4
Olney T v Irchester E 0-1
Long Buckby v Brackley 2-0
Stamford v Rothwell 2-1
Stevenage v Higham 5-1
Newport Pagnell v Bourne 3-1

SECOND ROUND

S&L Corby v Eynesbury R 2-3
Ampthill T v Stamford 3-2
Holbeach v Stevenage 3-0
Newport Pagnell v Desborough T 0-2
Long Buckby v Corby Gains 7-1
St Neots v Baldock 0-2
Buckingham T v British Timken A 4-0
Irchester E v Raunds 0-6

THIRD ROUND

Baldock v Holbeach 2-1
Desborough T v Long Buckby 3-2
Buckingham T v Eynesbury R 4-0
Ampthill T v Raunds 0-3

SEMI-FINALS

Desborough T v Raunds 1-3
Baldock v Buckingham T 1-2

FINAL

1st Leg Raunds v Buckingham T 0-0
2nd Leg Buckingham T v Raunds 3-1

UNITED COUNTIES LEAGUE — HAT TRICKS

PREMIER DIVISION

4 goals — T. Shrieves (Buckingham) v Rothwell 29.10.83
3 goals — R. Stonnell (Eynesbury) at Rothwell 27.8.83
— I. Ferguson (Baldock) at Raunds 3.9.83
— M. Kurila (Irthlingborough) v Eynesbury 13.9.83
— R. Pirsztuk (Rothwell) v Raunds 13.9.83
— J. Kenny (S&L) v Eynesbury 17.9.83
— T. Shrieves (Buckingham) v Eynesbury 18.10.83
— M. Harwood (Eynesbury) v Holbeach 22.10.83
— D. Genovese (Stamford) v Bourne 2.1.84
— T. Carter (Baldock) at Stamford 14.1.84
— M. Harwood (Eynesbury) v Rothwell 14.1.84
— R. Taylor (Holbeach) v Bourne 25.2.84
— M. Mitchell (Bourne) v Rothwell 21.4.84
— T. Shrieves (Buckingham) at Holbeach 23.4.84
— S. Hodge (Ampthill) v Baldock 10.5.84
— D. Genovese (Stamford) at Eynesbury 10.5.84
— A. Worthington (Long Buckby) at Bourne 12.5.84

DIVISION ONE

4 goals — D. Gow (Corby Gainsborough) at Towcester 11.2.84
— A. West (Northampton Spencer) at Ford Sports 10.3.84
— M. Newell (Timken Athletic) at Ford Sports 7.4.84
3 goals — P. Jelley (ON Chenecks) at Olney 22.10.83
— J. Henderson (Kempston) at Irchester 21.1.84
— M. Newell (Timken Athletic) v Towcester 25.2.84
— J. Connor (Cottingham) at Shanbrook 14.4.84
— N. Green (Timken Dustan) at Towcester 14.4.84
— L. Isom (Ford Sports) at Olney 14.4.84
— M. Newell (Timken Athletic) v Corby Gainsborough 14.4.84

KNOCK-OUT CUP

3 goals — S. Holmes (Buckingham) v Timken Athletic 25.10.83
— N. Roberts (Buckingham) v Eynesbury 13.3.84

UNITED COUNTIES LEAGUE KNOCK—OUT CUP

Preliminary Round

Brit Timken Dust (Ingman)	1	Kempston Rovers (Ragan, Fossey)	2
Higham Town (Whitehead, Smart, Dunbar)	3	ON. Chenecks (Harrold 2)	2
Rothwell Town (Norman, Barrowman 2)	3	Towcester Town	0

First Round

Arlesey Town (Reynolds)	1	Holbeach Utd (Maltby)	1 aet
Baldock Town (Daintree, Ferguson 2, Gettings 2)	5	Potton United (Cran)	1
Buckingham Town (Russell, Heap)	2	Kempston Rovers	0
Burton P.W. (Minard, Amos)	2	Brit Timken Athletic (D. Haddon, Everiss, Thompson, Newell)	4
Desborough Town (Garner, Wilcox, Nee)	3	Wootton Blue Cross	0
Ford Sports	0	Stewart & Lloyds (Martin 2)	2
Long Buckby (Peach, Beecham)	2	Brackley Town	0
Newport Pagnell T (Resch, Horsley, og)	3	Bourne Town (og)	1 aet
Northampton Spencer (Eborall, Goodchild)	2	Eynesbury Rovers (Currington, Mattia)	2 aet
Olney Town	0	Irchester Eastfield (Williams)	1
Raunds Town (P. Walters, Taylor, 2 ogs)	4	Irthlingborough D (Ashby, Sargent)	2
St Neots Town (Hunter 2)	2	Cottingham	0
Sharnbrook	0	Corby Gainsborough (Duroe)	1
Stamford (Genovese, Blades)	2	Rothwell Town (Middleton)	1
Stevenage Borough (Marshall 2, Metcalfe 2, Lear)	5	Higham Town (Althorpe)	1
Thrapston Venturas (Starks, Bettles)	2	Ampthill Town (Harnaman 2, McMellon 2, Bridge, Targett)	6

Replays

Holbeach United (Gosling, M. Taylor, Bemrose)	3	Arlesey Town (Earl)	1
Eynesbury Rovers (Mattia, Stringer, Harwood, Cheesewright)	4	Northampton Spencer (Eborall)	1

Second Round

Ampthill Town (Harnaman, Turner 2)	3	Stamford (Rogers, og)	2 aet
Buckingham Town (Roberts, Holmes 3)	4	Brit Timken Athletic	0
Holbeach United (Maltby, Bemrose 2)	3	Stevenage Borough	0
Irchester Eastfield	0	Raunds Town (O'Riordan 2, Adams 2, Nestor 2)	6
Long Buckby (Pearson 2, Norris, Kingston 2, A. Worthington 2)	7	Corby Gainsborough (Gow)	1
Newport Pagnell T	0	Desborough Town (White 2)	2
St Neots Town	0	Baldock Town (Lawson 2)	2
Stewart & Lloyds (Martin, Parker)	2	Eynesbury Rovers (Harwood 2, Furness)	3

Third Round

Ampthill Town	0	Raunds Town (M. Walters 2, Adams)	3
Baldcock Town (Dance 2)	2	Holbeach United (Bemrose)	1
Buckingham Town (Liddle, Roberts 3)	4	Eynesbury Rovers	0
Desborough Town (Mee, Leah, White)	3	Long Buckby (Ross 2)	2 aet

Semi-finals

Baldcock Town (Beech)	1	Buckingham Town (Russell, Roberts)	2
Desborough Town (Wood)	1	Raunds Town (Simons, O'Riordan, Simmonds)	3

FINAL

First Leg:
Raunds Town 0 Buckingham Town 0

Raunds: Davenport, Redding, Humphries, Burt, Murphy, Burdett, Peasnall, Simons, Walters, O'Riordan, Moodie. Sub: Adams.

Buckingham: Hopps, Jones, Folds, Liddle, Goodeve, Pittam, Russell, Roberts, Heap, Shrieves, Large. Sub: Holmes.

Second Leg:
Buckingham Town (Shrieves, Folds, Goodeve) 3 Raunds Town (Moodie) 1 aet

Buckingham: Hopps, Heap, Folds, Liddle, Goodeve, Pittam, Russell, Roberts, Shrieves, Frost, Holmes. Sub: Kingston.

Raunds: Davenport, Redding, Humphries, Murphy, Burt, Peasnall, Walters, Simmons, O'Riordan, Moodie, Burdett. Sub: Adams.

Stamford's *Vase Final Squad pictured at Wembley before their match with Stansted. Back Row (L-R): Mick Lyon, Steve Blades, Ray Medwell (assistant manager), Chris Corby (manager), Linden Parslow, Alan McIlwain, John Mackin (captain), Robbie Chapman, John Waddicor, Glen Beech. Front Row (L-R): Barry Daff, Tommy Robson, Eddie Green, Dominic Genovese, Russ Allen, Mark Smitheringale, Steve Hines.*
Photo: Stamford Photographic Services (A. J. Story)

UNITED COUNTIES LEAGUE

	Leading Goalscorers	Hat Tricks	Penalties	Most Appearances
Ampthill Town	D. Harnaman 25 S. Hodge 16 R. Bridge 8 P. Targett 8			D. Harnaman 39 P. Magee 39 M. Filby 35 L. Caves 34
Bourne Town	Mark Mitchell 16 Nicky Papworth 15 Palmer, Piergianni 7 Kirkup 7			Jimmy Jackson 44 Dave Palmer 42 Chris Gardiner 41
Brackley Town	Terry Shreeve 42			
Desborough Town	Mick White 7 Paul Mee 7 Dave Barrett 4 Barry Wilcox 4		Peter Creamer (2) Barry Wilcox	Dave Barrett 40 Steve Birch 37 Adam Garner 35
Stamford	Dominic Genovese 32 John Waddicor 15 Russ Allen 14			Alan McIlwain 47 Mark Smitheringale 46 + 1 Dominic Genovese 46

AMPTHILL TOWN

President: H. E. Hoskins
Chairman: K. H. Thomson
Manager: B. J. Gill
Coach: B. Wainwright
Physiotherapist: P. Robinson
Secretary: C. Batchelor
Address & Tel No: Ampthill 402349 (H) Bedford 67400 x337 (B)
Commercial Manager:
Address & Tel No:
Press Officer & Tel No: E. Turner (Ampthill 403128)
Address & Tel No of ground: Ampthill Park, Woburn Road, Ampthill **Club shop:** Confectionery
Simple ground directions: A418 Ampthill to Woburn road
No of seats: 100 **Covered accommodation:** Stand 600 **Capacity:** **Floodlights:** Being built
Year formed: 1887 **Nickname:** None **Club sponsors:** John Eastaff
Previous names: None
Previous grounds: Station Road, Ampthill
Club colours: Gold/Red/Black
Change colours: Red/Black/Red
Day for midweek home matches: Tuesday/Wednesday
Record attendance: 1,250 v St Neots **Year:** 1959
Previous League: South Midlands
Clubhouse details: Comfortable brick-built
Programme details: 10p, 12 pages
Club metal badges: No
Local newspapers & Tel No: Bedfordshire Times, Ampthill Times, Luton News, Evening Post, Echo
Senior Honours: South Midlands League

ARLESEY TOWN

President: Derek Larman
Chairman: Maurice Crouch
Manager: Dave Mosley
Coach: Brian Williams
Physiotherapist: Jim Anderson/John Bryant
Secretary: Malcolm Skillings
Address & Tel No: 0462 732313 (H)
Commercial Manager:
Address & Tel No:
Press Officer & Tel No: Tony Smith (0462 54328)
Address & Tel No of ground: Lamb Meadow, Hitchin Road, Arlesey, Beds. 0462 731448 **Club shop:** No
Simple ground directions: Enter village from Hitchin, 200 yards past Biggs Wall on left hand side
No of seats: 40 **Covered accommodation:** 250 **Capacity:** **Floodlights:** Yes
Year formed: 1891 **Nickname:** The Blues **Club sponsors:** Bennett Swiftline
Previous names: None
Previous grounds: The Bury
Club colours: Light & Dark Blue
Change colours: Red & White
Day for midweek home matches: Tuesday
Record attendance: 2,000 v Luton Town Reserves, Beds Cup **Year:** 1906
Previous Leagues: Biggleswade & District, Beds County, South Midlands, Partheon, London
Clubhouse details: Open every evening, every lunchtime except Tuesday
Programme details: Free, 4 pages
Club metal badges: No
Local newspapers & Tel No: Biggleswade Chronicle, Hitchin Gazette
Senior Honours: Beds Senior Cup (2), South Midlands Premier League (2), South Midlands League K.O. Competition (2), Hinchingbrooke Cup (3), Beds Premier Cup

BALDOCK TOWN

President: T. Pulford
Chairman: R. L. Childerstone
Manager: Maurice Howkins
Coach: Robin Chandler
Physiotherapist: B. Dear
Secretary: David Stevenson
Address & Tel No: 85 High Street, Baldock, Herts 0462 895165
Commercial Manager: P. Hammond
Address & Tel No: 0462 892321
Press Officer & Tel No: Alan Thompson. 0462 893997
Address & Tel No of ground: Norton Road, Baldock, Herts. 895449 **Club shop:**
Simple ground directions: A505 Hitchin to Baldock, turn left into Norton Road. From Railway Station: West down Ickneild Way, right at gasometer into Norton Road and under railway bridge
No of seats: 100 **Covered accommodation:** 100 **Capacity:** 5,000 **Floodlights:** Yes
Year formed: 1889 **Nickname:** The Reds **Club sponsors:**
Previous Ground: Bakers Close to 1982
Club Colours All Red
Change colours: All Blue
Day for midweek home matches:
Record attendance: 1,250 v Arsenal, 6th March 1984
Previous Leagues: South Midlands, Parthenon, London
Clubhouse details: New club house, capacity 300, open lunchtimes and evenings
Programme details: 24 pages, with admission
Club metal badges:
Local newspapers & Tel No: Gazette (0462 51611), Comet (0462 31666)
Senior Honours: South Midland Premier Champions (4), Herts Charity Shield Winners, South Midland Trophy Winners (2)

BOURNE TOWN

President: E.C. Moody
Chairman: C. D. Notley
Manager: Mick Reilly
Assistant Manager: Stuart Hodson
Physiotherapist: Don Mitchell
Secretary: Peter Dowse
Address & Tel No: 10 Dovecote Estate, Rippingale, Bourne, Lincs PE10 0SY. (Dowsby 305)
Commercial Manager:
Address & Tel No:
Press Officer & Tel No: As Sec
Address & Tel No of ground: Abbey Lawn, Abbey Road, Bourne, Lincs. 0778 422292 **Club shop:** No
Simple ground directions: In market place, take road for Spalding. Ground 500 yards on right
No of seats: 250 **Covered accommodation:** 750 **Capacity:** 3,000 **Floodlights:** No
Year formed: 1883 Oct **Nickname:** The Wakes **Club sponsors:** Fossitt & Thorne Ltd
Previous names: None
Previous grounds: None
Club colours: All Red
Change colours: White or Yellow
Day for midweek home matches: Tuesday
Record attendance: not known **Year:**
Previous Leagues: Midland, Central Alliance, Peterborough & District
Clubhouse details: Small — open match days and for specific events
Programme details: 16 pages, 10p
Club metal badges: No
Local newspapers & Tel No: Stamford Mercury, Lincolnshire Free Press, Peterborough Evening Telegraph
Senior Honours: United Counties League (3), United Counties League Cup (1), Lincolnshire Senior 'A' Cup (1)

A brilliant action photo of Desborough goalkeeper Jim Ogilvie was taken by a local newspaper photographer.

A Holbeach forward goes close with a header but Ampthill won their home game 3-0. Photo: Mike Joss

Brackley Town — Division One champions.

BRACKLEY TOWN

President: C. Clifford
Chairman: N. Howard
Manager: Ray Styles
Coach: Phil Lines
Physiotherapist:
Secretary: R. Miles
Address & Tel No: 6 Hill Street, Brackley 0280 704896
Commercial Manager: P. Purdle
Address & Tel No: 28 Blencowe Drive, Brackley 0280 704504
Press Officer & Tel No: Tony Baker. 0280 702814
Address & Tel No of ground: St. James' Park, Churchill Way, Brackley. 0280 704077 **Club shop:**
Simple ground directions: Churchill Way, east off A43, south end of town
No of seats: 50 **Covered accommodation:** 400 **Capacity:** 3,500 **Floodlights:** No
Year formed: 1890 **Nickname:** Saints **Club sponsors:** SK Distributors (Skoda), Brackley
Previous names: None
Previous grounds: Buckingham Road
Club colours: Blue/Red/White
Change colours: Red/White
Day for midweek home matches:
Record attendance: not known **Year:**
Previous Leagues: Hellenic, North Bucks, Banbury & District
Clubhouse details: Lounge and main hall, open all week (extension to be built)
Programme details: 12 pages, 50p **Local newspapers & Tel No:**
Club metal badges:
Senior Honours: Hellenic League Div 1 KO Cup 1982-83, Buckingham Senior Charity Cup 1982-83, Runners-up 1979-80, 1983-84, United Counties Div 1 Champions 1983-84

BUCKINGHAM TOWN

President: Robin B. Taylor
Chairman: C. D. Lawrence
Manager: Gary Knibbs
Assistant Manager: Frank Holman
Physiotherapist: Vic Marsh
Secretary: P. E. Holman
Address & Tel No: 15 The Maltings, Chackmore, Buckingham
Commercial Manager: C. D. Lawrence
Address & Tel No: 'Newlands', Leckhampstead Road, Akeley, Buckingham. Lillingstone Dayrell 318
Press Officer & Tel No: D. A. Hacker, 7 Glynswood Road, Buckingham. 812176
Address & Tel No of ground: Ford Meadow, Ford Street, Buckingham. 816257 **Club shop:**
Simple ground directions: 400 yards from town centre, off Buckingham to Aylesbury road
No of seats: 100 **Covered accommodation:** Yes **Capacity:** 3,500 **Floodlights:** Yes
Year formed: 1883 **Nickname:** "Robins" **Club sponsors:** various
Previous names: None
Previous grounds: None
Club colours: All Red, White trim
Change colours: All White, Red trim
Day for midweek home matches: Tuesday
Record attendance: 2,000 v Barton Rovers, F.A. Vase **Year:**
Previous Leagues: Hellenic, South Midlands, North Bucks, Aylesbury & District
Clubhouse details: Open 7 days a week and Fri, Sat, Sun lunchtimes. Concert room with stage for hire, capacity 240. Bingo, domino, ladies and mens darts teams
Programme details: 12 to 16 pages, 10p **Local newspapers & Tel No:**
Club metal badges: No
Senior Honours: 1983-84 Centenary Season. Berks & Bucks Senior Cup Winners, Premier Division UCL Champions, League Knock-out Cup Winners, Buckingham Senior Charity Cup Winners

DESBOROUGH TOWN

President:
Chairman: V. Panter
Manager: Maurice Murray
Coach:
Physiotherapist:
Secretary: R. Coe
Address & Tel No: Kettering (0536) 760386 (H)
Commercial Manager:
Address & Tel No:
Press Officer & Tel No: I. Tortoishell. Kettering (0536) 760873
Address & Tel No of ground: Waterworks Field, Braybrooke Road, Desborough **Club shop:** No
Simple ground directions: Half mile west of A6
No of seats: 250 **Covered accommodation:** Yes **Capacity:** 8,000 **Floodlights:** Yes
Year formed: 1896 **Nickname:** Ar Tarn **Club sponsors:** None
Previous names: None
Previous grounds: None
Club colours: All Blue
Change colours: All Yellow
Day for midweek home matches: Monday
Record attendance: 8,000 v Kettering Town **Year:**
Previous League:
Clubhouse details: 2 lounges, bar and games room, open 7 days a week. Telephone Kettering (0536) 761350
Programme details: Free, 16 pages
Local newspapers & Tel No: Evening Telegraph, Chronicle and Echo, Northants Post
Senior Honours: United Counties League Champions (9). Current holders of the Desborough, Market Harborough and Wellingbrough Charity Cups and the United Counties Reserve KO Cup
Programme Editor: John Lee **Player of the Year (1983-84):** Dave Barrett

EYNESBURY ROVERS

President: W. A. Stephenson
Chairman: A. H. Eddy
Manager: B. Abraham
Coach: P. Sussams
Physiotherapist: Miss B. Abraham
Secretary: D. G. Irons
Address & Tel No: 12 Hadleigh Close, Bedford Bedford 68111
Commercial Manager:
Address & Tel No:
Press Officer & Tel No:
Address & Tel No of ground: Hall Road, Eynesbury, St. Neots, Cambs. (Huntingdon 74041) **Club shop:**
Simple ground directions: Approx 2 miles from trunk road A1 on the south side of the St. Neots urban area
No of seats: 250 **Covered accommodation:** 250 **Capacity:** 3,450 **Floodlights:** Yes
Year formed: 1898 **Nickname:** **Club sponsors:** None
Previous names: None
Previous grounds: None
Club colours: Royal Blue & White
Change colours: Yellow & Green
Day for midweek home matches:
Record attendance: Friendly v Charlton **Year:** 1953
Previous Leagues: Eastern Counties
Clubhouse details: To accommodate 150 on ground
Programme details: 8 pages, 10p **Local newspapers & Tel No:**
Club metal badges:
Senior Honours: UCL Division One Champions 1976-77

Desborough goalkeeper Jim Ogilvie confidently catches a centre off the head of a visiting Stewarts and Lloyds striker. Photo: Mike Joss

Stevenage Town scores the only goal of the game, from the penalty spot, against Ampthill. Photo: Mike Joss

Raunds Town beat Stewart's and Lloyds 3-1; another picturesque view from Leo Hoenig.

HOLBEACH UNITED

President: Dr J. C. Hunter
Chairman: B. Paul
Manager: G. Steels
Physiotherapist:
Press Officer & Tel No: J. Eldridge. 23436
Secretary: Bryan Stamp
Address & Tel No: 22930 (H)
Address & Tel No of ground: Carters Park, Park Road, Holbeach, Lincs. 22381 **Club shop:** No
Simple ground directions: Second left at traffic lights in town centre, 200 yards down road on left
No of seats: 150 **Covered accommodation:** Stand **Capacity:** **Floodlights:** No
Year formed: 1927 **Nickname:** Tigers **Club sponsors:** None
Previous names: Lillywhites
Previous grounds: None
Club colours: Amber & Black
Change colours: Green & Black
Day for midweek home matches: Wednesday
Record attendance: 4,000 v Wisbech Town **Year:** 1956-57
Previous Leagues: Peterborough, UCL, Eastern Counties
Clubhouse details: Clubhouse large enough to hold dances and other forms of entertainment
Programme details: 10p, 4 pages
Local newspapers & Tel No: Lincolnshire Free Press, Spalding Guardian
Senior Honours: League KO Cup (1), Lincolnshire Cup 1983-84

IRTHLINGBOROUGH DIAMONDS F.C.

President: C. M. Jones
Chairman: A. C. Jones
Manager: Roger Ashby
Coach: Joe Kiernan
Physiotherapist: Rod Cooper
Press Officer & Tel No: As Secretary
Secretary: George Whiting
Address & Tel No: 5 Clare Walk, Higham Ferrers Rushden 56717 (H) Northampton 810700 (B)
Commercial Manager: As Secretary
Address & Tel No:
Address & Tel No of ground: Nene Park, Station Road, Irthlingborough. Wellingborough 650345 **Club shop:** No
Simple ground directions: Overlooks the main A6 trunk road
No of seats: 300 **Covered accommodation:** 350 standing **Capacity:** **Floodlights:** Yes
Year formed: 1947 **Nickname:** The Diamonds **Club sponsors:** Astraseal
Previous names: None
Previous grounds: The Recreation Ground
Club colours: Red/Blue/Red
Change colours: All Blue
Day for midweek home matches: Tuesday
Record attendance: 2,412 v Dagenham, F.A. Cup 4th Round Replay **Year:** 1970
Previous Leagues: Rushden & Dist Youth League, Rushden & Dist Junior League, Kettering Amateur League
Clubhouse details: Open, Mon Tues Thurs Fri evenings, Sun lunchtime to members. Disco Wed Sun. Private parties catered for Sat evenings
Programme details: 5p, 8 pages
Local newspapers & Tel No: Evening Telegraph, Northamptonshire Chronicle & Echo
Senior Honours: Northants Senior Cup (1), UCL Premier Division Champions (4), UCL Premier Division KO Cup Winners (2), Hinchingbrooke Cup Winners (3), Wellingborough Charity Cup Winners (1)

LONG BUCKBY

President: Tim Pearson
Chairman: A. Bruce
Manager: Chris Beckett
Coach: None
Physiotherapist: None
Press Officer & Tel No: R. Pryor
Secretary: E. M. Thresher
Address & Tel No: Long Buckby (0327) 842959 (H) Rugby 2121 ext 546 (B)
Commercial Secretary: Glyn Stanyon
Address & Tel No: Long Buckby 843122
Address & Tel No of ground: Station Road, Long Buckby. (0327) 842682 **Club shop:** No
Simple ground directions: Situated on the Daventry-Long Buckby road 400 yards from main Rugby to Northampton railway
No of seats: 50 **Covered accommodation:** 150 **Capacity:** **Floodlights:** No
Year formed: 1945 **Nickname:** The Bucks **Club sponsors:** Nene Group, Northampton
Previous names: Long Buckby Nomads
Previous grounds: None
Club colours: Blue/White/Blue
Change colours: Red/White/Red
Day for midweek home matches: Tuesday & Thursday
Record attendance: **Year:**
Previous Leagues: Rugby & District, Central Northants Football Combination
Clubhouse details: Bar and concert room
Programme details: 30p, 4 pages
Local newspapers & Tel No: The Chronicle & Echo, The Daventry Weekly Express
Senior Honours: United Counties League Div II & III

NEWPORT PAGNELL TOWN

President: Lt.Col. L. G. Payne
Chairman: B. G. Moore
Manager: M. Durrant
Assistant Manager: T. Ashton
Physiotherapist: J. Goodship
Secretary: J. Anderson
Address & Tel No: 48 Linford Avenue, Newport Pagnell Newport Pagnell (0908) 610453 (H), Bedford 870201 (B)
Commercial Manager: M. Stanton
Address & Tel No: Newport Pagnell 610164
Press Officer & Tel No: J. Anderson, Newport Pagnell 610453
Address & Tel No of ground: Willen Road, Newport Pagnell, 611993 **Club shop:** No
Simple ground directions: Willen Road, Newport Pagnell
No of seats: 20 **Covered accommodation:** 300 **Capacity:** **Floodlights:** No
Year formed: 1963 **Nickname:** None **Club sponsors:** Scottish & Newcastle Breweries
Previous names: Newport Pagnell Wanderers
Previous grounds: Bury Field and Youth Club
Club colours: Green/White
Change colours: Blue/White
Day for midweek home matches: Tuesday/Thursday
Record attendance: 2,000, Entertainers XI **Year:** 1982 **Programme Editor:** Secretary
Previous Leagues: North Bucks 1964-69, South Midlands 1970-76
Clubhouse details: On Ground, Willen Road. Bar & Lounge. Capacity 200
Programme details: Yes
Local newspapers & Tel No: Bucks Standard, Milton Keynes Gazette,
Senior Honours: None

POTTON UNITED

President: P. Hutchinson
Chairman: A. Hutchinson
Manager: T. King
Coach: T. Reedman
Physiotherapist: J. Page
Secretary: D. F. Inskip
Address & Tel No: Potton (0767) 260355 (H) Bedford 67433 (B)
Commercial Manager: Secretary
Address & Tel No:
Press Officer & Tel No: Secretary
Address & Tel No of ground: The 'Hollow', Biggleswade Road, Potton. (0767) 261100 **Club shop:** No
Simple ground directions: Outskirts of Potton on Biggleswade road
No of seats: 100 **Covered accommodation:** 150 **Capacity:** **Floodlights:** Yes
Year formed: 1943 **Nickname:** None **Club sponsors:** None
Previous names: None
Club colours: Royal Blue
Previous grounds: Recreation Ground
Change colours: Red/Black
Day for midweek home matches: Any
Record attendance: v Bedford Town **Year:**
Programme Editor: D. F. Inskip
Previous Leagues: South Midlands, Central Alliance
Clubhouse details: Small, for after match entertaining and functions. New one in pipeline
Programme details: 6 pages, 5p
Local newspapers & Tel No: Biggleswade Chronicle
Senior Honours: County Senior Cup, League Prem KO Cup

RAUNDS TOWN

President:
Chairman: Barry Burridge
Manager: J, Burt
Coach: A. Wright/M. James
Physiotherapist:
Press Officer & Tel No: F. R. Matson
Secretary: Frank R. Matson
Address & Tel No: 14 St Chads Close, Kettering, Northants. 0536 517055
Commercial Manager: D. Barker
Address & Tel No: Langham Road, Raunds, Northants 0933 622966
Address & Tel No of ground: Berristters, Raunds. 0933 623351
Simple ground directions: On entering Raunds from A6 travel through town and over pelican crossing (only one set in Raunds), first turn right, first left, road finishes on ground
No of seats: 50 **Covered accommodation:** 200 **Capacity:** 2,000 **Floodlights:** No
Year formed: **Nickname:** Shopmates **Club sponsors:** B & B Meats/Gateway Building Society/Thrapston Tyres
Previous names: None
Club colours: White/Red/Red
Previous grounds: None
Change colours: All Yellow
Day for midweek home matches:
Record attendance: not known **Year:**
Previous Leagues: Ruthden District, Northamptonshire Combination
Clubhouse details: On ground
Programme details: 10 pages, 10p (not every match)
Local newspapers & Tel No:
Senior Honours: United Counties Div I Winners 1982-83, NFA Junior Cup Winners 1982-83

ROTHWELL TOWN

President: J. Covington
Chairman: S. Andrews
Manager: D. Walker
Coach: J. Conde
Physiotherapist:
Secretary: W. L. Parker
Address & Tel No: 223 Rockingham Road, Kettering 82809
Commercial Manager:
Address & Tel No:
Press Officer & Tel No:
Address & Tel No of ground: Cecil Street, Rothwell, Northants. Kettering 710694 **Club shop:** No
Simple ground directions: Enter Rothwell on A6, turn into Bridge Street at Midland Bank, turn at third left (Tresham St) and ground is at top
No of seats: 400 **Covered accommodation:** 400 **Capacity:** 3,000 **Floodlights:** Yes
Year formed: 1896 **Nickname:** The Bones **Club sponsors:** City Electrics
Previous names: None
Club colours: Red
Previous grounds: None
Change colours: Yellow & Blue
Record attendance: 2,508 v Irthlingborough Diamonds **Year:** 1971
Previous Leagues: Kettering Amateur, Leicester Senior, Central Alliance
Clubhouse details: Large Sportsmans bar, Top of the Town ballroom and lounge for 200 dancers
Programme details: 20 pages, 10p
Club metal badges: No
Senior Honours: Northants Senior Cup 1960-61, UCL Cup 1970-71, 1971-72, Market Harboro Charity Cup 1981-82

ST NEOTS TOWN

President:
Chairman: Joe Wright
Manager: Melvyn Hancock
Coach: P. L. Walker
Physiotherapist: Jack Page
Secretary: John Delaney
Address & Tel No: 28 Sandwich Road, St. Neots 0480 218096
Commercial Manager: John Walker
Address & Tel No: 0480 77295
Press Officer & Tel No: As Secretary
Address & Tel No of ground: 'Shortsands', Cambridge Street, St Neots, Cambs PE19 2DA. 0480 72457 **Club shop:**
Simple ground directions: On A45 eastbound towards Cambridge. Entrance in Cambridge Street between the 'Bull' and 'Queen Victoria' public houses
No of seats: 150 **Covered accommodation:** Two sides of ground **Capacity:** 2,000 **Floodlights:** Training only
Year formed: 1879 **Nickname:** The Saints **Club sponsors:** James Paine & Co
Previous names: None
Club colours: Light and Dark Blue
Previous grounds: Recreation Ground
Change colours: White and Green
Day for midweek home matches: Monday or Wednesday
Record attendance: 2,000 v Wisbech F.A. Cup **Year:** 1966
Previous Leagues: Metropolitan, Eastern Counties
Programme Editor: Jim Allan (0487 813967)
Clubhouse details: Above dressing rooms
Local newspapers & Tel No: Hunts Post (0480 52571), St Neots Advertiser (0480 73136)
Programme details: Yes
Senior Honours: Metropolitan League Champions & Runners-up, Cup Winners & Runners-up (2), United Counties League Champions (2) & Runners-up & Div 1 Runners-up, UCL Cup Winners (3), Central Alliance League Cup Winners, Hunts Senior Cup Winners (36), Scott Gatty Cup (10), Hinchingbrooke Cup (8), Hunts Benevolent Cup (1)

STAMFORD

President:
Chairman: Vic Couzens
Manager: Chris Corby
Coach: Ray Medwell
Physiotherapist: Barry Cunnington
Press Officer & Tel No: See Secretary
Secretary: Jeremy Biggs
Address & Tel No: 'The Essendine', Essendine, Nr Stamford, Lincs PE9 4LD. 0780 63048
Commercial Manager: Kit Cameron-Allen
Address & Tel No: 2 Sutherland Way, Stamford. Tel 62445
Address & Tel No of ground: Wothorpe Road, Stamford. 63079 **Club shop:** No
Simple ground directions: Off A43 Kettering Road, one mile east of A1. Railway station 200 yards
No of seats: 250 **Covered accommodation:** 1,250 **Capacity:** 5,000 **Floodlights:** Yes
Year formed: 1896 **Nickname:** The Daniels **Club sponsors:** Jewsons, Aspec Car Audio
Previous names: None
Previous grounds: None
Club colours: All Red
Change colours: All White/All Sky Blue
Day for midweek home matches: Tuesday
Record attendance: 4,200 v Kettering FA Cup **Year:** 1953
Best performance in: **F.A. Cup:** 1913-14 5th Qual Round, lost 2-1 to Chatham
F.A. Trophy: 1973-74 3rd Qual Round, lost 1-0 to Bedworth
F.A. Vase: 1979-80 Winners, beating Guisborough 2-0
Present players with Football League experience: Tommy Robson, Russ Allen
Past players who progressed into the Football League: Teddy Tye (Chelsea), Reg Chester (Aston Villa), Alan Birchenall (Sheffield Utd, Chelsea, Leicester, C. Palace, Luton, Oldham, Hereford), Brian Stubbs (Notts County), Gerry Fell (Brighton, Southend, Torquay, York)
Previous Leagues: Northants, United Counties, Peterborough, Central Alliance, Midland Counties
Clubhouse details: Matches, functions, training nights
Programme details: 32-40 pages, 10p
Club metal badges: No
Local newspapers & Tel No: Stamford Mercury
Peterborough Evening Telegraph
Senior Honours: FA Vase Winners & Runners-up (2), United Counties League Champions (5), UC League Cup winners (4), Northants League Champions, Lincolnshire Senior Cup Winners 'A' (2), 'B' (2), Junior Cup Winners

STEWARTS AND LLOYDS F.C.

President: R. Baldwin
Chairman: D. Wilkinson
Manager: J. Hamill
Coach: C. Stacey
Physiotherapist:
Press Officer & Tel No:
Secretary: P. J. Mackay
Address & Tel No: 0536 761041 (H)
0536 520910 (B)
Commercial Manager:
Address & Tel No:
Address & Tel No of ground: Recreation Ground, Occupation Road, Corby, Northants. 05366 3231 **Club shop:** No
Simple ground directions:
No of seats: 100 **Covered accommodation:** Yes **Capacity:** **Floodlights:** No
Year formed: 1947 **Nickname:** None **Club sponsors:** None
Previous names: None
Previous grounds: None
Club colours: Amber shirts, Red shorts
Change colours: Light Blue shirts, Dark Blue shorts
Day for midweek home matches: Any
Record attendance: **Year:**
Previous League:
Clubhouse details: Licensed bar
Programme details: None
Local newspapers & Tel No: Evening Telegraph
Club metal badges: No
Senior Honours: None

STOTFOLD

President: E. Perrin
Chairman: J. R. Talbot
Manager: B. Lambert
Coach: L. Wood
Physiotherapist: D. Northern
Secretary: W. Clegg
Address & Tel No: 12 Common Road, Stotfold, Hitchin, Herts. 73042
Commercial Manager: Miss J. Longhurst
Press Officer: Miss J. Longhurst
Address & Tel No of ground: Roker Park, The Green, Stotfold, Hitchin, Herts. (Hitchin 730421)
Simple ground directions: A507 from A1: Turn right at traffic lights, right at T-junction; A507 from Bedford: Via Shefford, left at traffic lights, right at T-junction
No of seats: 50 **Covered accommodation:** Yes **Capacity:** 200 **Floodlights:** Yes
Year formed: 1904, reformed 1945 **Nickname:** Canaries **Club sponsors:** Icknield Instruments
Club colours: Amber/Black **Change colours:** White
Previous names: Stotfold O.B., Stotfold Hornets, Stotfold Athletic
Previous grounds: Hitchin Road Recreation Ground
Previous Leagues: Biggleswade League, North Herts, South Midlands **Programme:** 10 pages, free
Clubhouse details: Clubroom, bar, dressing rooms, physio room **Programme Editor:** Miss J. Longhurst
Major Honours: Beds Senior Cup 1964-65, Beds Premier Cup 1980-81, S.M.L. Premier Div 1980-81, S.M.L. Challenge Cup 1981-82, North Beds Charity Cup 1955-56, 1956-57, 1961-62

Another fine action photo from Mike Joss as he catches Irthlingborough Diamonds' second goal against Newport Pagnell.

Irthlingborough Diamonds, FA Vase Semi Finalists
Back Row (L-R): R Cooper (Physio), K Kurila, G Sargent, L Haines, G Smith, R Ashby (Player/Manager), P Phipps, A Lloyd. Front Row (L-R): J Gillespie, D Atkinson, M Garratt (Captain), M McGuire, T Mann. Inset: P York

Steve Holmes scores Buckingham Town's winner in their 3-2 victory over Stamford at home.
Photo: Mike Joss

WOOTTON BLUE CROSS

President: G. Robinson
Chairman: C. Fuller
Manager: Dave Skinn
Coach: Martin Bartlett
Physiotherapist: Ray Bridges
Secretary: R. T. C. Mynott
Address & Tel No: 9 Russell Way, Wootton, Beds Bedford 768374
Commercial Manager:
Address & Tel No:
Press Officer & Tel No: R. Howe. Bedford 852218
Address & Tel No of ground: Weston Park, Bedford Road, Wootton, Beds. Bedford 767662 **Club shop:** No
Simple ground directions: Four miles south of Bedford. Ground at rear of Post Office on main road through village
No of seats: **Covered accommodation:** 250 **Capacity:** 2,000 **Floodlights:** No
Year formed: 1890 **Nickname:** Blue Cross **Club sponsors:** G. Robinson Ltd (plumb & htg) & Manns Brewery
Previous names:
Previous grounds: Recreation Ground, Wootton
Club colours: White/Blue/Blue
Change colours: All Yellow
Day for midweek home matches:
Record attendance: 300 v Kempston Rovers, U.C.L. **Year:** 1980-81
Previous Leagues: Bedford & District, South Midlands
Clubhouse details: Main hall, bar, bingo, darts, pool, cabaret nights. Open every night, Sat & Sun lunchtime
Programme details: 4 pages, free
Club metal badges: No
Local newspapers & Tel No: Bedford Journal, Bedford Express, Bedfordshire Times
Senior Honours: UCL League Cup Winners, South Midlands League Champions, Beds Senior Cup Winners, Hinchingbrooke Cup Winners (5)

O'Keefe opens the scoring with a header in Rochester's 3-0 home victory over Higham. Photo: Mike Joss

British Timken Duston go two up as John Selley scores against O N Chenecks. Photo: Mike Joss

EASTERN COUNTIES FOOTBALL LEAGUE

President: J.A. Jones

Secretary: Dr G.P. Cubbin, 19 Emmanuel Road, Cambridge. Telephone: 315099

TWO DIVISIONS FOR EASTERN COUNTIES

If applications for membership are any yardstick for success, the Eastern Counties League is the most successful League in the country. For years the League has been turning away would-be members, because the single division of 22 clubs already creates too many fixtures. This year the League could have increased its size by 50%. So now the format of the League is to be changed in order to cope with demand, and from 1985 there will be two divisions. The fixture congestion caused by 42 League matches plus 6-10 cup ties will soon be a thing of the past.

Two divisions will also make the League more competitive. Last season's champions Braintree scored 125 goals, while three clubs at the bottom had over 100 scored against them. The two re-elected clubs were well short of 20 points. In the future there will be many fewer very high scores.

Despite these improvements, from which everybody will benefit, it will be hard to produce a more interesting season than last. Ely City produced a remarkable recovery at the foot of the table. After 15 games they had just two points, both from draws. With a change of manager they managed just short of a point a game for the next 27 games and ended up well clear of the re-election zone. Lowestoft twenty years ago used to treat the League as if they owned it, but this season started off with barely more than a point a game. Then somehow some of their old arrogance returned and they hit form in time to win the League Cup and gain prize money for fourth place in the table.

Doctors throughout East Anglia were kept busy with palpitations caused by the most exciting championship race for years. Colchester were the early leaders, but by Christmas the title seemed to be between Braintree, traditionally a struggling club, last season's Champions Saffron Walden, and perennial winners Wisbech. Then Saffron Walden gave notice that they would resign at the end of the season. Rather interestingly, they then took only 25 points from 25 games instead of the 40 needed, and finished only sixth. Perhaps someone in the Southern League put a jinx on them for having the temerity to prefer the Isthmian League. In 1983 Saffron Walden turned down the chance to join the Southern League.

Braintree and Wisbech had other things to think about than gremlins and jinxes because both were going hammer and tongs to grab some real live silverware to test out the weight-bearing qualities of their directors' sideboard legs. Wisbech always had more points, Braintree games in hand and a better goal-difference. When the two met at Wisbech at the end of April it could not have been more equal. The teams had shared four goals but in the last minute a further goal for Braintree seemed to have ended Wisbech's hopes for good. But that was the last match which Braintree won — and in the end the title was decided on goal difference in Braintree's favour. What an achievement by new manager Chris Symes.

There were many other causes for satisfaction. Chatteris and Stowmarket joined the clubs with floodlights bringing the days of compulsory floodlights that much closer. The league joined the Western, Southern and Isthmian as a Contributory League for referees living in the south. Everyone is looking forward to better things in the future, but it will be hard to beat the 1983/84 season for interest and progress all the way.

Membership changes 1984:
Saffron Walden to Isthmian. Harwich & Parkeston from Athenian.

Wisbech Town *Back Row (L-R): A. Thorn (trainer), M. Mattless, J. Brighty, W. Feary, K. Hudson, G. Rider, P. Ward, J. Gallagher. Front Row (L-R): P. Chadman, J. Scase, R. McManus (player/manager). I. Jones, W. Tyler.* Photo: Wisbech Standard

EASTERN COUNTIES LEAGUE

Final League Table

	P	W	D	L	F	A	Pts
Braintree T	42	29	9	4	125	45	67
Wisbech T	42	29	9	4	91	37	67
Colchester U Res.	42	26	7	9	94	41	59
Lowestoft T	42	24	7	11	77	46	55
Sudbury T	42	21	11	10	87	56	53
Saffron Walden T	42	22	8	12	88	47	52
Gorleston	42	18	16	8	73	47	52
Tiptree U	42	20	9	13	83	64	49
Gt Yarmouth T	42	19	10	13	75	51	48
Chatteris T	42	17	10	15	57	58	44
Brantham A	42	16	9	17	66	68	41
Newmarket T	42	16	9	17	62	73	41
Bury T	42	16	8	18	69	73	40
Felixstowe T	42	13	13	16	53	57	39
March T United	42	13	11	18	57	63	37
Histon	42	12	11	19	53	60	35
Haverhill R	42	16	3	23	68	91	35
Soham Town R	42	11	7	24	49	90	29
Stowmarket T	42	10	8	24	57	99	28
Ely C	42	7	8	27	45	108	22
Clacton T	42	6	4	32	47	120	16
Thetford T	42	6	3	33	43	125	15

LEADING GOALSCORERS

J. Tippett	Saffron Walden	35
P. Harrison	Tiptree	30
C Guy	Braintree	29
K. Ready	Gt Yarmouth	28
P. Chapman	Wisbech	26
R. Sainty	Chatteris	25
A. Ramsey	Saffron Walden	24
M. Chrissell	Sudbury	23
W. Woodhouse	Tiptree	22
I. Gooday	Braintree	21
M. Money	Lowestoft	21
M. Chapman	Lowestoft	20
R. Palmer	Newmarket	20
N. Ray	Gorleston	20
J. Bibby	Braintree	19
G. Jennings	Braintree	18
Mervyn Henry	Felixstowe	17
P. Smith	Sudbury	17
C. Oldfield	Colchester	16
B. Holmes	Haverhill	15
S. Low	Newmarket	15
M. Thorpe	Brantham	15

Bury Town (dark shorts) put the pressure on the Northwood defence in an extra preliminary round FA Vase match, but they lost at home 1-2. Photo: David Shute

EASTERN COUNTIES LEAGUE
SEASON 1983/84

	Braintree	Brantham	Bury	Chatteris	Clacton	Colchester	Ely	Felixstowe	Gorleston	Gt Yarmouth	Saffron Walden	Haverhill	Histon	Lowestoft	March	Newmarket	Soham	Stowmarket	Sudbury	Thetford	Tiptree	Wisbech
Braintree		2-2	2-0	2-0	3-0	3-1	4-0	3-0	0-0	3-0	2-1	4-0	2-0	2-2	2-1	7-2	3-0	6-2	2-2	7-1	6-0	0-0
Brantham	0-3		4-2	3-0	2-1	3-0	3-2	0-0	2-0	1-0	2-0	0-1	0-0	0-4	2-0	4-1	4-1	3-1	0-2	0-1	1-1	0-1
Bury	1-7	2-2		2-4	3-1	2-1	5-0	3-2	1-3	1-4	2-1	3-0	1-1	1-0	1-1	4-1	0-0	0-0	1-2	2-1	2-1	1-1
Chatteris	1-4	1-2	2-5		5-0	2-1	3-1	1-1	1-4	3-2	2-0	0-1	1-0	1-0	1-2	0-2	1-0	4-1	2-2	1-2	1-1	0-1
Clacton	0-1	3-3	0-2	1-2		0-2	1-1	3-2	3-4	0-4	0-2	4-0	1-2	1-1	1-0	2-3	1-3	0-3	1-6	1-4	2-3	0-2
Colchester	1-1	1-0	1-0	0-0	5-1		8-0	1-0	2-0	0-2	1-1	5-0	1-0	1-1	7-1	2-0	5-0	4-2	1-0	3-0	1-0	1-1
Ely	2-2	2-1	1-0	1-2	1-3	2-5		0-1	0-0	1-2	1-5	2-1	1-4	0-2	0-2	1-2	3-5	2-2	0-2	2-1	2-7	2-3
Felixstowe	1-3	4-2	0-2	1-0	4-1	2-3	0-1		0-0	0-0	0-0	1-3	1-2	0-1	3-1	1-1	5-1	6-2	2-0	1-0	2-2	0-4
Gorleston	3-5	2-2	4-1	1-1	4-3	0-0	4-0	1-1		0-2	4-1	2-1	3-0	2-1	0-0	2-1	0-0	1-0	3-0	8-1	1-2	0-0
Gt Yarmouth	1-1	3-1	3-1	1-1	2-0	2-1	0-2	2-2	1-1		1-1	4-0	2-2	1-0	3-1	3-3	4-0	0-1	0-1	5-0	2-1	1-1
Saffron Wald.	2-0	0-0	4-0	0-0	7-0	0-3	3-2	1-3	0-0	0-3		3-1	3-2	0-0	1-1	3-1	3-0	6-0	2-3	7-0	8-1	4-0
Haverhill	1-2	3-1	1-3	0-1	0-2	3-1	2-1	0-1	1-1	4-1	2-0		2-3	2-0	0-2	1-1	7-2	3-1	1-2	2-0	1-4	1-2
Histon	1-0	2-2	1-1	1-3	4-0	1-2	1-0	1-1	0-3	0-0	0-1	5-0		0-3	0-0	3-0	2-2	0-1	0-2	4-0	2-0	1-2
Lowestoft	4-2	3-0	3-1	3-1	6-1	0-2	4-2	0-0	2-1	0-0	0-1	2-2	3-0		0-1	3-1	2-1	3-0	2-4	2-1	0-4	3-2
March	2-5	4-3	1-3	0-0	6-0	1-0	1-1	0-0	1-1	1-2	0-1	4-2	2-1	2-4		0-1	0-2	1-1	1-3	8-2	1-1	1-1
Newmarket	3-2	2-1	1-0	2-2	5-1	2-4	1-1	1-2	0-1	1-3	0-4	5-1	1-0	0-1	2-0		2-0	2-0	1-2	1-1	3-3	0-2
Soham	1-5	0-4	2-1	0-1	2-0	0-3	2-0	2-0	0-0	3-1	1-3	2-0	1-1	0-1	0-3	0-1		2-5	2-2	2-0	2-4	0-1
Stowmarket	0-3	0-2	2-0	1-1	2-4	0-4	1-1	2-1	4-1	3-2	0-3	4-7	3-0	2-4	0-1	2-2	0-4		1-2	4-1	1-2	0-0
Sudbury	3-3	2-3	3-1	1-3	2-2	2-3	1-1	1-1	4-1	4-2	1-2	3-4	1-1	4-0	3-1	1-1	3-0	4-0		1-0	1-1	1-2
Thetford	0-5	3-0	2-6	1-2	1-0	2-4	0-2	0-1	1-4	0-2	1-3	2-3	1-3	0-4	1-0	1-2	2-2	1-1	0-4		2-4	2-5
Tiptree	1-1	4-1	1-0	1-0	4-1	1-1	4-0	5-0	1-2	2-1	3-0	1-4	3-0	0-2	0-2	0-1	3-1	3-1	0-0	4-3		0-1
Wisbech	3-4	4-0	2-2	4-0	2-1	3-2	8-1	1-0	1-1	2-1	4-1	4-0	4-2	0-1	2-0	2-0	4-1	3-1	2-0	3-1	1-0	

Saffron Walden have moved on to the Isthmian League but they scored five on their last visit to Ely City. Here John Clarke cracks in a shot with Ely Cathedral as a picturesque backing. Photo: Leo Hoeniig

Lowestoft Town *Back Row (L-R): R. Barratt, D. Evans, A. Arber, G. Brighton, R. Hatch, S. Ward. Front Row: P. Hartle, M. Money, N. Twaits, M. Chapman, R. Atterton, P. Lythgoe.* Photo: P. Calvert

EASTERN COUNTIES FOOTBALL LEAGUE CUP

FIRST ROUND

Sudbury v Colchester	3-1
Thetford v Braintree	0-2
Wisbech v Clacton	4-0
Soham v Stowmarket	2-1
Newmarket v March	3-2
Ely v Saffron Walden	0-4

SECOND ROUND

Lowestoft v Bury	3-0 (after 0-0 draw)
Gt Yarmouth v Newmarket	3-2
Sudbury v Chatteris	2-0
Haverhill v Felixstowe	0-3
Histon v Braintree	1-2
Soham v Brantham	5-3
Saffron Walden v Gorleston	0-1
Wisbech v Tiptree	1-2

THIRD ROUND

Soham v Lowestoft	0-4
Gt Yarmouth v Braintree	3-2
Tiptree v Sudbury	1-3
Gorleston v Felixstowe	0-2

SEMI-FINALS

Sudbury v Lowestoft	0-2
Great Yarmouth v Felixstowe	3-2

FINAL

Lowestoft v Great Yarmouth (at Gorleston)	2-1

Braintree 0 Wisbech 0. This was the very improbable scoreline when these two sides met at Braintree, but by the end of the season they had amassed 216 league goals between them! The leaping Gus Jennings (6) is the only Braintree attacker challenging the Wisbech defence on this occasion. Photo: David Shute

Holbeach travelled to Spartan League Crown & Manor in this FA Vase Third Round Replay but lost 0- 1 and if this photo is any guide, the home team seemed capable of crowding out the Holbeach attackers.
Photo: David Shute

Wisbech attack the Histon goal in a thrilling match where, as title challengers, they came back from a 1-2 half time deficit to win 4-2. Photo: Mike Joss

Action from Bury Town v Northwood, F.A. Vase. Northwood won 2-1.

Photo: Leo Hoenig.

BRAINTREE TOWN

President: P. Wicks
Chairman: A. Stewart
Manager: Chris Symes
Asst. Manager: Dave Ward
Coach: Keith Smith
Physiotherapist:
Secretary: T. Woodley
Address & Tel No: 19a Bailey Bridge Road, Braintree Braintree 26234
Commercial Manager: Chris Symes
Address & Tel No: 22 Greenacres, Colchester. 0206 851627
Press Officer & Tel No: Ron Webb
Address & Tel No of ground: Cressing Road, Braintree, Essex. 0376 45617
Simple ground directions: 1 mile from town centre on B1018 to Witham
No of seats: **Covered accommodation:** Yes **Capacity:** 200 **Floodlights:** Yes
Year formed: 1894 **Nickname:** Iron **Club sponsors:**
Club colours: Yellow, Blue trim **Change colours:** All Blue
Previous Names: Crittall Athletic **Previous Grounds:** None
Previous Leagues: London, Metropolitan
Record Attendance: 4,000 v Tottenham Hotspur **Year:** 1953-54
Programme Details: 34 pages, 15p
Clubhouse Details: Bar open evenings and weekends. Darts, pool table, etc.
Senior Honours: Eastern Counties League Champions (2), East Anglian Cup Winners (2), Metropolitan League Cup Winners

BRANTHAM ATHLETIC

President:
Chairman: D. White
Manager: B. O'Reilly
Coach:
Physiotherapist: E. Williamson
Secretary: J. Newton
Address & Tel No: 'Gurdons', Holbrook Road, Brantham, Manningtree, Essex. 0473 328821
Commercial Manager:
Press Officer & Tel No: R. Sparrow
Address & Tel No of ground: Brantham Athletic & Social Club, New Village, Brantham, Manningtree, Essex. 020 639 2506
Simple ground directions:
No of seats: 100 **Covered accommodation:** 100 **Capacity:** 1,500 **Floodlights:** None
Year formed: 1887 **Nickname:** Athletic **Club sponsors:** None
Club colours: Blue & White stripes **Change colours:** Red
Previous Names: None **Previous Grounds:** None
Previous Leagues: Essex-Suffolk Border
Record Attendance: Not known
Clubhouse Details: Open seven days a week during licensing hours.
Senior Honours: Suffolk Senior Cup 1976/7

BURY TOWN

President: C. G. Elsey
Chairman: R. Mingay
Manager: M. Spore
Coach: A. Davies
Physiotherapist: None
Secretary: Eric F. Barbrooke
Address & Tel No: Bury St Edmunds 4115
Commercial Manager: None
Address & Tel No:
Press Officer & Tel No: Secretary
Address & Tel No of ground: Ram Meadow, Cotton Lane. Tel 4721
Simple ground directions: Just off centre of town, on main car park
No of seats: 200 **Covered accommodation:** 1,000 **Capacity:** 5,000 **Floodlights:** Yes
Year formed: 1875 **Nickname:** The Blues **Club sponsors:** Hayes Publicity and Design
Club colours: Blue **Change colours:** Red/Red
Previous Names: Bury United **Previous Grounds:** Kings Road
Previous Leagues: Norfolk & Suffolk, Essex & Suffolk, Metropolitan, Southern
Record Attendance: 3,000 v Bournemouth, F.A. Cup 1st Round **Year:** 1968
Clubhouse Details: Discos, darts, cribbage, pool
Senior Honours: Suffolk Premier Cup (9), Suffolk Senior Cup (4)

CHATTERIS TOWN

President: A. Munns
Chairman: M. Munns
Manager: M. Simmons
Coach:
Physiotherapist: J. Tarry
Secretary: R. W. Salisbury
Address & Tel No: 16 Westbourne Road, Chatteris, Cambs. Chatteris 2144
Commercial Manager:
Press Officer & Tel No: R. Blake
Address & Tel No of ground: West Street, Chatteris. 2139
Simple ground directions: Enter Chatteris on the A141 from Huntingdon, turn right into West Street after going round bypass roundabout
No of seats: 250 **Covered accommodation:** 150 **Capacity:** 4,000 **Floodlights:** Yes
Year formed: 1920 **Nickname:** The "Lillies" **Club sponsors:**
Club colours: White trimmed Blue **Change colours:** All Yellow
Previous Names: None **Previous Grounds:** None
Previous Leagues: Peterborough Premier
Programme details: 6 pages, included with 50p admission
Clubhouse Details: Bar and Tea in clubhouse
Senior Honours: Peterborough Premier League (3), The Hinchingbrooke Cup (7)

CLACTON TOWN

President: None
Chairman: P. B. Ingham
Manager: F. Lock
Coach: B. McManus
Physiotherapist: Bill Gow
Secretary: A. R. Harvey
Address & Tel No: 4 Fairlop Close, Clacton-on-Sea. 0255 420219
Commercial Manager: None
Press Officer & Tel No: Secretary
Address & Tel No of ground: Clacton Stadium, Old Road Ground, Old Road, Clacton-on-Sea. Tel 432590
Simple ground directions: Tendring DC coach park is in front of ground, which is signposted from Colchester
No of seats: 750 **Covered accommodation:** 750 **Capacity:** 2,500 **Floodlights:** None
Year formed: 1892 **Nickname:** Seasiders **Club sponsors:** None
Club colours: White & Blue **Change colours:** All Blue (sometimes Red)
Previous Names: Lilywhites **Previous Grounds:** None
Previous Leagues: Essex & Suffolk Border, Southern
Record Attendance: 7,000 v Clapton Orient **Year:** 1945
Clubhouse Details: Supporters Social Club holds 150-200. Vice-President's Club holds 50-60
Senior Honours: Southern League Div1, Eastern Counties League & Cup, East Anglian Cup

COLCHESTER UNITED

President:
Chairman: M. J. Cadman
Manager: Cyril Lea
Reserve Player/Coach: Stewart Houston
Physiotherapist: C. Simpson
Secretary: Martin R. Bennet
Address & Tel No: Colchester 574042 (B)
Reserve Manager: Colin Henson
Press Officer & Tel No: H. Mason, Sudbury 74878
Address & Tel No of ground: Layer Road Ground, Colchester CO2 7JJ. Colchester 574042
Simple ground directions: 1½ miles south-west of town centre
No of seats: 1,143 **Covered accommodation:** 7,000 **Capacity:** 15,000 **Floodlights:** Yes
Year formed: 1937 **Nickname:** The "Us" **Club sponsors:** The Royal London Mutual Insurance Soc. Ltd.
Club colours: Royal Blue & White stripes/Royal Blue/White **Change colours:** Red/Black/Black
Previous Names: Colchester Town **Previous Grounds:** None
Previous Leagues: None
Record Attendance: 19,072 v Reading, F.A. Cup **Year:** 1948
Clubhouse Details: Licensed bar open 1 hour before and 1 hour after matches
Senior Honours: None

ELY CITY

President: D. Unwin
Chairman: A. B. Smith
Manager: Roger Crane
Coach:
Physiotherapist: Keith Peacock
Secretary: Roger Pauley AIMBM
Address & Tel No: 29 Upherds Lane, Ely, Cambs. 3086
Commercial Manager: None
Address & Tel No:
Press Officer & Tel No: Roger Pauley
Address & Tel No of ground: 'Paradise', New Barns Road, Ely. Tel 2035
Simple ground directions:
No of seats: 250 **Covered accommodation:** 500 **Capacity:** 3,750 **Floodlights:** No
Year formed: 1885 **Nickname:** The Robins **Club sponsors:** Vincents of Ely
Club colours: All Red **Change colours:** All White
Previous Names: None **Previous Grounds:** None
Previous Leagues: Cambs, Peterborough, Central Alliance
Record Attendance: 5,300 v Torquay **Year:** 1956
Clubhouse Details: On ground
Programme details: 4 pages, 10p
Senior Honours:

FELIXSTOWE TOWN

President: J. Nicholls
Chairman: D. Ashford
Manager: Paul Adams
Coach: T. Wardlaw
Physiotherapist: B. Simpson
Secretary: S. Page
Address & Tel No: Ipswich 712613
Commercial Manager: D. Pipe
Address & Tel No:
Press Officer & Tel No: S. Page
Address & Tel No of ground: Town Ground, Dellwood Ave, Felixstowe.
Simple ground directions: A45 into Felixstowe.
No of seats: 100 **Covered accommodation:** Yes **Capacity:** 2,000 **Floodlights:** No
Year formed: 1900 **Nickname:** Seasiders **Club sponsors:** Townsend Thoresen Ltd
Club colours: Red & Black/Black/Black **Change colours:** White shirts
Previous Names: None **Previous Grounds:** None
Previous Leagues: Essex and Suffolk Border League
Record Attendance: 500
Clubhouse Details: Bar/snack bar/T.V./darts/pool table.
Senior Honours: Suffolk Senior Cup Winners 1967 and 1975

GORLESTON

President: E. Paine
Chairman: R. Carter
Manager: S. Morgan
Coach: M. Antcliffe
Physiotherapist: M. Jermy
Secretary: E. W. H. Proudfoot
Address & Tel No: Lowestoft 730952
Commercial Manager: Z. Mobbs
Address & Tel No: Gt Yarmouth 728230
Press Officer & Tel No: M. Whurr
Address & Tel No of ground: Woodfarm Lane, Gorleston, Great Yarmouth 602802
Simple ground directions: 50 yards from Gorleston Church
No of seats: 400 **Covered accommodation:** 5,000 **Capacity:** 5,000 **Floodlights:** Yes
Year formed: 1908 **Nickname:** The Greens **Club sponsors:** None
Club colours: Green **Change colours:** Yellow
Previous Names: None **Previous Grounds:** None
Previous Leagues: Norfolk & Suffolk, Anglian Combination
Record Attendance: 6,000 v Leyton Orient, F.A. Cup **Year:** 1950
Clubhouse Details: Bar, colour TV, pool table, darts, snacks
Senior Honours: Eastern Counties League (4), Norfolk Senior Cup (12)

GREAT YARMOUTH TOWN

President: Gordon Edwards
Chairman: Derek Needham
Manager: Bill Punton
Coach: Bill Punton
Trainer: Eric Crouch
Physiotherapist: Melvin Jessup LCSP(Phys)
Secretary: Jack Pegg
Address & Tel No: 66 Louise Close, Gt Yarmouth. 842652
Commercial Manager: John Holmes
Address & Tel No: 21 Wellington Road, Gt Yarmouth. 855296
Press Officer & Tel No: Secretary
Address & Tel No of ground: Wellesley Road, Great Yarmouth 842936 (groundsman) and 843373 (clubhouse)
Simple ground directions: Just off Marine Parade, north of Britannia Pier
No of seats: 600 **Covered accommodation:** 2,000 **Capacity:** 5,000 **Floodlights:** Yes
Year formed: 1897 **Nickname:** Bloaters **Club sponsors:** Yartoft Supply Ltd
Previous Names: None
Previous Leagues: Norfolk & Suffolk
Club colours: Amber/Black
Change colours: Red
Day for midweek home matches: Tuesday
Previous Leagues: Norfolk & Suffolk
Record Attendance: 8,944 v Crystal Palace, F.A. Cup 1st Round Proper **Year:** 1953
Best performance in: **F.A. Cup:** 1952, 1953 2nd Round
F.A. Vase: 1983 Semi-final, v Rugby
Clubhouse Details: Built 1980. Bar, colour TV, pool table, darts, snacks, open weekday evenings and on match days, regular functions, capacity 150
Present players with Football League experience: Mike Sutton (Norwich), Kevin Ready (Aston Villa)
Past players who progressed into Football League: Mel Blyth and Nolan Keeley (Scunthorpe), Gary Butcher (Blackburn)
Programme details: 16 pages, 10p
Club metal badges: Yes
Local Newspapers & Tel No: Yarmouth Mercury 844201, Eastern Football News, Norwich 28311
Senior Honours: East Counties League, East Anglian Cup, Eastern Counties League Cup (3), Norfolk Senior Cup (11)

HARWICH & PARKESTON

President: J. Whitmore
Chairman: B. Thomas
Manager: S. Vox
Coach: B. Laflin
Physiotherapist: M. Jeffries
Secretaries: R. Bareham, Harwich 506129
C. Lowe, Harwich 504605
Commercial Manager: None
Address & Tel No:
Press Officer & Tel No: Carl Allen. Harwich 52510
Address & Tel No of ground: Royal Oak, Main Road, Harwich. Harwich 3649 **Club shop:** Yes
Simple ground directions: Take main road from Colchester. Ground is on the right as you enter Harwich
No of seats: 650 **Covered accommodation:** 1,000 **Capacity:** 5,000 **Floodlights:** Yes
Year formed: 1877 **Nickname:** Shrimpers **Club sponsors:** None
Previous names: None
Previous grounds: None
Club colours: Black & White
Change colours: Yellow or Blue
Day for midweek home matches: Tuesday
Previous Leagues: Athenian, Eastern Counties
Record attendance: 4,700 v Ipswich Town **Year:** 1936
Best performance in: **F.A. Cup:** 1935, 37, 54, 62, 64, 77 1st Round
F.A. Trophy/F.A. Vase: 1975-6 3rd Round/1981-2 3rd Round
Clubhouse details: Open 7 days a week. Normal Public House hours plus match days. Dances, bingo, darts and other functions
Present players with Football League experience: Gary Harvey (Colchester), P. Spurling (Colchester)
Past players who progressed into the Football League: None
Record transfer fee paid: None
Record transfer fee received: None
Programme details: 6 pages, 10p
Club metal badges: No
Local newspapers & Tel No: Harwich & Manningtree Standard (Harwich 3224)
Senior Honours: Essex Senior Cup (2), Amateur Cup Finalists (2)

HAVERHILL ROVERS

President: R. Carter
Chairman: R. Harding
Manager: T. Jenkinson
Coach: P. Dyer
Physiotherapist: D. Franklin
Secretary: M. J. Nunn
Address & Tel No: 0440 705596
Commercial Manager: None
Address & Tel No:
Press Officer & Tel No: Secretary
Address & Tel No of ground: Hamlet Croft, Haverhill 0440 702137
Simple ground directions:
No of seats: 200 **Covered accommodation:** 200 **Capacity:** 3,000 **Floodlights:** None
Year formed: 1888 **Nickname:** Rovers **Club sponsors:** None
Club colours: Red
Change colours: Blue
Previous Names: None
Previous Grounds: None
Previous Leagues: Essex & Suffolk Border
Record Attendance: 1,300 v Chatteris **Year:** 1978-9
Clubhouse Details: None
Senior Honours: Town & Country League 1978-79, Eastern Counties League Cup 1964-65

HISTON

President: G. P. Muncey
Chairman: J. Butler
Manager: Alan Doyle
Coach:
Physiotherapist: Bill Brignell
Secretary: P. Johnson
Address & Tel No: 6 Albemarle Way, Cambridge CB4 2SP Cambridge 314738 (H), 317935 (B)
Commercial Manager: None
Press Officer & Tel No: None
Address & Tel No of ground: Bridge Road, Impington, Cambridge. Tel Histon 2301
Simple ground directions: Situated on the B1049 Cambridge-Cottenham Road, approx ¼-mile from junction with A45
No of seats: 100 **Covered accommodation:** 200 **Capacity:** 2,000 **Floodlights:** None
Year formed: 1906 **Nickname:** None **Club sponsors:** Unwins Seeds
Club colours: Red & Blue **Change colours:** Green & Blue
Previous Names: Histon Institute **Previous Grounds:** New Road, Impington
Previous Leagues: Spartan, Delphian, Corinthian
Record Attendance: 4,500
Clubhouse Details: Bar/Lounge open Wednesdays to Sundays, evenings and Sunday lunchtime, plus matchdays and training nights
Senior Honours: Cambridgeshire Invitation Cup (2)

LOWESTOFT TOWN

President: R. Bishop
Chairman: R. Butcher
Manager: P. Chick
Coach: D. Pye
Physiotherapist: R. Wade
Secretary: M. J. Reeve
Address & Tel No: 15 Norfolk St, Lowestoft 0502 84335 (H)
Commercial Manager: As Secretary
Press Officer & Tel No: As Secretary
Address & Tel No of ground: Crown Meadow, Love Road, Lowestoft 0502 3818
Simple ground directions: North centre of town, ¾-mile from station
No of seats: 400 **Covered accommodation:** 400 **Capacity:** 400 **Floodlights:** Yes
Year formed: 1890 **Nickname:** The Blues **Club sponsors:** Sain Hook Sports
Club colours: Royal Blue Shirts **Change colours:** White shirts
Previous Names: None **Previous Grounds:** None
Previous Leagues: Norfolk & Suffolk
Record Attendance: 5,000 v Watford, F.A. Cup 1st Round **Year:** 1966
Clubhouse Details: Open every night, 7pm
Senior Honours: Eastern Counties League (10), Suffolk Premier Cup (6), League Cup (8), East Anglian Cup (4), FA Amateur Cup runners-up 1899/1900.

MARCH TOWN UNITED

President: None
Chairman: Mr. D. Warrington
Manager: B. Malpass
Coach: L. Kent
Physiotherapist: M. Miller
Secretary: C. R. Woodcock
Address & Tel No: 4817
Commercial Manager: None
Address & Tel No:
Press Officer & Tel No: None
Address & Tel No of ground: GER Ground, Robin Goodfellow's Lane
Simple ground directions: 5 mins from town, 15 mins from BR station
No of seats: 600 **Covered accommodation:** 650 **Capacity:** 3,000 **Floodlights:** No
Year formed: 1886 **Nickname:** Hares **Club sponsors:** Northlevel Motors
Club colours: Yellow & Navy Blue **Change colours:** White & Red
Previous Names: None **Previous Grounds:** None
Previous Leagues: U.C.L. & Peteboro Leauge & Isle of Ely League
Record Attendance: 7,500
Clubhouse Details: On ground. Bar and small room, seat approx 100
Senior Honours: None

NEWMARKET TOWN

President: A. C. Warren
Chairman: F. Trowsdale
Manager: G. Johnson
Coach: D. Stewart
Physiotherapist: As above
Secretary: D. Sadler
Address & Tel No: 22 Windsor Road. 663920
Commercial Manager: None
Press Officer: A. Pulford Greenacre, Nunery Green, Wickhambrooke, Nr N'mkt
Address & Tel No of ground:
Simple ground directions: From station, turn right into Green Road, right at crossroads, follow road round, turn left at top of hill, Cricket Field Road Ground is at bottom
No of seats: 150 **Covered accommodation:** 200 **Capacity:** 500 **Floodlights:** No
Year formed: 1888 **Nickname:** Jockeys **Club sponsors:** Anglia Fabrications
Club colours: Yellow/Blue/Blue **Change colours:** Red/Black/Red
Previous Names: None **Previous Grounds:** None
Previous Leagues: Peterborough District, Essex Border, Bury District
Record Attendance: 1,200 v Ely City (Peterborough League) **Year:** 1963-64
Clubhouse Details: **Programme details:** 12 pages, 10p
Senior Honours: None

SOHAM TOWN RANGERS

Chairman: K. Barber
Manager: S. Low
Coach: B. Manning
Physiotherapist: B. Manning
Secretary: John K. Pendrey
Tel No: 0353 720542
Commercial Manager: A. J. Mann
Press Officer: M. Gipp
Address & Tel No of ground: Julius Martin Lane, Soham. 0353 720732.
Simple ground directions: A142 from Ely (A10) or Newmarket (A11)
No of seats: 240 **Covered accommodation:** 240 **Capacity:** 2,500 **Floodlights:** Yes
Year formed: 1919 **Nickname:** None **Club sponsors:** C. J. Murfitt
Club colours: Emerald/White Stripes **Change colours:** All Emerald, White or Black shorts
Previous Leagues: Peterborough League
Record Attendance: 3000 Pegasus
Clubhouse Details: Main Hall 150, Boot Bar 25, Lounge Bar 75.
Major Honours: Cambs. Premier League and several Cambs. Cup wins.
Our club was a "County F.A." until the 1960's and, unlike most football clubs, has grown in stature, facilities and quality in the subsequent years of football regression. We consider this to be a major achievement as a result of our policies.

STOWMARKET TOWN

President: D. Hopgood
Chairman: J. Sutton
Manager: Don James
Coach: Vacant
Physiotherapist: Vacant
Secretary: John Doward
Address & Tel No: Deepland House, Stowupland, Stowmarket, Suffolk IP14 4DE. (0449) 612003 (H), (0449) 612318 (B)
Commercial Manager: None
Press Officer & Tel No: None
Address & Tel No of ground: "Greens Meadow", Bury Road, Stowmarket, Suffolk. Tel. Stowmarket (0449) 612533
Simple ground directions: Traffic lights in town centre, leave by Bury Street, continue to roundabout, Bury Road. Ground on right hand side
No of seats: 200 **Covered accommodation:** Yes **Capacity:** 2,500 **Floodlights:** Yes
Year formed: 1848 **Nickname:** None **Club sponsors:** Various
Club colours: Gold & Black **Change colours:** Red
Previous Names: Stowmarket Corinthians **Previous Grounds:** Cricket Meadow, Iliffe Way, Stowmarket (vacated 1.8.84)
Previous Leagues: Essex & Suffolk Border
Record Attendance: (old ground) 2,500, F.A. Cup **Year:** 1950
Clubhouse Details: Licensed bar, various meeting rooms, kitchen
Senior Honours: Suffolk Premier Cup 1978

Mangotsfield United and Pegasus Juniors (Hellenic) play out a 0-0 draw in the FA Vase.
Photo: Leo Hoenig

THETFORD TOWN

President: A. Barrell
Chairman: E. Cisban
Manager: Jim Lowe
Coach:
Physiotherapist:
Secretary:
Address & Tel No:
Commercial Manager: None
Address & Tel No:
Press Officer & Tel No:
Address & Tel No of ground: Murdford Road, Thetford, Norfolk. (No telephone)
Simple ground directions: Situated on Murdford Road, signposted via Lynn Downham Market
No of seats: 400 **Covered accommodation:** 400 **Capacity:** 1,400 **Floodlights:** No
Year formed: 1883 **Nickname:** None **Club sponsors:** Thetford Home Improvement Services
Club colours: Claret/Blue **Change colours:** Yellow
Previous Names: None **Previous Grounds:** Melford Common
Previous Leagues: Norfolk & Suffolk **Programme details:** 6 pages, 10p
Record Attendance: Not known
Clubhouse Details: Bar, Tea Bar for members and guests
Senior Honours: None

TIPTREE UNITED

President: L. Foakes
Chairman: M. Hunt
Manager: E. Rumney
Coach:
Physiotherapist:
Secretary: K. G. Pullon
Address & Tel No: 37 Blue Road, Tiptree. 0621 817610
Commercial Manager: None
Address & Tel No:
Press Officer & Tel No: None
Address & Tel No of ground: Chapel Road, Tiptree. 0621 815213
Simple ground directions:
No of seats: 100 **Covered accommodation:** 250 **Capacity:** 3,000 **Floodlights:** Yes
Year formed: 1933 **Nickname:** Jammakers **Club sponsors:** Chris Smith Transport
Club colours: White shirts, Red shorts
Change colours: Blue shirts, Blue shorts
Previous Names: None
Previous Grounds: None
Previous Leagues: Essex Senior
Record Attendance: **Year:**
Programme details: 16 pages, 10p
Clubhouse Details: Sports hall & licenced bar
Senior Honours: Eastern Counties League Champions 1981-82, Cup Winners 1981-82, Essex Senior Trophy 1980-81

WISBECH TOWN

President: A. Harrold
Chairman: A. S. Roseberry
Manager: R. McManus
Coach:
Physiotherapist: Bert Blackshaw
Secretary: M. E. Davis
Address & Tel No: Ely House, 158 Lynn Road, Wisbech, Cambs PE13 3EB. 0945 583567
Commercial Manager: As above
Press Officer & Tel No:
Address & Tel No of ground: Fenland Park, Lerowe Road, Wisbech, Cambs. 0945 584176
Simple ground directions: From Freedom Bridge roundabout (Junc A47 & A1101) take A47 direction Kings Lynn, approx ¾mile, turn right into Lerowe Road, Ground 300 yards on right
No of seats: 350 **Covered accommodation:** 4,000 **Capacity:** 7,500 **Floodlights:** Yes
Year formed: 1920 **Nickname:** Fenmen **Club sponsors:** Wiffen & Co
Club colours: Red
Change colours: Blue
Previous Names: None **Previous Grounds:** Wisbech Park, Walsoken Rectory Field, Harecroft Road
Previous Leagues: Peterborough, United Counties, Eastern Counties, Southern, Midland
Record Attendance: 8,044 v Peterborough United (Midland League) **Year:** 28 Aug, 1957
Programme details: 20 pages, 20p **Club metal badges:** £1
Clubhouse Details:
Senior Honours: FA Cup 2nd Rnd Proper (1), 1st Rnd Proper (5), CIC Winners (7), United Counties League Winners (4) & Runners-up, K.O., Cup Winners, Southern League Div 1 Winners, Midland League Runners-up, Eastern Counties League Winners (2), Runners-up (3), League Cup Winners (3)

Holbeach defend in strength in their away 1-1 draw with Arlesey Town.

Photo David Shute.

MIDLAND FOOTBALL COMBINATION

Chairman: P. Fellows

Hon. Gen. Secretary/Treasurer: L.W. James JP, 175 Barnett Lane, Kingswinford, Brierley Hill, West Midlands DY6 9QA. Tel: Kingswinford 3459

MIDLAND FOOTBALL COMBINATION

Premier Division

	P	W	D	L	F	A	Pts
Studley Sporting	38	22	8	8	83	49	52
Coleshill Town	38	22	7	9	77	43	51
West Midlands Police	38	20	10	8	82	52	50
Highgate United	38	17	14	7	70	41	48
Racing Club Warwick	38	21	4	13	79	66	46
Paget Rangers	38	15	15	8	55	35	45
Hurley Daw Mill	38	16	11	11	68	55	43
Evesham United	38	16	10	12	55	49	42
Stratford Town	38	16	6	16	58	71	38
Boldmere St Michaels	38	14	9	15	46	37	37
Northfield Town	38	14	9	15	63	56	37
Mile Oak Rovers	38	15	7	16	58	53	37
Solihull Borough	38	15	7	16	54	57	37
Chipping Norton Town	38	13	10	15	49	51	36
Kings Heath	38	11	14	13	50	59	36
Cinderford Town	38	12	9	17	51	63	33
Walsall Borough	38	13	6	19	54	58	32
Smethwick Highfield .	38	7	13	18	45	66	27
Southam United	38	7	8	23	35	76	22
Knowle North Star ..	38	3	5	30	34	129	11

Division 1

	P	W	D	L	F	A	Pts
New World	34	25	6	3	94	25	56
Polesworth N. Warwick	34	21	7	6	70	27	49
Bromsgrove Brookfield	34	17	6	11	51	42	40
Bridgnorth Town Res.	34	15	9	10	60	42	39
Kingsbury United ...	34	17	4	13	59	55	38
Moor Green Reserves	34	16	6	12	50	51	38
Bloxwich A.F.C.	34	14	8	12	54	58	36
Sutton Coldfield T. Res.	34	14	7	13	81	59	35
Oldbury United Res. .	34	12	9	13	55	48	33
Chelmsley Town	34	13	7	14	54	63	33
Alcester Town	34	14	3	17	52	62	31
Alvechurch Reserves .	34	9	12	13	42	52	30
Bournville Ath.	34	9	11	14	49	55	29
Wythall	34	12	5	17	44	61	29
Boldmere St Michaels R	34	10	7	17	29	51	27
Mile Oak Rovers Res.	34	8	9	17	39	64	25
Paget Rangers Res. ...	34	8	8	18	31	59	24
Highgate United Res.	34	7	6	21	47	87	20

Division 2

	P	W	D	L	F	A	Pts
Kingswinford Town .	36	23	7	6	89	38	53
Princes End United ..	36	23	5	8	91	43	51
Sedgley Rovers	36	22	7	7	82	47	51
Enville Athletic	36	21	6	9	63	29	48
Henley Forest of Arden	36	19	9	8	74	39	47
Whitesmore Old Boys	36	20	7	9	73	46	47
Northfield Town Res.	36	18	6	12	82	54	42
Smethwick Highfield R.	36	16	9	11	45	36	41
Coleshill Town Res. .	36	17	6	13	62	56	40
Colinthians '83	36	16	7	13	70	57	39
Racing Club Warwick R	36	16	5	15	62	59	37
Bolehall Swifts	36	15	3	18	57	69	33
Kings Norton O. Boys	36	11	10	15	52	55	32
Redditch United Res.	36	12	6	18	55	76	30
Earlswood Town	36	9	6	21	49	62	24
Ludlow Colts	36	6	9	21	42	98	21
Rockwood Albion ...	36	7	6	23	30	94	20
Witton Social	36	4	8	24	37	79	16
Stratford Town Res. .	36	3	6	27	31	109	12

Ashman of Coleshill beats the visiting Highgate goalkeeper but his shot hits the inside of the post and rebounds back into play. Photo: David Shute.

Evesham United *Back Row (L-R): Simon Moverley, Kenny Gwynne, Paul Hare, Neil Bradley, Andy Berry, Steve Barratt, Graham Crowe, Dave Thomson. Front Row (L-R): Steve Reed, Jon Spiers (skipper), Andy Winkett, Rob Candy, Mark Prescott.*
Photo: Evesham Journal.

MIDLAND COMBINATION

	Leading Goalscorers	Hat Tricks	Penalties	Most Appearances
Boldmere St Michaels	Maurice Wright 12 Robert Mowen 10 Darren Meredith 7		Darren Meredith 5	Stephen Clarke 44 Gary Beech 42 Robert Mowen 42
Coleshill Town	Roy Ashman 19 Steve Polack 15 Bob Dyer 10			Roy Ashman 38 Bob Dyer 32 Mark Bishop 32
Evesham United	Steve Reed 15 Paul Hare 9 Rob Candy 8 Mark Prescott 8	Steve Reed	Rob Candy (5) Paul Hare (2)	Andy Berry 47* Jon Spiers 41 Neil Bradley 41
Hurst Daw Mill	Mark Charnley 16 Eamon Pugh 12 Trevor Hubbard 10	Mark Neale Mark Charnley	D. Harvey K. Willis M. Charnley	Malcolm Randle 41 Paul London 39 David Harvey 37
Northfield Town	Robert Pedley 17 Ron Wingfield 8 Mark Wingfield 7 Alan McLaren 7	Alan McLaren	Bob Pedley (4) Gary Whild	Colin Burford 41* Bob Pedley 38 Alan Beardshaw 37 Ron Wingfield 37
Paget Rangers	Chris Sharp 16 Steve Wiseman 15 Gary Williams 11			Paul Edwards 48 Gary Williams 44 Steve Wiseman 44
Racing Club Warwick	Alan Bryan 24 Steve Edgington 21 Paul Coleman 9	Mark Charnley v Knowle A. Bryan v Cinderford	Paul Coleman (3)	Neil Humpney 33+1s Paul Coleman 33 Steve Cooper 28+2s
Smethwick Highfield	Eaton Gordon 9 Chris Mason 7 John Kreft 7	Eaton Gordon v Chipping Norton	John Kreft	Steve Stride 38 Chris Mason 38 Kevin Evans 36
Stratford Town	Jimmy Whitehouse 19 Nyrere Kelly 9 Steve Johnson 8	J. Whitehouse v Hurley Daw Mill	Ivor Pheasant	Jimmy Whitehouse 41 Keith Walton 40 Roy Osborne 39
Walsall Borough	Richard Brade 11 Nigel McCollin 10 David Haycock 9	David Haycock (2)	Ahah Ahiah Nigel McCollin Jon Owen	Richard Brade 35 Duval Palgrave 34 Bob Mallaband 33

Cinderford Town's Evans sets up their only goal of the game here, but Mile Oak came back to score twice and register a fine away victory. Photo: Mike Joss.

THORN-EMI LIGHTING FOOTBALL FLOODLIGHTING FINALS

GROUP A

Denaby United 1 *Watkin* — Shepshed Charterhouse 2 *Grewcock, Wharton*

Littlehampton Town 4 *Smith, Gibb 3* — Cray Wanderers 0

Denaby United 2 *Leary, Whitaker* — Cray Wanderers 1 *French*

Shepshed Charterhouse 6 *Lissaman, Grewcock 2, Wharton, Fearn, Jenas* — Littlehampton Town 1 *Smith*

Denaby United 6 *Deakin 2, Barnsley, Leary 2, Smith* — Littlehampton Town 2

Shepshed Charterhouse 4 *Grewcock 4* — Cray Wanderers 0

Group Result	Goals for	Against
1. Shepshed Charterhouse	12	2
2. Denaby United	9	5
3. Littlehampton Town	7	12
4. Cray Wanderers	1	10
	Total Goals: 29	

GROUP B

Three Bridges 2 *Palmer, Thomas* — Stamford 5 *Genovese 2, Robson 2, Blades*

Southall 5 *Jackson, Regan 2, Rowe, Powell* — Rainworth MW 1 *Comerford*

Three Bridges 7 *Bason 3, Millis 3, Welch* — Rainworth MW 4 *Comerford, Raine, Gray 2*

Stamford 5 *Genovese 3, Blades 2* — Southall 0

Three Bridges 8 *Thomas 2, Bason 2, Millis 3, Joselyn* — Southall 5 *Regan 2, Leather, Joseph, Exer*

Stamford 4 *McIlwain, Genovese, Blades 2* — Rainworth MW 7 *Comerford 2, Gray 3, Humphreys, Morton*

Group Result	Goals for	Against
1. Three Bridges	17	14
2. Stamford	14	9
3. Rainworth MW	12	16
4. Southall	10	14
	Total Goals: 53	

FINAL

Shepshed Charterhouse 9 *Grewcock 3, Jenas 4, Gould, Lissaman* — Three Bridges 0

TEAMS:

Shepshed Charterhouse: King, Gould, Wharton, Grewcock, Jenas, Lissaman. Subs: Thrower, Fearn.

Three Bridges: Norris, Thomas, Williamson, Palmer, Millis, Bason. Subs: Joselyn, McQueen.

Individual Scorers: 10 Grewcock (Shepshed Charterhouse)
6 Millis (Three Bridges)
Genovese (Stamford)

Stratford Town

Boldmere St Michael's on the attack away to West Midlands Police but Steve Clarke fires wide. Photo: Leo Hoenig.

Challenge Cup

First Round

Kings Heath v Smethwick Highfield 5-1
Wythall v Highgate United 1-3
Southam United v Racing Club Warwick . . . . . . 1-1 aet, 1-2
Kingsbury United v Walsall Borough 3-2
Solihull Borough v Bromsgrove Brookfield 4-1
New World v Mile Oak Rovers 2-0
Evesham United v West Midlands Police 3-0
Chipping Norton Town v Hurley Daw Mill 2-1
Chelmsley Town v Bournville Ath 2-3
Stratford Town v Knowle North Star 4-0
Polesworth North Warwick v Coleshill Town 4-1
Studley Sporting v Northfield Town 4-1
Cinderford Town v Bloxwich AFC 2-0
Byes
Alcester Town
Paget Rangers
Boldmere St Michaels

Second Round

Solihull Borough v Chipping Norton Town 2-1
Bournville Ath v Evesham United 2-3
Boldmere St Michaels v Racing Club Warwick 2-1
Studley Sporting v Kingsbury United 4-0
New World v Paget Rangers 1-2
Cinderford Town v Alcester Town 2-2,3-3,2-0
Polesworth North Warwick v Kings Heath 4-1
Highgate United v Stratford Town 2-1

Third Round

Solihull Borough v Studley Sporting 1-2
Paget Rangers v Highgate United 1-0
Boldmere St Michaels v Polesworth North Warwick . . . 2-3
Cinderford Town v Evesham United 2-2,2-2,1-2

Semi-Finals

Paget Rangers v Evesham United 0-1
Studley Sporting v Polesworth North Warwick 2-1,1-3
(Protest by Polesworth North Warwick upheld. Match ordered to be replayed)

Final

Evesham United v Polesworth North Warwick . . . . . 1-2 aet
(Score at 90 mins 1-1)

President's Cup Final

Polesworth North Warwick v Bridgnorth T Res 2-1

Challenge Vase Final

Northfield Town Res v Sedgley Rovers . . . . 3-2 aet

Redditch United reserves fielded over 100 players in their Midland Combination Division Two side during the 1983-84 season. Here their defence holds out against Enville Athletic but they conceded a goal to give the home side a 1-0 win, in the last four minutes. Photo: Leo Hoenig.

Cinderford Town, who have now left the Midland Combination to play in the Gloucestershire County League. Photo: Mike Joss.

Northfield Town *Back Row (L-R): C. Lowe (Secretary/Trainer), E.J. Rough (Chairman), P. Wainman, R. Young, R. Singh, M. Wingfield, P. Kavanagh, C. Burford, R. Pedley (Player/Manager). Front Row: R. Clark (Kit Man and Mascot), N. Ross, D. Barker, P. Dugmore, A. McLaren, A. Belcher, C. Lowe (Mascot).*

Paget Rangers *Back Row (L-R): R. Holmes (Physio), D. Loughran, M. Wooldridge, D. Clayton, S. Lippitt, J. Gittens, G. Harris, N. Evans, E. Caulfield (Manager). Front Row (L-R): N. Morgan, S. Wiseman, G. Williams, P. Edwards (Captain), S. Tucker, K. Douglas, Jason (Ball Boy).* Photo: L. Cox.

BOLDMERE ST. MICHAELS F.C.

Chairman: Harry Peakman
Manager: John Morris
Coach: Brian Hampson
Physiotherapist:
Secretary: J. D. Shaw
Tel No: 021-350 5869
Commercial Manager:
Press Officer:
Address & Tel No of ground: Church Road, Boldmere, Sutton Coldfield. 021-373 4435
Simple ground directions: A38 from Birmingham to Yenton lights, turn left on Chester Road then 5th right into Church Road
No of seats: None **Covered accommodation:** Yes **Capacity:** 100 **Floodlights:** No
Year formed: 1883 **Nickname:** The Mikes **Club sponsors:** None
Club colours: White/Black/Black
Change colours: Sky/Dark Blue/Gold
Record attendance: 3,000
Previous Leagues: Birmingham League, Worcester Comb
Clubhouse details: Bar and lounge open 7 nights and 4 lunchtimes
Major Honours: Midland Combination Challenge Cup Winners, F.A. Amateur Cup Semi-finalists
Programme Editor: Gerry Haggard
Club Captain (1983-84): Peter Spencer
Player of the Year (1983-84): Robert Mowen

COLESHILL TOWN F.C.

Chairman: H. Davies
Manager: H. Shrimpton
Ass. Manager: J. Gardner
Press Officer: J. Edkins
Secretary: Mrs S. Davies
Tel No: Coleshill 65486
Development Officer: L. Lindsay
Press Officer: Mrs. Carol Holder
Address & Tel No of ground: Pack Meadow, Packington Lane, Coleshill, Warks. Tel: Coleshill 63259
Simple ground directions: Exit Junction 4 on M6 signposted to Coleshill, take right hand lane to cross dual carriageway. Ground first on right approx 400 yds
No of seats: None **Covered accommodation:** approx 250 **Capacity:** 3,000 **Floodlights:** No
Year formed: 1894 **Nickname:** None **Club sponsors:** Metal Products
Club colours: Green/White/Green **Change colours:** White/Black/White
Record attendance: 1,000 **Previous Leagues:** Sutton Coldfield
Clubhouse details: Bar open seven nights per week and before and after matches. Bar Manager resides in cottage on ground
Major Honours: Wallsall Senior Cup Season 1982/83. Midland Comb. Runners-up 1983/84.
Club Captain: David Moore

EVESHAM UNITED F.C.

Chairman: Malcolm Davis
Manager: Vacant
Coach:
Physiotherapist:
Secretary: Richard Porter
Tel No: Evesham (0386) 47438
Commercial Manager: Vacant
Press Officer: Secretary
Address & Tel No of ground: Common Road, Evesham, Worcs. Tel: 0386 2303
Simple ground directions: From Birmingham on the A435 turn left into Swan Lane, down Conduit Hill, left into Common Road, turn right before the railway bridge
No of seats: 400 **Covered accommodation:** 400 **Capacity:** 4,000 **Floodlights:** No
Year formed: Reformed 1945 **Nickname:** None **Club sponsors:** Black & White Garages, Valmar Motor Co.
Club colours: All Red **Change colours:** White with Red Trim
Record attendance: **Previous Leagues:**
Clubhouse details: Clubhouse open Monday to Thursday eenings, Saturday and Sunday (match days)
Major Honours: Midland Combination Div. One Champions 1952/3, 1954/5, 1965/6, 1967/8, 1968/9, Worcs. Senior Urn 1976/77, 1977/78
Club Captain: Jon Spiers **Player of the Year:** Steve Reed

HURLEY DAW MILL F.C.

President: D.T. Childs
Chairman: A.J. Allton
Manager: K. Evans
Press Officer: K. Haskins
Secretary: A. Binnie
Address & Tel No: 24 Elm Grove, Hurley, Atherstone, Warks CV9 2NE. Tamworth 872128
Address & Tel No of ground: Daw Mill Sports & Social Club, Welfare Ground, Hurley Common, Atherstone, Warks. Tamworth 873415
Simple ground directions: Take Kingsbury Road from Birmingham, turn right on A51 Coventry-Tamworth Road, follow signposts for Hurley
No of seats: 100 **Covered accommodation:** Yes **Capacity:** 2,000 **Floodlights:** No
Year formed: 1962 **Nickname:** The Mill **Club sponsors:** None
Club colours: Amber/Black **Change colours:** Sky Blue
Record attendance: 599 v Coleshill Town 1983-84
Previous Names: Hurley Utd, Dawmill FC (amalgamated) **Previous Ground::** Hallaughton Grange
Previous Leagues: Tamworth & Trent Valley, Sutton League, Mercian A.F.A.
Clubhouse details: None **Programme:** No
Club Captain (83-84): Keith Evans **Player of the Year:** Des Brown
Major Honours: Midland Comb Div 2 Champions 1977/78, 1979/80, B'ham Junior Cup winners 1983-84, B'ham Junior Cup r/u 1980-81

KNOWLE NORTH STAR F.C.

Chairman: Ron Clarkeson
Manager: Mark Sutherland
Coach:
Physiotherapist:
Secretary: L. Shaw
Tel No: 560 77298
Commercial Manager:
Press Officer:
Address & Tel No of ground: Hampton Road, Knowle, Solihull. 56-79807
Simple ground directions: Main Warwick Road to Knowle from Birmingham, turn left at Wilsons pub, 200 yds on right
No of seats: None **Covered accommodation:** 200 **Capacity:** 3,000 **Floodlights:** No
Year formed: 1926 **Nickname:** Star **Club sponsors:** None
Club colours: Yellow, Black **Change colours:** Blue
Record attendance: 600
Previous Leagues: Birmingham Youth and Old Boys, B'ham Alliance
Clubhouse details: Seating for 60 bar, tea bar
Major Honours: 1971 Finalist B'ham County Junior Cup, 1982 Quarter Finalist F.A. Challenge Vase

MILE OAK ROVERS F.C.

Chairman: T. LLewellen
Secretary: Mr. Paul Blood
Manager: Mr. R. J. Bott
Tel No: Tamworth (0827) 289925
Coach: B. Kenning
Commercial Manager: D. Crump
Physiotherapist: A. Gee
Press Officer: L. Bretherton
Address & Tel No of ground: Recreation Ground, Price Ave, Mile Oak, Tamworth, Staffs. Tamworth 289614
Simple ground directions: Situated on the A5 from Mile Oak Hotel travelling south take third turning right, ground is 200 yds on the right
No of seats: 60 **Covered accommodation:** 300 **Capacity:** 2,500 **Floodlights:** Yes (by Sept. 1984)
Year formed: 1958 **Nickname:** The 'Oak' **Club sponsors:** Greenall Whitley
Club colours: Blue with Yellow trim
Change colours: All Yellow
Record attendance: 500
Previous Leagues: Trent Valley
Clubhouse details: A new £65,000 extension has just been completed and the club is now open every lunchtime and evening
Major Honours: Birmingham Junior Cup Winners

NORTHFIELD TOWN F.C.

Chairman: E. J. Rough
Secretary: C. B. H. Lowe
Manager: R. Pedley
Tel No: Bromsgrove 76913
Coach: Steve Busby
Commercial Manager: N. Harrison
Physiotherapist: A. Woods
Press Officer: E. Rough
Address & Tel No of ground: Northfield Town F.C., Shenley Lane, Birmingham B29. 021-475 5009
Simple ground directions: A38 (Bristol Road) to Northfield turn into Shenley Lane
No of seats: None fixed **Covered accommodation:** Yes **Capacity:** 3,500 **Floodlights:** No
Year formed: 1966 **Nickname:** "The Cross" **Club sponsors:** Den Caney
Club colours: Yellow/Blue/Yellow
Change colours: Blue/Yellow/Blue
Record attendance: 2,200
Previous Leagues: Worcester Combination
Clubhouse details: (Ready by December 1984). New, brick built, suite of four dressing rooms, referees room, showers etc, plus additional covered accommodation.
Major Honours: Birmingham Senior Amateur Cup 1974/75, Midland Football Combination League Champions 1975/76, Midland Football Combination Presidents Cup 1980/81, B'ham County Youth Cup 70, 71, 72, Worcs Youth Cup 4 times Winners, Midland Football Combination Challenge Vase winners 1983/4
Club Captain (83-4): Colin Burford
Player of the Year (83-4): Alan Beardshaw

PAGET RANGERS F.C.

Chairman: Mr. D. Culling
Secretary: L.A. Cox
Manager: Mr. E. Caulfield
Tel No: 378-2225
Coach: Mr. E. Caulfield
Commercial Manager:
Physiotherapist: Mr. R. Holmes
Press Officer: L.A. Cox
Address & Tel No of ground: Springfield Road, Walmley, Sutton Coldfield. 021-351 1563
Simple ground directions: 114 bus from Birmingham City centre to ground
No of seats: 150 **Covered accommodation:** Yes **Capacity:** 2,000 **Floodlights:** Yes
Year formed: 1938 **Nickname:** The "Ps" **Club sponsors:** None
Club colours: Yellow/Black/Yellow
Change colours: Red/Black/Red
Record attendance: 2,000
Previous Leagues: Worcestershire Combination
Clubhouse details: Licensed clubhouse with full social facilities. Open six evenings per week, Saturday and Sunday lunchtimes.
Major Honours: Midland Combination Champions, Midland Combination Cup Winners
Club Captain: Paul Edwards
Player of the Year: Gary Harris (club), Paul Edwards (supporters)
Programme Editor: Neil Griffin

POLESWORTH NORTH WARWICK F.C.

Chairman: E. D. Harris
Secretary: E. Guild
Manager: Eammon Hickey
Tel No: Tamworth (0827) 893690
Coach: Michael Russell
Commercial Manager: R. Wright
Physiotherapist:
Press Officer:
Address & Tel No of ground: Tamworth Road, Polesworth. Tamworth 892482
Simple ground directions: B5000 from Tamworth
No of seats: None **Covered accommodation:** Yes **Capacity:** 1,000 **Floodlights:** No
Year formed: 1966 **Nickname:** None **Club sponsors:** Coppice Car Sales
Club colours: Green and Yellow
Change colours: Tangerine and Black
Record attendance:
Previous Leagues: Mercian A.F.A.
Clubhouse details: Licenced bar, tea bar and refreshments
Major Honours: 1983-84 Midland Comb Challenge Cup, Presidents Cup, Invitation Cup, Div 1 Runners-up

RACING CLUB WARWICK F.C.

Chairman: Mr. E. G. Hainies
Manager: Mr. Dietmar Bruck
Coach: Mr. Ron Watkins
Physiotherapist: Mr. Ron Watkins
Secretary: P. J. A. Murphy
Tel No: Harbury 612675
Press Officer: P.J.A. Murphy
Address & Tel No of ground: Townend Meadow, Hampton Road, Warwick
Simple ground directions: Situated on B4095 Warwick to Redditch Road, follow signs for Warwick Race Course
No of seats: 50 **Covered accommodation:** 100 **Capacity:** 500 **Floodlights:** No
Year formed: 1919 **Nickname:** None **Club sponsors:**
Club colours: Old Gold shirts, Black shorts **Change colours:** White shirts, Black shorts
Previous Leagues: West Midlands Regional League, Warwickshire Combination
Clubhouse details: Open every night plus Sat, Sun, Mon and Fri lunchtimes
Club Captain: Paul Coleman **Player of the Year:** Alan Bryan
Programme Editor: P. Murphy

SMETHWICK HIGHFIELD F.C.

Chairman: B. Guest
Manager: D. Garratt
Coach: S. Garratt
Physiotherapist: None
Secretary: M. Stanley
Tel No: 021-544 5091
Commercial Manager: Mike Joyce (Dudley 235925)
Press Officer: M. Davenport
Address & Tel No of ground: Oldbury Sports Centre, Newbury Lane, Oldbury, Warley. 021-552 1795
Simple ground directions: A-Z ref. P60, A1
No of seats: 200 **Covered accommodation:** 600 **Capacity:** 3.000 **Floodlights:** Yes
Year formed: 1918 **Nickname:** Stags **Club sponsors:** Capri Construction
Club colours: White shirts, Black shorts **Change colours:** Amber shirts, Black shorts
Record attendance: 300 **Previous Leagues:** B'ham Alliance
Clubhouse details: Licensed lounge bar overlooking pitch. Extension planned. Open 6 nights (Mon-Sat)
Major Honours: B'ham Junior Cup, Presidents Cup **Day for midweek Home matches:** Wednesday
Programme Details: New programme planned for 84-85. Last year's programme was placed 9th in the Midland Football Combination section of The Wirrall Non-League Programme Review
Previous Name: Smethwick Town **Previous Ground:** Londonderry Playing Field **Club Captain:** David Parker

SOLIHULL BOROUGH F.C.

Chairman: Mr. W. C. Sutton
Manager: Mr. R. Corbett
Coach: Mr. G. Andrews
Physiotherapist: Mr. J. R. Bignell
Secretary: Mr. H. Cherry
Tel No: 021-707 4285
Commercial Manager:
Press Officer: P. Fletcher
Address & Tel No of ground: Widney Lane, Solihull, West Midlands. 021-705 3169
Simple ground directions: From Solihull town centre, follow Blossomfield Road for 2 miles, turn left at traffic lights into Widney Lane. Ground is 1 mile on right hand side
No of seats: None **Covered accommodation:** Yes **Capacity:** 200 **Floodlights:** No
Year formed: 1951 **Nickname:** The Borough **Club sponsors:** Permoglaze Industrial Finishes
Club colours: All Blue **Change colours:** Yellow/Blue/Yellow
Record attendance: **Previous Leagues:** Mercian Football Association
Clubhouse details: Clubhouse (and bar) on ground
Major Honours: None

STRATFORD TOWN F.C.

Chairman: G. Cutler
Manager: S. Keenan
Coach: L. Keenan
Physiotherapist/Trainer: T. Taylor
Secretary: P. W. Gardner
Tel No: Stratford-on-Avon 296002
Commercial Manager:
Press Officer: P. W. Gardner
Address & Tel No of ground: Masons Road, off Alcester Road, Stratford-on-Avon
Simple ground directions: Follow Worcester signs when in Stratford, Masons Road first right turn after passing railway bridge
No of seats: 200 **Covered accommodation:** **Capacity:** 4,000 **Floodlights:** No
Year formed: 1944 **Nickname:** None **Club sponsors:** None
Club colours: Tangerine/Black **Change colours:** Silver shirts, Black shorts
Record attendance: Not known **Programme Editor:** P.W. Gardner
Previous Leagues: Hellenic League, West Midlands League
Clubhouse details: Open 7 nights. Mon-Fri 7.30p.m.-11.00p.m., Sat 4.30p.m.-11.00p.m., Sun 7.30p.m.-10.30p.m.
Major Honours: Midland Football Combination Champions 1956/57, Birmingham C.F.A. Senior Cup Winners
Club Captain: Graham Ulyatt **Player of the Season:** Graham Ulyatt

WALSALL BOROUGH

President: R. Mee
Chairman: D. Preston
Manager: F. Ross
Club Captain: Nigel McCollin
Press Officer: J. Rousell
Secretary: B. Bishop
Address & Tel No: 12 Lindens Drive, Streetly, Sutton Coldfield. 021-353 5378
Commercial Manager: J. Bridgett
Address & Tel No of Ground: Oak Park, Lichfield Road, Walsall Wood, Brownhills. Brownhills 2223
Simple ground directions: From M6 to centre of Walsall, take A461 from Walsall and go through Rushall, Shelfield, Walsall Wood, then ground on the left at the corner of Oak Park Recreation car park
No of seats: 200 **Covered accommodation:** Yes **Capacity:** 3,000 **Floodlights:** Yes
Year formed: 1982 **Nickname:** None **Club sponsors:** Sportsco
Club colours: Red/White/Red **Change colours:** Yellow/Blue/Blue
Previous names: Walsall Wood and Walsall Sportsco (joined to form Walsall Borough)
Previous Leagues: None **Major honours:** None
Record attendance: 858 v Aston Villa FC, 24th April 1984 (official opening of floodlights)
Clubhouse details: Two clubrooms — one holds approx 100, the other approx 240, open seven nights a week

WEST MIDLANDS POLICE F.C.

President: Sir Philip Knight, Chief Constable
Chairman: Ass. Chief Constable L. Sharp
Manager: Colin Brookes
Coach: Vacant
Physiotherapist: Ray Northwood
Secretary: Brian Pigott
Tel No: 382 3958 (H); 359 5555 Ext 32 (B)
Commercial Manager: None
Press Officer: David Taylor
Address & Tel No of ground: West Midlands Police Sports Ground, "Tally Ho", Pershore Road, Edgbaston, B'ham. 472 2944
Simple ground directions: Pershore Road (A441) 200 yards on left hand side, past junction with Edgbaston Road travelling out of City
No of seats: Portable poss 300 **Covered accommodation:** Yes **Capacity:** 150 **Floodlights:** No
Year formed: 1974 **Nickname:** None **Club sponsors:** None
Club colours: Red/Black/Black **Change colours:** White/Green/Green
Record attendance: **Previous Leagues:**
Clubhouse details: Complex of three bars, snooker room, ballroom, large kitchen for catering
Major Honours: Challenge Cup Winners 1974-75, Midland Football Combination, Worcestershire Senior Urn Finalists 1981-82, Police National (B. Isles) Champions three times
Club Captain (1983-84): M. Buttress **Player of the Year (1983-84):** M. Buttress

TEBBUTT-BROWN CUP 1983/84

Round 1

Anstey N.	3	Holwell	0
Desford C.	2	Earl Shilton A.	3
Friar Lane	2, 2	Leic. Utd. Res.	2, 3
Newfoundpool	2	Melton T.	1
Oadby T.	1	Birstall	2
Quorn	0	Wigston T.	2
Thringstone	2, 0	Stapenhill	2, 3
Wigston F.	0, 0	Narborough	0, 4
Barwell	0	Hinckley T.	6
Houghton	2	Harborough	3
Kirby Muxloe	1	Rolls Royce	0
Thurmaston	0	Syston	1
Whetstone	0, 1	Hillcroft	0, 3
Lutterworth	4	Anstey T.	1
Leic. YMCA	2	Barrow T.	0
Sileby	0, 0, 1	Barlestone	0, 0, 2

Round 2

Anstey N.	0	Narborough	3
Earl Shilton	2	Birstall	1
Leic. Utd. Res.	2	Stapenhill	3
Wigston T.	4	Newfoundpool	1
Hillcroft	0	Harborough	4
Kirby Muxloe	5	Lutterworth	2
Hinckley T.	3	Barlestone	0
Syston St. P.	1, 1, 1	Leic. YMCA	1, 1, 0

Quarter Finals

Hinckley T.	3	Stapenhill	0
Narborough	2	Harborough	0
Earl Shilton	0	Wigston T.	1
Kirby Muxloe	3	Syston St. P.	2

Semi Finals

Hinckley T.	0	Wigston T.	3
Kirby Muxloe	0	Narborough	2

Final

Narborough	0	Wigston T.	1

LEICESTERSHIRE SENIOR LEAGUE

President: L. T. Shipman CBE, MBE
Secretary: P. Henwood, 450 London Road, Leicester, LE2 2PP
Tel: Leicester 704121

Consistent Melton Town win Championship

The championship of the premier division was won by Melton Town, who finished 9 points ahead of their nearest challengers, Narborough and Littlethorpe. During the early months of the season, Desford Colliery and Thringstone were very much in contention with Melton, but by the end of the year Melton were clear at the top and their results remained consistent as they progressed into the second half of the season, finally clinching the title on the last day of March, a month before the season ended.

Wigston Fields, who were pipped for the championship in the previous season by Anstey Nomads, had a disastrous start to the season, losing their manager John Perkins after 3 games. At the end of October, they appointed John Goodman as manager and recorded their first league win in 9 games, but their form improved from then on and they finished a respectable 6th in the table and went on to thrash Anstey Nomads 6-0 in the Leicestershire FA Challenge Cup, after having defeated Shepshed Charterhouse (Southern League) in the semi-final. Anstey Nomads despite losing the final, beat Hinckley Athletic (West Midlands League) in the quarter final and defeated Leicester United (Southern League) in the semi-final.

Stapenhill, who only collected 6 points by the end of the year, pulled themselves together and just avoided relegation by one point.

The unlucky teams to be relegated were Quorn and Holwell.

PREMIER DIVISION

	P	W	D	L	F	A	Pts
Melton Town	30	23	4	3	81	28	50
Narboro' & Littlethorpe	30	17	7	6	65	35	41
Anstey Nomads	30	16	8	6	58	34	40
Birstall United	30	15	9	6	54	37	39
Wigston Town	30	15	5	10	44	30	35
Wigston Fields	30	11	11	8	45	36	33
Friar Lane Old Boys	30	12	8	10	50	36	32
Oadby Town	30	9	13	8	49	47	31
Thringstone	30	10	8	12	44	54	28
Desford Colliery	30	12	3	15	54	73	27
Earl Shilton Albion	30	8	9	13	60	54	25
Leicester United Res	30	7	11	12	30	41	25
Newfoundpool WMC	30	8	10	12	61	62	24*
Stapenhill	30	5	7	18	46	92	17
Quorn	30	6	4	20	40	77	16
Holwell Works	30	5	5	20	30	55	15

DIVISION ONE

	P	W	D	L	F	A	Pts
Harborough Town	30	18	6	6	46	23	42
Hinkley Town	30	14	12	4	45	26	40
Kirby Muxloe	30	17	5	8	50	31	39
Anstey Town	30	12	12	6	50	44	36
Houghton Rangers	30	12	11	7	45	29	35
Syston St Peters	30	15	5	10	56	45	35
Lutterworth Town	30	11	10	9	40	37	32
Rolls Royce	30	13	5	12	70	53	31
Sileby Town	30	11	9	10	32	32	31
Leicester YMCA	30	11	8	11	45	39	30
Barrow Town	30	11	6	13	39	47	28
Thurmaston Town	30	8	8	14	34	55	24
Barlestone St Giles	30	5	13	12	42	56	23
Hillcroft	30	9	5	16	34	47	23
Parwell Athletic	30	7	3	20	38	61	17
Whetstone Athletic	30	4	6	20	22	63	14

PREMIER DIVISION	Anstey N	Birstall Utd	Desford Coll	Earl Shilton	Leicester Utd Res	Friar Lane	Holwell Works	Melton Town	Narborough	Newfoundpool	Oadby Town	Quorn	Stapenhill	Thringstone	Wigston Fields	Wigston Town
Anstey N	—	3-0	3-1	1-0	0-0	1-1	3-1	0-5	0-1	2-1	3-2	3-2	9-0	3-1	0-0	1-0
Birstall Utd	2-1	—	4-0	1-2	2-0	1-1	0-0	0-2	1-1	3-1	1-4	3-2	3-1	5-1	1-0	0-0
Desford Coll	0-2	1-3	—	4-1	2-3	3-2	1-0	1-1	1-4	1-1	2-2	0-1	4-0	1-3	1-3	1-3
Earl Shilton	2-4	2-2	1-3	—	0-2	3-2	6-2	0-3	2-3	2-1	1-1	2-3	1-2	3-1	2-3	0-0
Leicester Utd Res	2-1	0-1	0-2	0-0	—	0-1	1-1	1-3	4-3	5-1	1-1	1-1	1-1	0-1	2-2	0-2
Friar Lane	1-1	0-3	7-1	5-0	0-1	—	2-1	0-0	1-0	2-1	3-0	1-1	4-3	2-0	0-2	2-0
Holwell Works	0-2	0-2	1-2	0-1	0-0	0-2	—	2-3	1-1	0-1	2-3	4-0	4-2	0-1	1-3	1-0
Melton Town	2-1	3-3	5-1	4-1	1-2	3-2	2-0	—	0-1	2-0	2-1	9-0	6-1	3-0	2-0	4-0
Narborough	1-0	1-0	0-1	2-2	1-0	0-0	3-0	1-3	—	2-3	1-1	1-0	8-1	3-1	2-2	1-0
Newfoundpool	2-3	1-1	9-4	3-0	1-1	1-1	2-2	3-3	4-2	—	2-2	6-3	4-1	3-2	1-3	1-1
Oadby Town	1-1	2-2	1-3	2-2	2-0	2-1	3-0	1-2	1-3	1-1	—	1-0	2-0	1-1	2-1	3-1
Quorn	1-2	2-3	2-3	3-4	3-1	2-4	0-3	0-1	1-6	3-1	2-2	—	2-1	2-1	1-2	0-1
Stapenhill	3-3	4-2	2-3	2-5	1-1	3-3	1-2	1-2	1-6	4-3	2-2	2-1	—	2-4	3-2	0-2
Thringstone	2-2	2-2	3-2	1-1	1-1	1-0	3-2	4-1	1-2	2-0	2-0	1-1	1-1	—	0-0	1-4
Wigston Fields	0-0	0-1	2-3	1-1	3-0	1-0	3-0	0-2	2-2	0-3	2-2	4-1	1-1	2-1	—	0-0
Wigston Town	0-3	0-2	4-2	3-0	3-0	1-0	2-0	1-2	1-3	1-0	3-1	4-0	1-0	5-1	1-1	—

Leading Scorers

Premier Division		Division One	
Reeestone T. (Desford)	25	Sanderson (Rolls Royce7	26
Jackson (Melton Town)	19	Springthorpe (Kirby Muxloe)	18
Saxby (Melton Town)	18	Wilson (Hinckley Town)	18
Weston R. (Narborough)	18	Poole (Barlestone)	17
Raynor (Newfoundpool)	16		
Jarram (Anstey Nomads)	15		
Cockayne (Quorn)	15		

ANSTEY NOMADS (1948) **Chairman:** N. Perkins
Secretary: T. French, 6 James Street, Anstey, Leicester. Tel: 362838
Manager: **Previous Leagues:** East Midlands
Ground Address & Tel No: Cropston Road, Anstey. Tel: 364868
Directions to Ground: M1 Junc 22, A50 to Leicester, B5327 to Anstey, on right ½ mile from centre
Colours: All Red **Change colours:** All White
Programmes: 8 pages, included with admission **Clubhouse:** Yes **Floodlights:** No **Seating:** No

BIRSTALL UNITED (1961) **Chairman:** M. Whiteman
Secretary: S. Fisher, 24 Iris Avenue, Birstall. Tel: 677422
Manager: D. Smith **Previous Leagues:** Leicester Mutual
Ground Address & Tel No: Meadow Lane, Birstall. Tel: 671230
Directions to Ground: A6 Leicester to Loughborough main road, 3 miles out of Leicester
Colours: White shirts, Navy shorts **Change colours:** Blue shirts, Blue shorts
Programmes: No **Clubhouse:** Yes **Floodlights:** No **Seating:** No

DESFORD COLLIERY (1965-66) **Chairman:** M. Smedley
Secretary: 104 Preston Drive, New Bold Verdon, Leicester. Tel: Desford 2959
Manager: B. Airis **Previous Leagues:** Leicester District (Sat)
Ground Address & Tel No: Heath Road, Nr. Bagworth. Tel: Bagworth 7198
Directions to Ground: Leicester to Kirby Muxloe to Butchesterton to Heath Road, Bagworth
Colours: Yellow/Red/Red **Change colours:** White/Black/Black
Programmes: No **Clubhouse:** Yes **Floodlights:** No **Seating:** No

EARL SHILTON ALBION (Formed 1886, Reformed 1946) **Chairman:** A. Tillson
Secretary: B. Thompson, 18 Belle Vue Road, Earl Shilton. Tel: Earl Shilton 47141
Manager: D. Leaver **Previous Leagues:** South Leicester, Leicester Dist, Leicester Comb
Ground Address & Tel No: Stoney Croft, New Street, Earl Shilton. Tel: E/S 42826, 42056
Directions to Ground: New Street, Earl Shilton adjacent to A47
Colours: Green/White **Change colours:** Red/Black
Programmes: 8 to 10 pages, 40p including admission **Clubhouse:** Yes **Floodlights:** No **Seating:** No

FRIAR LANE OLD BOYS (1961) **Chairman:** Ivan Birchem
Secretary: Trevor James Knibbs, 75 Brighton Avenue, Wigston Fields, Leics LE8 1JB. Tel: 0533 888928 (H), 832287 ext 214 (W)
Manager: Dave White **Previous Leagues:** Leicester Mutual
Ground Address & Tel No: Knighton Lane East, Leicester. Tel: 0533 833629
Directions to Ground: Leave M69/M1 at Junc 21, take Narborough Road, turn right at first lights into Braunstone Lane. Left at next lights, then immediately right into Wigston Lane. Take first exit at roundabout into Saffron Lane then right at first set of traffic lights. Clubhouse on right, round bend
Colours: Black & /White stripes/Black/Black **Change colours:** Red with White pinstripe/White/Red
Programmes: No **Clubhouse:** Yes **Floodlights:** No **Seating:** No

HINCKLEY TOWN (1958) **Chairman:** E. Huddlestone
Secretary: M. Moore, 52 Eskdale Road, Hinckley, Leics. Tel: Hinckley 636296
Manager: Tony Bowden **Previous Leagues:** Nuneaton Amateur
Ground Address & Tel No: Hinckley Sports Club, Leicester Road, Hinckley, Leics. 615062
Directions to Ground: Midway between Leicester and Coventry on A47
Colours: Claret and Blue **Change colours:** White
Programmes: 8 pages, free with admission **Clubhouse:** Yes **Floodlights:** No **Seating:** No

LEICESTER UNITED (1900) **Chairman:** G. Smith
Secretary: G. C. Glover
Manager: D. Callow **Previous Leagues:** East Midlands
Ground Address & Tel No: George Street, Coleridge Drive, Enderby. 863154
Directions to Ground: Railway station – Narborough 1 mile from Motorway – A46 to Enderby roundabout, Co-operation Street, Shortridge Lane, George Street
Colours: Red/Black/Red **Change colours:** All Blue
Programmes: 10 pages **Clubhouse:** Yes **Floodlights:** Yes **Seating:** Yes

MELTON TOWN (1972)

Chairman: Nigel Vandyk
Secretary: Keith Harris, 27 Highfield Avenue, Melton Mowbray, Leics. Tel: M.M. 63389
Manager: Andy Westwood **Previous Leagues:** None
Ground Address & Tel No: Egerton Park, Leicester Road, Melton Mowbray. M.M. 60350
Directions to Ground: On right of Leicester Road just on edge of town
Colours: White with Red trim/Red/Red **Change colours:** All Yellow
Programmes: 8 pages, 5p **Clubhouse:** Yes **Floodlights:** No **Seating:** No

NARBOROUGH & LITTLETHORPE F.C. ( )

Secretary: Peter Jackson, 93 Cleveleys Avenue, Braunstone, Leicester **Chairman:** Martyn Gibson
Manager: David Callow **Previous Leagues:** Leicester City, Leicester Sunday, Leicester & District
Ground Address & Tel No: The Recreation Ground, Leicester Road, Narborough, Leicester
Directions to Ground: A46 south from Leicester for 6 miles.
Colours: Blue & White stripes/Royal Blue/Red **Change colours:** White shirts
Programmes: No **Clubhouse:** Yes **Floodlights:** No **Seating:** No

NEWFOUNDPOOL WMC F.C. (reformed 1945)

Chairman: S. Turland
Secretary: L. Wilson, 23 Tilton Drive, Oadby, Leics. Tel: Leics. 715892
Manager: R. James **Previous Leagues:** Leicester City
Ground Address & Tel No: Blenheim Road, Birstall, Leicester
Directions to Ground:
Colours: Green & Amber pinstripe/Green/Green **Change colours:** Red & White vertical stripe/Black/Red

OADBY TOWN F.C. (1945)

Chairman: J. E. Beaumont
Secretary: S. D. Young, 21 Orange Street, South Wigston, Leicester. 783300
Manager: S. D. Young **Previous Leagues:**
Ground Address & Tel No: Wigston Road, Oadby, Leicester. 715728
Directions to Ground: A5096 between Oadby and Wigston Magna
Colours: All Red **Change colours:** Sky Blue/Navy/Navy & Sky
Programmes: No **Clubhouse:** Yes **Floodlights:** No **Seating:** No

QUORN F.C. (1924)

Chairman: Geo. Blackshaw
Secretary: Len Sutton, 394 Park Road, Loughborough. Tel: 214434
Manager: Len Sutton **Previous Leagues:** Loughborough Alliance
Ground Address & Tel No:
Directions to Ground:
Colours: Red & White **Change colours:** All Blue
Programmes: No **Clubhouse:** Yes **Floodlights:** Yes **Seating:** Yes

STAPENHILL F.C. (1947-8)

Chairman: D. Wood
Secretary: F. A. Sleigh, 48 Long Street, Stapenhill, Burton-on-Trent. Tel: Burton 65957
Manager: S. Purcell **Previous Leagues:** Burton, Derby
Ground Address & Tel No: Edge Hill, Maple Grove, Stapenhill, Burton-on-Trent. Burton 62471
Directions to Ground: 300 yards off A444 Burton to Measham Road, turning right at "The Copperhearth" public house into Sycamore Road, 3 miles from Burton
Colours: Red/White/Red **Change colours:** Blue/White/Blue
Programmes: No **Clubhouse:** Under construction **Floodlights:** No **Seating:** No

THRINGSTONE F.C. ( )

Chairman: Vacant
Secretary: P. Allgood, 61 Swallowdale, Thringstone, Coalville. 222817
Manager: B. Harley **Previous Leagues:** Loughborough Alliance
Ground Address & Tel No: Homestead Road, Thringstone
Directions to Ground: From Loughborough follow road to Thringstone, take 2nd right past "Rangers Supporters Club", first right straight into ground
Colours: All Yellow **Change colours:** All Blue
Programmes: No **Clubhouse:** Yes **Floodlights:** No **Seating:** No

WIGSTON FIELDS F.C. (1947)

Chairman: D. Goacher
Secretary: K. M. Chatterton, 21 Claybrook Avenue, Braunstone, Leics LE3 2GY. Tel: Leics 896946
Manager: J. Goodman **Previous Leagues:**
Ground Address & Tel No: Windsor Avenue, Glen Parva, Leics. Leics 771039
Directions to Ground: Main A426 from Leicester, turn left at Beefeater Inn (A5096), ¾ mile turn right (follow W.F.F.C. signs)
Colours: All Red **Change colours:** All Yellow
Programmes: 8 pages, included in admission **Clubhouse:** Social clubhouse & player lounge **Floodlights:** No **Seating:** No

WIGSTON TOWN (1928)

Chairman: E. Phillips
Secretary: D. A. Young, 10 Willowpark Drive, Wigston, Leics
Manager: H. Riley **Previous Leagues:** Leicester & District Mutual, Leicester District
Ground Address & Tel No: Holmes Park, Dog & Gun Lane, Whetstone, Leics. 861521
Directions to Ground: M1 to Narborough then through Littlethorpe, Whetstone
Colours: Red **Change colours:** White
Programmes: 8 pages, inclusive with admission **Clubhouse:** Yes **Floodlights:** Yes **Seating:** Yes

Bedfordshire Senior Cup

First Round

Arlesey v Sandy Albion	1-0
Eaton Bray United v Biggleswade	2-0
Potton United v Ampthill Town	1-0
61 Club Luton v Kempston Rovers	4-1
Stotford v Vauxhall Motors	1-0
Waterlows v Shillington	1-2
Wootton Blue Cross v Barton Rovers	2-2,2-2,2-1

Second Round

Eaton Bray United v Arlesey Town	1-0
Potton United v 61 Club Luton	0-2
Shillington v Stotford	0-3
Wootton Blue Cross v Dunstable	2-0

Semi-Final

Stotford v Eaton Bray United	2-0
Wootton Blue Cross v 61 Club Luton	1-2

Final

61 Club Luton v Stotford	3-2

Northants Hillier Senior Cup

First Round

Wellingborough v Raunds Town	3-5
Rushden Town v Desborough Town	2-3
Rothwell Town v Long Buckby	0-4

Second Round

Desborough Town v Raunds Town	1-4
Long Buckby v S & L Corby	4-3
Irthlingborough D v Corby Town	0-1

Semi-Finals

Corby Town v Kettering Town	1-4
Raunds Town v Long Buckby	1-5

Final (two legs)

Kettering Town v Long Buckby	2-2
Long Buckby v Kettering Town	1-5

OXFORDSHIRE SENIOR CUP

Quarter Finals

Chipping Norton v Morris Motors	0-1
Banbury United v Witney Town	2-5*
Blackfriars Athletic v Oxford City	0-6
Headington Amateurs v Kidlington	1-2

Semi-Finals

Morris Motors v Witney Town	0-4
Oxford City v Kidlington	3-1*

Final

Witney Town v Oxford City	1-3

Corby Town *Back Row (L-R): Kevin McGuire, Derek Walker, Peter McDonald, Kevin Byrne, Kevin Johnson, Richard Paterson, Tony Ferns, Roy Clayton. Front Row (L-R): John Hamill, Elwyn Roberts, Andy McGowan, Malcolm Hird (manager), John Adkins, Gary Wood, Gordon Hall.*

Photo: Northamptonshire Evening Telegraph

THE COVENTRY SUBURBAN AND FOOTBALL ALLIANCE

General Secretary: R. H. Ashby,
214 Brownshill Green Road, Coventry CV6 2DW.
Tel: Keresley 2595.

PREMIER DIVISION ONE

	P	W	D	L	F	A	Pts	Linesmans Mks
Massey Ferguson	24	14	5	5	43	19	33	8.24
Sphinx FC	24	14	4	6	35	18	32	9.34
GEC Coventry	24	11	9	4	42	23	31	9.50
Bulkington	24	12	7	5	38	31	31	9.49
Talbot Cars	24	12	4	8	39	36	28	8.95
Nuneaton Griff	24	8	6	10	32	39	22	9.18
Bermuda WMC	24	8	5	11	27	26	21	9.31
Potterton Int.	24	7	7	10	29	31	21	8.95
AEI Rugby	24	7	7	10	33	40	21	9.72
Triumph	24	8	5	11	28	39	21	9.30
Folly Lane	24	6	8	10	18	26	20	8.84
Morris Sports	24	8	2	14	37	47	18	9.00
GEC Willans	24	6	2	16	31	58	14	9.05

PREMIER DIVISION TWO

	P	W	D	L	F	A	Pts	Linesmans Mks
Mancetter Sports	24	15	6	3	51	32	36	9.46
Municipal Sports	24	16	3	5	49	21	35	9.38
Alvis	24	13	7	4	53	27	33	8.67
Stockingford AA	24	11	7	6	63	40	29	9.12
Matrix	24	11	6	7	52	47	28	9.28
Wickmans**	24	12	4	8	45	36	26**	9.21
Coventry Coll	24	10	4	10	40	36	24	8.76
Jet Blades	24	10	3	11	34	36	23	9.29
Courtaulds	24	6	7	11	40	45	19	8.21
Herberts Ath	24	7	5	12	29	41	19	8.82
Lanchester Poly	24	6	2	16	42	62	14	5.29
Dunlop	24	5	4	15	29	64	14	8.05
Jaguar	24	3	4	17	16	54	10	9.05

**2 pts deducted.

BIRMINGHAM & DISTRICT AFA

Hon. Secretary: N L Worskett, 158 Blake Street,
Sutton Coldfield, West Midlands B74 4EU.
Telephone 021-353 6845

PREMIER DIVISION

	P	W	D	L	F	A	Pts
Sutton United	26	19	3	4	66	26	41
Old Wulfrunians	26	15	5	6	54	35	35
Walsall Phoenix	26	12	8	6	75	39	32
Parkfield	26	13	6	7	55	45	32
Wake Green Amtrs	26	11	8	7	36	31	30
Staffordshire Casuals	26	11	7	8	35	29	29
Fire Service	25	11	6	8	41	35	28
Darlaston O B	26	9	8	9	38	33	26
Arcadian	26	8	8	10	30	38	24
Handsworth GSOB	26	6	9	11	28	36	21
Silhill	26	6	9	11	34	53	21
Colinthians	26	4	7	15	30	68	15
Cresconians	26	3	8	15	25	50	14
Old Dudleians	25	4	6	15	25	54	14

Worcestershire Senior Cup

First Round

Alvechurch v Willenhall Town 1-2
Lye Town v Dudley Town 2-0
Redditch United v Oldbury United 2-1

Second Round

Gloucester City v Bromsgrove Rovers ..... 2-1 aet
Halesowen Town v Lye Town 6-0
Kidderminster Harriers v Willenhall Town 0-1
Worcester City v Redditch United 3-3,4-2

Semi-Finals

Gloucester City v Willenhall Town 2-1
Worcester City v Halesowen Town 4-0

Cup Final

Worcester City v Gloucester City
1st Leg at Gloucester 1-1
2nd Leg at Worcester 3-1
Worcester City won 4-2

Birmingham Senior Cup

First Round

Boldmere St Michaels v Coleshill Town 1-1, 6-0
Highgate United v Mile Oak Rovers 1-2
Northfield Town v Halesowen Town 0-7
Smethwick Highfield v Cradley Town 0-4
Walsall Borough v Racing Club Warwick 0-0,2-1
Wolverhampton United v Oldswinford 3-1

Second Round

Alvechurch v Wednesfield Social 6-1
Banbury United v Darlaston 2-1
Boldmere St Michaels v AP Leamington 1-3
Burton Albion v Tamworth 1-0
Dudley Town v Coventry Sporting 3-1
Halesowen Town v Cradley Town 3-0
Lye Town v Hednesford Town 1-2
Mile Oak Rovers v Bedworth United 0-3
Moor Green v Nuneaton Borough 1-1,0-1
Oldbury United v Bromsgrove Rovers 1-4
Stourbridge v Paget Rangers 1-0
Stratford Town v Redditch United 1-1,1-2
Sutton Coldfield Town v Solihull Borough 3-1
VS Rugby v Knowle North Star 4-0
Willenhall Town v Walsall Borough 4-0
Wolverhampton United v Tividale ..... 0-0,?-?

Third Round

Banbury United v Bedworth United 1-1,1-3
Bromsgrove Rovers v Redditch United 5-1
Burton Albion v Dudley Town 0-1
Halesowen Town v Alvechurch 2-0
Sutton Coldfield Town v AP Leamington 1-4
Tividale v Nuneaton Borough 0-1
VS Rugby v Hednesford Town 2-0
Willenhall Town v Stourbridge 1-1,3-2

Fourth Round

Bedworth United v VS Rugby 3-3,0-3
Dudley Town v Bromsgrove Rovers 3-2
Halesowen Town v Nuneaton Borough 3-2
Willenhall Town v AP Leamington 3-1

Fifth Round

Willenhall Town v Dudley Town 0-2
VS Rugby v Halesowen Town 1-4

Final

Dudley Town v Halesowen Town 0-1

LEICESTERSHIRE SENIOR CUP

Preliminary Round

Friar Lane O.B. v Anstey Nomads ... 3-3, 1-0
Ibstock Penistone R v Hillcroft ... 0-1
Stapenhill v Birstall United ... 2-0

First Round

Anstey Town v Desford Colliery ... 0-1
Barwell Athletic v Barlestone St Giles ... 1-0
Hinckley Town v Barrow ... 2-0
Holwell Works v Hillcroft ... 1-0
Houghton Rangers v Friar Lane O.B. ... 1-2
Kirby Muxloe v Thurmaston ... 1-2
Leicester United v Whetstone Ath ... 1-0
Leicester YMCA v Harborough ... 0-3
Lutterworth Town v Hinckley Athletic ... 1-2
Newfoundpool WMC v Sileby Town ... 2-1
Oadby Town v Stapenhill ... 5-0
Quorn v Earl Shilton Albion ... 2-0
Rolls Royce v Narborough & Littlethorpe ... 1-2
Syston St Peters v Shepshed Charterhouse ... 1-3
Thringstone v Melton Town ... 1-2
Wigston Fields v Wigston Town ... 3-0

Second Round

Desford Colliery v Friar Lane O.B. ... 1-0
Harborough Town v Quorn ... 3-2
Holwell Works v Hinckley Athletic ... 0-2
Narborough & Littlethorpe v Melton Town ... 2-0
Oadby Town v Leicester United ... 1-2
Shepshed Charterhouse v Hinckley Town ... 1-0
Thurmaston Town v Newfoundpool WMC ... 1-2
Wigston Fields v Barwell Athletic ... 4-0

Third Round

Desford Colliery v Harborough Town ... 2-1
Hinckley Athletic v Wigston Fields ... 3-1
Leicester United v Shepshed Charterhouse ... 0-2
Newfoundpool WMC v Narborough & Littlethorpe ... 0-1

Semi-Finals

Desford Colliery v Hinckley Athletic ... 0-4
Narborough & Littlethorpe v Shepshed Chart ... 1-3

Final

Hinckley Athletic v Shepshed Charterhouse ... 0-3

WALSALL SENIOR CUP

FIRST ROUND

Pelsall Villa v Bilston United ... 0-2
Blakenall v Atherstone ... 0-1
Rushall v Bloxwich AFC ... 1-1
(Bloxwich thrown out)
Smethwick v Chasetown ... 1-0
Hurley Daw Mill v Pelsall C and S ... 3-1
Aldridge v Wednesfield Social ... 0-1
Harrisons v Armitage ... 2-1
Chasewood v Gornal ... 1-4
Tividale v Great Wyrley ... 2-2, replay 3-2
Boldmere v Coleshill ... 2-1
Highgate v Paget ... 0-4
Walsall Borough v Cradley Town ... 0-1
Mile Oak v Darlaston ... 2-0
Tipton v Oldswinford ... 2-0
Hednesford v Wolverhampton United ... 0-3
Brereton Social v Bloxwich Town ... 5-0

SECOND ROUND

Bilston United v Cradley ... 0-1
Wednesfield v Smethwick ... 5-2
Mile Oak v Rushall ... 3-3, replay 1-2
Atherstone v Hurley Daw Mill ... 3-0
Brereton Social v Paget ... 4-1
Harrisons v Wolverhampton ... 1-1, replay 4-2
Tipton v Tividale ... 0-2
Gornal v Boldmere ... 5-1

QUARTER-FINALS

Gornal v Rushall ... 1-2
Harrisons v Cradley ... 3-3, replay 2-3
Tividale v Wednesfield ... 3-2
Brereton Social v Atherstone ... 1-2

SEMI-FINALS

Atherstone v Rushall ... 3-0
Tividale v Cradley ... 1-1, replay 3-3
(Cradley thrown out)

FINAL (at Walsall Borough FC)

Atherstone v Tividale ... 4-0

Staffordshire Senior Cup

Semi-Finals

Kidderminster Harriers v Sutton Coldfield Town ... 3-1
Northwich Victoria v Halesowen Town ... 1-2

Final

Halesowen Town v Kidderminster Harriers ... 1-2
Kidderminster Harriers v Halesowen Town ... 2-1

BIRMINGHAM & DISTRICT WORKS AND COMBINATION AFA

CHAMPIONS — DEWAR SHIELD
RUNNERS-UP — J. H. LLOYD MEM.

PREMIER DIVISION

	P	W	D	L	F	A	Pts
ANSELLS	22	14	7	1	59	33	35
Old Throstles	22	15	2	5	57	33	32
IMI Kynoch	22	12	4	6	54	35	28
Hughes Johnson Stpgs	22	11	5	6	58	48	27
Albright & Wilson	21	10	2	7	46	32	26
Burmans Social	21	10	3	8	41	34	23
Land Rover Solihull	19	7	9	3	28	27	23
TI Tubes Aston	21	6	4	11	29	43	16
W Midlands Pass Trans.	22	6	2	14	28	44	14
Lucas Batteries	20	5	3	12	30	43	13
Tube Products	22	4	4	14	33	61	12
Dudley Sports	22	2	3	17	31	61	7
	256	104	48	104	494	494	256

CHAMPIONS — TURNER & SIMPSON SHIELD
RUNNERS-UP — CORNWALL/TANGYES SHIELD

DIVISION ONE/A

	P	W	D	L	F	A	Pts
GROSVENOR PARK	17	14	2	1	59	20	30
Monica Star	20	13	4	3	62	25	30
New Manor	18	11	3	4	47	26	25
Delta Group	18	11	0	7	37	40	22
Rover Tyseley	17	8	3	6	31	22	19
Moor Green	19	6	3	10	37	49	15
Ansells Res	21	6	3	12	44	56	15
Formans Road	16	5	4	7	40	38	14
TI Reynolds	19	6	1	12	26	43	13
Bromsgrove Brookfield	20	6	1	13	34	63	13
Willies Wanderers*	8	2	3	3	16	16	7
BSA Sports*	11	0	1	10	8	43	1
	204	88	28	88	441	441	204

*Denotes Withdrawn

Shepshed Charterhouse win the Leicestershire Senior Cup. Photo: Leo Hoenig

Andy Gould (No 10) heads towards goal for Shepshed against Hinckley Athletic in their County Cup Final confrontation. Photo: David Shute

MIDLAND FLOODLIT CUP

Secretary: Keith Allen (0203-349989 (B), 0530-414894 (H))

FINAL LEAGUE TABLE

	P	W	D	L	F	A	Pts
Nuneaton B	6	5	0	1	17	4	67
Bedworth U	6	5	0	1	16	3	66
Stafford R	6	3	0	3	10	10	40
Irthlingborough D	6	3	0	3	7	10	37
Redditch U	6	2	1	3	11	13	36
Kettering T	6	1	2	3	5	10	25
AP Leamington	6	0	1	5	2	18	10

RESULTS

	AP Leamington	Bedworth U	Irthlingborough D	Kettering T	Nuneaton B	Redditch U	Stafford R
AP Leamington	—	0-3	—	—	—	0-3	1-3
Bedworth U	—	—	2-0	3-0	—	—	4-0
Irthlingborough D	2-0	—	—	2-0	0-1	—	—
Kettering T	1-1	—	—	—	3-0	1-1	—
Nuneaton B	6-0	3-1	—	—	—	—	2-0
Redditch U	—	0-3	6-1	—	5-0	—	—
Stafford R	—	—	1-2	3-0	—	3-1	—

Clubs only played each other once

10 points for a win
5 points for a draw
1 point for each goal scored

Top two teams in the league should play a two legged final.

This season a one legged final only was played on 7th May 1984 in front of 1,700 people including Muhamad Ali who presented the trophy.

Nuneaton Borough 1 v 1 Bedworth United
after extra time (score at 90 mins 1-1) the trophy being shared.

MIDLAND COUNTIES CHAMPIONSHIP

Group A — Bedfordshire 2 Cambridgeshire 2, Bedfordshire 1 Nottinghamshire 1, Cambridgeshire 2 Leicestershire 1, Cambs 4 Notts 3, Leics 5 Beds 1, Leics 1 Lincolnshire 1, Lincolnshire 0 Beds 1, Notts 1 Leics 2, Notts 4 Lincs 2, Lincs 0 Cambs 3.

Table

	P	W	D	L	F	A	Pts
Cambridgeshire	4	3	1	0	11	6	7
Leicestershire	4	2	1	1	9	5	5
Bedfordshire	4	1	2	1	5	8	4
Nottinghamshire	4	1	1	2	9	9	3
Lincolnshire	4	0	1	3	3	9	1

Group B — Herefordshire 2 Birmingham County 3, Birmingham 0 Staffordshire 0, Birmingham 4 Shropshire 0, Hereford 4 Staffs 5, Staffs 4 Shropshire 2, Shropshire 2 Hereford 1.

Table

Birmingham	3	2	1	0	7	2	5
Staffordshire	3	2	1	0	9	6	5
Shropshire	3	1	0	2	4	9	2
Herefordshire	3	0	0	3	7	10	0

FINAL at Butlin Road, Rugby (VS Rugby) on Thursday April 26th: Birmingham County FA 0 Cambridgeshire 3.

EAST MIDLANDS FOOTBALL ALLIANCE

1983/4 SEASON — REVIEW

Following their first League Championship in season 1982/3 Gretton F.C. confirmed their superiority by again winning the Premier Division. The Reserves of Alliance Premier league team, Kettering Town, were 7 points behind in second place with Kettering Nomads a further point behind in third place. The three teams were pace setters all season, but a devastating late run by Gretton put the issue beyond doubt, although Kettering Reserves were weakened by first team calls. Stamford Road Old Boys were placed fourth but had the consolation of winning the League K.O. Cup — the "Munton" Cup — at the expense of Corby Hazeltree. After 25 years Corby Gainsborough Res., who finished as wooden spoonists in the Premier Division, are terminating their association with the League. Weldon, also a long serving Club and despite ground improvements, also face the drop into Division 1, following a number of disappointing seasons. They will be replaced in the top flight by Corby Danesholme Albion & Rothwell Corinthians, winners and runners-up of Division 1, and whose pitches and facilities measure up to the Premier Division requirements. At the foot of Division 1 Kettering Avondale, League members for 36 years, have been relegated to Division 2 for the first time in their history, whilst bottom but one club Thrapston Res. are also departing the E.M.F.A. The two clubs relegated to Division 2 the previous year quickly regained their Division 1 status — Corby Locomotives Res. the only team to reach a century of goals were champions of the division, 5 points ahead of Titchmarsh F.C. League newcomers Kettering Buccleuch Wanderers were champions of Division 3, 2 points ahead of former Youth Club team F.C. Azetec. In Division 4 Corby Corinthian Rovers, also in their first year, were worthy champions.

The League, which embraces 70 teams this coming season, covers an area of mid-Northants, with the main areas around Kettering, Corby & Wellingborough, although clubs nearer to Northampton are now joining, as the League expands it's area.

East Midlands Football Alliance

Premier Division*

	P	W	D	L	F	A	Pts
Gretton	30	24	4	2	79	27	52
Kettering Town Res	30	19	7	4	80	37	45
Kettering Nomads	30	20	4	6	75	28	44
Stamford Road OB's	30	14	10	6	54	34	38
Corby Hazeltree	30	15	7	8	73	39	37
Brixworth	30	15	7	8	60	37	37
Corby Locomotives	30	14	8	8	55	47	36
Wellingbro T Res	30	10	11	9	45	42	31
FC Fisher, Corby	30	11	7	12	44	46	28
Wel'ngbro' Whitworths	30	10	4	16	60	73	24
Irthlingbro' Rangers	30	8	6	16	32	54	22
Wellingborough Utd	30	7	7	16	48	64	21
Corby Strip Mills	30	7	7	16	47	76	21
Woodford Stars	30	4	10	16	36	75	18
Weldon	30	5	4	21	31	75	14
Corby Gainsbro' Res	30	4	3	23	23	88	11

*Mears Ashby Sports (MAS) are joing the EMFA from the Rushden League for next season.

NFA Junior Cup Final
Cottingham 1 Brixworth 0

Munton Cup
Semi-Finals
Corby Hazeltree 0,3 FC Fisher 0,0
Kettering Town R. 0 Stamford Road OB's 1

Final
Stamford Road OB's 1 Corby Hazeltree 0
(At Corby Town FC). Attendance 400.

SUFFOLK & IPSWICH

Senior Division

	P	W	D	L	F	A	Pts
Westerfield	30	22	3	5	98	28	47
Ransomes	30	19	7	4	71	31	45
Cranes	30	18	8	4	89	44	44
Ipswich United	30	18	7	5	70	34	43
Grundisburgh	30	16	5	9	79	46	37
Haughley	30	15	4	11	50	44	34
Hadleigh	30	11	9	10	50	41	31
Halesworth	30	10	10	10	45	65	30
Coplestonians	30	10	6	14	47	52	26
Achilles	30	10	4	16	41	52	24
Stutton	30	10	4	16	36	57	24
Leiston	30	10	4	16	55	91	24
Nicholians	30	7	8	15	40	80	22
Old Newton	30	7	6	17	38	69	20
Caribbeans	30	5	7	18	36	75	17
Needham Mkt	30	5	2	23	26	73	12

Division One

	P	W	D	L	F	A	Pts
Leiston	26	18	5	3	53	13	41
Willis Faber	26	14	10	2	61	27	38
Murrayside	26	13	8	5	65	33	34
Whitton	26	14	5	7	60	37	33
Woodbridge	26	13	6	7	53	25	32
B.R.O.B.	26	11	9	6	50	33	31
British Telecom	26	11	7	8	42	32	29
Fonnereau	26	11	6	9	42	42	28
Alan Road	26	10	6	10	42	42	26
Framlingham	26	8	4	14	33	51	20
Murray Rangers	26	8	4	14	42	61	20
Wickham Market	26	6	8	12	35	56	20
Saxmundham	26	2	5	19	33	81	9
Electric Supply	26	1	1	24	18	99	3

ANGLIAN COMBINATION FOOTBALL LEAGUE

FINAL LEAGUE TABLE

	P	W	D	L	F	A	Pts
Wroxham	30	22	5	3	62	26	49
Hoveton	30	21	5	4	51	21	47
Newton Flot	30	18	8	4	61	33	44
Wells	30	12	11	7	55	44	35
St Andrew's	30	13	9	8	55	45	35
Fakenham	30	10	10	10	47	40	30
Lowestoft Reserves	30	13	4	11	48	44	30*
Dereham	30	11	8	11	53	54	30
Poringland	30	8	12	10	49	59	28
Diss	30	9	9	12	53	45	27
Watton	30	9	8	13	46	47	26
Wymondham Town	30	7	11	12	47	56	25
Yarmouth Reserves	30	9	7	14	40	54	25
Gorleston Reserves	30	6	7	17	36	53	19
Kirkley	30	4	8	18	38	74	16
Bungay	30	4	8	18	38	74	16

*Two points deducted

EAST MIDLANDS FOOTBALL ALLIANCE

PREMIER DIVISION

	P	W	D	L	F	A	Pts
Gretton	30	24	4	2	79	27	52
Kettering T Res	30	19	7	4	80	37	45
Kettering Nomads	30	20	4	6	75	28	44
Kettering Stamfd OB	30	14	10	6	54	34	38
Corby Hazeltree	30	15	7	8	73	39	37
Brixworth	30	15	7	8	60	37	37
Corby Locomotives	30	14	8	8	55	47	36
Wellingborough T Res.	30	10	11	9	45	52	31
Corby F.C. Fisher	30	11	7	12	44	46	29
Wellingborough Whit.	30	10	4	16	60	73	24
Irthlingborough Rgrs	30	8	6	16	32	54	22
Wellingborough Utd	30	7	7	16	48	64	21
Corby Strip Mills	30	7	7	16	47	76	21
Woodford Stars	30	4	10	16	36	75	18
Weldon	30	5	4	21	31	75	14
Corby Gainsborough R.	30	4	3	23	23	88	11

Suffolk Premier Cup

Brantham Ath v Newmarket Town 3-2
Felixstowe v Haverhill Rovers..................... 1-1
Lowestoft Town v Bury Town 4-1
Sudbury Town v Stowmarket 3-3,3-1

Semi-Finals

Haverhill Rovers v Brantham Ath............... 1-1,0-2
Lowestoft Town v Sudbury Town.................. 4-2

Final (at Ipswich Town FC)

Brantham Ath v Lowestoft Town 2-0

Suffolk Senior Cup

First Round

Leiston St Margaret v Needham Market............. 2-4
Nicholians v Kirkley 0-1
Lowestoft Town v Ransomes...................... 3-0
Felixstowe v Stutton 1-1,3-3,0-2
Sudbury v Waterside 3-1
Old Newton v Bungay 3-2
Coplestonians v Ipswich United 0-3
Haughley v Hadleigh.......................... 3-1
Stowmarket v Bury Town 2-0
Mildenhall v Sudbury Wanderers 1-0
Westerfield v Lakenheath 6-0
Achilles v Halesworth 2-1
Caribbeans v Haverhill Rovers 2-0
Crane Sports v Beccles.......................... 4-0
Brandon v Oulton Broad......................... ?-?
Brantham v Grundisburgh 1-2

Second Round

Caribbeans v Crane Sports........................ 1-4
Ipswich Town v Haughley........................ 2-0
Lowestoft T v Stutton 5-1
Needham Market v Kirkley....................... 1-2
Oulton Broad v Grundisburgh..................... 3-1
Stowmarket v Mildenhall 1-1,1-1,3-0
Sudbury v Old Newton 4-2
Westerfield v Achilles 4-2

Third Round

Crane Sports v Oulton Broad...................... 2-0
Kirkley v Lowestoft Town........................ 2-0
Stowmarket Town v Westerfield................... 0-3
Sudbury Town v Ipswich Town 0-3

Semi-Finals

Kirkley v Ipswich Town 0-1
Westerfield v Crane Sports........................ ?-?

Cup Final

Crane Sports v Ipswich Town .... ?-?

East Anglian Cup

GROUP 1
First Round

Kings Lynn v Bourne Town 2-1

Second Round

Cambridge City v Kings Lynn 4-2
Potton United v Soham T Rangers 2-1
Stotfold v Spalding United 0-1
Wisbech Town v Eynesbury Rovers 2-1

Semi-Finals

Cambridge City v Wisbech Town 5-1
Potton United v Spalding United .... Spalding W-O

GROUP 2
First Round

Ware v Royston Town 1-1,1-4

Second Round

Epping Town v Baldock Town 1-0
Hertford Town v Royston Town 3-0
Letchworth GC v Saffron Walden Town 0-2
Stevenage Boro v Hoddesdon Town 1-2

Semi-Finals

Saffron Walden T v Epping Town 0-1
Hertford Town v Hoddesdon Town 2-1

GROUP 3
First Round

East Thurrock United v Stansted 2-2,2-4
Woodford Town v Colchester U 1-2

Second Round

Billericay Town v Chelmsford C 1-2
Braintree v Stansted 0-1
Colchester United v Bishops Stortford 3-0
Heybridge Swifts v Tiptree United 0-1

Semi-Finals

Stansted v Tiptree United 2-1
Chelmsford City v Colchester United 0-1

GROUP 4
First Round

Diss Town v Ransomes 0-1
Gorleston v Brantham Ath 5-1

Second Round

Clacton Town v Haughley United 0-1
Crane Sports v Sudbury Town 1-3
Gorleston v Lowestoft Town 1-0
Witham Town v Ransomes 2-3

Semi-Finals

Gorleston v Ransomes 3-0
Sudbury Town v Haughley United 2-0

Area-Group Finals

Spalding United v Cambridge City 2-1
Hertford Town v Epping Town 1-0
Stansted v Colchester United 1-0
Gorleston v Sudbury Town 0-1

Semi-Finals Competition Proper

Spalding United v Stansted 1-1,1-4
Sudbury Town v Hertford Town 2-1

Final

Sudbury Town v Stansted 1-3

NORFOLK SENIOR CUP

FIRST ROUND

Dereham Town	v	Newton Flotman	1-3
Fakenham Town	v	Wymondham O B	4-3
Downham Town	v	Watton United	4-2
Diss Town	v	Thetford Rovers	5-0
St Andrews	v	Wymondham Town	4-0
Wroxham	v	Wells Town	4-0
Overstrand	v	Norman O B	2-0
Blofield United	v	Hoveton United	0-3
Poringland	v	Harleston Town	5-0
Kings Lynn Res	v	Lakeford Rangers	2-1
Holt United	v	Hellesdon	0-2

SECOND ROUND

Kings Lynn Res	v	Hellesdon	5-4
Poringland	v	Overstrand	0-2
Norwich City Res	v	St Andrews	4-0
Wroxham	v	Downham	6-0
Thetford Town	v	Gorleston	1-3
Hoveton	v	Diss Town	2-1
Loddon	v	Newton Flotman	0-0, 0-3
Gt Yarmouth Town	v	Fakenham Town	3-1

QUARTER FINALS

Overstrand	v	Gt Yarmouth Town	0-4
Newton Flotman	v	Gorleston	0-2
Hoveton	v	Norwich City Res	0-1
Wroxham	v	Kings Lynn Res	0-1

SEMI-FINALS

Kings Lynn Res	v	Gorleston	1-1, 0-3
Norwich City Res	v	Gt Yarmouth Town	1-2

FINAL (AT NORWICH CITY)

Gorleston	v	Great Yarmouth	2-0

PETERBOROUGH LEAGUE

FINAL LEAGUE TABLE

PREMIER DIVISION

	P	W	D	L	F	A	Pts
Yaxley	38	28	4	6	88	40	60
St Ives	38	23	10	5	90	39	56
B. Perkins	38	24	8	6	90	39	56
Ortonians	38	23	8	7	77	35	54
Pinchbeck	38	22	9	7	79	41	53
K. Lynn	38	21	10	7	90	45	52
B'stone	38	20	7	11	83	48	47
Perkins	38	18	10	10	71	56	46
Somersham	38	16	7	15	69	58	39
Wisbech	38	15	8	15	74	73	38
Leverington	38	14	9	15	56	52	37
Spalding	38	14	9	15	55	64	37
Eye	38	14	8	16	70	77	36
Whittlesey	38	13	5	20	51	65	31
Huntingdon	38	12	7	19	58	78	31
Ramsey	38	10	10	18	52	64	30
Downham	38	7	8	23	60	86	22
Warboys	38	3	7	28	23	104	13
Phorpres	38	3	5	30	26	106	11
P. Drove	38	2	7	29	25	117	11

KENT LEAGUE

Chairman: P. Wager. *Secretary:* D. D. Baker, 17 Sterling Road, Sittingbourne, Kent ME10 1SJ

From the beginning of November 1983, when Sittingbourne first went to the top of the table, there was never any doubt who was going to win this seasons League Championship. There was none of the excitement of the previous two seasons when the results of the last matches decided the League Championship. For the football they played Sittingbourne thoroughly deserved the title. The biggest surprise was that they did not win the double, losing an extraordinary semi-final to Sheppey at home 6-2 after extra time. Sheppey were themselves runners-up in the League in this their final season in the Kent League before joining the Southern League. They were also the runners-up to Cray Wanderers in the League Cup. At the beginning of November, Hythe Town were second from the bottom in the League and had it not been for this poor start to the season, one wonders where they may have finished, as it was, their third position was very creditable after such a start. Cray Wanderers improved on their League performances of last season, including a 10-1 home victory against Ramsgate. They won a very exciting Cup Final against Sheppey and their season culminated in reaching the finals of the Thorn/E.M.I. Floodlight Competition.

Between Tunbridge Wells in fifth position and Alma Swanley in thirteenth position, 9 points separated the two teams and they and the clubs between them were all very much of a muchness in ability, all of them at times playing well but lacking in consistency. The last three clubs were the same as the previous season, Kent Police this time finishing above Whitstable, leaving Ramsgate, as in the previous season, at the bottom.

It was interesting to note that even though the points system was changed this season to three points for a win, had the previous seasons points system been used, there would have been very little difference in the final table. It would only have meant Crockenhill, Faversham and Alma Swanley moving up one place. Whether it has anything to do with the new points system or not but only 47 games were drawn compared with 73 in the previous season.

In the Kent League Division II, newcomers Fisher Athletic Reserves won the title after an exciting finish, with Sittingbourne Reserves as the runners-up. The Division II League Cup was won by Erith & Belevedere Reserves.

In the national trophies Sittingbourne reached the third qualfying round of the F.A. Cup before losing to Dartford after a replay. In the F.A. Vase Crockenhill reached the fourth round, their run ending at Buckingham Town.

During the season Lea-Ray Insport Limited of Faversham agreed to sponsor a Manager of the Month award, the first winner being Alan Payne of Cray Wanderers.

The new Chairman presented, at the end of the season, a new Trophy to be presented to the team scoring the most goals in Division I, this to be called the Peter Wager Trophy and the first winners were Sittingbourne.

The Kent League Division I will be having two new clubs competing next season, Greenwich Borough and Metropolitan Police Division 4, but will be losing Sheppey United

Cray Wanderers
Back Row (L-R): Don Butterfill, Phil Williams, Kevin Walsh, Gary O'Neill, George Henning, Glen Cooper, Alan White. Front Row (L-R): Dave Quirke, Alan Payne, Neil Adams, Terry French, Peter Capuccio.

to the Southern League. The League are understandably unhappy as it assumed, under the pyramid system now operating, that one of the clubs coming out of the Southern League would join the Kent League. Apparently this is not to be. However, all in the Kent League wish Sheppey United success in their new competition.

Everyone concerned with the League was saddened during the season by the announcements of the deaths of President Eddie Butcher and Chairman Fred Round. Both men have contributed much to the League and will be greatly missed.

Division 1

	P	W	D	L	F	A	Pts
Sittingbourne	30	24	3	3	87	26	75
Sheppey	30	21	3	6	61	28	66
Hythe	30	17	5	8	63	39	56
Cray Wanderers	30	14	7	9	66	40	49
Tunbridge Wells	30	12	7	11	61	44	43
Crockenhill	30	11	10	9	37	34	43
Herne Bay United	30	13	4	13	42	43	43
Beckenham Town	30	12	6	12	56	54	42
Deal Town	30	13	3	14	54	54	42
Faversham Town	30	12	6	12	40	41	42
Slade Green	30	11	4	15	38	52	37
Darenth Heathside	30	9	8	13	44	50	35
Alma Swanley	30	8	10	12	39	50	34
Kent Police	30	8	6	16	27	63	30
Whitstable	30	4	9	17	37	62	21
Ramsgate	30	4	3	23	22	94	15

Division Two

	P	W	D	L	F	A	Pts
*Fisher Athletic	28	19	5	4	82	23	62
Sittingbourne	28	19	2	7	66	38	59
Chatham Town	28	13	8	7	43	31	47
Hythe Town	28	14	4	10	67	44	46
Beckenham Town	28	13	5	10	43	30	44
Hastings United	28	13	5	10	48	46	44
Erith & Belvedere	28	13	4	11	48	34	43
Ashford	28	13	4	11	40	35	43
Darenth Heathside	28	10	8	10	36	39	38
Faversham	28	10	6	12	52	57	36
Snowdown C.W.	28	9	7	12	35	44	34
Dover	28	9	5	14	37	46	32
Folkestone	28	9	3	16	41	56	30
Herne Bay	28	6	4	18	29	77	22
Whitstable Town	28	3	4	21	27	100	13

*Three points and six goals deducted for playing ineligible player.

KENT LEAGUE DIVISION I CUP — 1983-84

1st Round

Alma Swanley	1	Darenth Heathside	3
Deal Town	3	Faversham Town	3
	(A.E.T.)		
Hythe Town	1	Herne Bay	2
	(A.E.T.)		
Ramsgate	0	Cray Wanderers	3
Sheppey	4	Beckenham	2
	(A.E.T.)		
Slade Green	3	Kent Police	2
	(A.E.T.)		
Sittingbourne	3	Whitstable	1
Tunbridge Wells	2	Crockenhill	1

Replay

Faversham Town	0	Deal Town	2

2nd Round

Cray Wanderers	4	Tunbridge Wells	0
Darenth Heathside	2	Slade Green	2
	Slade played ineligible player		
Sheppey	5	Deal	1
Sittingbourne	2	Herne Bay	0

Replay

Darenth Heathside	3	Slade Green	1

Semi-Finals

Cray Wanderers	3	Darenth Heathside	2
	(A.E.T.)		
Sittingbourne	2	Sheppey	6
	(A.E.T.)		

Final

Cray Wanderers	4	Sheppey	3

at Sittingbourne, 5.5.84

Kent League Team

O'Neal	(Cray Wanderers)
Asplin	(Slade Green)
Hope	(Alma Swanley)
Turner	(Alma Swanley)
White	(Crockenhill)
Rogers	(Sittingbourne)
Haskins	(Crockenhill)
Woolford, Capt.	(Sheppey)
Williams	(Cray Wanderers)
Doe	(Sheppey)
McFaden	(Kent Police)

Kent League Manager was Wally Hill of Crockenhill

Herne Bay's Russell sends Whitstable Town goalkeeper, Gambrill the wrong way to score his side's third in a 3-1 win. Photo: Roland Reeve

KENT LEAGUE DIV 1 1983-84

		Alma Swanley	Beckenham Town	Cray Wanderers	Crockenhill	Darenth Heathside	Deal Town	Faversham Town	Herne Bay	Hythe Town	Kent Police	Ramsgate	Sittingbourne	Sheppey	Slade Green	Tunbridge Wells	Whitstable
Alma Swanley	H	—	0-2	1-1	1-1	0-4	3-1	0-1	2-2	0-0	2-2	5-0	0-2	2-1	1-2	2-3	1-1
	A	—	2-5	0-2	0-0	3-2	3-2	1-1	0-4	0-1	0-0	2-0	1-5	0-2	2-2	3-1	2-0
Beckenham Town	H	5-2	—	3-6	0-0	3-0	1-3	3-1	5-1	1-4	4-4	6-0	1-4	1-5	0-0	2-1	1-0
	A	2-0	—	0-2	0-0	1-1	1-3	1-1	3-1	1-3	1-2	3-0	0-2	3-2	1-2	0-2	3-2
Cray Wanderers	H	2-0	2-0	—	2-0	2-0	5-2	3-0	3-1	0-1	2-0	10-1	0-1	1-0	0-1	2-2	2-2
	A	1-1	6-3	—	0-0	3-3	3-1	0-1	0-2	1-2	1-0	3-0	3-4	3-4	1-3	2-2	3-3
Crockenhill	H	0-0	0-0	0-0	—	2-1	3-0	3-0	2-1	3-1	1-1	3-0	1-5	1-1	1-2	2-0	1-0
	A	1-1	0-0	0-2	—	1-2	1-2	1-0	0-0	2-2	1-2	3-0	1-4	0-3	1-3	1-0	1-1
Darenth Heathside	H	2-3	1-1	3-3	2-1	—	0-1	0-2	3-0	3-2	6-1	1-1	1-1	0-1	2-3	3-2	0-0
	A	4-0	0-3	0-2	1-2	—	2-1	0-4	0-0	0-2	2-1	3-0	0-4	2-4	1-1	1-3	1-1
Deal Town	H	2-3	3-1	1-3	2-1	1-2	—	2-3	1-2	2-1	3-2	4-2	2-1	3-1	3-1	2-2	1-1
	A	1-3	3-1	2-5	0-3	1-0	—	0-1	0-1	1-3	3-1	5-0	0-2	1-5	0-1	1-1	4-1
Faversham Town	H	1-1	1-1	1-0	0-1	4-0	1-0	—	3-1	0-3	0-0	1-0	1-2	2-5	0-1	2-0	1-0
	A	1-0	1-3	0-3	0-3	2-0	3-2	—	0-1	5-1	1-1	3-4	2-3	0-0	3-2	0-2	1-1
Herne Bay	H	4-0	1-3	2-0	0-0	0-0	1-0	1-0	—	2-1	5-0	1-1	0-1	0-1	1-0	1-3	3-1
	A	2-2	1-5	1-3	1-2	0-3	2-1	1-3	—	1-4	3-0	2-1	0-2	0-1	2-1	2-3	2-1
Hythe Town	H	1-0	3-1	2-1	2-2	2-0	3-1	1-5	4-1	—	6-0	3-0	0-0	1-0	2-0	2-1	5-2
	A	0-0	4-1	1-0	1-3	2-3	1-2	3-0	1-2	—	0-1	4-1	1-4	2-4	2-2	2-2	2-0
Kent Police	H	0-0	2-1	0-1	2-1	1-2	1-3	1-1	0-3	1-0	—	1-2	1-4	0-1	1-0	2-1	0-1
	A	2-2	4-4	0-2	1-1	1-6	2-3	0-0	0-5	0-6	—	2-1	0-4	0-3	1-0	0-1	1-0
Ramsgate	H	0-2	0-3	0-3	0-3	0-3	0-5	4-3	1-2	1-4	1-2	—	1-5	0-0	1-4	1-0	0-3
	A	0-5	0-6	1-10	0-3	1-1	2-4	0-1	1-1	0-3	2-1	—	0-7	1-2	2-1	1-4	1-3
Sittingbourne	H	5-1	2-0	4-3	4-1	4-0	2-0	3-2	2-0	4-1	4-0	7-0	—	0-1	5-0	2-2	5-2
	A	2-0	4-1	1-0	5-1	1-1	1-2	2-1	1-0	0-0	4-1	5-1	—	2-1	2-1	0-2	4-1
Sheppey	H	2-0	2-3	4-3	3-0	4-2	5-1	0-0	1-0	4-2	3-0	2-1	1-2	—	3-0	3-1	2-0
	A	1-2	5-1	0-1	1-1	1-0	1-3	5-2	1-0	0-1	1-0	0-0	1-0	—	2-1	2-1	1-0
Slade Green	H	2-2	2-1	3-1	3-1	1-1	1-0	2-3	1-2	2-2	0-1	1-2	1-2	1-2	—	0-4	3-1
	A	2-1	0-0	1-0	2-1	3-2	1-3	1-0	0-1	0-2	0-1	4-1	0-5	0-3	—	0-1	1-6
Tunbridge Wells	H	1-3	2-0	2-2	0-1	3-1	1-1	2-0	3-2	2-2	5-0	4-1	2-0	1-2	1-0	—	8-1
	A	3-2	1-2	2-2	0-2	2-3	2-2	0-2	3-1	1-2	1-2	0-1	2-2	1-3	4-0	—	2-2
Whitstable	H	0-2	2-3	3-3	1-1	1-1	1-4	1-1	1-2	0-2	0-1	3-1	1-4	0-1	6-1	2-2	—
	A	1-1	0-1	2-2	0-1	0-0	1-1	0-1	1-3	2-5	1-0	3-0	2-5	0-2	1-3	1-8	—

ALMA SWANLEY

President: Mrs M. Isley
Chairman: A. F. Sullivan
Manager: J. Kane
Coach: R. Sustins
Physiotherapist: None
Secretary: M. J. Dougherty
Address & Tel No: 10 Woodgers Grove, Swanley, Kent. 322 62054
Commercial Manager:
Press Officer & Tel No: None
Address & Tel No of ground: Greencourt Road, Crockenhill, Kent. (0322 66120)
Simple ground directions: Junction of M25 and A20 — one mile west of town
No of seats: None **Covered accommodation:** 200 **Capacity:** 3,000 **Floodlights:** No
Year formed: 1963 **Nickname:** Alma **Club sponsors:** None
Club colours: Red and Black stripes, Black shorts **Change colours:** Yellow and Blue
Previous Names: Alma United **Previous Grounds:** Recreation Ground, Swanley
Record attendance: 1,000 v Enfield L.S.C. **Year:** 1973
Previous Leagues: Spartan, Greater London, London Spartan, London Metropolitan **Programme:** 4 pages, 10p
Clubhouse details: Monday, Tuesday, Thursday, Friday and Saturday evenings. Sunday lunchtimes and Match Days
Club Honours: Metropolitan London Senior Div I Champions 1973-74, Metropolian London Senior Cup Winners 1973-74, Kent Senior Trophy Winners 1975-76

BECKENHAM TOWN

President: F. Starmer
Chairman: G. L. Ward
Manager: W. Proud
Coach: F. Sells
Physiotherapist: K. R. Simmons
Secretary: H. D. Smith
Address & Tel No: 85 Eden Park Avenue, Beckenham, Kent. 01-650 3667
Commercial Manager:
Press Officer & Tel No: G. L. Ward. 01-777 0125
Address & Tel No of ground: Eden Park Avenue, Beckenham, Kent. (01-650 1066)
Simple ground directions: 1 mile west of town, off A214
No of seats: 70 **Covered accommodation:** 70 **Capacity:** 5,000 **Floodlights:** Yes
Year formed: (Present club) 1971 **Nickname:** Town **Club sponsors:** Copers Cope Garage
Club colours: All Red **Change colours:** All Blue
Previous Names: None **Previous Grounds:** Stanhope Grove, Beckenham
Record attendance: 250 v Cray Wanderers **Year:** 1983
Previous Leagues: London Spartan 1975-82, London 1971-75 **Programme:** 8 pages, 50p entrance includes programme
Clubhouse details: Open 7 days a week
Senior Honours: Spartan League Cup Finalists 1977-78, 1978-79, Kent Senior Trophy Finalists 1981-82

CRAY WANDERERS FC

President: None
Chairman: R. Harsant
Manager: Alan Payne
Coach: D. Ruse
Physiotherapist: David Ruse
Secretary: D. A. Hargreaves
Address & Tel No: 19 Station Approach, Chelsfield, Orpington, Kent. 0689 58818
Commercial Manager: None
Press Officer & Tel No: Gerry Dowlin. 0689 25326
Address & Tel No of ground: Oxford Road, Sidcup, Kent. 01-300 9201
Simple ground directions: Between Sidcup High St. and Footcary High St.
No of seats: 20 **Covered accommodation:** 300 **Capacity:** 5,000 **Floodlights:** No
Year formed: 1860 **Nickname:** The Wands **Club sponsors:** Spiral Packs Ltd. Erith, Kent.
Club colours: Amber/Black **Change colours:** White/Black
Previous Names: None **Previous Grounds:** Grassmeade, St. Mary's Cray
Record attendance: 1,500 v Stamford F.C. 6th Round F.A. Vase **Year:** 1979-80
Previous Leagues: Greater London, London, London Spartan, Aetolian, London Met.
Clubhouse details: Open match days and Tues. and Thurs. evenings **Programme:** 8 pages, by donation
Club Honours: Kent League (2), London League (2) & League Cup, Aetolian League & League Cup, Greater London League & League Cup (2), Metropolitan London League & League Cup, London Spartan (2), Kent Amateur Cup (4), Kent League Div I Cup Winners 1983-84

Action from the Darenth Heath side & Alma Swanley match which resulted in a 3-2 victory for the visitors.
Photo: Leo Hoenig

Sheppey United have now joined The Southern League but here they are seen entertaining Whitstable in a game they won 2-0. Photo: Leo Hoenig

CROCKENHILL F.C.

President: H. Miller
Chairman: P. Meagan
Manager: P. Meagan
Coach: None
Physiotherapist: None
Secretary: C. J. A. Nicholls
Address & Tel No: 97 West View, Crockenhill, Swanley, Kent. 0322 62719
Commercial Manager: None
Press Officer & Tel No: None
Address & Tel No of ground: 'Wested', Eynesford Road, Crockenhill, Swanley, Kent. 0322 62097
Simple ground directions: Off main Swanley Road. Station – Swanley Junction. Bus 477 route
No of seats: 200 **Covered accommodation:** 500 **Capacity:** 3,500 **Floodlights:** No
Year formed: 1946 **Nickname:** Crocks **Club sponsors:** None
Club colours: Red & White stripes, Black shorts **Change colours:** Yellow shirts, Blue shorts
Previous Names: None **Previous Grounds:** None
Record attendance: 800 v Maidstone K.A.C. **Year:** 1948
Previous Leagues: Kent Amateur, Aetolian, Greater London **Programme:** 4 pages, 5p
Clubhouse details: Every Friday night, Saturday night and match days
Club Honours: Sevenoaks Charity Cup, West Kent Senior Cup, Kent Amateur Cup Finalists, Kent Senior Trophy

DARENTH HEATHSIDE F.C.

President: None
Chairman: B. W. Smith
Manager: None
Coach: A. G. Burke
Physiotherapist: None
B. R. Reed
Address & Tel No: 18 Belmont Road, Chislehurst, Kent. 01-467 6229
Commercial Manager: None
Press Officer & Tel No: M. S. Wiseman (Orpington 33083)
Address & Tel No of ground: Horton Road, South Darenth, Dartford, Kent (0689 863554)
Simple ground directions: A2 or A20 hence A225 and turn off at Farningham Road Station.
No of seats: 150 **Covered accommodation:** 150 **Capacity:** 2,000 **Floodlights:** No
Year formed: 1951 **Nickname:** None **Club sponsors:** None
Club colours: All Blue **Change colours:** All Red
Previous Names: Heathside Sports F.C. **Previous Grounds:** None
Record attendance: Approx 800 Silver Jubilee Match v Internationals XI. **Year:** 1976
Previous Leagues: Metropolitan 1971-75, Greater London 1968-71, London Spartan 1975-78
Clubhouse details: Open for match days and other events **Programme:** Single sheet, included in admission
Club Honours: Kent Intermediate Cup Finalists 1974-75, Kent League Div II Cup Finalists 1978-79, 1983-84, Kent League Div I Cup Finalists 1980-81

DEAL TOWN

President: None
Chairman: R. Dixon
Manager: D. Parsons
Coach: R. Prior
Physiotherapist: None
Secretary: V. Medus
Address & Tel No: 22 Marlborough Road, Margate, Kent. 0843 291829
Commercial Manager: None
Press Officer & Tel No: None
Address & Tel No of ground: Charles Sports Ground, Mill Road, Deal, Kent. 03045 5623
Simple ground directions: Get to Deal and ask
No of seats: 500 **Covered accommodation:** 1,000 **Capacity:** 4,000 **Floodlights:** Yes
Year formed: 1908 **Nickname:** Town **Club sponsors:** Southern Stock-taking Services Ltd
Club colours: Black and White **Change colours:** Yellow and Black
Previous Names: None **Previous Grounds:** None
Record attendance: 4,000 v Billy Wright Showbiz XI **Year:** 1961
Previous Leagues: Southern, Greater London, Aetolian **Programme:** 2 pages, free with admission
Clubhouse details: Open match days and for functions
Club Honours: Kent League Champions 1952-53, Kent League Div I Cup Winners 1955-56, 1981-82, Greater London Cup Winners 1967-68, Kent Senior Trophy Finalists 1982-83

FAVERSHAM TOWN

President: W. Brock
Chairman: Mrs A. MacDonald
Manager: R. Davis
Secretary: K. F. Hammond
Address & Tel No: 8 Sherwood Close, Faversham, Kent. 0795 535612
Commercial Manager, Address & Tel No: Ray Leader, 48 Blenheim Avenue, Faversham, Kent. 0795 535048
Address & Tel No of ground: Salters Lane, Faversham. 0795 532738
Simple ground directions: On A2. Just west of town.
No of seats: 200 **Covered accommodation:** 3,000 **Capacity:** 8,000 **Floodlights:** Yes
Year formed: 1901 **Nickname:** Town **Club sponsors:** Coast and Country Caravans
Club colours: All White
Change colours: Maroon shirts
Previous Names: None
Previous Grounds: Gordon Square
Record attendance: 950 v Sheppey. **Year:** 1979
Previous Leagues: Metropolitan, Athenian
Programme: 12 pages, 10p
Clubhouse details: Tues. & Thurs. evenings and Match Days
Club Honours: Kent Amateur Cup Winners 1957, 1959, 1972, 1973, 1974; Kent League Champions 1970, 1971, 1978; Kent League Cup Div I Winners 1971; Kent Senior Trophy Winners 1977, 1978

HERNE BAY F.C.

President: None
Chairman: J. Brownett
Manager: P. Clark
Coach: D. McFall
Physiotherapist: J. Hodgkinson
Secretary: Miss G. Carter
Address & Tel No: 17 Oxenden Park Drive, Herne Bay, Kent. 02273 2934
Commercial Manager: None
Press Officer & Tel No: None
Address & Tel No of ground: Winch's Field, Herne Bay, Kent. 02273 4156
Simple ground directions: Leave A299 at Herne Bay Roundabout second turning on left
No of seats: 250 **Covered accommodation:** 4,000 **Capacity:** 6,000 **Floodlights:** No
Year formed: 1886 **Nickname:** The Bay **Club sponsors:** Herne Bay Building Society
Club colours: All Blue
Change colours: All Red
Previous Names: Herne Bay United
Previous Grounds: None
Record attendance: 3,000 v Margate F.C. **Year:** 1970
Previous Leagues: Athenian
Programme: 4 pages, 10p
Clubhouse details: Match Days and Functions
Club Honours: Athenian League Cup Winners 1966-67; Kent Senior Cup Semi-finalists 1970; Athenian League Champions 1970-71; Kent Senior Trophy Winners 1979-80, Kent League Cup Finalists 1978-79

HYTHE TOWN

President: E. Whittlesea-Webster
Chairman: J. Robb
Manager: G. Dempsey
Coach: None
Physiotherapist: None
Secretary: Miss J. D. Bessell
Address & Tel No: 105 Dymchurch Road, Hythe, Kent. 0303 68362
Commercial Manager: None
Press Officer & Tel No: None
Address & Tel No of ground: Reachfields, Fort Road, Hythe, Kent. 0303 65658
Simple ground directions: A259i road to Folkestone, Dymchurch Road ¼ mile out of town
No of seats: 20 **Covered accommodation:** 200 **Capacity:** 2,500 **Floodlights:** No
Year formed: 1922 **Nickname:** None **Club sponsors:** Burlington Insurance
Club colours: White shirts, Black shorts
Change colours: Blue and White stripes, White shorts
Previous Names: None
Previous Grounds: None
Record attendance:
Previous Leagues: Kent Amateur
Programme: 4 pages, 10p
Clubhouse details: Match Days and every evening
Club Honours: Kent League Div I Runners-up 1978-79, 1982-83

KENT POLICE

President: None
Chairman: H. V. D. Hallett
Manager: P. Spittles
Coach: G. Harrison
Physiotherapist: None
Secretary: R. M. Jones
Address & Tel No: 1 Coverdale Avenue, Maidstone, Kent 0622 681740 (H)
Commercial Manager:
Press Officer & Tel No: None
Address & Tel No of ground: Police H.Q., Sutton Road, Maidstone, Kent. 0622 65432
Simple ground directions: Leave Maidstone on Hastings Road, then on to A274
No of seats: 40 **Covered accommodation:** 60 **Capacity:** 3,000 **Floodlights:** No
Year formed: 1951 **Nickname:** None **Club sponsors:** None
Club colours: All Royal Blue
Change colours: All Red
Previous Names: None
Previous Grounds: None
Record attendance: Not known **Year:**
Previous Leagues: Kent Amateur
Programme: None
Clubhouse details: Use HQ Bar on Match Days
Club Honours: Kent League Cup Div I Winners 1969/70; Kent League Div I Runner-up 1969/70

RAMSGATE F.C.

President: E. Butcher
Chairman: A. Blackley
Manager: S. Jest
Coaches: M. Williamson and B. Clifton
Physiotherapist: None
Secretary: P. Link
Address & Tel No: 53 Rydal Avenue, Ramsgate, Kent CT11 0PX. 0843 55125
Commercial Manager: R. Sacks
Press Officer & Tel No: None
Address & Tel No of ground: Southwood Football Ground, Prices Avenue, Ramsgate. 0843 51662
Simple ground directions: Coming from London A299 joining the A253 which takes you into Ramsgate.
No of seats: 1,000 **Covered accommodation:** 1,000 **Capacity:** 3,500 **Floodlights:** Yes
Year formed: 1946 **Nickname:** Rams **Club sponsors:** None
Club colours: All Red **Change colours:** All White
Previous Names: Ramsgate Athletic **Previous Grounds:** None
Record attendance: 7,500 v Margate F.C. **Year:** 1956-57
Previous Leagues: Southern 1959-75 **Programme:** 6 pages, 10p
Clubhouse details: Match days and functions
Club Honours: Kent League 1949-50, 1955-56, 1956-57, League Cup 1948-49; Kent Intermediate Cup 1954-55; Kent Senior Cup 1963-64, Thames Medway Cup 1960-61; Kent Senior Shield 1960-61; Kent Floodlight Trophy 1969-70

SHEPPEY UNITED

President: None
Chairman: V. E. Ward
Manager: Dave Perkins
Coach: A. Woolford
Physiotherapist: None
Secretary: G. E. Carpenter
Address & Tel No: 53 Cecil Avenue, Sheerness, Kent ME12 1DX. 0795 662013
Commercial Manager: P. Fagg
Address & Tel No: 0795 662301
Address & Tel No of ground: Botany Road, St. George's Avenue, Sheerness, Kent. 0795 665299
Simple ground directions: 200 yards from main shopping area of Sheerness
No of seats: 400 **Covered accommodation:** 2,000 **Capacity:** 7,000 **Floodlights:** Yes
Year formed: 1889 **Nickname:** Islanders **Club sponsors:** None
Club colours: Red and White shirts, Black shorts **Change colours:** All Light Blue
Previous Names: Sheppey Athletic **Previous Grounds:** None
Record attendance: 3,000 v Sittingbourne **Year:** 1922
Previous Leagues: Metropolitan, Greater London, Aetolian **Programme:** 4 pages, 5p
Clubhouse details: Open match day only
Club Honours: Kent Amateur Cup Winners 1946, 1952; Kent Senior Shield Winners 1978; Kent League Champions 1973, 1975, 1979; Kent League Div I Winners 1976, 1979, Finalists 1983-84

SITTINGBOURNE F.C.

President: D. Roberton
Chairman: S. Richardson
Manager: P. Laraman
Coach: J. Coyne
Physiotherapist: None
Secretary: L. Davies
Address & Tel No: 41 Murston Road, Sittingbourne, Kent 0795 25441
Commercial Manager: None
Press Officer & Tel No: Secretary
Address & Tel No of ground: Bull Ground, Sittingbourne, Kent. 0795 72884
Simple ground directions: Rear of High Street, Sittingbourne
No of seats: 500 **Covered accommodation:** 3,000 **Capacity:** 8,000 **Floodlights:** Yes
Year formed: 1881 **Nickname:** Brickies **Club sponsors:** None
Club colours: Red and Black stripes, Black shorts **Change colours:** All White
Previous Names: None **Previous Grounds:** None
Record attendance: 5,728 v Gravesend F.A.C. **Year:** 1956
Previous Leagues: Southern, Thames & Medway **Programme:** 2 pages, 5p
Clubhouse details: New Club House open every day
Club Honours: Kent League 1902-03, 1957-58, 1958-59, 1975-76, 1983-84; Kent League Cup 1954-55, 1980-81; Kent Senior Cup 1901-02, 1928-29, 1929-30, 1957-58; Kent Senior Shield 1926-27, 1927-28, 1953-54; Thames-Medway Cup 1955-56, 1958-59

SLADE GREEN F.C.

President: W. Dudley
Chairman: B. Smith
Manager: W. Palmer
Coach: K. Gurr
Physiotherapist: As above
Secretary: P. W. Harwood
Address & Tel No: 1b Elm Road, Slade Green, Erith, Kent 03224 48974
Commercial Manager:
Press Officer & Tel No: None
Address & Tel No of ground: The Glen, 35 Moat Lane, Slade Green, Erith, Kent. 03224 38381
Simple ground directions: Slade Green Station — 200 yards
No of seats: 100 **Covered accommodation:** 200 **Capacity:** 2,000 **Floodlights:** To be erected
Year formed: 1946 **Nickname:** The Green **Club sponsors:** To be arranged
Club colours: Green and Black stripes, Black shorts **Change colours:** Green and White stripes, White shorts
Previous Names: None **Previous Grounds:** None
Record attendance: Not known **Year:**
Previous Leagues: London, Kent Amateur **Programme:** 8 pages, included in admission
Clubhouse details: Every evening and match days
Club Honours: Kent League Cup Winners 1983

SNOWDOWN COLLIERY WELFARE

President: D. Hanson
Chairman: R. Payne
Manager: T. Comer
Coach: T. Norton
Physiotherapist: S. Causer
Secretary: K. W. Owen
Address & Tel No: 34 The Boulevard, Aylesham, Nr. Canterbury, Kent. 0304 841415
Commercial Manager: None
Press Officer & Tel No: Secretary
Address & Tel No of ground: Spinney Lane, Aylesham, Kent. 0304 840278
Simple ground directions: Leave A2 at Barham crossroads, take road to Aylesham
No of seats: 350 **Covered accommodation:** 350 **Capacity:** 5,000 **Floodlights:** No
Year formed: 1919 **Nickname:** Magpies **Club sponsors:** None
Club colours: Black and White **Change colours:** Red and White
Previous Names: None **Previous Grounds:** None
Record attendance: 4,000 v Folkestone K.L.C. Final **Year:** 1956
Previous Leagues: Greater London, Aetolian, Thames & Medway **Programme:** No
Clubhouse details: Open Match Days and functions
Club Honours: Kent League Div I Winners 1954-55; Kent League Cup Winners 1944-45, 1950-51; Kent Senior Cup 1950-51, 1955-56; Aetolian League Winners 1960-61 & League Cup 1961-62

TUNBRIDGE WELLS F.C.

President: None
Chairman: F. J. Oakley
Manager: R. Savage
Coach: None
Physiotherapist: None
Secretary: P. C. Wager
Address & Tel No: 46 Mereworth Road, Tunbridge Wells, Kent TN4 9PL. 0892 24182
Commercial Manager:
Press Officer & Tel No: R. Bonny. 0892 31898
Address & Tel No of ground: Culverden Stadium, Culverden Drive, Tunbridge Wells. 0892 20517
Simple ground directions: Leaving town on main Tonbridge Road turn left opposite Red Lion pub.
No of seats: 200 **Covered accommodation:** 700 **Capacity:** 5,000 **Floodlights:** No
Year formed: 1967 **Nickname:** Wells **Club sponsors:** None
Club colours: Red and White **Change colours:** All Blue
Previous Names: None **Previous Grounds:** None
Record attendance: 967 v Maidstone **Year:** 1969
Previous Leagues: None **Programme:** 8 pages, 10p
Clubhouse details: Match days and functions
Club Honours: Kent League Cup Winners 1974-75, 1977-78

WHITSTABLE TOWN

President: None
Chairman: P. R. Stevenson
Manager: D. Bosson
Coach: None
Physiotherapist: B. Smith
Secretary: A. R. Vinter
Address & Tel No: The Paddock, The Drive, Chestfield, Whitstable, Kent. 022779 2697
Commercial Manager: None
Press Officer & Tel No: None
Address & Tel No of ground: Belmont Road, Belmont, Whitstable. 0227 266012
Simple ground directions: From Thanet Way (A299) down Millstrood Road, ground at bottom. By train, 400 yards from station
No of seats: 400 **Covered accommodation:** 700 **Capacity:** 4,000 **Floodlights:** No
Year formed: 1886 **Nickname:** The Oystermen, The Reds **Club sponsors:** Continental Cabinets, Whitstable
Club colours: Red/White **Change colours:** All White
Previous Names: Whitstable F.C. **Previous Grounds:** None
Record attendance:
Previous Leagues: None **Programme:** 12 pages, 10p
Clubhouse details: Used for social and recreative purposes
Club Honours: Kent League Div II Champions 1927-28, 1933-34, 1949-50; Kent League Premier Division 1960-61; Kent Amateur Cup Winners 1928-29; Kent League Cup Winners 1979-80; Kent Senior Trophy Finalists 1978-79

SUSSEX COUNTY FOOTBALL LEAGUE

(sponsored by the Sussex County Building Society)

President: Dr John O'Hara.

Chairman and Hon. Fixtures Secretary: P. R. Bentley,

199 Chanctonbury Road, Burgess Hill, RH15 9HF. Tel: B. Hill 3181.

Hon Secretary: D. D. Welsh, 19 Dukes Rd, Lindfield, RH16 2JH (Lindfield 2400).

CHAIRMAN'S REPORT 1983-84

Whitehawk with an outstanding final run-in of 16 consecutive victories at the end of the season lifted the League title for the first time since 1963-64. Their final match on the morning of May Day Bank Holiday saw them only having to avoid defeat, but their emphatic 7-0 triumph in front of a crowd of over 800 meant that they had pipped at the post a Littlehampton Town side who had all season been odds on to win the championship for the first time in their history.

The third and fourth placed teams also contested a competitive League Challenge Cup Final at Wick on Good Friday before Steyning Town lifted the Trophy after extra time by two goals to one. Southwick were also runners-up in the Sussex County F.A. R.U.H. Cup losing 2-1 to Littlehampton at Lancing in front of a crowd of 1,300. Whitehawk completed 57 competitive League and Cup matches, Littlehampton 51 and Southwick and Peacehaven both 49, a credit to the stamina of both players and officials of those clubs.

In the Preliminary Round of the F.A. Cup no fewer than seven noteworthy victories were achieved by our clubs over teams from other Leagues. In the First Qualifying Round Hailsham then beat Eastbourne Town 1-0 in a local derby before losing 3-1 to Ashford Town. Horsham YMCA took Hertford Town to a third match before losing 2-0, Whitehawk won 2-1 at Whitstable Town, Pagham drew 1-1 at Thanet United but lost the replay by the only goal, while Three Bridges obtained the outstanding result beating Croydon 5-1, only to lose 3-0 at Sittingbourne in the next round. Our interest in the competition ended with Whitehawk, having beaten Walton & Hersham 4-1 at home, losing to Tooting & Mitcham in the third Qualifying Round by 3-0. Whitehawk were our most successful side in the FA Vase. They went to Tiptree United in the third round and won 4-1, before losing at Corinthian Casuals.

All First Round Vase teams were eligible for entry to a competition sponsored by Philips EMI, who were divided into eight sections with the winners calculated on goals scored in League matches and bonus points for further process in the F.A. Vase were totalled over ten matches. We were honoured by two of our Clubs winning their sections, Three Bridges and Littlehampton, who proceeded to the eight team finals in May at Birmingham. A depleted Littlehampton side gave a good account of themselves, but Three Bridges went right to the Final of the competition before losing to Southern Leaguers Shepshed Charterhouse. However they gained for themselves over £2,000 of electrical goods, as Runners-up.

In the Sussex Senior Cup Final Bognor continued to keep the Isthmian flag flying in creating a record breaking fifth consecutive final victory in defeating Littlehampton 1-0.

The success of our new Division Three formed by 13 of the more ambitious Clubs from Intermediate Leagues was one of the highlights in injecting more impetus into our Division Two, while at the same time providing an extremely competitive Division. The spirit and enthusiasm shown throughout the teams in the Division are the best possible response to its critics. The final outcome of the promotion and relegation between Division Two and Three has still to be confirmed, following classification of respective facilities. Lower Bevendean decided to withdraw at the end of the season, but the size of the Division will be increased by the inclusion of Cooksbridge, Ifield, Oakwood and Saltdean United, to all of whom we extend a warm welcome. The Sussex County Building Society donated an excellent trophy for the new Divisional Championships, and also a trophy for the Divisions Cup Competition.

PETER BENTLEY

SUSSEX COUNTY FOOTBALL LEAGUE
(Sponsored by Sussex County Building Society)

Division 1

	P	W	D	L	F	A	Pts	GD
Whitehawk	30	23	5	2	77	19	74	+58
Littlehampton	30	22	5	3	92	32	71	+60
Steyning	30	20	6	4	62	27	66	+35
Southwick	30	18	9	3	67	22	63	+45
Three Bridges	30	16	4	10	59	45	52	+14
Hastings Town	30	13	7	10	52	34	46	+18
Peachaven & Tels	30	12	7	11	50	37	43	+13
Ringmer	30	10	5	15	38	52	35	−14
Hailsham	30	10	3	17	35	66	33	−31
Eastbourne T	30	8	8	14	33	43	32	−10
Horsham YMCA	30	10	2	18	43	65	32	−22
Midhst & Easbrn	30	8	8	14	36	77	32	−41
Lancing	30	8	6	16	41	62	30	−21
Wick	30	6	8	16	31	57	26	−26
Burgess Hill T	30	4	9	17	29	56	21	−27
Pagham	30	4	4	22	26	78	16	−52

Division 2

	P	W	D	L	F	A	Pts	
Portfield	30	23	6	1	71	21	75	+55
Arundel	30	20	6	4	72	27	66	+45
Hassocks	30	18	5	7	66	38	59	+28
Wigmore	30	17	8	5	57	33	59	+24
Bexhill	30	17	7	6	65	31	58	+34
Chichester	30	15	4	11	54	39	49	+15
Haywards Hth	30	12	12	6	53	33	48	+20
East Grinstead	30	10	9	11	39	41	39	−2
Lingfield	30	10	8	12	47	42	38	+5
Sidley	30	9	6	15	52	58	33	−6
Albion	30	9	6	15	47	68	33	−21
Selsey	30	6	10	14	41	56	28	−15
Storrington	30	6	10	14	39	54	28	−15
Newhaven	30	7	5	18	31	58	26	−27
Shoreham	30	2	8	20	23	83	14	−60
Crowborough	30	1	6	23	22	92	9	−70

Division 3

	P	W	D	L	F	A	Pts	
East Preston	24	15	6	3	38	15	51	+23
Franklands V	24	13	11	0	48	19	50	+29
Ferring	24	13	8	3	53	15	47	+38
Bosham	24	11	5	8	50	38	38	+12
Langney Sports	24	10	8	6	43	36	38	+7
Westdene	24	10	4	10	42	32	34	+10
Broadbridge Hth	24	9	7	8	36	31	34	+5
Seaford Town	24	9	5	10	32	40	32	−8
Midway	24	10	1	13	40	35	31	+5
Hurstpierpoint	24	6	7	11	27	46	25	−19
Eastbourne R	24	7	2	15	31	52	23	−21
Lower Bevenden	24	3	5	16	24	61	14	−37
St Francis Hos	24	3	5	16	19	63	14	−44

Sponsorship Monies

Merit Table:	£1,000 as attached	
Leagues		
Division One	Winners	£250
	Runners-up	£150
Division Two	Winners	£150
	Runners-up	£100
Division Three	Winners	£100
	Runners-up	£50
Cups		
Challenge Cup	Winners	£100
	Runners-up	75
Div Two Cup	Winners	£75
	Runners-up	£50
Div Three Cup	Winners	£50
	Runners-up	£25

Manager of the Month Awards

September	Norman Cairns (Littlehampton)
October	Alan Pook (Southwick)
November	Brian Donnelly (Whitehawk)
December	John Bolingbroke (Peacehaven)
January	David Kew (Portfield)
February	David John (Haywards Hth)
March	Barry Youell (Steyning Town)
April	Barry Taylor (Hailsham Town)

Manager of the Season
Brian Donnelly (Whitehawk)

Whitehawk *Sussex League Champions.* Photo: Brighton & Hove Gazette & Herald.

SUSSEX COUNTY FOOTBALL LEAGUE DIVISION ONE SEASON 1983/84

	Burgess Hill Town	Eastbourne Town	Hailsham Town	Hastings Town	Horsham YMCA	Lancing	Littlehampton Town	Midhurst & Easebourne	Pagham	Peacehaven & Telscombe	Ringmer	Southwick	Steyning Town	Three Bridges	Whitehawk	Wick
Burgess Hill Town	—	0-0	0-2	1-3	5-2	1-1	1-1	0-2	2-0	0-2	1-0	1-2	0-1	1-3	0-6	0-1
Eastbourne Town	2-0	—	1-2	4-2	1-1	0-0	1-3	2-0	3-0	0-1	1-0	0-0	1-2	0-0	1-3	2-0
Hailsham Town	1-1	1-0	—	3-0	3-5	1-2	1-6	0-0	3-1	2-1	1-2	0-0	1-2	2-4	1-2	1-0
Hastings Town	1-1	3-1	4-0	—	5-0	2-1	2-2	8-0	3-0	0-1	2-0	0-2	0-1	3-0	1-2	1-1
Horsham YMCA	1-0	1-2	2-1	0-2	—	4-1	1-5	3-1	4-1	2-3	0-3	1-3	3-4	0-1	0-3	5-0
Lancing	0-0	2-0	2-0	1-2	0-1	—	0-2	1-1	4-1	2-0	1-2	1-2	2-4	4-2	2-8	2-1
Littlehampton Town	4-3	2-1	7-0	1-1	2-2	3-1	—	7-2	9-1	3-1	5-2	1-0	2-1	6-1	2-0	3-1
Midhurst & Easebourne	1-1	3-3	2-1	1-1	1-3	3-2	0-3	—	2-1	0-8	3-1	1-1	0-3	3-2	1-3	0-0
Pagham	3-2	0-0	0-1	0-2	1-0	3-3	0-3	1-3	—	2-0	3-5	0-2	2-1	1-4	1-3	0-2
Peacehave & Telscombe	2-0	1-0	0-1	0-0	4-0	2-3	1-2	2-0	5-1	—	0-2	1-1	0-3	3-0	2-2	5-2
Ringmer	1-1	1-1	0-3	1-1	1-0	1-0	1-4	3-1	3-1	1-1	—	1-3	0-2	1-2	0-2	4-2
Southwick	5-1	5-1	2-0	2-1	2-1	4-1	1-0	9-0	0-0	1-1	3-1	—	1-1	1-2	2-0	5-0
Steyning Town	2-1	5-2	4-1	4-1	2-0	5-1	1-1	3-0	1-0	1-0	1-1	2-2	—	2-1	0-0	0-1
Three Bridges	3-3	2-0	4-1	2-0	5-0	2-0	1-2	2-3	3-0	3-3	2-0	2-1	1-0	—	0-1	3-1
Whitehawk	3-0	1-0	7-0	2-0	3-0	3-0	2-0	3-2	3-0	3-0	4-0	0-0	1-1	2-1	—	3-0
Wick	1-2	2-3	5-1	0-1	0-1	1-1	2-1	0-0	2-2	0-0	1-0	1-5	1-3	1-1	2-2	—

DIVISION TWO

	Albion United	Arundel	Bexhill Town	Chichester City	Crowborough Athletic	East Grinstead	Hassocks	Haywards Heath	Lingfield	Newhaven	Portfield	Selsey	Shoreham	Sidley United	Storrington	Wigmore Athletic
Albion United	—	2-6	0-1	0-1	3-2	0-2	2-4	2-2	1-0	2-0	2-4	5-1	2-1	0-3	3-3	0-0
Arundel	3-0	—	2-0	3-2	5-0	4-2	0-2	2-1	3-0	1-0	0-2	3-0	3-0	2-1	3-0	2-4
Bexhill Town	6-1	1-1	—	2-0	9-1	2-2	2-2	0-2	1-0	1-1	1-5	4-3	9-0	2-1	3-1	0-0
Chichester City	4-1	1-3	1-0	—	3-1	2-1	1-2	1-2	3-2	2-0	2-2	1-0	8-2	4-1	0-0	0-2
Crowborough Athletic	0-3	0-5	0-4	0-1	—	3-4	1-2	0-5	0-0	2-3	0-5	1-6	0-1	1-1	1-2	0-2
East Grinstead	0-1	0-0	3-0	0-4	0-0	—	2-1	1-1	0-1	3-0	1-1	1-1	1-1	1-0	2-2	0-1
Hassocks	4-1	2-2	1-3	2-0	6-1	0-1	—	2-1	3-1	2-1	1-1	4-5	4-1	5-0	0-3	0-2
Haywards Heath	2-0	0-1	0-0	3-0	3-0	1-1	0-2	—	2-2	2-0	1-1	2-0	4-0	0-1	1-1	2-2
Lingfield	1-1	0-2	2-4	1-1	2-4	2-0	2-2	1-1	—	5-0	0-1	2-0	4-0	3-0	3-2	0-2
Newhaven	1-0	1-0	0-1	1-3	3-0	1-4	0-1	5-2	1-3	—	0-3	0-4	0-0	0-2	2-2	2-2
Portfield	4-1	0-0	1-0	2-1	6-1	3-0	2-0	1-1	0-1	4-1	—	1-0	1-0	1-0	3-0	3-2
Selsey	1-1	0-5	0-1	0-0	1-1	2-0	0-2	0-2	1-1	2-2	1-3	—	1-1	4-1	2-3	1-1
Shoreham	3-8	0-4	0-3	0-5	1-1	1-0	0-3	3-3	0-3	0-2	2-4	2-2	—	0-4	1-1	1-2
Sidley United	6-0	4-4	0-2	3-0	1-1	2-3	2-2	1-3	2-1	3-2	1-3	2-2	3-0	—	1-1	2-4
Storrington	2-4	0-1	0-0	1-3	3-0	1-2	1-4	1-1	2-2	0-2	0-1	0-1	3-2	3-2	—	0-2
Wigmore Athletic	1-1	2-2	1-3	2-0	2-0	3-2	0-1	2-3	3-2	2-0	1-3	4-0	0-0	4-2	2-1	—

DIVISION THREE

	Bosham	Broadbridge Heath	East Preston	Eastbourne Rangers	Ferring	Franklands Village	Hurstpierpoint	Langney Sports	Lower Bevendean	Midway	Seaford Town	St Francis Hospital	Westdeen
Bosham	—	1-2	1-2	5-1	2-1	2-2	2-1	3-4	3-0	2-4	2-1	4-2	4-2
Broadbridge Heath	1-1	—	0-2	1-2	2-1	1-1	6-2	1-1	3-0	0-1	0-3	2-1	0-1
East Preston	2-0	2-1	—	0-1	0-0	2-2	2-0	2-1	2-2	1-0	2-0	2-0	3-0
Eastbourne Rangers	2-4	3-2	1-2	—	1-2	3-5	3-2	0-3	0-1	2-0	3-3	1-0	2-4
Ferring	2-2	1-2	1-0	4-0	—	0-0	3-0	6-1	9-0	3-1	0-0	5-0	2-2
Franklands Village	1-0	1-1	1-1	2-0	1-1	—	4-0	0-0	3-0	4-1	3-2	1-1	1-1
Hurstpierpoint	2-1	1-1	1-0	1-0	0-1	1-1	—	1-4	1-1	1-1	2-1	2-2	0-0
Langney Sports	1-2	1-1	3-3	1-0	0-0	0-2	3-1	—	2-1	1-2	0-1	2-0	2-0
Lower Bevendean	2-2	1-2	0-1	1-3	0-1	0-1	1-1	4-4	—	1-3	1-3	4-1	1-4
Midway	0-2	1-0	0-3	5-1	1-2	0-1	0-1	3-4	4-0	—	5-0	0-2	1-2
Seaford Town	1-4	0-0	0-3	0-0	0-3	0-3	5-2	1-1	3-1	1-0	—	3-0	0-3
St Francis Hospital	1-1	1-4	0-0	1-0	0-5	0-5	1-4	2-2	0-2	1-6	1-2	—	0-5
Westdene	1-0	2-3	0-1	3-2	0-0	2-3	3-0	0-2	5-0	0-1	1-2	1-2	—

Steyning Town *(Sussex League Cup Winners) Back Row (L-R): Dave Mayne (Trainer), Paul Begent, Andy Reed, Alex Siveyer, Rod Wood, Mark Howells, Steve Burrows, John Green, Neale Phillips, Andy Horn, Tim Willows (Secretary), Barry Yowell (Manager). Front Row (L-R): Paul Yowell (Mascot), John Robson, Keith Perkins, Dave Clark, Dave Robinson, Chris Metcalfe (Captain), Graeme Gerry, Derek Steel.*

LEAGUE CHALLENGE CUP — 1983/84

First Round

Portfield (h)	v	Southwick (a)	2-1
Hastings T	v	Bexhill T	4-2
Whitehawk	v	Shoreham	3-0
Albion U	v	Hailsham T	0-2
Pagham	v	Arundel	1-0
Peacehaven & T	v	Sidley U	4-1
Horsham YMCA	v	Chichester	*3-1
East Grinstead	v	Eastbourne T	*1-1, 1-0
Burgess Hill	v	Lingfield	3-1
Storrington	v	Littlehampton	0-3
Wick	v	Crowborough	3-1
Haywards Heath	v	Three Bridges	1-4
Selsey	v	Midhurst & E	3-1
Steyning T	v	Hassocks	2-0
Wigmore Ath	v	Ringmer	2-1
Newhaven	v	Lancing	0-2

Second Round

Southwick	v	Hastings T	2-1
Whitehawk	v	Hailsham T	2-1
Pagham	v	Peacehaven & T	0-1
Horsham YMCA	v	East Grinstead	2-1
Burgess Hill	v	Littlehampton	0-2
Wick	v	Three Bridges	2-3
Selsey	v	Steyning T	0-2
Wigmore Ath	v	Lancing	*3-2

Third Round

Southwick	v	Whitehawk	2-1
Peacehaven & T	v	Horsham YMCA	*2-2, 1-0
Littlehampton	v	Three Bridges	3-0
Steyning T	v	Wigmore Ath	2-1

Semi-Finals

Southwick	v	Peacehaven	1-0
Littlehampton	v	Steyning T	*2-2, 0-2

Final

Southwick	v	Steyning T	*1-2

Final Man of the Match: Neil Phillips (Steyning Town).

* After extra time

LEADING LEAGUE GOALSCORERS
1983/84
10 or club highest

Division 1

Burgess Hill Town	Frank Wakeley 4
Eastbourne Town	Pip Facer 8
Hailsham Town	Stephen Richardson 9
Hastings Town	John Kemp 14
Horsham YMCA	Lee Mobsby, Alan Ricketts both 10
Lancing	David Stevens 13
Littlehampton Town	Ian Cole 26, Kevin Keehan 24
Midhurst & Easebourne	Simon Dummer 16
Pagham	Michael Bennett 4
Peacehaven & Tels.	Cyril 'Biz' Russell 13, Everton Ifill 12
Ringmer	Neill Ewen 12
Southwick	Geoff Pook 27
Steyning Town	Rodney Wood 14, Andrew Horn 12 (inc 5 for Pagham)
Three Bridges	David Gates 11
Whitehawk	Gerry Fell 22, Kevin Crooks 22 (inc 4 for Southwick), Stephen Gill 13 (inc 6 for Wigmore Athletic)
Wick	Paul Clarey 9

Leading goalscorers:

Geoff Pook (Southwick)	27
Ian Cole (Littlehampton T)	26
Kevin Keehan (Littlehampton T)	24

Division 2

Albion United	Terry Button 15
Arundel	Paul J Bennett 36
Bexhill Town	Peter Heritage 22
Chichester City	Neal Holder, Stephen White both 9
Crowborough Athletic	Rod Harmon 10
East Grinstead	Neil Hayes 11
Hassocks	Ian Rogers 14, Grant Paskins 12, Nigel Carr 12 (inc 3 for Burgess Hill Town)
Haywards Heath	Brian Welsh 12, Martin Bairdow 11
Lingfield	Robert North 18
Newhaven	Francis Haren 7
Portfield	James Davis 16, Gary James 13, Patrick Hynes 11
Selsey	Gary Wheatcroft 17 (inc 1 for Chichester City)
Shoreham	Steven Coleby 7
Sidley United	Kevin Bevis, Robin Watson both 12
Storrington	Paul Bradford 6
Wigmore Athletic	Lee Murphy 10

Leading goalscorers:

Paul J Bennett (Arundel)	36
Peter Heritage (Bexhill T)	22
Robert North (Lingfield)	18

SUSSEX COUNTY BUILDING SOCIETY

MERIT TABLE

SEASON 1983/84

	Games Played	Win Points	Draw Points	Goal Points	Points	Dismissals	TOTAL POINTS
Portfield	30	115	12	71	280		478
Arundel	30	100	12	72	290		474
Steyning Town	30	100	12	62	280		454
Littlehampton T	30	110	10	92	240	−10	442
Southwick	30	90	18	67	270	−10	435
Whitehawk	30	115	10	77	230		432
Haywards Heath	30	60	24	53	290		427
Hassocks	30	90	10	66	260		426
Hastings T	30	65	14	52	290		426
Chichester City	30	75	8	54	280		417
Bexhill Town	30	85	14	65	260	−10	414
Wigmore Athletic	30	85	16	57	260	−20	398
Three Bridges	30	80	8	59	250		397
East Grinstead	30	50	18	39	290	−10	387
Selsey	30	30	20	41	290		381
Storrington	30	30	20	39	280		369
Ringmer	30	50	10	38	280	−10	368
Albion United	30	45	12	47	260		364
Midh'st & Easebn	30	40	16	36	270		362
Sidley United	30	45	12	52	250		359
Peacehaven &Tel.	30	60	14	50	250	−20	354
Horsham YMCA	30	50	4	43	250		347
Lancing	30	40	12	41	250	−10	333
Newhaven	30	35	10	31	250		326
Hailsham Town	30	50	6	35	230		321
Burgess Hill T	30	20	18	29	250		317
Wick	30	30	16	31	240		317
Pagham	30	20	8	26	260		314
Lingfield	30	50	16	47	200		313
Eastbourne Town	30	40	16	33	230	−10	309
Crowborough Ath	30	5	12	22	250		289
Shoreham	30	10	16	23	200	−10	239

5 points for a win, 2 points for a draw and 1 point per goal. 10 points for a clean game and deduct 10 points for a dismissal.

SENIOR REPRESENTATIVE MATCHES 1983/84

9th November, 1983

v Kent League at Sittingbourne.

Micky Phillips (Littlehampton), Russell Rego (Three Bridges), Mark Dunk (Whitehawk), Frank Croney (Haywards Heath), Gary Williams (Whitehawk), Martin Bairdow (Haywards Hth), Phil Somers (Whitehawk), Mark Croft (Southwick), Brian Bason (Three Bridges), Dave Palmer (Three Bridges), Ian Cole (Littlehampton).

Manager Brian Donnelly (Whitehawk) Result: won 2-0

30th November, 1983

v Essex Senior League at Burgess Hill

Micky Phillips (Littlehampton), Russell Rego (Three Bridges), Frank Croney (Haywards Hth), Steve Welch (Three Bridges), Graham Farmer (Southwick), Liam Lyons (Haywards Heath), Martin Bairdow (Haywards Heath), Brian Bason (Three Bridges), Paul Brigden (Peacehaven), Dave Palmer (Three Bridges), Geoff Pook (Southwick).

Manager John Keehan Result: won 1-0

ARUNDEL

Chairman: Mick Monk
Manager: Mick Peters
Coach: Mick Peters
Physiotherapist: K. Scott
Secretary: Peter Wells
Tel No: Rustington 71146
Commercial Manager:
Press Officer: Colin Dobbs
Address & Tel No of ground: Mill Road, Arundel. Arundel 882548
Simple ground directions: A27 to Arundel, turn right into castle car park
No of seats: **Covered accommodation:** Yes **Capacity:** 2,000 **Floodlights:** No
Year formed: 1889 **Nickname:** The Mullets
Club colours: Red **Change colours:** Blue & White
Record attendance: 2,200 **Previous Leagues:** West Sussex
Clubhouse details: Bar, darts, pool table, food, committee room, dance floor, kitchen
Major Honours: County League Div 1 Winners 1957-58, 1958-59, Sussex RUR Cup Winners 1969, 1973, 1979, 1980, Division 2 League Cup Winners 1976-77, Reserve Section Cup 1978-79

BURGESS HILL TOWN F.C.

Chairman: A. G. Lake
Manager: H. Easton
Coach: F. Croney
Physiotherapist: B. Howell
Secretary: A. Gunn
Tel No: Burgess Hill ((04446) 44963
Commercial Manager: J. Collins
Press Officer: None
Address & Tel No of ground: Leylands Park, Burgess Hill. 044 46 42429
Simple ground directions: BR to Wivelsfield
No of seats: None **Covered accommodation:** 400 **Capacity:** 4,000 **Floodlights:** Yes
Year formed: 1882-83 **Nickname:** The Hillians **Club sponsors:** Claremont Travel
Club colours: Yellow/Green **Change colours:** White/Green
Clubhouse details: Club open 7 days a week. Two bars. Separate hall for functions
Major Honours: Sussex Senior Cup (3), Sussex County League, Sussex County League Cup, Sussex County Youth F.A. Cup

EASTBOURNE TOWN F.C.

Chairman: R. J. Hutchinson
Manager: T. J. Wood
Coach: P. Dallaway
Secretary: K. H. Trailor
Tel No: Eastbourne 27645
Commercial Manager: None
Address & Tel No of ground: The Saffrons, Eastbourne. 23734
Simple ground directions: 5 minutes from station
No of seats: 700 **Covered accommodation:** 500 **Capacity:** 5,000 **Floodlights:** No
Year formed: 1882 **Nickname:** The 'Bourne **Club sponsors:** Davies & Tate Ltd
Club colours: Yellow & Blue **Change colours:** Red & Black
Record attendance: Not known **Previous Leagues:** Corinthian, Athenian
Clubhouse details: Full restaurant and liquor licence
Major Honours: Sussex County League Winners 1976-77

HAILSHAM TOWN

Chairman: R. Soan
Manager: P. Lawrenson
Coach: None
Physiotherapist: Mrs M. Andrews
Secretary: Mrs J. Packham
Tel No: 844360
Commercial Manager: None
Press Officer: Mrs J. Packham
Address & Tel No of ground: Western Road Recreation Ground, Hailsham. 840446
No of seats: **Covered accommodation:** Yes **Capacity:** **Floodlights:** No
Year formed: 1885 **Club colours:** Green/Yellow **Change colours:** Royal Blue
Previous Leagues: Sussex Combination

HASTINGS TOWN

Chairman: P. Eastman
Manager: K. Barry
Secretary: R. T. Capon
Address & Tel No: 35 Park Drive, Hastings TN34 2PR (Hastings 713885)
Address & Tel No of ground: The Firs, Elphinstone Road, Hastings (Hastings 439165)
Simple ground directions: Via Seafront (A259). Turn left at traffic lights in centre of town into Queens Road, turn right under bridge
Colours: White with Red trim **Previous Leagues:** Hastings League
Seating: No **Clubhouse:** Yes **Floodlights:** Yes **Programmes:** 10 pages, 10p
Major Honours: Sussex County F.A. Senior, R.U.R. Charity, Intermediate & Junior Cup, Sussex County League Div 2, League Challenge and Div 2 Cup, Hastings & District F.A. Intermediate Cup

HORSHAM Y.M.C.A.

Chairman: G. Head
Manager: Tony Elkins-Green
Coach: Norman Dearlove
Physiotherapist:
Secretary: C. James
Tel No: Horsham 51818
Commercial Manager: Roy White
Press Officer: Roy White
Address & Tel No of ground: Gorings Mead, Horsham. 52689
Simple ground directions: A281 off Brighton Road, Horsham
No of seats: 80 **Covered accommodation:** 300 **Capacity:** 2,000 **Floodlights:** No
Year formed: 1898 **Record attendance:** 667 **Club sponsors:** Raben-Christensen
Club colours: Red & Black **Change colours:** White
Previous Leagues: Horsham & District, Brighton & District, Mid Sussex
Clubhouse details: Bar open Tuesday, Thursday, Friday, Saturday & Sunday. Hall available for functions

Three Bridges FC *Back Row (L-R): Paul Ranson, Trevor Wright, Dave Gates, Gary Brooker, Bill Norris, Steve Welch, Paul Taylor, Trevor Williamson. Front Row (L-R): Brian Bason, Bobby Nash, Russell Rego, Steve Thomas, Dave Palmer. Mascot Chris Brown in front.*

Lancing *Winners of the Sportsmanship Trophy.*

Littlehampton *(Runners up in Division One) Back Row (L-R): D. Treagus, R. Tiltman, J. Campbell, H. Smith, S. Piper, R. Cheal. Front Row (L-R): I. Gibb, I. Cole, K. Hotston, S. Bennett, R. Sopp, M. Phillips, T. Still.*

LANCING

Chairman: John Brown
Manager: Alf Ford
Physiotherapist: Don Stevens
Secretary: John Chisnall
Tel No: Lancing (0903) 763048
Press Officer: Len Ralph
Address & Tel No of ground: Culver Road, Lancing. 764398
Simple ground directions: 200 yards north of Lancing railway station
No of seats: 400 **Covered accommodation:** 400 **Capacity:** 3,000 **Floodlights:** Yes
Year formed: 1941 **Nickname:** **Club sponsors:** Eschmann
Club colours: Yellow shirts, Blue shorts **Change colours:** All Red
Record attendance: 2,591 v Tooting (Amateur Cup 4th Qual Round) **Year:** 1947
Previous Leagues: Brighton League **Clubhouse details:** Owned by Sussex County F.A.
Major Honours: Sussex County League Runners-Up 1949-50, 1964-65, Division Two Champions 1957-58, 1969-70, Runners-Up 1982-83, Division Two Cup Winners 1981-82, Sussex RUR Cup Winners 1965-66

LITTLEHAMPTON TOWN

Chairman: B. Wadsworth
Manager: N. Cairns
Coach: N. Cairns
Secretary: A. C. Wickens
Tel No: Littlehampton 717641
Press Officer: A. C. Wickens
Physiotherapist: P. Redmond
Address & Tel No of ground: Sportsfield Street, Floras Road, Littlehampton. 3944
Simple ground directions: A259 from Bognor. A284 from Arundel. A259 from Worthing
No of seats: 200 **Covered accommodation:** 500 **Capacity:** 2,000 **Floodlights:** No
Year formed: 1896 **Nickname:** Marigolds **Club sponsors:** Barry Wadsworth
Club colours: Amber with Red trim **Record attendance:** 1,200
Clubhouse details: Lounge bar and restaurant. Daily lunches and evening meals
Major Honours: Sussex Invitation Cup 1952-53, 1953-54, 1958-59, 1961-62, League Challenge Cup 1975-76, 1976-77, Sussex Senior Cup 1949, 1970, Sussex Intermediate 1949, Sussex RUR Charity 1947, 1970, 1971

MIDHURST & EASEBOURNE UNITED F.C.

Chairman: Robert Boxall
Manager: N. O'Boyle
Coach: N. O'Boyle
Secretary: E. S. Dummer
Tel No: Midhurst 3887
Press Officer: Rex Lane
Address & Tel No of ground: Rotherfield Sports Ground, Dodsley Lane, Easebourne, Midhurst, West Sussex
Simple ground directions: Take the A286 (London) road out of Midhurst town. Rotherfield is ¼ mile on left after River Bridge **No of seats:** 50 **Covered accommodation:** Yes
Year formed: 1946 **Club sponsors:** Lewis & Glue Electrical of Midhurst
Club colours: Royal Blue **Change colours:** Amber or All Red
Previous Leagues: West Sussex, Southern Counties Combination
Clubhouse details: Modern clubhouse with bar and canteen facilities
Major Honours: Sussex Intermediate Cup (5), Southern Counties Combination League Challenge Cup and Division Two Championship

PEACEHAVEN & TELSCOMBE

Chairman: J. Edwards
Manager: J. Bolingbroke
Secretary: Mrs P. Solomons
Address & Tel No: 186 Arundel Road, Peacehaven, Sussex (Peacehaven 5773)
Address & Tel No of ground: Piddinghoe Avenue, Peacehaven (Peacehaven 2471)
Simple ground directions: A259 Coastal road from Brighton. Piddinghoe Avenue is about 1 mile past the roundabout leading into the Meridan Centre **Programmes:** 12 pages, 10p
Year formed: 1923 **Colours:** White/Black **Clubhouse:** Yes
Major Honours: Sussex County F.A.R.U.R. Charity Cup, Sussex County Football League champions, Div 2 champions, Div 2 Cup winners and Whitbread Wessex 5-a-side Tournament winners

PORTFIELD

Chairman: J. Dowling
Manager: D. Kew
Physiotherapist: D. Kew
Secretary: R. A. Granger
Tel No: Haslemere 56268
Press Officer: Mrs V. Larner
Address & Tel No of ground: Church Road, Chichester. 779875
Simple ground directions: One mile east of city center on A27 (behind Wadham/Stringer Garage)
No of seats: **Covered accommodation:** **Capacity:** 250 **Floodlights:** No
Year formed: 1896 **Nickname:** 'Field' **Club sponsors:** Hargreaves Sports
Club colours: Black/Amber **Change colours:** White **Previous Leagues:** West Sussex
Clubhouse details: Seating for 160 people, dance floor and stage, two bars
Major Honours: Sussex County League Div 2 Champions

RINGMER F.C.

Chairman: D. M. Jeary
Manager: D. M. Bielkus
Coach: R. Ralfe
Secretary: Mrs J. M. Feltham
Tel No: Lewes 6341
Commercial Manager: None
Address & Tel No of ground: Caburn Ground, Ringmer. 812738
Simple ground directions: From Lewes Road turn into Springett Avenue, first left into Anchor Field, first left into Caburn ground
Year formed: 1910 **Covered accommodation:** Covered area **Capacity:** 400 **Floodlights:** No
Club colours: Light and Dark Blue **Change colours:** Red, White trim **Club sponsors:** David D. Construction
Record attendance: 948 **Previous Leagues:** Brighton
Clubhouse details: Main hall, bar, lounge, kitchen, toilets and committee room
Major Honours: County League Champions 1970-71, F.A. Cup First Round 1970-71, Sussex Senior Cup Winners 1972-73, Sussex Senior Cup Finalists 1980-81

STEYNING TOWN

Chairman: T. Davis
Manager: B. Youell
Coach: J. Robson
Physiotherapist: D. Mayne
Secretary: T. Willows
Tel No: Steyning 814430
Commercial Manager: D. Mayne
Press Officer: B. Barnard
Address & Tel No of ground: Shooting Field, Shooting Field Estate, Steyning. 812228.
Simple ground directions: Turn down Church Street from High Street, 2nd left and straight on, 4th on left entrance
No of seats: None **Covered accommodation:** 250 **Capacity:** 3,000 **Floodlights:** No
Year formed: 1900 **Club sponsors:** Bowyer Travel, Yovell Butchers, Chanctonbury Laundries
Club colours: Red/White/Red 1st XI; All Red 2nd XI **Change colours:** Blue/White/White
Previous Leagues: Brighton
Clubhouse details: Open 6 days a week. Entertainment on most Saturday evenings
Major Honours: Sussex County League runners-up and League Challenge Cup winners

THREE BRIDGES F.C.

Chairman: C. J. Steele
Manager: A. Knight
Coach/Asst Manager: A. Knight
Physiotherapist: J. McConnell
Secretary: C. Clark
Tel No: 26087
Commercial Manager: P. Terry
Press Officer: A. Blackler
Address & Tel No of ground: Jubilee Field, Three Bridges, Crawley. 30540
Simple ground directions: 200 yards BR Three Bridges
No of seats: None **Covered accommodation:** 350/400 **Capacity:** 2,500 **Floodlights:** No
Year formed: 1901 **Nickname:** The Bridges **Club sponsors:** Kingsland Paper, Fielddale Ltd, Brookes Sports
Club colours: Amber/Black **Change colours:** Red/White
Record attendance: 1,700 **Previous Leagues:** Not available
Clubhouse details: Bar open Monday to Saturday, Sunday lunchtimes
Major Honours: Sussex FA RUR Charity Cup Winners 1982-83, Sussex County League Invitation Cup Winners 1970-71

WHITEHAWK

Chairman: K. J. Powell
Manager: B. Reeves
Press officer: S. Galloway
Secretary: J. D. Rosenblatt
Tel No: Brighton 680322
Commercial Manager: D. Etheridge
Address & Tel No of ground: Whitehawk Football Ground, East Brighton Park, Brighton. 609736
Simple ground directions: North of Brighton Marina
No of seats: **Covered accommodation:** Stand **Capacity:** 500 **Floodlights:** No
Year formed: 1945 **Nickname:** Hawks **Club sponsors:** Etheridge Electrics
Club colours: Red & White **Change colours:** White
Record attendance: 1,500 **Previous Leagues:** Brighton, Hove & District
Clubhouse details: Capacity of 200, open every evening with bar facilities
Major Honours: Sussex County Div 1 1961-62, 1963-64, 1983-84, Div 2 1967-68, 1980-81; Sussex Senior Cup 1951, 1962; Sussex Intermediate Cup 1950; Sussex Junior Cup 1949, 1952; Brighton Charity Cup 1962; Sussex Youth Cup 1981-82, 1982-83

WICK

Chairman: Ken Gordon
Manager: Dave Thorpe
Coach: Mick Streeter
Secretary: Terence Davies
Tel No: Littlehampton 21887 (H)
Press Officer: As secretary
Address & Tel No of ground: Crabtree Park, Wick (Littlehampton 3535)
Simple ground directions: A27 to Crossbush, turn left at Cameillia Hotel, down road for approx 1 mile, over railway crossing, 1st left nextdoor to Locomotive public house, go up road at side
No of seats: 300 **Covered accommodation:** Yes **Capacity:** 300 seated **Floodlights:** Yes
Year formed: 1892 **Nickname:** Wickers **Programme:** 8 pages, 10p
Club colours: Red & Black striped shirts, Black shorts, Red socks **Change colours:** Yellow shirts, Black shorts
Record attendance: 1,000 **Previous Leagues:** Sussex County League
Clubhouse details: Lower floor – dressing rooms, referee's changing room, kitchen, store cupboard, toilets. Upper floor – bar and seating accommodation
Major Honours: Sussex County League Div 2 champions 1981-82; Sussex County League Div 2 League Cup runners-up 1981-82; Gilbert Rice Floodlight Cup runners-up 1980-81; 1981-82; Sussex County Building Society Merit Table winners 1981-82.

Peacehaven score to send Burgess Hill into the bottom two places. As Southwick decided to move into the Combined Counties League Burgess Hill were given a reprieve and were not relegated. Photo: G. Humphrey

Portfield *Champions of Division Two.*

East Preston *Champions of Division Three.*

Franklands Village *Runners up in Division Three and the only Sussex League club to remain unbeaten in the league all season.*

ALBION UNITED

Chairman: K. Cherry
Manager: R. Funnell
Secretary: Mrs Cherry
Address & Tel No: 3 Lewes Close, Bexhill, Sussex (0424 217191)
Address & Tel No of ground: Pear Tree Lane, Little Common, Cooden (5861)
Simple ground directions: From Brighton on A259, turn left at Little Common roundabout into Pear Tree Lane
Seating: No **Floodlights:** No **Programmes:** 4 pages, 10p
Club colours: Blue/Maroon **Change colours:** White
Year formed: 1966 **Clubhouse:** Yes

BEXHILL TOWN F.C.

Manager: J. Price
Physiotherapist: J. Sands
Secretary: R. W. Foster
Tel No: Hastings 432065
Commercial Manager: B. Crowhurst
Address & Tel No of ground: The Polegrove, Brockley Road, Bexhill-on-Sea. Bexhill 220732
Simple ground directions: Turn right to town centre from traffic lights to London Road from A27
No of seats: 200 **Covered accommodation:** 200 **Capacity:** 500 **Floodlights:** No
Club colours: Green shirts **Change colours:** Yellow
Record attendance: Not known **Club sponsors:** Glyne Gap Garage
Major Honours: Sussex County League 1956-57, 1965-66, 1966-67, Sussex RUR Charity Cup 1957-58, 1973-74

CHICHESTER CITY

Chairman: J. F. Hutter
Manager: N. Hillier
Secretary: J. F. Hutter
Tel No: Chichester 785839
Address & Tel No of ground: Oaklands Park, Chichester. 785978
Simple ground directions: Adjacent to Festival Theatre and City Centre
No of seats: None **Covered accommodation:** Yes **Capacity:** 2,500 **Floodlights:** No
Year formed: 1881 **Nickname:** City **Club sponsors:** None
Club colours: White shirts, Black shorts **Change colours:** Red shirts, White shorts
Record attendance: 2,500 v Dorchester (F.A. Cup) **Year:** 1960
Previous Leagues: Founder members of Sussex County League
Clubhouse details: Open matchdays and some evenings
Major Honours: Sussex County League (5), Sussex Senior Cup 1926, RUR Cup (2), League Cup (4)

EAST GRINSTEAD

Chairman: P. Cadman
Manager: C. White
Secretary: G. E. Tizzard
Tel No: East Grinstead 22167
Press Officer: Contact Secretary
Address & Tel No of ground: East Court, East Grinstead. 25885
No of seats: None **Covered accommodation:** 600 (standing) **Capacity:** **Floodlights:** No
Year formed: 1890 **Nickname:** The Wasps **Club sponsors:** None
Club colours: Amber/Black **Change colours:** Green
Record attendance: 2,002 **Previous Leagues:** Mid Sussex, Southern Amateur
Clubhouse details: Licensed bar

FERRING F.C.

Chairman: R. Relton **Manager:** P. Ebers
Secretary: S. H. Blake, 9 Fernhurst Drive, Goring by Sea BN12 5AS. Tel: Worthing 46436
Address & Tel No of ground: Glebelands Ground, Ferring. Worthing 43618
Simple ground directions: Turn south from A259 Worthing/Littlehampton road into either Ferring Lane or Langbury Lane. Cross Ferring railway crossing, turn right into Rife Way then left into Greystoke Road. Nearest railway station: Goring (1 mile)
Colours: Royal Blue wiht White pin stripe

FRANKLANDS VILLAGE F.C.

Chairman: G. Dixon
Manager: B. Waller
Secretary: D. Worsfold
Address & Tel No: 342 Franklands Village, Haywards Heath, W. Sussex (H.H. 416475)
Address & Tel No of ground: Reed Pond Walk, Frankland Village, Haywards Heath, W. Sussex (H.H. 412435)
Seating: No **Clubhouse:** Yes **Floodlights:** No
Colours: All Light Blue **Change colours:** All Red
Year formed: 1956 **Programmes:** Pages and prices yet to be decided for 1984-85
Previous Leagues: Southern Counties Comb, Brighton Hove & District, Crawley & District, Mid-Sussex & District

HASSOCKS F.C.

Chairman: M. A. Boxall
Manager: C. Smart
Coach: A. Lower
Secretary: R. Ward
Tel No: Hurstpierpoint 832036
Address & Tel No of ground: Adastra Park, Hassocks. 2668
Simple ground directions: BR Hassocks 250 yards due east
Covered accommodation: 200 **Nickname:** Robins **Floodlights:** No
Year formed: 1903 **Club colours:** Red/Black **Change colours:** White/Amber
Previous Leagues: Southern Counties Combination, Brighton & District, Mid Sussex
Clubhouse details: Changing rooms, showers, bar
Major Honours: Sussex Intermediate Cup Winners & Runners-Up, Southern Counties Combination League Champions & Cup Winners

HAYWARDS HEATH

Chairman: F. Hall
Secretary: P. Tuck
Manager: D. John
Tel No: Haywards Heath 451159
Coach: A. Hillman
Physiotherapist: D. B. Howell
Address & Tel No of ground: Hanbury Park Stadium, Allen Road, Haywards Heath, Sussex. 412837
Simple ground directions: One mile east from railway station
No of seats: 750 **Covered accommodation:** One stand **Capacity:** 5,000 **Floodlights:** No
Year formed: 1900 **Nickname:** The Bluebells **Club sponsors:** W. C. Hilton (Holdings) Ltd
Club colours: Royal Blue **Record attendance:** 4,000
Previous Leagues: Mid Sussex, Metropolitan
Clubhouse details: Bar, lounge, small dance floor, reception hall
Major Honours: Sussex Senior Cup 1957-58, RUR Charity Cup 1943-44, 1966-67, 1974-75, Sussex County League Champions 1949-50, 1950-51, 1969-70, Sussex County League Div 2 Cup 1984, Roy Hayden Trophy 1966-67, 1967-68, 1970-71, Mid Sussex Senior Charity Cup, 1978-79, Sussex County Youth Cup 1978-79, Southern Youth League Cup 1978-79

LINGFIELD

Chairman: P. Yeates
Secretary: J. Thomas
Manager: D. Moore
Address & Tel No: 24 Gun Pit Road, Lingfield, Surrey (Lingfield 832223)
Address & Tel No of ground: Godstone Road, Lingfield (Lingfield 834269)
Simple ground directions: A22 London to Eastbourne Road. 4 miles north of East Grinstead to the Mormon Temple roundabout. Take exit signposted Lingfield (B2028) Newchapel Road for 1½ miles into Lingfield. Turn left onto B2029, ground ½ mile on left
Seating: No **Clubhouse:** Yes **Floodlights:** Yes
Year formed: 1893 **Programmes:** 16 pages, 30p
Colours: Scarlet/Amber stripes

NEWHAVEN F.C.

Chairman: M. Godden
Secretary: Frank Dixon
Manager: Mick Pooley
Tel No: Peacehaven 5514
Coach: Brian Pooley
Press Officer: D. Lander
Address & Tel No of ground: Fort Road, Newhaven.
Simple ground directions: Follow one way traffic, turn left, South Way through to Fort Road
No of seats: 100 **Covered accommodation:** Yes **Capacity:** 3,000+ **Floodlights:** Part
Year formed: 1888 **Nickname:** The Dockers **Club sponsors:** Beacon Royal Hotel
Club colours: Red, White trim **Change colours:** Blue
Record attendance: 2,800+ **Clubhouse details:** Fairly large with bar
Major Honours: RUR Cup 1905, Sussex County League Champions 1953-54, 1973-74, Division 2 1971-72

PAGHAM

Chairman: I. Baker
Secretary: A. Tucker
Manager: J. Campbell
Tel No: Bognor 827978
Press Officer: R. Dewey
Commercial Manager: E. Nunn
Address & Tel No of ground: Nyetimber Lane, Pagham. 66112.
Simple ground directions: A27, Chichester-by-pass, turn off to Pagham, Nyetimber Lane 2 miles.
No of seats: 50 **Covered accommodation:** Yes **Capacity:** 2,000 **Floodlights:** No
Year formed: 1903 **Nickname:** None **Club sponsors:** Butlins
Club colours: White/Black **Change colours:** Red
Record attendance: 1,200 **Previous Leagues:** West Sussex
Clubhouse details: Members and Players bar open match days and Sunday lunchtime
Major Honours: Sussex County League Div 1 Champions, Runners-Up, Div 2 Cup Winners, FA Vase 4th Round

SELSEY

Chairman: D. Longworth
Secretary: D. Campbell
Manager: D. C. Lee
Tel No: Selsey 605172
Coach: Roly Schumacher
Press Officer: D. Fowler
Address & Tel No of ground: High Street Ground, Selsey. 603420
Simple ground directions: Through car park at rear of fire station
No of seats: 90 **Covered accommodation:** Yes **Floodlights:** No **Year formed:** 1908
Club colours: Blue shirts, White shorts **Change colours:** Red shirts, White shorts
Record attendance: Not known **Previous Leagues:** Chichester & District, West Sussex
Clubhouse details: Bar, snooker table, television, phone
Major Honours: Div 2 Champions (2), Final of Sussex Senior Cup

SHOREHAM F.C.

Chairman: G. Croydon
Secretary: J. Fairhall
Manager: A. Marchant
Tel No: Brighton 595091
Coach: B. Wells
Commercial Manager: G. Croydon
Press Officer: G. Croydon
Address & Tel No of ground: Middle Road, Shoreham-by-Sea
Simple ground directions: Up Kingston Lane from Coast Road in Shoreham, second left, along Middle Road, on the left
No of seats: **Covered accommodation:** Yes **Capacity:** 400 **Floodlights:** No
Year formed: 1893 **Club colours:** Blue **Change colours:** Yellow
Previous Leagues: County League Div I, West Sussex
Major Honours: Winners Division 2 Cup 1983

SIDLEY UNITED F.C.

Chairman: Bernard Sealy
Manager: Cyril Jeans
Secretary: Mrs G. Taylor
Address: 3 Buckholt Lane, Bexhill-on-Sea, E. Sussex
Address & Tel No of ground: Gullivers Sports Ground, North Rd/Glovers La, Sidley, Bexhill-on-Sea (Bexhill 217078)
Simple ground directions: A269 from Ninfield, turn left at Glovers Lane and 1st left into North Road. On A259 from Brighton, turn left at London Road to Sidley, left on A269, right at New Inn, left at North Road. Nearest station: Bexhill (½ mile)
Seating: No **Clubhouse:** Yes **Floodlights:** No
Previous Leagues: Hastings & District
Year formed: 1906
Colours: Royal Blue/White/Red
Programmes: 4 pages, 40p
Change colours: Red/Black (will be All White for 84/85)

STORRINGTON F.C.

Chairman: M. Wickenden
Manager: J. Suter
Secretary: R. Bishop
Tel No: Storrington 2393
Address & Tel No of ground: Storrington Recreation Ground, Storrington, Sussex
Simple ground directions: In main village just off Storrington-Pulborough road
No of seats: None **Covered accommodation:** Yes **Capacity:** 350 **Floodlights:** No
Year formed: pre 1920 **Nickname:** None **Club sponsors:** Alexander Timber Supplies Ltd
Club colours: Royal Blue
Record attendance: 620
Change colours: Red
Previous Leagues: Worthing & District, West Sussex
Clubhouse details: Bar/Social facilities etc
Major Honours: Hove & Worthing Cup, Worthing Charity Cup, Crowshaw Cup, Chichester Charity Cup, Worthing League Div 1 Champions, County League Div 2 Cup

WIGMORE ATHLETIC

Chairman: A. W. Angel
Manager: D. Barnard
Secretary: M. Flitt
Tel No: Worthing 203659
Address & Tel No of ground: Beeches Avenue, Worthing. 34466
Simple ground directions: From the Hill Barn roundabout, Worthing, proceed along A27 Upper Brighton Road (signposted to Brighton), Beeches Avenue is the 4th turning on left
No of seats: 60 **Covered accommodation:** 500 **Capacity:** 5,000 **Floodlights:** No
Year formed: 1948
Club colours: All Red
Record attendance: 3,000
Club sponsors: Manulife
Change colours: All Blue
Previous Leagues: Worthing & District
Major Honours: Sussex County League: Div 2 Champions 1952-53, 1973-74, Invitation Cup Winners 1959-60, Challenge Cup Winners 1974-75, Div 2 Invitation Cup Winners 1967-68

An excellent view of the main stand at Bexhill as the home side go down 0-2 to Haywards Heath. Photo: David Shute.

The Littlehampton substitute waits to come on as colleague Richard Tilton gains possession in the centre circle. Photo: David Shute.

Hastings Town

Ferring FC *First Winners of the Sussex League Third Division KO Cup.*

Chichester City
Back Row (L-R): Nigel Hillier (Team Manager), Howard Payne, Alan Parrott, Steve White, Terry Vick, Mark Wiseman, Dave Exall, Andy Campbell. Front Row (L-R): Dave Benham, Ian Pearce, Richard Keates, Dave Barnes, Nigel Offord, Neal Holder.

Midhurst & Easebourne United FC
Left to Right — Back Row: Robert Boxall (Chairman), Bern May, Joe Walker, Ken Boxall, Simon Gibson, Graeme Woodcock, Simon Dummer, Micky Farr, Ted Dummer (Secretary). Front Row (L-R): Adrian Holden, Jon Barrott, Andy Woodward, Neil O'Boyle (Player/Manager), Dennis Greenwood, Chris Slade, Bern Penny (Trainer), Chris Bowles.

BOSHAM F.C.
Chairman: D. G. Long **Manager:** R. L. Collyer
Secretary: R. D. Probe, 39 Arnold Way, Bosham, Chichester PO18 8NJ. Tel: Bosham 572570
Address & Tel No of ground: The Recreation Ground, Walton Lane. Bosham 574011
Simple ground directions: West from Chichester on A27, turn south at the roundabout by the White Swan public house and Swan Garage, continue south to the T-junction by the Berkeley Arms public house and turn left. Entrance is 50 yards on left
Colours: Red with White trim

BROADBRIDGE HEATH F.C.
Chairman: J. Martin **Manager:** R. Knight
Secretary: G. W. Manktelow, 110 Clarence Road, Horsham RH13 5SG. Tel: Horsham 53297
Address & Tel No of ground: Sports Centre, Broadbridge Heath. Horsham 65871
Simple ground directions: From the Broadbridge Heath By-pass, between roundabouts on the A24 and A264, take the only southerly turning (Wickhurst Lane) and then turn left into the Horsham District Sports Centre
Colours: Royal Blue

COOKSBRIDGE F.C.
Chairman: J. C. Mander **Manager:** W. Johnson
Secretary: D. Walter, 122 Blois Road, Landport, Lewes BN7 2TS. Tel: Lewes 2184
Address of ground: Recreation Ground, Beechwood Lane, Cooksbridge
Simple ground directions: 150 yards from Lewes side of the Railway Crosssing, sign posted to East Chiltington is Beechwood Lane
Colours: White with Green pin stripe

CROWBOROUGH ATHLETIC F.C.
Chairman: B. J. Sykes
Manager: F. Morriss
Secretary: H. J. Collick
Tel No: Crowboro 5565
Press Officer: J. Ridgway
Address & Tel No of ground: Alderbrook, Fermor Road, Crowborough. 61893
Simple ground directions: From Crowborough Cross through High Street, Croft Road, and Whitehill Road into Fermor Road, then second right
No of seats: **Covered accommodation:** 200 **Capacity:** 1,000 **Floodlights:** No
Year formed: 1894 **Nickname:** Crows **Club sponsors:** Sportique
Club colours: White/Blue/White **Change colours:** Blue shirts, White shorts
Clubhouse details: Members bar **Major Honours:** Winners Division 2 Cup 1978

EAST PRESTON F.C.
Chairman: D. Cooper **Manager:** B. Trode
Secretary: B. A. Withers, 7 Guildford Road, Rustington BN16 3JB. Tel: Rustington 72416
Address & Tel No of ground: Roundstone Drive Recreation Ground. Rustington 76026
Simple ground directions: Off the A259 at the Roundstone Hotel, 6 miles west of Worthing and 4 miles east of Littlehampton. Over the level crossing, turn left and first right is Roundstone Drive
Colours: White/Black

EASTBOURNE RANGERS F.C.
Chairman: B. Wiggins **Manager:** J. Scarrad
Secretary: A. Ross, 34 Priory Road, Langney, Eastbourne BN23 7AX. Tel: Eastbourne 764581
Address & Tel No of ground: Hinlands, Polegate. Polegate 2690
Simple ground directions: On A22 East Grinstead to Eastbourne road. Half mile past Polegate crossroads, turn left at bus stop layby into Brighton Polytechnic College complex
Colours: Yellow

HURSTPIERPOINT F.C.
Chairman: W. Marchant **Manager:** J. F. Weatherill
Secretary: J. Tobias, 152 Cuckfield Road, Hurstpierpoint. Tel: Hurstpierpoint 832392
Address of ground: Fairfield Recreation Ground
Simple ground directions: At Hurstpierpoint cross roads, proceed north into Cuckfield Road (B2117) for 1km. Entrance to ground between house numbers 158 and 160
Colours: Blue/White stripes

IFIELD F.C.
Chairman: D. Whinder **Manager:** B. Morton
Secretary: H. J. Stratton, 5 Bramber Close, Northgate, Crawley RH10 2HP. Tel: Crawley 515670
Address of ground: Ifield Green, Crawley
Colours: White

LANGNEY SPORTS F.C.
Chairman: D. Kenward **Manager:** P. Cherry
Secretary: C. Field, 17 Montague Way, Westham, East Sussex. Tel: Eastbourne 765859
Address & Tel No of ground: Priory Lane, Eastbourne. Eastbourne 766265
Simple ground directions: A22 to Polegate. Turn left on A27 to Stone Cross. Turn right on B2104 to Langney Precinct. Left on B2191 past Crematorium, first right into Priory Road, first left into Priory Lane
Colours: Red

MIDWAY F.C.
Chairman: B. Donnelly **Manager:** M. Neal
Secretary: B. J. Phillpott, 'Lathom', 14 Gorse Close, Portslade BN4 2YX. Tel: Brighton 410515
Address & Tel No of ground: Southwick Recreation Ground. Brighton 593428
Simple ground directions: Turn north from A259 (coast road) at the Pilot public house, Southwick, into Station Road. Under railway bridge, turn right into Croft Avenue. Nearest railway station: Southwick (1/4 mile)
Colours: Claret and Blue

OAKWOOD F.C.

Chairman: A. Bridges **Manager:** R. Conley
Secretary: Mrs L. E. Rooney, 23 Morrison Court, Henderson Road, Crawley RH11 9JJ. Tel: 513382
Address & Tel No of ground: Oakwood Sports & Social Club. Crawley 545742
Simple ground directions: From south on A23, turn left at traffic lights into Manor Royal. Pass first traffic lights, first roundabout then first right into Tinsley Lane. Ground 50 yards on left
Colours: Red/Black

SALTDEAN UNITED F.C.

Chairman: M. Walker **Manager:** R. Wedge
Secretary: T. Britton, 39 Stanmer Avenue, Saltdean BN2 8QL. Tel: Brighton 38630
Address of ground: Hill Park, Coombe Vale, Saltdean
Simple ground directions: Follow A259 to Arundel Drive West, alongside Saltdean Lido. Then follow Saltdean Vale to end
Colours: Red and Black stripes

SEAFORD TOWN F.C.

Chairman: M. Webster **Manager:** R. Knight
Secretary: Mrs M. Stone, 49 Saltwood Road, Seaford BN25 3SR. Tel: Seaford 894631
Address of ground: Crouch Gardens, Seaford
Simple ground directions: Enter Seaford on A259 and turn into Warwick Road (opposite the library). Proceed along into East Street taking the 2nd left into Mercread Road. Park at the end. Nearest railway station: Seaford
Colours: Red

ST FRANCIS HOSPITAL F.C.

Chairman: V. Stevens **Manager:** D. Kluge
Secretary: E. Toner, 163 Hoblands, Haywards Heath RH16 3SB. Tel: Haywards Heath 457798
Address of ground: St Francis Hospital, Haywards Heath
Simple ground directions: A272 Haywards Heath to Uckfield road, turn right into Colwell Road (about ¼ mile before the Birch Service Station)
Colours: Green/White

WESTDENE F.C.

Chairman: M. Plumstead **Manager:** R. Standen
Secretary: Mrs B. Plumstead, Flat 1, 38 Ventnor Villas, Hove, Sussex. Tel: Brighton 728209
Address & Tel No of ground: Withdean Sports Statium. Brighton 551638
Simple ground directions: On main London to Brighton road (A23), 1 mile north of Preston Park, turn left into Tongdean Lane and follow signposts
Colours: Red/White

Shoreham: *Back Row (L-R): Dave Skinn (Manager), Richard Bunker, Steve Byrne, Martin Baker, Keith Stapleton, John Richardson, Paulo Botrugno, Pete Fossey, Ray Bridges (Physio). Front Row (L-R): George Cleary, Neil Kirkup, Terry Smith, Philip Remblance, Mick Handy.*

Ringmer

SUSSEX COUNTY FOOTBALL LEAGUE

(Sponsored by the Sussex County Building Society
President: Dr John O'Hara
Chairman & Hon. Fixtures Secretary: P R Bentley
199 Chanctonbury Road, Burgess Hill, RH15 9HF.
(Tel: B Hill 3181)

DIVISION TWO CUP — 1983/84

First Round

Shoreham	v	Sidley U	3-1
Portfield	v	E Grinstead	2-1
Haywards H	v	Newhaven	5-1
Storrington	v	Arundel	0-4
Selsey	v	Hassocks	1-0
Crowborough	v	Lingfield	1-4
Wigmore A	v	Chichester C	*2-2, *4-4, 5-3
Albion U	v	Bexhill T	0-1

Second Round

Shoreham	v	Portfield	1-0
Haywards H	v	Arundel	2-1
Selsey	v	Lingfield	2-3
Wigmore A	v	Bexhill T	*2-1

Semi-Finals

Shoreham	v	Haywards H	0-4
Lingfield	v	Wigmore A	*1-1, *1-1, + 3-4

Final

Haywards H	v	Wigmore A	*1-1, *4-2

Final Man of the Match: Frank Croney (Haywards Heath)

DIVISION THREE CUP — 1983/84

First Round

Eastbourne Rangers	v	Langney Sports	0-0, 1-3, (1)-(3)
Lower Bevendean	bye		
East Preston	v	Broadbridge H	1-0, 2-1, (3)-(1)
St Francis Hosp	v	Seaford Town	0-2, 1-3, (1)-(5)
Bosham	v	Westdene	2-1, 2-4, (4)-(5)
Midway	v	Ferring	0-1, 3-4, (3)-(5)
Hurstpierpoint	bye		
Franklands Vill	bye		

Second Round

Langney Sports	v	Lower Bevendean	2-0, 6-3, (8)-(3)
East Preston	v	Seaford Town	0-0, 2-1, (2)-(1)
Westdene	v	Ferring	0-3, 2-4, (2)-(7)
Hurstpierpoint	v	Franklands Vill	2-4, 0-2, (2)-(6)

Semi-Finals

Langney Sports	v	East Preston	*0-1
Ferring	v	Franklands Vill	1-0

Final

East Preston	v	Ferring	1-2

Final Man of the Match: Tony Corona (Ferring)

* After extra time
+ Penalties

Other Cup Winners

Pre-season Six-a-Side Tournament

Whitehawk 2 Peacehaven 1 a.e.t

Mark Baldwin Trophy

Hastings T 2 League xi 2

RESERVE SECTION EAST: PEACEHAVEN
(Jack Taylor Trophy)

RESERVE SECTION WEST: SOUTHWICK
(Ernie White Trophy)

RESERVE PLAY-OFF: Peacehaven 3 Southwick 1

RESERVE SECTN CUP: Peacehaven 3 Littlehampton 1

VERNON WENTWORTH CUP: Southwick Res.

CRAWLOT SHIELD: Three Bridges Res.

YOUTH SECTN O/ALL CHAMPIONS: Crowborough R

YOUTH SECTN CUP: Whitehawk 1 Horsham YMCA ?

SPORTSMANSHIP TROPHY: Lancing

CLUB 'LINESMAN' AWARD: Miss Liza White.

Without doubt the best League magazine is produced by Alf Blackler for the Sussex County Football League. Within its sixteen A4 pages of quality paper all divisions are well covered and the reproduction of photographs is excellent. Priced at 40p it is available from Alf at 9 Ennerdale Close, Southgate West, Crawley RH11 8SF.

Arundel FC

Burgess Hill FC

Haywards Heath FC

HAMPSHIRE F.A. FOOTBALL LEAGUE

President: J. Barter

Chairman: K. Atkins

Secretary: R. G. Barnes, JP. Hampshire Football Association, 367 Winchester Road, Ashwood Gardens, Southampton SO9 2UA. Tel: 766884

Despite the fact that Pirelli General spent a large part of the season as league leaders, it was difficult to believe that in the end it would be anything but a two horse race, or that these two teams would be other than AFC Totton and Sholing Sports. It was these two again who had the successes in the FA Cup, with three Southern League sides losing to the big two.

In the Vase, it was Brockenhurst who made the early headlines, beating Wimbourne Town, one of the previous season's FA Cup heroes by 6-1! However, only Newport (IOW) and Eastleigh survived to the third round, with the islanders winning the clash between them, before going down at Old Georgians.

Sholing Sport's attempt to hold onto the Senior Cup, part of their 'treble' the previous year, was only foiled in a replay of the final with the cup returning to Farnborough Town, whereas an early meeting with RS Southampton saw them drop out of contention for the Russell Cotes Cup, where Blackfield & Langley provided the real cup surprises — beating Andover's Southern League team 4-0, and First Division Petersfield United and Waterlooville (Res) by 2-1 and 2-0 respectively — all away from home. It was only in the final that RS Southampton turned out to be too strong for the Division Two side, winning 3-1 at Sholing. Sadly Blackfield were the team to miss out when the top three in the division all finished on 53 points. Portals' goal difference of +63 giving them the championship, while Lymington's +45 meant they, rather than Blackfield (+37) moved into Division One.

The Division Three title went to Winchester Castle, who have missed out on promotion for the last few years, while two of the newcomers — Locksheath and Bashley — fought out the other place, and Locksheath (who also reached the semis of the Sutton Transformer Vase), won through by one point.

Once again no club has choosen the 'pyramid' route to attempt to get into the Southern League, but Petersfield have taken the opportunity to join the expanding Isthmians. Aldershot Services are to resign after one season, and neither Enham Alamien or BTC have been re-elected, but instead four new teams have been elected — three under the 'pyramid' system, being West Wight (Island League), Basing Rovers (North Hants) and AC Delco (Southampton), and the other, from the Combined Counties, is Alton Town.

Sholing Sports *Back Row (L-R): Malcolm Jones, David Lynch, Mark Barber, Paul Brown, Malcolm Ross, Ian Bampton, Mark Allen, Alan Long (coach). Front Row (L-R): Alan Weatherley, Steve Barnes, Kevin Roberts, Terry Morton, Trevor Roberts, Kevin Randall. Inset: R. French.* Photo: D. W. Hampton

Brockenhurst F.C. Back Row (left to right) Canford (Joint Manager), Thomas, Love, Wickision, Harvey, Bundy, Umburn, Biddle, Batchford (Trainer).
Front Row (left to right) Maskell, Fitzhenry, Talkes (Joint Manager), Taylor, Fell, Finn.

Division One

	P	W	D	L	F	A	Pts
Sholing Sports	38	28	8	2	81	22	64
AFC Totton	38	28	6	4	93	33	62
Pirelli General	38	19	10	9	49	29	48
Eastleigh	38	16	14	8	51	33	46
Portsmouth RN	38	17	9	12	62	44	43
Brockenhurst	38	18	6	14	68	63	42
Petersfield United	38	15	11	12	69	57	41
Newport	38	15	9	14	74	73	39
Southampton A	38	15	7	16	80	63	37
Horndean	38	15	6	17	53	57	36
Netley Central Sports	38	13	10	15	48	60	36
Portsmouth United	38	12	12	14	39	54	36
Bass (Alton)	38	11	13	14	53	55	35
Havant Town	38	12	10	16	54	63	34
Romsey Town	38	15	3	20	65	74	33
Waterlooville	38	10	11	17	47	71	31
Downton	38	7	15	16	56	85	29
East Cowes Vics	38	9	10	19	42	51	28
Fareham Town	38	8	6	24	49	74	22
Brading Town	38	6	6	26	40	112	18

Petersfield United have joined the Southern Isthmian League.

Division Two

	P	W	D	L	F	A	Pts
Portals Athletic	34	24	5	5	93	30	53
Lymington	34	25	3	6	76	31	53
Blackfield & Langley	34	24	5	5	61	24	53
Overton United	34	18	9	7	55	36	45
Ringwood Town	34	18	6	10	54	38	42
Folland Sports*	34	16	8	10	40	37	39
AFC Totton Reserves	34	15	7	12	43	30	37
Sway	34	13	10	11	54	45	36
Basingstoke Town	34	13	7	14	57	50	33
New Street	34	13	5	16	53	60	31
Christchurch	34	11	7	16	44	58	29
Eastleigh Reserves	34	10	7	17	32	53	27
B.A.T.	34	11	5	18	40	66	27
Warsash	34	7	11	16	34	58	25
McMurdo	34	10	4	20	49	77	24
Brockenhurst Res.	34	5	9	20	38	62	19
Sholing Sports Res.	34	6	7	21	43	73	19
Cowes Sports	34	7	5	22	46	84	19

Goalkeeper Steve Fisher who was once on Southampton's books as a teenager will be playing for Havant next season, or at least he thinks they are known by that name! For Steve played over 500 games for another Hampshire club. He signed on for Hawker Siddeley and without ever leaving he played for De Havilland, Strongs Sports, Moneyfields Sports and finally before they disbanded last season, Portsmouth United. The club played under five names, which must be some sort of record.

BASINGSTOKE TOWN (1896)

Chairman: D. Letts **Manager:** C. Stoker
Secretary: Bryan Banning, 7 White House Close, Basingstoke, Hants. Tel: 0256 64164
Ground Address & Tel No: Camrose Ground, Western Way, Basingstoke, Hants. 0256 64353
Directions to Ground: West Ringway A30, off Brighton Hill roundabout
Previous Leagues: Hants **Colours:** All Blue, Gold trimmings **Change colours:** All Yellow, Blue trimmings
Programmes: 12 pages, 20p **Clubhouse:** Yes **Floodlights:** Yes **Seating:** Yes

BROCKENHURST (1898)

Chairman: J. R. Lawford **Manager:** M. Hall
Secretary: S. Bartlett, 2 Martins Road, Brockenhurst, Hants SO4 7TQ. Tel: Lymington 22502
Ground Address & Tel No: Grigg Lane, Brockenhurst, Hants. Lymington 23544
Directions to Ground: ¼ mile from Brockenhurst Railway Station (SR), just off main shopping centre
Previous Leagues: New Forest, Bournemouth **Colours:** Blue, White trim **Change colours:** Yellow
Programmes: 8 pages, 10p **Clubhouse:** Open every day and after every game **Floodlights:** Yes **Seating:** 250 seat stand

EASTLEIGH (1946)

Chairman: J. C. Samson **Manager:**
Hon. Match Secretary: D. P. Broomfield, 52 Fairoak Road, Bishopstoke, Eastleigh, Hants. Tel: 0703 617759
Ground Address & Tel No: 'Ten Acres', Stoneham Lane, Eastleigh. 0703 613361
Directions to Ground: From north: On A33 Chandlersford Bypass, go past Eastleigh, turn off towards Southampton, at end of dual carriage turn left at roundabout into Bassett Green Road, proceed to traffic lights and turn left into Stoneham Lane, Ground is ¾ mile approx up Stoneham Lane on right. From east and west: Leave M27 Junc marked Eastleigh and at roundabout take exit marked Stoneham Lane, Ground on left but carry on to roundabout and come back down Stoneham Lane, opposite Concord Club turn right, Ground entrance is 400 yards on left
Previous Leagues: Southampton Junior, Southampton Senior (West), Hampshire (West)
Colours: Sky & Navy/Navy/Sky & Navy **Change colours:** White/Navy/White
Programmes: free on admission **Clubhouse:** Yes **Floodlights:** Yes **Seating:** Yes

DOWNTON (1905)

Chairman: R. E. Tanner **Manager:** D. Colgrave
Secretary: R. Deacon, 82 The Borough, Downton, Salisbury, Wilts SP5 3LY. Tel: Downton 21355
Ground Address & Tel No: Dr Whitehead Sports Ground, Wick Lane, Downton, Salisbury, Wilts
Directions to Ground: Turn into Wick Lane at Downton on A338, right turn from Salisbury, left turn from Bournemouth
Previous Leagues: Salisbury District, Bournemouth, Hants 2 & 3
Colours: Red shirts, White shorts **Change colours:** White shirts, Red or White shorts
Programmes: 16 pages, free with admission **Clubhouse:** Yes **Floodlights:** No **Seating:** No

HAVANT TOWN (1958)

Chairman: P. Wilson **Manager:** D. Pope
Secretary: T. V. Ashman, 3 Woodcot Crescent, West Leigh, Havant, Hants PO9 5LD. Tel: Havant 484871
Ground Address & Tel No: West Leigh Park, Martins Road, West Leigh, Havant, Hants. 455465
Directions to Ground: From London A3 to Peterfield, From west M27 from Southampton
Previous Leagues: Portsmouth **Colours:** Yellow/Black/Black **Change colours:** White/Black/Black
Programmes: 4 pages, 10p **Clubhouse:** Yes **Floodlights:** No **Seating:** No

HORNDEAN (1887)

Chairman: George Cable **Manager:** John Knight
Secretary: Trevor Brock, 2 Betula Close, Waterlooville. Tel: 67276
Ground Address & Tel No: Five Heads Park, Five Heads Road, Horndean
Directions to Ground:
Previous Leagues: Waterlooville & District, Portsmouthshire & District, Hampshire
Colours: Red shirts, Black shorts **Change colours:** Yellow shirts, Green shorts
Programmes: 8 pages, 10p **Clubhouse:** Open every evening, Sat & Sun lunchtimes **Floodlights:** Yes **Seating:** 50

LYMINGTON (1876)

Chairman: L. Crouch **Manager:** A. Farrar
Secretary: A. D. Longhurst, 36 Tithe Barn, Lymington, Hants SO4 9ED. Tel: Lymington 77301
Ground Address & Tel No: Southampton Road, Lymington
Directions to Ground: From Southampton to Lyndhurst, turn left, through Brockenhurst to Lymington
Previous Leagues: Hants II & III
Colours: Red with White pin stripes/Red/Red **Change colours:** White shirts Black trim
Programmes: 4 pages, included with admission **Clubhouse:** Yes **Floodlights:** Yes **Seating:** Yes, in stand

NEWPORT (IoW) ( )

Chairman: Tony Hunt **Manager:** John Rayner
Secretary: Chris Cheverton, 18 Windmill Close, Ryde IoW. Tel: Ryde 67355
Ground Address & Tel No: Church Litten, Newport IoW. 525027
Directions to Ground: From all ferry terminals proceed to bus station from which Church Litten is visible in south-easterly direction, 100 metres away
Previous Leagues: Isle of Wight **Colours:** Yellow with Blue sleeve/Blue/Yellow **Change colours:** All White
Programmes: 8 pages, 10p **Clubhouse:** Yes **Floodlights:** Yes **Seating:** 350

PIRELLI GENERAL ( )

Chairman: N. L. White **Manager:** R. W. Hawkins
Secretary: R. W. Hawkins, Pirelli General Social & Sports Club, The Pavilion, Dew Lane, Eastleigh, Hants. Tel: 612721
Ground Address & Tel No: The Jubilee Sports Club, Chestnut Avenue, Eastleigh, Hants. 0703 612725
Directions to Ground: Nearest Railway Station Eastleigh. Follow Southampton road, turn left into Chestnut Avenue, proceed for approx 2 miles, Ground on left
Previous Leagues: Hampshire & Southampton **Colours:** Blue and White **Change colours:** Yellow
Programmes: 10 pages, 10p **Clubhouse:** Yes **Floodlights:** Yes **Seating:** Yes

ROMSEY TOWN (1885)

Chairman: M. Beale **Manager:** M. Brown
Secretary: F. J. Matthews, 14 Eight Acres, Hillside Gardens, Romsey, Hants. Tel: Romsey (0794) 513825
Ground Address & Tel No: The By-Pass Ground, Romsey. 0794 512003
Directions to Ground: On A27 through Romsey at Southampton end of Romsey Bypass, adjacent to large roundabout
Previous Leagues: Southampton Premier, Hants Div 4, 3, 2, 1 **Colours:** Yellow & Blue **Change colours:** All Red
Programmes: 10 pages (larger this year) **Clubhouse:** Yes **Floodlights:** Yes **Seating:** No

PORTSMOUTH ROYAL NAVY ( )

Chairman: Captain A. Wheatley RN **Manager:** Lieutenant J. H. Millington RN
Secretary: Lt. D. W. Bridger RN, 2 Orion Close, Stubbington, Hants. Tel: Stubbington 667274
Ground Address & Tel No: Royal Navy Stadium, Burnaby Road West, Portsmouth. 822351 ext 24527
Directions to Ground: From Portsmouth Harbour Station, drive towards Southsea along "The Hard" Pass under the rail bridge, road is now St. Georges Road, Ground and entrance on left
Previous Leagues: **Colours:** Blue/White/Blue **Change colours:** All Red
Programmes: No **Clubhouse:** being built **Floodlights:** Yes **Seating:** Yes

SHOLING SPORTS (1914)

Chairman: G. Dunn **Joint Managers:** Len Wolfe/Tony Noble
Secretary: Steve Smith, 21 Whites Road, Bitterne, Southampton SO2 7NP. Tel: 0703 440345 (H), 738181 (B)
Ground Address & Tel No: Birch Lawn, Northeast Road, Sholing, Southampton. 0703 449381
Directions to Ground: M27 Junc 8 (Southampton East) follow A3024 towards Southampton, take 6th left into North East Road, Ground ¼ mile on right
Previous Leagues: Southampton Senior
Colours: Black & White stripes/Black/Black **Change colours:** Red & Black stripes/Black/Red
Programmes: 10-16 pages, free with admission **Clubhouse:** Yes **Floodlights:** Yes **Seating:** Yes

A.F.C. TOTTON (1886)

Chairman: A. Peckham **Manager:** R. Sherwood
Secretary: R. S. Sawyer, "Glen Rest", Bourne Road, Bartley, Southampton. Tel: Southampton 812156
Ground Address & Tel No: Testwood Park, Testwood Place, Totton, Southampton, Hants. Totton 868981
Directions to Ground: Off Testwood Lane, Totton
Previous Leagues: New Forest, Southampton **Colours:** Blue & White **Change colours:** Red & White
Programmes: 12 pages, 10p included in entrance fee **Clubhouse:** Yes **Floodlights:** Yes **Seating:** Yes

WATERLOOVILLE (1910)

Chairman: F. P. Faulkner **Manager:** E. Bradwell
Secretary:
Ground Address & Tel No: Jubilee Park, Aston Road, Waterlooville, Hants
Directions to Ground: Town bypass road, take right hand turning at roundabout, first turning right into Aston Road
Previous Leagues: Portsmouth **Colours:** All White **Change colours:** All Yellow
Programmes: 16 pages, 20p **Clubhouse:** Yes **Floodlights:** Yes **Seating:** 560

WESTERN LEAGUE

Exmouth Town. Top Row (left to right) Hook, Barrett, Sprague, Petersen, Hynds, Harris. Bottom Row (left to right) Thomas, Weeks, Gauntlett, Hooker, Weeks, Pym.

Premier Division

	P	W	D	L	F	A	Pts
Exmouth Town	38	21	11	6	59	35	53
Saltash United	38	22	7	9	72	39	51
Barnstaple Town	38	21	9	8	68	40	51
Frome Town	38	20	10	8	78	35	50
Liskeard Athletic	38	18	9	11	64	38	45
Bideford	38	16	10	12	71	49	42
Clevedon Town	38	16	8	14	55	56	40
Bristol Manor Farm	38	14	11	13	54	42	39
Plymouth Argyle	38	16	8	14	68	58	*38
Minehead	38	15	7	16	55	68	37
Shepton Mallet Town	38	14	9	15	55	74	37
Taunton Town	38	10	15	13	46	52	35
Mangotsfield United	38	12	10	16	47	48	34
Dawlish Town	38	13	8	17	38	43	34
Weston-super-Mare	38	13	8	17	46	54	34
Chippenham Town	38	13	8	17	44	56	34
Clandown	38	12	10	16	34	51	34
Melksham Town	38	9	11	18	49	66	29
Devizes Town	38	7	11	20	41	74	25
Wellington	38	4	8	26	29	95	16

*Two points deducted for playing ineligible players.

First Division

	P	W	D	L	F	A	Pts
Bristol City	40	26	8	6	96	36	60
Chard Town	40	22	8	10	82	44	52
Paulton Rovers	40	20	12	8	74	46	52
Swanage T. & Herston	40	19	12	9	89	61	50
Keynsham Town	40	19	11	10	50	36	49
Backwell United	40	18	13	9	47	42	49
Glastonbury	40	15	9	16	68	61	39
Welton Rovers	40	13	13	14	49	56	39
Portway-Bristol	40	13	12	15	57	49	38
Wimborne Town	40	14	10	16	51	60	38
Bath City	40	13	11	16	61	57	37
Warminster Town	40	15	7	18	61	67	37
Odd Down	40	12	13	15	60	66	37
Larkhall Athletic	40	12	12	16	50	55	36
Radstock Town	40	13	10	17	51	63	36
Heavitree United	40	14	8	18	66	80	36
Yeovil Town	40	11	13	16	65	72	35
Ottery St. Mary	40	14	7	19	42	58	35
Elmore	40	11	12	17	47	78	34
Weymouth	40	12	7	21	43	64	31
Tiverton Town	40	5	10	25	37	95	20

GREAT MILLS WESTERN LEAGUE CUP

League Cup First Round

Backwell United	v	Bristol City	0-2
Barnstaple Town	v	Shepton Mallet Town	2-0
Elmore	v	Welton Rovers	0-1
Odd Down	v	Liskeard Athletic	1-1
Odd Down won on penalties 5-4			
Ottery St Mary	v	Wellington	2-1
Portway Bristol	v	Minehead	2-1
Weston Super Mare	v	Dawlish Town	0-3
Swanage T & Herston	v	Heavitree United	2-3
Taunton Town	v	Bristol Manor Farm	2-0
Exmouth Town	v	Frome Town	0-1

Second Round

Bath City	v	Saltash United	1-3
Chard Town	v	Bideford	1-2
Clandown	v	Devizes Town	3-0
Mangotsfield United	v	Larkhall Athletic	4-1
Melkaham Town	v	Chippenham Town	3-1
Radstock Town	v	Warminster Town	0-5
Tiverton Town	v	Bridport	1-0
Barnstaple Town	v	Glastonbury	3-1
Bristol City	v	Clevedon Town	5-1
Heavitree United	v	Yeovil Town	4-3
Portway Bristol	v	Keynsham Town	2-1
Plymouth Argyle	v	Ottery St Mary	5-2
Taunton Town	v	Paulton Rovers	0-2
Welton Rovers	v	Odd Down	3-1
Weymouth	v	Frome Town	0-3
Wimborne Town	v	Dawlish Town	2-5

Third Round

Barnstaple Town	v	Bristol City	3-2
Heavitree United	v	Frome Town	1-3
Mangotsfield United	v	Bideford	0-2
Melksham Town	v	Dawlish Town	2-3
Tiverton Town	v	Odd Down	0-6
Plymouth Argyle	v	Paulton Rovers	0-2
Portway Bristol	v	Saltash United	0-1
Warminster Town	v	Clandown	0-4

Quarter Finals

Dawlish Town	v	Bideford	1-0
Odd Down	v	Frome Town	0-3
Paulton Rovers	v	Barnstaple Town	3-2
Saltash United	v	Clandown	1-0

Semi-Finals

Frome Town	v	Paulton Rovers	3-1
Dawlish Town	v	Saltash United	4-2

Final

Dawlish Town	v	Frome Town	-

One of the most useful publications I have seen is The 'Great Mills' Western League Travel Guide' produced by Rupert Metcalfe on behalf of the Plymouth Argyle Supporters Branch based in London. This excellent brochure costs £1 (postage free) from Rupert at 1A Gordon Road, London W5 9AD.

Action at Frome Town.

Frome Town

Bridgwater Town

Barnstaple Town, Meret Cup Winners, 1983/84.
Back Row (L-R): Alan Swift (ass. manager), Mark Hunt, Jon Beer, John Palmer, Steve Barker, Keith Manley (p/manager), Len Ellery, Dave Savage. Front Row (L-R): Richard Cardew, Billy Ferris, Kevin Skinner, Tony Schiller (capt), Steve West.

BARNSTAPLE TOWN A.F.C.

President: J. Symons
Chairman: V. Hamilton-Philip
Manager: Keith Manley
Ass. Manager: Alan Swift
Coach: None
Secretary: A. Sampson
Address & Tel No: 10 Harman Walk, Barnstaple, Devon EX32 8AL. 0271 77818
Commercial Manager: E. Woodhams
Physiotherapist: Vacancy
Address & Tel No of ground: 0271 43469 **Club shop:** Yes
Simple ground directions: Follow A361 Ilfracombe signs, turn left after Rolle Quay
No of seats: 400 **Covered accommodation:** 1,000 **Capacity:** 5,000 **Floodlights:** No
Year formed: 1906 **Nickname:** Barum **Club sponsors:**
Previous names: Barnstaple **Club colours:**
Previous grounds: Highfield Road **Change colours:**
Day for midweek home matches: Wednesday
Record attendance: 6,000 v Bournemouth, F.A. Cup **Year:** 1954
Previous Leagues: North Devon
Clubhouse details: New clubhouse (open August 1984)
Present players with Football League experience: Keith Manley
Past players who progressed into the Football League: H. Scott, P. Fewings, L. Pickard, B. Vassello
Record transfer fee paid: £1,000 **Record transfer fee received:** £3,000
Programme details:
Club metal badges: No
Local newspapers & Tel No: North Devon Journal Herald (Barnstaple 43064)
Senior Honours: Western League Champions 1952-53, 1979-80, Western League Meret Cup Winners 1974-75, 1983-84

BIDEFORD

President: E. Hopkins
Chairman: R. Harding
Manager: J. Hore
Coach: B. Hill
Physiotherapist: D. Hare
Secretary: J. A. Wenham
Address & Tel No: 168 Stucley Road, Bideford, Devon Bideford 78938 (H) Bideford 5501 (B)
Commercial Manager: N. J. Gross
Address & Tel No: Bideford 3713
Press Officer & Tel No: D. Henderson (Bideford 77946)
Address & Tel No of ground: Sports Ground, Kingsley Road, Bideford, Devon **Club shop:** Yes
Simple ground directions: On entering town follow signs towards Westward Ho and Northam, ground ½ mile on left
No of seats: 300 **Covered accommodation:** 1,500 **Capacity:** 6,000 **Floodlights:** Yes
Year formed: 1946 **Nickname:** The Robins **Club sponsors:** Bosher Insurance
Previous names: Bideford Town **Club colours:** Red & White
Previous grounds: None **Change colours:** Yellow & Green
Day for midweek home matches: Wednesday
Previous League: Southern
Record attendance: 6,000 v Bristol Rovers, F.A. Cup **Year:** 1971
Best performance in: F.A. Cup: 1963, 1971, 1978, 1981 1st Round Proper
F.A. Trophy: 1981 4th Qualifying Round
Clubhouse details: New club house, 2-storey, open every lunchtime and evening
Present players with Football League experience: J. Hore (Plymouth, Exeter), I. Pearson (Millwall, Exeter), R. Forbes (Exeter), S. Davey (Plymouth, Hereford, Portsmouth)
Past players who progressed into the Football League: None
Record transfer fee paid: None
Record transfer fee received: £15,000 for Peter Griffiths (Stoke City)
Programme details: 32 pages, 25p
Club metal badges: Yes
Local newspapers & Tel No: Bideford Gazette (2615) North Devon Journal (Barnstaple 3064)
Senior Honours: Western League (3)

BRISTOL MANOR FARM

President: Colin Howlett
Chairman: Mervyn Brown
Manager: Mike Fisher
Coach: Bobby George
Physiotherapist: Bert Weaver
Press Officer & Tel No: Iain Anderson, 0272 616426
Secretary: Iain Anderson
Address & Tel No: 182 Forest Road, Kingswood, Bristol BS15 2EN. 0272 616426 (H) 0272 508956 (B)
Commercial Manager: Mark Townsend
Address & Tel No: 17 Nicholettes, Millers Lodge, Warmley, Bristol BS15 5YF. Tel: Bitton 5997
Address & Tel No of ground: The Creek, Portway, Sea Mills, Bristol. 0272 683571
Simple ground directions: Leave M5 motorway at junction 18 (Avonmouth Bridge), sign for Bristol at first roundabout leads onto the Portway
No of seats: None **Covered accommodation:** Yes **Capacity:** 1,500 **Floodlights:** None
Year formed: 1964 **Nickname:** The Farm **Club sponsors:** None
Club colours: Red & Black **Change colours:** White & Blue
Record attendance: 500 v Portway-Bristol **Year:** 1978 **Programme:** 10 pages 40p
Best performance in F.A. Vase: 1983-84 5th Round
Clubhouse Details: Lounge bar, entertainments hall, skittle alley. Bar meals Thursday-Saturday. Open every evening, open lunchtime Saturday and Sunday
Present players with Football League experience: Billy Down (Bristol C)
Local Newspapers: Bristol Evening Post, Western Daily Press (Bristol 20080)
Senior Honours: Somerset Senior League Div 2 (2), League Cup, Somerset Senior League Division One, Great Mills Western League Division One

CHARD TOWN

President: F. Wilson
Chairman: B. Beer
Manager: P. Smith
Coach: None
Physiotherapist: C. Meek
Secretary: C. Dunford
Address & Tel No: Ilminster 3164 (H) Yeovil 23165 (B)
Commercial Manager: L. Norris
Address & Tel No: Chard 5895
Press Officer & Tel No: None
Address & Tel No of ground: Town Ground, Dening Sports Field, Zembard Lane, Chard
Simple ground directions: 150 yards town centre
No of seats: None **Covered accommodation:** Yes **Capacity:** Not known **Floodlights:** None
Year formed: 1920 **Nickname:** None **Club sponsors:** None
Club colours: White/White/Maroon **Change colours:** Yellow/Yellow/Royal Blue
Record attendance: Not known **Programme:** 24 pages, 15p
Clubhouse Details: Open every night 7-10.30 except Sunday. Open 12-2 Sundays and during football matches, usual hot food services
Local Newspapers: Chard & Ilminster News, Pulmans Weekly News
Senior Honours: Somerset Senior League (5), Somerset Senior Cup (2), Somerset Senior League K.O. Cup (3)

CHIPPENHAM TOWN

President: John Northover
Chairman: Doug Webb
Manager: Ken Owens
Coach: D. Sharland, V. Flippance
Physiotherapist:
Secretary: Tony Knee
Address & Tel No: 62 Sadlers Mead, Chippenham, Wilts SN15 3PL. Chippenham 50483 (H), 4141 (B)
Commercial Manager: D. Jones
Address & Tel No: 7 Picketleaze, Chippenham. 55264
Press Officer & Tel No: Tim Penwel (Trowbridge 3538)
Address & Tel No of ground: Hardenhuish Park, Bristol Road, Chippenham. Tel. 50400 **Club shop:** No
Simple ground directions: 15 mins walk from railway station on main A420 road
No of seats: 150 **Covered accommodation:** 350 **Capacity:** 4,000 **Floodlights:** No
Year formed: 1873 **Nickname:** Bluebirds **Club sponsors:** None
Previous names: None **Previous grounds:** Westmead, Lowden, Little George Lane, Malmesbury Road
Club colours: Royal Blue **Change colours:** Red
Day for midweek home matches: Wednesday
Record attendance: 4,800 v Chippenham United, Western League **Year:** 1948
Best performance in: F.A. Cup: 1951-2 v Leyton, 1st Round Proper, lost 0-1
F.A. Trophy: Not beyond 2nd Round
Previous Leagues: Hellenic, Wiltshire Senior, Wiltshire Premier
Clubhouse details: Clubhouse on ground above stand with bar, skittles, etc
Present players with Football League experience: Keith Nash (Bristol C, Burnley, Newport Co)
Past players who progressed into the Football League: R. Tilley (Plymouth, Swindon T,), George Walker (Bristol C, Carlisle)
Record transfer fee paid: Not known
Record transfer fee received: £1,000 A. Scarrott, WBA, 1963. R. Tilley, Plymouth, 1951
Programme details:
Club metal badges: No
Local newspapers & Tel No: Chippenham News, Wiltshire Gazette
Senior Honours: Western League 1951-52, Western League 1980-81, Wiltshire Senior Cup (8), Wiltshire Senior League (5), Wiltshire Pro Shield 1965-66
Programme Editor: Ian Monnery

CLANDOWN

President: S. Parfitt
Chairman: B. Pearce
Manager: E. Jordan
Coach: None
Physiotherapist: None
Press Officer & Tel No: None
Secretary: J. E. Pool
Address & Tel No: Midsomer Norton 415190 (H)
Midsomer Norton 413301 x2532 (B)
Commercial Manager: T. Gillard
Address & Tel No: Midsomer Norton 418448
Address & Tel No of ground: Radstock 34274
Club shop: No
Simple ground directions: Leave Bath on A367, follow signs to Radstock, turn right into Clandown village, ground 500 yards on top of hill
No of seats: 500 **Covered accommodation:** None **Capacity:** 4,000 **Floodlights:** Yes
Year formed: 1895 **Nickname:** None **Club sponsors:** Trend Furnishers
Previous names: None
Previous grounds: None
Club colours: Black/White stripes
Change colours: Blue
Day for midweek home matches: Tuesday
Record attendance: 4,000 v Paulton Rovers, F.A. Cup **Year:** 1946
Best performance in: F.A. Cup:
F.A.Trophy: 1979-80 1st Qualifying Round F.A. Vase 1977-8 3rd Round
Previous Leagues:
Wiltshire Premier,
Somerset Senior
Clubhouse details: Full social facilities, skittles, function room
Present players with Football League experience: None
Past players who progressed into the Football League: None
Record transfer fee paid: None
Record transfer fee received: None
Programme details: 16 pages, 10p
Club metal badges: No
Local newspapers & Tel No: Western Daily Press, Somerset Guardian, Bristol Evening Post
Senior Honours: Somerset Senior Cup (3), Western League Div 1 & Runners-up (2)

CLEVEDON TOWN

President: D. Hand
Chairman: L. Stacey
General Manager: D. J. Robbins
Team Manager & Coach: L. G. Stacey
Physiotherapist: L. Scapens
Press Officer & Tel No: T. Bidwell (0272-87 7735)
Secretary: T. E. Oliver
Address & Tel No: Clevedon 0272-87 1617 (H&B)
Commercial Manager: P. Davis
Address & Tel No: 0272-85 7725
Address & Tel No of ground: Teignmouth Road, Clevedon, Avon. Telephone 0272-87 1636
Club shop: Yes
Simple ground directions: 3 mins from M5 motorway, junction 20
No of seats: 24 **Covered accommodation:** 1,500 **Capacity:** 3,000 **Floodlights:** Yes
Year formed: 1880 **Nickname:** Seasiders **Club sponsors:** Ampep
Previous names: None
Previous grounds: None
Club colours: White shirts Green collars, Black shorts/socks
Change colours: Royal Blue shirts, White shorts, Blue socks
Day for midweek home matches: Tuesday
Record attendance: 2,300 v Bath City **Year:** 1951
Best performance in: F.A. Cup: 1947 v Merthyr Tydfil away (10,000 gate)
F.A. Amateur Cup: 1952-3 3rd Round
Previous Leagues:
Somerset
Bristol Charity
Clubhouse details: Open every mid-day and evenings. Separate skittle alley on ground
Present players with Football League experience: T. Stanton (Liverpool, Bristol R)
Past players who progressed into the Football League: None
Record transfer fee paid: £250, D. Wiltshire, Frome Town
Record transfer fee received: £1,000, C. Cureton to Minehead
Programme details: 30 pages, 15p
Local newspaper & Tel No: South Avon Mercury
Club metal badges: No
Senior Honours: Somerset League, Bristol Charity League

DAWLISH

President: G. Rodgers
Chairman: M. Swift
Manager: A. Chown
Coach: J. Webber
Physiotherapist: C. Moyse
Press Officer & Tel No: J. Batten (86557)
Secretary: G. R. Turner
Address & Tel No: 862438 (H)
Commercial Manager: R. Carter
Address & Tel No: 864952
Address & Tel No of ground: Playing Fields, Exeter Road, Dawlish
Club shop: No
Simple ground directions: Playing Fields, main Exeter Road
No of seats: 200 **Covered accommodation:** 50 **Capacity:** 2,000 **Floodlights:** No
Year formed: 1889 **Nickname:** None **Club sponsors:** None
Previous names: None
Previous grounds: None
Club colours: Green & White
Change colours: Red & Blue
Day for midweek home matches: Tuesday
Record attendance: 1,500 v Heavitree, Devon Cup Quarter Final **Year:**
Best performance in: F.A. Cup:
F.A. Trophy: 2nd Qualifying Round
Previous Leagues:
Devon & Exeter
Clubhouse details: Open 1st May 1982
Present players with Football League experience: R. Crabtree (Bristol R), K. Ford (Exeter)
Past players who progressed into the Football League: None
Record transfer fee paid: None
Record transfer fee received: None
Programme details: 16 pages, 20p
Club metal badges: No
Local newspapers & Tel No: Express & Echo (Exeter)
Dawlish Gazette
Senior Honours: Western League Challenge Cup, Devon Premier Cup

EXMOUTH TOWN

President: D. Scott
Chairman: R. Clements
Manager: Bob Davis
Coach: Peter Amos
Physiotherapist:
Secretary: G. Morris
Address & Tel No: 34 Salterton Road, Exmouth 72141 (H), 4356 (B)
Commercial Manager: A. Jones
Address & Tel No: 74100
Press Officer & Tel No: A. Wilson. 74977
Address & Tel No of ground: King George V Ground, Southern Road, Exmouth. Tel 3348
Club shop: No
Simple ground directions: On right side of main Exeter to Exmouth Road (town bypass)
No of seats: 100 **Covered accommodation:** 100 **Capacity:** 1,500 **Floodlights:** No
Year formed: 1933 **Nickname:** Town **Club sponsors:** None
Previous names: None
Previous grounds: Maer Sports Ground
Club colours: Royal Blue & White
Change colours: Red & White shirts, Black shorts
Day for midweek home matches: Tuesday
Record attendance: 500 v Torpoint, Amateur Cup **Year:** 1966
Previous Leagues: Devon & Exeter
Best performance in: F.A. Cup:
F.A. Trophy: 1974-5 Prelim. Round F.A. Vase 1978-9 2nd Round
Clubhouse details: Function room & lounge bar open every night. Cabaret Saturdays. Skittles, darts, pool teams
Present players with Football League experience: Graham Weeks (Exeter City)
Past players who progressed into the Football League: None
Record transfer fee paid: None
Record transfer fee received: None
Programme details: 12 pages, 10p
Club metal badges: Yes
Local newspapers & Tel No: Exmouth Journal, Exmouth Herald, Express & Echo
Senior Honours: Devon County Cup (3), Great Mills Western League Champions 1983-84

FROME TOWN

President: E. G. Berry
Chairman: E. G. Berry, ABAA
Manager: S. D'Arcy
Coach: H. Adams
Physiotherapist: J. Fuller
Secretary: Peter M. Bishop
Address & Tel No: 0373 61794 (H) 0373 62201 (messages only)
Commercial Manager: None
Address & Tel No:
Press Officer & Tel No: Secretary
Address & Tel No of ground: Badgers Hill, Berkeley Road, Frome. Tel: 0373 64087
Club shop: Yes
Simple ground directions: Locate Vine Tree Inn (Bath Road), ground 100 yards from Inn
No of seats: 250 **Covered accommodation:** 500 **Capacity:** 7,500 **Floodlights:** Yes
Year formed: 1904 **Nickname:** Robins **Club sponsors:** None
Previous names: None
Previous grounds: None
Club colours: Red
Change colours: Sky Blue
Day for midweek home matches: Wednesday
Record attendance: 7,500 v L. Orient, F.A. Cup 1st Rnd **Year:** 1954
Previous League: Wiltshire Premier
Best performance in: F.A. Cup: 1954 v L. Orient, 1st Round
F.A. Trophy: 1980-1 v Yeovil, 1st Round Proper (replay)
Clubhouse details: Built 1974. Modern ballroom holds 400. Open every evening. Two skittle alleys, three bars
Present players with Football League experience: None
Past players who progressed into the Football League: None
Record transfer fee paid: £1,000
Record transfer fee received: £6,000 approx for D. Wiffil, now with Manchester City
Programme details: 16 pages, 15p
Club metal badges: Yes
Local newspapers & Tel No: Western Daily Press Somerset Standard
Senior Honours: Western League, Alan Young Cup, Western League Challenge Cup, Somerset Professional Cup, Wilts Premier League, Western League Subsidiary Cup

LISKEARD ATHLETIC

President: E. K. Brown
Chairman: Adrian Wilton
Manager: Brian Hodge
Coach: Stuart Brace
Reserve Team Manager: John Maynard
Secretary: A. James
Address & Tel No: 59 Higher Cut St, Liskeard 43862 (H) & (B)
Commercial Manager: Alan Mayne
Address & Tel No:
Press Officer & Tel No: P. Broad (42174)
Address & Tel No of ground: Lux Park, Liskeard
Club shop: Yes
Simple ground directions: Take the Tavistock road (A390) from town centre, after ½ mile turn left on the St Cleer road and the ground is 200 yards on the left.
No of seats: 100 **Covered accommodation:** 700 **Capacity:** 2,000 **Floodlights:** Yes
Year formed: **Nickname:** The Blues **Club sponsors:** Castle Motors
Previous names: None
Previous grounds: None
Club colours: Blue
Change colours: White
Day for midweek home matches: Tuesday
Record attendance: 2,000 v Bournemouth (friendly) **Year:**
Best performance in: F.A. Cup: 1981-2 3rd Qualifying Round
F.A. Trophy: Not entered
Previous Leagues: East Cornwall, Plymouth & District, South-Western
Clubhouse details: Open seven days a week. Dancing, food.
Present players with Football League experience: None
Past players who progressed into the Football League: None
Programme details: 12 pages, 10p
Club metal badges: No
Local newspaper & Tel No: The Cornish Times
Senior Honours: South Western League (2), Cornwall Charity Cup, South-Western League Cup (2), Pratten Cup, Western League Merit Cup, Cornwall Senior Cup 1983

This picture shows a presentation award from Great Mills for Manager of the Month award. It is being accepted by Mr C E Packer (Chairman) on behalf of Ralph Miller, the Mangotsfield manager, who was unfortunately ill. Photo: Rex Conway

MANGOTSFIELD UNITED

President: A. Hill
Chairman: C. E. Packer
Manager: R. S. J. Miller
Physiotherapist: Mike Hamilton
Secretary: Paul Britton
Address & Tel No: 41 South Road, Kingswood, Bristol 676229
Commercial Manager: Barry Tilling
Press Officer & Tel No:
Address & Tel No of ground: Cossham Street, Mangotsfield, Bristol. (560119) **Club shop:**
Simple ground directions: From M32 through Downend to Mangotsfield
No of seats: 200 **Covered accommodation:** 1,000 **Capacity:** 2,500 **Floodlights:** Yes
Year formed: 1950 **Nickname:** "The Field" **Club sponsors:** Design Windows (Longwell Green, Bristol)
Day for midweek home matches: Wednesday
Record attendance: 2,000 **Year:** 1976
Best performance in: F.A. Cup:
F.A. Trophy:
Previous League: Bristol & District, Avon Combination
Clubhouse details: Large function room with separate lounge and kitchen facilities
Present players with Football League experience: Wayne Powell, Mike Simmons, Paul Crowley
Past players who progressed into the Football League: Gary Megson, Steve White
Programme details:
Programme Editor: Barry Tilling
Local newspapers & Tel No: Bristol Evening Post, Western Daily, 20080
Senior Honours: Gloucester Senior Cup Winners, Avon Combination Winners, Hungerford Cup Winners

MINEHEAD

President: A. C. Copp
Chairman: N. R. Elston
Manager: Tom Middleton-Smith
Secretary: M. W. Crichton
Address & Tel No: 12 Bernard Crescent, Minehead, Somerset TA24 5EJ. Minehead 3112 after 6pm 4191 messages
Coaches: M. Crichton/B. Hurford
Physiotherapist: Brian Hurford
Press Officer & Tel No: Jim Walder. Minehead 2692
Commercial Manager: B. Hurford
Address & Tel No: M. AFC, Summerland Ave, Minehead Minehead 5348
Address & Tel No of ground: The Recreation Ground, Alexandra Road, Minehead 5573 (Office M), 4989 (Club)
Simple ground directions: On entering town follow road to town centre, look out for "Coach Park/Car Park" signs pointing to the right, this will lead you into the car park at the entrance to ground **Club shop:** Yes
No of seats: 500 **Covered accommodation:** 750 **Capacity:** 4,500 **Floodlights:** Yes
Year formed: 1889 **Nickname:** The Blues or Seasiders **Club sponsors:** Butlins
Previous names: None
Previous grounds: None
Club colours: All Sky Blue
Change colours: All Yellow
Day for midweek home matches: Wednesday
Record attendance: 3,200 v Exeter City F.A. Cup **Year:** 1978
Best performance in: F.A. Cup: 1976-7, 1977-8 2nd Round
F.A. Trophy: 1973-4, 1978-9 2nd Round
Previous Leagues: Somerset Senior, Western
Clubhouse details: Clubhouse open every day. Skittles, bingo, darts, pool, discos on Fri nights, dances on Sats
Present players with Football League experience: W. Brown, W. Powell
Past players who progressed into the Football League: N. Johns (Millwall), A. Ford (Bournemouth)
Record transfer fee paid: £1,100 to Yeovil for Brian Durbin
Record transfer fee received: £7,000 from Bath for Brian Durbin
Programme details: 20 pages, 15p
Club metal badges: Yes
Local newspapers & Tel No: West Somerset Free Press Williton 32731; County Gazette, Taunton 85361
Senior Honours: Southern League Div 1 (South), Southern League Premier, Southern League Merit, Somerset Professional Cup (3)

Melksham Town FC *Back Row (L-R): T. Woodward, C. Shipman (trainer), M. Trowbridge, G. Broom, D. Bartlett, R. Pratt, C. Stevens, M. Bennett, M. Gingell (manager). Front Row (L-R): S. Harvey, R. Radcliffe, R. Legg (captain), A. Beasley, P. Fielding, D. Miluk.*

MELKSHAM TOWN

President: L. Crook
Chairman: H. J. Goodenough
Manager: Mel Gingell
Asst Manager: Mike Downs
Secretary: M. J. Perrin
Address & Tel No: Melksham 704523
Commercial Manager: M. Tanner
Address & Tel No:
Physiotherapist: Colin Shipman
Press Officer & Tel No: Dave Phillips (Melksham 706904)
Address & Tel No of ground: The Conigre, Melksham, Wilts. Melksham 702843 **Club shop:** No
Simple ground directions: Turn into car park in the town market place, then left into Melksham House grounds, proceed up drive, ground is to the left
No of seats: 500 **Covered accommodation:** 3 stands on 2 sides **Capacity:** 3,000 **Floodlights:** No
Year formed: 1876 **Nickname:** Town **Club sponsors:** None
Previous names: Melksham & Avon United **Club colours:** Old Gold/Black/Black
Previous grounds: Bear Field **Change colours:** Blue/White/Blue
Day for midweek home matches: Tuesday
Record attendance: 2,821 v Trowbridge Town, F.A. Cup 3rd Qualifying Round **Year:** 1957-8
Best performance in: **F.A. Cup:** 1957-8 3rd Qualifying Round
F.A. Vase: 1981-2 3rd Round
F.A. Trophy: 1982-83 2nd Qualifying Round
Previous League: County
Clubhouse details: Open every night of the week and on Saturday and Sunday lunchtimes
Present players with Football League experience: None
Past players who progressed into the Football League: Archie Stephens, Simon Panes
Record transfer fee paid: None
Record transfer fee received: £3,000 from Bristol Rovers for Archie Stephens
Programme details: 20 pages, 10p
Programme Editor: Dave Phillips (M. 706904)
Club metal badges: No
Local newspapers & Tel No: Wiltshire Times (Trowbridge 2532), Bath Evening Chronicle (Bath 63051)
Senior Honours: Wiltshire League Winners, Runners-up (3), Wiltshire Senior Cup (3), Runners-up (3), Wiltshire Professional Shield (2), Western League Div 1, Wiltshire Subsidiary Cup, Wiltshire Combination Runners-up (2)

PLYMOUTH ARGYLE RESERVES

President: G. H. Gillan
Chairman: S. W. Dawe
Manager: John Hore
Secretary: Graham Little
Commercial Manager: W. E. Pearce
Coach: Martin Harvey
Address & Tel No of ground: Home Park, Plymouth, Devon PL2 3DQ. 0752 52561
Simple ground directions: Special buses from Plymouth bus station at Bretonside
Seats: 5,000 **Covered accommodation:** 20,000 **Capacity:** 38,000 **Floodlights:** Yes
Year formed: 1886 **Nickname:** Argyle
Club colours: Green with Black trim, White shorts **Chaange colours:** All Yellow

TAUNTON TOWN

President: Rt. Hon. Edward du Cann
Chairman: T. F. Ellis
Manager: C. Porter
Coach:
Physiotherapist: Jimmy Green
Press Officer & Tel No:
Secretary: Mrs Joan Ellis
Address & Tel No: Ground, Taunton (0823) 78191
Commercial Manager: D. O. Marriott
Address & Tel No: Ground, Taunton (0823) 87191
Club Shop: Yes
Address & Tel No of ground: Denmans Park, Wordsworth Drive. Taunton (0823) 78191; Taunton (0823) 89608 (Social Club)
Simple ground directions: Leave M5 at junction 25. Ground ½-mile from junction on main road leading to town centre
No of seats: 250 **Covered accommodation:** 1,000 **Capacity:** 4,000 **Floodlights:** Yes
Year formed: 1947 **Nickname:** The Peacocks **Club sponsors:** None
Previous names: None
Club colours: Sky Blue/Claret pin stripe shirts, Claret shorts
Previous grounds: Rose Meadows, Denmans Park
Change colours: Yellow shirts, Blue shorts
Day for midweek home matches: Wednesdays
Record attendance: 2,800 v Torquay **Year:** 1956
Previous League: Southern League
Best performance in: F.A. Cup: 1981-82 1st Rnd v Swindon (A) 1-2
F.A. Trophy: 1969-70, 1972-3, 1973-4, 1978-9, 1980-1 1st Rnd
Clubhouse details: Social club to accommodate 300. Full bar facilities. Separate bar and hall for private functions
Present players with Football League experience: None
Past players who progressed into the Football League: C. Rutter (Cardiff C.), S. Brace (Plymouth A.), P. Rogers (Exeter City), J. Sherwood (Bristol R.)
Record transfer fee paid: None
Record transfer fee received: D. Singleton (Weymouth) £6,500
Programme details: 28 pages, 15p
Club metal badges: Yes
Local newspapers & Tel No: Somerset County Gazette Taunton (0823) 85361; Western Daily Press

WESTON SUPER MARE

President: D. Usher
Chairman: S. Gillard
Manager: H. Thomas
Coach: J. Coles
Physiotherapist: Ian Pitt
Press Officer & Tel No:
Secretary: B. T. White
Address & Tel No: 13 Milton Ave, WSM. 31974 (H)
Commercial Manager: W. H. Hill
Address & Tel No: 8 Salisbury Rd. 25255
Address & Tel No of ground: Woodspring Pk. Winterstoke Rd. 21618 **Club shop:** No
Simple ground directions: From M5 southbound, 1st set traffic lights turn left proceed half a mile. From M5 northbound proceed along Bristol route, over 1st bridge, last turning on roundabout proceed quarter of a mile.
No of seats: None **Covered accommodation:** 400 **Capacity:** 8,000 **Floodlights:** No
Year formed: 1948 **Nickname:** Seasiders **Club sponsors:** Quality Carpets
Previous names: None
Club colours: Royal Blue and White
Previous grounds: The Great Ground + Langford Rd.
Change colours: Red shirts, Black shorts
Day for midweek home matches: Tuesday
Record attendance: 2,500 v Bridgwater Town, F.A. Cup 1st Round Proper **Year:** 1961-2
Previous Leagues: None
Best performance in: F.A. Cup: 1961-2 1st Round Proper
F.A. Trophy: 1982-83 1st Round Proper v Weymouth
Clubhouse details: Open every night, social activities, refreshments, 2 skittle alleys, 3 bars
Present players with Football League experience: John Palmer
Past players who progressed into the Football League: Ian Maine, John Palmer
Record transfer fee paid: None
Record transfer fee received: None
Programme details: 16 pages, 10p
Club metal badges: No
Local newspapers & Tel No: Bristol Evening Post, Western Daily Press, Weston Mercury
Senior Honours: League K.O. Cup, Somerset Senior Cup, Western Senior Cup, Western League Merit Cup (2)

BACKWELL UNITED

President: C. W. Jones
Chairman: D. Lester
Manager: John Southern
Coach: Ade Britton
Physiotherapist: Not yet appointed
Secretary: W. G. Coggins
Address & Tel No: 34 Westfield Road, Backwell, Bristol BS19 3ND. 027 583 3424
Commercial Manager: Not yet appointed
Press Officer & Tel No: None
Address & Tel No of ground: Backwell Recreation Grounds, Backwell, Nr Bristol, Avon. (027 583 2616)
Simple ground directions: A370 Bristol to Weston-s-Mare road
No of seats: **Covered accommodation:** 150 **Capacity:** 600 **Floodlights:** None
Year formed: 1911 **Nickname:** Reds **Club sponsors:** None
Club colours:
Change colours:
Record attendance: 450 **Year:** 1984
Programme:
Clubhouse Details:
Local Newspapers:
Previous Leagues: Bristol leagues, Somerset Senior
Senior Honours: Somerset Senior Champions (5), Somerset Challenge & League Cup Winners, Sutton Transformer Vase

DEVIZES TOWN

President: E. B. Springford
Chairman: E. J. Chivers
Manager: P. A. Lloyd
Coach: P. A. Lloyd
Physiotherapist: R. Collins
Press Officer & Tel No: J. Whittingstall (Devizes 77159)
Secretary: R. W. Booth
Address & Tel No: Devizes 2145 (H)
Commercial Manager: J. L. Hinder
Address & Tel No: Devizes 4415
Address & Tel No of ground: Nursteed Road, Devizes. Telephone 2817
Club shop: Yes
Simple ground directions: ½-mile along A342 Devizes, Upavon Road, on the right
No of seats: 370 **Covered accommodation:** 450 **Capacity:** 3,000+ **Floodlights:** No
Year formed: 1883 **Nickname:** None **Club sponsors:** G. Pearce & Sons Ltd, Wadworths Brewery
Previous names: Southbroom F.C.
Club colours: Red/White stripes, Black shorts, Red socks
Previous grounds: Quakers Walk, Devizes
Change colours: Sky Blue
Day for midweek home matches: Wednesday
Previous Leagues: Wiltshire County Premier
Record attendance: 2,000 v Vauxhall Motors **Year:** 1957-8
Best performance in: F.A. Amateur Cup: 1957-8 2nd Round Proper
F.A. Trophy F.A. Vase: 1980-1 v Whickham, 6th Round (Quarter Finals)
Clubhouse details: Social club, lounge bar, main bar with dance floor, skittle alley, office, toilets, gymnasium
Present players with Football League experience: K. Newman (Aldershot, York), (capt, 7 England schoolboy caps)
Past players who progressed into the Football League: None
Record transfer fee paid: None
Record transfer fee received: None
Programme details: 14 pages, 15p
Club metal badges: Yes
Local newspapers & Tel No: Wiltshire Times & News, Wiltshire Gazette & Herald, Devizes News
Senior Honours: Western League, Western League Div 1 Runners-up, Western League Subsidiary Cup, Western League Cup Runners-up, Western League Amateur Trophy (6), Wilts Premier League (2), Wilts Premier League Challenge Cup (4), Wilts Senior Cup (13), Wilts Senior Cup Runners-up (8)

HEAVITREE UNITED

President: O. W. Taylor
Chairman: D. J. Henson
Manager: D. M. Carpenter
Coach:
Physiotherapist:
Secretary: Mrs M. L. Toze
Address & Tel No: 8 Masefield Road, Exeter. 67496 (H)
Commercial Manager:
Address & Tel No:
Press Officer & Tel No: None
Address & Tel No of ground: Wingfield Park, East Wonford Hill, Exeter (73020)
Simple ground directions:
No of seats: 150 **Covered accommodation:** 150 **Capacity:** 2,500 **Floodlights:** None
Year formed: 1885 **Nickname:** The Heavies **Club sponsors:** None
Club colours:
Change colours:
Record attendance: Not known
Programme:
Clubhouse Details:
Local Newspapers: Sunday Independent, Express & Echo, Western Morning News
Senior Honours: Devon & Exeter League Premier Division Winners, Devon Senior Cup, East Devon Senior Cup

PAULTON ROVERS

President: R. Carter
Chairman: B. Lewis
Manager: L. Alderman
Coach: None
Physiotherapist: None
Secretary: K. Simmons
Address & Tel No: 1 Underhill Lane, Midsomer Norton 0761 418030
Commercial Manager: Secretary
Press Officer & Tel No: Secretary
Address & Tel No of ground: Winterfield Road, Paulton, Bristol. 0761 412907
Simple ground directions: From Bristol approx 15 miles south towards Wells. From Bath approx 10 miles south west towards Wells
No of seats: None **Covered accommodation:** 200 approx **Capacity:** 4,000 approx **Floodlights:** Yes
Year formed: 1881 **Nickname:** Rovers **Club sponsors:** None
Club colours: White/Black/Black
Change colours: Red or Blue/White/Maroon
Record attendance: Not known
Programme: 8 pages, free
Present players with Football League experience: D. Gillies, G. Sweeney, W. Hughes, S. Strong
Clubhouse Details: Bar, lounge, skittle alley, dance hall for 400
Local Newspapers: Bath Evening Chronicle, Bristol Evening Post, Western Daily Press
Senior Honours: Somerset Senior Cup (12), Somerset Senior League (7)

TIVERTON TOWN

President: D. McCauley
Chairman: A. Butler
Manager: Mike Southcott
Coach: Johnny Owen
Physiotherapist: Gavin Haig (F.R.C.S. Eng.)
Secretary: A. Disney
Address & Tel No: 56 Melbourne Street, Tiverton 253829
Commercial Manager: Phil Chant
Press Officer & Tel No: None
Address & Tel No of ground: "Ladysmead", Bolham Road, Tiverton (252397)
Simple ground directions: Leave M5 at junction 27, Ground on A396, ¼ mile town centre
No of seats: 300 **Covered accommodation:** 300 **Capacity:** 3,000 **Floodlights:** None
Year formed: 1920 **Nickname:** Tivvy **Club sponsors:** None
Club colours: **Change colours:**
Record attendance: Not known **Programme:**
Clubhouse Details: New, opened Dec 1983. Functions room holds 250, food available at all times. Lounge, Bar and separate Skittle Alley
Past players who have progressed into Football League: Mike Franklin (Charlton), Hedley Steele (Exeter City)
Present players with Football League experience: Mike Franklin
Local Newspapers: Tiverton Gazette, Bampton St. 252725
Senior Honours: Devon County Senior Cup Winners 1955-56, 1965-66, League Champions 1926-27, 1928, 1933-34, 1964-65, 1965-66

WELLINGTON

President: Alan Baker
Chairman: Doug Northam
Manager: Selwyn Aspin
Coach:
Physiotherapist: None
Press Officer & Tel No: None
Secretary: Tony Brown
Address & Tel No: 2920 (H) 2439 (B)
Commercial Manager: None
Address & Tel No:
Address & Tel No of ground: Wellington Playing Field, North Street, Wellington. Wellington 4810 **Club shop:** No
Simple ground directions: From north: leave M5 at junction 26, follow A38 into Wellington, turn right at traffic lights into North Street and take first left in North Street by fire station. From south: leave M5 at junction 27, follow A38 into Wellington, turn left at traffic lights into North Street and take first left in North Street by fire station
No of seats: None **Covered accommodation:** 250 **Capacity:** 3,000 **Floodlights:** No
Year formed: 1892 **Nickname:** None **Club sponsors:** None
Previous names: None
Previous grounds: None
Club colours: Tangerine
Change colours: All Blue
Day for midweek home matches: Wednesday
Record attendance: Not known **Year:**
Best performance in: F.A. Cup: Not known
F.A. Vase: 1974-5 1st Round
Previous Leagues: Taunton Saturday, Somerset Senior
Clubhouse details: Modern clubhouse with lounge bar, dance hall, TV room and skittle alley
Present players with Football League experience: None
Past players who progressed into the Football League: None
Record transfer fee paid: None
Record transfer fee received: None
Programme details: 10 pages, 10p **Local newspaper & Tel No:** Wellington Weekly News
Club metal badges: No
Senior Honours: Somerset Senior League Div 2, Western League Div 1 Runners-up

Bristol Manor Farm
Back Row (L-R): Bert Weaver, Bobby George, Paul Williams, Steve Garrett, Dave Parsons, Gary Bray, Terry Pocock, Mark Savage, Mike Fisher. Front Row (L-R): Lee Holbrook, Mark Johns, Chris Rex, Carmelo Micciche, Billy Down, Paul Hawkes.

Clandown F.C.
Back Row (L-R): Terry Gillard (Gen. Manager), Duncan Atkinson, Nigel Brimble, Bob Andrews, Bob Farmer, Eric Jordon (Team Manager), Mark Bartlett. Front Row (L-R): Phil McCloughlin, Alan O'Leary, Nigel Sandquest, Colin Goatley, Ian Pope, Clive Herron, (Mascot) Duncan James.
Photo: Eric Marsh

Wimborne's Robson clears a Warminster attack, but his side lost 2-3 in the end. Photo: Leo Hoenig

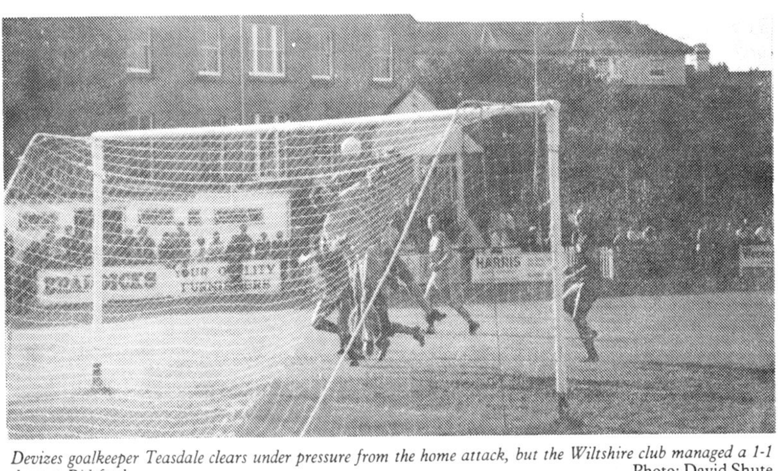

Devizes goalkeeper Teasdale clears under pressure from the home attack, but the Wiltshire club managed a 1-1 draw at Bideford. Photo: David Shute

Frome's Derek Bryant crashes a shot against the Exmouth bar and the Devon side went on to win 2-1 and clinch the championship. Photo: David Shute

SOUTH WESTERN FOOTBALL LEAGUE

Chairman: T.H. Scott *President:* G. Gillin

Secretary: G. Gazzard, 6 Coastguard Crescent, Penzance. Tel: Penzance 61397

	P	W	D	L	F	A	Pts
Newquay	38	26	8	4	87	26	60
Launceston	38	24	6	8	99	54	54
Millbrook	38	22	8	8	79	37	52
Bugle -5	38	24	9	5	68	33	52
St Austell	38	22	6	10	85	49	50
Newton Abbot	38	21	6	11	83	51	48
St Blazey	38	17	13	8	88	64	47
Appledore BAAC	38	20	6	12	76	54	46
Wadebridge Town	38	18	8	12	74	56	44
Torpoint	38	16	10	12	66	65	42
Plymouth C Service	38	17	5	16	78	58	39
Torrington	38	13	9	16	57	56	35
Truro City -3	38	14	9	15	63	75	34
Tavistock	38	13	4	21	52	69	30
Holsworthy	38	11	6	21	51	65	28
Clyst Rovers	38	10	8	20	61	77	28
Teignmouth	38	9	7	22	50	89	25
Penzance	38	5	7	26	43	94	17
Plymouth Command	38	3	5	30	40	130	11
Bodmin Town	38	3	4	31	45	145	10

St Austell FC

Photo: Leo Hoenig

THE BAYLY BARTLETT SOUTH-WESTERN FOOTBALL LEAGUE

President: G. H. Gillin *Chairman:* T. H. Scott

Hon. Secretary: G. Gazzard, 6 Coastguard Crescent, Penzance. *Tel:* Penzance 61397

APPLEDORE/BAAC, Marshford
Secretary: E. G. Nichols, 30 Stucley Road, Bideford, Devon. (Bideford 5493)
Colours: Yellow, Blue trim, Blue shorts

BODMIN TOWN, Priory Park
Secretary: R. Butler, 3 Agar Terrace, Dennison, Road, Bodmin, Cornwall. (2946)
Colours: Amber and Black, Black shorts Floodlights

BUGLE, Molinnis
Secretary: B. Penhall, 134 Phernyssick Road, Boscoppa, St. Austell. (St. A. 63023)
Colours: Black & White, Black shorts

CLYST ROVERS, Waterslade Park, Clyst Honiton
Secretary: B. Harvey, Sapele, Farthing Down, Holywell Lake, Wellington, Somerset. (Greenham 672483)
Colours: All Blue

FALMOUTH TOWN, Bickland Park. (75156)
Secretary: M. Rowe, 9 Treveryn Parc, Budock Water, Falmouth, Cornwall. (73017)
Colours: Black and Amber, Black shorts Floodlights

HOLSWORTHY, Upcott Field
Secretary: M. Goodenough, Rose Cottage, Horrelsford, Milton Damerel, Holsworth. (Milton Damerel 402)
Colours: Black & White stripes, Black shorts

LAUNCESTON, Pennygillam. (3279)
Secretary: C. Bradshaw, 4 Poltamar, Tavistock Road, Launceston. (4355)
Colours: Claret & Blue

MILLBROOK, Sports Ground
Secretary: B. Harvey, 27 Hounster Drive, Millbrook, Cornwall. (Plymouth 822066)
Colours: Black & White stripes, Black shorts

NEWQUAY, Mount Wise. (2935)
Secretary: B. A. Biggin, 8 Michell Avenue, Newquay, Cornwall. (5623)
Colours: Red & White stripes, Black shorts

NEWTON ABBOT, Centrax Sports Field
Secretary: R. Perkins, 21 Prospect Terrace, Newton Abbot, Devon. (61596)
Colours: Yellow shirts with Blue trim, Black shorts

PENZANCE, Penlee Park. (61964)
Secretary: D. R. Ferris, 96 Polmor Road, Crowlas, Penzance, Cornwall. (Cockwells 740585)
Colours: Black & White stripes, Black shorts Floodlights

PLYMOUTH CIVIL SERVICE, Beacon Down
Secretary: J. Tottel, 13 Arden Grove, Pennycross, Plymouth, Devon. (777979)
Colours: Blue shirts, White shorts

ST. AUSTELL, Poltair. (66099)
Secretary: P. Beard, 24 Alexandra Road, St. Austell, Cornwall. (64138)
Colours: White shirts, Black shorts

ST. BLAZEY, Station Road, St. Blazey. (Par 4110)
Secretary: P. A. Coad, 31 Porthmeor Road, Holmbush, St. Austell, Cornwall. (St. Austell 64589)
Colours: Green & Black shirts, Green shorts

TAVISTOCK, Langsford Park. (4447)
Secretary: R. Lowe, Panorama, Lamerton, Tavistock, Devon. (3516)
Colours: White shirts with Black trim, Black shorts

TEIGNMOUTH, Coombe Valley
Secretary: W. Parker, 23 Higher Coombe Drive, Teignmouth, Devon. (4277)
Colours: White shirts, Black shorts

TORPOINT ATHLETIC, The Mill Field. (812889)
Secretary: J. Millward, 92 Woodland Way, Torpoint, Cornwall. (Plymouth 813447)
Colours: Royal Blue shirts, White shorts

TRURO CITY, Treyew Road. (78853)
Secretary: A. Rowe, 5 Lander Court, Truro, Cornwall. (78853)
Colours: Red shirts, Black shorts

WADEBRIDGE TOWN, Bodieve Park
Secretary: L. George, 32 Wellington Place, Wadebridge, Cornwall. (2503)
Colours: Red shirts, White shorts

DETAILS OF HONOURS LIST 1983-84 SEASON

Champions NEWQUAY
Runners-up LAUNCESTON

S.W.L. Challenge Cup
Winners BUGLE
Runners-up TAVISTOCK

Sporting Club Trophy
Joint Winners NEWQUAY and PENZANCE

Jack Hawke Trophy for Leading Goalscorer
Joint Winners P. RYDER (Newquay) 31
T. JOURNEAUX (St. Austell) 31

Devon Premier Cup
Winners APPLEDORE/BAAC

Cornwall Charity Cup
Winners ST. BLAZEY

A picturesque view of the lovely St Blazey ground. Photo: David Shute

LYDNEY TOWN F.C.

President: Vic Hale
Chairman: Sid Barnfield
Manager: Mike Kear
Coach: None
Physiotherapist: None
Secretary: R. A. Sansom
Address & Tel No: (H) 0594 43210 (B) 0594 42235
Commercial Manager: None
Address & Tel No:
Press Officer & Tel No: R. Morgan (0594 562 243)
Address & Tel No of ground: Lydney Recreation Trust Ground, Lydney, Glos (0594 42765)
Simple ground directions: Enter Lydney on A48 from Gloucester, turn left into Swan Rd, continue along this Road to ground.
No of seats: None **Covered accommodation:** None **Capacity:** 2,000 **Floodlights:** No
Year formed: 1900 **Nickname:** The Town **Club sponsors:**
Club colours: All Sky Blue
Change colours: White
Previous Names:
Previous Grounds: Bathurst Park, Lydney
Record attendance: 750 v John Macey XI. Year: 1981
Programme: 10 pages, 25p
Previous Leagues: North Gloucester League 1971-72. Glos Northern Senior League 1972-80
Clubhouse details: Lounge bar + Skittle Alley/Function Room.
Major Honours: Glos NSL Div 1 Winners 1979-80, Runners-Up 1977-78, 1978-79, Malvern Invitation Trophy Winners 1979

Action in the Sutton Transformer Vase as Cadbury Heath's Phil Steeds blocks an AFC Totton attack.

Photo Leo Hoenig.

BRIDPORT

President: Campbell Edwards, OBE, JP
Chairman: M. A. Guyer
Manager: T. Cotton
Coach: B. Williams
Physiotherapist: P. House
Secretary: S. D. Miles
Address & Tel No: 56636 (H) 862404 (B)
Commercial Manager: K. Morgan
Address & Tel No: 25113
Press Officer & Tel No: S. D. Miles (tel. as Secretary)
Address & Tel No of ground: St. Mary's Field, South Street, Bridport. Tel. 23834 **Club shop:** Yes
Simple ground directions: Towards West Bay via South St, 1st right at Brewery Hill, 1st right again into club car park
No of seats: 200 **Covered accommodation:** 200 **Capacity:** 1,500 **Floodlights:** No
Year formed: 1887 **Nickname:** The Bees **Club sponsors:** Stevenson's Garage, Bridport
Previous names: None
Previous grounds: Brewery Ground
Club colours: Black/Red
Change colours: Amber
Day for midweek home matches: N/A
Record attendance: 1,150 v Exeter City **Year:** 1981
Previous Leagues: Dorset, Dorset Combination
Best performance in: F.A. Cup:
F.A.Trophy: 1971-2 3rd Qualifying Round F.A. Vase 1975-6 3rd Round
Clubhouse details: Bar, Dance Hall, darts etc.
Present players with Football League experience: Terry Cotton
Past players who progressed into the Football League: None
Record transfer fee paid: None
Record transfer fee received: £1,000
Programme details: 12 pages, 15p
Club metal badges: No
Local newspapers & Tel No: Dorset Echo, Bridport News
Senior Honours: Western League Challenge Cup (4), Mark Frowde Cup, Dorset Senior Challenge Cup (4)

GLOUCESTERSHIRE FOOTBALL ASSOCIATION COUNTY LEAGUE

Chairman: A.C. Barrett

Hon Secretary: L.V. James, 5 Anbrook Crescent, Hucclecote, Gloucester GL3 3HL

Tel: Gloucester 68671

FIRST CHAMPIONSHIP FOR SHARPNESS

Sharpness carted off the league title for the first time, establishing a new points total of 62, seven points more than runners-up and last season's champions, Old Georgians, and an impressive goal difference of +90. Old Georgians reached the quarter-finals of the FA Vase while Wotton Rovers were defeated in the semi-final of the Gloucestershire FA Challenge Trophy.

We regret losing yet another team to the Hellenic League in Sharpness, though we wish them every success in their new league. This, once again, emphasises the urgent need for some pyramid system over and above the County League whereby there is an exchange of clubs of a like standard. To that end a meeting of representatives of the Wiltshire County League, the Somerset Senior League and the Gloucestershire County League was held in June and a further meeting is to be held in October after reporting back to the leagues.

Two new clubs for the coming season will increase the membership to 19. Ellwood, runners-up in the Gloucestershire Northern Senior League, qualify under the pyramid system operating in this county while past members of the league, Cinderford Town, are welcomed back after many seasons in the Midland Combination.

	P	W	D	L	F	A	Pts
Sharpness	34	29	4	1	116	26	62
Old Georgians	34	24	7	3	76	29	55
Bristol St George	34	17	9	8	61	40	43
Port of Bristol	34	14	11	9	50	41	39
Avon St Philips	34	15	8	11	65	59	38
Lwrnce Wstn Hallen	34	16	4	14	54	51	36
Hambrook	34	14	6	14	43	46	34
Frampton Athletic	34	15	3	16	61	60	33
Oldland Decora	34	12	9	13	59	61	33
Hanham Mt Hill Ath	34	12	9	13	47	50	33
Harrow Hill	34	11	9	14	40	48	31
Wotton Rovers	34	10	10	14	43	51	30
Wilton Rovers	34	10	9	15	41	61	29
Frampton United	34	9	9	16	43	58	27
Newent Town	34	10	7	17	48	65	27
Lydbrook Ath	34	10	6	18	57	63	26
Cadbury Heath	34	6	10	18	35	64	22
Stonehouse	34	4	6	24	38	104	14

Leading goalscorers:
D. Rock (Sharpness) 31.
R. Humphris (Frampton Athletic), G. Twose (Oldland Decora) 21.
M. Rigg (Sharpness) 20.
D. Bruno (Avon St Philips), M. Grimshaw (Bristol St George) 19.

GLOUCESTERSHIRE COUNTY LEAGUE SEASON 1983/84

	Avon St Philips	Bristol St George	Cadbury Heath	Frampton Athletic	Frampton United	Hambrook	Hanham Mount Hill Athletic	Harrow Hill	Lawrence Weston Hallen	Lydbrook Athletic	Newent Town	Old Georgians	Oldland Decora	Port of Bristol	Sharpness	Stonehouse	Wilton Rovers	Wotton Rovers
Avon St Philips		2-0	3-1	1-3	4-3	3-2	2-1	4-1	0-1	2-2	1-0	2-2	3-0	2-1	1-2	5-0	4-0	2-4
Bristol St George	1-1		4-1	1-1	4-2	1-1	2-0	4-1	1-0	6-1	4-0	1-3	1-0	2-0	4-2	2-2	0-1	1-4
Cadbury Heath	1-3	0-2		1-2	0-1	0-3	1-0	0-0	2-0	1-0	1-3	0-4	1-3	2-3	0-6	7-1	0-1	1-1
Frampton Athletic	5-1	1-2	1-1		0-2	0-2	0-2	3-2	2-5	2-2	1-2	0-2	1-2	2-3	1-3	4-1	5-1	3-1
Frampton United	2-2	1-1	0-0	0-1		1-3	3-0	0-1	0-1	2-1	0-0	0-1	1-2	2-2	0-3	1-2	2-2	2-0
Hambrook	1-0	0-0	3-1	2-0	1-2		2-1	2-0	1-1	2-1	2-1	0-2	1-2	1-0	1-3	2-0	0-1	2-0
Hanham Mount Hill Athletic	2-2	1-1	1-1	1-2	2-2	2-1		0-0	2-1	2-3	0-0	0-3	2-2	4-1	0-3	3-1	4-2	2-2
Harrow Hill	3-0	2-1	2-1	4-3	2-0	0-1	3-0		0-2	2-1	1-1	0-2	2-2	1-0	1-1	1-2	2-2	0-0
Lawrence Weston Hallen	2-3	1-0	1-1	1-2	3-1	5-1	1-0	2-1		1-0	1-0	0-3	1-2	1-1	0-1	7-0	3-0	1-0
Lydbrook Athletic	0-2	2-4	1-1	2-5	3-4	1-0	0-1	4-0	2-1		1-2	1-3	4-0	0-0	1-1	6-0	2-0	4-0
Newent Town	1-5	2-1	1-1	2-4	1-3	0-0	1-3	0-3	5-0	1-2		1-2	2-2	2-1	0-1	5-2	1-2	0-0
Old Georgians	1-1	0-1	0-0	1-0	3-0	2-1	2-0	2-0	4-1	4-2	4-1		2-1	0-1	3-4	3-0	1-1	2-1
Oldland Decora	3-1	1-2	1-1	1-2	3-0	1-1	0-0	2-1	1-4	2-3	2-3	3-3		1-2	0-2	3-1	6-2	2-0
Port of Bristol	4-1	2-2	3-0	4-1	2-2	2-0	0-2	0-0	1-1	1-1	3-1	0-0	2-1		1-4	3-1	1-0	2-2
Sharpness	6-0	3-1	4-0	2-0	5-0	5-2	5-0	2-0	6-1	2-0	8-2	2-2	5-2	1-0		6-1	2-0	1-1
Stonehouse	1-1	0-1	2-3	1-2	0-2	4-0	0-5	1-2	1-2	4-3	1-3	3-5	2-2	1-1	1-7		0-3	0-0
Wilton Rovers	1-1	0-1	2-1	1-2	1-1	3-1	0-1	0-0	3-1	3-1	2-4	1-4	2-2	0-2	0-3	1-1		1-1
Wotton Rovers	2-0	2-2	2-3	1-0	2-1	1-1	1-3	3-2	4-1	2-0	1-0	0-1	1-2	0-1	0-5	3-1	1-2	

AVON ST. PHILIPS (1951)

Chairman: E. J. Jones **Manager:** R. Quinton
Secretary: P. G. Mitchell, 168 Main Road, Cleeve, Bristol BS19 4PP. Tel: Flax Bourton 2017
Ground Address & Tel No: Bristol Rovers Training Ground, Hambrook, Bristol. 573687
Directions to Ground: M4 Junc 19 to M32 Junc 1. Ground just off M32 Junc 1 behind Eurocrest Hotel. Nearest railway station Parkway, on A4174 to Filton
Previous Leagues: County of Avon Premier Combination, Bristol & District, Bristol Downs
Colours: Red shirts/Black shorts **Change colours:** Sky Blue shirts, shorts
Programmes: No **Clubhouse:** Licenced club on ground, belonging to Bristol Rovers FC **Floodlights:** No **Seating:** No

BRISTOL ST. GEORGE (1884)

Chairman: R. Higgins **Manager:** R. Grimshaw
Secretary: A. W. Abbott, 4 Dragon Walk, St. George, Bristol BS5 7RZ. Tel: 613873
Ground Address & Tel No: Butler Memorial Ground, Whiteway Road, St. George, Bristol
Directions to Ground: Nearest Rail Station – Temple Meads, Bristol. Leave M4 Junc 19, directions Bristol East to Downend – St. George
Previous Leagues: **Colours:** White/Black/White **Change colours:** Yellow & Black/Black/White
Programmes: 8 pages, 30p **Clubhouse:** Yes **Floodlights:** No **Seating:** No

CINDERFORD TOWN (1922)

Chairman: G. R. Bevan **Manager:** Len Hill
Secretary: T. R. Peates, 128 Church Road, Cinderford, Glos GL14 3ER. Tel: Dean 22603 (H), Dean 542421 (B)
Ground Address & Tel No: Causeway Ground, Hilldene, Cinderford, Glos
Directions to Ground: From centre of town take Heywood Road, Ground is in centre of Hilldene Housing Estate
Previous Leagues: Midland Combination
Colours: White shirts/Black shorts **Change colours:** Royal Blue shirts and shorts
Programmes: Yes **Clubhouse:** Yes **Floodlights:** No **Seating:** Yes

FRAMPTON ATHLETIC (1949)

Chairman: M. Williams **Manager:** R. Burns
Secretary: K. W. Potter, 94 Goldcrest Road, Chipping Sodbury, Bristol BS17 6XN. Tel: 0454 313704
Ground Address & Tel No: Beesmoor Road, Frampton Cotterell, Bristol. (no phone at Ground – messages 0454 772122, Greens newsagents)
Directions to Ground: From Bristol take M32, leave at the Hambrook-Filton exit, follow Yate signs. Take A432 through Winterbourne into Frampton Cotterell, turn right at the traffic lights (V.M.W. Garage) into Church Road, go past church to brow of hill, turn right at P.O. into Ryecroft Road, follow road, Ground at bottom of hill, turn left at Golden Lion
Previous Leagues: County of Avon Premier Combination, Bristol & District
Colours: Red with Black pinstripe shirts/Black shorts **Change colours:** White with Black pin stripe shirts
Programmes: 16 pages, 20p **Clubhouse:** Yes **Floodlights:** No **Seating:** No

LAWRENCE WESTON HALLEN (1948)

Chairman: F. Fairman **Manager:** C. Baldwin
Secretary: B. L. Phillips, 145A Station Road, Bristol BS10 7LZ. Tel: 0272 501754
Ground Address & Tel No: Hallen Playing Field Association, Moorhouse Lane, Hallen, Bristol
Directions to Ground: Signposted from M5 Junc 17
Previous Leagues: County of Avon Premier Comb, Bristol District
Colours: Blue/Black/Blue **Change colours:** All Green
Programmes: 4 pages, 20p **Clubhouse:** No **Floodlights:** No **Seating:** No

LYDBROOK (1919)

Chairman: D. G. Knight **Manager:** P. Brain
Secretary: J. A. Price, 'Wobage', 4th Avenue, Greytree, Ross-on-Wye. Tel: 0989 63788
Ground Address & Tel No: Reeds, Lower Lydbrook, Glos
Directions to Ground: On B4228 Ross-on-Wye – Coleford road
Previous Leagues: Herefordshire, Glos Northern Senior, Warwickshire Comb, Worcester & District, Midland Comb
Colours: Black/White **Change colours:** Yellow
Programmes: No **Clubhouse:** Yes **Floodlights:** No **Seating:** No

OLD GEORGIANS (1947)

Chairman: Geoff Cleak **Manager:** Dave Fear
Secretary: Brian Latchem, 87 Vicarage Road, Whitehall, Bristol BS5 9AQ. Tel: 556292 (H), 823681 (B)
Ground Address & Tel No: St. George School, Johnsons Lane, Whitehall, Bristol. 516888
Directions to Ground: M32 Junc 2, turn left into Muller Road, left at mini roundabout into Fishponds Road, travel 300 yds, turn right at traffic lights into Royate Hill, follow into Gordon Road, right at lights, first right into Whitehall Gardens, Ground at top of road
Previous Leagues: Bristol & Suburban **Colours:** Light Blue/Navy/Navy **Change colours:** Red/Navy/Red
Programmes: Usually cup matches, 8 or 12 pages, free **Clubhouse:** Yes **Floodlights:** No **Seating:** No

WOTTON ROVERS (1959)

Chairman: Arthur David Bushell **Manager:** Ernie Calder
Secretary: Martyn Peter Excell, 94 Bearlands, Wotton under Edge, Glos. Tel: 0453 845178
Ground Address & Tel No: Synwell Playing Field, Wotton under Edge, Glos. Dursley (0453) 8442929
Directions to Ground: From War Memorial in Wotton under Edge, down hill towards Potters Pond, follow road up Synwell Lane, Ground on left
Previous Leagues: Glos Northern Senior **Colours:** Royal Blue shirts, shorts **Change colours:** Yellow shirts, Black shorts
Programmes: 12 pages, 20p **Clubhouse:** Yes **Floodlights:** No **Seating:** No

Geoff Hall (No 11) scores the only goal of the match to give Bristol St George a victory over Lawrence Weston Hallon. Photo: Leo Hoenig

GLOUCESTERSHIRE COUNTY LEAGUE

CADBURY HEATH Springfield, Cadbury Heath Road, Cadbury Heath, Bristol. Tel: 675731
Hon. Sec. T. Mitchell, 134 Parkwall Road, Cadbury Heath, Bristol BS15 5AH. Tel: 612707
Colours: Red & White shirts, White shorts **Change Colours:** Yellow shirts, Black shorts

ELLWOOD Bromley Road, Ellwood, Coleford, Glos. Tel: Dean 32927
Hon. Sec. D. A. Haviland, 34 Lakeside, Lydney, Glos GL15 5PY. Tel: Dean 42182
Colours: Blue shirts, Blue shorts **Change Colours:** Red shirts, Black shorts

FRAMPTON UNITED Bell Field, Frampton-on-Severn, Gloucester
Hon. Sec. H. G. Tudor, "Ad Extremum", Frampton-on-Severn, Gloucester GL2 7EA. Tel: Gloucester 740224
Colours: Blue and White striped shirts, Blue shorts **Change Colours:** White shirts, Blue shorts

HAMBROOK Whiteshill Common, Hambrook, Bristol. Tel: Bristol 566820
Hon. Sec. D. P. Andrews, 8 Grove Avenue, Fishponds, Bristol BS16 2DJ. Tel: Bristol 650884
Colours: Red & White striped shirts, Red shorts **Change Colours:** White shirts, Black shorts

HANHAM ATHLETIC Avon Valley Park, Vicarage Road, Hanham, Bristol. Tel: Bristol 678820
Hon. Sec. J. A. Jacobs, 3 Lydiard Croft, Hanham, Bristol BS15 3LU. Tel: Bristol 611845
Colours: White shirts, White shorts **Change Colours:** Sky Blue shirts, White shorts

HARROW HILL Larksfield Road, Harrow Hill, Drybrook, Glos. Tel: Dean 543873
Hon. Sec. R. C. Beckett, "Sunny View", Bridge Road, Harrow Hill, Drybrook, Glos GL17 9JT. Tel: Dean 543390
Colours: Claret and Blue shirts, Blue shorts **Change Colours:** Blue shirts and shorts

NEWENT TOWN Wildsmiths Meadow, Malswick, Gloucester Road, Newent, Glos. Tel: Newent 821509
Hon. Sec. R. T. Knowles, 4 Chedworth, Bury Bar, Newent, Glos GL18 1SE. Tel: Newent 821506
Colours: Blue shirts, Blue shorts **Change Colours:** Tangerine shirts, Blue shorts

OLDLAND DECORA Atchison Memorial Field, Castle Road (off High Street), Oldland Common, Bristol
Hon. Sec. R. Hamblin, 41 Siston Park, Kingswood, Bristol BS15 4PE. Tel: Bristol 674569
Colours: Blue & White striped shirts, Blue shorts **Change Colours:** Yellow & Blue striped shirts, Yellow shorts

PORT OF BRISTOL Port of Bristol Sports Ground, Nibley Road, Shirehampton, Bristol. Tel: Avonmouth 823927
Hon. Sec. M. B. Brown, 33 Park Road, Northville, Bristol BS7 0RH. Tel: Bristol 695487
Colours: Red shirts, Black shorts **Change Colours:** Yellow shirts, Red shorts

STONEHOUSE Oldend Lane, Stonehouse, Glos
Hon. Sec. F. V. Wilks, 9 Glenthorn Close, Stonehouse, Glos GL10 2EF. Tel: Stonehouse 3708 (Mrs R. Bilton)
Colours: Black & White striped shirts, Black shorts **Change Colours:** Red shirts, Red shorts

WILTON ROVERS Gala Club, Fairmile Gardens, Tewkesbury Road, Gloucester. Tel: Gloucester 24447
Hon. Sec. P. Allen, 74 Oxstalls Lane, Gloucester GL2 9HX. Tel: Gloucester 20524
Colours: Orange shirts, Navy shorts **Change Colours:** Yellow or White shirts, Yellow or White shorts

Somerset Senior League

Premier Division

	P	W	D	L	F	A	Pts
Robinson's DRG	34	26	5	3	79	22	57
Brislington	34	21	8	5	71	27	50
Bristol Manor Farm	34	21	6	7	78	43	48
Redwood Dundry	34	16	9	9	61	42	41
Watchet Town	34	14	12	8	63	50	40
Avon Police	34	17	5	12	65	57	39
Peasedown Ath.	34	16	6	12	61	49	38
Timsbury Ath.	34	13	10	11	70	63	36
Burnham United	34	13	8	13	69	73	34
Hengrove Ath.	34	14	4	16	57	67	32
East Worle	34	9	13	12	34	49	31
Mangotsfield United	34	9	11	14	57	55	29
Imperial (Bristol)	34	9	11	14	49	59	29
Abbotonians	34	9	9	16	40	57	27
Shirehampton	34	8	11	15	32	50	27
Nailsea United	34	9	7	18	44	65	25
Bridgwater	34	6	3	25	34	99	15
Portishead	34	6	2	26	37	74	14

Division One

	P	W	D	L	F	A	Pts
Bishop Sutton	34	28	2	4	102	35	58
Castle Cary	34	22	5	7	64	37	49
Clevedon United	34	20	8	6	64	31	48
Brislington Res.	34	20	6	8	84	53	46
Bristol Hospitals	34	18	6	10	74	45	42
Tunley Ath.	34	15	6	13	64	55	36
Wells City	34	11	12	11	57	45	34
Westland United	34	13	8	13	52	40	34
Shepton Mallet	34	13	8	13	64	74	34
Bath University	34	11	9	14	45	42	31
Imperial (Bristol) Res.	34	10	10	14	50	53	30
Wellington	34	12	6	16	51	71	30
Clandown	34	9	9	16	42	66	27
Harptree United	34	9	9	16	43	69	27
Odd Down	34	7	9	18	35	61	23
Saltford	34	6	10	18	30	56	22
Yatton Ath.	34	8	6	20	41	73	22
Keynsham Cricketers	34	7	5	22	43	99	19

League K.O. Cup winners: Peasedown Athletic
League K.O. Cup runners-up: Robinson's DRG.

Dorset Football Combination League

	P	W	D	L	F	A	Pts
Parley Sports	34	24	7	3	99	28	55
Portland United	34	24	7	3	94	41	55
Blandford United	34	24	4	6	109	31	52
Sturminster Newton	34	20	7	7	64	34	47
Sherborne Town	34	20	6	8	79	47	46
Westland Sports	34	18	8	8	65	35	44
Bridport	34	14	5	15	63	57	33
Dorchester T. Res.	34	12	8	14	56	55	32
Wareham Rangers	34	11	10	13	63	65	32
Hamworthy United	34	11	10	13	59	65	32
Poole Town Res	34	11	9	14	52	49	31
Flight Refuelling	34	11	8	15	50	65	30
Shaftesbury	34	11	7	16	44	70	29
Bournem'th Water	34	9	5	20	46	70	23
Holt United	34	8	5	21	41	109	21
Swanage & Hin. R.	34	6	8	20	43	85	20
Wimborne T Res.	34	4	7	23	35	94	15
Gillingham Town	34	4	7	23	36	98	15

To seek re-election: Wimborne Town Res, Gillingham Town.

Dorset Combination Cup Final
Westland Sports 3, Parley Sports 0

BRISTOL & SUBURBAN LEAGUE

PREMIER DIVISION 1

	P	W	D	L	F	A	Pts
1 Barr Utd	34	23	3	8	95	53	49
2 Lockleaze CA	34	20	9	5	80	60	49
3 Stockwood Green	34	19	9	6	85	45	47
4 Teyfant Ath.	34	17	9	8	79	60	43
5 Glenside St Gabriels	34	15	12	7	80	52	42
6 P&W Utd	34	18	4	12	68	56	40
7 Broad Plain House	34	15	9	10	72	59	39
8 Eagle House Utd	34	15	8	11	78	52	38
9 Wessex Glass	34	16	5	13	80	76	37
10 Exeter Utd.	34	14	5	15	80	69	33
11 The Mill YC	34	12	9	13	58	54	33
12 Avonmouth	34	11	9	14	53	55	31
13 Port of Bristol Res.	34	11	5	18	51	69	27
14 St Aldhelms	34	12	3	19	52	78	27
15 Bristol St Andrews	34	11	3	20	38	65	25
16 Avon Fire Brigade	34	7	7	20	37	64	21
17 Bristol Crusaders	34	6	6	22	45	88	18
18 Old Georgians Res	34	4	5	25	38	108	13

PREMIER DIVISION 2

	P	W	D	L	F	A	Pts
1 St Josephs	32	22	5	5	63	33	49
2 De Veys	32	21	5	6	69	33	47
3 Dynamo	32	20	4	8	63	32	44
4 Longwell Green	32	14	9	9	71	48	37
5 Hartcliffe BC	32	16	5	11	80	56	37
6 Totterdown Ath	31	15	6	10	65	46	36
7 Filwood Crusaders	32	14	7	11	46	46	35
8 Yate Town Res	32	13	6	13	69	59	32
9 Bristol Waterworks	32	14	4	14	56	68	32
10 Electricity Sports	32	13	3	16	39	61	29
11 Bristol Telephones	31	9	8	14	39	58	26
12 Southmead Ath	32	10	6	16	39	61	26
13 Melbury Utd	29	8	7	14	39	56	23
14 Cadbury Heath Res.	31	7	9	15	34	62	23
15 SAC Technology	32	7	8	17	42	65	22
16 Portway Bristol Res.	32	7	7	18	52	63	21
17 Avon Dynamo	30	6	7	17	34	73	19

The Cornwall Combination League 1983-84
Final Table

	P	W	D	L	F	A	Pts
Falmouth Town	36	28	3	5	108	28	59
Penryn Athletic	36	24	8	4	104	31	56
Mousehole	36	24	5	7	82	44	53
RNAS Culdrose	36	19	11	6	74	43	49
Illogan R.B.L.	36	23	3	10	84	63	49
Porthleven	36	20	7	9	86	42	47
*St Just	36	20	6	10	83	57	44
*Mullion	36	19	5	12	88	50	39
Truro City	36	16	7	13	66	54	39
Pendeen Rovers	36	17	4	15	57	71	38
Newquay	36	14	5	17	66	69	33
Helston Athletic	36	11	8	17	80	86	30
Perranwell	36	12	3	21	62	75	27
Ludgvan	36	8	8	20	42	75	24
Penzance	36	9	4	23	47	97	22
Falmouth Docks	36	6	7	23	47	91	19
*St Agnes	36	7	6	23	42	99	19
Holmans SC	36	6	7	23	46	107	19
Marazion	36	3	5	28	27	109	11

*points deducted.

The Cornwall Combination League Cup 1983-4
Final Tie
Penryn Athletic 1 Porthleven 3

SOUTH WEST COUNTIES CHAMPIONSHIP RESULTS AND TABLES 1983/1984

SENIORS

GROUP 'A'

Cornwall	1	Devon	1
Glos	1	Somerset	2
Somerset	0	Cornwall	1
Devon	3	Army	1
Glos	0	Cornwall	0
Somerset	1	Devon	0
Cornwall	1	Army	2
Somerset	0	Army	1
Devon	0	Glos	2
Army	3	Glos	4

	P	W	D	L	F	A	Pts
Glos	4	2	1	1	7	5	5
Cornwall	4	1	2	1	3	3	4
Somerset	4	2	—	2	3	3	4
Army	4	2	—	2	7	8	4
Devon	4	1	1	2	4	5	3

GROUP 'B'

Wilts	2	Dorset	1
Sussex	2	Dorset	0
Hants	0	Sussex	0
Wilts	0	Hants	3
Hants	0	RN	1
RN	2	Sussex	2
Dorset	1	RN	2
RN	4	Wilts	1
Dorset	0	Hants	1
Sussex	1	Wilts	0

	P	W	D	L	F	A	Pts
RN	4	3	1	—	9	4	7
Sussex	4	2	2	—	5	2	6
Hants	4	2	1	1	4	1	5
Wilts	4	1	—	3	3	9	2
Dorset	4	—	—	4	2	7	0

Final: Gloucestershire 1 Royal Navy 2

South West Counties Representative Matches

South West Counties XI v F.A.XI. at The Dell, Southampton. Won 2-1.

Teasdale (Wiltshire), Brown (Hampshire), Lowe (Royal Navy), Swiggs (Devon), Harriss (Hampshire), Hurford (Somerset & Avon), Mills (Wiltshire), Herring (Wiltshire), Clark (Hampshire), Ryder (Cornwall), Burns (Dorset), Slattery (Wiltshire).

South West Counties XI v Western League at Dawlish. Lost 1-3.

Philp (Cornwall), Berry (Cornwall), Tummon (Cornwall), Beer (Devon), Hurford (Somerset & Avon), Monnery (Wiltshire), Clark (Hampshire), Thomas (Cornwall), Ryder (Cornwall), Slattery (Wiltshire), Bailey (Gloucestershire).

Gloucestershire Senior Trophy

First Round

Moreton Town v Bristol Manor Farm . . . 2-1
Cinderford Town v Cadbury Heath . . . 6-0
Wotton Rovers v Avon St Philips . . . 3-2
Lawrence Weston Hallen v Bristol St George . . . 1-2
Frampton Utd v Stonehouse . . . 2-1
Yate Town v Robinsons DRG . . . 1-2
Shortwood Utd v Port of Bristol . . . 3-1*
Shirehampton v Hambrook . . . 1-2
Glenside St Gabriels v Cheltenham Rs . . . 0-3
Wilton Rovers v Cirencester Town . . . 2-2,1-2
Harrow Hill v Sharpness . . . 1-2
Oldland v Lydbrook Athletic . . . 1-0
Newent Town v Frampton Athletic . . . 3-2
Mangotsfield U v Almondsbury Greenway . . . 0-1*
Old Georgians v Fairford Town . . . 2-0
Portway Bristol v Hanham MH Athletic . . . 2-2,4-1

Second Round

Wotton Rovers v Frampton United . . . 2-0
Oldland v Bristol St George . . . 2-2,0-3
Moreton Town v Cinderford Town . . . 1-0
Sharpness v Robinsons DRG . . . 2-4
Old Georgians v Portway Bristol . . . 0-2
Cirencester Town v Almondsbury Greenway . . . 0-4
Cheltenham Town Res v Shortwood United . . . 2-3
Newent Town v Hambrook . . . 2-3

Third Round

Moreton Town v Almondsbury Greenway . . . 3-2
Portway Bristol v Bristol St George . . . 3-2
Shortwood United v Hambrook . . . 3-0
Wotton Rovers v Robinson DRG . . . 3-2

Semi-Finals

Wotton Rovers v Portway Bristol . . . 2-3*
Shortwood United v Moreton Town . . . 0-0,0-0
(Shortwood United won on penalties)

Final

Portway Bristol v Shortwood United . . . 0-1
*After extra time.

Somerset Senior Cup

First Round

Westland Sports v Saltford . . . 1-0
Brislington v Watchet . . . 2-2
Redwood Dundry v Bridgwater Res . . . 2-0
Peasedown v Robinsons DRG . . . 0-1
Imperial United v Congresbury . . . 5-1
Highbridge v Keynsham Cricketer . . . 1-1
Mangotsfield Res v Castle Cary . . . 2-1
Wells v Ilminster . . . 2-2
Imperial Bristol v Timsbury . . . 2-0
Bishop Sutton v Tunley . . . 2-3
Bristol Spartak v Harptree . . . 5-0
Long Sutton v Odd Down . . . 2-2
Hengrove Athletic v Weston St Johns . . . 3-1
Radstock v Bristol Gen Hosp . . . 3-0
Backwell United v Larkhall Athletic . . . 0-3
Frys v Nailsea . . . 5-1

Second Round

Brislington v Tunley . . . 9-0
Larkhall Athletic v Keynsham Cricketers . . . 5-0
Wells v Odd Down . . . 2-1
Mangotsfield United v Robinsons DRG . . . 3-2
Radstock Town v Westland Sports . . . 2-0
Imperial Bristol v Frys . . . 1-1,2-1
Imperial United v Redwood Dundry . . . 2-2,1-2
Hengrove Athletic v Bristol Spartak . . . 5-2

Third Round

Imperial Bristol v Hangrove Athletic . . . 1-2
Larkhall Athletic v Mangotsfield Utd . . . 1-0
Redwood Dundry v Brislington . . . 1-0
Wells v Radstock Town . . . 1-5

Semi-Finals

Redwood Dundry v Hengrove Athletic . . . 0-1
Radstock Town v Larkhall Athletic . . . 3-0

Final

Hengrove Athletic v Radstock Town . . . 1-0

WILTSHIRE COUNTY FOOTBALL LEAGUE

President: D. S. Paget, Esq.
Chairman: J. R. Nunn, Esq.
Hon. Gen. Sec: Mr P. J. Ackrill, 3 Dallas Avenue, Swindon, Wilts SN3 3NP
Tel: Swindon 20334

1983/84

DIVISION 1

	P	W	D	L	F	A	Pts
Penhill	30	22	5	3	73	24	49
Bemerton Athletic	30	21	7	2	69	28	49
Amesbury Town	30	14	9	7	71	36	37
Park	30	15	7	8	54	42	37
Calne Town	30	14	8	8	49	41	36
Avebury	30	12	10	8	69	48	34
Tisbury United	30	12	10	8	49	41	34
Sanford	30	11	11	8	52	47	33
Purton	30	11	9	10	51	52	31
Highworth Town*	30	11	7	12	55	51	29
Meadowcroft	30	11	6	13	50	52	28
Melksham Town Res	30	8	8	14	46	62	24
Chippenham T Res	30	8	2	20	39	71	18
Westbury United*	30	4	8	18	41	80	16
Devizes Town Res	30	3	8	19	30	85	14
St. Josephs**	30	3	5	22	20	58	11

LEADING GOALSCORERS

J. Rushton (Bemerton Athletic)	21
D. Perry (Amesbury Town)	19
C. Valters (Park)	19
K. Willis (Westbury United)	19
M. Tutton (Bemerton Athletic)	18
T. Diaper (Amesbury Town)	17

*Withdrawing from league
**Relegated clubs
§Promoted clubs

Ghia Senior Cup
Winners Wootton Bassett Town **Runners-Up** Sanford

Ghia Junior Cup
Winners Plessey Sports **Runners-Up** Kington Langley

Subsidiary Cup — Division 2
Winners Warminster Town R. **Runners-Up** Wroughton

Senior Clubs to be admitted to League
Burmah House, Old Manor and Westbury United Reserves

DIVISION 2

	P	W	D	L	F	A	Pts
The Wills FC§	26	19	3	4	59	21	41
Aldbourne§	26	18	4	4	85	29	40
Wroughton§	26	17	6	3	58	31	40
Wootton Bassett	26	15	6	5	47	24	36
Warminster Res.	26	14	6	6	62	31	34
Burbage Sports	26	12	6	8	48	41	30
Marlborough Town	26	9	6	11	46	51	24
Shrewton United	26	7	9	10	45	50	23
Terry Warner	26	6	7	13	35	62	19
Walcot Athletic	26	6	6	14	38	55	18
Pewsey Vale	26	7	3	16	40	62	17
Dorcan	26	4	7	15	26	60	15
Corsham Town	26	3	8	15	25	54	14
Ferndale Athletic	26	3	7	16	20	63	13

LEADING GOALSCORERS

N. Mapstone (Wroughton)	21
M. Baker (Aldbourne)	18
N. Offer (Burbage Sports)	16
M. Perrett (Aldbourne)	15
C. Bagwell (Wills)	15
S. Murden (Warminster Town Res)	14

WILTSHIRE SENIOR CUP

(PREL ROUND)

Supermarine v Westbury United ... 3-0

FIRST ROUND

Pewsey Vale v Meadowcroft ... 0-4
Sanford v Wills ... 1-4
Warminster Town v Melksham Town ... 0-3
Highworth Town v Supermarine ... 1-3
Aldbourne v Purton ... 3-1
Marlborough Town v St Josephs* ... 0-0
Corsham Town v Tisbury Utd ... 0-2
Burbage Sports v Shrewton Utd ... 4-1
Calne Town v Avon Bradford ... 3-0
Penhill v Downton ... 5-1
Walcot Athletic v Ferndale Athletic ... 2-3
Dorcan v Amesbury Town ... 0-2
Wootton Bassett* v TW Pinehurst ... 2-2
Avebury v Park ... 1-2
Devizes Town v Bemerton Athletic ... (Away team won)
Chippenham T v Walton ... (Home team won)

SECOND ROUND

Bemerton Athletic v Wills ... 2-1*
Calne Town v St Joseph ... 2-0
Burbage Sports v Aldbourne ... 2-3
Meadowcroft v Wootton Bassett ... 1-2
Melksham Town v Amesbury Town ... 3-5
Penhill v Supermarine ... 2-1
Tisbury United v Ferndale Athletic ... 7-0
Park v Chippenham T ... (Away team won)

THIRD ROUND

Amesbury v Calne Town ... 4-0
Bemerton Athletic v Chippenham Town ... 1-3
Tisbury v Aldbourne ... 1-2*
Wootton Bassett v Penhill ... 2-2*, 1-2*

SEMI-FINALS

Amesbury v Chippenham Town ... 0-0, 2-0
Aldbourne v Penhill ... 0-4

FINAL

Amesbury v Penhill ... 2-1

*after extra time

DEVON & EXETER LEAGUE
PREMIER DIVISION

	P	W	D	L	F	A	Pts
Budleigh Salterton	30	23	0	7	103	39	46
Exeter C Services	30	20	2	8	71	35	42
Exeter City 'A'	30	17	5	8	83	38	39
Exeter University	30	16	7	7	67	33	39
Honiton Town	30	17	3	10	76	43	37
Dawlish Res	30	13	10	7	64	45	36
Willeys	30	14	5	11	56	47	33
Alphington	30	14	4	12	56	57	32
Exmouth T Res -2	30	13	6	11	72	61	30
Cullompton	30	10	9	11	59	55	29
Willand	30	12	5	13	57	55	29
Feniton	30	12	3	15	48	60	27
Clyst Valley	30	8	5	17	41	66	21
Chulmleigh	30	6	5	19	44	87	17
Sidmouth Town -2	30	5	4	21	33	90	12
Dolphin	30	2	3	25	25	153	7

Sussex Royal Ulster Rifles Charity Cup

First Round

Midhurst-Easebourne v Littlehampton Town	0-5
Portfield v Horsham YMCA	0-1
Chichester City v Steyning Town	0-1
Wick v Lancing	1-2(A),0-2
Selsey v Pagham	1-1,2-1
Wigmore Athletic v Southwick	0-3
Shoreham v Storrington	1-0
Rye United v East Grinstead	EG W-O
Newhaven v Crowborough Ath	0-1
Haywards Heath v Sidley United	1-2
Burgess Hill Town v Eastbourne Town	2-0
Whitehawk v Ringmer	1-1,4-0
Hailsham Town v Albion United	6-0
Hassocks v Peacehaven & T	1-1,0-1
Hastings Town v Three Bridges	2-1
Arundel	Bye

Second Round

Arundel v Horsham YMCA	3-0
Selsey v Littlehampton Town	1-4
Southwick v Steyning Town	2-0
Lancing v Shoreham	3-1
Burgess Hill Town v Hastings Town	4-6
Peacehaven & Tels v Crowborough Ath	10-1
Sidley United v East Grinstead	3-1
Hailsham Town v Whitehawk	0-1

Third Round

Hastings Town v Southwick	1-3
Arundel v Peacehaven & T	2-2,1-0
Littlehampton Town v Whitehawk	1-1,3-2
Lancing v Sidley United	6-1

Semi-Finals

Southwick v Arundel	3-2
Lancing v Littlehampton Town	0-4

Final at Culver Road, Lancing FC

Littlehampton Town v Southwick	2-1

Sussex Senior Cup

Preliminary Round

Arundel v Chichester City	1-2
East Grinstead v Albion United	2-1
Hassocks v Rye United	w-o Hassocks
Haywards Heath v Storrington	2-1
Portfield v Bexhill Town	1-3
Newhaven v Sidley United	2-2,4-3
Shoreham v Crowborough Athletic	4-3
Wigmore Athletic v Selsey	2-1

First Round

Burgess Hill Town v Hastings United	2-4
Chichester City v Bexhill Town	0-1
Crawley Town v Pagham	4-2
Eastbourne Town v Lancing	1-0
East Grinstead v Midhurst & Easebourne	1-1,1-3
Hassocks v Bognor Regis Town	0-1
Hastings Town v Brighton & Hove A	1-3
Haywards Heath v Worthing	0-8
Horsham v Three Bridges	1-1,1-2
Horsham YMCA v Southwick	1-2
Lewes v Eastbourne United	6-1
Newhaven v Peacehaven & Telscombe Cliffs	0-2
Ringmer v Hailsham Town	2-3
Shoreham v Littlehampton	2-3
Steyning Town v Whitehawk	1-1,1-1,1-2
Wigmore Athletic v Wick	1-3

Second Round

Bexhill Town v Hastings United	2-1
Bognor Regis Town v Worthing	3-1
Crawley Town v Peacehaven TC	0-2
Eastbourne Town v Whitehawk	0-0,0-0,1-2
Lewes v Hailsham Town	5-1
Midhurst & Easebourne v Brighton & Hove A	0-2
Three Bridges v Littlehampton Town	0-1
Southwick v Wick	1-0

Third Round

Bognor Regis Town v Bexhill Town	5-1
Lewes v Whitehawk	4-1
Peacehaven TC v Brighton & Hove A	2-1
Southwick v Littlehampton Town	1-1,1-3

Semi-Finals

Bognor Regis Town v Peacehaven TC	3-0
Lewes v Littlehampton Town	0-1

Final

Bognor Regis Town v Littlehampton Town	1-0

Goalmouth action as Lewes attack the Peacehaven goal in an early season cup-tie at 'The Dripping Pan'.
Photo: Leo Hoenig

Farnborough Town with the Hampshire Senior Cup, which they have won three times in the last nine years.
Photo: Eric Marsh

Hampshire Senior Cup

Preliminary Round

Cove v Gosport Borough .... w-o Cove
Vale Recreation v Alton Town 2-1
Portals Athletic v BAT 4-0
Andover v Hartley Wintney 3-3,2-1
Cowes Sports v Christchurch 0-1
Basingstoke v First Tower United 2-1
Ringwood Town v Sway 2-0
RS Southampton v Overton United 2-0

First Round

Hartley Wintney reinstated — ineligible player
AFC Totton v Warsash 4-2
Cove v Portsmouth RN 1-0
Christchurch v Netley Central Sp 2-3
Brading Town v Farnborough Town 0-5
Portsmouth United v Havant Town 0-0,2-0
Portals Athletic v Southampton 'A' 1-3
Fareham Town Res v Horndean 1-2
Basingstoke Town v Bass Alton 1-2
East Cowes Vics v Romsey Town 0-0,1-3
Pirelli General v Vale Recreation 0-3
Fleet Town v Waterlooville 2-1
RS Southampton v Petersfield United 2-0
Eastleigh v Brockenhurst 0-2
Blackfield Langley v Downton 2-0
Hartley Wintney v Newport IOW 3-0
Ringwood Town v Sholing Sports 0-3

Second Round

Cove v AFC Totton 0-3
Netley Central Sp v Horndean 3-2
Sholing Sports v Portsmouth United 5-0
Brockenhurst v Farnborough Town 0-8
Bass Alton v Hartley Wintney 3-1
RS Southampton v Fleet Town 2-0
Romsey Town v Vale Recreation 1-2
Blackfield & Lang v Southampton 'A' 0-4

Third Round

Farnborough Town v AFC Totton 4-2
Sholing Sports v Netley Central Sp 3-1
Southampton 'A' v RS Southampton 3-0
Vale Recreation v Bass Alton 0-4

Semi-Finals

Southampton 'A' v Sholing Sports 1-3
Bass Alton v Farnborough Town 1-3

Final (at Southampton FC)

Farnborough Town v Sholing Sports 2-2,3-0
Replay at Fareham Town FC

Hampshire FA Russell Cotes Cup

First Round

Andover v Warsash 5-0
Awbridge v Sholing Sports 1-4
Portsmouth United v Brockenhurst 1-6
Alton Town v Bass Alton 2-4
Havant Town v Horndean 2-1
Petersfield United v Netley Central Sp 3-2
Portsmouth RN v East Cowes Vics 1-0
Fareham Town v Romsey Town 2-1
Cowes Sports v RS Southampton 1-5
Eastleigh v New Street 4-0

Second Round

Andover v Blackfield & Langley 0-4
Havant Town v Portsmouth RN 2-2,0-3
Ringwood Town v Petersfield United 1-3
Waterlooville Res v Fleet Town 2-1
Sholing Sports v RS Southampton 1-2
Brokenhurst v Fareham Town 3-2
Bass Alton v Eastleigh .... -
AFC Totton v Pirelli General 1-3

Third Round

Blackfield & Langley v Petersfield United 1-1,2-1
Waterlooville Res v Pirelli General 2-1
RS Southampton v Portsmouth RN .... w-o Southampton
Bass v Brockenhurst 2-0

Semi-Finals

Bass Alton v RS Southampton 0-5
Blackfield & Langley v Waterlooville 1-1,2-0

Final (at Sholing Sports FC)

RS Southampton v Blackfield & Langley 3-1

South West Counties Sutton Transformer Vase

First Round

Horndean v Abbotonians United .... w-o Abbotonians
P & W United v AFC Totton 0-2

Second Round

Yate Town v Clump Inn 2-1
Wotton Rovers v Locks Heath 0-1*
Calne Town v Oldlands Decora 1-0
Paulton Rovers v Sharpness 3-1
RS Southampton v Thornbury Town 9-0
Pucklechurch v Holsworthy 3-2
Cadbury Heath v Kilkhampton 3-0
AFC Totton v Abbotonians United 2-1

Third Round

Cadbury Heath v AFC Totton 1-3
Locks Heath v Calne Town 2-0
Paulton Rovers v Yate Town 1-3
RS Southampton v Pucklechurch 1-0

Semi-Finals

Locks Heath v RS Southampton 1-1,0-1
AFC Totton v Yate Town 2-0

Final (two legs)

RS Southampton v AFC Totton 0-0
AFC Totton v RS Southampton 1-3

Gloucestershire Amateur Cup — North

First Round

Borough United v Shipton Oliffe	5-1
Bymarks v Shortwood United Res	4-1
Huntley v Hilldene	2-1
Newnham United v Tuffley	1-0
Bourton v Cheltenham Saracens	2-3
Mitcheldean v Minchinghampton	3-2
Lydney Town v Chalford	4-0
Brockworth v Berkley Town	2-4
Campden Town v Worrall Hill	2-1
Shardington v St Marks	0-5
Smiths Athletic v College St Pauls	3-1
Cinderford Town Res v The Herd	0-4
Dursley Town v Dowty Dynamo	1-0
Ellwood v Hardwicke	3-0
Dowty Staverton v Wilton Rovers Res	3-2
Badminton Pickson v Dowty Ashchurch	1-4
Cam v Longlevens	1-3
Kingstanley v Bishop's Cleeve	0-2
Tewkesbury YMCA v Sharpness Res	1-2

Second Round

Bishop's Cleeve v Coleford United	5-3
Bymarks v Smiths Athletic	2-3
Ellwood v St Marks	4-5
Brimscombe & Thrupp v Dowty Staverton	0-2
Borough United v Viney St Swithens	3-5
Longlevens v Sharpness Res	4-1
Newnham United v Frampton United Res	2-1
Lydney Town v Huntley	2-1
Broadwell v Cheltenham Saracens	2-4
The Herd v Woodmancote	2-0
Campden Town v Forest Green Rovers Res	3-0
Bilbury v Charfield	1-4
Dursley Town v Dowty Ashchurch	0-2
Moreton Town Res v Cope Chat	6-1
Newent Town Res v Berkley Town	2-5
Mitcheldene	Bye

Third Round

Cheltenham Saracen v Moreton Town Res	2-3
Longlevens v Dowty Staverton	4-1
Berkley Town v Newnham United	6-1
Smiths Athletic v Mitcheldean	2-1
Lydney Town v Dowty Ashchurch	1-0
St Marks v The Herd	5-1
Campden Town v Bishop's Cleeve	1-0
Charfield v Viney St Swithens	0-1

Fourth Round

Longlevens v Smiths Athletic	3-0
Lydney Town v Moreton Town Res	0-2
St Marks v Campden Town	0-0,0-3
Viney St Swithens v Berkley Town	1-0

Semi-Finals

Longlevens v Campden Town	1-0
Moreton Town v Viney St Swithens	0-1

Final (at Gloucester City FC)

Longlevens v Viney St Swithens	0-1

Gloucestershire Amateur Cup — South

Preliminary Round

SAC Technology v Hambrook Res	0-7
Stapleton v Staple Hill	1-1,4-3
Hillfields OB v Totterdown Athletic	1-3
Olveston United v Robinsons DRG Res	3-6
Bristol St Andrews v De Veys	4-0

First Round

Avon Fire Brigade v P & W United	0-3
Avonmouth v Exeter United	1-3
Sun Life v The Mill	2-1
Totterdown Athletic v Bristol Crus	2-2,6-1
Stapleton v Yate Town Res	3-2
Bristol Union v Filton Town	3-4
Sea Mills Park v Gardeners	2-2,5-4
Henbury Athletic v Patchway	3-2
Henbury OB v Port of Bristol Res	4-0
Made For Ever v Bishop Rovers SB	1-6
Winterbourne United v St Josephs	3-1
Cots v Hanham Mnt Hill Res	3-1
Thornbury Town v Shaftsbury Crusader	1-3
Hartcliffe BC v Melbury United	1-3
Bristol St Andrews v Lawrence Rovers	5-0
Iron Acton v Bristol Waterworks	6-0
Pucklechurch Sports v Dynamo	2-1
Manor Farm BC v RWP	2-3
Bristol Manor Farm R v Abbotonians United	0-1
Hambrook Res v St Aldhems	0-1
Portway Bristol R v Longwell Green	1-4
Southmead Athletic v Eden Grove	1-5
Filwood Crusaders v Hillfields Park	3-4
Avon Dynamo v Electricity	3-1
Nicholas Wanderers v Soundwell	1-5
Almondsbury Gway R v Wick	0-1
Bitton v Barr United	1-3
Telephones v Old Georgians Res	3-0
Wessex Glass v St Vincents	4-6
Saints v St Pancras	3-0
Lockleaze CA v Robinsons DRG Res	0-3
St Phillips MAS v Cadbury Heath Res	1-0

Second Round

Wessex Glass v St Phillips MAS	2-5
Telephones v Cots	2-0
Avon Dynamo v Henbury OB	0-8
Eden Grove v Filton Town	6-4
Hillfields Park v P & W United	3-2
RWP v Totterdown Athletic	3-3
Sea Mills Park v Winterbourne United	0-4
Soundwell v Sun Life	2-1
Henbury Athletic v Pucklechurch Sports	3-3
Stapleton v Longwell Green	0-2
St Aldhems v Bristol St Andrews	2-1
Shaftsbury Crus v Exeter United	3-4
Saints v Iron Acton	0-7
Melbury United v Abbotonians United	3-2
Barr United v Robinsons DRG Res	0-3
Wick v Bishop Rovers SB	3-0

Third Round

Exeter United v St Phillips MAS	0-3
St Aldhems v Pucklechurch Sports	0-1
Hillfields Park v Iron Acton	2-2,0-2
Eden Grove v Robinsons DRG Res	2-1
Longwell Green v Winterbourne United	0-1
Wick v Telephones	3-0
Hanbury OB v Totterdown Athletic	2-0
Soundwell v Melbury United	1-0

Semi-Finals

Pucklechurch Sport v Eden Grove	3-1
Iron Acton v Henbury Old Boys	0-1

Final

Pucklechurch Sport v Henbury Old Boys	-

Another beautiful setting for a football match as Wotton Rovers entertain Robinsons DR and win 3-2 in the Gloucestershire Senior Trophy.

Photo: Leo Hoenig

Bideford keeper Neil Fowler punches clear in the Devon Challenge Cup tie at Heavitree which they won 1-0.

Photo Leo Hoenig.

NORTHERN PREMIER FOOTBALL LEAGUE

President: N. White, F.S.C.A.
Chairman: K. Marsden
Secretary and Treasurer: R.D. Bayley, 22 Woburn Drive, Hale Altrincham, Cheshire WA15 8LZ. Tel. 061 980 7007 (home) 061 834 8600 (business)
Telegraphic Address "Norprem, Altrincham".

A Merrier Mix

The 1983/84 season was dominated by three clubs as far as the Northern Premier League was concerned, Champions Barrow, FA Trophy semi-finalists Marine and Bass Northern Premier League and Liverpool Senior Cup winners South Liverpool.

Yes, I know that the rest played their part. Who can forget the joy that Hyde United's Chairman Peter Pluck must have felt to see his side challenge Third Division big spenders Burnley in the First Round of the FA Cup . . . and surely that pleasure would be enhanced with a video recording of the game for posterity? Maybe so but oh the heartache when, after taking the only copy home, his ten year old daughter Justine lost her innocent status when she taped over it — Tom and Jerry cartoons no less.

Such was one of the more whimsical stories of the NPL year. There was of course the usual turn over in managers, which, by now, goes without saying. Colin Clarke (Stafford), Alex Gibson (Southport), Les Rigby (Morecombe) and Mick Davies (Buxton) were all dismissed. John Saunders stepped down at Worksop, Kevin Randall quit Goole just before the start of the season and Bob Murphy ended a six year spell at Mossley by taking over at Southport. Indeed, 1984 was a memorable time for the NPL's most successful manager, winning the McKenzie Manager of the month award for a record tenth time when he scooped the pool for April.

And if it is records you want then last season was able to supply just that. Workington's Presidents Cup success was their first ever honour, as was Barrow's first NPL Championship. Barrow's average home attendance hit the 1,000 mark whilst the gate at Barrow for the representative match between the NPL and an FAX1 was a record for such fixtures involving the FA and any representative side from any semi professional League.

Other comings and goings saw Ken Roberts relieved of his managerial duties at Oswestry, his place being taken over by Stuart Mason who managed to save the Shropshire outfit from a plea for re-election with a tremendous late flurry of results including a 3-0 win against Barrow, one of only three defeats suffered by the Cumbrians as they stormed to title honours by a massive 20 points.

EX-NORTHERN PREMIER LEAGUE FOOTBALL LEAGUE XI

Gary Pierce
(Mossley, Huddersfield T, Wolves, Barnsley, Blackpool)

Joe Hinnigan
(S Liverpool, Newport Co, Sunderland, PNE)

Chris Nichol
(Witton A, Halifax T, Luton T, Aston Villa, Southampton, Grimsby T, N Ireland)

Geoff Twentyman
(Chorley, Preston NE)

Steve Buckley
(Burton A, Luton T,, Derby Co)

Steve Galliers
(Chorley, Wimbledon, C Palace, Wimbledon)

Jimmy Case
(S Liverpool, Liverpool, Brighton, England U23)

Eamonn O'Keefe
(Stalybridge Celtic, Plymouth, Mossley, Everton, Wigan Ath, Port Vale, Eire)

John Aldridge
(S Liverpool, Newport Co, Oxford U)

Paul Mariner
(Chorley, Plymouth Arg, Ipswich T, England)

Tony Galvin
(Goole T, Tottenham H, Eire)

Chorley and South Liverpool take the honours for supplying some quality players amongst the thirty ex NPL stars who played with Football League clubs last season.

Bob Mountain, who has scored 77 goals for Matlock Town in only two seasons, finds the back of the Workington net with a crisp header. Photo: Derbyshire Times.

Leading Goalscorers — Season 1983-84:
(Northern Premier League and Cup games only)
37 Barry Diamond (Barrow).
27 Bob Gauden (Gainsborough Trinity, Les Harris (Buxton).
22 Tommy Smith (Witton Albion).
21 Colin Cowperthwaite (Barrow), Peter Coyne (Hyde United).
19 Andy Brolly (Gainsborough Trinity), Frank Gamble (Barrow).
18 Andy Jones (Rhyl).
17 Grant Lightbown (Chorley), Paul Moss (Horwich), Bob Mountain (Matlock Town), John Smith (Workington), Jimmy Thornton (Marine).
16 Martin Hanchard (Stafford Rangers), David Leadbeater (Grantham), Ray Redshaw (Horwich).
15 Paul Meachin (Marine), Peter Moore (Worksop Town).

What of Marine then? The Merseysiders went ever so close to gleaning a Wembley Trophy place against Bangor. Having fought off the challenges of the likes of Scarborough, Fisher and Telford and then gaining a 1-1 draw in the away leg of the semi final against Northwich, Roly Howard (honoured by replacing Bob Murphy as the NPL team manager) must have been left with few nerves as his team spluttered to a 2-0 home defeat a week later.

Fellow Scousers South Liverpool had a magnificent season too. Their final place in the NPL of 3rd was the highest ever for the Holly Park club, managed by John King and George Rooney at the start of the term before the two left for King's old club Altrincham. In their place came Bryan Griffiths, a veteran of the non-league scene around Merseyside. His qualifications were simple. He had performed miracles by steering North West Counties Burscough to a Championship the season before, working on a limited budget . . . and that is precisely what he had at Holly Park, very little money to utilize. Nevertheless he kept up the momentum and steered South to a NPL Cup final win, albeit on penalties, at Manchester City's Maine Road Ground and followed that up with a splendid win at Holly Park against a strong Everton XI in the Final of the Liverpool Senior Cup.

Finally, what a great season for Barrow! Out of their 42 games, they won a staggering 29, drew 10 and lost a modest 3. 92 NPL goals were scored in the process, out of which Barrow's front three of Barry Diamond, Colin Cowperthwaite and Frank Gamble scored a mammoth 75 goals between them. Barrow also conceded the least number of goals last term, with keeper Peter McDonnell righly earning the tag as semi professional football's best goalkeeper.

Barrow's success in the field in the NPL earned its just reward off the field, attracting large crowds away from home, including over 1,600 at Burton and the biggest gate in the league of the season with 1,700 plus to witness the Boxing Day derby against Workington.

Ironically, the end of season saw many more changes. Bryan Griffiths quit South Liverpool, Vic Halom, after his first season in management at Barrow, left to take over the same job at Fourth Division Rochdale and Barrow, promoted to the Gola League, were replaced, somewhat ironically by former NPL Champions and FA Trophy finalists, Bangor City . . . I suspect that season 1984/85 will prove just as stimulating, just as busy and, as ever, just as interesting.

NORTHERN PREMIER LEAGUE

	Home						Away					
	P	W	D	L	F	A	W	D	L	F	A	Pts
Barrow	42	17	4	0	57	16	12	6	3	35	22	97
Matlock Town	42	13	3	5	38	18	10	5	6	34	30	77
South Liverpool	42	14	5	2	31	16	8	6	7	24	28	77
Grantham	42	12	4	5	40	21	8	4	9	24	30	68
Burton Albion	42	9	4	8	34	24	8	9	4	27	23	64
Macclesfield Town	42	12	4	5	38	26	6	6	9	27	29	64
Rhyl	42	11	2	8	35	23	8	4	9	29	32	63
Horwich RMI	42	11	5	5	35	23	7	4	10	29	36	63
Gainsborough Town	42	9	9	3	48	26	8	2	11	34	40	62
Stafford Rangers	42	9	7	5	37	23	6	10	5	28	29	62
Hyde United	42	9	3	9	29	28	8	5	8	32	35	59
Marine	42	8	6	7	37	32	8	4	9	26	36	58
Witton Albion	42	11	5	5	38	23	3	9	9	26	34	56
Chorley	42	6	6	9	34	36	8	5	8	34	29	53
Workington	42	9	5	7	33	24	5	4	12	20	33	51
Southport	42	9	5	7	32	28	5	3	13	25	46	50
Worksop Town	42	7	4	10	32	37	6	4	11	25	37	47
Goole Town	42	6	7	8	36	38	6	3	12	23	42	46
Morecambe	42	9	6	6	35	25	2	6	13	24	50	45
Oswestry Town	42	7	5	9	38	47	4	3	14	28	50	41
Buxton	42	6	3	12	24	34	5	3	13	28	57	39
*Mossley	42	5	6	10	26	35	4	3	14	21	39	33

*Three points deducted for fielding ineligible player.

Total goals scored — 1,390 in 462 matches (average 3.008)

NORTHERN PREMIER LEAGUE SEASON 1983/84

Home team / Away team:	Barrow	Burton Albion	Buxton	Chorley	Gainsborough Trinity	Goole Town	Grantham	Horwich RMI	Hyde United	Macclesfield Town	Marine	Matlock Town	Morecambe	Mossley	Oswestry Town	Rhyl	South Liverpool	Southport	Stafford Rang.	Witton Albion	Workington	Worksop Town
Barrow		5-0	2-0	2-2	3-0	4-3	1-0	2-0	2-2	2-0	4-0	3-0	4-1	3-1	4-0	1-0	2-1	5-1	1-1	2-2	3-1	2-1
Burton Albion	0-0		4-1	2-4	0-2	0-0	0-2	1-2	1-2	0-2	1-2	3-0	1-0	1-1	4-0	2-1	0-1	3-1	2-2	2-0	3-0	4-1
Buxton	1-2	0-1		1-0	1-4	1-2	1-0	0-2	0-1	1-3	2-2	0-1	3-3	2-3	1-0	1-2	0-1	3-2	2-2	1-0	3-1	0-2
Chorley	0-2	0-2	4-0		3-4	4-1	1-3	2-2	1-1	4-2	0-2	4-4	2-1	1-0	3-2	0-1	1-1	1-2	1-1	0-0	1-3	1-2
Gainsborough Trinity	1-2	1-1	3-2	1-1		0-1	3-1	0-2	4-1	2-2	2-2	1-1	1-1	4-1	5-1	1-1	5-0	1-1	3-1	1-1	3-1	6-2
Goole Town	2-3	0-0	2-2	0-0	6-3		3-1	2-0	2-4	0-2	1-1	2-3	2-2	0-0	3-3	1-4	1-2	3-1	2-0	2-5	0-2	2-0
Grantham	1-1	1-2	4-2	1-1	2-1	2-0		2-1	1-3	2-1	4-0	0-1	1-0	2-1	0-1	4-0	1-1	3-0	0-1	4-1	0-0	5-3
Horwich RMI	0-0	0-0	3-0	3-4	2-1	4-0	1-2		2-1	1-1	1-0	0-1	3-1	2-0	4-2	0-3	1-1	2-1	2-1	1-1	1-0	2-3
Hyde United	0-0	0-0	3-1	4-1	1-2	2-1	2-1	2-0		2-0	0-2	0-2	3-1	1-3	2-0	2-4	0-2	0-3	0-1	2-2	1-2	2-0
Macclesfield Town	1-3	2-0	1-2	3-1	0-2	1-2	2-2	2-2	1-3		4-1	2-2	1-0	2-0	2-1	3-1	2-1	2-0	2-2	2-0	2-1	1-0
Marine	2-3	1-3	2-2	0-3	3-1	4-1	2-0	0-1	5-2	2-1		1-1	1-1	2-1	0-1	1-1	1-1	5-2	2-2	1-3	1-0	1-2
Matlock Town	1-2	1-1	2-1	0-1	3-1	5-2	0-0	1-0	2-2	2-1	0-1		2-0	3-0	4-1	3-1	2-3	1-0	3-0	0-1	2-0	1-0
Morecambe	2-1	1-1	4-0	1-2	1-2	1-4	1-0	1-1	2-0	1-1	4-1	2-0		1-0	2-1	0-1	1-3	1-2	0-0	2-2	2-2	5-1
Mossley	1-1	1-1	2-4	1-4	0-2	2-0	1-1	1-2	0-1	1-1	3-0	0-5	5-1		1-0	0-2	0-0	2-2	2-3	2-0	1-2	0-3
Oswestry Town	3-0	2-3	3-3	2-1	2-1	2-1	0-2	0-6	2-2	2-0	0-4	1-1	4-4	0-2		5-2	0-1	2-3	1-4	3-3	3-0	1-4
Rhyl	0-1	2-4	1-2	1-0	0-0	1-0	2-3	3-0	2-0	1-2	0-2	2-1	6-1	1-2	3-1		3-0	0-0	1-2	2-1	3-1	1-0
South Liverpool	3-0	0-0	2-0	0-2	2-1	1-1	1-1	1-0	1-1	1-0	2-1	1-2	2-1	1-0	1-0	2-1		4-2	4-3	1-0	1-0	0-0
Southport	1-3	2-0	0-1	0-4	2-1	1-2	0-1	2-2	2-1	2-0	3-0	1-2	0-2	4-2	3-3	3-0	1-0		1-1	2-1	1-1	1-1
Stafford Rang.	1-1	1-1	1-2	0-0	3-1	4-0	4-0	3-1	0-2	1-3	1-2	2-1	4-0	3-2	1-4	2-1	1-1	4-0		1-1	0-0	0-0
Witton Albion	1-3	2-1	4-1	2-1	3-1	0-2	1-2	7-1	2-0	1-1	3-1	2-3	1-1	1-1	2-1	0-0	0-1	2-1	0-0		2-1	2-0
Workington	1-3	0-1	6-1	2-1	0-1	0-0	4-1	3-1	1-2	0-3	1-1	2-0	2-0	1-0	3-4	0-2	4-2	2-0	0-0	1-1		0-0
Worksop Town	0-4	1-5	4-1	3-1	3-3	3-0	0-1	1-3	2-1	1-1	0-1	1-3	2-3	4-1	2-2	1-1	2-1	0-1	0-1	2-1	0-2	

NORTHERN PREMIER LEAGUE

No. of clubs competing:	20	20	22	24	24	24	24	24	23	24	23	22	22	22	22	22
Season	68/69	69/70	70/71	71/72	72/73	73/74	74/75	75/76	76/77	77/78	78/79	79/80	80/81	81/82	82/83	83/84
1 Altrincham	9	12	8	10	4	3	3	7	10	5	2	—	—	—	—	—
2 Ashington	18	—	—	—	—	—	—	—	—	—	—	—	—	—	—	—
3 Bangor City	6	8	7	9	13	9	19	8	4	3	12	—	—	1	—	—
4 Barrow	—	—	—	—	23	22	22	23	21	13	16	—	—	—	—	1
5 Boston U.	14	3	4	2	1	1	12	5	1	1	6	—	—	—	—	—
6 Bradford P.A.	—	—	14	18	5	21	—	—	—	—	—	—	—	—	—	—
7 Burton Albion	—	—	—	—	—	—	—	—	—	—	—	4	6	7	3	5
8 Buxton	—	—	—	—	—	18	16	17	18	23	22	6	4	16	12	21
9 Chorley	19	—	10	13	—	—	—	—	—	—	—	—	—	—	4	14
10 Ellesmere P.T.	—	—	—	16	11	—	—	—	—	—	—	—	—	—	—	—
11 Fleetwood	10	13	18	20	24	14	24	24	—	—	—	—	—	—	—	—
12 Frickley Athletic	—	—	—	—	—	—	—	—	20	12	19	3	—	—	—	—
13 Gainsborough Tr.	4	6	11	7	7	10	20	14	16	16	17	14	5	18	17	9
14 Gateshead (1)	11	20	—	—	—	—	—	—	—	—	—	—	—	—	—	—
15 Gateshead (2)	—	—	—	—	—	—	—	—	—	17	21	16	11	4	1	—
16 Gateshead U.	5	5	13	8	20	6	7	16	8	—	—	—	—	—	—	—
17 Goole T.	8	19	22	23	19	13	8	10	6	14	9	11	8	14	16	18
18 Grantham	—	—	—	—	—	—	—	—	—	—	—	9	14	6	14	4
19 Great Harwood	—	17	19	15	16	20	10	21	17	15	—	—	—	—	—	—
20 Horwich R.M.I.	—	—	—	—	—	—	—	—	—	—	—	—	—	—	—	8
21 Hyde U.	7	11	—	—	—	—	—	—	—	—	—	—	—	—	8	11
22 King's Lynn	—	—	—	—	—	—	—	—	—	—	—	—	19	5	9	—
23 Kirkby T.	—	—	21	24	—	—	—	—	—	—	—	—	—	—	—	—
24 Lancaster C.	—	—	15	14	22	23	18	12	7	11	11	12	16	17	—	—
25 Macclesfield T.	1	1	5	6	10	8	17	15	19	22	23	8	13	10	5	6
26 Marine	—	—	—	—	—	—	—	—	—	—	—	10	3	9	6	12
27 Matlock T.	—	18	17	12	21	19	11	4	3	10	3	5	15	21	10	2
28 Morecambe	3	15	12	17	15	17	13	20	15	21	18	17	21	20	13	19
29 Mossley	—	—	—	—	14	15	6	9	9	9	1	1	2	2	2	22
30 Netherfield	16	10	16	19	9	24	23	19	23	18	15	18	17	22	22	—
31 Northwich Victoria	13	9	6	5	8	16	9	11	2	6	10	—	—	—	—	—
32 Oswestry T.	—	—	—	—	—	—	—	—	—	—	—	13	18	15	18	20
33 Rhyl	—	—	—	—	—	—	—	—	—	—	—	—	—	—	—	7
34 Runcorn	15	14	20	22	18	7	2	1	12	8	7	15	1	—	—	—
35 Scarborough	17	4	3	4	2	5	5	3	5	4	4	—	—	—	—	—
36 Skelmersdale U.	—	—	—	11	12	12	21	18	—	—	—	—	—	—	—	—
37 South Liverpool	12	16	9	21	17	11	15	22	22	24	20	20	9	13	19	3
38 Southport	—	—	—	—	—	—	—	—	—	—	5	19	20	8	15	16
39 Stafford R.	—	7	2	1	6	4	4	2	11	7	8	—	—	—	—	10
40 Tamworth	—	—	—	—	—	—	—	—	—	—	—	22	22	19	20	—
41 Wigan Ath.	2	2	1	3	3	2	1	6	14	2	—	—	—	—	—	—
42 Witton Albion	—	—	—	—	—	—	—	—	—	—	—	2	7	3	11	13
43 Workington	—	—	—	—	—	—	—	—	—	19	14	21	10	11	7	15
44 Worksop T.	20	—	—	—	—	—	14	13	13	20	13	7	12	12	21	17

NORTHERN PREMIER LEAGUE 1968-84

		P	W	D	L	F	A	Pts*	%	Best Pos.	Seasons
1	Wigan Athletic	438	236	120	82	761	404	592	67.5	1st (2)	68-78
2	Boston U.	482	257	126	99	804	457	640	66.3	1st (4)	68-79
3	Stafford R.	486	242	131	113	826	495	615	63.2	1st	69-79 & 83-84
4	Scarborough	482	237	128	117	792	512	602	62.4	2nd	68-79
5	Burton Albion	210	104	45	61	359	258	253	60.2	3rd	79-84
6	Witton Albion	210	100	52	58	380	245	252	60.0	2nd	79-84
7	Mossley	528	257	119	152	938	683	633	59.9	1st (2)	72-84
8	Altrincham	482	225	127	130	836	581	577	59.8	2nd	68-79
9	Marine	210	88	59	63	339	280	235	55.9	3rd	79-84
10	Bangor City	524	231	124	169	958	743	586	55.9	1st	68-79 & 81-84
11	Northwich Victoria	482	206	125	151	791	679	537	55.7	2nd	68-79
12	Runcorn	566	234	146	186	898	741	614	54.2	1st (2)	68-81
13	Horwich R.M.I.	42	18	9	15	64	59	45	53.5	8th	83-84
14	Gateshead U.	392	167	84	141	655	526	418	53.3	5th (2)	68-77
15	Hyde U.	160	66	37	57	282	250	169	52.8	7th	68-70 & 82-84
16	Grantham	210	85	51	74	306	293	221	52.6	4th	79-84
17	Rhyl	42	19	6	17	64	55	44	52.3	7th	83-84
18	King's Lynn	126	44	43	39	169	145	131	51.9	5th	80-83
19	Macclesfield T.	692	268	181	243	964	930	717	51.8	1st (2)	68-84
20	Matlock T.	654	254	164	236	1,063	1,017	672	51.3	2nd	69-84
21	Gateshead (2)	258	101	63	94	401	367	265	51.3	1st	77-83
22	Chorley	210	76	57	77	315	309	209	49.7	4th	68-69 70-72 82-84
23	Ellesmere Port T.	92	35	20	37	119	127	90	48.9	11th	71-73
24	Frickley Athletic	176	63	42	71	281	292	168	47.7	3rd	76-80
25	Gainsborough Tr.	692	238	181	273	1,054	1,049	657	47.4	4th	68-84
26	Bradford Park Avenue	180	56	53	71	213	278	165	45.8	5th	70-74
27	Goole T.	692	231	172	289	946	1,104	634	45.8	6th	68-84
28	Southport	254	79	74	101	312	386	232	45.6	5th	78-84
29	Workington	300	103	66	131	403	459	272	45.3	7th	77-84
30	Lancaster C.	532	170	137	225	725	842	477	44.8	7th	70-82
31	Skelmersdale U.	230	75	55	100	277	343	205	44.5	11th	71-76
32	Buxton	482	155	110	217	575	759	420	43.5	4th	73-84
33	Worksop T.	474	146	120	208	606	764	412	43.4	7th	68-69 & 74-84
34	South Liverpool	692	203	192	297	863	1,144	598	43.2	3rd	68-84
35	Morecambe	692	202	187	303	905	1,131	591	42.7	3rd	68-84
36	Barrow	360	114	74	172	443	615	302	41.9	1st	72-79 83-84
37	Great Harwood	400	111	113	176	560	731	335	41.8	10th	69-78
38	Oswestry T.	210	60	49	101	275	382	169	40.2	13th	79-84
39	Gateshead (1)	76	19	21	36	79	142	59	38.8	11th	68-70
40	Ashington	38	10	8	20	48	74	28	36.8	18th	68-69
41	Netherfield	650	167	137	346	729	1,181	471	36.2	9th	68-83
42	Fleetwood	348	77	91	180	351	648	245	35.2	10th	68-76
43	Tamworth	168	34	38	96	139	306	106	31.5	19th	79-83
44	Kirkby T.	88	12	25	51	95	197	49	27.8	21st	70-72

*2pt for a win. 1pt for a draw.

Morecambe F.C.

There are more than two teams on Merseyside as South Liverpool will proudly testify. Here they pose for the cameras following their Bass Northern Premier League Cup success at Maine Road, Manchester, over Hyde United which went to a penalty shoot-out after extra-time with the teams locked together at 1-1.

Photo: John Rooney

NORTHERN PREMIER LEAGUE CHALLENGE CUP — Season 1983/84

1st Round — 1st Leg

Grantham	2	Gainsborough Tr.	0
Morecambe	0	Horwich	0
Oswestry Town	0	South Liverpool	1
Southport	1	Barrow	3
Stafford Rangers	2	Rhyl	1
Worksop Town	5	Goole Town	1

1st Round — 2nd Leg

Gainsborough Tr.	1	Grantham	1
Horwich	4	Morecambe	2
South Liverpool	2	Oswestry Town	0
Barrow	1	Southport	1
Rhyl	0	Stafford Rangers	0
Goole Town	2	Worksop Town	3

2nd Round

Grantham	0	Hyde United	0
Macclesfield Town	2	Matlock Town	2
Horwich	1	Burton Albion	1
South Liverpool	0	Mossley	0
Barrow	2	Buxton	0
Witton Albion	0	Chorley	1
Workington	2	Marine	1
Worksop Town	2	Stafford Rangers	1

Replays

Hyde United	1	Grantham	0
Matlock Town	1	Macclesfield Town	2
Burton Albion	1	Horwich	2
Mossley	1	South Liverpool	2

3rd Round

Barrow	1	Worksop Town	1
Horwich	0	Hyde United	2
Workington	1	Chorley	2
South Liverpool	3	Macclesfield Town	1

Replay

Worksop Town	1	Barrow	0

Semi Final — 1st Leg

Hyde United	1	Worksop Town	1
South Liverpool	4	Chorley	2

Semi Final — 2nd Leg

Worksop Town	1	Hyde United	2
Chorley	1	South Liverpool	1

Final at Manchester City FC

Hyde United	1	South Liverpool	1

(South Liverpool won 7-6 on penalties) AET

NORTHERN PREMIER LEAGUE 'PRESIDENT'S' CUP — Season 1983/84

1st Round — 1st Leg

Matlock Town	4	Burton Albion	2
Chorley	0	Workington	0
Hyde United	1	Macclesfield Town	1
Mossley	4	Marine	4

1st Round — 2nd Leg

Burton Albion	3	Matlock Town	0
Workington	2	Chorley	1
Macclesfield Town	1	Hyde United	2
Marine	1	Mossley	0

Semi Final — 1st Leg

Hyde United	0	Marine	1
Workington	2	Burton Albion	0

Semi Final — 2nd Leg

Marine	2	Hyde United	1
Burton Albion	1	Workington	0

Final — 1st Leg

Marine	1	Workington	1

Final — 2nd Leg

Workington	0	Marine	0

(Workington won on away goals rule) AET

NORTHERN PREMIER LEAGUE
FIRST TEAM MATCH STATISTICS 1983-84

	Leading Goalscorers	Hat Tricks	Penalties	Most Appearances
Bangor City	Mark Carter 31 Bruce Urquhart 21 Kevin Westwood 9	B. Urquhart v Cefn A M. Carter v AP Leamington	A. Morris (3) B. Urquhart (3) M. Carter (3)	J. Cavanagh 64* M. Carter 58 M. Gray 54
Burton Albion	Doug Newton 10 Gary Marrow 9 Paul Froggatt 8	P. Fisher Andy Harrison Gary Marrow	Gary Marrow (4) Pat Lally (2) Andy Harrison (2) Doug Newton	David Vaughan 57 Doug Newton 57 Paul Froggatt 55
Buxton	Les Harris 33 Ian Rogers 11 Lenny Yates 5	Les Harris	Steve Guest	Les Harris 58* Lenny Yates 56 Steve Guest 54
Chorley	Grant Lightbrown 24 Chris Hunter 13 Gary Buckley 10	Grant Lightbrown (2)	Chris Hunter (2)	Simon Westwell 56 Jim Clayton 56 Gary Butcher 53
Goole Town	Mark Mailton 13 Jimmy Seal 8 Gary Brattan 8			Gary Brattan 49 Duncan Milner 48 Steve Worsfeld 47
Grantham	David Leadbeater 28 Phil Boyer 20 David Stewart 12	David Leadbeater (2)	Dave Adamson (4)	Phil Boyer 75 Stuart Franklin 75 Gary Elliman 68
Horwich	Paul Moss 17 Ray Redshaw 16 Neil McLacklan 8	Paul Moss	Alan Froggatt (4) Vernon Lang (2)	Ray Silous 51 Steve Waywell 51 Tommy McMahon 43
Hyde United	Peter Coyne 32 Steve Johnson 14 Barry Howard 7 Jimmy Golder 7	Peter Coyne v Tranmere R (Cheshire SC)	Jimmy Golder (6) Colin Skillen (2) Gary Riley	Terry Cook 62 Steve Johnson 62 Peter Coyne 60
Macclesfield T	'Chalkie' White 15 Nigel Shaw 11 Brian Griffin 9	Kevan Keelan 4 v Tamworth FAC Colin Kersley v Congleton FAC	Neil Fairclough (4) 'Chalkie' White	Neil Fairclough 57* Graham Tobin 57* Ian Elsby 52 + 1s
Matlock Town	Bob Mountain 28 Graham Vardy 17 Kevin Woods 13 Wayne Biggins 13	Bob Mountain		Mark Broughton 59 Graham Vardy 59 Mick Fenoughty 57 David Burrows 57 Alan Lukasik 54
Morecambe	John Beasley 17 Tommy Quinn 12 Keith Galley 11		Derek Brownbill (2) A. Quinn (2)	John McKenna 54 James Weston 52 Kenneth Pym 51
Mossley	Tibor Szabo 15 Martin Gill 5 Greg Brown 4		Jimmy O'Connor (2)	Jimmy O'Connor 49 Tibor Szabo 48 Mike Halliday 44
Oswestry Town	Terry Farrell 14 Gary Simpson 13 Steve Hanlon 11	Mark Joseph		Steve Hanlon 53* Terry Farrell 48 Paul Needham 44
Rhyl	Andy Jones 18 Selwyn Morris 11 Brian Davies 8		Les Armur (2)	Dave Wignall 44* Barry Horne 43 Andy Jones 40
South Liverpool	Phil McFerran 67 Kevin O'Brien 66 Gary Anderson 65	Paul Wilkinson v Southport	John Donnelly (2) Lawrence Iro (2) John Lawler (2) G. Anderson	Phil McFerran 67 Kevin O'Brien 66 Gary Anderson 65
Southport	Joe Strong 13 Gary Cooper 8 John McMahon 7		Ian Hodge (2) Alan Wilson (2)	Jay McCombe 64 Joe Strong 60 Paul Evans 60
Stafford Rangers	Martin Hanchard 21 Andy Lee 12 Chris Arnot 11	M. Hanchard P. Carr	Andy Lee (12)	Kevan Mooney * Paul Upton Derek Goulding
Witton Albion	Tommy Smith 24 Don Graham 12 Tony Quinn 7	Tommy Smith (3)	Don Graham (9) Jimmy Golder	Don Graham 44 Tommy Smith 41 Mickey Kilduff 41
Workington	John Smith 19 John Roach 12 Allan Curruthers 10		John Smith (3) Wayne Harrison	Martin Harris 56 Allan Curruthers 55 Vaughan Williams 51
Worksop *Ever present	Mark Smith 20 Peter Moore 18 Paul Cavell 15	Peter Moor 4 v Goole T	Martin Hardy (5) Bryna Kent	Steve Adams 58 David Cunnington 57 Martin Hardy 53

NORTHERN PREMIER LEAGUE

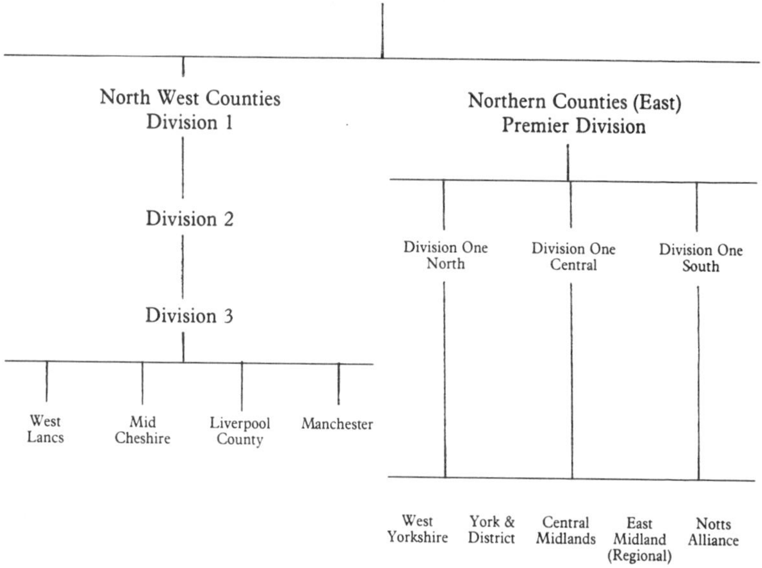

The northern section of the 'pyramid' involves a large number of competitors but at the lower level negotiations to set up official promotion and relegation are still in the discussion stage. However it is a great encouragement for many small clubs that their leagues are being considered and a real chance is being set up for their progressive members.

Hyde United's Peter Coyne shoots for goal during the first half of the Northern Premier League Challenge Cup Final with South Liverpool at Maine Road, Manchester. Photo: John Rooney

NORTHERN PREMIER LEAGUE PLAYERS 1984

(Football League appearances in brackets)

BANGOR CITY
Goalkeepers
Glan Letheran: Scarborough, Oxford City, Swansea City (21), Chesterfield (63), Leeds United (1)
Gareth Hughes: Local

Defenders
Jerry Banks: Caernarfon Town
John Cavanagh: Altrincham, Preston NE
Mark Gray: Local
Gwyn Peris-Jones: Local
Phil Lunn: Chester City, Bangor City

Midfield
Jim Smith: Oswestry Town, Stafford Rangers, Bangor City, Everton
Alan Morris: Caernarfon Town
Steve Craven: Altrincham, Northwich Victoria, Crewe Alexandra (29-3), Tranmere Rovers (114-17)
Paul Whelan: Local
Bruce Urquhart: Wrexham
Andy Puddle: Local

Forwards
Peter Sutcliffe: Chester (109-7), Port Vale (50-6), Stockport County (27-2), Manchester United
Ian Howat: Crewe Alexandra (17-1), Chester (57-10)
Kevin Westwood: Stafford Rangers, Nantwich Town
Mark Carter: South Liverpool, Liverpool
Graham Murphy: Local

BURTON ALBION
Goalkeeper
Paul Evans: Macclesfield Town, Worksop Town, Mansfield Town (6), Worksop Town, Kiveton Park

Defenders
Steve Dolby: Local
Kenny Blair: Southport (17), Halifax Town (43-4), Derby County
Clive Arthur: Local
David Vaughan: Mossley, Boston FC
Ian Vaughan: Rotherham United (6-1)
Pat Lally: Doncaster Rovers (122), Swansea City (160-10), York City (72-5), Millwall (1)

Midfield
Nigel Simms: Local
Mick Fletcher: Derby County
Iain Maclain: Local
Doug Newton: Belper Town, Alfreton Town, Eastwood Town
Kevin Sheldon: Wigan Athletic (39-1), Stoke City (15)

Forwards
Paul Froggatt: Worksop Town, Sheffield Wednesday, Manchester City
Dennis Leman: Scunthorpe United (40-2), Sheffield Wednesday (117-10), Manchester City (20-2)
David Sunley: Stafford Rangers, Tsun Wan (Hong Kong), Stockport County (83-6), Lincoln City (41-6), Hull City (69-11), Sheffield Wednesday (133-21)
Terry Mulholland: Local
Gary Kemm: Gresley Rovers

Non-Contract
Jon Whiteley: Alfreton Town, Matlock Town, Buxton
Darryl Chapman: Alfreton Town, Crewe Alexandra (6-2), Heanor Town, Derby County

BUXTON
Goalkeeper
Des Finch: Spalding United, Belper Town, Worksop Town, Gainsborough Trinity, Skegness Town, Worksop Town, Mansfield Town

Defenders
Steve Goldstraw: Local
John Reynolds: Rowntree Mackintosh
Steve Guest: Local
Carl Swan: Goole Town, Chesterfield, Doncaster Rovers (17-1), Burton Albion, Buxton
Mark Stanley: Winterton Rangers, Spalding United
Greg Mitchell: Sheffield United

Midfield
Lenny Yates: Worksop Town, Sheffield United
Wayne Oxley: Hallam
Mark Orritt: Whaley Bridge, Sheffield Wednesday
Peter Telling: Heanor Town, Staveley, Sutton Town, Staveley
Richard Davis: Sutton Town, Alfreton Town
Mark Hearn: Alfreton Town, Buxton, Mansfield Town

Forwards
Les Harris: Burton Albion, Gainsborough Trinity, Buxton, Barnsley (26-2)
Malcolm Wagstaffe: Marine, Mossley, Marine, Irlam Town
Martin Haughton: Hallam
Steve Kulic: Winterton Rangers, Belper Town, Mexborough Town Athletic, Matlock Town, Rotherham United, Goole Town, Denaby United
Ian Rogers: Boston FC, Worksop Town

CHORLEY
Goalkeeper
John Wood: Altrincham, Rossendale United, Great Harwood

Defenders
Dave Fitzharris: Ashton United
Peter Nicholson: Lytham, Carlisle United (1), Bolton (318-12), Blackpool (6)
Simon Westwell: Preston NE (74-1)
Mick Richmond: Barrow, Lancaster City, Preston NE
Howard Taylor: Local
Neil Cudworth: Morecambe
John Fielding: Local
John Hughes: Witton Albion, Bury (1)

Midfield
Gary Buckley: Preston NE (38-2), Manchester City (8)
Chris Hunter: Preston NE (1)
Ian Galliers: Local
Neil Hanson: Halifax Town, Preston NE
Jimmy Clayton: Lancaster City, Morecambe, Netherfield
Wayne Lancaster: Horwich RMI, Irlam Town

Forwards
Grant Lightbown: Darwen, Blackburn Rovers
Andy Stafford: Mossley, Rochdale, Stockport County (25-1), Halifax Town (41-1)
Gary Butcher: Blackburn Rovers, Norwich City, Great Yarmouth Town
Peter Devine: Blackburn Rovers (5), Bristol City (28-1), Vancouver Whitecaps, Chorley, Bury

GAINSBOROUGH TRINITY
Goalkeeper
Gary Ingham: Rotherham United

Defenders
Ashley Taylor: Rotherham United (23)
Richard Beaumont: Sheffield Wednesday
Dave Senescall: Appleby Frodingham
Ian Bennyworth: Hull City (1)
Andy Lodge: Blackburn Rovers, Ashby Town
Graham Jones: Bradford City (4)

Midfield
Gary Clayton: Spalding United, Rotherham United
Andy Brolly: Frechville Community, Bristol Rovers, Rotherham United
Trevor Thompson: Lincoln City (80-1), Newport County (35-2), WBA (20)
Tony Henson: Chesterfield (28-2), Alfreton Town, Sheffield Wednesday

Forwards
Jimmy Snee: Appleby Frodingham, Gainsborough Trinity
Bob Guaden: Burton Albion, Scarborough, Buxton
Russell Simpson: Sheffield United

GOOLE TOWN
Goalkeepers
Paul Blackburn: Gainsborough Trinity, Goole Town, Gainsborough Trinity, Bridlington Trinity
Chris Marples: Bradford City

Workington (white shorts) are on the attack away to Goole Town and achieve a 2-0 win in their NPL meeting last season. Photo: David Shute

Defenders
Chris Dale: Scarborough
Duncan Milner: Sheffield FC
Steve Worsfold: Frickley Athletic
Peter Holmes: Bridlington Trinity, Hull City
Tommy Stanley: Scarborough, York City (18)
Chris Jackson: Local

Midfield
David Pugh: Doncaster Rovers (6), York City (77-2), Rotherham United (58), Halifax Town (96-3), Chesterfield (213-12), Newport County (78-9)
Gary Brattan: Hall Road Rangers, Bridlington Trinity, Hull City
David Holmes: Bridlington Trinity, Hull City
John Black: Scarborough, Hereford United (5), Bradford City (60-15), Wolves (6)
Ian Thompson: Worksop Town, Gainsborough Trinity, Huddersfield Town
Steve Roberts: Pontefract Colliery
Chris Gaffney: Worksop Town

Forwards
Mark Hamilton: Leeds Ashley Road
Jimmy Seal: Gainsborough Trinity, Rochdale (53-4), Darlington (122-19), York City (161-43), Barnsley (43-12), Wolves (1)
John Woodall: Frickley Athletic, Scarborough, Rotherham United, York City, Sheffield Wednesday
Stuart Lowe: Sheffield FC
Dean Lancaster: Local

GRANTHAM
Goalkeeper
Graham Hempsall: Yorkshire Main

Defenders
Stuart Franklin: Belper Town, Alfreton Town
Dave Adamson: Chester-le-Street, Boston United, Hatfield Main, South Shields, Doncaster Rovers
Mick Daley: Gainsborough Trinity, Boston FC, Scarborough, Sheffield Wednesday
Steve Richards: Lierse SK (Bel), Hull City (61-2)
Gary Elliman: Burton Albion, Buxton, Skegness Town, Boston FC, Sunderland
Rob Forman: Boston FC, Grantham
Graham Neal: Boston FC

Midfield
Dave Stewart: Goole Town, Kanberra Denmark, Scunthorpe United (97-19), Chelsea, Hull City (51-7) *(N.Ire)
Stuart Chapman: Nottingham Forest
Peter Barker: Boston FC, Spalding United
Nicky Jarvis: Long Eaton United, Grantham, Scunthorpe United (21), Grantham
Stan Farley: Harworth Colliery Institute, Denaby United

Forwards
Phil Boyer: Bulova (Hong Kong), Manchester City (20-2), Southampton (138-49), Norwich City (116-34), AFC Bournemouth (141-46), York City (109-27), Derby County *(England)
Paul Edmunds: Bentley Victoria, AFC Bournemouth (14-2), Leicester City (8-2)
Andy Ryder: Local
Gary Wilkinson: Eastwood Racing, Sheffield United
Dave Leadbeater: Bridlington Trinity, Hull City, Bridlington Trinity
Kevin Harris: Local

HORWICH RMI
Goalkeeper
Tony McMahon: Glossop, Droylsden, Chorley, Horwich RMI

Defenders
Dave Griffiths: Glossop, Witton Albion, South Liverpool, Formby
Ray Silous: Macclesfield Town, Horwich RMI, Bedford Town
Steve Waywell: Chorley, Darwen, Stalybridge Celtic
Ian Edwards: Chester
Joe Nichol: Irlam Town

Midfield
Gly Stephens: Leyland Motors
Allan Froggatt: Local
Vernon Lang: Chorley, Horwich RMI
Dennis Haslam: Local

Forwards
Paul Moss: Winsford United, Stalybridge Celtic, Darwen
Ray Redshaw: Glossop, Southport, Hyde United, Glossop, Prestwich Heys
Jimmy Garrett: Witton Albion, Chorley, Prestwich Heys, Lancaster City, Wigan Athletic
Dave Liptrot: Stockport County
Neil McLachlan: Morecambe

HYDE UNITED
Goalkeepers
Colin Darcy: Altrincham, Bury (4), Everton
Mark Deaville: Leek Town, Stafford Rangers

Defenders
Paul Knight: Chorley, Stalybridge Celtic
David Lees: Chorley, Ashton United, Stoke City
John Bingham: Chorley, Middlewich Athletic
Brian Hart: Southport, Horwich RMI, Bangor City, Glossop, Northwich Vics, Rochdale (78), Bolton
Gary Blore: Stalybridge Celtic, Hyde United, Leek Town, Hyde United, Macclesfield Town
Tony Steenson: Winsford United, Mossley

Midfield
Kevin Gorman: Mossley, Droylsden, Bacup Borough, Barrow
Colin Jackson: Chorley, Glossop
Steve Johnson: Stockport County, Manchester City
Terry Cook: Chorley, Stalybridge Celtic, Leek Town, Mossley, Stockport C
Paul Cruickshank: Altrincham, Bury (17-1), Blackpool

Forwards
Colin Skillen: Stalybridge Celtic, Macclesfield Town, Rochdale
Peter Coyne: Rio Ave Oporto (Port), Hyde United, Crewe Alexandra (134-47), Ashton United, Manchester United (2-1)
Barry Howard: Altrincham, Stockport County, Runcorn, Hyde United
Gary Riley: Stalybridge Celtic, Hyde United

MACCLESFIELD TOWN
Goalkeeper
Mike Sherlock: Mossley, Macclesfield Town, Altrincham

Defenders
Ian Elsby: Port Vale (43-1)
Neil Fairclough: Stalybridge Celtic
Mark Fielding: Runcorn, Witton Albion, Preston NE, Witton Albion
Craig Wardle: Bolton W
Graham Tobin: Altrincham, Burscough
David Kay: Bolton W

Midfield
Nigel Shaw: Congleton Town
Phil Marsden: Stafford Rangers, Prestwich Heys, Bolton W
George Urquhart: Wigan Athletic (68-6), Glasgow Rangers
Geoff Gay: Bangor City, Southport, Wigan Athletic (1), Southport (40-5), Macclesfield Town, Bolton W
Dave Goodwin: Stafford Rangers, Stoke City (22-3)
John White: Witton Albion

Forwards
Brian Griffin: Witton Albion, Nantwich Town
Syd Nolan: Burscough
Colin Kersley: Stafford Rangers, Leek Town
John Walker: Witton Albion, Nantwich Town, Leek Town, Macclesfield Town, Chester

MARINE
Goalkeepers
Brian Parkinson: South Liverpool, Marine, Los Angeles Aztecs (USA), Witton Albion, Winsford United
Dave Griffiths: Aintree Villa, South Liverpool

Defenders
Paul Dawson: Winsford United
Keith Johnson: Prescot Town
Paul Edwards: Local
Peter Smith: Los Angeles Aztecs (USA), Marine, Wrexham
Ray Mawson: Southport, Dingle Rail

Midfield
Tony Edwards: Witton Albion, Skelmersdale United, Liverpool
Alan Wilson: Southport, IFK Norrkoping (Swe), Northwich Victoria, Torquay United (42-2), Southport (134-13), Everton (2)
Dave Kelly: Witton Albion, Runcorn, Adelaide City (Aust), Oswestry Town, Everton
Mike Scott: Runcorn, Morecambe, Wigan Athletic, Everton

Forwards
Derek McClatchey: Barrow, Liverpool
Jimmy Thornton: South Liverpool
Paul Meachin: New Brighton, Southport
Jimmy Williams: Witton Albion, Oswestry Town, Liverpool
Mike Macauley: Local

MATLOCK TOWN
Goalkeeper
Mark Broughton: Scarborough, Burton Albion, Goole Town

Defenders
Ian Travis: Heanor Town, Matlock Town, Lincoln City
Colin Smith: Bury
Alan Lukasik: Oxley Park, Matlock Town
Richard Warburton: Buxton
Steve Cam: Norton Woodseats
Paul Tindle: Worksop Town, Scarborough, Lincoln City, Rotherham United
Andy Bircumshaw: King's Lynn, Mansfield Town

Midfield
Kevin Woods: Worksop Town, Tulsa Roughnecks (USA), Chesterfield
Nick Fenoughty: Buxton, Stafford Rangers, Matlock Town, St Georges Budapest (Aus), Matlock Town
Mark Jones: Worksop Town, Bentley Victoria, Frickley Athletic, Doncaster Rovers (13)
Ian Helliwell: BSC (Parkgate)
Mick Fenoughty: Crook Town, Goole Town, Sheffield United

Forwards
Bob Mountain: Alfreton Town, Grantham, Bridlington Trinity, Mexborough Town Athletic, Frickley Athletic, Bolton W, Huddersfield Town
Graham Vardy: Worksop Town
Dave Burrows: Heanor Town, King's Lynn, Lincoln City (1)
Paul Haycock: Local

MORECAMBE
Goalkeepers
John McKenna: Formby, Everton
Tod Hunter: Local

Defenders
David Carter: Lancaster City, Morecambe, Everton
John Curtis: Wigan Athletic (32), Blackburn Rovers (10), Blackpool (102)
Mark Holmes: Lancaster City, Morecambe
Kenny Tym: Marine, St Helens Town
Jack Trainer: Rochdale (7), Morecambe, Bury (1), Hong Kong Rangers, Halifax Town (105-5), Cork Hibs
Mark Baron: Lancaster City
Jimmy Weston: Wigan Athletic (69-2), Torquay United (41-1), Blackpool (112-8), Skelmersdale United
Martin Eatough: Southport, Barrow, Morecambe, Great Harwood Town

Midfield
Steve Yates: Cape Town City (SA), Morecambe, Chorley
Colin Edwards: Southport, Marine
Mark Wignal: Wigan Athletic (34)
David Lever: Local
Lee Richardson: Local

Forwards
Keith Galley: Netherfield, Morecambe, Southport (60-11), Rochdale, Telford United, Morecambe
Derek Brownbill: Oswestry Town, Stafford Rangers, Wigan Athletic (48-8), Port Vale (92-13), Liverpool (1)
Tony Quinn: Witton Albion, HJK Helsingfors (Fin), Wigan Athletic (43-14)
Bobby Grimshaw: Stalybridge Celtic, Horwich RMI, Rossendale United, Darwen
Chris O'Donnell: Wren Rovers

MOSSLEY
Goalkeeper
Andy Gray: Curzon Ashton

Defenders
Simon Gallagher: Morecambe, Lancaster City, Manchester City
Chris Conway: Glossop, Morecambe
Paul Webb: Mexborough Town Athletic, Alfreton Town, Worksop Town, Gainsborough Trinity, Bishop's Stortford, Dartford, Dagenham, Tooting & Mitcham United
Jim Curran: Local
Peter Jamieson: Glossop
Chris Hewitt: Stalybridge Celtic

Midfield
Brian Clegg: Glossop, Droylsden
Tony Keyes: Southport, Witton Albion, Ashton United, Stafford Rangers, Stockport County, Witton Albion
Mike Halliday: Prestwich Heys, Stockport County, Manchester United
Neil Wheelton: Bacup Borough, Glossop, Ashton United, Droylsden, Mossley, Wycombe Wanderers, Loughborough College
Jimmy O'Connor: Droylsden, Runcorn, Macclesfield Town, Mossley, Bury
Denzil Hart: Prestwich Heys, Ashton United
Mick Lacey: Hyde United, Leek Town, Hyde United
Mark Hoolickin: Local

One of the most successful NPL sides of recent years suffered a disappointing season for the first time for many seasons. The action here is from their 1-2 defeat at home to Workington. Photo: Leo Hoenig

Forwards
Gary Collins: Glossop, Macclesfield Town, Stalybridge Celtic
Greg Brown: Stalybridge Celtic
Tibor Szabo: Macclesfield Town, Bradford City (13-1)
Rod Bates: Local
Kevin Scarborough: Stalybridge Celtic, Hyde United
Barry Hadfield: Local
David Moore: Chester

OSWESTRY TOWN
Goalkeeper
Simon Wright: Harrisons

Defenders
Stuart Mason: Bangor City, Crewe Alexandra (4-1), Chester (137-7), Wrexham (158-3), Doncaster Rovers (1), Liverpool, Wrexham (28)
Paul Needham: Chester (60-1)
Gary Evans: Wrexham, Liverpool
Alan Hill: Wrexham (239-7)
Bob Delgado: Colwyn Bay, Oswestry Town, Dallas Tornados (USA), Port Vale (41), Chester (128-8) Rotherham United (70-5), Carlisle United (35-3), Luton Town
Nigel Edwards: Chester (9-1), Aldershot (154-6), Chester (330-3), Blackburn Rovers

Midfield
David Burns: Scarborough, Chester (78-1)
Mark Cartwright: Wrexham
David Young: Wigan Athletic (3)
Terry Farrell: Whitchurch Alport
Mark Joseph: Wrexham
Bernard Purdie: Bangor City, Crewe Alexandra (16), Huddersfield Town (46-1), Crewe Alexandra (213-44), Chester (63-14), Wrexham (10-3)

Forwards
Trevor Phillips: Stockport County (54-5), Chester (66-11), Hull City (24-3), Rotherham United (363-92)
Keith Sudlow: Local
Barry Wellings: Tranmere Rovers, Northwich Victoria, Tranmere Rovers (16-3), Rochdale (92-25), York City (47-9), Everton
Gary Simpson: Bangor City, Chester (70-18), Chesterfield (51-9)
Steve Hanlon: Yaro (Fin), Nantwich Town, Crewe Alexandra (18)
Steve Blakemore: Local
Mike Bradbourne: Wrexham

RHYL
Goalkeepers
Paul Searle: Runcorn
Trevor Ball: Local

Defenders
David Dodds: Bangor City
Robert Hughes: Local
Terry Nugent: Local
Barry Roberts: Bangor City
Paul Harrison: Local
Steve Cruse: Local

Midfield
Gary Wynne: Local
Dave Wignall: Gainsborough Trinity, Colchester United, Doncaster Rovers (41-1), Preston NE
Les Armor: Colwyn Bay
Craig Le Cornu: Oswestry Town, Tranmere Rovers (6), Everton
Richie Gendall: Oswestry Town, Chester (5)

Forwards
Andy Jones: Wrexham
Selwyn Morris: Local
Brian Davies: Winsford United, St Helens Town
Keith Warner: Local

SOUTH LIVERPOOL
Goalkeeper
Kevin O'Brien: Runcorn, Chorley, Oswestry Town, Burscough, Rhyl, New Brighton, Maghull, Everton

Defenders
Keith Featherstone: Local
Russell Hooton: Stockport County
Lawrence Iro: Altrincham, Southport, Wigan Athletic
John Carroll: Local
John Lawler: Ford Motors

Midfield
Kevin Hawkins: Altrincham
Phil McFerran: Bootle, Burscough, South Liverpool, Macclesfield Town, Witton Albion, Marine
John McInnes: Southport, Liverpool
Tony Scott: Chorley
Barry Williams: Local

Forwards
Ian Gibson: Altrincham, Nairn County
Jeff Swede: Skelmersdale United, Northwich Victoria
Paul Wilkinson: St Georges Budapest (Australia)
Alvin McDonald: Ashton United
Danny Atwere: Liverpool
Dave Martindale: Liverpool

SOUTHPORT
Goalkeeper
Paul Evans: Blackpool

Defenders
Shaun Teale: Ellesmere Port
Andy Reid: Witton Albion, Worksop Town
Ben Seddon: Macclesfield Town, Runcorn, Stafford Rangers, Wigan Athletic, Tranmere Rovers
Jay McComb: Witton Albion, South Liverpool
Kenny Freeman: Skelmersdale United
Ian Claque: Oswestry Town, Bangor City
Rob Sturgeon: Formby
Phil Warrilow: Skelmersdale United

Midfield
John McMahon: Everton
John Gauntry: Bolton W
Kevin Humphreys: Tranmere Rovers
Keith Tierney: Everton
John Millar: High Park
Neil Wood: South Liverpool, Scarborough, South Liverpool, Bridlington Town
Steve Jones: Everton
Andy Mutch: Everton

South Liverpool defenders rise to the occasion to clear a Hyde United attack in the NPL Cup Final at Maine Road. The Merseysiders went on to win on penalties.

Forwards
Billy Hughes: Mossley, Prestwich Heys, Mossley, Buxton, Droylsden, Aston Villa
John Beesley: Morecambe, Southport, Morecambe, Southport
Ray Thomas: Marine
Joe Strong: Netherfield, Mapoel Marmark (Israel), Netherfield
Ian Hodge: Witton Albion, Tranmere Rovers
Andy Sinclair: Fleetwood Hesketh
Gary Cooper: Rochdale (91-14), Horwich RMI

STAFFORD RANGERS
Goalkeepers
Barry Alcock: Witton Albion, Burton Albion, Stoke City
Carl Austin: Port Vale

Defenders
Steve Austin: Port Vale
Paul Upton: Bedworth United, Coventry Sporting
Derek Goulding: Bangor City, Altrincham, Prescot Cables
Kevin Mooney: Tranmere Rovers (25-3), Telford United, Bury (1), Bangor City
Andy Lee: Oswestry Town, Bangor City, Wrexham, Liverpool
Jos Williams: Oxford United

Midfield
Peter Carr: Burton Albion, Gainsborough Trinity, Rotherham United (36-3)
Paul Johnson: Altrincham, Chester (21-1), Stoke City (60)
Martyn Gill: Mossley, Frickley Athletic, Bridlington Trinity, Worsborough
Stuart Chapman: Port Vale

Forwards
Paul Fisher: Burton Albion, Macclesfield Town, Worksop Town, Sheffield Wednesday
Martin Hanchard: Stoke City
Steve Burr: Lichfield, Atherstone United
Chris Arnot: Hereford United

WITTON ALBION
Goalkeeper
Drew Brand: Leeds United, Hereford United (54), Everton (2)

Defenders
Benny Phillips: Mossley, Stalybridge Celtic, Bury (14), Crewe Alexandra
Noel Bradley: Mossley, Chester (35), Bury (28-1), Manchester City
Trevor Brissett: Stafford Rangers, Darlington (12), Port Vale (55), Stoke City
Micky Kilduff: Runcorn, Oswestry Town, Marine, Telford United, Oswestry Town, Bangor City
Mick Hill: Southport, Workington, Droylsden
Simon Darby: Local

Midfield
Bryn Jones: Oswestry Town, Bangor City, Scarborough, Chester City (162-17)
David Esser: Altrincham, Hyde United, Karlskrona (Swe), Apol (Cyprus), Rochdale (180-24), Everton
Franny Firth: Bury (35-4), Halifax Town (171-19), Huddersfield Town (31-4)
Don Graham: Barrow, Bury (7), Hyde United, Macclesfield Town, New Mills
Reece Moses: WBA
Graham Holder: Hyde United
Kevin Tully: Morecambe, Barrow, Bury (10-1), Chorley, Port Vale (13-2), Crewe Alexandra (86-4), Cambridge United (44-8), Blackpool (11)

Forwards
Tommy Smith: Emley, Huddersfield Town (4-1), Sheffield United
Tony Whelan: Atlanta Chiefs (USA), Fort Lauderdale Strikers (USA), Rochdale (124-20), Manchester City (6), Manchester United
Jimmy Golder: Hyde United, Stockport County
Peter Henderson: Macclesfield Town, Runcorn, Telford United, Chester (28-5), Gillingham (7-3), Chester (64-10), Witton Albion
David Holt: Mossley, Hyde United, Stalybridge Celtic, Luton Town
Steve Burns: Manchester City

WORKINGTON
Goalkeepers
John Rush: Carlisle United, Blackpool (11)
Gerard Fisher: Morecambe

Defenders
Martin Gaffney: Bury, Workington, Hartlepool
Vaughan Williams: Lancaster City, Everton
Keith Glover: Penrith, Workington
Neil McDonald: Barrow, Workington (6), Barrow
Ian Johnston: Local

Midfield
Gary Quinn: Sunderland, Wolves
Alan Carruthers: Penrith, Netherfield, Carlisle Spartans, Coventry City
John Reach: Durham City
Keith Sawyers: Penrith, Carlisle United (9)
John Smith: Halifax Town (28-6), Preston NE (91-4)

Forwards
Wayne Harrison: Blackpool (86-6), Sheffield Wednesday, Workington (4), Everton
Martin Harris: Scarborough, Hartlepool (1), Workington (106-13), Grimsby Town
Graham Gill: KTV Kokkola (Fin), Lancaster City, Netherfield, Leyland Motors
Gary Benfold: Lancaster City

Non-Contract
Dennis Wann: Morecambe, York City, Blackpool (19), Rochdale (67-7), Darlington (121-13), York City (66-7), Blackpool (17)

WORKSOP TOWN

Goalkeeper

Gil Hopkinson: Sheffield United, Spalding United, Winterton Rangers, Retford Town, Cambridge United

Defenders

Bryan Kent: Workington, Burton Albion, Nottingham Forest

John Stokes: Eastwood Town, Belper Town

Phil Annable: Grantham, Burton Albion, Boston United, Burton Albion, Mansfield Town

Tony Moore: Sheffield FC, Sheffield United (29), Burton Albion

Dave Cunnington: Local

Tracey Pettinger: Local

Andy Radford: Heanor Town, Matlock Town, Alfreton Town

Midfield

Steve Adams: Rotherham United

Martin Hardy: Notts County

Craign Thompson: King's Lynn, Gainsborough Trinity, Boston United

Craig Howard: Sheffield Wednesday, Leeds United

Martin Fox: Local

Mark Marrow: Local

Forwards

Peter Moore: Sheffield United

Steve Hiner: Maltby Miners Welfare

Mark Smith: Sheffield United

Paul Cavell: Local

N.P.L. 'Bass' Challenge Cup — Final

HYDE UNITED..........1,	SOUTH LIVERPOOL...1

(After extra time. South Liverpool won 7-6 on penalties)

N.P.L. 'President's' Cup — Final

MARINE.....................1,	WORKINGTON...........1
WORKINGTON..........0,	MARINE......................0

(After extra time. Workington won on away goals rule)

N.P.L. Challenge Shield

BURTON ALBION......2,	GATESHEAD...............0
(League Cup Winners)	(League Champions)

Manager of the Month Awards

(Sponsored by P. MacKenzie & Co. Distillers Ltd.)

Presented by Mr J.G. Watson, National Sales Manager

August 1983	VIC HALOM — Barrow
September 1983	NEIL WARNOCK — Burton Albion
October 1983	JOHN KING — South Liverpool
November 1983	PETER WRAGG — Hyde United
December 1983	BOB DUNCAN — Grantham
January 1984	BRIAN BOOTH — Macclesfield T
February 1984	MICK FENOUGHTY — Matlock T
March 1984	BRIAN GRIFFITHS — S Liverpool
April 1984	BOB MURPHY — Southport

Kevin Gorman scores from the spot for Hyde United against South Liverpool in the NPL Cup Final at Maine Road. This was the first of a series of penalty kicks which resulted in the Merseysiders winning 7-6. At least the competition lasted longer than the two European cup competitions that were decided in the same manner. Photo: John Rooney

Bangor City *Back Row (L-R): Len Davies (trainer), Alan Morris, Gareth Hughes, Glan Letheren, Jerry Banks, Phil Lunn, Paul Whelan, Steve Craven. Front Row (L-R): Kevin Westwood, Bruce Urquhart, Mr John Ross-Jones (chairman), Mark Carter, Dave Elliott, John Cavanagh, Peter Sutcliffe, Ian Howat.*
Photo: Bangor Weekly News

BANGOR CITY

Chairman: T. Owen
Manager: Dave Elliott
Coach: Dave Elliott
Physiotherapist: Len Davies
Secretary: Ken Pritchard
Address & Tel No: 0248 355836 (H)
Commercial Manager: Roy Williams
Address & Tel No: c/o Club
Press Officer & Tel No: Keith Evans (0248 712464)
Address & Tel No of ground: Farrar Road, Bangor. Tel. Bangor 351716
Club shop: Yes
Simple ground directions: To centre of town, on left by station
No of seats: 1,200 **Covered accommodation:** 6,000 **Capacity:** 10,000 **Floodlights:** Yes 192 Lux
Year formed: 1876 **Nickname:** The City **Club sponsors:** Various
Previous names: None
Club colours: Navy Blue shirts, socks and shorts
Previous grounds: Maes-y-Dref
Change colours: All Red
Day for midweek home matches: Tuesday
Previous Leagues: Lancashire Combination, Cheshire, NPL
Record attendance: 15,000 Manchester United v Wales **Year:** 1969
Best performance in: **F.A. Cup:** 1972-73, 1983-84 2nd Round
F.A. Trophy: 1983-84 Final
Clubhouse details: Open seven nights and days. Live entertainment three nights. Full snacks.
Present players with Football League experience: Bruce Urquhart (Wrexham), Ian Howat (Chester), Peter Sutcliffe (Chester), B. Purdie (Crewe)
Past players who progressed into the Football League: John McClleland (Mansfield), Kevin Mooney (Bury), Barry Ashworth (Southend)
Record transfer fee paid: Mark Carter (South Liverpool)
Record transfer fee received: £10,000 J. McClleland (Mansfield)
Programme details: 20 pages, 20p
Local newspapers & Tel No: Chronicle 352051, Daily Post 712464, Weekly News 362747
Club metal badges: Yes
Senior Honours: Northern Premier League, Northern Premier League Cup, Welsh Cup (3), Lancashire Combination Cup

Club Captain (1983-84): Mark Carter
Player of the Year (1983-84): Mark Carter
Programme Editor: Keith Evans

Matlock Town player/manager Mick Fenoughty proudly displays the Derbyshire Senior Cup which his team won for the first time in six years by beating Northern Premier League rivals Buxton 4-1 on aggregate in the final. Matlock also lifted the NPL runners-up trophy for the first time in their history while Fenoughty was named the NPL's first ever 'Manager of the Year'. The Matlock players are pictured, back-row (L-R): Colin Smith, Nick Fenoughty, Alan Lukasik (captain), Mark Jones, Mark Broughton, Graham Vardy, Andy Bircumshaw, Simon Dwyer and Kevin Woods. Front: Paul Haycock, Ian Travis, David Burrows, Steve Cam, Mick Fenoughty (player/manager), Ian Helliwell and Bob Mountain.

Photo: Derbyshire Times.

MATLOCK TOWN

President: D.T. Carr
Chairman: C. Britland
Manager: M. Fenoughty
Coach:
Physiotherapist: Peter Ruane
Secretary: K. F. Brown
Address & Tel No: Matlock 4231 (H) Parwich 301 (B)
Commercial Manager: Mrs S. Tomlinson
Address & Tel No: Matlock 3866
Press Officer & Tel No: G. M. Tomlinson (Matlock 3763)
Address & Tel No of ground: Causeway Lane, Matlock, Derbyshire. Matlock 55362 3866 **Club shop:** Yes
Simple ground directions: 500yds from Town Centre on road to Alfreton
No of seats: 200 **Covered accommodation:** 2,000 **Capacity:** 7,500 **Floodlights:** Yes
Year formed: 1885/86 **Nickname:** The Gladiators **Club sponsors:** None
Previous names: None
Previous grounds: Park Head, Matlock
Club colours: Royal Blue shirts/socks, White shorts
Change colours: Yellow shirts/socks, Blue shorts
Day for midweek home matches: Tuesdays
Record attendance: 5,123 v Burton Alb Trophy S-Final **Year:** 1975
Best performance in: F.A. Cup: 1976-7 3rd Round
F.A. Trophy: 1974-5 Winners
Previous Leagues: Matlock District, Central Alliance, Midland League
Clubhouse details: Gladiators social club situated on ground. Open six nights a week.
Present players with Football League experience: M. Fenoughty (Sheffield Utd), C. Smith (Bury)
Past players who progressed into the Football League: Wayne Biggins (Burnley, 1984)
Record transfer fee paid: £300 to Grantham for Mick Chambers
Record transfer fee received: Wayne Biggins — Burnley
Programme details: 12 pages, 10p
Programme Editor: Dennis Philips
Local newspapers: Matlock Mercury, Derbyshire Times
Club metal badges: Yes (£1)
Senior Honours: FA Challenge Trophy, N.P.L. Cup, N.P.L. Shield, Derbyshire Senior Cup (4)
Club Captain (83-84): Alan Lukasik
Player of the Year (83-4): Mark Broughton

South Liverpool's 1983/84 *squad face the camera. Back Row (L-R): Len Hawksford (trainer), Phil McFerran, Danny Atwere, Kevin O'Brien, John Carroll, John Donnelly, Lawrence Iro, George Rooney (assistant manager). Front Row: Barry Williams, Jeff Swede, John McInnes (captain), John King (manager), Gary Anderson, Tony Scott.*

SOUTH LIVERPOOL

President: J. E. Hesketh
Chairman: J. B. Smith
Manager: B. Griffiths
Asst. Manager: D. Maloney
Physiotherapist: L. Hawksford
Secretary: J. C. Stanway
Address & Tel No: 10 Olive Vale, Liverpool L15 8JH.
Tel. 051-733 1286 (H) 0253 856123 ext 374 (B)
Commercial Manager: Secretary
Address & Tel No: c/o Club
Press Officer & Tel No: M. J. Flanagan (051-734 0928)
Address & Tel No of ground: Holly Park, Garston, Liverpool 19. 051-427 7372 (Match days)
Club shop: Yes
Simple ground directions: M62, left Queens Drive, left Allerton Road, right Mather Avenue, adj. Allerton stn
No of seats: 300 **Covered accommodation:** 2,000 **Capacity:** 6,000 **Floodlights:** Yes
Year formed: 1934 **Nickname:** 'The South' **Club sponsors:** MSS
Previous names: None
Previous grounds: None
Club colours: White/Black/Red & Black
Change colours: Red & Black striped/White/Black
Day for midweek home matches: Tuesday
Record attendance: 13,000 v Nigerian XI **Year:** 1949
Best performance in: F.A. Cup: 1936-7 v QPR, 1937-8 v Brighton, 1964-5 v Workington – 2nd Rnd
F.A. Trophy: 1973-4 v Goole 2nd Rnd Proper Replay
Previous Leagues: Lancashire Combination, Cheshire League
Clubhouse details: Members club with entertainment 7 nights a week. Opening times 1.30-5.00pm, 7.00-10.30pm
Present players with Football League experience: None
Past players who progressed into the Football League: Billy Jones (Bolton), Jimmy Case (Liverpool), Joe Hinnigan (Wigan), Peter Houghton (Wigan), John Aldridge (Newport), Jim Tansey (Captain of Australia)
Record transfer fee paid: None
Record transfer fee received: £3,200 for John Aldridge to Newport
Programme details: 16 pages, 20p
Programme Editor: Alan Bartlam
Local newspapers & Tel No: Liverpool Daily Post
Liverpool Echo
Club metal badges: Yes
Senior Honours: Lancs Comb (4), Lancs Comb Cup (3), Welsh Cup, Lancs Junior Cup (4), Liverpool S.N.L. Cup, NPL Cup, Liverpool Senior Cup
Club Captain (1983-84): John Carroll **Player of the Year (1983-84)** Gary Anderson

BURTON ALBION

President: T. Bradbury
Chairman: W. H. Royall
Manager: Neil Warnock
Coach:
Physiotherapist: Chris Stanley
Press Officer & Tel No: As Secretary
Secretary: Dave Mellor
Address & Tel No: 175 Ashby Road, Burton on Trent, Staffs DE15 0LG. 0283 63394 (H) 0283 812333 (B)
Commercial Manager: Eton Park, Shakespeare Rd, Horninglow, Burton-on-Trent
Address & Tel No: 0283-65938
Address & Tel No of ground: Eton Park, Shakespeare Road, Horninglow, Burton on Trent, Staffs DE14 2RU. 0283-65938
Simple ground directions: A50 from Town Centre to Uttoxeter/Stoke, after Derby turn 4th on right. At end of road
No of seats: 300 **Covered accommodation:** 4,000 **Capacity:** 10,000 **Floodlights:** Yes
Year formed: 1950 **Nickname:** The Brewers **Club sponsors:** Ind Coope Brewery, Burton
Club shop: Yes
Club colours: Yellow/Black/Yellow
Change colours: White/Red/Red
Day for midweek home matches: Wednesday
Record attendance: 5,860 v Weymouth Southern League Cup Final 2nd leg **Year:** 1964
Best performance in: F.A. Cup: 1956 v Charlton Athletic 3rd Round
F.A. Trophy: 1974-5 v Matlock Semi-Final
Previous Leagues: Birmingham, Southern
Clubhouse details: Open to all on match days, evenings and Sunday lunchtimes
Present players with Football League experience: Kenny Blair, Pat Lally
Past players who progressed into the Football League: Barker, Buckley, Corrigan, Pollock, Potter, Swan, Ward, Richard Jobson (Watford)
Record transfer fee paid: £2,250 for Carl Swan from Buxton
Record transfer fee received: £15,000 for Richard Jobson to Watford
Programme details: 24 pages, 20p
Programme Editor: Rex Page
Club metal badges: Yes
Local newspapers & Tel No: Burton Daily Mail 0283-43311
Senior Honours: Southern League Cup 1964, Bass Charity Vase 1981, Birmingham Sen. Cup, Staffordshire Sen. Cup Bass Challenge Cup
Club Captain (83/84): David Vaughan **Player of the year:** (83-84) Paul Evans

BUXTON

President: F. Pyle
Chairman: E. Lampard
Manager: E. M. Sutherland
Coach: K. Fogg
Physiotherapist: None
Secretary: Ronald A. Malpass
Address & Tel No: 20 Alport Avenue, Fairfield, Buxton. Tel. (0298) 3443 (H)
Commercial Manager:
Address & Tel No:
Address & Tel No of ground: The Silverlands, Buxton, Derbyshire. Tel. (0298) 4733 **Club shop:** No
Simple ground directions: From Buxton Market Place opposite the County Police HQ and TA Drill Hall
No of seats: 654 **Covered accommodation:** 2,500 **Capacity:** 6,500 **Floodlights:** Yes
Year formed: 1877 **Nickname:** The Bucks **Club sponsors:** None
Previous names: None
Previous grounds: Wyelands, Buxton
Club colours: White shirts/socks, Blue shorts
Change colours: Amber shirts/socks, White shorts
Day for midweek home matches: Tuesday
Record attendance: 6,000+ v Barrow F.A. Cup 1st Round **Year:** 1962-3
Best performance in: F.A. Cup: 1951-2 v Doncaster R. 3rd Round
F.A. Trophy: 1970-1, 1971-2 Quarter-Finals
Previous Leagues: Combination, North Derbyshire, East Cheshire, Manchester, Cheshire C.
Clubhouse details: Marstons beers, all spirits, bingo, darts and dominoes. Every night, Sunday morning. Run by committee. Two tea bars. Tel. 0298 3197
Present players with Football League experience: A. Cooper, L. Harris, C. Swan
Past players who progressed into the Football League: Tony Parkes, John Froggart, Jack Gaskell, Billy Haylock
Record transfer fee paid: £2,000 by Manchester City for Billy Haydock
Record transfer fee received: £2,500 for R. Gauden from Burton Albion
Programme details: 6 pages, 10p
Club metal badges: Yes
Local newspapers & Tel No: Buxton Advertiser, (0298) 2118/2119. Matlock Mercury (Matlock 2432/3)
Senior Honours: Manchester League Champions (2), Cheshire League Champions 1972/73, Derbyshire Senior Cup Winners (6), The Presidents Cup 1981/82, Cheshire League Cup Winners (3)
Club Captain (83-84): Steve Guest
Player of the year (83-84): Wayne Oxley (Players) Les Harris (Supporters)

Buxton *Back Row (standing, L-R): K. Perrin (trainer), M. Stanley, M. Naughton, W. Oxley, A. Cooper, L. Yates, L. Haris, M. Hearn, G. Hodgkinson, M. Davis (manager). Front Row: I. Rogers, J. Denby, R. Davis, S. Guest (captain), M. Orritt, M. Hill, R. Pollard*

Burton Albion *Back Row (L-R): Neil Warnock (manager), Gary Marrow, Paul Froggatt, Steve Dolby, Ian Vaughan, Paul Evans, Nigel Simms, Doug Newton, John Whiteley, Terry Mulholland. Front Row (L-R): Ken Blair, Clive Arthur, David Vaughan (captain), Dennis Leman, David Sunley.*

CHORLEY

President: Dr P. J. Wren
Chairman: W. Conway
Manager: Tommy Haworth
Coach:
Physiotherapist: T. Lomax
Secretary: M. Wearmouth
Address & Tel No: Victory Park, Chorley. 02572 63406
Commercial Manager: None
Address & Tel No:
Press Officer & Tel No: John Newman 0254-73822 (evenings), 02572 75236 Press box
Address & Tel No of ground: Victory Park, Duke Street, Chorley PR7 3DU 02572-63406, 02572-75662 (Social Club)
Simple ground directions: A6 Manchester to Blackpool, Duke Street is off Bolton Street, half a mile from Chorley town centre
No of seats: 700 **Covered accommodation:** 4,000 **Capacity:** 15,000 **Club Shop:** On ground
Year formed: 1883 **Nickname:** Magpies **Club sponsors:** Multipart (Leyland Vehicles)
Previous names: None
Club colours: Black/White stripes, Black shorts/socks
Previous grounds: St. George's Park, Dole Lane, Rangletts
Change colours: Red
Day for midweek home matches: Tuesday
Previous Leagues: Cheshire League, Lancashire Combination, Lancashire League, Lancashire Alliance
Record attendance: 9,679 v Darwen **Year:** 1931/32
Best performance in: **F.A. Cup:** 1899-1900, 1938-9, 1945-6, 1963-4, 1978-79, 1st Round proper
F.A. Trophy: 1976-77 Quarter-finals
Clubhouse details: Open every evening, snacks available, entertainment at weekends
Present players with Football League experience: Simon Westwell (Preston NE)
Past players who progressed into the Football League: Teddy Hodgson (Burnley), Roger Heywood (Leicester), Arthur Cunliffe (Blackburn, England), Charlie Ashcroft (Liverpool, England "B"), Derek Hogg (Leicester), Paul Mariner (Plymouth, Ipswich, England), Steve Galliers (Wimbledon, Crystal Palace), Geoff Twentyman (Preston NE)
Record transfer fee paid: £900 for Geoff Twentyman from Formby
Record transfer fee received: £22,500 for Paul Mariner from Plymouth
Programme details: 12 pages, 20p
Programme Editor: Colin White
Local newspapers & Tel No: Chorley Guardian 02572 67859, Lancashire Evening Post 0772 54841
Club metal badges: Yes
Senior honours: Champions, Lancashire Alliance, Lancashire League, Lancashire Combination (Division 1 and 2). Runners-up: Lancashire Alliance, Lancashire Combination, Cheshire League. Winners ATS Lancashire FA Junior Cup (13 times), Lancashire Combination Cup, Lancashire FA Floodlit Cup. Finalists: ATS Lancashire FA Junior (12 times), Combination Cup, Cheshire League Cup, Lancashire and Cheshire Inter-League Cup
Club Captain (1983-4): Jim Clayton **Player of the Year (1983-4):** Simon Westwell

Chorley *A 1983 centenary year photograph of Chorley FC. Standing (L-R): Tom Haworth (manager), Ian Hanson (assistant manager), Andy Stafford, Simon Westwell, Colin Jackson, John Wood, Ronnie Brooks, Paul Round, Paul Knight, Terry Lomax (physio). Seated (L-R): Gary Butcher, Micky Graham, Grant Lightbown, Lienne Nowell (Centenary Princess), Jim Clayton, Chris Hunter.*

GAINSBOROUGH TRINITY

President: C. H. Caldicott, B.E.M.
Chairman: J. M. Davis
Chief Coach: Brian Fidler
Physiotherapist:
Secretary/Director: K. Marsden
Address & Tel No: Gainsborough (0427) 2577 (H) 2405 (B)
Commercial Manager: R. Hearn
Address & Tel No: Gainsborough 4307 or 3295
Press Officer & Tel No: As Secretary
Address & Tel No of ground: The Northolme, Gainsborough, Lincs (G 3295) **Club shop:** No
Simple ground directions: From town centre to General Post Office. Ground in North St 300yds from Post Office
No of seats: 400 **Covered accommodation:** 6,000 **Capacity:** 10,000 **Floodlights:** Yes
Year formed: 1873 **Nickname:** The Blues **Club sponsors:** None
Previous names: None
Previous grounds: None
Club colours: Royal Blue/White/White
Change colours: Red, Yellow
Day for midweek home matches: Tuesday
Record attendance: 9,760 v Scunthorpe Utd **Year:** 1948
Best performance in: F.A. Cup: 1959-60, 1st Round Replay v Doncaster
F.A. Trophy: 1975-6 2nd Round Replay
Previous Leagues: Football League, Midland Counties
Clubhouse details: Open every day, entertainment, food on certain nights. Steward D. Rawson. Gainsborough 3688
Present players with Football League experience: A. Lodge (Blackburn), A. Taylor (Rotherham U), T. Henson (Chesterfield)
Past players who progressed into the Football League:
Record transfer fee paid: £1,500 to Matlock for R. Barrett
Record transfer fee received: £4,000 from Sheffield Utd for S. Evans
Programme details: 12 pages, 20p
Club metal badges: Yes
Local newspapers & Tel No: Gainsborough News, Lincolnshire Echo
Senior Honours: Midland Counties League Champions & Cup Winners, N.P.L. Cup Winners, Lincolnshire Senior Cup
Club Captain (1983-84): Andy Lodge **Player of the Year (1983-84):** Bob Gauden

GOOLE TOWN

President: E. K. Holt
Chairman: S. R. Ullathorn
Manager: David Pugh
Coach: None
Physiotherapist: Stan Steadman
Press Officer & Tel No: As Secretary
Secretary: H. Harrison
Address & Tel No: 8 Devonshire Drive, Goole DM14 6PJ. Tel. 0405 4172 (H), 0405 5141 ext. 271 (B)
Commercial Manager: C. J. Raywood
Address & Tel No: 10 Woodfield Road, Goole. Goole 2476
Address & Tel No of ground: Victoria Pleasure Ground, Carter Street, Goole. Tel. Goole 2794 **Club shop:** Yes
Simple ground directions: Entering Goole, turn right at traffic lights. Carter Street is 6th street on the right
No of seats: 200 **Covered accommodation:** 4,000 **Capacity:** 8,000 **Floodlights:** Yes
Year formed: 1900 **Nickname:** Town **Club sponsors:** Autotrams (Renault)
Previous names: None
Previous grounds: None
Club colours: Blue, White, Red
Change colours: Red, White, Red
Day for midweek home matches: Tuesday
Record attendance: 8,700 v Scunthorpe **Year:** 1950
Best performance in: F.A. Cup: 1957 3rd Round Proper v Nottm Forest (A)
F.A. Trophy: 1978 Quarter-Final
Previous Leagues: Yorkshire League
Clubhouse details: None
Present players with Football League experience: K. Randall, J. Seal, J. Woodhall (Rotherham, York C)
Past players who progressed into the Football League: I. Pearson (Plymouth), J. Kaye (Scunthorpe), T. Galvin (Tottenham)
Record transfer fee paid: None
Record transfer fee received: £10,000 from Tottenham for T. Galvin
Programme details: 4 pages, 10p
Programme Editor: Secretary
Local newspapers & Tel No: Goole Times, 3391; Hull Mail, 2647
Senior Honours: West Riding Cup (10), Yorkshire Cup (4), Yorkshire League (5)
Club Captain (1983-84): Chris Jackson **Player of the Year (1983-84):** Duncan Milner

Hyde United
Back Row (L-R): Kevin Gorman, Peter Coutts, Gary Blore, Steve Johnson, Colin Jackson, Colin Darcy, Joe Connor, Brian Hart, Mark Deaville, Paul Knight, Peter Wragg (Manager). Front Row (L-R): Peter Coyne, Tony Steenson, Barry Howard, David Lees, Colin Skillen, Terry Cook.
Photo: North Cheshire Herald

Grantham *Back Row (L-R): Jock Turnbull (assistant trainer), Gary Elliman, Steve Richards, David Stewart, Grahame Hempsall, Stuart Franklin, Mick Daley, Nicky Jarvis, Terry Vallance (coach), Howard Kilbourn (secretary/director). Front Row (L-R): Robert Don-Duncan (player/manager), Phil Boyer, Stuart Chapman, Graham Neal, Peter Barker, David Leadbeater, Nigel Marshall (trainer).*
Photo: Copyright Nottingham Evening Post & Football Post

GRANTHAM F.C.

President: P.M. The Rt Hon Mrs Margaret Thatcher
Chairman (Acting): John Toon
Manager: Bob Duncan
Asst. Manager/Coach: Terry Vallance
Secretary: G. Howard Kilbourn
Address & Tel No: 35 Cliff Road, Carlton, Nottingham. Tel. 0602 876463 (H), 0602 623892 (B)
Physiotherapist: Bill Watt MSF
Commercial Manager: (Lottery) W. H. Parkinson 0476 77333; (Advertising) T. Smart 0476 68664
Press Officer & Tel No: Club Secretary
Trainer: Nigel Marshall
Address & Tel No of ground: London Road Ground, Grantham, Lincs. 0476 2011 (office), (G. 62011) **Club shop:** Yes
Simple ground directions: BR station ¼ mile. North or west to town centre, follow A52 Boston/A1 Stamford.
No of seats: 1,000 **Covered accommodation:** On three sides **Capacity:** 7,500 **Floodlights:** Yes
Year formed: 1876 **Nickname:** The Gingerbreads **Club sponsors:** Capitol Batteries, Yale Lift Trucks, Spittalgate Motors
Previous names: Grantham Town
Previous grounds: None
Club colours: Black & White stripes/Black/White
Change colours: Yellow/Black/Yellow
Day for midweek home matches: Monday
Record attendance: 6,578 v Middlesborough F.A. Cup 3rd Round **Year:** 1974
Best performance in: F.A. Cup: 1974 v Middlesborough 3rd Round
F.A. Trophy: 1971-2 v Yeovil. Quarter-Final. Lost 1-0
Previous Leagues: Midland Counties, Southern
Clubhouse details: Open 7 days a week. Licence on match day afternoons to 6.00pm. Re-open 7.00-11.00pm.
Present players with Football League experience: Phil Boyer (England, Norwich, Southampton, Manchester C), David Stewart (Northern Ireland, Chelsea, Hull City, Scunthorpe), David Adamson (England Semi Prof International, Doncaster R), Mick Daley (Sheffield Wed), Steve Richards (Hull), Paul Edmunds (Leicester, Bournemouth), Nick Jarvis (Scunthorpe), David Leadbeater (Hull City), Gary Elliman (Sunderland)
Past players who progressed into the Football League: Archie Burgin (Tottenham), Thompson (Peterborough), Jim Raynor (Notts Co.), David Dall (Scunthorpe), Robbie Cooke (Peterborough), Nicky Jarvis (Scunthorpe)
Record transfer fee paid: £2,500 for David Leadbeater from Bridlington Trinity
Record transfer fee received: £12,000 by Peterborough for Robbie Cooke
Programme details: 30 pages, 30p
Programme Editor: M. C. Korawski
Club metal badges: Yes
Local newspapers & Tel No: Grantham Weekly Shopper, 0476 67541/2; Nottingham Evening Post, 0476 3232, 0602 45521; Lincoln Echo; Grantham Journal, 0476 2291
Senior Honours: Midland League (3), Southern League Div 1 N. (2), Lincs County Cup (2), Lincs Senior Cup (8)
Club Captain (1983-84): Phil Boyer **Player of the Year (1983-84):** Phil Boyer

HORWICH R.M.I.

President: G. H. Fisher
Chairman: C. J. Healey
Manager: Ken Wright
Coach:
Physiotherapist:
Press Officer & Tel No: D. Wood (593003)
Secretary: D. J. Wood
Address & Tel No: 45 Bradshaw Meadows, Bradshaw, Bolton, Lancs. Bolton 593003
Commercial Manager: Mrs. J. McMahon
Address & Tel No: 124 Chorley Road, Adlington. 0257 482748
Address & Tel No of ground: Victoria Road, Horwich. Tel: 66908 **Club shop:** No
Simple ground directions: Ground at side of Horwich Leisure Centre
No of seats: 500 **Covered accommodation:** 3 sides **Capacity:** 6,000 **Floodlights:** Yes
Year formed: 1896 **Nickname:** Railwaymen **Club sponsors:** Cambrian Soft Drinks Ltd
Previous names: None
Previous grounds: None
Club colours: Blue & White stripes/ Blue/Blue
Change colours: All Yellow
Day for midweek home matches: Monday
Record attendance: Not known **Year:**
Best performance in: F.A. Cup: 1928, 1983 1st Round Proper
F.A. Trophy: 1978-9 1st Round Proper
Previous Leagues: Lancashire Combination, Cheshire County, North West Counties
Clubhouse details: Open each evening
Present players with Football League experience: None
Past players who progressed into the Football League: Frank Wignall (Everton, Nottm Forest, Derby C, England), Tony Caldwell (Bolton Wanderers)
Record transfer fee paid: Not known
Record transfer fee received: £2,000 from Bolton Wanderers for Tony Caldwell in 1983
Programme details: 26 pages, 20p
Programme Editor: David Wood
Club metal badges: No
Local newspapers & Tel No: Bolton Evening News Bolton 22345
Senior Honours: Lancashire Combination, Cheshire County League, Lancashire Junior Cup
Club Captain (1983-84): Vernon Lang **Player of the Year (1983-84):** Ray Redshaw

HYDE UNITED

President: Fred Pye
Chairman: Peter Pluck
Manager: Peter Wragg
Coach: Peter Wragg
Physiotherapist: Tommy Buckley
Press Officer & Tel No: Secretary
Secretary: David Goodwin
Address & Tel No: 3 Everest Close, Hyde. 061-368 6689
Commercial Manager: None
Address & Tel No:
Address & Tel No of ground: Ewen Fields, Miles Street, Hyde, Cheshire. 061-368 1031 **Club shop:** Yes
Simple ground directions: From Hyde town centre take A57 (signposted Sheffield/Barnsley), turn right at Bankfield Hotel into Grange Road, up the hill, turn right into Miles Street. Ground car park at end of street
No of seats: 650 **Covered accommodation:** 3,500 **Capacity:** 6,000 **Floodlights:** Yes
Year formed: 1919 **Nickname:** The Tigers **Club sponsors:** Boston Motors Ltd, Hyde
Day for midweek home matches: Monday **Club colours:** All Red
Record attendance: 9,500 **Year:** 1952 **Change colours:** White shirts/Black shorts/White socks
Best performance in: **F.A. Cup:** 1954 v Workington, 1st Round Proper; 1st Round 1983 v Burnley
F.A. Trophy: 1975-6, 1981-2, 2nd Round Proper
Clubhouse details: Open most nights. Full facilities, seats 180
Present players with Football League experience: C. Darcy (Everton, Bury), P. Coyne (Man U, Crewe)
Past players who progressed into the Football League: D. Constantine (Bury), D. Graham (Bury), G. Oghani (Bolton), K. Glendon (Burnley)
Record transfer fee paid: £600 for Paul Knight **Record transfer fee received:** £5,000 for David Constantine
Programme details: 20 pages, 20p
Programme Editor: M. Pavasovic
Local newspapers & Tel No: North Cheshire Herald & Hyde Reporter 061-368 3595/6, Advertiser 061-308 2621
Club metal badges: Yes
Senior Honours: Cheshire League, Cheshire Cup, Cheshire Shield, Cheshire Senior Cup
Club Captain (83-84): Tony Steenson **Player of the year (83-84):** Peter Coyne (Supporters) Terry Cook (Players)

MACCLESFIELD TOWN

Chairman: A. Brocklehurst
Manager: B. Booth
Coach: D. Berry
Psysiotherapist: M. Whiteside GP
Press Officer & Tel No: Alan Brocklehurst (0625-25141)
Secretary: John Whittaker
Address & Tel No: 7 Haddon Close, Macclesfield, Cheshire (0625-611380)
Commercial Manager: Mrs A. Messam
Address & Tel No: 5 Vine Close, Macclesfield 0625-21213 (H), 0625-24324 (B)
Address & Tel No of ground: Moss Rose Ground, London Road, Macclesfield, Cheshire. Tel. Macclesfield 24324
Simple ground directions: At south end of town on London Road to Leek (A523) **Club shop:** Yes
No of seats: 600 **Covered accommodation:** 2,000 **Capacity:** 10,000 **Floodlights:** Yes
Year formed: 1875 **Nickname:** The Silkmen **Club sponsors:** Peavdouce
Club colours: Blue/White **Change colours:** All Yellow
Day for midweek home matches: Tuesdays
Record attendance: 8,900 v Stockport County FA Cup 2nd Rnd **Year:** 1968-9
Previous League: Cheshire County
Best performance in: **F.A. Cup:** 1968-9 v Fulham 3rd Round
Clubhouse details: Match days, social club on ground under main stand
Present players with Football League experience: I. Elsby (Port Vale), N. Griffiths (Port Vale, Crewe A), G. Urquhart (Wigan A), D. Goodwin (Stoke C, Mansfield, Rochdale, Crewe A)
Past players who progressed into the Football League: G. Collier (Notts County)
Record transfer fee paid: £2,000 to Crewe for P. Connelly
Record transfer fee received: £4,000 for G. Collier from Notts Co.
Programme details: 12 pages, 15p
Club metal badges: No
Local newspapers & Tel No: Macclesfield Express, Macclesfield 24445
Senior Honours: FA Trophy Winners 1970, Cheshire League (6), N.P.L. 1968-9, 1969-70, Cheshire Senior Cup (15)
Club Captain (83-84): George Urquhart **Player of the season (83-84):** Graham Tobin

MARINE

President: D. Lucas
Chairman: P. T. Culshaw
Manager: Roly Howard
Coach: Frank O'Brien
Physiotherapist: Roger Patience
Press Officer & Tel No: John Wildman
Secretary: W. Read
Address & Tel No: 76 Sunnyside Road, Crosby, Liverpool 23. 051-924 8469
Commercial Manager: None
Address & Tel No:
Address & Tel No of ground: Rossett Park, College Road, Crosby, Liverpool 23. 051-924 4046 **Club shop:** Yes
Simple ground directions: Merseyrail N. Line, Blundellsands & Crosby station (10 min walk) Off A565 road (signposted)
No of seats: 400 **Covered accommodation:** 1,500 **Capacity:** 4,000 **Floodlights:** Yes
Year formed: 1894 **Nickname:** Mariners **Club sponsors:** Ignition Sports
Previous names: None **Club colours:** White shirts, Black shorts/socks
Previous grounds: Waterloo Park **Change colours:** Yellow shirts/socks, Blue shorts
Day for midweek home matches: Tuesday
Record attendance: 4,000 v Nigeria **Year:** 1947 **Club metal badges:** Yes
Best performance in: **F.A. Cup:** 1975-6 v Hartlepool 2nd Round
F.A. Trophy: 1983-84 Semi-Final
Previous Leagues: Liverpool Izingari, Liverpool County Comb, Lancs Comb, Cheshire
Clubhouse details: Concert room with stage for hire seats 250. Lounge bar open all week seats 150, snooker room with bar
Past players who progressed into the Football League: M. Kearney
Record transfer fee received: £23,000 for Mark Kearney (Everton)
Programme details: 20 pages, 15p
Programme Editor: John Wildman
Local newspapers & Tel No: Crosby Herald 71-36655, Liverpool Echo 051-227 2000
Senior Honours: F.A. Amateur Cup Finalists, Cheshire County League (3), Lancashire Combination Cup (3), Lancashire Junior Cup, Liverpool Senior Cup
Club Captain (1983-84): Mike Scott **Player of the Year (1983-84):** Tony Edwards

Marine *Back Row (L-R): D. Coleman, P. Meachin, B. Parkinson, M. Scott (captain), J. Thornton. Middle Row (L-R): F. O'Brien (coach), A. Wilson, P. Smith, T. Edwards, R. Patience (trainer). Front Row (L-R): J. Williams, K. Johnson, R. Howard (manager), P. Edwards, D. McClatchey.*

MORECAMBE

President: G. W. Newsham
Chairman: G. Gill
Manager: S. Gallacher
Coach: D. Edge
Physiotherapist: W. C. Carlton
Secretary: K. D. Ormrod
Address & Tel No: 0524 415324 (H) 0524 55611 x 220 (B)
Commercial Manager: L. Taylor
Address & Tel No: 0524 52593
Press Officer & Tel No: F. Weldrake
Address & Tel No of ground: Christie Park, Lancaster Road, Morecambe LA4 5TJ. 0524 411797 **Club shop:** Yes
Simple ground directions: Main Road to Town Centre
No of seats: 1,300 **Covered accommodation:** Three sides **Capacity:** 9,000 **Floodlights:** Yes
Year formed: 1920 **Nickname:** Shrimps **Club sponsors:**
Previous names: Seasiders (nickname) **Club colours:** Red shirts, Red shorts/socks
Previous grounds: Woodhill Lane **Change colours:** White shirts, Black shorts/socks
Day for midweek home matches: Tuesdays **Previous Leagues:** Lancashire Combination
Record attendance: 12,000 F.A. Cup 3rd Round v Weymouth **Year:** 1962
Best performance in: F.A. Cup: 1962 3rd Round v Weymouth **F.A. Trophy:** 1974 Winners
Clubhouse details: Open every night. New World Cup '82 Bar.
Present players with Football League experience: J. Weston (Blackpool/Wigan Ath.)
Past players who progressed into the Football League: R. Charnley (Blackpool), A. Taylor (Rochdale/West Ham)
Record transfer fee paid: £400 for K. Galley (Netherfield), N. Halsall, (Chorley)
Record transfer fee received: £2,500 from Rochdale for Alan Taylor
Programme details: 24 pages, 20p **Local newspapers & Tel No:** Morecambe Visitor 0524 414531
Programme Editors: L. Taylor and S. Middlesbrough
Club metal badges: No
Senior Honours: FA Trophy, Lancs Comb. (5), Lancs Junior Cup (3), Lancs Senior Cup, Lancs Comb. Cup (3)
Club Captain: Bob Grimshaw **Player of The Year:** Mark Baron

MOSSLEY

President: N. Brooke
Chairman: J. Wharmby **Manager:** Brian Grundy
Physiotherapist: P. Ward
Secretary: Brian Cowburn
Address & Tel No: 159 Great Norbury Street, Hyde, Cheshire SK14 1HU. 061-368 9693
Press Officer & Tel No: Secretary
Address & Tel No of ground: Seel Park, Mossley, Aston-u-Lyne, Lancs. Mossley 2369 **Club shop:** Yes
Simple ground directions: Off M62 via Saddleworth or Oldham
No of seats: 300 **Covered accommodation:** 2,000 **Capacity:** 8,000 **Floodlights:** Yes
Year formed: 1909 **Nickname:** Lilywhites **Club sponsors:** Universal Steels Ltd
Previous names: None **Club colours:** White/Black/White
Previous grounds: Luzley Park 1909-12 **Change colours:** Amber/Black/Black or Amber/Amber/Amber
Day for midweek home matches: Monday **Previous Leagues:** Ashton League, S.E. Lancs, Manchester Amateur, Lancs Comb, Cheshire C
Record attendance: 7,000+ v Stalybridge Celtic **Year:** 1950
Best performance in: F.A. Cup: 1949, 1980 2nd Round
F.A. Trophy: 1980 Final
Clubhouse details: Open every evening, Saturday and Sunday lunch, snacks available
Present players with Football League experience: Jimmy O'Connor (Bury), Tibor Szabo (Bradford)
Past players who progressed into the Football League: Arthur Tyrer (Leeds Utd), Peter Tilley (Arsenal, Bury), Don Megson (Sheffield Wed), Harvey McCreadie (Hibernian), Alan Roberts (Bradford), Gary Pierce (Huddersfield T., Wolves, Barnsley), Eamonn O'Keefe (Everton, Wigan Ath), David Young (Wigan Ath)
Record transfer fee paid: £2,300 Phil Wilson (Altrincham), £2,000 Tibor Szabo (Macclesfield), £2,000 Faz Page (Netherfield)
Record transfer fee received: £25,000 Eamonn O'Keefe (Everton), £9,000 Ian Smith (Scarborough), £3,500 Leo Skeete (Runcorn)
Programme details: 28 pages, 25p **Local newspapers & Tel No:** Mossley & Saddleworth Reporter 061-330 5311
Club metal badges: Yes
Senior Honours: FA Trophy Finalists, NPL Champs (2), NPL Runners-Up (3), NPL Cup Winners, NPL Cup Runners-Up (2), NPL Shield Runners-Up (4)
Club Captain (1983-84): Jimmy O'Connor **Players of the Year (1983-84):** Jimmy O'Connor and Tibor Szabo (joint)

OSWESTRY TOWN

Chairman: A. Jones
Manager: S. Mason
Coach:
Physiotherapist:
Press Officer & Tel No: Secretary
Secretary: W. B. Jones
Address & Tel No: 146 Whitchurch Road, Shrewsbury SY1 4EJ. 0743 3243
Commercial Manager: S. Billson
Address & Tel No: c/o Club
Address & Tel No of ground: Victoria Road, Oswestry, Shropshire. Tel. 0691 653800 **Club shop:** Yes
Simple ground directions: From north: M6, M56-Chester by-pass to Wrexham and Oswestry, through town to traffic lights, turn left, ground on right. From south: A5, turn left at Queens Head onto A5083, ground 4 miles ahead
No of seats: 500 **Covered accommodation:** 1,500 **Capacity:** 5,500 **Floodlights:** Yes
Year formed: 1860 **Nickname:** The Blues **Club sponsors:** Yes
Previous names: Oswestry United
Previous grounds: None
Club colours: Sky Blue/Royal Blue
Change colours: All Yellow
Day for midweek home matches: Wednesday
Record attendance: 5,500 v Hereford Utd FA Cup 3rd Qual Rnd **Year:** 1950
Best performance in: F.A. Cup: 1927 v Stockport, 1957 v Bournemouth (att 5,368), 1959 v Southend, 1974 v Doncaster (att 2,600) 1st Round
F.A. Trophy: 1979 2nd Round
Previous Leagues: The Combination, Lancs Combination, Welsh National, Birmingham, Cheshire Co., Southern
Present players with Football League experience: T. Storton (Chester)
Past players who progressed into the Football League: G. Williams, E. Potts, S. Sharratt, H. Roberts, G. Antonio, G. Pulley, K. Thomas, N. Hobson, B. Shadbolt, C. Sear, F. Morris, P. Bebbington, I. Hughes, J. Quinn
Record transfer fee paid: £2,000 for Jim Smith from Stafford Rangers
Record transfer fee received: £5,000 from Sheffield Wednesday for Billy Shadbolt (1953)
Programme details: 16 pages, 20p
Programme Editor: W. M. Clarke
Local newspapers & Tel No: Shropshire Star, 0691 654251; Border Counties Advertiser, 0691 655321
Senior Honours: Welsh Cup (3), Shropshire Senior Cup (10), Birmingham League, Cheshire League Cup & Shield, Border Counties Floodlit League Champions
Club Captain (1983-84): Steve Hanlon **Player of the Year (1983-84):** Steve Hanlon

Rhyl *Back Row (L-R): Paul Harrison, Brian Davies, Paul Searle*, Andy Jones, Steve Cruse, Dave Wignall. Front Row: Les Armor, Barry Horne, Dave Dodds, Gary Wynne*, Karl Lewis*, Selwyn Morris.*
** Now with Caernarfon Town FC.*
As this was an early season photograph, some regulars were not included above, namely: Trevor Ball (goalkeeper), Terry Nugent (left back), Barry Roberts (centre back), Steve Ludgam (midfield), Richie Gendall (midfield).

RHYL

Chairman: David Rhodes
Manager: Ray Jones
Physiotherapist:
Secretary: John B. Williams
Address & Tel No: 50566 (H)
Press Officer & Tel No: W. H. Prandle (37409)
Address & Tel No of ground: Belle Vue, Grange Road, Rhyl. 38327 **Club shop:** Yes
Simple ground directions: Opposite Rhyl High School
No of seats: 200 **Covered accommodation:** 2,000 **Capacity:** 6,000 **Floodlights:** Yes
Year formed: 1928 **Nickname:** Beavers **Club sponsors:** Egatube Ltd, St. Asaph, Clwyd
Previous names: Lilywhites
Previous grounds: None
Club colours: White/Blue/White
Change colours: Blue/White/Blue
Day for midweek home matches: Tuesday
Record attendance: 10,000 **Year:**
Best performance in: F.A. Cup: Please refer to 100th Cup Final programme (Rhyl F.C. were featured) 4th Round. Hold record for most consecutive appearances for Non League Club 1st Round Proper
Previous Leagues: NW Counties
Clubhouse details: Fully equipped social club
Present players with Football League experience: M. Adams, R. Gendall
Past players who progressed into the Football League: I. Edwards, G. Millington, B. Lloyd
Record transfer fee paid: None
Record transfer fee received: £2,000
Programme details: 16 pages, 20p
Local newspapers & Tel No: Rhyl Journal, Rhyl 51515
Programme Editors: Mike Newman and Arthur Johnson
Senior Honours: NW Counties League Div 1 Runners-Up 1982-83, Welsh Cup Winners 1952, 1953
Club Captain (1983-84): David Dodds
Player of the Year (1983-84): Barry Horne (supporters) Trevor Ball (players)

Southport *Back Row (L-R): R. Murphy (manager), B. Hedley (reserve team manager), S. Teale, W. Hughes, R. Sturgeon, A. Mutch, J. Beesley, N. Wood, J. Strong, A. Reid, A. Gibson (coach), C. Powell (trainer). Front Row (L-R): J. Gautrey, J. McMahon, B. Seddon, J. McComb, G. Cooper. Kneeling: Emlyn Marchant (mascot).*

SOUTHPORT

Chairman: G. Culshaw
Manager: Bob Murphy
Coach: Alex Gibson
Physiotherapist: C. Powell
Press Officer & Tel No: Peter Williams
Secretary: Peter Williams
Address & Tel No: 3 Sunnyside, Southport Merseyside PR8 2EE. 0704 66646
Commercial Manager: Charlie Clapham
Tel No: 0704 44170 (H), 051-486 6101 (B)
Address & Tel No of ground: Haig Avenue, Southport. Tel. 0704 33422. Social Club 0704 30930 **Club shop:** Yes
Simple ground directions: Signposted on all roads into Southport
No of seats: 1,576 **Covered accommodation:** Three sides **Capacity:** 15,000 **Floodlights:** Yes
Year formed: 1881 **Nickname:** The Sandgrounders **Club sponsors:** None
Previous names: Southport Vulcan, Southport Central
Club colours: Old Gold & Black
Previous ground: Ash Lane
Change colours: Blue/White trim
Day for midweek home matches: Wednesday
Previous League: Football League
Record attendance: 20,000 v Newcastle United, FA Cup **Year:** 1932
Best performance in: F.A. Cup: 1930-1 6th Round (as Football League club)
F.A. Trophy: 1978-9 1st Round
Clubhouse details: Directors', Ladies', VIP Lounges. Club on ground. (0704 30930)
Present players with Football League experience: Gary Cooper, Ben Seddon
Past players who progressed into the Football League: Numerous
Record transfer fee paid: £6,000 for Malcolm Russell
Record transfer fee received: £16,000 for Tony Field
Programme details: 24 pages, 30p
Programme Editor: Simon Williams
Club metal badges: Yes (£1 inc postage)
Local newspapers & Tel No: Southport Visitor 0704 36655 Southport Star 0704 34237 Liverpool Daily Post & Echo (051-227 2000)
Senior Honours: Division Four Champions & Runners-up
Club Captain (1983-4): Ben Seddon
Player of the Year (1983-4): Jay McComb

STAFFORD RANGERS

President: R. N. Heath
Chairman: Ed Weetham
Manager: Ron Reid 0742-471017 (H)
Physiotherapist: Mr P. S. B. Whittaker
Press Officer & Tel No: Angela Meddings 0785-52339
Secretary: G. D. Swinton
Address & Tel No: 9 Cameo Way, Stafford, Stafford 0785 58062
Commercial Manager: J. Scriven
Address & Tel No: 0785 40267
Address & Tel No of ground: Marston Road, Stafford. 0785 42750 **Club shop:** Yes
Simple ground directions: Leave at exit 14 off M6 motorway to the A34 into Stafford. First turn left over railway bridge into Co-operative Street. Ground at the end of this street
No of seats: 426 **Covered accommodation:** 3,000 **Capacity:** 9,500 **Floodlights:** Yes
Year formed: 1876 **Nickname:** The Boro **Club sponsors:** Bass + Evode
Previous names: None
Club colours: Black/White stripes
Previous grounds: Lammascotes
Change colours: Yellow
Day for midweek home matches: Tuesday
Previous Leagues: Birmingham & Dist, North Staffs, Birmingham Comb., Cheshire, Alliance Premier
Record attendance: 8,523 v Rotherham **Year:** 1975
Best performance in: F.A. Cup: 1973-4 v Peterborough 4th Round
F.A. Trophy: 1971-2 and 1978-9 Winners
Clubhouse details: Open daily. Bar, snacks, Saturday night entertainment
Present players with Football League experience: S. Chapman (Port Vale), K. Mooney (Tranmere Rovers)
Past players who progressed into the Football League: M. Aleksic (Tottenham), J. Arnold (Blackburn), R. Williams (Port Vale), M. Cullerton (Port Vale), Ken Barnes (Man C.), McIllvenny (WBA), E. Cameron (Exeter), G. Bullock (Barnsley), K. Mottershead (Doncaster)
Record transfer fee paid: £10,000 T. Dance
Record transfer fee received: £20,000 J. Arnold
Programme details: 20 pages, 20p
Programme Editor: Angela Meddings
Club metal badges: Yes
Local newspapers & Tel No: Stafford Newsletter 57700 Express & Star 52192. Sentinel 51139 Local Radio stations: Beacon Radio, Radio Stoke, Radio Signal
Senior Honours: Birmingham Combination League, Birmingham & District League, Northern Premier League, Staffs Senior Cup (7), Cheshire League Cup, F.A. Trophy (2)
Club Captain (83-84): Stuart Chapman
Player of the year (83-84): Kevan Mooney

Stafford Rangers *Back Row (L-R): Martyn Gill, Mal Meddings (assistant manager), Paul Fisher, Paul Upton, Barry Alcock, Martin Hanchard, Derek Goulding, Peter Carr, Barry Whittaker (physio). Front Row (L-R): Bob Walters (trainer), Paul Johnson, Chris Arnot, Ron Reid (manager), Kevan Mooney, Steven Burr, Andy Lee.*

WITTON ALBION

Chairman: Paul Broadhurst
Manager: Les Sutton
Coach: Kevin Tully
Physiotherapist: Eric Campbell
Press Officer & Tel No: Secretary
Secretary: D. M. Leather
Address & Tel No: 34 Grosvenor Avenue, Hartford, Northwich, Cheshire. Tel. 0606 76488 (H)
Commercial Manager:
Address & Tel No:
Address & Tel No of ground: The Central Ground, Albion Way, off Witton Street, Northwich. Tel. 0606 3008
Simple ground directions: Behind Plaza bingo hall which is situated in Witton Street, Northwich **Club shop:** Yes
No of seats: 690 **Covered accommodation:** 1,500 **Capacity:** 9,500 **Floodlights:** Yes
Year formed: 1890 **Nickname:** Albion **Club sponsors:** None
Previous names: None
Previous grounds: None
Club colours: Red/White stripes/Black/Red
Change colours: White/White/Black
Day for midweek home matches: Tuesday
Record attendance: v Northwich Victoria **Year:** 1948
Previous League: Cheshire County
Best performance in: F.A. Cup: 1951-2 v Workington 2nd Round Proper
F.A. Trophy: 1978-9, 1981-2 3rd Round Proper
Clubhouse details: Concert room, lounge. Open 7 nights per week + match days. Steward: Betty McCormick 0606 3493
Present players with Football League experience: Tommy Smith (Huddersfield T), Benny Phillips (Bury), Noel Bradley (Chester), Dave Esser (Rochdale), Drew Brand (Everton)
Past players who progressed into the Football League: Peter Mellor, Chris Nichol, Peter Henderson
Record transfer fee paid: £800 for Mick Brennan from Oswestry T.
Record transfer fee received: £10,500 for Peter Henderson from Chester
Programme details: Albion Review, 24 pages, 25p
Programme Editors: Steve Conneely, Keith Jump
Club metal badges: Yes
Local newspapers & Tel No: Northwich Guardian, 0606 3333; Northwich Chronicle, 0606 2272
Senior Honours: Cheshire County League (3), Cheshire County FA Cup (5)
Club Captain (1983-4): Benny Phillips **Player of the Year (1983-4):** Tommy Smith

Witton Albion *Back Row (L-R): Micky Kilduff, Paul Cruikshank, Tommy Smith, Trevor Brissett, Drew Brand, Stuart Parker, Noel Bradley, Franny Firth, Graham Holder, Les Sutton (manager). Front Row (L-R): Dave Holt, Jimmy Golder, Benny Phillips (captain), Don Graham, Dave Esser, Kevin Tully (coach). Inset: Derek Fortune.* Photo: Northwich Chronicle

WORKINGTON

President: E. D. Smith
Chairman: P. M. Gunn
Manager: J. Wojciechowioz
Coach: I. Wodeson
Physiotherapist: R. Lockwood
Secretary: K. Nelson
Address & Tel No: 20 College View, Whitehaven. Tel. 0946 3438 (H), 0946 65947 (B)
Commercial Manager: G. Payne
Address & Tel No: 0900 2871
Press Officer & Tel No: As Secretary
Address & Tel No of ground: Borough Park, Workington. Tel. 2871 **Club shop:** Yes
Simple ground directions: On entering Workington turn left then right at traffic lights, straight through to ground
No of seats: 1200 **Covered accommodation:** 12,000 **Capacity:** 20,000 **Floodlights:** Yes
Year formed: 1884 **Nickname:** Reds **Club sponsors:** None
Previous names: None
Previous grounds: None
Club colours: Red/Blue
Change colours: Blue/Red
Day for midweek home matches: Tuesday
Previous League: Football League
Record attendance: 21,000 v Manchester United **Year:** 1958
Best performance in: F.A. Cup: 1934 4th Round
F.A. Trophy: 1977-8
Clubhouse details: Full bar facilities, usual opening hours. Voluntary staffing
Present players with Football League experience: I. Johnston, J. Smith, M. Harris, N. McDonald, W. Harrison, K. Sawyers
Past players who progressed into the Football League: Numerous
Record transfer fee paid: B. Donaghy from WBA
Record transfer fee received: I. McDonald to Liverpool
Programme details: 16 pages, 20p
Programme Editor: Steve Durham
Local newspapers & Tel No: Workington Times and Star, 0946 5801
Club metal badges: Yes
Senior Honours: Promotion from Division Four, Cumberland Cup Winners
Club Captain (1983-84): John Reach **Player of the Year (1983-84):** John Reach

WORKSOP TOWN

President:
Chairman: L. Ferrand
Manager: T. Spencer
Physiotherapist:
Secretary: A. A. Ridsdale
Address & Tel No: 1 Wharfedale, Worksop, Notts 0909 475008 (H) 0709 582261 (B)
Commercial Manager:
Address & Tel No:
Address & Tel No of ground: Central Avenue, Worksop. Tel. 0909 480783 or 480784 **Club shop:** Yes
Simple ground directions: Opposite bus station – town centre
No of seats: 300 **Covered accommodation:** 2,000 **Capacity:** 6,000 **Floodlights:** Yes
Year formed: 1861 (Reformed 1893) **Nickname:** The Tigers **Club sponsors:** None
Previous names:
Previous grounds:
Club colours: Amber/Black
Change colours: Blue/White
Day for midweek home matches: Wednesday
Previous Leagues: Midland Counties
Record attendance: 8,171 v Chesterfield F.A. Cup **Year:** 1925
Best performance in: F.A. Cup: 1956, 1979 3rd Round
F.A. Trophy: 1971 2nd Round
Clubhouse details: "The Tigers" newly renovated offering cabaret, bar snacks and disco. Parties catered for
Present players with Football League experience: Tom Spencer (Rotherham, Lincoln, Workington), Trevor Thompson (Lincoln, Newport)
Past players who progressed into the Football League: Jack Brown (Sheffield Wed, England), Alan Hodgkinson (Sheffield Utd, England)
Record transfer fee paid:
Record transfer fee received: £2,000 from Nottingham Forest for Bert Bowrey
Programme details: 20 pages, 20p
Programme Editor: A. A. Ridsdale
Local newspapers & Tel No: Worksop Guardian 0909 474747. Worksop Star 0909 486355
Club metal badges: Yes
Senior Honours: Midland League Champions (3), Sheffield & Hallamshire Senior Cup (6), Mansfield Charity Cup
Club Captain (1983-84): David Cunnington **Player of the Year (1983-84):** Gil Hopkinson

Worksop *Back Row: John Stokes, Phil Annable, John Storey, Martin Hardy, Gil Hopkinson, Steve Hiner, Mark Marrow, David Cunnington, Trevor Thompson, Tommy Spencer (manager). Front Row: Andy Radford, Mark Smith, Paul Cavell, Peter Moore, Steve Adams, Bryan Kent, Craig Thompson.*
Photo: Worksop Guardian Series

Horwich R.M.I. F.C. *Back Row (L-R): Joe Nicholl, Steve Waywell, Alan Froggatt, Glyn Stephens, Tony McMahon, Ray Silous, Dave Liptrott, Harold Taylor (Trainer). Front Row (L-R): Wayne Lancaster, Ian Edwards, Ray Redshaw (now at Wigan), Vernon Lang, Dennis Haslam.*

Mossley *Back Row (L-R): V. Philbin, P. Webb, J. Curran, A. Grey, G. Brown, F. Page, B. Clegg, R. Partridge. Front Row: P. Ward, M. Halliday, T. Szabo, C. Hewitt, J. O'Connor, B. Hadfield, S. Gallagher.* Photo: Ashton Reporter Group of Newspapers

A floodlit scene at Causeway Lane, home of Matlock Town, where around £20,000 has been spent on ground improvements over the past year. Brand new lights have been installed and a stand has been built at the town end of the ground. Photo: Derbyshire Times.

THE NORTH WEST COUNTIES FOOTBALL LEAGUE

President: Canon J. R. Smith, MA *Chairman:* J. E. Hinchcliffe, TD
Secretary: C. R. Mahood, Burscough Nurseries, Ring O'Bells Lane, Lathom, Ormskirk, Lancashire, L40 5US. Telephone: Burscough (0704) 892150 (Business), Rufford (0704) 822688 (Home).

STALYBRIDGE CELTIC WORTHY CHAMPIONS

The second season of the new League was completed with very few problems, and a much less severe winter meant that the fixture programme was only slightly disrupted around the half-way stage.

The League Championship was won, by five clear points, by Stalybridge Celtic. Penrith clinched runners-up spot in their final match of the season when they defeated Curzon Ashton. Radcliffe Borough were waiting in the wings, as a win for Curzon would have put them in second place. Burscough, Curzon, and Radcliffe had been pressing Stalybridge hard all season.

All those connected with the league, and especially people involved with Stalybridge, were extremely disappointed when, at the Annual General Meeting of The Northern Premier League on 16th June, the Tameside Club failed in its bid for election. Ambitious clubs in the league are becoming increasingly frustrated with the delay in the introduction of automatic promotion and relegation between the Leagues in the north. Every effort is to be made during the next twelve months to try to put this right.

A magnificent effort by Fleetwood Town brought them the Second Division Championship by an eight point margin over Potteries side Eastwood Hanley. It was 18th February when Fleetwood lost their first league game of the campaign, and they dropped only twelve points in the whole season. Eastwood only pipped Irlam Town for second place at the last gasp. However, the main aim of Fleetwood and Eastwood was to gain promotion to the First Division, and this was achieved.

Clitheroe took the Third Division title, finishing five points ahead of Padiham. Here again the second position was not known until the last match of the season. Clitheroe and Padiham will compete in the Second Division in the 1984-85 season.

For the second year in succession a Second Division side reached the final of the League Challenge Cup Competition; this time it was Ellesmere Port & Neston. However, the Cheshire side went one better than did Skelmersdale United last year, defeating Stalybridge Celtic in an excellent match at Gigg Lane, Bury, by 4-2 on penalties; the match having ended in stalemate after two hours play.

Stalybridge avenged this Cup Final defeat by taking the League Champions v Cup Winners Trophy at Bower Fold by convincingly beating Ellesmere Port 3-0. This trophy had been won during the first week of the season by Burscough, the 1982-83 Champions, who defeated the 1982-83 Cup Winners Darwen. During the year it had been decided that this match would be better played at the end rather than at the beginning of each season.

The Reserve Division was increased for 1983-84, twenty-five clubs taking part. The Division was divided into two, and a subsidiary Cup Competition was run alongside the league fixtures. Irlam Town emerged as Division I Champions with Curzon Ashton finishing in runners-up position. Fleetwood Town completed a 'double' by winning the Reserve Division II, and Maghull came in second. The Reserve Division Challenge Cup was won by Skelmersdale United in a splendid final at Burscough when Curzon Ashton were the losing finalists.

There was not a great deal of success in National and County Competitions, but the following are certainly worthy of mention:

Penrith — who reached the First Round Proper of the F.A. Cup, losing at home by 0-2 to Hull City

Curzon Ashton — who won the Manchester Premier Cup, defeating fellow NWCFL side Droylsden in the final

Warrington Town — who reached the fourth round of the FA Vase, suffering 0-3 at the hands of Guiseley. The club also reached the semi-final stage of the Cheshire Senior Cup competition, only losing by the odd goal in three against Alliance Premier League team Northwich Victoria in a very entertaining final at Runcorn.

Accrington Stanley — who reached the Final of the ATS Lancashire Junior Cup Competition, losing 1-2 to NPL side South Liverpool at Wigan after a very hard-fought game

Daisy Hill — who reached the final of the Lancashire Amateur Shield, only to lose 1-2, at Victory Park, Chorley at the hands of Lonsdale.

Maghull — who lost in the Final of the Liverpool Challenge Cup by 2-3 against St Dominic's at Marine's College Road ground.

Due to the movement of clubs owing to grading standards etc, Lytham have been relegated to the Third Division; Prescot BI and Vulcan Newton have left the league; Nantwich Town and Salford have retained Second Division status. At the annual meeting Ashton Athletic and Newton gained re-election, and Colwyn Bay and Kirkby Town were admitted to the league.

Here's looking forward to the 1984-85 season. . . . Best of luck to everyone.

CHRIS MAHOOD
Secretary — NWCFL

North West Counties League

First Division

	P	W	D	L	F	A	Pts
Stalybridge Celtic	38	26	8	4	81	30	60
Penrith	38	23	9	6	88	39	55
Radcliffe Borough	38	26	3	9	79	41	55
Burscough	38	22	8	8	87	47	52
Curzon Ashton	38	21	5	12	74	51	47
Lancaster City	38	21	3	14	76	56	43*
Accrington Stanley	38	17	8	13	67	60	42
St. Helens Town	38	17	7	14	69	55	41
Congleton Town	38	18	5	15	64	50	41
Prescot Cables	38	17	6	15	72	45	40
Leek Town	38	14	10	14	56	64	38
Winsford United	38	12	12	14	49	54	36
Formby	38	14	7	17	48	61	35
Caernarfon Town	38	11	12	15	46	55	34
Glossop	38	11	11	16	38	61	33
Bootle	38	11	7	20	46	69	27*
Leyland Motors	38	9	9	20	44	79	27
Netherfield Motors	38	5	11	22	27	73	21
Ashton United	38	7	9	22	47	86	19**
Darwen	38	2	2	34	29	111	6

Second Division

	P	W	D	L	F	A	Pts
Fleetwood Town	34	24	8	2	73	24	56
Eastwood Hanley	34	21	6	7	69	35	48
Irlam Town	34	19	8	7	67	41	46
Warrington Town	34	18	7	9	65	45	43
Droylsden	34	19	5	10	59	42	43
Colne Dynamoes	34	16	9	9	55	37	41
Ellesmere P & Neston	34	12	10	12	49	38	34
Chadderton	34	14	6	14	56	46	34
Atherton L.R.	34	11	11	12	37	41	33
Wren Rovers	34	11	10	13	45	47	32
Skelmersdale United	34	13	6	15	60	63	32
Ford Motors	34	9	9	16	38	53	27
Prescot B.I.	34	9	9	16	50	66	27
Lytham	34	13	3	18	56	81	27*
Rossendale United	34	10	6	18	53	84	26
Great Harwood Town	34	5	12	17	36	60	22
Salford	34	5	11	18	24	60	21
Nantwich Town	34	8	2	24	44	73	18

Third Division

	P	W	D	L	F	A	Pts
Clitheroe	34	22	7	5	79	29	51
Padiham	34	19	8	7	58	34	46
Ashton Town	34	19	7	8	54	42	45
Oldham Dew	34	17	9	8	63	37	43
Daisy Hill	34	19	3	12	54	40	41
Maghull	34	16	8	10	60	50	40
Blackpool Mechanics	34	17	5	12	70	49	39
Atherton Collieries	34	14	9	11	54	50	37
Vulcan Newton	34	15	8	11	64	54	36*
Prestwich Heys	34	15	5	14	61	59	33*
Whitworth Valley	34	11	8	15	45	53	30
Bolton S.T.	34	10	10	14	49	64	30
Bacup Borough	34	11	9	14	65	60	27**
Nelson	34	8	10	16	49	55	26
Cheadle Town	34	9	8	17	39	67	26
Urmston Town	34	7	9	18	35	67	23
Newton	34	8	4	22	33	63	20
Ashton Athletic	34	4	3	27	30	89	11

Each asterisk denotes the deduction of two points for Breach of Rule.

NORTH WEST COUNTIES FOOTBALL LEAGUE

FIRST DIVISION RESULTS — SEASON 1983/1984

	Accrington Stanley	Ashton United	Bootle	Burscough	Caernarfon Town	Congleton Town	Curzon Ashton	Darwen	Formby	Glossop	Lancaster City	Leek Town	Leyland Motors	Netherfield	Penrith	Prescot Cables	Radcliffe Borough	St Helens Town	Stalybridge Celtic	Winsford United
Accrington Stanley	—	3-1	1-1	2-4	1-0	3-1	1-1	5-1	2-2	3-0	2-0	1-1	1-1	5-0	2-1	2-1	2-3	2-4	0-1	1-0
Ashton United	0-2	—	1-3	2-2	0-1	1-4	0-3	2-0	3-1	1-2	0-1	3-1	1-1	1-2	0-3	1-0	3-3	3-3	1-6	0-0
Bootle	1-2	3-1	—	0-4	1-1	2-1	0-3	4-1	1-2	0-1	1-1	0-1	0-0	2-1	2-6	1-1	1-2	1-3	0-2	2-0
Burscough	3-1	4-1	4-2	—	1-2	2-0	0-1	4-1	2-0	1-1	3-2	4-1	6-0	3-0	2-3	0-2	3-1	0-0	0-0	2-1
Caernarfon Town	2-2	2-1	0-2	1-2	—	0-1	3-1	4-2	2-1	0-0	2-2	0-1	1-0	0-0	1-1	0-0	1-3	1-4	0-2	1-1
Congleton Town	3-0	5-1	5-1	2-1	3-0	—	1-3	3-1	0-1	3-0	0-1	4-1	2-3	4-0	0-3	1-0	4-1	3-2	1-2	0-1
Curzon Ashton	2-3	5-2	3-1	1-2	2-1	4-3	—	7-1	2-0	1-0	2-3	2-1	2-0	4-2	2-0	0-3	1-0	2-2	3-1	0-1
Darwen	0-2	1-3	1-3	1-4	0-2	0-0	1-2	—	0-1	3-2	1-2	3-1	2-3	1-1	1-3	2-4	0-2	0-4	0-4	0-1
Formby	5-1	2-0	1-0	2-3	4-2	1-1	0-1	2-1	—	2-1	5-2	2-0	3-2	1-4	1-1	0-2	1-1	0-2	0-1	0-0
Glossop	1-3	1-1	0-1	2-2	1-1	1-0	1-1	3-1	0-1	—	2-0	0-1	3-1	1-1	0-3	1-1	2-1	0-5	1-1	1-1
Lancaster City	1-0	3-1	3-1	2-1	2-0	0-1	1-0	6-0	2-1	0-2	—	4-2	3-1	1-1	1-2	0-5	2-1	2-3	1-0	7-1
Leek Town	4-3	2-0	4-1	1-2	2-2	1-2	2-2	2-1	2-1	0-0	2-1	—	0-0	0-0	3-1	0-3	1-4	4-3	2-2	3-0
Leyland Motors	2-3	4-1	1-1	1-2	0-1	0-1	1-2	3-1	1-1	2-0	0-8	3-0	—	0-0	2-2	1-3	0-1	4-3	0-3	2-1
Netherfield	0-0	0-2	2-0	1-1	0-5	1-2	0-4	2-0	1-1	1-2	1-3	1-1	1-1	—	0-5	0-2	0-3	0-2	0-4	1-2
Penrith	5-1	4-1	0-0	5-2	0-0	1-1	4-1	5-0	3-1	6-0	0-2	3-1	2-1	1-0	—	1-4	0-1	2-1	2-2	2-0
Prescot Cables	1-2	6-3	0-2	1-1	3-0	1-1	3-2	5-0	8-0	0-1	3-1	0-2	1-2	3-1	0-2	—	1-3	0-1	0-1	0-0
Radcliffe Borough	2-0	1-1	4-0	0-2	3-2	3-0	3-1	2-0	3-0	1-2	2-1	3-1	4-0	1-0	1-2	2-1	—	2-0	2-1	4-2
St Helens Town	2-1	2-2	0-2	0-0	0-1	1-0	2-0	2-0	1-2	3-2	3-1	1-3	2-1	1-2	0-2	2-3	0-4	—	0-0	3-0
Stalybridge Celtic	2-1	0-2	4-2	4-3	4-2	6-1	2-1	4-1	2-0	2-0	2-0	1-1	5-0	1-0	0-0	2-0	2-0	1-1	—	1-0
Winsford United	1-1	0-0	2-1	0-5	2-2	0-0	0-0	2-0	1-0	6-1	2-4	1-1	6-0	3-0	2-2	4-1	1-2	2-1	2-3	—

SECOND DIVISION RESULTS — SEASON 1983/1984

	Atherton LR	Chadderton	Colne Dynamoes	Droylsden	Eastwood Hanley	Ellesmere Port & Neston	Fleetwood Town	Ford Motors	Great Harwood Town	Irlam Town	Lytham	Nantwich Town	Prescot BI	Rossendale United	Salford	Skelmersdale United	Warrington Town	Wren Rovers
Atherton LR	—	0-3	1-0	2-0	0-1	0-2	1-4	0-0	1-0	1-1	5-0	1-0	1-1	1-1	1-1	1-1	1-0	2-1
Chadderton	1-0	—	3-1	0-1	0-2	0-0	0-1	0-1	2-2	0-1	2-0	4-1	3-3	0-0	2-3	1-1	2-3	3-2
Colne Dynamoes	2-1	1-0	—	3-1	0-0	0-1	0-0	2-1	2-0	4-0	3-1	1-0	4-3	4-1	3-0	2-1	2-2	1-0
Droylsden	3-0	2-4	1-1	—	1-0	2-0	1-1	3-0	3-2	3-5	0-1	3-1	3-1	2-0	3-0	2-1	0-0	2-0
Eastwood Hanley	0-1	0-4	2-1	1-1	—	2-1	1-4	3-0	2-0	1-1	2-0	6-2	2-4	5-0	4-0	2-1	3-0	3-1
Ellesmere Port & Neston	4-2	3-0	1-1	2-0	0-1	—	0-2	5-2	0-0	3-3	3-1	3-0	2-3	4-0	0-0	3-0	1-2	1-1
Fleetwood Town	1-1	0-1	1-0	4-0	2-1	2-0	—	2-0	4-0	0-3	2-0	2-0	2-1	1-1	3-0	3-0	3-3	2-1
Ford Motors	3-0	1-0	1-1	1-2	1-2	1-0	1-1	—	0-0	1-2	3-1	2-0	3-2	0-1	2-3	4-4	3-2	1-2
Great Harwood Town	3-2	0-3	1-1	1-1	0-2	2-3	1-2	1-1	—	0-2	1-1	1-1	4-1	2-3	3-2	1-1	0-1	1-1
Irlam Town	2-1	4-2	0-4	0-2	0-0	0-0	0-2	1-0	1-1	—	0-1	4-2	2-0	4-0	4-0	3-1	1-1	2-1
Lytham	3-1	2-0	4-1	2-1	1-1	3-2	1-5	4-1	4-1	1-3	—	3-5	4-1	3-7	1-1	2-0	0-4	0-2
Nantwich Town	1-1	0-1	0-4	0-1	3-5	0-1	1-3	3-0	2-1	2-3	3-0	—	2-1	2-4	1-2	3-4	2-3	0-1
Prescot BI	0-2	1-1	1-1	2-0	0-1	1-1	0-4	0-0	1-1	2-4	1-4	1-0	—	2-0	4-1	3-3	1-2	1-1
Rossendale United	1-1	2-5	0-3	3-7	3-8	3-2	1-1	1-2	0-1	2-4	3-4	1-3	2-1	—	1-1	2-1	0-1	1-3
Salford	1-1	2-4	1-0	0-2	0-2	0-0	1-1	1-1	1-2	0-0	1-0	0-1	0-1	0-2	—	1-4	0-2	0-0
Skelmersdale United	0-1	3-1	1-0	1-3	1-3	3-1	0-1	1-0	3-1	0-7	4-0	4-2	1-3	2-3	4-1	—	1-0	4-2
Warrington Town	0-0	0-3	6-1	1-0	2-1	1-0	3-5	2-0	5-2	2-0	6-1	0-1	4-1	2-3	0-0	0-3	—	1-1
Wren Rovers	0-3	3-1	1-1	2-3	0-0	0-0	0-2	1-1	1-0	1-0	6-3	2-0	1-2	2-1	1-0	1-1	3-4	—

THIRD DIVISION RESULTS — SEASON 1983/1984

	Ashton Athletic	Ashton Town	Atherton Collieries	Bacup Borough	Blackpool Mechanics	Bolton ST	Cheadle Town	Clitheroe	Daisy Hill	Maghull	Nelson	Newton	Oldham Dew	Padiham	Prestwich Heys	Urmston Town	Vulcan Newton	Whitworth Valley
Ashton Athletic	—	0-2	0-1	1-0	0-1	1-3	0-0	0-1	1-5	2-6	0-4	3-2	1-2	0-2	0-5	2-2	2-0	2-3
Ashton Town	1-1	—	1-0	3-3	0-4	0-0	2-1	2-2	2-1	3-2	0-0	1-0	0-3	1-0	2-1	2-0	3-2	4-1
Atherton Collieries	4-1	2-2	—	1-1	1-2	0-1	3-1	2-2	1-1	1-1	1-0	2-0	0-6	2-1	3-1	3-0	2-2	1-0
Bacup Borough	0-5	0-1	2-4	—	1-2	6-3	8-2	1-3	1-2	3-1	1-0	1-1	2-2	4-0	1-3	5-0	1-2	4-1
Blackpool Mechanics	4-0	4-3	4-1	1-1	—	0-1	5-2	0-3	2-3	7-1	1-0	4-0	1-2	1-0	2-3	3-0	1-2	4-0
Bolton ST	6-3	0-0	1-4	2-0	3-2	—	1-0	1-3	1-1	2-2	2-2	1-2	0-5	1-1	4-3	3-3	0-4	3-0
Cheadle Town	2-1	1-2	0-2	1-2	1-0	1-1	—	0-0	2-1	2-1	3-1	3-2	2-1	3-5	0-0	1-3	1-4	0-2
Clitheroe	10-0	1-0	4-0	0-0	2-3	0-0	3-0	—	1-0	2-1	2-2	4-0	0-0	3-0	2-0	3-1	4-0	1-0
Daisy Hill	2-0	2-1	1-0	2-4	2-0	2-1	0-1	2-0	—	0-1	1-0	3-1	2-1	0-1	4-2	1-0	2-3	1-0
Maghull	1-0	0-2	2-0	2-1	5-2	1-0	2-1	2-1	3-1	—	4-2	1-2	2-2	2-2	0-0	0-0	2-2	0-0
Nelson	4-1	1-3	1-4	0-0	1-1	1-3	2-2	1-4	3-1	0-1	—	3-1	2-1	0-0	0-1	1-4	1-2	2-1
Newton	2-0	0-3	2-2	2-3	2-1	1-0	0-2	0-2	0-1	1-3	2-0	—	1-3	0-0	0-1	2-1	0-2	0-1
Oldham Dew	4-0	2-1	2-2	3-1	1-1	1-0	3-0	1-2	0-1	1-0	3-3	0-0	—	1-0	3-3	3-1	0-0	2-0
Padiham	1-0	4-0	2-0	3-1	4-1	6-2	0-0	4-2	1-1	3-2	2-1	4-2	2-0	—	2-0	2-0	2-1	1-0
Prestwich Heys	3-1	1-2	2-0	4-1	0-0	3-1	2-0	0-5	1-4	2-3	1-6	3-2	2-0	0-1	—	5-1	4-0	2-2
Urmston Town	1-0	1-3	1-3	0-3	0-0	2-0	1-1	0-2	1-3	0-3	1-1	2-1	1-3	1-1	1-0	—	1-1	2-1
Vulcan Newton	2-0	2-1	2-1	1-1	3-4	2-0	5-1	3-4	3-1	1-2	0-0	1-2	4-1	1-0	2-3	2-2	—	1-1
Whitworth Valley	3-2	0-1	1-1	2-2	1-2	2-2	2-2	3-1	1-0	2-1	1-4	2-0	0-1	1-1	4-0	3-1	4-2	—

Stalybridge Celtic. Top Row (left to right) O'Brien (Manager), Roberts, Keelan, Stewart, Brown, Simpson, Pawsey, Stewardson, Garmory.
Front Row (left to right) Dodd (Trainer), Mather, Butterworth, Morgan, Lutkevitch, Lutkevitch, Morley, Malcolm (Mascot).

League Challenge Cup Results 1983/1984

First Round

Ashton Athletic	0	Ford Motors	0
Ashton Town	1	Clitheroe	2
Atherton Collieries	6	Skelmersdale U	2
Bolton ST	1	Daisy Hill	1
Chadderton	3	Blackpool Mechanics	3
Eastwood Hanley	1	Nantwich Town	3
Irlam Town	1	Newton	1
Nelson	1	Oldham Dew	2
Prescot BI	1	Padiham	0
Vulcan Newton	2	Rossendale U	1
Whitworth Valley	0	Bacup Borough	1
Wren Rovers	1	Lytham	2

(Wren Rovers through by default)

Replays

Blackpool Mechanics	2	Chadderton	3
Daisy Hill	3	Bolton ST	0
Ford Motors	3	Ashton Athletic	0
Newton	2	Irlam Town	2

(Irlam Town through on Away Goals Rule)

Second Round

Atherton Collieries	0	Great Harwood Town	1
Atherton LR	0	Vulcan Newton	2
Chadderton	2	Wren Rovers	3
Cheadle Town	0	Ellesmere Port & N	2
Clitheroe	2	Irlam Town	1
Colne Dynamoes	3	Oldham Dew	0
Fleetwood Town	2	Droylsden	0
Nantwich Town	1	Ford Motors	1
Prestwich Heys	3	Maghull	1
Salford	1	Bacup Borough	1
Urmston Town	0	Prescot BI	3
Warrington Town	6	Daisy Hill	1

Replays

Bacup Borough	5	Salford	0
Ford Motors	5	Nantwich Town	0

Third Round

Accrington Stanley	5	Formby	2
Ashton United	2	Prescot Cables	1
Caernarfon Town	2	Wren Rovers	0
Clitheroe	0	St Helens Town	0
Colne Dynamoes	1	Congleton Town	1
Curzon Ashton	3	Burscough	1
Ellesmere Port & N	2	Bootle	1
Ford Motors	0	Glossop	0
Leek Town	0	Fleetwood Town	1
Leyland Motors	5	Darwen	1
Prescot BI	1	Warrington Town	1
Prestwich Heys	1	Netherfield	1
Radcliffe Borough	1	Penrith	1
Salford	0	Lancaster City	4
Stalybridge Celtic	6	Great Harwood Town	0
Vulcan Newton	1	Winsford United	0

Replays

Congleton Town	1	Colne Dynamoes	0
Netherfield	1	Prestwich Heys	0
Penrith	1	Radcliffe Borough	0
St Helens Town	2	Clitheroe	2

(Clitheroe through on Away Goals Rule)

Warrington Town	0	Prescott BI	2

Fourth Round

Accrington Stanley	2	Fleetwood Town	1
Ashton United	0	Ellesmere Port & N	0
Clitheroe	2	Netherfield	1
Curzon Ashton	0	Stalybridge Celtic	0
Lancaster City	2	Congleton Town	0
Penrith	3	Caernarfon Town	2
Prescot BI	1	Ford Motors	0
Vulcan Newton	3	Leyland Motors	1

Replays

Ellesmere Port & N	2	Ashton United	1
Stalybridge Celtic	2	Curzon Ashton	0

Quarter-Finals

Accrington Stanley	5	Prescot BI	0
Penrith	3	Clitheroe	0
Stalybridge Celtic	2	Lancaster City	1
Vulcan Newton	0	Ellesmere Port & N	1

Semi-Finals

Accrington Stanley	3	Ellesmere Port & N	4
Stalybridge Celtic	1	Penrith	0

Final

(played at Gigg Lane, Bury)

Ellesmere Port & N	0	Stalybridge Celtic	0

After Extra Time

Ellesmere Port & Neston won 4-2 on Penalties

HONOURS LIST
SEASON 1983-1984

First Division	Champions	Stalybridge Celtic
First Division	Runners-Up	Penrith
Second Division	Champions	Fleetwood Town
Second Division	Runners-Up	Eastwood Hanley
Third Division	Champions	Clitheroe
Third Division	Runners-Up	Padiham
Reserve Division I	Champions	Irlam Town
Reserve Division I	Runners-Up	Curzon Ashton
Reserve Division II	Champions	Fleetwood Town
Reserve Division II	Runners-Up	Maghull
League Challenge Cup	Winners	Ellesmere Port & Neston
League Challenge Cup	Finalists	Stalybridge Celtic
Reserve Division Cup	Winners	Skelmersdale United
Reserve Division Cup	Finalists	Curzon Ashton
League Champions v Cup Winners (1982/83)	Winners	Burscough
	Runners-Up	Darwen
League Champions v Cup Winners (1983/84)	Winners	Stalybridge Celtic
	Runners-Up	Ellesmere Port & Neston

NATIONAL AND COUNTY CUP COMPETITIONS

FA Challenge Cup	First Round Proper	Penrith
FA Challenge Trophy	Third Round Qualifying	Lancaster City
		Radcliffe Borough
		Stalybridge Celtic
FA Challenge Vase	Fourth Round	Warrington Town
Cheshire Senior Cup	Semi-Finalists	Warrington Town
Lancashire Junior Cup	Finalists	Accrington Stanley
Lancashire Amateur Shield	Finalists	Daisy Hill
Liverpool Challenge Cup	Finalists	Maghull
Manchester Premier Cup	Winners	Curzon Ashton
Manchester Premier Cup	Finalists	Droylsden

Stalybridge Celtic Skipper Dave Stewart receiving The League Champions v Cup Winners Trophy from League President Mr Eric Hinchliffe following the 3-0 triumph over Ellesmere Port & Neston. The League Challenge Cup can be seen in the background in the hands of Ellesmere Port players.

Photo: The Ashton-under-Lyne Reporter Series

Fleetwood Town — Full playing staff and officials with The Second Division Championship Trophy and Reserve Division II Championship Shield. Photo: Blackpool Gazette & Herald Ltd

The North West Counties Football League — List of clubs in division order 1984/85

FIRST DIVISION
Accrington Stanley, Bootle, Burscough, Caernarfon Town, Congleton Town, Curzon Ashton, Eastwood Hanley, Fleetwood Town, Formby, Glossop, Lancaster City, Leek Town, Leyland Motors, Netherfield, Penrith, Prescot Cables, Radcliffe Borough, St Helens Town, Stalybridge Celtic, Winsford United.

SECOND DIVISION
Ashton United, Atherton LR, Chadderton, Clitheroe, Colne Dynamoes, Darwen, Droylsden, Ellesmere Port & Neston, Ford Motors, Great Harwood Town, Irlam Town, Nantwich Town, Padiham, Rossendale United, Salford, Skelmersdale United, Warrington Town, Wren Rovers.

THIRD DIVISION
Ashton Athletic, Ashton Town, Atherton Collieries, Bacup Borough, Blackpool Mechanics, Bolton ST, Cheadle Town, Colwyn Bay, Daisy Hill, Kirkby Town, Lytham, Maghull, Nelson, Newton, Oldham Dew, Prestwich Heys, Urmston Town, Whitworth Valley.

NORTH WEST COUNTIES

	Leading Goalscorers	Hat Tricks	Penalties	Most Appearances
Accrington Stanley	Dave Hargreaves 35 Steve Parry 22 John Blackburn 9	Steve Parry David Hargreaves Errol Williams	D. Hargreaves (4)	D. Mooney 54 M. Higgins 54 D. Adams 52
Ashton United	Alvin McDonald 10 Mark Capstick Stephen Sanders		Alvin McDonald (3)	Stephen Saunders Alvin McDonald Ian Meadowcroft
Burscough	John Coleman 30 Mike Fagan 19 Tommy Duffy 13	Steve Skeete	Mike Fagan (5) John Coleman	Peter Murphy 48* Dick Johnson 47 John Coleman 46
Caernarfon Town	Meilir Owen 12 Karl Lewis 9 Billy Windle 4		Alan Morris (2)	Mike Lewis * Alan Jones * Meilir Owen *
Darwen	Martin Horsfield 10 Nigel Tebay 5		Ian Whittaker (2) Martin Horsfield	Ian Jepson 35 Ian Whittaker 34 Chris Rigly 30
Droylsden	Steve Jennings 16 Kevin Duigan 13 Mark Gledhill 10	Jennings 5 v Rossendale Gledhill 3 v Maine RD		Mark Gledhill 38 Steve Jennings 38 Mark Fallon 34
Glossop	Gary Collins 8 Ray Redshaw 7 Steve Stobart 6		Dave Ahern (2)	Mickey Brooke 45* Steve Bradley 45* Dave Ahern 34
Lancaster City	Dave Barnes 48 Andy Graham 26 Paul Fox 11 Derek Hartley 11	Dave Barnes (5) Andy Graham	Dave Barnes (5) Phil Haslam	Dave Barnes 55* Lawrie Walsh 53 Andy Graham 51
Leek Town	Andy Birch-Machin 12 Bob Horton 8 Andy Morgan 6		Gary Pearce (4)	Gary Pearce 41 Chris McMullen 41 Andy Morgan 40
Penrith	Billy Armstrong 18 Bill Gilmour 18 Les Armstrong 14	Billy Armstrong Bill Gilmour	Billy Armstrong (8)	W. Armstrong * L. Armstrong * Laurie Coulthard *
Prescot Cables	Garry Jones 13 Steve Skeete 11 Syd Nolan 6	Peter Doyle Bobby Pascoe Garry Jones (2)	Garry Jones Tony Kelly	Peter Orr 42 Joe Kelly 39 Limmy Horrocks 38
Radcliffe Borough	Gary Haworth 35 Earl Thompson 16 Darren Lloyd 13	Gary Haworth (3) Earl Thompson	Darren Lloyd (3) Steve Walton (2)	Andy Hills 49* Ian Sampson 49* Gary Haworth 43

THE NORTH WEST COUNTIES FOOTBALL LEAGUE

Leading Goalscorers by Division
Season 1983-84

Name	Club	League	League Cup	Total
FIRST DIVISION				
Barnes, D. W.	Lancaster City	32	4	36
Haworth, G.	Radcliffe Borough	31	1	32
Hargreaves, D.	Accrington Stanley	24	5	29
Coleman, J.	Burscough	25	—	25
Biddle, M.	Congleton Town	22	1	23
Morley, A.	Stalybridge Celtic	23	—	23
Armstrong, W.	Penrith	20	1	21
Edwards, J. M.	St Helens Town	20	1	21
SECOND DIVISION				
Hughes, S.	Warrington Town	23	1	24
(plus 2 goals in Reserves)				
Moran, N.	Fleetwood Town	19	3	22
Eastham, C.	Atherton L.R.	20	—	20
(plus 4 goals in Reserves)				
Shields, V.	Wren Rovers	18	2	20
Jennings, S.	Droylsden	16	—	16
White, E. A.	Eastwood Hanley	15	1	16
THIRD DIVISION				
O'Brien, F.	Bacup Borough	23	4	27
Cain, I.	Blackpool Mech	23	1	24
Ennis, C.	Prestwich Heys	20	3	23
Cheetham, M.	Padiham	22	—	22
(plus 1 goal in Reserves)				
Taylor, J.	Clitheroe	19	3	22
Proos, D.	Clitheroe	20	1	21

(D. Lunt of Ashton Town scored 14 First Team and 13 Reserve Team goals during the season)

			Reserve Cup	
RESERVE DIVISIONS				
Brewer, W.	Fleetwood Town	14	11	25
(plus 2 goals in First Team)				
Wallwork, D.	Curzon Ashton	14	11	25
(plus 2 goals in First Team)				
Dunford, G.	Radcliffe Borough	10	14	24
(plus 2 goals in First Team)				
Gibson, T.	Prescot B.I.	19	2	21
Geoghegan, M.	Irlam Town	13	6	19
Clarke, A.	Warrington Town	14	4	18
(plus 4 goals in First Team)				

NORTH WEST COUNTIES

	Leading Goalscorers	Hat Tricks	Penalties	Most Appearances
Atherton L R				
Chadderton	Stuart Anderson 14 Tony Blackman 14 Dave Gregory 11	Tony Blackman (2) Stuart Anderson Dave Gregory		Robin Smith 42* John Pemberton 41 Stuart Anderson 41
Colne Dynamoes	T. McGovern 13 P. Gregory 10 R. Walker 9	T. McGovern v Droysden	S. McKavett (3)	S. McKavett 38 A. Samuels 38 M. Byrom 36 S. Hartley 36
Ellesmere Port & Neston	Robert Owen 25 Gary Bishop 15 Kenneth Hulme 6		Gary Smith (6)	Robert Owen* Stephen Jackson Kenneth Hulme
Fleetwood Town	Norman Moran 24 Kevin Brown 20 Jimmy Hall 11	Kevin Brown Norman Moran P. Sanderson	Jimmy Hall (5) Roy Whitehouse (2)	Stewart Robinson 44 Roy Whitehouse 43 Roy Dobson 42
Ford Motors	Brian Gilligan 9 Tony McVey 8 Ritchie Longworth 5	Brian Gilligan	Tony McVey (1)	Angus Jamieson 27 Tony McVey 23 Brian Gilligan 22
Great Harwood Town	Stuart Lally 7 Paul Whittaker 4 John Kenton 4		Paul Whittaker (2)	Philip Maher 39 Kevin Dobson 36 Stuart Lally 36
Lytham	Frank Towers 15 Mel Totton 13		Frank Towers (6)	Frank Towers 26 Mick Fuller 20 Jimmy Houagan 19
Nantwich Town	Alan Young 9 Adrian Zidak 6 Ian Cooke 6		Ian Cooke (6)	Mick Smith 30 Lee Prince 22
Prescot B I				
Rossendale United	David Stones 13 David Nuggent 8 Graham Walton 7		David Stones (4)	Graham Walton 30 Bob Barras 29 Michael Gardner 29
Salford				Carl Hodgert* John Redgate* David Bates*
Wren Rovers Sports Club	Vic Shields 22 Rob Thomas 12 Clayton Smith11			Rob Thomas

ACCRINGTON STANLEY

President: J. C. Prescott
Chairman: J. S. Alty
Manager:
Coach: Gerry Keegan
Physiotherapist: A. A. Clements
Press Officer & Tel No: c/o Secretary
Secretary: M. Turner
Tel No: 'Craigholme', Blackburn Road, Clayton-le-Moss, Accrington, Lancs. 061-797 4066 (B), Accrington 31938 (H)
Commercial Manager: Rod Kenyon
Address & Tel No: 061-797 4066
Address & Tel No of ground: Crown Ground, Whalley Rd, Accrington. Tel: 383235 **Club shop:** No
Simple ground directions: From M66, take A680 to Acc. Ground two miles from town centre, behind the Crown Pub
No of seats: 80 **Covered accommodation:** 1,000 **Capacity:** 3,000 **Floodlights:** No
Year formed: 1968 **Nickname:** Stanley **Club sponsors:** Mafco Ltd
Previous names: None
Previous grounds: None
Club colours: All Red
Change colours: Yellow/Green
Day for midweek home matches: Wednesday
Record attendance: 1,200 v Blackburn Rovers **Year:** 1978
Best performance in: F.A. Cup: 1975 4th Qualifying Round
F.A. Trophy: 1972 & 1979 1st Round Proper
Previous Leagues: Lancashire Comb, Cheshire County
Clubhouse details: Open three nights a week and match days
Present players with Football League experience: D. Hargreaves (Blackburn Rovers)
Past players who progressed into the Football League: None
Record transfer fee paid: None
Record transfer fee received: Undisclosed, for D. Hargreaves (Blackburn Rovers)
Programme details: 32 pages, 20p
Programme Editor: Mark Turner
Local newspapers: Accrington Observer, Lancashire Evening Telegraph
Club metal badges: Yes
Senior Honours: Cheshire County League Div 2, Lancashire Combination (2)
Club Captain (1983-84): Ronnie Brooks **Player of the Year (1983-84):** Daryl Adams

BOOTLE

President: A. Roberts M.P.
Chairman: S. Heaney
Manager: Frank Doran
Coach: J. Horrocks
Physiotherapist: F. Brady
Secretary: Edward Lyons
Address & Tel No: 26 Dooley Drive, Netherton, Bootle L30 8RS
Commercial Manager:
Address & Tel No: 051-526 1850
Press Officer & Tel No: P. Carr (051-526 1850) **Club shop:** No
Address & Tel No of ground: Bucks Park, Northern Perimeter Road, Netherton, Merseyside. 051-526 1850
Simple ground directions: Rail: Old Roan Aintree, approx ½ mile walk to ground. Road: end of M57
No of seats: None **Covered accommodation:** 500 **Capacity:** 6,000 **Floodlights:** No
Year formed: 1952 **Nickname:** The Bucks **Club sponsors:** None
Previous names: Langton
Previous grounds: Orrell Mount Park, Bootle
Club colours: Royal Blue
Change colours: Amber
Day for midweek home matches: Wednesday
Record attendance: 750 v Carshalton, F.A. Trophy 2nd Round **Year:** 1981
Best performance in: F.A. Cup: None
F.A. Trophy: 1980-1 2nd Round Proper
Previous Leagues: Liverpool County Comb, Liverpool Shipping, Lancashire County Comb, Cheshire
Clubhouse details: Licensed bar, refreshments, entertainment
Present players with Football League experience: None
Past players who progressed into the Football League: None
Programme details: 4 pages, 10p
Local newspapers & Tel No: Bootle Times
Club metal badges: Yes
Senior Honours: Liverpool County F.A. Challenge Cup, Lancashire Amateur Cup

BURSCOUGH

President: D. Hunter
Chairman: F. Parr
Manager: M. McKenzie
Coach: W. Jaycock
Physiotherapist:
Press Officer & Tel No: Secretary
Secretary: K. Hilton
Address & Tel No: 58 Higgins Lane, Burscough, Ormskirk, Lancs. 0704 894504 (H), 0704 840775 (B)
Commercial Manager: W. Tyrer
Address & Tel No: 1 Stanley Court, Burscough, Ormskirk, Lancs. 0704 894693
Address & Tel No of ground: Victoria Park, Mart Lane, Burscough **Club shop:** Yes
Simple ground directions: 300 yards from Main Liverpool/Preston Road (A59), 3 miles north of Ormskirk
No of seats: 400 **Covered accommodation:** Main stand + one end **Capacity:** 3,500 **Floodlights:** Yes
Year formed: 1946 **Nickname:** The Linnets **Club sponsors:** None
Previous names: None
Previous grounds: None
Club colours: Green/White
Change colours: Navy Blue/Light Blue
Day for midweek home matches: Tuesday
Record attendance: 3,500 v Crewe Alexandra, F.A. Cup 1st round **Year:** 1947
Best performance in: F.A. Cup: 1959, 1977, 1979, 1980 1st Round
F.A. Trophy:
Previous Leagues: Liverpool County Comb, Lancashire Comb, Cheshire County
Clubhouse details: None
Present players with Football League experience: Dick Johnson (Tranmere)
Past players who progressed into the Football League: F. Gamble (Derby County)
Record transfer fee paid: None
Record transfer fee received: None
Programme details: 6 pages, 10p
Programme Editor: Mark Parr
Local newspapers & Tel No: Ormskirk Advertiser, Liverpool Echo, Liverpool Daily Post, Ormskirk Star
Senior Honours: Cheshire County League Cup, Cheshire County League Runners-up, Liverpool Senior Non-League Cup, Lancs Comb (2) Lancs Junior Cup (3), North West Counties Div 1
Club Captain (1983-84): Mike Fagan **Player of the Year (1983-84):** Mike Fagan

CAERNARFON TOWN

President: H. Jones
Chairman: R. A. Roberts

Secretary: H. H. Williams
Address & Tel No: 36 High Street, Caernarfon 4080 or 5325

Manager: R. Hunt
Coach: None
Physiotherapist: Ian Humphreys
Press Officer & Tel No: Mr. Griffiths. Caernarfon 3019

Commercial Manager: Mr D. Williams
Address & Tel No: Caernarfon 5906

Address & Tel No of ground: The Oval, Marcus St, Caernarfon. Tel Caernarfon 5002 **Club shop:** No
Simple ground directions: A4087 off Inner Relief Road, turn right top of the hill.
No of seats: 250 **Covered accommodation:** 1,000 **Capacity:** 4,000 **Floodlights:** Yes
Year formed: 1886, Reformed 1977 **Nickname:** Canaries **Club sponsors:** Caernarfon Motors
Previous names: Caernarfon Athletic **Club colours:** Red shirts/White shorts
Previous grounds: None **Change colours:** All Yellow
Day for midweek home matches: Wednesday
Record attendance: 6,000 v Bournemouth, F.A. Cup 2nd Round **Year:** 1929
Best performance in: F.A. Cup: 1929 2nd Round Proper, 1981-2 4th Qual Round
F.A. Trophy: 1981-2 3rd Qualifying Round
Previous Leagues: Welsh, Lancashire Comb
Clubhouse details: On the ground, run by Supporters Club
Present players with Football League experience: None
Past players who progressed into the Football League: Tommy Walley
Record transfer fee paid: None
Record transfer fee received: £1,000 for Tom Walley from Arsenal
Programme details: 24 pages, 20p
Club metal badges: No
Local newspapers & Tel No: Caernarfon & Denbigh Herald, Liverpool Daily Post
Senior Honours: Welsh League (4), Welsh Intermediate Cup, Lancashire Combination Cup, Lancashire Combination League Champions

CONGLETON TOWN

President: B. Sandbach
Chairman: J. A. Cooke
Manager: Colin Moss
Manager: D. Nixon
Coach: D. Buckley
Physiotherapist: C. Powner
Press Officer & Tel No: P. Hallett (Congleton 71234)

Secretary: R. Stanley
Address & Tel No: 61 Sandbach Road, Congleton, Cheshire Congleton (026 02) 3458 (H)
Commercial Manager: None
Address & Tel No:

Address & Tel No of ground: Booth Street, off Crescent Road, Congleton. Congleton 4022 **Club shop:** No
No of seats: 250 **Covered accommodation:** 3 stands **Capacity:** 5,000 **Floodlights:** Yes
Year formed: 1900 **Nickname:** The Town **Club sponsors:** None
Previous names: None **Club colours:** Black/White stripes, black shorts/socks
Previous grounds: None **Change colours:** Gold
Day for midweek home matches: Tuesday
Record attendance: 7,000 v Macclesfield Town **Year:** 1953/54
Best performance in: F.A. Cup: Not known
F.A. Vase: 1980-1 Round 5
Previous Leagues: Cheshire County, Mid Cheshire
Clubhouse details: Open only on match days
Present players with Football League experience: None
Past players who progressed into the Football League: L. Hamlet, D. Frost
Record transfer fee paid: None
Record transfer fee received: £5,000 for D. Frost from Leeds United
Programme details: 20/24 pages, 15p
Club metal badges: No
Local newspapers & Tel No: Congleton Chronicle, Staffs Evening Sentinel, 3737
Senior Honours: Mid Cheshire League (3) Runners-up, Cheshire Saturday Cup, County League Div 2, Cheshire Senior Cup Runners-Up 1982-83

CURZON ASHTON

President: M. Rubin
Chairman: H. Twamley
Manager: Kevin Bryan
Coach: None
Physiotherapist:
Press Officer & Tel No: None

Secretary: J. Barlow
Address & Tel No: 9 Harefield Drive, Didsbury, Manchester 061 445 7174 (H & B)
Commercial Manager: D. Brown
Address & Tel No:

Address & Tel No of ground: National Park, Katherine St, Ashton-U-Lyne 061 330 6033 **Club shop:** No
No of seats: 350 **Covered accommodation:** 350 **Capacity:** 8,000 **Floodlights:** No
Year formed: 1963 **Nickname:** Curzon **Club sponsors:** Marlyn Homes Centre
Previous names: None **Club colours:** Blue/White
Previous grounds: None **Change colours:** White/Blue
Day for midweek home matches: Monday
Record attendance: 1,826 v Stamford **Year:** 1980
Best performance in: F.A. Cup: 1981 3rd Qualifying Round
F.A. Vase: Semi-final
Previous Leagues: Manchester Amateur, Manchester, Cheshire County
Clubhouse details: Open Tue-Thur — Match Days — Social Events
Present players with Football League experience: None
Past players who progressed into the Football League: Gordon Taylor, Steve Wigley
Record transfer fee paid: None
Record transfer fee received: £2,000 for Steve Wigley (Notts Forest)
Programme details: 15p
Club metal badges: No
Local newspapers & Tel No: Ashton Reporter
Senior Honours: None

EASTWOOD HANLEY

President: P. Goel
Chairman: K. Finney
Manager: Kevin Roche
Commercial Manager: G. Eccleston
Address & Tel No: 20 Redcar Road, Trentham, Stoke-on-Trent. 0782 644063 (H), 0782 47187 (B)
Trainer: G. Plant
Secretary: C. R. Plant
Address & Tel No: 44 Rothsay Avenue, Sneyd Green, Stoke-on-Trent, Staffs ST1 6EZ. 0782 273275 (H) 0782 29581 (B)
Press Officer & Tel No: C. R. Plant
Address & Tel No of ground: Berryhill Fields, Trentmill Road, Hanley, Stock-on-Trent. 0782 29174
Simple ground directions: M6 to A500 (Junction 16) via Stoke Road, Cauldon Road and Leek Road
No of seats: 100 **Covered accommodation:** 1,000 **Capacity:** Not known **Floodlights:** Probably by Dec '83
Year formed: 1946 **Nickname:** The Potters **Club sponsors:** VGT & Graisley Trucks
Club colours: Blue/White/Blue
Change colours: All Red or All White
Previous Names: None
Previous Grounds: None
Record attendance: 5,000 v Stoke City, Brooke Brothers Testimonial **Year:** 1978
Previous Leagues: Mid Cheshire, Manchester, West Midlands Premier, Cheshire County **Programme:** From Aug '83

FLEETWOOD TOWN

Chairman: Frank Whelan
Managers: K. Byrne/A. Tinsley
Physiotherapist: M. Sillis
Press Officer & Tel No: Secretary
Secretary: J. Lawrenson
Address & Tel No: 0253 825192
Commercial Manager: Mrs R. Brand
Address & Tel No: 0253 852702
Address & Tel No of ground: Highbury Stadium, Highbury Avenue, Fleetwood, Lancs. Tel Fleetwood 6443
Simple ground directions: M6 to Broughton, M55 to A585 to Fleetwood, ground behind fire station
No of seats: 250 **Covered accommodation:** 400 **Capacity:** 4,500 **Floodlights:** Oct 84
Year formed: 1977 **Nickname:** Fishermen **Club sponsors:** None
Club colours: Red
Change colours: Blue
Previous Names: Fleetwood F.C.
Previous Grounds: None
Record attendance: v Chorley **Year:** 1978-9
Programme: Yes
Programme Editor: Mrs M. Whelan
Previous Leagues: Local, Cheshire County, Lancs Comb, NPL
Club Captain (1983-84): Keith Bowey
Player of the Year (1983-84): Stewart Robinson

FORMBY

President: R. Formby
Chairman: Chris Welsh
Manager: R. Smith
Coach: H. McAuley
Physiotherapist: G. Lloyd
Secretary: Mrs S. Welsh
Address & Tel No: 38 Green Loons Walk, Formby, Merseyside L37 2LE. Formby (07048) 77414
Commercial Manager: Secretary
Fixture Secretary: Sheila Welsh. 77414
Press Officer & Tel No: Chairman
Youth Development Officer: Vic Manning
Address & Tel No of ground: Brows Lane, Formby. Tel: Formby 72603 **Club shop:** No
Simple ground directions: Entrance in Elbow Lane, centre of Formby
No of seats: 200 **Covered accommodation:** 300 **Capacity:** 3,000 **Floodlights:** No
Year formed: 1919 **Nickname:** The Squirrels **Club sponsors:** None
Previous names: None
Club colours: Gold/Blue/Blue
Previous grounds: None
Change colours: Blue & White stripes/Blue/Blue
Day for midweek home matches:
Record attendance: 2,500 v Oldham Athletic, F.A. Cup 1st Round **Year:** 1973
Best performance in: **F.A. Cup:** 1973 1st Round Proper
F.A. Trophy:
Previous Leagues: Lancashire Combination, Cheshire
Clubhouse details: Open every night, 8.00-10.30 (except Sunday)
Present players with Football League experience: H. McAuley
Past players who progressed into the Football League: None
Record transfer fee paid: None
Record transfer fee received: £800
Programme details: New this season
Local newspaper & Tel No: Formby Times, 72237
Club metal badges: Pennants
Senior Honours: None

GLOSSOP

President: T. Boak
Chairman: A. J. McCarthy
Manager: Tony Webber
Coach:
Physiotherapist:
Secretary: Peter Hammond
Address & Tel No: 15 Longmoor Road, Simmondley, Glossop, Derbyshire SK13 9NH. Glossop 63852
Commercial Manager: None
Address & Tel No:
Press Officer & Tel No: Frank Wood (Glossop 65426)
Address & Tel No of ground: Surrey Street, Glossop. Glossop 5469 **Club shop:** Yes
Simple ground directions: Quarter-mile town centre.
No of seats: 300 **Covered accommodation:** Yes **Capacity:** 500 **Floodlights:** No
Year formed: 1886 **Nickname:** The Hillmen **Club sponsors:**
Previous names: None
Previous grounds: North Road, Glossop
Club colours: Royal Blue/Yellow trim
Change colours: Yellow/Blue trim
Day for midweek home matches: Tuesday
Record attendance: Not known **Year:**
Best performance in: F.A. Cup: Quarter-Final
F.A. Vase: 1980-1 3rd Round
Clubhouse details: Licensed. Open 6 days per week
Present players with Football League experience: None
Previous Leagues: Football League (Div 1 & 2), Manchester, Lancs Combination, North Cheshire, Cheshire County
Past players who progressed into the Football League: Ray Redshaw (Wigan)
Programme details: 20 pages, 15p
Programme Editor: Frank Wood
Local newspapers & Tel No: Glossop Chronicle & Advertiser 061-330 5311
Club metal badges: No
Senior Honours: Cheshire League Div 2 Runners-up, Football League Div 2 Runners-up
Club Captain (1983-84): Barry Kershaw **Player of the Year (1983-84):** Barry Kershaw

LANCASTER CITY

Chairman: R. Hanley
Manager: R. Danson
Coach:
Physiotherapist: A. Sweeney
Secretary: B. Roberts
Address & Tel No: 231 Bowerham Road, Newlands, Lancaster. 0524 67654
Commercial Manager: None
Address & Tel No:
Press Officer & Tel No: None
Address & Tel No of ground: Giant Axe Field, West Road, Lancaster. 0524 382238 **Club shop:** No
Simple ground directions: A6 thru' city centre, follow signs for station, immed. right over bridge, follow road to ground
No of seats: 250 **Covered accommodation:** 1,000 **Capacity:** 5,000 **Floodlights:** Yes
Year formed: 1905 **Nickname:** The Dollies **Club sponsors:** None
Previous names: Lancaster Town
Previous grounds: None
Club colours: Blue/White/Blue
Change colours: Yellow/Red/Red
Day for midweek home matches: Monday
Record attendance: 7,509 v Carlisle **Year:** 1936
Best performance in: F.A. Cup: 1972-3 v Notts County, 2nd Round Proper
F.A. Trophy: 1974-5, 1975-6
Previous League: Lancashire Combination, Northern Premier
Clubhouse details: None
Present players with Football League experience: None
Past players who progressed into the Football League: Brendan O'Callaghan, Alan Taylor
Record transfer fee paid: None
Record transfer fee received: £7,500
Programme details: Reintroduced 1984-85
Club metal badges: No
Local newspapers & Tel No: Lancaster Guardian (0524) 2525, Lancs Evening Post
Senior Honours: North West Counties League Div 1
Club Captain (1983-84): Dave Barnes

LEEK TOWN

President: B. Joyce
Chairman: G. P. Littlehales
Manager: Mike Pejic
Coach:
Physiotherapist: Mark Leather
Secretary: J. L. Reid
Address & Tel No: 2 Northam Road, Sneyo Green, Stoke-on-Trent, 0782 279062 (H) 0782 22341 (B)
Commercial Manager: None
Address & Tel No:
Press Officer & Tel No: None
Address & Tel No of ground: Hamil Park, Macclesfield Road, Leek, Staffs. Leek 383744 **Club shop:** Yes
Simple ground directions: Main Leek to Macclesfield Road (A523)
No of seats: 200 **Covered accommodation:** 1,000 **Capacity:** 5,000 **Floodlights:** Yes
Year formed: 1948 **Nickname:** Blues **Club sponsors:** Style Sports
Previous names: Leek Lowe Hamil
Previous grounds: None
Club colours: Blue shirts/socks, White shorts
Change colours: All Yellow with Red Trim
Day for midweek home matches: Tuesday
Record attendance: 3,500 v Macclesfield **Year:** 1973
Best performance in: F.A. Cup: 1975-6 4th Qualifying Round
F.A. Trophy: 1973 1st Round Proper
Previous Leagues: Staffs County, Birmingham, Manchester
Clubhouse details: Open on match days and available for hire
Present players with Football League experience: Mark Bright (Port Vale)
Past players who progressed into the Football League: Bill Summerscales
Record transfer fee paid: None
Record transfer fee received: £2,000 from Stafford Rangers for Colin Kersley
Programme details: 8 pages, 15p
Programme Editor: John Reid
Local newspapers & Tel No: Leek Post & Times, Evening Sentinel
Senior Honours: Cheshire League, Challenge Shield
Club Captain (1983-84): Andy Morgan **Player of the Year (1983-84):** Andy Birch-Machin

LEYLAND MOTORS

President: L. Southworth
Chairman: K. Kirby
Manager: T. Challenor
Coach: A. Timmins
Physiotherapist:
Secretary: J. Hickson
Address & Tel No: 395 Leyland Lane, Leyland, Lancs (07744) 31066 (H & B)
Commercial Manager: None
Address & Tel No:
Press Officer & Tel No: T. Challiner (07744) 32940
Address & Tel No of ground: Thurston Road, Leyland (STD 07744) 22400 (office hours only) **Club shop:** No
Simple ground directions: M6, exit 28, follow road into centre of Leyland (3 mins from motorway)
No of seats: 80 **Covered accommodation:** 500 **Capacity:** 5,000 **Floodlights:** Yes
Year formed: 1920 **Nickname:** Tigers **Club sponsors:** Station Garage (Leyland) Ltd
Previous names: None
Previous grounds: None
Club colours: Amber/Blue/Amber
Change colours: All Blue
Day for midweek home matches: Wednesday
Record attendance: 4,000 v Manchester City **Year:** 1981
Best performance in: F.A. Cup: 1980 2nd Qualifying Round
F.A. Vase: 1981 3rd Round
Previous Leagues: West Lancashire, Lancashire Combination, Cheshire County
Clubhouse details: Large clubhouse offering weekend entertainment, 3 bars and catering facilities
Record transfer fee paid: None
Record transfer fee received: None
Programme details: None
Club metal badges: No
Senior Honours: Lancashire Combination Cup
Local newspapers & Tel No: South Ribbe Guardian Chorley 74911

NETHERFIELD

President: J. R. Peat
Chairman: Vacant
Manager: M. Burgess
Coach: G. Inchmore
Physiotherapist: Keith Edmondson
Secretary: Pauline Bainbridge
Address & Tel No: 2 Howgill Close, Bumeude, Kendal, Cumbria. Tel. 0539 21723 (H), 0539 20028 (B)
Commercial Manager: N. Wilkinson
Address & Tel No: c/o Club
Press Officer & Tel No: T. Wilson (K. 22278 evenings)
Address & Tel No of ground: Parkside Road, Kendal, Cumbria. Tel. 0539 22278 **Club shop:** Yes
Simple ground directions: Parkside Road adjacent to "K" Shoe Factory, Kendal
No of seats: 300 **Covered accommodation:** 2,000 **Capacity:** 6,000 **Floodlights:** Yes
Year formed: 1920 **Nickname:** Field **Club sponsors:** None
Previous names: None
Previous grounds: None
Club colours: Black & White stripes/Black/Red
Change colours: All Amber
Day for midweek home matches: Tuesdays
Record attendance: 5,200 v Wrexham F.A. Cup **Year:** 1955
Best performance in: F.A. Cup: 1963 v Barnsley 2nd Round
F.A. Trophy: 1980-1 Second Round
Previous Leagues: Westmorland, West Lancashire, Lancashire Combination
Clubhouse details: Daily 1pm-5pm, 7pm-11pm. Steward: E. Forrest, Kendal 22278. Two bars seating 250.
Present players with Football League experience: None
Past players who progressed into the Football League: Michael Graham (Bolton), Jeff Wright (Wigan), John Simpson (Gillingham), Peter McDonnell (Oldham)
Record transfer fee paid: £2500 for T. Brownlee from Bradford City
Record transfer fee received: £4500 from Bradford City for T. Brownlee
Programme details: 8 pages, 15p
Club metal badges: No
Senior Honours: Lancashire Combination (2)
Local newspapers & Tel No: Westmorland Gazette 0539 20555

PENRITH

President: None
Chairman: D. Johnston
Manager: B. Williams
Coach: P. Dunne
Physiotherapist: None
Secretary: L. N. Bailey
Address & Tel No: 20 Brougham St, Penrith, Cumbria 0768 64664 (H)
Commercial Manager: None
Address & Tel No:
Press Officer & Tel No: Club Secretary
Address & Tel No of ground: Southend Road, Penrish. Tel 0768 63212 **Club shop:** No
Simple ground directions: Turn off M6 at junction 40, onto dual carriageway to Appleby & Scotch Corner, then turn off at next roundabout, approx ½-mile, into Penrish, follow A6 into town taking 1st left, for ground
No of seats: 200 **Covered accommodation:** 1,000 **Capacity:** 4,000 **Floodlights:** Yes
Year formed: 1894 **Nickname:** The Blues **Club sponsors:** Kleg Engineering
Previous names: None
Previous grounds: None
Club colours: Blue/White/Blue
Change colours: All Red
Day for midweek home matches: Wednesday
Record attendance: 4,000 v West Auckland, F.A. Amateur Cup **Year:** 1961
Best performance in: F.A. Cup: 1981-2 v Doncaster Rovers, 2nd Round
F.A. Trophy: 1980-1 1st Round
Previous Leagues: None
Clubhouse details: Open on all match days, evenings and Sunday lunchtime (Tel 0768 63212)
Present players with Football League experience: K. Sawyers, G. Mossop, G. Fell (all Carlisle)
Past players who progressed into the Football League: None
Record transfer fee paid: for A. Carruthers to Netherfield
Record transfer fee received: for B. Brown from Queen of the South
Programme details: 16 pages, 10p
Programme Editor: D. Johnston
Club metal badges: No
Local newspapers & Tel No: Cumberland & Westmorland Herald, Penrith 0768 62313. Cumberland News, Carlisle 0228 23488
Senior Honours: North West Counties League Div 1 Runners-up 1983-84
Club Captain (1983-84): Graham Mossop **Player of the Year (1983-84):** W. Gilmour

Accrington Stanley FC. Photo: John Barry

Fleetwood Town *Standing (L-R): R. Apperley (dir), F. Whelan (chairman), B. McLaughlin (groundsman), M. Rudd, C. O'Donnell, S. Robinson, R. Whitehouse, L. Milligan, K. Brown, R. Dobson, H. Furnival (coach), K. Byrne (manager), D. Lloyns (dir), J. Lawrenson (sec). Kneeling: M. Sillis (physio), D. Wann, J. Hall, M. Strachan, A. Tinsley (player/manager), K. Bowey (capt), N. Moran, A. Kennerley, Ian Meeson (mascot).*

PRESCOT CABLES

President: B. F. Taylor
Chairman: Paul Orr
Manager: G. Tansey
Coach: G. Byrne
Physiotherapist: H. Moore
Press Officer & Tel No: B. Taylor (051-426 6105)
Secretary: A. Finnigan
Address & Tel No: 24 Coronation Drive, Prescot, L35 5ER 051-426 9400 (H)
Commercial Manager: J. Richards
Address & Tel No: 10 Seascale Avenue, St. Helens 74-36845
Address & Tel No of ground: Hope Street, Prescot, Merseyside. 051-426 6819, 051-426 1286 **Club shop:** No
Simple ground directions: M6-M62 junction 7, A57 Prescot
No of seats: 600 **Covered accommodation:** 4,000 **Capacity:** 10,000 **Floodlights:** No
Year formed: 1884 **Nickname:** The Tigers **Club sponsors:** Dave Wright Sports & Speedy Fixings
Previous names: Prescot Athletic
Club colours: Yellow/Black
Previous grounds: None
Change colours: All Red
Day for midweek home matches: Wednesday
Record attendance: 8,122 **Year:** 1932
Best performance in: F.A. Cup: 1952-3, 1953-4 1st Round Proper
F.A. Vase: 1978-9, last 16
Previous Leagues: Lancashire Comb, Mid-Cheshire, Cheshire County
Clubhouse details: Concert room with bar, lounge and committee room with bar
Present players with Football League experience: Garry Jones (Bolton)
Past players who progressed into the Football League: Frank Soo (Stoke City), Eddie Kilshaw (Bury, Sheffield Wed), Bill Watkinson (Liverpool), John Quinn (Sheffield Wed), John Butler (Wigan Athletic), Tony Kelly (Wigan Athletic)
Programme details: 24 pages, 20p
Programme Editor: John Richards
Club metal badges: No
Local newspapers & Tel No: Liverpool Echo, Prescot, Huyton & Knowsley Reporter
Senior Honours: Lancs Comb Cup, Lancs Comb League, Liverpool Senior Non-League Cup (4), Liverpool Challenge Cup (6)
Club Captain (1983-84): S. Nolan
Player of the Year (1983-84): P. Orr

RADCLIFFE BOROUGH F.C. (1980)

President: C. P. Yates
Chairman: R. McLaughlin
Manager: D. Morris
Coach: Frank O'Kane
Physiotherapist: Keith Hardman
Press Officer & Tel No: S. Baguley (061-724 0343)
Secretary: G. E. Fielding
Address & Tel No: 93 Callender Street, Ramsbottom, Bury, Lancs BL0 9DU. Ramsbottom 5299
Commercial Manager: J. Pickford
Address & Tel No: 34Coronation Road, Radcliffe, Lancs 061-723 2295
Address & Tel No of ground: Stainton Park, Pilkington Road, Radcliffe, Lancs. 061-723 4181 **Club shop:** No
Simple ground directions: M62 junction 17, follow signs for Radcliffe & Whitefield
No of seats: 200 **Covered accommodation:** 5,000 **Capacity:** 5,000 **Floodlights:** No
Year formed: 1980 (Radcliffe Borough formed 1949) **Nickname:** 'Boro' **Club sponsors:** Morleys (Estate Agents)
Previous names:
Club colours: All Blue
Previous grounds: Bright Street
Change colours: All Yellow
Day for midweek home matches: Wednesday
Record attendance: 1,465 v Caernarfon Town **Year:** 1983
Best performance in: F.A. Cup:
F.A. Vase:
Previous Leagues: SE Lancs, Lancs Comb, Cheshire County
Clubhouse details: Public House "The Footballers" on ground
Record transfer fee received: £1,500 John Denham to Northwich Victoria, 1980
Programme details: 16 pages, 10p
Local newspapers & Tel No: Bury Times
Programme Editor: Miss F. Carr
Club metal badges: No
Senior Honours: NW Counties Div 2 Champions 1982-83
Club Captain (1983-84): Ian Sampson
Player of the Year (1983-84): Chris Lilley

ST HELENS TOWN

President: R. Southcote
Chairman: J. Jones
Manager: A. Wellens
Coach: S. Tickle
Physiotherapist: Dave Bingham
Press Officer & Tel No:
Secretary: W. Burrows
Address & Tel No: 48 Fisher Street, Sutton, St Helens, Merseyside WA9 3PU. 0744 811856
Commercial Manager: None
Address & Tel No:
Address & Tel No of ground: Hoghton Road, Sutton, St. Helens, Merseyside (0744 812721 – Social Club, 817225 – Secs Office) **Club shop:** No
Simple ground directions: Nr St Helens Junction station, approx 4 miles M6, M62 and M67
No of seats: 200 **Covered accommodation:** 1,000 **Capacity:** 8,000 **Floodlights:** No
Year formed: 1946 **Nickname:** Town Ground **Club sponsors:** C.M.A. (Cycles)
Previous names: None
Club colours: Blue/White/Blue
Previous grounds: None
Change colours: All Amber (or Red)
Day for midweek home matches: Tuesday
Record attendance: 4,000 **Year:**
Best performance in: F.A. Cup: 1977-8
F.A. Trophy: 1977-8
Previous Leagues: Liverpool County Comb, Lancs Combination, Cheshire County
Clubhouse details: Social club seats 850. Artistes, bingo, dances, darts, dominoes and snooker
Present players with Football League experience: Steve Murfin
Past players who progressed into the Football League: None
Record transfer fee received: None
Programme details: 10 pages,
Club metal badges: No
Senior Honours: Lancashire Combination Cup
Club Captain (1983-84): Steve Murfin
Programme Editor: Jim Barrett
Local newspapers & Tel No: St Helens Reporter, St Helens Star, Liverpool Daily Post, St. Helens Leader, Liverpool Echo
Player of the Year (1983-84): John Bendon

STALYBRIDGE CELTIC

President: J. Knott
Chairman: R. Connor
Vice Chairman: J. Hammersley
Manager: Peter O'Briern
Coach: W. Dodd
Physiotherapist: L. Brown
Press Officer & Tel No: D. Norton (Mottram 64808)
Secretary: J. Dillon
Address & Tel No: 12 Moorland Road, Carr Brook, Stalybridge, Cheshire 04575 2593 (H) 061-368 1961 (B)
Commercial Manager: J. M. Hall
Address & Tel No: 39 Bardsley Gate Avenue, Stalybridge Cheshire. Mottram 65634
Address & Tel No of ground: Bower Fold, Mottram Road, Stalybridge, Cheshire. Tel: 061-338 2828 **Club shop:** Yes
Simple ground directions: On A6108 Ashton to Glossop Road. Nearest rail station, Stalybridge (1 mile away). Bus 236 from Stalybridge bus station stops at ground (service every ½-hour)
No of seats: 500 **Covered accommodation:** 4,000 **Capacity:** 7,500 **Floodlights:** Yes
Year formed: 1909 **Nickname:** Celtic **Club sponsors:** Barcrest & Longendale Mastiffs
Previous names: None
Previous grounds: None
Club colours: All Blue
Change colours: All Red
Day for midweek home matches: Tuesday
Record attendance: 13,000 v Dick Kerr's Ladies XI **Year:**
Best performance in: F.A. Cup: 1923 v WBA, 1st Round, lost replay 0-2
F.A. Trophy: 1979-80 v Dagenham, 2nd Round, lost 0-5
1982-83 v Scarborough, 2nd Round, lost 3-1
Previous Leagues: Football League Div 3, Central, Lancashire Combination, Southern, Lancashire & Cheshire, Manchester Amateur
Clubhouse details: Bistroteque on ground, open 8pm-2am Wed, Thur, Fri & Sat. Converted railway carriage with licensed bar open on match days for spectators. Three refreshment kiosks on ground
Present players with Football League experience: R. Simpson (Stockport Co), P., Morgan (Manchester City), D. Lutkevitch (Blackburn R.), V. Garmory (Manchester City), G. Butterworth (Rochdale), A. Morley (Blackburn R.)
Past players who progressed into the Football League: E. O'Keefe (Everton), J. Anderson (Everton & Chester), E. Kerfoot (Leeds U)
Record transfer fee paid: £500 each for N. Nicklin (Droylesden), D. Bourne (Leek Town)
Record transfer fee received: £4,000 for E. Kerfoot (Leeds Utd)
Programme details: 24 pages, 20p
Prrogramme Editor: J. M. Hall
Local newspapers & Tel No: Reporter 061-330 5311, Advertiser 061-339 7611
Club metal badges: Yes
Senior Honours: Cheshire League & Shield, Cheshire Senior Cup, N W League Div 1 & Trophy Winners (all once each)
Club Captain (1983-84): P. Brown **Player of the Year (1983-84):** P. Brown

WINSFORD UNITED

President: J. Deans
Chairman: T. Cartwright
Manager: Mike Pickup
Coach: K. Davies
Physiotherapist: J. W. Dale
Press Officer & Tel No: None
Secretary: P. Warburton
Address & Tel No: 3 Massey Avenue, Winsford, Cheshire 06065 54295 (H)
Commercial Manager: None
Address & Tel No:
Address & Tel No of ground: Barton Stadium, Winsford, Cheshire. Tel: 06065 2054 **Club shop:** No
Simple ground directions: From north: Junction 19 (M6), take A533 thru' Davenham. From south: Junction 18, take A54 for Middlewich. Barton Stadium is less than ¼-mile off these main roads in the Wharton area of Winsford
No of seats: 300 **Covered accommodation:** 2,500 **Capacity:** 8,000 **Floodlights:** Yes
Year formed: 1883 **Nickname:** United **Club sponsors:** None
Previous names: None
Previous grounds: None
Club colours: Blue shirts, White trim/shorts/socks
Change colours: White with Navy trim
Day for midweek home matches: Wednesday
Record attendance: 7,000 v Witton Albion **Year:** 1947
Previous Leagues: None
Best performance in: F.A. Cup: 1975 v Peterborough Utd, 1st Round
F.A. Trophy: 1977-8 Quarter Final
Clubhouse details: Open every night. Entertainments, snacks. Steward: Mrs Edith Nancollis (3021)
Present players with Football League experience: None
Past players who progressed into the Football League: W. Hughes, J. Richardson (Sheff Utd), R. Walters (Shrewsbury), N. Southall (Bury), B. Sutton (West Ham)
Record transfer fee paid: None
Record transfer fee received: £6,000 for Nevile Southall from Bury
Programme details: 16 pages, 10p
Club metal badges: No
Local newspapers & Tel No: Winsford Guardian (2888), Winsford Chronicle
Senior Honours: Cheshire County League Champions 1976-77, Runners-Up 1979-80, Challenge Cup Winners 1949-50, 1955-56, 1959-60, 1976-77, 1978-79, 1979-80, 1980-81

DIVISION TWO

ASHTON UNITED

President:
Chairman: C. H. Buxton
Manager: Bill Chell
Coach: D. Thornley
Physiotherapist: R. Manton
Assistant Manager: Gerry Clewse
Secretary: Malcolm Smart
Address & Tel No: 55 Derby Road, Ashton-under-Lyne OL6 6PF. 061-330 3761
Commercial Manager: M. Smart
Address & Tel No: 55 Derby Road, Ashton-under-Lyne. 061-330 3761
Press Officer & Tel No: D. C. N. Jones. 061-330 3442
Address & Tel No of ground: Surrey Street, Hurst Cross, Ashton-Under-Lyne. Tel: 061-330-1511 **Club shop:** No
Simple ground directions: From town centre: up Mossley Rd, left into Queens Rd, left at X-roads on Skyline, turn left and through side streets to the ground
No of seats: 400 **Covered accommodation:** 4,000 **Capacity:** 12,000 **Floodlights:** Yes
Year formed: 1878 **Nickname:** The Robins **Club sponsors:** Smith Knight and Fay
Previous names: Hurst F.C. **Club colours:** Red & White
Previous grounds: None **Change colours:** Royal Blue shirts/socks, White shorts
Day for midweek home matches: Monday
Record attendance: 11,750 v Halifax, F.A. Cup 1st Rnd Proper **Year:** 1952-3
Best performance in: F.A. Cup: 1952-3 v Halifax, 1954-5 v Southport, 1st Rnd Proper
F.A. Trophy: 1977-8 v Wigan Athletic, 1st Round Proper
Previous Leagues: Cheshire Co, Midland Co, Lancs Comb, Manchester
Clubhouse details: Members Club. Open every day except Wed. Beers, all spirits, bingo, pool, darts, electronic games.
Present players with Football League experience: Gary Fitzgerald (Manchester City)
Past players who progressed into the Football League: Alan Ball, John Mahoney, Alf Arrowsmith, John Platt
Record transfer fee paid: Not disclosed
Record transfer fee received: £4,000 for Barnie Daniels from Manchester City
Programme details: 8 pages, 10p
Programme Editor: Stephen Jones
Local newspapers & Tel No: Ashton-U-Lyne Reporter & Advertiser
Club metal badges: No
Senior Honours: Manchester Senior Cup, Manchester League (2), Lancs Comb. Cup, Lancs Comb Div 2, Manchester Senior Cup, Reporter Cup, Manchester Premier Cup & Runners-up
Club Captain (1983-84): Stephen Saunders **Player of the Year (1983-84):** James Irvine

ATHERTON L.R.

President: J. Sumner
Chairman: A. Grundy
Manager: H. Crilly
Coach: H. Crilly
Physiotherapist: B. Dandy
Secretary: B. Seddon
Address & Tel No: 18 First Avenue, Atherton, Manchester 870872 (H)
Commercial Manager:
Press Officer & Tel No: None
Address & Tel No of ground: Crilly Park, Greendale, (Atherton 883950)
Simple ground directions: From Bolton: left at Upton Road, left Springfield Road, Left Hillside to ground.
No of seats: None **Covered accommodation:** 100 **Capacity:** 5,000 **Floodlights:** No
Year formed: 1950 **Nickname:** None **Club sponsors:** None
Club colours: Tangerine **Change colours:** Blue
Previous Names: Laburnum Rovers **Previous Grounds:** Hag Fold Playing Fields
Record attendance: Not known
Previous Leagues: Bolton Combination **Programme:** None

CHADDERTON

President: L. F. Conroy
Chairman: N. H. McDonnell
Manager: R. Ashton
Coach:
Physiotherapist: None
Secretary: John Regan
Address & Tel No: 3 Hill Top, Healds Green, Chadderton, Oldham OL1 2SB. 061-624 3307 (H), 061-834 4079 (B)
Commercial Manager:
Address & Tel No:
Press Officer & Tel No: R. T. Barber (061-620 7507)
Address & Tel No of ground: Broadway, Chadderton (061-624 9733) **Club shop:** No
Simple ground directions: M62 to junction 20, A627(M) to ground
No of seats: None **Covered accommodation:** 200 **Capacity:** Not known **Floodlights:** No
Year formed: 1947 **Nickname:** None **Club sponsors:** Focus TV & Video Rentals Ltd
Previous names: Millbrow, North Chadderton Amateurs **Club colours:** Red/Navy/Red
Previous grounds: None **Change colours:** Blue/Black stripes, Blue shorts
Day for midweek home matches: Tuesday or Wednesday
Record attendance: 1,500 v Guinness Export, F.A. Amateur Cup **Year:** 1969
Best performance in: F.A. Cup: Unknown
F.A. Vase: 1980 3rd Round
Previous Leagues: Oldham Amateur, South East Lancs, Manchester Amateur, Manchester, Lancs Comb
Clubhouse details: Players lounge, refreshment room, licensed bar, toilets
Present players with Football League experience: None
Past players who progressed into the Football League: Graham Bell (Oldham Ath, Preston North End, Bolton Wanderers), Paul Hilton (Bury, West Ham)
Record transfer fee paid: None
Record transfer fee received: None
Programme details: 18 pages, 10p **Local newspaper & Tel No:** Oldham Evening Chronicle
Club metal badges: No
Senior Honours: Manchester League Gilgryst Cup
Club Captain (1983-84): Tony Blackman **Player of the Year (1983-84):** Stuart Anderson

CLITHEROE

Chairman: C. H. Whiteside
Manager: Eric Whalley
Secretary: C. Wilson
Address & Tel No: 4 Moss Street, Clitheroe, Lancs Clitheroe 24370
Address & Tel No of ground: Shawbridge, Clitheroe. 23344
Club colours: Royal Blue with thin White stripe/Royal Blue/Royal Blue
Programme: Yes
Change colours: Red with thin White stripes/Red/Red

COLNE DYNAMOES

President:
Chairman: H. Pickup
Manager: G. L. White
Coach: G. L. White
Physiotherapist: S. Parkinson
Secretary: P. Terry
Address & Tel No: Colne 866768
Commercial Manager: None
Press Officer: None
Address & Tel No of ground: Holt House, Colne. 862335
Club shop: No
Simple ground directions: Go to top of Harrison Drive, Colne
No of seats: 25 **Covered accommodation:** 200 **Capacity:** 2,000 **Floodlights:** No
Year formed: 1962 **Nickname:** Dynamoes **Club sponsors:** Riddiough's Timber (Raab Marcher) Colne
Previous names: None
Previous grounds: None
Club colours: All Red
Change colours: All Sky Blue
Day for midweek home matches: Wednesday
Record attendance: 1,200 **Year:** 1979
Best performance in: F.A. Cup: Unknown
F.A. Vase:
Clubhouse details: None
Previous Leagues: Lancs Combination, West Lancs, Burnley Comb, Nelson & Colne Prem
Present players with Football League experience: None
Past players who progressed into the Football League: Kevin Hird
Record transfer fee paid: None
Record transfer fee received: None
Programme details:
Club metal badges: No
Local newspaper & Tel No: Nelson Leader/Colne Times, Nelson 62561
Senior Honours: NW Counties Div 3 Champions 1982-83, Lancashire Combination Runners-Up 1980-81, 1981-82
Club Captain (1983-84): Andrew Samuels

DARWEN

President: J. Watson
Chairman: J. D. Jepson
Manager: N. Bell
Coach:
Physiotherapist: C. H. Bishop
Press Officer & Tel No: None
Secretary: A. R. McCombe
Address & Tel No: 162 Belthorn Road, Belthorn, Blackburn BB1 2NY. 0254 52406 (H)
Commercial Manager:
Address & Tel No:
Address & Tel No of ground: Anchor Ground, Anchor Road, Darwen, Lancs BB3 0BB.
Club shop: Yes
Simple ground directions: Just off the main A666 twixt Bolton/Blackburn, approx 1 mile north of Darwen town centre
No of seats: 80 approx **Covered accommodation:** 4,500 **Capacity:** 9,000 **Floodlights:** No
Year formed: 1875 **Nickname:** The Anchormen **Club sponsors:** Various
Previous names: None
Previous grounds: Barley Bank
Club colours: Maroon/Sky Blue
Change colours: Navy/White
Day for midweek home matches: Tuesday
Record attendance: 9,000 v Luton, F.A. Cup **Year:** 1909
Best performance in: F.A. Cup: 1881 Semi-Final
F.A. Trophy: 1978-9, 2nd Qualifying Round
Clubhouse details: Light refreshments available matchdays. Bar facilities available
Previous Leagues: Football Alliance, Football League Div 1, Div 2, Lancashire Combination, Cheshire County
Present players with Football League experience: Norman Bell (Wolves, Blackburn Rovers), Lammie Robertson (Exeter C)
Past players who progressed into the Football League: S. Mullen (Bury), A. Whitehead (Brentford), P. Devine (Burnley), J. Waddington (Blackburn Rovers), R. Jackson (Bury), H. Jackson (Burnley), T. Prest (Burnley), T. Haslam (Manchester U)
Record transfer fee paid: None
Record transfer fee received: £3,000 for S. Mullen
Programme details: 15p
Club metal badges: No
Local newspapers & Tel No: Darwen Advertiser & News, Lancashire Evening Telegraph
Senior Honours: Lancashire Combination (4), NW Counties Cup Winners
Club Captain (1983-84): Ian Whittaker
Player of the Year (1983-84): Chris Rigby

DROYLSDEN

President:
Chairman: W. J. Mercer
Manager: J. Cooke
Coach: D. W. Jackson
Physiotherapist:
Secretary: A. S. Fenna
Address & Tel No: 277 Manchester Road, Audenshaw, Manchester M34 5SQ. 061-370 1299 (H), 061-832 2274 (B)
Commercial Manager:
Address & Tel No:
Press Officer & Tel No: J. Kennedy. 061-344 2470 (H)
Address & Tel No of ground: Butchers Arms, Market Street, Droylsden, Manchester. 061-370 1426 **Club shop:**
Simple ground directions: Four miles east of Manchester via A662 Ashton New Road, ground is directly behind the Butchers Arms Hotel in Droylsden town centre
No of seats: 200 **Covered accommodation:** 1,000 **Capacity:** 3,500 (reduced in 1982) **Floodlights:** Yes
Year formed: 1866 **Nickname:** The Bloods **Club sponsors:** Buxton Lane Estates
Previous names: Droylsden United
Previous grounds: None
Club colours: All Red
Change colours: White/Blue/Blue
Day for midweek home matches:
Record attendance: 4,250 v Grimsby Town, F.A. Cup First Round **Year:** 1976
Best performance in: **F.A. Cup:** 1978 2nd Round Proper (lost 0-2 to Altrincham)
F.A. Trophy: 1972, 1976, 1979 3rd Qualifying Round
Previous Leagues: Lancashire Combination, Manchester, Cheshire County
Clubhouse details: Open six evenings a week and Saturday afternoon match days. Bingo Wednesday, Friday, Saturday, Sunday. Entertainment Saturday, Sunday. Bars in Lounge and Games Room
Present players with Football League experience: None
Past players who progressed into the Football League: Harry Johnston (Blackpool), Kevin Randall (Notts C, York C), Peter Litchfield (Preston NE)
Record transfer fee paid: £700 to Macclesfield Town for Jimmy O'Connor, 1977
Record transfer fee received: £10,000 from Preston North End for Peter Litchfield, 1979
Programme details: 16 pages, 15p
Programme Editor: Tony Glennon
Local newspapers & Tel No: Droylsden Reporter 061-370 8118
Senior Honours: Cheshire County League Runners-up (2), Cheshire County League Challenge Cup Winners & runners-up, Manchester Senior Cup Winners (3), Runners-up (3), Manchester Challenge Shield Winners (2) & Runners-up, Manchester Intermediate Cup Winners (3), Runners-up (3), Manchester Premier Cup Winners & Runners-up
Club Captain (1983-84): Mark Gledhill **Player of the Year (1983-84):** Mark Fallon

ELLESMERE PORT + NESTON

President: J. F. Price
Chairman: H. Thelwell
Manager: G. Byrne
Coach/Asst Manager: J. Keeling
Physiotherapist: G. Hammond
Secretary: L. Jones
Address & Tel No: 15 Ure Court, Overpool, E. Port 051-356 2308
Commercial Manager: P. Hunwicks
Address & Tel No: 28 Warren Drive, E. Port. 051-355 2308
Press Officer & Tel No: Secretary
Address & Tel No of ground: Thornton Road Stadium, Thornton Road, Ellesmere Port, Wirral 355 7475
Simple ground directions: Junction 10 M56, ground about 2 miles away, follow signs to Stadium
No of seats: 700 **Covered accommodation:** 1,500 **Capacity:** 5,500 **Floodlights:** Yes
Year formed: 1979 **Nickname:** None **Club sponsors:** None
Club colours: All Yellow **Change colours:** All Green
Previous Names: Ellesmere Port Town **Previous Grounds:** York Road
Record attendance: Not known
Programme: 6 pages, 10p
Previous Leagues: Clwyd, Northern Premier, Cheshire County
Programme Editor: Len Jones
Senior Honours: North West Counties Challenge Cup Winners 1983-84
Club Captain (1983-84): Robert Owens

FORD MOTORS (LIVERPOOL)

President: Charles Wyatt
Chairman: Keith Houghton
Manager: Robert Campbell
Coach: Jack Williams
Physiotherapist: Jack Williams
Secretary: John Pilkington
Address & Tel No: 051-226 9435 (H) 051-3900 6827 c/o Jack Williams (B)
Commercial Manager:
Press Officer & Tel No: None
Address & Tel No of ground: Ford Sports & Social Club, Cronton Lane, Widnes. 051-424 7078/4615
Simple ground directions: M62 junction 7, road to Liverpool Airport off Bland, pick up A5080 to Liverpool, ground behind Hillcrest Motel, Cromton Lane, Widnes
No of seats: None **Covered accommodation:** 300 **Capacity:** 2,000 **Floodlights:** None
Year formed: 1967 **Nickname:** The Motors **Club sponsors:** Glebe Garages
Programme: 10 pages, 10p
Programme Editor: John Williams
Previous Names: None
Club colours: Blue/Black/Blue
Change colours: White/Black/Red
Previous Grounds: None
Record attendance: Not known
Previous Leagues: Liverpool Shipping, Lancashire Comb., Cheshire County
Club Captain (1983-84): Peter Doyle **Player of the Year (1983-84):** Tony McVey

GREAT HARWOOD TOWN

President: None
Chairman: Dave Holden
Manager: Dick Mitchell
Coach: Richard Mitchell
Physiotherapist: Mick Dunn
Secretary: Stefan Mankowski
Address & Tel No: 69 James St, Gt. Harwood 0254 884714 (H) or 885918 (B)
Commercial Manager: None
Address & Tel No:
Press Officer & Tel No: Dave Holden (Gt Harwood 884255)
Club shop: No
Address & Tel No of ground: Cloggers S.C., Showground, Wood Street, Great Harwood (Gt Harwood 888103)
Simple ground directions: Look for gas holder, ground 100 yds away
No of seats: 220 **Covered accommodation:** 1,000 **Capacity:** 4,000 **Floodlights:** Yes
Year formed: 1966 **Nickname:** Arrad **Club sponsors:** Ashworth & Young
Previous names: Great Harwood Wellington
Club colours: Red with White band/Red/Red
Previous grounds: Memorial Park, Gt Harwood
Change colours: All Blue
Day for midweek home matches: Wednesday
Record attendance: 500 v Heskin, Lancs Amateur Shield Semi-Final **Year:** 1978
Best performance in: F.A. Cup: Not entered
F.A. Vase: 1981-2 2nd Qualifying Round
Previous Leagues: Blackburn Comb., West Lancashire Lancs Comb
Clubhouse details: Cloggers Social Club, licensed bar and refreshments
Present players with Football League experience: John Kenyon (Blackburn Rovers)
Past players who progressed into the Football League: None
Record transfer fee paid: None
Record transfer fee received: None
Programme details: None
Club metal badges: No
Local newspapers & Tel No: Lancashire Evening Telegraph, Accrington Observer
Senior Honours: Lancashire Combination Cup

IRLAM TOWN

President: J. Sanderson
Chairman: W. Veldhoven
Manager: Peter Mayo
Coach: Barry Thomas
Physiotherapist: None
Secretary: D. Murray
Address & Tel No: 8 Marston Drive, Irlam, Manchester 061-775 7509
Commercial Manager: None
Press Officer & Tel No: D. Murray (061-775 7509)
Address & Tel No of ground: Silver Street, Irlam. 061-775 5599
Simple ground directions: M6 exit 21A, onto A57, five miles to ground
No of seats: None **Covered accommodation:** 500 **Capacity:** 3,000 **Floodlights:** None
Year formed: 1965 **Nickname:** The Town **Club sponsors:** Bass Charrington
Club colours: Royal Blue & White
Change colours: Red & White
Previous Names: None
Previous Grounds: None
Record attendance: Not known
Previous Leagues: Manchester
Programme: Programme of the Year 1983

NANTWICH TOWN

President: Dr K. Kay
Chairman:
Manager: E. Blunstone
Coach:
Physiotherapist:
Secretary: J. Lindop
Address & Tel No: 13 Park View, Nantwich, CW5 6EP Tel: N. 626458 (H) 255125 x2645 (B)
Commercial Manager: None
Address & Tel No:
Press Officer & Tel No: None
Address & Tel No of ground: Jackson Avenue, Nantwich. Tel: N. 624098
Club shop: Yes
Simple ground directions: 4 miles from Crewe Railway Station on main road to Nantwich
No of seats: 200 **Covered accommodation:** 1,500 **Capacity:** 5,000 **Floodlights:** No
Year formed: 1884 **Nickname:** The Dabbers **Club sponsors:** None
Previous names: Nantwich
Club colours: Green shirts, Green shorts
Previous grounds: London Road, Kingsley Fields London Road, Baroney Park London Road
Change colours: Yellow shirts, White shorts
Day for midweek home matches: Tuesday
Record attendance: 5,121 v Winsford united (Cheshire Senior Cup) **Year:** 1920-21
Best performance in: F.A. Cup: 4th Qualifying Round
F.A. Trophy: 1973-4 1st Round
Previous Leagues: Mid-Cheshire, Manchester Crewe Amateur Comb Cheshire County
Clubhouse details: Light refreshments available
Present players with Football League experience: None
Past players who progressed into the Football League: None
Record transfer fee paid: None
Record transfer fee received: £2,750 for Paul Mayman (Northwich Victoria)
Programme details: 12 pages, 15p
Programme Editor: Michael Chatwin
Local newspapers & Tel No: Nantwich Chronicle, 65698. Evening Sentinel, Stoke-on-Trent 29511
Club metal badges: No
Senior Honours: Cheshire Senior Cup, Cheshire League Champions 1980-81
Club Captain (1983-84): M. Smith

PADIHAM

Chairman: R. M. Armstrong
Manager: Vacant
Secretary: M. Higgin
Address & Tel No: 272 Sycamore Avenue, Burnley, Lancs Burnley 27262
Address & Tel No of ground: The Arbories Memorial Ground, Well Street, Padiham. 0282 73742
Club colours: Navy Blue with Red sash/White/Navy Blue **Change colours:** Red with Black stripes/Black/Red
Programme: Yes

ROSSENDALE UNITED

President: C. Barcroft, J.P.
Chairman: D. Hutchinson
Manager: Glyn Watson
Assist Manager: Dave Thornley
Physiotherapist:
Secretary: R. M. Jones
Address & Tel No: 0706 213446 (H)
Commercial Manager: None
Address & Tel No:
Press Officer & Tel No: None
Address & Tel No of ground: Dark Lane, Newchurch, Rawtenstall, Rossendale, Lancashire. 0706 213296
Simple ground directions: Newchurch Road on to Staghills Road, 1¼ miles from Rawtenstall centre
No of seats: 380 **Covered accommodation:** 200 **Capacity:** 5,000 **Floodlights:** Yes
Year formed: 1898 **Nickname:** Stags **Club sponsors:** J. A. Taylor Ltd (Ford Dealers) Rawtenstall
Club colours: All Blue **Change colours:** All Yellow
Previous Names: None **Previous Grounds:** None
Record attendance: 12,100 v Bolton, F.A. Cup 2nd Round **Year:** 1971
Previous Leagues: Lancashire Combination, Cheshire County **Programme:** 12 pages, 10p
Clubhouse details: Open every night, Saturday and Sunday dinner, cabaret weekends
Club Captain (1983-84): Michael Gardner **Programme Editor:** Gordon Hurst

SALFORD

President:
Chairman: Harold Brearley
Manager: David Entwistle
Asst. Manager/Coach: Eric Haslam
Physiotherapist: Alan Raw
Secretary: Michael McKeown
Address & Tel No: 061-794 1095
Commercial Manager: None
Trainer: David Bell
Press Officer & Tel No: Chairman
Address & Tel No of ground: Moor Lane Ground, Nevile Road, Kersal, Salford 7. 061-792 6287 and 061-773 3310
Simple ground directions: Take Bury road out of Manchester (Bury New Road), Moor Lane 3 miles from Cathedral (Deansgate), Nevile Road first left
No of seats: 200 **Covered accommodation:** 600 **Capacity:** **Floodlights:** No
Year formed: 1937 **Nickname:** Ammies **Club sponsors:** None
Club colours: Orange/Black/White **Change colours:** Maroon/Blue/Blue
Previous Names: None **Previous Grounds:** None
Record attendance: 1,500 on Ground. At Old Trafford, Lancs Cup Final, 13,000
Previous Leagues: Manchester **Programme:** 12 pages, 10p
Clubhouse details: None
Major Honours: Lancashire Amateur Cup 1973, 1975, 1977, Manchester Premier Cup (Senior) 1973, 1974, 1976, Manchester County Champion of Champions 1975, Manchester League, Champions 1975, 1976, 1977, 1979, Runners-Up 1971, 1973, 1978, First Division & Cup Winners 1969
Club Captain (1983-84): David Bates **Programme Editor:** John Redgate

SKELMERSDALE UNITED

President:
Chairman: R. Glover
Manager: G. McIntyre
Coach: None
Physiotherapist: None
Secretary: T. Rogers
Address & Tel No: 19 Loxton Crescent, Worsley Mesnes, Wigan, Lancs. Wigan 38474
Fixture Secretary: R. Hadwin
Address & & Tel No: 0695 33081 (H)
Address & Tel No of ground: White Moss Park, White Moss Road, Skelmersdale
Simple ground directions:
No of seats: 350 **Covered accommodation:** Yes **Capacity:** 10,000 **Floodlights:** Yes
Year formed: 1882 **Nickname:** Skem **Club sponsors:** None
Club colours: Blue/White/Blue **Change colours:** All Yellow
Previous Names: None **Previous Grounds:** Sandy Lane, Skelmersdale
Record attendance: 7,000 v Slough, F.A. Amateur Cup **Year:** 1967 **Programme:** 18 pages, 15p
Previous Leagues: Liverpool County Comb., Lancashire Comb., Northern Premier, Cheshire County

WARRINGTON TOWN

President:
Chairman: R. Hennessey
Manager: D. Taylor
Coach: E. Shaw
Physiotherapist: None
Secretary: R. Smith
Address & Tel No: 6 Holly Bank, Cherry Lane, Lymm Cheshire WA13 0NT. Lymm 2943 (H), 061-499 4029 (B)
Commercial Manager: R. Smith, 0695 33081 (H)
Press Officer & Tel No: R. Smith
Address & Tel No of ground: Common Lane, off Loushers Lane, Latchford, Warrington, Cheshire. 31932
Simple ground directions: From Warrington centre via A49, turn left into Loushers Lane, 2 miles from town centre
No of seats: **Covered accommodation:** 200 **Capacity:** 3,000 **Floodlights:** No
Year formed: 1949 **Nickname:** Wires **Club sponsors:** Hiross GB Ltd
Club colours: Yellow/Blue/Yellow
Change colours: All Blue
Previous Names: None
Previous Grounds:
Record attendance: 1,500 **Year:**
Previous Leagues: Mid Cheshire, Cheshire
Programme:
Clubhouse details: Excellent clubhouse with 2 bars, concert room and players lounge
Major Honours: Mid Cheshire League Champions 1959-60, NWFCL Third Div Runners-Up 1982-83

WREN ROVERS SPORTS CLUB

President: J. P. Sutton
Chairman: J. Flatters
Manager: Mike Emery
Coach: Dave Furnival
Physiotherapist: J. Burke
Press Officer & Tel No:
Secretary: P. Kimberley
Address & Tel No: 0253 49853 (H), 0253 737464 (B)
Commercial Manager: None
Address & Tel No:
Address & Tel No of ground: School Road, Marton, Blackpool 68425 **Club shop:** No
Simple ground directions: Follow "Airport" signs from M55 or A583 to South Shore
No of seats: 104 **Covered accommodation:** 400 **Capacity:** 4,000 **Floodlights:** No
Year formed: 1931 **Nickname:** Wrens **Club sponsors:** Many
Previous names: None
Previous grounds: None
Club colours: Red/White
Change colours: All Blue
Day for midweek home matches: Tuesday and Thursday
Record attendance: Not known
Best performance in: F.A. Cup: Not known
F.A. Trophy: 1982-3
Previous Leagues: Blackpool Amateur, West Lancashire
Clubhouse details: Members lounge bar, visiting officials lounge
Present players with Football League experience: J. Sutton, Rob Thomas, John Armfield
Past players who progressed into the Football League: Mark Lawrenson (Liverpool)
Record transfer fee paid: None
Record transfer fee received: None
Programme details: 8 pages
Programme Editor: Paul Kimberley
Club metal bades: No
Local newspapers & Tel No: Blackpool Evening Gazette
Senior Honours: Lancashire Combination League (2), Lancashire F.A. Challenge Shield Winners (2), Lancashire Combination Cup (1) (League and Cup Double 1979)
Club Captain (1983-84): Gary Robinson
Player of the Year (1983-84): Mark Jones

NORTH WEST COUNTIES — DIVISION THREE CLUBS

Floodlights F
Clubhouse C
Programme P
Shop S
Badges B

Club	*Secretary*	*Ground*	*Colours*	*Previous Leagues*	
ASHTON ATHLETIC	J. Tattum 0942 716174	Brocstedes Road, North Ashton	Yellow	Warrington, Lancs Comb	C P
ASHTON TOWN	L. Massam 0942 729307	Edge Green St, Ashton-in-Makerfield	Black & White	Warrington, Lancs Comb	C P
ATHERTON COLLIERIES	W. Shaw 0942 53863	Alder Street, Atherton	Black & Red	Cheshire County Bolton Comb, Lancs Comb, Cheshire County	C P
BACUP BOROUGH	D. Whatmough Bacup 875001	Blackthorn, Bacup	Black & White	Lancs Comb	C
BLACKPOOL MECHANICS	D. Cain 0253 46243	Common Edge Road, Blackpool	Green	Lancs Comb	C
BOLTON S T	W. Roberts 0204 32082	Holy Harbour St, Halliwell, Bolton	Red	Bolton Comb, Lancs Comb	C
CHEADLE TOWN	R. M. Walker 061-427 3454	Park Road, Cheadle, Cheshire	Royal Blue	Manchester	C P
COLWYN BAY	A. J. Banks C.B. 516941	Llandian Rd, Old Colwyn	Sky Blue & Maroon		
CLITHEROE	C. Wilson 0200 24370	Shawbridge, Shaw, Clitheroe	Blue	North Lancs, Lancs Comb	C P
DAISY HILL	R. Naylor 0942 813720	St. James Street, Westhoughton	Sky Blue & Navy	Bolton Comb, Lancs Comb	C
KIRKBY TOWN	J. Smith 051-548 0780	Simonswood Lane	White and Navy Blue		
LYTHAM	J. E. Berry Stannes 711126	Ballam Road	Red and White		
MAGHULL	D. Sherlock 051-526 2306	Hall Lane, Maghull	Blue	Liverpool Comb, Lancs Comb	C P
NELSON	R. Codd 0282 37667	Victoria Park, Lomeshaye Road	Blue Red Trim	Cheshire County Football League, Lancs Comb	C
NEWTON	V. T. Hulmes N-le-W 28358	Vista Road, Newton-le-Willows	Sky Blue	Mid Cheshire	P
OLDHAM DEW	L. M. Charnock 061 620 2976	Norden's Road, Chadderton, Oldham	Blue & White	Manchester, Lancs Comb	C P
PRESTWICH HEYS	J. Pheby 061 773 3310	Heys Road, Prestwich	Red & White, Black	Manchester, Lancs Comb, Cheshire County	C P
URMSTON TOWN	S. Entwistle 061 747 9937	Shawe Road, Flixton M/C	Red	Manchester	C
WHITWORTH VALLEY	A. Hampton 070 685 3237	Rawstron Street, Whitworth	Blue & Navy Blue	Rochdale Am, S.E. Lancs, Lancs Comb	

An excellent photo by Chris Davies catches Steve Berisford scoring the only goal of the match for Congleton Town at Caernarvon.

Droylesden *Back Row (L-R): John Cooke (Manager), Alan Armstrong, Steve Jennings, Mark Fallon, Neil Colbourne, Ricky Burgess, Steve Smith, Kevin Duignan, Nick Hayward, Denis Jackson (Assistant Manager). Front Row (L-R): John Flanagan, Steve Wright, Victor Owusu, Mike Sweeney, Mark Gledhill.*
Photo: Droylesden Reporter

Radcliffe Borough *Back Row (L-R): Dave Morris (Manager), Pete Barrow, Gary Haworth, Gary Dunford, Chris Lilley, Andy Hills, Darren Lloyd, Bobby Pizelis, Earl Thompson, John Ratcliffe, Keith Hardman (Physio). Front Row (L-R): Ian Wood, Dave Mahon, Charlie Gisbourne, Steve Walton, Ian Sampson (Captain), Ian McCool, Vic Dougherty, Gary Smith, Stewart Wilson.*

THE ISMAIL WEST LANCASHIRE FOOTBALL LEAGUE

Chairman: D. Procter

Secretary: W. Carr, 60 Selby Avenue, Blackpool. Tel: (B) 48450

EXCITING CHAMPIONSHIP TRIUMPH FOR DALTON UNITED

The race for the championship honours in the three divisions of The Ismail West Lancashire Football League proved to be very exciting. It took until the last games of the season to decide them.

The first division had seven clubs breaking away from the pack. They kept jockeying for top place. With about half a dozen games to go all but two started to fall by the wayside.

The two clubs left were Burnley United and Dalton United. Neither side had an easy run in. Dalton had a few more games left than Burnley but Burnley had the points. The task facing Dalton was one of having to win their remaining games and increase the goal difference. This they did.

For Burnley to have won the championship it meant Dalton losing their last game by a margin of at least seven goals. The game was lost by by only one goal.

BAC Preston had a very interesting but frustrating season. In their first ten games they lost eight but in the remaining twenty four they were defeated twice.

The fortunes of the three promoted clubs varied considerably. Middleton had for a short while headed the division. They faded towards the end and finished in a creditable mid-table position. ICI Thornton experienced a long run of bad luck. They played well for most of the season but the run of the ball went against them. They won the fight against relegation with several games to spare. College suffered the ignomy of being relegated in their first ever season in the first division. Colne British Legion and Barnoldswick Park Rovers will join College in the second division next season.

Colne Dynamoes Reserves won the second division championship in fine style. The mild winter prevented a fixture backlog, a feature in previous seasons, and helped the continuity. After a short while in the second division Wigan College and Trimpell both won promotion. In their last game, Wigan won the runners-up spot.

Sympathy must go to Anchor Cables. Once again they failed, in the home run, to win promotion. Rumour has it that they are trying to emulate Plymouth Argyle's six consecutive seasons of just missing promotion. Penwortham Hill Rovers are another side that were in the running until the late stage of the season. Another year in division two will help them strengthen their team.

The reserve division saw newcomers Kirkham Town head the table for quite a while. Injuries and first team call ups prevented them from seeing their challenge bear fruit. The experience and skill of Anchor Cables and Longridge United put these two teams in a class of their own. In only their third season in this particular division Anchor Cables won the championship. Longridge did give them a fright when they beat them with a couple of games left. Anchor needed a point from their visit to Haslingden to clinch top spot. They achieved this and during the course of the season they scored over a hundred goals.

The Richardson Cup, sponsored by Speedwell Tool Company of Preston, produced a surprise semi-finalist, Holker Old Boys. For the whole of the season Holker battled against relegation but somehow found the ability to produce surprise results.

Burnley United reached the final for the first time in their history. They had appeared in six semi-finals before this season. Whilst injuries prevented Burnley from fielding their strongest side, they were beaten by a better and more experienced side on the night. Blackpool Rangers have a good record in this competition.

This final saw The League renew its aquaintance with Preston North End who staged it.

The final of the President's Cup produced one of the best spectacles for a long time. The two teams are new to the League. Kirkham Town and ROF Blackburn met at Christie Park and scored five goals. They kept the crowd on edge until the final whistle. Kirkham won this great game by the odd goal in five.

Longridge United met Blackpool Rangers in the final of The Houston cup and ran out easy winners. Blackpool took the lead against the run of play and this spurred United on to take complete control of the game.

The weather was very kind to football this season. The only month that was affected was January.

Sponsorship:
The League Competition: Ismail Tea Company of Blackpool.
The Richardson Cup: Speedwell Tool Company of Preston.
The Presidents Cup: British Nuclear Fuels of Preston.
The Houston Cup: G. Bamber Esq of Preston.

Compiled by C. Barwise
Fixtures and Referees Appointments Secretary

Division 1

Dalton United	34	23	6	5	88	43	52
Burnley United	34	22	8	4	73	33	52
Haslingden	34	20	6	8	71	44	46
Feniscowles	34	17	10	7	57	37	44
BAC Preston	34	18	6	10	75	43	42
Blackpool Rangers	34	18	6	10	69	42	42
Longridge United	34	19	4	11	75	53	42
Vickers SC (Barrow)	34	15	6	13	54	50	36
Middleton (Heysham)	34	13	9	12	55	44	35
Freckleton	34	13	9	12	52	55	35
Poulton	34	11	9	14	60	69	31
Squires Gate	34	8	12	14	47	56	28
Lansil (Lancaster)	34	10	8	16	40	57	28
ICI Thornton	34	9	9	16	54	67	27
Holker Old Boys (Barrow)	34	9	8	17	44	68	26
College FC (Morecambe)	34	5	11	18	39	65	21
Colne British Legion	34	7	4	23	45	81	18
Barnoldswick Pk R	34	2	3	29	29	120	7

Division 2

Colne Dynamoes Res	32	22	6	4	70	29	50
Wigan College	32	21	5	6	96	36	47
Trimpell (Morecambe)	32	22	3	7	69	29	47
Kirkham Town	32	19	5	8	75	43	43
BAe Warton	32	18	7	7	70	44	43
Anchor Cables (Leigh)	32	18	6	8	73	38	42
Penwortham HR	32	18	6	8	62	31	42
ROF Blackburn	32	16	4	12	70	45	36
Lucas SC (Burnley)	32	13	6	13	56	59	32
Mill Hill St Peters	32	12	7	13	65	55	31
Wren Rovers Res	32	12	7	13	63	65	31
Springfields	32	10	8	14	50	54	28
Galgate	32	6	7	19	47	85	19
Wigan Rovers	32	7	3	22	33	76	17
*Lancaster City Res	32	8	3	21	39	89	17
Wesham	32	3	7	22	39	90	13
Carnforth Rangers	32	1	2	29	34	143	4

* 2 points deducted.

The Speedwell Richardson Cup

Preliminary Round

Colne British Legion	1	Lansil	0
ICI Thornton	2	Longridge United	4

First Round

Barnoldswich Park R	1	Holker Old Boys	5
Blackpool Rangers	5	Colne British Legion	0
Dalton United	2	BAC Preston	0
Vickers	2	Freckleton	0
College	0	Feniscowles	1
Middleton	2	Poulton	1
Squires Gate	2	Haslingden	2
Longridge United	1	Burnley United	3

Replay

Squires Gate	0	Haslingden	1

Second Round

Dalton United	2	Vickers	0
Blackpool Rangers	1	Middleton	0
Feniscowles	1	Burnley United	3
Holker Old Boys	1	Haslingden	0

Semi-Finals

Blackpool Rangers	2	Holker Old Boys	0
Burnley United	2	Dalton United	1

Final

Blackpool Rangers	2	Burnley United	0

The Presidents Cup

Preliminary Round

Penwonham Hill R	6	Lancaster City R	2

First Round

Colne Dynamoes Res	3	Wigan Rovers	0
Galgate	0	Anchor Cables	5
Kirkham Town	3	BAe Warton	1
Lucas	2	Wesham	1
Mill Hill St Peters	4	Springfields	0
ROF Blackburn	7	Carnforth Rangers	0
Trinpell	5	Wren Rovers Res	0
Wigan College	3	Penwonham Hill R	0

Second Round

Kirkham Town	2	Anchor Cables	0
Mill Hill St Peters	3	Colne Dynamoes Res	2
ROF Blackburn	3	Lucas	2
Wigan College	1	Trinpell	3

Semi-Finals

Kirkham Town	2	Trinpell	1
ROF Blackburn	2	Mill Hill St Peters	0

Final

Kirkham Town	3	ROF Blackburn	2

The Houston Cup

Preliminary Round

College	2	Springfields	0

First Round

Anchor Cables	2	Burnley United	0
BAC Preston	5	Squires Gate	0
BAe Warton	1	Kirkham Town	0
Blackpool Ranger	3	Penwonham Hill R	2
Freckleton	0	Feniscowles	5
Longridge United	2	Haslingden	0
Mill Hill St Peters	2	Trinpell	3
Poulton	1	College	0

Second Round

Blackpool Rangers	1	Anchor Cables	4*
BAC Preston	2	Longridge United	3
BAe Warton	3	Feniscowles	1
Poulton	0	Trinpell	1

Semi-Finals

Blackpool Rangers	3	BAe Warton	2
Longridge United	5	Trinpell	1

Final

Blackpool Rangers	2	Longridge United	5

* Anchor Cables expelled from competition for a breach of rules.

DIVISION 1
RESULTS 1983-84

	BAC Preston	Barnoldswick Park R	Blackpool Rangers	Burnley United	College	Colne British Legion	Dalton United	Feniscowles	Freckleton	Haslingden	Holker Old Boys	ICI Thornton	Lansil	Longridge United	Middleton	Poulton	Squires Gate	Vickers
BAC Preston	—	4-1	1-3	1-4	3-0	5-1	1-1	2-0	1-2	2-3	5-1	7-2	4-0	1-2	2-1	1-3	4-1	2-1
Barnoldswick Park R	0-4	—	1-1	2-3	1-1	1-4	1-4	0-3	1-2	1-4	1-3	0-2	2-0	0-5	0-5	0-8	0-3	2-3
Blackpool Rangers	0-1	7-0	—	0-2	1-0	1-0	2-3	1-0	2-1	1-2	0-2	0-0	3-2	4-1	4-0	4-0	4-3	5-1
Burnley United	2-3	2-1	0-0	—	4-1	3-0	4-0	1-1	2-3	2-1	1-1	2-1	5-0	2-1	3-2	3-1	2-1	1-1
College	1-6	3-0	1-1	2-4	—	1-0	1-3	0-1	1-2	2-1	0-2	1-1	1-1	1-2	1-1	2-2	1-1	2-3
Colne British Legion	1-1	6-3	2-3	0-1	1-1	—	2-4	2-1	3-2	0-4	1-3	0-0	0-1	1-8	1-5	4-1	1-0	1-3
Dalton United	3-0	6-0	1-3	2-2	2-1	2-1	—	2-2	3-0	3-0	1-0	5-1	1-0	4-0	2-2	5-2	2-1	2-1
Feniscowles	1-3	2-0	2-1	0-1	3-3	2-1	1-3	—	0-0	2-0	4-0	3-2	1-1	2-0	2-1	1-1	1-1	2-0
Freckleton	0-0	3-0	0-3	1-1	2-1	2-1	2-0	3-4	—	3-2	2-0	1-1	1-1	0-2	3-2	1-2	1-3	1-1
Haslingden	0-0	5-2	2-1	1-2	2-1	4-1	5-4	0-0	2-2	—	1-1	1-0	2-2	3-1	2-0	3-2	1-0	3-1
Holker Old Boys	1-1	0-3	0-0	0-4	2-3	3-0	0-2	0-2	0-3	2-3	—	3-4	0-1	1-0	1-0	1-1	3-2	1-3
ICI Thornton	0-3	2-2	2-2	1-6	3-0	5-1	0-2	0-1	2-0	1-3	2-4	—	0-1	0-2	1-1	4-2	1-1	3-1
Lansil	3-1	4-1	0-2	0-1	2-0	2-1	1-5	3-3	0-0	1-0	5-1	1-3	—	1-4	0-3	2-0	2-2	0-0
Longridge United	1-2	4-1	3-2	0-1	0-2	3-2	0-0	0-0	1-1	1-3	7-3	1-4	3-2	—	3-1	6-2	4-1	2-1
Middleton	2-1	4-0	0-1	0-0	3-0	3-3	2-1	2-0	3-1	0-2	2-2	1-1	1-0	1-2	—	2-1	1-0	0-1
Poulton	1-1	3-0	2-1	1-1	1-1	2-0	2-5	1-2	1-3	0-5	2-2	4-2	1-0	2-3	2-2	—	3-2	2-0
Squires Gate	0-2	4-0	1-2	2-1	2-1	0-3	2-2	0-5	4-2	1-1	1-1	2-1	3-1	1-1	0-0	0-0	—	2-2
Vickers	1-0	3-0	4-2	2-0	2-2	1-0	1-3	2-3	5-2	2-0	1-0	3-1	2-0	1-2	1-2	0-2	0-0	—

LANCASHIRE JUNIOR CUP

FIRST ROUND

Atherton Colliers v Netherfield 6-1
Atherton LR v Bacup Borough 3-2
Blackpool Mechanics v Great Harwood Town 0-1
Clitheroe v South Liverpool 0-1
Darwen v Lancaster City 2-2, 1-3
Lytham v Accrington Stanley 2-4
Marine v Rossendale United 5-1
Nelson v Ratcliffe Borough 1-1, 0-4
Wren Rovers v Prestwich Heys 2-0
Fleetwood Town v Burscough 6-7

SECOND ROUND

Atherton Collieries v Atherton LR 2-1
Barrow v Wren Rovers 4-1
Burscough v Sth Liverpool 1-1, 0-1
Horwich RMI v Radcliffe Boro' 5-0
Leyland Motors v Chorley 1-3
Marine v Great Harwood Town 5-0
Morecambe v Lancaster City 0-1
Southport v Accrington Stanley 1-2

THIRD ROUND

Horwich RMI v Accrington Stanley 1-1, 0-1
Lancaster City v Barrow 1-2
South Liverpool v Marine 0-0, 2-1
Chorley v Atherton Coll's 4-0

SEMI-FINALS

Accrington Stanley v Chorley 3-2
Barrow v South Liverpool 1-2

FINAL

Accrington Stanley v South Liverpool 1-2

WEST CHESHIRE LEAGUE SEASON 1983/84

	P	W	D	L	F	A	Pts
Cammell Lairds	31	25	5	1	90	26	55
Vauxhall Motors	32	24	3	5	76	29	51
Poulton Vics	32	22	3	7	85	39	47
West Kirby	31	18	4	9	73	45	40
Van Leer	31	16	7	8	75	35	39
Heswall	32	15	9	8	49	39	39
Newton -2	32	15	4	13	56	49	32
Stork -2	31	12	6	13	48	56	28
Christleton	32	11	6	15	52	71	28
General Chemical	32	9	7	16	52	57	25
Willaston	32	9	7	16	38	56	25
Port Sunlight	32	7	7	18	40	76	23
Ashville	32	9	4	19	32	55	22
Bromsboro' Pool	32	7	8	17	45	77	22
Cadbury's	32	7	7	18	42	73	21
Hoylake Ath	32	8	5	19	46	80	21
Moreton	32	6	8	18	29	65	20

NORTHERN AMATEUR

	P	W	D	L	F	A	Pts
Winlaton Queens H	28	22	2	4	81	29	46
Clarke-Chapman	28	16	5	7	69	40	37
Whitley Bay Res	28	16	5	7	55	52	37
Lobley Hill	28	14	6	8	50	34	34
Proctor & Gamble	28	13	6	9	55	48	32
Longbenton	28	10	8	10	43	42	28
Annitsford Welfare	28	9	9	10	65	63	27
Routefinder St C	28	10	6	12	47	49	26
Belford	28	9	6	13	53	51	24
North Co OB	28	9	6	13	41	50	24
Ashington Res -2	28	11	4	13	52	62	24
NEI Parsons	28	7	10	11	49	60	24
Bohemians	28	9	5	14	57	68	23
Tyne Athletic	28	8	6	14	54	73	22
DHSS	28	4	2	22	28	81	10
Dixons Sports	Record Expunged						

MANCHESTER LEAGUE

PREMIER DIVISION

	P	W	D	L	F	A	Pts
Maine Road	30	23	3	4	92	31	49
Northern Nomads	30	19	7	4	68	34	45
Waterloo	30	20	5	5	59	34	45
Flixton	30	15	10	5	60	32	40
Dukinfield Town	30	13	9	8	64	53	35
Highfield United	30	12	9	9	55	40	33
Wythenshawe Amateurs	30	10	11	9	51	34	31
Mount Pleasant	30	13	4	13	46	46	30
Walkden Town	30	10	9	11	49	46	29
Milton	30	9	10	11	32	48	28
North Withington	30	9	6	15	47	52	24
Abbey Hey	30	8	7	15	38	61	23
Little Lever	30	6	9	15	31	58	21
ICL	30	6	8	16	31	51	20
Old Altrinchamians*	30	5	10	15	29	60	20
Robinsons*	30	2	3	25	22	94	7

* Relegated clubs

DIVISION 1

	P	W	D	L	F	A	Pts
Shell Carrington**	22	15	3	4	55	21	33
Moravian**	22	14	6	2	56	25	*32
Glossopians	22	14	4	4	57	27	32
Urmstonians	22	15	1	6	58	34	31
Eccles Town	22	10	4	8	54	45	24
Coldhurst United	22	8	4	10	52	48	20
Hollinwood	22	6	7	9	32	46	19
Clifton	22	4	8	10	39	51	16
Trafford South	22	6	4	12	30	43	16
Mirrlees	22	5	5	12	30	49	15
Glossop Hillmen	22	4	7	11	29	49	15
Manchester University	22	2	5	15	25	79	9

* Moravian: Two points deducted from points total for breach of rules

** Promoted clubs

TROPHY WINNERS — 1983/84 SEASON

		Winners	D/Finalist
Gilgryst Cup	(Premier Division Cup)	Maine Road	Flixton
Murray Trophy	(Division 1 Cup)	Urmstonians	Glossopians
Open Trophy	(Reserves Divs. Cup)	Milton Res	Dukinfield Town Res

COMPOSITION OF LEAGUE — 1984/5 SEASON

One club leaving league from Division 1 — Trafford South

*Four clubs joining league:	Little Hulton	From Bolton Combination
	Clarksfield	From South East Lancs League
	Sacred Heart	From South East Lancs League
	Pennington	New Club

* Subject to acceptance at AGM on 25th June 1984

MANCHESTER PREMIER CUP

FIRST ROUND

Ashton United v Irlam Town 0-1
Chadderton v Maine Road 1-2
Droylsden v Oldham Dew 2-0
Salford v Curzon Ashton 2-5

SEMI-FINALS

Curzon Ashton v Irlam Town 4-0
Droylsden v Maine Road 3-1

FINAL

Curzon Ashton v Droylsden 1-0

LANCASHIRE AMATEUR LEAGUE

PREMIER DIVISION

	P	W	D	L	F	A	Pts
Rossendale Amateurs	30	21	6	3	80	29	48
Old Mostonians	30	21	5	4	86	38	47
Broughton Amateurs	30	19	4	7	74	34	42
Burnley Belvedere	30	17	7	6	67	38	41
Bury Amateur	30	18	4	8	77	42	40
Southport Amateur	30	16	8	6	69	41	40
Old Boltonians	30	17	5	8	59	40	39
Walshaw Sports Club	30	11	5	14	45	67	27
Old Blackburnians	30	8	8	14	51	62	24
Old Rivingtonians	30	8	8	14	51	68	24
Oldham Hulmeians	30	11	2	17	45	73	24
Bury GSOB	30	7	8	15	40	59	22
Hesketh Casuals	30	9	4	17	40	64	22
Nelson GSOB	30	6	7	17	41	67	19
Whalley Range	30	4	6	20	40	69	14
Newman College	30	1	5	24	24	98	7

DIVISION ONE

	P	W	D	L	F	A	Pts
Old Gregorians	28	24	3	1	93	26	51
Burnley GSOB	28	18	8	2	70	19	44
Stanley United	28	16	3	9	67	56	35
Rochdale St Clements	28	12	9	7	68	43	33
Old Smithillians	28	14	5	9	49	38	33
Old Chaddertonians	28	13	4	11	70	57	30
Chorley Amateurs	28	10	10	8	58	59	30
Lymm Old Boys	28	11	6	11	68	59	28
Ashton GSOB	28	9	10	9	51	55	28
Bolton County	28	8	5	15	60	73	21
Little Lever Sports Club	28	9	3	16	42	64	21
Preston GSA	28	8	4	16	44	65	20
Leigh Athletic	28	5	8	15	31	56	18
Hayward	28	7	2	19	45	92	16
Middleton	28	2	8	18	31	85	12

DIVISION TWO

	P	W	D	L	F	A	Pts
Fulwood Amateurs	24	18	3	3	92	29	39
Old Sladians	24	15	4	5	56	33	34
Old Mancunians	24	15	2	7	46	37	32
Accrington Amateurs	24	13	5	6	58	37	31
Burnage HSOB	24	13	3	8	57	45	29
Thornleigh College OB	24	13	2	9	57	44	28
Hathershaw School OB	24	8	7	9	40	39	23
Bolton Wyresdale	24	9	2	13	44	50	20
North Manchester HSOB	24	7	5	12	44	70	19
Old Salfordians	24	6	6	12	32	47	18
Old Chorltonians	24	5	6	13	38	55	16
Manchester YMCA	24	5	5	14	35	46	15
Radcliffe Amateurs	24	3	2	19	24	91	8

CARLISLE & DISTRICT LEAGUE

DIVISION ONE

	P	W	D	L	F	A	Pts
1 Haig Colliery	18	14	3	1	57	17	31
2 Cleator Moor Celtic	18	11	3	4	48	18	25
3 Aspatria	18	11	2	5	53	42	24
4 Harraby Star	18	7	4	7	43	31	18
5 Carlisle United Res	18	8	2	8	30	38	18
6 Gretna	18	7	3	8	39	26	17
7 Carlisle Utd SC	18	7	3	8	28	34	17
8 Wigton	18	4	4	10	25	52	12
9 Canonbie	18	2	5	11	25	52	9
10 Abbeytown	18	3	3	12	20	58	9

LIVERPOOL COUNTY FOOTBALL COMBINATION

DIVISION ONE

		P	W	D	L	F	A	Pts
1	BRNESC	30	21	6	3	99	37	48
2	St Dominics	30	18	8	4	92	42	44
3	Plessey	30	15	10	5	52	26	40
4	Earle*	30	16	10	4	59	34	38
5	Waterloo Dock	30	15	7	8	66	49	37
6	Ayone	30	17	2	11	53	54	36
7	Uniasco	30	13	8	9	63	43	34
8	Aintree SS	30	11	9	10	49	47	31
9	South Liverpool Res	30	11	6	13	43	43	28
10	Ford Motor Res	30	13	1	16	41	59	27
11	Yorkshire Imperial	30	9	8	13	38	57	26
12	AC Sparks*	30	10	6	14	32	44	22
13	Royal Seaforth	30	7	4	19	40	77	18
14	Marine Res	30	6	4	20	30	72	16
15	Crawfords UB	30	3	8	19	33	68	14
16	Garswood Utd	30	3	7	20	37	70	13

Leading goalscorer: T. Malloy (BRNESC)

DIVISION TWO

		P	W	D	L	F	A	Pts
1	LMT*	32	25	6	1	101	29	54
2	Littlewoods Ath	32	24	6	2	100	33	54
3	Evans	32	23	3	6	100	43	49
4	Plessey Res*	32	17	7	8	77	55	39
5	Cheshire Lines	32	17	4	11	70	49	38
6	Fleetwood Hesketh	32	14	6	12	63	50	34
7	Avon Ath	32	14	6	12	63	60	34
8	Dunlop (Speke)	32	13	7	12	72	54	33
9	Kraft	32	13	7	12	70	55	33
10	Ward Blenkinsop	32	15	3	14	71	68	33
11	Electric Supply	32	13	5	14	54	49	31
12	Rainford NE	32	8	8	16	54	72	24
13	Lucas Sports	32	8	6	18	42	59	22
14	ICI (Widnes)	32	9	3	20	53	100	21
15	Bottle Res	32	7	5	20	58	76	19
16	Garswood United Res	32	3	6	23	35	136	12
17	Liverpool Transport	32	3	4	25	35	129	10

18 Palmers Record Expunged
* Points deducted for a rule infringement
New clubs in 1984-85: Beesix, Kirkby Town

T.S.B. LORD WAVERTREE CUP
Winners: LMT
Finalists: Kraft

LIVERPOOL COUNTY FA CHALLENGE CUP
Winners: St Dominics

AMATEUR CUP
Winners: Plessey
Finalists: Cheshire Lines

MID CHESHIRE LEAGUE

	P	W	D	L	F	A	Pts
Rylands Rec	34	25	8	1	94	30	58
Barnton	34	21	8	5	78	36	50
Alsager Town	34	21	8	5	78	36	50
Linotype	34	21	7	6	75	38	49
Newcastle Town	34	17	7	10	49	35	41
Knutsford	34	16	7	11	56	34	39
USC Sale	34	16	6	12	47	38	38
Hanley Town	34	15	8	11	54	47	38
Sandbach Ramblers	34	17	4	13	49	42	38
Winnington Park	34	15	5	14	51	54	35
Bramhall	34	12	9	13	56	49	33
Kidsgrove Ath	34	11	10	13	51	41	32
Middlewich Ath	34	10	8	16	46	56	28
Pilkington Rec	34	10	7	17	56	65	27
Styal	34	9	7	18	33	60	25
Crewe Rolls Royce	34	9	6	19	48	64	24
Northwich V Res	34	8	2	24	32	56	18
Whitchurch Alport	34	2	1	31	31	21	5

WESTMORLAND ASSOCIATION FOOTBALL LEAGUE

DIVISION 1

	P	W	D	L	F	A	Pts
Wetheriggs	28	20	6	2	69	29	46
Shap	28	19	5	4	82	31	43
Keswick	28	18	6	4	91	40	42
Staveley United	28	16	7	5	64	29	39
Burneside	28	15	6	7	74	41	36
Ambleside	28	15	5	8	92	43	35
Kent	28	14	6	8	67	46	34
Coniston	28	10	8	10	50	45	28
Kendal County	28	10	6	12	62	62	26
Ibis	28	8	5	15	43	62	21
Appleby	28	9	2	17	45	72	20
Kirkby Stephen	28	7	4	17	42	77	18
Kirkoswald	28	7	4	17	33	74	18
Netherfield Res	28	4	4	20	31	78	12
Kendal United	28	—	2	26	21	137	2

DIVISION 2

	P	W	D	L	F	A	Pts
Keswick Res	32	25	6	1	89	28	56
Windermere SC	32	23	5	4	102	38	51
Burneside Res	32	16	10	6	82	40	42
Ullswater United	32	17	8	7	82	47	42
Shap Res	32	14	10	8	90	66	38
Endmoor KGR	32	15	7	10	80	63	37
Esthwaite Vale	32	14	7	11	75	60	35
Appleby Res	32	13	8	11	85	68	34
Sedbergh	32	15	4	13	80	64	34
Thirlmere	32	12	7	13	59	73	31
Graystoke	32	10	9	13	63	77	29
Ambleside Res	32	10	6	16	63	86	26
Kirkoswald Res	32	7	10	15	50	82	24
Endmoor United	32	10	2	20	83	113	22
Windermere QPR	32	6	4	22	44	97	16
Langwathby	32	8	—	24	73	129	16
Lunesdale United	32	4	3	25	37	106	11

High Sheriffs Cup:
Winners: Staveley United
Runners-up: Shap

Mason & Freeman Cup:
Winners: Sedbergh
Runners-up: Shap Res

East Lancashire League

	P	W	D	L	F	A	Pts
Clitheroe Res	26	18	3	5	76	32	39
Padiham Wdrs	26	18	3	5	68	40	39
Oswaldtwistle Imm	26	15	5	6	75	43	35
Bacup Boro' Res	26	14	6	6	63	32	34
Trawden Celtic	26	14	5	7	66	39	33
Gt Harwood Town Res	26	14	5	7	55	41	33
Waddington	26	11	6	9	67	48	28
Whalley Arms Celtic	26	10	6	10	46	37	26
Pendle Forest	26	9	5	12	57	57	23
Keighley Green	26	8	6	12	46	58	22
Mansfield	26	7	5	14	43	64	19
Chatburn	26	3	6	17	32	64	12
Colne Legion Res	26	5	2	19	36	103	12
Whalley	26	2	5	19	24	92	9

East Lancashire League's Presidents Cup
First Round
Padiham Wanderers 1 Clitheroe Res 5
Pendle Forest 5 Whalley 2
Oswaldtwistle Imm 1 Mansfield 0
Whalley Arms Celtic 2 Keighley Green 1
Trawden Celtic 5 Waddington 1
Gt Harwood Town Res 2 Colne Legion Res 1
Byes — Bacup Boro' Res and Chatburn.

Cheshire Senior Cup

First Qualifying Round

No Ties

Second Qualifying Round

Alsager Town v Ellesmere Port & Nelson 1-3
Bramhall v Dukinfield Town 1-0
Chester City v Nantwich town 4-3
Middlewich Athletic v Barnton 1-0
Barnton through, Middlewich disqualified
Tranmere Rovers v Cheadle Town 3-0
West Kirby v Knutsford 4-1

Third Qualifying Round

Bramhall v Chester City 2-1
Ellesmere Port v Neston & Barton 1-0
Warrington Town v Vauxhall 0-0,5-3
West Kirby v Tranmere Rovers 1-2

First Round Proper

Altrincham v Winsford United 2-0
Cammell Laird v Crewe Alexandra 2-1
Congleton Town v Macclesfield Town 0-1
Northwich Victoria v Ellesmere Port 4-0
Stalybridge Celtic v Runcorn 3-3,1-2
Stockport County v Hyde United 2-5
Tranmere Rovers v Witton Albion 2-0
Warrington Town v Bramhall 3-2

Second Round

Altrincham v Warrington Town 2-3
Cammell Laird v Northwich Victoria 1-2
Runcorn v Macclesfield Town 1-0
Tranmere Rovers v Hyde United 0-4

Semi-Finals

Hyde United v Runcorn 0-2
Northwich Victoria v Warrington 2-1

Final (at Altrincham FC)

Northwich Victoria v Runcorn 3-0

Third Round

Davenport	v	Burmah Castrol	1-0
Alsager Town	v	Linotype	0-3*
Bramhall	v	USC Sale	4-0
Christleton	v	Chester College	2-1
Grove United	v	Shell Carrington	6-3
Highfield	v	Cadbury	1-6
Helsby BI	v	Adswood Amt	2-1*
Hoylake Athletic	v	Styal	4-0
Knutsford	v	Middlewich Ath	1-2
Moreton	v	Cammell Laird	0-6
Newton Athletic	v	Mersey Royal	3-5
Newton	v	Heswall	1-2
Sandbach Ramblers	v	Alderley St Phillip	5-0
St Werberghs	v	Port Sunlight	0-3
Van Leer	v	Vauxhall	3-0
West Kirby	v	Poulton Vics	4-1

Fourth Round

Bramhall	v	Heswall	3-2
Cadbury	v	Port Sunlight	5-1
Davenport	v	Grove United	1-0
Hoylake Athletic	v	Linotype	2-2,0-2
Mersey Royal	v	Christleton	3-4
Middlewich Ath	v	Helsby BI	3-1
Sandbach Ramblers	v	Van Leer	1-1,0-1
West Kirby	v	Cammell Laird	0-1,1-1

(First game ordered to be replayed due to short time 40 minutes each way) 2-1

Fifth Round

Bramhall	v	Davenport	2-0
Christleton	v	Middlewich Ath	1-0
Cadbury	v	Linotype	0-3
West Kirby	v	Van Leer	0-2

Semi-Finals

Bramhall	v	Christleton	2-0
Linotype	v	Van Leer	0-1

Final

Bramhall	v	Van Leer	2-1

CHESHIRE SATURDAY CUP

First Round

Adswood Amateurs	v	Blacon YC	2-1
Barnton	v	Prestbury	3-0
Bramhall	v	Ashville	5-2
Bromborough Pool	v	Crewe Rolls Ro'	2-2,3-2
Cheadle Hulme	v	Cheadle Heath Nomads	0-5
Chester College	v	Lostock Gralam	8-1
Chester Nomads	v	Willaston (Wirral)	0-3
Davenport	v	Wilmslow Albion	2-1
General Chemicals	v	Old Stoconians	2-0
Hazel Grove	v	Northwich Vics Res	0-3
Knutsford	v	Stockport Georgians	2-1
Malpas	v	Old Altrinchamians	3-1
Mirrlees	v	Helsby BICC	1-2
Old Stopfordians	v	Crewe Villa	3-2
Rivacre SC	v	Wythenshawe College	8-1
Sandbach Ramblers	v	Barrow	2-1
Shell (Wirral)	v	Poynton	6-0
Shell Carrington	v	Crewe LMR	5-0
Tattenhall	v	Adlington	0-3
Winnington Park	v	Port Sunlight	0-2

Second Round

Adlington	v	Knutsford	1-1,0-2
Adswood Amt	v	Cheadle Heath Nomads	5-0
Bramhall	v	Norwest Gas	7-0
Barnton	v	St Werberghs	1-2
Bromborough Pool	v	Davenport	2-1
Chester College	v	Malpas	4-3
Helsby BICC	v	Rivacre Social Club	1-0
Heswall	v	Old Stopfordians	2-1
Lymm OB	v	Alderley St Phillips	0-1
Newton Athletic	v	Stork	1-0
Port Sunlight	v	Northwich Vics Res	6-1
Sandbach Ramblers	v	General Chemical	4-3
Shell	v	Van Leer	1-3
Strafford South	v	Styal	1-3
Willaston	v	Shell Carrington	1-3
Woodley	v	Middlewich Athletic	1-7

CUMBERLAND SENIOR CUP

FIRST ROUND

Windscales United v Hearts of Liddlesdale 4-1
Abbeytown v Marchon 5-4
Wigton v Langwathby 5-1
Haig Colliery v Cleator Moor Celtic 3-0
Parton v British Steel Corp 4-3
Haig Social v Carlisle City 2-1
North Bank v Gretna 0-3
Workington v Canonbie 5-0
Kirkoswald v Thirlmere 1-3
Keswick v Cumbria Police 3-1
Alston v Wetheriggs 0-2
Silloth v Cleator United 1-2
Greystoke v Kirkpatrick Fleming 0-5

SECOND ROUND

Gretna v Keswick 6-1
Workington v Parton 1-0
Thirlmere v Kirkpatrick Fleming 1-2
Abbeytown v Sportsman 1-1, 1-2
Wetheriggs v Haig Colliery 1-2
Aspatria Spartans v Carlisle Supporters 3-1
Haig Social v Wigton 2-3
Cleator United v Windscales Utd 0-2

THIRD ROUND

Sportsman v Kirkpatrick Fleming 6-0
Windscales United v Wigton 2-1
Aspatria Spartans v Workington 2-0
Gretna v Haig Colliery 3-0

SEMI-FINALS

Windscales Utd v Sportsman 3-1
Aspatria Spartans v Gretna 1-3

FINAL

at Borough Park, Workington FC, 8th May 1984
Gretna v Windscales 1-3

Lancashire Floodlight Trophy

Chairman: L. T. Rigby
Secretary/Treasurer: J. V. Heyes Esq

The Lancashire Floodlight Trophy was formed in Season 1983/84, and consisting of nine senior non-league clubs, five from the Northern Premier League and four from the North West Counties League. These clubs were split into two sections, the 'North Section' consisting of: Great Harwood Town; Horwich RMI; Lancaster City; and Morecambe FC. The Southern Section contained: Leyland Motors; Marine; Skelmersdale United; South Liverpool; and Southport FC. Fixtures were arranged on a home and away basis, these being played usually on Monday or Tuesday evenings during the months of November to April. An away win counted as three points, and the top team in each section competed in the Trophy Final which was played at Deepdale the home of Preston North End FC. Southport defeated Horwich RMI in the Final to become the first holders of a very attractive Trophy sponsored and provided by Dairy Crest Milk.

A feature of the league is the rule which states that clubs must play a minimum of six and a maximum of eight players who played in their club's previous Saturday league fixture; this prevents clubs fielding complete reserve sides in midweek floodlight fixtures, and helps keep faith with their paying supporters. It also enables team managers to include two or three reserve and youth team players in their senior side giving them the experience of playing under floodlights in a first team environment.

Final League Tables — Season 1983-84

Section A (North)

	P	W	D	L	F	A	Pts
Horwich RMI	6	5	0	1	16	11	13
Lancaster City	6	4	1	1	16	7	11
Morecambe	6	2	1	3	9	10	6
Grat Harwood	6	0	0	6	2	15	0

Section B (South)

	P	W	D	L	F	A	Pts
Southport	8	5	1	2	14	9	14
South Liverpool	8	4	2	2	12	8	12
Leyland Motors	8	3	2	3	13	15	9
Marine	8	3	1	4	16	14	8
Skelmersdale	8	2	0	6	10	19	5

Results of Matches

Section A

	Home Team	1	2	3	4
1	Great Harwood Town		0-1	0-1	1-2
2	Horwich RMI	3-0		2-5	3-2
3	Lancaster City	6-0	2-4		2-1
4	Morecambe	2-1	2-3	0-0	

Section B

	Home Team	1	2	3	4	5
1	Leyland Motors		4-4	1-0	3-1	1-3
2	Marine	3-0		5-3	0-1	0-1
3	Skelmersdale United	1-3	1-3		2-0	0-3
4	South Liverpool	1-1	2-0	3-0		2-2
5	Southport	2-0	2-1	1-3	0-2	

Pride of Lancashire in the Trophy were Marine, who reached the semi-final before losing at home to Northwich Victoria. Here Northwich put the pressure on the home side at a corner. Photo: Leo Hoenig

F.A. TROPHY GOES TO THE NORTH WEST

Skipper Ken Jones of Northwich Victoria holds aloft the F.A. Trophy in triumph.

Another view of Colin Chester's penalty at the Victoria Ground, Stoke. Both Photos: Leo Hoenig

NORTHERN COUNTIES (EAST) FOOTBALL LEAGUE

Chairman: Cliff Morris
General Secretary: B. Wood, 6 Restmore Ave, Guiseley, Leeds LS20 9DG.
Tel: 0943 74558

SPALDING WIN THRILLING CHAMPIONSHIP PLACE

Having lost two sides from the Premier Div. at the end of the previous season it was considered right to operate the Division with 18 clubs rather than offer promotion to sub-standard clubs. A glance at the early League tables shows that Winterton Rangers took up the early running followed by Ilkeston Town — once again, it was difficult to predict any likely championship contender due to the different number of matches played. However, as the season progressed Winterton suffered some player problems and slipped out of the race whilst with just 3 weeks of the season remaining any of 7 clubs could still see a realistic chance of the championship. Both Arnold and Emley were setting the pace but Spalding had matches in hand. With pressure mounting in what was a classic championship 'cliff hanger', Spalding were left with their final match at Guiseley — win the game and they were Champions; a draw meant the Championship for Arnold and defeat would push the club into 3rd place behind Emley. A nail-biting 1-0 victory gave the Lincolnshire club the Trophy with 48 points and full credit for sticking to their task in the final weeks of the season. In the lower reaches of the Division competition was no less intense with Bridlington Trinity and Mexborough Town finally emerging from the bottom places to leave Bentley VW and Heanor Town propping up the Division.

At Regional level there were plenty of close challenges but it was the two promoted clubs — Rowntree Mackintosh and Pontefract Colls — who always looked likely candidates for honours in Div 1 (N). In this Division it is worthwhile recording that Farsley Celtic did not play a League fixture for *14 weeks* due to cup commitments and postponements, and may, under different circumstances, have been able to stake a claim on the championship. As it was Pontefract held off the York side's challenge and the two sides changed places following the previous season's campaign for them both in Div 2 (N). At the bottom Liversedge were only able to get off bottom spot at the end when Ossett Town occupied that position.

In Div 1 (S) there was no holding Borrowash Victoria, another promoted club, for they led the Division for long periods pressured by Woolley MW and Sheffield both of whom had costly lapses in the spring which left the way clear for Denaby United to move into 2nd position. Credit goes to the Derbyshire side in taking honours in two successive campaigns and to Denaby who now accept a position in the Premier Division as the suitably graded Div 1 (S) runners-up. Bottom positions were occuped by Norton Woodseats and Harworth CI.

Div 2 (N) saw a remarkable resurgence in the fortunes of Harrogate Railway when they compensated admirably for their miserable 82/83 season. This year they took the Championship from newcomers, Armthorpe Welfare, who were the other chief contenders. A crucial game for Armthorpe was when they turned up at Harrogate with a depleted team and lost 4-0. In the race, too, were Selby Town and Yorkshire Amat whilst at the bottom Tadcaster Albion had an uncharacteristically poor season with fellow club, Brook Sports.

The success of Retford Town in Div 2 (S) was well-deserved and reminiscent of their better Midland League days. As the new club they set the pace but Kimberley Town will be well pleased with an honours position after being relegated the previous season. Retford Rail and Sutton Trinity were at the bottom with the latter side unable to win a single League game. In fact, the Rail themselves had to wait until 11th February to record their first win — against Sutton Trinity!

In the old days of the Yorkshire League Reserve Div, the reserve sides of Emley and Thackley could usually be relied upon to be amongst the honours although this season the final honours had to rely on goal difference. Both sides finished level on 45 points with Emley taking the championship with a Goal Diff of +53 to Thackley's +43.

The Fletcher Motors Cup competition was a victory for the Regional Divisions with a number of surprising results — surprising, that is, to those who may be unsure of the quality of football played at Regional level. Particularly noteworthy was the feat of Ossett Albion, the final winners, who eliminated Prem Div sides Heanor Town, Spalding United and Emley on the way to the Final. On a poor night for weather Ilkeston Town were the Yorkshire side's opponents but after equalising Ossett's early second half goal it was the Albion who won the match 2-1 providing them with exemption to Rd 3 of next season's competition.

The Reserve Div Cup final over two legs was contested by two local rivals — Fryston CW Res and Pontefract Colls Res. Both clubs won on their opponent's grounds with the aggregate score of 3-2 in Fryston's favour. Our congratulations are due to all finalists and particularly to Peter Fletcher of Fletcher Motors for kindly sponsoring the League Cup competition.

In National competitions I must echo my remarks of last year by saying that our clubs tried hard without just making that breakthrough into National prominence. In the FA Cup, the best run was that of Eastwood Town, finally going out in the replay of the 4th Qual Rd at Wycombe Wanderers 2-1 after an excellent match at Eastwood. Two of our clubs did well to reach the 1st Round proper of the FA Trophy when Sutton Town fell at home to Frickley Ath and Arnold were defeated by Barrow. In the lesser FA Vase competiton 6th round progress was made by Staveley before they went out to the eventual finalists Stamford. However, there were some notable victories by other NCE sides in the earlier rounds of the competition. My hope as always is that we can produce a Wembley finalist — preferably in the FA Cup!

At County FA level our clubs achieved successes as follows:

Derbys Divsl Cup (South)	Winners — Graham St Prims
Lincs County Senior Cup	Runners-up — Spalding United
North Riding Sat County Cup	Winners — York RI
Notts Saturday Senior Cup	Winners — Eastwood Town
Sheff & H Senior Cup	Winners Emley, Runners-up — Frecheville CA
West Riding County Cup	Winners — Farsley Celtic, Runners-up — Guiseley

For the second year the League also had finalists in the Thorn-EMI Floodlighting Competition played in Birmingham when Denaby Utd represented the League.

NORTHERN COUNTIES EAST FOOTBALL LEAGUE

Allocation of Clubs to Divisions
Season 1984/85

PREMIER DIVISION

Alfreton Town, Appleby Frodingham, Arnold, Belper Town, Bentley VW, Boston, Bridlington Trinity, Denaby United, Eastwood Town, Emley, Guisborough Town, Guiseley, Heanor Town, Ilkeston Town, Mexborough Town, Pontefract Colls, Spalding United, Sutton Town, Thackley, Winterton Rangers.

DIVISION ONE (N)

Bradley Rangers, Bridlington Town, Collingham, Farsley Celtic, Garforth Miners, Hall Road Rangers, Harrogate Railway, Harrogate Town, Liversedge, North Ferriby, Phoenix Park (BFD), Pickering Town, Rowntree Mackintosh, Selby Town, Tadcaster Albion, York RI, Yorkshire Amateurs.

DIVISION ONE (C)

Armthorpe Welfare, Brigg Town, BSC (Parkgate), Fryston CW, Grimethorpe MW, Hatfield Main, Maltby MW, Ossett Albion, Ossett Town, Pilkington Recs, Stockbridge Works, Thorne Colliery, Wombwell SA, Woolley MW, Worsbrough Bridge MW, Yorkshire Main Colliery.

DIVISION ONE (S)

Arnold Kingswell, Blidworth Welfare, Borrowash Victoria, Dronfield United, Frecheville CA, Graham St Prims, Hallam, Harworth CI, Kimberley Town, Kiveton Park, Lincoln United, Long Eaton United, Oakham United, Retford Town, Sheffield, Staveley.

NORTHERN COUNTIES EAST FOOTBALL LEAGUE

Premier Division

	P	W	D	L	F	A	Pts
Spalding United	34	20	8	6	76	43	48
Arnold	34	22	3	9	82	37	47
Emley	34	20	7	7	59	32	47
Alfreton Town	34	18	6	10	56	32	42
Eastwood Town	34	17	7	10	75	49	41
Ilkeston Town	34	14	11	9	49	38	39
Guiseley	34	14	11	9	54	48	39
Guisborough Town	34	16	6	12	58	54	38
Thackley	34	14	6	14	61	54	34
Winterton Rangers	34	13	7	14	48	42	33
Belper Town	34	12	8	14	47	46	32
Boston	34	10	12	12	46	57	32
Sutton Town	34	10	7	17	36	63	27
Appleby Frodingham	34	8	9	17	51	75	25
Mexborough Town	34	6	12	16	34	68	24
Bridlington Trinity	34	7	9	18	40	60	23
Heanor Town	34	7	9	18	31	68	23
Bentley VW	34	6	6	22	45	82	18

Division One North

	P	W	D	L	F	A	Pts
Pontefract Colls	26	17	5	4	43	24	39
Rowntree Mackintosh	26	16	2	8	59	43	34
Farsley Celtic	26	12	6	8	51	33	30
Bradley Rangers	26	12	6	8	35	36	30
Ossett Albion	26	10	9	7	44	30	29
Garforth Miners	26	10	8	8	45	33	28
Harrogate Town	26	12	4	10	43	31	28
Scarborough	26	9	7	10	42	43	25
North Ferriby	26	8	8	10	33	35	24
York RI	26	9	6	11	35	45	24
Bridlington Town	26	7	9	10	30	50	23
Hatfield Main	26	6	7	13	38	45	19
Liversedge	26	5	7	14	29	53	17
Ossett Town	26	4	6	16	34	60	14

Division One South

	P	W	D	L	F	A	Pts
Borrowash Victoria	26	18	3	5	61	24	39
Denaby United	26	16	4	6	58	28	36
Woolly MW	26	14	6	6	61	33	34
Sheffield	26	12	6	8	44	38	30
Lincoln United	26	11	7	8	39	30	29
Maltby MW	26	11	7	8	36	29	27*
BSC Parkgate	26	11	5	10	29	29	27
Staveley	26	10	5	11	41	34	25
Hallam	26	8	7	11	28	39	23
Long Eaton United	26	7	8	11	24	38	22
Frecheville CA	26	6	10	10	33	48	22
Arnold Kingswell	26	7	7	12	30	44	21
Norton Woodseats	26	5	4	17	23	59	14
Harworth CI	26	5	3	18	19	53	13

* 2 points deducted

Division Two North

	P	W	D	L	F	A	Pts
Harrogate Railway	26	19	6	1	72	23	44
Armthorpe Welfare	26	17	5	4	48	26	39
Yorkshire Amateur	26	14	7	5	42	21	35
Selby Town	26	12	7	7	48	30	31
Phoenix Park (BFD)	26	12	7	7	49	36	31
Pickering Town	26	13	2	11	36	34	28
Fryston CW	26	10	6	10	48	41	26
Thorne Colliery	26	10	6	10	43	41	26
Grimethorpe MW	26	8	9	9	38	39	25
Hall Road Rangers	26	5	8	13	36	57	18
Collingham	26	5	6	15	26	47	16
Pilkington Recs	26	4	7	15	33	55	15
Tadcaster Albion	26	3	9	14	23	56	15
Brook Sports	26	5	5	16	27	63	15

Division Two South

	P	W	D	L	F	A	Pts
Retford Town	24	18	3	3	63	22	39
Kimberley Town	24	16	4	4	39	21	36
Graham St Prims	24	15	3	6	58	37	33
Brigg Town	24	13	6	5	44	30	32
Oakham United	24	12	3	9	44	28	27
Yorkshire Main Colly	24	12	3	9	44	37	27
Worsbrgh Br MW	24	12	3	9	51	46	27
Wombwell SA	24	7	6	11	28	37	20
Blidworth Welfare	24	8	3	13	32	52	19
Kiveton Park	24	7	4	13	31	41	18
Stockbridge Works	24	6	5	13	40	44	17
Retford Rail	24	5	4	15	27	53	14
Sutton Trinity	24	0	3	21	21	74	3

Pontefract Colliers *Div 1 champions Northern Counties (East) meet the press.*

SEASON 1983-84 N.C.E. LEAGUE PREMIER DIVISION	Alfreton Town	Appleby Frodingham	Arnold	Belper Town	Bentley VW	Boston	Bridlington Trinity	Eastwood Town	Emley	Guisborough Town	Guiseley	Heanor Town	Ilkeston Town	Mexborough Town	Spalding United	Sutton Town	Thackley	Winterton Rangers
Alfreton Town		1-1	4-2	2-2	0-1	2-0	2-1	1-2	2-1	0-1	0-1	4-1	1-0	1-0	1-2	3-0	1-2	1-0
Appleby Frodingham	0-2		1-1	0-5	2-3	2-2	2-2	2-1	1-4	2-3	0-2	1-0	0-0	0-1	2-3	1-1	3-2	0-0
Arnold	1-1	1-1		3-0	6-3	3-0	3-0	3-0	1-0	3-2	1-2	0-2	2-1	1-0	4-2	4-0	3-0	3-2
Belper Town	0-1	2-2	0-1		3-0	3-1	2-1	2-1	0-2	1-0	1-2	2-0	2-3	0-1	0-0	1-0	0-2	1-3
Bentley VW	0-3	1-6	2-4	2-0		1-3	3-0	0-1	2-3	3-3	2-3	1-1	1-1	0-1	4-5	4-5	1-1	1-2
Boston	2-1	5-3	0-4	1-1	1-1		1-0	3-1	0-0	0-2	1-1	1-1	1-0	2-2	2-1	0-2	1-2	1-1
Bridlington Trinity	0-4	2-0	1-2	2-2	3-0	1-1		3-0	0-2	0-2	2-2	0-0	0-1	1-1	0-2	4-0	5-2	3-2
Eastwood Town	0-4	2-1	3-2	3-0	4-0	6-1	6-0		1-2	2-0	0-2	7-1	2-2	3-1	6-0	5-2	0-0	2-1
Emley	2-0	3-1	1-0	0-2	3-0	1-1	2-2	1-3		4-0	1-1	2-0	0-0	2-0	2-1	1-1	4-2	2-1
Guisborough Town	3-1	3-2	1-4	0-1	4-2	1-1	1-0	3-2	0-2		0-3	4-1	1-1	1-1	1-1	1-2	2-1	2-2
Guisley	0-0	1-2	1-0	2-2	2-0	0-4	2-2	2-2	1-1	2-5		1-1	3-3	1-2	0-1	3-0	1-0	0-1
Heanor Town	0-3	2-3	0-4	1-4	1-0	2-1	0-2	0-0	1-2	2-3	0-4		0-0	0-0	0-3	0-2	0-4	2-1
Ilkeston Town	3-0	4-1	2-1	3-1	3-0	0-1	3-0	1-1	2-1	2-0	1-4	1-1		3-0	0-2	0-0	4-0	0-1
Mexborough Town	1-1	2-5	0-7	1-1	3-3	1-1	1-1	0-4	0-2	2-5	1-3	5-2	0-0		0-4	1-1	1-0	0-1
Spalding United	1-3	7-2	3-2	2-1	1-0	2-4	1-0	2-2	2-0	3-1	1-1	1-1	6-0	4-0		6-0	2-1	1-1
Sutton Town	0-2	0-1	0-2	2-1	1-2	3-2	2-1	0-0	0-2	1-0	4-1	1-2	1-2	2-0	0-2		0-0	2-2
Thackley	2-2	3-1	2-1	1-3	2-0	3-1	4-1	7-2	3-2	0-2	3-0	1-2	3-1	3-3	1-1	4-1		0-1
Winterton Rangers	0-2	4-0	0-3	1-1	1-2	3-0	2-0	0-1	1-2	0-1	4-0	0-4	1-2	3-2	1-1	3-0	2-0	

SEASON 1983-84 N.C.E. LEAGUE DIVISION 1 (NORTH)	Bradley Rangers	Bridlington Town	Farsley Celtic	Garforth Miners	Harrogate Town	Hatfield Main	Liversedge	North Ferriby	Ossett Albion	Ossett Town	Pontefract Collieries	Rowntree Mackintosh	Scarborough	York RI
Bradley Rangers		1-1	1-0	1-1	2-2	2-2	2-2	1-0	3-2	3-0	0-1	0-1	1-2	3-1
Bridlington Town	0-1		2-2	1-1	1-0	1-0	1-1	1-1	0-0	3-1	0-2	1-0	1-2	1-1
Farsley Celtic	1-0	7-0		2-3	3-0	4-3	4-1	2-0	2-2	1-1	0-1	5-0	2-2	3-2
Garforth Miners	0-1	1-2	1-0		1-2	0-0	2-0	0-1	1-4	1-1	0-1	3-1	2-1	6-1
Harrogate Town	0-2	5-0	3-0	0-3		4-1	1-1	1-0	2-0	3-1	1-1	2-5	4-3	4-0
Hatfield Main	1-2	4-4	3-0	0-2	1-0		3-0	4-2	1-1	1-1	0-2	1-2	1-2	0-0
Liversedge	1-2	2-3	2-1	1-1	2-0	1-4		1-2	1-0	2-2	1-1	1-4	3-2	0-2
North Ferriby	1-1	3-0	1-1	3-0	0-4	1-0	3-0		3-3	2-1	1-1	1-2	4-0	0-0
Ossett Albion	5-0	3-1	0-2	0-0	0-2	1-3	3-0	0-0		2-1	0-0	3-1	1-0	1-1
Ossett Town	1-2	6-1	1-3	0-6	0-3	2-2	4-1	1-0	0-2		2-3	3-4	1-1	2-0
Pontefract Collieries	2-0	2-1	1-0	2-6	1-0	2-0	2-0	4-2	2-1	6-1		0-1	1-2	2-0
Rowntree Mackintosh	6-1	2-1	1-3	5-1	1-0	3-2	0-2	4-0	2-2	1-0	1-1		0-1	6-3
Scarborough	2-1	1-1	1-1	2-2	0-0	4-1	3-2	1-1	1-4	4-0	1-2	3-4		0-1
York RI	1-2	1-2	1-2	1-1	2-0	2-0	1-1	2-1	1-4	3-1	3-0	3-2	2-1	

SEASON 1983-84 N.C.E. LEAGUE DIVISION 1 (SOUTH)	Arnold Kingswell	Borrowash Victoria	BSC (Parkgate)	Denaby United	Frecheville CA	Hallam	Harworth CI	Lincoln United	Long Eaton United	Maltby MW	Norton Woodseats	Sheffield	Staveley	Woolley MW
Arnold Kingswell		1-3	3-1	1-5	1-1	1-1	3-0	1-0	0-3	2-3	1-1	2-2	1-0	1-3
Borrowash Victoria	1-0		0-1	1-0	3-1	5-0	8-0	3-0	3-0	4-1	5-2	1-1	1-1	2-0
BSC (Parkgate)	1-0	2-4		0-2	1-1	1-0	0-2	1-0	1-2	0-2	4-0	3-1	0-0	1-0
Denaby United	4-0	2-1	2-1		7-1	1-2	2-0	1-1	4-0	3-0	1-0	1-2	1-3	0-0
Frecheville CA	0-2	0-2	1-1	1-3		2-2	1-0	2-2	2-1	1-1	0-1	0-2	2-1	3-3
Hallam	2-1	0-3	1-1	2-4	1-2		3-0	0-0	1-1	0-0	2-0	1-2	0-5	2-1
Harworth CI	1-1	3-0	0-1	1-5	0-0	0-1		2-0	2-2	0-1	4-0	0-1	0-1	1-2
Lincoln United	3-0	2-2	1-0	2-0	2-0	2-1	4-0		3-0	1-1	3-1	3-2	4-0	1-2
Long Eaton United	1-0	1-3	2-1	1-1	1-1	1-0	0-1	1-1		1-3	0-0	1-2	0-0	0-4
Maltby MW	1-2	1-0	1-2	1-1	1-1	3-0	2-0	4-1	3-0		1-2	0-1	1-1	1-1
Norton Woodseats	2-4	0-1	3-2	2-4	2-5	0-0	2-1	1-3	2-0	0-2		0-2	0-2	0-4
Sheffield	1-1	0-2	0-0	4-1	3-1	1-3	4-0	1-1	0-0	2-0	5-0		0-4	1-3
Staveley	3-0	1-2	0-1	0-1	1-2	0-2	3-0	4-0	0-4	2-0	1-1	5-1		1-2
Woolley MW	1-1	4-1	1-2	1-2	4-2	2-1	6-1	0-0	1-1	1-2	2-1	5-3	8-2	

Spalding United FC *pictured at Guiseley before their final championship game on 12.5.84. Back (L-R): Jack Pateman (trainer), Carl Shutt, Kevan Lancaster, Jack Hobson, Nathan Procter, Graham Cawthorne, Dave Birkinshaw, Gary Hull, Mick Hennigan (manager). Front (L-R): David Stenson, Wayne Roebuck, Martin Johnson, Steve Taylor (capt), Rob Haddrell.*

SEASON 1983-84 N.C.E. LEAGUE DIVISION 2 (NORTH)	Armthorpe Welfare	Brook Sports	Collingham	Fryston CW	Grimethorpe MW	Hall Road Rangers	Harrogate Railway	Phoenix Park (BFD)	Pickering Town	Pilkington Recs	Selby Town	Tadcaster Albion	Thorne Colliery	Yorkshire Amateurs
Armthorpe Welfare		1-0	1-0	1-0	1-1	1-1	2-2	2-1	3-0	6-0	1-1	3-0	0-2	1-3
Brooks Sports	1-5		0-0	1-0	3-0	0-3	0-4	1-5	0-1	0-2	0-2	2-2	2-2	0-2
Collingham	0-1	1-2		3-1	3-1	3-2	2-3	0-2	0-2	0-2	0-0	2-1	1-2	0-2
Fryston CW	1-2	7-0	4-2		0-1	1-1	1-4	1-2	5-1	1-0	1-0	1-1	2-1	3-1
Grimethorpe MW	0-3	4-3	2-0	0-0		6-2	1-1	1-2	1-2	4-2	0-0	1-1	4-0	1-4
Hall Road Rangers	1-2	3-2	3-2	1-1	1-1		0-3	1-1	1-3	2-2	2-2	0-1	1-3	2-2
Harrogate Railway	4-0	5-1	1-1	2-1	2-2	6-2		2-1	1-0	3-1	1-1	5-1	1-0	3-0
Phoenix Park (BFD)	1-1	6-1	2-2	5-3	2-0	4-1	0-2		1-2	3-2	2-1	1-1	2-0	2-2
Pickering Town	0-2	0-0	4-0	2-3	0-2	4-0	1-2	1-0		3-1	1-0	0-1	1-1	0-1
Pilkington Recs	3-4	2-0	2-2	1-1	0-2	1-3	2-3	1-1	0-3		1-4	0-0	1-1	0-0
Selby Town	0-1	1-4	5-1	2-3	3-0	1-0	0-3	1-1	4-1	5-2		2-1	3-0	1-1
Tadcaster Albion	0-2	0-4	0-1	3-3	1-1	1-2	0-8	1-2	3-0	0-3	0-3		3-3	1-1
Thorne Colliery	1-2	5-0	0-0	0-2	2-1	2-0	1-1	3-0	2-3	3-2	3-5	5-0		1-0
Yorkshire Amateurs	3-0	0-0	2-0	4-2	1-1	2-1	2-0	3-0	0-1	1-0	0-1	1-0	4-0	

SEASON 1983-84 N.C.E. LEAGUE DIVISION 2 (SOUTH)	Blidworth Welfare	Brigg Town	Graham St Prims	Kimberley Town	Kiveton Park	Oakham United	Retford Rail	Retford Town	Stockbridge Works	Sutton Trinity	Wombwell SA	Worsbrough Bridge MW	Yorkshire Main Colly
Blidworth Welfare		0-3	2-4	1-0	3-4	0-6	3-1	1-3	0-0	2-1	1-0	1-2	0-3
Brigg Town	0-2		3-1	2-1	2-1	0-1	2-1	1-1	4-2	3-0	1-1	2-2	1-2
Graham St Prims	3-2	1-1		0-2	4-1	2-0	0-0	2-1	3-1	6-1	3-1	4-0	4-4
Kimberley Town	1-0	1-1	1-3		1-0	1-0	1-0	0-0	2-2	2-0	2-0	3-1	3-1
Kiveton Park	3-0	1-2	0-3	2-3		2-2	1-3	0-1	0-0	3-2	0-1	1-2	1-0
Oakham United	1-2	6-0	3-0	0-1	2-0		1-0	0-4	2-0	1-0	3-0	2-2	1-2
Retford Rail	4-4	2-1	1-2	0-1	1-2	0-3		0-5	1-3	3-0	0-3	4-1	1-4
Retford Town	6-2	2-2	3-0	5-2	1-0	4-2	4-1		3-1	1-0	2-0	5-1	3-0
Stocksbridge Works	2-0	0-2	1-2	1-2	1-4	1-3	7-1	2-0		3-0	2-2	1-3	0-2
Sutton Trinity	2-5	1-4	2-5	0-2	1-1	0-3	2-2	2-4	0-5		1-1	1-3	1-3
Wombwell SA	0-0	0-1	0-3	0-4	3-0	1-1	3-0	1-2	1-1	3-1		2-1	1-3
Worsbrough Bridge MW	0-1	1-4	4-3	1-1	2-3	4-0	0-1	2-0	3-1	6-3	4-1		3-1
Yorkshire Main Colly	3-0	0-2	3-0	1-2	1-1	2-1	0-0	0-3	4-3	3-0	1-3	1-3	

Ossett Albion's triumphant team which won the Fletcher Motors Cup last Thursday, beating Ilkeston 2-1 in the final. Pictured are (back row, from left) Tony Ogden, Steve Hockett, Nigel Yarrow, David Ingham, Tony Smith, Keith Cusworth, Tony Gavin (manager). Front row, from left, Lindsay Dawson, Adrian Patterson, Peter Eaton (captain), Neil Easter (mascot), Paul Hargreaves, Brian Crowther and Gary Brook.
Photo: Ossett Observer

NORTHERN COUNTIES EAST LEAGUE CUP 83/84

First Round

Armthorpe Welfare v Garforth Miners	1-2
Brigg Town v Sheffield	2-1
B.S.C. (Parkgate) v Selby Town	0-3
Collingham v Long Eaton United	4-2
Farsley Celtic v Pontefract Colls	2-2, 0-2
Hatfield Main v Harworth CI	5-1
Kimberley Town v Hallam	1-3
Maltby MW v Arnold Kingswell	0-1
Norton Woodseats v North Ferriby	0-2
Phoenix Park (BFD) v Hall Road Rgrs	1-3
Pickering Town v Thorne Colliery	2-0
Pilkington Recs v Grimethorpe MW	2-3
Liversedge v Bridlington Town	2-1
Rowntree Mackintosh v Yorkshire Main	5-0
Staveley v Fryston CW	4-2
Stocksbridge Works v Brook Sports	5-0
Sutton Trinity v Blidworth Welfare	2-0
Tadcaster Albion v Denaby United	0-4
Wombwell SA v York RI	1-3
Woolley MW v Bradley Rangers	3-4
Worsbrough Bridge v Ossett Albion	2-4
Yorks Amat v Ossett Town	1-0
Harrogate Railway v Retford Rail	3-1
Kiveton Park v Graham St Prims	1-5
Oakham United v Borrowash Victoria	2-3
Harrogate Town v Scarborough	3-1
Retford Town v Frecheville CA	3-1

Second Round

Graham St Prims v Staveley	1-0
Hatfield Main v Hallam	2-0
Denaby United v Harrogate Railway	4-2
Brigg Town v Harrogate Town	2-0
Arnold Kingswell v Liversedge	2-1
Grimethorpe MW v Retford Town	1-4
Ossett Albion v Bradley Rangers	7-1
Yorkshire Amat v Borrowash Victoria	2-3
Lincoln United v York RI	3-1
Sutton Trinity v Garforth Miners	0-2
Collingham v North Ferriby	1-2
Stocksbridge Works v Pontefract Colls	0-1
Pickering Town v Hall Road Rangers	1-0
Rowntree Mackintosh v Selby Town	3-2

Third Round

Heanor Town v Ossett Albion	1-2
Sutton Town v Arnold	2-5
Mexborough Town v Spalding United	1-1, 1-7
Bridlington Trinity v Retford Town	3-1
Denaby United v Ilkeston Town	0-1
Winterton Rgrs v Alfreton Town	2-0
Belper Town v Pontefract Colls	0-2
Borrowash Victoria v Eastwood Town	2-3
Pickering Town v Thackley	0-2
Appleby Frodingham v Boston	2-3
Emley v Lincoln United	2-2, 2-1
Garforth Miners v North Ferriby	2-0
Graham St Prims v Bentley VW	3-2
Hatfield Main v Rowntree Mackintosh	1-3
Arnold Kingswell v Guisborough Tn	3-1
Brigg Town v Guiseley	2-2, 0-2

Fourth Round

Spalding United v Ossett Albion	1-2
Bridlington Trinity v Arnold Kings	1-2
Boston v Eastwood Town	3-1
Garforth Miners v Rowntree Mack	0-0, 1-3
Arnold v Ilkeston Town	1-3
Thackley v Winterton Rangers	1-2
Pontefract Colls v Guiseley	1-0
Emley v Graham St Prims	1-1, 2-1

Fifth Round

Ilkeston Town v Winterton Rangers	1-0
Ossett Albion v Pontefract Colls	1-0
Rowntree Mackintosh v Boston	1-2
Emley v Arnold Kingswell	5-2

Semi-Finals

Emley v Ossett Albion	0-0, 1-3
Boston v Ilkeston Town	0-5

Final

Ossett Albion v Ilkeston Town	2-1

(at Eastwood Town)

NORTHERN COUNTIES EAST FOOTBALL LEAGUE

LEADING SCORERS – LEAGUE & LEAGUE CUP – SEASON 1983/84

Premier Division

	gls.
M. S. Johnson (Spalding Utd)	30
C. S. Shutt (Spalding Utd)	25
M. Twigger (Arnold)	23
R. V. Baker (Guiseley), W. Rayner (Thackley)	20
M. A. Davis (Guisborough Town), Jeff Webster (Ilkeston Town)	19
D. Cook (Emley)	17
C. Townsend (Arnold)	16
R. I. Wetton (Belper Town)	15
S. T. Matthews (Boston), P. Saunders (Arnold)	14
P. Doidge (Bentley VW), L. G. Richards (Ilkestone Town)	13
G. Cooper (Emley)	12
G. Daniels (Appleby Frodingham), R. Lawson (Guiseley), J. T. Mullins Guisborough Town)	11
Daryl Brook (Emley), T. Jones (Alfreton Town), M. D. Richardson (Eastwood Town)	10

Division 1 North

A. Smith (Ossett Albion)	30
E. Jarrett (Farsley Celtic), K. A. Matthews (Garforth Miners)	17
R. Mortimer (Bradley Rangers), P. Nelson (Rowntree Mackintosh)	16
C. Mulhall (York RI)	14
S. P. Brown (Scarborough), G. D. Elliott (Pontefract Colls), P. Howarth (Rowntree Mackintosh)	13
A. Billingham (Ossett Town), J. Reid (Rowntree Mackintosh), P. Taylor (Garforth Miners), C. Teare (York RI)	11

Division 1 South

R. Guest (Woolley MW)	26
P. M. Acklam (Borrowash Vict)	22
P. Brown (Lincoln United)	19
C. M. Beresford (Denaby United, M. Rodgers (Borrowash Vict)	15
S. R. Cant (Borrowash Vict), G. Smith Denaby United)	13

Division 2 North

A. Canham (Harrogate Railway)	26
M. Couzens (Phoenix Park)	18
D. M. Penney (Fryston CW)	16
I. Mitchell (Selby Town), W. Ward Yorkshire Amat)	14
J. Barnett (Selby Town), C. Spurr (Harrogate Railway)	13
A. R. Martin (Hall Road Rangers), J. North (Grimethorpe MW)	12
C. Frank (Pickering Town)	11
M P Hart (Armthorpe Welfare), D. Whyte (Harrogate Railway)	10

Division 2 South

K. Hutchinson (Retford Town)	21
S. Littlewood (Worsbrough Bridge)	16
P. Hilliard (Graham St Prims), G. Keena (Brigg Town), R. Lewis (Graham St Prims)	15
D. A. Smith (Yorkshire Main)	13
I. W. Whyte (Brigg Town)	12
M. C. Frid (Worsbrough Bridge), G. Mozley (Retford Town), I. Preston (Retford Town), R. P. Radzki (Oakham United)	11

Reserve Division

M. P. Dolan (Thackley)	18
J. Kennedy (Ossett Albion), M. Ripley (Farsley Celtic)	14
M. Clark (Fryston CW)	13
R. B. Sadler (Harrogate Railway), A. Ellis (Pontefract Colls)	12
P. A. Baron (Garforth Miners), J. A. Hannah (Garforth Miners), T. Pritchard (Ossett Town), M. R. Ramsey (Emley), R. B. Whisker (Emley)	11
J. S. Beaumont (Emley), C. D. Helliwell (Emley), R. Kitching (Guiseley), H. Lee (Garforth Miners), P. Murphy (Ossett Town), N. C. Ramsey (Harrogate Town)	10

Boston FC *Back Row (L-R): (Team Trainer), Dave Belton, Paul Lockwood, Steve Chamberlain, Neil Ellis, John Arnold, Brendon Blythe, Sean Farrow, Martyn Boyers. Front Row (L-R): Kev Scrupps, Trevor Hall, Lee Rippin, Sean Matthews, John Spall, Ricky Greenhough, Chris Runnalls.*

Photo: Courtesy Lincolnshire Standard

NORTHERN COUNTIES (EAST)

Club	Leading Goalscorers		Hat-Tricks	Penalties	Most Appearances	
Alfreton Town	J. Whiteley	12	K. Okine (1)	C. Prophett (3)	J. Whiteley	43
	T. Jones	11			C. Prophett	41
	K. Okine	10			D. Markham	40
Appleby Frodingham	G. Daniels	14	–	D. Whiteman (3)	M. O'Neill	36/39
	S. Smith	7			D. Whiteman	36/39
	D. Whiteman	7			M. Muldon	33/39
Arnthorpe Welfare	M. Hart	12	P. Rushton (1)	G. Leighton (2)	G. Leighton	30
	M. Downing	8	(4 goals)		(all matches)	
	P. Rushton	8			G. Hancock	29
					D. Ridley	27
Arnold	Martin Twigger	23	–	–	Trevor Thompson	33
	Chris Townsend	16			Billy Millar	34
	Phil Saunders	14			St Clair Edwards	32
Arnold Kingswell	P. Naisbitt	7	None	P. Dean (3)	M. Waitt	32
	M. Waitt	7		D. Osborn (2)	P. Naisbitt	31
	R. Farrow	4			S. Rann	31
	J. Pass	4				
Belper Town	R. Whetton	16	D. Daley (1)	T. Brown (5)	S. Mann	42/45
	T. Brown	11		R. Downing (1)	P. Mann	42/45
	P. Mann	10			T. Brown	42/45
Bentley V.W.	P. Doidge	13	–	M. Bates (3)	K. Ripley	
	P. Lloyd	5			K. Locke	
	S. Robinson	4			S. Robinson	
Blidworth M.W.	J. Coupe	7	–	J. Coupe (2)	A. Goward	(26)
	A. Locker	6		A. Locker (1)	(all matches)	
	K. Smith	6			T. Buckley	26
					(all matches)	
					S. Geary	25
Borrowash Victoria	P. M. Acklam	22	–	–	G. Cooney	32
	M. Rodgers	15			P. Turner	32
	S. R. Cant	13			I. Grostate	32
					N. Kellogg	32
					S. Cant	32
					P. Acklam	32
Boston	S. Matthews	15	S. Matthews (1)	S. Matthews (4)	J. Arnold	41
	D. Belton	8			D. Belton	40
	S. Chamberlain	7			S. Farrow/J. Spall	38
Bradley Rangers	B. Mortimer	19	–	P. Gibson (2)	A. Hebditch	
	P. Gibson	8			B. Mortimer	
	M. Reid	5			M. Harrold	
	M. Farrer	5				
	T. Hotte	5				
Bridlington Town	J. Speake	7	–	D. Bowman (1)	J. Gosling	24
	I. Hare	4		J. Speake (1)	(all matches)	
	D. Fenton	4			D. Bowman	23
					J. Speake/N. Tate	22
Bridlington Trinity	D. Lancaster	9	D. Lancaster (1)	M. Parker (1)	D. Lancaster	38
	C. McLocklan	8			T. Hood	36
	A. Sugden	8			S. Rodgers	35
Brigg Town	G. Keena	16	G. Keena (1)	G. Keena (5)	S. Guilliatt	
	A. Gibbons	12			D. Othen	
	I. Whyte	10			A. Gibbons	
B.S.C. (Parkgate)	D. Whitehouse	12	D. Whitehouse (1)	–	D. Whitehouse	31
	P. Kay	9	P. Kay (1)		G. Marshall	30
	D. Sykes	7			S. Lill	29
Collingham A.F.C.	G. Ibbetson	6	–	I. Herendi (2)	I. Herendi	27
	J. Dickson	6			K. Wetherop	26
	I. Herendi	5			G. Ibbetson	24
Denaby United	C. Beresford	19	S. Leary (1)	P. Watkin (2)	A. Barnsley	35
	G. Smith	15			C. Beresford	35
	S. Leary	13			G. Smith	33
Dronfield United	D. Herbert	14	D. Herbert (1)	–	D. Herbert	23
	P. Rodgers	6			A. King	23
					M. Lindley	23
Eastwood Town	M. Buxton	15	M. Richardson (1)	S. Johnson (6)	K. Shaw	46/47
	K. Walters	13	M. Wright (1)		S. Johnson	46/47
	M. Richardson	12	G. Collier		J. Eaton	44/47
			(1×4 goals)		G. Wright	44/47
Emley	G. Cooper	25	Three	S. Skirrow (4)	S. Fielding	51
	D. Cook	20			S. Skirrow	50
	D. Brook	13			D. Nichols	47
Farsley Celtic	E. Jarrett	22	E. Jarrett (3)	–	W. Ingleson	41
	J. Carvill	11			T. Rockett	40
	B. Ingleson	10			E. Jarrett	40
Frecheville Community	S. Parkin	7	–	P. Scholey (2)	P. Wareing	31
	P. Wareing	7			(all matches)	
	C. Gaffney	5			P. Scholey	30
					S. Totty	29

Borrowash Victoria *Back Row (L-R): A. Crofts, G. Taylor, I. Grostate, M. Taplin, M. Rofgers. Front Row: P. Turner, M. Dick, A. Dodsworth, D. Leake, N. Dorsett, Scant, N. Kellog.*

Fryston Colliery	C. Betteridge	8	–	C. Betteridge (2)	M. Coulson	31
	K. Waite	7	–	R. Norman (1)	D. Winter	30
	A. Turner	5			A. Turner	29
Garforth Miners	K. Matthews	18	K. Matthews (3)	P. Copley (3)	T. Ward	33
	P. Taylor	13			C. Greenbank	32
					H. Randkins	29
Graham St Prims	P. Hilliard	12	G. Leblond	A. Forster (5)	C. Rees	36/37
	R. Lewis	18	(1×4 goals)	S. Adcock (3)	W. Thompson	34/37
	G. Leblond	9	P. Hilliard (1)		P. Hilliard	34/37
	A. Forster	9	R. Lewis (1)			
Grimethorpe M.W.	J. North	12	J. North (1)	S. Senior (1)	J. Rowley (all matches)	
	T. Wainwright	8			J. North	
	J. Rushforth	7			T. Wainwright	
Guisborough Town						
Guiseley	R. Baker	26	–	–	J. McPhee	43
	B. Lawson	14			J. Kudlentilky	40
	J. McPhee	5			J. Armfield	38
Hall Road Rangers	A. Martin	14	–	–	C. Moody	30/30
	J. Walker	8			J. Walker	29/30
					A. Martin	28/30
Hallam	P. Ellis	11	J. Whitham (2)	G. McHale (1)	S. Phelan	33/33
	J. Whitham	11			S. Green	31/33
	C. Wilson	4			I. Green	31/33
					C. Wilson	31/33
Harrogate Railway Athletic	T. Canham	29	T. Canham (4)	D. Whyte (2)	P. Render	31
	D. Whyte	14	C. Spurr (1)		P. Docking	31
	C. Spurr	13			D. Whyte	30
Harrogate Town	M. Margis	13	–	No record	M. Parker	41/41
	S. Ferebee	10			S. Ferebee	41/41
	D. Ballantyne	7			C. King	40/41
	J. Reynard	7			M. Margis	40/41
					J. Deacey	40/41
Harworth Colliery	M. Bennett	3	M. Bennett (1)	–	J. Perry	26/26
	J. Perry	2			P. Dudley	22/26
	N. Cowans	2				
Hatfield Main						
Heanor Town	P. Haycock	5	–	K. Betts (1)	P. Smalley	26
	K. Betts	4			T. Kerry	23
	N. Clough	4			A. Ball	22
Ilkeston Town	J. Webster	22	J. Webster (2)	J. Webster (5)	T. Cuthbert	43/44
	L. Richards	15			S. Barrett	42/44
	A. Lambert	9			K. Ford	39/44
Kimberley Town	A. Cowlishaw	8	–	C. Francis (3)	K. Mihaly (all matches)	
	C. Francis	7		A. Cowlishaw (2)	C. Smith (all matches)	
	C. Smith	5			A. Cowlishaw	
Kiveton Park						
Lincoln United	P. Brown	27	P. Brown (1)	G. Crosby (2)	M. Walker	46
	S. Brown	9		P. Brown (1)	S. Brown	45
	K. Whitehead	8			P. Brown	45

Retford Town FC *Back Row (L-R): Trainer John Kirk, Nigel Tucker, John Day, Ian Hutchinson, Malcolm Gregory, Keith Hutchinson, Robert Needham, Mark Burrell, Assistant Trainers Keith Revill and Michael Higginson. Seated: Gary Mozley, John Reed, Manager Paddy Buckley, Capt Ken Burton, Michael McCairns, Ian Preston and Patrick Nelson.* Photo: Bob Burgess

Liversedge	C. McFadzean	7	–	J. Cairney (2)	J. Cairney	29/29
	K. Milner	6		C. McFadzean (1)	J. Curley	28/29
	P. Barstow	5		M. Saville (1)	K. Milner	27/29
Long Eaton Utd	D. Hailwood	5	–	D. Hailwood (3)	N. Whitehead	31/31
	W. Robertson	4			M. Baines	30/31
	D. Chapman	4			W. Robertson	29/31
Maltby M.W.F.C.	M. Steventon	13	–	G. Waller (2)	R. Habbin	21
	G. Waller	10		M. Steventon (2)	G. Waller	19
	R. Habbin	6			D. Trickett	19
Mexborough Town	M. Roscoe	7	–	M. Palmer (2)	P. Mellor	34
Athletic	P. Webb	7			K. Powell	33
	S. Dwyer	5			S. Mellor	32
North Ferriby						
Oakham Utd	R. Radzki	14	R. Radzki (1)	R. Radzki (3)	P. Elrich	30/30
	A. Wheatley	9			N. Campion	29/30
	J. Martin	5			R. Radzki	29/30
	P. Elrick	5				
	A. Pack	5				
Osset Albion	A. Smith	34	–	–	N. Yarrow	37
	A. Patterson	12			S. Hockett	36 (1)
					B. Crowther	35 (1)
Ossett Town A.F.	A. Billingham	11	One	–	S. Whiteley	
& S.C.	S. Whiteley	6			(all matches)	
	B. Noble	3			B. Noble	
					P. Wakefield	
Phoenix Park (BFD)	M. Couzens	18	M. Couzens (2)	–	M. Couzens	28/28
	J. Kowal	8			J. Kowal	28/28
	S. Watson	6			P. Devanney	25/28
Pickering Town	C. Frank	12	–	–	P. Bower	31/31
	R. Denney	7			R. Denney	31/31
					D. Chapman	29/31
Pilkington Recreation	S. Bell	15	–	D. Travis (4)	A. Townsend	30/30
	G. Hodgett	8			S. Ostle	29/30
	S. Ostle	6			G. Hodgett	29/30
Retford Town	K. Hutchinson	22	Four	N. Tucker (1)	M. Burrell (all matches)	
	G. Mozley	11		G. Mozley (1)	I. Preston	
	I. Preston	11			P. Nelson	
Rowntree Mackintosh	P. Nelson	22	P. Nelson (2)	J. Reid (5)	J. Reid	38/38
(York)	P. Howarth	16	P. Howarth (1)		P. Nelson	35/38
	J. Reid	13			T. Stanley	31/38
Selby Town	I. Mitchell	15	–	–	I. Robb	32/32
	J. Barnett	14			D. Wilkinson	31/32
	M. Barnett	8			S. Alaster	31/32
Sheffield						
Spalding Utd	M. Johnson	35	M. Johnson (1)	D. Stenson (6)	C. Short	48/48
	C. Short	28	C. Short (1×6,		D. Stenson	46/48
	D. Stenson	8	1×4, 1×3)		M. Johnson	43/48
Staveley	D. Vernon	13	–	–	A. Alkinson	30
	S. Quigley	8			P. Dennis	30
	C. De Giralamo	6			P. Hardy	28

Stocksbridge Works	P. Thompson R. Holley J. Benbow	9 6 5	—	—	R. Moorhouse 20 A. Turner 19 R. Holley 18
Sutton Town	K. Fisher S. Shaw P. Cooper	9 6 6	—	G. Brown (3)	P. Fisher 43/43 S. Lamb 39/43 M. Tasker 38/43
Tadcaster Albion	P. McNamara R. Booth D. Fenton	10 9 4	—	P. McNamara (4)	K. Dwyer (all matches) M. Myers D. Dewsnap
Thackley	W. Rayner R. Bennett M. Driver	21 14 8	W. Rayner (1)	No record	R. Bennett 40 W. Rayner 38 M. Driver 37
Thorne Colliery					
Winterton Rangers	B. Shrimpton B. Mooney G. McNally	10 10 7	—	B. Shrimpton (1)	B. Shrimpton 44/44 P. Markham 37/44 G. McNally 34/44
Wombwell	I. Mann G. Crew J. Levitt P. Angle	4 4 3 3	—	J. Levitt (2)	P. Waller 26 J. Levitt 26 P. Angel 23
Woolley M.W.	R. Guest J. Edgar C. Kendrick	26 10 8	R. Guest (2)	P. Greenwood (1) S. Blakey (1) R. Horbury (1)	C. Kendrick 27/27 K. Holmes 26/27 R. Guest 25/27 G. Parkin 25/27 I. Williams 25/27
Worsbrough Bridge M.W.	S. Littlewood M. Frid K. Brown	19 11 5	S. Littlewood (1) M. Frid (1)	S. Littlewood (2) K. Brown (1)	S. Littlewood 29 D. Snape 27 P. Shaw 26
Yorkshire Amateurs	W. Ward J. McPhee B. Bligh G. Fozzard	17 11 5 5	W. Ward (2)	J. McPhee (3)	J. McPhee 32 A. Parry 30 S. Roberts 30
Yorkshire Main Colliery	D. Smith S. Aldridge P. Dewick	16 11 7	—	M. Duncan (6)	G. Lockwood (all matches) M. Duncan (all matches) L. Dutt
York Railway Institute	C. Mulhall C. Tease B. Mason	15 12 7	—	—	G. Mulhall 30/30 T. Metcalfe 30/30 G. Green 29/30 N. Sanderson 29/30 T. Brandon 29/30

A match to remember for Belper's Mick Williamson when Appleby-Frodingham were the visitors. He took over in goal for ten minutes while the goalkeeper received treatment then reverted to centre forward and scored two in two minutes. Photo: Leo Hoenig

ALFRETON TOWN

President: C. Thornton
Chairman: G. Worth
Manager: G. Worth
Coaches: K. Knowles & C. Prophett
Physiotherapist: K. Knowles
Press Officer & Tel No: None
Secretary: T. McRoy
Address & Tel No: 12 Alma Street, Alfreton. Alfreton 834707
Commercial Manager: None
Address & Tel No:
Address & Tel No of ground: North Street, Alfreton. 832819 **Club shop:** No
Simple ground directions: North Street, off Nottingham Road, Alfreton
No of seats: 120 **Covered accommodation:** 2,000 **Capacity:** 8,500 **Floodlights:** Yes
Year formed: 1959 **Nickname:** Reds **Club sponsors:** Alfreton Sports
Previous names: None
Previous grounds: None
Club colours: Red/White/Red
Change colours: All Yellow
Day for midweek home matches: Wednesday
Record attendance: 5,023 v Matlock Town, Central Alliance **Year:** 1960
Best performance in: F.A. Cup: 1969-70, 1973-4 1st Round Proper
F.A. Trophy: 1983-84 3rd Round Qual
Previous Leagues: Midland Counties, Central Alliance
Clubhouse details: Separate social club committee (Kimberley Breweries)
Present players with Football League experience: C. Prophett
Past players who progressed into the Football League: None
Record transfer fee paid: None
Record transfer fee received: £1,500 for Tony Henson from Chesterfield
Programme details: 12 pages, 10p
Programme Editor: W. Draper
Club metal badges: No
Local newspapers & Tel No: Derbyshire Times, Derby Evening Telegraph, Notts Evening Post, Ripley & Heanor News
Senior Honours: Midland League (3), Derbyshire Senior Cup (5), Midland League Cup (3)

APPLEBY FRODINGHAM

President: J. B. Clayton
Chairman: C. Allen
Manager: R. Clayton
Coach:
Physiotherapist: J. Stallard
Press Officer & Tel No: None
Secretary: G. Spencer
Address & Tel No: 0724 843117 (H) 0724 853378 (B)
Commercial Manager: None
Address & Tel No:
Address & Tel No of ground: Brumby Hall, Ashby Road, Scunthorpe. 0724 843024 **Club Shop:** No
Simple ground directions: M180, M181, A18, take 1st exit out at Queensway roundabout, ground 300 yds on left
No of seats: None **Covered accommodation:** 300 **Capacity:** 4,000 **Floodlights:** No
Year formed: 1920 **Nickname:** Steelmen **Club sponsors:** Cherry Mill Ltd
Previous names: None
Previous grounds: None
Club colours: Amber/Black/Amber
Change colours: Blue & White stripes/White/Black
Day for midweek home matches: Wednesday
Record attendance: Not known **Year:**
Best performance in: F.A. Cup: 1977-78, 1982-83 4th Qualifying Round
F.A. Vase: 1978-79, 1981-82, 1982-83, 1983-84 3rd Round
Previous Leagues: Scunthorpe Lindsey, Lincolnshire
Clubhouse details: Bar open match days (Saturday) 12.00-5.30pm, Midweek 6.30-10.30pm
Present players with Football League experience: None
Past players who progressed into the Football League: None
Record transfer fee paid: None
Record transfer fee received: £1,500 each, S. Earl to Scunthorpe Utd & P. Wainwright to Grimsby Town
Programme details: None
Programme Editor: G. Spencer
Club metal badges: No
Local newspapers & Tel No: Scunthorpe Evening Telegraph, Scunthorpe Star
Senior Honours: Midland League Cup, Lincs League (3), Lincs League Challenge Cup (4), Lincs Senior B Cup (3)
Club Captain (1983-84): Tony Hoodless **Player of the Year (1983-84):** G. Daniels

ARNOLD

Chairman: J. Martin
Manager: J. Harrison
Coach: I. Hollett
Physiotherapist: I. Long (Tel: 266854)
Secretary & Tel No: M. Leivers. 878258 (home), 266440 (business)
Commercial Manager: C. Wilkinson
Press Officer & Tel No: J. Brace. 207227
Address & Tel No of ground: Gedling Road, Arnold. 266330
Simple ground directions: Rear of Arnold Market
No of seats: 250 **Covered accommodation:** 1,000 **Capacity:** 4,000 **Floodlights:** Yes
Club colours: Maroon shorts, Gold shirts & stockings **Change colours:** Red shirts, White shorts
Nickname: Saints **Club sponsors:** Hanger Motors
Previous Leagues: Central Alliance, Midland Counties
Previous names: Arnold St Marys **Club Shop:** No
Record attendance: 3,850 v Bristol Rovers, Nov 1967
Clubhouse details: Arnold Football & Sportsman's Club, 144 St Albans Road, Arnold
Best year in FA Cup: 1st Round Proper, 1967 & 1977 **Best year in FA Trophy:** 3rd Round, 1970, v Wigan Ath
Present players with Football League First Team experience: None
Local Newspapers: Nottingham Evening Post **Club Metal Badges:** No **Midweek match day:** Tuesday
Senior honours won: Notts Senior Cup (7 times)

A lot of hot air at Stavely Works! Photo: Leo Hoenig

Long Eaton's Steve Hawley heads for goal at Hanworth Colliery Institute. Photo: David Keward

Norton Woodseats are now known as Dronfield United. This is their very pleasant enclosed ground at 'The Hare and Hounds'. Photo: David Keward

BELPER TOWN

President: G. Glossop
Chairman: R. Kirkland
Manager: Neville Morton
Coach: Joe Mulholland
Physiotherapist: Graham Sanderson
Secretary: P. Herrett
Address & Tel No: 75 Dovedale Crescent, Belper. 077382 2282 (H), 4181 (B)
Commercial Manager: Kevin Hall
Address & Tel No: 7 Leamington Street, Ripley, Derbys. Ripley 47676
Press Officer & Tel No: Richard Kirkland. Belper (077382) 6090 (H), 5517 (B)
Club shop: No
Address & Tel No of ground: Christ Church Meadow, Bridge Street, Belper, Derbyshire. Tel: 077382 5549
Simple ground directions: Junction 28 off M1, A38 to A610, A610 to A6. Ground on A6 at junction with A517
No of seats: 100 **Covered accommodation:** 1,000 **Capacity:** 3,000 **Floodlights:** Yes
Year formed: 1951 **Nickname:** The Nailers **Club sponsors:** Alan Ward Sportswear & various match sponsors
Previous names: None
Previous grounds: None
Club colours: Gold/Black/Gold
Change colours: All White
Day for midweek home matches: Tuesday
Record attendance: 3,600 v Ilkeston Town **Year:** 1951
Best performance in: F.A. Cup: 1957-58 4th Qualifying Round
F.A. Trophy: 1982-83 3rd Qualifying Round
Previous Leagues: Central Alliance, Midland Counties
Clubhouse details: Open Thurs & Fri evenings, match days and training nights
Record transfer fee received: £700 for Brian Hall to Mansfield Town
Programme details: 12 pages, 15p
Programme Editor: B. Kirkland
Local newspapers & Tel No: Belper News, Belper 5517, Derby Evening Telegraph
Club metal badges: No
Senior Honours: Midland League, Derbyshire Senior Cup
Club Captain (1983-84): Steve Mann
Player of the Year (1983-84): Mark Thornley

BENTLEY VICTORIA WELFARE

President:
Chairman: G. Jennings
Manager: N. Brandon
Coach: M. Hunt
Physiotherapist: As coach
Secretary: Mrs. E. Follows
Address & Tel No: Doncaster 873546
Commercial Manager:
Address & Tel No:
Press Officer & Tel No:
Address & Tel No of ground: Bentley Colliery Ground, The Avenue, Bentley, Doncaster
Club Shop: No
Simple ground directions: A19 from Doncaster (2 miles) to bottom of High St, right at Arksey Lane, first left into Avenue
No of seats: None **Covered accommodation:** 200 **Capacity:** 8,000 **Floodlights:** This season
Year formed: 1930 **Nickname:** Vics **Club sponsors:** None
Previous names: Bentley Victoria
Previous grounds: Bentley Park
Club colours: All White
Change colours: Red/Black/Red
Day for midweek home matches: Tuesday & Thursday
Record attendance: 900 v Emley S.Final Lge Cup **Year:** 1982
Best performance in: F.A. Cup: None
F.A. Vase: 4th Rnd 1978-79
Previous Leagues: Yorkshire
Record transfer fee received: None
Programme details: 8 pages, 15p
Programme Editor: Paul Follows
Local newspapers & Tel No: Doncaster Evening Post
Club metal badges: No
Senior Honours: Yorks Division 2, Runners Up, Yorks Division 3, Champions.
Club Captain (1983-84): Keith Ripley
Player of the Year (1983-84): John Faulkner

BOSTON

President: W. Jackson
Chairman: W. M. Stanwell
Manager: M. Boyers
Coach:
Physiotherapist: K. Vincent
Secretary: R. Gell
Address & Tel No: (0205) 723381 (H) (0205) 63078 (B)
Commercial Manager: None
Address & Tel No:
Press Officer & Tel No: J. Ashberry. (0205) 67551
Address & Tel No of ground: Tattershall Road, Boston (0205) 65470
Club shop: No
Simple ground directions: From the inner relief road take the Horncastle road (B1183), turn first left and at the sluice bridge turn right into Tattershall Road
No of seats: 450 **Covered accommodation:** 950 **Capacity:** 6,600 **Floodlights:** No
Year formed: 1963 **Nickname:** Poachers **Club sponsors:** Roosters
Previous names: None
Previous grounds: Mayflower
Club colours: White shirts, Navy shorts, White/Navy socks
Change colours: All Red
Day for midweek home matches: Tuesday
Record attendance: 2,700 v Boston Utd, F.A. Cup **Year:** 1970
Best performance in: F.A. Cup: 1976-7 v Barnsley, 1st Round Proper, 1-3 (A)
F.A. Trophy: 1979-80 v Mossley, 2nd Round Proper, 0-0 3-6
Previous Leagues: Lincolnshire, Central Alliance, Eastern Co, Midland Co
Clubhouse details: Open during match hours
Present players with Football League experience: None
Past players who progressed into the Football League: None
Record transfer fee paid: None
Record transfer fee received: £2,000 for Mark Cox from Boston Utd
Programme details: 16 pages, 15p
Programme Editor: Jeremy Ashberry
Local newspapers & Tel No: Lincolnshire Standard, Lincolnshire Echo
Club metal badges: No
Senior Honours: Lincolnshire League, Central Alliance League, Lincolnshire Senior Cup (4), Midland Counties League (3), Midland Counties League Cup
Club Captain (1983-84): Sean Farrow
Player of the Season (1983-84): David Belton

Denaby United *Back Row (L-R): Dave Moxon, John Whittaker, Steve Eamer, David Brown, Colin Beresford, Andrew Barnsley, Gary Kay, Mick Leng. Front Row (L-R): Tim Seville, Kevin Deakin, Gary Smith, Mick Horne, Roy Ford (manager), Phil Watkin, Steve Leary, John Bukovina.*

Eastwood Town *Back Row: D. Myatt (trainer), A. Kirk, P. Fletcher, J. Eaton, K. Shaw, M. Richardson, N. Lovell, K. Walters, R. James (asst trainer). Front Row: G. Collier, M. Buxton, G. Wright, S. Johnson, B. Hunter, B. Jeffrey (manager).*

BRIDLINGTON TRINITY

President: Ian Brackenbury
Chairman: H. (Frank) Catt
Manager: Colin McLocklan
Coach:
Physiotherapist:
Secretary: Arthur W. Petch
Address & Tel No: 18 Midway Avenue, Bridlington, E. Yorks YO16 4NU. 0262 670448
Commercial Manager: None
Address & Tel No:
Press Officer & Tel No: None
Club shop: No
Address & Tel No of ground: Queensgate Football Ground, Queensgate, Bridlington. 0262 603879 (match days only)
Simple ground directions: A166 to Bridlington, turn left at traffic lights, over railway bridge to next set of lights and turn right into Queensgate, Ground 400 yds on right
No of seats: 350 **Covered accommodation:** 300 **Capacity:** 3,000 **Floodlights:** No
Year formed: 1935 **Nickname:** Emerald Greens **Club sponsors:** None
Previous names: None
Club colours: Green/White/White
Previous grounds: None
Change colours: Blue/White/Blue
Day for midweek home matches: Wednesday
Record attendance: Unknown **Year:**
Best performance in: F.A. Cup: Unknown
F.A. Trophy: 1969-70, 1973-74 1st Round
Previous Leagues: East Riding Amateur, Yorkshire, Midland Counties
Clubhouse details: Blenheim Road, Bridlington. Open licence hours
Present players with Football League experience: None
Past players who progressed into the Football League: Paul Olberg (Scunthorpe)
Record transfer fee paid: None
Record transfer fee received: £2,500, David Leadbeater, Grantham
Programme details: 8 pages, 10p
Programme Editor: H. F. Carr
Club metal badges: No
Local newspapers & Tel No: Hull Daily Mail 0262 672327, Sports Mail 0482 27111, Bridlington Free Press 0262 677305
Senior Honours: Yorkshire League Div 1 (3), Midland Counties Cup, Midland Counties League Runners-up, East Riding Senior Cup & Runners-up
Club Captain (1983-84): Dave Adams

DENABY UNITED

President: A. Wilson
Chairman: F. Martin
Manager: R. Ford
Coach: J. Kirk
Physiotherapist: J. Scott
Secretary: A. Jones
Address & Tel No: Rotherham 866316
Commercial Manager: M. Hemmingway
Address & Tel No:
Press Officer & Tel No: None
Address & Tel No of ground: Tickhill Square, Denaby Main
Simple ground directions: From Mexborough: Hill Top Road, Bolton Street, Wheatley Street. From: Conisbrough-Wadsworth Street
No of seats: 750 **Covered accommodation:** 250 **Capacity:** 6,000 **Floodlights:** No
Year formed: 1902 **Nickname:** None **Club sponsors:** Cadeby Colliery
Club colours: Red and White/Red/Red
Change colours: Green and Yellow stripes/Green/Yellow
Previous Names: None
Previous Grounds: None
Record attendance: v Voldham Ath, F.A. Cup 1st Round Proper **Year:** 1958
Previous Leagues: Midland
Programme: 12 pages, free
Programme Editor: David Green
Club Captain (1983-84): John Whittaker
Player of the Year (1983-84): Colin Beresford

EASTWOOD TOWN

President: D. Pettitt
Chairman: G. H. Belshaw
Manager: W. G. Jeffrey
Coach:
Physiotherapist: G. C. Haslam
Press Officer & Tel No: Secretary
Secretary: P. Farrell
Address & Tel No: 0773 715500 (H) 0602 470451 (B)
Commercial Manager: R. Cheatle
Address & Tel No: 07737 69431
Address & Tel No of ground: Coronation Park, Eastwood, Notts. 07737 2301
Club shop: Yes
Simple ground directions: M1 (exit 27 from north, 26 from South) ground behind fire station, enter from Chewton Street
No of seats: 100 **Covered accommodation:** 1,000 **Capacity:** 6,600 **Floodlights:** Yes
Year formed: 1953 **Nickname:** Badgers **Club sponsors:** Fryer Group of Derby
Previous names: Eastwood Colliery
Club colours: Black/White stripes, Black shorts/socks
Previous grounds: None
Change colours: All Yellow/All White
Day for midweek home matches: Tuesday or Wednesday
Record attendance: 2,500 v Wealdstone **Year:** 1967-8
Best performance in: F.A. Cup: 1975-6 3rd Qualifying Round
F.A. Trophy: 1978-9 1st Round Proper
Previous Leagues: Notts Alliance, Central Alliance, East Midlands
Clubhouse details: Open normal licenced hours except Sat (11.00-2.30pm, 5.00-11.00pm). Meals, snacks and sandwiches always available. Steward: Keith Burton, 07737 5823
Present players with Football League experience: Martin Wright (Chesterfield, Torquay)
Past players who progressed into the Football League: None
Record transfer fee paid: None
Record transfer fee received: £500
Club metal badges: No
Programme details: 2+ pages, 10p
Programme Editor: Paddy Farrell
Local newspapers & Tel No: Eastwood & Kimberley Advertiser, Notts Even. Post, Derby Even. Telegraph
Senior Honours: Midland League & Runners-up (2), Midland League Cup (2), Notts Senior Cup (4), Northern Counties East Runners-Up
Club Captain (1983-84): Graham Wright
Player of the Year (1983-84): Neil Lovell

EMLEY

President: Peter Maude
Chairman: Alec F. Hardy
Manager:
Coach: Michael Pamment
Physiotherapist: Alan Graham
Press Officer & Tel No: None
Secretary: Gordon Adamson
Address & Tel No: 219 Rowley Lane, Lepton, Huddersfield HD8 0EH. Huddersfield 602720
Commercial Manager: None
Address & Tel No:
Club shop: No
Address & Tel No of ground: Emley Welfare Sports Ground, Emley, Huddersfield. Tel: Wakefield 848398
Simple ground directions: M1 to junction 38, follow Huddersfield signs to roundabout, turn left onto A636 for approx ¾-mile, turn right, 1 mile into Emley
No of seats: None **Covered accommodation:** 1,000 **Capacity:** 5,000 **Floodlights:** Yes
Year formed: 1903 **Nickname:** None **Club sponsors:** Fleet Steel Services
Previous names: None
Previous grounds: None
Club colours: Maroon & Blue/Blue/Blue
Change colours: Blue/Maroon/Maroon
Day for midweek home matches: Tuesday
Record attendance: 5,134 v Barking, F.A. Amateur Cup **Year:** 1969
Best performance in: F.A. Cup: 1974-5, 1976-7 3rd Qualifying Round
F.A. Trophy: 1979-80 1st Round Proper
Previous Leagues: Huddersfield, Yorkshire
Clubhouse details: Open 7 days. Bingo, dancing, artists, food supplied
Present players with Football League experience: Daryl Brock (Huddersfield Town)
Past players who progressed into the Football League: Graham Cooper (Huddersfield Town)
Programme details: 8 pages, 10p
Programme Editor: Gordon Adamson
Local newspapers & Tel No: Huddersfield Examiner 0484 37444, Huddersfield Chronicle 0484 862219
Senior Honours: Yorkshire League, Yorkshire League Cup, Sheffield Senior Challenge Cup
Club Captain (1983-84): Dennis Brookes **Player of the Year (1983-84):** Gerry Quinn

GUISBOROUGH TOWN

President: J. Morgan, MBE
Chairman: J. Mapplebeck
Manager: S. Fellows
Coach: D. Aldridge
Physiotherapist: G. Miller
Press Officer & Tel No: As Secretary
Secretary: T. B. Milward
Address & Tel No: Guisborough 35901 (H) 0642 56728 (B)
Commercial Manager: None
Address & Tel No:
Address & Tel No of ground: King George V, Howlebeck Road, Guisborough. Tel: 37904 **Club shop:** Yes
Simple ground directions: Upon entering Guisborough from Middlesbrough turn left at 2nd set traffic lights into Park Lane, proceed 400 yds and turn left into Howlebeck Road and straight on
No of seats: None **Covered accommodation:** Yes **Capacity:** 5,000 **Floodlights:** Yes
Year formed: 1973 **Nickname:** Priorymen **Club sponsors:** Friar Tuckers, Guisborough
Previous names: None
Previous grounds: None
Club colours: All Red with White trim
Change colours: All Yellow
Day for midweek home matches: Wednesday
Record attendance: 3,100 v Hungerford Town **Year:** 1980
Best performance in: F.A. Cup: None
F.A. Vase: 1980 Finalists
Previous Leagues: Middlesbrough & District, South Bank, Northern Alliance
Clubhouse details: Completion for 1984 season
Present players with Football League experience: A. McCreesh (Middlesbrough), G. Forster (Hartlepool)
Past players who progressed into the Football League: Mark Robinson (Hartlepool), Paul Wood (Portsmouth), Mark Forster (Leicester), Frank Harrison (Middlesbrough)
Programme details: 24 pages, 15p
Programme Editor: M. Hodgson
Local newspapers & Tel No: Middlesbrough Sports & Evening Gazette, 0642 245401
Senior Honours: South Bank League & Cup, N. Riding Senior Cup, Northern Alliance League & Cup, F.A. Vase Finalists
Club Captain (1983-84): P. Aldridge **Player of the Year (1983-84):** M. Taylor

GUISELEY

President: N. Threapleton
Chairman: N. Threapleton
Manager: M. Beck
Coach: M. Beck
Physiotherapist: J. Clark
Press Officer & Tel No: H. Pittendreigh. Leeds 677207
Secretary: C. E. Waite
Address & Tel No: 23 Netherfield Road, Guiseley, Leeds. Guiseley 74097
Commercial Manager: M. Schofield
Address & Tel No: Leeds 587003
Address & Tel No of ground: Nethermoor Ground, Otley Road, Guisley. Guis. 72872 **Club shop:** Yes
Simple ground directions: A65 from Leeds direct to ground, 10 miles from Leeds
No of seats: 400 **Covered accommodation:** 600 **Capacity:** 4,000 **Floodlights:** No
Year formed: 1909 **Nickname:** None **Club sponsors:** Various
Previous names: None
Previous grounds: None
Club colours: All White
Change colours: Yellow/Blue/Yellow
Day for midweek home matches: Wednesday
Record attendance: 2,000 v Willenhall Town, F.A. Vase Quarter-Final **Year:** 1980-1
Best performance in: F.A. Cup: None
F.A. Vase: 1980-1 6th Round
Previous Leagues: West Riding County Amateur, West Yorkshire Yorkshire
Clubhouse details: Social club open evenings and weekends
Present players with Football League experience: Harney, Baker, Gartland, Harrison
Past players who progressed into the Football League: K. Walwyn (York City)
Programme details: Free
Programme Editor: Mike Schofield
Local newspapers & Tel No: Bradford Telegraph & Argus, Yorkshire Eve. Post, Airedale & Wharfedale Ob'ver
Club metal badges: No
Senior Honours: West Riding County Cup (4), Yorkshire League Cup Winners, Yorkshire League Runners-up
Club Captain (1983-84): Dave Houlston **Player of the Year (1983-84):** Paul Cartland

HEANOR TOWN

President: H. Holmes
Chairman: J. Woolley
Manager: D. Berresford
Company Secretary: K. Costello
Coach:
Physiotherapist:
Secretary: S. Wilton
Address & Tel No: "Haven Holme", 57 Main Road, Smalley, Derbyshire DE7 6DS. 0332 880199
Commercial Manager: S. Wilton
Address & Tel No:
Press Officer & Tel No: S. Wilton
Club shop: No
Address & Tel No of ground: The Town Ground, Mayfield Avenue, Heanor, Derbyshire. Board Room: Langley Mill (0773) 713742. Social Club: Langley Mill (0773) 715815
Simple ground directions: M1 Junc 27 – A 608 Mansfield – Derby, approx 6 miles. M1 Junc 26 – A 610 – Ripley, approx 9 miles. Ground is 200 yards from Market Square
No of seats: 200 **Covered accommodation:** 2,500 **Capacity:** 6,000 (terraced) **Floodlights:** Yes
Year formed: 1883 **Nickname:** Lions **Club sponsors:** None
Previous names: None
Club colours: White/Black/White
Previous grounds: Midland Road
Change colours: All Red
Day for midweek home matches: Monday or Wednesday
Record attendance: 6,511 v Carlisle Utd, F.A. Cup 1st Round **Year:** 15 Nov, 1958
Best performance in: **F.A. Cup:** 1892, 1894, 1899, 1902, 1959, 1963 1st Round
F.A. Trophy: 1971, 1981 2nd Qualifying Round
Previous Leagues: Central Combination, Notts Alliance, Central Alliance, Midland Counties, West Midlands (Regional), Northern Counties East Premier Division
Clubhouse details: Open 12.00-3.00pm, 7.30-11.00pm daily. Open until 5.30 on match days
Present players with Football League experience: Keith Betts (Sheffield U), Vince Duffy (Scunthorpe U)
Past players who progressed into the Football League:
Record transfer fee paid: None
Record transfer fee received: £10,000 from Shrewsbury Town for Nigel Pearson
Programme details: 32 pages, 5p
Programme Editor: S. Wilson
Club metal badges: No
Local newspapers & Tel No: Nottingham Evening Post, Derby Evening Telegraph, Ripley & Heanor News, Derbyshire Times
Senior Honours: Central Alliance Champions 1956-57, 1957-58, Runners-up (2), Midland League Runners-up (2), Derbyshire Senior Challenge Cup Winners (6), Runners-up (3), West Midlands Regional League Runners-up (1)
Club Captain (1983-84): Perry Smalley
Player of the Year (1983-84): Perry Smalley

ILKESTON TOWN

Joint Presidents: Garry Birtles/Robert Lindsay
Chairman: J. Raynor
Manager: T. Cuthbert
Coach: None
Physiotherapist: F. Fearn
Secretary: A. J. Jackson
Address & Tel No: 26 Milton Street, Ilkeston, Derbys 0602 322565
Commercial Manager: None
Address & Tel No:
Press Officer & Tel No: Norman Stevenson. Nottm 301831
Address & Tel No of ground: Manor Road, Ilkeston. Tel Ilkeston 324094 **Club shop:** On ground
Simple ground directions: Via M1, A52, A609, A608
No of seats: 400 **Covered accommodation:** 600 **Capacity:** 10,000 **Floodlights:** None
Year formed: 1945 **Nickname:** Robins **Club sponsors:**
Previous names: None
Club colours: Red/White/Red
Previous grounds: None
Change colours: Blue or White/Black or White/White or Red
Day for midweek home matches: Wednesday
Record attendance: 10,000 v Rochdale, F.A. Cup **Year:** 1951
Best performance in: **F.A. Cup:** 1951
F.A. Trophy: 1982-83 (last 16)
Previous Leagues: Central Alliance, Midland
Clubhouse details: None
Present players with Football League experience: A. Lambert, J. Parry, L. Richards
Past players who progressed into the Football League: G. Barrowcliffe, J. Tudor, J. Parry
Record transfer fee paid: None
Record transfer fee received: £5,000
Programme details: 4 pages, 10p
Programme Editor: John Raynor
Club metal badges: No
Local newspapers & Tel No: Ilkeston Advertiser, Derby Telegraph, Nottingham Post
Senior Honours: Midland League, Derbyshire Senior Cup
Club Captain (1983-84): Lloyd Richards
Players of the Season (1983-84): Paul Gregory (Players), Scott Barrett (Club)

MEXBOROUGH TOWN ATHLETIC

President: Tony Sleight
Chairman: Graham Calland
Manager: Steve Mellor
Coach:
Physiotherapist: J. Scott
Press Officer & Tel No: Secretary
Secretary: William Stones
Address & Tel No: 0709 586939
Commercial Managers: D. Trickett & W. Stones
Address & Tel No: 0709 586939
Address & Tel No of ground: Hampden Road, Mexborough, South Yorkshire (0709) 586479/583426 **Club shop:** Yes
Simple ground directions: Just off the A6023 (Conisbrough – Mexborough Road)
No of seats: 250 **Covered accommodation:** Stand **Capacity:** 5,000 **Floodlights:** No
Year formed: 1962 **Nickname:** The Boro' **Club sponsors:** Tony Sleight Car Sales
Previous names: Mexborough Town
Club colours: Royal Blue/White
Previous grounds: None
Change colours: Green or Yellow/Black
Day for midweek home matches: Tuesday
Record attendance: 1,800 v Scarborough, F.A. Trophy 3rd Round **Year:** 1972-3
Best performance in: F.A. Cup: 1975-6 4th Qualifying Round
F.A. Trophy: 1972-3 3rd Round Proper (last 16)
Previous Leagues: Yorkshire, Midland Counties
Clubhouse details: Mexborough Athletic Club & Miners' Welfare
Present players with Football League experience:
Past players who progressed into the Football League: Billy Whitehurst
Record transfer fee paid: Not disclosed by club
Record transfer fee received: £1,800 from Hull City for Billy Whitehurst
Programme details: 20 pages, 10p
Programme Editor: Bill Stones
Local newspapers & Tel No: South Yorkshire Times, Sheffield "Green-un"
Club metal badges: Yes
Senior Honours: Yorkshire League Div 1, Yorkshire League Cup, Sheffield Senior Cup (8), Yorkshire League Double 1972-3
Club Captain (1983-84): John Tandy

Mexborough Town Athletic *Back Row (L-R): W. Smith (trnr), K. Powell, S. Smith, P. Webb, P. Mellor, K. Murphy, R. Batham, M. Palmer, G. Rowbotham (asst man). Front Row (L-R): G. Parkin, S. Mellor (magr), A. Rose, J. Tandy (capt), P. Piearcey, S. Battams.*

PONTEFRACT COLLERIES F.C.

President: R. Blatherwick
Chairman: T. Dunwell
Manager: P. Cooper
Coach: P. Cooper
Physiotherapist: D. Sharp
Secretary: S. Mason
Address & Tel No: (707756)
Commercial Manager: None
Address & Tel No:
Press Officer & Tel No: T. Bullock (Pontefract 700239)
Address & Tel No of ground: Skinner Lane, Pontefract. (0977 702180)
Simple ground directions: Exit Junction 32 from M62. Left at first traffic lights to ground
No of seats: None **Covered accommodation:** Yes **Capacity:** 250 **Floodlights:** No
Year formed: 1958 **Nickname:** The Colls **Club sponsors:** None
Club colours: All Blue
Change colours: Red
Previous Names: None
Previous Grounds: None
Record attendance: 500 v Winterton Rangers YL Cup Qtr Final **Year:** 1981
Previous Leagues: West Yorkshire
Programme: 16 pages, 20p
Clubhouse details: Licensed bar
Programme Editor: Terry Bullock
Club Captain (1983-84): Alan Thaler
Player of the Season (1983-84): Andrew Butterwick

SPALDING UNITED

President:
Chairman: A. H. Porter
Manager: M. Hennigan
Coach:
Physiotherapist:
Secretary: C. A. Feakes
Address & Tel No: 0775 67190 (H)
0775 2677 (B)
Commercial Manager: A. Newton
Address & Tel No: 0775 5300
Press Officer & Tel No: C. A. Feakes 0775 67190
Address & Tel No of ground: Sir Halley Stewart Field, Winfrey Avenue, Spalding. 0775 4957 **Club shop:** No
Simple ground directions: Town centre off A16, adjacent bus station
No of seats: 350 **Covered accommodation:** 2,500 **Capacity:** 7,000 **Floodlights:** Yes
Year formed: 1921 **Nickname:** The Tulips **Club sponsors:** None
Previous names: None
Previous grounds: None
Club colours: Blue & White hoops
Change colours: All White
Day for midweek home matches: Tuesday
Record attendance: 6,972 v Peterborough Utd, F.A. Cup **Year:** 1952
Best performance in: F.A. Cup: 1964-5 v Newport Co, 1st Round, 3-5 (a)
F.A. Trophy: 1974-5 v Worksop, 3rd Qualifying Round, 2-3 (a)
Previous Leagues: United Counties, Eastern Counties, Central Alliance
Clubhouse details: Open matchdays
Present players with Football League experience: G. Cawthorne (Doncaster Rovers)
Past players who progressed into the Football League: None
Record transfer fee paid: None
Record transfer fee received: None
Programme details: 16 pages, 10p
Programme Editor: Colin Feakes
Club metal badges: Yes
Local newspapers & Tel No: Spalding Guardian, Lincolnshire Free Press 0775 5021
Senior Honours: United Counties Premier League 1954-55, 1974-75, Northern Counties (East) Premier 1983-84
Club Captain (1983-84): Steve Taylor **Player of the Season (1983-84):** Martin Johnson

Sutton Town *Back Row: Ken Burton (trainer), Pete Cooper, Sean Kay, Mick Tasker, Steve Chadbourne, Rick Knowles, Alan Ogrizovic, Paul Fisher, John Flint. Front Row: Steve Shaw, Dave Roberts, Geoff Brown, Steve Lamb, Gary Timmins.*

SUTTON TOWN

President: P. Moody
Chairman: Colin Straw
Manager: Daryl Claypole
Coach: Ken Peck
Assist. Manager: Mick Taylor
Secretary: Derek Skinner
Address & Tel No: 7 Forest Street, Annesley, Woodhouse, Kirkby-in-Ashfield, Notts. 0623 752798 (H), 0623 555000 (B)
Commercial Manager: Jack Swinbourne
Address & Tel No: 0623 34222
Press Officer & Tel No: Steve Jarvis, 0623 34466
Address & Tel No of ground: Lowmoor Road, Kirkby-in-Ashfield, Notts. Tel: 0623 752181
Club shop: Yes, 159 Sheepbridge Lane, Mansfield, Notts
Simple ground directions: M1 Junction 27, follow signs Mansfield into Kirkby-in-Ashfield, 2nd left, across traffic lights, ground at rear of Lowmoor Inn
No of seats: None **Covered accommodation:** 400 **Capacity:** 8,000 **Floodlights:** Yes
Year formed: 1885 **Nickname:** The Snipes **Club sponsors:** Hardwick Motors, Knighthood Quickprint
Previous names: None
Club colours: White shirts, Black shorts
Previous grounds: Russell St, The Avenue Gnd, Skegby M.W., Priestsic Rd
Change colours: All Red
Day for midweek home matches: Wednesday
Record attendance: 1,562 v Leeds Utd, opening of floodlights **Year:** 1980
Best performance in: F.A. Cup: 1933-34 2nd Round Proper
F.A. Trophy: 1983-84 1st Round Proper
Previous Leagues: Midland, Central Alliance, Notts Alliance, Central Comb, Derbys Sen., Midland Comb, Notts & Derbys, Notts & Dist
Clubhouse details: None at present
Present players with Football League experience: Phil Orton (Mansfield)
Past players who progressed into the Football League: Ivan Hollett (Mansfield), Colin Walker (Barnsley)
Record transfer fee paid: None
Record transfer fee received: £300 for Ivan Hollett to Mansfield Town
Programme Editor: Steve Jarvis.
Programme details: 20 pages, 15p
Club metal badges: Yes, 25p
Local newspapers & Tel No: Notts Free Press, Sutton & Kirkby News
Senior Honours: Notts Senior Cup (17), Notts & District League (2), Derbyshire Senior League (3), Central Alliance
Club Captain (1983-84): Paul Fisher

THACKLEY

President: Councillor P. Hockney
Chairman: D. Brayshaw
Manager: J. Mackay
Coach: J. Mackay
Physiotherapist: M. Atkinson
Press Officer & Tel No: As Secretary
Secretary: S. Willingham
Address & Tel No: Bradford (0274) 598589
Commercial Manager:
Address & Tel No:
Address & Tel No of ground: Dennyfield, Ainsbury Avenue, Thackley, Bradford. Tel: Bradford 615571 **Club shop:** No
Simple ground directions: From centre of Thackley – Thackley Road, turn right, Ainsbury Avenue
No of seats: 300 **Covered accommodation:** 300 **Capacity:** 4,500 **Floodlights:** Yes
Year formed: 1930 **Nickname:** None **Club sponsors:** Sports Shoes Unlimited
Previous names: Thackley Wesleyians
Previous grounds: None
Club colours: Red & White striped shirts, Black shorts
Change colours: Blue & White striped shirts, Blue shorts
Previous Leagues: Bradford Amateur, West Riding County, West Yorkshire, Yorkshire
Day for midweek home matches: Tuesday
Record attendance: 1,500 v Leeds United **Year:** 1984
Best performance in: F.A. Cup:
F.A. Vase: 1980-81 5th Round
Clubhouse details: Open every night except Monday
Present players with Football League experience:
Past players who progressed into the Football League: Tony Brown (Leeds Utd)
Record transfer fee paid: None
Record transfer fee received: None
Programme details: 8 pages, 10p
Programme Editor: S. L. Willingham
Local newspapers & Tel No: Bradford Telegraph & Argus
Club metal badges: No
Senior Honours: West Riding County Cup (2), Yorkshire League Div 2
Club Captain (1983-84): Micky Driver

Hallam FC

Long Eaton United *Back Row, left to right: Willie Robinson, Pete McGurk, David Hailwood, Nigel Whitehead, Steve Hawley, Andy Brown. Front Row: Kevin Jackson, Mick Bains, Richard Davis, Paul Tomlin, Paul Broughton, Darrel Chapman.* Photo: David Keward

DIVISION ONE (NORTH)

BRADLEY RANGERS

President:
Chairman: G. Murphy
Manager: A. Pearce
Coach: J. Inglesby
Physiotherapist: R. Bates
Secretary: David Platt
Address & Tel No: 0484 656422 (H) 0484 24283 (B)
Commercial Manager: None
Address & Tel No:
Press Officer & Tel No: H. Stephenson. 513346
Address & Tel No of ground: Warrenside, Beighton, Huddersfield. 0484 42044
Simple ground directions: Leave M62 at junction 25 to Huddersfield (East), turn right at lights, then left on Keldregate to Warrenside road
No of seats: None **Covered accommodation:** 100 **Capacity:** 6,000 **Floodlights:** None
Year formed: 1946 **Nickname:** Rangers **Club sponsors:** Pizzeria Sole Mio
Club colours: White & Black
Change colours: Green & White
Previous Names: None
Previous Grounds: None
Record attendance: v Emley **Year:** 1982
Programme: 16 pages, 15p
Previous Leagues: Huddersfield, West Yorks, Yorks
Programme Editor: H. Stephenson
Club Captain (1983-84): Mark Harold
Player of the Season (1983-84): Alan Hebditch

BRIDLINGTON TOWN

President: M. Taylor
Chairman: C. Skinner
Manager: P. Johnson
Coach: None
Physiotherapist: None
Secretary: D. W. Pearce
Address & Tel No: 75400
Commercial Manager: None
Address & Tel No:
Press Officer & Tel No: C. Skinner
Address & Tel No of ground: Queensgate Football Ground
Simple ground directions: A166 from Driffield to Bridlington, over bridge to Quay Road, Queensgate on right
No of seats: 300 **Covered accommodation:** 150 **Capacity:** 3,000 **Floodlights:** None
Year formed: 1925 **Nickname:** None **Club sponsors:** None
Club colours: White
Change colours: Yellow
Previous Names: Bridlington Central
Previous Grounds: None
Record attendance: Not known
Previous Leagues: Yorkshire
Programme: 6 pages, 10p

COLLINGHAM A.F.C

President: P. Fletcher
Chairman: P. Fletcher
Manager: K. Parkin
Coach: K. Parkin
Physiotherapist: B. Hillyard
Secretary: R. Fox
Address & Tel No: (B) 0532-444531
Commercial Manager: None
Address & Tel No:
Press Officer & Tel No: E. Stentiford
Address & Tel No of ground: Harewood Road, Collingham (Coll. Bridge 72207
Simple ground directions: From Leeds: A58 to Collingham, left on Harewood Road 50yds
No of seats: None **Covered accommodation:** None **Capacity:** 500 **Floodlights:** No
Year formed: 1947 **Nickname:** None **Club sponsors:** None
Club colours: All Sky Blue
Change colours: White/Red socks
Previous Names: None
Previous Grounds: None
Record attendance: None **Year:**
Programme: Yes
Previous Leagues: None
Programme Editor: E. Steniford
Clubhouse details: Large clubhouse with bar facilities
Player of the Season (1983-84): I. Herendi

FARSLEY CELTIC A.F.C.

President: G. Dunkerley
Chairman: F. Chappell
Manager: D. Metcalf
Coach: P. Wigglesworth/R. Brown
Physiotherapist: T. Gregg
Secretary: B. Falkingham
Address & Tel No: 0532 564366 (H)
Commercial Manager: None
Address & Tel No:
Press Officer & Tel No:
Address & Tel No of ground: Throstle Nest, Newlands, Farsley, Pudsey, West Yorkshire. 0532 561517
Simple ground directions: M62 Junction 28, turn right into Leeds Ring Road to A647, turn right at roundabout then left, down New Street to Newlands Ground at bottom of road
No of seats: **Covered accommodation:** 1,000 **Capacity:** 5,000 **Floodlights:** None
Year formed: 1908 **Nickname:** Village Lads **Club sponsors:** Ceramic Tiles (Leeds)
Club colours: Sky Blue & White stripes
Change colours: Red & White
Previous Names:
Previous Grounds: None
Record attendance: Not known
Programme: Yes
Previous Leagues: Leeds Red Triangle
Programme Editor: S. Broughton
Senior Honours: West Riding County Cup (4)
Club Captain (1983-84): Terry Rockett
Players of the Season (1983-84): Terry Rockett (Players)
W. Ingleson (Club)

Garforth Miners *Back Row (L-R): Stuart Wilson, Phil Matthews, Chris Greenbank, Rob Hunt, Peter Taylor, Keith Matthews, Leigh Appleton. Front Row (L-R): Peter Ryder, Paul Copley, Tony Ward (capt), Kevin Clarkson, Phil Hart.*

Harrogate Railway

Collingham *K. Parkin (manager), G. Smickersgill, I. Herendi, G. Ibberson, K. Wetherop, G. Gordon, G. Batley, B. Latto (committee), T. Learoyd, C. Annan, S. Hussey, A. Leamonth, D. Goodman.*

GARFORTH MINERS

President: None
Chairman: J. Hill
Manager: R. Johnson
Coach: R. Johnson
Physiotherapist: J. Abbott
Secretary: W. S. Hayle
Address & Tel No: 17 Richmondfield Lane, Barwick-in-Elmet. Leeds 812548 (H), 704941 (B)
Commercial Manager: W. S. Hayle
Press Officer & Tel No: J. Griffiths. Leeds 871702
Address & Tel No of ground: Brierlands Lane, Garforth, Leeds
Simple ground directions: Off Aberford Road (A642), Garforth
No of seats: None **Covered accommodation:** 1,000 **Capacity:** 2,000 **Floodlights:** None
Year formed: 1964 **Nickname:** The Miners **Club sponsors:** Mike Dobson & Son/Patrick Forbes Sports
Club colours: Green shirts, Black shorts
Change colours: Blue and White stripes
Previous Names: Miners Arms A.F.C.
Previous Grounds: None
Record attendance: Not known
Programme: 20 pages, 16p
Previous Leagues: Leeds Sunday, West Yorkshire, Yorkshire
Programme Editor: Stephen Hayle
Club Captain (1983-84): Tony Ward
Player of the Season (1983-84): Stuart Wilson

HALL ROAD RANGERS

President: None
Chairman: T. Norrie
Manager: Ted Richardson
Coach: Mike Osborne
Physiotherapist: A. Wilson
Secretary: E. Richardson
Address & Tel No: 0482 43781 (H) 26104 (B)
Commercial Manager: D. Walker
Address & Tel No: 0482 801973
Press Officer & Tel No: R. Balmforth, 0482 821279
Address & Tel No of ground: Dene Park, Dene Close, Dunswell, Near Hull (0482) 850101
Simple ground directions: On Hull to Beverley Road (A1079 and A1174)
No of seats: None **Covered accommodation:** None **Capacity:** 400 **Floodlights:** None
Year formed: 1959 **Nickname:** Rangers **Club sponsors:** None
Club colours: Blue & White hoops
Change colours: All Green
Previous Names: None
Previous Grounds: Hull Co-Op Ground
Record attendance: 250 v North Ferriby United
Programme: Yes
Previous Leagues: East Riding County
Programme Editor: D. Walker
Club Captain (1983-84): Colin Moody
Player of the Season (1983-84): Chris Heard

HARROGATE RAILWAY ATHLETIC

President: J. Blakey
Chairman: D. Bentley
Manager: F. Cliffe
Coach: J. O'Byrne
Physiotherapist: D. Whitehead
Secretary: A. Potter
Address & Tel No: (H) 0423-62317. (B) 60441
Commercial Manager: J. Robinson
Address & Tel No: (H) 0423-863077. (B) 863124
Press Officer & Tel No: J. Render (0423 883467)
Address & Tel No of ground: Station View, Starbeck, Harrogate, No. Yorks. (0423-883104)
Simple ground directions: A59 Harrogate to Knaresboro Road at Starbeck Pelican crossing turn left
No of seats: None **Covered accommodation:** 350 **Capacity:** 4,000 **Floodlights:** No
Year formed: 1935 **Nickname:** The 'Rail' **Club sponsors:** Smith & Robinson/Various
Club colours: Red/Black
Change colours: Yellow
Previous Names: Starbeck L.N.E.R
Previous Grounds: None
Record attendance: 4,000 v Penrith **Year:** 1952
Programme: 4 pages, 10p
Previous Leagues: W. Yorks, Harrogate District
Programme Editor: Alan Potter
Clubhouse details: Games, TV room & Lounge. Beers, spirits and snacks available
Club Captain (1983-84): Neil Parker
Player of the Season (1983-84): Tony Canham

HARROGATE TOWN

President: Cecil Margolis
Chairman: Colin Court
Player/Manager: Alan Smith. 521066 (B)
Coach: Terry Dolan
Physiotherapist: John Townrow
Secretary: Peter Robinson
Address & Tel No: Harrogate 521363 (H)
Commercial Manager: None
Address & Tel No:
Press Officer & Tel No: None
Address & Tel No of ground: Wetherby Road, Harrogate. 883671
Simple ground directions: From Leeds turn right at traffice lights (Appleyards Garage) into Hookstone Road, continue until Woodlands Hotel (traffic lights), turn left into Wetherby Road, ground on right
No of seats: 300 **Covered accommodation:** One covered stand **Capacity:** 5,000 **Floodlights:** Yes
Year formed: 1936 **Nickname:** None **Club sponsors:** Not yet known for 1984-85 season
Club colours: Amber & Black/Black/Black
Change colours: All Blue
Previous Names: Harrogate Hotspurs
Previous Grounds: None
Record attendance: 3,208 v Starbeck LNER, Whitworth Cup Final **Year:** 1948
Previous Leagues: West Yorkshire, Yorkshire
Programme: 20 pages, 20p
Programme Editor: Ken Welford
Club Captain (1983-84): Mick Parker
Players of the Season (1983-84): Mick Parker (Players)
Chris King (1st Team)

LIVERSEDGE

President: H. Summerscales
Chairman: C. Ferrier
Manager: Mick Ferrier
Coach: Bob Gawthorpe
Physiotherapist: Ian Northrop
Secretary: M. Balmforth
Address & Tel No: 5 Victoria Road, Gomersal, Cleckheaton, West Yorkshire BD19 4RG
Press Officer & Tel No: As above
Address & Tel No of ground: Clayborn, Quaker Lane, Hightown Road, Cleckheaton
Simple ground directions: Into Cleckheaton, turn along top side of Memorial Park, under railway bridge then first left. Quaker Lane is about ¼-mile up on the left and leads down to ground
No of seats: None **Covered accommodation:** 500 **Capacity:** 2,000 **Floodlights:** None
Year formed: 1920 **Nickname:** The Sedge **Club sponsors:** None
Club colours: Blue & White shirts, White shorts
Change colours: Red shirts, Navy Blue shorts
Previous Names: None
Previous Grounds: None
Record attendance: Not known
Programme: 12 pages
Previous Leagues: Spen Valley, W.R. County Amateur
Programme Editor: Secretary
Past players who progressed into the Football League: Gary Briggs (Oxford Utd), Martyn Hirst (Bristol City)
Club Captain: Jim Cairney

Garforth Miners leading goalscorer Keith Matthews and Peter Taylor (dark shirts) attack the North Ferriby goal.

NORTH FERRIBY UNITED

President: J. R. Bingham
Chairman: K. S. Alexander
Secretary: R. Wallis
Address & Tel No: 60 Spring Gardens, Anlaby Common, Hull. 0482 55639
Manager: Stuart Blampey
Coach: D. Milne
Physiotherapist: None
Commercial Manager: K. Dobbins
Address & Tel No: 67 Southfield Drive, North Ferriby 0482 632165
Press Officer & Tel No: R. Wallis
Address & Tel No of ground: Church Road, North Ferriby, N. Humberside. 0482 634601
Simple ground directions: Ferriby 8 miles west of Hull on A63 – Ground 100 yards past church
No of seats: 40 **Covered accommodation:** 1 stand **Capacity:** 200 **Floodlights:** None
Year formed: 1934 **Nickname:** United **Club sponsors:** Humber Electrical Engineering Co Ltd
Club colours: Green/White
Change colours: Blue/Blue/Red
Previous Names: None
Previous Grounds: None
Record attendance: 1,100 v Nottingham Forest Reserves (clubhouse opening) **Year:** 1980
Previous Leagues: Church, East Riding Amateur, Yorkshire
Clubhouse details: Bar, lounge, TV, pool
Programme: No
Major Honours: East Riding Senior Cup Winners (4), Yorkshire League Cup 1974-75, Yorkshire League Div II Champions 1970-71

PHOENIX PARK (BFD)

President: M. Barraclough
Chairman: None
Manager: J.L. Price
Coach: M. Couzens
Physiotherapist: G. Bottomley
Press Officer & Tel No: R. Maule
Secretary: S. Marlow
Address & Tel No: 0274 575083 (H)
Commercial Manager: M. Couzens
Address & Tel No: 20 Brae Avenue, Bolton, Bradford 0274 639975
Address & Tel No of ground: Dick Lane, Thornbury BFD
Simple ground directions: On the Leeds side of Bfd — just off the Leeds Ring Road — Bradford Road
No of seats: None **Covered accommodation:** Yes **Capacity:** 1,000 **Floodlights:** No
Year formed: None **Nickname:** The Park **Club sponsors:** None
Club colours: Yellow/Red
Change colours: Sky Blue
Previous Names: None
Previous Grounds: None
Record attendance: 400 v Bfd City (pre-season) **Year:** 1981
Programme: 16 pages, 30p
Previous Leagues: West Riding County Amateur
Programme Editor: M. Couzens
Clubhouse details: 3 Bars, Ind Lounge, Games Rm. Dressing Rms underneath
Club Captain (1983-84): Paul Devanney

PICKERING TOWN

President: J. P. Jeninson
Chairman: J. Ewbank
Manager: D. Chapman
Coach: A. Lee
Physiotherapist: None
Secretary: D. L. Jemison
Address & Tel No: 0751 73210
Commercial Manager: None
Address & Tel No:
Press Officer & Tel No: None
Address & Tel No of ground: Recreation Ground, Malton Road (Pickering 73317)
Simple ground directions: A169 from Malton, first left past Pickering Police Station
No of seats: 50 **Covered accommodation:** One stand **Capacity:** 200 **Floodlights:** No
Year formed: 1890 **Nickname:** Pikes **Club sponsors:** Simon Ball
Club colours: All Royal Blue
Change colours: Red/White/White
Previous Names: None
Previous Grounds: None
Record attendance: None **Year:** None
Previous Leagues: Yorkshire, York & District
Programme: 8pages, 10p
Clubhouse details: Bar, TV, pool table
Programme Editor: David Chapman
Club Captain (1983-84): Peter Bower
Player of the Season (1983-84): Peter Bower

ROWNTREE MACKINTOSH (YORK)

President: K. H. Thompson
Chairman: D. Bunce
Manager: J. T. Collis
Coach: Colin Sanderson
Physiotherapist: G. Calpin
Secretary: M. E. Hodgson
Address & Tel No: (H) 0904 26519. (B) 0904 53071. Ext 2488
Commercial Manager: G. B. Shaw
Address & Tel No:
Press Officer & Tel No: C. J. Swanton. 0904 793384
Address & Tel No of ground: Mile Crux, Haxby Road, York (0904 23933)
Simple ground directions: Through city centre from south, ground on north side of city 1 mile from city centre, off the B1363 Helmsley Road
No of seats: No **Covered accommodation:** No **Capacity:** 1,000 **Floodlights:** No
Year formed: 1900 **Nickname:** The Trees **Club sponsors:** Rowntree Mackintosh & Data Dart
Club colours: White/Blue/White
Change colours: Gold/White/Gold
Previous Names: Rowntrees F.C.
Previous Grounds: None
Record attendance: None **Year:**
Programme: 15p
Previous Leagues: York & District
Programme Editor: Chris Swanton
Clubhouse details: On Ground, refreshments, no licence
Club Captain (1983-84): Jimmy Reid

SELBY TOWN A.F.C.

President: A. Williams
Chairman: E. S. Henry
Manager: G. Shepherd
Coach: G. Shepherd
Physiotherapist: None
Secretary: M. N. Seguss
Address & Tel No: 41 St Marys Avenue, Hemingbrough, Selby. Selby 638827 (H)
Commercial Manager: None
Address & Tel No:
Press Officer & Tel No: None
Address & Tel No of ground: Flaxley Road Ground, Selby
Simple ground directions: Via Scott Road, Richard Street
No of seats: 250 **Covered accommodation:** 500 **Capacity:** 5,000 **Floodlights:** Yes
Year formed: 1920 **Nickname:** The Robins **Club sponsors:** Gowthorpe Travel
Club colours: All Red
Change colours: All White
Previous Names: Robins
Previous Grounds: None
Record attendance: 6,500 v Bradford Park Avenue, F.A. Cup 2nd Round Proper **Year:** 1955
Previous Leagues: Yorkshire
Programme: Price/Pages None
Clubhouse details: None
Club Captain (1983-84): David Wilkinson
Player of the Season (1983-84): I. Robb

Phoenix Park *Back Row (L-R): M. Marshall (secretary), J. L. Price (manager), P. Mitchell, K. Fieldhouse, A. Low, B. Robinson, S. Watson, P. Horne, G. Bottomley (trainer). Bottom Row (L-R): J. Kowal, B. Bilaszewski, D. Jeng, P. Devanney, J. Price, G. Watson, M. Couzens.*
Photo: Telegraph & Argus

Rowntree Mackintosh FC *Back Row: P. Howarth, A. Clements, R. Tatterton, J. Reynolds, A. Tuite, C. Wordsworth, J. Reid, J. Collis (manager). Front Row: T. Brandon, C. Jones, J. Hodgson, H. Brittain, S. Smythe, G. Green.*

York RI *Back Row (L-R): T. Forward, J. Gill, G. Green, T. Metcalfe, C. Teare, D. Patterson. Front Row: R. Mason, T. Brandon, A. Kamara (capt), N. Sanderson, P. Holder, C. Mulhall.*

TADCASTER ALBION

President: K. Gilbertson
Chairman: Tony Dawson
Manager: Dennis Hawkins
Coach: Dennis Hawkins
Physiotherapist: Mrs S. Stuart
Secretary: E. Brown
Address & Tel No: (H) 832844. (B) 833213
Commercial Manager: K. Derry
Address & Tel No: (0937 832037)
Press Officer & Tel No: H. Clarke (0937 832361)
Address & Tel No of ground: The Park, Ings Lane, Tadcaster (0937 834119)
Simple ground directions: On entering Tadcaster turn through John Smiths Brewery
No of seats: None **Covered accommodation:** Yes **Capacity:** 2,000 **Floodlights:** No
Year formed: 1926 **Nickname:** None **Club sponsors:** Permisome Homes
Club colours: Yellow and blue/Blue/Yellow
Change colours: White and black/Black/White
Previous Names: None
Previous Grounds: None
Record attendance: 1,000 v Winterton Rangers F.A. Vase **Year:** 1977
Previous Leagues: Yorkshire
Programme: 6 pages, 10p
Clubhouse details: On Ground with John Smiths beer
Programme Editor: Leslie West
Club Captain (1983-84): Martin Myers
Player of the Season (1983-84): Martin Myers

YORK RAILWAY INSTITUTE

President: None
Chairman: F. Webster
Manager: R. Mollett
Coach: R. Mollett
Physiotherapist: None
Secretary: F. Webster
Address & Tel No: 0904 798055 (H)
Commercial Manager: None
Address & Tel No:
Press Officer & Tel No: None
Address & Tel No of ground: Railway Institute Sports Ground, New Lane, Acomb, York. 0904 798930
Simple ground directions:
No of seats: None **Covered accommodation:** None **Capacity:** 1,500 **Floodlights:** None
Year formed: 1912 **Nickname:** None **Club sponsors:** Micklegate Sports, York
Club colours: White/Navy
Change colours: Blue/White
Previous Names: None
Previous Grounds: None
Record attendance: Not known
Programme: Yes
Previous Leagues: York & District
Programme Editor: Mike Barker
Club Captain (1983-84): Alan Kamara
Player of the Season (1983-84): Neil Sanderson

Yorkshire Amateurs *Back Row (L-R): Eric Smith (Asst Manager), Dave Light (Physio), Simon Roberts, Gary Fozzard, Sean Jennings, Steve Jackson (now Harrogate Rail), Warren Ward, Craig Sidda, Barrie Walker (Manager). Front Row: Anthony White, Alan Parry, John MacPhee (captain), Neil Haynes, Alan Thurman and Andy Nicholson. Line up v Norton & Stockton Ancients, FA Vase 1st Rnd, 1983/84.*

YORKSHIRE AMATEURS

President: A. Pishhorn
Chairman: P. L. Chapman
Manager: B. Walker
Coach: E. Smith
Physiotherapist: D. Light
Secretary: V. Thurman
Address & Tel No: 22 Parkwood Road, Leeds 11. 770159
Commercial Manager: Eric Batley
Address & Tel No: 41 Conway Drive, Leeds LS8 5JG 487425 (H), 431224 (O)
Address & Tel No of ground: "Bracken Edge", Sycamore Avenue, Leeds LS7 4JF. Leeds 674093
Simple ground directions: Off Harehills Lane
No of seats: 1,000 **Covered accommodation:** Yes **Capacity:** 8,000 **Floodlights:** No
Year formed: 1919 **Nickname:** Hammers **Club sponsors:** Christopher Paul Curtains
Club colours: White/Blue/Red
Change colours: Blue/White/Blue
Previous Names: None
Previous Grounds: Elland Road
Record attendance: 4,500 v Wimbledon **Year:** 1932
Programme: 8 pages, 10p (1st Team), 4 pages, 10p (Res)
Previous Leagues: Yorkshire
Programme Editor: Andrew Wilkinson
Clubhouse details: Fully licensed, seating 125, games room, refreshment bar
Club Captain (1983-84): John MacPhee
Player of the Season (1983-84): Warren Ward

DIVISION ONE (CENTRAL)

ARMTHORPE WELFARE

President:
Chairman: Alan Bell
Manager: Joe Johnson
Coach: As above
Physiotherapist: John McKeown
Secretary: John Lawson
Address & Tel No: Doncaster (0302) 831871
Commercial Manager: Charlie Dunn
Address & Tel No:
Press Officer & Tel No: As above
Address & Tel No of ground: Armthorpe Welfare, Church Street, Armthorpe. 0302 831871
Simple ground directions: From Doncaster A630 towards Thorne, turn right at Royal Infirmary to Armthorpe. Ground behind Plough Inn on main street. From M18 Junction 4 to Doncaster, left at first roundabout
No of seats: None **Covered accommodation:** 300 **Capacity:** 3,000 **Floodlights:** No
Year formed: 1976 **Nickname:** The Welfare **Club sponsors:** None
Club colours: White, Navy trim/Navy/Navy
Change colours: Red shirts/Black shorts
Previous Names: None
Previous Grounds: None
Record attendance: 1,500 **Year:**
Programme: Yes
Previous Leagues: Doncaster Senior
Programme Editor: Charlie Dunn
Clubhouse details: Use of Armthorpe Miners Welfare Club adjoining ground
Club Captain (1983-84): Carl Leighton
Player of the Season (1983-84): Steve Woodhouse

BRIGG TOWN

President: B. Robins
Chairman: J. Colby
Manager: J. Wilkinson
Coach: R. Rivron
Physiotherapist: D. Newton
Secretary: R. B. Taylor
Address & Tel No: Brigg 52284
Commercial Manager: H. Williams
Address & Tel No: 53195
Press Officer & Tel No: B. Robins (53905)
Address & Tel No of ground: The Hawthorns, Hawthorn Avenue, Brigg. 52767
Simple ground directions: A15/A18 to Brigg; through Brigg on Grimsby Road; turn left at Recreation Ground
No of seats: 400 **Covered accommodation:** 2 Stands **Capacity:** 4,000 **Floodlights:** No
Year formed: 1864 **Nickname:** Zebras **Club sponsors:** Robert Clark (Roofing)
Club colours: Black/White stripes
Change colours: All Green
Previous Names: None
Previous Grounds: Brocklesby Ox, Manor House Convent
Record attendance: 2,500 v Boston F.C. **Year:** 1953
Programme: 12 pages, 10p
Previous Leagues: Lindsey, Lincolnshire
Programme Editor: J. Wilkinson
Clubhouse details: Licensed social club open on match days
Club Captain (1983-84): Ian Whyte
Player of the Season (1983-84): Dave Othen

B.S.C. (PARKGATE)

President: M. Sharpe
Chairman: B. Lovell
Manager: B. Tonks
Coach:
Physiotherapist: I. Hill
Secretary: R. Mortimer
Address & Tel No: Rotherham 523150
Commercial Manager: K. Swancott
Address & Tel No: Rotherham 523751
Press Officer & Tel No: B. Lovell
Address & Tel No of ground: Green Lane, Rawmarsh, Rotherham (Rotherham 523471)
Simple ground directions: From Rotherham to Rawmarsh down Green Lane for 800 yds
No of seats: None **Covered accommodation:** Yes **Capacity:** None **Floodlights:** No
Year formed: 1969 **Nickname:** The Gate **Club sponsors:** None
Club colours: All Blue
Change colours: Yellow/Black
Previous Names: None
Previous Grounds: None
Record attendance: v Worksop **Year:** 1982
Programme: 12 pages, 10p
Previous Leagues: Yorkshire
Programme Editor: K. Swancott
Clubhouse details: None.
Club Captain (1983-84): David Markham
Player of the Season (1983-84): John Wheeler

FRYSTON COLLIERY

President: J. C. Kirkwood
Chairman: F. Isles
Manager: T. Winter
Coach: Jim Kenyon
Physiotherapist: None
Secretary: B. Bennett
Address & Tel No: 60a Park Avenue, Allerton Bywater, Castleford, Yorks WF10 2AS. 0977 558531
Commercial Manager: None
Press Officer & Tel No: Secretary
Address & Tel No of ground: Fryston Colliery Welfare, Askham Road, Ferry Fryston, Castleford. 0977 553413. (Saturday mornings 0977 550982 Mr Binks)
Simple ground directions: Left at Airdale Hotel (B6136) into Fryston Rd, Elizabeth Drive, Watling Rd, Borrowdale Drive and Askham Rd.
No of seats: None **Covered accommodation:** Stand **Capacity:** 200 **Floodlights:** No
Year formed: 1910 **Nickname:** Colliery/Colliers **Club sponsors:** Castlevision Television Specialists
Club colours: Red/White
Change colours: Yellow/Green
Previous Names: None
Previous Grounds: Milners Farm; Pit Pony Field
Record attendance: Not known
Programme Editors: Frank Machlachlan/Terry Watson
Previous Leagues: Castleford District, Pontefract, West Yorkshire **Programme:** 8 pages, 15p
Clubhouse details: Welfare Club on ground, open until 3.30pm and evenings, and for visiting teams after each match
Club Captain (1983-84): Neil Bennett
Player of the Season (1983-84): Alan Turner

GRIMETHORPE M.W.

President: J. Blundell
Chairman: K. Donkin
Manager: D. North
Coach: T. Stevenson
Physiotherapist: None
Secretary: H. Livett
Address & Tel No: (0226) 710774
Commercial Manager: None
Address & Tel No:
Press Officer & Tel No: None
Address & Tel No of ground: Grimethorpe Miners Welfare, Cemetery Road, Grimethorpe (0226) 711544
Simple ground directions: From Barnsley A628 to Grimethorpe
No of seats: None **Covered accommodation:** 150 **Capacity:** 5,000 **Floodlights:** No
Year formed: 1920 **Nickname:** None **Club sponsors:** Appleyards Bros
Club colours: Blue/White
Change colours: Red/White
Previous Names: None
Previous Grounds: None
Record attendance: 3,000 Leeds All Stars Charity Match **Year:** None
Previous Leagues: Barnsley & Doncaster Premier
Programme: 8 pages, 10p
Clubhouse details: None
Programme Editor: Keith Donkin
Club Captains (1983-84): T. Reed/T. Wainwright

HATFIELD MAIN

President: J. Deeming
Chairman: D. Willis
Manager: J. Reed
Coach: As above
Physiotherapist: J. Kirk
Secretary: W. A. Jones
Address & Tel No: 26 Hampton Road, Broadway, Dunscroft, Doncaster. 0302 843388
Commercial Manager: None
Press Officer & Tel No: As above
Address & Tel No of ground: Dunscroft Welfare Grounds, Dunscroft, Nr Doncaster
Simple ground directions: From Doncaster: A18 Scunthorpe Road, turn left at Flarepath Hotel in Dunsville. Ground half mile down Broadway on the right
No of seats: None **Covered accommodation:** Being erected **Capacity:** 300 **Floodlights:** No
Year formed: 1936 **Nickname:** None **Club sponsors:** None
Club colours: White/Red/White
Change colours: All Blue
Previous Names: None
Previous Grounds: None
Record attendance: 450 v Bishop Auckland (F.A. Trophy) **Year:** Not known
Previous Leagues: None
Programme: 10 pages, 10p
Clubhouse details: Open every evening

MALTBY M.W. F.C.

President:
Chairman: L. Henson
Manager: Alan Turner
Coach: Richard Habbin
Physiotherapist: Brian Waller
Secretary: Peter Kenny
Address & Tel No: Rotherham 813675
Commercial Manager:
Address & Tel No:
Press Officer & Tel No: None
Address & Tel No of ground: Muglet Lane, Maltby
Simple ground directions: Situated on Muglet Lane opposite Maltby Miners Welfare Club
No of seats: None **Covered accommodation:** Yes **Capacity:** 250 **Floodlights:** No
Year formed: 1970 **Nickname:** **Club sponsors:** None
Club colours: White shirts/Black shorts
Change colours: Yellow shirts/Blue shorts
Previous Names: None
Previous Grounds: None
Record attendance: 940 **Year:**
Previous Leagues: Yorkshire, Sheffield County Senior
Programme:
Clubhouse details: None
Club Captain (1983-84): Richard Habbin
Player of the Season (1983-84): John Biggs

OSSETT ALBION

President: J. B. Burrows
Chairman: N. A. Wigglesworth
Manager: A. J. Gavin
Coach:
Physiotherapist:
Secretary: D. R. Chambers
Address & Tel No: (0924) 276004 (H), (0924) 275421 (B)
Commercial Manager: None
Address & Tel No:
Press Officer & Tel No: None
Address & T l No of ground: Dimple Wells, Ossett. Wakefield (0924) 273618
Simple ground directions: Leave M1 at Junction 40, take Wakefield Road for 200 yards, turn right at the Post House Hotel, down Queens Drive to the end, turn right, then second left down Southdale Road, turn right at end, then first left down Dimple Wells.
No of seats: None **Covered accommodation:** 200 **Capacity:** 2,000 **Floodlights:** No
Year formed: 1944 **Nickname:** None **Club sponsors:** Burmatex Ltd/Post House Hotel
Club colours: Old Gold/Black
Change colours: Blue/White
Record attendance: **Year:**
Local newspaper: Ossett Observer
Previous Leagues: Yorkshire
Programme: 8 pages, 10p
Clubhouse details: Full bar facilities open 7 days
Major Honours: Yorkshire League Champions 1975, Yorkshire League Cup Winners 1976, 1977, Fletcher Motors Cup Winners 1984

OSSETT TOWN AF & SC

Chairman: J. Leathley
Manager: B. Moran
Coach: D. Heeley
Physiotherapist: J. Garlick
Address & Tel No of ground: Ingfield. Ossett 272960
Simple ground directions: Exit 40 M1 to town centre
No of seats: **Covered accommodation:**
Year formed: 1936 **Nickname:** None
Club colours: Red/White
Record attendance: Not known
Clubhouse details: None
Major Honours: West Riding County Cup (twice)
Club Captain (1983-84): S. Whitelam

Secretary: F. Lloyd
Address & Tel No: Barnsley 382415
Commercial Manager: G. Firth
Press Officer: J. Carter

Capacity: **Floodlights:**
Club sponsors: Woodheads & Post House Hotel
Change colours: White/Navy
Previous Leagues: Yorkshire League

Fryston Colliery *Back (L-R): D. Dixon, D. Winter, R. Carley, M. Smithson, A. Arlotte, I. Atkinson, W. Everitt. Front (L-R): K. Waite, P. Robinson, M. Locker (Capt), J. Kenyon, A. Turner.*
Photo: Pontefract & Castleford Express

Fryston Colliery's Carley and Waite (stripes) appear outnumbered by Thorne defenders in the opening game Northern Counties East game at Fryston. Photo: Pontefract & Castleford Express

PILKINGTON RECREATION

President:
Chairman: C. Antwis
Manager: Paul Ostle
Coach: Mick Hughes
Physiotherapist: Graham Brierley
Secretary: Brian Wood
Address & Tel No: (H) 0405. (B) 812001
Commercial Manager: John Brown
Address & Tel No: 14 Milcroft Cres, Hatfield, Don 843577
Press Officer & Tel No: As above
Address & Tel No of ground: Moor Lane, Kirk Sandall, Doncaster. Doncaster 883391
Simple ground directions: Take A18 from Doncaster Town Centre. At Wheatley Hotel take left fork to Kirk Sandall, over railway bridge. Ground 2nd entrance on left
No of seats: None **Covered accommodation:** Stand **Capacity:** 500 **Floodlights:** No
Year formed: 1921 **Nickname:** Pilks **Club sponsors:** None
Club colours: White trimmed Red
Change colours: Blue/Black
Previous Names: None
Previous Grounds: None
Record attendance: 498 v Swinton Athletic **Year:** 1974/5
Programme: 20 pages, 50p (including admission)
Previous Leagues: Yorkshire, Sheffield County Senior
Programme Editor: J. Elward
Clubhouse details: Lounge, dance room, pool room, darts room, licensed bar opens 2.00pm, match days until 11.00 pm
Club Captain (1983-84): Steve Ostle
Player of the Season (1983-84): Steve Ostle

STOCKSBRIDGE WORKS

President: None
Chairman: D. Sedgwick
Secretary: M. Grimmer
Address & Tel No: 48 Hole House Lane, Stocksbridge, Sheffield S30 5BP. (Sheffield 886470)
Manager: G. Cotton
Coach: M. Grimmer
Physiotherapist: None
Commercial Manager: None
Address & Tel No:
Press Officer & Tel No: None
Address & Tel No of ground: Bracken Moor, Stocksbridge (Sheffield 882045)
Simple ground directions: From Manchester A616, Leeds exit 36, M1. 500yds uphill from clock tower in Stocksbridge
No of seats: 150 **Covered accommodation:** 150 **Capacity:** 2,500 **Floodlights:** No
Year formed: 1932 **Nickname:** The Foxes **Club sponsors:** Manulife
Club colours: All Blue
Change colours: None
Previous Names: None
Previous Grounds: None
Record attendance: Unknown
Previous Leagues: Yorkshire
Programme: Price/Pages None
Clubhouse details: None
Club Captain (1983-84): Martin Morton

WOMBWELL SPORTING ASSOCIATION

President: J. Illidge
Chairman: G. Littlewood
Secretary: P. Schofield
Address & Tel No: 57 Ashdene Avenue, Crofton, Wakefield WFA 1LY (Wakefield 864719)
Manager: H. Winstanley
Coach: None
Physiotherapist: None
Commercial Manager: None
Address & Tel No:
Press Officer & Tel No: None
Address & Tel No of ground: The Stadium, Station Road, Wombwell (Barnsley 752128)
Simple ground directions: From Wombwell Town Hall take Darfield Road for 300yds. Ground on left
No of seats: None **Covered accommodation:** None **Capacity:** None **Floodlights:** No
Year formed: 1906 **Nickname:** None **Club sponsors:** None
Club colours: Black/White stripes
Change colours: None
Previous Names: Wombwell Athletic
Previous Grounds: None
Record attendance: None **Year:** None
Programme: 30p
Previous Leagues: Midland, Yorkshire
Programme Editors: Secretary/Chairman
Clubhouse details: New 1983-84
Club Captain (1983-84): Jim Levitt
Player of the Season (1983-84): P. Waller

WOOLLEY MINERS WELFARE

President: G. C. Biggins
Chairman: J. B. Senior
Manager: G. Bedford
Coach: C. Chambers
Physiotherapist: None
Secretary: G. A. Britton
Address & Tel No: (H) Barnsley (0226 384277. (B)
Commercial Manager: None
Address & Tel No:
Press Officer & Tel No: None
Address & Tel No of ground: Colliery Road, Woolley Colliery
Simple ground directions: Via M1 Exit 38 follow Woolley Colliery signs. Ground 2 miles from Exit 38
No of seats: 200 **Covered accommodation:** None **Capacity:** 2,000 **Floodlights:** No
Year formed: 1965 **Nickname:** None **Club sponsors:** Wheelsbrook Services (Yorks) Ltd
Club colours: Amber/Black
Change colours: Blue/White
Previous Names: None
Previous Grounds: None
Record attendance: 10,000 approx. Elmley v Frickley Sheffield Sen Cup Final **Year:**
Previous Leagues: None
Programme: Yes
Clubhouse details: None
Programme Editor: J. H. Howard
Club Captain (1983-84): George Swallow
Player of the Season (1983-84): Robert Guest

Woolley MW FC *Back Row (L-R): J. Edgar, K. Paddon, G. Lofthouse, A. Davis, C. Chambers (trainer), I. Williams, R. Horbury, G. Bedford (manager). Front Row (L-R): G. Parkin, K. Holmes, J. Schofield, C. Kendrick, S. Blakey, T. Malkin, R. Gillespie.*

WORSBROUGH BRIDGE M.W.

President: D. Walton JP
Chairman: J. Wright
Manager: Colin Robinson
Coach: None
Physiotherapist: None
Secretary: D. Smith
Address & Tel No: 18 Shield Avenue, Worsbrough Bridge, Barnsley, South Yorks S70 5BQ (Barnsley 43418)
Commercial Manager: None
Address & Tel No:
Press Officer & Tel No: None
Address & Tel No of ground: Park Road, Worsbrough Bridge, Barnsley (Barnsley 84452)
Simple ground directions: A61 Barnsley to Sheffield Road. 2 miles south of Barnsley opposite Grimes Garage
No of seats: 200 **Covered accommodation:** 200 **Capacity:** **Floodlights:** No
Year formed: 1921 (reformed 1945) **Nickname:** None **Club sponsors:** None
Club colours: All Red **Change colours:** Yellow & Blue
Previous Names: Worsbrough Bridge St. James, Worsbrough Bridge Athletic **Previous Grounds:**
Record attendance: 2,300 v Blyth Spartans (F.A. Amateur Cup) **Year:** 1971
Previous Leagues: Barnsley, Sheffield County Senior, Yorkshire **Programme:**
Clubhouse details: Refreshment room, lounge for visiting officials
Club Captain (1983-84): Des Snape

YORKSHIRE MAIN COLLIERY

President: None
Chairman: F. Arrowsmith
Manager: G. D. Vipond
Coach: G. D. Vipond
Physiotherapist: S. Reid
Secretary: A. Summers
Address & Tel No: Doncaster 834907
Commercial Manager: None
Address & Tel No:
Press Officer & Tel No:
Address & Tel No of ground: Yorkshire Main Miners Welfare, Edlington, Doncaster
Simple ground directions: Leave A1M Junction with A630, travel towards Sheffield, take B6376 at Warmsworth traffic lights, ground approxc ¼ mile on left
No of seats: None **Covered accommodation:** **Capacity:** **Floodlights:** No
Year formed: 1940 **Nickname:** Main **Club sponsors:** Allguard Footwear
Club colours: Red shirts, Black shorts **Change colours:** White/Black/White
Previous Names: None **Previous Grounds:**
Record attendance: 1,000 **Year:**
Previous Leagues: Sheffield & Hallam County Senior, Doncaster Senior, Bentley **Programme:** Yes
Clubhouse details: Private club on grounds, Players lounge **Programme Editor:** Andy Summers
Club Captain (1983-84): Lal Dutt **Player of the Season (1983-84):** Gary Lockwood

---

DIVISION ONE (SOUTH)

ARNOLD KINGSWELL

President: Fred Thompson
Chairman: Robert Simpson
Manager: John Bower
Coach: John Sargent
Physiotherapists: Trevor Whitt & Les Bell
Secretary: Terence Stevens
Address & Tel No: 0602 204395
Commercial Manager: T. Bicknell
Address & Tel No: c/o Ground
Press Officer & Tel No: Ian Burton
Address & Tel No of ground: Nottingham Road Ground, Arnold, Nottingham. 0602 264722
Simple ground directions: A60, 3 miles from Nottingham
No of seats: None **Covered accommodation:** – **Capacity:** – **Floodlights:** No
Year formed: 1962 **Nickname:** Kings **Club sponsors:** Pioneer Estates
Club colours: Blue/Yellow/Blue **Change colours:** Yellow/Black/Yellow
Previous Names: None **Previous Grounds:** None
Record attendance: 600 **Year:**
Previous Leagues: Notts Youth, Notts Amateur, Notts Spartan, East Midlands Regional, Midlands Counties, Northern Counties East **Programme:** 10 pages
Clubhouse details: Bar

BLIDWORTH MINERS WELFARE

President: B. Turner
Chairman: J. Booth
Manager: J. Todhunter
Coach: None
Physiotherapist: None
Secretary: D. Sheldon
Address & Tel No: Mansfield 796729
Commercial Manager: None
Address & Tel No:
Press Officer & Tel No: Mrs. M. Fowler (Mans. 642671)
Address & Tel No of ground: Blidworth Miner Welfare, Mansfield Road, Blidworth, Notts
Simple ground directions: On B6020 outskirts of Blidworth, twixt Larch Farm on main Nottingham Rd and Rainworth
No of seats: None **Covered accommodation:** None **Capacity:** None **Floodlights:** No
Year formed: 1982 **Nickname:** Welfare **Club sponsors:** Rufford Motor Company
Club colours: Blue & White/Blue/Blue **Change colours:** Yellow & Green/Green/Green
Previous Names: Folk House Old Boys **Previous Grounds:** Chesterfield Road, Mansfield
Record attendance: Unknown
Previous Leagues: None **Programme: Price/Pages** None
Clubhouse details: None
Club Captain (1983-84): Trevor Buckley

BORROWASH VICTORIA

President: I. Anderson
Chairman: W. K. Tyler
Manager: N. A. Kellogg
Coach: T. Keogh
Physiotherapist: E. Leek
Secretary: W. I. Collins
Tel No: home: (0332) 678016, bus: (0332) 662441 ext 15
Commercial Manager: P. Vincent
Tel No: (0332) 671738
Address & Tel No of ground: Spondon Leisure Centre, Borrowash Road, Spondon. (0332) 668656
Simple ground directions: Via M1, turn-off at Junction 25 onto A52 to Derby. Take 3rd turning left onto Borrowash road. Ground entrance on left hand side
No of seats: ** **Covered accommodation:** ** **Capacity:** ** **Floodlights:** **
** All in process of being built as new
Year formed: 1911 **Nickname:** The Vics **Club sponsors:** M. J. Milward
Club colours: Red & White striped shirts with Black collars, Black shorts with Red & White trim, Black stockings
Change colours: Yellow shirts, Green shorts, Green Stockings
Previous Grounds: Deans Drive, Borrowash **Club shop:** No
Previous Leagues: Northern Counties East, Midland Counties, East Midlands Regional, Central Alliance, Football Combination, Welfare League
Midweek match day: Wednesday **Club metal badges:** No **Programme:** 6 pages, 10p
Local Newspapers: Derby Evening Telegraph, Derby Football Special
Clubhouse details: Bar open match days 10.30-2.30, 6.00-11.00; midweek 6.00-11.00; plus snacks available
Senior honours won: Northern Counties East F.L. Championship (Div 1 South) 83/84, Midland Counties League Div 1 League & Cup double 80/81

DRONFIELD UNITED

President: D. Dooley
Chairman: D. Dooley
Manager: D. Wickens
Coach: None
Physiotherapist: D. Newbould
Hon. Secretary: David Taylor
Address & Tel No: 1 Lowedges, Chesterfield Road South, Sheffield S8 8LW. 376121
Commercial Manager: None
Address & Tel No:
Press Officer & Tel No: None
Address & Tel No of ground: Coach & horses, Dronfield
Simple ground directions: Sheffield-Dronfield Road
No of seats: None **Covered accommodation:** 200 **Capacity:** 1,500 **Floodlights:** No
Year formed: 1911 **Nickname:** None **Club sponsors:** None
Club colours: Green **Change colours:** Blue
Previous Names: Norton Woodseats **Previous Grounds:** None
Record attendance: 4,800 v Enfield **Year:** 1947
Previous Leagues: None **Programme: Price/Pages** None
Clubhouse details: None
Club Captain (1983-84): David Gillott **Player of the Season (1983-84):** Andrew King

FRECHEVILLE COMMUNITY

President: None
Chairman: K. James
Manager: T. Dale
Coach: R. Jones
Physiotherapist: Dr. Little
Secretary: G. C. Warman
Address & Tel No: (H) 0742 390728. (B) 0742 344204
Commercial Manager: None
Address & Tel No:
Press Officer & Tel No: R. Green (396395)
Address & Tel No of ground: Silkstone Road, Frecheville, Sheffield 12. 396395
Simple ground directions: Opposite Birley Hotel and shops on A616 Sheffield to Newark Road, 4 miles from Sheffield
No of seats: None **Covered accommodation:** Yes **Capacity:** 5,000 **Floodlights:** No
Year formed: 1947 **Nickname:** Villa **Club sponsors:** Heineken Breweries
Club colours: Blue
Change colours: Yellow/Blue
Previous Names: None
Previous Grounds: None
Record attendance: 1,507 v Emley FC (Senior Cup Tie) **Year:** 1968
Previous Leagues: None
Programme: 8 pages, 10p
Clubhouse details: Two social clubs
Programme Editor: G. C. Warman
Club Captain (1983-84): Paul Scholey
Player of the Season (1983-84): Dave Battams

GRAHAM ST. PRIMS

President: C. McBride
Chairman: L. Astle
Manager: D. Holmes
Coach: J. Page
Physiotherapist: V. Bolan
Secretary: J. B. Ballington
Address & Tel No: (0332) 792745 (H) 42442 x2777 (B)
Commercial Manager: None
Address & Tel No:
Press Officer & Tel No:
Address & Tel No of ground: Derby County Training Ground (Ramarena), Raynesway, Derby (0332 672697)
Simple ground directions: Ground situated off Derby Ring Road (A511) between suburbs Chaddesden (north end Derby) Alvaston (south end Derby)
No of seats: None **Covered accommodation:** None **Capacity:** None **Floodlights:** No
Year formed: 1953 **Nickname:** Prims **Club sponsors:** Pennine Electrical (Derby)
Club colours: Yellow/Green
Change colours: Blue & White/Blue
Previous Names: None
Previous Grounds: None
Record attendance: None **Year:** None
Previous Leagues: None
Programme: 8 pages, 10p
Clubhouse details: Bar and refreshments
Programme Editor: Jim Ballington
Club Captain (1983-84): Leslie Wright

HALLAM

President: T. Stones
Chairman: W. Powall
Manager: Jack Whitham
Coach: John Fantham
Physiotherapist: John Brachell
Secretary: G. L. Holland
Address & Tel No: (H) 0742 381899. (B) Ditto
Commercial Manager: None
Address & Tel No:
Press Officer & Tel No: P. Gill (0742 304274)
Address & Tel No of ground: Sandygatge Road, Sheffield 20 (0742 301802)
Simple ground directions: Off A57 Crosspool, Sheffield 10
No of seats: None **Covered accommodation:** 250 **Capacity:** 2,000 **Floodlights:** No
Year formed: 1862 **Nickname:** None **Club sponsors:** Hallamshire Inc Services
Club colours: All Blue
Change colours: All Red
Previous Names: None
Previous Grounds: None
Record attendance: 3,000 v Evenwood Town, Amateur Cup **Year:** 1955
Previous Leagues: None
Programme: Yes
Clubhouse details: None
Programme Editor: Barry Holmes
Club Captain (1983-84): Cliff Wilson
Player of the Season (1983-84): Stephen Phelan

HARWORTH COLLIERY F.C.

President: G. Griffin
Chairman: K. Evans
Secretary: T. A.B. Rogan
Address & Tel No: 30 Lindsey Road, Harworth. 0302 750132
Manager: D. Birkinshaw
Coach: B. Higham
Physiotherapist: H. Farnsworth
Commercial Manager: S. Tucker
Address & Tel No: 27 Harewood Court, Bircotes 0302 744660
Address & Tel No of ground: Scrooby Road, Harworth, nr Doncaster
Simple ground directions: From Aim Blyth A614 to Bircotes approx 2 miles from Blyth
No of seats: None **Covered accommodation:** None **Capacity:** None **Floodlights:** No
Year formed: 1931 **Nickname:** Reds **Club sponsors:** None
Club colours: Red/Black
Change colours: Yellow/Green & Blue/White
Previous Names: None
Previous Grounds: None
Record attendance: None **Year:** None
Programme: 20 pages, 30p
Previous Leagues: Yorkshire, Sheffield County Senior, Doncaster Senior
Programme Editor: S. Owen
Club Captain (1983-84): Phil Dudley
Player of the Season (1983-84): John Perry

Kimberley Town *Back Row (L-R): Dave Brunell (manager), Arnie Bucknall, Dean Brunell, Richard Jones, Kevan Mihaly, Rob Stone, Tony Webster, Carl Francis. Front Row (L-R): Ian Liddle, Kevin Hall, Andy Cowlishaw, Steve Szep (capt), Clive Smith, Darren Whyley.*

Photo by courtesy of Nottingham Evening Post

KIMBERLEY TOWN

President: R. J. Penney
Chairman: George Giddens
Manager: Dave Brunell
Coach:
Physiotherapist: Harry Bethell
Secretary: H. Hibbert
Address & Tel No: (H) 383382. (B) (0602)
Commercial Manager: C. Buxton
Address & Tel No: Langley Mill 69755
Press Officer & Tel No: N. Hibbert (0602) 383382
Address & Tel No of ground: Stag Ground, Nottingham Road, Kimberley (382788)
Simple ground directions: M1 south Exit 26. B6010 via Nuthall
No of seats: None **Covered accommodation:** Yes **Capacity:** 3,000 **Floodlights:** No
Year formed: 1948 **Nickname:** Stags **Club sponsors:** Granby Motors
Club colours: Royal Blue/White
Change colours: Red/Black/White
Previous Names: Kimberley YMCA
Previous Grounds: None
Record attendance: 1,122 v Eastwood Town **Year:** 1976
Previous Leagues: Notts Amateur, Central Alliance, East Midlands, Midland Counties
Programme: Yes
Programme Editor: Neil Hibbert
Club Captain (1983-84): Steve Szep
Player of the Season (1983-84): Kevan Mihaly

KIVETON PARK

President: None
Chairman: E. Banks
Manager: John Warnock
Coach:
Physiotherapist:
Secretary: John Holden
Address & Tel No: 184 Wales Road, Kiveton Park, Sheffield S31 8RE. Worksop 770558
Commercial Manager:
Press Officer & Tel No:
Address & Tel No of ground: Kiveton Park, Miners Welfare Ground, Hard Lane, Kiveton Park, Nr Sheffield
Simple ground directions: From north or south on the M1, Junction 31, signposted Worksop, after ¼ mile turn right down Goosecar Lane, through Todwick Village to Hard Lane Crossroad. Ground 200 yards on right
No of seats: 200 **Covered accommodation:** Stand **Capacity:** 200 **Floodlights:** No
Year formed: 1890s **Nickname:** Park **Club sponsors:**
Club colours: All Red
Change colours: All Blue
Previous Names: Kiveton Park Colliery United
Previous Grounds: None
Record attendance: None **Year:** None
Previous Leagues: Yorkshire
Programme: None
Clubhouse details: None
Major Honours: Yorkshire League Div 2 Champions 1977-78

Lincoln United

LINCOLN UNITED

President: A. Rylatt
Chairman: A. Simpson
Manager: F. Green (28771)
Coach: R. Townsend
Physiotherapist: H. Spencer
Secretary: F. Green
Address & Tel No: 0522 28771 (H)
Commercial Manager: None
Address & Tel No:
Press Officer & Tel No: B. Smith (682559)
Address & Tel No of ground: Ashby Avenue, Hartsholme, Lincoln (690674)
Simple ground directions: From Worksop: right at Saxilby Bridge, Skellingthorpe Road, Ashby Avenue. From Lincoln: High Street, Dixon Street, Tritton Road, Skellingthorpe Road, Ashby Avenue.
No of seats: 200 **Covered accommodation:** Seating stand and standing shelter **Capacity:** 2,000 **Floodlights:** No
Year formed: 1938 **Nickname:** United **Club sponsors:** Ironstone Roofing Ltd., Lincoln
Club colours: White and red
Change colours: All Red
Previous Names: Lincoln Amateurs
Previous Grounds: Skellingthorpe Road, Skew Bridge
Record attendance: 1,500 v Crook Town **Year:** 1968
Programme: 8 pages, 10p
Previous Leagues: Lincolnshire
Programme Editor: Fred Green
Clubhouse details: Social area and bar, colour TV, pool table; planned extensions for later this year
Club Captain (1983-84): Benny Williams
Player of the Season (1983-84): Keith Ellis

LONG EATON UNITED

President: J. C. Fairley
Chairman: J. C. Fairley
Manager: P. Johnson
Coach: None
Physiotherapist:
Secretary: G. W. Whitehead
Address & Tel No: (H) 033917 2849. (B) 0602 861994
Commercial Manager: J. C. Fairley
Address & Tel No: 0602 735700
Press Officer & Tel No: Secretary
Address & Tel No of ground: Grange Park, Station Road, Long Eaton, Nottingham (Long Eaton 5700)
Simple ground directions: M1 Exit 25. To centre of Long Eaton. Take Nottingham Road. Turn left into Station Road
No of seats: None **Covered accommodation:** Yes **Capacity:** 5,000 **Floodlights:** No
Year formed: 1956 **Nickname:** Blues **Club sponsors:** Topfare & Western Savings Bank Ltd
Club colours: All Blue
Change colours: Yellow and Green
Previous Names: None
Previous Grounds: None
Record attendance: v Matlock Town (Derbyshire Snr Cup Final) **Year:** 1977
Previous Leagues: None **Programme:** 24 pages, 15p **Programme Editor:** G. W. Whitehead
Clubhouse details: Clubroom open after all matches, also Tues., Wednes. and Thurs. evenings. General refreshments

OAKHAM UNITED

President: D. Concannon, PC, MP
Chairman: W. Gillies
Manager: B. Chambers
Coach: W. Newson
Physiotherapist: None
Secretary: J. M. Martin
Address & Tel No: Notts (0602) 200660 (H)
Commercial Manager: None
Address & Tel No:
Press Officer & Tel No: None
Address & Tel No of ground: Mansfield Hosiery Mills Sports Ground, Sutton Road, Mansfield, Notts
Simple ground directions: M1 junct 28, join A38, straight thru' Sutton-in-Ashfield, 1½ miles on left
No of seats: None **Covered accommodation:** One stand **Capacity:** 600 **Floodlights:** No
Year formed: 1969 **Nickname:** None **Club sponsors:** Five Star Driving School
Club colours: White/Blue/White
Change colours: All Yellow
Previous Names: None
Previous Grounds: None
Record attendance: 450 v Sutton Trinity 2nd Leg Midland Lge KO Cup Final **Year:** None
Previous Leagues: None
Programme: 4 pages, 10p
Club Captain (1983-84): Steven Renshaw
Programme Editor: W. Newson

RETFORD TOWN F.C.

President:
Chairman: A. Zaccaria
Manager: P. Buckley
Coach: P. Buckley
Physiotherapist:
Secretary: G. Hilton
Address & Tel No: Retford 705538
Commercial Manager: None
Address & Tel No:
Press Officer & Tel No: None
Address & Tel No of ground: River Lane, Retford, Notts.
Simple ground directions: A638 from Doncaster or A1 onto A620 to Retford roundabout where ground is signposted. Left hand side of A620 relief road
No of seats: 500 **Covered accommodation:** 2,000 **Capacity:** **Floodlights:** No
Year formed: 1950 **Nickname:** Shamrocks **Club sponsors:** None
Club colours: Green
Change colours: White
Previous Names: None
Previous Grounds: None
Record attendance: Unknown
Previous Leagues: Derby Premier, Retford
Programme: Yes
Clubhouse details: All new facilities
Programme Editor: John Bramley
Club Captain (1983-84): Ken Burton
Player of the Season (1983-84): John Needham

SHEFFIELD

President: Keith Healey
Chairman: Keith Healey
Manager: To be appointed
Coach:
Physiotherapist:
Secretary: R. Salt
Address & Tel No: 3 Den Bank Crescent, Sheffield
Commercial Manager:
Address & Tel No:
Press Officer & Tel No:
Address & Tel No of ground: Abbeydale Park, Sheffield (0742 362040)
Simple ground directions: 4½ miles from City Centre on A621 (Sheffield – Bakewell Rd). Sheffield Amateur Sports Club ground, on right after passing Abbeydale Garden Centre
No of seats: None **Covered accommodation:** Yes **Capacity:** 60 **Floodlights:** No
Year formed: 1857 **Nickname:** None **Club sponsors:** None
Club colours: Red/Black/Black
Change colours: Blue/White/Blue
Previous Names: None
Previous Grounds: None
Record attendance: None **Year:** None
Previous Leagues: Yorkshire **Programme:** (whenever possible) 4 pages included with admission
Major Honours: Amateur Cup Winners 1903-04, F.A. Vase Finalists 1976-77

STAVELEY

President: A. Colleyshaw, BSc
Chairman: D. Howitt
Manager: G. Clarke
Coach: C. Millward
Physiotherapist: M. Sargerson
Secretary: M. A. Wake
Address & Tel No: Chesterfield 475994
General Manager: N. Newstead
Address & Tel No:
Press Officer & Tel No: N. Newstead
Address & Tel No of ground: Handley Wood Sports Ground, Barrow Hill. Chesterfield 77251
Simple ground directions: M1 North Junction 30. From South Junction 29, then A619 to Staveley
No of seats: None **Covered accommodation:** Yes **Capacity:** 2,000 **Floodlights:** Yes
Year formed: **Nickname:** **Club sponsors:**
Club colours: Red/Black/Black
Change colours: All Blue
Previous Names: None
Previous Grounds: None
Record attendance: 1,105 **Year:** 1982-83
Previous Leagues: Midlands Div I, East Midland, Chesterfield
Programme: Yes
Clubhouse details: Licensed
Programme Editor: Dave Howitt
Club Captain (1983-84): Paul Dennis
Player of the Season (1983-84): Neil Hardy

Staveley Works *Back Row (L-R): M. Sargerson, A. Atkinson, D. Quigley, B. Hemstalk, R. Turner, M. Collins, C. Millward, K. Hardy, R. Gilbert. Front Row: C. De Giralamo, D. Hardy, D. Vernon, K. Lee, P. Dennis (capt).*

NOTTS FOOTBALL ALLIANCE

President: R J Leafe
Chairman: J W Stokeld
General Secretary Registrar: E R Rudd

First Championship for Meadows Albion

The Senior Division was not dominated by any one club as in the past by Rainworth Miners Welfare, although Rainworth Miners Welfare and the Hucknall Miners Welfare did have good runs in the FA Vase, both being knocked-out in the sixth round, and Rainworth finished runners-up after winning the title for the past six years.

The table kept changing at the top with Keyworth United, Meadows Albion and Plessey FC taking their turn to head the table. Rainworth with a late run in at one stage were 12 games behind but battled on to finish the season one point behind Meadows Albion, who took the title for the first time in their history. Keyworth United had the best chance of taking the title but dropped 4 points in their last 4 games.

Notts Police struggling with fixtures due to the Picket duty at the Pits finally completed their programme, but finished at the foot of the table with John Player FC second from bottom.

The League Senior Cup went to Plessey FC, who in a hard fought Cup Final against City Sherwood Hospitals, came out winners by 3-1, this being the first time Plessey had won the Senior League Cup.

The Division One title race was just as close as the Senior Division both Leagues being decided on the last games, with Clifton All Whites finally taking the League Title on goal difference over Hucknall Colliery Welfare Reserves. Dunkirk had the best chance of winning the title but went down to Hucknall Colliery Welfare Reserves in their last game by 4-2 to put them in 3rd position.

Parliament Street Meths and Gedling Colliery Welfare Reserves finished at the bottom of the table. Gedling Reserves were promoted from Division Two last season but went straight back down this season.

In the County Cups Hucknall Colliery Welfare reached the final of the Notts Senior Cup finally losing to Eastwood Town.

Bulwell Forest Villa reached the final of the Notts Intermediate Cup losing to the holders Arnold Town Reserves.

Collingham FC reached the final of the Notts Junior Cup losing to their neighbours Balderton Wanderers.

To reach three finals in the County Cup and not win one is unbelieveable but that is football.

In the FA Vase the outstanding game of the season must have been Hucknall Colliery Welfare v VS Rugby (holders), Hucknall winning by 2-0.

Rainworth Miners Welfare reached the Thorn Electric's 5-a-side Competition for the second year in succession.

E R Rudd
Secretary

League Senior Cup Winners
Plessey FC

Finalists
City Sherwood Hospitals

League Intermediate Cup Winners
Hucknall Colliery Welfare Res

Finalists
Meadows Albion Reserves

Notts Senior Cup Finalists
Hucknall Colliery Welfare

Notts Intermediate Cup Finalists
Bulwell Forest Villa

Notts Junior Cup Finalists
Collingham FC

Leading Goalscorers

	Lge	Cup
C Guy, Rainworth MW	25	1
C Parkes, Boots Ath	17	1
A Raine, Rainworth MW	15	1
P Johnson, Southwell	14	—
Division One		
D Elliot, Clifton AW	38	2
R Johnson, Hucknall Res	30	4
P Foster, Clifton AW	27	—
G Larvin, Bulwell FV	23	—
R Farrell, Dunkirk FC	19	2
C Giscombe, BF Villa	19	—

Senior Division

	P	W	D	L	F	A	Pts
Meadows Albion	30	20	5	5	60	23	45
Rainworth MW	30	21	2	7	79	39	44
Keyworth Utd	30	19	6	5	59	26	44
City Sher Hosp	30	16	5	9	55	37	37
Clipstone MW	30	16	4	10	65	54	36
Plessey FC	30	14	7	9	55	39	35
Hucknall CW	30	13	6	11	53	41	32
Southwell City	30	12	7	11	58	57	31
Carlton Ath	30	7	12	11	35	62	27
Boots Athletic	30	8	10	12	48	55	26
Worthington Simp	30	11	4	15	35	47	26
Thorseby CW	30	10	4	16	41	54	24
Gedling CW	30	9	3	18	28	44	21
Nottm Acads	30	8	4	18	32	61	20
John Player FC	30	7	5	18	46	66	17*
Notts Police	30	5	4	20	26	70	14

* Denotes 2 points deducted

Division One

Clifton AW	30	19	6	5	96	45	44
Hucknall CW Res	30	20	4	6	79	39	44
Dunkirk FC	30	17	9	4	73	32	43
Meadows Alb Res	30	16	6	8	56	36	38
Collingham FC	30	14	9	7	57	29	37
Bulwell FV	30	13	11	6	92	59	36
Plessey FC Res	30	15	4	11	63	58	34
Keyworth Utd Res	30	13	8	9	48	45	34
Worthington Res	30	12	5	13	54	58	29
Rainworth MW Res	30	11	4	15	52	73	26
Clipstone MW Res	30	11	3	16	56	71	25
John Player Res	30	9	7	14	43	73	25
Greenwood FC	30	7	5	18	50	86	19
Basford Utd	30	5	8	17	48	77	18
Gedling CW Res	30	4	6	20	38	77	14
Parliament St Meth	30	3	7	20	50	97	13

CITY & SHERWOOD HOSPITALS F.C.

Chairman: A. Korol
Manager: S. Throssell
Secretary: B. Richards
Address & Tel No: 1 Rectory Rd, Cotgrave, Nottingham (N'ham 892661)
Ground address & Tel No: C.O.D. Army Ground, Chilwell, Nottingham
Simple ground directions: Main Nottingham to Long Eaton road approx 3 miles from City
Colours: Green & White hoops, Green shorts & socks
Change colours: All Yellow
Year formed: 1955
Programmes: No
Club house: No
Floodlights: No
Seating: No

HUCKNALL C.W.

President: J. Hand
Chairman: P. Hunt
Manager: J. Nixon
Coach: D. Kendall
Secretary: E. Jackson
Address & Tel No: 43 Florence Street, Hucknall, Notts (Nottingham 634321)
Press Officer: E. Jackson
Physiotherapist: H. Cutts
Address of ground: Hucknall Colliery Welfare Sports Ground, Watnall Road, Hucknall, Notts
Simple ground directions: From Nottingham, A611 into Hucknall (7 miles), Hucknall High Street, turn left onto Watnall Road, 1 mile on ground on right opposite old colliery
Covered accommodation: 200
Capacity: 2,000
Floodlights: No
Year formed: 1946
Nickname: Colliers
Club sponsors: None
Club colours: Orange shirts, Black shorts, Orange socks
Change colours: All Red
Previous grounds: Wigwam Lane, Hucknall
Programme: 6 pages, only at big games
Record attendance: 906 v VS Rugby, 4th Round FA Vase, 1983/84
Previous Leagues: Bulwell-District, Nottingham Spartan
Clubhouse details: Welfare at Portland Road, Hucknall (1 mile from ground)
Major honours: Notts Football Alliance — Champions 1976-77, Senior Cup Winners 1978-79, Div One Champions 1980-81, Intermediate Cup Winners 1979-1980-1981; Notts Senior Cup beaten finalists 1983-84

JOHN PLAYER F.C.

Chairman: R. Springthorpe
Manager: D. K. France
Secretary: R. H. Walton
Address & Tel No: 6 Watson Avenue, Bakersfields, Nottingham NG3 7BL (504631)
Ground address & Tel No: Aspley Lane, Nottingham. (293213 — Groundsman)
Simple ground directions: Corner of Aspley Lane and Western Boulevard on the outer ring road of Nottingham
Colours: Yellow shirts & socks, Green shorts
Change colours: Red or Blue shirts, Black shorts & socks
Year formed: 1904
Programmes: No
Club house: Yes
Floodlights: No
Seating: No

KEYWORTH UNITED

President: J. Hartley
Chairman: A. Gatter
Manager: A. Oldham
Secretary: M. Simpson
Address & Tel No: 30 Main Street, Keyworth (Plumtree 4689)
Address of ground: Platt Lane Playing Fields, Keyworth
Simple ground directions: Off A606 Nottingham to Melton road
Year formed: 1910
Nickname: The Greens
Club sponsors: Rancliffe Arms
Club colours: Green shirts, Black shorts
Change colours: All White
Previous grounds: Nottingham Road, Keyworth
Previous Leagues: Spartan League
Major honours: Notts Intermediate Cup Winners 1978/79; Notts Alliance — Winners Div 1 1979/80, Winners Div 2 1978/79, Runners-up Senior Div 1982/83

RAINWORTH MINERS WELFARE

President: G. Edwards
Chairman: D. Cope
Manager: B. Philips
Coach:
Physiotherapist: P. Manock
Secretary: A. Wright
Address & Tel No: Mansfield 0623 24379 (H) 553237 (B)
Commercial Manager: None
Address & Tel No:
Press Officer & Tel No: Miss E. Widdison
Address & Tel No of ground: Kirklington Road, Rainworth, Mansfield, Notts. **Club shop:** No
Simple ground directions: A617, Mansfield to Newark Road
No of seats: None **Covered accommodation:** None **Capacity:** 6,000 **Floodlights:** No
Year formed: 1922 **Nickname:** None **Club sponsors:** None
Previous names: Rufford Colliery **Club colours:** All White
Previous grounds: None **Change colours:** All Red
Day for midweek home matches: Tuesday and Thursday
Record attendance: 5,071 v Barton Rovers, F.A. Vase Semi-Final **Year:**
Previous Leagues: None
Best performance in: **F.A. Cup:** Not known
F.A. Vase: 1981-2 Final
Clubhouse details: Miners' Welfare Club
Present players with Football League experience: None
Past players who progressed into the Football League: None
Record transfer fee paid: None
Record transfer fee received: None
Programme Editor: Secretary
Programme details: 20 pages, 10p
Local newspapers & Tel No: Chronicle, Advertiser
Club metal badges: No
Senior Honours: League Champions (5), Notts Senior Cup (2), League Cup

RYECROFT F.C.

Chairman: D. Jones
Manager: S. Withers
Secretary: P. Drew
Address & Tel No: 1 Hemlock Ave, Stapleford, Notts NG9 8DN (Sandiacre 390165)
Ground address & Tel No: Hickings Lane Recreation Ground, Hickings Lane, Stapleford, Notts
Simple ground directions: M1, exit 25 Sandiacre, take A52 towards Nottingham to Bramcote. Take 2nd exit from roundabout towards Ilkeston, ½ mile down turn left at Jaguar pub, this is Hickings Lane, ground down at bottom on left
Colours: All Blue **Change colours:** Red shirts, Blue shorts, socks
Year formed: 1950 **Programmes:** No
Club house: No **Floodlights:** No **Seating:** No
Previous Leagues: Teams in Notts Amateur and in Notts Youth Leagues

SNEINTON F.C.

Chairman: R. Smith
Manager: P. Shelton
Secretary: J. W. Stokeld
Address & Tel No: 4 Baker Ave, Arnold, Nottingham (263681)
Ground address & Tel No: Burton Joyce 2726
Simple ground directions: Rear of Ferry Boat Inn, Stoke Bardolph, Burton Joyce, Notts
Colours: Green & Blue striped shirts, Blue shorts & socks **Change colours:** Red shirts, Black shorts & socks
Year formed: 1904 **Programmes:** No
Club house: Planning consent for one **Floodlights:** No **Seating:** No
Previous Leagues: Notts Amateur Football League

SOUTHWELL CITY

Chairman: G. Allen
Managers: R. Cottam, C. Watson, C. Barratt
Secretary: P. K. Johnson
Address & Tel No: 63 The Ropewalk, Southwell, Notts. (812594)
Ground address: War Memorial Recreation Ground, Bishop's Drive, Southwell
Simple ground directions: War Memorial Recreation Ground, off Bishop's Drive, Westgate
Colours: Black/White striped shirts, Black shorts **Change colours:** Red shirts
Year formed: 1955 **Programmes:** First team only, 12 pages, 15p
Club house: Yes **Floodlights:** No **Seating:** No
Previous Leagues: Notts Spartan, Notts & District, Newark & District

WORTHINGTON SIMPSON

Chairman: L. Tindall
Manager: P. Grummitt
Secretary: G. Brooks
Address: 39 Russell Ave, New Balderton, Newark
Ground address & Tel No: Lowfields, New Balderton, Newark (Newark 702672)
Simple ground directions: From Newark Hospital turn right at lights onto Bowbridge Road. Follow road for 1 mile, turn left by timber yard, over railway bridge, turn right to Worthington Simpson, ground on left opposite car park
Colours: Burgundy/Blue **Change colours:** Blue/Burgundy
Year formed: 1935 **Programmes:** No
Club house: Yes **Floodlights:** No **Seating:** Yes
Previous Leagues: Newark & District

CENTRAL MIDLANDS FOOTBALL LEAGUE 1983/84

Chairman: Frank Harwood
General Secretary: A. E. Goodacre, 6 Madison Avenue, Chaddesden, Derby.
Tel: Derby 672986

THREE CHAMPIONSHIPS DECIDED ON GOAL DIFFERENCE

At the completion of the League's first season under its new title The Central Midlands League produced high excitement with three of the four divisions being decided on goal difference with the Premier and Senior Divisions Titles being decided on the last day of the season.

The Premier Division was reclaimed by Shepshed Charterhouse who have now won it twice in three seasons. They also became the first holders of the Manns Premier Cup. This Cup Competition is sponsored by Manns Brewery of Northampton and the Free Trade Sales Director, Martin Finneran, became the League Patron. The Final of the Manns Premier Cup saw Shepshed beat Belper Town 1-0 at the Baseball Ground (by kind permission of Derby County FC), watched by nearly 800 spectators. Long Eaton Grange beat Mickleover Royal British Legion in the 3rd/4th place "Shoot out" during the half-time interval.

Former Champions and Cup Holders Arnold FC had to be content with the Runner Up spot, although they did collect the Nottinghamshire Intermediate County Cup for the second season in a row beating Bulwell 5-1. Readord Olympic did well to finish 3rd in their first season in the League. They are a progressive club who have just signed a 21 year lease on their own new ground. Dave Nicholson finished 3rd highest scorer with 31 goals.

In Premier One, Rolls Royce took the title at the first attempt and will now be promoted to the Premier Division. They clinched the Championship in fine style and won their last 17 League Games. They also sported the League top goal scorer in Norman Owers, who cracked in 34 goals, and the club can be happy with the results of their first season in the League. Retford Town snatched 2nd spot on goal difference from new boys Rossington Main; both finished on 67 points, Rossington will be promoted to the Premier Division and they put the "icing" on the cake by lifting the Premier One League Cup with a 3-2 victory over Riddings St James. The League wish to thank Worksop Town FC for the use of the facilities for this Final. Kilburn Miners Welfare did well to finish in 4th place and are considered one of the favourites for the title next season. They won the Belper Nursing Cup for a well deserved Trophy.

The Senior Division produced the tightest finish with FC Ashbourne taking the title on goal difference from Holbrook Miners Welfare. Ashbourne had to win their last match with Rolls Royce Reserves for the Championship and a close game saw them triumph 2-1. Ashbourne also got the better of Holbrook when they met in the Final of the B.E. Webbe Challenge Cup and won 3-0. In the Senior Division League Cup Final, Radford Olympic Reserves rounded off a fine season for the club with a 3-1 victory over Rolls Royce. One must feel sorry for Castle Donington Town who had led the table for most of the season only to finish in 4th place behind Alfreton & District ASC who are promoted with Ashbourne and Holbrook.

In Division One, Clay Cross Works and Swanwick Pentrich Road had been together all season and all depended on the last game which saw Swanwick win 2-0 but lose the Championship to Clay Cross on goal difference. They did, however, win the Ripley Charity Cup which helped to ease their League disappointment.

The Division One League Cup was won by Riddings St James Reserves, who beat Draycott FC by 1-0 at the Manor Ground, Ilkeston.

Next season the Central Midlands League are revising their Divisions with 1st teams only making up the Premier Division. Premier One has been upgraded to Supply Status and will accommodate the Reserve Teams of Senior Clubs from Football League and Contributory Leagues. A New Division named the Central Division is being formed to take the clubs from last season's Premier One.

The League have again accepted a number of Top Senior local clubs which proves the standard is what clubs are seeking. Nuthall FC, Stanton FC, Slack & Parr, Carriage & Wagon Welfare (all East Midland Regional), Sutton Trinity (Northern Counties East), Thorpe Acre (North Leicestershire), Blackwell Miners Welfare (Sutton & Skegby) have all joined with their respective reserve teams, plus Chesterfield FC (Central League), Hinckley Athletic (Leicestershire District), and Lincoln United Reserves (Lincolnshire League). It is also hoped that Worksop Town and Tamworth FC will be entering Reserve Teams in Premier One. Three member clubs, Rossington, Denby Drury Lowe and Brailsford are also entering new reserve teams for next season.

The revised league layout is in preparation for the 85-86 season when the League Executive hope to finalise a new division for the top senior clubs within a 50 mile radius.

The League have their first Honorary Life Member and this was presented to Mr H.L.P. Holmes, Secretary of the Derbyshire County Football Association, at the League's Annual Dinner/Dance Presentation Evening.

CENTRAL MIDLANDS FOOTBALL LEAGUE

Premier Division

	P	W	D	L	F	A	Pts
Shepshed Charterhouse	34	25	4	5	104	32	79
Arnold F.C.	34	25	4	5	96	35	79
Radford Olympic	34	19	11	4	81	32	68
Long Eaton Grange	34	19	6	9	68	41	63
Borrowash Victoria	34	17	9	8	59	51	60
Belper Town	34	14	9	11	54	31	51
Staveley Town	34	14	6	14	55	64	48
Denby Drury Lowe	34	14	6	14	49	58	48
Eastwood Town	34	13	7	14	63	59	46
Gresley Rovers	34	14	4	16	45	62	46
Newhall United	34	12	8	14	68	65	44
Clay Cross Works	34	11	8	15	75	82	41
Mickleover RBL	34	11	6	17	58	72	39
Swanwick Pentrich Rd	34	10	9	15	55	74	39
Alvaston & Boulton	34	9	8	17	41	69	35
Ilkeston Town	34	8	8	18	43	81	32
Ibstock Penistone Rov	34	5	6	23	35	87	21
Attenborough	34	4	5	25	29	83	17

LEADING GOAL SCORERS

N. Owers	34	Rolls Royce
A. Henshall	32	Valley Park
D. Nicholson	31	Radford Olympic
G. Walker	29	Arnold FC
G. Millington	24	Clay Cross Works
C. Betts	23	Shepshed Charterhouse
T. Kelsall	23	Swanwick Pentrich Road
J. Maslauskas	23	FC Ashbourne
B. Stone	23	Holbrook Miners Welfare
R. Hardy	21	Rossington Main
B. Marcer	20	Castle Donington Town

Premier Divison One

	P	W	D	L	F	A	Pts
Rolls Royce	30	24	2	4	104	32	74
Retford Town	30	21	4	5	80	24	67
Rossington Main	30	21	4	5	83	43	67
Kilburn Miners Welfare	30	17	5	8	54	44	56
Smalley Villa	30	14	6	10	54	47	48
Alfreton Town	30	12	7	11	62	52	43
Ridding St James	30	12	5	13	59	73	41
Valley Park	30	12	5	13	78	93	41
Graham St Prims	30	9	8	13	47	50	35
Brailsford FC	30	9	7	14	49	63	34
Sandiacre Town	30	9	5	16	61	76	32
Draycott FC	30	8	7	15	48	66	31
Long Eaton United	30	7	9	14	44	68	30
Mickleover RBL Res	30	6	10	14	39	57	28
Hilton Athletic	30	7	7	16	46	79	28
Ashfield Glass Trinity	30	5	3	22	39	80	18

Senior Division

	P	W	D	L	F	A	Pts
FC Ashbourne	26	18	5	3	71	31	59
Holbrook Miners Wel	26	18	5	3	61	27	59
Alfreton & Dist ASC	26	17	5	4	56	22	56
Castle Donington T	26	17	3	6	64	31	54
Radford Olympic Res	26	14	6	6	61	39	48
Midlectron FC	26	13	4	9	43	38	43
Attenborough FC Res	26	10	4	12	43	47	34
Melbourne FC	26	9	4	13	41	62	31
Tansley FC	26	8	6	12	48	48	30
Newhall Labour Club	26	8	4	14	40	57	28
Rolls Royce Res	26	7	6	13	42	52	27
Shardlow St. James	26	3	8	15	33	50	17
Alvaston & Boulton Res	26	4	4	18	35	68	16
Pegasus	26	3	2	21	31	97	11

CUP FINALS 1983-84

MANNS PREMIER CUP FINAL

Belper Town 0 Shepshed Charterhouse 1
Referee: G. Short. Linesmen: T. Nutt, I. Wright.

PREMIER ONE CUP FINAL

Rossington Main 3 Ridding St James 2
Referee: B. Rudkin. Linesmen: A. Clarke, J. Oldknow.

SENIOR DIVISION CUP FINAL

Radford Olympic Res 3 Rolls Royce Res 1
Referee: G. Clarke. Linesmen: S. Baker, N. Frost.

DIVISION ONE CUP FINAL

Draycott FC Res 0 Ridding St James Res 1
Referee: I. Reed. Linesmen: R. J. Fleming, B. Meynall.

B E WEBBE CHALLENGE CUP FINAL

FC Ashbourne 3 Holbrook Mnrs Welfare 0
Referee: D. Thorp. Linesmen: G. Belcher, R. Rawson.

CENTRAL MIDLANDS FOOTBALL LEAGUE

PREMIER DIVISION	Alvaston	Arnold	Attenborough	Belper	Borrowash	Clay Cross Works	Denby Drury Lowe	Eastwood	Gresley	Ibstock	Ilkeston	Long Eaton Grange	Mickleover	Newhall	Radford	Shepshed	Staveley	Swanwick
Alvaston	—	1-3	5-0	1-1	0-1	4-3	3-2	2-1	0-0	0-0	3-0	0-2	1-5	3-3	0-1	0-3	3-1	3-5
Arnold	5-0	—	3-0	0-1	0-1	4-0	2-0	5-1	5-0	2-0	2-0	4-3	3-2	2-1	2-4	3-4	1-1	3-1
Attenborough	1-1	1-3	—	0-4	2-3	1-2	1-0	2-4	0-1	1-1	0-4	3-0	0-1	0-4	1-3	0-2	2-5	2-0
Belper	1-3	0-1	2-0	—	2-2	2-0	3-0	0-0	2-1	6-0	1-1	0-0	3-0	1-2	0-2	0-1	4-1	0-2
Borrowash	1-1	0-1	2-0	0-1	—	2-0	2-0	2-1	1-2	2-0	1-1	1-1	2-1	1-5	2-2	1-1	4-0	3-1
Clay Cross Works	5-0	1-6	1-1	1-1	4-4	—	1-2	4-3	1-3	4-2	8-0	1-3	9-1	5-2	0-2	1-3	1-2	3-2
Denby Drury Lowe	2-1	1-1	2-1	2-1	2-5	2-4	—	1-1	2-0	3-1	2-0	2-4	2-1	2-1	2-2	0-2	4-2	1-1
Eastwood	1-2	1-5	4-0	0-4	1-2	5-0	2-0	—	2-1	4-0	2-1	4-2	2-5	1-0	0-1	2-3	1-1	4-0
Gresley	1-0	1-4	3-0	1-5	0-1	3-3	0-1	1-2	—	2-0	3-2	2-1	0-3	4-1	1-7	0-3	5-1	3-2
Ibstock	1-1	0-4	4-0	0-0	1-5	2-2	3-1	4-1	0-1	—	5-2	0-1	0-4	2-0	0-3	0-7	1-3	2-2
Ilkeston	7-1	2-3	2-0	1-0	1-1	3-2	0-2	0-0	1-1	1-0	—	0-4	2-0	1-1	0-4	1-4	1-6	0-0
Long Eaton Grange	3-0	0-3	4-1	1-0	5-2	0-1	0-1	2-1	4-0	4-0	3-2	—	4-1	3-1	3-0	1-1	1-1	1-1
Mickleover	0-0	1-4	1-1	2-3	1-2	2-2	1-1	0-0	1-0	4-0	4-0	2-0	—	3-1	0-8	2-5	1-2	1-1
Newhall	2-1	2-2	4-1	1-1	3-1	3-3	3-3	3-2	5-2	4-0	2-2	1-2	3-2	—	1-2	1-1	1-2	2-0
Radford	4-0	0-0	3-1	1-1	4-0	0-1	2-0	2-2	0-0	5-1	5-0	1-1	0-1	3-0	—	2-1	1-1	3-3
Shepshed	0-1	1-2	2-0	2-1	6-0	8-1	1-0	0-0	0-2	3-2	9-1	3-0	5-3	5-0	3-0	—	7-1	4-1
Staveley	1-0	0-5	1-4	1-0	0-1	0-0	5-0	2-3	0-1	2-1	2-0	1-3	3-2	2-0	2-2	0-2	—	3-1
Swanwick	3-0	4-3	2-2	1-3	1-1	4-1	1-4	2-5	2-0	3-2	0-4	0-2	3-0	0-5	2-2	3-2	1-0	—

PROPOSED DIVISIONS FOR SEASON 1984-85

PREMIER DIVISION: Carriage and Wagon Welfare, Nuthall FC, Stanton FC, Slack and Parr, Sutton Trinity, Radford Olympic, Long Eaton Grange, Staveley Town, Denby Drury Lowe, Newhall United, Mickleover Royal British Legion, Alvaston & Boulton, Rolls Royce, Rossington Main, Clay Cross Works, Swanwick Pentrich Road.

CENTRAL DIVISION: Graham St Prims Reserves, Rossington Main Reserves, Long Eaton United Reserves, Attenborough FC, Ibstock Penistone Rovers, Thorpe Acre FC, Holbrook Miners Welfare, Alfreton and District ASC, Ridding St James, Kilburn Miners Welfare, Smalley Villa, Valley Park FC, Brailsford FC, Sandiacre Town, Draycott FC, FC Ashbourne.

SENIOR DIVISION: Swanwick Pentrich Road Reserves, Mickleover RBL Reserves, Hilton Athletic, Sutton Trinity Reserves, Kilburn Miners Welfare Reserves, Castle Donington Town, Radford Olympic Reserves, Midlectron FC, Attenborough FC Reserves, Melbourne FC, Blackwell Miners Welfare, Carriage and Wagon Reserves, Nuthall FC Reserves, Stanton FC Reserves, Rolls Royce Reserves, Clay Cross Works Reserves.

DIVISION ONE: Shardlow St James, Alvaston & Boulton Reserves, Pegasus FC, Draycott FC Reserves, Ridding St James Reserves, Smalley Villa Reserves, Holbrook Miners Welfare Reserves, FC Ashbourne Reserves, Hilton Athletic Reserves, Valley Park Reserves, Castle Donnington Town Reserves, Brailsford FC Reserves, Denby Drury Lowe Reserves, Thorpe Acre FC Reserves.

CENTRAL MIDLANDS FOOTBALL LEAGUE

PROPOSED NEW PREMIER ONE: Alfreton Town, Arnold FC, Belper Town, Eastwood Town, Gresley Rovers, Hinckley Athletic, Ilkeston Town, Retford Town, Shepshed Charterhouse, Chesterfield FC, Lincoln United, Tamworth FC, Worksop Town, Borrowash Victoria (Subject to Ground).

CARRIAGE & WAGON WELFARE F.C. (1935)

Chairman: R.J. Probert **Managers:** D.J. Scattergood, R.G. Shapcott
Secretary: Adrian Harris, 93 Violet Street, Cavendish. Derby DE3 8SR
Ground Address & Tel No: Carriage & Wagon Welfare Sports Ground, Long Bridge Lane, off Ascot Drive, Wilmorton, Derby DE2 8ST. Tel: Derby 71376
Directions to Ground: Take A6 (London Rd) for 2 miles south of Derby City Centre. To first island at Wilmorton. Turn right at island into Ascot Drive. Long Bridge Lane is 2nd turn on right off Ascot Drive
Previous Leagues: Derby Amateur, Central Alliance, Derby Senior, Derby Combination, South Derbyshire Premier, East Midlands (Regional)
Colours: Red with Blue and White stripe/Red/Red **Change colours:** Royal Blue with White stripe/Blue/Blue
Programmes: No **Clubhouse:** Yes **Floodlights:** on training areas only **Seating:** No
Reserves Team Secretary: A. Harris, 93 Violet Street, Cavendish, Derby DE3 8SR. Tel: Derby 764741

NUTHALL (1978)

Chairman: David Poxon **Manager:** Ivor Pacey
Secretary: Colin Cooper, 9 Foxglove Road, Newthorpe, Notts NG16 2BG. Tel: Langley Mill 713627
Ground Address & Tel No: Maple Drive, Nuthall, Notts
Directions to Ground: Ground located at rear of Nuthall Church which is situated approx ½ mile from M1 Motorway, exit 26
Previous Leagues: East Midlands Regional, Central Alliance **Colours:** All Red **Change colours:** White/Blue/Red

---

STANTON (early 1900)

Chairman: R. Gregory **Manager:** J. Parry
Secretary: A. W. Hall, 12 Thoresby Road, Long Eaton, Notts NG10 3NP. Tel: L.E. 735443
Ground Address & Tel No: Stanton Club, Hallam Fields, Ilkeston, Derbyshire. Ilkeston 323244
Directions to Ground: Hallam Fields is a small area within Ilkeston Town. Major approach roads to Ilkeston from most directions. M1, junc 25 from south, junc 26 from north. A52 bypass from Derby to Nottingham
Previous Leagues: Notts Amateur, Derby Senior, Central Alliance, East Midlands Regional
Colours: All Yellow **Change colours:** All Red
Programmes: No **Clubhouse:** Yes **Floodlights:** No **Seating:** No

---

CLAY CROSS WORKS SPORTS (1952) **Chairman:** W. Deakin **Manager:**

Secretary: A. Kilcline, 4 Deerpark Cres., Wingerworth, Chesterfield, Ches 76707, work 862151 ext 45 (9 to 4pm)
Ground Address & Tel No: John Street, Clay Cross
Directions to Ground: John St, off Market St, Clay Cross
Previous Leagues: Sutton & Skegby **Colours:** All Yellow **Change colours:** All Blue

SLACK & PARR (1956) **Chairman:** C. Marrable **Manager:** P. Williams

Secretary: R. W. Withers, 1 Meynell Road, Long Eaton, Notts. Tel: L.E. 726170 (H)
Ground Address & Tel No: Slack & Parr Ltd, Long Lane, Kegworth, Derby
Directions to Ground: Motorway turnoff 24 onto A6 — ½ mile before entering Kegworth Village turn left opposite Westminster Bank Computer Centre, Long Lane is ½ mile on left
Previous Leagues: Notts Football Alliance, East Midlands Regional, Central Alliance
Colours: Blue & White stripes/Blue/Blue **Change colours:** Red/Black/Red

RADFORD OLYMPIC (1964) **Chairman:** Reg Davis **Manager:** Terry Lack

Secretary: K. Brailsford, 94 Woolmer, Road, Nottingham
Ground Address & Tel No: New Ground, Ilkeston Road, Lenton Boulevard, Radford, Notts
Directions to Ground: M1 (junction 25) — A52 Derby - Nottingham, left onto Lenton Boulevard to corner A609, Ilkeston Road
Previous Leagues: East Midlands Regional **Colours:** Claret/SkyBlue/Claret **Change colours:** Yellow/Green/Green

DENBY DRURY LOWE (1979) **Chairman:** R. Haslam **Manager:** W. Alton

Secretary: M. Turner, 68 Warmwells Lane, Ripley, Derbys DE5 8JB. Tel: Ripley 46851
Ground Address & Tel No: Derby Road, Denby, Derbs
Directions to Ground: Situated on A61 ½ mile north of Kilburn traffic lights, 3 miles south of Ripley
Previous Leagues: Derbyshire Premier
Colours: Red & White stripes/Black/Red **Change colours:** Blue & White striped/White/White

NEWHALL UNITED (1947) **Chairman:** I. Bennett **Joint Manager:** J. Wain and K. Yates

Secretary: D. Hackett, 15 Renshaw Drive, Newhall, Burton-on-Trent, Staffs DE11 0RY. Tel: Burton 212981
Ground Address & Tel No: Hawfields Ground, Oversetts Road, Newhall
Directions to Ground: Two entrances to Ground, either from Oversetts Road or St. Johns Drive
Previous Leagues: East Midlands, Central Alliance, Burton & District
Colours: Blue & White shirts/Blue shorts **Change colours:** Maroon shirts/White shorts

MICKLEOVER R.B.L.F.C. (1946) **Chairman:** T. Annis **Manager:** P. Shone

Secretary: G. Trueman, 145 Brisbane Road, Mickleover. Tel: 513241 (H), 661461 (B)
Ground Address & Tel No: Ypres Lodge, Western Road, Mickleover, Derbys
Directions to Ground: Uttoxeter Road onto Western Road, Mickleover
Previous Leagues: East Midlands Regional **Colours:** All Blue **Change colours:** All Red

ALVASITON & BOULTON (1961) **Chairman:** K. Orchard **Manager:** M. Froggatt

Secretary: S. Bettridge, 47 Collingham Gdns, Derby DE3 4FR, Derby 43170
Ground Address & Tel No: Alvasiton & Boulton Sports Club, Raynesway, Derby, Derby 664279
Directions to Ground: Southern end of Derby ring road
Previous Leagues: Derby Football Combination, Derby Welfare League, Derbyshire Premier League
Colours: White/Blue/Blue **Change colours:** All Blue

ROLLS ROYCE F.C., DERBY (1918)

Chairman: P. Caswell **Manager:** W. Chetwyn
Secretary: J. C. Lynch, 32 Seymour Close, Kingsway, Derby DE3 3FG. Tel: 362044
Ground Address & Tel No: Rolls Royce Recreational, Moor Lane, Derby
Directions to Ground: Derby Ring Road – Osmaston Park Road, left turn at traffic lights on to Moor Lane approaching from Nottingham end
Previous Leagues: East Midlands Regional, Derbyshire Premier
Colours: Blue & White stripes/Blue/Blue **Change colours:** All Red

ROSSINGTON MAIN (1920) **Chairman:** R. Hinton **Manager:** R. Hinton

Secretary: N. Peach, 21 St. Michaels Avenue, Rossington, Doncaster DN11 0UB. Tel: Doncaster 868246
Ground Address & Tel No: Rossington Miners Welfare Ground, Rossington, Doncaster
Directions to Ground: M1 to M18, then A631 to Bawtry, after Tickhill, B6463 to Rossington
Previous Leagues: Yorkshire, Doncaster Senior
Colours: Yellow & Green/Green/Yellow **Change colours:** Blue & White stripe/Blue/Blue

SWANWICK PENTRICH ROAD (1965)

Chairman: Mrs Jean Gwatkin **Manager:** Peter Walters
Secretary: Mrs Dorothy Walters, 14 Western Avenue, Swanwick, Derbys. Tel: Leabrooks 604483
Ground Address & Tel No: Sports Ground, Highfield Road, Swanwick, Derbyshire. Leabrooks 604483
Directions to Ground: From Swanwick traffic lights take road to Pentrich, proceed up the green, turn left down Pentrich Road to end of village, turn left down Highfield Road
Previous Leagues: Matlock & District, Derbyshire Comb, Derbyshire Premier
Colours: White/Black/White **Change colours:** All Red

WHITBREAD COUNTY SENIOR LEAGUE

(Sanctioned by Sheffield-Hallamshire County FA)

Chairman: M. Matthews

A SUCCESSFUL FIRST SEASON

This was the first season of the newly formed Whitbread County Senior League, and despite some behind-the-scenes difficulties it can be looked back upon with success.

Windsor dominated the premier division early on but faded in the run-in. However they had a sufficient points cushion, and they duly won the title by obtaining a goalless draw in their last game. Swinton Athletic, who were in the bottom three at the turn of the year, had a tremendous run in 1984 that lifted them to be eventual runners-up to Windsor. Consistent performances came from Oughtibridge, Ecclesfield Red Rose and Rotherham Club. Penistone Church had a disastrous season, but with new management and coaching staff they will be looking for a quick return to premier football. As Stocksbridge Works have withdrawn, Old Edwardians were the only other relegated side.

Crookes and Ash House overran most opposition in division 1 and were worthy of promotion to the premier division. A late winning run by Pilkington Recreation saw them gain the third promotion place. Worsbrough Bridge M.W. and Kiveton Park were relegated whilst Norton Woodseats and Phoenix did just enough in the latter games to ensure they remained in division one.

Woodsetts Welfare and Arthur Lea SC were the outstanding sides in division two and were promoted to division one. Joining them in the higher division next season will be Firparmians, who by winning their last seven games pipped Sheffield Bankers on goal difference for the third promotion place. Elsecar Main will be the only relegated team from this division.

Stella and Aurora were dominant in division three with Stella winning the championship on goal difference. They wil be joined in division two next season by Oxley Park who pulled clear of Kilnhurst Colliery in the closing stages of the season.

Swinton Athletic gained some reward for their excellent recovery in the second half of the season by winning the league KO cup competition. After drawing the first game with Rotherham Club at Millmoor, they won the replay at BSC Parkgates ground decisively.

WHITBREAD COUNTY SENIOR

PREMIER DIVISION

	P	W	D	L	F	A	Pts
Windsor	26	13	9	4	64	36	35
Swinton Athletic	26	13	8	5	59	31	34
Rotherham Club	26	15	2	9	53	43	32
Oughtibridge	26	10	11	5	48	33	31
Ecclesfield Red Rose	26	9	13	4	41	30	31
BSC Parkgate	26	11	8	7	52	37	30
Mexborough Main St	26	10	9	7	45	33	29
Maltby MW	26	12	4	10	53	59	28
Stocksbridge Works	26	11	5	10	46	49	27
Centralians	26	7	7	12	53	51	21
Frecheville CA	26	9	3	14	38	41	21
Treeton Welfare	26	8	5	13	43	59	21
Old Edwardians	26	6	8	12	35	42	20
Penistone Church	26	0	4	22	26	112	4

DIVISION ONE

	P	W	D	L	F	A	Pts
Crookes	26	24	0	2	109	20	48
Ash House	26	20	3	3	65	28	43
Pilkington Recs	26	14	3	9	60	53	31
Jubilee Sports	26	12	6	8	62	61	30
East Dene	26	12	4	10	67	42	28
Davy McKee	26	12	4	10	46	47	28
Hallam	26	12	3	11	58	48	27
Sheffield Club	26	10	6	10	45	48	26
Forgemasters	26	9	5	12	39	69	23
Oughtibridge Res.	26	6	8	12	36	58	20
Phoenix	26	5	8	13	35	47	18
Norton Woodseats	26	5	8	13	40	58	18
Kiveton Park	26	5	6	15	38	69	16
Worsbro' Bridge	26	2	4	20	37	89	8

GOALSCORERS

League only

Premier:	K. Pressley (Windsor)	21
	S. Johnson (Swinton Athletic)	19
Div 1:	S. Marshall (Crookes)	47
	H. Pennington (East Dene)	27
Div 2:	P. Gibb (Firparnians)	20
	C. Oxley (Woodsetts Welfare)	18
Div 3:	M. Coles (Stella)	25
	D. Smith (Stella)	24
	K. Buttery (Stella)	19

League Cup only

K. Brown (Rotherham Club) 11

Sporting Award was won by Penistone Church Reserves.

CLUB DIRECTORY FOR THE WHITBREAD COUNTY SENIOR LEAGUE

Club	Ground	Capacity	Seats	Covered Accom	Clubhouse
Ash House (GC)	Lordens Hill, Dinnington	700	Nil	75	at Dinnington RUFC
Aurora United	Bawtry Road, Rotherham	700	Nil	200	Yes
Bahco Record Sports	Waverley Lane, Handsworth	1000	Nil	200	Yes
Crookes WMC	Bawtry Road, Rotherham	700	Nil	200	Yes
Elsecar Main	Armroyd Lane, Elsecar	2000	200	Seats only	Yes
Hallam	Sandygate Road, Sheffield	2000	Nil	250	No
Firparmians	Lordens Hill, Dinnington	700	Nil	75	at Dinnington RUFC
James Fairley Steels	Hemsworth Road, Norton	600	Nil	Nil	Yes
Maltby Miners Welfare	Miners Welfare, Maltby	1000	Nil	250	Yes
Midland Bank	Hathersage Road, Dore	700	20	Seats only	Yes
Norton Woodseats	Coach and Horses, Dronfield	1500	Nil	220	No
Old Edwardians	Bawtry Road, Sheffield	800	Nil	150	No
Oughtibridge WMSC	Station Lane, Oughtibridge	800	Nil	Nil	Yes
Penistone Church	Memorial Ground, Penistone	1200	Nil	300	at Planning Stage
Swinton Athletic	Park Road, Swinton	1500	Nil	30	Yes
Windsor	Ferrars Road, Tinsley	600	Nil	Nil	Yes
Woodsetts Welfare	Recreation Ground, Woodsetts	700	Nil	Nil	Yes
Worsbrough Bridge	Park Road, Worsbrough	2000	200	Seats only	Yes

None of the member clubs issued programmes and only the newly admitted Staveley Works have floodlights.

WHITBREAD C. SENIOR LEAGUE

PREMIER DIVISION SEASON 1983/84

	B.S.C. (Park Gate)	Ecclesfield Red Rose	Frechville C.A.	Maltby M.W.	Mexborough Main St.	Old Edwardians	Oughtibridge W.M.S.C.	Penistone Church	Rotherham Club	Sheffield Centralians	Stockbridge Works	Swinton Athletic	Treeton Welfare	Windsor
B.S.C. (Park Gate)		1-1	2-0	4-2	3-1	2-0	2-2	5-1	2-1	2-0	1-1	4-5	1-2	3-3
Ecclesfield Red Rose	2-1		4-0	2-1	0-1	1-1	3-3	1-1	3-0	3-1	2-1	0-0	2-2	1-1
Frechville C.A.	2-1	0-1		2-2	0-0	2-1	0-1	2-1	0-1	4-2	2-3	3-1	2-3	2-4
Maltby M.W.	3-3	1-0	2-1		1-0	1-3	0-2	4-2	4-5	2-1	2-2	2-2	3-1	2-0
Mexborough Main St.	1-1	1-2	1-0	1-2		2-2	1-1	1-1	1-2	3-1	3-2	0-0	5-2	1-1
Old Edwardians	1-0	1-1	0-2	1-4	3-2		0-2	3-1	3-0	3-3	1-2	0-1	0-1	1-1
Oughtibridge W.M.S.C.	1-2	1-1	0-1	2-3	0-0	2-2		5-2	4-1	1-1	5-0	2-0	2-1	1-4
Penistone Church	0-2	1-1	0-5	0-4	1-8	1-1	0-3		1-6	1-2	1-3	0-8	1-6	2-7
Rotherham Club	2-1	4-1	2-0	6-1	2-4	1-0	2-2	1-0		3-1	1-1	2-0	4-1	0-2
Sheffield Centralians	3-2	2-2	1-5	6-0	2-3	2-1	1-1	10-1	1-2		1-4	0-1	6-1	1-1
Stockbridge Works	0-2	0-0	3-1	3-2	0-1	4-3	2-0	7-2	0-5	2-3		0-4	3-0	0-0
Swinton Athletic	1-1	2-1	2-2	3-0	0-1	2-1	2-2	5-0	5-0	1-1	2-1		2-2	2-5
Treeton Welfare	1-1	0-3	2-0	3-4	1-1	0-1	1-2	5-3	3-0	1-1	0-1	1-6		3-0
Windsor	1-3	3-3	1-0	4-1	3-2	2-2	1-1	7-2	2-0	1-0	5-1	0-2	5-0	

WHITBREAD C. SENIOR LEAGUE

DIVISION ONE SEASON 1983/84

	Ash House G.C.	Crookes W.M.C.	Davy McKee	East Dene	Hallam	Jubilee Spts.	Kiveton Park	Norton Woodseats	Oughtibridge Res.	Phoenix	Pilkington Rec.	Sheffield Club	Sheff. Forgemasters	Worsbrough Bridge
Ash House G.C.		0-1	6-2	2-0	4-2	4-3	6-2	4-0	3-0	0-0	2-1	1-1	2-0	4-2
Crookes W.M.C.	0-1		2-0	2-0	4-0	12-2	7-1	4-0	3-1	3-0	5-1	2-1	8-1	8-0
Davy McKee	2-3	1-8		3-2	1-0	1-2	2-1	2-2	1-1	0-1	6-1	2-1	3-0	4-2
East Dene	2-1	0-3	4-0		2-3	0-3	2-2	5-1	2-3	2-2	1-4	8-0	1-0	5-2
Hallam	2-5	0-1	1-2	1-6		1-1	5-0	4-2	2-2	2-1	2-1	2-0	0-2	5-0
Jubilee Spts.	1-4	4-3	1-2	4-2	2-5		3-2	2-2	8-1	4-1	2-3	1-3	1-1	3-2
Kiveton Park	1-2	3-4	1-5	0-4	0-0	2-2		1-1	3-1	1-0	1-2	1-0	1-2	3-3
Norton Woodseats	0-2	1-4	0-0	1-1	0-2	0-2	5-1		1-1	1-5	2-3	4-0	1-3	5-1
Oughtibridge Res.	0-1	2-3	0-4	1-0	3-2	2-3	1-2	1-0		0-0	2-1	0-1	2-2	4-1
Phoenix	0-1	1-2	1-1	0-5	2-1	0-0	2-3	2-5	1-1		2-3	1-1	4-0	1-3
Pilkington Rec.	2-2	0-4	1-0	0-0	2-1	5-2	3-1	5-1	7-2	1-0		1-5	4-1	3-3
Sheffield Club	3-1	0-4	4-0	1-2	1-2	1-1	2-1	0-0	4-4	3-2	3-2		2-2	0-3
Sheffield Forgemasters	1-3	0-3	1-0	1-8	2-9	1-3	4-3	2-2	2-0	2-2	2-0	1-4		4-2
Worsbrough Bridge	0-1	0-9	1-2	2-3	2-4	1-2	1-1	1-3	1-1	2-4	1-4	0-4	1-2	

THE WEST YORKSHIRE ASSOCIATION FOOTBALL LEAGUE

PREMIER DIVISION

	P	W	D	L	F	A	Pts
Otley Town (LCW)	26	19	–	7	68	42	38
Farnley WMC	26	14	7	5	60	30	35
East End Park WMC	26	13	7	6	60	39	33
Altofts	26	14	4	8	50	36	32
Whitkirk Wanderers	26	14	3	9	47	33	31
Baildon (CRU)	26	14	2	10	63	49	30
Carlton Athletic	26	11	7	8	41	37	29
Glasshoughton Welfare	26	10	5	11	54	53	25
Horsforth St Margaret's	26	11	3	12	39	39	25
Walton Miners' Welfare	26	10	4	12	43	47	24
Ripon City	26	10	1	15	51	75	21
Ferrybridge Amateurs	26	7	4	15	29	56	18
Robin Hood Athletic	26	7	3	16	26	49	17
BBA	26	2	2	22	21	67	6

HAMBRO LIFE LINCOLNSHIRE FOOTBALL LEAGUE PREMIER DIVISION

	P	W	D	L	F	A	Pts
Ross Sports	34	21	9	4	94	38	51
Louth United	34	20	10	4	66	30	50
Immingham Town	34	21	6	7	66	32	48
Barton Town	34	21	4	9	80	49	46
Sleaford Town	34	18	10	6	65	39	46
Lincoln Claytons	34	16	5	13	66	58	37
Gainsborough United	34	14	7	13	49	63	35
Crowle United	34	12	10	12	62	56	34
Ruston Sports	34	13	8	13	50	48	34
Ruston Bucyrus	34	11	11	12	38	50	33
Grimsby Pelham	34	13	6	15	70	63	32
Gainsborough Town	34	11	7	16	52	68	29
Boston United	34	12	6	16	42	50	28
Nettleham	34	10	7	17	41	57	27
Skegness Town	34	13	2	19	58	64	25
Market Rasen Town	34	6	9	19	49	85	21
Messingham Trinity	34	7	5	22	42	78	19
Scunthorpe Desert Rat	34	3	6	25	23	85	12

Nottinghamshire Senior Cup

First Round

Oakham United v John Player FC . . . 4-1
Hucknall CW v Blidworth Welfare . . . 2-1
Nottingham Academicals v Boots Ath . . . 4-2
Ruddington v British Rail Newark . . . 1-5
Brinsley v City & Sherwood Hospitals . . . 0-3
Keyworth Utd v Attenborough . . . 6-0
Calverton Rangers v Notts Police . . . 1-3
Arnold v Southwell City . . . 2-3
Arnold Kingswell v Retford Town . . . 1-2
Newstead MW v Plessey FC . . . 0-1
Calverton Welfare v Thoresby CW . . . 0-8
Rainworth MW v Meadows Albion . . . 1-0*
Gedling CW v Carlton Athletic . . . 1-2
Kimberley Town v Eastwood Town . . . 1-5
Sutton Town v Worthington Simpsons . . . 1-0
Sutton Trinity v Clipstone Welfare . . . 1-3

Second Round

British Rail Newark v Hucknall CW . . . 3-4
Carlton Athletic v Plessey FC . . . 2-1
Clipstone MW v Notts Police . . . 7-0
Nottingham Academicals v Eastwood Town . . . 1-5
Oakham United v Keyworth Utd . . . 2-0*
Rainworth MW v Retford Town . . . 1-0
Sutton Town v City & Sherwood Hospitals . . . 0-1
Thoresby CW v Southwell City . . . 2-0

Third Round

Eastwood Town v Rainworth MW . . . 3-1
Hucknall CW v Clipstone Welfare . . . 2-1*
Oakham United v Carlton Athletic . . . 4-1*
Thoresby CW v City & Sherwood Hospitals . . . 4-1*

Semi-Finals

Oakham United v Eastwood Town . . . 0-5
Thoresby CW v Hucknall CW . . . 1-2*

Final (at Arnold FC)

Eastwood Town v Hucknall CW . . . 6-1

EAST MIDLANDS (REGIONAL) LEAGUE

PREMIER DIVISION

	P	W	D	L	F	A	Pts
Eastwood Racing FC	26	17	8	1	59	21	42
Carriage & Wagon	26	18	2	6	56	20	38
Kingswell FC	26	15	4	7	51	33	34
Stanton FC	26	11	9	6	51	46	31
Harrowby United	26	14	1	11	53	50	29
New Villa	26	13	3	10	46	51	29
Belper United	26	12	4	10	43	42	28
Stapleford OB	26	11	4	11	55	47	26
Slack & Parr	26	9	6	11	58	57	24
International Combustion	26	8	7	11	48	58	23
Brinsley FC	26	5	8	13	36	53	18
Holbrook St Michaels	26	4	7	15	41	58	15
Folk House FC	26	5	4	17	32	62	14
Gameworld Villa	26	5	3	18	28	59	13

League Knock-Out Cup Winners:
Grantham United
League Knock-Out Cup Runners-Up:
Eastwood Racing FC

DERBYSHIRE SENIOR CUP

First Round

Long Eaton Grange v Clay Cross Works . . . 2-6
Alfreton Town v Stapenhill . . . 4-0
Matlock v Heanor Town . . . 3-0
Borrowash Vics v Mickleover RBL . . . 4-0
Gresley Rovers v Staveley Town . . . 3-0
Buxton AFC v Newhall United . . . 4-0
Belper Town v Long Eaton United . . . 5-0
Ilkeston Town v Glossop . . . 5-0

Second Round

Belper Town v Clay Cross Works . . . 1-0
Gresley Rovers v Alfreton Town . . . 1-1, 0-1
Ilkeston Town v Matlock Town . . . 1-1, 1-3
Buxton AFC v Borrowash Vics . . . 2-2, 1-0

Semi-Finals

Matlock Town v Alfreton Town . . . -
Belper Town v Buxton AFC . . . -

Final

Buxton v Matlock Town . . . 1-1
Matlock Town v Buxton . . . 3-0
Matlock Town won 4-1 on aggregate.

CUP FINAL RESULTS

Sheffield & Hallamshire FA Senior Cup Final (at Barnsley)
Emley v Frechville Community Association 2-0

Notts Saturday County Cup Final (at Arnold FC)
Eastwood Town v Hucknall Colliery Welfare 6-1

North Riding Saturday County Cup Final (at Darlington RA)
Northallerton Town v York Railway Institute 1-2

West Riding County Cup Final (at Thackley)
Farsley Celtic v Guiseley 1-1, 1-0

Lincolnshire County Senior Cup Final (at ?x?x?)
Grantham v Spalding United

DRYBROUGHS NORTHERN LEAGUE

Chairman: A Clark
Secretary: G Nicholson, 99 Watling Road, Bishop Auckland, Co. Durham
Tel: 0388 602176

DRYBROUGH NORTHERN LEAGUE LEAGUE CHALLENGE CUP

PRELIMINARY ROUND

Northallerton T v Billingham Synthonia	0-5
Peterlee Newtown v Consett	0-1
South Bank v Esh Winning	5-0
Billingham Town v Blyth Spartans	1-4

FIRST ROUND

Horden CW v Darlington Res	3-1
Whitley Bay v Spennymoor Utd	1-2
Gretna v Darlington C Br	4-1
Ashington v Whitby Town	0-4
Durham City v Bishop Auckland	0-2
Crook Town v South Bank	1-0
Willington v Shotton Comrades	1-2
Ferryhill Athletic v Billingham Synthonia	1-0
Evenwood v Ryhope CA	4-0
Alnwick Town v West Auckland Town	5-3*
Langley Park v Brandon United	0-3
Chester Le Street v North Shields	1-0
Bedlington Terrier v Seaham Red Star CW	0-4
Shildon v Hartlepool Utd Res	4-2
Tow Law Town v Consett	1-0
Norton & Stockton v Blyth Spartans	1-2

SECOND ROUND

Horden CW v Ferryhill Ath (8-7 on Pen)	3-3
Spennymoor Utd v Whitby Town	0-1
Bishop Auckland v Brandon U	1-0
Chester Le Street v Gretna	1-4
Blyth Spartans v Tow Law Town	4-1
Seaham Red Star v Evenwood	2-0
Shildon v Alnwick Town	3-1
Shotton Comrades v Crook Town	0-3

THIRD ROUND

Whitby Town v Bishop Auckland	
Blyth Spartans v Shildon	
Gretna v Horden CW	
Crook Town v Seaham Red Star	

SEMI-FINALS

....

FINAL

Horden CW v Blyth Spartans ....

EX-DRYBROUGH'S NORTHERN LEAGUE FOOTBALL LEAGUE XI

David Clarke
(ex-Newcastle U)**

Gerry Forrest
(South Bank, Rotherham U)

John Wile
(Durham C, Sunderland, Peterborough, WBA, Peterborough)

Steve Carney
(Blyth Spartans, Newcastle U)

Alan Barber
(Bishop Auckland, Hartlepool)

Peter Cartwright
(North Shields, Newcastle U, Darlington)

Keith Houghton
(Blyth Spartans, Carlisle U, Lincoln C)

Chris Waddle
(Tow Law T, Newcastle U)

Les Mutrie
(Blyth Spartans, Hull C, Colchester U)

Malcolm Poskett
(Whitby T, Hartlepool U, Brighton, Watford, Carlisle U)

Alan Shoulder
(Blyth Spartans, Newcastle U, Carlisle U)

There were over twenty ex-Northern League players on the staffs of League clubs including three in our 'team' who made their name with the famous Blyth Spartans FA Cup giant killing side of 1977-78.

**Clarke is not playing for a Football League side now but is selected here in the absence of any other candidates as his ability justifies it.

DIVISION ONE

	P	W	D	L	F	A	Pts
Blyth Spartans	34	23	9	2	74	22	78
North Shields	34	21	6	7	81	51	69
Whitby Town	34	20	7	7	79	33	67
Tow Law Town	34	19	8	7	72	44	65
Bishop Auckland	34	19	7	8	80	39	64
South Bank	34	18	7	9	62	35	61
Billingham Syn	34	14	8	12	56	54	50
Gretna	34	15	7	12	65	58	49*
Whitley Bay	34	14	5	15	37	60	47
Horden Colliery Wel	34	12	7	15	48	59	43
Spennymoor United	34	10	9	15	41	58	39
Consett	34	10	8	16	43	58	38
Peterlee Newtown	34	11	5	18	50	78	38
Crook Town	34	9	10	15	38	50	37
Shildon	34	10	6	18	50	63	36
Ferryhill Athletic	34	9	6	19	47	61	33
Ashington	34	7	8	19	59	71	26*
Evenwood Town	34	1	5	28	27	95	8

League Cup Winners: Horden Colliery Welfare
League Cup Finalists: Blyth Spartans
J. R. Cleator Cup Winners: Blyth Spartans

DIVISION TWO

	P	W	D	L	F	A	Pts
Chester-le-Street Town	34	25	7	2	84	21	82
Ryhope Com Assoc	34	23	6	5	66	33	75
Seaham CW Red Star	34	23	5	6	69	30	74
Brandon United	34	20	6	8	67	37	66
Durham City	34	16	11	7	61	38	59
Darlington Cleveland B.	34	15	9	10	60	53	54
Hartlepool United Res	34	18	5	11	73	52	53**
Bedlington Terriers	34	14	7	13	52	41	49
Esh Winning	34	13	10	11	49	55	49
Billingham Town	34	13	6	15	63	51	45
Darlington Reserves	34	12	4	18	47	69	40
Northallerton Town	34	12	6	16	48	52	39*
Langley Park Welfare	34	9	8	17	46	76	35
Alnwick Town	34	7	12	15	49	53	33
Shotton Comrades	34	9	5	20	55	76	32
Norton & Stockton Anc.	34	6	10	18	30	55	28
West Auckland Town	34	7	3	24	36	83	24
Willington	34	2	4	28	27	107	10

*denotes three points deducted
**denotes six points deducted.

North Riding Senior Cup Winners: South Bank
Cumberland Senior Cup Winners: Gretna.

DRYBROUGHS NORTHERN LEAGUE AWARDS 1983-84

	Final League Placings	Goal Scoring Awards	Three Goal Wins	TOTAL
Ashington	—	—	£50	£50
Billingham Synth	—	£300	£150	£450
Bishop Auckland	—	£700	£450	£1150
Blyth Spartans	£1500	—	£450	£1950
Consett	—	—	£50	£50
Crook Town	—	—	£100	£100
Evenwood Town	—	—	—	—
Ferryhill Athletic	—	—	£200	£200
Gretna	—	£500	£150	£650
Horden CW	—	—	£150	£150
North Shields	£1000	—	£300	£1300
Peterlee	—	—	£100	£100
Shildon	—	—	£200	£200
South Bank	—	£400	£400	£800
Spennymoor	—	—	£100	£100
Tow Law	£700	—	£400	£1100
Whitby Town	£800	—	£600	£1400
Whitley Bay	—	—	£50	£50
Alnwick Town	—	—	£150	£150
Bedlington Terriers	—	—	£120	£120
Billingham Town	—	£300	£150	£450
Brandon United	£400	—	£210	£610
Chester-Le-Street T	£800	—	£330	£1130
Darlington Reserves	—	—	£30	£30
Darlington Cleve B	—	£100	£120	£220
Durham City	—	£200	£150	£350
Esh Winning	—	—	£30	£30
Hartlepools Utd Res	—	£400	£210	£610
Langley Park Welf	—	—	£60	£60
Northallerton Town	—	—	£120	£120
Norton & Stock Anc	—	—	£30	£30
Ryhope Com Assoc	£600	—	£150	£750
Seaham CW Red Star.	£500	—	£210	£710
Shotton Comrades	—	—	£120	£120
West Auckland T	—	—	£60	£60
Willington	—	—	£30	£30

INDIVIDUAL GOAL SCORING AWARDS

First Division:
RUSSELL BLACK (Gretna) — 32 goals — £300
Second Division:
COLIN COWAN (Ryhope CA) — 24 goals — £200

DRYBROUGH CUP AWARDS 1983-84

Winners: HORDEN COLLIERY WELFARE £200
Runners-up: BLYTH SPARTANS £100

In addition, all 36 clubs received playing equipment from this sponsorship to the total value of £3,000.

DNL GOOD CONDUCT AWARDS 1983-84

DURHAM, EVENWOOD TOWN, RYHOPE CA and LANGLEY PARK

All four clubs receive a set of shirts, shorts and stockings.

NO OF CLUBS COMPETING:	20	20	20	19	20	20	20	20	20	20	20	19	18
SEASON:	71/72	72/73	73/74	74/75	75/76	76/77	77/78	78/79	79/80	80/81	81/82	82/83	83/84
1 Ashington	18	9	8	9	7	9	15	2	4	5	18	16	17
2 Billingham Synth	15	4	5	14	14	18	12	11	15	9	6	6	7
3 Bishop Auckland	17	2	4	3	4	8	4	10	6	3	7	4	5
4 Blyth Spartans	2	1	2	1	1	5	2	4	1	1	1	1	1
5 Consett	5	11	13	6	9	2	5	5	7	13	16	9	12
6 Crook T	16	17	17	16	15	4	10	3	5	18	13	10	14
7 Durham C	4	10	10	7	13	12	8	9	18	17	8	17	—
8 Evenwood T	9	12	12	15	10	15	19	20	13	15	14	15	18
9 Ferryhill Ath	11	6	14	13	18	14	18	17	17	6	11	12	16
10 Gretna	—	—	—	—	—	—	—	—	—	—	—	—	8
11 Horden CW	—	—	—	—	11	13	6	8	3	12	12	3	10
12 North Shields	10	19	6	11	8	6	7	6	16	14	10	7	2
13 Penrith	14	14	9	17	12	20	20	19	14	10	15	—	—
14 Peterlee Newtown	—	—	—	—	—	—	—	—	—	—	—	—	13
15 Shildon	6	8	15	18	16	19	16	13	9	7	9	14	15
16 South Bank	13	20	18	10	19	10	13	7	8	8	3	11	6
17 Spennymoor United	1	5	1	2	3	1	1	1	2	2	5	5	11
18 Stanley United	20	18	20	—	—	—	—	—	—	—	—	—	—
19 Tow Law Town	8	15	7	8	5	17	17	12	12	4	4	8	4
20 West Auckland Town	19	16	19	19	20	16	11	16	10	16	17	18	—
21 Whitby Town	7	13	16	5	6	3	3	14	11	11	2	2	3
22 Whitley Bay	3	7	11	12	17	7	14	15	20	19	19	13	9
23 Willington	12	3	3	4	2	11	9	18	19	20	20	19	—

WHITBY TOWN'S RESULTS, 1983-84

Northern League Results				F	A	(H.T.)	GOALSCORERS FOR WHITBY	ATTEND
Aug 27	Bishop Auckland	H	D	3	3	(2-1)	Linacre, Smith & Sills	464
29	Evenwood Town	H	W	6	2	(5-0)	Linacre (2) Sills (2) Granycome & Gollogly	381
Sep 3	South Bank	H	D	2	2	(1-2)	Granycome & Hampton	351
7	Peterlee N. Town	A	W	2	0	(1-0)	Linacre & Walker	—
10	Ferryhill Athletic	A	D	1	1	(1-1)	Sills	—
14	Billingham Syn.	H	W	3	1	(2-0)	Lilley (2) & Sills	432
20	Whitley Bay	A	W	4	0	(2-0)	Linacre (2) Lilley & S. Coleby	—
24	Spennymoor United	A	W	4	1	(3-1)	T. Smith (3) & Sills	—
28	Ferryhill Athletic	H	W	5	2	(2-1)	Linacre (2) Sills (2) & Opp. Own Goal	461
Oct 5	Crook Town	H	W	3	0	(0-0)	Lilley (2) & Linacre	582
8	Shildon	A	L	1	3	(0-2)	Hampton	—
22	Horden C.W.	H	W	1	0	(1-0)	Linacre	538
Nov 5	Peterlee N. Town	H	W	4	1	(2-1)	Hampton (2) T. Smith & Sills	571
12	Evenwood Town	A	W	3	0	(2-0)	Sills (2) & Linacre	—
26	Bishop Auckland	A	W	3	1	(2-1)	Linacre, Lawrence & Walker (pen)	—
Dec 3	Blyth Spartans	H	D	1	1	(1-1)	S. Coleby	1,005
17	Shildon	H	W	4	0	(1-0)	Coleby, Lilley, Sills, Walker (pen)	372
26	South Bank	A	W	2	0	(0-0)	Gollogly & Sills	—
31	Billingham Syn.	A	D	0	0	(0-0)		—
Jan 7	Tow Law Town	A	L	1	3	(1-0)	Lilley	—
21	Whitley Bay	H	D	1	1	(1-1)	T. Smith	561
Feb 18	Crook Town	A	L	0	1	(0-0)		—
Mar 3	Gretna	H	W	2	0	(0-0)	Granycome & Hampton	666
10	North Shields	A	L	2	4	(1-2)	T. Smith & Escritt	380
28	Spennymoor Utd.	H	W	3	0	(1-0)	Logan (2) & Sills	404
31	Consett	A	L	1	2	(1-1)	Lilley	—
Apr 9	Ashington	A	L	1	2	(1-1)	Sills	—
14	Blyth Spartans	A	L	0	1	(0-0)		450
17	Horden C.W.	A	W	3	0	(1-0)	Hampton (2) & Andrews	—
20	Consett	H	D	0	0	(0-0)		451
21	Gretna	A	W	2	0	(1-0)	Granycome & Sills	—
23	Ashington	H	W	5	0	(3-0)	Sharkey (3) Gollogly & Opp. Own Goal	354
25	Tow Law Town	H	W	3	1	(2-0)	Sharkey, T. Smith & Andrews	411
28	North Shields	H	W	3	0	(2-0)	Smith, Hampton, Sharkey	452

Whitby Town's Season and Attendance Record

When a club press officer bothers to compile his clubs records and send them for editorial consideration we make no apology for including them in the 'Directory' if we think they are of interest to the rest of the country's football followers. In Whitby Town's case considering they are geographically situated on the North East coast I am sure their attendances alone are of particular interest and our thanks go to **Gerry Trowsdale** for sending us the well presented feature which does his club and the Drybrough's Northern League great credit.

Turnbull Attendence

Home Attendence	81/82	82/83	83/84
Ashington	270	336	354
Billingham Syn.	541	361	432
Bishop Auckland	437	464	464
Blyth Spartans	393	344	1,005
Consett	289	303	451
Crook Town	321	301	582
Evenwood Town	339	286	381
Ferryhill Athletic	401	420	461
Gretna	—	—	666
Horden C.W.	399	512	538
North Shields	347	302	452
Peterlee N. Town	—	—	571
Shildon	285	320	372
South Bank	403	308	351
Spennymoor Utd.	372	465	404
Tow Law Town	382	410	411
Whitley Bay	311	284	561
TOTAL =	5,496	5,416	8,456
Average =	366	361	497.4

F.A. CUP 1983/84

Oct 19	Lancaster City	1,018
29	Bishop Auckland	1,115
		2,133

F.A. TROPHY 1983/84

Jan 17	Blyth Spartans	961
Feb 25	Frickley Athletic	1,853
Mar 21	Dagenham	2,688
		5,502

DNLC 1983/4

Feb 29	Bishop Auckland	706
Apr 4	Horden C.W.	629
		1,335

NRSC 1983/4

Mar 7	Nunthorpe Ath	813
Apr 7	South Bank	555
		1,368

Combined Total 1983/84 18,794
Average 722.8

DIVISION ONE	Ashington	Billingham S	B. Auckland	Blyth	Consett	Crook	Evenwood	Ferryhill	Gretna	Horden	N. Shields	Peterlee	Shildon	S. Bank	Spennymoor	Tow Law	Whitby	Whitley Bay
Ashington	—	2-1	0-0	0-4	3-2	1-2	3-0	0-1	2-1	0-1	0-2	2-2	1-2	1-2	0-0	0-0	2-1	2-1
Billingham S.	1-1	—	0-3	0-0	1-1	3-1	2-0	2-1	3-1	3-4	4-1	1-0	3-0	1-2	3-2	5-3	0-0	2-0
B. Auckland	4-1	2-1	—	0-1	5-1	1-1	5-1	3-0	4-2	3-1	2-0	1-0	2-0	3-0	4-2	2-2	1-3	1-2
Blyth	3-2	3-0	2-0	—	0-1	1-0	3-1	5-0	6-2	3-1	2-2	4-1	5-1	0-0	1-0	0-0	1-0	2-1
Consett	4-0	1-1	0-0	0-0	—	2-2	2-0	0-0	0-2	3-3	1-3	3-2	2-4	2-0	1-2	0-3	2-1	1-2
Crook	2-2	4-1	2-1	1-3	0-2	—	1-1	1-1	1-0	1-1	2-2	0-1	1-1	1-2	3-0	1-0	1-0	2-3
Evenwood	1-1	0-5	0-6	1-3	2-1	1-1	—	0-3	2-3	1-4	1-5	1-2	0-3	1-3	2-2	1-2	0-3	0-1
Ferryhill	2-1	0-1	0-2	0-2	4-0	1-3	4-1	—	1-1	0-2	4-3	2-2	2-1	0-3	3-1	0-1	1-1	7-0
Gretna	2-1	5-0	3-1	1-2	4-2	1-1	2-1	4-2	—	2-1	4-0	3-2	2-0	3-3	4-4	0-4	0-2	1-0
Horden	3-4	0-0	0-6	2-1	2-4	1-0	3-1	0-0	1-1	—	0-1	0-2	4-1	0-2	3-0	1-4	0-3	0-1
N. Shields	3-2	2-1	2-2	1-1	2-1	3-1	3-1	3-1	3-2	5-1	—	5-1	2-0	1-0	2-0	3-3	4-2	4-1
Peterlee	3-0	2-3	0-4	0-0	1-2	2-1	4-3	3-1	1-1	5-2	0-4	—	4-1	1-4	0-0	0-3	0-2	2-1
Shildon	3-0	2-2	2-3	0-3	1-0	2-0	3-0	3-2	2-3	0-2	1-1	4-1	—	1-2	1-1	2-2	3-1	2-4
S. Bank	5-0	0-2	1-1	0-2	3-0	3-0	1-0	2-1	0-1	1-1	2-0	4-1	1-1	—	1-2	2-3	0-2	6-1
Spennymoor	1-1	2-1	1-2	1-1	3-0	0-1	3-0	1-0	2-1	0-2	2-1	1-3	2-1	0-1	—	0-4	1-4	0-0
Tow Law	3-2	5-1	3-2	0-3	1-0	1-0	1-1	3-1	2-1	0-0	2-4	6-0	1-0	0-4	3-3	—	3-1	0-1
Whitby	5-0	3-1	3-3	1-1	0-0	3-0	6-2	5-2	2-0	1-0	3-0	4-1	4-0	2-2	3-0	3-1	—	1-1
Whitley Bay	2-0	1-1	2-1	1-6	1-2	3-0	1-0	1-0	0-0	0-2	1-4	3-1	3-1	0-0	0-2	0-3	0-4	—

	Alnwick	Bedlington	Billingham T	Brandon	Chester Le St	Darlington	Darl'n C.B	Durham	Esh	Hartlepool	Langley Park	Northallerton	Norton	Ryhope	Seaham	Shotton	W. Auckland	Willington
Alnwick	—	0-1	0-0	1-1	1-3	1-0	2-3	2-2	1-3	1-2	4-1	2-2	0-0	3-0	1-1	1-2	4-0	1-2
Bedlington	1-4	—	0-2	1-2	1-2	1-2	2-0	2-0	1-0	1-1	3-2	2-2	0-0	1-2	1-1	2-0	3-0	2-0
Billingham T.	1-0	0-4	—	1-0	2-2	2-0	1-1	4-0	2-1	1-2	6-0	2-1	6-0	1-1	0-2	1-0	6-0	3-2
Brandon	1-4	2-0	2-1	—	0-2	5-1	0-0	3-1	2-0	3-0	2-3	1-0	0-0	0-1	0-1	4-2	2-2	4-1
Chester Le St	3-0	1-0	4-2	1-1	—	4-2	2-0	1-1	5-0	3-1	4-0	2-0	4-0	1-2	1-1	2-2	3-0	3-0
Darlington	1-1	0-2	2-0	1-6	0-1	—	2-4	2-1	1-3	0-2	1-1	2-1	1-1	1-3	2-1	2-4	2-1	3-0
Darl'n C.B	1-1	3-2	4-2	3-0	0-5	3-1	—	1-1	1-2	1-4	2-2	3-1	1-0	1-2	0-3	2-0	3-0	5-1
Durham	2-1	2-0	2-1	0-1	0-1	5-1	1-1	—	2-1	0-0	3-1	3-1	3-1	1-1	1-0	3-1	2-2	1-1
Esh	2-0	0-0	2-2	0-4	0-0	3-2	0-1	1-1	—	1-0	1-1	2-2	2-1	0-3	0-0	4-2	2-0	2-1
Hartlepool	2-2	2-3	3-0	0-1	1-2	1-3	4-0	0-3	6-1	—	5-1	1-0	3-2	1-2	2-0	3-2	5-2	2-1
Langley Park	0-0	3-1	3-2	0-2	0-6	2-3	2-1	1-5	0-0	1-1	—	2-5	2-1	0-1	0-4	1-1	5-1	1-1
Northallerton	2-1	3-0	1-0	3-3	0-1	2-1	0-0	0-1	1-0	1-4	3-2	—	0-1	1-2	0-2	4-1	1-2	1-1
Norton	2-1	0-0	1-1	1-2	0-3	1-3	1-1	1-1	1-1	0-1	2-1	0-2	—	1-2	1-3	3-0	1-0	1-1
Ryhope	2-0	3-3	2-1	2-0	1-1	3-0	2-2	0-0	1-2	4-2	1-2	3-1	2-1	—	0-2	2-1	2-0	4-1
Seaham	4-1	1-0	2-1	3-4	3-1	1-1	3-1	3-0	1-2	4-2	1-0	3-0	1-0	1-0	—	2-1	5-1	5-0
Shotton	3-3	1-2	4-1	0-3	0-3	1-0	2-5	2-3	4-4	2-2	0-2	0-1	3-2	1-4	5-2	—	1-2	3-0
W. Auckland	0-0	0-4	3-2	0-1	0-2	1-2	1-2	0-4	6-3	0-2	2-0	0-2	3-2	0-1	1-2	1-2	—	5-2
Willington	3-5	0-7	0-6	1-5	0-5	1-2	0-1	0-5	0-4	1-6	1-4	1-4	0-1	1-4	0-1	0-2	3-0	—

Chester-le-Street *Back Row (L-R): P Reach, T Callaghan, K Cuskeran, G Davison, A Armstrong, G Wright, P Teasdale, P Harding, P Ward. Front Row (L-R): P Stronach, P Nixon, B Hill, D Adamson, D Norton, N Howie, A Gibson.*

DRYBROUGHS NORTHERN LEAGUE

DIVISION ONE

Club	Leading Goalscorers		Hat-Tricks	Penalties	Most Appearances	
Bishop Auckland	Kevin Cross	15	Cross	Andy McKinnell	David Johnson	45*
	Harry Dunn	14	McKinnell	5 including a	Harry Dunn	44
	Andy McKinnell	14	Johnson	hat trick	Phil Owers	43
					Malcolm Newton	43
Blyth Spartans	Tony McFadden	29	Hart (2)		Dave Clarke	48
	Geoff Hart	20	Grigg		Ian Chester	46
	Paul Grigg	13			Tommy Dixon	45
	Bob Scaife	13				
Chester-le-Street	Paul Nixon	29	Nixon (2) 4 + 3		Tony Gibson	48*
	Paul Teasdale	16	Howie (2) 4 + 3		George Davison	42
	Neil Howie	16	Teasdale		Kevin Cuskeran	40
			Maddison		Brian Hill	40
Consett	Barrie Fowler	17	Fowler	Fowler (2)	Brian Fowler	41*
	Gary Bell	9	Bell		Paul McArdle	41*
	Paul McArdle	4			Brian Hardy	40
Gretna	Russell Black	50	Russell Black (4)	Russell Black (6)	Stuart Rome	39
	Donald Peattie	18			Tony Monaghan	39
	Tony Monaghan	10			Don Peattie	38
Horden C.W.	Gerry Hogan	18	Jeff Lloyd		Gerry Hogan	49
	Paul Dobson	13+			Garry Lormor	47
	Paul Walker	13			Paul Brown	46
North Shields	Jim Pearson	34	Jim Pearson	Jim Pearson (2)	Mike Carroll	51*
	Mike Carroll	25	Paul Ross	Paul Ross	George Dickson	50
	Paul Ross	25			Brian Pilkington	50
Ryhope C.A.	Colin Cowan	25	Colin Cowan	Colin Cowan (3)	Colin Cowan	38*
	Peter Harding	10			Steve Moore	37
	Jeff Simpson	9			John Burrell	35
Shildon	Mick Omoni	13	Kevin Clarke	Colin Smith (4)	Lou Christie	43
	Phil Omoni	8		Peter Graham	Paul Burton	36
	Kevin Clarke	6		Mick Omoni	Phil Omoni	35
South Bank	Tony Boylan	19	One		Charlie Butler	45
	Colin Bickerstaff	13			Tony Sharkey	42
	Charlie Butler	9			Ged Hartley	41
					Kevin Taylor	41
Spennymoor United	Kevin Berry	10		David Curry (3)	Robin Gill	41*
	David Curry	8			Jack Sheekey	39
	Ken Heslop	4			Kevin Berry	39
	Stuart Regan	4				
Tow Law Town	Paul Haley	18	Paul Haley	Danny Wheatley	Mike Haley	34*
	Steve Turner	12		(3)	Kevin Campbell	34*
	Danny Wheatley	10			Stephen Webb	34*
Whitby Town	Ronnie Sills	29	Phil Linacre (2)	Richie Walker (5)	Derek Hampton	52
	Trevor Smith	13	5 + 4	Neal Grannycome	Richie Walker	52
	Phil Linacre	27+	Smith (1)	David Coleby	Grannycome	51
			Paul Sharkey (1)		D. Coleby	51

*Ever present

DIVISION TWO

Club	Leading Goalscorers		Hat-Tricks	Penalties	Most Appearances	
Alnwick Town	Colin Chambers Steve Wright David Brown	12 8 6		David Willis Colin Chambers	Colin Chambers* Ronnie Blacklin George Parker	
Ashington	Kevin Fulbeck Clinton Sage Howard Smith Graeme Wilson	12 9 4 4	Kevin Fulbeck	Graeme Wilson (1)	Tommy Dodds Clinton Sage Graeme Wilson + 3 subs	38 35 33
Billingham Town	Graham Jones Mark Puttick Bernard Grainger	15 8 7	Graham Jones Mark Steel Steve Bates	Mike Taylor Andrew McCreash	Vincent Jacques Gary Popple Mark Puttick	41* 40 40
Brandon United	Bryan Jennings John Thomson William Moat	28 12 8	Bryan Jennings (2) Paul Dixon	Bryan Jennings (3)	Matt Hillary Keith Brown Steve Forster Bryan Jennings	45 43 43 43
Darlington Reserves	John Hannah David Young Brian Lynn Steve Bailes Phil Shute	6 6 4 4 4	Phil Shute		Brian Lynn Kevin Wolfe Graham Morgan	34 28 26
Darlington Cleveland Bridge	G. Stanford S. Hope D. Towers	12 12 9	Graham Stanford David Towers		D. Hardy D. Hutton J. Gilsenan	36* 35 33
Durham City	Ian Mulholland Paul Main John Jackson	19 15 9	Paul Main	I. Mulholland (4) P. Main	Paul Malcolm Geoff Morgan Albert Hickman	44 44 38
Esh Winning	Terry Allen Steve McDermott Henry Crampton	16 8 7		Steve McDermott (3)	Henry Crampton Paul Bailes Gary Cranston	
Evenwood Town	Steve Weldon David McGinn John Clark	5 5 4		David McGinn (4) Steve Weldon	Ian Campbell John Clark Darren Elliott	40* 39 34
Langley Park Welfare	Steward Ogden Peter Donelly David McGinn	11 7 6	S. Ogden	D. McGinn (3) P. Donnelly (2)	Stuart Birkenfield David Robson Peter Donnelly	32 31 31
Norton & Stockton Ancients	Jimmy Horton Chris Smith Geoff Brookes	7 3 3		J. Horton (2)	Sean O'Brien Peter Cain Stephen Bates	42* 40 34
Seaham Red Star	Keith Robertson Tom Henderson Nigel Greghorn	30 15 15	K. Robertson	K. Robertson (5)	Vincent Elwick Keith Robertson Ken Mitchell Keith Guy	44 42 41 41
Shotton Comrades	Keith Willetts Peter Cockburn Stuart Pearn	18 14 10	K. Willetts	Lenny Worral (3)	Peter Cockburn Ron Brown Lenny Worral	36* 32 30
Willington	Colin Goodchild Ken Riley David Taylor	7 7 3		Ken Riley (2)	John Dixon Tony Hopkins David Todner Billy Todner	33 29 28 28

*Ever present

BILLINGHAM SYNTHONIA

President: L. Cattermole
Chairman: P. E. Lax
Manager: E. Nobbs
Coach: E. Nobbs
Physiotherapist:
Secretary: J. Dunlop
Address & Tel No: 0642 533008 (H)
Commercial Manager:
Address & Tel No:
Press Officer & Tel No: Secretary
Address & Tel No of ground: The Stadium, Central Avenue, Billingham (Tel Ground: Stock. 552358) **Club shop:** No
Simple ground directions: Adjoins main ICI building at Junction of Central Avenue and Cowper Lane, south end of town
No of seats: 3,000 **Covered accommodation:** 3,000 **Capacity:** 8,000 **Floodlights:** Yes
Year formed: 1923 **Nickname:** Synners **Club sponsors:** None
Previous names: None
Previous grounds: None
Club colours: Green & White
Change colours: White
Day for midweek home matches: Wednesday
Record attendance: Not known
Previous Leagues: Teesside, South Bank
Best performance in: F.A. Cup: 1948-9 v Crewe, 1950-1 Stockport, 1951-2 Scunthorpe, 1956-7 Carlisle, all 1st Round Proper
F.A. Trophy: 1980-1 3rd Qualifying Round
Clubhouse details: Billingham Synthonia recreation club (11,000 members)
Present players with Football League experience: J. Roddy (Queen of the South, Sunderland)
Past players who progressed into the Football League: None
Record transfer fee paid: None
Record transfer fee received: None
Programme details: None
Club metal badges: No
Local newspaper & Tel No: Middlesbrough Evening Gazette
Senior Honours: Drybrough Northern League & Runners-up (3), Drybrough Northern League Cup, North Riding Senior Cup, Vaux Floodlight League
Club Captain (1983-84): A. Harbron
Player of the Year (1983-84): Mark Kirton

BISHOP AUCKLAND

President: W. B. Botcherby
Chairman: G. H. Metcalfe
Manager: B. T. Newton
Coach: J. Lee
Physiotherapist: D. Robertson
Secretary: F. W. Jobson
Address & Tel No: Aycliffe 313537 (H)
Commercial Manager: H. Young
Address & Tel No:
Press Officer & Tel No: Secretary
Address & Tel No of ground: Kingsway, Bishop Auckland, Co. Durham. Tel B.A. 603686 **Club shop:** No
Simple ground directions: Leave A167 at Thinford (near Ferryhill), follow signposts for Bishop Auckland, travelling west through town centre ground on nearside
No of seats: 1,080 **Covered accommodation:** 1,000 **Capacity:** 8,500 **Floodlights:** Yes
Year formed: 1886 **Nickname:** The Bishops **Club sponsors:** None
Previous names: None
Previous grounds: None
Club colours: Dark & Light Blue/Dark Blue/D. & L. Blue
Change colours: Red & White/White/Red & White
Day for midweek home matches: Wednesday
Record attendance: v Coventry City **Year:** 1952-3
Previous Leagues: Northern
Best performance in: F.A. Cup: 1954-5 v York City, 4th Round
F.A. Trophy: 1978-9 v Stafford, 1981-2 v Wycombe 4th Round
Clubhouse details: Open for members/visitors before and after games. Normal opening 6.30-10.30pm daily
Present players with Football League experience: P. Owers (Darlington)
Past players who progressed into the Football League: Very many including: Seamus O'Connell (Chelsea, Middlesborough), Jack Major (Hull City), Bob Paisley (Liverpool), Tomy Sword (Stockport County), Warren Bradley (Manch U), Billy Ayre (Halifax, Hartlepool, Mansfield); also Lawrie McMenemy was manager of Bishop in 1966-67 and progressed to manage Grimsby, Doncaster and Southampton
Record transfer fee paid: None
Record transfer fee received: £6,000 for Thomas Sword from Stockport County
Programme details: 12 pages, 20p
Programme Editor: Secretary
Local newspapers & Tel No: Northern Echo, Newcastle Journal, Evening Despatch
Club metal badges: £1.50
Senior Honours: F.A. Amateur Cup (10) Runners-up (8), Durham Benevolent Bowl (9) Runners-up (4), Northern League (17), Northern League Challenge Cup (6) Runners-up (6)
Club Captain (1983-84): Harry Dunn
Player of the Year (1983-84): Harry Dunn

BLYTH SPARTANS

President: Jackie Milburn
Chairman: J. A. Turney
Manager:
Coach:
Physiotherapist:
Press Officer & Tel No: Secretary
Secretary: G. Watson
Address & Tel No:
Commercial Manager: M. Turnbull
Address & Tel No: Blyth 2373
Address & Tel No of ground: Croft Park, Blyth. Office: Blyth 352373, Clubhouse: Blyth 354818 **Club shop:** Yes
Simple ground directions: Near to town centre
No of seats: 300 **Covered accommodation:** 2,500 **Capacity:** 8,500 **Floodlights:** Yes
Year formed: 1899 **Nickname:** Spartans **Club sponsor:** Universal Building Society
Previous names: None
Club colours: Green & White
Previous grounds: None
Change colours: Yellow
Day for midweek home matches: Tuesday
Record attendance: 42,000 (at Newcastle) v Wrexham **Year:** 1978
Best performance in: F.A. Cup: 1977-8 5th Round Proper Replay
F.A. Trophy: 1980-1 Quarter-Final
Previous Leagues: Northumberland, N. Alliance, North Eastern, Midland, N. Counties
Clubhouse details: Open every night, Sunday lunch, Saturday lunch on match days
Present players with Football League experience: D. Clarke (Newcastle), P. Robinson (Burnley), R. Scaife (Middlesborough), A. McFadden (Darlington), J. Stirk (Ipswich)
Past players who progressed into the Football League: A. Shoulder (Carlisle), S. Carney (Newcastle), K. Houghton (Colchester), L. Mutrie (Doncaster)
Record transfer fee paid: None
Record transfer fee received: £30,000 for L. Mutrie from Hull City
Programme details: 20 pages, 15p
Programme Editor: P. Hindmarsh
Local newspapers & Tel No: Blyth News (Blyth 66347)
Club metal badges: Yes
Senior Honours: N.F.A. Senior Cup (18), Amateur Cup Semi-Final, Northern League
Club Captain (1983-84): Tommy Dixon **Player of the Year (1983-84):** P. Robinson

CHESTER-LE-STREET TOWN

President: G. Newton
Chairman: R. Bell
Manager: M. Moore
Coach: R. Mulvaney
Physiotherapist:
Press Officer: Malcolm Pratt 0385 883565
Secretary: J. D. Burlison
Address & Tel No: 4 Carrowmore Road, Chester-le-Street, Co. Durham DH2 3DY. 0385 884607
Commercial Manager: D. Weetman
Address & Tel No: 3 Surtees Drive, Crossgate Moor, Durham. 0385 65604
Address & Tel No of ground: Points North, Chester Moor, Chester-le-Street. Tel. 0385 883363
Simple ground directions: Travel on A167 road between Durham and Newcastle-upon-Tyne, ground is situated approximately 1 mile south of Chester-le-Street on this dual carriageway
No of seats: 200 (approx) **Covered accommodation:** under construction **Capacity:** 4,000 **Floodlights:** being installed
Year formed: 1972 **Nickname:** Cestrians **Club sponsors:** North East Daf Trucks
Club colours: Blue/White/Blue hose
Change colours: All Yellow
Previous Names: Garden Farm F.C.
Previous Grounds: Ropery Lane
Record attendance: 473 v Barrow F.C. F.A. Cup **Year:** 1983-84 **Previous Leagues:** Vaux Wearside League
Clubhouse details: Lounge/bar downstairs, games room upstairs and bar
Programme details: 10 pages 10p
Programme Editor: George Ford
Major Honours: Dryboroughs Northern League Div II Champions 1983-84, Vaux Wearside League Winners 1980-81, Runners-up 1982-83
Club Captain (1983-84): Bill Lisco **Player of the Year (1983-84):** Bill Lisco

CONSETT

President: M. Murray
Chairman: Brian Suddes
Manager: Gordon Hindson
Coach: Gordon Hindson
Physiotherapist: H. Burgess
Press Officer & Tel No: Secretary
Secretary: Alan Shearer
Address & Tel No: Lanchester 520895 (H)
Commercial Manager: None
Address & Tel No:
Address & Tel No of ground: Belle Vue Park, Consett. 503788 **Club shop:** Yes
Simple ground directions: 12 miles north of Durham on A691, ¼ mile north side of town
No of seats: 500 **Covered accommodation:** 2,000 **Capacity:** 10,000 **Floodlights:** Yes
Year formed: 1899 **Nickname:** Steelmen **Club sponsors:** None
Previous names: Consett Celtic
Club colours: Red/White/Red
Previous grounds: Vicarage Field, Consett
Change colours: Sky Blue/Royal Blue/Sky Blue
Day for midweek home matches: Wednesday
Record attendance: 7,500 v Bishop Auckland, Durham Challenge Cup **Year:** 1947-8
Best performance in: F.A. Cup: 1954 v Doncaster 1st Round
F.A. Trophy: 1976-7, 1977-8 1st Round Proper
Previous Leagues: North Eastern, Wearside, Midland Counties, Northern Counties
Clubhouse details: Open match days only
Present players with Football League experience: G. Hindson
Past players who progressed into the Football League: P. Noble, J. Wilson, C. Nattrass
Record transfer fee paid: None
Record transfer fee received: £1,000 for Peter Noble from Newcastle Utd
Programme details: 12 pages, 10p
Programme Editor: Secretary
Local newspapers & Tel No: Consett Guardian, Consett Chronicle
Club metal badges: No
Senior Honours: North Eastern League, Northern Counties League, Durham Challenge Cup (5)
Club Captain (1983-84): Brian Fowler **Player of the Year (1983-84):** Brian Hardy

CROOK TOWN

President: T. Oates
Chairman: H. Hutchinson
Manager: Clive Nattress
Coach: D. Wake
Physiotherapist:
Secretary: Eric Burton
Address & Tel No: 12 West End Villas, Crook 0388 762026
Commercial Manager:
Address & Tel No:
Press Officer & Tel No: Secretary
Address & Tel No of ground: Millfield Ground, Crook. (Bishop Auckland 762959)
Club shop: Yes
Simple ground directions: 300 yards from Market Place on Tow Law Road
No of seats: 200 **Covered accommodation:** 500 **Capacity:** 2,000 **Floodlights:** Yes
Year formed: 1889 **Nickname:** Black Ambers **Club sponsors:** Oates Garage (Willington)
Previous names: None
Club colours: Amber shirts, Black shorts
Previous grounds: None
Change colours: White
Day for midweek home matches: Wednesday
Previous Leagues: None
Record attendance: Not known
Best performance in: F.A. Cup: 1931-32 v Leicester C, 3rd Round
F.A. Trophy: 1976-77 2nd Round
Clubhouse details: Yes
Present players with Football League experience: C. Nattress (Darlington)
Past players who progressed into the Football League: None
Record transfer fee paid: None
Record transfer fee received: None
Programme Editor: J. Pascoe
Programme details: Yes
Local newspaper & Tel No: Northern Echo
Club metal badges: No
Senior Honours: Amateur Cup Winners (5), Northern League (5), Northern League Cup (3)
Club Captain (1983-84): C. Hallimond
Player of the Year (1983-84): D. Pinkney

FERRYHILL

President: Trevor Southern
Chairman: John Gornett
Manager: Geoff Wade
Coach: John Foster
Physiotherapist: T. Morris
Secretary: D. H. James
Address & Tel No: Ferryhill (0740) 51177 (H)
Commercial Manager:
Address & Tel No:
Press Officer & Tel No:
Address & Tel No of ground: Darlington Road Football Ground. 51937
Club shop: No
Simple ground directions: A167 main road, left-hand side travelling north
No of seats: 200 **Covered accommodation:** Yes **Capacity:** 6,000 **Floodlights:** Yes
Year formed: 1921 **Nickname:** None **Club sponsors:** Trevor Southern Estate Agents
Previous names: Dean Bank Villa
Club colours: Amber & Black
Previous grounds: None
Change colours: All Blue
Day for midweek home matches: Wednesday
Previous League: Palatine
Record attendance: 10,000 v Bishop Auckland, F.A. Cup **Year:** 1953
Best performance in: F.A. Cup: 1951-2 1st Round Proper
F.A. Trophy: None
Clubhouse details: Bar, lounge in progress
Present players with Football League experience: None
Past players who progressed into the Football League: None
Record transfer fee paid: None
Record transfer fee received: None
Programme Editor: Manager
Programme details: 10 pages, 10p
Local newspapers & Tel No: Northern Echo, Evening Despatch
Club metal badges: No
Senior Honours: None
Club Captaion (1983-84): Ian Mohan
Player of the Year (1983-84): Shaun Mayers

GRETNA

President: I. B. Dalgleish
Chairman: W. Kerr
Manager: W. Gill and R. Thompson
Coach: B. Oaks
Physiotherapist: K. Speak
Secretary: K. Rhodes
Address & Tel No: 8 Grantwey, Gretna, Carlisle (04613) 447
Commercial Manager:
Press Officer: Secretary
Address & Tel No of ground: Raydale Park, Gretna. Tel. (04613) 602
Simple ground directions: 6 miles north of Carlisle on the A74
No of seats: 100 **Covered accommodation:** 1,000 **Capacity:** 5,000 **Floodlights:** Yes
Year formed: 1946 **Nickname:** Black & Whites **Club sponsors:** S & N
Club colours: Black & White
Change colours: Green
Record attendance: 2,000
Previous Leagues: Carlisle & District
Clubhouse details: 1,800 members, entertainment Fri., Sat., Sun.
Major Honours: Cumberland Cup Winners 1983, 1984 Runners up Drybrough's 2nd Division 1982-83
Club Captain (1983-84): James Hamilton
Player of the Year (1983-84): Russell Black

HORDEN C.W.

President: L. S. Patterson
Chairman: E. Walker
Manager: J. Coddington
Coach: J. Coddington
Physiotherapist: S. Kirkup
Press Officer & Tel No: Secretary
Secretary: Ray Matthews
Address & Tel No: 16 Ninth Street, Horden, Peterlee, Co. Durham. Tel. Peterlee 870727
Commercial Manager: L. S. Patterson
Address & Tel No: 0783 866441
Address & Tel No of ground: Welfare Park Ground, Park Road, Horden. Tel 0783 861493 **Club shop:** No
Simple ground directions: Off A19 signposted Horden
No of seats: 300 **Covered accommodation:** 400 **Capacity:** 4,500 **Floodlights:** Yes
Year formed: 1908 **Nickname:** Colliers **Club sponsors:** Kevco Products
Previous names: None **Club colours:** Red/White/White
Previous grounds: None **Change colours:** Blue & White/Black/Black
Day for midweek home matches: Tuesday
Record attendance: 8,000 **Year:** 1937
Best performance in: F.A. Cup: 1952-3, 1953-4, 1954-5, 1981-2 1st Round Proper
F.A. Trophy: 1970-1, 1972-3, 1979-80, 1981-2 1st Rnd Proper
Previous Leagues: Wearside, Midlands, North Eastern
Clubhouse details: Open 7 nights a week. Disco, players functions plus canteen facilities
Present players with Football League experience: Stuart Sherwood (Sunderland), John Honour (WBA, Hartlepool), Gerry Hogan (Leeds), Dave Evans (Hartlepool), Paul Brown (Sunderland), Jackie Hather (Aberdeen, Blackpool)
Past players who progressed into the Football League: Paul Dobson (Hartlepool U)
Senior Honours: Wearside League, Durham Challenge Cup
Club Captain (1983-84): Paul Walker **Player of the Year (1983-84):** Paul Walker

NORTH SHIELDS

President: G. Bilclough
Vice Presidents: C. R. Munro, F. Brennan
Chairman: Len Murphy
Manager: Bob Elwell
Coach: To be appointed
Physiotherapist: Jimmy Florance
Press Officer & Tel No: Ken Green 0632 579044
Secretary: Bruce Speller
Address & Tel No: 7 Stoneyhurst Road, Newcastle-u-Tyne NE3 1PR. 091 285771 (H), 0632 610111 (B)
Commercial Manager: Peter Grieve
Address & Tel No:
Address & Tel No of ground: Appleby Park, Hawkey's Lane, North Shields, Tyne & Wear **Club shop:** Yes
Simple ground directions: From Metro Station proceed up Nile Street to Albion Road, turn left, pass Spring Gardens P.H. and then turn right into Hawkeys Lane. Ground ½-mile up on left
No of seats: 800 **Covered accommodation:** 4,500 **Capacity:** 8,500 **Floodlights:** Yes
Year formed: 1898 **Nickname:** The Robins **Club sponsors:** Pils from Holsten
Previous names: North Shields Ath, Preston Colliery **Club colours:** All Red
Previous grounds: None **Change colours:** White shirts, Black shorts
Day for midweek home matches: Tuesday
Record attendance: 12,500 v South Shields, North Eastern League **Year:** 1956
Best performance in: F.A. Cup: 1933-34, 1982-83 2nd Round Proper
F.A. Trophy: 1983-84, 2nd Round Proper
Previous Leagues: North Eastern, Midland Counties, Northern Counties
Clubhouse details: Open 7 days a week including lunchtime. Three bars
Present players with Football League experience: A. Harrison (Carlisle, Southport), M. Carroll (Chesterfield)
Past players who progressed into the Football League: P. Cartwright (Newcastle), S. Carney (Newcastle) B. Joicey (Coventry)
Club metal badges: Yes
Senior Honours: F.A. Amateur Cup, European Amateur Cup Winners Cup, Northumberland Senior Cup, Northern League, Northern League Cup (2) & Runners-up
Club Captain (1983-84): David Varty **Player of the Year (1983-84):** Mike Carroll

PETERLEE NEWTOWN

President: D. J. Brown
Chairman: Brian Hall
Manager: S. Summerill
Coach: T. Turnbull
Physiotherapist: R. C. Park
Press Officer & Tel No: Secretary & Gordon Low
Secretary: D. Cassidy
Address & Tel No: 23 Melbury Street, Seaham, Co. Durham. Seaham (0783) 814591 (H)
Commercial Manager:
Address & Tel No:
Club shop: No
Address & Tel No of ground: Edenlane Playing Fields, Edenlane, Peterlee, Co. Durham. Tel Peterlee 863004
Simple ground directions: Travel on A19 dual carriageway to Peterlee roundabout then follow B1320 to town centre roundabout, straight on when past fire station on right, take next left into Edenhill Road, straight on until T-junction, turn right into Robson Avenue, left next junction then sharp right into ground
No of seats: None (stand being built) **Covered accommodation:** 300 **Capacity:** 6,000 **Floodlights:**
Year formed: 1976 **Nickname:** Newtowners **Club sponsors:** Peterlee Development Corporation
Previous names: None **Club colours:** Blue & White stripes/White/White
Previous grounds: None **Change colours:** All Yellow
Day for midweek home matches: Wednesday
Record attendance: 450 v Newcastle United Reserves **Year:** 1977
Best performance in: F.A. Cup: 1980-1 2nd Qualifying Round
F.A. Vase: 1981-2 3rd Round
Previous Leagues: Northern Alliance, Vaux Wearside
Clubhouse details: Open normal hours lunchtimes and evenings all week (Steward: J. Moore)
Present players with Football League experience: Bobby Park (Aston Villa, Wrexham), Gordon Larkin (Hartlepool), Mickey Bartlett (Huddersfield), T. Bainbridge (Hartlepool), B. Honour (Darlington)
Senior Honours: Vaux Wearside League Runners-up, Magnet & Southern North Eastern Floodlit League and Cup
Club Captain (1983-84): K. Bendelow **Player of the Year (1983-84):** T. Radestock (Player), K. Charlton (Supporters)

RYHOPE CA

Chairman: E. Carlin
Manager: J. Clark
Coach: H. Clark
Physiotherapist: T. Brace
Secretary: David Hall
Address & Tel No: 0783 286712
Commercial Manager:
Press Officer & Tel No: N. Taylor
Address & Tel No of ground: 'Meadow Park', Ryhope, Sunderland. 236555
Simple ground directions: South end of village, off road leading to Ryhope hospitals
No of seats: **Covered accommodation:** Yes **Capacity:** 200 **Floodlights:** Yes
Year formed: 1961 **Nickname:** **Club sponsors:**
Club colours: Royal Blue **Change colours:** White
Record attendance: 1,018
Previous Leagues: Northern Alliance **Programme Editors:** N. Taylor, D. Hall, J. Clark
Senior Honours: Northern Alliance Challenge Cup Winners & League Runners-up
Club Captain (1983-84): Jim Osher

Shildon *Back Row (L-R): Trevor Hogg, Peter McCabe, Mick Seddon, Lou Christie, Rob Wheatley, Steve Williams, Iain Leckie. Front Row (L-R): Derek Green, Peter Grahqm, Colin Smith (Capt), Ian Hogan, Paul Burton.*

SHILDON

President: C. Attwood
Chairman: A. B. Chipchase
Manager: Tom Smith
Coach: Alan Williamson
Physiotherapist: Alva Caygill
Secretary: J. M. Armitage
Address & Tel No: Aycliffe 316322 (H) Darlington 57257 (B)
Commercial Manager:
Address & Tel No:
Press Officer & Tel No: J. M. Armitage. Aycliffe 316322
Address & Tel No of ground: Dean Street, Shildon. Tel Bishops Auckland 773877 **Club shop:** No
Simple ground directions: Town centre
No of seats: 500 **Covered accommodation:** One stand **Capacity:** 4,000 **Floodlights:** No
Year formed: 1892 **Nickname:** Railwaymen **Club sponsors:** None
Previous names: None
Previous grounds: None
Club colours: All Red
Change colours: All White or All Sky Blue
Day for midweek home matches: Wednesday
Record attendance: 14,000 Schools Match
Previous Leagues: North Eastern
Best performance in: **F.A. Cup:** 1939 2nd Round Proper
F.A. Trophy: 1974-5 3rd Qualifying Round
Clubhouse details: Under grandstand. Open 7.30pm-10.30pm every night, 1.30-5.30 Sat afternoon, 12-2 Sun afternoon
Present players with Football League experience: None
Past players who progressed into the Football League: Kevin Stonehouse (Blackburn)
Record transfer fee paid: None
Record transfer fee received: None
Programme details: None
Club metal badges: Yes
Local newspapers & Tel No: Northern Echo, Evening Despatch, Evening Gazette
Senior Honours: Northern League (5), Northern League Challenge Cup (6), Durham County Challenge Cup (3), Durham Benevolent Bowl (2)
Club Captain (1983-84): Colin Smith **Player of the Year (1983-84):** Paul Burton

SOUTH BANK

President: C. Bugg
Chairman: D. Dawkins
Manager:
Coach: T. Harrison
Physiotherapist: R. O'Brien
Secretary: R. J. Kidd
Address & Tel No: Middlesbrough 243412 (H)
Commercial Manager:
Address & Tel No:
Press Officer & Tel No: Chris Wood, 0388 605181 **Club shop:** No
Address & Tel No of ground: Normanby Road Ground, South Bank, Middlesbrough. 0642 453193 (Club house)
Simple ground directions: Approach South Bank along main Normanby Road, ground on right side about 400 yds from Bennets Corner traffic lights
No of seats: 400 **Covered accommodation:** Stand and terrace **Capacity:** 400 + terrace **Floodlights:** Yes
Year formed: 1868 **Nickname:** Bankers **Club sponsors:** Royal Tours
Previous names: None
Previous grounds: None
Club colours: Red & White stripes/Black/Red
Change colours: White/Red or White/White
Day for midweek home matches: Wednesday
Record attendance: 10,000 v Bishop Auckland **Year:** Pre-war
Best performance in: F.A. Cup: 1925-6, 1933-4 1st Round Proper
F.A. Trophy: 1974-5 2nd Round Proper
Previous Leagues: None
Clubhouse details: Clubhouse open 7 days a week and afternoons. Lounge and bar/concert room. Entertainment Thursday and Sunday nights, bingo and raffles nightly
Present players with Football League experience: Maurice Gormley, Tony Sharkey
Past players who progressed into the Football League: G. Forrest (Rotherham)
Record transfer fee paid: None
Record transfer fee received: None
Programme details: 8 pages, 10p
Programme Editor: Mick Reid
Local newspapers & Tel No: Evening Gazette
Club metal badges: Yes
Senior Honours: F.A. Amateur Cup (1) Runners-up (2), North Riding Senior Cup (6), Northern League Cup (2)
Club Captain (1983-84): Tony Lynch

SPENNYMOOR UNITED

President: K. G. Newell
Chairman: J. B. Hindmarch
Manager: W. Bell
Coach:
Physiotherapist: D. Lumley
Secretary: T. A. Metcalfe
Address & Tel No: 23 Tangmere, Spennymoor Spennymoor 811561 (H)
Commercial Manager: C. M. Whitehouse
Address & Tel No:
Press Officer & Tel No: J. B. Hindmarch, Spennymoor 815168
Address & Tel No of ground: The Brewery Field, Durham Road, Spennymoor. 0388 814100 **Club shop:** Yes
Simple ground directions: From town centre ground situated about ¼-mile on left of Durham Road
No of seats: 320 **Covered accommodation:** 1,500 **Capacity:** 7,500 **Floodlights:** Yes
Year formed: 1901 **Nickname:** The Moors **Club sponsors:** G.T. Leisure Automatics Ltd
Previous names: None
Previous grounds: None
Club colours: Black & White stripes/Black/Black
Change colours: All Red, All White or All Yellow
Day for midweek home matches: Wednesday
Record attendance: Not known
Best performance in: F.A. Cup: 1937 v West Bromwich, 3rd Round
F.A. Trophy: 1977-8 Semi-Final
Previous Leagues: Northern, North Eastern, Midland Counties
Clubhouse details: 12.00-3pm & 7-10.30pm Monday-Saturday, 12-2pm & 7-10.30pm Sunday
Present players with Football League experience: D. A. Young
Past players who progressed into the Football League: (postwar) D. Crampton, E. Hulme, Bill Gates, L. Walker, T. Atkinson, J. McGeorge, A. Harding
Programme details: 8 pages, 10p
Programme Editor: G. O. Smith
Local newspapers & Tel No: Northern Echo, Northern Despatch, Evening Gazette
Club metal badges: Yes
Senior Honours: Northern Eastern League (4), Northern League (6) & Runners-up (3), Durham Challenge Cup (11), Northern League Cup (4), F.A. Trophy Semi-Finalists, Durham Benevolent Bowl (4), J R Cleator Trophy
Club Captain (1983-84): David Curry
Player of the Year (1983-84): Robin Gill

TOW LAW TOWN

President: John Wright
Chairman: Harry Hodgson
Manager: Stuart Leeming
Physiotherapist:
Secretary: Bernard Fairbairn
Address & Tel No: Darlington 50743 (H) Bishop Auckland 772636 (B)
Commercial Manager:
Address & Tel No:
Press Officer & Tel No: Secretary
Address & Tel No of ground: Ironworks Road. Bishop Auckland 730325 **Club shop:** Yes
Simple ground directions: High Street into Grove Road, left into Ironworks Road
No of seats: 300 **Covered accommodation:** Yes **Capacity:** 8,000 **Floodlights:** No
Year formed: 1890 **Nickname:** Lawyers **Club sponsors:** None
Previous names: None
Previous grounds: None
Club colours: Black & White stripes/Black/White
Change colours: All Red
Day for midweek home matches: Tuesday
Record attendance: 5,000 v Mansfield **Year:** 1967
Previous Leagues: None
Best performance in: F.A. Cup: 1967-8 **F.A. Trophy:** 1977-78, 1982-83 1st Round
Clubhouse details: Small bar and lounge area
Present players with Football League experience: None
Past players who progressed into the Football League: Chris Waddle (Newcastle)
Record transfer fee paid: None
Record transfer fee received: None
Programme details: None
Local newspaper & Tel No: Northern Echo
Club metal badges: Yes
Senior Honours: Northern League
Club Captain (1983-84): Kevin Campbell
Player of the Year (1983-84): Kevin Campbell

Ashington stage a rare attack during their 0-5 defeat at Whitby. Photo: Mark Heron

Ashington's Kevin Fulbeck shoots just wide at Peterlee. Photo: Mark Heron

Turner, the Tow Law centre forward (on ground), just gets his foot to the ball to beat the tackle of Evenwood's Rogers. The ball also slid beyond the diving Butler in the Evenwood goal but went past the post. Photo: Galdon

WHITLEY BAY

President: C. E. Fuller
Chairman: A. Moor
Manager: J. Connelly
Coach: W. Colwill
Physiotherapist: Joe Jabs
Press Officer & Tel No: S. Cope
Secretary: R. Harding
Address & Tel No: 24 Cambridge Avenue, Whitley Bay, Tyne & Wear. Whitley Bay 515179
Commercial Manager: None
Address & Tel No:
Address & Tel No of ground: Hillheads Park, Whitley Bay 513680 **Club shop:** No
Simple ground directions: Leave St Paul's Church, head south, turn right at roundabout, 3rd left, ground rear of ice rink
No of seats: 450 **Covered accommodation:** 200 **Capacity:** 5,000 **Floodlights:** Yes
Year formed: 1897, reformed 1957 **Nickname:** The Bay **Club sponsors:** Crohscrew Ride
Previous names: Whitley Bay Athletic **Club colours:** White/Royal Blue
Previous grounds: None **Change colours:** Yellow
Day for midweek home matches: Tuesday
Record attendance: 7,301 v Hendon **Year:** 1964-5
Previous League: Northern Alliance
Best performance in: F.A. Cup: 1958-9, 1971-2 4th Qualifying Round
F.A. Trophy: 1975-6, 1977-8, 1980-1, 1981-2 1st Qual Round
Clubhouse details: Bar room, concert room
Present players with Football League experience: None
Past players who progressed into the Football League: John Richie, Gary Haire, Mark Miller
Record transfer fee paid: None
Record transfer fee received: None
Programme details: None **Local newspaper & Tel No:** Whitley Bay Guardian
Club metal badges: No
Senior Honours: League (2) & Runners-up (4), League Cup (2) & Runners-up, Northumberland Senior Cup (9) & Runners-up (4)

Whitby Town *Back Row (L-R): S Coleby, R Walker, R Gormer (Physio), F Storr (Trainer), P Sharkey, D Coleby, J Gollogly, A Escritt, D Logan, G Lilley, M Lawrence, Tony Lee (Team Manager), A N Other. Front Row (L-R): A Kell, L Bell, B Andrews, N Granycome, A Watson (Mascot), L Scott, T Smith, R Sills, D Hampton, G & A Lee (Manager's Sons).* Photo: David O'Donnell

WHITBY TOWN

President: D. Dunwell
Chairman: J. Metcalfe
Manager: Tony Lee
Coach:
Physiotherapist: None
Secretary: R. Scaife
Address & Tel No: 4 Waterstead Lane, Whitby, N. Yorks 0947 600776 (H), 0947 603443 (B)
Commercial Manager:
Address & Tel No:
Press Officer & Tel No: Gerry Trowsdale, 49 Ingham Close, Sleights, Whitby. 0947 810469
Address & Tel No of ground: Turnbull Ground, Upgang Lane, Whitby, N. Yorks. 0947 604847 **Club shop:** No
Simple ground directions: Take A174 road from town centre, ground on offside travelling towards Sandsend
No of seats: 200 **Covered accommodation:** 400 **Capacity:** 4,000 **Floodlights:** Yes
Year formed: 1896 **Nickname:** The Seasiders **Club sponsors:** Universal Garage
Previous names: Whitby United **Club colours:** All Blue
Previous grounds: None **Change colours:** All White
Day for midweek home matches: Wednesday
Record attendance: 4,000 v Scarborough **Year:** 1965-66
Previous Leagues: None
Best performance in: F.A. Cup: 1983-84 v Wigan Athletic, 2nd Round
F.A. Trophy: 1983-84 v Dagenham, Quarter Finals 2nd Round Proper
Clubhouse details: Open nightly 7-11pm, Saturdays 1.30-6pm, 7-11pm, Sundays 12.00am-2.00pm, 7-10.30pm
Present players with Football League experience: D. Hampton, T. Smith, J. Gollogly, M. Lawrence
Past players who progressed into the Football League: M. Poskett (Hartlepool, Brighton, Watford, Carlisle), Sammy Kemp (Huddersfield), Jimmy Mulvaney (Hartlepool, Barrow, Stockport), Bobby Veart (England Amateur International, Hartlepool), Derek Hampton, Trevor Smith (both Hartlepool, now returned to Whitby), John Linacre (Hartlepool), Mark Hine (Grimsby T), Phil Linacre (Hartlepool)
Record transfer fee paid: None
Record transfer fee received: None
Programme details: 12 pages, 20p
Programme Editor: Gerry Trowsdale
Local newspaper & Tel No: Whitby Gazette, Tel 0947 602836
Club metal badges: Yes
Senior Honours: North Riding Senior Cup, Northern League Cup, Rothmans Knock-out Overseas Cup (2)
Club Captain (1983-84): Les Scott **Supporters Player of the Year:** Derek Hampton **Runner up:** Neal Granycome

ALNWICK TOWN

Chairman: D. G. Kent
Manager: Ray Ellison
Coach: Ray Ellison
Asst Manager: Ken Prior
Secretary: A. Brown
Address & Tel No: 49 North End, Long Houghton
Long Houghton 396 (H), Alnwick 602080 (B)
Press Officer & Tel No: Cyril E. J. Cox, 0632 366456
Address & Tel No of ground: St James Park, Alnwick, Northumberland. 0665 603162
Simple ground directions: Turn sharp left at column monument entering town from south
No of seats: 100, including Director's Box **Covered accommodation:** Yes **Capacity:** 100 **Floodlights:** No
Year formed: 1879/80 **Nickname:** **Club sponsors:**
Club colours: Black & White shirts, Black shorts **Change colours:** Red & White shirts, White shorts
Record attendance: 800 **Programme Editor:** Cyril Cox
Clubhouse details: Full length panorama window overlooking pitch with bar and directors box
Previous Leagues: Northern Alliance, Durham Central
Senior Honours: Northern Alliance Challenge Cup Winners (4), Northumberland Senior Cup Runners-up, Northumberland Amateur Cup, Northern Alliance League Champions (9) & Runners-up (3), Durham Central League Cup & Runners-up, Northern Alliance Subsidiary Cup
Club Captain (1983-84): Michael Anderson

ASHINGTON

President: H. Turner
Chairman: D. Peary
Manager: P. Chambers
Coach: R. Scott
Physiotherapist: T. Rigg
Secretary: V. Donnelly
Address & Tel No: 31 Doctor Terrace.
Bedlington 829464
Commercial Manager: P. Morton
Address & Tel No: 76 Mildurn Road, Ashington. 819278
Press Officer & Tel No: P. Cunningham, Ashington. 817092
Address & Tel No of ground: Portland Park, Ashington. Tel 812240 **Club shop:** Yes
Simple ground directions: Lintonville Tce-Ashington, near town centre
No of seats: 315 **Covered accommodation:** 4,000 **Capacity:** 15,000 **Floodlights:** Yes
Year founded: 1883, formed 1902 **Nickname:** The Colliers
Club sponsors: C. C. Grigg (Domestic & Electrical Appliances)
Previous names: None **Previous grounds:** Recreation Ground, Farmers Field, Ashington
Club colours: Black & White stripes/Black/Black & White **Change colours:** All Red
Day for midweek home matches: Wednesday
Record attendance: 13,199 v Rochdale, F.A. Cup **Year:** 1950-51
Best performance in: F.A. Cup: 1926-27 3rd Round
F.A. Trophy: 1979-80, 1980-81, 1982-83 2nd Round
Clubhouse details: Supporters Club. Tel 812240
Previous Leagues: Northern Premier, North Regional Football League Div 3 North North Eastern League, Wearside, Northern Alliance, Midlands, Northern Counties
Present players with (Scottish) Football League experience: Graeme Wilson, Mark Cameron
Past players who progressed into the Football League: Tony Lowery (now Mansfield), Les Mutrie (now Colchester), R. Cummins (Aberdeen, Newcastle)
Record transfer fee paid: None
Record transfer fee received: £3,500 for Tony Lowery from W.B.A.
Programme details: 28 pages, 15p **Local newspaper & Tel No:** News Post/Leader
Programme Editors: Paddy Cunningham, Alf Marchetti
Club metal badges: Yes
Senior Honours: Northumberland Senior Cup (9), Northumberland Challenge Bowl (6), North East League Cup (2) Northern Alliance
Club Captain (1983-84): Tommy Dodds **Player of the Year (1983-84):** Andy Gowens

BEDLINGTON TERRIERS

Chairman: Brian Richmond
Manager: Robert Graham
Coach: John Armstrong
Physiotherapist: Alan Locke
Secretary: Terry Allen
Address & Tel No: 21A Victoria Terrace, Bedlington
0670 829839
Commercial Manager:
Address & Tel No of ground: Dr. Pitt Welfare Park, Bedlington, Northumberland. Bedlington (0670) 824046
Simple ground directions:
No of seats: Being built **Covered accommodation:** Being built **Capacity:** 2,500 **Floodlights:** No
Club colours: Red/Black/Red **Change colours:** Blue/Blue/White or Blue
Programme: Yes **Programme Editor:** Chairman

BILLINGHAM TOWN

President: S. Linton
Chairman: J. Driver
Manager: Ray Halliday
Coach: D. Bice
Physiotherapist: Dave Smith
Press Officer & Tel No: Secretary
Secretary: T. V. Donnelly
Address & Tel No: 1 Shotley Close, Billingham, Cleveland. Stockton-on-Tees 565767
Commercial Manager: D. Sparrow
Address & Tel No: 22 Stokesley Crescent, Billingham. Stockton-on-Tees 531596
Address & Tel No of ground: Bedford Terrace Football Ground, Billingham. Stockton-on-Tees 560043
Simple ground directions: Arrive in Billingham on A19, leave A19 on 1027, turn left from north, right from south, continue over two roundabouts into Central Avenue, then left at next roundabout, over bridge, first left and first left again into Bedford Terrace
No of seats: 200 **Covered accommodation:** 200 (under construction) **Capacity:** 5,000-6,000 **Floodlights:** No
Year formed: 1968 **Nickname:** The Social **Club sponsors:** Billingham Social Club
Club colours: All Royal Blue **Change colours:** All Red
Record attendance: 1500 Billingham Telstar v Billingham Cons, Cup Final, 1983
Programme details: None until 1984-85 **Programme Editor:** D. Sparrow
Clubhouse details: Billingham Social, 3,000 members
Previous Leagues: Stockton & District, Teesside League **Previous Names:** Billingham Social Club
Senior Honours: Durham Trophy Winners 1976-77, Teesside League Winners, 1977-78-82, North Riding Finalists 1977-1982
Club Captain (1983-84): Mark Puttick **Player of the Year (1983-84):** Mark Puttick

BRANDON UNITED

Chairman: N. Green
Manager: P. Feenan
Coach: R. Gowan
Physiotherapist: B. Wrightson
Secretary: A. Waggott
Address & Tel No: Durham 781778
Commercial Manager: M. Richardson
Press Officer & Tel No: Secretary
Address & Tel No of ground: Welfare Ground. 782957
Simple ground directions:
No of seats: 50 **Covered accommodation:** 400 **Capacity:** 6,000 **Floodlights:** Yes
Year formed: **Nickname:** **Club sponsors:** Masters & Milburn 'Volvo'
Club colours: All Blue **Change colours:** Red
Record attendance: 3,500 **Club Captain (1983-84):** Keith Brown
Previous Leagues: Vaux Wearside **Player of the Year (1983-84):** Keith Brown
Senior Honours: All England Sunday Cup Winners **Programme Editor:** T. Gallagher

DARLINGTON RESERVES

President: J. L. Moore
Chairman: K. W. Warne
Manager: Brian Swift
Coach: Brian Swift
Physiotherapist: Bob Farrelly
Secretary: David A. Thorne
Address & Tel No: Darlington 465097/467712
Commercial Manager: Alice Burton
Press Officer: Secretary
Address & Tel No of ground: Feethams Ground, Darlington, DL1 5JB
Simple ground directions: A66 to town centre, Feethams to the south of town adjacent to the Ring Road
No of seats: **Covered accommodation:** **Capacity:** 15,000 **Floodlights:** Yes
Year formed: 1883 **Nickname:** The Quakers **Club sponsors:** None
Club colours: White/Black/Black **Change colours:** All Red or All Blue

DARLINGTON CLEVELAND BRIDGE F.C.

President: W. Tennet
Chairman: C. Bellwood
Manager: W. Shevels
Coach: G. Moore
Physiotherapist:
Secretary: D. Shevels
Address & Tel No: 202 North Road, Darlington Darlington 402753
Commercial Manager:
Address & Tel No:
Press Officer & Tel No: D. Shevels
Address & Tel No of ground: Neasham Road, Darlington (469735) **Club shop:**
Simple ground directions: Turn left at Skippers Garage, turn right Station Bridge, leads into Neasham Ground at top of road
No of seats: **Covered accommodation:** stand being erected **Capacity:** 5,000 **Floodlights:** Yes
Year formed: 1903 **Nickname:** The Bridge **Club sponsors:**
Previous names: None **Club colours:** Gold shirts, Black shorts
Previous grounds: None **Change colours:** All Red **Previous Leagues:** Darlington & District, Northern Alliance
Record attendance:
Best performance in: F.A. Cup: N/A
F.A. Trophy: N/A
Clubhouse details: Yes on ground **Programme Editor:** D. Shevels
Present players with Football League experience:
Past players who progressed into the Football League: Jeff Wealands (Birmingham C, Manchester U)
Record transfer fee paid:
Record transfer fee received: £400 for Tony Swainston to Crook Town
Programme details: Yes **Local newspaper & Tel No:**
Club metal badges: No
Senior Honours: North Riding County Cup Winners, Northern Alliance League Champions
Club Captain (1983-84): Jim Gilsenan **Player of the Year (1983-84):** Dean Hardy

Durham City *Back Row (L-R): D Mason (Coach), K Dowd, T Cochrane, J Jackson, G Morgan, P Malcolm, N Gibbons, P Main, B Rutledge, K Anderson. Front Row (L-R): I Harrison, T Richardson, G Sheldon, A Hickman (Player-Manager), T Rosethorn, P Ray.*

Evenwood Town *Back Row (L-R): Smith, Coulthard, Campbell, Butler, McGinn, Rogers, Forster. Front Row (L-R): Sharpe, Elliott, Clarke, Weldon, Dobson, Hilditch.* Photo: Galdon

Darlington Cleveland Bridge

DURHAM CITY

President: N. Miller
Chairman: D. W. Asbery
General Manager: J. Rayner
Team Manager: A. Hickman
Coach: D. Mason
Physiotherapist: D. Mason
Secretary: A. Young
Address & Tel No: Durham 730727 (H)
Durham 853121 (B)
Commercial Manager: G. Grainger
Address & Tel No: Durham 64082
Press Officer & Tel No: A. Young, Durham 730727
Address & Tel No of ground: Ferens Park, The Sands, Durham DH1 1JY. Durham 69616
Club shop: No
Simple ground directions: Down G.P.O. Bank, along riverside, on right
No of seats: 300 **Covered accommodation:** 300 **Capacity:** 6,300 **Floodlights:** Yes
Year formed: 1949 **Nickname:** Citizens **Club sponsors:**
Previous names: None
Previous grounds: None
Club colours: Gold/Blue/Gold
Change colours: All Blue
Day for midweek home matches: Tuesday
Previous Leagues: Wearside,
Record attendance: 6,000 v Tranmere Rovers **Year:** 1956
Best performance in: F.A. Cup: 1955-56 2nd Round
F.A. Trophy: 1983-84 1st Round
Clubhouse details: Open week nights and matchdays
Present players with Football League experience:
Past players who progressed into the Football League: None
Record transfer fee paid: None
Record transfer fee received: None
Programme details: 8 pages, free
Club metal badges: No
Programme Editors: D. W. Asbery & A. Young
Local newspapers & Tel No: Durham Advertiser, Northern Echo
Senior Honours: Durham Benevolent Bowl, Northern League Runners-up
Club Captain (1983-84): Keith Anderson
Player of the Year (1983-84): Paul Malcolm

ESH WINNING A.F.C.

President: Jack Lumsden
Chairman: C. A. Ryan
Manager: Douglass Robson
Coach: Not yet appointed
Physiotherapist: Not yet appointed
Secretary: Dennis R. Fort
Address & Tel No: 8 Durham Road, Esh Winning, Durham DH7 9NW. Durham 734292
Commercial Manager: Not yet appointed
Press Officer: Jim Potts
Address & Tel No of ground: West Terrace, Waterhouses, Esh Winning, Durham. Durham 733872
Simple ground directions: Take main Crook Road from Durham City to Nevilles Cross, continue on Crook Road after Nevilles Cross traffic lights, take first right, follow road through Broompark and Ushaw Moor to Esh Winning. Pass straight through Esh Winning for ½ mile to Waterhouses
No of seats: 200 **Covered accommodation:** 2 stands **Capacity:** 3,000 **Floodlights:** Yes
Year formed: 1967-68 **Nickname:** "Esh" **Club sponsors:** Lumsden and Carroll
Previous names: Esh Winning "Pineapple" AFC
Previous grounds: None
Club colours: Yellow shirts, Green shorts
Change colours: All Green or All Red
Record attendance: 900 approx, Liverpool Fantail, 1978-79
Programme details: 6 pages, 10p
Programme Editor: Jimmy Potts
Clubhouse details: 17yds × 8yds, approx 120 seats
Previous Leagues: Durham & District Sunday, Northern Football Alliance
Senior Honours: DDSL Div 1 Champions 1978-79, 1979-80, Staffieri Cup Winners 1974-75, Gaurdscup Winners 1972-73,Durham County Sunday Cup Runners-up 1978-79
Club Captain (1983-84): Gary Cranston

EVENWOOD

President: H. P. Proctor
Chairman: R. Simpson
Manager: R. Sharp
Coach: R. Sharp
Physiotherapist: B. Tray
Secretary: D. R. Reynolds
Address & Tel No: 58 High Grange, Crook, Co. Durham DL15 8AT. Bishop Auckland 766332 (H)
Commercial Manager: A. Harrison
Address & Tel No:
Press Officer & Tel No: A. Harrison, Bishop Auckland 603554
Address & Tel No of ground: Welfare Ground, Evenwood, Co. Durham
Club shop: No
Simple ground directions: A68 Darlington to West Auckland, off A688 Bishop Auckland to Barnard Castle
No of seats: 250 **Covered accommodation:** 250 **Capacity:** 3,000 **Floodlights:** No
Year formed: 1931 **Nickname:** None **Club sponsors:** LEC — Lou Elliott Contractors
Previous names: None
Previous grounds: None
Club colours: Blue/Blue/White
Change colours: Yellow/Green/Yellow
Day for midweek home matches: Wednesday
Previous Leagues: None
Record attendance: 2,300 v Hendon, F.A. Amateur Cup
Best performance in: F.A. Cup: 1936 1st Round
F.A. Trophy: Not known
Clubhouse details: No clubhouse
Present players with Football League experience: None
Past players who progressed into the Football League: None
Record transfer fee paid: None
Record transfer fee received: None
Programme details: 1984-85
Local newspaper & Tel No: Northern Echo
Club metal badges: No
Senior Honours: Northern League (2), Northern League Challenge Cup, Durham Challenge Cup
Club Captain (1983-84): Tony Coulthard
Player of the Year (1983-84): Ian Campbell

HARTLEPOOL UNITED RESERVES

President: E. Leadbetter M.P.
Chairman: J. W. Smart
Manager: Billy Horner
Coach: J. Bird
Physiotherapist: T. Johnson
Secretary: Mrs Linda Holmes
Tel No: (0429) 72584
Commercial Manager: S. Lavelle
Press Officer: Secretary
Address & Tel No of ground: The Victoria Ground, 18 Scarborough St., Hartlepool
Simple ground directions: The ground is only a few hundred yards from the station
No of seats: 3,000 **Covered accommodation:** 6,000 **Capacity:** 18,000 **Floodlights:** Yes
Year formed: 1908 **Nickname:** 'The Pool' **Club sponsors:** None
Club colours: Blue and White shirts, White shorts, Blue stockings **Change colours:** All Red with White trim

Lancelot Park *Back Row (L-R): T Taylor, S G Ogden, B Richardson, A Morris, D J Harrison, S J Page, G Taylor, M R McVittie, D C Robson, J Davis, S Birkenfield, E Gregory, P Donnelly, D Bell. Missing from line-up: S Newstead, A Gonsalves, V Boyd, D McGinn, and Manager B Suddes.*

LANGLEY PARK WELFARE

President: Bobby Robson (England Manager)
Chairman: Brian Smarr
Manager: Brian Suddes
Coach: Brian Richardson
Physiotherapist: Terry Taylor
Secretary: Jeff Dover
Address & Tel No: 39 Quebec Street, Langley Park, Durham. 731381
Commercial Manager: Secretary
Press Officer: Secretary
Address & Tel No of ground: Low Moor Road, Langley Park, Durham. Durham 731526
Simple ground directions: Take the main Durham to Consett road, through Witton Gilbert, next left into Langley Park, approx 5 miles from Durham
No of seats: in progress **Covered accommodation:** 300 **Capacity:** 3,000 **Floodlights:** No
Year formed: 1982 (as a Saturday Club) **Nickname:** **Club sponsors:**
Previous names: Langley Park Rams Head (Sunday League) **Previous grounds:** None
Club colours: All Blue **Change colours:** Orange/Black/Black
Record attendance:
Programme details: 16 pages, 10p **Programme Editor:** Jeff Dover
Clubhouse details: Licenced, lounge/games room and concert room
Previous Leagues: Durham & District Sunday, Durham City & District
Senior Honours: F.A. "All England" Sunday Cup
Club Captain (1983-84): Brian Richardson **Player of the Year (1983-84):** Stuart Birtenfield

NORTHALLERTON

Chairman:
Manager: Christopher Topping
Coach:
Physiotherapist: Alan Locke
Secretary: Peter Coulson
Address & Tel No: 19 Ainderby Road, Romanby, Northallerton, North Yorks. 0609 779354
Address & Tel No of ground: Ainderby Road, Romanby, Northallerton, North Yorks. 0609 2193
Simple ground directions:
Club colours: Amber/Black **Change colours:** Red/White
Programme: 12 pages, 15p **Programme Editor:** Secretary

Norton & Stockton Ancients

NORTON & STOCKTON ANCIENTS

President: W. Lawson
Chairman: B. Lee
Manager: Peter Mulcaster
Coach: Alex Smith
Physiotherapist: Arthur Shepherd
Secretary: Richard Scott
Address & Tel No: 3 Keld Grove, Fairfield, Stockton-on-Tees, Cleveland. Stockton 581360
Commercial Manager: Secretary
Press Officer: Secretary
Address & Tel No of ground: Station Road, Norton, Stockton-on-Tees. 0642 554031
Simple ground directions: Off A19 at Billingham Motor's roundabout, take road to Norton Village, at next roundabout turn into Junction Road, take first right into Station Road
No of seats: 50 **Covered accommodation:** 200 **Capacity:** 2,000 **Floodlights:** No
Year formed: 1959 **Nickname:** Ancients **Club sponsors:** Rowney Roofing
Previous names: Norton CCT **Previous grounds:** None
Club colours: Amber shirts, Black shorts **Change colours:** Blue shirts, White shorts
Record attendance:
Programme details: 4 to 6 pages, free **Programme Editor:** Richard Scott
Clubhouse details:
Previous Leagues: Teesside
Senior Honours: Drybrough League Cup Winners 1982-83
Club Captain (1983-84): Stephen Bates **Player of the Year (1983-84):** Sean O'Brien

SEAHAM RED STAR

President: M. English
Chairman: T. M. English
Manager: L. Phillips
Coach: M. Harrison/C. Copeland
Physiotherapist: A. Black
Secretary: H. C. Hobson
Address & Tel No: 43 General Graham Street, Pallion, Sunderland. 79472
Commercial Manager:
Press Officer: Secretary
Address & Tel No of ground: Seaham C.W. Ground, Seaham.
Simple ground directions: A19 from South to Murton/Seaham turn off, ground approx 3 miles opposite Mill Inn pub. From North A19 Seaham turn off right at Lodge Garage, ground first left.
No of seats: **Covered accommodation:** 300 **Capacity:** 2,000 **Floodlights:** Yes
Year formed: 1973 **Nickname:** The Star **Club sponsors:** None
Club colours: Red & White/Black/Black & Red **Change colours:** White/Red/White
Record attendance: 1,500 v S/land Res. **Previous Leagues:** Northern Alliance, Vaux Wearside
Clubhouse details:
Programme details: 8 pages, 10p **Programme Editor:** Secretary
Major Honours: 1979 Phillips National Floodlight Trophy Winners, 1980 Durham Challenge Cup Winners, 1980 Monkwearmouth Cup Finalists, 1982 Vaux Wearside League Champions, 1982 Vaux Wearside League Challenge Cup Winners
Club Captain (1983-84): Bob Huntingdon **Player of the Year (1983-84):** Keith Guy

SHOTTON COMRADES

President: G. Bennett
Chairman: A. Stoutt
Manager: T. Tuttle
Coach: W. Banks
Physiotherapist: Dr De-Silva
Secretary: Paul Farn
Address & Tel No: 17 Milton Lane, Easington, Co. Durham. Easington 272237
Commercial Manager: Secretary
Press Officer: Secretary
Address & Tel No of ground: Shotton Recreational Ground, Shotton Colliery, Co. Durham. Hetton 262859
Simple ground directions: Take exit marked Shotton off roundabout on A19, follow road into village, turn right at 'T' junction, ground is 500 yards ahead on right
No of seats: **Covered accommodation:** 400 **Capacity:** 7,500 **Floodlights:** No
Year formed: 1973 **Nickname:** 'Comrades' **Club sponsors:** Bennett & Gibson Construction
Club colours: Sky Blue/Royal **Change colours:** Red/White
Record attendance: 1,726 v Dennis Waterman XI
Programme details: 20 pages, 15p **Programme Editor:** Paul Farn
Clubhouse details:
Previous Leagues: Peterlee Sunday, Houghton & District, Northern Alliance
Senior Honours: 1978-79 Houghton League Champions, Hetton Charity Cup Winners, League Cup Runners-up
Club Captain (1983-84): Ron Brown **Player of the Year (1983-84):** Ron Brown

WILLINGTON

President: D. Giblin
Chairman: D. H. Warner
Manager: A. Gouden
Coach: J. Ryans
Physiotherapist: N. Fields
Press Officer & Tel No: Secretary
Secretary: W. Holborn
Address & Tel No: Bishop Auckland 663043
Commercial Manager:
Address & Tel No:
Address & Tel No of ground: Hall Lane, Willington, Crook. Tel Willington 746221 **Club shop:** Yes
Simple ground directions: Hall Lane from Main Street
No of seats: 500 **Covered accommodation:** Yes **Capacity:** 500 **Floodlights:** Yes
Year formed: 1911 **Nickname:** None **Club sponsors:** None
Club Colours: Blue & White/Blue/Blue **Change colours:** Yellow/Green/Yellow
Day for midweek home matches: Wednesday
Record attendance: v Bromley **Year:** 1951
Previous Leagues: None
Best performance in: F.A. Cup: 1974 1st Round Proper
F.A. Trophy: 1976 3rd Round
Local Newspaper & Tel No: Northern Echo
Clubhouse details: Club house open every night and match days
Senior Honours: Amateur Cup, Northern League Cup, Durham Benevolent Bowl, League
Club Captain (1983-84): Billy Todner

WEST AUCKLAND TOWN

President: L. Nevison
Chairman: G. Curtis
Manager: S. Alderson
Coach: V. Suddes
Physiotherapist: F. Patrick
Press Officer & Tel No: Secretary
Secretary: N. Ayton
Address & Tel No: 3 Derrness Road, Bishop Auckland
Bishop Auckland (0388) 604375 (H)
Commercial Manager: G. Curtis
Address & Tel No:
Address & Tel No of ground: Darlington Road Ground, West Auckland **Club shop:** No
Simple ground directions: On A68 road on south side of village
No of seats: 200 **Covered accommodation:** 400 **Capacity:** 6,000 **Floodlights:** Yes
Year formed: 1908 **Nickname:** West **Club sponsors:** None
Previous names: None
Previous grounds: None
Club colours: Amber with pinstripe
Change colours: White & Black with Amber trim
Day for midweek home matches: Wednesday
Record attendance: 6,500 v Dulwich
Previous Leagues: None
Best performance in: F.A. Cup: 1959, 1962 1st Round
F.A. Trophy: 1978 3rd Round
Clubhouse details: Light refreshments only (unlicensed)
Present players with Football League experience: None
Past players who progressed into the Football League: None
Record transfer fee paid: None
Record transfer fee received: None
Programme details: None
Club metal badges: No
Local newspapers & Tel No: Northern Echo, Evening Despatch, Sunday Sun
Senior Honours: Northern League, Durham Challenge Cup, Northern League Cup, Durham Benevolent Bowl, Sir Thomas Lipton Trophy

The Langley Park goalkeeper punches clear following a corner at Norton & Stockton Ancients.
Photo: Mark Herron

North Shields
Back Row (L-R): Jimmy Florance (Physio), Jimmy Harmison, Paul Ross, Tony Harrison, Mike Coady, Chris Kelly, George Dickson, David Thompson, Beele McCaffrey, Micky Carroll. Front Row (L-R): Colin Ayre, Brian Pilkington, Jim Pearson, Steve Atkinson, Jeff Peters, David Varty.

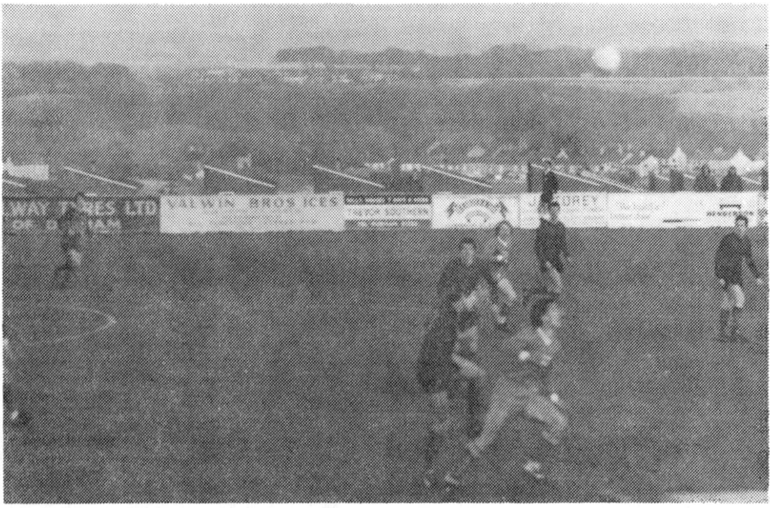

Action at Brandon when United entertained Darlington Cleveland Bridge in the Durham Senior Cup.
Photo: Mark Herron

VAUX WEARSIDE FOOTBALL LEAGUE

Secretary: M. G. Gordon, 9 Cliffe Park, Seaburn, Sunderland, Tyne & Wear SR6 9NS
Tel: 0783 490414

BLUE STAR WIN THRILLING CHAMPIONSHIP

The past season was one of the more memorable ones as far as the League Championship was concerned in that Blue Star retained the title by beating Easington, one of their nearest challengers, on the last day of the season; and a victory by Coundon in their final match by seven clear goals if Blue Star and Easington had drawn would have given Coundon the title in only their second season in the League.

On the FA Vase scene Whickham were very unlucky to lose in the second leg of the semi final to the eventual winners Stansted FC, when it appeared to everyone involved that the second leg at home would be a formality after they had drawn at Stansted the previous week. Blue Star, who were one of the favourites for the Vase, were in fact eliminated from the competition by Farsley Celtic in early January much to the disappointment of their supporters.

Also on the cup scene Blue Star and Coundon carried off a unique double for the League by both clubs winning their respective County Trophies with Coundon defeating Dryboroughs Northern League side Norton and Stockton Ancients in the Durham Challenge Cup Final at Darlington; and Blue Star retained their Northumberland Senior Cup by defeating Blyth Spartans in a Final replay at North Shields.

As far as the domestic cups within the League were concerned Blue Star retained the Vaux League Challenge Cup by beating South Shields in a repeat of the 1983 Final; and Coundon won the Shipowners Cup by beating South Shields in the Final after extra time; and Wingate after a very successful season in the League beat Murton CW in the Final of the Monkwearmouth Charity Cup at Murton CW.

As far as Vaux Breweries are concerned as sponsors of the League they have always encouraged good sportsmanship and this past season was no exception for the League with Coundon, Boldon CA and Washington FC all sharing first prize in the sportsman awards with only four points deducted each for cautions throughout the season and to each of these clubs credit must be given to both the players and the team managers and coaches.

As far as the new season is concerned the League will be operating with 20 clubs as both Newton Aycliffe FC and Gateshead Clarke Chapman FC were elected to the League for the new season and in both cases the newcomers will prove an asset to the League as both clubs can offer first class playing facilities along with excellent clubhouses attached to these facilities.

On a rather sad note the League's President, Mr Bob Wood, has retired from the position after 52 years with the League as a player, assistant secretary, secretary and chairman; and at the recent AGM he was elected a life member in view of his services that will never be surpassed.

In July of last year John Walsh resigned as League Secretary after 12 years in order that he could take up the office of full time Secretary of the Durham Football Association; and he was replaced by Michael Gordon who in turn has been involved in non league football throughout the past 19 years in the North East as a Class One Referee; and Mr J C Thomas was elected as President of the League, and Mr Ian Walker is still the League's Chairman.

Darlington AFC Reserve Team *Back Row (L-R): Brian Swift (Manager), Alan Plant, Charles Morrison, John Hannah, Jeff Wilson, Graham Morgan, Kevin Wolfe, Andrew Larkin, Terry Baker (Trainer). Front Row (L-R): Michael Ord, Peter Bowman, Phil Shute, Nigel Foster, David Young, Brian Lynn.*

VAUX WEARSIDE LEAGUE

		P	W	D	L	F	A	Pts
1	Blue Star	34	27	3	4	94	24	57
2	Coundon	34	27	2	5	93	29	56
3	Easington CW	34	24	7	2	79	34	55
4	Wingate	34	19	5	10	66	37	43
5	Whickham	34	18	6	10	66	44	42
6	South Shields	34	17	7	10	61	41	41
7	Annfield Plain	34	16	8	10	50	42	40
8	Washington	34	16	7	11	53	44	39
9	Boldon CW	34	11	12	11	55	54	34
10	Eppleton CW	34	13	5	16	66	50	31
11	Stockton	34	12	6	16	54	61	30
12	Dawdon CW	34	8	10	16	42	64	26
13	Murton CW	34	6	10	18	35	67	22
14	Ryhope CW	34	6	10	18	33	66	22
15	Gateshead Res	34	8	6	20	50	83	22
16	Reyrolles	34	5	8	21	42	88	18
17	Roker	34	6	6	22	41	105	18
18	South Hetton	34	5	6	23	28	75	16

ANNFIELD PLAIN

President: C. Errington
Chairman: J. Peadon
Manager: S. Bell
Coach: B. Dunn
Physiotherapist: None
Secretary: M. H. Lawson
Address & Tel No: Stanley 35879
Commercial Manager: None
Address & Tel No:
Press Officer & Tel No: None
Address & Tel No of ground: Derwent Park, West Road, Annfield Plain, Co. Durham
Simple ground directions: On A693 road to Consett, 200 yds west of junction with A6067
No of seats: 20 **Covered accommodation:** 200 **Capacity:** 6,000 **Floodlights:** No
Year formed: 1890 **Nickname:** The Plain **Club sponsors:** None
Club colours: Claret & Blue/Sky/Claret **Change colours:** Sky Blue/Sky/Sky
Previous Names: None **Previous Grounds:** None
Record attendance: 7,200 v Southport, F.A. Cup 1st Round Proper **Year:** 1928
Previous Leagues: North Eastern **Programme: Price/Pages** None
Clubhouse details: None

BLUE STAR

President: F. S. Brown
Chairman: Bill Dryden
Manager: Colin Richardson
Coach: Graham Defty
Physiotherapist: Derek Sayers & Billy Thompson
Secretary: R. Hunter
Address & Tel No: Newcastle 732655 (H) Wallsend 628941 x282 (B)
Commercial Manager: None
Address & Tel No:
Press Officer & Tel No: None
Address & Tel No of ground: Wheatsheaf Sports Ground, Woolsington, Newcastle. Newcastle 860425
Simple ground directions: Half-mile before Newcastle Airport on Jedburgh Road, A696
No of seats: None **Covered accommodation:** Yes **Capacity:** 250 **Floodlights:** No
Year formed: 1932 **Nickname:** None **Club sponsors:** None
Club colours: Blue/White/White **Change colours:** All Red
Previous Names: None **Previous Grounds:** None
Record attendance: v Almondsbury Greenway, F.A. Challenge Vase Semi-final 2nd Leg **Year:** 1977-8
Previous Leagues: Northern Combination **Programme: Price/Pages** 15p, 16 pages
Clubhouse details: Refreshment lounge, 80 seats. Sauna baths and small training room

BOLDON COMMUNITY ASSOCIATION

President: T. S. Snowdon
Chairman: W. Wilson
Manager: J. Compton
Coach: J. Carney
Physiotherapist: J. Carney
Secretary: W. Davison
Address & Tel No: 35 Byron Avenue, Boldon Colliery, Tyne & Wear. Boldon 362240 (Home); 368085 (Headqtrs) and Newcastle 816144 (B)
Commercial Manager: B. Storey
Address & Tel No: Boldon Community Centre, New Road, Boldon Colliery, Tyne & Wear
Press Officer & Tel No: B. Storey (Boldon 368085)
Address & Tel No of ground: Welfare Ground, Boldon Colliery
Simple ground directions: From Newcastle: Buses 528 or 530. From Sunderland: Buses 540. From South Shields: Buses 530, 531, 533. From Jarrow: Bus 540
No of seats: None **Covered accommodation:** None **Capacity:** 2,000 **Floodlights:** Training only
Year formed: 1903 **Nickname:** The Villa **Club sponsors:** Boldon Villa, Boldon Colliery Welfare
Club colours: Blue/White/Blue & White **Change colours:** Red/White/Red & White
Previous Names: Boldon Villa, Boldon Colliery Welfare **Previous Grounds:** Station Road
Record attendance: 1,550 v Stockton, Durham Challenge Cup **Year:** 1934
Previous Leagues: None **Programme: Price/Pages** None
Clubhouse details: Modern pavillion on ground

COUNDON T.T.

President:
Chairman: Dennis Donohue
Manager: Paul Adams
Coach: Kevin Rielly
Physiotherapist:
Secretary: Maurice Flint
Address & Tel No: Bishop Auckland 601155
Commercial Manager: None
Address & Tel No:
Press Officer & Tel No: Maurice Flint
Address & Tel No of ground: Leeholme School, Leeholme Road, Bishop Auckland
Simple ground directions: From Eden Arms, Rushyford, Bishop Auckland Road, approx 2 miles pass crossroads, turn next right, then left at Welfare Hall about 300 yards behind Co-op
No of seats: None **Covered accommodation:** None **Capacity:** 2,400 **Floodlights:** No
Year formed: 1976 **Nickname:** None **Club sponsors:** None
Club colours: Red **Change colours:** Blue
Previous Names: None **Previous Grounds:** None
Record attendance: 800 **Year:**
Previous Leagues: Auckland District, Durham District **Programme: Price/Pages**
Clubhouse details: None **Club Captain:** John Wren
Major Honours: Auckland League 1977, 1978, 1979, 1980; Auckland Charity Winners 1979, 1981, 1982; Durham District 1981, 1982; (2), Durham Trophy Winners 1981, Durham Minor Cup 1979, Weardale Cup 1977, Durham Hospital 1979, 1982; Auckland League Cup 1978, 1979; Durham League Cup 1981, 1982; Brancepeth Cup 1979, 1980, 1981, 1982

DAWDON C.W.F.C.

President:
Chairman: A. Carr
Manager: I. Arthur/N. Kelly
Coach: G. Dale
Physiotherapist:
Secretary: R. Pigg
Address & Tel No: Seaham 815382
Commercial Manager: None
Address & Tel No:
Press Officer & Tel No: N. Kelly
Address & Tel No of ground: Dawdon Welfare, Green Drive, Dawdon
Simple ground directions:
No of seats: None **Covered accommodation:** 100 **Capacity:** 3,000 **Floodlights:** No
Year formed: 1977 **Nickname:** None **Club sponsors:** Hays Travel
Club colours: Blue & White stripes/White/Blue **Change colours:** Red & White/White/Red
Previous Names: None **Previous Grounds:** None
Record attendance: Not known **Programme Editor:** Norman Kent
Previous Leagues: Houghton & District, Washington SaveCentre **Programme: Price/Pages**
Clubhouse details: None
Club Captain (83-4): Leslie Dodd **Player of the Year (83-4):** Paul Morse

EASINGTON COLLIERY

President: Joseph Oliver
Chairman: P. Pygall
Managers: Lol Jones, Terry Dunster
Coach: Terry Dunster
Physiotherapist: Fred Wellburn
Secretary: David Elliott
Address & Tel No: 17 Cotswold Place, Peterlee, Co. Durham. 867581
Commercial Manager: None
Press Officer & Tel No: Secretary
Address & Tel No of ground: Welfare Park, Easington Colliery, Peterlee, Co. Durham. Easington 270395 (Groundsman's house)
Simple ground directions: Approx two miles east of A19 trunk road, north of Peterlee
No of seats: None **Covered accommodation:** None **Capacity:** 1,000 **Floodlights:** No
Year formed: 1920 **Nickname:** The Colliery **Club sponsors:** F & D Welding, Mick Emery Motors Ltd
Club colours: Green/White **Change colours:** Tangerine/Black
Previous Names: None **Previous Grounds:** None
Record attendance: 4,500 v Tranmere **Year:** 1955
Previous Leagues: None **Programme: Price/Pages** None
Clubhouse details: None

EPPLETON C.W.

Chairman: Councillor J. Storey
Secretary, Address & Tel No: F. Browell, 98 Houghton Road, Hetton-le-Hole, Tyne & Wear. 0783 263618 (H)
Address & Tel No of ground: Eppleton C.W. Ground, 0783 261048
Club colours: Tangerine/Black/Tangerine **Change colours:** All Green
Programme: Yes

GATESHEAD RESERVES

President:
Chairman: E. G. Hill
Manager: R. Wilkie
Coach: J. Tudor
Physiotherapist:
Secretary: H. Fairley
Address & Tel No: 0632 604311 (H), Low Fell 878822 ext 6221 (B)
Commercial Manager: E. J. Hall
Address & Tel No:
Press Officer & Tel No: P. McDonough
Address & Tel No of ground: Wardley Park, West Crescent, Wardley, Gateshead, Tyne & Wear
Simple ground directions: A6115 to A195 intersection, West Crescent is third on left below garage
No of seats: None **Covered accommodation:** 200 **Capacity:** 3,000 **Floodlights:** Yes
Year formed: 1983 **Nickname:** None **Club sponsors:** None
Club colours: Red shirts, White shorts **Change colours:** Blue shirts, Blue shorts
Previous Names: None **Previous Grounds:** None
Record attendance: **Year:**
Previous Leagues: **Programme: Price/Pages**
Clubhouse details: None

GATESHEAD CLARKE CHAPMAN F.C.

President: J.F. Howey
Chairman: L. Crossley
Manager: J. Wales
Coach: G. Langley
Physiotherapist: W. Thompson
Secretary: G.T. Castlehow
Address & Tel No: 53 Burnhope Road, Barmston Village, Washington, Tyne & Wear. (091) 4160106
Commercial Manager: Secretary
Press Officer: Secretary
Address & Tel No of ground: Clarke Chapman Sports Ground, Old Ford, Gateshead. 782555/781220
Simple ground directions: Old Ford-Gateshead A6115 (Felling By-Pass), road to ground opposite Gateshead International Stadium
Year formed: 1949
Nickname: Clarkie's
Club colours: Sky Blue shirts & shorts
Change colours: Red shirts, Black shorts
Previous Leagues: Washington Amateur League, Northern Amateur League
Major Honours: Washington League Champions 1966, Gateshead Charity Cup Winners 1966 & 1982, Heddon Homes Charity Cup Winners 1983

HEBBURN REYROLLE

President: None
Chairman: J. Minto
Manager: Brian Hudson
Coach: Malcolm Leask
Physiotherapist: None
Secretary: J. Baker
Address & Tel No: 88 Cherwell Sulgrave, Washington, Tyne & Wear. 832441 (H), 471033 (B)
Commercial Manager: None
Address & Tel No:
Press Officer & Tel No: Secretary
Address & Tel No of ground: Reyrolle Sports Ground, Victoria Road West, Hebburn, Tyne & Wear
Simple ground directions: Next to the works on Victoria Road West, Hebburn
No of seats: 200 **Covered accommodation:** 400 **Capacity:** 2,000 **Floodlights:** No
Year formed: 1912 **Nickname:** None **Club sponsors:** None
Club colours: Blue & White stripes/Black/Blue
Change colours: Yellow/Blue/Yellow
Previous Names: None
Previous Grounds: None
Record attendance: Not known
Previous Leagues: None
Programme: Price/Pages None
Clubhouse details: None
Club Captain: Paul McIntyre
Player of the Year: Joe Calvert

NEWTON AYCLIFFE F.C.

President: S. Wood B.E.M.
Chairman: R.M. Blair
Manager: G. Farley
Coach: D. Hall
Physiotherapist: R.M. Blair
Secretary: D. Southern
Address & Tel No: 9 Witton Road, Ferryhill, Co Durham. Ferryhill 53432
Commercial Manager: None
Press Officer: D. Southern
Address & Tel No of ground: Sports Club, Moore Lane, Newton Aycliffe, Co Durham
Simple ground directions: From the A1(M) Bradbury Interchange onto the A689 Bishop Auckland road. Turn onto the A167 to Darlington, take the first right into Newton Aycliffe, then left at the first roundabout. Take the third turn on the left into Creighton Road, then right into Moore Lane. Sports Club on the right
No of Seats: None **Covered accommodation:** None **Capacity:** 2,000 **Floodlights:** None
Year formed: 1968 **Nickname:** The Acorns **Club sponsors:** None
Club colours: Navy Blue & White stripes, Navy Blue shorts & socks
Change colours: All Yellow **Previous names:** Newton Aycliffe Sports Club Rangers
Record attendance: 300 v Shildon BR, Cup semi-final, 1975
Previous Leagues: Auckland District League, Teesside League
Clubhouse details: Bar, lounge, snug, concert room **Programme:** 20 pages, 20p
Major honours: Bp. Auckland & District Div 2 Champions, Brancepeth Aged Miners Cup, Bp. Auckland & District League Cup, Bp. Auckland Charity Cup, Weardale Cup, Bp. Auckland & District Div 1 Champions

MURTON F.C.

Chairman: W. Gunn
Coach: Ray Lish
Ground: Recreation Park, Murton
Capacity: 4,000
Record attendance: 3,500 v Sunderland, 1948
Colours: All Yellow
Previous League: North Eastern
Secretary: J.T. Pratt
Address & Tel No: 8 Church Lane, Murton, Seaham, Co Durham (Hetton 261962)
Sponsors: Murton Parish Council
Change Colours: All Red

ROKER

President: P. Graham
Chairman: P. Wall
Secretary: D. Worthy
Address & Tel No: 0783 293587

Manager: T. Middlemist
Coach: Not yet appointed
Physiotherapist: T. Middlemist
Commercial Manager: None
Address & Tel No:
Press Officer & Tel No: None
Address & Tel No of ground: Silksworth Recreation Park. Sunderland 211951 **Club shop:** Yes
Simple ground directions: Behind Co-operative Store, Silksworth. Bus service No 133 from Park Lane, Sunderland; service No 111 from Ryhope or Herrington to Police Station. Ground 300 yards.
No of seats: None **Covered accommodation:** None **Capacity:** 2,000 **Floodlights:** Yes
Year formed: 1961 **Nickname:** None **Club sponsors:** None
Club colours: All Red
Change colours: All White
Previous Names: None
Previous Grounds: None
Record attendance: 1,000 v Sunderland, Friendly **Year:** 1980
Club Captain: Steve Hunter
Player of the Season: Derek Holden

RYHOPE COLLIERY WELFARE

President: R. Surtees
Chairman:
Manager: K. Johnstonne
Coach: A. Harding
Physiotherapist: P. Vincent
Secretary: J. Errington
Address & Tel No: (0783) 287668 (H)
Commercial Manager: Mrs E. A. Errington
Address & Tel No: (0783) 287668
Press Officer & Tel No: Julie Ann Errington (Sunderland 287668)
Address & Tel No of ground: Ryhope Recreation Park, Ryhope, Sunderland (0783) 212843
Simple ground directions: On B1286 at Brick Row, Ryhope
No of seats: None **Covered accommodation:** None **Capacity:** 2,000 **Floodlights:** Yes
Year formed: 1957 **Nickname:** The Welfare **Club sponsors:** None
Club colours: Red/White stripes, Blue/Blue
Change colours: All Yellow and All Sky Blue
Previous Names: Ryhope Blue Star, Ryhope Villa
Previous Grounds: None
Record attendance: 1,600 v Workington, F.A. Cup 1st Round **Year:** 1967
Previous Leagues: North Eastern, Houghton and District
Programme: 6 pages, 30p
Clubhouse details: Now open with Vaux's Beer (Sunderland 210091)
Club Captain: Billy Youren
Programme Editor: Julie Errington

SOUTH SHIELDS

President: Martin Ford
Chairman: John Rundle
Secretary: Ian Joice
Address & Tel No: Newcastle 653567 (H) South Shields 567611 x244 (B)

Manager: Colin Revell
Coach: Wally Carmichael
Physiotherapist: Wally Carmichael
Commercial Manager: John Rundle
Address & Tel No:
Press Officer & Tel No: None
Address & Tel No of ground: Jack Clark Park, Horsley Hill Road, South Shields **Club shop:** Yes
Simple ground directions: Quarter-mile east of Ingham Informary
No of seats: None **Covered accommodation:** None **Capacity:** 2,000 **Floodlights:** No
Year formed: 1974 **Nickname:** Mariners **Club sponsors:** Hearn's Leisure + various others
Club colours: White & Orange/Orange/White
Change colours: Orange/Black/Orange
Previous Names: None
Previous Grounds: None
Record attendance: 1,500 v Brigg Town, F.A. Vase **Year:** 1976
Previous Leagues: Northern Alliance
Programme: Price/Pages Free, 4 pages
Clubhouse details: None

SPORTING CLUB VAUX
(formerly SOUTH HETTON F.C.)

President:
Chairman: John Mair
Manager:
Coach:
Physiotherapist: Brian Hill
Secretary: Trevor Whitehead
Address & Tel No: Sunderland 285366
Commercial Manager: Alan Bosher
Address & Tel No:
Press Officer & Tel No: George Hunter
Address & Tel No of ground: Vaux Sports Ground, Glenesk Road, Sunderland
Simple ground directions: A690 to Houghton-le-Spring. A182 for 4 miles to South Hetton Colliery, first left under bridge
No of seats: None **Covered accommodation:** None **Capacity:** 2,000 **Floodlights:** No
Year formed: 1968 **Nickname:** **Club sponsors:** A.G. Gibbons
Club colours: Red with Gold Trim/Red/Red
Change colours: Yellow with Red Trim/Yellow/Yellow
Previous Names: None
Previous Grounds: None
Record attendance: **Year:**
Previous Leagues: North Eastern Amateur, Tyne-Wear
Programme: No
Clubhouse details: Private club
Major Honours: North Eastern Amateur League, Division 1 Champions (2), Division 2 Champions (4), Shield Winners (3), Leukaemia Cup Winners, Tyne-Wear League Champions (2), Cup Winners (2)

STOCKTON

President: None
Chairman: Keith Wren
Manager: J. Hope
Coach: J. Hope
Physiotherapist: J. Smith (Snr)
Secretary: Glenn Youngman
Address & Tel No: 587871 (B) 587871 (B)
Commercial Manager: None
Address & Tel No:
Press Officer & Tel No: J. Smith (584593)
Address & Tel No of ground: Teesdale Park, Acklam Road, Thornaby, Cleveland (Stockton 606803)
Simple ground directions: 1 mile from Thornaby station **Club shop:** No
No of seats: None **Covered accommodation:** None **Capacity:** 3,000 **Floodlights:** No
Year formed: 1980 **Nickname:** None **Club sponsors:** Classic Cars
Club colours: White shirts, Black shorts, White socks
Change colours: Green shirts, White shorts, Black socks
Previous Names: None
Previous Grounds: Stockton Sports Centre, Stockton
Record attendance: 1,000
Programme Editor: J.M. Smith
Previous Leagues: Stockton & District
Programme: Price/Pages 20p, 20 pages
Club Captain: Les Bibok
Player of the Year: Glenn Shepherd

WASHINGTON

President: D. Davies
Chairman: W. Blevins
Manager: T. Boylen
Coach: D. Armstrong
Physiotherapist: H. Ellerington
Secretary: D. Benson
Address & Tel No: 461658 (H) 650411 x314 (B)
Commercial Manager: J. Crook
Address & Tel No: 463634
Press Officer & Tel No: T. McBurnie (461558)
Address & Tel No of ground: Albany Park, Spout Lane, Concord, Washington **Club shop:** No
Simple ground directions: Concord, Distric 11, Washington
No of seats: None **Covered accommodation:** None **Capacity:** 3,000 **Floodlights:** No
Year formed: 1947 **Nickname:** Mechanics **Club sponsors:** Washington Coachworks
Club colours: Royal Blue
Change colours: Red
Previous Names: Washington Mechanics
Previous Grounds: Usworth Park, Glebe Welfare
Record attendance: 3,800 v Bradford Park Ave, F.A. Cup **Year:** 1970
Previous Leagues: Northern Alliance, Washington Amateur **Programme: Price/Pages** 20p, 6 pages
Clubhouse details: Plans passed for new clubhouse at Albany Park

WHICKHAM

President: Michael Anderson
Chairman: A. Hutchinson
Manager:
Coaches: M. Chapman, M. Barkess
Physiotherapist: W. Thompson
Secretary: J. T. Gilbert
Address & Tel No: Newcastle 4882853
Commercial Manager: None
Address & Tel No:
Press Officer & Tel No: None
Address & Tel No of ground: Glebe Ground (4883054) **Club shop:** No
Simple ground directions: Newcastle to Whickham, proceed 300 yds up Rectory Lane, ground on right
No of seats: None **Covered accommodation:** None **Capacity:** 5,000 **Floodlights:** No
Year formed: 1944 **Nickname:** None **Club sponsors:** Vaux
Club colours: Black & White/Black/White
Change colours: Red & White/Red/Black
Previous Names: Axwell Park C.W.
Previous Grounds: None
Record attendance: 4,400 v Windsor & Eton, Semi-Final
Previous Leagues: Derwent Valley, Northern Combination **Programme: Price/Pages** 10p, 4 pages
Clubhouse details: Bar and Lounge
Major Honours: Winning F.A. Vase at Wembley

WINGATE

President: To be appointed
Chairman: T. Lenehan
Team Managers: J. Maddison, D. Buckle
Coach: J. Costello
Physiotherapist: R. Wolfe
Treasurer: G. Wood
Secretary: R. Hayes
Address & Tel No: 78 Newholme Est, Station Town, Wingate, Co Durham (Wellfield 838946)
Commercial Officer & Tel No: Derek Knapp (Washington 091-417-1266)
Press Officer: Secretary
Address & Tel No of ground: Community Association Ground, Wingate (Wellfield 838318 — club house)
Simple ground directions: On Front Street, Wingate, turn at Queens Head P.H., ground is approx 400 yds west
No of seats: None **Covered accommodation:** None **Capacity:** 5,000 **Floodlights:** Training only
Year formed: 1947 **Nickname:** None **Club sponsors:** Camerons Brewery (Hansa Lager Bier)
Club colours: Silver shirts, Black shorts, Silver socks
Change colours: All Red
Previous Names: Wingate St Marys (until 1967)
Previous Grounds: None
Record attendance: Not known
Programme Editor: R. Hayes
Previous Leagues: Hartlepool and District
Programme: 16 or 20 pages, 15p
Clubhouse details: Bar and Lounge. Entertainment Saturday and Sunday nights. Bar meals Friday, Saturday and Sunday nights. Bar open nightly
Local newspapers: Hartlepool Mail, Sunderland Echo, Northern Echo, Peterlee Times
Club Captain: Jim Costello
Player of the Year: Paul Harrisskit
Club Honours: Monkwearmouth Charity Cup Winners 1978 & 1984, runners-up 1972; Wearside League Cup Winners 1970, runners-up 1979; Wearside League runners-up 1979; Durham Challenge Cup runners-up 1973; Sunderland Shipowners Cup runners-up 1968 & 1979

South Shields F.C. *Back Row: Colin Revel (Manager), Les Tatum, Graham Dickinson, Barry Goodwin, Kevin Bruce, Paul Hedley, Bobby Doig, Alan Fletcher (Coach). Front Row: David Taws, Ian Potts, Joe O'Harrow, Tony Cornfoot, Paul O'Connor, Mark Cass, Ray Banks.* Photo: Shields Gazette

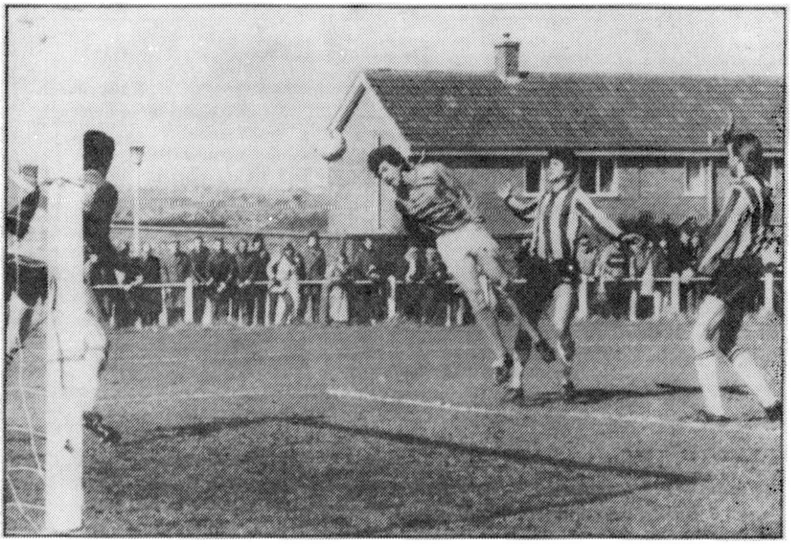

Stansted's Steve Cooper just fails with a header in the second leg at Whickham.

Northumberland Senior Cup

First Round

Alnwick Town v Newcastle Town . . . 0-2
Dudley Welfare v Seaton Terrace . . . 2-3
North Shields v Ashington . . . 4-0
Ponteland United v Percy Main Amateurs . . . 5-4

Second Round

Blue Star v Seaton Terrace . . . 6-1
North Shields v Newcastle United . . . 1-0
Ponteland United v Blyth Spartans . . . 0-1
Whitley Bay v Prudhoe East End . . . 1-2

Semi-Finals

Blyth Spartans v Prudhoe East End . . . 2-1
North Shields v Blue Star . . . 0-0,0-1

Final (at Newcastle United FC)

Blue Star v Blyth Spartans . . . 0-0,4-2*
Replay at North Shields FC

Northumberland Senior Benevolent Bowl

First Round

Morpeth Town v Longbenton . . . 5-2
Gosforth St Nicholas v Lindisfarne Walls . . . 1-3
Bedlington Terriers v Newcastle University . . . 3-0
Hirst Progressive v Wallington . . . 2-1
Stobswood Welfare v Annitsford Welfare . . . 6-1
Forest Hall v Bohemian . . . 5-3
West Allotment Celtic v Wallsend Town . . . 1-1,1-2

Second Round

Forest Hall v Stobswood Welfare . . . 0-1
Hirst Progressive v Wallsend Town . . . 1-1,0-2
Lindisfarne Walls v Morpeth Town . . . 0-3
NEI Parsons v Bedlington Terriers . . . 2-1

Semi-Finals

Wallsend Town v Stobswood Welfare . . . 2-2,3-2
Morpeth Town v NEI Parsons Athletic . . . 0-1

Final (at Blyth Spartans FC)

Parsons Athletic v Wallsend Town . . . 2-1

Durham County Cup

First Qualifying Round

Coundon Three Tuns v Crawcrook OB . . . 6-0

Second Qualifying Round

Crook Town v Whickham . . . 1-0
Darlington Rail A v Ferryhill John Dee . . . 0-3
Dunston Mechanics v Hartlepool BW . . . 2-2
Durham City v Langley Park . . . 3-2
Eppleton v Boldon . . . 2-0
Ferryhill Athletic v Clarke Chapmans . . . 6-1
Esh Winning v Shotton Comrades . . . 3-1
Willington v Roker . . . 2-3
Philadelphia cW v Billingham Town . . . 0-2
Ryhope CW v Coundon Three Tuns . . . 1-3
Seaham Red Star v Reyrolle . . . 2-2,3-0
Shildon United v Norton & Stockton Ancients . . . 1-4
Stockton v Newton Aycliffe . . . 1-2
Stockton Town v Swalwell . . . ?-?
Ushaw Moor v Wingate . . . 2-5
West Auckland v Dawden CW . . . 2-2,2-3

First Round Proper

Brandon United v Darlington Cl Br . . . 0-4
Chester le Street v Ryhope CA . . . 4-3
Crook Town v Stockton Town . . . 2-1*
Dawden CW v Dunston Mechanics . . . 4-3
Easington Colliery v Consett . . . 1-0*
Eppleton CW v Roker . . . 3-0
Esh Winning v Durham City . . . 1-2*
Ferryhill Athletic v Billingham Town . . . 1-3
Ferryhill John Dee v Coundon Three Tuns . . . 0-2
Murton CW v Horden CW . . . 2-4
Newton Aycliffe v Wingate . . . 1-2
Peterlee Newtown v South Shields . . . 0-2
Seaham Red Star v Billingham Synth' . . . 3-2
Shildon v Annfield Plain . . . 2-0
Spennymoor United v Washington . . . 1-0
Norton & Stockton Ancients v Evenwood Town . . . 2-0

Second Round

Chester le Street v Seaham Red Star . . . 1-1,3-0
Darlington Cl Br v Wingate . . . 1-0
Crook Town v Horden CW . . . 1-3
Dawden CW v Billingham Town . . . 1-1*,0-6
Durham City v Norton & Stockton Ancients . . . 0-1
Easington Colliery v South Shields . . . 1-2
Eppleton CW v Coundon Three Tuns . . . 0-1
Spennymoor United v Shildon . . . 0-2

Third Round

Horden CW v South Shields . . . 0-2
Norton & Stockton Ancients v Darlington Cl Br . . . 2-0
Chester le Street v Billingham Town . . . 3-1
Shildon v Coundon Three Tuns . . . 1-3

Semi-Finals

South Shields v Norton & Stockton Ancients . . . 0-1*
Coundon Three Tuns v Chester le Street . . . 1-0*

Final (at Darlington FC)

Norton & Stockton Ancients v Coundon Three Tuns . . 1-2*

* After extra time

North Riding Senior Cup

Quarter-Finals

Scarborough v Middlesbrough Res . . . 3-2
Whitby Town v Nunthorpe Athletic . . . 3-1
Guisborough Town v South Bank . . . 1-2
York City v Wilton ICI . . . 2-3

Semi-Finals

Whitby Town v South Bank . . . -
Wilton ICI v Scarborough . . . -

NORTHERN ALLIANCE FOOTBALL LEAGUE

	P	W	D	L	F	A	Pts
1 Morpeth Town	26	16	6	4	63	32	38
2 Dudley Welfare	26	13	6	7	49	34	32
3 Stobswold Welfare	26	12	7	7	63	42	31
4 Seaton Terrace	26	11	9	6	49	39	31
5 West Allotment	26	10	10	6	41	34	30
6 Prudhoe	26	12	5	9	45	42	29
7 Wigton	26	10	8	8	51	45	28
8 Seaton Delaval	26	8	7	11	37	34	23
9 Ponteland United	26	7	9	10	38	38	23
10 Wallsend Town	26	8	7	11	40	50	23
11 Haltwhistle CP	26	8	5	13	44	58	21
12 Forest Hall	26	6	8	12	32	51	20
13 Percy Main	26	7	5	14	33	66	19
14 Carlisle City	26	4	8	14	27	47	16

NORTHERN COMBINATION

	P	W	D	L	F	A	Pts
Swalwell	28	25	1	2	96	20	51
Dunston Mechanics	28	20	3	5	71	30	43
Gateshead-Tyne S	28	18	2	8	69	33	38
Parsons Athletic	28	13	5	10	57	55	31
Prudhoe East End	28	11	8	9	46	41	30
New Kyo United	28	10	10	8	43	48	30
Winlaton Hallgarth	28	11	5	12	44	41	27
Wallsend Rising Sun	28	9	8	11	58	63	26
Newcastle Univ -2	28	9	10	9	50	58	26
Ryton	28	9	5	14	49	70	23
Lindisfarne Wa'end	28	6	10	12	43	59	22
Gateshead Ath	28	7	7	14	55	66	21
Gosforth St Nic'	28	6	8	14	55	53	20
Crawcrook OB	28	6	3	19	39	79	15
N'umberland Police	28	5	5	18	29	88	15

TEESSIDE FOOTBALL LEAGUE SEASON 1983/84 FINAL LEAGUE TABLE

PREMIER DIVISION

	P	W	D	L	F	A	Pts
Nunthorpe Athletic	34	24	5	5	83	36	53
Wilton ICI	34	23	6	5	82	31	52
Cassel Works	34	21	8	5	72	33	50
Hartlepool BWOB	34	20	7	7	79	50	47
Brotton Teescomp	34	18	4	12	64	55	40
Newton Aycliffe	34	14	8	12	69	65	36
Grangetown BC	34	12	10	12	60	54	34
Fishburn Park	34	16	1	17	65	66	33
Darlington RA	34	13	6	15	55	53	32
Marske United	34	13	6	15	59	53	32
Wolviston	34	12	6	16	57	59	30
Stockton Town	34	9	10	15	51	60	28
Teeside Poly	34	10	6	18	44	66	26
Smiths Dock	34	10	6	18	48	87	26
Dormans Ath	34	9	7	18	48	74	25
Acklam Works	34	9	6	19	44	80	24
New Marske SC	34	7	9	18	42	56	23
Redcar Albion	34	10	3	21	63	103	23

NON-LEAGUE CLUBS IN THE SCOTTISH CUP

There was only one distinguished Non-League effort this past season in the Scottish Cup — but what an effort! Team of the last two seasons, Inverness Caledonian, went as far as the Fourth Round before bowing out at home to the might of Rangers from Ibrox by six clear goals, but prior to that Albion Rovers and Stirling Albion through a late extra-time goal by Urquhart (at Stirling in a replay) had to give best to 'Caley'. The latter match only took place a few days before the Rangers game and the home team might well claim that but for fatigue the result might have been closer.

Results:

First Round:

Cowdenbeath	3	**Vale of Leithen**	0
Dalbeattie Star	1	Arbroath	5
Elgin City	0	Queen's Park	2
Forfar Athletic	4	**Spartans**	1
Inverness Caledonian	2	Albion Rovers	1

Second Round:

East Stirlingshire	3	**Fraserburgh**	1
Gala Fairydean	0	**Inverness Caledonian**	2
Peterhead	1	Berwick Rangers	2

Third Round:

Inverness Caledonian	0	Stirling Albion	0

Replay:

Stirling Albion (After extra-time)	1	**Inverness Caledonian**	2

Fourth Round:

Inverness Caledonian	0	Glasgow Rangers	6

THE HIGHLAND LEAGUE

	P	W	D	L	F	A	Pts
Inverness Caledonian	30	21	5	4	85	28	68
Keith	30	20	6	4	62	30	66
Peterhead	30	17	6	7	45	21	57
Elgin City	30	17	5	8	59	31	56
Buckie Thistle	30	14	8	8	74	65	50
Inverness Thistle	30	15	3	12	60	51	48
Brora Rangers	30	10	10	10	55	42	40
Fraserburgh	30	11	7	12	58	55	40
Forres Mechanics	30	12	4	14	53	60	37
Huntly	30	9	7	14	45	51	34
Inverness Clachnacuddin	30	9	7	14	55	63	34
Nairn County	30	8	9	13	57	57	33
Ross County	30	7	9	14	51	63	30
Deveronvale	30	8	5	17	38	67	29
Rothes	30	6	5	19	43	97	23
Lossiemouth	30	6	4	20	26	82	22

SOUTH OF SCOTLAND LEAGUE SEASON 1983-84

	P	W	D	L	F	A	Pts
Annan	18	13	4	1	74	23	30
Dalbeattie	18	13	4	1	49	17	30
Stranraer	18	12	3	3	56	21	27
Threave	18	7	5	6	52	39	19
Wigtown	18	8	2	8	51	46	18
Girvan	18	7	3	8	36	50	17
St. Cuthberts	18	6	3	9	48	53	15
Newton	18	5	1	12	40	63	11
Creetown	18	2	4	12	23	57	8
Tarff	18	2	1	15	20	80	5

SCOTTISH QUALIFYING CUP FINAL

Inverness Caledonian	2	Elgin City	1
Davidson 71 min		Armstrong 34 min	
Robertson 75 min			

Caledonian: Macdonald, Davidson, Mann, Lisle, Summers, Corbett, Dewar, Mackintosh, Urquhart, Docherty, Robertson. Subs: Gibson, Christie.

Elgin City: McHattie, Brown, Maclennan, Slavin, Bremner, McHardy, F Kallas, Anderson, Armstrong, Masson, Guyan. Subs: N Kallas, Dunbar.

Referee: Mr D Hope (Glasgow).

COCHRANE EAST OF SCOTLAND LEAGUE

	P	W	D	L	F	A	Pts
Spartans*	30	22	4	4	103	37	48
Gala Fairydean	30	21	6	3	89	30	48
Selkirk	30	19	5	6	85	45	43
Hawick Royal Albert	30	19	4	7	81	48	42
Craigroyston	30	16	7	7	62	32	39
Vale of Leithen	30	15	8	7	72	34	38
Postal United	30	16	6	8	76	39	38
Civil Service Strollers	30	16	3	11	63	43	35
Whitehill Welfare	30	13	7	10	57	43	33
Kelso United	30	11	4	15	51	48	26
Eyemouth United	30	9	6	15	51	63	24
Easthouses M. W.	30	7	9	14	45	58	23
Heriot-Watt Univ.	30	6	4	20	45	100	16
Edinburgh Univ.	30	6	2	22	27	78	14
Peebles Rovers	30	2	4	24	26	135	8
Coldstream	30	2	1	27	19	122	5

* Won on goal difference

McEWANS NORTH OF SCOTLAND CUP FINAL

Inverness Thistle	1	Inverness Caledonian	4
A. MacDonald		Docherty (pen), Lisle, Summers, Robertson	

Caledonian: Macdonald, Davidson, Mann, Gibson, Summers, Corbett, Lisle, Dewar, Urquhart, Docherty, Robertson. Subs: Baxter, N Mackintosh.

Thistle: George, Skinner, B Black, Maclean, Milroy, Andrew, A Black, Wilson, Macdonald, Oliver, Watt. Subs: Bennett, Calder.

Referee: Mr G Black (Castletown).

CENTRAL LEAGUE

	P	W	D	L	F	A	Pts
Petershill	26	18	4	4	67	22	40
Pollok	26	18	4	4	71	27	40
Baillieston	26	14	5	7	41	34	33
Yoker Athletic	26	10	10	6	42	35	30
Larkhall Thistle	26	11	4	11	46	43	26
Benburb	26	10	5	11	48	57	25
East Kilbride Thistle	26	10	3	13	46	50	23
Blantyre Vics	26	8	7	11	42	49	23
Lesmahagow	26	9	5	12	51	61	23
Port Glasgow	26	7	8	11	40	48	22
Neilston	26	9	3	14	42	50	21
Kirkintillock Rob Roy	26	8	5	13	44	54	21
Kilsyth Rangers	26	9	2	15	42	61	20
Forth Wanderers	26	6	5	15	25	58	17

AYRSHIRE LEAGUE

	P	W	D	L	F	A	Pts
Cumnock	20	15	2	3	48	16	32
Auchinleck	20	14	4	2	39	17	32
Irvine M.	20	13	3	4	44	28	29
Kello	20	8	5	7	39	26	21
Annbank	20	8	5	7	39	30	21
Glenalton	20	8	5	7	26	29	21
Darvel	20	8	2	10	32	37	18
Kilbirnie	20	7	2	11	34	43	16
Whitletts	20	6	2	12	25	40	14
Muirkirk	20	4	4	12	29	46	12
Craigmark	20	2	0	18	22	65	4

FIFE REGION LEAGUE 1983-84

	P	W	D	L	F	A	Pts
Glenrothes	34	28	1	5	102	42	57
Oakley United	34	19	13	2	65	30	51
Halbeath	34	22	5	7	83	40	49
Kelty Hearts	34	20	6	8	84	50	46
St. Andrews United	34	16	9	9	71	46	41
Hill of Beath Hawthorn	34	16	9	9	61	45	41
Leven	34	14	9	11	57	48	37
Crossgates Primrose	34	14	9	11	62	57	37
Dundonald Bluebell	34	13	10	11	59	47	36
Kirkcaldy YM	34	10	13	11	57	56	33
Tulliallan Thistle	34	11	7	16	72	77	29
Jubilee Athletic	34	12	4	18	58	67	28
Thornton Hibs	34	10	8	16	52	64	28
Clackmannan	34	7	12	15	47	63	26
Lochgelly Albert	34	7	9	18	51	84	23
Lochore Welfare	34	6	10	18	49	74	22
Newburgh	34	8	5	21	44	75	21
Comrie Colliery	34	2	3	29	21	130	7

SCOTLAND LEAGUE

SECTION A

	P	W	D	L	F	A	Pts
Linlithgow	22	18	3	1	53	14	39
Broxburn	22	14	4	4	42	27	32
Ormiston	22	12	3	7	41	34	27
Bo'ness	22	12	2	8	43	34	26
Newtongrange	22	10	4	8	50	37	24
Arniston	22	8	6	8	32	28	22
Haddington	22	8	4	10	31	34	20
Fauldhouse	22	8	3	11	31	40	19
Tranent	22	7	4	11	35	40	18
Dalkeith	22	6	5	11	22	34	17
Camelon	22	3	4	15	26	55	10
Penicuik	22	2	6	14	24	53	10

SECTION B

	P	W	D	L	F	A	Pts
Bonnyrigg	26	19	4	3	73	22	42
Whitburn	26	16	6	4	49	34	38
Sauchie	26	17	3	6	60	29	37
Bathgate	26	14	7	5	50	29	35
Musselburgh	26	12	5	9	45	32	29
Armadale	26	12	5	9	38	35	29
Dunbar	26	7	9	10	43	46	23
West Calder	26	8	7	11	41	48	23
Livingston	26	8	6	12	37	51	22
Bonnybridge	26	7	7	12	35	49	21
Blackburn	26	6	7	13	36	59	19
Preston	26	5	8	13	30	47	18
Stoneyburn	26	5	7	14	35	56	17
Polkemmet	26	2	7	17	39	74	11

JUNIOR INTERNATIONALS

October 1 1983, Griffith Park, Dublin

Rep of Ireland	0	Scotland Dickson, Myles, Malarkey	3

Hendrie (Shotts), Martin (Shotts), Young (Auchinleck), Strachan (Sunnybank), Auld (Pollok), Jamieson (Pollok), Malarkey (Manyhill), Myles (Bonnyrigg), Carvil (Ashfield), Reilly (E. Kilbride), Dickson (Glenaftan). Subs: Paterson (Ashfield), Roos (Whittletts), Bentley (Cumnock), Dunlevie (Bo'ness).

April 14, Somerset Park, Ayr

Scotland Webster 2, Moffat 3	5	Wales	0

Hendrie, Dunlevie, Wishart (Pollok), Auld, Roos, Myles, Morrison (Auchinleck), Moffat (Halbeath), Ferguson (Auchinleck), Webster (Sunnybank), Dickson. Subs: Docherty, Strachan, Reilly, Dailly (Petershill).

SCOTTISH JUNIOR CUP
(last 16)

Round 5

Bo'ness	2	Cumnock	0
Darvel	2	Ardrossan W.R.	0
Whitburn	0	Auchinleck	3
Glenboig	1	Petershill	2
Pollok	2	Benburb	1
Rob Roy	0	Ballieston	1
Broxburn	2:2	Banks O'Dee	2:3
Fauldhouse	1:1	Dunipace	1:0

Round 6

Petershill	0	Darvel	3
Pollok	1	Ballieston	3
Auchinleck	3	Banks O'Dee	0
Bo'ness	2:2	Fauldhouse	2:1

Semi-Finals

Auchinleck	1	Ballieston	4

(Rugby Park, Kilmarnock)

Bo'ness	2	Darvel	0

(Brockville Park, Falkirk)

SCOTTISH JUNIOR CUP FINAL

Sunday, 10th June, 1984, Ibrox Park, Glasgow. Attendance: 15,000.

BAILLIESTON 0 — BO'NESS UNITED 2
Shields 2. HT 0-0.

With Hampden Park now no longer the venue for Junior Cup Finals — they do not like to have such matches played there on Sundays — Ibrox has become the new home for this big occasion and in a thrilling match the Cup went East for the first time since 1978 when Bo'ness wing-man, Lex Shields, scored twice in the last fifteen minutes — the second with only five minutes remaining. It was fitting that the little man, who lost an eye as a child, should have been the hero as he had been the match's star long before his final two acts of virtuosity. The Central League monopoly on the Cup was broken by his efforts.

Up to the moment of the first goal it had been a very hard rather than brilliant match with Bo'ness slightly the better team. Baillieston's best chance came in the 62nd minute when Andy Walker, a nineteen-year-old, hit a post with Kirkwood beaten, but the goalkeeper was not in any other real trouble as he played competently as did Carroll, Breen, Sinnet, Fairlie and, of course, Shields for the winners.

Both goals were exceptional solo efforts. For the first Shields picked up the ball just inside the Baillieston half and beat five members of the opposition before slipping it past Boles. For the second he did almost the same thing after accelerating into a solo run which ended with the bemused Boles again having to bend his back to recover the ball from his own net.

It was not all fun for Shields. He along with Baillieston's Quigley was booked during the game, but he is unlikely to remember that part of his afternoon for long!

Teams:-
Baillieston: Boles; Quigley, McCabe, Innes, Murphy, Lamont, A. Walker, Doctor, Baptie, Clark, Donaldson. Subs: T. Walker, Donaldson.
Bo'ness: Kirkwood; Dunlevie, Breen, Carroll, Caldwell, Reid, Shields, Beaton, Sinnet, Fairlie, Wilson. Subs: Balanowski, Robertson.
Referee: Mr. H. Goud, Coupar.

Drybrough Cup Final: Pollok 3, Benburb 2 (at Shettleston).

Bo'ness United

Baillieston

WELSH LEAGUES

It is hoped to expand the Welsh section to include club directories for 1985/86. League secretaries will be circulated but any help with compilation of a much more comprehensive Welsh section will be greatly appreciated. T.W.

NATIONAL DIVISION

	P	W	D	L	F	A	Pts
Barry Town	30	21	5	4	85	24	68
Caerleon	30	19	5	6	58	28	62
Maesteg Park	30	15	8	7	62	37	53
Haverfordwest County	30	14	7	9	59	41	49
Blaenrhondda	30	14	7	9	55	44	49
Briton Ferry Athletic	30	14	6	10	46	36	48
Bridgend Town	30	14	6	10	39	30	48
Llanelli	30	13	8	9	35	26	47
Ton Pentre	30	13	6	11	43	40	45
Brecon Corinthians	30	13	4	13	49	42	43
Caerau	30	11	5	14	40	52	38
Cwmbran Town	30	10	4	16	40	50	34
Pontllanfraith	30	9	7	14	37	57	34
Pembroke Boro'	30	7	8	15	31	47	29
Ebbw Vale	30	4	3	23	25	88	15
Milford United	30	3	3	24	19	81	12

PREMIER DIVISION

	P	W	D	L	F	A	Pts
Sully	36	26	6	4	89	32	77*
Cardiff Corinthians	36	21	9	6	60	35	72
Port Talbot Athletic	36	20	11	5	69	33	71
Lake United	36	16	10	10	52	34	58
Newport YMCA	36	18	4	14	56	46	58
Merthyr Tydfil	36	17	6	13	75	56	57
BP (Llandarcy)	36	15	9	12	73	56	54
Morriston Town	36	15	9	12	58	47	54
S. Glamorgan Institute	36	14	8	14	75	68	50
Spencer Works	36	12	10	14	54	64	46
Ferndale Athletic	36	12	9	15	52	60	45
Ammanford Town	36	13	6	17	48	63	45
Tondu Robins	36	12	8	16	51	60	44
Abercynon Athletic	36	12	7	17	54	55	43
Pontardawe Athletic	36	11	7	18	34	59	40
Clydach United	36	12	4	20	41	68	40
Treharris Athletic	36	10	7	19	45	72	37
Taffs Well	36	10	6	20	54	70	36
Garw Athletic	36	6	4	26	38	100	22

*Denotes 7 points deducted.

DIVISION ONE

	P	W	D	L	F	A	Pts
Pontlottyn	36	28	3	5	99	36	87
Newport County	36	26	4	6	121	38	82
Blaenavon Blues	36	26	3	7	102	28	81
Afan Lido	36	20	8	8	76	41	68
Carmarthen Town	36	19	9	8	64	36	66
Tynte Rovers	36	19	6	11	77	54	63
Abergavenny Thursdays	36	18	4	14	73	49	58
Seven Sisters	36	15	7	14	65	56	52
Skewen Athletic	36	15	7	14	61	77	52
Tonyrefail Welfare	36	14	8	14	47	56	50
Ynysybwl	36	11	6	19	49	85	39
Aberaman	36	11	5	20	47	95	38
Panteg	36	9	9	18	40	46	36
Blaina West Side	36	9	9	18	39	66	36
Swansea University	36	10	6	20	42	71	36
Trelewis	36	9	7	20	53	75	34
Pontyclun	36	8	9	19	51	63	33
Lewistown	36	8	4	24	62	127	28
Tredomen Works	36	6	8	22	43	94	26

S.A. Brain Challenge Cup — Winners: Lake United. Runners-up. Ammanford Town. No. 33 — 83/84.

WELSH NATIONAL LEAGUE (CENTRAL WALES SECTION)

	P	W	D	L	F	A	Pts
Aberystwyth Town	28	21	6	1	85	20	48
Knighton Town	28	18	8	2	51	18	44
Caersws	28	20	3	5	87	35	43
Welshpool Town	28	17	5	6	68	35	39
Llanidloes Town	28	15	7	6	58	27	37
Newtown	28	14	8	6	67	38	36
Presteigne	28	12	5	11	51	54	29
Llandrindod	28	10	7	11	47	57	27
Rhayader	28	10	5	13	40	49	25
Brecon C	28	10	2	16	49	68	22
Penrhyncoch	28	10	1	17	49	81	21
Carno	28	5	4	19	34	67	14
Kington	28	4	6	18	31	66	13
U.C.W.	28	3	2	23	36	97	8

MONTGOMERY AMATEUR LEAGUE

DIVISION ONE

	P	W	D	L	F	A	Pts
Bettws	22	13	5	4	32	20	31
Llanfair	22	13	4	5	61	27	30
Llansanffraidd	22	14	2	6	49	23	30
Caersws R	22	13	4	5	53	32	30
Welshpool R	22	11	6	5	54	31	28
Berriew	22	10	7	5	39	24	27
Four Crosses	22	10	5	7	46	34	25
Waterloo Rovers	22	7	3	12	34	45	17
R & Q Sports	22	7	3	12	37	55	17
Llanfyllin	22	5	4	13	29	60	14
Guilsfield	22	3	3	16	20	57	9
Llangedwynn	22	3	0	19	30	77	6

DIVISION TWO

	P	W	D	L	F	A	Pts
Forden	22	17	2	3	67	18	36
Trewern	22	14	5	3	77	39	33
Llanwyddyn	22	14	4	5	74	32	32
Llanfechain	22	14	3	5	76	36	31
Abermule	22	13	4	5	66	35	30
Manafan	22	9	6	7	59	47	24
Llanfyllyn R	22	10	2	10	35	53	22
Welshpool Allian.	22	3	8	11	32	58	14
Kerry	22	4	4	14	34	68	12
Meifod	22	2	8	12	22	55	12
Llanrhaedr	22	4	4	14	34	68	12
Montgomery A	22	1	2	19	18	97	4

Welsh National League Champions: **Barry Town.** Photo: Mike Joss

Central Wales League Champions: **Aberystwyth Town.** Photo: Mike Joss

Cwmbran Town: *Welsh National League.* Photo: Mike Joss

Action in The Valleys as Cardiff Corinthians win 3-0 at Garw. Photo: Leo Hoenig

Bridgend on the attack and they won this game at Ebbw Vale 7-3. Photo: Mike Joss

Brendan Dowd scores Caerlon's first goal in their 2-0 win at Llanelli. Photo: Mike Joss

Craig Richards (No 10) scores Briton Ferry's first goal in their 2-1 home victory over Llanelli. Photo: Mike Joss

Ian Blythe Knighton's third goal in their 3-1 home win over Caldicot in the Welsh Intermediate Cup.
Photo: Mike Joss

Briton Ferry Athletic Photo: Mike Joss

The match that attracted 'The Loonies' Connam Quay Nomads take on Shrewsbury Town (the eventual winners) in The Welsh Cup. Photo: Peter Burrin

The home goalkeeper makes a fine penalty save in the Llanidloes v Rhyl Welsh Cup match which was drawn 0-0. Photo: Mike Joss

Brecon Corinthians. Photo: Mike Joss

LEAGUE OF IRELAND (EIRE)

FINAL TABLE 1983-84

	P	W	D	L	F	A	Pts
Shamrock Rovers	26	19	4	3	64	15	42
Bohemians	26	13	10	3	39	20	36
Athlone Town	26	15	4	7	44	28	34
Limerick City	26	13	7	6	38	26	33
Shelbourne	26	9	10	7	41	34	28
UCD	26	9	10	7	24	23	28
Dundalk	26	9	9	8	38	31	27
Waterford	26	10	6	10	34	34	26
Finn Harps	26	8	8	10	36	46	24
St Patrick's Ath	26	8	7	11	36	37	23
Drogheda Utd	26	10	2	14	37	54	22
Galway Utd	26	6	9	11	26	33	21
Home Farm	26	4	4	18	16	54	12
Sligo Rovers	26	2	4	20	20	58	8

EIRE Results 1983-84

FAI CUP FINAL
UCD 0
Shamrock Rovers 0

REPLAY
UCD 2 (Hanrahan, O'Doherty)
Shamrock Rangers 1 (McDonagh)

UCD: O'Neill, Lawlor, Moran, O'Doherty, Dunning, Gaffney, Murphy, Hanrahan, Cullen, Devlin, Dignam. *Shamrock Rovers:* Byrne, Whelan, McDonagh, Keely, King, Byrne, Steedman, Campbell, Buckley, Coady, Neville.

LEAGUE CUP FINAL
Drogheda Utd 3 (Dillon 2, Martin)
Athlone Town 1 (Collins)

SHIELD FINAL
Limerick City 1 (Hulmes)
UCD 1 (O'Doherty) aet
Limerick won 3-0 on penalties

IRISH LEAGUE (NORTHERN IRELAND)

FINAL TABLE 1983-84

	P	W	D	L	F	A	Pts
Linfield	26	22	1	3	76	23	45
Glentoran	26	18	6	2	65	19	42
Cliftonville	26	12	7	7	28	23	31
Ards	26	9	11	6	32	26	29
Coleraine	26	11	6	9	44	34	28
Ballymena	26	10	8	8	32	30	28
Glenavon	26	10	7	9	41	33	27
Crusaders	26	11	5	10	38	41	27
Distillery	26	11	4	11	35	42	26
Portadown	26	9	6	11	28	31	24
Newry Town	26	8	3	15	30	47	19
Bangor	26	4	6	16	24	57	14
Larne	26	7	1	18	25	58	13*
Carrick Rangers	26	3	3	20	24	57	9

* Two points were deducted from Larne for playing an ineligible player against Bangor.

NORTHERN IRELAND Results 1983-84

BASS IRISH CUP FINAL
Ballymena Utd 4 (Fox, Crockard, Harrison, Speak)
Carrick Rangers 1 (Fellowes)
Ballymena: Platt, McCreery, Fox, Harrison, Crockard, Burns, Sloan, Ring, Speak, Guy, Wright.
Carrick Rangers: Coburn, Fraser, Smyth, Blair, McCullough, Bowyer, Conville, Fellowes, Hardy, Thompson, Richardson.

HENNESSY GOLD CUP FINAL
Linfield 3 (Anderson 2, McGaughey)
Glentoran 1 (Blackledge)

MORANS ULSTER CUP FINAL
Glentoran 5 (Blackledge 4, McDowell o.g.)
Coleraine 2 (O'Kane, McCoy)

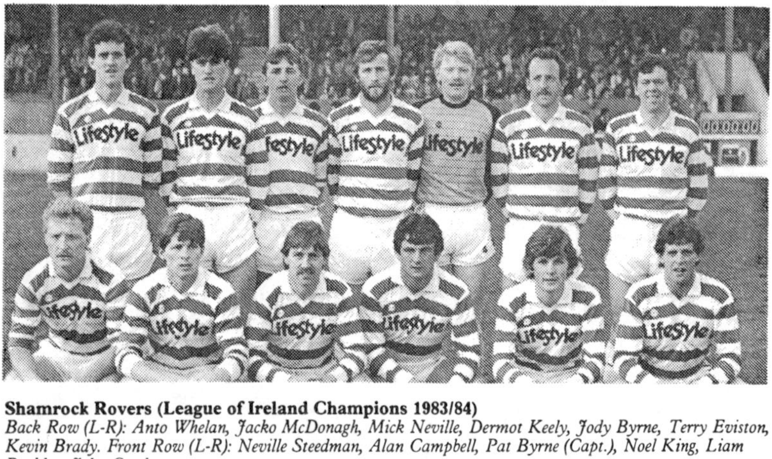

Shamrock Rovers (League of Ireland Champions 1983/84)
Back Row (L-R): Anto Whelan, Jacko McDonagh, Mick Neville, Dermot Keely, Jody Byrne, Terry Eviston, Kevin Brady. Front Row (L-R): Neville Steedman, Alan Campbell, Pat Byrne (Capt.), Noel King, Liam Buckley, John Coady.

SERVICES FOOTBALL

COMBINED SERVICES (KENTISH CUP)

British Armed Forces v. French Armed Forces at Aldershot on 25 Jan. 1984. (CSFA 1, French 0).

CSFA C Lomas (Army), M Bowen (Army), J Woodward (Army), D Dodds (RAF), J O'Connell (R Navy), D Wood (RAF), J Hancocks (RAF), G Torrance (Army), A Brown (Army), S Butler (Army), P White (Army), M Edwards (RAF), G Holland (R Navy), J Nesbitt (R Navy), N McGregor (Army), D Bragg (RAF).
French Osmond, Goussett, Sonor, Buisine, Lopez, Cobos, Spadiny, Colin, Philippe, Stefanini, Thomas, Morgante, Danio, Robert, Rousset.

British Armed Forces v. Belgian Armed Forces at Elsden on 6 Feb. 1984. (CSFA 2, Belgians 1).

CSFA Lomas, Bowen, O'Connell, Dodds, Woodward, Wood, Hancocks, Torrance, White, Butler, Brown, Edwards, Holland, Nesbitt, McGregor, Bragg.
Belgians de Wilde, Wegria, Verboven, Cloquet, Schoofs, Austen, Noe, Verspaille, van Genechten, Meeus, Claes, Hanouille, M'Buyu, Suply, Schoenaers, d'Hondt, Geldof, van Raamdonk.

This competition used to be competed for by the Army alone until 1980 when it went over to Combined Services. The last time the British Army won the Kentish Cup was in season 69/70 so this victory was the first British success for fourteen years.

The wonderful achievement of winning The Kentish Cup is celebrated by skipper Lance Corporal White (REME, Army). Phil scored one of the goals in the 2-1 victory over the Belgian forces, who like their French counterparts are full professionals.
Photo: Eric Marsh

Inter Services Championship.

Royal Navy	0	Royal Air Force	3
Royal Air Force	2	Army	0
Army	0	Royal Navy	2

Royal Air Force ...	2	2	0	0	5-0
Royal Navy	2	1	0	1	2-3
Army	2	0	0	2	0-5

FISHER ATHLETIC WIN TROPHIES IN ITALY

The Fisher Athletic successful first team squad. Photo: Derek Rowe

The Fisher trophies, 1983-84. Photo: Derek Rowe

Fisher Athletic won two cups in the Anglo Italian tournament by being the most successful English club and finishing third. Results were:

Francavilla	3	Fisher A	2
Teramo	2	Kings Lynn	1
	3rd place match		
Fisher A	3	Kings Lynn	0
	Final		
Francavilla	1	Teramo	0

CHANNEL ISLANDS FOOTBALL

ROTHMANS JERSEY FOOTBALL COMBINATION

DIVISION ONE

	P	W	D	L	F	A	Pts
First Tower Utd	16	13	2	1	45	9	41
St Paul's	16	9	4	3	44	26	31
Springfield	16	8	4	4	40	19	28
Jersey Scottish	16	7	3	6	27	20	24
St Peter	16	7	3	6	27	29	24
Wanderers	16	7	2	7	31	31	23
Beeches Old Boys	16	7	2	7	21	30	23
St Ouen	16	2	2	12	15	37	8
St Lawrence	16	1	0	15	10	59	3

ROTHMANS GUERNSEY PRIAULX LEAGUE

	P	W	D	L	F	A	Pts
Vale Rec	18	12	3	3	50	19	39
St Martin's	18	12	1	5	26	19	37
Rangers	18	7	6	5	30	20	27
Sylvans	18	7	5	6	30	30	26
North	18	7	4	7	35	28	25
Rovers	18	3	3	12	13	36	12
Belgraves	18	3	2	13	20	52	11

In the Channel Islands, the 1983-84 soccer season was dominated by Jersey who accomplished a clean sweep of the major inter-island trophies.

There was a sensational finish to the most important match of the season — the Muratti Cup final — which was played at Springfield in Jersey in May.

With less than 10 minutes of extra time to go and the score standing at 2-2, a replay in Guernsey three days later seemed inevitable.

But, at that point, Football League referee Trevor Spencer, of Salisbury, awarded Jersey a highly-controversial penalty. It was duly converted and, in the remaining minutes, substitute Peter Fleury, who had taken the field in the first half of the additional period, 'went mad' and scored the quickest hat-trick in the 79-year history of the competition.

The final score was 6-2 to Jersey but the Guernsey players and supporters were convinced they had been 'robbed' by the referee and that no penalty offence had, in fact, been committed.

Jersey had got away to a flying start with two goals in the first 11 minutes but Guernsey had fought back to equality by half time.

And the 'green-and-whites' just failed to win in the dying minutes of normal time when a post came to Jersey's rescue.

Jersey's victory means that the coveted trophy — known as the 'Vase' — has now been won 33 times by each island. Their new right-winger, Jerry Guest, won the man-of-the-match award.

In the semi-final, played in Alderney, Guernsey had overwhelmed the home island 6-0 with 18-year-old Mark Culverwell having celebrated his first cap with two of the goals.

Jersey also won the Upton Park and Wheway and Jeremie Cups — the Wheway and Jeremie trophies both being carried off by St Peter who beat fellow Jersey club St Paul's in the final of the former and Guernsey's St Martin's in that of the latter.

In the 'Upton', played at The Track in Guernsey, Jersey champions First Tower United beat Guernsey champions Vale Recreation 3-1 to win the trophy for the 10th time.

It was the second year running Tower had defeated the Rec. and the result represented Vale's third consecutive Upton defeat.

After Tower had taken an early lead, Vale equalised with a 'fluke' goal before half time — a halfway-line free-kick by their Daryl Tapp bouncing in the Tower goalmouth and shooting over the outrushing keeper into the top of the net — but Tower dominated the second half.

Tower had qualified for the match by winning the Jersey League by a 10-point margin; Vale having just managed to hold off an unexpected challenge from St Martin's to win the Guernsey league by two points only.

St Ouen and St Lawrence finished in the last two places in the Jersey League and thus were relegated. Playing in their places in the 1984-85 season will be St Clement and St John, the latter having acquired First Division status for the first time.

The quickest hat trick ever scored in a 'Muratti' was recorded this year by Peter Fleury. He had come on for the extra-time period as substitute and scored all his goals in the last ten minutes. Here he is seen scoring his first.
Photo: Guernsey Press

MURATTI CUP SEMI-FINAL (*Attendance:* 0,000)
Alderney 0 Guernsey 6 (Culverwell 2, Fallaize, Graham, C Le Tissier, Dyer) Referee: A Phillips (Jersey)
Alderney: D Oakman. P Burland, M Richardson, T Pasquire, H Aldcroft, W Bohan, P Concanen, D Mitchell, I MacFarlane, S Davies, S Parry. Subs: T Bohan and N Rose.
Guernsey: C Hamon, C Hargreaves, P Blondel, K Le Gallez, D Mahoney, L Graham, C Dyer, N Laine, M Culverwell, C Fallaize, C Le Tissier. Subs: D Tapp and D Martel.

MURATTI CUP FINAL (*Attendance:* 3,400)
Jersey 6 (Fleury 3, Pitman, Guest, Vincenti pen) **Guernsey 2** (Fallaize, Le Gallez) aet Referee: T Spencer (Salisbury)
Jersey: M Le Blancq, J Carney, W Richardson, P Duffy, G Westwood, D Corrigan, P Vincenti, P Carberry, J Guest, S Dewhurst, B Pitman. Subs: P Harzo and P Fleury.
Guernsey: C Hamon, C Hargreaves, P Blondel, D Mahoney, M Le Tissier, K Le Gallez, C Dyer, N Laine, L Graham, C Fallaize, C Le Tissier. Subs: A Bougourd and M Culverwell.

The victorious Jersey 'Muratti' squad with their new coach Jimmy Reeves (right). Photo: Barbara Pitman

Hampshire Senior Cup

Entering the Hampshire Senior Cup for the first time, Vale Rec. won through three rounds before being beaten 4-0 at home by Bass (Alton) at the quarter-final stage.

Vale had defeated Alton Town 2-1 at home; Pirelli General 3-0 away and Romsey Town 2-1 away.

A happy First Tower team celebrate after their 'Upton Park Trophy' victory over Guernsey League Champions Vale Recreation. Photo: Guernsey Press

UPTON PARK CUP (*Attendance:* 680)
Vale Rec 1 (Tapp) **First Tower United 3** (Petulla, Dewhurst, Murphy) Referee: N Midgley (Salford)
Vale Rec: C Hamon, C Hargreaves, D Tapp, M Le Tissier, D Blanchard, M Marley, C Dyer, L Graham, A Bougourd, P Blondel, C Le Tissier. Sub: N Laine.
First Tower: M Le Blancq, J Carney, B Birch, R Kearsey, G Westwood, J Murphy, R Crick, P Carberry, S Petulla, S Dewhurst, B Pitman.

CUP FINAL RESULTS
Wheway Cup: St Peter 4, St Paul's 1
Jeremie Cup: St Martin's 2, St Peter 4
Rothmans Le Riche Cup: First Tower 7, St Paul's 4
Stranger Cup: Vale Rec 4, Sylvans 1

GUERNSEY REPRESENTATIVE MATCHES
Guernsey 0. Royal Naval Air Command 2
Guernsey 0, Sunderland 9

Leading goalscorers
For the second season running, Carl Le Tissier (Vale Rec) was the leading scorer in Guernsey senior football, though his total dropped from 43 to 26. His brother Kevin (North) was second highest scorer with 21.

YOUTH INTER-INSULAR MATCHES
Guernsey Juniors 0, Jersey Juniors 0 (aet)
Jersey Schoolboys 0, Guernsey Schoolboys 3
'Pompey' Trophy: Jersey Wanderers Juniors 1, Guernsey Belgraves Juniors 2 (aet)

Guernsey conceded a hotly disputed penalty in extra time. Here Jersey's Peter Vincenti scores despite a superb effort by Guernsey goalkeeper Chris Hamon. Photo: Guernsey Press

ISLE OF MAN FOOTBALL

SEASON 1983/84

DIVISION ONE

		HOME					AWAY					
	P	W	D	L	F	A	W	D	L	F	A	Pts
Peel	20	9	1	0	44	8	8	1	1	41	16	36
Rushen U	20	7	3	0	35	9	7	2	1	34	10	33
DHSOB	20	4	3	3	22	19	6	1	3	22	16	24
Castletown	20	5	1	4	23	23	4	4	2	16	15	23
Ramsey	20	4	2	4	21	21	5	2	3	31	28	22
Gymnasium	20	5	1	4	25	24	5	1	4	22	20	22
St George's	20	4	3	3	26	23	5	0	5	21	22	21
Ayre U	20	4	2	4	16	21	2	1	7	16	30	15
Corinthians	20	2	1	7	16	38	2	3	5	18	29	12
Malew	20	2	1	7	16	28	0	2	8	12	35	7
St Mary's	20	0	1	9	13	33	1	2	7	14	36	5

BOWRING TYSON LEAGUE DIVISION TWO

		HOME					AWAY					
	P	W	D	L	F	A	W	D	L	F	A	Pts
Union Mills	22	10	0	1	48	19	9	1	1	37	15	39
Ronaldsway	22	8	0	3	37	18	8	0	3	37	17	32
RYCOB	22	8	0	3	34	20	5	1	5	25	30	27
Marown	22	5	2	4	27	25	6	2	3	38	20	26
Braddan	22	4	3	4	21	24	5	3	3	32	22	24
Colby	22	3	3	5	24	23	6	2	3	30	23	23
Pulrose	22	4	1	6	18	24	4	3	4	26	29	20
Onchan	22	3	4	4	25	36	3	3	5	27	32	19
Laxey	22	2	5	4	25	28	3	3	5	19	24	18
Michael U	22	4	0	7	23	36	3	2	6	23	31	16
St John's U	22	2	3	6	31	37	3	2	6	23	26	15
Pot Black	22	2	1	8	16	43	0	0	11	16	60	5

EASTER FESTIVAL: CROXETH 2, ALLERTON 2
(Croxeth won 4-2 on penalties)

JUNIOR INTERNATIONAL:
ISLAND UNDER 21 2, DUBLIN CIVIL SERVICE 2

SENIOR INTERNATIONAL:
ISLAND XI 1, MANCHESTER UTD RESERVES 2

LEADING SCORERS

MYLCHREESTS
DIVISION ONE

24 — Neil Shimmin (Rushen), 19 — David Craine (Peel), 18 — Chris Bass (DHSOB), Alan Gawne (Gymns) 15 — Andrew Hudgeon (Ramsey), Kevin Middleton (Peel), Paul Quayle (St George's), 14 — Karl Clare (Rushen)

DIVISION TWO

34 — David Cannell (Union Mills), 24 — Paul Beattie (Ronaldsway), 19 — Tony Edmonds (Oncham), 16 — Tony McMullin (St John's), 15 — Roger Chadwick (St John's), 14 — Ian Aire (Marown), Quentin Kelly (Braddan), Stef McKay (Pulrose)

LEADING SCORERS IN ALL COMPETITIONS

DIVISION ONE

	LGE	Rail Cup	F.A. Cup	Hosp. Cup	Total
Chris Bass (DHSOB)	18	—	8	9	35
Neil Shimmin (Rushen)	24	—	—	3	27
David Craine (Peel)	19	—	1	1	21
Alan Gawne (Gymns)	18	1	2	—	21
Andrew Hudgeon (Ramsey)	15	—	—	5	20

DIVISION TWO

	LGE	Woods Cup	F.A. Cup	Hosp. Cup	Total
David Cannell (U. Mills)	34	—	—	1	35
Paul Beattie (Ronaldsway)	24	2	—	4	30
Roger Chadwick (St John's)	15	6	—	1	22
Tony Edmonds (Oncham)	19	—	1	1	21
Ian Aire (Marown)	14	3	1	2	20

CUP WINNERS 1983-84

RAILWAY CUP: RUSHEN 1, DHSOB 0

WOODS CUP: ST JOHN'S 2, COLBY 1 (after 1-1)

OFFICE EQUIPMENT F.A. CUP:
PEEL 1, DHSOB 0

IND COOPE HOSPITAL CUP:
DHSOB 3, RUSHEN 2

IOM STEAM PACKET JUNIOR CUP:
RUSHEN 5, CASTLETOWN 0

COWELL CUP: GYMNASIUM 6, PEEL 1

OTHER AFFILIATED ASSOCIATIONS

	Secretary	Address	Tel. No.
Cambridge University	Dr. S.C. Aston	22 Topcliffe Way, Cambridge CB1 4SH	
English Schools	A. Rice	4a Eastgate Street, Stafford ST16 2NN	(0785) 51142 (B)
Guernsey	G.R. Skuse	Ar-Hyd-Y-Nos, Courtil Ollivier Castel, Guernsey, CI	(0481) 56719 (H) (0481) 26241 (B)
Isle of Man	Mrs J.F. Shaw	120 Bucks Road, Douglas, Isle of Man	(0624) 6349
Jersey	B. Ahier	Sunbrayton, Route Orange, St Brelade, Jersey, CI	
Oxford University			

COUNTY DIRECTORY 1983-84

County	Secretary	Address	Tel. No.
AFA	W.P. Gross	Room 33, 6 Langley Street, London WC2H 9JA	01-638 0923 (H) 01-240 3837/8 (B) — county office
Army	Major A Dobson MBE	Army F.A. ASCB MOD, Clayton Barracks, Aldershot, Hants GU11 2BG	(0252) 24431 (B) x2571
Bedfordshire	R.G. Berridge	The Limes, 14 Bedford Road, Sandy, Beds SG19 1EL	(0767) 80417 (H)
Berks & Bucks	W.J. Gosling	County Office, 15a London Street, Faringdon, Oxon SN7 8AG.	(0367) 22099 (B) — county office
Birmingham	M. Pennick	County Office, Ray Hall Lane, Great Barr, Birmingham B43 6JE.	021-357 4278/9/0 (B) — county office
Cambridgeshire	R.E. Rogers	20 Aingers Road, Histon, Cambs. CB4 4JP	(022 023) 2803 (H) (0223) 358977 x266 (B)
Cheshire	A. Collins	50 Ash Grove, Timperley, Altrintham, WA15 6UX	061-980 4706 (H)
Cornwall	F.H. Malone	59 Bosmeor Park, Illogan, Redruth, Cornwall TR15 3JN	(0209) 214979 (H)
Cumberland	R Johnson	72 Victoria Road, Workington, Cumbria, CA14 2QT	(0900) 3979 (H) — county office
Derbyshire	H.L.P. Homes	82 Friar Gate, Derby, DE1 1FL	(0332) 769835 (H) (0332) 361422 (B) — county office
Devon	C.H. Norsworthy, DSM, BEM	8 Belair Road, Peverell, Plymouth, Devon PL2 3QH	(0752) 773550 (H) — county office
Dorset	P.S. Hough	110 Dorchester Road, Oakdale, Poole, Dorset. BH15 3SD	(0202) 746244 (H) — county office
Durham	J.R. Walsh	'Codeslaw', Ferens Park, Durham, DH1 1JZ	(0385) 486563 (B) — county office
East Riding	C. Branton	83 Belvedere Road, Hessle, N. Humberside, HU13 9JH	(0482) 649294 (H) (0482) 27065 x245 (B)
Essex	M.S. Jeffers	54a Eastwood Road, Goodmayes, Ilford, Essex, IG3 8XA	01-590 7893 (H)
Gloucestershire	E.J. Marsh	46 Douglas Road, Horfield, Bristol, BS7 0JD	(0272) 519435 (H)
Hampshire	R.G. Barnes, JP	367 Winchester Road, Ashwood Gardens, Southampton, Hants. SO9 2UA	(0703) 766884/766561 — county office
Herefordshire	E.R. Prescott	7 Kirkland Close, Hampton Park, Hereford, HR1 1XP	(0432) 51134 (H) (0432) 761555 x264
Hertfordshire	G.W. Daulby, DFC	158 Hazelwood Drive, St Albans, Herts. AL4 0UZ	(0727) 52601 (H&B)
Huntingdonshire	M.M. Armstrong	1 Chapel End, Great Gidding, Huntingdon, Cambs. PE17 5NP	(083 23) 262 (H) (0733) 240215 (B)
Kent	K.T. Masters	69 Maidstone Road, Chatham, Kent, ME4 6DT	(0634) 43824 (B) — county office
Lancashire	J. Kenyon	31a Wellington Street, St Johns, Blackburn, BB1 8AU	(0254) 46201 (H) (0254) 64333/4 (B) — county office
Leics. & Rutland	R. Barston	Holmes Park, Dog & Gun Lane, Whetstone, Leics LE8 3LJ	(0533) 880312 (H) (0533) 867828 (B) — county office
Lincolnshire	F.S. Richardson	PO Box 26, 12 Dean Road, Lincoln, LN2 4DP	(0522) 26788 (H) (0522) 24917 (B) — county office
Liverpool	S.A. Rudd	23 Greenfield Road, Liverpool L13 3BN	051-526-9515 (H) 051-220-6089 (B) — county office
London	A.F. Monger	4 Aldworth Grove, London SE13	01-690 9626 (B) — county office
Manchester	S. Holliday	87 Hart Road, Fallowfield, Manchester, MI4 7AE	061-224-5185 (H) 061-224-2804 (B)
Middlesex	S. Bowen	25 Melthorne Drive, South Ruislip, Middlesex HA4 0TS	01-845 1629 (H) 01-200 2147 (B)
Norfolk	Ray Kiddell, JP	39 Beaumont Road, Costessey, Norwich, NR5 0HG	(0603) 742421 (H) (0603) 20316 (B)
Northamptonshire	B. Walden	County Office, 37 Harding Terrace, Northampton	(0536) 81451 (H) (0604) 39584 (B) — county office
North Riding	P. Kirby	284 Linthorpe Road, Middlesbrough, Cleveland TS1 3QU	(0642) 818767 (H) (0642) 224585 (B) — county office

COUNTY DIRECTORY 1983-84

County	Secretary	Address	Tel. No.
Northumberland	J.A. Forster	30 St Marys Place, Newcastle-u-Tyne, NE1 7PG	(091) 4132680 (H) (0632) 610779 (B) — county office
Nottinghamshire	W.T. Annable	7 Clarendon Street, Nottingham NG1 5HS	(0602) 874200 (H) (0602) 418954 — county office
Oxfordshire	P.J. Ladbrook	3 Wilkins Road, Cowley, Oxford, OX4 2HY	(0865) 775432 (H) (0865) 726249 (B)
RAF	Sqn.Ldr. A.V. Heron, RAF	24 Chiltern Close, Princes Risborough, Bucks HP17 0EA	(0844) 4875 (H) (0494) 26200 x2153 (B)
Royal Navy	Lt.Cdr. H.A. Sheppard, RN	HMS Temeraine, Portsmouth, Hants PO1 3HH	(0705) 812967 (H) (0705) 822351 x22671 (B) — county office
Sheffield & Hallamshire	G. Thompson	'Clegg House', 253 Pitsmoor Road, Sheffield S3 9AQ	(0742) 27817 (B) — county office
Shropshire	A.W. Brett	10-11 High Street, Shrewsbury, Shrops. SY1 1SG	(0743) 56066 (H) (0743) 62769 — county office
Somerset & Avon (South)	L.G. Webb	32 North Road, Midsomer Norton, Bath, Avon. BA3 2QQ	(0761) 413716 (H) — county office
Staffordshire	T. Myatt	County Office, 2 Miller Street, Newcastle, Staffs. ST5 1HB	(0782) 312372 (H) (0782) 622585 (B) — county office
Suffolk	B.A.H. Collings	15 Taunton Close, Henley Rise, Ipswich, Suffolk. IP1 6SX	(0473) 43666 (H)
Surrey	L.F.J. Smith	2 Fairfield Avenue, Horley, Surrey. RH6 7PD	(02934) 4945 (H) (0372) 373543 (B) — county office
Sussex	R.F. Reeve	County Office, Culver Road, Lancing, Sussex. BN15 9AX	(0903) 753545 (B) — county office
Westmorland	J.R. Plumbe	24 Crescent Green, Kendal, Cumbria. LA9 6DR	(0539) 23227 (H) — county office
West Riding	R.M. Robin	77 Great George Street, Leeds. LS1 3BR	(0532) 452444 (B) — county office
Wiltshire	F.J. Peart	161 Grange Drive, Stratton St Margaret, Swindon Wilts. SN3 4JY	(0793) 822239 (H) — county office
Worcestershire	P. Rushton	84 Windermere Drive, Warndon, Worcester. WR4 9JB	(0905) 51166 (H) (0905) 612336/7 (B)

A.F.A. CLUBS BEST F.A. VASE PERFORMANCES

Club	League	Round	Season	Clubs Defeated	Eliminating Club
EAST BARNET O.G.	S.A.L.	1st Rd	1975-76		Harefield U. (A) 1-4
KEW ASSOCIATION	S.A.L.	3rd Rd	1976-77	Fleet Town (A) 2-0, Uxbridge (A) 1-0	Molesey (H) 0-2
MIDLAND BANK	S.A.L.	1st Rd R	1983-84	Eastbourne U (A) 5-1	Southwick (A) 1-1, (H) 2-4
NORSEMEN	S.A.L.	3rd Rd	1982-83	Haringey Borough (H) 0-0 (A) 4-0 Kempston Rovers (A) 2-1	Brantham (H) 0-2
OLD ALOYSIANS	O.B.L.	1st Rd	1976-77		Alma Swanley (H) 0-5
OLD ESTHAMIANS	S.A.L.	1st Rd	1979-80 1981-82	Crown Manor (A) 4-3	Tiptree U. (H) 0-3
OLD SALESIANS	O.B.L.	1st Rd	1975-76 1981-82 1982-83	Royal Arsenal Sports (A) 1-0 1975-76	Feltham (H) 1-3 1975-76
OLD SUTTONIANS	O.B.L.	Prelim Rd	1977-78		
WEST WICKHAM	S.A.L.	3rd Rd	1978-79	Darenth Heathside (A) 2-0 Tansley (H) 2-0 Redhill (A) 2-0	Farnborough T (H) 2-2 aet 2-3 (A)
CIVIL SERVICE	S.A.L.	2nd Rd	1976-77	Chobham (A) 4-3	Camberley (A) 1-3
TANSLEY	N.A.L.	1st Rd	1978-79	Stotfold (H) 2-1	West Whickham (A) 0-2

S.A.L. = Southern Amateur League. OBL = Old Boys League. N.A.L. = Nemean Amateur League.

AFA SENIOR CUP

FIRST QUALIFYING ROUND

Latymer OB.	3	Chertsey O. Salesians	1
Mill Hill Village	2	Cuaco	1
London Airways	0	O. Parkonians	6
Ulysses	6	O. Carthusians	1
Parkfield	6	Wood Green O.B.	2
O. Brentwoods	2	O. Bealonians	2 aet
O. Plaistovians	0	O. Salvatorians	6
Royal Bank of Scotland	2	St Mary's College	1
Economicals	1	Lloyds Bank	7
O. Meadonians	1	O. Grammarians	0
Temple Bar	1	O. Uxonians	3
Duncombe Sports	0	O. Tollingtonians	2
Civil Service	1	O. Cholmeleians	0
O. Aldenhamians	2	O. Westminsters	1
O. Manorians	0	O. Monovians	3
Wandsworth Borough	2	O. Chigwellians	3
Ol. Hamptonians	1	Catford Wanderers	3
Alexandra Park	2	O. Reptonians	1
Hampstead Heathens	3	City of London Poly	1
Inland Revenue	0	O. Elizabethans	6

FIRST QUALIFYING ROUND REPLAY

Old Bealonians	3	Old Brentwoods	1

SECOND QUALIFYING ROUND

Williams & Glyns	2	Old Elizabethans	1
Mill Hill Village	2	Kew Association	1
Merton	2	Old Westhamians	3
Wake Green	3	Fulham Co O.B.	0
Old Stationers	5	Old Salvatorians	0
Old Fincunians	3	Tansley	0
Old Camdenians	1	Old Owens	4
Phoenicians	2	Lloyds Bank	5
Reigate Priory	3	G.W.R.	1
Old Tollingtonians	1	Old Bealonians	3
Old Greenfordians	3	Hampstead Heathens	0
Old Parmiterians	8	Old Foresters	3
Polytechnic	6	Mayfield Athletic	0
Parkfield	3	Old Isleworthians	1
Ibis	1	John Fisher O.B.	3
Old Tiffinians	—	Catford Wanderers	—
Old Woodhouseians	0	Old Paludians	1
Old Aloysians	3	Old Malvernians	2 aet
Old Salesians	6	Old Kingsburians	1
Crouch End Vampires	0	Centymca	1
Old Minchendenians	2	Hale End Athletic	3
Old Sinjuns	1	Witan	2
Orange Hill O.B.	2	Old Wokingians	1 aet
Old Uxonians	0	Pearl Assurance	5
Old Latymerians	4	Old Monovians	0
Old Actonians	4	Royal Bank of Scotland	2
Old Colfeians	1	Old Parkonians	2
Old Aldenhamians	0	Lancing O.B.	2
Southgate Olympic			Walkover
Old Suttonians	2	Nat. West. Bank	0
British Petroleum	1	Old Westminster Citz	4
Garflac	0	Alleyn O.B.	7
Derbyshire Amateurs			Walkover
Cardinal Manning O.B.	2	Lensbury	2 aet
Bourneside Sports	0	Latymer O.B.	2
Broomfield	2	Barclays Bank	2 aet
Brentham	7	Old Addeyans	2
Old Buckwellians	3	Old Edmontonians	0
Ulysses	1	Ealing Association	6
Patcham	1	Civil Service	2
Shene O.G.	0	Winchmore Hill	2
Albanian	0	Old Esthameians	1
Glynn O.B.	3	Old Tenisonians	1
Old Hendonians	4	Alexandra Park	2
Old Elysians	2	Old Chigwellians	3
Old Offingtonians	3	Old Wilsonians	2
Leyton Co O.B.	3	London Welsh	0
Old Meadonians	5	Southgate County	0

SECOND QUALIFYING ROUND REPLAYS

Barclays Bank	0	Broomfield	4
Old Tiffinians	0	Catford Wanderers	1

FIRST ROUND

Old Parmiterians	0	Broomfield	1
Hale End	0	Nottinghamshire	3
Enfield O.G.	6	Old Meadonians	1
Old Salesians	1	Parkfield	1 aet
Leyton Co. O.B.	2	Pearl Assurance	8
Old Owens	1	Norsemen	3
Latymer O.B.	0	Old Paludians	2
Old Esthameians	4	Wake Green	0
East Barnet O.G.	1	Old Lyonians	0
Mill Hill Village	2	Old Fairlopians	1
Derbyshire Amateurs	4	Ealing Association	4 aet
Southgate Olympic	3	Old Actonians	2
Alleyn O.B.	2	Old Westhamians	0
Old Hendonians	2	Carshalton	5
Old Chigwellians	1	Witan	3
Old Parkonians	1	Lloyds Bank	0
Brentham	2	Bank of England	1
Corinthians	4	Centymca	2
Glyn O.B.	1	Old Bromleians	2
South Bank Poly	2	Winchmore Hill	2 aet
John Fisher O.B.	1	O. West. Citizens	2
Old Buckwellians	2	Old Fincunians	3
Polytechnic	1	Old Aloysians	1
Old Stationers	5	Old Latymerians	1
Catford Wanderers	3	Reigate Priory	0
Old Finchleians	7	Old Uffingtonians	2
West Wickham	3	Old Vaughanians	1
Old Bealonians	2	Cardinal Manning O.B.	3
Orange Hill O.B.	0	William & Glyns Bank	2
Civil Service	1	Old Suttonians	2
Old Greenfordians	0	Midland Bank	6
Lancing O.B.	3	Old Ignatians	0

FIRST ROUND REPLAYS

Parkfield	1	Old Salesians	2
Ealians Assn.	3	Derbyshire Amateurs	4
Polytechnic	1	Old Aloysians	3
Winchmore Hill	2	South Bank Poly	5

SECOND ROUND

Derbyshire Amts	1	Enfield O.G.	3
Old Suttonians	2	Catford Wanderers	0
Norsemen	2	Carshalton	1
Corinthian	3	Alleyn O.B.	4
South Bank Poly	0	Old Parkonians	3
Broomfield	3	Lancing O.B.	3 aet
East Barnet O.G.	4	Mill Hill Village	1
Williams & Glyns	2	Old Paludians	0
Nottinghamshire	2	Old Finchleians	3 aet
Old Aloysians	4	Old Stationers	0
Midland Bank	3	Cardinal Manning	0
West Wickham	3	Brentham	2 aet
Pearl Assurance	1	Old Westminster Citz.	0
Witan	1	Old Bromleians	2
Old Fincunians	4	Southgate Olympic	1
Old Salesians	0	Old Esthameians	3

REPLAY

Lancing O.B.	6	Broomfield	0

THIRD ROUND

Pearl Assurance	3	Old Finchleians	4 aet
Alleyn O.B.	3	Old Suttonians	1 aet
Lancing O.B.	0	Old Aloysians	1
Williams & Glyns	0	Norsemen	2
Old Bromleians	2	Old Parkonians	0
Old Esthameians	1	West Wickham	1 aet
East Barnet O.G.	1	Midland Bank	3
Enfield O.G.	1	Old Fincunians	1 aet

REPLAYS

West Wickham	3	Old Esthameians	4 aet
Old Fincunians	2	Enfield O.G.	1 aet

SEMI FINALS

Old Esthameians	2	Norsemen	1
Midland Bank	0	Old Aloysians	2

FINAL

Old Esthameians	2	Old Aloysians	0

AFA Representative XI
Back Row (L-R): J Wilson (Secretary), G Shaw (Norseman), D O'Grady (O Ignatians), S Norris (West Wickham), K Francis (Brentham), M Walker (Midland Bank), I Broadbridge (O Esthamians), P Rees (Norton Rose), M Perks (Chairman). Front Row (L-R): A Howe (O Fairlopians), C Scott (O Fincunians), R Gonzales (O Bromleians), P Mitchell (O Parmiterians), D Malone (Kew Association), R Horner (O Esthamians).

CUP COMPETITION FINALS

SENIOR			
Old Esthameians	2	Old Aloysians	0
ESSEX SENIOR			
Old Fairlopians	1	Corinthian	0
MIDDLESEX SENIOR			
Old Aloysians	2	E.Barnet O.Grammarians	1
SURREY SENIOR			
Old Bromleians	1	British Petroleum	0
AUTHUR DUNN			
Lancing Old Boys	2	Old Carthusians	0
INTERMEDIATE			
Nat. West. Bank 2nd	2*	Bromfield 2nd	0*
ESSEX INTERMEDIATE			
Old Chigwellians 2nd	2	Old Monovians 2nd	1
KENT INTERMEDIATE			
Old Bromleians 2nd	2*,3	Coutts Bank	2*,0
MIDDLESEX INTERMEDIATE			
Winchmore Hill 2nd	1	Old Hamptonians 2nd	0
SURREY INTERMEDIATE			
Kew Association 2nd	0*,3	Nat. West. Bank 2nd	0*,1
JUNIOR			
Crouch End Vampires 3rd	2	Old Stationers 3rd	0
MINOR			
Old Wokingians 4th	4	Old Bealonians 4th	3
SENIOR NOVETS			
Polytechnic 5th	2*	South Bank Poly 5th	1*
JUNIOR NOVETS			
Nat. West. Bank "D"	3	Carshalton 6th	1
VETERANS'			
Corinthian-Casuals	2*,2	Old Salvatorians	2*,0

* After extra time

REPRESENTATIVE MATCHES

RESULTS 1983-84

v	The Army	Won	2-1
v	Oxford University	Won	6-2
v	Cambridge University	Draw	2-2
v	Kent F.A.	Lost	1-2
v	Royal Air Force	Draw	1-1
v	London University	Won	3-0
v	Sussex F.A.	Lost	2-3
v	New England Universities	Won	3-0
v	Royal Navy	Won	4-0
v	Football Association XI		cancelled

PLAYERS GAINING REPRESENTATIVE TIES

J. Bayer (Norsemen)
P. Rees (Norton Rose)
K. Fincunane (Lovell White & King)
G. Shaw (Norsemen)

REPRESENTATIVE MATCHES

LONDON BANKS

(H)	v	Old Boys' League	Lost	2-3
(H)	v	L.U. "Sidonians"	Draw	0-0
(H)	v	S. Olympians League	Lost	1-4
(H)	v	Nemean League	Won	3-1
(A)	v	Insurance Offices F.A.	Won	1-0

UNITED BANKS

(H)	v	Stock Exchange	Won	3-1
(H)	v	London University	Lost	3-4
(A)	v	Royal Marines	Draw	1-1
(A)	v	Stock Exchange	Lost	1-3

THE 100TH UNIVERSITY MATCH

Oxford University **2** (1) **Cambridge University** **2** (1)
Varty, Husselbee Aspinall 2

After 100 games, Cambridge University have won 41, Oxford 37 with 22 drawn.
Andy Husselbee's goal was his fifth in three Wembley appearances.
Teams as below:*

***Oxford** K Rutledge (St Cuthberts, Newcastle & Wadham), N Metaxa (Eton & Wadham), S Craft (Westminster & St Anne's), L Barrass (Harrogate Granby Comp & Lincoln), A Huse (Bishop Luffa C of E Comp, Chichester & Lincoln), R Edbrooke (Queen Elizabeth's Hospital Bristol & Hertford), C Grant (Barton Peveril Coll. Eastleigh & Queen's), R Smyth (Bilborough Coll. Nottingham & St Edmunds Hall), K Varty (Trinity Hall, Leamington Spa & Hertford), A Husselbee (Wolverhampton GS & St John's), S Zneimer (British School of Brussels & Queen's).

Cambridge M D Potts (Haberdashers' Aske's Elstree & Queens'), A J Pollock (Shrewsbury & Trinity), W J Rentoul (Wolverhampton GS & King's), J C Ironside (St Edmunds, Canterbury & Trinity Hall), D W Hudson (Handsworth GS & Trinity Hall), A P Marshall (Queen Elizabeth GS, Gainsborough & St Catherine's), G D Harper (Abingdon & St John's), A A Whyte (Wolverhampton GS & Trinity Hall), C Aspinwall (Hutton GS, Preston & Homerton), G J Walsh (Barrow 6th Form Coll & Trinity Hall), J N Cook (King Edwards GS, Chelmsford & Homerton), Subs: T C Knight (Batley GS & St Catherine's), C Evans (Wolverhampton GS & Fitzwilliam).

Record to date: Cambridge 41; Oxford 37; Draws 22.

SOUTHERN AMATEUR LEAGUE

SENIOR SECTION

DIVISON ONE

	P	W	D	L	F	A	Pts
Winchmore Hill	22	12	7	3	46	28	31
South Bank Poly	22	11	5	6	52	29	27
Norsemen	22	10	7	5	27	25	27
West Wickham	22	10	6	6	32	24	26
Midland Bank	22	10	5	7	37	28	25
Old Esthameians	22	11	3	8	37	31	25
Crouch End Vampires	22	8	6	8	29	39	22
Nat West Bank	22	6	7	9	31	35	19
East Barnet Old Gramm	22	6	7	9	32	37	19
Lensbury	22	6	7	9	22	33	19
Old Bromleians	22	5	6	11	15	33	16
Kew Association	22	1	6	15	21	59	8

Division Two

	P	W	D	L	F	A	Pts
Old Stationers	22	13	7	2	50	17	33
Carshalton	22	14	2	6	44	19	30
Old Parkonians	22	12	5	5	41	21	29
Civil Service	22	12	2	8	45	31	26
Polytechnic	22	7	10	5	24	21	24
Alleyn Old Boys	22	10	3	9	25	31	23
Old Westminster Citizens	22	8	5	9	26	28	21
Lloyds Bank	22	6	9	7	30	38	21
Southgate Olympic	22	4	10	8	36	44	18
Old Lyonians	22	5	8	9	23	31	18
Barclays Bank	22	6	5	11	27	35	17
British Petroleum	22	0	4	18	18	73	4

Division Three

	P	W	D	L	F	A	Pts
Old Salesians	22	16	3	3	69	22	35
Brentham	22	15	5	2	53	13	35
Pearl Assurance	22	15	2	5	55	29	32
Old Actonians Assoc	22	13	2	7	53	36	28
Bank of England	22	11	2	9	50	34	24
Reigate Priory	22	10	1	11	50	37	21
Cuaco	22	8	3	11	25	45	19
Broomfield	22	7	3	12	42	53	17
Merton	22	7	3	12	27	52	17
Old Latymerians	22	5	6	11	30	45	16
Alexandra Park	22	6	2	14	27	46	14
Ibis	22	2	2	18	18	87	6

MIDLAND AMATEUR ALLIANCE

DIVISION ONE

	P	W	D	L	F	A	Pts
Wollaton	22	15	4	3	51	22	34
Peoples College	22	14	4	4	55	23	32
Old Elizabethans	22	11	6	5	53	32	28
Nottinghamshire	22	12	4	6	46	35	28
Derbyshire Amateurs	22	5	11	6	30	33	21
Chilwell	22	7	6	9	35	34	20
Wilford	22	7	5	10	39	41	19
Brunts Old Boys	22	6	7	9	36	53	19
Sherwood Amateurs	22	7	4	11	27	38	18
Heanor Amateurs	22	7	4	11	38	55	18
Mapperley Park	22	6	4	12	38	58	16
Woodthorpe	22	3	5	14	34	58	11

DIVISION TWO

	P	W	D	L	F	A	Pts
Wollaton 2nd	20	13	3	4	62	30	29
Hall Park	20	13	1	6	63	40	27
Magdala Amateurs	20	10	6	4	42	24	26
Old Elizabethans 2nd	20	10	6	4	47	33	26
Lady Bay	20	10	3	7	43	37	23
Old Bemrosians	20	9	2	9	50	52	20
Nottinghamshire 2nd	20	9	1	10	39	43	19
Chesterfield Ramblers	20	6	5	9	39	58	17
Kingswood	20	6	3	11	40	48	15
Derbyshire Amateurs 2nd	20	6	1	13	30	51	13
Civil Service	20	2	1	17	30	69	5

DIVISION THREE

	P	W	D	L	F	A	Pts
Peoples College 2nd	22	11	7	4	58	26	29
Beeston O.B.A.	22	13	3	6	61	37	29
Wilford 2nd	22	14	1	7	49	28	29
Magdala Amateurs 2nd	22	12	5	5	61	43	29
Brunt's Old Boys 2nd	22	11	2	9	71	47	24
Heanor Amateurs 2nd	22	9	6	7	50	43	24
Old Elizabethans 3rd	22	10	3	9	29	45	23
W. Bridgford Casuals	22	11	1	10	60	61	23
Nottinghamshire 3rd	22	8	3	11	48	50	19
Sherwood Amateurs 2nd	22	5	6	11	45	54	16
Hall Park	22	6	2	14	48	81	14
Ilkeston Electric	22	2	1	19	20	115	5

DIVISION FOUR

	P	W	D	L	F	A	Pts
Charnos	22	15	4	3	74	19	34
Bassingfield	22	15	3	4	76	36	33
Old Mundellians	22	15	3	4	79	46	33
F.C. Toton	22	14	2	6	66	47	30
Derbyshire Amateurs 3rd	22	12	4	6	61	50	28
Chilwell 2nd	22	11	2	9	52	45	24
Mapperley Park 2nd	22	7	3	12	39	58	17
Old Bemrosians 2nd	22	6	4	12	48	66	16
County NALGO	22	5	4	13	49	63	14
Woodthorpe 2nd	22	5	4	13	41	62	14
W. Bridgford Casuals 2nd	22	4	6	12	50	76	14
Civil Service 2nd	22	2	3	17	22	89	7

DIVISION FIVE

	P	W	D	L	F	A	Pts
Lady Bay 2nd	20	13	3	4	55	32	29
Wollaton 2nd	20	13	2	5	62	25	28
Magdala Amateurs 3rd	20	12	2	6	45	24	26
Nottingham Spartan	20	11	1	8	56	34	23
Sherwood Amateurs 3rd	20	10	1	9	44	45	21
Charnos 2nd	20	8	4	8	55	44	20
Brunt's Old Boys 3rd	20	9	2	9	44	43	20
Kingswood 2nd	20	8	1	11	37	47	17
Old Bemrosians 3rd	20	7	2	11	36	67	16
Beestopn O.B.A. 2nd	20	5	2	13	32	65	12
Bassingfield 2nd	20	3	2	15	26	66	8

H.B. Poole Trophy — Nottinghamshire
Challenge Trophy — Peoples College
Senior Cup — Peoples College
Intermediate Cup — Nottinghamshire 2nd
Minor Cup — Old Elizabethans 3rd
Senior Supplementary — Wollaton 2nd
Junior Supplementary Cup — Wollaton 3rd

NEMEAN LEAGUE

DIVISION ONE

	P	W	D	L	F	A	Pts
Albanian	20	16	0	4	55	34	32
Old Isleworthians	20	12	2	6	52	35	26
Parkfield	20	11	3	6	48	34	25
Old Hendonians	20	10	4	6	48	52	24
Ealing Association	20	11	1	8	60	43	23
Tansley	20	7	7	6	35	30	21
Old Hamptonians	20	6	6	8	41	47	18
Hampstead Heathens	20	4	9	7	34	39	17
Old Greenfordians	20	6	4	10	39	38	16
Old Tiffinians	20	3	5	12	37	50	11
Economicals	20	2	3	15	23	70	7

DIVISION TWO

	P	W	D	L	F	A	Pts
Wood Green Old Boys	20	13	5	2	62	29	31
Albanian 2nd	20	13	3	4	51	34	29
Hale End Athletic	20	13	1	6	57	27	27
Old Greenfordians 2nd	20	10	5	5	46	27	25
Parkfield 2nd	20	10	0	10	49	41	20
Old Hamptonians 2nd	20	9	2	9	30	23	20
Old Isleworthians 2nd	20	9	1	10	33	41	19
Tansley 2nd	20	7	4	9	41	50	18
Duncombe Sports	20	6	2	12	27	60	14
London Airways	20	3	4	13	29	47	10
Ealing Association 2nd	20	2	3	15	22	68	7

DIVISION THREE

	P	W	D	L	F	A	Pts
Old Elysians	20	16	3	1	79	24	35
Economicals 2nd	20	11	5	4	56	35	27
Old Greenfordians 3rd	20	11	3	6	58	41	25
Parkfield 3rd	20	10	3	7	45	44	23
Wood Green Old Boys 2nd	20	8	5	7	59	53	21
Old Hendonians 2nd	20	8	4	8	49	40	20
Hale End Athletic 2nd	20	8	2	10	38	44	18
Old Tiffinians 2nd	20	7	4	9	35	42	18
Albanian 3rd	20	5	5	10	44	54	15
Hampstead Heathens 2nd	20	4	4	12	36	57	12
Ulysses 3rd	20	2	2	16	23	88	6

DIVISION FOUR

	P	W	D	L	F	A	Pts
Old Isleworthians 3rd	22	18	3	1	72	20	39
Albanian 4th	22	17	4	1	73	32	38
Old Hamptonians 3rd	22	12	3	7	62	37	27
Old Elysians 2nd	22	9	5	8	44	51	23
Tansley 3rd	22	9	4	9	47	43	22
Parkfield 4th	22	8	5	9	50	44	21
Hale End Athletic 3rd	22	8	4	10	56	55	20
International Students House	22	7	3	12	44	72	17
Ealing Association 3rd	22	6	4	12	41	62	16
Duncombe Sports 2nd	22	5	4	13	38	62	14
Wood Green Old Boys 3rd	22	5	4	13	17	46	14
Eastcote-Regeians	22	5	3	14	47	67	13

Division Five *(9 Teams)*
won by Old Tiffinians 3rd
Division Six *(9 Teams)*
won by Parkfield 6th
Division Seven *(9 Teams)*
won by Old Tiffinians 4th

Challenge Cup — won by Tansley
Memorial Cup — won by Economicals 2nd
Bruce Cup — won by Hale End Athletic 3rd
Brixton Cup — won by Old Greenfordians 4th
Renowden Cup — won by Ealing Association 5th

LONDON INSURANCE FOOTBALL LEAGUE

DIVISION ONE

	P	W	D	L	F	A	Pts
Sun Alliance	20	16	4	0	74	19	36
Granby	20	12	5	3	34	33	29
Liverpool Victoria	20	11	4	5	72	43	26
Gaflac	20	11	4	5	49	42	26
Sedgwick	20	10	4	6	51	47	24
Temple Bar	20	8	2	10	32	49	18
Bowring	20	6	5	9	45	45	17
Hill Samuel I.S.	20	7	3	10	31	34	17
Thistle	20	6	2	12	41	63	14
Eagle Star	20	3	3	14	31	56	9
Bardhill	20	2	0	18	24	85	4

DIVISION TWO

	P	W	D	L	F	A	Pts
Colonial Mutual	16	12	3	1	60	16	27
Phoenix	16	11	3	2	21	12	25
Guardian Royal Exchange	16	10	2	4	53	30	22
Medical Sickness	16	7	3	6	23	22	17
Sun Alliance 2nd	16	4	6	6	30	39	14
Temple Bar 2nd	16	5	3	8	40	39	13
Bowring 2nd	16	5	3	8	26	41	13
Temple Bar 3rd	16	3	2	11	20	55	8
Gaflac 2nd	16	1	3	12	20	42	5

DIVISION THREE

	P	W	D	L	F	A	Pts
Liverpool Victoria 2nd	16	14	0	2	76	12	28
Namulus	16	11	3	2	71	33	25
Sedgwick 2nd	16	10	2	4	60	41	22
Hill Samuel I.S. 2nd	16	8	3	5	50	42	19
Norwich Union	16	7	2	7	59	42	16
Confed. Life Ins. Co.	16	6	2	8	58	58	14
Granby 2nd	16	4	2	10	27	44	10
Eagle Star 2nd	16	3	0	13	29	95	6
Temple Bar 4th	16	2	0	14	27	90	4

DIVISION FOUR

	P	W	D	L	F	A	Pts
Bardhill 2nd	16	12	3	1	52	22	27
Sedgwick 3rd	16	12	1	3	46	23	25
Municipal	16	11	1	4	54	36	23
Sun Alliance 3rd	16	8	1	7	44	37	17
Colonial Mutual 2nd	16	6	3	7	32	39	15
Gaflac 3rd	16	5	4	7	48	46	14
Asphalia	16	6	1	9	34	37	13
Bowring 3rd	16	3	1	12	36	61	7
Sun Alliance 4th	16	1	1	14	23	68	3

DIVISION FIVE

	P	W	D	L	F	A	Pts
Guardian Royal Exchange 2nd	14	13	1	0	69	11	27
Liverpool Victoria 3rd	14	7	3	4	48	29	17
Gaflac 4th	14	8	0	6	35	32	16
Pearl 6th	14	6	2	6	40	28	14
Medical Sickness 2nd	14	6	2	6	35	34	14
Hill Samuel I.S. 3rd	14	6	0	8	50	41	12
Colonial Mutual 3rd	14	3	1	10	29	76	7
Pearl 7th	14	2	1	11	25	80	5

CHALLENGE CUP
Sun Alliance 1 Granby 0
CHARITY CUP
Pearl Assurance 4 Gaflac 0
JUNIOR CUP
Pearl Assurance 4th 2 Liverpool Victoria 2nd 1
MINOR CUP
Ibis 4th 2 Pearl Assurance 6th 1
W.A. JEWELL MEMORIAL TROPHY
(Five-a-Side)
Winners: Liverpool Victoria
Runners-Up: Pearl Assurance
SPORTSMANSHIP TROPHY:
Colonial Mutual

SOUTHERN OLYMPIAN LEAGUE

SENIOR SECTION

DIVISION ONE

	P	W	D	L	F	A	Pts
Old Fairlopians	18	13	4	1	58	25	30
Catford Wanderers	18	9	4	5	44	31	22
Old Grammarians	18	5	7	6	37	34	17
Old Woodhouseians	18	6	5	7	31	30	17
Mill Hill Village	18	5	7	6	24	28	17
Old Parmiterians	18	7	3	8	35	42	17
Old Bealonians	18	5	6	7	29	31	16
Bourneside	18	6	4	8	27	38	16
Witan	18	5	4	9	26	37	14
Old Finchleisns	18	5	4	9	30	45	14

DIVISION TWO

	P	W	D	L	F	A	Pts
St. Mary's College	18	13	3	2	42	21	29
Fulham Compton Old Boys	18	11	4	3	58	25	26
Old Wilsonians	18	9	6	3	38	24	24
Wandsworth Borough	18	9	3	6	55	42	21
Old Colfeians	18	6	6	6	23	26	18
Centymca	18	7	2	9	39	44	16
Old Monovians	18	5	5	8	33	34	15
London Welsh	18	5	5	8	18	35	15
Southgate County	18	3	4	11	31	61	10
Old Owens	18	1	4	13	23	48	6

DIVISION THREE

	P	W	D	L	F	A	Pts
City of London Poly OSA	16	12	1	3	52	21	25
Conoco	16	11	3	2	53	25	25
Old Edmontonians	16	11	2	3	46	27	24
Mayfield Athletic	16	9	1	6	42	35	19
G.W.R.	16	6	5	5	32	30	17
Birkbeck College	16	5	2	9	40	48	12
Old Plaistovians	16	4	1	11	32	47	9
Brent	16	3	2	11	19	45	8
Inland Revenue	16	2	1	13	19	57	5

JUNIOR SECTION
Division One *(10 Teams)*
won by Wandsworth Borough 2nd
Division Two *(10 Teams)*
won by St Mary's College 2nd
Division Three *(10 Teams)*
won by Witan 3rd
Division Four *(10 Teams)*
won by Old Wilsonians 3rd

MINOR SECTION
Division "A" *(10 Teams)*
won by Old Parmiterians 4th
Division "B" *(10 Teams)*
won by Old Parmiterians 5th
Division "C" *(10 Teams)*
won by Old Parmiterians 6th
Division "D" *(9 Teams)*
won by Old Wilsonians 4th
Division "E" *(10 Teams)*
won by Wandsworth Borough 4th
Division "F" *(10 Teams)*
won by Old Parmiterians 7th
Division "G" *(10 Teams)*
won by Old Parmiterians 8th
Division "H" *(8 Teams)*
won by Old Finchleians 7th

CHALLENGE BOWL

Bournside	3	Old Wilsonians	2 (aet)

JUNIOR CUP

Old Bealonians 2nd	4	St. Mary's College 2nd	1

MINOR CUP

Old Wilsonians 3rd	3	Catford Wanderers 3rd	2
Centymca 4th	4	Mayfield Ath 4th	0

BURNTWOOD TROPHY

Old Bealonians 5th	2	Witan 4th	1

THOMAS PARMITER CUP

Mill Hill Village 7th	0	Old Parmiterians 8th	3

VETERANS' CUP

Distillers	4	Witan	1

RADIO TIMES CUP (six-a-side)

F. Compton O.B.	3	Bourneside	1

UNIVERSITY OF LONDON INTER-COLLEGIATE LEAGUE

PREMIER DIVISION

	P	W	D	L	F	A	Pts
King's College	18	13	3	2	45	18	29
Goldsmiths' College	18	13	1	4	69	18	27
University College	18	10	5	3	49	20	25
London Sch. Economics	18	10	2	6	71	49	22
Bedford College	18	10	2	6	40	32	22
Wesminster Hospital M.S.	18	5	3	10	34	63	13
The London Hospital M.C.	18	5	2	11	27	43	12
Middlesex Hospital M.S.	18	5	1	12	26	52	11
Imperial College	18	4	2	12	26	47	10
King's College Hosp. M.S.	18	3	3	12	25	70	9

DIVISION ONE

	P	W	D	L	F	A	Pts
St. Thomas's Hospital M.S.	18	13	3	2	63	19	28
Goldsmiths' College 2nd	18	12	2	4	46	38	26
Queen Mary College	18	11	3	4	62	31	23
Royal Holloway College	18	8	3	7	31	29	19
University College 2nd	18	7	4	7	47	36	18
Chelsea College	18	8	1	9	50	43	17
St. Bartholomew's Hosp. M.C.	18	7	2	9	32	35	16
School of Pharmacy	18	6	1	11	33	58	13
University College Hospital	18	6	1	11	23	57	13
St. Mary's Hospital M.S.	18	1	2	15	19	60	4

DIVISION TWO

	P	W	D	L	F	A	Pts
Queen Elizabeth College	18	17	1	0	112	14	35
St. George's Hospital M.S.	18	11	1	6	43	31	23
King's College 2nd	18	9	3	6	42	33	21
University College 3rd	18	9	2	7	37	47	20
Imperial College 2nd	18	7	3	8	33	35	17
Westfield College	18	8	0	10	45	46	16
London Sch. Economics 2nd	18	6	3	9	32	38	15
Royal School of Mines	18	6	3	9	32	53	15
Charing Cross Hospital M.S.	18	6	2	10	26	55	14
Royal Veterinary College	18	1	2	15	14	64	4

DIVISION 1R

	P	W	D	L	F	A	Pts
Bedford College 2nd	16	13	0	3	53	23	26
Royal Free Hospital S.M.	16	9	3	4	38	18	21
Queen Mary College 2nd	16	9	2	5	38	29	20
Guy's Hospital M.S.	16	8	3	5	55	32	19
Goldsmiths' College 3rd	16	7	3	6	49	37	17
Imperial College 3rd	16	7	0	9	27	34	14
Sch. Slav. & E. Eur. Studies	16	5	1	10	29	54	11
London Sch. Economics 3rd	16	4	2	10	28	52	10
Imperial College 4th	16	2	2	12	24	52	6

DIVISION 2R

	P	W	D	L	F	A	Pts
Queen Mary College 3rd	16	13	2	1	59	17	28
King's College 3rd	16	13	1	2	61	17	27
University College 4th	16	11	2	3	63	25	24
R. Holloway College 2nd	16	7	3	6	37	35	17
London Hospital M.C. 2nd	16	6	2	8	56	50	14
King's Coll. Hosp. M.S. 2nd	16	5	2	9	53	55	12
Imperial College 5th	16	5	1	10	32	57	11
R. Holloway Coll. 3rd	16	3	0	13	17	59	6
Chelsea College 2nd	16	2	1	13	22	85	5

DIVISION 3R

	P	W	D	L	F	A	Pts
Queen Mary College 4th	16	11	4	1	59	21	26
Bedford College 3rd	16	9	2	5	63	43	20
Univ. Coll. Hosp. 2nd	16	8	3	5	49	45	19
Guy's Hospital 2nd	16	8	2	6	50	44	18
University College 5th	16	7	3	6	54	54	17
St. Barts. Hosp. 2nd	16	6	3	7	38	28	15
R. Sch. Mines 2nd	16	4	2	10	40	58	10
Ch. Cross Hosp. 2nd	16	4	2	10	25	54	10
Queen Mary College 5th	16	3	3	10	33	64	9

DIVISION 4R

	P	W	D	L	F	A	Pts
Lon. Sch. Economics 4th	14	9	3	2	53	25	21
Queen Elizabeth College 2nd	14	9	1	4	50	21	19
University College 6th	14	8	2	4	40	31	18
The London Hosp. 3rd	14	8	2	4	25	18	18
Imperial College 6th	14	6	2	6	37	31	14
St. George's Hosp. 2nd	14	6	1	7	40	30	13
St. Mary's Hospital 2nd	14	3	1	10	25	59	7
Kings Coll. Hosp. 3rd	14	1	0	13	11	66	2

DIVISION 5R

	P	W	D	L	F	A	Pts
Middlesex Hospital 2nd	14	12	1	1	53	19	25
St. Thomas's Hospital 2nd	14	7	3	4	22	23	17
King's College 4th	14	7	2	5	33	24	16
Westminster Hospital 2nd	14	7	1	6	38	29	15
Imperial College 7th	14	5	2	7	39	40	12
London Sch. Economics 5th	14	4	3	7	34	31	11
Guy's Hospital 3rd	14	5	0	9	20	61	10
Charing Cross Hosp. 3rd	14	3	0	11	24	36	6

CHALLENGE CUP

Westminster Hospital 3 Queen Elizabeth College 1

UPPER RESERVES CUP

Queen Mary College 2nd 1 Imperial College 3rd 0

LOWER RESERVES CUP

St. Georges's Hospital 0,3* London Hospital 0,3

(* won 5-4 in penalty competition)

LONDON BANKS F.A.

DIVISION ONE

	P	W	D	L	F	A	Pts
Williams & Glyn's Bank	18	14	3	1	70	21	31
Royal Bank of Scotland	18	10	5	3	52	26	25
Bankers Trust Co	18	10	2	6	46	35	22
Morgan Guaranty	18	9	3	6	34	30	21
Citibank	18	8	4	6	38	35	20
Nat. Westminster Bank "A"	18	8	1	9	41	42	17
Coutts & Co	18	6	3	9	45	39	15
Standard Chartered Bank	18	5	4	9	33	37	14
Hong Kong Bank	18	3	2	13	28	71	8
Bank of America	18	1	5	12	29	80	7

DIVISION TWO

	P	W	D	L	F	A	Pts
Williams & Glyn's Bank Res	16	12	2	2	50	22	26
Manufacturers Hanover Trust	16	10	2	4	49	33	22
Nat. Westminster Bank "B"	16	7	4	5	30	22	18
Swiss Bank Corp	16	8	2	6	48	42	18
Lloyds Bank International	16	6	4	6	32	31	16
Chase Manhattan Bank	16	6	3	7	38	41	15
Samuel Montagu	16	5	2	9	14	29	12
Grindlays Bank	16	3	3	10	19	43	9
Hill Samuel	16	3	2	11	39	56	8

DIVISION THREE

	P	W	D	L	F	A	Pts
Mitre (C. Hoare)	18	12	3	3	69	35	27
Midland Bank "A"	18	12	3	3	49	29	27
Citibank Res	18	11	4	3	54	25	26
Coutts & Co Res	18	7	5	6	39	40	19
Nat. Westminster Bank "C"	18	7	3	8	44	43	17
Bank of America Res	18	8	1	9	45	55	17
Kleinwort Benson	18	6	4	8	35	51	16
Royal Bank of Scotland Res	18	5	2	11	36	62	12
Williams & Glyn's Bank 3rd	18	5	0	13	39	53	10
Westpac Banking Corp	18	3	3	12	33	49	9

Division Four *(10 Teams)*
won by Bank of Scotland
Division Five *(10 Teams)*
won by Bank of Ireland
Division Six *(10 Teams)*
won by Bank of Credit & Commerce
Division Seven *(10 Teams)*
won by Credit Lyonnais
Challenge Cup
won by Midland Bank
Senior Cup
won by Royal Bank of Scotland
Sportsmans Cup
won by Trustee Savings Bank
Minor Cup
won by National Westminster Bank "5th"
Junior Cup
won by National Westminster Bank "D"
Bonner Shield *(VI-a-Side)*
won by Barclays Bank

THE OLD BOYS' FOOTBALL LEAGUE

PREMIER DIVISION

	P	W	D	L	F	A	Pts
Old Aloysians	20	16	3	1	55	12	35
Old Fincunians	20	12	6	2	45	22	30
Enfield Old Grammarians	20	9	7	4	36	20	25
Old Suttonians	20	9	5	6	21	27	23
Old Ignatians	20	8	5	7	34	27	21
Old Wokingians	20	7	5	8	25	25	19
Old Buckwellians	20	7	3	10	46	44	17
Old Meadonians	20	6	5	9	27	40	17
Old Sinjuns	20	4	5	11	23	44	13
Strand Hollingtonian O.B.	20	4	3	13	19	40	11
Latymer O.B.	20	2	5	13	20	50	9

SENIOR DIVISION ONE

	P	W	D	L	F	A	Pts
Phoenix O.B.	20	14	4	2	14	20	32
Orange Hill O.B.	20	13	4	3	35	16	30
Old Tollingtonians	20	11	6	3	49	26	28
Old Camdenians	20	12	3	5	46	25	27
Old Tenisonians	20	6	6	8	29	35	18
Old Joesphians	20	5	7	8	21	26	17
Old Addeyans	20	5	6	9	30	32	16
Old Highburians	20	6	2	12	28	43	14
Old Minchendenians	20	2	10	8	28	39	14
Clapham O. Xaverians	20	4	5	11	40	54	13
Old Manorians	20	3	4	13	29	66	10

SENIOR DIVISION TWO

	P	W	D	L	F	A	Pts
Old Salvatorians	20	13	4	3	43	29	30
Old Kingsburians	20	12	3	5	47	24	27
Old Uxonians	20	12	3	5	43	28	27
Old Sinjuns 2nd	20	9	4	7	43	35	22
Old Vaughanians	20	9	4	7	38	30	22
Old Paludians	20	10	0	10	41	36	20
Old Westhamians	20	7	5	8	44	37	19
Old Camdenians 2nd	20	7	3	10	39	60	17
Leyton County O.B.	20	6	3	11	36	41	15
Glyn O.B.	20	7	1	12	32	45	15
Old Wokingians 2nd	20	2	2	16	17	58	6

SENIOR DIVISION THREE

	P	W	D	L	F	A	Pts
Cardinal Manning O.B.	22	16	5	1	55	18	37
Old Danes	22	11	6	5	57	39	28
Shene Old Grammarians	22	12	3	7	55	37	27
Chertsey O. Salesians	22	10	4	8	52	39	24
Enfield O. Grammarians 2nd	22	9	5	8	51	40	23
Old Uffingtonians	22	10	2	10	31	45	22
Clapham O. Xaverians 2nd	22	9	3	10	40	48	21
Old Thorntonians	22	8	5	9	46	52	21
Old Ignatians 2nd	22	8	4	10	39	43	20
Old Aloysians 2nd	22	7	4	11	42	49	18
Old Fincunians 2nd	22	4	5	13	25	52	13
Old Pelhamians	22	3	4	15	29	60	10

Intermed. Division North *(12 Teams)*
won by Old Tollingtonians 2nd
Division One North *(12 Teams)*
won by Old Buckwellians 3rd
Division Two North *(11 Teams)*
won by Old Minchendenians 4th
Division Three North *(10 Teams)*
won by Old Camdenians 6th
Division Four North *(10 Teams)*
won by Leyton County OB 5th
Division Five North *(10 Teams)*
won by Old Westhamians 6th
Intermed. Division South *(12 Teams)*
won by John Fisher OB
Division One South *(11 Teams)*
won by Old Thorntonians 2nd
Division Two South *(11 Teams)*
won by Old Sinjuns 4th
Division Three South *(11 Teams)*
won by Old Guildfordians
Division Four South *(12 Teams)*
won by Old Tensionians 4th
Division Five South *(12 Teams)*
won by Glyn OB 6th
Division Six South *(11 Teams)*
won by Old Reigatians 4th
Intermed. Division West *(12 Teams)*
won by Orange Hill OB 2nd
Division One West *(12 Teams)*
won by Phoenicians
Division Two West *(11 Teams)*
won by Old Vaughanians 4th
Division Three West *(10 Teams)*
won by Old Danes 3rd
Division Four West *(11 Teams)*
won by Old Uxonians 5th
Division Five West *(10 Teams)*
won by Old Vaughanians 6th

LONDON OLD BOY'S CUP COMPETITION

Senior Cup *(62 entries)*

Old Fincunians	3	Phoenix OB	0

Intermediate Cup *(57 entries)*

Enfield O Gram Res	3	Old Chigwellians Res	2 (aet)

Junior Cup *(57 entries)*

Old Aloysians 3rd	2	Old Vaughanians 3rd	1

Minor Cup *(52 entries)*

Old Parmiterians 4th	2	Old Meadonians 4th	0

Senior Novets *(46 entries)*

Old Tollingtonians 5th	2:1	Enfield O Gramm 5th	2:1

(Trophy shared)

Junior Novets *(56 entries)*

Old Camdenians 6th	8	Salesians 6th	1

Veterans' *(30 entries)*

E Barnet O Gramm	3	O Edmontonians	2

STOCK EXCHANGE FOOTBALL ASSOCIATION

Individual Cup

Cazenove	4	Phillips & Drew	0

Combined Cup

*Phillips & Drew	5	Smith Bros	5

Rossage Cup

Rowe & Pitman	3	Akroyd & Smithers	1

Six-a-Side

Stock Exchg Settmnt Ser	4	T. C. Coombs	0

(*won on kicks from the penalty mark)

ARTHURIAN LEAGUE FINAL TABLES 1983/84

PREMIER DIVISION

	P	W	D	L	F	A	Diff	Pts
Lancing	16	12	3	1	40	17	+23	27
Carthusians	16	10	1	5	41	22	+19	21
Malvernians	16	7	5	4	21	14	+7	19
Chigwellians	16	7	3	6	34	31	+3	17
Brentwoods	16	6	3	7	32	29	+3	15
Cholmeleians	16	5	4	7	27	29	−2	14
Foresters	16	6	2	8	31	39	−8	14
Harrovians	16	4	2	10	22	40	−18	10
Bradfieldians	16	2	3	11	15	41	−26	7

DIVISION ONE

	P	W	D	L	F	A	Diff	Pts
Westminsters	16	11	2	3	38	20	+18	24
Aldenhamians	16	9	3	4	38	24	+14	21
Reptonians	16	8	4	4	40	26	+14	20
Salopians	16	8	4	4	37	25	+12	20
Wellingburians	16	5	3	8	33	39	−6	13
Wykehamists	16	4	5	7	28	38	−10	13
Ardinians	16	4	3	9	28	41	−13	11
Citizens	16	5	1	10	29	43	−14	11
Etonians	16	4	3	9	18	33	−15	11

All eyes on the ball in the Rainworth M W goalmouth at Staveley Works in the FA Vase 5th Round.

Bromley goalkeeper John Vincent makes a fine save under pressure from Carshalton players (L-R): Tommy Tuite, Tony Tagg (5) and Chris Lewington (8).

Photo: Wallington and Carshalton Advertiser.

AROUND THE CLUBS

Harrow Borough thoroughly enjoyed their first ever Isthmian championship which they won by seventeen points! Manager Mike Tomkys was in his seventh season while eleven members of the squad have now made over 100 first team appearances and three over 350! Having lost on the first Saturday of the season, Borough didn't lose another Saturday League game all season and finished the season with an unbeaten run of 31 league games without defeat from 25th October.

Having planned for their centenary in 1985 **Bognor Regis Town**were surprised, to say the least, when club historian Frank Davies and Vice Chairman visited a British newspaper library in London and found that the club had been formed in October 1883. This news was discovered, however, and 'The Rocks' enjoyed their centenary year last season.

Sutton United won and lost two trophies last season as they triumphed in the Surrey Senior and Hitachi cups but burglars stole a great deal of their silverware from the clubhouse during the season.

The fine clubhouse at Imber Court, the home of **Metropolitan Police**, was built from funds collected in recognition of the police force's excellent work in 1926 during the General strike. Following the heroic efforts of the Midland Police perhaps their regional sides in that area will be given the freedom of the City ground Nottingham.

Half of the **Leyton-Wingate Club (the Leyton half)** is the oldest club in London and one of the oldest surviving clubs outside the football league. As Matlock Swifts the club was formed in 1868.

Billericay Town hold a unique record having played three oldest clubs in football in three different FA competitions within five years.

v Sheffield (Founded 1857) FA Vase Final at Wembley in 1977
v Cray Wanderers (Founded 1860) FA Cup, 19 September 1981
v Hitchin Town (Founded 1865) FA Trophy, 8 November 1980

Willenhall's star player during their climb up 'the pyramid' **Garry Matthews** holds three records at the club; most goals in a season, 58 in 1980-81; most goals in a career, 354; and most appearances 435.

Tony Mahoney has now played 202 consecutive games for **Gosport Borough**.

Tommy Welsh scored 561 goals for **Holyhead** in the Welsh League (North) Division one before January 1964. He also went on to score many more for **Colwyn Bay** but does anyone know how many he had collected by the time he retired?

Former professional players to appear in the **United Counties League** during the 1983-84 season included: Ian Fergusson (ex Wimbledon) of Baldock; Stuart Hodson (ex Peterborough) of Bourne; Andy Kingston (Oxford), Dave Liddle (Northampton), Ken Goodeve (Manchester United, Brighton, Luton, Watford), Bobby Folds (Gillingham and Northampton) of Buckingham; Jimmy Husband (Everton and Luton) of Eynesbury; Dick Kwiatkowski

Gresley Rovers *latest recruit Roger Davies faces the camera with ex-Derby and England team mates player manager David Nish and Kevin Hector, before his West Midland Leage debut against Chasetown.*
Photo: Derrick Kinsey

Can you name the two challengers in this photo?

Answers on the back page.

Camberley suffered a sad loss last year when 'Pop' Howarth their programme seller for many years died at the age of 90. Photo: Eric Marsh

(Peterborough) of Holbeach; Brian Knight (Huddersfield and Northampton), Gary Sargent (Norwich, Scunthorpe, Peterborough and Northampton) of Irthlingborough; Des Waldock (Northampton), Russ Ashenden (Northampton) of Long Buckby; Tommy Robson (Northampton, Chelsea, Newcastle, Peterborough), Russ Allen (Tranmere, Mansfield) of Stamford; Graham Cox (Cambridge) of Stevenage; George Cleary (Cambridge) of Wootton.

David Nish in his second season at **Gresley Rovers** propelled the West Midland League outfit to a very creditable fourth place; this was easily Gresley's highest position since joining the league nine years ago.

Former Derby County and England internationals **Roger Davies** and **Kevin Hector** also joined the Moat Street club; at the time of writing talks were being held with another ex-Derby pro **Bruce Rioch**. If the former Scottish international signs he will be the sixth ex-Derby pro to join the club.

A few centenary programmes are still available from Derrick Kinsey, 92, Midway Road, Midway, Burton-on-Trent, sae plus 20p in stamps.

Steve Waller, aged 34, has just completed his 14th successive season as **Boreham Wood's** goalkeeper. He has made a total of 575 first team appearances, which is a club record.

Gary Hand made his 600th appearance for **Hendon** in their Middlesex Senior Cup Final appearance verus Wembley at Harrow Borough FC on Easter Monday.

In their 43 competitive matches in 1983-84 **Epsom and Ewell's** reserve side, who play in the Suburban League, used no fewer than 13 different goalkeepers:—

(Games played in brackets) Andy Abel (1), Paul Brook (4), Steve Chapman (4), Gary Cook (19), Bobby Knock (2), Grant Long (2), Steve May (1), Barry Smith (4), Frank Wheatland (1), Simon Wilkinson (2) and Terry Wilson (1) were all recognised goalkeepers, and in addition defenders Gary Kent (1) and Richard Strong (1) played full games between the sticks.

In 1952-53, **Bill Goddard** of **Epsom FC** scored 20 goals in six consecutive games, including five consecutive hat-tricks:

Oct 18 — Grays Athletic (A) 2-2	Corinthian League	Goddard scored 2
Oct 25 — Guildford (H) 7-0	Surrey Senior Cup	Goddard scored 5
Nov. 1 — Chesham (H) 6-1	Corinthian League	Goddard scored 4
Nov. 8 — Hounslow (H) 4-1	Corinthian League	Goddard scored 3
Nov. 15 — Hounslow (A) 6-2	Corinthian League	Goddard scored 3
Nov. 22 — Malden Town (H) 7-2	Surrey Senior Cup	Goddard scored 3

Daryl Lucas is the secretary of **Gravesend & Northfleet FC** and he is believed to be the youngest secretary in the country at the age of 18. He is still at school and is at present studying for A-levels at St George's School. Prior to his appointment he was the club's reserve team secretary. As well as his club duties he is also a qualified football referee.

Almost 100%. Liphook FC *of Aldershot Senior League 33 wins out of 34 games (83/84) with one drawn, with over 100 goals and a 2-nil victory over Petersfield United at Aldershot FC in Aldershot AFA Cup Final, which Barry Woodger their goalkeeper won "man of match". Back Row (L-R): Gray (manager), P Sturt, M. Marshall, R. Williams, P. Hunt, B. Woodger, P. Roberts, R. Ward (capt). Front Row (L-R): D. Williams, C. Matthews, A. Cooper, C. Gatcum, J. Ray.*

Four **Merthyr Tydfil** players were selected to play against England in the first Non-League International played by Wales. Keith Pontin was picked to captain the Welsh team but had to withdraw through injury. Phil Fisher, Peter Jones and Ian Love all played in the match at Newtown which Wales won 2-1.

Caernarfan Town did not compete in the FA Cup for 49 years as a result of an administrative blunder. The Caernarfan club fielded 10 men at Winsford on 20/9/30 and shortly afterwards went into liquidation. When the club restarted officials always believed that the FA had fined Caernarfan and because this fine was unpaid the club were barred from the FA Cup.

In 1978 new chairman Jack Thomas established with the FA that Caernarfan owed no fine, and on 15/9/79 the club again played in the FA Cup against Northwich Victoria — after an interval of 49 years!

Past **Nantwich Town** players who have progressed into the Football League: G. Green (Bury), S. Barnett, W. Cartwright, H. Champion, H. Crawford, R. Keay, E. Williams, H. Sandland (all to Crewe Alex). H. Boston (Bolton, WBA), W. Betteley (Stockport). F. Chesworth (Glossop). G. Clarke (Stoke). H. Cotton (Burslem Port Vale). S. Davies (Bury, Luton). G. Spencer (WBA, Brighton), W. Weaver, H. Simpson, F. Mellor, G. Tatton (all to Bolton). F. Worrall (Oldham, Portsmouth, Crewe). H. Clayton (Tranmere). R. Ryder (Gillingham).

Around the Clubs

In the year that Melksham Town won the Western League Division One Championship in 1979-1980 they played 9 games and 20 minutes without conceding a goal — a total of 830 minutes. Is this a record?

Midweek afternoon kick-off at Connahs Quay Nomads brought those intrepid travellers (L-R): Mick Burt (nearly 1,000 grounds), Alan Wiggins (some 700-odd) and elder statesman of the hobby, Tony Smith. Says Glossop-based Tony "I've now done more grounds than I have hairs!!" Photo: Peter Burrin

THE FOOTBALL MANIACS DIARY OF 83-4
by LEO HOENIG

AUGUST

The starting date of the season is no longer a straightforward occasion, because since the Football League put back it's own start date to the last weekend of the month the others have been unsure whether to follow suit. Most leagues now start a week before the Football League, but a few start a week before this, and at least for the neutral supporter this is where the season must start. It is a busy time, as for the first few weeks all leagues tend to play mid-week as well as Saturday fixtures and this gives the opportunity to visit some of the more local grounds even without floodlights for their early evening kick-offs. Added to this, on the last Sunday of the month, **Odd Down** entertained **Liskeard Athletic** in the Western League Cup; unfortunately neither side did a great deal to entertain the large neutral contingent at the match, with no goals in the first 90 minutes. Both sides got one in extra time, although the visitors needed an own goal, and **Odd Down** equalised from the penalty spot. In the penalty decider it was eventually left to David Lamborn, who scored the own goal, to put his side (Odd Down) through. The next day was Bank Holiday Monday, so one match just wasn't good enough; so off we went to the East to see **Canvey Island**, **Basildon**, and **Dagenham**, and just to make the point I saw a 6.30 kick-off in Dorset on Tuesday and a 6.15 back in London on the Wednesday, but still found some time to go to work! Incidently, with the match at New Street (near **Andover**) on the Saturday this means 7 matches in 5 days, a journey of 800 miles and 24 goals; only one of the matches **Dagenham v Enfield** was on a ground I had visited before. Very satisfactory!

SEPTEMBER

487 clubs enter the F.A. Cup, but only the 44 that start their run in January can have any realistic chance of reaching Wembley; in fact almost half the clubs will drop out during September, for only 250 survive, and there is no shortage of surprise results in the Preliminary and First Qualifying rounds. Still the Preliminary on 3rd September was dominated by the result at **St Albans City**, where the home side put ten past the hapless **Banstead Athletic** defence. Meanwhile, **Lye Town** beat **Willenhall Town** by 1-0, and **Metropolitan Police** lost by the same score at home to Sussex League **Horsham YMCA**; another Sussex League side, **Peacehaven**, also travelled to Surrey and came home with the spoils with a 5-0 win over **Chertsey** (Athenian), while over in East London **Clapton** were surprised by **Cray Wanderers** (Kent), who won 3-2. (Still it rubs both ways: before the month was out I saw **Clapton** beat **Slough Town** from the Premier Division of the Isthmian by 1-0). Two Southern League sides, **Coventry Sporting** and

On a parched ground in August, Mark Hunt puts Barnstaple ahead against visitors Wellington. The home side went on to win this Western League match 4-0. Photo: Great Mills

Autumn is setting in Sussex and here home keeper Tony Chad makes a fine save for Hassocks in their cup tie against Peacehaven which was drawn 1-1. Photo: R.U.R.

Banbury United each took the lead in their visits to **Wigston Fields** (Leicester) and **Racing Club (Warwick)** (Mid Comb) respectively, but both home sides recovered in the second half to win by 3-1; I had spent most of the week trying to decide which of these games to see, and eventually chose **Racing Club** (I think it was because Dave Shate offered me a lift!).

Two weeks later and the same theme of surprises can be followed with **Chester-le-Street** (D. Northern Div 2) beating **Barrow**, the future Northern Prem champions, by 1-0, while **King's Lynn** got a real hammering at **Halesowen Town** by 6-0. **Basildon** were going well in the Isthmian Div 2, too well for **Leytonstone**, who lost 1-0 to their Essex rivals. Two Southern League sides went down to Hampshire League opposition. **Salisbury**, by 2-1 at **Sholing Sports**, and **Andover** lost at home to **AFC Totton** by 3-1. My chances of seeing another shock ended in a classic at **Hastings Town** with the home side 2-1 up at half time, but **Tooting & Mitcham United** came back to score the winner at 4-3 just 3 minutes from time. The two biggest shocks saw Alliance League **Trowbridge** go down 4-2 at **Clandown**, whereas **Spennymoor Utd**, no stranger to cup glory themselves, lost 4-1 to **Yorkshire Amateurs** of the Northern Counties (East), Division Two (North).

Replays gave an unusual double for fans in **Horsham** (actually, I know that some came from at least as far as Birmingham to see it). The town's Sussex League club, **YMCA**, didn't have floodlights, so they kicked off at 5pm in the match against **Hertford Town**. Still it was getting dark and murky when substitute Keith Hurran gained the **YM's** a second replay with only 4 minutes of extra time to play. The match finished at about 7.20; and Isthmian League **Horsham** kicked off their replay against Kent League **Sittingbourne** at 7.45pm. The club may well have collected more in gate money if they had put a man in to collect from those who clambered through the fence between the two grounds; perhaps that would have been some consolation as they lost 2-1 to a side reduced to ten men before the scoring had started, as Carl Laraman was sent off (for dissent in the 23rd minute, after having already been booked for the same offence).

Sandwiched between the two cup rounds the two non-league competitions started with 20 matches in the Preliminary of the Trophy, most notable of which was **Weston-Super-Mare's** 1-0 replay victory at **Forest Green Rovers**, and 5 matches in the extra Preliminary Round of the Vase. Off the field, **Stafford** became one of the first sides to sack their manager with Colin Clarke being dismissed with former Matlock assistant manager Ron Reid taking over.

OCTOBER

Once again the month is dominated by the F.A. Competitions, with F.A. Cup rounds on the 1st, 15th and 29th, the F.A. Vase playing on the 8th, and the Trophy on the 22nd. The first of the month was not a good day for the Alliance as **Bath City** lost 1-0 at home to **Merthyr** (Southern, Mid Div), and **Runcorn** went down 3-0 at **Hyde Utd** (NPL), with **Gateshead** lasting only a little longer, losing a home replay to **Accrington Stanley**; still it was a great time for the N. Western Counties League, for as well as **Accrington's** great result 3 Northern Premier teams went out to the league's teams, **Rhyl** losing 2-0 at **Stalybridge**, **Oswestry Town** 3-0 at **Congleton** and **Glossop** beat **Goole Town** by 4-0; and to wrap it up Southern League **Shepshed** went down 3-1 at **Winsford**.

Down in the Midlands forwards predominated particularly at **Sutton Coldfield**, who beat **Shifnal** 5-4, while the **Lye** v **A.P. Leamington** and **Thame United** v **Moor Green** matches both ended in 4-4 draws. Both these matches were replayed on the Tuesday, with **Moor Green** kicking off at 4pm for their 4-2 a.e.t. victory (4 of the goals and two sendings off (both Thames players) came in extra-time); and **Leamington** started their replay at 7.30 so that some enterprising supporters could go on from Moor Green to 'the brakes' 4-0 victory, or they could have followed my route over to **Dudley** v **Willenhall** (a Southern League Cup tie), which the away side won 1-0. Going back to the Saturday the Southern League also lost **Alvechurch**, 2-1 at **Buckingham**, and **Dudley Town**, 3-2 at **March**; while down on the South Coast **AFC Totton** took another scalp with a 3-0 win at **Fareham Town**, while Sussex League

Whitehawk, who include a number of **ex-Brighton** players in their side, beat **Walton & Hersham** 4-1, perhaps partially avenging the defeat their more illustrious neighbours suffered at Walton ten years before.

With 160 matches it is impossible to analyse the Preliminary Round of the Vase, so I shall settle for mentioning one minor surprise. Isthmian League **Epping Town** lost 2-0 at home to one of their Essex Senior neighbours — **Stansted**.

The third qualifying round of the cup was played on a day when gale force winds and torrential rain swept the country, causing two matches to be abandoned in the Cup and some others were postponed, but we also saw most of the smaller clubs (**Accrington, Stalybridge, Congleton, Glossop, Winsford, Buckingham, March** and **Whitehawk**) go out. **Whitehawk** protested when a light was blown down in the wind and caused the substitute to be injured without playing at **Tooting**, but it wasn't upheld. **AFC Totton** came close to upsetting **Waterlooville**; 1-0 up when the first match was abandoned, they again led in the re-match two days later but **'Ville'** drew level after a penalty was missed by Totton. A further failure from the spot in the replay when Waterlooville were one down signalled the end of the Hampshire League's interest in the season's contest. **Sittingbourne**, too, may have thought they had a chance after drawing 2-2 at **Dartford**, but the Southern League side proved too powerful at the Ball Ground and **Sittingbourne** went down 4-1. **Corinthian Casuals** from Division Two of the Isthmian gained the biggest upset with a 3-1 victory over high-riding Premier side **Bognor Regis**, whereas the goals came in a replay at **Whitby**, where the home side, having been held to a 2-2 draw at **Lancaster**, won by 7-3.

When the Trophy got under way the form book seemed to rule, although after two replays **Belper** of the Northern Counties (East) beat **Buxton**, Northern Premier. Another of **Belper's** league rivals, **Alfreton**, beat **Willenhall** by 3-1, and **King's Lynn's** poor cup form was shown again when they lost by the only goal at **Maidenhead**.

The final qualifying round of the cup sees 20 of the 'elite' join the 36 clubs who have got through the last two months. Possibly the biggest clash was in East London where **Harrow Borough** and **Fisher Athletic** drew 1-1, the Isthmians winning the replay 4-2. Two clubs relegated the previous season to the Southern division of the Southern League won home ties against Isthmian Premier opposition. **Poole** beating **Slough** 3-0, while **Waterlooville** won 3-2 against **Wokingham**.

Off the field, it was a bad month to be the manager of a struggling club, and the biggest name to go was Don Masson, replaced at **Kettering** by Dave Needham; while Graham Allner resigned from **A.P. Leamington**, the side he led to the Southern League championship last term, to take up the reins at **Kidderminster** in the Alliance. **Milton Keynes City**, meanwhile, no strangers in the lower reaches of the Southern League and also managerless, won a match after 51 consecutive failures when they beat local rivals **Milton Keynes Borough** in the second replay of a Berks & Bucks senior cup tie. Western League side **Bridport**, having played 6 games and lost them all, resigned from the league as they were unable to raise a team.

NOVEMBER

By this stage of the season it is possible to see which way the various leagues are going; in the Alliance **Nuneaton** and **Runcorn** led and had opened up a small gap over **Altrincham** and **Northwich Vics**. **Worthing** were ahead of the field in the Isthmian. **Barrow** already had a big lead over all their rivals in the Northern Premier and **King's Lynn** were also ahead in the Southern, although all their rivals had games in hand. Perhaps the most unhappy town in the football world was **Biggleswade**, which has two sides, Town & United, in the lower division of the S. Midlands League; after 14 matches each they filled the bottom two places in the league with only one win between them (by Town).

Alan Fogarty returned to non-league management by replacing Tony Freeley at **Stourbridge**; after experience with **Wealdstone, Nuneaton** and **Tamworth**, he had been scouting for **Wimbledon**. Meanwhile West Midlands League side **Gresley Rovers** thought they had made a big signing in ex-Derby player Roger Davies, but he moved on to **Darlington** without playing a match.

At the beginning of the month there were a number of high scores, particularly the away wins by **Bridgnorth** (8-1 at **Oldswinford**) and **Corinthian Casuals** (9-2 at **Chertsey**). I won't complain though, as I saw **Newquay** win 6-2 at **Glenside St. Gabriels** and after a few minutes' cycle ride I also took in the second half and extra time of **Mangotsfield's** scoreless draw with **Pegasus**. Other results saw previous finalists **Sheffield** lose 3-1 at **Hatfield Main**, while **Sholing** won the big Hampshire league clash, beating **AFC Totton 1-0. Horsham** lost 4-2 at home to Kent League **Tonbridge Wells**, wheras **Erith & Belvedere** also lost at home, beaten 2-1 by **Arundel** (Sussex Div 2).

When the First Round was played, four more entries were added to the roll of honour of non-league clubs to have beaten league sides in the Cup. Pride of place went to **Whitby Town**, who gained their first scalp with a 3-2 away win at **Halifax**. **Telford** easily saw off **Stockport County**, by 3-0 at Buck's Head ground, while **Maidstone** and **Worcester** both had away draws, both 1-1, at **Exeter** and **Aldershot** respectively, and both gained 2-1 victories in the replays. Another four sides (**Macclesfield, Barnet, Corinthian-Casuals** and **Poole Town**) drew 0-0 at home to league opposition, but went down in the replays to **York City** 2-0, **Bristol Rovers** 3-1, **Bristol City** 4-0, and **Newport County** 3-1 respectively. **Dagenham** had a similar fate, going down 2-1 in a replay at **Brentford**, after a 2-2 draw, whereas **Northampton** and **Waterlooville** drew 1-1 on each of their grounds, before the league side won 2-0 in the third match.

On the last weekend of the month the last two sides to make the drop from the football league drew 0-0 in the F.A. Trophy, with **Workington** winning the replay 1-0 at **Southport**. The two biggest shocks involved teams from the Northern Counties (East), with **Arnold** beating **Oswestry** by 2-0 and **Alfreton** knocked out **Bedworth** by the same score. I went to one of the most picturesque settings for a football match to see **Matlock** beat **Sutton Coldfield Town** 4-0. The month ended, for me, and some other 'travellers' with a 2pm Wednesday afternoon kick off at **Connahs Quay Nomads**, where the Clwyd league side lost 1-0 to **Shrewsbury Town** in a Welsh cup match.

DECEMBER

The first Saturday in December was the day that all the exempted clubs joined in the F.A. Vase and certainly the holders, **V.S. Rugby**, had no problems in making a further stop along the way, beating **Skegness** by 7-1. **Halesowen**, beaten finalist last season, had some more trouble, but eventually came up victors against Leicestershire Senior League side **Wigston Fields**. One of the previous season's semi-finalists went down, though, **Burnham** losing 1-0 at Grays, while the day's two biggest shocks saw Western League leaders **Clevedon Town** lose 1-0 at **Old Georgians** and one of the favourites, **Shepshed Charterhouse**, lost 3-1 at **Lincoln United**; with **Shepshed** moving up to the Premier Division of the Southern League, and hence almost certainly transferring to the Trophy, this was probably the last chance for one of the competition's successes to reach Wembley.

After the second round of the Cup on December 10th only two clubs survived to fly the non-league flag; one of these two was **Maidstone United**, who beat another Alliance side by 3-2, while **Telford United** added to their reputation by beating **Northampton Town** 3-2 in a replay after a 1-1 draw. Three other teams gained draws. **Altrincham** drew 0-0 at **Darlington** but they then went down 2-0 at home. **Windsor & Eton** went by the same score in their replay at **AFC Bournemouth** after originally drawing 0-0 at the Stag Meadow. As the original match in this tie had been postponed to the Tuesday I know of at least one person that saw this and the match at **Bangor City**, where Bruce Urquhart scored a last minute equaliser to give his side a replay at **Blackpool**, but unfortunately they too went down, by 2-1 in the re-match.

The following Saturday was the final qualifying round of the Trophy. Some of the Alliance clubs start at this stage, but there were few major surprises — Alliance League **Kettering** lost by the odd goal in seven at **Dulwich** and last term's surprise team, **Ilkeston Town**, went down 5-0 at home in their first match to **Witton Albion**. I saw **Arnold** (Northern Counties (East)) pull off the biggest coup of the

The winter weather was reasonably good this year but no doubt this goal, Staveley's fourth, scored by Darren Vernon against Rainworth Miners Welfare in the FA Vase, warmed the home supporters on a bleak January day.

day beating **Burton Albion** with a single first half goal by Bob Norris. (I guess some of **Albion's** fans can remember his name; when **Burton** and **Grantham** were both in the Southern League he always topped the goalscoring charts for the Lincolnshire club.) Bad weather, particularly down South, affected this round, so for the 'loony' like myself, especially as I was staying in London for the holiday period, there was a chance to see two more matches after Christmas.

Christmas is of course a bonanza for the Football 'loony', and this season there were two bank holidays after Christmas Day, one being for the New Year, and as an extra bonus there was the possibility of 'doubles' (i.e. Morning and Afternoon fixtures) on both Christmas and New Year's Eve, so it wasn't at all difficult to see at least a dozen matches over the period. One club that didn't show the Christmas spirit though was **Cheltenham** sacking manager **Alan Wood** in the week prior to the holiday with **John Murphy** one of their full backs taking over.

As you may have gathered, my choice of fixture in the Vase 3rd Round on News Year's Eve was decided by the discovery that some Essex Senior League matches were to kick off at 11am, so I ended up seeing **Stansted** beat **Wivenhoe** 2-0; otherwise I was trying to choose between trips to **Denaby United** where **Halesowen** suffered only their second defeat of the season (the first was in the F.A. Cup, at **Oldbury**) or to **Rothwell**, where the home side beat **Dorking** 4-3. The other shock results saw **Great Yarmouth** go down 3-0 at **Baldock**, and **Old Georgians** claimed their second victim from the Western League, beating **Devizes** 1-0, while **Blue Star** lost 1-0 to **Farsley Celtic** in a replay.

JANUARY

The month started as December ended, with a Bank Holiday 'double'; still it could have been a 'treble' if the continuous rain had not caused the cancellation of the evening match between **Wycombe** and **Slough Town**.

After this busy period games became thinner on the ground, although I did manage to maintain my two-games-a-week minimum throughout. I didn't however see a third round F.A. Cup match which **Maidstone Utd** lost 4-1 at **Darlington**, but **Telford Utd** cruised through, winning by the same result at **Rochdale**. In the following midweek I think I saw one of the most amazing matches, when **Cwmbran Town** met **Hereford Utd** in the Welsh Cup; the league side (and it was their full league eleven) went ahead in just 5 seconds and were 2-0 ahead after only two minutes, but over the next thirty minutes the Welsh League side completed an amazing turn around with two goals by Phil Cole and one by Mark Gripton. It didn't last though; Hereford were level by half-time and ahead just four minutes from time.

The best of the action stayed in Wales in the First Round of the Trophy, when Alliance League Champions **Enfield** visited **Merthyr Tydfil**, going down to goals at each end of the second half from Chris Williams. Meantime, **Scarborough**, who have three victories at Wembley to their credit, were losing 2-1 at **Marine**, and **Altrincham**, losers to **Enfield** in the '82 final, were beaten at home 2-0 by **Kidderminster**, the start of a run that was to take the **Harriers** clear of the relegation zone.

At the same time the Vase future of **Rainworth M.W.** was saved by a clever piece of work with a tape measure, the Nottinghamshire club putting in a protest about the size of **Rylands** pitch before their hosts had kicked off a 4-1 victory. The protest was upheld and given a home replay **Rainworth** scored the only goal to go through 1-0. In the fourth round **Rainworth** did not need a tape measure, but didn't find their delayed trip (due to weather) to **Rothwell** easy, still going through though on account of a 3-3 a.e.t. draw and a narrow 3-2 victory in the return. Neither **Denaby Utd** nor **Farsley Celtic** went further, as both were drawn away in the far North East, **Denaby** losing 3-2 at **Whickham**, while **Farsley** were on the wrong end of a 2-1 scoreline at **Brandon Utd**, so the minor surprises were left to **Baldock**, beating **Grays** by 1-0, to **Bristol Manor Farm** (1-0 victors at **Newbury**) and **Old Georgians**, who celebrated another home draw by beating **Newport** (IOW) by 3-2; the major shock, however, saw **Hacknall Colliery Welfare** score two goals in the first 25 minutes against holders **V.S. Rugby** and hang on to this scoreline against relentless pressure from the Southern League side.

More managers on the move in January saw John Adams leaving **Alvechurch** to be replaced by ex-**Kidderminster** boss John Chambers (a busy man, since leaving **Kidderminster** he had a spell as a player at **Cheltenham),** while John Lagton left **Trowbridge** and Tony Saunders left **Altrincham**. Up at **Willenhall** a bid by manager Graham Newton to lead a consortium and make the club a limited company failed to get through despite the cash boost this could have provided to a club whose success on the field was not always matched in the 'financial stakes'. In the wake of this manager Graham Newton resigned to be replaced by **Sutton Coldfield's** Ian Cooper and secretary Tony Turpin, who had been at the club for 27 years in one capacity or another, left his post, although he did tell me that this was not entirely due to the consortium business and he continued with the club as a supporter until joining **Dudley** as assistant secretary at the end of the season. (In fact at the end of the season **Willenhall** did become a limited company!)

Another strange story saw **Gloucester City** manager put his entire team up for sale after heavy defeats by **Cheltenham** and **Witney**. There were no takers, but it did improve the results for a while and to put the story in context read on to the events at the club in May. Meanwhile **Milton Keynes City** started 1984 with something they did not obtain in 1983 — a league win! **Coventry Sporting** were the victims and, although the home side were ahead in 2 minutes through Phil Nardiello, two goals by Phil Burrell and one from John Adams gave **Milton Keynes** their first league victory since the end of 81-2 season!

FEBRUARY

On February the First the F.A. Cup match between **Derby** and **Telford**, postponed the previous Saturday, took place, and, although **Telford** didn't give up without a fight, they went down 3-2; Telford's goalscorers were Steve Eaton and Mark Bailey, while a hat-trick from Bobby Davison saw **Derby** through. All the complaining from manager Stan Storton, who claimed that one of **Derby's** goals was offside and that his side should have had a penalty in the dying minutes (can't anyone lose with some sportsmanship these days?), cannot take the edge off **Telford's** performance – their best ever in the F.A. Cup (in fact, Telford's first victory over a league side was against Wigan in 82-83).

The big story of the month, however, was not this, nor was it the signing of **A.P. Leamington's** full back Mark Baukland by **Wolverhampton** (he went straight from Southern League to Division One playing for **Wolves** against **Birmingham** in his first week), but undoubtedly the dismissal by **Worcester City** of manager Nobby Clark, the Alliance League's longest serving manager, who had almost ten years to his credit. Nobby had led the club to many trophys, Southern League Div 1 (North) 1977, Southern League Champions 1979, and the challenge match that year against the Northern Premier Champions, plus the Worcestershire Senior Cup in 78, 80 and 82, the Staffordshire Cup in 77, the prestigious Birmingham Senior Cup in 1976, and a big handful of ties against league opposition in the F.A. and Welsh Cups. For those of us that were there in the 7,500 crowd when the **City's** 3-0 victory over **Kettering** gave them the Southern League Championship at the end of the 1978-9 season there can have been few more emotional atmospheres; the crowd sang the name of Bobby Clark that day. Bobby Shinton, the former **Wrexham** striker, was given the unenviable task of trying to improve on Nobby's record.

Other managerial appointments saw John King get the **Altrincham** job and Steve Coles, formerly at **Clandown**, was given the task of keeping **Yeovil** clear of relegation from the Alliance, while Rhys Davies got the job at **Sutton Coldfield**. Still off the field two Alliance chairmen were in trouble; at **Kettering Town** John Murphy fought off an attempt by a consortium to buy up the club and replace him; his new board included three members of the supporters club, surely a progressive move when so many clubs ignore the people coming through the gate. Still this was nothing compared to the problems in Kent, as Jim Thompson ousted by his fellow directors took legal action to try and regain his place.

All this off the field action gives little chance to remember what was happening on the pitch in a month that included two rounds of the Trophy and one for the Vase, starting, as the month did, with the second round of the Trophy, where Northern Premier leaders **Barrow** crashed 5-2 at **Frickley** (my choice of match); **Telford** beat **Runcorn** 2-1 to show they weren't suffering a hangover from the previous week's exertions at **Derby**. **Nuneaton**, leaders of the Alliance, needed a home replay against **Maidstone Utd**, a side whose games in hand still gave them a good crack at the championship. The major result saw **Wycombe Wanderers** lose 2-0 at **Bromsgrove**, while **Dulwich** needed three matches to beat **Chorley**. The weather hit this round with the **Carshalton** v **Gateshead** match being held over till the following Tuesday afternoon, while up in the North East things were only just starting to move again. One match in this round **Windsor** v **Fisher** was a repeat of a second round match the previous term in the Vase! Although the match was again drawn at **Windsor**, this time it was **Fisher** who won through.

Only 8 ties in the fifth round of the Vase, and not a replay in sight! News had reached me from the South that **R.S. Southampton** (Southern League) and **Corinthian Casuals** (Isthmian) may have been the teams to watch, but **R.S.** were not having the luck of the draw and went out at **Leyton-Wingate**, while **Corinthian Casuals** lost to a fine comeback, **Stamford** winning 4-2 a.e.t. I personally favoured the chances of **Brandon Utd**, who won 1-0 at **Guiseley**, while **Whickham** (2-0 victors over **Hucknall**) certainly looked on course for a return to Wembley. **Old Georgians** continued to enjoy home draws and beat **Baldock** 1-0; a sixth successive home draw meant they would face **Stansted** in the quarter-finals after the Essex club had seen off **Bristol's** other representatives (Western League **Manor Farm**) by 2-1. In the big all United

Counties clash **Irthlingborough** beat league leaders **Buckingham**, by 1-0, and hopes of a 'single league' final were kept up when they stayed apart from **Stamford** in the quarter final draw. Finally up at **Staveley Works** (as indeed I was) the home side won an interesting match by 4-2 against a Nottinghamshire side (**Rainworth**), seemingly at a loss for a tape measure.

So back to the Trophy and **Bromsgrove**, heroes of the last round, had the most difficult task, travelling to holders **Telford**, where goals by Dean Edwards and Eddie Hogan saw the Southern League side drop out, while **A.P. Leamington** beat **Chelmsford City** 4-0. Few people expected the result at **Fisher**, where **Marine** won through by a single goal, while **Bangor City** were 2-0 down at **Gateshead** and left it until the last 5 minutes before striking twice and gaining a replay, which they won 2-0. **Kidderminster** led at **Barnet**, but went down 2-1, while **Nuneaton** were a little lucky not to lose at home to **Dagenham**; instead they lost away, 1-0 after a 2-2 draw. **Frickley Athletic** had to go to **Whitby**, where the season's F.A. Cup heroes beat their Alliance opponents by 2-0. The remaining tie, so I'm told, was marred by dull defensive football, as only one goal was scored in 300 minutes of football to see **Northwich Vics** beat **Dulwich** 1-0 (2nd replay, after 0-0, and 0-0 a.e.t.).

To tell the truth I missed all this, travelling instead to **Abingdon United**, where the home side, members of the Hellenic League, did themselves credit to beat **Wokingham T** (Isthmian, Premier) by 2-1. In the Berks & Bucks Cup, Sean Sunderland scored in the 19th & 21st minutes to put his side 2-0 ahead and **Wokingham's** only reply, despite dominating the second half, came from Neil Stanley ten minutes from time.

MARCH

The quarter finals of the Vase make up the first round with a national draw, and the point was proved by sending both the North Eastern sides down south. **Whickham** won the honours by being the only away side to win, 1-0 at **Leyton-Wingate** after extra time. **Brandon Utd**, however, left **Irthlingborough Diamonds** somewhat shell shocked by the power of Gary Sargent, a striker with league experience at Northampton and Peterborough, and one of Barry Fry's stars, lining up for him at Bedford and Barnet. Sargent got three in the **Diamond's** 5-0 win. The luck ran out for **Old Georgians** of the Gloucestershire County League, when they had to travel to **Stansted** after a 1-1 draw. Not used to travelling they went down 2-0. As for **Stamford**, whom I saw beat **Staveley** 3-0 at Wothorpe Road, all I can say is they looked good and they were the first side I had seen that looked capable of going to Wembley (of course, of the semi-finalists, the only other one I'd seen was **Stansted**). Russ Allen gained two goals, after Tommy Robson had put his side ahead in the 52nd minute.

When the Trophy reached the same stage two weeks later it was **A.P. Leamington** who had to suffer, and **Bangor City's** Mark Carter was the hat-trick hero as his side beat their hosts by 6-1. I saw a competent, but uninspiring, **Northwich Victoria** survive considerable pressure from

Barnet to win 1-0 through Colin Chesters, while I had difficulty in believing the news on the radio that **Marine** were 3-0 up at **Telford**! It was true, but somehow **Telford** clawed it all back and earned a replay; still I did not imagine they'd lose their second chance, but **Telford** lost 2-0 in the replay at **Marine**. **Dagenham** also surprised a lot of people by winning their replay 3-0 at **Whitby**, after being held to a 2-2 draw at home. Some consolation for **A.P. Leamington**! Their defeat at home to **Bangor City** coincided with the news that their survival was guaranteed for another season, as they had been given another year on the Windmill Ground. The Vase Semi-Finals paired two United Counties League clubs, **Irthlingborough Diamonds** and **Stamford**. **Stamford** had already beaten their rivals twice in the league, 2-1 at Nene Park and 2-0 on their own ground. In the Vase they repeated these results to reach Wembley. **Stansted** meanwhile could only draw 1-1 at home to **Whickham**, so when I went up to the second leg I found the home side full of confidence for a return to Wembley. However, I found that **Stansted** were a different side to the one I'd seen in the third round three months before. They certainly had learned a great deal during their run and goals at the beginning of each half saw them through. What happened at the end was I think due to the frustration of the home players and the belief that the referee held, with all his league experience of league football, that this was going to be an easy match. So as the match got tougher **Trelford Mills** appeared to let it go too far before bringing the book out and in the final minutes sending off both Keith Knox and Geoffrey Mayne.

Between these two matches, the **English Non-League XI** suffered the sort of blow normally reserved for the senior side losing 2-1 to **Wales** at **Newtown FC**. Ossie Smith put England ahead, but goals from Alan Jones (**Rhyl**) and Paul Hughes (**Aberystwyth**) turned the scores around.

APRIL

The month starts with most competitions still needing the answers to the championship, promotion and relegation issues to be decided, and ends with little left to be done. The first two Saturdays are taken off by the Trophy semi-finals, both of which had several twists to them. **Bangor City** led 1-0 after playing their home leg against **Dagenham**, while **Marine** achieved a 1-1 draw at **Northwich Victoria**. Seeing the second leg of the match at **Marine**, I expected the Northern Premier League side to deal with the **Vics**, as they had earlier dealt with **Telford**, but their tactics consisted merely of high crosses into a goalmouth where the **Northwich** defence could have mopped them up until the Cows came home; still it took a cruel own goal to put the visitors ahead. Once ahead, **Vics** never looked in trouble and near the close Colin Chesters made certain that they would return to Wembley.

In the Alliance League, **Maidstone United** had taken the lead but **Nuneaton** and **Runcorn** were still close on their tails, while at the other end **Trowbridge's** relegation was made certain by the middle of the month, while **Bangor City** came through their second leg of the Trophy at **Dagenham** with a score of 2-2 a.e.t., knowing that between that match and the Trophy final they would have a lot of work to do to avoid relegation. **Harrow Borough** had already confirmed their position as champions of the Isthmians, and **Worthing** needed only to do reasonabaly in their games in hand to be runners-up. **Bromley** were bottom and finished their games early, while **Tooting** were in real trouble as well. Like **Harrow**, **Barrow** were well clear of the field in the Northern Premier League, but for **Dartford** (favourites) and **Fisher** the battle for the title still had a way to go.

For the non-league 'loony' April is the start of the 'silly season', as almost every evening there is a match on somewhere, giving the true fanatic many chances to see a large number of matches. Plus, as an extra bonus, the Easter bank holiday gives two bank holidays, although few leagues still play on Good Friday, and it is sometimes difficult to make a full day of the first of the holidays. Still, there is one guarantee with the South Midlands League Challenge Trophy final being over two legs played on the evenings of Good Friday and Easter Monday.

The month ended with the Vase Final. The match was a credit to football, but no doubt it is well covered elsewhere in the Directory.

The moment they have dreamt about for three years. Northwich Victoria lift the FA Trophy in triumph and not a little relief!

MAY

The end of the season, but still full of matches and much more happening off the field! During the first two weeks the 'silly season' continues, and football was still findable on most nights of the week. The Bank Holiday weekend was an obvious and busy core, as an evening fixture in the Leicestershire Senior Cup final meant it was possible to do two matches on May 5th; looking around I counted people who had been to **West Bromwich**, **Leicester**, **Ilkeston**, **Boots Athletic**, and **Alfreton Town** converging on Holmes Park for the fixture to see **Shepshed** beat **Hinckley Ath** 3-0. The following day there were two fixtures in the Welsh League, and not far apart being at **Lake Utd**, and at **Taffs Well** — sadly they both kicked off at 3pm; then of course a further two or for those luckier than myself (stuck in a town when the first train is at 9am), three matches. Still, it wasn't over with further fixtures on Tuesday, Wednesday and Thursday before the Trophy Final. Sadly the trophy did not live up to the excitement given to us by the Vase, and the replay didn't entirely help to rectify the position. Again, I think the story of **Vics** win appears elsewhere, but I hope that next season the show-piece of non-league football can be more exciting, and I would like to hope for better crowds. I think these matches are losing out somewhat by clashing with important league fixtures, especially the Vase, where clubs in both United Counties and Essex League played the same day, and **Stansted's** numbers were probably cut down by the fact that **Spurs**, **B. Stortford** and **Enfield** all played that day. I would like to see a "non-league" jamboree, with the two finals being played on a single day and preferably, at that, on a Sunday (Vase kick-off 1pm, Trophy 4pm?). Any takers?

For me the last fixture was the day before the Cup Final, when Vase winners **Stansted**, who still had 5 matches to play, visited **Wivenhoe Town** and won 1-0.

Many decisions were still to be made at that time though, including another manager for **Worcester City** after Bobby Shinton quit the post. Tony Freely, sacked as manager by **Stourbridge** earlier in the season, was appointed as the new manager at **Gloucester City**; this angered the outgoing Bob Marcell, who thought it ought to have been offered to Gerry Sweeney and hence resigned as director, as well as manager, moving to **Trowbridge** and probably taking some of **Gloucester City's** most experienced players with him (7 of the highest paid were released immediately by Freely, including Sweeny). Freely, who has since signed top **Bromsgrove** striker M. Langford to lead the strike force next season, can reflect that his replacement, Alan Fogarty, at **Stourbridge** did not last long — he was replaced by Graham Newton in March.

JUNE & JULY

As I wait for news on how the make-up of the leagues will change before next season (and there are so many ifs and buts there is no point in speculating), I shall attempt to answer the question I am always asked: what does a football 'loony' do in the summer? The anwers are various — some go into other sports, notably Speedway or Cricket, others (if they can afford it) go and watch Soccer abroad, but most of us hibernate until the cold weather comes again!

The amusing photographs included in my last two Non-League publications have proved very popular. And the winner of last years caption competition will be sent a copy of this book as a prize. This year's selection should give you plenty of ideas for amusing captions and we will send copies of the 1986 edition to those who send in the best entries. Wembley's resident photographer (that's Wembley F.C. of the Isthmian League not the Stadium!) Peter Burrin has supplied four of this years photos — it proves that watching Wembley can bring a smile to your face!

Andy McGonigle (Wembley) Peter Burrin.

Brian Parkinson Marine's goalkeeper against Fisher Athletic in the Trophy.
Photo: Eric Marsh.

Could it be the Wembley goalkeeper? Peter Burrin.

(above): Wembley defensive setpiece!
Peter Burrin.

(right): A scene in the Southern League somewhere in Kent. Photo: R. Barrett.

(below): Wembley early season game.
Peter Burrin.

CLUB CAREER GOALSCORING RECORDS WITH ONE CLUB – QUALIFICATION: 250 GOALS

D. Spendlove	Rhyl	650
S. Fisher	Lambourn	600
T. Welsh	Holyhead	561
J. Woodley	Oxford City	544
T. Horseman	Wycombe Wanderers	525
G. Brown	Bromley	510
P. Wassall	Kidderminster	448
G. Wiggin	Rushall Olympic	445
J. Bartley	Welling United	437
J. Bentley	Telford United	431
B. Ellis	Irthlingborough D.L.	428
E. Kail	Dulwich Hamlet	427
W. Dodge	Ashford Town	425
J. Lewis Jnr	Walthamstow Avenue	417
P. Ellis	Hallam	400
M. Tooley	Lowestoft	383
R. Lawton	Curzon Ashton	380
W. Lindsay	Kings Lynn	380
A. Morse	Bridgend	374
P. Watson	Chorley	372
W. Wright	Whitley Bay	365
J. McCartney	Grantham	362
D. Keeton	Arnold Kingswell	350
R. Scott	Rossendale	350
T. Broadbent	Bangor City	340
T. Tuite	Epsom & Ewell	328
*G. Matthews	Willenhall	354
T. Gorringe	Three Bridges	310
J. Burcher	Arnold	305
R. Livermore	Tilbury	305
M. Pamment	Emley	305
J. Harrison	Alfreton Town	303
G. Duggins	Gresley R.	302
J. Harrison	Alfreton	301
S. Diamond	Ashton United	300
P. Ellis	Halesowen Town	300
R. Parker	Tooting & Mitcham	300
A. Roscoe	Daisy Hill	300
D. Lewis	Cheltenham	299
R. Castle	Pirton	296
H. Lewis	V.S. Rugby	294
J. Martin	Oakham United	292
T. Glasscock	Royston	289
E. Hewitt	Sutton Coldfield Town	288
P. Farren	Feltham	287
K. Palmer	Alvechurch	282
G. Cairns	Carshalton	282
D. Hargreaves	Accrington Stanley	277
W. Haines	Weymouth	275
M. Clausen	Minehead	274
P. Nolan	Vulcan Newton	270
B. Wassall	Kidderminster	269
T. Langham	Kimberley	261
H. Brand	Grays Athletic	260
P. Hempel	Blackpool Rangers	260
R. Endacott	Wadebridge	258
C. Vaughan	Sutton United	255
G. Duck	Wealdstone	251
M. Streeter	Worthing	251
M. Kielty	Epping	250
J. Roscoe	South Liverpool	250
J. Swindells	Altrincham	250
R. Weaver	Gloucester City	250
C. Vaughan	Sutton United	250+

*Still playing for club

LEADING PRESENT DAY CAREER GOALSCORERS

John Bartley (Welling United and Maidstone United)	518
George Duck (Wealdstone, Dagenham and Harrow Borough)	401
Tommy Tuite (Epsom & Ewell and Carshalton Ath)	380
Gary Matthews (Willenhall)	354

Carshalton Athletic 1, Barking 2 *(Isthmian League) 14.4.84. Tommy Tuite challenges Barking 'keeper Dave Root.* Photo: Wallington & Carshalton Advertiser

CLUB APPEARANCE RECORDS '600' CLUB

*M. Wright	Kings Lynn	1,143
J. Campion	Olney Town	1,122
A. Hobson	Weymouth	1,076
J. Wallace	Hemel Hempstead	1,012
G. Kempthorne	Illogan R.B.L.	1,008
P. Burraway	Wootton Blue Cross	1,004
*P. Wood	St. Albans City	1,016
D. Moore	Dagenham	932
*P. Giggle	Hitchin Town	910
J. Woodley	Oxford City	904
T. Horseman	Wycombe Wanderers	900
G. Wade	Horden C.W.	895
J. Huttley	Dagenham	884
J. Foster	Horden C.W.	870
W. Fisher	Hendon	865
K. Palmer	Alvechurch	842
H. Dunn	Scarborough	859
K. Jones	Northwich Victoria	838
J. Bentley	Telford United	835
C. Hooper	Bromsgrove Rovers	835
T. Clausen	Minehead	830
G. Brown	Bromley	820
B. Chapman	Wadebridge	820
*T. Payne	Taunton Town	826
J. Clarke	Rossendale	809
L. Burns	Dartford	800
J. Maggs	Crawley Town	800
D. Seedhouse	Tamworth	800
H. Grisedale	Prescot Cables	780
L. Pritchard	Sutton United	765
A. Rowley	Eastwood Town	765
G. Smith	Robinsons D.R.G.	763
J. Sergeant	Stafford Rangers	750
P. Probert	Met Police	750
J. Price	Prescot B.I.	750
F. Bradley	Royston	733
H. Jeavons	Coventry Sporting	727
G. Broadhead	Oswestry Town	720
J. Evans	Rhyl	720
B. Fitch	Salisbury	713
D. Turner	Hitchin Town	709
R. Thorndale	Cheltenham Town	701
S. Logan	Kidderminster Harriers	700
M. Keenan	Cambridge City	700
C. Prior	Didcot Town	700
L. Harris	Yeovil Town	691
R. Nicholls	Uxbridge Town	691
G. Cooper	Erith & Belvedere	690
B. Wassall	Kidderminster Harriers	686
L. Wallace	Clitheroe	670
M. Brown	Gainsborough Trinity	669
A. Clay	Grantham	664
R. Ashby	Kettering Town	662
C. Gardner	Grantham	660
R. Smith	Harwich & P	660
M. Davis	Buxton	657
S. Unwin	Frecheville Com	653
D. Jones	Egham	652
B. Oakley	Whitley Bay	651
N. Gladwin	Harlow T.	651
H. Brockington	Sittingbourne	650
T. Monkhouse	Evenwood	650
S. Page	Harwich & Parkeston	650
H. Morris	Chelmsley Town	648
D. May	Bideford	646
I. Kettlewell	Emley	636
W. Wright	Whitley Bay	634
J. Granson	Horden C.W.	630
J. Binding	Totternhoe	630
C. Peck	Lowestoft Town	629
W. Chater	Whitley Bay	627
P. Wassall	Kidderminster Harriers	621
R. Burgess	Welling United	619
D. Huddart	Ramsgate	617
S. Carter	Minehead	612
W. Clarkson	Wisbech	612
J. Tredwell	Folkestone	612
H. Carradice	Colne Dynamoes	611
M. Thomas	Weston Super Mare	610
J. Goryl	Witton Albion	605
C. Priestly	Ramsgate	605
S. Unwin	Frecheville C.	605
T. Broadbent	Bangor City	601
M. Astley	Eastwood Hanley	600
C. Bate	Kidsgrove Athletic	600
M. Brown	Gainsborough T.	600
R. Campbell	Congleton	600
P. Ellis	Hallam	600
M. Gladwin	Harlow Town	600
G. Keegan	South Liverpool	600
M. Perrin	Melksham	600
R. Rodgers	Norton Woodseats	600
D. Stroud	Malden Vale	600
D. Ward	Netherfield	600

*Still Playing

There must have been a few thousand appearances accumulated by this squad: Charles Hughes, Keith Mead, Mickey Preston, John Swannell, John Delaney, Ted Powell, D. Gubbage (Physio), David Reid. Front Row: Tony Horseman, Chris Kelly, Larry Pritchard, Ray Eaton, Rod Haider, Paul Birdseye, Mickey Hollifield. Has anyone kept records for these players? Incidentally, do any readers know when this photo was taken?

The present day leading goalscorers could well be under pressure very soon from Worthing's goalscoring sensation Micky Edmonds (above right) who has now scored 178 goals in 200 matches and Hungerford Town's Ian Farr (below) who has registered 201 in 270 games. Both players are in their early twenties and, if they can keep their present form as they move into the peak of their careers, they should give a great deal of pleasure to their clubs's supporters in the seasons ahead. However, if reliability is to be guaranteed then Steve Price of Almondsbury Greenway must be the best bet, for over the years he has scored at Wembley, scored in local Cup Finals regularly (including all three in last season's Hellenic League Final) and has recorded a grand total of 265 in 246 games for the club. Granted the first five years were spent in the Gloucestershire County League but that is marksmanship of the highest order in any company. Watch out for these three next season.

Photos: Worthing Gazette & Herald and Newbury Weekly News

Hectic action in the Bangor City v. Northwich Victoria F.A. Trophy Final Replay.

John Davison's amazing FA Cup Record

The Altrincham FA Cup record over the last eleven years has never been bettered for consistency by a Non-League club and during that time John Davison a player who joined them from UAU football and is now a schoolteacher has been a regular either in mid field on the left hand side or at left back. John is also the leading goalscorer and equal leading appearance maker for the England semi-professional International team and last season won one of our special Yearbook awards. His personal FA Cup record in the competition proper (First Round Proper onwards) is:-

1973-1974	First Round	v	Hartlepool United	(h)	2-0	(Dickenson, Windsor)	2,923
	Second Round	v	Blackburn Rovers	(a)	0-0		8,564
	Replay	v	Blackburn Rovers	(h)	0-2		5,500
1974-1975	First Round	v	Scunthorpe United	(a)	1-1	(Hughes J)	2,627
	Replay	v	Scunthorpe United	(h)	3-1	(Morris, Davison, Hughes J)	3,500
	Second Round	v	Gateshead United	(h)	3-0	(Hughes J, Hughes R, Morris)	4,000
	Third Round	v	Everton	(a)	1-1	(Hughes J)	34,519
	Replay	v	Everton (at Old Trafford)		0-2		35,530
1975-1976	First Round	v	Halifax Town	(a)	1-3	(Moore)	4,077
1976-1977	First Round	v	Rotherham United	(a)	0-5		5,969
1977-1978	Altrincham lost 1-2 at Runcorn in the 4th Qualifying Round						
1978-1979	First Round	v	Southport	(h)	4-3	(Johnson 2, Bailey, Rodgers)	2,153
	Second Round	v	Droylsden	(a)	2-0	(Johnson, Brooke)	2,875
	Third Round	v	Tottenham Hotspur	(a)	1-1	(Johnson)	31,081
	Replay	v	Tottenham Hotspur (at Maine Road)		0-3		27,878
1979-1980	First Round	v	Crewe Alexandra	(h)	3-0	(Rogers, Whitbread, Wilson)	5,001
	Second Round	v	Rotherham United	(a)	2-0	(Bailey, Howard)	6,083
	Third Round	v	Orient	(h)	1-1	(Whitbread)	7,844
1980-1981	First Round	v	Burscough	(a)	2-1	(Johnson, Rogers)	1,207
	Second Round	v	Scunthorpe United	(a)	0-0		3,672
	Replay	v	Scunthorpe United	(h)	1-0	(Davison, pen)	5,176
	Third Round	v	Liverpool	(a)	1-4	(Heathcote, pen)	37,170
1981-1982	First Round	v	Sheffield United	(a)	2-2	(Rogers 2)	12,433
	Replay	v	Sheffield United	(h)	3-0	(Howard 2, Heathcote)	5,137
	Second Round	v	York City	(a)	0-0		3,786
	Replay	v	York City	(h)	4-3	(Goulding, Rogers, Whitbread 2)	3,088
	Third Round	v	Burnley	(a)	1-6	(Howard)	10,174
1982-1983	First Round	v	Rochdale	(h)	2-1	(Davison, Howard)	3,053
	Second Round	v	Huddersfield Town	(h)	0-1		5,800
1983-1984	First Round	v	Frickley Athletic	(a)	1-0	(Gardner)	2,267
	Second Round	v	Darlington	(a)	0-0		2,634
	Replay	v	Darlington	(h)	0-2		2,142

Record in Competition Proper 1973-1984: P 31, W 12, D 8, L 11, F 41, A 43

PUBLICATIONS AND PUBLICITY

The saddest aspect of the game's publicity last season was the loss of 'Around Football'. In last season's edition I wrote of the importance of supporting the publication and I was very sorry that the directors of Corvus Publishing were forced to close the magazine down.

However, the lack of a monthly national 'non-league' publication seems to have inspired one or two enthusiasts to produce their own very enjoyable periodicals.

The most comprehensive of these so far has been 'The Bureau of Non-League Football', which has now been published for three seasons. It is a monthly magazine which attempts to give up-to-date league tables and cup progress for all competitions throughout Britain. Subscription rates are £5.50 (UK), £7 (Europe) and £10 (International) for nine issues from Mike Ford, 173 Leytonstone Road, London E15.

A brand new periodical is 'The Midlands Non-League Digest' produced fortnightly by Mike Berry. He has also invited Steve Whitney, who produced 'Sidelines' last season, to help him next season when the Digest will be produced fortnightly as three regional issues covering the Midlands, the North and London and the South.

The price will be 30p an issue or £7.50 for the season and subscriptions should be sent to Mike Berry at Idsworth, Fair Close, Frankton, Nr Rugby, Warwickshire CV23 9PL.

I strongly recommend both 'The Bureau' and 'The Digest' for all Non-League football enthusiasts and hope that early subscriptions to these publications will give their editors the encouragement and inspiration their hard work deserves.

There is no better publication for the game's statisticians than the monthly magazine published by Ray Spiller for his vastly successful 'Association of Football Statisticians'. For details of next year's subscriptions and for all the excellent publications produced by the Association, you should write to Ray, at 22 Bretons, Basildon, Essex SS15 5BY.

Tony Incenzio wrote a thoroughly enjoyable review of the 1982-83 FA Vase competition, 'Tansley to Wembley' and hopes to produce a similar book on the 1983-84 FA Trophy season. Tony can be contacted at 31 Tarling Road, East Finchley, London N2 8LB.

Two counties have their own annuals. 'A Review of Non-League Football in Herts 1983-84' (55p) by Derek Fieldsend covers every senior game played in the county. The editorial office is at 42 Rodney Crescent, Hoddesdon, Herts EN11 9EW. Sussex are also well served by Peter Wallis's fine production 'A Sussex Non-League Football Annual 1983-84' (9 Stockwell Court, London Road, Burgess Hill, West Sussex RH15 9RS). Next season's edition will be even more comprehensive. For details please contact Peter at Burgess Hill.

The ever progressive United Counties League produced an enterprising wall calendar last season and indeed more and more leagues are sending out the most comprehensive and interesting news bulletins. League secretaries should be contacted concerning the availability of these. Last season the Alliance and the Northern Premier Leagues produced weekly bulletins, while the North West Counties introduced the most detailed monthly newsletters. The Sussex County League magazine 'Score' is another great success, and The Gloucestershire Northern Senior League history by Colin Timbrell is most impressive.

However, the book of the year for non-League football must be Bob Barton's 'A History of League and Cup Football'. It costs £4.99, plus 55p postage and packing, from 18 Southwood Gardens, Kenton, Newcastle upon Tyne NE3 3BU. I thoroughly enjoyed reading it and am looking forward to Bob's next publication featuring the FA Amateur Cup.

David Stacey's 'Football Programme Directory' costs £5.50 for 12 issues (overseas £6.50) and features programme news, adverts, members' letters, and details of programme fairs and collectors' meetings. The editorial office is at 66 Southend Road, Wickford, Essex SS11 8EN. This is an excellent magazine which is now well established.

Last year I included details of the Association of Football Badge Collectors but failed to include their address. It is: Barry White, 46 Ellington Drive, Gershwin Road, Brighton Hill Rise, Basingstoke, Hampshire RG22 4EZ.

Details of the Wirral Programme Club Awards for the season are shown elsewhere and our congratulations go to all the winners. The standard of the publications has again improved and the amount of information included in many of them is quite staggering. Programme editors throughout the country are doing a great job for the promotion of semi-professional clubs, and they should send copies of next season's issues to Ian Runham, Wirral Programme Club, 3 Tansley Close, Newton, West Kirby, Wirral, Merseyside L48 9XH, if they wish to enter next season's competition.

One of these dedicated editors is Stamford's Jeremy Biggs (this year's winner) who has also produced a super FA Vase Final souvenir booklet (£1 + stamped addressed envelope) and copies of this can be ordered from Jeremy at 'The Essendine', Essendine, nr Stamford, Lincs PE9 4LD.

Another book which is still available is the fascinating 'Goodall's FA Cup Non-League Giant Killers' (£2.95), from Goodall Publications Ltd, PO Box No 201, 12 Liverpool Street, London EC2M 7BS.

Publicity for semi-professional football is certainly improving but what a pity the later stages of the FA Trophy and FA Vase are not given better coverage. Surely the attendances for these games warrant at least the goalscorers, crowd figures and prominent score lines in the 'nationals'. However Neil Scott (*Daily Telegraph*), Michael Melaniphy (*Daily Mail*), Paul Walker (*Daily Star*), Paul Newman (*The Times*) and Ronald O'Connor (*Daily Telegraph*) all feature regular non-League columns in their papers, and John Bowles has continued his sterling work for the game at the Exchange Telegraph.

The regional Saturday night football 'specials' are still a source of enjoyment to the fans of semi-professional clubs and again I can highly recommend Birmingham's *Sports Argus*, Nottingham's *Football Post*, the South Coast editions of *The Sports Mail*, Reading's *Sports Post* and the Manchester and Liverpool specials.

For Scottish football enthusiasts, *The Scottish Football Historian* is a very enjoyable read and this can be ordered from John Litster, 34 Coldstream Drive, Rutherglen, Glasgow G73 3LH.

Another club production is being produced by Michael Chatwin, Oak Tree House, Hearns Lane, Faddiley, Nantwich, Cheshire. He is writing a 'Centenary History of Natwich Town', and anyone interested should contact him direct. A special newspaper tribute to Folkestone was also produced to celebrate their centenary.

STOP PRESS: Additional New Publications

Fisher Athletic are launching a new magazine to cover non-league football fortnightly called **'The Pyramid Magazine'**. It will be edited by their new commercial manager Tony Incenzo and should be very popular throughout the game at 25p a copy (36 pages). Orders should be sent to the club who are prepared to send a free copy of the first issue on request.

Steve Adamson and the **Scarborough** Supporters Association will have copies of the new club **yearbook** (£1.00 postage free) from Steve at 40 St. Leonards Crescent, Scarborough, North Yorkshire YO12 6SP.

Cray Wanderers (fortnightly) and **South Shields** (yearbook) are two more clubs with excellent publications and enquiries for these should be sent to the respective clubs.

A very impressive and now well established magazine is **The Programme Monthly** available at 50p + 16p postage from John Litster, 35 Gowing Road, Mulbarton, Norwich NR15 8AT. This A5 sized booklet has fifty pages, is well illustrated and has a glossy cover.

Enquiries for **The Gloucestershire Football Guide 1984-85** (£1.00 inc. postage) should be sent to Leo Hoenig, Basement Flat, 8 Lansdown Place, Cheltenham, Gloucestershire.

The **Ashington Programme catalogue** will be available throughout season 1984-85 advertising hundreds of programmes and souvenirs.

One of the most impressive club magazines I have ever seen is **'Touchliner'** produced for Sutton United every month by Dave Farebrother, 24 Lunley Road, Cheam, Surrey. (Cost 25p)

BEST NON LEAGUE PROGRAMME NATIONALLY 1983/4

1st: STAMFORD
2nd: Boston United
3rd: Three Bridges

THE NATIONAL TOP 30

1. Stamford, 2. Boston U., 3. Three Bridges, 4. Badminton Picksons, 5.= Port of Bristol, St. Neots T., 7. Lancing, 8. Farnborough T., 9. Moor Green, 10. Ash U., 11. Didcot T., 12. North Shields, 13.= Yeovil T., Wembley, Grantham, 16. Oxford City, 17.= Sutton U., Aylesbury U., Basingstoke T., 20.= V.S. Rugby, Hinckley Ath., 22.= Weymouth, Metropolitan Police, Highgate U., Bristol Manor Farm, 26.= St. Albans City, Stalybridge Celtic, 28. Barnstaple T., 29.= Banstead Ath., Hartley Wintney.

INDIVIDUAL LEAGUE RESULTS. TOP 3

League	First	Second	Third
Alliance Premier	Boston U.	Yeovil T.	Weymouth
Isthmian	Farnborough	Wembley	Oxford C.
Northern Premier	Grantham	Mossley	Matlock
Southern	Moor Green	Aylesbury, Basingstoke =	
Athenian	Banstead A.	Ruislip M.	Berkhamsted, Chertsey =
Northern	North Shields	Ashington	Shotton
North West Counties	Stalybridge	Atherton	Irlam
Northern Co. East	Harrogate T., Heanor T. =		Sutton T.
West Midlands	Hinckley A.	Gresley R.	Wednesfield
Kent	Beckenham T.	Faversham	Cray W.
Midland Comb.	Highgate U.	Evesham U.	Northfield
Western	Bristol M.F.	Barnstaple	Clevedon
Sussex	Three Bridges	Lancing	Bosham
Eastern Counties	Wisbech T.	Braintree	Stowmarket
Hampshire	Romsey T.	Horndean	Portsmouth U.
Wearside	Blue Star	Wingate	Eppleton
Hellenic	Badminton P.	Didcot T.	Supermarine, Lydney =
South Midlands	Winslow U., Biggleswade T. =		Totternhoe
Welsh Leagues	Newtown	Port Talbot	Blaenau F
Scottish Leagues	Caledonian	Keith	Troon
Combined Co.	Ash U.	Hartley W.	Godalming
Surrey Premier	Ashford T.	Chipstead	Worcester, Frinton R. =
United Co.	Stamford	St. Neots T.	Irthlingboro
Glos. Co.	Port of Bristol	Old Georgians	Frampton
London Spartan	Bracknall T.	Malden Vale	Barkingside
Leicestershire	Anstey N.	Thurmaston	Lutterworth
Herts Co.	St. Margaretsbury	Mount Grace	Wellcome
Essex Senior	Canvey Is.	Witham T.	Heybridge
Staffs Co.	Hednesford P	Ettingshall	Pelsall CS
West Sussex	Rustington	Wittering	Billingshurst
Other Leagues	Old Altrinchanians	Pinchbeck U.	Marske
Sunday clubs	Billericay TSC, Bournville Southern =		Central Eight, Southend USC =

'Best Non-League Special'

Ian Runham's Wirral Programme Club awards for 1983-84 were given to:

1st Stamford v Irthlingborough Diamonds
2nd Harrow Borough v Manchester United
3rd Heanor Town v Emley

1983-84 ACTION

Basildon United's John Reeves jumps just higher than his Dorking opponent to win this midfield battle. Photo: Steve Lindwell.

First meetings of 'The Greens'. Moor Green (stripes) entertain Forest Green Rovers. Photo: Solihull News

Paul Whelan celebrates after scoring Bangor City's goal against Dagenham in the F.A. Trophy Semi-Final First Leg.

J. Berry scores Newquay's second goal in their 6-2 away victory at Glenside St Gabriels in the First Round. Photo: Mike Joss

Rayners Lane skipper Phil Robson clears during his side's 1-0 home win over Harrow Borough Reserves in the Middlesex Premier Cup semi-final. Lane's Alan Williams, Val Boyle and Paul Abell (striped shirts) look on.

Photographer Eric Marsh certainly had a good game himself when he covered the Corinthian-Casuals v Stamford Vase match. It was also one of the most exciting ties of the whole competition and here we see Russ Allen beautifully balanced as he crashes a drive through the Casuals' defence. Photo: Eric Marsh

OTHER USEFUL ADDRESSES

National Federation of Football Supporters Clubs	Lottery Office: 1 Saville Row, Bath, Avon BA1 2QP 0225 312247 (B) General Secretary: Malcolm Gamlen, 69 Fourth Avenue, Chelmsford, Essex (0245) 63305 (B)
National Playing Fields Association	Col R. Satterthwaite OBE, 578b Catherine Place, London SW1
The Scottish Football Commercial Managers Association	Chairman: J.E. Hillier, c/o Keith FC Promotions Office, 60 Union Street, Keith, Banffshire, Scotland
British Olympic Association	R.W. Palmer, 1 Church Row, Wandsworth Plain, London SW18 1EH 01-874 4764 (B)
Universities Athletic Union	I. Grant, 28 Woburn Square, London WC1 0AA 01-637 4828 (B)
Central Council of Physical Recreation	General Secretary, 70 Brompton Road, London SW3 1HE 01-584 6651 (B)
Referees' Association	W.J. Taylor, Cross Offices, Summerhill, Kingswinford, West Midlands Kingswinford (0384) 288386
Wirral Programme Club	I.R.W. Runham, 3 Tansley Close, Newton, West Kirby, Merseyside L48 9XH 051-625 9554 (H)
The Bureau of Non-League Football	M. Ford, 173 Leytonstone Road, London E15
Midlands Non-League Digest	M. Berry, Idsworth, Fair Close, Frankton, Nr Rugby, Warks CV23 9PL Warwick (0926) 632708 (H)
The Association of Football League Referees and Linesmen	J.B. Goggins, 1 Tewkesbury Drive, Lytham St Annes, Lancs FY8 4LN
Women's Football Association	Miss L. Whitehead, 11 Portsea Mews, Portsea Place, London W2 01-402 9388 (B)
The Association of Provincial Football Supporters Clubs in London	E. Norfolk, 79 Dellow Close, Ilford, Essex
The Association of Football League Commercial Managers	G.H. Dimbleby, Secretary, WBA, F.C., The Hawthorns, Halfords Lane, West Bromwich B71 4LF
The Association of Football Statisticians	R.J. Spiller, 5 Hempstalls, Basildon, Essex 0268 282556 (H)
The Football Programme Directory	D. Stacey, 'The Beeches', 66 Southend Road, Wickford, Essex SS11 8EN Wickford 2041 (H)
England Football Supporters Association	Hon. Publicity Officer, D. Stacey, 'The Beeches', 66 Southend Road, Wickford Essex SS11 8EN Wickford 2041 (H)
The Football League Executive Staffs Association	P.O. Box 52, Leamington Spa, Warwickshire
The Ninety-Two Club	104 Hilda Crescent, Whitchurch, Bristol BS14 9LD
Wembley Stadium Ltd	Wembley Stadium, Wembley, Middlesex HA9 0DW 01-902 8833 (B) Box Office: 01-902 1234
Thorn EMI Football Floodlighting Competition	Competition Organiser, 299-300 Upper Street, Islington, London N1 2TU 01-359 7271 (B)

EX NON-LEAGUE FOOTBALL LEAGUE XI

Over eighty players from Non-League clubs represented League clubs last season apart from the 130 who we have already mentioned in the APL, Isthmian, Southern, NPL and Northern League sections. The 'team' on this page is selected from those 80 players.

Neville Southall
(Winsford U, Bury, Everton, Wales)

Colin Tartt
(Alsager T, Port Vale)

Richard Money
(Lowestoft T, Scunthorpe U, Fulham, Liverpool, Luton T, Portsmouth)

Martin Hicks
(Stratford T, Charlton A, Reading)

Stuart Mell
(Appleby, Frodingham, Doncaster R)

Brian Horton
(Hednesford T, Port Vale, Brighton, Luton T)

Glen Cockerill
(Louth U, Lincoln C, Swindon T, Lincoln C, Sheffield U)

Anton Otulakowski
(Ossett Trinity, Barnsley, West Ham U, Millwall)

Brian Stein
(Edgware T, Luton T, England)

Gary Birtles
(Long Eaton U, Nott'm F, Manchester U, Nott'm F)

Bobby Davison
(Seaham CW, Huddersfield T, Halifax T, Derby Co)

NON-LEAGUE CLUB EXEMPTIONS
1984-85

Four Semi-Professional clubs have again been given exemptions until the First Round Proper of the FA Cup. They are the FA Trophy finalists — Northwich Victoria and Bangor City — and the two other clubs considered to be most worthy of the honour by The Football Association: Altrincham and Telford United.

20 clubs to the Fourth Round Qualifying

Barking	Dartford	Maidstone United	Windsor & Eton
Barnet	Enfield	Mossley	Worcester City
Bishop's Stortford	Harrow Borough	Penrith	Workington
Boston United	Kettering Town	Scarborough	Wycombe Wanderers
Dagenham	Macclesfield Town	Weymouth	Yeovil Town

CHALLENGE TROPHY COMPETITION SEASON 1984-85 EXEMPTIONS

32 clubs to the First Round Proper

Altrincham	Dartford	Leytonstone/Ilford	Runcorn
Bangor City	Dulwich Hamlet	AP Leamington	Scarborough
Barnet	Enfield	Maidstone United	Telford United
Barrow	Fisher Athletic	Marine	Wealdstone
Bath City	Frickley Athletic	Matlock Town	Whitby Town
Blyth Spartans	Gateshead	North Shields	Worcester City
Chorley	Harrow Borough	Northwich Victoria	Worthing
Dagenham	Kidderminster H.	Nuneaton Borough	Wycombe Wanderers

32 clubs to the Third Round Qualifying

Aylesbury United	Chelmsford City	Hendon	Spennymoor United
Barking	Croydon	Hordon Colliery W	Sutton United
Bishop Auckland	Dorchester Town	Kettering Town	Trowbridge Town
Bishop's Stortford	Gloucester City	Merthyr Tydfil	Welling United
Boston United	Grantham	Mossley	Weymouth
Bromsgrove Rovers	Gravesend & N'fleet	Rhyl	Windsor & Eton
Burton Albion	Hastings United	Slough Town	Witton Albion
Carshalton Athletic	Hayes	South Liverpool	Yeovil Town

62 clubs not required to play in the Preliminary Round

Alfreton Town	Epsom & Ewell	Leatherhead	Stalybridge Celtic
Alvechurch	Fareham Town	Macclesfield Town	Sutton Town
Arnold	Ferryhill Athletic	Minehead	Tilbury
Ashington	Folkestone	Morecambe	Tooting & Mitcham U
Bedworth United	Frome Town	Oswestry Town	Tow Law Town
Billericay Town	Gainsboro' Trinity	Peterlee Newtown	Walthamstow Ave
Billingham Synthonia	Goole Town	Poole Town	Walton & Hersham
Bognor Regis Town	Gretna	RS Southampton	Wembley
Bromley	Hampton	Salisbury	Whitley Bay
Buxton	Harlow Town	Shepshed C'house	Willenhall Town
Cheltenham Town	Hitchin Town	Shildon	Witney Town
Consett	Horwich RMI	South Bank	Woking
Corby Town	Hyde United	Southport	Wokingham Town
Crawley Town	Ilkeston Town	Stafford Rangers	Workington
Crook Town	Kings Lynn	Staines Town	Worksop Town
Durham City	Lancaster City		

Clubs who competed in the FA Trophy last season but are now considered more suitable for the FA Vase for season 1984-85 are:
Bilston Town, Boston, Bridport Town, Cheshunt, Cinderford Town, Emley, Keynsham Town, Lowestoft Town, Nantwich Town, Sudbury Town, West Auckland Town and Willington.

Clubs who competed in the FA Vase last season but are now considered more suitable for the FA Trophy for season 1984-85 are:
Basildon United, RS Southampton and Shepshed Charterhouse.

New entries accepted into the FA Trophy for season 1984-85 are:
Corby Town, Leyland Motors, Llanelli and St Helens Town.

FA VASE EXEMPTIONS
1984-85

32 clubs to the Second Round

Appleby Frodingham	Corinthian-Casuals	Irthlingborough D	Shortwood United
Atherstone United	Devizes Town	Leyton-Wingate	Stamford
Blue Star	Frechevillie Com	Marlow	Stansted
Bracknell Town	Grays Athletic	Newbury Town	Staveley Works
Brandon United	Gt Yarmouth Town	Old Georgians	Three Bridges
Bristol Manor Farm	Guisborough Town	Ossett Albion	VS Rugby
Buckingham Town	Halesowen Town	Rainworth MW	Whickham
Burnham	Heybridge Swifts	Shifnal Town	Wivenhoe Town

32 clubs to the First Round

Abingdon Town	Cray Wanderers	Harefield United	Sholing Sports
Alma Swanley	Crockenhill	Hemel Hempstead	Skegness Town
Almondsbury G'way	Desborough Town	Hucknall CW	Southall
Arlesey Town	Eppleton CW	Irlam Town	Tiptree United
Baldock Town	Friar Lane OB	Lincoln United	AFC Totton
Barton Rovers	Gorleston	Newport IOW	Whyteleafe
Brantham Athletic	Guiseley	Rothwell Town	Wigston Fields
Clitheroe	Hallam	Ruislip Manor	Wren Rovers

38 new clubs accepted into the Competition

Alnwick Town	Eynesbury Rovers	Long Buckby	Shefford Town
Armthorpe Welfare	Frampton Athletic	Maltby MW	Shotton Comrades
Ashton Town	GKN Sankey	Molesey	Swanage T & Herston
Avon St Philips	Greenwich Borough	Newport Pagnell Tn	Tees Components
Blandford United	GS Ashcroft Co-op	Newton Aycliffe	Riverton Town
Bridlington Town	Harrogate RA	Ortonians	Washington Town
Brimsdown	Hurley Daw Mill W	Rayners Lane	W Allotment Celtic
Bristol St George	Keyworth United	Retford Town	Wigmore Athletic
Collier Row	Langley Pk Welfare	St Ivey Town	
Darlington CB	Liversedge		

FA CHALLENGE CUP COMPETITION — SEASON 1984-1985

Preliminary Round — 1st September 1984

First Round Qualifying — 15th September 1984

Second Round Qualifying — 29th September 1984
(for all Divisions)
Winners match 2 v Winners match 3
Winners match 1 v Winners match 4

Third Round Qualifying — 13th October 1984
(for all Divisions)
Winners match 2 or Winners match 3
v
Winners match 1 or Winners match 4

DIVISION 1

Prel Round
Shildon v Crook Town
Brandon United v Harrogate Town
Yorkshire Amateur v Consett

1st Round Qual
1 Blue Star v Horden CW
2 Shildon or Crook Town v Durham City
3 Yorkshire Amateur or Consett v Gateshead
4 Billingham Synthonia v Brandon U or Harrogate T

DIVISION 2

Prel Round
Ferryhill Athletic v Guiseley
Esh Winning v Guisborough Town

1st Round Qual
1 Seaham CW Red Star v Tow Law Town
2 Ferryhill Athletic or Guiseley v West Auckland Town
3 Netherfield v South Bank
4 Blyth Spartans v Esh Winning or Guisborough T

DIVISION 3

Prel Round
Peterlee Newton v Eppleton CW
Chester-le-Street v Lancaster City
Thackley v Darwen

1st Round Qual
1 Ashington v Whitley Bay
2 Peterlee Newtown or Eppleton CW v Evenwood T
3 Thackley or Darwen v Gretna
4 Bishop Auckland v Chester-le-Street or Lancaster C

DIVISION 4

Prel Round
Bridlington Trinity v Easington Colliery
Billingham Town v Coundon TT

1st Round Qual
1 Willington v Whitby Town
2 Bridlington Trin or Easington Colliery v Wren R
3 Ryhope CA v Spennymoor United
4 North Shields v Billingham Town or Coundon TT

DIVISION 5

Prel Round
Nantwich Town v Droylsden
Colwyn Bay v Lytham
Rossendale Unitedc v Denaby United

1st Round Qual
1 Bootle v Marine
2 Nantwich Town or Droylsden v Fleetwood Town
3 Rossendale United or Denaby United v Buxton
4 Barrow v Colwyn Bay or Lytham

DIVISION 6

Prel Round
Burscough v Emley
Alfreton Town v Eastwood Hanley

1st Round Qual
1 Leyland Motors v Southport
2 Burscough or Emley v Skelmersdale United
3 Leek Town v Runcorn
4 Morecambe v Alfreton Town or Eastwood Hanley

DIVISION 7

Prel Round
Radcliffe Borough v Clitheroe
Caernarfon Town v Garforth Miners
Shifnal Town v Chadderton

1st Round Qual
1 Belper Town v Rhyl
2 Radcliffe Borough or Clitheroe v Farsley Celtic
3 Shifnal Town or Chadderton v Oswestry Town
4 Frickley Athletic v Caernarfon T or Garforth Miners

DIVISION 8

Prel Round
Long Eaton United v Curzon Ashton
Arnold v Ilkeston Town
Prescot Cables v Ashton United

1st Round Qual
1 Armitage v Witton Albion
2 Long Eaton U or Curzon Ashton v Hednesford T
3 Prescot Cables or Ashton United v Hyde United
4 Accrington Stanley v Arnold or Ilkeston Town

DIVISION 9

Prel Round
Ossett Albion v Formby
Blakenall v Mile Oak Rovers
St Helens Town v Coleshill Town

1st Round Qual
1 Bilston Town v South Liverpool
2 Ossett Albion or Formby v Lye Town
3 St Helens Town or Coleshill Town v Congleton T
4 Chorley v Blakenall or Mile Oak Rovers

DIVISION 10

Prel Round
Dudley Town v Heanor Town
Appleby Frodingham v Glossop

1st Round Qual
1 North Ferriby United v Winsford United
2 Dudley Town or Heanor Town v Paget Rangers
3 Hinckley Athletic v Stalybridge Celtic
4 Horwich RMI v Appleby Frodingham or Glossop

DIVISION 11

Prel Round
Walsall Borough v Gresley Rovers
Brigg Town v Tamworth
Wednesfield Social v Friar Lane OB

1st Round Qual
1 Boston v Matlock Town
2 Walsall Borough or Gresley Rovers v Lincoln United
3 Wednesfield Social or Friar Lane OB v Goole Town
4 Eastwood Town v Brigg Town or Tamworth

DIVISION 12

Prel Round
Desborough Town v Racing Club Warwick
Boldmere St Michaels v Halesowen Town

1st Round Qual
1 Tividale v Worksop Town
2 Desborough T or Racing Club Warwick v Wigston F
3 Stourbridge v Sutton Town
4 Grantham v Boldmere St Michaels or Halesowen T

DIVISION 13

Prel Round

Stamford v Irthlingborough Diamonds
Chatteris Town v Oldswinford
Wisbech Town v Evesham United

1st Round Qual

1 Bromsgrove Rovers v Shepshed Charterhouse
2 Stamford or Irthlingborough D v Leicester U
3 Wisbech T or Evesham United v Nuneaton Borough
4 Gainsborough Trinity v Charteris T or Oldswinford

DIVISION 14

Prel Round

Milton Keynes City v Rothwell Town
Malvern Town v Redditch United

1st Round Qual

1 Rushden Town v Stafford Rangers
2 Milton Keynes City or Rothwell T v Wolverton T
3 Rushall Olympic v Kidderminster Harriers
4 Bridgnorth Town v Malvern Town or Redditch U

DIVISION 15

Prel Round

Stevenage Borough v Holbeach United
Coventry Sporting v Spalding United
Wootton Blue Cross v Histon

1st Round Qual

1 Banbury United v Willenhall Town
2 Stevenage Bor or Holbeach U v Soham Town R
3 Wootton Blue Cross or Histon v Burton Albion
4 Bedworth United v Coventry Sporting or Spalding U

DIVISION 16

Prel Round

Ampthill Town v Barton Rovers
Abingdon Town v Baldock Town

1st Round Qual

1 Hertford Town v Sutton Coldfield Town
2 Ampthill Town or Barton Rovers v Oxford City
3 Chalfont St Peter v Oldbury United
4 Moor Green v Abingdon Town or Baldock Town

DIVISION 17

Prel Round

Sudbury Town v Edgware
Boreham Wood v Haverhill Rovers
Wembley v Bourne Town

1st Round Qual

1 Berkhampstead Town v VS Rugby
2 Sudbury Town or Edgware v Flackwell Heath
3 Wembley or Bourne Town v AP Leamington
4 Alvechurch v Boreham Wood or Haverhill Rovers

DIVISION 18

Prel Round

Bury Town v Great Yarmouth Town
Arlesey Town v Cheshunt

1st Round Qual

1 Newmarket Town v Wellingborough Town
2 Bury T or Gt Yarmouth T v Saffron Walden T
3 Hemel Hempstead v Kings Lynn
4 Corby Town v Arlesey Town or Cheshunt

DIVISION 19

Prel Round

Stowmarket v Gorleston
Cambridge City v Hoddesdon Town
Tilbury v Epping Town

1st Round Qual

1 Aveley v March Town United
2 Stowmarket or Gorleston v Haringey Borough
3 Tilbury or Epping United v Lowestoft Town
4 Billericay Town v Cambridge City or Hoddesdon T

DIVISION 20

Prel Round

Finchley v Hornchurch
Felixstowe Town v Harwich & Parkeston

1st Round Qual

1 Tiptree United v Harlow Town
2 Finchley or Hornchurch v Woodford Town
3 Royston Town v Chelmsford City
4 Basildon U v Felixstowe T or Harwich & Parkeston

DIVISION 21

Prel Round

Bromley v Cray Wanderers
Braintree Town v Hillingdon
Leyton-Wingate v Burnham

1st Round Qual

1 Aylesbury United v Hayes
2 Bromley or Cray Wanderers v Heybridge Swifts
3 Leyton-Wingate or Burnham v Chesham United
4 Buckingham Town v Braintree Town or Hillingdon

DIVISION 22

Prel Round

Crockenhill v Grays Athletic
Clapton v Dunstable

1st Round Qual

1 Hounslow v Wealdstone
2 Crockenhill or Grays Athletic v St Albans City
3 Harefield United v Sutton United
4 Hendon v Clapton or Dunstable

DIVISION 23

Prel Round

Southall v Maidenhead United
Erith & Belvedere v Rainham Town
Tring Town v Kingsbury Town

1st Round Qual

1 Beckenham Town v Hitchin Town
2 Southall or Maidenhead United v Potton United
3 Tring Town or Kingsbury Town v Hampton
4 Fisher Athletic v Erith & Belvedere or Rainham T

DIVISION 24

Prel Round

Chatham Town v Metropolitan Police
Addlestone & Weybridge T v Letchworth Gard City

1st Round Qual

1 Uxbridge v Welling United
2 Chatham Town or Metropolitan Police v Ware
3 Tunbridge Wells v Leytonstone/Ilford
4 Corinthian Cas v Addlest. & Wey T or Letch G C

DIVISION 25

Prel Round

Steyning Town v Redhill
Horley Town v Ruislip Manor
Tonbridge AFC v Molesey

1st Round Qual

1 Herne Bay v Walthamstow Avenue
2 Steyning Town or Redhill v Ringmer
3 Tonbridge AFC or Molesey v Folkestone
4 Crawley Town v Horley Town or Ruislip Manor

DIVISION 26

Prel Round

Haywards Heath v Merstham
Chertsey Town v Lancing

1st Round Qual

1 Whyteleafe v Staines Town
2 Haywards Heath or Merstham v Woking
3 Thanet United v Sittingbourne
4 Carshalton Athletic v Chertsey Town or Lancing

DIVISION 27

Prel Round

Littlehampton Town v Canterbury City
Banstead Athletic v Lewes
Whitstable Town v Burgess Hill Town

1st Round Qual

1 Arundel v Worthing
2 Littlehampton T or Canterbury C v Faversham T
3 Whitstable Town or Burgess Hill Town v Croydon
4 Ashford Town v Banstead Athletic or Lewes

DIVISION 28

Prel Round

Dover Athletic v Horsham
Deal Town v Hastings Town

1st Round Qual

1 Sheppey United v Whitehawk
2 Dover Athletic or Horsham v Three Bridges
3 Pagham v Leatherhead
4 Hastings United v Deal Town or Hastings Town

DIVISION 29

Prel Round

Southwick v Egham Town
Chichester City v Kingstonian
Walton & Hersham v Eastbourne United

1st Round Qual

1 Bracknell Town v Tooting & Mitcham United
2 Southwick or Egham Town v Hailsham Town
3 Walt & Hersham or Eastbourne U v Gravesend & N
4 Dulwich Hamlet v Chichester City or Kingstonian

DIVISION 30

Prel Round

Camberley Town v Eastbourne Town
Basingstoke Town v Dorking

1st Round Qual

1 Horsham YMCA v Wokingham Town
2 Camberley Town or Eastbourne Town v Wick
3 Horndean v Epsom & Ewell
4 Bognor Regis Town v Basingstoke Town or Dorking

DIVISION 31

Prel Round

Salisbury v Marlow
Fleet Town v Petersfield United
Thame United v Hungerford Town

1st Round Qual

1 Eastleigh v AFC Totton
2 Salisbury or Marlow v Newport IOW
3 Thame United or Hungerford T v Gosport Borough
4 Farnborough T v Fleet T v Petersfield United

DIVISION 32

Prel Round

Brockenhurst v Chippenham Town
Andover v Calne Town

1st Round Qual

1 Newbury Town v Slough Town
2 Brockenhurst or Chippenham Town v Sholing Spts
3 Melksham Town v RS Southampton
4 Fareham Town v Andover or Calne Town

DIVISION 33

Prel Round

Wellington v Devizes Town
Chard Town v Shepton Mallet Town
Welton Rovers v Clevedon Town

1st Round Qual

1 Bridgend Town v Witney Town
2 Wellington or Devizes Town v Glastonbury
3 Welton Rovers or Clevedon Town v Waterlooville
4 Poole Town v Chard Town v Shepton Mallet Town

DIVISION 34

Prel Round

Clandown v Haverfordwest County
Cinderford Town v Forest Green Rovers

1st Round Qual

1 Mangotsfield United v Highgate United
2 Clandown or Haverfordwest County v Moreton T
3 Llanelli v Gloucester City
4 Barry Town v Cinderford Town or Forest Green Rov

DIVISION 35

Prel Round

Bridgwater Town v Dorchester Town
Bideford v Bristol Manor Farm

1st Round Qual

1 Ton Pentre v Trowbridge Town
2 Bridgwater T or Dorchester T v Weston-Super-Mare
3 Saltash United v Merthyr Tydfil
4 Cheltenham Town v Bideford or Bristol Manor Farm

DIVISION 36

Prel Round

Paulton Rovers v Taunton Town
Barnstaple Town v St Blazey

1st Round Qual

1 Wadebridge Town v Minehead
2 Paulton Rovers or Taunton Town v Wimborne Town
3 Torrington v Frome Town
4 Bath City v Barnstaple Town or St Blazey

THE FOOTBALL ASSOCIATION

FIXTURE PROGRAMME
SEASON 1984-1985

August 1984
Sat 11 Official Opening of Season
Sat 18 FA Charity Shield
Sat 25 Canon League Season starts
Wed 29 Milk Cup (1) 1st Leg

September 1984
Sat 1 FA Cup (P)
Wed 5 Milk Cup (1) 2nd Leg
Sat 8 FA Trophy (P)
FA Vase (EP)
FA Youth Cup (P)*
Wed 12 Iceland v Wales (WC)
Northern Ireland v Rumania (WC)
England v East Germany (F)
Scotland v Yugoslavia (F)
Sat 15 FA Cup (1Q)
Wed 19 European Cups (1) 1st Leg
Wed 26 Milk Cup (2) 1st Leg
Sat 29 FA Cup (2Q)
FA Youth Cup (1Q)*

October 1984
Wed 3 European Cups (1) 2nd Leg
Sat 6 FA Vase (P)
Sun 7 FA Sunday Cup (1)
Wed 10 Milk Cup (2) 2nd Leg
Cambridgeshire FA v FA XI
Sat 13 FA Cup (3Q)
Tue 16 England v Finland (U-21)
Wed 17 England v Finland (WC)
Scotland v Iceland (WC)
Spain v Wales (WC)
Sat 20 FA Trophy (1Q)
FA Youth Cup (2Q)*
Wed 24 European Cups (2) 1st Leg
Isthmian League v FA XI
Sat 27 FA Cup (4Q)
FA County Youth Cup (1)*
Wed 31 Milk Cup (3)

November 1984
Sat 3 FA Vase (1)
Sun 4 FA Sunday Cup (2)
Wed 7 European Cups (2) 2nd Leg
Oxford University v FA XI
Tue 13 England v New Zealand (B)
Turkey v England (U-21)
Wed 14 Turkey v England (WC)
Northern Ireland v Finland (WC)
Scotland v Spain (WC)
Wales v Iceland (WC)
Sat 17 FA Cup (1P)
FA Youth Cup (1P)
Wed 21 Milk Cup (4)
Sat 24 FA Trophy (2Q)
Wed 28 UEFA Cup (3) 1st Leg
Cambridge University v FA XI

December 1984
Sat 1 FA Vase (2)
Sun 2 FA Sunday Cup (3)
Wed 5 England v Australia (B)
Northern Premier League v FA XI
Sat 8 FA Cup (2P)
FA County Youth Cup (2)*
Wed 12 UEFA Cup (3) 2nd Leg
Sat 15 FA Trophy (3Q)
FA Youth Cup (2P)*
Sat 22 FA Vase (3)

January 1985
Sat 5 FA Cup (3P)
Sun 6 FA Sunday Cup (4)
Sat 12 FA Trophy (1P)
FA Youth Cup (3P)*
Wed 16 Milk Cup (5)
Combined Services v FA XI
Sat 19 FA Vase (4)
Wed 23 London University v FA XI
Sat 26 FA Cup (4P)
FA County Youth Cup (3)*

February 1985
Sat 2 FA Trophy (2P)
Sun 3 FA Sunday Cup (5)
Wed 6 Milk Cup (SF) 1st Leg
British Colleges v FA XI
Sat 9 FA Vase (5)
FA Youth Cup (4P)*
Wed 13 Milk Cup (SF) 2nd Leg
Sat 16 FA Cup (5P)
Wed 20 Universities Athletic Union v FA XI
Sat 23 FA Trophy (3P)
Wed 27 Northern Ireland v England (WC)
Spain v Scotland (WC)

March 1985
Sat 2 FA Vase (6)
Wed 6 European Cups (3 & 4) 1st Leg
Northern League v FA XI
Sat 9 FA Cup (6P)
FA Youth Cup (5P)*
FA County Youth Cup (4)*
Sat 16 FA Trophy (4P)
Sun 17 FA Sunday Cup (SF)
Wed 20 European Cups (3 & 4) 2nd Leg
Amateur Football Alliance v FA XI
Sat 23 FA Vase (SF) 1st Leg
Sun 24 Milk Cup Final
Wed 27 Scotland v Wales (WC)
Sat 30 FA Vase (SF) 2nd Leg

April 1985
Wed 3 Western League v FA XI
Sat 6 FA Trophy (SF) 1st Leg
FA Youth Cup (SF)*
Wed 10 European Cups (SF) 1st Leg
Sat 13 FA Cup (SF)
FA Trophy (SF) 2nd Leg
FA County Youth Cup (SF)
Wed 17 Suffolk FA v FA XI
Wed 24 European Cups (SF) 2nd Leg
Sat 27 FA Vase Final (Wembley Stadium)
Sun 28 FA Sunday Cup Final
Tue 30 Wales v Spain (WC)
Rumania v England (U-21)

May 1985
Wed 1 Rumania v England (WC)
Northern Ireland v Turkey (WC)
Sat 4 FA Youth Cup Final*
FA County Youth Cup Final (Fixed Date)
Wed 8 UEFA Cup Final 1st Leg
Sat 11 FA Trophy (Wembley Stadium)
Wed 15 European Cup Winners' Cup Final
Sat 18 FA Cup Final (Wembley Stadium)
Tue 21 Finland v England (U-21)
Wed 22 UEFA Cup Final 2nd Leg
Finland v England (WC)
Tue 28 Iceland v Scotland (WC)
Wed 29 European Champion Clubs' Cup Final

Key
* = Closing Date for Round
P = Preliminary Round
EP = Extra Preliminary Round
F = Friendly International
1Q = First Qualifying Round
1P = First Round Proper
U-21 = UEFA Under-21 Competition
WC = World Cup
B = "B" International
SF = Semi-Final

GOLA LEAGUE
LEAGUE FIXTURES
1984/85

	Altrincham	Barnet	Barrow	Bath City	Boston United	Dagenham	Dartford	Enfield	Frickley Athletic	Gateshead	Kettering T	Kidderminster H	Maidstone U	Northwich Vic	Nuneaton Boro	Runcorn	Scarborough	Telford U	Wealdstone	Weymouth	Worcester C	Yeovil Town
Altrincham	—	6.4	26.12	5.1	4.5	29.12	27.6	23.3	27.8	1.10	18.8	3.11	6.10	9.2	1.9	10.9	24.11	8.12	9.3	20.10	24.9	15.9
Barnet	8.9	—	26.1	4.5	16.3	8.4	24.11	27.8	22.12	30.3	29.9	8.12	20.4	22.9	4.9	3.11	23.2	18.8	26.12	5.1	16.2	13.10
Barrow	1.1	23.3	—	9.3	9.2	20.4	8.9	3.11	29.9	8.4	8.12	24.11	13.4	29.12	15.12	27.8	2.4	20.10	2.3	18.8	19.1	4.5
Bath City	22.9	10.11	25.8	—	2.3	8.9	29.12	16.2	30.3	6.10	1.12	4.9	20.8	27.4	27.10	16.3	20.10	15.12	29.9	8.4	26.12	19.1
Boston United	30.3	22.8	6.10	23.2	—	9.3	20.10	27.4	26.12	8.12	16.2	26.1	25.8	3.11	19.9	20.3	8.4	5.1	8.9	22.9	24.11	13.4
Dagenham	2.3	9.2	6.4	3.11	13.10	—	8.12	26.12	18.8	19.1	23.3	22.12	17.9	15.9	23.2	5.1	13.4	4.5	27.8	24.11	1.9	29.9
Dartford	29.9	15.12	16.3	26.1	1.12	16.2	—	18.9	5.1	4.5	27.8	16.10	26.12	23.3	10.11	6.4	18.8	1.9	2.10	3.11	15.9	23.2
Enfield	25.8	25.9	22.9	13.4	29.12	1.1	8.4	—	1.9	9.2	26.1	4.5	1.12	20.10	20.8	6.10	30.3	23.4	10.11	9.3	15.12	26.3
Frickley Athletic	13.4	20.10	17.11	8.12	1.1	26.3	25.8	16.3	—	25.9	3.11	8.9	26.1	23.2	29.12	27.4	19.1	24.11	15.12	6.4	16.2	23.3
Gateshead	15.12	27.4	27.10	23.3	27.8	1.12	9.3	8.9	13.10	—	29.10	13.4	16.2	11.3	6.4	17.9	1.1	22.9	26.1	20.4	18.8	2.3
Kettering T	19.1	2.3	22.12	1.9	10.11	22.8	30.3	24.11	20.4	20.10	—	9.2	23.2	25.8	1.1	26.9	22.9	3.10	4.5	13.3	6.10	8.4
Kidderminster H	10.11	6.10	23.2	10.9	1.9	22.9	19.1	18.8	9.3	5.1	27.4	—	15.12	1.12	30.3	20.10	29.12	26.12	16.2	27.8	8.4	24.9
Maidstone U	16.3	12.9	27.4	22.12	29.9	26.9	1.11	13.12	2.3	3.11	15.9	6.4	—	1.9	19.1	18.8	4.5	27.3	8.4	8.12	9.2	24.11
Northwich Vic	13.10	19.1	5.1	27.8	1.4	15.12	6.12	2.3	8.4	24.11	15.4	16.3	30.3	—	24.9	26.12	17.9	16.2	18.8	8.9	10.9	10.11
Nuneaton Boro	8.4	13.4	16.2	18.8	23.3	15.12	2.3	5.1	22.9	22.12	26.12	29.9	20.10	8.12	—	24.11	16.3	27.8	20.4	6.10	3.11	8.9
Runcorn	4.9	1.12	20.8	13.10	19.1	10.11	22.9	20.4	9.2	29.9	8.9	2.3	9.3	1.1	25.8	—	15.12	8.4	27.10	17.11	23.3	29.10
Scarborough	16.2	1.9	26.9	20.4	22.12	6.10	13.12	15.9	10.11	26.12	6.4	27.3	23.3	22.8	1.12	8.12	—	26.1	5.1	27.4	2.3	25.8
Telford U	27.10	29.12	1.12	6.4	15.9	25.8	9.2	19.1	18.9	10.11	13.4	1.1	8.9	29.9	13.10	22.12	9.3	—	23.3	23.2	27.4	20.8
Wealdstone	22.12	1.1	13.10	24.11	25.9	27.4	20.8	8.12	19.2	1.9	16.3	25.8	29.12	6.4	11.9	30.3	9.2	3.11	—	19.1	20.10	19.3
Weymouth	26.1	15.9	30.3	26.9	6.4	16.3	20.2	22.12	4.5	25.8	13.10	22.8	10.11	13.4	9.2	1.9	29.9	2.3	1.12	—	29.12	1.1
Worcester C	20.8	25.8	10.11	1.1	20.4	30.3	13.4	29.9	1.12	23.2	9.3	13.10	5.1	22.12	4.5	26.1	8.9	16.3	22.9	17.9	—	8.12
Yeovil Town	1.12	9.3	1.9	9.2	18.8	20.10	22.12	6.4	6.10	16.3	5.1	20.4	22.9	26.1	27.4	16.2	3.11	30.3	19.9	26.12	27.8	—

NB. Fixtures are subject to alterations for reasons of weather, cup-ties etc.

SERVOWARM ISTHMIAN LEAGUE PREMIER DIVISION 1984/85

	Barking	Billericay Town	Bishops Stortford	Bognor Regis Town	Carshalton Athletic	Croydon	Dulwich Hamlet	Epsom & Ewell	Harlow Town	Harrow Borough	Hayes	Hendon	Hitchin Town	Leytonstone/Ilford	Slough Town	Sutton United	Tooting & Mitcham	Walthamstow Ave	Windsor & Eton	Wokingham Town	Worthing	Wycombe Wanderers
Barking	—	26.12	18.9	12.1	2.10	22.9	25.8	16.3	8.9	13.11	27.4	5.1	2.3	29.12	19.1	1.12	3.11	26.3	17.11	2.2	16.2	13.4
Billericay Town	1.1	—	4.9	10.11	12.1	9.3	29.12	27.10	9.2	23.2	26.1	20.4	6.4	8.12	6.10	20.11	25.8	4.12	8.9	4.5	9.4	23.3
Bishops Stortford	24.11	2.4	—	9.2	8.9	6.4	20.10	26.1	27.4	23.3	9.3	28.8	29.12	1.1	8.12	10.11	20.4	25.8	9.4	11.9	22.9	23.2
Bognor Regis Town	3.9	30.3	16.2	—	1.12	5.1	26.11	12.11	4.5	27.4	1.10	3.11	16.3	13.4	2.3	25.8	17.11	6.10	2.2	19.1	26.12	8.9
Carshalton Athletic	11.9	3.11	2.2	6.4	—	26.12	13.11	26.3	2.3	22.9	13.4	1.9	27.4	24.11	4.9	29.1	16.3	5.1	20.10	16.2	8.12	17.11
Croydon	9.2	16.3	13.4	8.12	26.1	—	1.1	29.12	25.8	20.4	24.11	12.1	6.10	3.9	8.9	15.10	1.4	29.10	2.3	4.5	10.11	20.10
Dulwich Hamlet	2.4	22.9	19.1	30.10	28.8	1.12	—	2.3	20.4	5.1	26.3	17.4	10.11	11.9	16.3	16.2	26.12	2.2	3.11	1.9	15.12	6.10
Epsom & Ewell	20.4	2.2	6.10	23.2	27.11	27.4	2.10	—	1.9	17.11	25.9	16.2	3.11	29.1	6.4	26.12	16.10	8.9	1.12	23.3	5.1	9.3
Harlow Town	6.4	5.1	26.12	23.3	6.11	28.8	27.10	23.4	—	30.3	10.11	19.1	11.9	9.3	27.11	23.2	8.12	16.10	16.2	13.4	2.2	22.9
Harrow Borough	29.9	16.10	13.10	26.1	9.2	2.10	8.9	13.4	29.12	—	6.11	11.9	1.1	15.12	10.11	20.10	6.4	16.3	25.8	30.10	2.3	8.12
Hayes	6.10	1.12	3.11	22.9	18.12	12.2	6.4	30.10	16.3	26.12	—	2.2	17.11	23.3	9.4	20.4	5.1	16.2	19.1	2.3	1.9	4.9
Hendon	10.11	2.3	30.10	2.4	29.12	30.3	4.9	8.12	6.10	18.9	20.10	—	25.8	26.1	1.1	18.12	8.9	13.4	16.3	23.4	24.11	9.2
Hitchin Town	8.12	19.1	5.1	1.9	9.3	23.3	13.4	30.3	.11	2.2	28.8	26.12	—	23.2	20.11	27.10	16.2	27.11	22.9	20.4	27.4	9.4
Leytonstone/Ilford	28.8	17.4	2.3	9.4	20.4	16.2	30.3	6.11	30.10	6.10	8.9	27.4	1.12	—	25.8	2.2	13.11	26.12	5.1	16.3	19.1	3.11
Slough Town	20.10	16.2	1.4	10.9	23.3	17.11	24.11	22.9	3.11	28.8	30.3	23.2	30.10	4.12	—	9.3	2.2	20.4	26.12	5.1	13.4	22.9
Sutton United	26.1	13.4	16.3	29.12	1.1	26.3	23.3	11.9	17.11	2.3	8.12	22.9	9.2	1.9	12.1	—	4.12	3.11	27.4	28.8	6.10	24.11
Tooting & Mitcham	23.2	11.9	1.12	23.4	20.11	27.10	9.3	1.1	26.1	1.9	9.2	23.3	12.1	22.9	29.12	19.3	—	18.12	13.4	10.11	28.8	30.3
Walthamstow Ave	9.3	6.11	30.3	28.8	23.2	1.9	8.12	10.11	1.1	1.12	12.1	6.4	26.1	27.10	9.2	4.9	27.4	—	19.3	22.9	11.9	29.12
Windsor & Eton	1.9	28.8	15.9	9.3	30.3	11.4	26.1	9.2	12.1	24.11	23.2	6.11	4.9	10.11	12.2	6.4	6.10	23.3	—	8.12	20.4	1.1
Wokingham Town	30.3	27.4	17.11	16.4	6.10	3.11	23.2	12.1	4.9	9.3	1.1	1.12	6.11	9.12	26.1	8.9	26.3	9.4	29.12	—	19.3	25.8
Worthing	23.3	23.4	4.5	1.1	25.8	23.2	9.2	4.9	16.4	3.11	29.12	9.3	8.9	20.10	1.12	30.3	6.11	17.11	30.4	6.4	—	26.1
Wycombe Wanderers	15.9	1.9	29.9	20.4	10.11	2.2	27.4	28.8	1.12	16.2	11.9	26.3	2.4	6.4	6.11	5.1	2.3	19.1	13.10	26.12	16.3	—

NORTHERN PREMIER LEAGUE FIXTURES 1984/85

	Bangor City	Burton Albion	Buxton	Chorley	Gainsborough Trin	Goole T	Grantham	Horwich R.M.I	Hyde Utd	Macclesfield T	Marine	Matlock T	Morecambe	Mossley	Oswestry T	Rhyl	S. Liverpool	Southport	Stafford Rangers	Witton Albion	Workington	Worksop T
Bangor City	—	1.9	18.8	15.12	6.10	29.12	20.10	30.3	27.4	20.4	27.8	24.11	8.4	15.9	16.10	1.1	9.10	9.3	11.9	25.9	23.3	26.1
Burton Albion	4.5	—	25.9	9.3	5.9	10.10	19.9	12.1	8.9	22.8	13.4	8.4	16.2	20.10	29.12	1.12	23.3	25.8	1.1	19.1	17.11	31.10
Buxton	16.3	30.3	—	19.1	9.3	21.8	11.9	15.12	13.4	16.2	22.9	1.1	1.9	2.10	25.8	8.4	20.4	17.11	9.10	27.10	12.1	23.10
Chorley	8.9	6.10	6.4	—	25.8	2.2	3.12	26.11	18.9	16.10	25.9	20.4	30.10	21.8	16.3	23.2	5.1	16.2	17.11	27.4	4.9	29.12
Gainsborough Trin	13.4	26.1	27.8	27.10	—	11.9	23.10	17.11	4.5	15.12	23.2	25.9	12.1	9.10	8.4	30.3	22.9	29.12	1.9	16.3	18.8	1.1
Goole T	6.4	5.1	30.10	27.8	16.10	—	26.12	4.5	6.10	2.10	1.9	18.9	8.9	30.3	26.1	18.8	16.3	3.11	15.12	1.12	16.2	20.4
Grantham	16.2	15.10	26.1	13.4	20.8	1.1	—	20.4	9.3	12.1	27.10	3.9	17.11	29.12	22.9	16.3	1.12	6.10	24.9	6.4	8.9	27.8
Horwich R.M.I	19.1	10.9	27.4	8.4	23.3	27.10	18.8	—	1.12	22.9	9.3	5.11	27.8	22.10	1.1	29.12	23.2	1.10	13.4	15.10	17.9	1.9
Hyde Utd	22.9	16.3	29.12	22.10	1.10	23.2	8.10	2.2	—	1.1	15.12	27.10	20.8	8.4	1.9	19.1	25.8	30.3	10.11	17.11	20.4	10.9
Macclesfield T	29.9	2.2	4.9	1.12	18.9	19.1	30.10	5.1	26.12	—	18.8	23.3	16.3	13.10	23.2	23.10	8.9	27.4	27.8	6.10	6.4	25.9
Marine	2.10	24.11	3.11	1.1	8.9	8.4	25.8	6.10	4.9	30.3	—	27.4	4.5	16.3	21.8	16.10	19.1	18.9	30.10	16.2	29.12	17.11
Matlock T	23.2	27.8	26.12	1.9	30.10	23.10	2.10	5.1	16.3	11.9	2.2	—	15.12	22.9	30.3	17.11	20.10	13.4	26.1	18.8	4.5	9.10
Morecambe	1.12	22.9	23.2	11.9	6.4	23.3	19.1	25.9	3.11	29.12	9.10	25.8	—	2.2	13.11	27.10	23.10	4.9	27.4	20.4	1.1	18.8
Mossley	5.1	3.11	15.10	24.11	16.2	24.9	23.3	3.9	27.8	9.3	20.4	8.9	17.9	—	17.11	6.10	13.4	12.1	18.8	26.12	29.9	6.4
Oswestry T	5.9	27.10	23.3	18.8	1.12	27.4	4.5	8.9	16.2	10.10	24.10	6.10	5.1	19.1	—	27.8	26.12	7.11	6.4	19.9	9.3	13.4
Rhyl	26.12	6.4	8.9	20.10	5.1	12.1	24.11	9.10	25.9	25.8	23.3	16.2	13.4	4.5	30.10	—	4.9	21.8	9.3	6.11	26.1	22.9
S. Liverpool	18.9	18.8	6.10	4.5	27.4	17.11	2.2	30.10	12.1	3.11	6.4	9.3	30.3	1.9	11.9	2.10	—	1.1	29.12	27.8	16.10	16.2
Southport	27.10	23.2	4.5	9.10	19.1	22.9	5.1	6.4	18.8	1.9	26.12	1.12	16.10	11.9	20.4	2.2	25.9	—	16.3	30.10	27.8	15.12
Stafford Rangers	2.2	26.12	5.1	23.3	20.4	25.8	30.3	16.2	8.12	8.4	1.12	16.10	6.10	23.2	2.10	18.9	21.8	8.9	—	4.9	3.11	12.1
Witton Albion	21.8	23.10	2.2	22.9	3.11	9.3	1.9	25.8	23.3	13.4	20.10	29.12	2.10	1.1	12.1	11.9	24.11	8.4	4.5	—	9.10	23.2
Workington	13.10	27.4	1.12	3.10	2.2	13.4	23.2	22.8	31.10	15.9	12.9	19.1	26.12	25.8	15.12	1.9	8.4	24.10	22.9	5.1	—	16.3
Worksop T	25.8	3.10	19.9	30.3	26.12	5.9	8.4	3.11	17.10	4.5	5.1	22.8	9.3	1.12	2.2	27.4	27.10	23.3	19.1	8.9	6.10	—

FIXTURES

Due to bad weather or Cup commitments all fixture dates may have to be changed, so it is advisable to check them in the National or Local Press.

SOUTHERN FOOTBALL LEAGUE PREMIER DIVISION FIXTURES 1984-85

	AP Leamington	Alvechurch	Bedworth	Chelmsford	Cheltenham	Corby	Crawley	Fareham	Fisher	Folkestone	Gloucester	Gravesend	Hastings	King's Lynn	RS Southampton	Shepshed Charterhouse	Trowbridge	Welling United	Willenhall	Witney Town
AP Leamington	—	1.1	8.4	19.1	22.9	9.3	6.10	1.9	1.12	23.3	9.2	20.10	6.4	4.5	3.11	23.2	22.12	18.8	17.11	27.4
Alvechurch	24.11	—	12.1	20.4	16.2	27.4	22.9	6.10	26.12	18.8	8.12	2.3	1.9	30.3	2.2	15.12	27.10	10.11	5.1	23.3
Bedworth	26.12	9.3	—	1.9	6.10	24.11	22.12	10.11	23.2	13.4	18.8	6.4	22.9	27.8	8.12	2.2	19.1	5.1	23.3	27.10
Chelmsford	10.11	29.12	30.3	—	26.1	23.3	1.1	23.2	16.2	27.10	9.3	13.4	2.2	6.10	27.4	22.9	24.11	12.1	25.8	8.12
Cheltenham	5.1	29.9	9.2	8.9	—	8.12	10.11	24.11	2.2	1.9	26.12	18.8	19.1	3.11	13.10	6.4	27.4	23.3	13.4	2.3
Corby	29.9	13.10	2.3	3.11	30.3	—	19.1	22.12	15.12	29.12	6.4	9.2	17.11	16.3	8.9	5.1	25.8	1.12	23.2	20.4
Crawley	16.2	6.4	8.9	13.10	16.3	18.8	—	12.1	8.4	2.3	5.1	17.11	26.12	1.12	29.9	3.11	23.3	1.9	2.2	15.12
Fareham	2.3	16.3	15.12	17.11	20.4	16.2	30.3	—	8.9	19.1	13.10	3.11	5.1	25.8	26.12	1.12	29.9	27.4	26.1	9.2
Fisher	16.3	3.11	17.11	20.10	29.12	6.10	24.11	6.4	—	22.12	1.9	1.1	2.3	22.9	19.1	27.4	4.5	9.2	8.12	18.8
Folkestone	15.12	17.11	1.12	26.12	9.3	2.2	26.1	4.5	29.9	—	3.11	16.3	20.4	16.2	5.1	25.8	23.2	13.10	6.4	8.9
Gloucester	27.10	23.2	16.3	1.12	8.4	22.9	25.8	1.1	26.1	30.3	—	6.10	16.2	29.12	22.12	17.11	27.8	2.2	12.1	13.4
Gravesend	26.1	8.9	25.8	29.9	22.12	27.10	23.2	9.3	23.3	10.11	20.4	—	27.4	2.2	4.5	16.2	1.12	26.12	13.10	5.1
Hastings	8.9	26.1	29.12	8.4	25.8	1.1	13.4	27.10	13.10	24.11	10.11	8.12	—	12.1	30.3	23.3	9.2	29.9	9.3	23.2
King's Lynn	13.10	22.12	29.9	5.1	23.2	26.12	9.2	23.3	9.3	8.12	8.9	24.11	18.8	—	1.9	13.4	10.11	27.10	27.4	19.1
RS Southampton	13.4	25.8	20.4	9.2	15.12	10.11	9.3	8.4	27.10	22.9	23.3	12.1	1.12	26.1	—	6.10	1.1	23.2	29.12	24.11
Shepshed Charterhouse	8.12	9.2	13.10	16.3	27.10	8.4	20.4	18.8	10.11	12.1	19.1	29.12	22.12	1.1	2.3	—	8.9	24.11	29.9	1.9
Trowbridge	30.3	13.4	16.2	18.8	12.1	26.1	8.12	2.2	5.1	6.10	2.3	1.9	20.10	6.4	17.11	9.3	—	22.9	3.11	26.12
Welling United	25.8	19.1	3.11	6.4	17.11	13.4	29.12	8.12	27.8	1.1	20.10	30.3	16.3	2.3	16.2	26.1	20.4	—	8.9	6.10
Willenhall	20.4	8.4	1.1	2.3	1.12	1.9	27.10	22.9	30.3	9.2	24.11	19.1	6.10	15.12	18.8	26.12	16.3	22.12	—	10.11
Witney Town	2.2	1.12	26.1	22.12	1.1	12.1	4.5	29.12	25.8	8.4	29.9	22.9	3.11	17.11	16.3	30.3	13.10	9.3	16.2	—

CLUB & LEAGUE INDEX

The vast majority of clubs entering the Trophy and Vase are featured individually in the Yearbook with a few more listed only in league tables. The leagues in which clubs play are shown in a code in the Trophy and Vase lists. All clubs can be traced by looking up their respective league pages.

CHALLENGE TROPHY CLUBS

List of 215 Clubs accepted into the Competition for Season 1983-84

Accrington Stanley (NWC)
Addlestone & Weybridge T (SL)
Alfreton Town (NCE)
Altrincham (GL)
Alvechurch (SL)
Andover (SL)
Arnold (NCE)
Ashford Town (SL)
Ashington (NE)
Ashton United (NWC)
Aveley (I)
Aylesbury United (SL)

Banbury United (SL)
Bangor City (NP)
Barking (I)
Barnet (GL)
Barnstaple Town (WL)
Barrow (GL)
Basildon United (I)
Basingstoke Town (SL)
Bath City (GL)
Bedworth United (SL)
Belper Town (NCE)
Bideford (WL)
Billericay Town (I)
Billingham Synthonia (NE)
Bishop Auckland (NE)
Bishop's Stortford (I)
Blyth Spartans (NE)
Bognor Regis Town (I)
Bootle (NWC)
Boreham Wood (I)
Boston United (GL)
Bridgend Town (SL)
Bridgwater Town (SL)
Bridlington Trinity (NCE)
Bromley (I)
Bromsgrove Rovers (SL)
Burscough (NWC)
Burton Albion (NP)
Buxton (NP)

Caernarfon Town (NW)
Cambridge City (SL)
Canterbury City (SL)
Carshalton Athletic (I)
Chatham Town (SL)
Chelmsford City (SL)
Cheltenham Town (SL)
Chesham United (I)
Chorley (NP)
Clandown (WL)
Clapton (I)
Colwyn Bay (NWC)
Congleton T (NWC)
Consett (NE)
Corby Town (SL)
Crawley Town (SL)
Crook Town (NE)
Croydon (I)
Curzon Ashton (NWC)

Dagenham (GL)
Dartford (GL)
Dorchester Town (SL)
Dover Athletic (SL)
Dudley Town (SL)
Dulwich Hamlet (I)
Dunstable (SL)
Durham City (NE)

Eastwood Town (NCE)
Enfield (GL)
Epsom & Ewell (I)
Evenwood Town (NE)

Fareham Town (SL)
Farnborough Town (I)
Ferryhill Athletic (NE)
Fisher Athletic (SL)
Folkestone (SL)
Forest Green R (SL)
Formby (NWC)
Frickley Athletic (GL)
Frome Town (WL)

Gainsborough Trinity (NP)
Gateshead (GL)
Glossop (NWC)
Gloucester City (SL)
Goole Town (NP)
Grantham (NP)
Gravesend & Northfleet (SL)
Gretna (N)

Hampton (I)
Harlow Town (I)
Harrow Borough (I)
Hastings United (SL)
Hayes (I)
Heanor Town (NCE)
Hednesford Town (SL)
Hendon (I)
Hertford Town (I)
Highgate United (MFC)
Hillingdon Borough (SL)
Hitchin Town (I)
Horden Colliery Welfare (NE)
Hornchurch (I)
Horwich RMI (NWC)
Hounslow (M)
Hyde United (NP)

Ilkeston Town (NCE)

Kettering Town (GL)
Kidderminster Harriers (GL)
Kings Lynn (NP)
Kingstonian (I)

Lancaster City (NPL)
AP Leamington (SL)
Leatherhead (I)
Leek Town (NWC)
Leicester United (SL)
Lewes (I)
Leyland Motors (NWC)
Leytonstone & Ilford (I)
Llanelli (NEL)
Lye Town (WM)

Macclesfield Town (NP)
Maesteg Park (WEL)
Maidenhead United (I)
Maidstone United (GL)
Marine (NP)
Matlock Town (NP)
Melksham Town (WL)
Merthyr Tydfil (SL)
Metropolitan Police (I)
Mexborough Town Ath (NCE)
Milton Keynes City (SL)
Minehead (SL)
Moor Green (MFC)
Morecambe (NP)
Mossley (NP)

Netherfield (NP)
North Shields (NE)
Northwich Victoria (GL)
Nuneaton Borough (GL)

Oldbury U (SL)
Oswestry Town (NP)
Oxford City (I)

Penrith (NWC)
Peterlee Newtown (N)
Poole Town (SL)
Prescot Cables (NWC)

Radcliffe Borough (NWE)
Redditch United (SL)
Rhyl (NWC)
RS Southampton (SL)
Runcorn (GL)

St. Albans City (I)
St. Helens Town (NWC)
Salisbury (SL)
Scarborough (GL)
Sheppey United (SL)
Shepsted Charterhouse (SL)
Shepton Mallet Town (WL)
Shildon (NE)
Sittingbourne (K)
Slough Town (I)
South Bank (NE)
South Liverpool (NP)
Southport (NP)
Spalding United (NCE)
Spennymoor United (NE)
Stafford Rangers (NP)
Staines Town (I)
Stalybridge Celtic (NWC)
Stourbridge (SL)
Sutton Coldfield Town (SL)
Sutton Town (NCE)
Sutton United (I)

Tamworth (NP)
Taunton Town (SL)
Telford United (GL)
Thanet United (SL)
Tilbury (I)
Tonbridge AFC (SL)
Tooting & Mitcham United (I)
Tow Law Town (SE)
Trowbridge Town (SC)

Walthamstow Avenue (I)
Walton & Hersham (I)
Waterlooville (SL)
Wealdstone (GL)
Wellingborough Town (SL)
Welling United (SL)
Wembley (I)
Weston-super-Mare (WL)
Weymouth (GL)

Whitby Town (NE)
Whitley Bay (NE)
Willenhall (SL)
Windsor & Eton (I)
Winsford United (NWC)
Witney Town (SL)

Witton Albion (NP)
Woking (I)
Wokingham Town (I)
Worcester City (GL)
Workington (NP)

Workshop Town (NP)
Worthing (I)
Wycombe Wanderers (I)

Yeovil Town (GL)

Code for Trophy Club's Leagues: NWC - NW Counties; SL - Southern League; GL - Gola League; H - Hellenic; I -Isthmian; NCE - Northern Counties East; NE - Northern League; IS - Isthmian Second Division; WL - Western League; WL - Western League; WEL - Welsh League; NP - Northern Premier; K - Kent; WM - West Midlands; EC - Eastern Counties; MFC - Midland Football Combination.

FA CHALLENGE VASE COMPETITION

List of 409 Clubs accepted into the Competition for Season 1984-85

Abingdon Town (Hell)
Alma Swanley (K)
Almondsbury Greenway (Hell)
Alnwick Town (N)
Amersham Town (LS)
Amesbury Town (Wilts)
Ampthill Town (UC)
Anstey Nomads (Le)
Appleby Frodingham (NE)
Arlesey Town (UC)
Armitage (WM)
Armthorpe Welfare (NE)
Arnold Kingswell (NE)
Arundel (Sx)
Ashton Town (NW)
Ash United (CC)
Atherstone United (WM)
Atherton Collieries (NW)
Atherton LR (NW)
Avon (Bradford) (Hell)
Avon St Philips (G)

Backwell United (W)
Baldock Town (UC)
Banstead Athletic (I)
Barton Rovers (I)
Barton Town (Lincs)
Beaconsfield United (LS)
Beckenham Town (K)
Beckton United (LS)
Bedlington Terriers (N)
Bentley Victoria (NE)
Berkhamstead Town (I)
Bicester Town (Hell)
Billingham Town (N)
Bilston Town (WM)
Birstall United (Le)
Blackpool Mechanics (NW)
Blakenall (WM)
Blandford United (D)
Blue Star (Wear)
Boldmere St Michaels (MCB)
Boston (NE)
Bourne Town (UC)
Bowers (Ex)
Bracknell Town (I)
Bradley Rangers (NE)
Braintree Town (EC)
Brandon United (N)
Brantham Athletic (EC)
Brereton Social (WM)
Bridgnorth Town (SL)
Bridlington Town (NE)

Bridport Town (D)
Brigg Town (NE)
Brightlingsea United (Ex)
Brimsdown (LS)
Brislington (Som)
Bristol Manor Farm (N)
Bristol St George (G)
British Aerospace (Weybridge) (CC)
BSC (Parkgate) (NE)
Brockenhurst (Ha)
Buckingham Town (UC)
Burgess Hill Town (Sx)
Burnham (LS)
Burnley Belvedere (LA)
Bury Town (EC)

Calne Town (Wilts)
Camberley Town (I)
Chadderton (NW)
Chalfont St Peter (I)
Chatteris Town (EC)
Cheadle Town (NW)
Chertsey Town (I)
Cheshunt (I)
Chester-le-Street Town (N)
Chichester City (Sx)
Chippenham Town (W)
Chobham (CC)
Cinderford Town (G)
Cirencester Town (Hell)
Clacton Town (EC)
Clanfield (Hell)
Clay Cross Works (CM)
Cleator Moor Celtic (CD)
Clevedon Town (N)
Clipstone Welfare (NA)
Clitheroe (NW)
Cobham (CC)
Coggeshall Town (Ex)
Coleshill Town (MCB)
Collier Row (LS)
Corinthian-Casuals (I)
Coundon TT (Wear)
Coventry Sporting (WM)
Cradley Town (MCB)
Cray Wanderers (K)
Crockenhill (K)
Crown & Manor (LS)

Daisy Hill (NW)
Darenth Heathside (K)
Darlington Cleveland Bridge (N)
Darlington Railway Athletic (T)

Deal Town (K)
Denaby United (NE)
Desborough Town (UC)
Devizes Town (W)
Didcot Town (Hell)
Diss Town (AC)
Dorking (I)
Droylsden (NW)

Easington Colliery (Wear)
Eastbourne Town (Sx)
Eastbourne United (I)
East Grinstead (Sx)
Eastleigh (Ha)
Eastwood Hanley (NW)
Eaton Bray United (SM)
Edgware (LS)
Egham Town (I)
Ellesmere Port & Neston (NW)
Ely City (EC)
Emley (NE)
Epping Town (I)
Eppleton CW (N)
Erith & Belvedere (S)
Esh Winning (N)
Evesham United (MCB)
Exmouth Town (W)
Eynesbury Rovers (UC)

Fairford Town (Hell)
Farnham Town (CC)
Farsley Celtic (NB)
Faversham Town (K)
Felixstowe Town (EC)
Finchley (I)
Flackwell Heath (I)
Fleet Town (CC)
Fleetwood Town (NWC)
Flight Refuelling (D)
Ford Motors (Liverpool) (NW)
Ford United (London) (Ex)
Frampton Athletic (G)
Frecheville Community (NE)
Friar Lane OB (Le)
Frimley Green (CC)
Fryston CW (NE)

Garforth Miners (NE)
GKN Sankey (WM)
Glastonbury (W)
Glenside St Gabriels (B)
Godalming Town (CC)
Gorleston (EC)

Graham St Prims (NE)
Grays Athletic (I)
Great Yarmouth Town (EC)
Greenwich Borough (K)
Gresley Rovers (WM)
Grimthorpe MW (NE)
GS Ashcroft Co-op (SM)
Guisborough Town (NE)
Guiseley (NE)

Hadleigh United (Suff)
Haig Colliery (CD)
Hailsham Town (Sx)
Halesowen Town (WM)
Hallam (NE)
Hall Road Rangers (NE)
Halstead Town (Ex)
Harefield United (I)
Haringey Borough (I)
Harrogate Railway Athletic (NE)
Harrogate Town (NE)
Harwich & Parkeston (EC)
Hastings Town (Sx)
Hatfield Main (NE)
Hatfield Town (SM)
Havant Town (Ha)
Haverhill Rovers (EC)
Haywards Heath (Sx)
Hazells (Aylesbury) (Hell)
Hebburn Reyrolle (Wear)
Hemel Hempstead (I)
Hengrove Athletic (Som)
Herne Bay (K)
Heswall (WC)
Heybridge Swifts (I)
Hinckley Athletic (WM)
Histon (EC)
Hoddesdon Town (SM)
Holbeach United (UC)
Horley Town (CC)
Horndean (Ha)
Horsham (I)
Horsham YMCA (Sx)
Hucknall CW (NA)
Hungerford Town (I)
Hurley Daw Mill Welfare (MCB)
Hythe Town (K)

Immingham Town (Lincs)
Irlam Town (NW)
Irthlingborough Diamonds (UC)

Keynsham Town (W)
Keyworth United (NA)
Kimberley Town (NE)
Kingsbury Town (I)
Knowle North Star (MCB)

Lancing (Sx)
Langley Park Welfare (N)
Larkhall Athletic (W)
Lawrence Weston Hallen (G)
Letchworth Garden City (I)
Leyton-Wingate (I)
Lincoln (NE)
Linotype (MC)
Littlehampton Town (Sx)
Liversedge (NE)
Long Buckby (UC)
Long Eaton United (NE)
Louth United (Lincs)
Lowestoft Town (EC)
Lytham (NU)

Maghull (NW)
Maidenhead Town (Hell)
Maine Road (M)
Malden Town (CC)
Malden Vale (CC)
Maldon Town (Ex)
Maltby Miners Welfare (NE)
Malvern Town (WM)
Mangotsfield United (W)
March Town United (EC)
Marlow (I)
Melton Town (Le)
Merstham (CC)
Midland Bank (SA)
Mile Oak Rovers & Youth (MCB)
Milton Keynes Borough (SM)
Mirrless Blackstone (UC)
Molesey (I)
Moreton Town (Hell)

Nantwich Town (NW)
Nelson (NW)
Newbury Town (I)
Newhall United (D)
Newmarket Town (EC)
Newport (IOW) (Ha)
Newport Pagnell (UC)
Newquay (SW)
Newton Aycliffe (Wear)
Norsemen (SA)
Northallerton Town (N)
North Ferriby United (NE)
Northfield Town (MCB)
North Withington (M)
Northwood (LS)
Norton & Stockton Ancients (N)
Nunthorpe Athletic (T)

Oadby Town (Le)
Oakham United (NE)
Odd Down (W)
Old Esthameians (SA)
Old Georgians (G)
Oldswinford (WM)
Ortonians (P)
Ossett Albion (NE)
Ossett Town (NE)
Ottery St Mary (W)

Paget Rangers (MCB)
Pagham (Sx)
Paulton Rovers (W)
Pegasus Juniors (Hell)
Petersfield United (I)
Pilkington Recreation (NE)
Pirelli General (Ha)
Pirton (SM)
Portfield (Sx)
Port of Bristol (G)
Portway Bristol (N)
Potton United (UC)
Prescot BI (NW)
Prestwich Heys (NW)

Racing Club Warwick (MCB)
Radstock Town (W)
Rainham Town (I)
Rainworth MW (NA)
Ransomes (Suff)
Rayners Lane (Hell)
Redhill (LS)
Retford Town (NE)
Ringmer (Sx)
Romsey Town (Ha)
Rossendale United (NW)
Rothwell Town (UC)
Rowntree Mackintosh (NE)
Royston Town (I)
Ruislip Manor (I)
Rushall Olympic (WM)
Rushden Town (UC)
Ryhope CA (N)
Rylands (MC)

Saffron Walden Town (I)
St Dominics (Le)
St Ives Town (P)
St Neots Town (UC)
Sawbridgeworth Town (Ex)
Seaham CW Red Star (Hell)
Seaton Delaval Seaton Trr (NA)
Selby (SM)
Sharpness (Hell)
Sheffield (EC)
Shefford Town
Shifnal Town (WM)
Shillington (SM)
Sholing Sports (Ha)
Shortwood United (Hell)
Shotton Comrades (N)
61 FC (Luton) (SM)
Skegness Town (NE)
Skelmersdale United (NW)
Slade Green Athletic (K)
Smethwick Highfield (MCB)
Soham Town Rangers (EC)
Solihull Borough (MCB)
Somersham Town (P)
Southall (I)
South Shields (Wear)
Southwick (CC)
Stamford (UC)
Stansted (Ex)
Stapenhill (Le)
Staveley Works (NE)
Stevenage Borough (I)
Steyning Town (Sx)
Stockton (Wear)
Stotfold (UC)
Stowmarket Town (EC)
Stratford Town (MCB)
Sudbury Town (EC)
Supermarine (Hell)
Swanage Town & Herston (W)
Swanley Town (LS)

Tadcaster Albion (NE)
Tansley (Nemean)
Tees Components (T)
Thackley (NE)
Thame United (Hell)
Thatcham Town (LS)
Thetford Town (EC)
Three Bridges (Sx)
Tiptree United (EC)
Tiverton Town (W)
Tividale (WM)
Torrington (W)
AFC Totton (Ha)
Tring Town (I)
Tunbridge Wells (K)

Uxbridge (I)

Vauxhall Motors (SM)
VS Rugby

Wallingford Town (Hell)
Walsall Borough (MCB)
Wantage Town (Hell)
Ware (I)
Warminster Town (Wilts)
Warrington Town (NW)
Washington (Wear)
Waterloo Dock (Lp)
Waterlows (SM)
Watton United (AC)
Wednesfield Social (WM)
Wellington Town (W)
Welton Rovers (W)
Welwyn Garden City (SM)
West Allotment Celtic (NA)
West Auckland Town (N)
Westbury United (W)
West Midlands Police (MCB)
West Wickham (SA)
Whickham (Wear)
Whitehawk (Sx)
Whitstable Town (K)
Whyteleafe (I)
Wick (Sx)
Wigmore Athletic (Sx)
Wigston Fields (Le)
Wigton (WC)
Willington (N)
Wilton Rovers (G)
Wimborne Town (W)
Winchmore Hill (SA)
Wingate (Wear)
Winslow United (SM)
Winterton Rangers (NE)
Wisbech Town (EC)
Witham Town (Ex)
Wivenhoe Town (Ex)
Wolverhampton United (WM)
Wolverton Town (I)
Woodford Town (S)
Woolley MW (NE)
Wootton Blue Cross (WC)
Worsborough Bridge MW (NE)
Wren Rovers (NW)
Wythemshawe Amateurs (M)

Yate Town (Hell)
Yaxley (P)
York Railway Institute (NE)
Yorkshire Amateur (NE)

Code for Vase Club's Leagues: A - Athenian; AC - Anglian Combination; B - Bristol & Suburban; CC - Combined Counties; CD - Carlisle & District; CM - Central Midlands; D - Dorset Combination; EC - Eastern Counties; Ex - Essex Senior; G - Gloucestershire; Ha - Hampshire; Hell - Hellenic; I - Isthmian; K - Kent; LA - Lancashire Amateur; Le -Leicestershire Senior; Lincs - Lincolnshire; Lp - Liverpool Combination; LS - London Spartan; M - Manchester; MC - Mid-Cheshire; MCB - Midland Combination; N - Northern; NA - Notts Alliance; NAII - Northern Alliance; Nemean - Nemean Amateur; NE - Northern Counties East; NW - North West Counties; OB - Old Boys; P - Peterborough & District; S -Southern; SM - South Midlands; Som - Somerset Senior; SA - Southern Amateur; Sx - Sussex County; Staffs - Staffordshire Co (North); Suff - Suffolk & Ipswich; T - Teesside; United Counties; WC - West Cumberland; W - Western; Wear -Wearside; Westmorland - Westmorland; West Lancs - West Lancashire; West Rid - West Riding County Amateur; Wilts -Wiltshire; WChes - West Cheshire; WM - West Midlands.

Quiz answer back page

Did you recognise them? ITV's Jim Rosenthal challenges Hampton's manager Roger Charland in a friendly match. Photo: Peter Burrin